VALUATION

**MEASURING AND
MANAGING THE
VALUE OF
COMPANIES**

The Wiley Finance series contains books written specifically for finance and investment professionals as well as sophisticated individual investors and their financial advisors. Book topics range from portfolio management to e-commerce, risk management, financial engineering, valuation and financial instrument analysis, as well as much more. For a list of available titles, visit our website at www.WileyFinance.com.

Founded in 1807, John Wiley & Sons is the oldest independent publishing company in the United States. With offices in North America, Europe, Australia and Asia, Wiley is globally committed to developing and marketing print and electronic products and services for our customers' professional and personal knowledge and understanding.

VALUATION

MEASURING AND MANAGING THE VALUE OF COMPANIES

EIGHTH EDITION

McKinsey & Company

Tim Koller
Marc Goedhart
David Wessels

WILEY

Published by John Wiley & Sons, Inc., Hoboken, New Jersey.
Published simultaneously in Canada.

For general information on our other products and services or for technical support, please contact our Customer Care Department within the United States at (800) 762-2974, outside the United States at (317) 572-3993 or fax (317) 572-4002.

Wiley also publishes its books in a variety of electronic formats. Some content that appears in print may not be available in electronic formats. For more information about Wiley products, visit our web site at www.wiley.com.

Identifiers: LCCN 2025905243 | ISBN 978-1-394-27941-8 (Cloth edition) | ISBN 978-1-394-27942-5 (ePub) | ISBN 978-1-394-27943-2 (ePDF) | ISBN 978-1-394-27947-0 (University edition) | ISBN 978-1-394-27951-7 (Cloth edition with DCF Model download) | ISBN 978-1-394-27944-9 (Workbook) | ISBN 978-1-394-27950-0 (DCF Model Web download)

Cover Design: Jon Boylan
Cover Image: © starlineart/stock.adobe.com

SKY10101913_040425

Contents

About the Authors

The authors are all current or former consultants of McKinsey & Company's Strategy & Corporate Finance Practice. Together, they have more than 100 years of experience in consulting and financial education.

* * *

Tim Koller is a partner in McKinsey's Denver, Colorado, office and spent most of his career in the firm's New York office. He is a founder of McKinsey's Strategy and Corporate Finance Insights team, a global group of corporate-finance expert consultants. In his 40 years in consulting, Tim has served clients globally on corporate strategy and capital markets, acquisitions and divestitures, and strategic planning and resource allocation. He leads the firm's research activities in valuation and capital markets. Before joining McKinsey, he worked with Stern Stewart & Company and with Mobil Corporation. He received his MBA from the University of Chicago.

* * *

Marc Goedhart is a senior knowledge expert in McKinsey's Amsterdam office and an endowed professor of corporate valuation at Rotterdam School of Management (RSM), Erasmus University. Over the past 30 years, Marc has served clients across Europe on portfolio restructuring, M&A transactions, and performance management. He received his PhD in finance from Erasmus University.

* * *

David Wessels is an adjunct professor of finance at the Wharton School of the University of Pennsylvania. Named by *Bloomberg Businessweek* as one of America's top business school instructors, he teaches courses on corporate valuation and private equity at the MBA and executive MBA levels. David is also a director in Wharton's executive education group, serving on the executive development faculties of several Fortune 500 companies. A former consultant with McKinsey, he received his PhD from the University of California at Los Angeles.

* * *

McKinsey & Company is a global management consulting firm, working with clients across the private, public, and social sectors. McKinsey combines bold strategies and transformative technologies to help organizations innovate more sustainably, achieve lasting gains in performance, and build workforces that will thrive for this generation and the next.

Preface

The first edition of *Valuation* appeared in 1990, and we are encouraged that it and the subsequent editions have continued to attract readers around the world. We believe the book appeals to readers everywhere because the approach it advocates is grounded in universal economic principles. While we continue to improve, update, and expand the text as our experience grows and as business and finance continue to evolve, those universal principles do not change.

In the 35 years since that first edition, managers and executives have dealt with major economic challenges, including the COVID-19 pandemic, the economic crisis of the late 2000s, and the fallout from the internet boom at the turn of the century. All these events have strengthened our conviction that the core principles of value creation are general economic rules that continue to apply in all market circumstances. Thus, the extraordinarily high anticipated profits represented by stock prices during the internet bubble never materialized, because there was no "new economy." Similarly, the extraordinarily high profits seen in the financial sector for the two years preceding the start of the 2007–2009 financial crisis were not "real," in the sense that they didn't adequately set aside reserves for loan losses. The laws of competition should have alerted investors that those extraordinary profits couldn't last and might not be real.

Over time, we have also seen that, for some companies, some of the time, the stock market may not be a reliable indicator of value. At the time of this writing, ten different companies had market capitalizations greater than $1 trillion. We cannot predict whether all these companies can grow enough and maintain their profits and cash flows sufficiently to justify these values. Knowing that value signals from the stock market may occasionally be unreliable makes us even more certain that managers must always understand the underlying, intrinsic value of their companies—and thus how they can create more value. In our view, clear thinking about valuation and skill in using valuation to guide business decisions are prerequisites for company success.

Furthermore, there remains confusion about what it means to truly create value for shareholders. As we explain in Chapter 1, creating value for shareholders is not the same as pumping up today's share price. Rather, it means creating value for the collective of current and future shareholders by applying the techniques explained in this book. As they do so, companies will thrive, and ultimately, society as a whole will benefit.

WHY THIS BOOK

If CEOs and other executives are to do their jobs well and fulfill their responsibilities, they need to understand how value is created. This book's practical focus reflects its origins as a handbook for McKinsey consultants. We publish it for the benefit of current and future managers who want their companies to create value and also for investors. It aims to demystify the field of valuation and clarify the linkages between strategy and finance. So while it draws on leading-edge academic thinking, it is primarily a how-to book and one we hope you will use again and again. This is no coffee-table tome: if we have done our job well, it will soon be full of underlining, marginal notations, and highlighting.

The book's messages are simple: Companies thrive when they create real economic value for their shareholders. Companies create value by investing capital at rates of return that exceed their cost of capital. These two truths apply across time and geography. The book explains why these core principles of value creation are genuine and how companies can increase value by applying them.

The technical chapters of the book aim to explain, step-by-step, how to do valuation well. We spell out valuation frameworks that we use in our consulting work, and we illustrate them with detailed case studies that highlight the practical judgments involved in developing and using valuations. Just as important, the management chapters discuss how to use valuation to make good decisions for a company—specifically, by helping with the following tasks:

- Decide among alternative business strategies by estimating the value of each strategic choice
- Develop a corporate portfolio strategy, based on which business units a corporate parent is best positioned to own and which might perform better under someone else's ownership
- Assess major transactions, including acquisitions and divestitures
- Improve a company's strategic planning and resource allocation so the company's parts are aligned to execute strategic priorities and create value

- Communicate effectively with investors
- Design a capital structure that supports the corporation's strategy and minimizes the risk of financial distress

STRUCTURE OF THE BOOK

In this eighth edition, we continue to expand the practical application of finance to real business problems, reflecting past economic events, new accounting rules, new developments in academic finance, and our own experiences. The edition is organized into five parts, each with a distinct focus.

Part One, "Foundations of Value," provides an overview of value creation. We make the case that managers should focus on long-term value creation for current and future shareholders, not just some of today's shareholders looking for an immediate pop in the share price. We explain the two core principles of value creation: (1) the idea that return on invested capital and growth drive cash flow, which in turn drives value, and (2) the conservation-of-value principle, which says anything that doesn't increase cash flow doesn't create value (unless it reduces risk). We devote a chapter each to return on invested capital and to growth, including a new discussion of strategic principles and empirical insights for companies based in Europe.

Part Two, "Core Valuation Techniques," is a self-contained handbook for using discounted cash flow (DCF) to value a company. The reader will learn how to analyze historical performance, forecast free cash flows, estimate the appropriate opportunity cost of capital, identify sources of value, and interpret results. We also show how to use multiples of comparable companies to supplement DCF valuations.

Part Three, "Advanced Valuation Techniques," explains how to analyze and incorporate in a valuation such complex issues as taxes, pensions, leases, capital-light business models, inflation, and foreign currency. It also discusses alternative return-on-capital measures and applications.

Part Four, "Managing for Value," applies the value creation principles to practical decisions that managers face. It explains how to design a portfolio of businesses, how to run effective strategic-planning and resource allocation processes, how to create value through acquisitions and divestitures, how to construct an appropriate capital structure and payout policy, and how companies can improve their communications with the financial markets. New to the eighth edition are chapters on how to apply a value creation focus to issues of sustainability and new digital innovations.

Part Five, "Special Situations," is devoted to valuation in more complex contexts. It explores the challenges of valuing leveraged buyouts, venture capital, high-growth companies, companies in emerging markets, cyclical companies, and banks. In addition, it shows how uncertainty and flexibility affect value and how to apply option-pricing theory and decision trees in valuations.

Finally, our nine appendixes provide a full accounting of our methodology in this book. They provide theoretical proofs, mathematical formulas, and underlying calculations for chapters where additional detail might be helpful in the practical application of our approach. Appendix I, in particular, pulls into one place the spreadsheets for the comprehensive valuation case study of Costco featured in this edition.

VALUATION SPREADSHEET

An Excel spreadsheet valuation model is available via Web download. This valuation model is similar to the model we use in practice. Practitioners will find the model easy to use in a variety of situations: mergers and acquisitions, valuation of business units for restructuring or value-based management, and tests of the implications of major strategic decisions on a company's value. We accept no responsibility for any decisions based on your inputs to the model. If you would like to purchase the model (ISBN 978-1-394-27950-0), please call (800) 225-5945, or visit www.wileyvaluation.com.

Acknowledgments

No book is solely the effort of its authors. This book is certainly no exception, especially since it grew out of the collective work of McKinsey's Strategy & Corporate Finance Practice and the experiences of its consultants throughout the world.

Most important, we would like to thank the late Tom Copeland and Jack Murrin, two of the coauthors of the first three editions of this book. We are deeply indebted to them for establishing the book's early success, for mentoring the current authors, and for their hard work in providing the foundations on which this edition builds.

Ennius Bergsma deserves our special thanks. Ennius initiated the development of McKinsey's Strategy & Corporate Finance Practice in the mid-1980s. He inspired the original internal McKinsey valuation handbook and mustered the support and sponsorship to turn that handbook into a real book for an external audience.

Connor Guy, our lead editor, ensured that our ideas were expressed clearly and concisely. Jonathon Berlin and his team edited and oversaw the production of more than 400 exhibits, ensuring that they were carefully aligned with the text. Karen Schenkenfelder provided careful editing and feedback throughout the process. We are indebted to her excellent eye for detail.

The intellectual origins of this book lie in the present-value method of capital budgeting and in the valuation approach developed by Nobel laureates Merton Miller and Franco Modigliani in their 1961 *Journal of Business* article titled "Dividend Policy, Growth, and the Valuation of Shares." Others have gone far to popularize their approach. In particular, Professor Alfred Rappaport (Northwestern University, professor emeritus) and the late Joel Stern (Stern Stewart & Co.) were among the first to extend the Miller-Modigliani enterprise valuation formula to real-world applications.

We would like to acknowledge those who have personally shaped our careers and knowledge of valuation, corporate finance, and strategy. For their support, teachings, and inspiration, we thank Buford Alexander, Tony Bernardo, Chris Bradley, Richard Dobbs, the late Mikel Dodd, Bernie Ferrari, Dick Foster, Martin Hirt, Bob Holthausen, Bill Huyett, Rob Kazanjian, John Kelleher, Dan Lovallo, Michael Gibbons, Ofer Nemirovsky, Eduardo Schwartz, Chandan Sengupta, Sven Smit, the late Jaap Spronk, the late Joel Stern, Bennett Stewart, Robert Uhlaner, Sunil Wahal, Ivo Welch, and Loek Zonnenberg.

Tim and Marc are founders of McKinsey's Strategy & Corporate Finance Insights team, a group of dedicated corporate-finance experts who influence our thinking every day. A special thank-you to Bernie Ferrari, who initiated the group and nurtured its development, and to the earliest members of the team who stuck with it and became its leaders, including Susan Nolen Foushee, Jean-Hugues Monier, and Werner Rehm. Other leaders we are indebted to include Haripreet Batra, Alok Bothra, Josue Calderon, Marc de Jong, Dago Diedrich, Prateek Gakhar, Abhishek Goel, Anuj Gupta, Chetan Gupta, Peeyush Karnani, Tarun Khurana, David Kohn, Ankit Mittal, Chris Mulligan, Siddharth Periwal, Abhishek Saxena, and Zane Williams.

We wish to thank the following colleagues, who coauthored or provided analytical support to individual chapters:

- Chapter 1, "Why Value Value?": Michael Birshan and Andy West
- Chapter 5, "The Alchemy of Stock Market Performance": Rosen Kotsev
- Chapter 6, "The Stock Market and Economic Fundamentals": Vartika Gupta and Peter Stumpner
- Chapter 7, "The Stock Market Is Smarter Than You Think": Marc Silberstein
- Chapter 8, "Return on Invested Capital": Susan Nolen Foushee
- Chapter 9, "Growth": Rebecca Doherty and Laura Laberge
- Chapter 28, "Corporate Portfolio Strategy": Jamie Koenig, Paul Morgan, and Justin Sanders
- Chapter 30, "Strategic Management: Governance, Processes, and Decision Making": Aaron de Smet, Zuzanna Kraszewska, and Derek Schatz
- Chapter 31, "Acquisitions," Patrick McCurdy and Liz Wol, with support from Riccardo Andreola
- Chapter 32, "Divestitures": Jamie Koenig and Anna Mattsson, with support from Raghav Kapur and Mariola Ndrio
- Chapter 34, "Sustainability": Robin Nuttall, Werner Rehm, and Claudia Rexhausen, with support from Alex Harman
- Chapter 36, "Investor Communications": John Evers and Werner Rehm

- Chapter 37, "Leveraged Buyouts": Caleb Carter
- Chapter 41, "Emerging Markets": Anuj Gupta
- Chapter 42, "Cyclical Companies": Marco de Heer, whose dissertation formed the basis for this chapter
- Chapter 43, "Banks": Alok Bothra and Zane Williams

We extend thanks also to the Capabilities and Insights team, led by Rosen Kotsev. The team, which helped significantly in preparing analyses for us, includes Rafael Araya, Roerich Bansal, Satvik Bansal, Martin Barboza, Aya Benlakhder, Margarida Carrasqueira, Pedro Catarino, Abhranil Das, Carlo Eyzaguirre, Igor Ferreira, Jyotsna Goel, Gaukhar Janburshina, Raghav Kapur, Dilpreet Kaur, Kumari Monika, Carolina Oreamuno, Victor Rojas, Sapna Sharma, José Afonso Silva, Isaac Silvestre, and Ricardo Solis Arley. Other consultants who contributed include Andre Gaeta, Paulo Guimaraes, Daniel Guzman, and Martin Perez.

We've made extensive use of McKinsey Value Intelligence (MVI), led by Peter Stumpner and Vartika Gupta, which provided data and analyses in this book. MVI is a large curated database of company financial information, which includes both raw data and synthesized insights. Dick Foster, a former McKinsey colleague and mentor, inspired the development of McKinsey Value Intelligence.

Michael Cichello, professor of finance at the Smith School of Business at the University of Maryland, expertly prepared the teaching materials that accompany this book, including the syllabus, end-of-chapter problems and answers for the university edition, and exam questions and answers. These teaching materials are an essential supplement for professors and students using this book for finance courses. Thank you to our Capabilities and Insights team for their help in preparing and answering questions for these materials.

Of course, we could not have devoted the time and energy to this book without the support and encouragement of McKinsey's Strategy & Corporate Finance Practice leadership, particularly Michael Birshan and Andy West. Also, Raju Narisetti and Lucia Rahilly ensured that we received superior editorial support from McKinsey's external publishing team. Thanks also to Sneha Vats, Ramya DRozario, and their team, who facilitated the approvals process for mentions of specific company names.

We would like to thank again all those who contributed to the first seven editions. We owe a special debt to Dave Furer for help and late nights developing the original drafts of this book more than 35 years ago. Bill Javetski was our rigorous thought partner and editor for the fourth through seventh editions, honing our writing skills. Dennis Swinford edited and managed the more than 300 exhibits in those editions. The first seven editions and this edition drew upon work, ideas, and analyses from Carlos Abad, Paul Adam, Ashish Kumar Agarwal, Buford Alexander, Petri Allas, Alexandre Amson,

André Annema, the late Pat Anslinger, Vladimir Antikarov, Ali Asghar, Bill Barnett, Dan Bergman, Olivier Berlage, Peter Bisson, the late Joel Bleeke, Bing Cao, Nidhi Chadda, Carrie Chen, Steve Coley, Kevin Coyne, Bas Deelder, Marco de Heer, Johan Depraetere, Marijn de Wit, Pieter de Wit, the late Mikel Dodd, Lee Dranikoff, Will Draper, David Ernst, Bill Fallon, George Fenn, Susan Nolen Foushee, Russ Fradin, Gabriel Garcia, Richard Gerards, Alo Ghosh, Irina Grigorenko, Fredrik Gustavsson, Keiko Honda, Alice Hu, Régis Huc, Ritesh Jain, Mimi James, Mauricio Jaramillo, Bin Jiang, Chris Jones, William Jones, Mary Beth Joyce, Phil Keenan, Phil Kholos, David Krieger, Shyanjaw Kuo, Michael Kuritzky, Bill Lewis, Kurt Losert, Harry Markl, Yuri Maslov, Perry Moilinoff, Fabienne Moimaux, Jean-Hugues Monier, Mike Murray, Terence Nahar, Rafic Naja, Juan Ocampo, Martijn Olthof, Neha Patel, Vijen Patel, John Patience, Bill Pursche, Rishi Raj, S. R. Rajan, Werner Rehm, Frank Richter, Eileen Kelly Rinaudo, David Rothschild, Michael Rudolf, Yasser Salem, Antoon Schneider, Ram Sekar, Meg Smoot, Silvia Stefini, Konrad Stiglbrunner, Saravanan Subramanian, Ahmed Taha, Bill Trent, David Twiddy, Valerie Udale, Sandeep Vaswani, Kim Vogel, Christian von Drathen, Jon Weiner, Jack Welch, Gustavo Wigman, David Willensky, Zane Williams, Jonathan Witter, David Wright, Yan Yang, and Angela Zhang.

For help in coordinating the flow of Zoom meetings, e-mail, and phone calls, we owe our thanks to our assistants, Kate Anderson and Zofia Wisniewska.

We also extend thanks to the team at John Wiley & Sons, including Bill Falloon, Susan Cerra, Katherine Cording, Steve Kyritz, Jean-Karl Martin, and Tom Nery.

Finally, thank you to Melissa Koller, Monique Donders, Kate Wessels, and our children: Katherine, Emily, and Juliana Koller; Max, Julia, and Sarah Goedhart; and Adin, Aurora, Jacob, Lillia, and Nathaniel Wessels. Our wives and families are our true inspirations. This book would not have been possible without their encouragement, support, and sacrifice.

VALUATION

MEASURING AND MANAGING THE VALUE OF COMPANIES

Part One

Foundations of Value

1

Why Value Value?

Among the most important decisions executives face is the question of how to allocate their organizations' resources. Many leaders find themselves overwhelmed by the technicalities and nuances, often resorting to rules of thumb rather than robust analysis. This text aims to demystify how these highly complex decisions should be made by providing a clear, systematic approach to measuring value and a comprehensive understanding of how and why it is created.

In addition to the math of value creation, we show how to apply a value creation perspective to the complicated decisions that frequently arise in the course of managing a business—decisions such as whether to enter a new market, invest in product development, build a new plant, acquire another company, or divest a business.

While these questions can be daunting, the core concept behind business value creation is refreshingly simple: companies that grow and earn a return on capital that exceeds their cost of capital create value. Articulated as early as 1890 by Alfred Marshall,[1] the concept has proven to be both enduring in its validity and elusive in its application.

Nevertheless, managers, boards of directors, and investors sometimes ignore the foundations of value because of weak analyses or misaligned incentives. The tulip mania of the early 1600s, the collapse of Japan's economy in the 1990s, the internet bubble, and the mid-2000s real estate frenzy that touched off the financial crisis of 2007–2008 can all, to some extent, be traced to a misunderstanding or misapplication of this guiding principle. We see individual companies regularly misapplying the core principles of valuation—to get bigger, to beef up short-term earnings per share (often at the expense of long-term value creation), or to avoid hard choices.

This chapter was coauthored by Michael Birshan and Andy West.

[1] A. Marshall, *Principles of Economics* (New York: Macmillan, 1890), 1: 142.

Today, phenomena such as global climate change, the distribution of wealth within advanced economies, and the rise of corporations that are more highly valued than any in history are fueling debates about shareholder-oriented capitalism. These are important topics, but the discussion sometimes risks muddling two distinct issues: the perils of short-termism and the question of what responsibilities a company has beyond lawful operations and value creation for shareholders. Much, though not all, of the criticism of shareholder-oriented capitalism is really a critique of companies' short-term behavior.

If we are to truly understand the challenges we face, we must untangle these two issues. Doing that requires a deeper understanding of value, so this chapter begins by describing what value creation does and does not mean. We then discuss the dangers of short-term behavior, followed by the task of reconciling the competing interests of shareholders and other stakeholders. The chapter closes with an overview of what will be covered in the remainder of the book.

WHAT IT MEANS TO CREATE VALUE FOR SHAREHOLDERS

Particularly at this time of reflection on the role of business in society, it's critical that managers and board directors have a clear understanding of what value creation means. For value-minded executives, the definition cannot be limited to simply maximizing today's share price. Rather, a better objective is maximizing a company's collective value to all its shareholders, now and in the future.

In the first decade of this century, some banks acted as if maximizing short-term profits would maximize value—a mistake that ultimately precipitated a financial crisis and destroyed billions of dollars of shareholder value while also hurting non-shareholders, including employees who lost their jobs, borrowers who were taken advantage of, communities where homebuilding ground to a halt, and taxpayers to the extent they funded bailouts. Similarly, companies whose short-term focus leads to environmental disasters destroy shareholder value by incurring cleanup costs and fines and by inflicting lingering reputational damage. While these might be extreme examples, the best managers don't skimp on safety, don't make value-destroying decisions just because their peers are doing so, and don't use accounting or financial gimmicks to boost short-term profits, nor do they underinvest in their people.[2] Such actions undermine the interests of all stakeholders, including shareholders. They are the antithesis of value creation.

If a company's investors knew as much about its operations as its managers do, maximizing its current share price might be equivalent to maximizing its value over time. But in the real world, investors have only a company's

---

[2] A. Madgavkar, B. Schaninger, D. Maor, et al., "Performance through People: Transforming Human Capital into Competitive Advantage," McKinsey Global Institute, February 2, 2023, www.mckinsey.com.

published financial results and their own assessment of the quality and integrity of its management team. Investors in most companies don't know what is really going on inside the company or what decisions managers are making. They can't know, for example, whether the company is improving its margins by finding more efficient ways to work or by underinvesting in important areas such as product development, human capital development, maintenance, or marketing.

Since investors have limited information, companies can pump up their share price in the short to medium term. One global consumer product company consistently generated annual growth in earnings per share (EPS) between 11 and 16 percent for seven years. Managers attributed the company's success to improved efficiency. Impressed, investors pushed the company's share price above those of its peers—unaware that the company was shortchanging its investments in product development and brand building to inflate short-term profits even as revenue growth declined. Finally, managers had to admit what they'd done. Not surprisingly, the company went through a painful period of rebuilding. Its stock price took years to recover.

It would be a mistake, however, to conclude that the stock market is not "efficient" in the academic sense that it incorporates all public information. Markets do a great job with public information, but markets are not omniscient. In other words, they cannot take into account information they don't have. Think about the analogy of selling an older house. The seller may know that the boiler makes a weird sound sometimes or that some of the windows are a bit drafty. But unless the seller discloses those facts, a potential buyer may have great difficulty detecting them, even with the help of a professional house inspector—and these problems would not be incorporated into the market value of the house.

Overall, the evidence suggests that companies with a long strategic horizon create more value than those run with a short-term mindset.[3] Banks that had the insight and courage to forgo short-term profits during the real estate bubble of the 2000s, for example, earned much better total shareholder returns (TSR) over the longer term. In fact, when we studied the patterns of investment, growth, earnings quality, and earnings management of hundreds of companies across multiple industries over a 14-year period, we found that companies with a long-term focus tended to generate superior TSR, with a 50 percent greater likelihood of being in the top quartile by the end of the period studied.[4] In separate research, we've found that long-term revenue growth is the most important driver of shareholder returns for companies with high

---

[3] The studies we cite in this paragraph acknowledge that correlation is not causation. In fact, one could argue there is reverse causation—that is, companies' satisfactory financial performance gives them the luxury to place greater emphasis on long-term concerns.

[4] *Measuring the Economic Impact of Short-Termism*, McKinsey Global Institute, February 2017, www.mckinsey.com.

returns on capital.[5] In our 2023 survey of 721 executives, respondents who said their companies prioritize long-term value creation over short-term profits were 2.3 times more likely than other respondents to describe their company as more innovative than its peers and 2.5 times more likely to say their five-year revenue growth exceeded that of their peers. What's more, investments in research and development (R&D) correlate powerfully with long-term TSR.[6] Further evidence on employee and customer satisfaction indirectly supports the benefits of a long-term orientation.[7]

What this means is that managers who create value for the long term will not take actions to increase today's share price if those actions are likely to damage the company down the road. For example, they don't shortchange product development or reduce product quality. When considering investments, they take into account likely future changes in regulation or consumer behavior, especially with regard to environmental and health issues. All of this is easier said than done. Making long-term value-creating decisions requires courage and often a mindset that extends beyond one's own time in a specific role. But the fundamental task of management and the board is to demonstrate this courage, despite the possibility of short-term consequences.

SHORT-TERMISM RUNS DEEP

Despite evidence that what investors really want is long-term value creation,[8] too many managers continue to plan and execute strategy—and then report their performance—against shorter-term measures, particularly earnings per share (EPS). The widespread occurrence of short-termism presents challenges to managers but also a set of opportunities for companies and investors with greater foresight.

The Pressure on Managers

As a result of their focus on short-term EPS, major companies often pass up long-term value-creating opportunities. The CFO of one very large company instituted a standing rule: every year, every business unit must increase its profits faster than its revenues. Some of the units had profit margins above

---

[5] B. Jiang and T. Koller, "How to Choose between Growth and ROIC," *McKinsey on Finance*, no. 25 (Autumn 2007): 19–22, www.mckinsey.com. However, we didn't find the same relationship for companies with low returns on capital.

[6] We've performed the same analyses for 15 and 20 years and with different start and end dates, and we've always found similar results.

[7] A. Edmans, *Grow the Pie: How Great Companies Deliver Both Purpose and Profit* (Cambridge University Press, 2020), chap. 4.

[8] R. N. Palter, W. Rehm, and J. Shih, "Communicating with the Right Investors," *McKinsey Quarterly* (April 2008), www.mckinsey.com. Chapter 36 of this book also examines the behaviors of intrinsic and other investor types.

30 percent and returns on capital of 50 percent or more. Increasing margins every year sounds great if your horizon is the next annual report. But for units that already have high margins and a high return on capital, such a rule may incentivize passing up attractive future growth opportunities.

This example is by no means an isolated case. In a seminal survey of 400 chief financial officers in 2006, two Duke University professors found that fully 80 percent of the CFOs said they would reduce discretionary spending on potentially value-creating activities such as marketing and R&D in order to meet their short-term earnings targets.[9] In 2023, when we surveyed 721 executives working in various roles, only 35 percent said their organization prioritizes long-term value creation over short-term profit targets. In 2017, researchers published a paper showing that CEOs tended to reduce R&D spending and increase EPS guidance around the times when their stock options were vesting.[10] That's no way to run a railroad—or any other business.

Some analysts and some short-term-oriented investors will always clamor for short-term results. However, even though a company bent on growing long-term value will not be able to meet their demands all the time, this continuous pressure has the virtue of keeping managers on their toes. Sorting out the trade-offs between short-term earnings and long-term value creation is part of a manager's job. Perhaps even more important, it is up to corporate boards to investigate and understand the economics of the businesses in their portfolio well enough to judge when managers are making the right trade-offs and, above all, to protect managers when they choose to build long-term value at the expense of short-term profits.

THE STAKEHOLDER CONUNDRUM

One concern that has been posed consistently to business leaders for decades is skepticism over whether they are adequately considering the impact of their actions on others, beyond just shareholders. In some places, such as certain European countries, the interests of other stakeholder groups are embedded in corporate governance structures. Similarly, in many jurisdictions, companies are now required to be more transparent about their greenhouse gas emissions and the risks that climate change poses to their financial health.

We agree that for most companies around the world, creating long-term shareholder value requires satisfying other stakeholders as well. You can't create long-term value by ignoring the needs of your customers, suppliers, and

---

[9] J. R. Graham, C. R. Harvey, and S. Rajgopal, "Value Destruction and Financial Reporting Decisions," *Financial Analysts Journal* 62, no. 6 (2006): 27–39.

[10] A. Edmans, V. W. Fang, and K. A. Lewellen, "Equity Vesting and Investment," *Review of Financial Studies* 30, no. 7 (July 2017): 2229–2271, doi.org/10.1093/rfs/hhx018.

employees and the impact on the environment and climate. And investing for sustainable growth should and often does result in stronger economies, higher living standards, and more opportunities for individuals.

When Interests Collide

Research has shown that many corporate social-responsibility initiatives create shareholder value.[11] Inevitably, though, there will be times when the interests of a company's stakeholders are not entirely complementary. Strategic decisions involve trade-offs, and the interests of different groups can be at odds with one another. These are times for managers to lead, and in many cases the most pragmatic approach is to focus on the long-term interests of shareholders—subject to law and regulation, of course, which are the primary mechanisms for ensuring that the activity of companies is aligned with the overall interests of society. As we will show in the next section, long-term value creation leads to better resource allocation across the economy and better economic health, which ultimately creates more jobs and a higher standard of living for all. While skilled managers focus on the long-term interests of shareholders above all, they must also actively consider a broad set of priorities when making difficult decisions.

Consider employee stakeholders. A company that tries to boost profits by providing a shabby work environment or underpaying employees will have trouble attracting and retaining productive employees. Operating with less capable or motivated employees can result in lower-quality products, reduced demand, and damage to the brand reputation. Given these circumstances, many companies choose to pay wages that are high enough to attract suitable employees and keep them motivated and productive. Companies, then, must strike a careful balance, calibrating compensation so it is competitively attractive but not significantly above the market rate.

Similarly, consider pricing decisions. Here, too, the interests of customers are not entirely aligned with the interests of shareholders. When considering any adjustments to prices, managers must weigh the value of a lower price to buyers against the value of a higher price to shareholders and perhaps other stakeholders.

Economy-Wide Benefits of Prioritizing Value Creation

Value creation also plays a meaningful role in the health of an economy. When we examined employment from 2014 to 2023, we found that the U.S. and European companies that created the most shareholder value, measured as total shareholder returns, showed stronger-than-average employment growth

---

[11] S. Bonini, T. Koller, and P. H. Mirvis, "Valuing Social Responsibility Programs," *McKinsey Quarterly* (July 2009), www.mckinsey.com.

EXHIBIT 1.1 **Companies Creating More Shareholder Value Create More Jobs**

Correlation between total shareholder returns (TSR) and employment growth[1]

Compound annual growth rate, 2014–2023

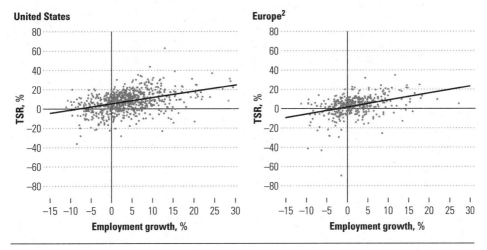

[1] Sample includes companies with real revenues greater than $1,000 million and excludes 2% top and bottom outliers in employment growth.

[2] Includes companies from EU27, United Kingdom, and Switzerland.

Source: Corporate Performance Analytics by McKinsey.

(Exhibit 1.1). This finding suggests an association between long-term corporate success and employment.[12]

Yet this is not the full picture. Sometimes, managers face unhappier circumstances. For example, companies in mature, competitive industries may have to grapple with whether to keep open high-cost plants (which support employment and local suppliers even as they sometimes lose money). In some cases, investing in innovation, productivity, and differentiation can justify higher-cost locations and create a win-win situation. In others, however, securing a future for the company as a whole—and all who depend on it—requires tough choices. In our experience, managers carefully weigh shareholder value impact *and* agonize over decisions that have pronounced consequences on workers' lives and community well-being.

For those making these difficult trade-offs, it's important to also consider who ultimately benefits from shareholder value creation. It is comforting to know that shares in most listed companies are held by retail investors, pension funds, and mutual funds. The ultimate beneficiaries are mostly people saving for retirement. In fact, a recent report found that the portion of shares owned by individuals—whether direct or indirect holdings—has continued to

---

[12] We've performed the same analyses for 15 and 20 years and with different start and end dates, and we've always found similar results.

EXHIBIT 1.2 **Increasing Percentage of American Households Owning Stocks**

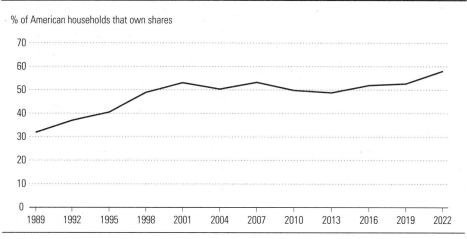

% of American households that own shares

[1] Sum of direct and indirect stock holdings. Examples of indirect holdings are pooled investment funds, retirement accounts, and other managed assets. Indirect holdings, particularly through tax-deferred retirement accounts, are much more common than direct holdings.

Source: Board of Governors of the Federal Reserve System, Survey of Consumer Finances (SCF), federalreserve.gov, accessed Jan. 2024.

increase and reached an all-time high of just under 60 percent in 2022, compared with 30 percent in 1989 (Exhibit 1.2).[13]

We can observe the importance of long-term value creation to the overall economy in widespread improvements to the standard of living in advanced economies such as the United States, where access to conveniences such as air conditioning, automobiles, and mobile phones has steadily increased over time. In 2020, almost 90 percent of U.S. homes had air conditioning.[14] In the 1940s and 1950s, such conveniences were far less common. In 1900, the agriculture sector required almost 40 percent of the workforce to feed the country's population. By 1950, thanks to technological advances and improvements in efficiency, that number had dropped to just over 10 percent, and it has since fallen below 2 percent.[15]

In their 2022 book, *Superabundance: The Story of Population Growth, Innovation, and Human Flourishing on an Infinitely Bountiful Planet*, authors Marian Tupy and Gale Pooley measure economic progress in terms of time prices—the hours of work required to buy a certain quantity of goods. They report, "Between 1980 and 2020, while [global] population grew by 75 percent, time prices of the 50 key commodities that sustain life dropped by

[13] H. Miao, "More Americans than Ever Own Stocks," *Wall Street Journal*, December 18, 2023, www.wsj.com.
[14] "Nearly 90% of U.S. Households Used Air Conditioning in 2020," *Today in Energy* (U.S. Energy Information Administration), May 31, 2022, www.eia.gov.
[15] "Changes in Agriculture, 1900 to 1950," in *1950 Census of Agriculture*, vol. 5, *Special Reports* (US Census Bureau, 1952), available at www.census.gov.

75 percent."[16] For example, in emerging markets like India, the time price of rice as food for a day has dropped from seven hours in 1960 to under an hour today.[17]

CONSEQUENCES OF FORGETTING VALUE CREATION PRINCIPLES

When companies forget the simple value creation principles, the negative consequences to the economy can be huge. One example of many executives failing in their duty to focus on true value creation is the internet bubble of the 1990s.

During the internet bubble, managers and investors lost sight of what drives return on invested capital (ROIC); indeed, many forgot the importance of this ratio entirely. Multiple executives and investors either forgot or threw out fundamental rules of economics in the rarefied air of the internet revolution. The notion of "winner takes all" led companies and investors to believe that all that mattered was getting big fast, on the assumption they could wait until later to worry about creating an effective business model. At the same time, the logic of achieving ever-increasing returns was mistakenly applied to areas such as online pet supplies, grocery delivery services, and others where a growing customer base would require investing (unsustainably, eventually) in more drivers, trucks, warehouses, and inventory. When the laws of economics prevailed, as they always do, it became clear that many internet businesses lacked the unassailable competitive advantages required to earn even modest returns on invested capital. Although the internet has revolutionized the economy (as have other innovations), it did not and could not render obsolete the rules of economics, competition, and value creation.

THIS BOOK

This book is a guide to how to measure and manage the value of a company. The faster companies increase their revenues and deploy more capital at attractive rates of return, the more value they create. The combination of growth and return on invested capital (ROIC), relative to its cost, is what drives cash flow and value. Anything that doesn't increase ROIC or growth at an attractive ROIC doesn't create value, such as when a company changes the ownership of claims to cash flows or uses accounting techniques that change the timing of profits without actually changing cash flows.[18]

---

[16] G. Pooley and M. L. Tupy, *Superabundance: The Story of Population Growth, Innovation, and Human Flourishing on an Infinitely Bountiful Planet* (Washington, DC: Cato Institute, 2022).
[17] Ibid.
[18] See Chapter 3 for more details.

This guiding principle of value creation links directly to competitive advantage, the core concept of business strategy. Only if companies have a well-defined competitive advantage can they sustain strong growth and high returns on invested capital. To the core principles, we add the empirical observation that creating sustainable value is a long-term endeavor—one that must take into account wider social, environmental, technological, and regulatory trends.

Competition tends to erode competitive advantages and, with them, returns on invested capital. Therefore, to create long-term value, companies must continually seek and exploit new sources of competitive advantage. To that end, managers must resist short-term pressure to take actions that create illusory value quickly at the expense of the real thing in the long term. Creating value is not the same as, for example, meeting the analysts' consensus earnings forecast for the next quarter. It does not come from ignoring the effects of decisions made today that may create greater costs down the road, such as the cost of retrofitting plants to meet future pollution regulations or attracting talent despite a tarnished reputation. It means balancing near-term financial performance against what it takes to develop a healthy company that can create value for decades ahead—a demanding challenge.

This book explains both the economics of value creation (for instance, how competitive advantage enables some companies to earn higher returns on invested capital than others) and the process of measuring value (for example, how to calculate return on invested capital from a company's accounting statements). With this knowledge, companies can make wiser strategic and operating decisions, such as what businesses to own and how to make trade-offs between growth and return on invested capital. Equally, this knowledge will enable investors to calculate the risks and returns of their investments with greater confidence.

Applying the principles of value creation requires making decisions based on long-term outcomes, which sometimes involves going against the crowd. It means accepting that there are no free lunches. It means relying on data, thoughtful analysis, a deep understanding of the competitive dynamics of your industry, and a broad, well-informed perspective on how society continually affects and is affected by your business. We hope this book provides readers with the knowledge that helps them throughout their careers make and defend decisions that will create value for investors and for society at large.

2

Finance in a Nutshell

Companies create value when they earn a return on invested capital (ROIC) greater than their opportunity cost of capital.[1] If the ROIC is at or below the cost of capital, growth may not create value. Companies should aim to find the combination of growth and ROIC that drives the highest discounted value of their cash flows. In so doing, they should consider that performance in the stock market may differ from intrinsic value creation, generally as a result of changes in investors' expectations.

To illustrate how value creation works, this chapter uses a simple story. Our heroes are Lily and Nate, who start out as the owners of a small chain of trendy clothing stores. Success follows. Over time, their business goes through a remarkable transformation. They develop the idea of expanding their stores into a new line called Lily's Emporium. To fund the expansion, they take their company public. Encouraged by the resulting gains, they develop more retail concepts, including Lily's Furniture and Lily's Garden Supplies. In the end, Lily and Nate are faced with the complexity of managing a multibusiness retail enterprise.

THE EARLY YEARS

When we first met Lily and Nate, their business had grown from a tiny boutique into a small chain of trendy, midpriced clothing stores called Lily's Dresses. They met with us to find out how they could assess their financial results. We told them they should measure their business's return on invested capital: after-tax operating profits divided by the capital invested in working capital and property, plant, and equipment. Then they could compare the

---

[1] A simple definition of return on invested capital is after-tax operating profit divided by invested capital (working capital plus property, plant, and equipment). ROIC's calculation from a company's financial statements is explained in detail in Chapters 10 and 11.

ROIC with what they could earn if they invested their capital elsewhere—for example, in the stock market.

Lily and Nate had invested $10 million in their business, and in 2025 they earned about $1.8 million after taxes, with no debt. So they calculated their return on invested capital as 18 percent. They asked what a reasonable guess would be for the rate they could earn in the stock market, and we suggested they use 10 percent. They easily saw that their money was earning 8 percent more than that, so they were pleased with their business's performance.

We commented that growth also is important to consider in measuring financial performance. Lily told us that the business was growing at about 5 percent per year. Nate added that they discovered growth can be expensive; to achieve that growth, they had to invest in new stores, fixtures, and inventory. To grow at 5 percent and earn 18 percent ROIC on their growth, they reinvested about 28 percent of their profits back into the business each year. The remaining 72 percent of profits was available to withdraw from the business. In 2025, therefore, they generated cash flow of about $1.3 million.

Lily and Nate were satisfied with 5 percent growth and 18 percent ROIC until Lily's cousin Logan told them about his aggressive expansion plans for his own retail business, Logan's Stores. Based on what Logan had said, Lily and Nate compared the expected faster growth in operating profit for Logan's Stores with their own company's 5 percent growth, as graphed in Exhibit 2.1. Lily and Nate were concerned that Logan's faster-growing profits signaled a defect in their own vision or management.

"Wait a minute," we said. "How is Logan getting all that growth? What about his ROIC?" Lily and Nate checked and returned with the data shown in

EXHIBIT 2.1 **Expected Profit Growth at Logan's Stores Outpacing Lily's Dresses**

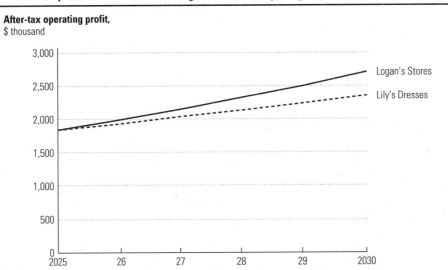

EXHIBIT 2.2 **Lily's Dresses Outperforming in Return on Invested Capital (ROIC) and Cash Flow**

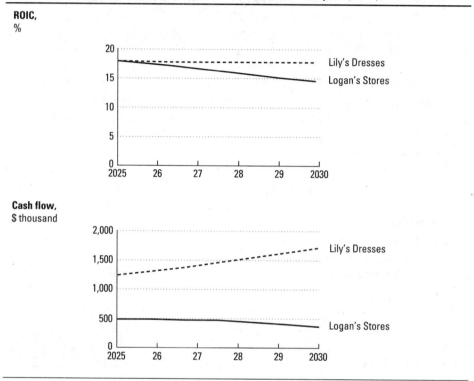

Exhibit 2.2. As we had suspected, Logan was achieving his growth by investing heavily. Despite all the growth in operating profit, his company's ROIC was declining significantly, so cash flow was slipping downward.

We asked the two why they thought their stores earned higher returns on capital than Logan's. Nate said one reason was that their products were unique and cutting-edge fashion, so their customers were willing to pay higher prices for their dresses than for the products at many other dress shops. Lily added that each of their stores attracted more customers than Logan's did, so their sales per square foot (and therefore coverage for fixed costs) were greater than Logan's. As they saw it, Logan's products were not much different from those of his competitors, so he had to match his prices to theirs and had less customer traffic in his stores. This discussion helped Nate and Lily appreciate that it was beneficial to consider ROIC along with growth.

A NEW CONCEPT

Several years later, Lily and Nate called us with a great idea. They wanted to develop a new concept, which they called Lily's Emporium. Lily's Emporium would operate larger stores carrying a wider assortment of clothes and accessories that their talented designers were working on. But when they looked at the projected results (they now had a financial analysis department), they found that all the new capital investment needed to convert their stores would reduce ROIC and cash flow for four years, even though revenue and profits would be growing faster, as shown in Exhibit 2.3. After four years, cash flow would be greater, but they didn't know how to trade off the short-term decline in ROIC and cash flow against the long-term improvement.

We affirmed that these were the right questions and explained that answering them would require more sophisticated financial tools. We advised them to use discounted cash flow (DCF), a measure that is also known as present value. DCF is a way of collapsing the future performance of the company into a single number. Lily and Nate needed to forecast the future cash flow of the company and discount it back to the present at the same opportunity cost of capital we had used for our earlier comparisons.

We helped Lily and Nate apply DCF to their new concept, discounting the projected cash flows at 10 percent. We showed them that the DCF value of their company would be $53 million if they did not adopt the new concept. With the new concept, the DCF value would be greater: $62 million. (Actually, on our spreadsheet, we rounded to the nearest thousand: $61,911,000.) These numbers gave them confidence in their idea for Lily's Emporium.

EXHIBIT 2.3 **Expansion's Impact on ROIC and Cash Flow**

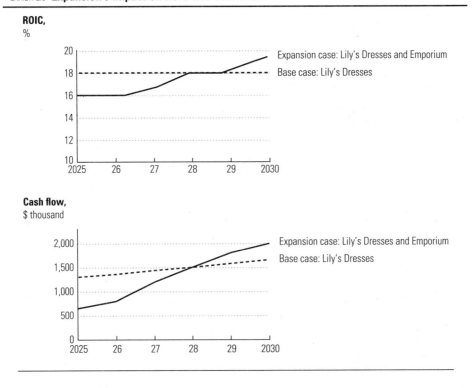

SHOULD LILY AND NATE TRY TO MAXIMIZE ROIC?

As they saw how these financial measures could help them build a more valuable business, Lily and Nate began to formulate more questions about measuring value. Lily asked whether their strategy should be to maximize their return on invested capital. She pointed to the fact that some stores outperformed others. For example, some were earning an ROIC of only 14 percent. If the business closed those lower-performing stores, they could increase their average return on invested capital.

Our advice was to focus not on the ROIC itself, but on the combination of ROIC (versus cost of capital) and the amount of capital. A tool for doing that is called economic profit. We showed them how economic profit applies to their business, using the measures in Exhibit 2.4.

We defined economic profit as the spread between ROIC and cost of capital multiplied by the amount of invested capital. In Lily and Nate's case, their economic profit forecast for 2029 would be the 8 percent spread multiplied by $12 million in invested capital, or $960,000. If they closed their low-returning stores, their average ROIC would increase to 19 percent, but their economic profit would decline to $855,000. This is because even though some stores earn a lower ROIC than others do, the lower-earning stores are still earning more than the cost of capital. Using this example, we made the case that Lily and Nate should seek to maximize economic profit, not ROIC, over the long term.

For Nate, though, this analysis raised a practical concern. With different methods available, it wasn't obvious which one to use. He asked, "When do we use economic profit, and when do we use DCF?"

"Good question," we said. "In fact, they're the same." We prepared Exhibit 2.5 to show Nate and Lily a comparison, using the DCF we had previously estimated for their business: $61,911,000. To apply the economic-profit method, we discounted the future economic profit at the same cost of capital we had used with the DCF. Then we added the discounted economic profit to the amount of capital invested today. The results for the two approaches are the same—exactly, to the penny.[2]

EXHIBIT 2.4 **Economic Profit Is Higher with Lower-Performing Stores in the Mix**

	ROIC, %	Cost of capital, %	Spread, %	Invested capital, $ thousand	Economic profit, $ thousand
Entire company	18	10	8	12,000	960
Without lower-performing stores	19	10	9	9,500	855

[2] See Chapter 10 for a detailed discussion of these two valuation approaches.

EXHIBIT 2.5 **Identical Results from DCF and Economic-Profit Valuation**

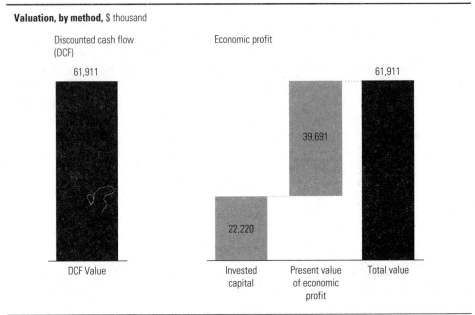

GOING PUBLIC

Now Lily and Nate had a set of tools to guide their important strategic decisions. Lily's Emporium was successful, and the next time they called us, they talked excitedly about new ambitions. "We need more capital to build more stores more quickly," Nate said. "Besides, we want to provide an opportunity for some of our employees to become owners. So we've decided to go public." They asked us to help them understand how going public would affect their financial decision making.

"Well," we said, "now's the time to learn about the distinction between financial markets and real markets and how they are related to each other. You'll want to understand that good performance in one market does not necessarily mean good performance in another."

Up until this point, we'd been talking with Lily and Nate about the real market. How much profit and cash flow were they earning relative to the investments they were making? Were they maximizing their economic profit and cash flow over time? In the real market, the decision rule is simple: choose strategies or make operational decisions that maximize the present value of future cash flow or future economic profit.

When a company enters the capital market, the decision rules for the real market remain essentially unchanged. But life gets more complicated, because management must simultaneously deal with the financial market.

When a company goes public and sells shares to a wide range of investors who can trade those shares in an organized market, the interaction (or trading activity) between investors and market speculators sets a price for those shares. The price of the shares is based on what investors think those shares are worth. Each investor decides what he or she thinks the value of the shares should be and makes trades based on whether the current price is above or below that estimate of the intrinsic value.

This intrinsic value is based on the future cash flows or earnings power of the company. This means, essentially, that investors are paying for the performance they expect the company to achieve in the future, not what the company has done in the past (and certainly not the cost of the company's assets).

Lily asked us how much their company's shares would be worth. "Let's assume," we said, "that the market's overall assessment of your company's future performance is similar to what you think your company will do. The first step is to forecast your company's performance and discount the future expected cash flows. Based on this analysis, the intrinsic value of your shares is $20 per share."

"That's interesting," said Nate, "because the amount of capital we've invested is only $7 per share." We told them that this difference meant the market should be willing to pay their company a premium of $13 over the invested capital for the future economic profit the company would earn.

"But," Lily asked, "if they pay us this premium up front, how will the investors make any money?"

"They may not," we said. "Let's see what will happen if your company performs exactly as you and the market expect. Let's value your company five years into the future. If you perform exactly as expected over the next five years and if expectations beyond five years don't change, your company's value will be $32 per share. Let's assume that you have not paid any dividends. An investor who bought a share for $20 per share today could sell the share for $32 in five years. The annualized return on the investment would be 10 percent, the same as the discount rate we used to discount your future performance. The interesting thing is that as long as you perform as expected, the return for your shareholders will be just their opportunity cost. But if you do better than expected, your shareholders will earn more than 10 percent. And if you do worse than expected, your shareholders will earn less than 10 percent."

"So," said Lily, "the return that investors earn is driven not by the performance of our company, but by its performance relative to expectations."

"Exactly!" we said.

Lily paused and reflected on the discussion. "That means we must manage our company's performance in the real markets and the financial markets at the same time."

We agreed and explained that if they were to create a great deal of value in the real market—say, by earning more than their cost of capital and growing fast—but didn't do as well as investors expected, the investors would be disappointed. Managers have a dual task: to maximize the intrinsic value of the company and to properly manage the expectations of the financial market.

"Managing market expectations is tricky," we added. "You don't want investor expectations to be too high or too low. We've seen companies convince the market that they will deliver great performance and then not deliver on those promises. Not only does the share price drop when the market realizes that the company won't be able to deliver, but regaining credibility may take years. Conversely, if the market's expectations are too low and you have a low share price relative to the opportunities the company faces, you may be subject to a hostile takeover."

After exploring these issues, Lily and Nate felt prepared to take their company public. They went forward with an initial public offering and raised the capital they needed.

EXPANSION INTO RELATED FORMATS

Lily and Nate's business was successful, growing quickly and regularly beating the expectations of the market, so their share price was a top performer. They were comfortable that their management team would be able to achieve high growth in their Emporium stores, so they decided next to try some new concepts they had been thinking about: Lily's Furniture and Lily's Garden Supplies. But they were growing concerned about managing the business as it became more and more complex. They had always had a good feel for the business, but as it expanded and they had to delegate more decision making, they were less confident that things would be managed well.

They met with us again and told us that their financial people had put in place a planning and control system to closely monitor the revenue growth, ROIC, and economic profit of every store and division. Their team set revenue and economic-profit targets annually for the next three years, monitored progress monthly, and tied managers' compensation to economic profit against these targets. Yet they told us they weren't sure the company was on track for the long-term performance that they and the market expected.

"You need a planning and control system that incorporates forward-looking measures alongside backward-looking financial measures," we told them.

"Tell us more," Nate said.

"As you've pointed out," we said, "the problem with any financial measure is that it cannot tell you how your managers are doing at building the business for the future. For example, in the short term, managers could improve their financial results by cutting back on customer service, such as by reducing the number of employees available in the store to help customers, by cutting into employee training, or by deferring maintenance costs or brand-building expenditures. You need to make sure that you build in measures related to customer satisfaction or brand awareness—measures that let you know what the future will look like, not just what the current performance is."

Lily and Nate both nodded, satisfied. The lessons they so quickly absorbed and applied have placed their company on a solid foundation. The two of them still come to see us from time to time, but only for social visits. Sometimes they bring flowers from their garden supplies center.

SOME LESSONS

While we have simplified the story of Lily and Nate's business, it highlights the core ideas around value creation and its measurement:

1. In the real market, you create value by earning a return on your invested capital greater than the opportunity cost of capital.
2. The more you can invest at returns above the cost of capital, the more value you create. That is, growth creates more value as long as the return on invested capital exceeds the cost of capital.
3. You should select strategies that maximize the present value of future expected cash flows or economic profit. The answer is the same regardless of which approach you choose.
4. The value of a company's shares in the stock market equals the intrinsic value based on the market's expectations of future performance, but the market's expectations of future performance may not be the same as the managers'.
5. The returns that shareholders earn depend on changes in expectations as much as on the actual performance of the company.

In the next chapter, we develop a more formal framework for understanding and measuring value creation.

3

Fundamental Principles of Value Creation

Companies create value for their owners by investing cash now to generate more cash in the future. The amount of value they create is the difference between cash inflows and the cost of the investments made, adjusted to reflect the fact that tomorrow's cash flows are worth less than today's because of the time value of money and the riskiness of future cash flows. As we illustrated in Chapter 2, the conversion of revenues into cash flows—and earnings—is a function of a company's return on invested capital (ROIC) and its revenue growth. That means the amount of value a company creates is governed ultimately by its ROIC, revenue growth, and ability to sustain both over time. Keep in mind that a company will create value only if its ROIC is greater than its cost of capital.[1] Moreover, only if ROIC exceeds the cost of capital will growth increase a company's value. Growth at lower returns actually reduces a company's value. Exhibit 3.1 illustrates this core principle of value creation.[2]

Understanding all these principles helps managers decide which strategies and investments will create the most value for shareholders in the long term. The principles can also help investors assess the potential value of companies they might consider investing in. This chapter explains the relationships that tie together growth, ROIC, cash flows, and value, and explains

---

[1] The cost of capital is an opportunity cost for the company's investors, not a cash cost. See Chapter 4 for a more detailed explanation.

[2] In its purest form, *value* is the sum of the present values of future expected cash flows—a point-in-time measure. *Value creation* is the change in value due to company performance (changes in growth and ROIC). Sometimes we refer to value and value creation based on explicit projections of future growth, ROIC, and cash flows. At other times, we use the market price of a company's shares as a proxy for value, and total shareholder returns (share price appreciation plus dividends) as a proxy for value creation.

EXHIBIT 3.1 **Growth and ROIC Drive Value**

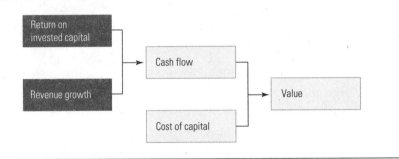

how managers can analyze these relationships to help decide among different investments or strategies. For example, we will show that high-ROIC companies typically create more value by focusing on growth, while lower-ROIC companies create more value by increasing ROIC. We'll also explore the principle, often forgotten by executives, that anything that doesn't increase cash flows, such as noncash accounting charges or changes in accounting methods, won't create value. And we'll introduce a simple equation that captures the essence of valuation in practice.

One might expect universal agreement on the definition of a concept as fundamental as value, but this isn't the case: many executives, boards, and financial media still treat accounting earnings and value as one and the same and focus almost obsessively on improving earnings. However, while earnings and cash flow are often correlated, earnings don't tell the whole story of value creation. Focusing too much on earnings or earnings growth often leads companies to stray from a value-creating path.

For example, earnings growth alone can't explain why the shoe company Skechers, with sales of $7.4 billion in 2022, and Brown-Forman, the producer of Jack Daniels and other alcoholic beverages, with sales of $3.9 billion the same year, earned similar shareholder returns (dividends plus appreciation in the share price) over the period from 2002 to 2022. These two successful companies had very different growth rates. During this period, revenues for Skechers grew by 10 percent per year on average, while those of Brown-Forman grew by an average rate of 4 percent annually. This means that revenues for Skechers in 2022 were seven times larger than in 2002, while revenues at Brown-Forman were only two times larger. Skechers, with its fast growth, earned average annual shareholder returns of 14 percent. Brown-Forman was growing much more slowly, yet its annual shareholder returns were also 14 percent. The reason Brown-Forman could create the same value as Skechers, despite much slower growth, was that Brown-Forman earned a 31 percent ROIC (typical for a branded consumer products company), while Skecher's ROIC was 12 percent.

As we'll show later, Brown-Forman's higher ROIC meant that it didn't need to invest as much of its profits back into the business as Skechers. The differences in growth rates and ROIC cancel each other out, leading to similar relative cash flow generation.

The difference in how Brown-Forman and Skechers create value also shows that both growth and ROIC are important. One is not necessarily preferable to the other—although, as we will see in Chapters 8 and 9, companies are typically better at sustaining high ROIC than high growth.

To be fair, if all companies in an industry earned the same ROIC, then earnings growth *would* be the sole differentiating metric in determining companies' cash flow. For reasons of simplicity, analysts and academics have sometimes made this assumption. But as Chapter 8 will demonstrate, returns on invested capital can vary considerably, not only across industries but also between companies within the same industry and across time.

THE RELATIONSHIP OF GROWTH, ROIC, AND CASH FLOW

Disaggregating cash flow into revenue growth and ROIC helps illuminate the underlying elements that power a company's performance. Say a company's cash flow was $100 last year and will be $115 this year. This doesn't tell us much about its economic performance, since the $15 increase in cash flow could come from many sources, including revenue growth, a reduction in capital spending, or a reduction in marketing expenditures. But if we told you that the company was generating revenue growth of 7 percent per year and would earn a return on invested capital of 15 percent, then you would be able to evaluate its performance. You could, for instance, compare the company's growth rate with the growth rate of its industry or the economy, and you could analyze its ROIC relative to peers, its cost of capital, and its own historical performance.

Growth, ROIC, and cash flow are mathematically linked. To see how, consider two companies, Value Inc. and Volume Inc., whose projected earnings, investment, and resulting cash flows are displayed in Exhibit 3.2. Earnings, in this illustration, are expressed as net operating profit after taxes (NOPAT), a term we use throughout the book. Both companies earned NOPAT of $100 million in year 1 and are expected to increase their revenues and earnings at 5 percent per year, so their projected earnings are identical. If the popular view that value depends only on earnings were true, the two companies' values also would be the same. But this simple example demonstrates how wrong that view can be.[3]

Almost all companies need to invest in plant, equipment, or working capital to grow. Free cash flow is what's left over for shareholders once these investments have been subtracted from earnings. Value Inc. generates higher free cash flows with the same earnings because it invests only 25 percent of its profits—its investment rate—to achieve the same profit growth as Volume

---

[3] What holds for NOPAT also holds for earnings per share (EPS). If both companies had the same number of shares outstanding, their EPS would also be identical, yet their values and price-to-earnings multiples would be different.

EXHIBIT 3.2 **Tale of Two Companies: Same Earnings, Different Cash Flows**

$ million

Value Inc.	Year 1	Year 2	Year 3	Year 4	Year 5
NOPAT[1]	100	105	110	116	122
Investment	(25)	(26)	(28)	(29)	(31)
Cash flow	75	79	82	87	91

Volume Inc.	Year 1	Year 2	Year 3	Year 4	Year 5
NOPAT[1]	100	105	110	116	122
Investment	(50)	(53)	(55)	(58)	(61)
Cash flow	50	52	55	58	61

[1] Net operating profit after taxes.

Inc., which invests 50 percent of its profits. Value Inc.'s lower investment rate results in 50 percent higher cash flows each year than those of Volume Inc., while generating the same level of profits.

We can value the two companies by discounting their future free cash flows to reflect what investors expect to earn from investing in the companies—that is, their cost of capital. For both companies, we assumed their growth and investment rates were perpetual, and we discounted each year's cash flow to the present at a 10 percent cost of capital. So, for example, Value Inc.'s year 1 cash flow of $75 million has a present value of $68 million today (see Exhibit 3.3). We summed each year's results to derive a total present value of all future cash flows: $1,500 million for Value Inc. and $1,000 million for Volume Inc.

The companies' values can also be expressed as price-to-earnings ratios (P/Es). Divide each company's value by its first-year earnings of $100 million. Value Inc.'s P/E is 15, while Volume Inc.'s is only 10. Despite identical earnings and growth rates, the companies have different earnings multiples because their cash flows are so different. Value Inc. generates higher cash flows because it doesn't have to invest as much as Volume Inc. does.

EXHIBIT 3.3 **Value Inc.: DCF Valuation**

$ million

	Year 1	Year 2	Year 3	Year 4	Year 5	Year X	Sum
			Value Inc.				
NOPAT[1]	100	105	110	116	122	...	
Investment	(25)	(26)	(28)	(29)	(31)	...	
Cash flow	75	79	82	87	91	...	
Value today	68	65	62	59	56	...	1,500

Present value of 75 discounted at 10% for 1 year

Present value of 87 discounted at 10% for 4 years

[1] Net operating profit after taxes.

Differences in ROIC—defined here as the incremental NOPAT earned each year relative to the prior year's investment—are what drive differences in investment rates. In this case, Value Inc. invested $25 million in year 1 to increase its profits by $5 million in year 2. Its return on new capital is 20 percent ($5 million of additional profits divided by $25 million of investment).[4] In contrast, Volume Inc.'s return on invested capital is 10 percent ($5 million in additional profits in year 2 divided by an investment of $50 million).

Growth, ROIC, and cash flow (as represented by the investment rate) are tied together mathematically in the following relationship:

$$\text{Growth} = \text{ROIC} \times \text{Investment Rate}$$

Applying the formula to Value Inc.:

$$5\% = 20\% \times 25\%$$

Applying it to Volume Inc.:

$$5\% = 10\% \times 50\%$$

As you can see, Volume Inc. needs a higher investment rate to achieve the same growth.

Another way to look at this comparison is in terms of cash flow:

$$\text{Cash Flow} = \text{Earnings} \times (1 - \text{Investment Rate})$$

In this equation, the investment rate is equal to growth divided by ROIC:

$$\text{Cash Flow} = \text{Earnings} \times \left(1 - \frac{\text{Growth}}{\text{ROIC}}\right)$$

For Value Inc.:

$$\$75 = \$100 \times (1 - 5\%/20\%)$$
$$= \$100 \times (1 - 25\%)$$

For Volume Inc.:

$$\$50 = \$100 \times (1 - 5\%/10\%)$$
$$= \$100 \times (1 - 50\%)$$

Since the three variables are tied together mathematically, you can describe a company's performance with any two variables. We generally describe a company's performance in terms of growth and ROIC because, as mentioned earlier, you can analyze growth and ROIC across time and against peers.

---

[4] We assumed that all the increase in profits is due to the new investment, with the return on Value Inc.'s existing capital remaining unchanged.

EXHIBIT 3.4 **Translating Growth and ROIC into Cash Flow Available for Distribution**

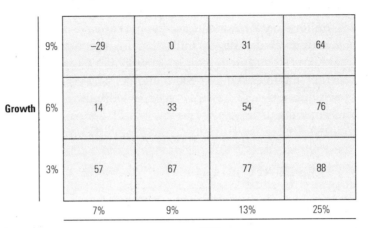

% of NOPAT

Growth		7%	9%	13%	25%
	9%	−29	0	31	64
	6%	14	33	54	76
	3%	57	67	77	88

ROIC

Exhibit 3.4 shows how different combinations of growth and ROIC generate different levels of cash flow that can be paid out to investors. The numbers in the boxes represent cash flow as a percentage of NOPAT, which represents the profits available for distribution to investors. You can see that as growth slows at any level of ROIC, the cash generated per dollar of NOPAT increases. That explains why even maturing companies with slow growth (and moderate ROIC) can pay out large amounts of their earnings to investors. Mature companies, even in tech and pharmaceuticals, are routinely criticized for paying out large amounts of cash to shareholders. But because they generate much more cash flow than they can reinvest at attractive returns on capital, they don't really have a choice.

Near-term cash flow by itself may not be a meaningful performance indicator. Consider what would happen if Value Inc. were to find more investment opportunities at a 25 percent ROIC and were thus able to increase its growth to 8 percent per year. Exhibit 3.5 shows the projected NOPAT and cash flow in such a scenario. Because it would be growing faster, Value Inc. would need to invest more of its earnings each year, so its cash flow at 8 percent growth would be lower than at 5 percent growth until year 9. However, its value, which at 5 percent growth would be $1.5 billion, would double at 8 percent growth to $3 billion because its cash flows would be higher in the long term.

If you simplify some assumptions—for example, that a company grows at a constant rate and maintains a constant ROIC—you can reduce the discounted cash flow to a simple formula. We call this the value driver formula. Here, NOPAT represents the net operating profit after taxes, g is the growth rate of the company, and WACC is the cost of capital.

EXHIBIT 3.5 **Value Inc.: Lower Initial Cash Flow at Higher Growth Rate**

$ million

5% growth

	Year 1	Year 2	Year 3	Year 4	Year 5	Year 6	Year 7	Year 8	Year 9	Year 10	Year 11	Year 12
NOPAT	100	105	110	116	122	128	138	141	148	155	163	171
Net investment	(25)	(26)	(28)	(29)	(30)	(32)	(34)	(35)	(37)	(39)	(41)	(43)
Cash flow	75	79	83	87	91	96	101	106	111	116	122	128

8% growth

	Year 1	Year 2	Year 3	Year 4	Year 5	Year 6	Year 7	Year 8	Year 9	Year 10	Year 11	Year 12
NOPAT	100	108	117	126	136	147	159	171	185	200	216	233
Net investment	(40)	(43)	(47)	(50)	(54)	(59)	(63)	(69)	(74)	(80)	(86)	(93)
Cash flow	60	65	70	76	82	88	95	103	111	120	130	140

Higher growth rate initially generates less cash flow

$$\text{Value} = \frac{\text{NOPAT}_{t=1}\left(1 - \frac{g}{\text{ROIC}}\right)}{\text{WACC} - g}$$

Using this equation, you can see that value is driven by growth, ROIC, and the cost of capital, just as we described in the example. In practice, we rarely use this formula by itself, because of its assumption that growth and ROIC will remain constant indefinitely. Still, we find it useful as a reminder of the elements that drive value. Note that improving ROIC, for any level of growth, always increases value because it reduces the investment required for growth. The impact of growth, however, is ambiguous, as it appears in both the numerator and the denominator. In the next section, we'll show that faster growth increases value only when a company's ROIC is greater than its cost of capital. At the end of this chapter, we'll also show how this equation is derived.

BALANCING ROIC AND GROWTH TO CREATE VALUE

It is possible to create a matrix that shows how different combinations of growth and ROIC translate into value (Exhibit 3.6). Each cell in the matrix represents the present value of future cash flows under each of the assumptions of growth and ROIC, discounted at the company's cost of capital. This case assumes a 9 percent cost of capital and a company that earns $100 in the first year.[5]

[5] We made explicit cash flow forecasts for the first 15 years and assumed that growth after that point converges on 4.5 percent in all scenarios. If a company grew faster than the economy forever, it would eventually overtake the entire world economy.

EXHIBIT 3.6 **Translating Growth and ROIC into Value**

Value,[1] $

Growth				
9%	400	1,100	1,900	2,700
6%	600	1,100	1,600	2,100
3%	800	1,100	1,400	1,600
	7%	9%	13%	25%

ROIC

[1] Present value of future cash flows, assuming year 1 earnings of $100 and a 9% cost of capital. After 15 years, all scenarios grow at 4.5%.

Observe that for any level of growth, value increases with improvements in ROIC. In other words, when all else is equal, a higher ROIC is always good, because it means that the company doesn't have to invest as much to achieve a given level of growth. The same can't be said of growth. When ROIC is high, faster growth increases value. But when ROIC is lower than the company's cost of capital, faster growth destroys value. When return on capital is lower than the cost of capital, growing faster means investing more at a value-destroying return. Where ROIC equals the cost of capital, we can draw the dividing line between creating and destroying value through growth. On that line, value is neither created nor destroyed, regardless of how fast the company grows. It's as if management were on a treadmill. They're working hard, but after their workout, they are right where they started.

From the exhibit, you can also see that a company with high ROIC and low growth may have a similar or higher valuation than a company with higher growth but lower ROIC. It is easiest to show this with companies with different business models and economics. For example, at the end of 2022, Skechers (the athletic shoe company) and Ralph Lauren (the fashion company) were both valued with the same ratio of enterprise value to pretax operating profits (EBITA): 10 times. Yet Skechers had grown at 12 percent over the prior five years, while Ralph Lauren had grown at about 1 percent per year. Ralph Lauren made up for its lower growth with a higher ROIC of 23 percent in 2022, versus 12 percent for Skechers.

We sometimes hear the argument that even low-ROIC companies should strive for growth. The logic is that if a company grows, its ROIC will naturally increase. However, we find this is true only for young, start-up businesses.

Most often in mature companies, a low ROIC indicates a flawed business model or unattractive industry structure. Don't fall for the trap that growth will lead to scale economies that automatically increase a company's return on capital. It almost never happens for mature businesses.

SOME EXAMPLES

The logic laid out in this section reflects the way companies perform in the stock market. Recall the earlier explanation of why shareholder returns for Skechers and Brown-Forman were the same even though earnings for Skechers grew much faster. Another example of the relative impact of growth and ROIC on value is Rockwell Automation, which provides integrated systems to monitor and control automation in factories. Rockwell's total shareholder returns (TSR) from 1995 to 2021 were 15 percent per year, placing it in the top quartile of industrial companies. During this period, Rockwell's revenues actually shrank from $13 billion in 1995 to $7 billion in 2021 as it divested its aviation and power systems divisions. The major factor behind its high TSR was its success in increasing ROIC (including goodwill), from about 12 percent in the mid-1990s to about 21 percent in 2021. While this was partially accomplished by divesting lower-margin ancillary businesses, the majority of the improvement came from operational improvement in industrial automation. The company publicly reiterated its focus on cost and capital productivity many times during the period.

Clearly, the core valuation principle applies at the company level. We have found that it applies at the sector level, too. Consider the consumer packaged-goods sector, for example. Even though well-known names in the sector such as Procter & Gamble and Colgate-Palmolive are modest-growth companies, the market values them at average or higher earnings multiples because of their high returns on invested capital.

In aggregate, large packaged-goods companies increased their revenues 1 percent a year from 2014 to 2019, slower than the aggregate growth of 3 percent for all Standard & Poor's (S&P) 500 companies, excluding financial institutions. Yet at the end of 2019, the aggregate P/E of consumer packaged-goods companies was about 19, slightly higher than the aggregate for the S&P 500. The valuations of companies in this sector rested on their high ROICs—in aggregate above 40 percent, compared with an aggregate ROIC of 20 percent for the S&P 500 in 2019.[6]

To test whether the core valuation principle also applies at the level of countries and the aggregate economy, we compared large companies based in Europe and the United States. In 2022, the aggregate trailing P/E ratio for large U.S. companies was 24 times, versus 15 for large European companies.

---

[6] We stopped this analysis in 2019 because COVID-19 caused a temporary jump in the performance of consumer packaged-goods companies. An analysis at the end of 2023 using forward growth estimates (rather than historical) shows similar results.

The difference in valuation relative to invested capital is even more extreme. The median enterprise value to invested capital for U.S. companies was 4.2, versus 2.4 for European companies. Some executives assume the reason is that investors are simply willing to pay higher prices for shares of U.S. companies (an assumption that has prompted some non-U.S. companies to consider moving their share listings to the New York Stock Exchange in an attempt to increase their value). But the real reason U.S. companies trade at higher multiples is that they typically earn higher returns on invested capital. Large U.S. companies earned a 21 percent ROIC (before goodwill and intangibles) in 2020–22, while the large European companies earned 16 percent.

A large part of this difference can be explained by the different mix of industries in each place; the United States, for example, has many more high-ROIC pharmaceutical, medical-device, and technology companies than Europe does. These broad comparisons also hide the fact that some European companies—for example, Robert Bosch in auto parts and LVMH in luxury goods—outperform many of their U.S. counterparts.

More evidence showing that ROIC and growth drive value appears in Chapter 7.

IMPLICATIONS FOR MANAGERS

We'll dive deeper into the managerial dimensions of ROIC and growth in Chapters 8 and 9, respectively. For now, we outline several lessons managers should learn for strategic decision making.

Start by referring back to Exhibit 3.6, because it contains the most important strategic insights for managers concerning the relative impact that changes in ROIC and growth can have on a company's value. In general, companies already earning a high ROIC can generate more additional value by increasing their rate of growth, rather than their ROIC. For their part, low-ROIC companies will generate relatively more value by focusing on increasing their ROIC.

For example, Exhibit 3.7 shows that a typical high-ROIC company, such as a branded consumer packaged-goods company, can increase its value by 10 percent if it increases its growth rate by one percentage point, while a

EXHIBIT 3.7 **Increasing Value: Impact of Higher Growth and ROIC**

Change in value, %

	High-ROIC company Typical packaged-goods company	Moderate-ROIC company Typical retailer
1 percentage point higher growth	10%	5%
1 percentage point higher ROIC	6%	15%

typical moderate-ROIC company, such as the average retailer, will increase its value by only 5 percent for the same increase in growth. In contrast, the moderate-ROIC company gets a 15 percent bump in value from increasing its return on invested capital by one percentage point, while the high-ROIC company gets only a 6 percent bump from the same increase in return on invested capital.

The general lesson is that high-ROIC companies should focus on growth, while low-ROIC companies should focus on improving returns before growing. Of course, this analysis assumes that achieving a one-percentage-point increase in growth is as easy as achieving a one-percentage-point increase in ROIC, everything else being constant. In reality, achieving either type of increase poses different degrees of difficulty for different companies in different industries, and the impact of a change in growth and ROIC will also vary between companies. However, every company needs to conduct the analysis to set its strategic priorities.

Until now, we have assumed that all growth earns the same ROIC and therefore generates the same value, but this is clearly unrealistic: different types of growth earn different returns on capital, so not all growth is equally value-creating. Each company must understand which types of growth are best positioned to create value given its industry and company type.

Exhibit 3.8 shows the value created from different types of growth for a typical consumer packaged-goods company.[7] These results are based on cases with which we are familiar, not on a comprehensive analysis. Still, we believe they reflect the broader reality.[8] The results are expressed in terms of value created for $1.00 of incremental revenue. For example, $1.00 of additional revenue from a new product creates $1.75 to $2.00 of value. The most important implication of this chart is the rank order. New products typically create more

EXHIBIT 3.8 **Value Creation by Type of Growth**

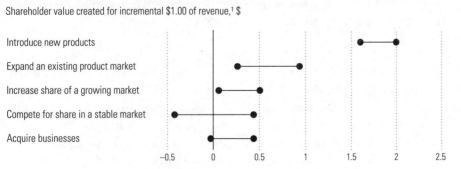

Shareholder value created for incremental $1.00 of revenue,[1] $

Introduce new products	
Expand an existing product market	
Increase share of a growing market	
Compete for share in a stable market	
Acquire businesses	

−0.5   0   0.5   1   1.5   2   2.5

[1] Value for a typical consumer packaged-goods company.

[7] This exhibit will look different for different industries.
[8] We identified examples for each type of growth and estimated their impact on value creation. For instance, we obtained several examples of the margins and capital requirements for new products.

value for shareholders, while acquisitions typically create the least. The key to the difference between these extremes is differences in returns on capital for the different types of growth.

In many industries, growth strategies based on the organic development of new products tend to have the highest returns because they don't require much new capital; companies can add new products to their existing factory lines and distribution systems. Furthermore, the investments to produce new products are not all required at once. If preliminary results are not promising, future investments can be scaled back or canceled.

Acquisitions, by contrast, require that the entire investment be made up front. The amount of the up-front payment reflects the expected cash flows from the target plus a premium to stave off other bidders. So even if the buyer can improve the target's performance enough to generate an attractive ROIC, the rate of return is typically only a small amount higher than its cost of capital.

To be fair, this analysis doesn't reflect the risk of failure. Most product ideas fail before reaching the market, and the cost of failed ideas is not reflected in the numbers. By contrast, acquisitions typically bring existing revenues and cash flows that limit the downside risk to the acquirer. But including the risk of failure would not change the basic fact that new products tend to create more value than acquisitions.

The interaction between growth and ROIC is a key factor to consider when assessing the likely impact of a particular investment on a company's overall ROIC. For example, we've found that some very successful high-ROIC companies in the United States are reluctant to invest in growth if it will reduce their returns on capital. One technology company had a 30 percent operating margin and ROIC of more than 50 percent, so it didn't want to invest in projects that might earn only 25 percent returns, fearing this would dilute its average returns. But as the first principle of value creation would lead you to expect, even an opportunity with a 25 percent return would still create value as long as the cost of capital was lower, despite the resulting decline in average ROIC.

The evidence backs this up. We examined the performance of large companies with high ROIC (greater than 20 percent) over three time periods: 1996–2005, 2010–2017, and 2015–2019.[9] Not surprisingly, the companies that created the most value, measured by total shareholder returns, were those that grew fastest and maintained their high ROICs (see the first column in Exhibit 3.9). But the second-highest value creators within this group were those that grew fastest even though they experienced moderate declines in their ROICs. They created more value than companies that increased their ROICs but grew slowly.

We've also seen companies with low returns pursue growth on the assumption that this will also improve their profit margins and returns, reasoning that growth will increase ROIC by spreading fixed costs across more revenues.

---

[9] B. Jiang and T. Koller, "How to Choose between Growth and ROIC," *McKinsey on Finance*, no. 25 (Autumn 2007): 19–22. Updated to include 2010–2017 and 2015–2019 data by the authors of this book.

EXHIBIT 3.9 **Impact of Growth and ROIC on High- and Low-ROIC Companies**

Median annualized TSR vs. S&P 500, 2015–2019,[1] %

Drivers of performance		Performance, by high vs. low ROIC	
Growth	**Change in ROIC[2]**	**Companies with ROIC over 20%**	**Companies with ROIC of 6%–9%**
Above average	Increased	15	5
Above average	Decreased	5	−11
Below average	Increased	4	2
Below average	Decreased	−6	−11

[1] US nonfinancial companies above $2 billion market cap at any point in 1995–2022. Analysis is updated until 2019 to remove COVID-19 impact.

[2] Significant change in ROIC defined as change of + or − 1.5 percentage points (i.e., a company has increased ROIC if change >1.5% or decreased ROIC if change <−1.5%).

Source: McKinsey Value Intelligence.

As mentioned earlier in this chapter, however, except at small start-up companies, faster growth rarely fixes a company's ROIC problem. Low returns usually indicate a poor industry structure (as is the case with airlines in Europe and Asia),[10] a flawed business model, or weak execution. If a company has a problem with ROIC, the company shouldn't grow until the problem is fixed.

The evidence backs this up as well. We examined the performance of large low-ROIC companies (the right column in Exhibit 3.9). The companies that had low growth but increased their ROICs outperformed the faster-growing companies that did not improve their ROICs.

One final factor for management to consider is the method by which it chooses to improve ROIC. A company can increase ROIC by either improving profit margins or improving capital productivity. With respect to future growth, it doesn't matter which of these paths a company chooses to prioritize. But for current operations, at moderate ROIC levels, a one-percentage-point increase in ROIC through margin improvement will have a moderately higher impact on value relative to improving capital productivity. At high levels of ROIC, the effect is amplified: improving ROIC by increasing margins will create much more value than an equivalent ROIC increase by improving capital productivity. Exhibit 3.10 shows how this works for a company that has a 9 percent cost of capital.

---

[10] Airlines have traditionally suffered from overcapacity and lack of differentiation, leading to price competition and low returns. Recently, U.S. airlines, after a wave of consolidation, have been disciplined about adding capacity and creating ways to charge for services, such as checking bags, with the result that returns on capital are higher than in the past.

EXHIBIT 3.10 **Impact on Value of Improving Margin vs. Capital Productivity**

| | Increase in value from improving ROIC by 1 percentage point[1] % change | | |
ROIC, %	Through margin improvement	Through capital productivity	Ratio of margin impact to capital productivity impact
10	20.0	16.4	1.2x
20	6.7	2.9	2.3x
30	4.0	1.2	3.4x
40	2.9	0.6	4.6x

[1] For a company with a 9% cost of capital.

The reason for this relationship is best explained by an example. Consider a company with zero growth, $1,000 of revenues, $100 of profits, and $500 of invested capital (translating to a 10 percent margin, a 50 percent ratio of invested capital to revenues, and ROIC of 20 percent). One way to increase ROIC by one percentage point is to increase the profit margin to 10.5 percent, increasing profits by $5. Since the company is not growing, the $5 of extra profits translates to $5 of cash flow each year going forward. Discounting at a 10 percent cost of capital, this represents a $50 increase in value. The company could also increase ROIC by reducing working capital. If it reduced working capital by $24, ROIC would increase to 21 percent ($100 divided by $476). The company's value would increase only by the $24 one-time cash inflow from reducing working capital. Future cash flows would not be affected.

ECONOMIC PROFIT COMBINES ROIC AND SIZE

You can also measure a company's value creation using economic profit, a measure that combines ROIC and size into a currency metric (here we use the U.S. dollar). Economic profit measures the value created by a company in a single period and is defined as follows:

$$\text{Economic Profit} = \text{Invested Capital} \times (\text{ROIC} - \text{Cost of Capital})$$

In other words, economic profit is the spread between the return on invested capital and the cost of capital times the amount of invested capital. Value Inc.'s economic profit for year 1 is $50 (Value Inc. must have $500 of starting capital if it earns $100 at a 20 percent return in year 1):

$$\begin{aligned} \text{Economic Profit} &= \$500 \times (20\% - 10\%) \\ &= \$500 \times 10\% \\ &= \$50 \end{aligned}$$

Volume Inc.'s economic profit in year 1 is zero (Volume Inc. must have $1,000 of starting capital if it earns $100 at a 10 percent return in year 1):

$$\text{Economic Profit} = \$1,000 \times (10\% - 10\%)$$
$$= \$1,000 \times 0\%$$
$$= \$0$$

You can also value a company by discounting its projected economic profit at the cost of capital and adding the starting invested capital. Value Inc. starts with $500 of invested capital. Its economic profit in year 1 is $50, which grows at 5 percent. Discounting the growing economic profit at a 10 percent discount rate gives a present value of economic profit of $1,000.[11] Use these amounts to solve for value:

$$\text{Value} = \text{Starting Invested Capital} + \text{PV(Projected Economic Profit)}$$
$$= \$500 + \$1,000$$
$$= \$1,500$$

The value of Value Inc. using the economic-profit approach is $1,500, exactly the same as with the discounted-cash-flow (DCF) approach.

Economic profit is also useful for comparing the value creation of different companies or business units. Consider Value Inc.'s economic profit of $50. Suppose Big Inc. had $5,000 in invested capital but earned only a 15 percent return on capital (and assume it doesn't have investment opportunities with higher returns on capital). Its economic profit would be $250. Clearly, creating $250 of economic profit is preferable to creating $50.

Finally, measuring performance in terms of economic profit encourages a company to undertake investments that earn more than their cost of capital, even if their return is lower than the current average return. Suppose Value Inc. had the opportunity to invest an extra $200 at a 15 percent return. Its average ROIC would decline from 20 percent to 18.6 percent, but its economic profit would increase from $50 to $60.

CONSERVATION OF VALUE

A corollary of the principle that DCF drives value is the conservation of value: anything that doesn't increase cash flows doesn't create value. That means value is conserved, or unchanged, when a company changes the ownership

[11] The present value of economic profit for a growing perpetuity is economic profit in year 1 divided by the cost of capital minus the growth rate. For Value Inc., the present value of economic profit is therefore $50/(10% – 5%).

of claims to its cash flows but doesn't change the total available cash flows—for example, when it substitutes debt for equity or issues debt to repurchase shares. Similarly, changing the appearance of the cash flows without actually changing the cash flows—say, by changing accounting techniques—doesn't change the value of a company.[12] While this principle may seem obvious, it is worth emphasizing because executives, investors, and pundits so often forget it, as when they hope that one accounting treatment will lead to a higher value than another or that some fancy financial structure will turn a mediocre deal into a winner.

The battle over how companies should account for executive stock options illustrates the extent to which executives continue to believe (erroneously) that the stock market is unaware of the conservation of value. Even though there is no cash effect when executive stock options are issued, they reduce the cash flow available to existing shareholders by diluting their ownership when the options are exercised. Under accounting rules dating back to the 1970s, companies could exclude the implicit cost of executive stock options from their income statements. In the early 1990s, as options became more material, the Financial Accounting Standards Board (FASB) proposed a change to the accounting rules, requiring companies to record an expense for the value of options when they are issued. A large group of executives and venture capitalists thought investors would be spooked if options were brought onto the income statement. Some claimed that the entire venture capital industry would be decimated because young start-up companies that provide much of their compensation through options would show low or negative profits.

The FASB issued its new rules in 2004,[13] more than a decade after taking up the issue and only after the bursting of the dot-com bubble. Despite dire predictions, the stock prices of companies didn't change when the new accounting rules were implemented, because the market already reflected the cost of the options in its valuations of companies.[14] One respected analyst told us, "I don't care whether they are recorded as an expense or simply disclosed in the footnotes. I know what to do with the information."

But executives needn't have worried that the changes in stock option accounting would negatively affect their share price—and the conservation of value principle explains why. It can also shed light on several other important and related questions. For instance, does an acquisition create value simply

---

[12] In some cases, a company can increase its value by reducing its cost of capital by using more debt in its capital structure. However, even in this case, the underlying driver is the reduction of taxes, but the overall pretax cost of capital doesn't change. See Chapter 35 for further discussion.

[13] Financial Accounting Standard 123R, released in December 2004, effective for periods beginning after June 15, 2005.

[14] D. Aboody, M. Barth, and R. Kasznik, "Firms' Voluntary Recognition of Stock-Based Compensation Expense," *Journal of Accounting Research* 42, no. 2 (December 2004): 123–150; D. Aboody, M. Barth, and R. Kasznik, "SFAS No. 123 Stock-Based Compensation Expense and Equity Market Values," *Accounting Review* 79, no. 2 (2004): 251–275; M. Semerdzhian, "The Effects of Expensing Stock Options and a New Approach to the Valuation Problem" (working paper, SSRN, May 2004).

because reported earnings increase? Should a company return cash to share-holders through share repurchases instead of dividends? Does financial engineering really create value? In each case, executives should focus on increasing cash flows rather than finding gimmicks that merely redistribute value among investors or make reported results look better. Executives should also be wary of financial engineering proposals that claim to create value unless they're clear about how their actions will materially increase the size of the pie. If you can't pinpoint the tangible source of value creation, you're probably looking at an illusion, and you can be sure that's what the market will think, too.

Conserving Value: A Brief History

The value conservation principle is described in the seminal textbook *Principles of Corporate Finance*, by Richard Brealey, Stewart Myers, and Franklin Allen.[15] One of the earliest applications of the principle can be found in the pioneering work of Nobel Prize winners Franco Modigliani and Merton Miller, financial economists who in the late 1950s and early 1960s questioned whether managers could use changes in capital structure to increase share prices. In 1958, they showed that the value of a company shouldn't be affected by changing the structure of the debt and equity ownership unless the overall cash flows generated by the company also change.[16]

Imagine a company that has no debt and generates $100 of cash flow each year before paying shareholders. Suppose the company is valued at $1,000. Now suppose the company borrows $200 and pays it out to the shareholders. Our knowledge of the core valuation principle and the value conservation principle tells us that the company would still be worth $1,000, with $200 for the creditors and $800 for the shareholders, because its cash flow available to pay the shareholders and creditors is still $100.

In most countries, however, borrowing money does change cash flows because interest payments are tax deductible. The total taxes paid by the company are lower, thereby increasing the cash flow available to pay both shareholders and creditors. In addition, having debt may induce managers to be more diligent (because they must have cash available to repay the debt on time) and, therefore, increase the company's cash flow. On the downside, having debt could make it more difficult for managers to raise capital for attractive investment opportunities, thereby reducing cash flow. The point is that substituting debt for equity isn't consequential in and of itself; it matters only if the substitution changes the company's cash flows through tax reductions or if doing so prompts management to make different decisions that change cash flows.

[15] R. Brealey, S. Myers, and F. Allen, *Principles of Corporate Finance*, 12th ed. (New York: McGraw-Hill/Irwin, 2017).
[16] F. Modigliani and M. H. Miller, "The Cost of Capital, Corporation Finance and the Theory of Investment," *American Economic Review* 48, no. 3 (1958): 261–297.

In a similar vein, finance academics in the 1960s developed the idea of efficient markets. While the meaning and validity of market efficiency are subjects of continuing debate, especially after the bursting of the dot-com and real estate bubbles, one implication of efficient-market theory remains: the stock market isn't easily fooled when companies undertake actions to increase reported accounting profit without increasing cash flows. One example is the market's reaction to changes in accounting for employee stock options, as described in the previous section of this chapter. And when the FASB eliminated goodwill amortization effective in 2002 and the International Accounting Standards Board (IASB) did the same in 2005, many companies reported increased profits, but their underlying values and stock prices didn't change, because the accounting change didn't affect cash flows. The evidence is overwhelming that the market isn't fooled by actions that don't affect cash flow, as we will show in Chapter 7.

A Tool for Managers

The conservation of value principle is extremely useful because it tells us what to look for when analyzing whether an action will create value: the cash flow impact and nothing else. This principle applies across a wide range of important business decisions, such as accounting policy, acquisitions (Chapter 31), corporate portfolio decisions (Chapter 28), dividend payout policy (Chapter 35), and capital structure (also Chapter 35).

This section provides three examples where applying the conservation of value principle can be useful: share repurchases, acquisitions, and financial engineering.

Share Repurchases   Share repurchases have become a popular way for companies to return cash to investors (see Chapter 35 for more detail). Until the early 1980s, more than 90 percent of the total distributions by large U.S. companies to shareholders were dividends, and less than 10 percent were share repurchases. But since 1998, about 50 percent of total distributions have been share repurchases.[17]

While buying back shares is often a good thing for management to do, a common fallacy is that share repurchases create value simply because they increase earnings per share (EPS).[18] For example, assume that a company with $700 of earnings and 1,000 shares outstanding borrows $1,000 to repurchase 10 percent of its shares. For every $1,000 of shares repurchased, the company will pay, say, 5 percent interest on its new debt. After tax savings of 25 percent, its total earnings would decline by $37.50, or 5.4 percent. However, the number of

---

[17] T. Koller, "Are Share Buybacks Jeopardizing Future Growth?," *McKinsey on Finance*, no. 56 (October 2015), www.mckinsey.com.

[18] O. Ezekoye, T. Koller, and A. Mittal, "How Share Repurchases Boost Earnings without Improving Returns," *McKinsey on Finance*, no. 58 (April 2016), www.mckinsey.com.

shares has declined by 10 percent, so earnings per share (EPS) would increase by about 5 percent.

A 5 percent increase in EPS without working very hard sounds like a great deal. Assuming the company's P/E ratio doesn't change, its market value per share also will increase by 5 percent. In other words, you can get something for nothing: higher EPS with a constant P/E.

Unfortunately, this doesn't square with the conservation of value, because the total cash flow of the business has not increased. While EPS has increased by 5 percent, the company's debt has increased as well. With higher leverage, the company's equity cash flows will be more volatile, and investors will demand a higher return. This will bring down the company's P/E, offsetting the increase in EPS.

Moreover, you must consider where the company could have invested the cash rather than returning it to shareholders. If the return on capital from the investment exceeded the company's cost of capital, it's likely that the longer-term EPS would be higher from the investment than from the share repurchases. Share repurchases increase EPS immediately but with the consequence of possibly lowering long-term earnings.[19]

However, even if cash flow isn't increased by a buyback, some have rightly argued that repurchasing shares can reduce the likelihood that management will invest the cash at low returns. If this is true and it is likely that management would otherwise have invested the money unwisely, then you have a legitimate source of value creation, because the operating cash flows of the company would increase. Said another way, when the likelihood of investing cash at low returns is high, share repurchases make sense as a tactic for avoiding value destruction. But they don't create value on their own.

Some argue that management should repurchase shares when the company's shares are undervalued. Suppose management believes that the current share price of the company doesn't reflect its underlying potential, so it buys back shares today. One year later, the market price adjusts to reflect management's expectations. Has value been created? Once again, the answer is no, value has not been created; it has only been shifted from one set of shareholders (those who sold) to the shareholders who did not sell. So while the holding shareholders may have benefited, the shareholders as a whole were not affected. Buying back shares when they are undervalued may be good for the shareholders who don't sell, but studies of share repurchases have shown that companies aren't very good at timing share repurchases, often buying when their share prices are high, not low.[20]

---

[19] Ibid.

[20] B. Jiang and T. Koller, "The Savvy Executive's Guide to Buying Back Shares," *McKinsey on Finance*, no. 41 (Autumn 2011): 14–17. The results here are counter to academic studies that were based on earlier samples and included many small companies. Our study included only companies in the S&P 500. When share buybacks were rare, announcements were made with great fanfare and often provided strong signals of management's concern for capital discipline. Most of the fanfare has faded because companies now regularly repurchase shares, so announcements aren't a surprise to the market anymore.

As a rule, executives need to exercise caution when presented with transactions such as share repurchases that appear to create value by boosting EPS. Always ask, "Where is the source of the value creation?" Some research and development (R&D)–intensive companies, for example, have searched for ways to capitalize R&D spending through complex joint ventures, hoping to lower expenses that reduce EPS. But does the joint venture create value by increasing short-term EPS? No, and in fact it may destroy value because the company now transfers upside potential—and risk, of course—to its partners.

Acquisitions   Chapter 31 covers acquisitions in more detail, but for now, we can say that acquisitions create value only when the combined cash flows of the two companies increase due to cost reductions, accelerated revenue growth, or better use of fixed and working capital.

To give you a sense of how a good transaction might work, we'll use the example of United Rentals' purchase of RSC (another equipment rental company) for $1.9 billion in 2011. Within several years, they had achieved more than $250 million of annual cost savings. We conservatively estimated that the cost savings were worth over $1.5 billion in present value. That's equivalent to about 80 percent of the purchase price.

For an example of a transaction that accelerated revenue, consider the automotive company BMW, which acquired the Mini brand through its acquisition of the Rover Group in 1994. BMW revived the brand by modernizing the product, marketing it, and adding variations to the core model (e.g., the Mini Clubman). All in all, BMW increased the sales of Mini cars from 20,000 in 1995 to 295,000 in 2023.

The common element of both acquisitions was radical performance improvement, not marginal change. But sometimes we have seen acquisitions justified by what could only be called magic.

Assume, for example, that Company A is worth $100 and Company B is worth $50, based on their respective expected cash flows. Company A buys Company B for $50, issuing its own shares. For simplicity, assume that the combined cash flows are not expected to increase. What is the new Company AB worth?

Immediately after the acquisition, the two companies are the same as they were before, with the same expected cash flows, and the original shareholders of the two companies still own the shares of the combined company. So Company AB should be worth $150, and the original A shareholders' shares of AB should be worth $100, while the original B shareholders' shares of AB should be worth $50.

As simple as this seems, some executives and financial professionals will still see some extra value in the transaction. Assume that Company A is expected to earn $5 next year, so its P/E is 20 times. Company B is expected to earn $3 next year, so its P/E is 16.7 times. What then will be the P/E of Company AB?

A straightforward approach suggests that the value of Company AB should remain $150. Its earnings will be $8, so its P/E will be about 18.8, between A's and B's P/Es. But here's where the magic supposedly happens. Many executives and bankers believe that once A buys B, the stock market will apply A's P/E of 20 to B's earnings. In other words, B's earnings are worth more once they are owned by A. By this thinking, the value of Company AB would be $160, a $10 increase in the combined value.

There are even terms for this: *multiple expansion* in the United States and *rerating* in the United Kingdom. The notion is that the multiple of Company B's earnings expands to the level of Company A's because the market doesn't recognize that perhaps the new earnings added to A are not as valuable. This must be so, because B's earnings will now be all mixed up with A's, and the market won't be able to tell the difference.

Another version of the multiple-expansion illusion works the other way around. Now suppose Company B purchases Company A. We've heard the argument that since a company with a lower P/E is buying a higher-P/E company, it must be getting into higher-growth businesses. Higher growth is generally good, so another theory postulates that because B is accelerating its growth, its P/E will increase.

If multiple expansion were true, all acquisitions would create value because the P/E on the lower-P/E company's earnings would rise to that of the company with the higher P/E, regardless of which was the buyer or seller. But no data exist that support this fallacy. Multiple expansion may sound great, but it is an entirely unsound way of justifying an acquisition that doesn't otherwise have tangible benefits.

Every corporate leader must know this. So why are we discussing such obvious fallacies? The answer is that companies often do justify acquisitions using this flawed logic. Our alternative approach is simple: if you can't point to specific sources of increased cash flow, the stock market won't be fooled.

Financial Engineering   Another area where the value conservation principle is important is financial engineering, which unfortunately has no standard definition. For our purposes, we define financial engineering as the use of financial instruments or structures other than straight debt and equity to manage a company's capital structure and risk profile.

Financial engineering can include the use of derivatives, structured debt, securitization, and off-balance-sheet financing. While some of these activities can create real value, most don't. Even so, the motivation to engage in non-value-added financial engineering remains strong because of its short-term, illusory impact.

Consider that many of the largest hotel companies in the United States don't own most of the hotels they operate. Instead, the hotels themselves are owned by other companies, often structured as partnerships or real estate investment trusts (REITs). Unlike corporations, partnerships and REITs don't pay U.S. income taxes; only their owners do. Therefore, an entire layer of taxation is eliminated by placing hotels in partnerships and REITs in the United States. This method of separating ownership and operations lowers total income taxes paid to the government, so investors in the ownership and operating companies are better off as a group, because their aggregate cash flows are higher. This is an example of financial engineering that adds real value by increasing cash flows.

In contrast, sale-leaseback transactions have rarely created value for investment-grade companies. Sale-leaseback transactions were popular until the FASB and IASB changed the lease accounting rules effective for the 2019 calendar year, stipulating that all leases greater than one year must be capitalized. In their heyday, sale-leaseback transactions would work like this: a company would sell an asset it owned but wanted to continue using, such as an office building, to a buyer who would then lease the asset back to the company. Often, the company was able to structure the lease such that it was treated as a sale for accounting purposes, and then would remove the asset from its balance sheet. It could also use the sale proceeds to pay down debt. Thus, the company could appear to have fewer assets and less debt. Rental expense replaced future depreciation and interest expense (though rental expenses were typically higher than the sum of depreciation and interest expense).

For larger investment-grade companies, the implied interest rate on the lease was often higher than the company's regular borrowing rate because the lessor would use the creditworthiness of the lessee to finance its purchase. In addition, the company buying the asset would have to cover its cost of equity and its operating costs.

In cases when the company intended to use the asset for its remaining life by renewing the lease, the transaction would make the company appear less capital-intensive and to have lower debt, but still would not create any value. In fact, in such a case, the company would have destroyed value because the cost of the lease was higher than the cost of borrowing. The company would also have incurred its own transaction costs and may have had to pay taxes on any gain from the sale of the asset. What's more, other creditors and rating agencies would have been likely to treat the lease as a debt equivalent anyway.

In some situations, it is possible that a sale-leaseback transaction would have created value—if, for instance, the company had wanted the ability to stop using the asset before its remaining life was expected to expire in order to eliminate the risk that the value of the asset would be lower when it decided to stop using the asset.

Sale-leaseback transactions may also have created value in situations when the lessor was better able to use the tax benefits associated with owning the asset, such as accelerated depreciation. This would not have violated the conservation of value principle, because the total cash flows to the companies involved would have increased—at the expense of the government.

THE MATH OF VALUE CREATION

Earlier in this chapter, we introduced the value driver formula, a simple equation that captures the essence of valuation. For readers interested in the technical math of valuation, this section will show how we derive the formula. Let's begin with some terminology that we will use throughout the book (Part Two defines the terms in detail):

- *Net operating profit after taxes (NOPAT)* represents the profits generated from the company's core operations after subtracting the income taxes related to those core operations.
- *Invested capital* represents the cumulative amount the business has invested in its core operations—primarily property, plant, and equipment and working capital.
- *Net investment* is the increase in invested capital from one year to the next:

$$\text{Net Investment} = \text{Invested Capital}_{t+1} - \text{Invested Capital}_t$$

- *Free cash flow (FCF)* is the cash flow generated by the core operations of the business after deducting investments in new capital:

$$\text{FCF} = \text{NOPAT} - \text{Net Investment}$$

- *Return on invested capital (ROIC)* is the return the company earns on each dollar invested in the business:

$$\text{ROIC} = \frac{\text{NOPAT}}{\text{Invested Capital}}$$

ROIC can be defined in two ways: as the return on all capital or as the return on new, or incremental, capital. For now, we assume that both returns are the same.

- *Investment rate (IR)* is the portion of NOPAT invested back into the business:

$$\text{IR} = \frac{\text{Net Investment}}{\text{NOPAT}}$$

- *Weighted average cost of capital (WACC)* is the rate of return that investors expect to earn from investing in the company and therefore the appropriate discount rate for the free cash flow. WACC is defined in detail in Chapter 15.
- *Growth (g)* is the rate at which the company's NOPAT and cash flow grow each year.

Assume that the company's revenues and NOPAT grow at a constant rate and the company invests the same proportion of its NOPAT in its business each year. Investing the same proportion of NOPAT each year also means that the company's free cash flow will grow at a constant rate.

Since the company's cash flows are growing at a constant rate, we can begin by valuing a company using the well-known cash flow perpetuity formula:

$$\text{Value} = \frac{\text{FCF}_{t=1}}{\text{WACC} - g}$$

This formula is well established in the finance and mathematics literature.[21] Next, define free cash flow in terms of NOPAT and the investment rate:

$$\begin{aligned} \text{FCF} &= \text{NOPAT} - \text{Net Investment} \\ &= \text{NOPAT} - (\text{NOPAT} \times \text{IR}) \\ &= \text{NOPAT}(1 - \text{IR}) \end{aligned}$$

Earlier, we developed the relationship between the investment rate (IR), the company's projected growth in NOPAT (g), and the return on investment (ROIC)[22]:

$$g = \text{ROIC} \times \text{IR}$$

Solving for IR, rather than g, leads to:

$$\text{IR} = \frac{g}{\text{ROIC}}$$

Now build this into the definition of free cash flow:

$$\text{FCF} = \text{NOPAT}\left(1 - \frac{g}{\text{ROIC}}\right)$$

Substituting for free cash flow in the cash-flow perpetuity formula gives the key value driver formula[23]:

$$\text{Value} = \frac{\text{NOPAT}_{t=1}\left(1 - \frac{g}{\text{ROIC}}\right)}{\text{WACC} - g}$$

This formula underpins the DCF approach to valuation, and a variant of the equation lies behind the economic-profit approach. Chapter 10 describes in depth these two mathematically equivalent valuation techniques. You might

[21] For the derivation, see T. E. Copeland and J. Fred Weston, *Financial Theory and Corporate Policy*, 3rd ed. (Reading, MA: Addison-Wesley, 1988), Appendix A.
[22] Technically, we should use the return on new, or incremental, capital, but for simplicity, we assume that the ROIC and incremental ROIC are equal.
[23] Technically, this formula should use the return on new invested capital (RONIC), not the company's return on all invested capital (ROIC). For convenience throughout this book, we frequently use ROIC to denote both the return on all capital and the return on new invested capital.

go so far as to say this formula represents all there is to valuation. Everything else is mere detail.

Substituting the forecast assumptions given for Value Inc. and Volume Inc. in Exhibit 3.2 into the key value driver formula results in the same values we came up with when we discounted their cash flows:

Company	NOPAT$_{t=1}$, $	Growth, %	ROIC, %	WACC, %	Value, $
Value Inc.	100	5	20	10	1,500
Volume Inc.	100	5	10	10	1,000

In most cases, we do not use this formula in practice. The reason is that in most situations, the model is overly restrictive, as it assumes a constant ROIC and growth rate going forward. For companies whose key value drivers are expected to change, we need a model that is more flexible in its forecasts. Nevertheless, while we generally do not use this formula in practice, it is extremely useful as a reminder to focus on what drives value.

Until now, we have concentrated on how ROIC and growth drive the DCF valuation. It is also possible to use the key value driver formula to show that ROIC and growth determine the multiples commonly used to analyze company valuation, such as price-to-earnings and market-to-book ratios. To see this, divide both sides of the key value driver formula by NOPAT:

$$\frac{\text{Value}}{\text{NOPAT}_{t=1}} = \frac{\left(1 - \frac{g}{\text{ROIC}}\right)}{\text{WACC} - g}$$

As the formula shows, a company's earnings multiple is driven by both its expected growth and its return on invested capital.

You can also turn the formula into a value-to-invested-capital formula. Start with the identity:

$$\text{NOPAT} = \text{Invested Capital} \times \text{ROIC}$$

Substitute this definition of NOPAT into the key value driver formula:

$$\text{Value} = \frac{\text{Invested Capital} \times \text{ROIC} \times \left(1 - \frac{g}{\text{ROIC}}\right)}{\text{WACC} - g}$$

Divide both sides by invested capital[24]:

$$\frac{\text{Value}}{\text{Invested Capital}} = \text{ROIC}\left(\frac{1 - \frac{g}{\text{ROIC}}}{\text{WACC} - g}\right)$$

[24] If ROIC and incremental ROIC are the same, this equation simplifies to:

$$\frac{\text{Value}}{\text{Invested Capital}} = \frac{(\text{ROIC} - g)}{(\text{WACC} - g)}$$

Now that we have explained the logic behind the DCF approach to valuation, you may wonder why analysts' reports and investment banking pitches so often use earnings multiples, rather than valuations based on DCF analysis. The answer is partly that earnings multiples are a useful shorthand for communicating values to a wider public. A leading sell-side analyst told us that he uses discounted cash flow to analyze and value companies but typically communicates his findings in terms of implied multiples. For example, an analyst might say Company X deserves a higher multiple than Company Y because it is expected to grow faster, earn higher margins, or generate more cash flow. Earnings multiples are also a useful sanity check for your valuation. In practice, we always compare a company's implied multiple based on our valuation with those of its peers to see if we can explain why its multiple is higher or lower in terms of its ROIC or growth rates. See Chapter 18 for a discussion of how to analyze earnings multiples.

SUMMARY

This chapter has explored how expected cash flows, discounted at a cost of capital, drive value. Cash flow, in turn, is driven by expected returns on invested capital and revenue growth. Companies create value only when ROIC exceeds their cost of capital. Moreover, higher-ROIC companies should typically prioritize growth over further improving ROIC, as growth is a more powerful value driver for them. In contrast, lower-ROIC companies should prioritize improving ROIC, as it is a stronger value driver for them.

A corollary of this is the conservation of value: anything that doesn't increase cash flows doesn't create value. So changing the appearance of a company's performance through, say, accounting changes or write-ups or write-downs, without changing cash flows, won't change a company's true value. Risk enters into valuation both through the company's cost of capital and in the uncertainty of future cash flows. Because investors can diversify their portfolios, the only risk that affects the cost of capital is the risk that investors cannot diversify, a topic we take up in Chapters 4 and 15.

4

Risk and the Opportunity
Cost of Capital

In valuing companies or projects, the subjects of risk and the cost of capital are essential, inseparable, and fraught with misconceptions. These misconceptions can lead to damaging strategic mistakes. For example, when a company borrows money to finance an acquisition and applies only the cost of debt to the target's cash flows, it can easily overestimate the target's value by as much as two times. Conversely, when a company adds an arbitrary risk premium to a target's cost of capital in an emerging market, it can underestimate the value of the target by half.

A company's cost of capital is also critical for determining value creation and for evaluating strategic decisions. It is the rate at which you discount future cash flows for a company or project. It is also the rate you compare with the return on invested capital to determine whether the company is creating value. The cost of capital incorporates both the time value of money and the risk of investment in a company, business unit, or project.

In this chapter, we'll explain why the cost of capital is *not* a cash cost, but an opportunity cost. The opportunity cost is based on what investors could earn by investing their money elsewhere at the same level of risk. This is always an option for publicly listed companies.[1] Only certain types of risks—those that cannot be eliminated by holding a well-diversified portfolio—affect a company's cost of capital. Risks that can be eliminated in this way should only be reflected in the cash flow forecast using multiple cash flow scenarios.

---

[1] As a reminder from Chapter 2, the amount of value that companies create is the amount they earn above their cost of capital. That is, companies create value only when they can invest funds at higher returns than their investors can earn themselves.

We'll also discuss how much cash flow risk to take on. Companies should take on all investments that have a positive expected value,[2] regardless of their risk profile, unless the projects are so large that failure would threaten the viability of the entire company. Most executives are reluctant to take on smaller risky projects even if the returns are very high. By aggregating projects into portfolios, rather than assessing them individually, executives can often overcome the well-documented bias of loss aversion.

Our focus in this chapter will be on key principles. Chapter 15 provides detail on how to measure the cost of capital.

COST OF CAPITAL IS AN OPPORTUNITY COST

The cost of capital is not a cash cost. It is an opportunity cost. To illustrate, when one company acquires another company, the alternative might have been to return that cash to shareholders, who could then reinvest it in other companies. So the cost of capital for the acquiring company is the price investors charge for bearing risk—what they could have earned by reinvesting the proceeds in other investments with similar risk.[3] Similarly, when valuing individual business units or projects for strategic decision making, the correct cost of capital is what a company's investors could expect to earn in other similarly risky projects, not necessarily the whole company. The core principle is that the cost of capital is driven by investors' opportunity cost, because the executives leading the company are the investors' agents and have a fiduciary responsibility to the company's investors.[4] That's why the cost of capital is also referred to as the investors' required return or expected return. Some of these terms may be more or less appropriate in different contexts, but for the most part, you can use cost of capital, required return, and expected return interchangeably.

Chapter 15 describes in detail how to estimate a company's opportunity cost of capital. Most practitioners use a weighted average cost of capital (WACC), meaning the weighted average of the cost of equity capital and the

---

[2] This is often referred to as net present value (NPV); we prefer the term *expected value* because it emphasizes the riskiness of underlying cash flows.

[3] To be more precise, the cost of capital is the return investors can earn from investing in a well-diversified, "efficient" portfolio of investments with similar risk.

[4] In some countries, executives also have a duty to the "company," but that concept is typically vaguely defined and does not provide executives with much guidance. For the most part, even in those countries, the opportunity cost for investors is the best calculation to make. In the United States, a recent innovation is the "benefit" corporation, whose charter includes additional objectives that executives can weigh against the interest of shareholders, including positive impact on society, workers, communities, and the environment. The concept is relatively new; not many large, listed companies are benefit corporations, the conversion to which requires a shareholder vote.

cost of debt capital.[5] For now, it's enough to say that a company's cost of equity capital is what investors could earn by investing in a broad portfolio of companies (say, the S&P 500), adjusted for the riskiness of the company relative to the average of all companies.

Within a company, individual business units can have different costs of capital if their risk profiles differ. The company's overall cost of capital is simply a weighted average of its business units' costs of capital. In banking, for example, risky trading operations carry much higher costs of capital than more stable retail banking units.

Executives often fail to adequately incorporate the idea of opportunity cost in thinking about their cost of capital. Sometimes they mix up the opportunity cost of capital by associating different funding streams with different investments. For example, when one company acquires another, the buyer might raise enough debt to pay for the entire company. It is tempting to say that the cost of capital for the acquisition is the cost of the debt. But this would be a fundamental mistake, because the risk of the target's free cash flows does not equal the risk of the bondholders' cash flows.

To illustrate, say Company A is considering buying Company B. Both operate in the same product area with similar risk. Company A has no debt and an opportunity cost of capital of 8 percent. Suppose Company A can borrow at 4 percent after taxes. If Company B is growing at 3 percent with $1 billion in earnings and a 15 percent return on capital, its value would be $80 billion at a 4 percent cost of capital and $20 billion at an 8 percent cost of capital. To get a sense of how absurd it would be to use the 4 percent cost of capital, consider that the implied price-to-earnings ratio (P/E) at 4 percent is 80, compared with 20 at an 8 percent cost of capital. Companies growing at 3 percent don't trade at a P/E of 80.

In addition, if you apply the cost of debt to the acquisition, you end up with a perverse situation: Company A's existing businesses are assigned an 8 percent cost of capital, and the acquired business is assigned a 4 percent cost of capital. In addition, the only reason Company A can borrow 100 percent of the cost of the acquisition is that Company B is benefiting from the unused debt capacity in Company A's other businesses. And don't forget, the cost of capital is determined by the acquired company's riskiness, not that of the parent company (although their risk profiles are likely to be the same if they are in the same industry).

---

[5] The use of WACC is a practical solution. In theory, the opportunity cost of capital is independent of capital structure (a company's amount of debt versus equity) except for the tax benefit of debt. An alternative is to estimate the opportunity cost of capital as the company's cost of equity (what equity investors expect to earn) if it had no debt, adjusted directly for the tax benefit of debt. In theory, the two approaches should yield the same result.

COMPANIES HAVE LITTLE CONTROL OVER THEIR COST OF CAPITAL

It might be surprising to learn that the cost of capital for a company with steady revenues, such as Procter & Gamble, isn't that different from a company such as LyondellBasell, a commodity chemical company in an industry known for having more variable earnings and cash flows. In 2024, most large companies' WACC fell in the range of 7 to 9 percent. The range is small because investors purposely avoid putting all their eggs in one basket. The ability of investors to diversify their portfolios means that only nondiversifiable risk such as exposure to economic cycles affects the cost of capital. Furthermore, because nondiversifiable risk also generally affects all companies in the same industry in the same way, a company's industry is what primarily drives its cost of capital. Companies in the same industry will have similar costs of capital.

Stock market investors, especially institutional investors, may hold hundreds of different stocks in their portfolios. Even the most concentrated investors have at least 50. As a result, their exposure to any single company is limited. Exhibit 4.1 shows how the total risk of a portfolio of stocks declines as more shares are added to the portfolio. The risk declines because companies' cash flows are not perfectly correlated. Over any period of time, some will increase while others decline.

One of the durable tenets of academic finance concerns the effect of diversification on the cost of capital. If diversification reduces risk to investors and it is not costly to diversify, then investors will not demand a higher return for any risks that can be eliminated through diversification. They require compensation only for risks they cannot diversify away.

Since most of the risks that companies face are, in fact, diversifiable, most risks don't affect a company's cost of capital. One way to see this in practice is to note the relatively narrow range of P/Es for large companies. Most large companies have P/Es between 12 and 20. If the cost of capital varied

EXHIBIT 4.1 **Volatility of Portfolio Return Declines with Diversification**

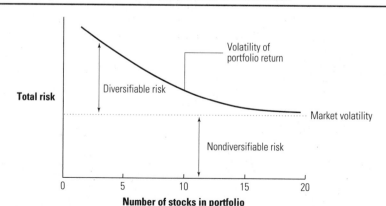

from 5 to 15 percent instead of 7 to 9 percent, many more companies would have P/Es below 8 and above 25.

Whether a company's cost of capital is 7 percent or 9 percent or somewhere in between is a question of great dispute (as we explore in Chapter 15). For decades, the standard model for measuring differences in costs of capital has been the capital asset pricing model (CAPM). The CAPM has been challenged by academics and practitioners, but so far, no practical competing model has emerged.[6] At any rate, when returns on capital across companies vary from less than 5 percent to more than 30 percent (sometimes even within the same sector), a one-percentage-point difference in the cost of capital seems hardly worth arguing about.

The unique risks that any company faces—say, product obsolescence and new competition—are not priced into the cost of capital. That does not mean a company's value is immune to these risks; they do affect expected cash flows and therefore expected value. Companies certainly do need to worry about the effects of such risks, as we discuss later in this chapter.

It is a common misconception that the cost of capital is company-specific, rather than a function of the industries in which a company operates and the specific investments it makes. For the most part, companies have scant influence over the cost of capital of their individual business units or their company as a whole. There are some ways that companies might conceivably reduce their cost of capital by transferring risk to others, but the cost of doing so will typically be larger than the benefits. For example, a company could outsource production to lower fixed costs and therefore reduce the volatility of cash flows. If you can achieve lower volatility than your peers, your cost of capital will be slightly lower. But it's unlikely that the change in the cost of capital will be large enough relative to other strategic considerations of outsourcing manufacturing.

Some companies have shortened the duration of their debt to try to reduce their cost of capital. This thinking is flawed. What these companies fail to recognize is that this actually increases the risk of financial distress because of the possibility that interest rates will be higher when the shorter-term debt is rolled over or that the company may have difficulty refinancing the debt at all.[7]

---

[6] Many in the academic community use the Fama-French three-factor model, but mostly for capital market research rather than business valuation. With this model, a stock's excess returns are regressed on excess market returns (like the CAPM), the excess returns of small stocks minus big stocks (SMB), and the excess returns of high book-to-market stocks minus low book-to-market stocks (HML). In 2015, the authors expanded the model to five factors, adding operating profitability and investment. See E. Fama and K. French, "The Cross-Section of Expected Stock Returns," *Journal of Finance* (June 1992): 427–465; E. Fama and K. French, "Common Risk Factors in the Returns on Stocks and Bonds," *Journal of Financial Economics* 33 (1993): 3–56; and E. Fama and K. French, "A Five-Factor Asset Pricing Model," *Journal of Financial Economics* 116 (2015): 1–22.

[7] Some in private equity argue that their preferential borrowing versus competitors lowers their cost of capital. However, the opportunity cost of capital is not about borrowing; it is about what you can earn in an alternative investment with similar risk. If a company does have preferential borrowing, we believe this should be valued separately using the adjusted present value (APV) method. For more on adjusted present value, see Chapter 10.

CREATE BETTER FORECASTS, NOT AD HOC RISK PREMIUMS

Certain projects carry what many investors see as high risk.[8] These include large capital projects in politically unstable countries (common among companies in the mining and oil and gas sectors), speculative R&D projects in high tech and pharmaceuticals, and acquisitions of unproven technologies or businesses in a wide range of industries. The potential returns for such investments are alluring, but what if the projects or companies fail? The answer is not to ignore these risks but to explicitly model them in your cash flow forecasts, not the cost of capital. The preferred way is to develop multiple cash flow scenarios.

It's not unusual for companies to bump up the assumed cost of capital to reflect the uncertainty of risky projects. In doing so, however, they often unwittingly set these rates at levels that even substantial underlying risks would not justify—and end up rejecting good investment opportunities as a result.[9] What many don't realize is that assumptions of discount rates that are only three to five percentage points higher than the cost of capital can significantly reduce estimates of expected value. Adding just three percentage points to an 8 percent cost of capital for an acquisition, for example, can reduce your estimate of present value by 30 to 40 percent.

Moreover, increasing the discount rate embeds into the valuation process opaque risk assumptions that are often based on little more than a gut sense that the risk is higher. The problem arises because companies take shortcuts when they estimate cash flows. To calculate expected value, project analysts should discount the expected cash flows at an appropriate cost of capital. In many cases, though, they use only estimates of cash flow that assume everything goes well. Managers, realizing this, increase the discount rate to compensate for the possibility that cash flows are overstated.

A better approach for determining the expected value of a project is to develop multiple cash flow scenarios, value them at the unadjusted cost of capital, and then apply probabilities for the value of each scenario to estimate the expected value of the project or company. Exhibit 4.2 provides an example. For simplicity, we assume just two scenarios, one with a present value of $1,000 and the other with a present value of $1,667, based on each scenario's expected cash flow. Assuming a 50 percent probability for each scenario leads to an expected value of $1,333.

---

[8] This section is adapted from R. Davies, M. Goedhart, and T. Koller, "Avoiding a Risk Premium That Unnecessarily Kills Your Project," *McKinsey on Finance*, no. 44 (Summer 2012).

[9] M. Goedhart and P. Haden, "Are Emerging Markets as Risky as You Think?" *McKinsey on Finance*, no. 7 (Spring 2003).

EXHIBIT 4.2 **Scenario Approach to Incorporating Nondiversifiable Risk**

Expected net present value (NPV), $	Probability of scenario	NPV at 8% WACC, $	Cash flows, $			
			Year 1	Year 2	Year 3	...
1,333 ←	Base case: 50%	1,667	100	102	104	
	Downside case: 50%	1,000	60	61	62	

Using scenarios has several advantages:

- It provides decision makers with more information. Rather than looking at a project with a single-point estimate of expected value (say, $100 million), decision makers know that there is a 20 percent chance that the project's value is –$20 million and an 80 percent chance it is $120 million. Making implicit risk assumptions explicit encourages dialogue about the risk of the project.

- It encourages managers to develop strategies to mitigate specific risks, because it explicitly highlights the impact of failure or less than complete success. For example, executives might build more flexibility into a project by providing options for stepwise investments—scaling up in case of success and scaling down in case of failure. Creating such options can significantly increase the value of projects.

- It acknowledges the full range of possible outcomes. When project advocates submit a single scenario, they need it to reflect enough upside to secure approval but also be realistic enough that they can commit to its performance targets. These requirements often produce a poor compromise. If advocates present multiple scenarios, they can show a project's full upside potential and realistic project targets they can truly commit to while also fully disclosing a project's potential downside risk.

Managers applying the scenario approach should be wary of overly simplistic assumptions—say, a 10 percent increase or decrease to the cash flows. A good scenario analysis will often lead to a highly successful case that is many multiples of the typical base case. It will often also include a scenario with a negative value. In addition, there may not be a traditional base case. For many projects, there is only big success or failure, with low likelihood that a project will just barely earn more than the cost of capital.

Consider an extreme example. Project A requires an up-front investment of $2,000. If everything goes well with the project, the company earns $1,000 per year forever. If not, the company gets zero. (Such all-or-nothing projects are not unusual.) To value project A, finance theory directs you to discount the expected cash flow at the cost of capital. But what is the expected cash flow in this case? If there is a 60 percent chance of everything going well, the expected cash flows would be $600 per year. At a 10 percent cost of capital, the project would be worth $6,000 once completed. Subtracting the $2,000 investment, the net value of the project before the investment is made is $4,000.

But the project will never generate $600 per year. It will generate annual cash flows of either $1,000 or zero. That means the present value of the discounted cash flows will be either $10,000 or nothing, making the project net of the initial investment worth either $8,000 or −$2,000. The probability of it being worth the expected value of $4,000 (that is, $6,000 less the investment) is zero. Rather than trying to identify the expected value, managers would be better off knowing that the project carries a 60 percent chance of being worth $8,000 and a 40 percent risk of losing $2,000. Managers can then examine the scenarios under which each outcome prevails and decide whether the upside compensates for the downside, whether the company can comfortably absorb the potential loss, and whether they can take actions to reduce the magnitude or risk of loss. The theoretical approach of focusing on expected values, while mathematically correct, hides some important information about the range and exclusivity of particular outcomes.

Moreover, some companies don't apply the expected-value approach correctly. Few companies discuss multiple scenarios, preferring a single-point forecast on which to base a yes-or-no decision. Most companies would simply represent the expected cash flows from this project as being $1,000 per year, the amount if everything goes well, and allow for uncertainty in the cash flow by arbitrarily increasing the discount rate. While you can get to the right answer with this approach, it has two flaws. First, there is no easy way to determine the cost of capital that gives the correct value. In this case, using a 16.7 percent cost of capital instead of 10 percent results in a project value of $6,000 before the investment and $4,000 after the investment. But the only way to know that this is the correct value would be to conduct a thorough scenario analysis. Companies sometimes arbitrarily add a risk premium to the cost of capital, but there is no way for them to know whether the amount they add is even reasonably accurate. Second, the decision makers evaluating a project with cash flows of $1,000 per year and a 16.7 percent cost of capital are still not thinking through the 40 percent risk that it might generate no cash at all.

If for some reason you must use a single cash flow scenario, you can analytically estimate the equivalent risk premium for different probability levels of failure, as in Exhibit 4.3. The exhibit shows the amounts by which you would increase the cost of capital instead of using cash flow scenarios for different combinations of the probability of failure, as represented on the vertical axis, and the size of loss relative to the base case, as represented by the horizontal axis. For example, if there was a 50 percent chance of failure in which

EXHIBIT 4.3 **Example of Equivalent Risk Premiums for Different Probability Levels of Failure**

			Size of cash flow reduction, %		
		20	40	60	80	100
	10	0.1	0.2	0.4	0.5	0.7
	20	0.2	0.5	0.8	1.1	1.5
Probability of lower cash flow, %	30	0.4	0.8	1.3	1.9	2.6
	40	0.5	1.1	1.9	2.8	4.0
	50	0.7	1.5	2.6	4.0	6.0

A 1.5% risk premium is required, assuming even odds that an investment will lose 40% of its value

Note: This particular example is for a company with an indefinite life, assuming a smooth cash flow profile, 8% weighted average cost of capital, and 2% terminal growth. The cost of capital adjustments would be larger for a project with a short life.

Source: R. Davis, M. Goedhart, and T. Koller, "Avoiding a Risk Premium That Unnecessarily Kills Your Project," *McKinsey Quarterly* (August 2012).

case the project would be worth 40 percent less than expected, the equivalent additional risk premium would be 1.5 percent. Notice in this exhibit that the additional risk premiums are small relative to what most people expect. To justify a 3 percent extra risk premium, for example, you'd have to believe there was a 50 percent chance of failure and a 60 percent reduction in cash flows associated with failure. To get to a 5 percent additional risk premium, you'd have to believe there is a 50 percent chance of failure and more than an 80 percent reduction in cash flows.[10]

Adding ad hoc risk premiums is a crude way to include project-specific uncertainty in a valuation. Scenario-based approaches have the dual appeal of better answers and more transparency regarding the assumptions embedded within them.

DECIDE HOW MUCH CASH FLOW RISK TO TAKE ON

Now let's turn to cash flow risk. When we talk about total cash flow risk, we mean the uncertainty that a company faces about its future cash flows, whether for the company as a whole, a business unit, or a single project. Finance theory provides guidance on pricing the nondiversifiable part of cash flow risk in the cost of capital. In theory, a company should take on all projects or growth opportunities that have positive expected values even if there is high likelihood of failure, as long as the project is small enough that failure will not put

---

[10] Note that the risk premium will be determined not just by the probability and magnitude of loss, but also by the duration of the project or company and pattern of cash flows.

the company in financial distress. In practice, we've found that companies tend to place disproportionate emphasis on the impact of losses from smaller projects, thereby missing opportunities for value creation.

For instance, how should a company think through whether to undertake a project—let's call it project A—with a 60 percent chance of earning $8,000, a 40 percent chance of losing $2,000, and therefore an expected value of $4,000? Theory says to take on all projects with a positive expected value, regardless of the upside-versus-downside risk. A company is likely to have many small projects like project A, which means that the risk for each one is small in the context of the entire enterprise. In other words, the risk of a project itself is not important; what matters is how it shifts the overall level of risk that the entire company faces across all of its projects. In fact, you could argue that if some projects don't fail, the company is not taking on enough risk.

But what if the company instead has one large project that would bankrupt the company if it fails? Consider an electric power company with the opportunity to build a nuclear power facility for $15 billion. Suppose the company has $25 billion in existing debt and $25 billion in equity market capitalization. If the plant is successfully constructed and brought on line, there is an 80 percent chance it will be worth $28 billion, for a net value of $13 billion. But there is a 20 percent chance it will fail to receive regulatory approval and be worth zero, leading to a loss of $15 billion. The expected value is $7 billion net of investment.[11] Failure will bankrupt the company, because the cash flow from the company's existing plants would be insufficient to cover its existing debt plus the debt on the failed plant. In this case, the economics of the nuclear plant spill over onto the value of the rest of the company. Failure would wipe out all the equity of the company, not just the $15 billion invested in the plant.

In this example, if the company were to file for bankruptcy under Chapter 11 of the United States Bankruptcy Code, it would be able to continue operating as normal while its debt and equity are restructuring. But the nuclear plant's financial failure may negatively affect the company in other ways, too. In addition to making it impossible for the company to service its entire debt, the nuclear plant's financial failure may also reduce the operating cash flows from the company's existing plants, because they may face new demands from suppliers or find it challenging to secure long-term contracts with existing customers. For all these reasons, companies considering large investments—especially when they are financed through debt—must carefully consider the degree to which the projects' failure could threaten cash flows from their existing business. At the same time, companies should not avoid even large risks if they don't threaten the ability of the rest of the company to operate normally.

---

[11] The calculation is ($13 billion × 80%) + (−$15 billion × 20%).

Executives making decisions for their companies should think about the company's risk profile, not their own.[12] After all, that's the job of corporations; they are designed to take risks and overcome the natural loss aversion of individuals. The earliest corporations were the British and Dutch East India shipping companies. With those, if a ship sank, all shareholders would lose a tolerable amount instead of having one ship owner lose his entire fortune.

Professors Daniel Kahneman and Amos Tversky have demonstrated that most people place greater weight on the potential economic losses from their decisions than on the potential equivalent gains. In a McKinsey survey of 1,500 global executives across many industries,[13] we presented the executives with the following scenario: You are considering making a $10 million investment that has some chance of returning, in present value, $40 million over three years, with some chance of losing the entire investment in the first year. What is the highest loss you would tolerate and still proceed with the investment?

A risk-neutral executive would be willing to accept a 75 percent chance of loss and a 25 percent chance of gain. One-quarter of $40 million is $10 million, which is the initial investment, so a 25 percent chance of gain creates an expected risk-neutral value of zero. But most survey respondents demonstrated extreme loss aversion;[14] they were willing to accept only a 19 percent chance of loss to make this investment, nowhere near the risk-neutral answer of 75 percent. In fact, only 9 percent of respondents were willing to accept a 40 percent or greater chance of loss. Informally, we've asked groups of executives the same question at even lower levels of investment and found similar results. Our findings echo those from Professor Ralph O. Swalm, going back to 1966.[15]

This phenomenon has serious consequences for hierarchical organizations. Executives are just as loss-averse when the bets are small as they are when the gambles are large, even though small gambles do not raise the same issues of survival or ruin that provide a rationale for aversion to large risks. What's more, small gambles offer opportunities for the risk-reducing effects of aggregation.

---

[12] "The remainder of this section is adapted from D. Lovallo, T. Koller, R. Uhlaner, and D. Kahneman, "Your Company Is Too Risk-Averse," *Harvard Business Review* (March–April 2020), hbr.org.

[13] T. Koller, D. Lovallo, and Z. Williams, "Overcoming a Bias against Risk," McKinsey & Company (August 2012), www.mckinsey.com.

[14] Note that loss aversion and risk aversion are different. Loss aversion is a cognitive bias that often arises from how a decision is framed and leads people to weigh losses more heavily than gains. Risk aversion is not a bias; it is a tendency to avoid risk. For example, a risk-averse investor might choose preservation of capital by investing in government bonds instead of higher-return stocks that are more volatile.

[15] These results build on a 1966 *Harvard Business Review* article, "Utility Theory: Insights into Risk Taking," by Ralph O. Swalm. He studied executives with varying levels of spending authority and found that risk-preference profiles were very similar for executives at different levels of the organization.

To overcome loss aversion and make better investment decisions, individuals and organizations must learn to *frame* choices in the context of the entire company's success, not the individual project's performance. In practice, this means looking at projects as a portfolio by aggregating them, rather than focusing on the risk of individual projects. It might also mean altering incentives for individual executives to overcome the wrong framing of the decision.

One technology company successfully used a portfolio approach to assess its projects. First, executives estimated the expected return of each project proposal (measured as expected present value divided by investment) and the risks associated with each (measured as the standard deviation of projected returns). Executives then built portfolios of projects and identified combinations that would deliver the best balance between return and risk. When they viewed portfolios of projects in the aggregate (Exhibit 4.4), executives could see that portfolios of projects had higher returns than most of the individual projects and much lower risk compared with most of the individual projects.

It's worth pointing out that even though a portfolio of projects has lower risk, the use of portfolios does not lower a company's cost of capital. That's because the portfolio, by definition, cannot reduce the nondiversifiable risk, which is the risk embedded in the cost of capital.

EXHIBIT 4.4 **Aggregating Projects Reduces Risk While Achieving High Expected Returns**

Projects	Return, ratio of present value to investment	Risk, standard deviation of expected return, %	Expected net present value, $ million
Portfolio of selected projects A–Q	4.5	15	8,100
A	15.4	64	200
B	12.4	104	500
C	7.5	66	50
D	4.7	22	5
E	4.7	150	200
F	4.4	52	500
G	3.7	37	30
H	3.7	29	400
I	2.7	58	900
J	2.6	31	400
K	2.5	150	300
L	2.3	20	220
M	1.9	18	520
N	1.5	20	300
O	1.1	13	850
P	0.9	5	2,000
Q	0.3	5	850

DECIDE WHICH TYPES OF RISK TO HEDGE

There are also risks that investors are eager for companies to take. For example, investors in gold-mining companies and oil production companies buy those stocks to gain exposure to often-volatile gold or oil prices. If gold and oil companies attempt to hedge their revenues, that effort merely complicates life for their investors, who then must guess how much price risk is being hedged and how and whether management will change its policy in the future. Moreover, hedging may lock in today's prices for two years, the time horizon within which it is possible to hedge those commodities, but a company's present value includes the cash flows from subsequent years at fluctuating market prices. So while hedging may reduce the short-term cash flow volatility, it will have little effect on the company's valuation based on long-term cash flows.

Some risks, such as the commodity price risk in this example, can be managed by shareholders themselves. Other, similar-looking risks—for example, some forms of currency risk—are harder for shareholders to manage. The general rule is to avoid hedging the first type of risk but hedge the second if possible.

Consider the effect of U.S. dollar currency risk on Heineken, the global brewer. For the U.S. market, Heineken produces its flagship brand, Heineken, in the Netherlands and ships it to America. In most other markets, it produces and sells in the same country. So, for most markets, an exchange rate change affects only the translation of local profits into their reporting currency. For example, for most markets, a 1 percent change in the value of the local currency relative to the euro translates into a 1 percent change in revenues and a 1 percent change in profits as well. Note that the effect on revenues and profits is the same, because all the revenues and costs are in the same currency. There is no change in operating margin.

The U.S. market is different. When the dollar/euro exchange rate changes, Heineken's revenues in euros are affected, but its costs are not. If the dollar declines by 1 percent, Heineken's euro revenues also decline by 1 percent. But since its costs are in euros, those don't change. Assuming a 10 percent margin to begin with, a 1 percent decline in the dollar will reduce Heineken's margin to 9 percent, and its profits reported in euros will decline by a whopping 10 percent.

Because Heineken's production facilities are in a different country and it is unable to pass on cost increases because it is competing with locally produced products, its currency risk is larger for its U.S. business than for its other markets. Hedging might be much more important for Heineken's U.S. business than for other markets, because a rise or fall in the dollar/euro exchange rate has a much greater impact on its business.

SUMMARY

To avoid unfavorable strategic decisions, executives must have a deep understanding of the dynamic relationship between the cost of capital and risk. Risk enters valuation both through the company's cost of capital (an opportunity cost) and through the uncertainty surrounding future cash flows. Because investors can diversify their portfolios, a company's cost of capital is for the most part determined by the industry in which it operates.

Valuations that use multiple cash flow scenarios better reflect diversifiable risks than those that adjust the cost of capital. Executives tend to shy away from risky projects even if the potential return is high. This excessive loss aversion can be overcome by examining portfolios of projects, rather than individual ones.

5

The Alchemy of Stock Market Performance

A commonly used measure for evaluating the performance of a company and its management is total shareholder returns (TSR), defined as the percent increase in share price plus the dividend yield over a period of time.[1] In fact, in the United States, the Securities and Exchange Commission requires that companies publish in their annual reports their TSR relative to a set of peers over the last five years. That sounds like a good idea: if managers focus on improving TSR to win performance bonuses, then their interests and the interests of their shareholders should be aligned. The evidence shows that this is indeed true over long periods—at a minimum, 10 to 15 years. But TSR measured over shorter periods may not reflect the actual performance of a company, because TSR is heavily influenced by changes in investors' expectations, not just the company's performance.

Earning a high TSR is much harder for managers leading an already-successful company than for those leading a company with substantial room for improvement. That's because a company performing above its peers will attract investors expecting more of the same, pushing up the share price. Managers then must pull off herculean feats of real performance improvement to exceed those expectations and outperform on TSR. We call their predicament the "expectations treadmill." For high-performing companies, TSR in isolation can unfairly penalize their high performance. Another drawback is that using TSR by itself, without understanding its components, doesn't help executives or their boards understand how much of the TSR comes from operating performance, nonoperating items, and changes in expectations.

This chapter was coauthored by Rosen Kotsev.

[1] Later in this chapter, we'll show that we also need to consider the impact of share repurchases as a significant source of cash distributions.

The widespread use of TSR over short periods as a measure of management performance can create perverse incentives. Managers running full tilt on the expectations treadmill may be tempted to pursue ideas that give an immediate bump to their TSR at the expense of longer-term investments that will create more value for shareholders over a longer horizon. In addition, TSR may rise or fall across the board for all companies because of external factors beyond managers' control, such as changing inflation rates. Strictly speaking, such factors should play no part in managers' compensation.

This chapter starts by explaining the expectations treadmill. It then shows an approach to analyzing TSR that isolates how much TSR comes from revenue growth and improvements in return on invested capital (ROIC)—the factors that drive long-term value creation—versus changes in expectations and nonoperating items. Managers, boards of directors, and investors can learn much more about company performance from this granular breakdown of TSR.

WHY SHAREHOLDER EXPECTATIONS BECOME A TREADMILL

As we described in Chapter 2, the return on capital that a company earns is not the same as the return earned by every shareholder. Suppose a company can invest $1,000 in a factory and earn $200 a year, which it pays out in dividends to its shareholders. The first investors in the company pay $1,000 in total for their shares, and if they hold the shares, they will earn 20 percent per year ($200 divided by $1,000).

Suppose that after one year, all the investors decide to sell their shares, and they find buyers who pay $2,000 for the lot. The buyers will earn only 10 percent per year on their investment ($200 divided by $2,000). The first investors will earn a 120 percent return ($200 dividends plus $1,000 gain on their shares versus their initial investment of $1,000). The company's return on capital is 20 percent, while one group of investors earns 120 percent, and the other group earns 10 percent. All the investors collectively will earn, on a time-weighted average, the same return as the company. But individual groups of investors will earn very different returns, because they pay different prices for the shares, based on their expectations of future performance.

As mentioned in this chapter's introduction, one way of understanding the effects of this dynamic is through the analogy of a treadmill, the speed of which represents the expectations built into a company's share price. If the company beats expectations, and if the market believes the improvement is sustainable, the company's stock price goes up, in essence capitalizing the future value of this incremental improvement. But it also means that managers must run even faster just to maintain the new stock price,[2] let alone improve it further: the speed of the treadmill quickens as performance improves. So a company with low expectations of success among shareholders at the beginning of a period may have an easier time outperforming the stock market, simply because low expectations are easier to beat.

The treadmill analogy is useful because it describes the difficulty of continuing to outperform the stock market. At some point, it becomes almost impossible for management to deliver on accelerating expectations without faltering, just as anyone would eventually stumble on a treadmill that keeps moving faster.

Consider the case of Terry Turnaround, a fictional character based on the experiences of many CEOs. Terry has just been hired as the CEO of Prospectus, a company with below-average returns on capital and growth relative to competitors. Because of this past performance, the market doesn't expect much, so the value of Prospectus is low relative to competitors. Terry hires a topnotch team and gets to work. After two years, Prospectus is gaining ground on its peers in margins and return on capital, and its market share is rising. Prospectus's TSR is double that of its peers because the market wasn't expecting the company's turnaround.

Terry and her team continue their hard work. After two more years, Prospectus has become the industry leader in operating performance, with the highest growth and return on capital. Because of its low starting point, the company's TSR over this two-year period has been four times the rate of the industry average. Given Prospectus's new trajectory and consistent performance, the market expects continued above-average returns on capital and revenue growth.

As time goes by, Prospectus maintains its high return on capital and leading market share. But two years later, Terry notes with frustration that her company's shares are now doing no better than those of its peers, even though the company has outperformed its rivals. At this point, Terry is trapped on the expectations treadmill: she and her team have done such a good job that the expectation of continued high performance is already incorporated into the company's share price. As long as Prospectus delivers results in line with the market's expectations, its share price performance will be no better or worse than average.

This explains why extraordinary managers may deliver only ordinary TSR: even for the extraordinary manager, it can be extremely difficult to keep beating high expectations. It also explains why managers of companies with low performance expectations might easily earn a high TSR, at least for a short

---

[2] Theoretically, if a company's performance exactly matches expectations, its TSR will equal the cost of equity. In practice, however, with continual changes in interest rates, inflation, and economic activity, comparison to the broader market is sometimes preferable.

time. They can create a higher TSR by delivering performance that raises share-holder expectations to the level of expectations for their peers in the sector.

The danger for companies whose shareholders already have high expectations is that in their quest to achieve above-peer TSR, they may resort to misguided actions, such as pushing for unrealistic earnings growth or pursuing big, risky acquisitions. Consider the electric power boom at the end of the 1990s and in the early 2000s. Deregulation led to high hopes for power generation companies, so deregulated energy producers were spun off from their regulated parents at extremely high valuations. Mirant, for instance, was spun off from Southern Company in October 2000 with a combined equity and debt capitalization of almost $18 billion, a multiple of about 30 times earnings before interest, taxes, and amortization (EBITA)—quite extraordinary for a power generation company. To justify its value, Mirant expanded aggressively, as did similar companies, investing in power plants in the Bahamas, Brazil, Chile, China, Germany, the Philippines, and the United Kingdom, as well as 14 U.S. states. The debt burden from these investments quickly became too much for Mirant to handle, and the company filed for bankruptcy in July 2003. The expectations treadmill pushed Mirant into taking enormous risks to justify its share price, and it paid the ultimate price.

The expectations treadmill is the dynamic behind the adage that a good company and a good investment may not be the same. In the short term, good companies may not be good investments, because future great performance might already be built into the share price. Smart investors may prefer weaker-performing companies, because they have more upside potential, as the expectations expressed in their lower share prices are easier to beat.

THE TREADMILL'S REAL-WORLD EFFECTS

In this section, we'll compare two successful companies to illustrate how the expectations treadmill works in the real world. Walmart is the world's largest retailer, with $642 billion in revenues in 2023. Ulta Beauty—the largest beauty retailer in the United States, selling both mass and prestige cosmetics, fragrances, and skin care products—generated $11 billion in revenues that same year. From 2018 to 2023, Ulta Beauty grew its revenues by 11 percent per year, while Walmart grew its revenues at 5 percent, which is exceptional for such a large company. In 2023, Ulta Beauty's ROIC was 35 percent, and the ROIC for Walmart was 17 percent—both high for retailers, though Ulta Beauty's is exceptional. Despite Ulta Beauty's higher growth and higher ROIC, the TSR for Walmart's shareholders was slightly higher, at 13 percent, versus 12 percent for Ulta (see Exhibit 5.1).

The expectations treadmill explains the mismatch between TSR and the underlying value created by the two companies. Using the ratio of enterprise value (EV) to net operating profit after taxes (NOPAT) as a proxy for market

EXHIBIT 5.1 **Walmart vs. Ulta Beauty: Growth, Return on Invested Capital (ROIC), and Total Shareholder Returns (TSR)**

Dec 2018–Dec 2023, %

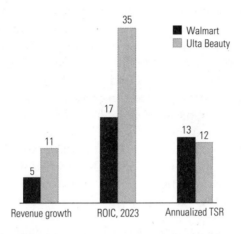

expectations, we can see that Ulta Beauty's EV/NOPAT started the period at 28 times, compared with 21 times for Walmart. Both treadmills were already running fast, with high expectations built into the share price. By the end of 2023, Ulta Beauty's multiple had come down to 19 times, still high for a retailer, while that of Walmart increased to 25 times.

Ulta Beauty also increased its margins from 14 to 16 percent, while Walmart's were flat at 4 percent. Ulta Beauty, though, didn't have to invest as much to achieve its growth as Walmart did.

Which company did a better job? Both did extremely well. Ulta Beauty outperformed on growth and ROIC, but its expectations for future performance fell from an extremely high level to something more typical of a retailer. Most likely, investors saw a declining growth trajectory: revenue growth in 2022 was 18 percent, versus 10 percent in 2023. Walmart's multiple increased, perhaps reflecting investor views of new growth opportunities, such as e-commerce, or opportunities to increase ROIC. For TSR to provide deeper insight into a company's true performance, we need a finer-grained look inside this measure.

DECOMPOSING TSR

We recommend analyzing TSR by decomposing it and quantifying its components in the manner outlined in this section. Doing so serves two purposes. First, when managers, boards of directors, and investors understand the sources of TSR, they are better able to evaluate management. For example, it's important to know that Ulta Beauty's TSR, though slightly lower than that of Walmart, reflects strong underlying performance against high expectations. Second, decomposing TSR can help with setting future targets.

The traditional approach to analyzing total shareholder returns is mathematically correct, but it does not link TSR to the true underlying sources of value creation. The decomposition we recommend gives managers a clearer understanding of the elements of TSR they can change, those that are beyond their control, and the speed at which their expectations treadmill is running. This information helps managers focus on creating lasting value and communicate to investors and other stakeholders how their plans are likely to affect TSR in the short and long terms.

Decomposition of TSR begins with its definition as the percent change in a company's market value plus its dividend yield (for simplicity, we assume the company has no debt and distributes all its excess cash flow as dividends each year):

$$\text{TSR} = \text{Percent Change in Market Value} + \text{Dividend Yield}$$

The change in market value is the change in net income plus the change in a company's price-to-earnings ratio (P/E).[3] Adding the dividend yield gives the following equation for TSR:

$$\begin{aligned} \text{TSR} = \ &\text{Percent Change in Net Income} \\ &+ \text{Percent Change in P/E} + \text{Dividend Yield} \end{aligned}$$

This equation expresses what we refer to as the "traditional" approach to analyzing TSR. While technically correct, however, this expression of TSR misses some important factors. For example, a manager might assume that all forms of net-income growth create an equal amount of value. Yet we know from Chapter 3 that different sources of earnings growth may create different amounts of value, because they are associated with different returns on capital and therefore generate different cash flows. For example, growth from acquisitions may reduce future dividend growth because of the large investments required.

A second problem is that this approach assumes that the dividend yield can be increased without affecting future earnings and dividends, as if dividends themselves create value. But dividends are merely a residual. For example, if a company pays a higher dividend today by taking on more debt, that simply means future dividends must be lower because future interest expense and debt repayments will be higher. Similarly, if a company manages to pay a higher dividend by forgoing attractive investment opportunities, then future dividends will suffer, as future cash flows from operations will be lower.

---

[3] Technically, there is an additional cross-term, which reflects the interaction of the share price change and the P/E change, but it is generally small, so we ignore it here.

Finally, the traditional expression of TSR fails to account for the impact of financial leverage: two companies that create underlying value equally well could generate very different TSR, simply because of the differences in their debt-to-equity ratios and the resulting differences in the risk to their investors.

To avoid these problems, we can decompose the traditional TSR components into ones that provide better insight into understanding the underlying sources of value creation. Exhibit 5.2 shows this graphically.

The derivation works as follows. Assume a company with no debt pays out all its cash flow as dividends. Start with the traditional definition:

$$\text{TSR} = \text{Percent Change in Net Income}$$
$$+ \text{Percent Change in P/E} + \text{Dividend Yield}$$

The percent increase in earnings can be decomposed into the increase in revenues and the change in profit margin[4]:

$$\text{Percent Change in Net Income} = \text{Percent Increase in Revenues}$$
$$+ \text{Impact of Increase in Profit}$$
$$\text{Margin on Net Income}$$

EXHIBIT 5.2 **TSR Driven by Revenue Growth, Margin, ROIC, and Changes in Expectations**

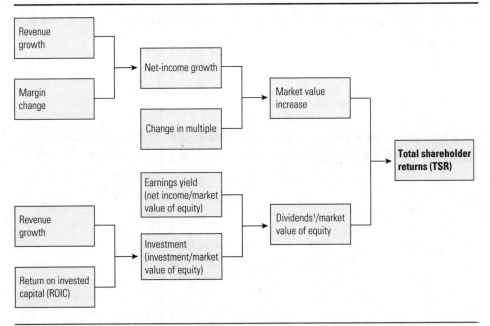

Note: Assumes company has no debt and no share repurchases.

[1] Dividends = Net Income – Investment.

[4] To be precise, there is an additional cross-term that reflects the interaction of these two effects. We have omitted it to focus on the key points.

The dividend yield also can be decomposed as:

$$\text{Dividend Yield} = \frac{\text{Dividends}}{\text{Market Value}}$$

In this simplified example, where the company pays out all its cash flow as dividends, dividends will equal net income less investment. Therefore, the dividend yield can be expressed as the earnings yield (net income divided by market value) less the percent of market value invested back into the business:

$$\text{Dividend Yield} = \frac{\text{Net Income}}{\text{Market Value}} - \frac{\text{Investment}}{\text{Market Value}}$$

Putting these components together gives the following expression for TSR:

$$\text{TSR} = \text{Percent Change in Revenue} - \frac{\text{Investment}}{\text{Market Value}}$$
$$+ \text{Impact of Change in Profit Margin}$$
$$+ \frac{\text{Net Income}}{\text{Market Value}} + \text{Percent Change in P/E}$$

To summarize, TSR is driven by these five factors:

1. Revenue growth
2. Investment required to achieve that revenue growth
3. Impact of a change in margin on net income growth
4. Starting ratio of net income to market value (which is the inverse of the P/E ratio)
5. Change in P/E ratio

The investment required for growth is a function of growth and ROIC, as described in Chapter 3:

$$\text{Investment} = \text{Net Income} \times \text{Growth/ROIC}$$

The percent of market value invested therefore equals

$$\frac{\text{Investment}}{\text{Market Value}} = \frac{\text{Net Income} \times \text{Growth/ROIC}}{\text{Market Value}}$$
$$= \frac{\text{Net Income}}{\text{Market Value}} \times \frac{\text{Growth}}{\text{ROIC}}$$

The ratio of net income to market value is just the inverse of the P/E ratio; therefore,

$$\frac{\text{Investment}}{\text{Market Value}} = \frac{1}{\text{P/E}} \times \text{Growth/ROIC}$$

EXHIBIT 5.3 **Traditional vs. Enhanced TSR Decomposition**

Company A financials				Decomposition of TSR		
$ million	Base year	1 year later		%	Traditional	Enhanced
Invested capital	100.0	107.0		Growth	7.0	7.0
Earnings	12.5	13.4		Required investment	–	(5.6)
				TSR from performance	7.0	1.4
P/E, multiple	10.0	10.3				
Equity value	125.0	137.5		Earnings yield	–	10.0
Dividends	5.0	5.5		Change in P/E	3.0	3.0
				Dividend yield	4.4	–
TSR, %		14.4		TSR, %	14.4	14.4

Now we can see how TSR is driven by growth and ROIC, adjusted by the beginning P/E.

Exhibit 5.3 uses the financials of hypothetical Company A to compare the traditional method of TSR decomposition with our enhanced approach.[5] Looking at the two decomposition approaches on the right side of the exhibit, the traditional approach indicates that Company A has a 14.4 percent TSR, based on 7 percent earnings growth, a 3 percent change in the company's P/E (a proxy for changed expectations), and a 4.4 percent dividend yield. The enhanced approach breaks down the TSR of Company A into three of the four parts of our full process of decomposition. (For simplicity, in this example, Company A does not increase its margins.) This shows that not much of the 14.4 percent TSR reflects the creation of new value. First, the reinvestment required to achieve 7 percent growth in earnings consumed most of the earnings growth itself, leaving TSR arising from performance at only 1.4 percent. Another 3 percent of TSR comes from a change in shareholder expectations (reflected in the P/E multiple increase), rather than performance. And the remaining 10 percent is simply the earnings yield, reflecting what the TSR would have been with zero growth and if investors had not changed their expectations.

We have found that many people struggle with the earnings yield (zero-growth return) part of this decomposition. Here's a simple example of how this works. Suppose you have two companies, H and L, each with $100 of earnings and zero growth. Since the companies aren't growing, they don't need to invest, so dividends to shareholders would equal earnings. Company H has a P/E of 20, and Company L has a P/E of 15. Exhibit 5.4 shows why the inverse of the P/E, the earnings yield, is the return the companies would earn if they didn't grow and their P/Es didn't change.

---

[5] The example assumes no changes in profit margins for both companies so that earnings growth can arise only from investments.

EXHIBIT 5.4 **Earnings Yield: TSR with Zero Growth**

	Company H		Company L	
	Year 0	Year 1	Year 0	Year 1
Earnings, $	100	100	100	100
× P/E	20	20	15	15
= Value, $	2,000	2,000	1,500	1,500
Dividends (equals earnings), $		100		100
Value plus dividends, $		2,100		1,600
TSR, %		5.0		6.7
Inverse of P/E, %		5.0		6.7

In the example, you can see that the TSR of Company H is 5.0 percent, exactly equal to the inverse of the P/E, the earnings yield. Similarly, Company L's TSR of 6.7 percent equals the inverse of its P/E. Note also that Company H, with the higher P/E, has the lower earnings yield (or zero-growth TSR). This demonstrates that companies with higher P/Es must achieve greater growth or improvements in ROIC to outperform the TSR of companies with lower P/Es.

The next example shows the impact of debt financing on the TSR decomposition. Suppose you own a house worth $500,000 and you've borrowed $200,000 against the house. If the house increases in value to $550,000, your equity value would increase from $300,000 to $350,000. A 10 percent increase in the value of the house leads to a 17 percent return on your equity.

The same concept applies to companies. Consider Company B, which is identical to Company A (our simpler example in Exhibit 5.3) except for its debt financing. As detailed in Exhibit 5.5, the difference in financing means Company B generated a higher TSR of 18 percent. The traditional approach to decomposing TSR suggests that Company B's shareholders benefited from a higher dividend

EXHIBIT 5.5 **Enhancing TSR Decomposition to Uncover Effects of Leverage**

Company B financials			Decomposition of TSR		
$ million	Base year	1 year later	%	Traditional	Enhanced
Enterprise value	125.0	137.5	Growth	7.0	7.0
Debt[1]	(25)	(25)	Required investment	–	(5.6)
Equity value	100.0	112.5	TSR from performance	7.0	1.4
Dividends		5.5	Earnings yield	–	10.0
			Change in P/E[2]	5.5	3.0
P/E (multiple)	8.0	8.4	Impact of financial leverage	–	3.6
			Dividend yield	5.5	–
TSR, %		18.0	TSR, %	18.0	18.0

[1] Assumes, for illustrative purposes, that debt carries no interest.

[2] Change in P/E multiple for traditional approach vs. change in unlevered P/E multiple in enhanced approach (enterprise value/earnings).

yield and a stronger increase in expectations. However, our more fundamental decomposition of Company B, based on earnings yield (zero-growth TSR) and changed expectations measured by the unlevered P/E (ratio of enterprise value to earnings), shows that the first three parts of the company's decomposed TSR are in fact identical to those of Company A. The additional 3.6 percent TSR for Company B arises from the higher proportion of debt in its capital, rather than any newly created value. Adjusting for the higher financial risk associated with higher debt shows that Company B did not in fact create more value than Company A—an important fact for investors and the companies' executives.

We can apply this approach to our earlier comparison of Walmart and Ulta Beauty. Exhibit 5.6 shows the TSR decomposition for the two companies. While the 13 percent annual TSR that Walmart achieved in the period from 2018 to 2023 was slightly higher than Ulta Beauty's 12 percent, Ulta Beauty outperformed Walmart on the TSR derived from growth: growth, net of investments, contributed 13 percent to its TSR, versus 4 percent for Walmart. (Note that for Ulta Beauty in this period, investment improved capital productivity, so it amplified growth.)

Ulta Beauty's margin went up, contributing three percentage points to TSR, while Walmart's was slightly down. Ulta Beauty's margin in 2023 was 16 percent, extremely high for a retailer, while Walmart's was 4 percent, reflecting the nature of its business as a discount retailer.

The big negative for Ulta Beauty was the decline in its EV/NOPAT multiple from 28 to 19 times—which, to be clear, is still a high number. You could say that the expectations treadmill caught up with Ulta Beauty.

UNDERSTANDING EXPECTATIONS

As the examples in this chapter have shown, investors' expectations at the beginning and end of the measurement period have a big effect on TSR. A crucial issue for investors and executives to understand, however, is

EXHIBIT 5.6 **Walmart vs. Ulta Beauty: TSR Decomposition, 2018–2023**

% annualized

	Walmart	Ulta Beauty	Difference
Revenue growth	5	11	(6)
Investment for growth	(1)	2	(3)
Change in margin	(1)	3	(4)
TSR from performance	3	16	(13)
Earnings yield (zero-growth return)	4	4	0
Change in earnings multiple	4	(9)	13
Nonoperating cash flows	2	1	1
TSR	13	12	1

that a company whose TSR has consistently outperformed the market will reach a point where the company will no longer be able to satisfy expectations reflected in its share price. From that point, TSR will be lower than it was in the past, even though the company may still be creating huge amounts of value. Managers need to realize and communicate to their boards and to investors that a small decline in TSR is better for shareholders in the long run at this juncture than a desperate attempt to maintain TSR through ill-advised acquisitions or new ventures.

This was arguably the point that Home Depot had reached in 1999. Earlier, we used earnings multiples to express expectations, but by reverse engineering the share price, you can also translate those multiples into the revenue growth rate and ROIC required to satisfy current shareholder expectations. Such an exercise can also help managers assess their performance plans and spot any gaps between their likely outcome and the market's expectations. At the end of 1999, Home Depot had a market value of $132 billion, with an earnings multiple of 47. Using a discounted-cash-flow model that assumes constant margins and return on capital, Home Depot would have had to increase revenues by 26 percent per year over the next 15 years to maintain its 1999 share price. Home Depot's actual revenue growth through 2006 averaged a very healthy 13 percent per year—an impressive number for such a large company but far below the growth required to justify its share price in 1999. It's no surprise, therefore, that Home Depot's shares underperformed the S&P 500 by 8 percent per year over the period. (Weakness in the housing market also played a significant role in keeping the company's growth slower during this time.) Since then, Home Depot's revenues would fall from $90 billion in 2006 to $66 billion in 2010, before recovering and ultimately reaching $153 billion in 2023—an annualized increase of 3 percent per year.

What should Home Depot's board of directors have done immediately after 1999, given the company's high market value? Celebrating is definitely not the answer. Some companies would try to justify their high share prices by considering all sorts of risky strategies. But given Home Depot's size, the chances of finding enough high-ROIC growth opportunities to justify its 1999 share price were virtually nil.

Realistically, there wasn't much Home Depot could have done except prepare for an inevitable decline in share price: Home Depot's market value dropped from $130 billion in December 1999 to $80 billion in December 2006 (it has since increased to over $330 billion, as of mid-2024). Some companies can take advantage of their high share prices to make acquisitions. But that probably wasn't a good idea for Home Depot because of its high growth—a large enough management challenge to maintain, even without considering that the retail industry doesn't have a track record of making large acquisitions successfully.

Home Depot's situation in 1999 was unusual. Most companies, most of the time, can satisfy the shareholder expectations expressed in their current share price simply by performing as well as the rest of their industry. We have reverse engineered hundreds of companies' share prices over the years, using discounted cash flows. Except during the Internet bubble era (1999–2000), at least 80 percent of the companies' share prices have had built-in performance expectations that are in line with industry growth expectations and returns on capital. For a company among these 80 percent, TSR is unlikely to be much different from the industry average unless the company performs significantly better or worse than expected, relative to its industry peers. The other 20 percent, however, should brace themselves for a significantly faster or slower ride on the treadmill. Managers who reverse engineer their share prices to understand expectations of their ROIC and growth can benefit from seeing on which side of this 80/20 divide they fall.

IMPLICATIONS FOR MANAGERS

The expectations treadmill makes it difficult to use TSR as a performance measurement tool. As we saw in the examples of Walmart and Ulta Beauty, a relatively small difference in TSR can mask big differences in operating performance and changes in expectations. In Home Depot's case, living up to the expectations was virtually impossible, as no company can run that fast for very long.

As a result of the expectations treadmill, many executive compensation systems tied to TSR do not reward managers according to their performance, since the majority of a company's short-term TSR is driven by movements in its industry and the broader market. That was the case for the many executives who became wealthy from stock options in the 1980s and 1990s, a time when share prices increased primarily because of falling inflation and interest rates, rather than anything those managers did. Conversely, many stock option gains were wiped out during the 2008 financial crisis. Again, the causes of these gains and losses were largely disconnected from anything managers did or didn't do (except for managers in financial institutions).

Instead of focusing primarily on a company's TSR over a given period, effective compensation systems should focus on growth, ROIC, and TSR performance relative to peers. That would eliminate much of the TSR that is not driven by company-specific performance.

In addition to fixing compensation systems, executives need to become much more sophisticated in their interpretation of TSR, especially short-term TSR. If executives and boards understand what expectations are built into their own and their peers' share prices, they can better anticipate how their actions might affect their own share prices when the market finds out about them. For example, if you're executing a great strategy that will create significant value, but the market already expects you to succeed, you can't expect to outperform on TSR. The management team and board need to know this, so the board will take a long-term view and continue to support management's value-creating priorities, even if these do not immediately strengthen the share price.

Executives also need to give up incessantly monitoring their stock prices. It's a bad habit. TSR is largely meaningless over short periods. In a typical three-month time frame, more than 50 percent of companies experience a share price increase or decrease of over 10 percent,[6] movements that are nothing more than random. Therefore, executives shouldn't even try to understand daily share price changes unless prices move over 2 percent more than the peer average in a single day or 10 percent more in a quarter.

Finally, be careful what you wish for. All executives and investors like to see their company's share price increase. But once your share price rises, it's hard to keep it rising faster than the market average. The expectations treadmill is virtually impossible to escape, and we don't know any easy way to manage expectations down.

---

[6] Share price movement for a sample of approximately 1,300 nonfinancial companies with greater than $1 billion revenue, measured during 2013–2023.

6

The Stock Market and Economic Fundamentals

The stock market's volatility has always raised questions about the link between stock prices and economic fundamentals. American investor Bill Gross claimed in 2012 that the last 100 years of U.S. stock returns "belied a commonsensical flaw much like that of a chain letter or yes—a Ponzi scheme."[1] Other commentators, including some Nobel laureates, have expressed similar sentiments.[2] In this chapter, we provide evidence to the contrary. The long-term return on stocks is driven by economic fundamentals: growth and return on capital. For the most part, individual company and industry valuations are aligned with their performance as well. Yes, stocks are volatile and periodic bubbles arise, but overall, the market works as it should. For this reason, managers should continue to make decisions based on these fundamental drivers of value.

In this chapter, we'll explain how a market with different types of investors can lead to rational prices most of the time, even if some of the investors don't make decisions based on economic fundamentals. Then we'll show the empirical evidence that growth and return on invested capital (ROIC) are, in fact, the key drivers of value. Finally, we'll explode the myths behind some commonly accepted beliefs that are at odds with the fundamental principles of valuation.

This chapter was coauthored by Vartika Gupta and Peter Stumpner.

[1] W. H. Gross, "Cult Figures," *Investment Outlook* (PIMCO), August 2012, www.pimco.com.
[2] P. Krugman, "Crashing Economy, Rising Stocks: What's Going On?" *New York Times*, April 30, 2020, www.nytimes.com; J. Smialek, "Nobel Economist Thaler Says He's Nervous about Stock Market," *Bloomberg News*, October 10, 2017, www.bloomberg.com; R. Shiller, "When a Stock Market Is Contagious," *New York Times*, October 18, 2014, www.nytimes.com.

MARKETS AND FUNDAMENTALS: A MODEL

We use a straightforward model to illustrate how market trading by both fundamental, or informed, investors and nonfundamental investors (what we call "noise traders") will produce prices that are generally in line with intrinsic value but can still be volatile.[3] These prices may even deviate significantly from intrinsic value under certain, albeit rare, conditions.

Assume a basic market where trading is limited to one company's stock and, for comparison, a risk-free asset. Two types of investors trade in this market. Informed investors develop a point of view about the intrinsic value of the company's shares based on its underlying fundamentals, such as return on capital and growth. They base their buy and sell decisions on this informed point of view. They may not all agree on the intrinsic value. Some may believe the company's shares are worth $40, others $50, and others $60. Because of transaction costs and uncertainty about the intrinsic value, they will trade only if the stock price deviates by more than 10 percent from their value estimates.

The other investors in this market are the noise traders. These traders may be news oriented, trading on any event they believe will move the share price up or down in the near term, without having a point of view on the company's intrinsic value. Noise traders can also trade on momentum, basing their trades only on price trends: when shares are going up, they buy, assuming the price will continue to increase, and when prices are going down, they sell.[4] Unfortunately, retail investors often behave like momentum traders, just not very good ones; they buy when stocks are high and sell when they are low.

Say trading starts when the price of a single share in the market is $30. Informed investors start buying shares because they believe the shares should be worth $40 to $60. Such buying drives up the share price. Some noise traders notice the rising share price and begin to purchase as well. This accelerates the share price increase, attracting more and more noise traders. As the share price increases, the informed investors gradually slow their purchases. At $44, the most pessimistic begin to sell. Once the price passes $66, all informed investors are selling. Momentum declines, which some of the noise traders sense, so they begin to sell as well. The selling pressure builds, and the stock price begins to fall. The noise traders accelerate the fall, but this slows as more and more informed investors begin to buy, until at $36, all informed investors are buying again, and the fall is reversed.

The pattern continues, with the share price oscillating within a band whose boundaries are set by the informed investors, as shown in Exhibit 6.1.

---

[3] Nonfundamental investors, or noise traders, could also be called "irrational" because they don't make decisions based on an economic analysis of a company. We call them nonfundamental, because their strategies might be rational and sophisticated, even though not based on fundamentals.

[4] Our two investor groups are similar to feedback traders and smart-money investors, as in W. N. Goetzmann and M. Massa, "Daily Momentum and Contrarian Behavior of Index Fund Investors," *Journal of Financial and Quantitative Analysis* 37, no. 3 (September 2002): 375–389.

EXHIBIT 6.1 **Model of Share Price Trading Boundaries**

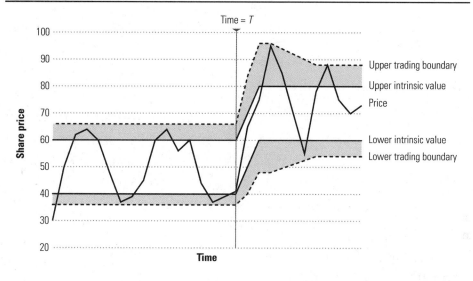

If the noise traders act not only on price movements but also on random, insignificant events, there will also be price oscillations within the band. The band itself can change over time, depending on changes in the assessment of the company's intrinsic value by informed investors. For example, product launches or successes in research and development can lead informed investors to increase their value estimates as well as their trading bandwidth. As a result, price volatility will be temporarily higher while investors are absorbing the new information, as shown in the period after time T in Exhibit 6.1.

In this model, prices will move within the band if there is enough informed capital. This mechanism can break down, but not often. For example, when informed investors are vastly outnumbered by noise traders, their sales of stocks might not be able to stop a price rally. Such circumstances are rare, given the amounts of capital managed by sophisticated, professional—that is to say, informed—investors today.[5] Nevertheless, if informed investors believe the shares are overvalued, once they have sold all the overvalued shares, some may be reluctant to engage in short sales for fear of losing significant amounts before prices revert to lower levels. Others can face institutional or regulatory restrictions. As a result, the price rally might continue. But noise traders cannot push share prices above their intrinsic levels for prolonged periods; at some

---

[5] This is also what the academic literature predicts: informed investors outweigh and ultimately survive noise traders. See, for example, L. Blume and D. Easley, "Market Selection and Asset Pricing," *in Handbook of Financial Markets: Dynamics and Evolution*, ed. T. Hens and K. Hoppe (Amsterdam: Elsevier, 2009); and J. De Long, A. Shleifer, L. Summers, and R. Waldman, "The Survival of Noise Traders in Financial Markets," *Journal of Business* 64, no. 1 (1991): 1–19.

point, fundamentals prevail in setting prices in the stock market. In extreme cases, such as the technology bubble of the 1990s, this could take a few years, but the stock market always corrects itself to align with the underlying fundamental economics.

MARKETS AND FUNDAMENTALS: THE EVIDENCE

The empirical evidence supports the idea that growth and ROIC are the key drivers of value. In this section, we examine some of this evidence. For instance, by looking at stock returns and valuation levels over a very long period, from 1962 to 2023, we can see clearly that they are linked to growth and ROIC. We show that sector and company valuations are aligned with growth and ROIC. Finally, we show that differences in the valuation of U.S. and European companies are the result not of superficial factors but of these same market fundamentals—growth and ROIC.

Many conventional and widely held beliefs about the stock market posit alternative explanations as to why it behaves as it does and why it is sometimes erratic. However, these are not supported by the evidence. For example, some investors and analysts like to think of company stocks as either "value" or "growth" stocks. However, as shown on the left side of Exhibit 6.2, many so-called growth companies don't grow that fast compared with "value" companies. How can this be? It's because companies are typically classified

EXHIBIT 6.2 **Distribution of Growth Rates and ROIC for Growth and Value Stocks**

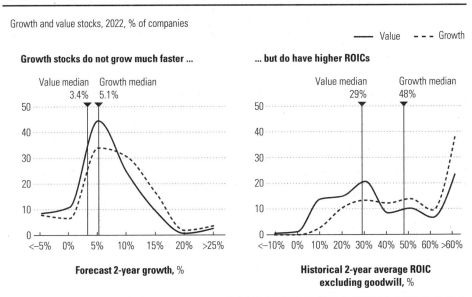

Source: Standard & Poor's; McKinsey Value Intelligence database.

as growth or value based on P/Es and market-to-book ratios (M/Bs), not on underlying growth. The implicit assumption is that faster-growing companies have higher P/Es and higher M/Bs, but a slow-growing company can have a higher P/E and high M/B if it has a high ROIC. This is consistent with the right side of Exhibit 6.2, which shows that companies called growth companies often have higher ROICs.

Sixty Years of Stock Returns Linked to Economic Fundamentals

Market bubbles and crashes have always captured public attention, fueling the belief that the stock market moves in chaotic ways, detached from economic fundamentals. The rise and decline of technology stocks between 2020 and 2022, the 2008 financial crisis, the technology bubble of the 1990s, the Black Monday crash of October 1987, the leveraged-buyout (LBO) craze of the 1980s, and of course, the Wall Street crash of 1929 appear to confirm such ideas. But if we look at the long view, as Exhibit 6.3 shows, we can see clearly that U.S. equities over the past 200 years have delivered decade after decade of consistent returns to shareholders of about 7 percent annually, adjusted for inflation.

The origins of this 7 percent total shareholder return (TSR) lie in the fundamental performance of companies and the long-term cost of equity.

EXHIBIT 6.3 **Stock Performance Against Bonds in the Long Run, 1801–2023**

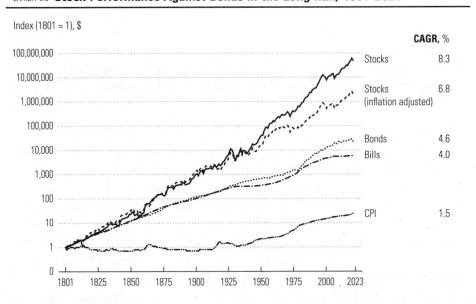

Source: J. J. Siegel, *Stocks for the Long Run: The Definitive Guide to Financial Market Returns and Long-Term Investment Strategies* (New York: McGraw-Hill, 2014); R. G. Ibbotson, *2019 SBBI Yearbook* (Duff & Phelps) (data points for 1801–1927); A. Damodaran, Damodaran Online, pages.stern.nyu.edu/~adamodar (data points from 1928 onward).

EXHIBIT 6.4 **Economic Fundamentals Explain Long-Term Total Shareholder Returns**

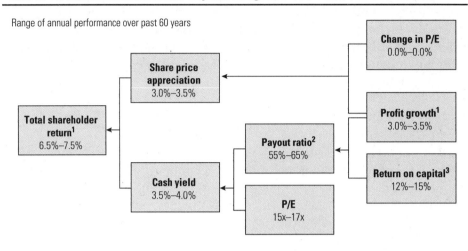

Range of annual performance over past 60 years

[1] Measured in real terms.

[2] Estimated as (1 − growth)/ROIC, where growth is real-terms profit growth plus inflation at 2.0%–2.5%.

[3] Long-term average return on equity. Recent years have been above average levels.

TSR is simply the sum of the share price appreciation plus the cash yield (see Exhibit 6.4). During the past 60 years (the period for which we have the most reliable data), share price appreciation in real terms has been in the range of 3.0 to 3.5 percent per year, and total cash yields have been around 3.5 to 4.0 percent. Hence the total real returns of about 7 percent.

Share price appreciation is driven by U.S. corporate profit growth of about 3.0 to 3.5 percent per year in real terms and no significant change in the median P/E when spread over 60 years.[6] Moreover, corporate America has typically reinvested about 35 to 45 percent of profits every year to achieve this profit growth, leaving the remainder to be paid to shareholders as dividends and share repurchases (55 to 65 percent of profits).

This ratio is not random. From Chapter 3, we know that the reinvestment rate is the growth rate in nominal terms divided by the return on equity (ROE). With 3.0 to 3.5 percent real growth and 5 to 6 percent nominal growth and 12 to 15 percent ROE, it follows that the reinvestment rate should be 35 to 45 percent. That leads to a cash payout ratio of 55 to 65 percent. That cash payout ratio translates to a cash yield on the value of the shares of around 3.5 to 4.0 percent, assuming a long-term P/E of 15 to 17. The math is the payout ratio times the inverse of the P/E ratio. Adding the cash yield of 3.5 to 4.0 percent to the annual 3.0 to 3.5 percent share price appreciation results in total real shareholder returns of about 6.5 to 7.5 percent per year—which, for simplicity, we will call 7 percent.

[6] Note that the P/E is stable if long-term growth rates, returns on capital, and costs of equity are stable.

Some analysts miss an important element of stock returns: that gains are driven by both share price appreciation and cash yields. As they see it, share prices cannot increase faster than corporate profits. But this perspective erroneously misses the cash distributions entirely. Other analysts have been too pessimistic about the share price appreciation component because they've predicted declines in the P/E. They estimate that P/Es will decline far below the range of 15 to 17 that we've used, because they incorporate the 1970s and 1980s in their estimates of long-term P/E ratios—a time when P/Es were severely depressed because of exceptionally high inflation levels.[7]

P/Es Are Also Linked to Economic Fundamentals over Time

We can also see the fundamental performance of companies reflected in the movement of P/E ratios over time. To demonstrate this close relationship, we estimated a fundamental P/E for the U.S. stock market for each year from 1962 to 2023, using a simple equity discounted-cash-flow (DCF) valuation model, following the value driver formula first presented in Chapter 3. We estimated what the price-to-earnings ratios would have been for the U.S. stock market for each year, had they been based on these fundamental economic factors. Exhibit 6.5 shows how well even a simple fundamental valuation model fits the stock market's actual P/E levels over the past decades, despite periods of extremely high economic growth in the 1960s and 1990s, as well as periods of low growth and high inflation in the 1970s and 1980s and again in the early 2020s. By and large, the U.S. stock market has been reasonably priced, with the median P/E oscillating around our estimated fundamental P/Es. Note that the aggregate P/E—which is the ratio most often referenced in the news media—is not a reliable indicator of the pricing level of most companies, because it is often skewed by highly valued, very large companies (as we will discuss later in this chapter). We conducted a similar analysis of the European stock markets and obtained similar results—albeit with P/Es generally at lower levels than for the U.S. market because of lower growth and return on capital.

Note that since 2010, the actual P/Es have been slightly higher than in previous decades. Part of the explanation lies in steadily increasing returns on capital, and another part in excess cash balances held by large companies. Cash has a high implied P/E because it carries little after-tax interest. We find that correcting for the excess cash balance in corporate P/Es typically lowers the ratio for the market as a whole by one to two points.[8]

---

[7] In addition, Robert Shiller's measure of the current P/E is overestimated because it does not exclude extraordinary losses such as goodwill impairments. See J. Siegel, "Don't Put Faith in Cape Crusaders," *Financial Times*, August 20, 2013; "Siegel vs. Shiller: Is the Stock Market Overvalued?" Knowledge@ Wharton, September 18, 2018, knowledge.wharton.upenn.edu.

[8] See, for example, R. Gupta, B. Jiang, and T. Koller, "Looking behind the Numbers for US Stock Indexes," *McKinsey on Finance*, no. 65 (January 2018): 11–15.

EXHIBIT 6.5 **Estimating Fundamental Market Valuation Levels**

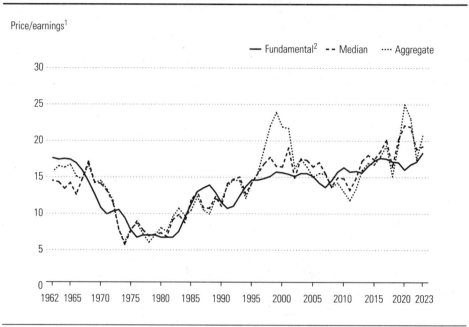

[1] Price-to-earnings ratio on 12-month forward-looking earnings for the 500 largest U.S.-based companies by market capitalization.

[2] Moving-average over 3 years.

Stock Market Eras: 1960–2023

It would be hard to argue that the market's movements over one hour, one day, one week, or one month can be explained by anything other than a random process. There are simply too many moving parts, and as we saw in Chapter 5, short-term market movements are as much about changes in expectations as they are about actual performance. Short-term prices are also influenced by purely technical factors, such as large investors selling shares to rebalance their portfolios.

So if we can't explain the market over one month but we can explain it over 100 years, what sort of time frame might provide a useful basis for understanding the market's movements? One common practice is to examine the stock market from peak to trough or vice versa, because this shows the greatest extremes in performance and makes for better headlines. But this practice may distort our understanding of the underlying economic events. In Exhibit 6.6, we adopt an alternative method, identifying seven eras over the past 60 years that merit distinction based on the fundamental forces driving the U.S. economy and stock market:

1. *Carefree 1960s (1960–68).* During this period, the economy grew at a steady rate, as did corporate profits, and interest rates and inflation

EXHIBIT 6.6 **U.S. Equity Markets: Seven Eras**

Total shareholder return for S&P 500, inflation adjusted, index (Jan. 1960 = 100)

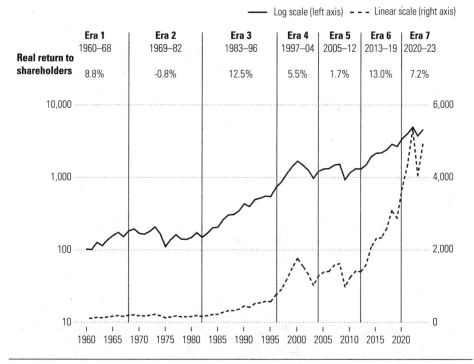

—— Log scale (left axis)   - - - Linear scale (right axis)

	Era 1	Era 2	Era 3	Era 4	Era 5	Era 6	Era 7
	1960–68	1969–82	1983–96	1997–04	2005–12	2013–19	2020–23
Real return to shareholders	8.8%	-0.8%	12.5%	5.5%	1.7%	13.0%	7.2%

were low and stable. It should be no surprise, then, that the real return to shareholders was 8.8 percent, comfortably above the long-term average.

2. *Great Inflation (1969–82).* High inflation led investors to reduce P/Es from 17 in 1968 to 9 in 1982, leading to negative real returns for investors over this miserable 14-year period.

3. *Return to Normalcy (1983–96).* P/Es and economic growth recovered as inflation was brought under control, leading to impressive real returns of 12.5 percent for investors.

4. *Technology Bubble (1997–2004).* From beginning to end of this era, real returns and economic growth were near normal levels, with real returns averaging 5.5 percent. But most accounts of this period have focused on the negative returns following the bubble in the middle.

5. *Leveraging and Credit Crisis (2005–12).* The financial sector's reckless-ness in this era wiped out corporate profits, leading to real returns of less than 2 percent per year, well below the long-term average.

6. *Growth in Profits and Rise of Technology (2013–19).* Earnings growth accelerated to an annualized real rate of 6.7 percent, driven partly by growth in the high-tech and life sciences sectors. This led to real shareholder returns of 13 percent annualized—almost double the long-term average return.

7. *Pandemic and Recovery (2020–24).* Corporate earnings were depressed in 2020 by the COVID-19 pandemic but quickly recovered in the following years. Market returns averaged 7.2 percent in real terms, despite an increase in inflation. Again, the large tech stocks were important drivers of market returns, with the seven largest accounting for 28 percent of the index at the end of 2023.

Sector and Company Valuations Also Are in Line with Fundamental Performance

What holds for the stock market as a whole also holds across industries. To demonstrate this, we used the 2022 and 2023 ROIC for the largest listed companies in the world, grouped by industry, as a proxy for each industry's expected future returns and used the analysts' consensus estimate of their two-year growth outlook as a proxy for long-term expected growth (see Exhibit 6.7).[9] Industries with higher ratios of market value to capital or market value to earnings also have higher growth and/or higher ROIC, driven by better operating profit margins and capital turnover. Life science and technology companies had the highest valuation levels, thanks to having the highest ROIC combined with superior growth. Other companies, including healthcare providers, receive high valuations from strong growth at average levels of ROIC. Companies in oil and gas and in metals and mining were valued at low market-value-to-capital multiples because of their low returns on capital and low expected growth. Note that the ratios of market value to earnings show less variation across sectors, reflecting investor expectations of converging earnings growth in the long term.

The same principles apply to individual companies. We compared the ratios of market value to capital of all the companies in the same sample versus their expected ROIC and growth. Exhibit 6.8 shows that, for a given level of growth, higher rates of ROIC generally lead to higher market values, and above a given level of ROIC, higher growth also leads to higher value. Although the empirical results do not fit the theoretical model perfectly, they still clearly demonstrate that the market values companies based on growth and ROIC.[10]

---

[9] This sample comprises listed companies (excluding financial institutions) with revenues exceeding $1 billion from the European Union, Switzerland, the United Kingdom, and the United States.

[10] The lowest ROIC cohort is omitted in the chart for market-value-to-earnings because it includes companies with low earnings levels that distort the cohort multiple (for example, cyclical companies).

EXHIBIT 6.7 **Market Value vs. ROIC and Growth: Selected Industry Sectors**

Sector median of 2022–2023 company averages, U.S. and European companies with real revenues > $1 billion

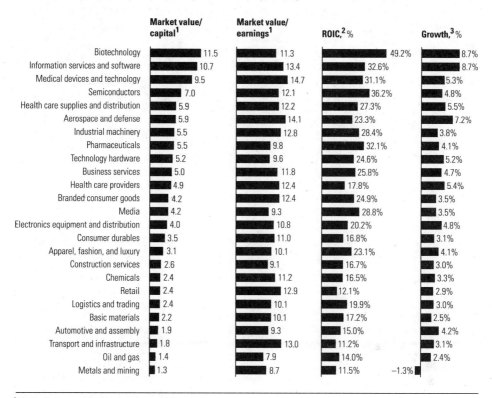

	Market value/capital[1]	Market value/earnings[1]	ROIC,[2] %	Growth,[3] %
Biotechnology	11.5	11.3	49.2%	8.7%
Information services and software	10.7	13.4	32.6%	8.7%
Medical devices and technology	9.5	14.7	31.1%	5.3%
Semiconductors	7.0	12.1	36.2%	4.8%
Health care supplies and distribution	5.9	12.2	27.3%	5.5%
Aerospace and defense	5.9	14.1	23.3%	7.2%
Industrial machinery	5.5	12.8	28.4%	3.8%
Pharmaceuticals	5.5	9.8	32.1%	4.1%
Technology hardware	5.2	9.6	24.6%	5.2%
Business services	5.0	11.8	25.8%	4.7%
Health care providers	4.9	12.4	17.8%	5.4%
Branded consumer goods	4.2	12.4	24.9%	3.5%
Media	4.2	9.3	28.8%	3.5%
Electronics equipment and distribution	4.0	10.8	20.2%	4.8%
Consumer durables	3.5	11.0	16.8%	3.1%
Apparel, fashion, and luxury	3.1	10.1	23.1%	4.1%
Construction services	2.6	9.1	16.7%	3.0%
Chemicals	2.4	11.2	16.5%	3.3%
Retail	2.4	12.9	12.1%	2.9%
Logistics and trading	2.4	10.1	19.9%	3.0%
Basic materials	2.2	10.1	17.2%	2.5%
Automotive and assembly	1.9	9.3	15.0%	4.2%
Transport and infrastructure	1.8	13.0	11.2%	3.1%
Oil and gas	1.4	7.9	14.0%	2.4%
Metals and mining	1.3	8.7	11.5%	−1.3%

[1] Market value is enterprise value, capital is invested capital excluding goodwill, and earnings is earnings before interest, taxes, depreciation, and amortization (EBITDA).

[2] Return on invested capital excluding goodwill.

[3] Analyst consensus forecast of annual revenue growth for next 2 years.

Source: McKinsey Value Intelligence database.

The Last 15 Years: Divergence between the United States and Europe

As shown in Exhibit 6.9, European and U.S. stocks performed similarly from the 1970s into the late 2000s: the MSCI Europe and S&P 500 indices both delivered returns of around 5.25 percent in real terms per year on average. These returns were below long-term average levels, due to the oil crises of the 1970s and the subsequent inflation in the 1980s (nominal returns were around 10 percent). But around 2012, as the fifth era—the Leveraging and Credit Crisis—came to an end, this pattern changed fundamentally. Over the following two eras, from 2013 to 2024, U.S. stocks returned over 10 percent per year while European stocks returned less than 4 percent, more than six points below U.S. stocks (all in real terms).

This development has led some to believe that European stocks trade at lower multiples and provide lower returns simply because they are European—and that relisting in the United States can boost shareholder

EXHIBIT 6.8 **Market Value, ROIC, and Growth: Empirical Relationship Across Companies**

Sector median of 2022–2023 company averages, U.S. and European companies with real revenues > $1 billion

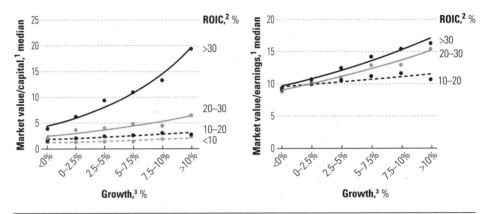

[1] Market value is enterprise value, capital is invested capital excluding goodwill, and earnings is earnings before interest, taxes, depreciation, and amortization (EBITDA).

[2] Return on invested capital excluding goodwill.

[3] Analyst consensus forecast of annual revenue growth for next 2 years.

Source: McKinsey Value Intelligence database.

EXHIBIT 6.9 **Diverging Returns in U.S. and European Equity Markets**

Total shareholder return, S&P 500 and MSCI Europe, inflation adjusted, index (Jan. 1970 = 100)

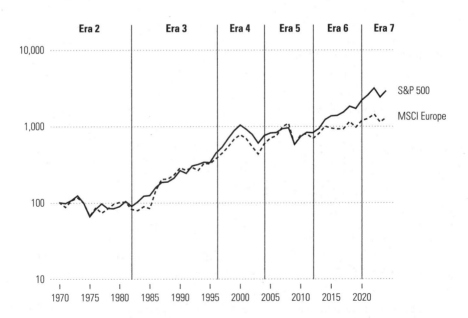

returns. However, the true explanation is again found in the underlying fundamentals, which improved significantly in the high-tech and pandemic recovery eras for U.S. companies but did not for European companies. Three reasons explain why U.S. stocks have outperformed European stocks on aggregate:

1. Across industries, U.S. companies on average deliver higher returns on capital than European companies and have been able to increase profit margins at a much higher rate than European companies. (For more on this, see Chapter 8.)

2. U.S. companies grow faster and invest more than European companies. Over the last decade, total invested capital (the capital stock) of U.S. public companies has grown by four percentage points more per year, across industries, than its European counterpart. This has played a major role in faster revenue growth for large companies in the United States versus those in Europe (for more on this, see Chapter 9).

3. The United States is home to significantly more highly profitable, fast-growing technology and life science companies and is where the small number of the most successful companies are based. Europe does not have any companies that have achieved this level of industry leadership. The success of these and other life science and technology companies has changed the industry composition of the U.S. economy, making it seem as though its higher return on capital and growth prospects are the result of structural factors (for more on this, see Chapter 8).

The combined effect of these differences in industry composition, return on capital, and growth explains the divergence in capital market valuation for the U.S. and the European economies, including the United Kingdom and Switzerland. Exhibit 6.10 combines return on capital and growth for U.S. and European economies into a single number for value creation: economic profit (for more on this, see Chapter 3). This clearly shows that the growth in aggregate economic profit for the largest companies in the United States and Europe between 2013 and 2023 has driven the divergence in equity market valuations. In terms of economy-wide growth of economic profit, the United States clearly outpaced Europe by more than four percentage points per year over the decade, with high-tech and life sciences sectors driving most of that difference. Again, all of this is the result of underlying economic fundamentals.

BUBBLES IN THE STOCK MARKET

If the most sophisticated investors (that is, informed investors) drive share prices, are there stock market bubbles and, if so, why do they occur? The short answer is that, yes, there are bubbles, but they're generally confined

EXHIBIT 6.10 **Economic Profit Growth and Market Capitalization: U.S. and European Companies, 2013–2023**

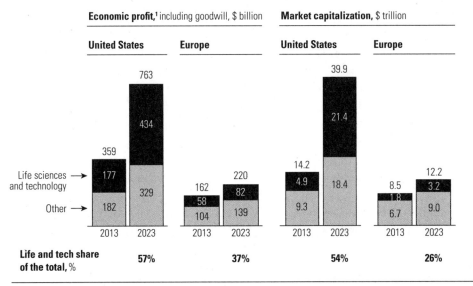

U.S. and European companies with revenues > $ 1 billion

Economic profit,[1] including goodwill, $ billion

Market capitalization, $ trillion

United States | Europe | United States | Europe

Life and tech share of the total, %: 57% | 37% | 54% | 26%

[1] Average economic profit of past and current year for 2013 and 2023.

to industry sectors or individual companies, not the entire market. And they occur because informed investors are sometimes unable to offset the behavior of less rational investors.

It's important to first distinguish stock market bubbles from stock price declines in reaction to new information. Unlike other assets, such as art or cryptocurrencies, a corporate stock is unique in that its owners are entitled to a stream of profit and cash flow generated by the company. Stocks therefore have intrinsic value, and the price at which the stocks trade in the market will eventually reflect that value. There is, however, uncertainty about what that value is, because future cash flows are uncertain. Understanding this allows us to analyze stock prices and, at least in hindsight, determine whether there was a bubble.

For example, one can reasonably assert that a shoe-making company shouldn't be worth $1 trillion because the market for shoes simply isn't large enough to generate cash flows worth $1 trillion. So if the stock of a shoe company were trading in the stock market at $1 trillion and then dropped to $50 billion, we could reasonably assert that it was in a price bubble at $1 trillion. But when stock prices drop sharply in the face of uncertainty and new information, this is not necessarily evidence of a bubble. For example, when a pharmaceutical company announces that a promising new drug has failed in clinical trials, the share price of the company will usually drop considerably. The steep decline in this case doesn't indicate that the price was originally at a bubble level. The price prior to the announcement likely reflected a reasonable estimate of the company's value based upon a reasonable estimate of probability for the drug's success.

We define a bubble as a time when the stock price of a company is far above the level at which rational, informed investors would value the company. The prices of some dot-com companies in the late 1990s are good examples of bubbles. For some companies, it was impossible to imagine any reasonable cash flow scenario that could justify their price. This can be a good litmus test for assessing whether a bubble is occurring: Can you come up with a reasonable, even if highly optimistic, cash flow scenario that is in line with the stock price? If not, there is a good chance that a bubble is the cause.

Why Bubbles Form

Mainstream academic finance has been criticized for years because some of its underlying assumptions are clearly not true. For example, most finance theories assume that all investors are rational. It's clearly not true that all behave rationally, and a growing body of literature (loosely categorized as behavioral finance or behavioral economics) describes the irrational decisions that investors make.

But the irrational behavior of some investors doesn't necessarily lead to a market with a lot of mispriced shares and bubbles. For bubbles to occur, individual investor irrationality must be combined with herding behavior and structural constraints. As long as irrational investors behave randomly, they should cancel each other out.

Even so, there are times when large groups of investors exhibit the same behavior and push a company's share price above or below rational levels. Following the market model discussed in the first section of this chapter, that should create opportunities for informed investors to take an opposite position, pushing the share price back toward a rational level. But structural impediments sometimes prevent the informed investors from countering the irrational ones in case of overpricing.

To correct overpricing, rational investors need to sell shares short (that is, sell shares they don't own but borrow, typically from a broker). But in addition to obstacles imposed by governments and stock exchanges, short selling comes with certain risks that can be difficult to manage. First, there is no limit to the potential loss for the short seller if the share price increases. (In contrast, for a long position, any loss from a declining share price maxes out at 100 percent of the investment.) The second risk is liquidity. The broker who lent the shares will require the short seller to make a cash deposit equal to the market value of the shares borrowed, with deposits to be added (returned) if the share price increases (decreases).

For a simple example of what can go wrong, suppose you believe the shares of Company A are worth only $50 while they are currently selling at $100. You sell short 10,000 shares for $1 million. Two years later, the share price drops to $50, so you repurchase the shares at $50, paying $500,000. You initially received $1 million and paid out $500,000 three years later, for a profit of $500,000—in theory. But what if the share price first goes up before coming down? Assume that the share price rises first to $200 before declining to $50. When the share price hits $200, the shares you have borrowed are worth $2 million, but the government bonds you have on deposit with the broker are worth only $1 million. The broker asks for another $1 million in collateral. If you don't have another $1 million to put up, you are out of business, and the broker takes your collateral. Even though your assessment of the shares' ultimate value was correct, you lose $1 million instead of gaining $500,000. Shorting is risky without sufficient liquidity to weather adverse movements in the company's share price. In contrast, the long investor can sit tight and wait until proven right.

Market Bubbles

Bubbles that affect the broad market in developed economies are rare. On the surface, over the last 60 years in the United States, there appear to have been three periods that might be considered market bubbles: the early 1970s, 1997–2001, and 2007–09. Digging deeper, however, even these bubbles weren't broad based but were concentrated in segments of the market.

The apparent bubble in the 1970s mainly involved a small number of high-capitalization companies. Several established companies traded at extremely high multiples. For example, in 1972, Kodak traded at a P/E multiple of 37 times, Xerox traded at 39 times, and McDonald's traded at 58 times. These companies were part of the so-called Nifty 50, a group of 50 large-cap stocks you could supposedly buy and hold forever. The simplicity of the Nifty 50 influenced many investors to follow the herd, leading to inflated share prices.

The technology market boom in the late 1990s was a classic valuation bubble, in which stocks were priced at earnings multiples that underlying fundamentals could not justify. When Netscape Communications became a public company in 1995, it saw its market capitalization soar to $6 billion on an annual revenue base of just $85 million. As investors quickly became convinced that the internet would change the world, they sent the Standard & Poor's (S&P) 500 index to a new peak in 2000. By 2003, the index had tumbled back to half that level.

However, although the valuation of the market overall was affected, the bubble was concentrated in technology stocks and certain very large stocks (so-called megacaps) in other sectors. Before and after the bubble, the P/Es of the 30 largest companies were about the same on average as those of the other 470 companies in the S&P 500 (see Exhibit 6.11). However, in 1999, the average

EXHIBIT 6.11 **Impact of Largest Stocks on Overall Market Valuation**

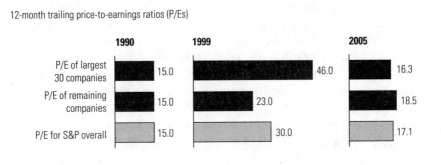

12-month trailing price-to-earnings ratios (P/Es)

top-30 company had a P/E of 46 times, compared with an average of 23 times for the other 470 companies. As a result, the weighted average P/E for the market overall reached 30 times.

Most of the large-capitalization companies with high P/Es during this period were clustered in just three sectors: technology, media, and telecommunications. Of course, some of the companies born in this era (including Amazon and eBay) have created substantial economic value. But for every solid, innovative new business idea, there were dozens of companies that forgot or purposely threw out fundamental rules of economics.

By 2007, stock markets around the world had more than recovered from the technology bubble fallout, and the S&P 500 reached a new peak. Meanwhile, the largest property boom and credit expansion in U.S. and European history drove corporate earnings to exceptional levels that ultimately proved unsustainable. Although all companies were affected, this bubble too was mainly driven by a few sectors. The financial, energy, utilities, and materials sectors showed sharply inflated earnings, from 41 percent of total S&P earnings in 1997 to 51 percent in 2006. But in 2007, a chain reaction of collapsing funding structures for mortgages and other forms of credit brought financial institutions across the world into distress. U.S. and European stock markets lost more than half of their value as the world's economy experienced the steepest downturn since the 1930s. From the end of 2006, the S&P 500 dropped by about 50 percent in early 2009. Fueled by strong increases in returns on capital and revenue growth, it rebounded to its previous high by 2012. It's not clear, though, that we should call this a bubble, because it was driven by events in the real economy, rather than investor irrationality.

Sector and Company Bubbles

Sector and company valuation bubbles are more frequent than apparent market-wide bubbles, but they're still rare. One example of a sector bubble is the market valuation of biotechnology companies in the United States in

2005 and 2006, when the sum of the market capitalizations of all the listed biotech companies was about $450 billion (excluding the traditional large pharmaceutical companies, most of which were also investing in biotech). Making reasonable assumptions about future margins, we estimate that these companies as a group would have needed $600 billion in revenues in 2025 to justify such a valuation level (all in 2006 dollars). Given that all listed U.S. pharmaceutical companies combined earned about $600 billion of revenues in 2006, that was not very realistic.

Likewise, company-specific bubbles are not widespread—at least for sizable companies. We examined 3,560 U.S.-based companies that traded at a minimum market capitalization of $1 billion in any year between 1982 and 2007. Of those, only 123 could be considered to have experienced a bubble in their stock price at a given time during those 25 years.[11] Of those 123, the vast majority—92—were technology, media, or telecom companies that experienced their bubbles during the tech bubble of 1999–2001. That leaves only 31 other companies, less than 1 percent of the sample, that might have experienced independent bubbles in their share prices.

The COVID-19 pandemic did create some unusual overreactions by investors. Peloton, the maker of interactive exercise bikes, is a good example. Its share price was $26 at the beginning of 2020. As the pandemic hit and demand for the company's products increased, its share price shot up to $151 by October of that year. Of course, that wasn't aligned with the company's true economic potential, and by the end of 2021, Peloton's share price was back down to $26.

Bubbles Reinforce the Need to Focus on Long-Term Value Creation

While valuation bubbles do occur, they are rare and short-lived, so they do not invalidate the principles of this book. Paradoxically, given such market deviations, it's even more important for corporate managers and investors to understand the true, intrinsic value of companies. While there may be some tactical opportunities to use overvalued shares to make acquisitions, managers should be skeptical of analyses claiming to find market deviations for a company's shares. After careful analysis, most of the alleged deviations we've encountered have turned out to be insignificant or even nonexistent.

As long as your company's share price will eventually return to its long-run, intrinsic discounted cash flow (DCF) value, you should rely on using the DCF approach for making strategic decisions. What matters is the long-term behavior of your company's share price, not whether it's 5 or 10 percent undervalued this week.

---

[11] We considered a company to have experienced a bubble in its share price when the following conditions were met: (1) its P/E reached twice the P/E of the S&P 500 or at least 40 when the S&P 500 P/E was greater than 20; (2) the drop in the company's share price after the peak year was not due to a substantial decline in earnings; and (3) the share price dropped by 30 percent or more after its peak P/E.

SUMMARY

Volatile share prices sometimes lead people to suggest that valuations and long-term TSR are divorced from economic fundamentals. In this chapter, we presented evidence from multiples angles showing that the stock market, in the long run, is clearly linked to economic fundamentals: growth and ROIC. Over the past six decades, this has applied consistently both to the market as a whole and to individual sectors and companies. It also applies outside the United States, particularly in Europe.

At times, markets deviate from fundamentals and experience bubbles, but these tend to be short-lived and isolated to specific sectors or companies. Such bubbles can occur even in otherwise well-functioning, developed markets, mostly because of structural barriers to intervention by informed investors—for example, a lack of perfect liquidity.

In the next chapter, we explore and debunk many myths about how the stock market works in practice, showing that the fundamental theory provides better guidance than much conventional wisdom does for guiding management decisions and creating value in companies.

7

The Stock Market Is Smarter Than You Think

As we discussed in the previous chapter, there is compelling evidence that the stock market's valuations of individual companies and industries are sound and generally reflect the fundamental performance of the company or industry, measured in return on invested capital (ROIC) and growth. True, there are times when valuations deviate from fundamentals, but these rarely last long.

Despite this, some managers and finance professionals erroneously believe that these deviations are systemic and can be used to outsmart the stock market. In this chapter, we'll explore some of the myths that perpetuate this belief and explain why they are at odds with the fundamental principles of value creation. One group of myths suggests that stock markets are focused above all on a company's accounting earnings, or earnings per share (EPS)—leading some to believe, for example, that when managers must decide between share repurchases or acquisitions, they should always pick the option that is most favorable for EPS growth, even though the facts clearly show that ROIC and growth are much more important for value creation than EPS. Another group of myths contends that companies can create value in the stock market simply by meeting certain targets or analyst expectations. Again, this is simply not true. There is no reward for earnings management. Other myths posit that value creation benefits can be derived from attributes such as company size, diversification, index membership, cross-listing, and cash returns to shareholders.

The evidence presented in this chapter is clear: these myths do not stand up to scrutiny. Instead of looking for shortcuts, managers should continue making decisions based on fundamental drivers of value.

This chapter was coauthored by Marc Silberstein.

MYTHS ABOUT EARNINGS

We believe strongly that the best course for managers is to focus their energy on growth at an attractive ROIC. Yet some companies go to great lengths to achieve a certain earnings per share (EPS) number or to smooth out their earnings. This is wasted energy. The evidence shows that these efforts aren't worth it, and they may actually hurt the company.

We're not saying EPS doesn't matter. Companies that create value often have attractive earnings growth, and earnings will equal cash flow over the life span of the company. But not all earnings growth creates value. Consider the three most important drivers of EPS growth: revenue growth, margin improvement, and share repurchases. As we've pointed out, revenue growth (especially organic growth) is a powerful driver of value if it generates a return on invested capital exceeding the cost of capital. Margin improvements coming purely from cost cutting are not sustainable in the long term and might even hurt a company's future growth and value creation—if, for example, investments in research or marketing are cut back. Share repurchases typically increase EPS but also increase a company's debt or reduce its cash. In either case, this leads to a decline in a company's P/E, which neutralizes the increase in EPS so that value per share does not change. Consider German engineering and steel company Thyssenkrupp, which had around €6.6 billion in liquid assets in 2023. The liquid assets are low risk and low return, so they have a high P/E (higher than for Thyssenkrupp's operating assets). Paying out the liquid assets would reduce the proportion of high-P/E assets relative to lower-P/E assets, reducing the overall (weighted-average) P/E for Thyssenkrupp as a whole.

In this section, we'll show that the sophisticated investors who drive stock market values dig beneath a company's accounting information to understand the underlying economic fundamentals. A classic example is the share price reaction to changes in inventory accounting by U.S. companies in the 1960s and 1970s. Because of rising price levels in these years, changing from first-in-first-out (FIFO) to last-in-first-out (LIFO) accounting decreased reported profits as well as taxable income. But the investor reaction reflected by the share price was typically positive, because investors understood that free cash flows would be higher as a result of lower taxes.[1] Time and again, we find that stock markets correctly interpret changes in accounting, whether this concerns elimination of goodwill amortization, expensing of stock options at fair value, or capitalization of operating leases. As finance theory predicted, none of these changes affected company valuations, even though the impact on earnings per share was sometimes significant.

[1] G. Biddle and F. Lindahl, "Stock Price Reactions to LIFO Adoptions: The Association between Excess Returns and LIFO Tax Savings," *Journal of Accounting Research* 20, no. 2 (1982): 551–588.

Sometimes investors have difficulty detecting the true economic situation behind accounting information. For example, investors found it hard to assess the true risks and returns on capital of many financial institutions prior to the 2008 credit crisis because the financial reports were so opaque. Some companies, including Enron and WorldCom, misled stock markets by purposely manipulating their financial statements. But all managers should understand that markets can be mistaken or fooled for only so long. Sooner or later, share prices need to be justified by cash flows rather than accounting earnings.

EPS Growth from Share Repurchases

Even though EPS is not a reliable indicator of value creation, many companies still use it as a key measure of financial performance and an important input for executive compensation. Not surprisingly, we find that executives pursue share repurchase programs mainly because they believe the resulting EPS growth creates value for shareholders. But savvy markets see through such moves with a gimlet eye. One company managed to create strong growth in EPS while its net income was falling, simply by retiring its shares even faster.[2] When investors understood that business results were declining, the company's share price dropped by 40 percent relative to the overall market change.

The empirical evidence is clear. At face value, there appears to be a correlation between shareholder value creation and the intensity of a company's share repurchase program. But that is simply because companies with higher returns on capital and growth also tend to pay out more cash to shareholders. After we control for differences in growth and return on capital, no relationship is left between share repurchases and shareholder value creation (see Exhibit 7.1).[3]

Earnings from Mergers and Acquisitions

There is yet another way for companies to increase their earnings: buying another company. Say a company has $1 billion of excess cash. It uses the cash to buy another company earning $50 million per year at a P/E multiple of 20 times. Its earnings will increase by $50 million, less the forgone interest it was earning on the excess cash; assuming that equals $5 million (at a 0.5 percent after-tax return on cash), the net increase is $45 million. Though the company's earnings have increased, we can't tell whether it has created value. At a 20 P/E purchase price, it will be earning only 5 percent on its invested capital. If it has

---

[2] See O. Ezekoye, T. Koller, and A. Mittal, "How Share Repurchases Boost Earnings without Improving Returns," *McKinsey on Finance*, no. 58 (2016): 15–24.

[3] If companies could time share repurchases when share prices are truly low, they could create value for shareholders who do not sell. However, as we discuss in Chapter 35, most companies do not time repurchases effectively.

EXHIBIT 7.1 **Relationship Between Share Repurchases and Shareholder Returns**

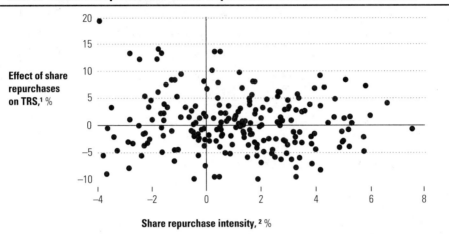

[1] Effect of share repurchases on total shareholder return (TSR) is measured by residuals of multivariate regression. Variables are share repurchase intensity and economic-profit growth. Economic-profit growth is a measure that combines earnings growth and return on capital (relative to cost of capital). This regression shows that the effect of share repurchase intensity is not statistically significant.

[2] Difference between EPS growth and net income growth used as proxy for degree of share repurchase intensity.

Source: Corporate Performance Analytics by McKinsey (with a sample of >250 nonfinancial S&P 500 companies).

a 10 percent cost of capital, it will need to double the earnings of the acquired company to earn its cost of capital on the $1 billion it just invested.

Investors see through the accounting earnings. Chapter 31 shows that whether an acquisition increases or decreases earnings in the first year or two after the acquisition has no significant correlation with the stock market's reaction to the transaction.

Investors also see through the illusion of "multiple expansion," as we discussed in Chapter 3. There is no empirical evidence or economic logic to support the idea that the stock market will value an acquired business at the earnings multiple of the acquiring business. The earnings multiple of two combined businesses will simply equal the weighted average of the individual earnings multiples. Any value increase must come from additional cash flows over and above those of the individual businesses.

Write-Downs

Executives are often reluctant to take the earnings hit from writing down the value of assets, assuming investors will react negatively. But investors don't respond mechanically to write-downs. Rather, they assess what information the write-down conveys about the future performance of the company.

We looked at 40 of the largest goodwill impairments since 2013 by companies in the United States and Europe. In each case, the company had written off at least $2 billion of impaired goodwill against its profits. As Exhibit 7.2 shows, there was no meaningful drop in share prices in the days after the write-off

EXHIBIT 7.2 **No Market Reaction to Announcement of Goodwill Impairment**

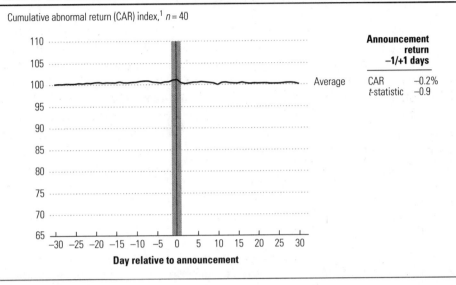

Cumulative abnormal return (CAR) index,[1] $n = 40$

Average

	Announcement return −1/+1 days
CAR	−0.2%
t-statistic	−0.9

Day relative to announcement

[1] For 40 large impairments (write-offs of $2 billion or more) at companies in Europe and the United States since 2013.

Source: SEC filings; Datastream; Bloomberg.

announcement. We found similar results in earlier research that looked at the largest goodwill impairments in the United States and Europe from 2007 to 2012, and 2002 to 2004.[4] The pattern is remarkably consistent over the past two decades. Markets already anticipated the lower benefits from past acquisitions and reduced the share prices long before the write-off announcements. For example, prices jumped nearly 10 percent when Boston Scientific announced a $2.7 billion write-down associated with its 2006 acquisition of Guidant.

Stock markets clearly look at the underlying cash flows and business fundamentals rather than reported earnings and goodwill impairments. In fact, of the European write-offs that we considered in our earlier 2007 to 2012 sample, only one analyst report issued after one announcement even commented on the size of the impairment. Analysts did, however, pay a great deal of attention to indications of how the company would move forward, carefully tracking signals about future operating earnings, the outlook for certain business units, and any management actions or plans to address changing conditions.

Employee Stock Options

In the early 2000s, proposed new accounting rules requiring employee stock options to be expensed in the income statement caused much concern. Some executives and venture capitalists claimed that expensing stock options would

[4] See prior editions of this book and B. Cao, M. Goedhart, and T. Koller,. "Goodwill Shunting: How to Better Manage Write-Downs," *McKinsey on Finance*, no. 50 (Spring 2014): 13–15.

reduce the earnings of small high-growth companies so much that they would not be able to take the companies public.

Of course, there was no need for concern, because stock prices are driven by cash flows, not reported earnings. Academic research has shown that the stock market already took account of employee options in its valuation of companies that give full information about their options schemes—even when the option values are not explicitly expensed in the companies' income statements.[5] In fact, companies that voluntarily expensed their employee options before doing so became mandatory experienced no decrease in share price, despite the negative implications for reported earnings.[6] The market already had the relevant information on the option plans and was not confused by a change in reporting policy.

Different Accounting Standards

Share price data for companies that report different accounting results in different stock markets provide additional evidence that stock markets do not take reported earnings at face value. Prior to 2008, non-U.S. companies that had securities listed in the United States and did not report under U.S. Generally Accepted Accounting Principles (GAAP) or International Financial Reporting Standards (IFRS), for example, were required to report equity and net profit under U.S. GAAP.[7] These could have provided results that differed significantly from the equity and net profit reported under their domestic accounting standards. We analyzed a sample of 50 European companies that began reporting reconciliations of equity and profit to U.S. GAAP after obtaining U.S. listings between 1997 and 2004. The differences between net income and equity under U.S. and local accounting standards were often quite large; in more than half the cases, the gap exceeded 30 percent.

Many executives probably worried that lower earnings under U.S. GAAP would translate directly into a lower share price. But this was not the case. Even though two-thirds of the companies in our sample reported lower earnings following U.S. disclosure, the stock market reaction to their disclosure was positive. At that time, in the late 1990s and early 2000s, following U.S. GAAP standards also generally meant disclosing more information than required by local standards. Evidently, improved disclosure outweighed any artificial accounting effects.

---

[5] D. Aboody, M. Barth, and R. Kasznik, "SFAS No. 123 Stock-Based Compensation Expense and Equity Market Values," *Accounting Review* 79, no. 2 (2004): 251–275.

[6] D. Aboody, M. Barth, and R. Kasznik, "Firms' Voluntary Recognition of Stock-Based Compensation Expense," *Journal of Accounting Research* 42, no. 2 (December 2004): 251–275.

[7] Since March 2008, non-U.S. companies reporting under IFRS are no longer required to reconcile financial statements to U.S. GAAP in their Securities and Exchange Commission (SEC) filings.

MYTHS ABOUT EARNINGS MANAGEMENT

On July 17, 2019, internet entertainment service company Netflix reported second-quarter earnings of $0.56 per share, just four cents short of the $0.60 analyst consensus expectations. In addition, it had generated $4.92 billion in revenues, 25 percent higher than for the same quarter the year before, but missed analyst revenue targets by $10 million. On the same day, its share price dropped by more than 10 percent. But the trigger for the price decline was not the company's missing its earnings or revenue targets. Rather, investors were concerned about the company's long-term outlook because of a decline in U.S. subscribers when an increase was expected, as well as significantly lower growth in international subscribers. Still, events such as this have led many managers to believe that stock markets are increasingly sensitive to short-term earnings that undershoot analysts' expectations or to volatility in earnings generally. As we'll show, events such as these are not driven by the earnings announcement itself but by other information that accompanies the earnings, such as the underlying subscriber base growth in the case of Netflix. Furthermore, investors are not much concerned by earnings volatility and offer no rewards for predictable earnings or earnings guidance.

Earnings Volatility

Some managers believe investors will pay a premium for steady earnings growth. Indeed, executives regularly cite stabilizing earnings growth as a motivating factor in explaining their actions. For example, the CEO of Conoco once justified a pending merger with Phillips Petroleum in part by asserting that the merger would offer greater earnings stability over the commodity price cycle.[8]

In contrast, academic research has found that earnings variability has either limited or no impact on market value and shareholder returns. Ratios of market value to capital are diminished by cash flow volatility but not by earnings volatility. Investors see through earnings smoothing that is unconnected to cash flow.[9] In 30 years of U.S. profit data, there is no correlation between variability in EPS and a company's market value.[10] Some researchers find a statistically significant but practically negligible relationship between the two: between the 1 percent of companies with the lowest earnings volatility and the 1 percent with the highest lies a difference in market-to-book ratios of less than 10 percent.[11]

---

[8] Analyst teleconference, November 19, 2001.

[9] See B. Rountree, J. Weston, and G. Allayannis, "Do Investors Value Smooth Performance?" *Journal of Financial Economics* 90, no. 3 (December 2008): 237–251.

[10] J. McInnis, "Earnings Smoothness, Average Returns, and Implied Cost of Equity Capital," *Accounting Review* (January 2010) 85(1): 315–341.

[11] R. Barnes, "Earnings Volatility and Market Valuation: An Empirical Investigation," LBS Accounting Subject Area Working Paper ACCT 019, 2003. The difference was 0.2, and the average market-to-book ratio for the entire sample was around 2.

EXHIBIT 7.3 **Earnings Growth of Least Volatile Companies: Not So Smooth**

Earnings growth,[1] %

	Accenture	Costco	Philip Morris	Home Depot	UnitedHealth Group
2013	28	19	2	25	4
2014	−9	0	−9	25	3
2015	5	15	−7	16	6
2016	35	−1	1	18	21
2017	−16	14	−13	13	49
2018	16	17	31	34	14
2019	16	16	−9	5	17
2020	7	9	12	16	12
2021	16	25	13	30	13
2022	17	17	0	7	17

[1] Earnings per share before extraordinary items, adjusted for goodwill impairment.

Source: S&P Capital IQ.

Part of the explanation for the results is that smooth earnings growth is a myth. Almost no companies demonstrate smooth earnings growth. Exhibit 7.3 shows the earnings growth of the five firms among the largest listed U.S. companies that had the least volatile earnings growth from 2012 to 2022.[12] Of the companies examined, Home Depot and UnitedHealth Group were the only ones with ten years of steady earnings growth. Most companies with relatively stable earnings growth follow a pattern similar to the three other companies: several years of steady growth interrupted by a sudden decline in earnings.

Meeting Consensus Earnings Estimates

When a high-profile company misses an earnings target, it certainly makes headlines, but the impact of short-term earnings on share prices should not be overstated. For example, empirical research has shown that earnings surprises explain less than 2 percent of share price volatility in the four weeks surrounding the announcements.[13] Investors place far more importance on a company's economic fundamentals than on reported earnings. For instance, surveys have shown that more than 85 percent of investors do not consider it essential for a company to consistently beat its EPS consensus.[14] Sometimes, however, short-term earnings are the only data investors have on which to

[12] These were the 500 largest nonfinancial U.S. companies by market capitalization in 2022.
[13] W. Kinney, D. Burgstahler, and R. Martin, "Earnings Surprise 'Materiality' as Measured by Stock Returns," *Journal of Accounting Research* 40, no. 5 (December 2002): 1297–1329.
[14] McKinsey & Company Long Term Voices Survey, 2015.

base their judgment of fundamental corporate performance. In these cases, investors may interpret a missed EPS target as an omen of a decline in long-term performance and management credibility, so they lower the company's share price accordingly. As we describe in more detail in Chapter 36, the announcement of lower-than-expected earnings generally drives share prices down only when those results are accompanied by downward revisions of long-term fundamental prospects.

Similarly, share prices do not rise if the market believes a positive earnings surprise is simply the result of some imaginative accounting, such as deliberate timing of book gains from asset divestments or acceleration of sales from deep discounts to customers. For such accruals-dependent earnings increases, subsequent shareholder returns are poor, relative to peers.[15] And investors are wise to be wary when accruals contribute substantially to earnings, because this typically indicates that a company has reached a turning point and will post lower earnings in the future.

Earnings Guidance

Many companies believe that providing guidance on their expected earnings for the upcoming quarter or year can lead to higher valuations, lower share price volatility, and greater market liquidity for their shares at what they perceive to be limited costs. Unfortunately, there is no evidence that guidance delivers any of these benefits. As we discuss in Chapter 36, some 65 percent of the S&P 500 companies do not provide any quarterly or annual EPS guidance. For Eurostoxx 300 companies, the portion is even higher. The reason so many companies eschew such guidance is that they know it does not affect their earnings multiples, returns to shareholders, or share price volatility. The impact of guidance on a stock's liquidity, if any, typically disappears in the following year, making it practically irrelevant from a shareholder's perspective.[16] However, earnings guidance could lead to significant but hidden costs. Companies at risk of missing their own forecasts could be tempted to artificially improve their short-term earnings. As described previously, that is not likely to convince the market and could come at the expense of long-term value creation. When providing guidance at all, companies are therefore better off if they present ranges rather than point estimates and if they present these for underlying operational performance (for example, targets for volume and revenue, operating margins, and initiatives to reduce costs), rather than for earnings per share.

[15] K. Chan, L. Chan, N. Jegadeesh, et al. (2006). "Earnings Quality and Stock Returns," *Journal of Business* 79 (3): 1041–1082.
[16] See T. Koller, B. Jiang, and B. Raj, "Three Common Misconceptions about Markets," *Journal of Applied Corporate Finance* 25, no. 3 (2006): 32–38.

MYTHS ABOUT DIVERSIFICATION

Diversification is intrinsically neither good nor bad; rather, it all depends on whether the parent company is the best owner of the businesses in its portfolio. But several myths about diversification persist among finance practitioners. Interestingly enough, two of the most common myths contradict one another.

First, some executives believe diversification brings benefits, such as more stable aggregate cash flows, tax benefits from higher debt capacity, and better timing of investments across business cycles. However, as we discuss in Chapter 28, there is no evidence of such advantages in developed economies. Yet the evidence does point to *costs* of diversification: the business units of diversified companies often underperform their focused peers because of added complexity and bureaucracy, which leads corporate costs to drag.

The contrary misconception, also about diversification, is that it leads to so-called conglomerate discounts to the fair value of the business. According to this viewpoint, spin-offs and other forms of divestment are effective instruments to unlock these conglomerate discounts. Those who hold this view note that share price reactions to divestment announcements are typically positive, which is taken as evidence that such transactions are an easy solution to low valuations.

Typically, this misunderstanding is based on a misleading sum-of-the-parts calculation, in which analysts estimate the value of each of a company's businesses based on the earnings multiples of each business's industry peers. If the value of the sum of the businesses exceeds the company's current market value, the analysts assume the market value includes a conglomerate discount. However, as we discuss in Chapter 19, the analyses are often based on industry peers that are not actually comparable in terms of performance or sector. When the analysis uses true industry peers, the conglomerate discount disappears. We find that conglomerates tend to underperform when compared with more focused companies in terms of growth or ROIC. The underlying causes are typically inadequate management focus, poor operational efficiency, and suboptimal capital allocation.[17]

Positive share price reactions to divestment announcements therefore do not represent any correction of undervaluation or oversight by investors. The reactions simply reflect investor expectations that performance will improve at both the parent company and the divested business once each has the freedom to change its strategies, operating model, people, and capital allocation.

[17] J. Cyriac, T. Koller, and J. Thomsen, Testing the Limits of Diversification, *McKinsey on Finance*, no. 42 (Winter 2012): 1–5; J. Koenig, T. Koller, and A. Luu, "When Bigger Isn't Always Better," McKinsey & Company, December 2021, www.mckinsey.com.

A large body of empirical evidence shows that investors are correct in anticipating performance step-ups.[18]

MYTHS ABOUT COMPANY SIZE

Many executives are tempted by the illusion that the absolute size or scale of a company brings benefits in the form of either higher share prices in the stock market or higher ROIC and growth in the businesses. Academics and practitioners have claimed that larger companies are in higher demand by investors because they get more coverage from equity analysts and media. Or they say the cost of capital is lower because large companies are less risky and their stocks more liquid. Higher demand and lower cost of capital should lead to higher valuation in the market.

However, there is no evidence that size matters past a certain point. The cutoff probably lies in the range of a market capitalization between $250 million and $500 million.[19] Only below that range is there any indication of higher cost of capital, for example. Whether a company has a market capitalization of $1 billion, $5 billion, or more does not matter for its relative valuation in the market.

The same holds for any positive effect a company's size might have on its ROIC and growth. Under rare circumstances, some business models can capture ongoing improvements in operating margins, capital efficiency, or both as they grow larger. For example, as we discuss in Chapter 8, this applies to businesses with scalable product or service offerings or even so-called network effects—such as Microsoft's Office product range. But such cases are the exception, not the rule. In most businesses, economies of scale make a difference only up to a certain size of the business. Large (and medium-size) companies have typically already extracted maximum benefits from such economies of scale. For example, it is tempting to believe that package delivery companies such as UPS can easily process more packages at limited additional costs (the planes and trucks are already in place). But the networks of these companies are finely tuned and optimized for minimum unused capacity. Increasing volume by 10 percent might in fact require 10 percent more planes and trucks.

[18] See, for example, J. Miles and J. Rosenfeld, "The Effect of Voluntary Spin-Off Announcements on Shareholder Wealth," *Journal of Finance* 38 (1983): 1597–1606; K. Schipper and A. Smith, "A Comparison of Equity Carve-Outs and Seasoned Equity Offerings: Share Price Effects and Corporate Restructuring," *Journal of Financial Economics* 15 (1986): 153–186; K. Schipper and A. Smith, "Effects of Recontracting on Shareholder Wealth: The Case of Voluntary Spin-Offs," *Journal of Financial Economics* 12 (1983): 437–468; J. Allen and J. McConnell, "Equity Carve-Outs and Managerial Discretion," *Journal of Finance* 53 (1998): 163–186; and R. Michaely and W. Shaw, "The Choice of Going Public: Spin-Offs vs. Carve-Outs," *Financial Management* 24 (1995): 5–21.

[19] See R. McNish and M. Palys, "Does Scale Matter to Capital Markets?" *McKinsey on Finance* (Summer 2005): 21–23.

For most companies, increases in size alone no longer automatically bring further improvements in performance but just generate more complexity. Growth often means adding more business units and expanding geographically, which lengthen the chain of command and involve more people in every decision. Smaller, nimbler companies can well end up with lower costs. Whether size helps or hurts—whether it creates scale economies or diseconomies—depends on the unique circumstances of each company.

MYTHS ABOUT MARKET MECHANICS

Conventional wisdom has long held that companies can capture benefits for their shareholders without any improvements to underlying cash flows by having their stock included in a key market index, listing it in multiple markets, or splitting their stocks. And it is true that a company from an emerging market in Asia securing a U.S. listing or a little-known European company joining a leading global stock index might secure some appreciable uplift. But at the same time, well-functioning capital markets are entirely focused on the fundamentals of cash flow and revenue growth.

Index Membership

Becoming a member of a leading stock market index such as the S&P 500 or FTSE 100 appeals to managers because many large institutional investors track these indexes. Managers believe that when institutional investors rebalance their portfolios to reflect the change of index membership, demand will shift dramatically, boosting the share price.

But empirical evidence shows that such changes are typically short-lived. On average, share prices of companies excluded from a major stock index do indeed decrease after the announcement. But this fall is fully reversed within one or two months.[20] Surprisingly, the evidence on the impact of index inclusions appears less conclusive; while they generally produce an effect analogous to that of exclusions—an initial increase in share price, followed by a slower reversal—several publications have reported that these price increases are only partly reversed over time.[21] However, recent findings do not confirm such patterns and suggest that even the initial price reactions have diminished over the years.[22]

---

[20] H. Chen, G. Noronha, and V. Singal, "The Price Response to S&P 500 Index Additions and Deletions: Evidence of Asymmetry and a New Explanation," *Journal of Finance* 59, no. 4 (August 2004): 1901–1929.
[21] See also, for example, L. Harris and E. Gurel, "Price and Volume Effects Associated with Changes in the S&P 500: New Evidence for the Existence of Price Pressures," *Journal of Finance* 41 (1986): 815–830; and R. A. Brealey, "Stock Prices, Stock Indexes, and Index Funds," *Bank of England Quarterly Bulletin* (2000): 61–68.
[22] H. Preston, "What Happened to the Index Effect? A Look at Three Decades of S&P 500 Adds and Drops," S&P Global, September 2021, www.spglobal.com.

EXHIBIT 7.4 **Effects of Inclusion and Exclusion Disappear**

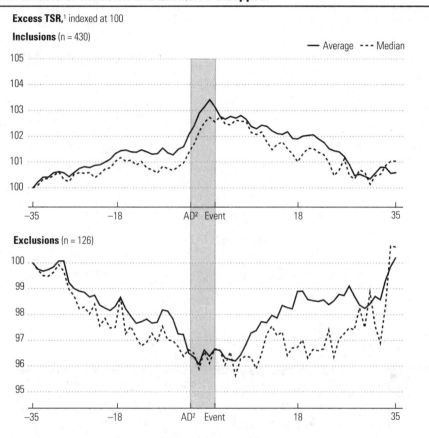

Excess TSR,[1] indexed at 100

Inclusions (n = 430)

— Average --- Median

Exclusions (n = 126)

[1] Excess total shareholder return (TSR) is calculated using the buy and hold abnormal returns (BHAR) method. The benchmark for excess TSR is the S&P 500 Index return.

[2] Event is the day of inclusion/exclusion and set at 0. Announcement date (AD) set at −4. Using as proxy the median days between announcement and event date from H. Preston and A. M. Soe, "What Happened to the Index Effect? A Look at Three Decades of S&P 500 Adds and Drops," S&P Global, Sept. 2021, www.spglobal.com.

Our own research indicates a full reversal. We analyzed the effect on share price of 430 inclusions and 126 exclusions from the S&P 500 between 2002 and 2023.[23] As Exhibit 7.4 shows, new entrants to the index experienced only a short-lived increase in share price that largely disappeared after 35 days. As investors adjust their portfolios to changes in the index, share prices of new entrants initially increase but then revert to normal once portfolios are rebalanced. For companies ejected from the S&P 500, we found similar patterns of temporary price change. The pressure on their prices following exclusion from the index typically lifted within a month. All in all, our findings indicated that this pattern of initial price reaction followed by gradual reversal was unchanged for both inclusions and exclusions over the two decades analyzed.

[23] For further details, see T. Koller et al., "The Myth of an Enduring Index Premium," McKinsey & Company, May 2024, www.mckinsey.com; and M. Goedhart and R. Huc, "What Is Stock Membership Worth?" *McKinsey on Finance*, no. 10 (Winter 2004): 14–16.

EXHIBIT 7.5 **Delisting from U.S./UK Exchanges: No Value Impact on Companies from Developed Markets**

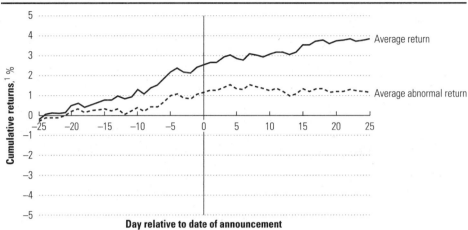

[1] Sample of 229 delistings from New York Stock Exchange, NASDAQ, or London International Main Market. Announcement dates between December 31, 2002, and December 31, 2007.

Source: Reuters; Bloomberg; Datastream.

Cross-Listing

For years, many academics, executives, and analysts believed companies cross-listing their shares on exchanges in the United States, London, and Tokyo could realize a higher share price and a lower cost of capital.[24] Cross-listed shares, they supposed, would benefit from more analyst coverage, a broader shareholder base, improved liquidity, higher governance standards, and better access to capital.

But our analysis does not find any significant impact on shareholder value from cross-listings for companies in the developed markets of North America, Western Europe, Japan, and Australia.[25] We found no decline in share price when companies announced a delisting from U.S. or UK stock exchanges (Exhibit 7.5).[26] In fact, most announcements in our sample produced hardly any reaction from analysts and investors. In 2008 and again in 2023, we did not find any valuation premium for companies with cross-listings in New York or London relative to companies without any cross-listing, once we corrected for differences in return on invested capital (Exhibit 7.6).

[24] See, for example, C. Doidge, A. Karolyi, and R. Stulz, "Why Are Foreign Firms That List in the U.S. Worth More?" *Journal of Financial Economics* 71, no. 2 (2004): 205–238; and M. King and U. Mittoo, "What Companies Need to Know about International Cross-Listing," *Journal of Applied Corporate Finance* 19, no. 4 (Fall 2007): 60–74.

[25] For further details, see R. Dobbs and M. Goedhart, "Why Cross-Listing Shares Doesn't Create Value," *McKinsey on Finance*, no. 29 (Autumn 2008): 18–23.

[26] We analyzed the stock market reactions to 229 voluntary delistings between 2002 and 2008.

EXHIBIT 7.6 **U.S. Cross-Listing: No Impact on Valuation of Developed-Market Companies**

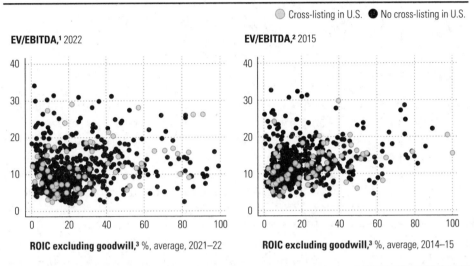

○ Cross-listing in U.S.   ● No cross-listing in U.S.

EV/EBITDA,[1] 2022

EV/EBITDA,[2] 2015

ROIC excluding goodwill,[3] %, average, 2021–22

ROIC excluding goodwill,[3] %, average, 2014–15

[1] Enterprise value (2022, year end) divided by EBITDA (2022, year end).

[2] Enterprise value (2015, year end) divided by EBITDA (2015, year end).

[3] Return on invested capital average. Return on equity (ROE) for financial institutions.

Source: S&P Capital IQ; McKinsey Value Intelligence database.

In fact, we found no evidence for any of the ostensible benefits from cross-listings. After correcting for size, cross-listed European companies have only marginally more analyst coverage than those not cross-listed.[27] Institutional investors from the United States do not require the foreign companies in which they want to invest to be listed in the United States.[28] There is no meaningful impact on liquidity, as cross-listed shares of European companies in the United States—American depositary receipts (ADRs)—typically account for only a small fraction of these companies' total trading volumes. Corporate governance standards across the developed world have converged with those in the United States and the United Kingdom. There is hardly any benefit from better access to capital, given that three-quarters of the U.S. cross-listings of companies from the European Union have never involved raising any new capital in the United States.[29]

[27] See, for example, M. Lang, K. Lins, and D. Miller, "ADRs, Analysts, and Accuracy: Does Cross Listing in the U.S. Improve a Firm's Information Environment and Increase Market Value?" *Journal of Accounting Research* 41, no. 2 (May 2003): 317–345.

[28] For example, CalPERS, a large U.S. investor, has an international equity portfolio of around 2,400 companies, but less than 10 percent of them have a U.S. cross-listing.

[29] Based on 420 depositary receipt issues on the New York Stock Exchange, NASDAQ, and American Stock Exchange from January 1970 to May 2008. Data from the Bank of New York Mellon Corporation, www.adrbnymellon.com.

For companies from the emerging world, however, the story might be different. These companies might benefit from access to new equity and more stringent corporate governance requirements through cross-listings in U.S. or UK equity markets.[30]

Stock Splits

Although their numbers have come down significantly over the past decade, each year some listed companies in the United States increase their number of shares through a stock split to bring a company's share price back into the "optimal trading range."[31] A recent example is Tesla, which split its stock in a five-for-one exchange on August 31, 2020, and in a three-for-one exchange on August 25, 2022, in order "to make stock ownership more accessible to employees and investors."[32] But fundamentally, stock splits can't create value, because the size of the pie available to shareholders does not change. For example, after a two-for-one stock split, a shareholder who owned two shares worth $5 apiece ends up with four shares, each worth $2.50. In the case of Tesla's stock splits, share price reactions even turned out to be negative. But some managers and academics claim that the lower price should make the stock more attractive for capital-constrained investors, thereby increasing demand, improving liquidity, and leading to higher returns for shareholders.[33]

In many cases, a stock split is indeed accompanied by positive abnormal returns to shareholders in the months prior to the split (see Exhibit 7.7).[34] The abnormal returns have nothing to do with the split as such but are simply a function of self-selection and signaling. Self-selection is the tendency of companies to split their stocks into lower denominations because of a prolonged rise in their share price.

A more consequential phenomenon is the abnormal return that occurs for the three days around the announcement of the stock split, which researchers

[30] See R. Newell and G. Wilson, "A Premium for Good Governance," *McKinsey Quarterly*, no. 3 (2002): 20–23.

[31] R. D. Boehme and B. R. Danielsen report over 6,000 stock splits between 1950 and 2000: "Stock-Split Post-Announcement Returns: Underreaction or Market Friction?" *Financial Review* 42 (2007): 485–506. D. Ikenberry and S. Ramnath report over 3,000 stock splits between 1988 and 1998: "Underreaction to Self-Selected News Events: The Case of Stock Splits," *Review of Financial Studies* 15, no. 2 (2002): 489–526.

[32] "Tesla Announces a Five-for-One Stock Split," press release, Tesla, August 11, 2020, www.ir.tesla.com.

[33] There is ample evidence to show that this is not the case: after a split, trading volumes typically decline, and brokerage fees and bid-ask spreads increase, indicating lower liquidity, if anything. See T. Copeland, (1979) "Liquidity Changes Following Stock Splits," *Journal of Finance* 34, no. 1 (March 1979): 115–141.

[34] E. Fama, L. Fisher, M. Jensen, and R. Roll, "The Adjustment of Stock Prices to New Information," *International Economic Review* 10 (1969): 1–21.

EXHIBIT 7.7 **Cumulative Average Abnormal Returns Around Stock Splits**

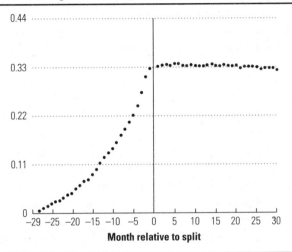

Source: E. Fama, L. Fisher, M. Jensen, and R. Roll, "The Adjustment of Stock Prices to New Information," *International Economic Review* 10 (1969): 1–21.

have found to be about 3 percent, on average.[35] When managers announce a stock split, they are also signaling that they expect further improvement in economic fundamentals. Indeed, two-thirds of companies reported higher-than-expected earnings and dividends for the entire year following a stock split. When performance improvements followed the split, the stock market did not react, indicating that investors had already factored them into their decisions at the time of the stock split announcement. Consistent with this pattern, companies that did not improve performance as expected in the year after a stock split saw their share prices fall.[36]

MYTHS ABOUT VALUE DISTRIBUTION

Another common misconception among executives is that share repurchases and dividends create value for shareholders. This view is often reinforced by both private and public demands from investors for companies to return more cash to shareholders, particularly as share repurchases. If you dig deeper into understanding investor demands, though, you will typically find that

[35] Some researchers have reported positive abnormal returns not only in the days around but in the entire year following a split announcement. They conclude that the market is inefficient by under-reacting to stock splits; see Ikenberry and Ramnath, "Underreaction to Self-Selected News Events." Others find that these abnormal returns do not lead to any arbitrage opportunities and that the market is efficient; see Boehme and Danielsen, "Stock-Split Post-Announcement Returns"; and J. Conrad and G. Kaul, "Long-Term Market Overreaction or Biases in Computed Returns?" *Journal of Finance* 48, no. 1 (March 1993): 39–63.

[36] See Fama et al., "Adjustment of Stock Prices."

investors want more cash distributed, not because the cash distribution itself creates value, but because investors are concerned that companies will squander excess cash and debt capacity on value-destroying investments. They view cash distributions as a way to impose discipline on the company's use of its cash.[37]

More important, companies create value when they generate cash flows. Distributing those cash flows to shareholders cannot create additional value. That would be double-counting and akin to violating principles such as the conservation of matter in physics.

So why do companies' share prices often increase on the announcement of share repurchases or dividend increases? In some cases, investors interpret dividend increases as a sign that management is confident enough about future cash flow generation to commit to a higher dividend level. In other cases, investors are relieved that management is less likely to spend cash on value-destroying investments. The result is that investors raise their expectations of future cash flows. If these expectations are not met, the companies' share prices will decline later.

Dividends and share repurchases are merely instruments for distributing cash generated by the company's operations. Furthermore, as we discuss in Chapter 35, decisions about cash distribution should not drive a company's investment decisions; they should be an integral part of a company's capital allocation that matches its investment needs, financing opportunities, and desired level of risk.

SUMMARY

There is compelling evidence that valuation levels for individual companies and the stock market as a whole clearly reflect the underlying fundamental performance in terms of return on capital and growth. Nevertheless, myths that persist among managers and finance professionals assert various rationales for the supposed deviation of valuations from fundamentals. With few exceptions, these myths are erroneous.

We find that executives are often overly focused on earnings and earnings growth. Earnings don't drive value in their own right; only cash flows do. Of course, companies with attractive growth and returns on invested capital will also generate good earnings. But the market sees through earnings that aren't backed up by solid fundamentals, such as earnings increases from share repurchases or from mergers and acquisitions that don't earn adequate returns on capital. Managers should also not be concerned about noneconomic events that reduce earnings, such as asset write-downs or the effects of

---

[37] See, for example, M. Goedhart and T. Koller, "How to Attract Long-Term Investors: An Interview with M&G's Aled Smith," *McKinsey on Finance* 46 (Spring 2013): 8–13.

changes in accounting rules. Nor should they be concerned about delivering smooth earnings or meeting short-term consensus earnings forecasts.

Finally, other myths assert that the market values companies based on various measures unrelated to the companies' economic performance. None of these stand up to scrutiny. There is no value premium from diversification, from cross-listing, or from size for size's sake. Conversely, there is no conglomerate discount, only a performance discount for many diversified companies. Dividends and share repurchases don't create value, but markets react positively when management signals it will be disciplined about future investments.

8

Return on Invested Capital

As Chapter 3 explains, the higher a company can raise its return on invested capital (ROIC), and the longer it can earn a rate of return on that capital greater than its cost of capital, the more value it will create. Therefore, every strategic and investment decision requires an ability to understand and predict what drives and sustains ROIC.

Why do some companies develop and sustain much higher returns on capital than others? Take the examples of International Workplace Group (IWG, formerly known as Regus) and Airbnb. As of 2019, the equity value of IWG was around $4 billion, and Airbnb's value was estimated to be approximately $30 billion to $35 billion.[1] Both companies have digital business models offering their customers real estate for rent (office space in the case of IWG and residential rentals in the case of Airbnb). Over the preceding ten years, IWG had increased its revenues at an average rate of 9 percent each year to $3.5 billion, while Airbnb had grown its revenues from practically zero to $4.8 billion. Nevertheless, just a couple of years later, IWG ended up in financial difficulty, while Airbnb was still thriving with a market capitalization close to $100 billion.

What explains the difference? Perhaps most importantly, since it started business in 1989, IWG (then known as Regus) has traditionally entered into long-term lease contracts for office space, which it then sublets to individuals and other companies for shorter time periods. Airbnb, in contrast, does not own or lease any real estate but instead serves as a real estate marketplace through which owners can connect with travelers in need of accommodations.

This chapter was coauthored by Susan Nolen Foushee.

[1] Airbnb was not publicly listed at the time. The value was estimated from Airbnb's Series F round in 2016, valued at $31 billion. IWG was listed at the time under the name of Regus plc.

These differences resulted in very different returns on capital and very different levels of risk.

IWG's business model requires significant capital to meet its long-term lease commitments, which it could not easily reduce or cancel when faced with lower occupancy rates (as eventually came to pass during the 2020 pandemic). Almost inevitably, IWG ended up generating a low return on capital—less than 5 percent—even as its annual revenues grew to $3.5 billion in 2019. IWGs' business model has always been unlikely to achieve high returns on capital, given that its costs and rent per square foot have remained largely constant amid intense competition from other real estate companies. Furthermore, IWG's most likely option for growth has involved investing more capital by taking on more lease commitments, creating little opportunity for increasing returns with scale.

Airbnb has not required any capital for the accommodations it provides. Its early-mover advantage helped it attract additional owners and travelers to its marketplace, reducing the number available to other such platforms (although a few became large). The combination of low capital and limited competition led to very high returns on capital. Airbnb also enjoyed clear scale advantages: it could serve additional owners and travelers at almost no additional cost. By 2023, Airbnb earned a return on capital in excess of 30 percent on revenues of $10 billion. Airbnb was also able to weather the COVID-19 pandemic, thanks to its low capital investment and relatively low fixed costs, whereas the pandemic proved devastating to IWG's model.

The importance of ROIC is universal: it applies to companies as well as to businesses within companies. For example, within its retail business model, Amazon creates substantial revenues from the third-party sellers that use its online platform. Platform sales by third parties generate increasingly greater returns to scale than Amazon's direct sales. Platform sales require little invested capital, and Amazon's marginal cost of additional transactions is minimal, so platform sales have become an important driver of value creation in online retail for Amazon and many other players.

This chapter explores how rates of return on invested capital depend on competitive advantage and market attractiveness. We examine how strategy drives competitive advantage, which when properly fitted to industry structure and competitive behavior can produce and sustain a superior ROIC. This explains why some companies earn only a 10 percent ROIC while others earn 50 percent. The final part of the chapter presents ROIC data by industry over 60 years for the United States and 30 years for the European Union, Switzerland, and the United Kingdom. This analysis shows how ROIC varies across different regions and industries—and how rates of ROIC fluctuate or remain stable over time.

WHAT DRIVES ROIC?

To understand how strategy, competitive advantage, industry attractiveness, and return on invested capital are linked, consider the following representation of ROIC:

$$ROIC = (1 - \text{Tax Rate}) \frac{\text{Price per Unit} - \text{Cost per Unit}}{\text{Invested Capital per Unit}}$$

This version of ROIC simply translates the typical formula of net operating profit after taxes (NOPAT) divided by invested capital into a per unit calculation: price per unit, cost per unit, and invested capital per unit.[2] To a large extent, a company's ROIC is driven by the industry in which it operates: some industry structures provide companies with better opportunities than others to generate favorable returns. To earn a higher ROIC in a given industry, a company needs a competitive advantage that enables it to charge a price premium or produce its products more efficiently than other companies (at lower cost, lower capital per unit, or both). A company's ROIC therefore depends on the industry in which it operates and the strategy it has chosen to create a competitive advantage.

The economic model that underlies our thinking about how strategy drives competitive advantage and ROIC is the structure-conduct-performance (SCP) framework. According to this framework, the structure of an industry influences the conduct of the competitors, which in turn drives the performance of the companies in the industry. Originally developed in the 1930s by Edward Mason, this framework was not widely influential in business until Michael Porter published *Competitive Strategy* (Free Press, 1980), applying the model to company strategy. According to Porter, the intensity of competition in an industry is determined by five forces: the threat of new entry, pressure from substitute products, the bargaining power of buyers, that of suppliers, and the degree of rivalry among existing competitors. Companies need to choose strategies that build competitive advantages to mitigate or change the pressure of these forces and achieve superior profitability. Because the five forces differ by industry, and because companies within the same industry can pursue different strategies, there can be significant variation in ROIC across and within industries.

There have been extensions and variations of the SCP model, such as the resource-based theory and, more recently, theories on value creation and

---

[2] We introduce "units" to encourage discussion regarding price, cost, and volume. The formula, however, is not specific to manufacturing. Units can represent the number of hours billed, patients seen, transactions processed, and so on.

value capture.[3] Resource-based theories state that competitive advantages are driven not only by a company's strategic choices, but also by its unique resources (which can be tangible, such as location for an airport or reserves for an oil company, and intangible, such as superior innovation capabilities in a semiconductor design company). Value capture theory provides deeper insights into the way that competition determines what share of total value creation is captured by companies or by customers (where total value creation is defined as the difference between a buyer's willingness to pay for a product or service and a supplier's opportunity cost to provide it). Note that, following this logic, our definition of value creation aligns with the "value captured" by companies. Although these theories do add new insights into what drives a company's performance, Porter's framework is probably still the most widely used for thinking about strategy.

Exhibit 8.1 underlines the importance of industry structure to ROIC. It compares the median return on invested capital over approximately 30 years in two sectors: branded consumer goods and extraction industries (such as mining and oil and gas). Consumer goods have earned consistently higher ROICs than extraction companies. In addition, the returns of extraction-based companies have been highly volatile.

EXHIBIT 8.1   **Company Profitability: Industry Matters**

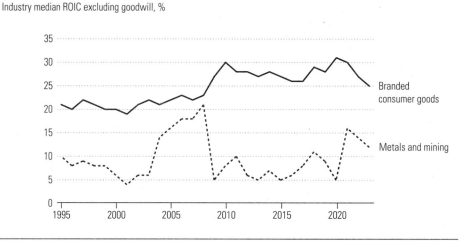

Industry median ROIC excluding goodwill, %

Source: McKinsey Value Intelligence database.

[3] For resource-based theory, see, for example, R. M. Grant, "The Resource-Based Theory of Competitive Advantage: Implications for Strategy Formulation," *California Management Review* 33, no. 3 (1991): 114–135; J. Barney, "Resource-Based Theories of Competitive Advantage: A Ten-Year Retrospective on the Resource-Based View," *Journal of Management* 27 (2001): 643–650. For value capture theory, see, for example, A. M. Brandenburger and H. W. Stuart Jr., "Value-Based Business Strategy," *Journal of Economics and Management Strategy* 5, no. 1 (1996): 5–24; D. P. Lepak, K. G. Smith, and M. S. Taylor, "Value Creation and Value Capture: A Multilevel Perspective," *Academy of Management Review* 32, no. 1 (2007): 180–194.

The reason for this difference in the industries' performance lies mainly in differences between their competitive structures. In the branded-consumer-goods industry, companies such as Nestlé, Procter & Gamble, and Unilever developed long-lasting brands with high consumer loyalty that made it difficult for new competitors to gain a foothold. Building on these advantages, these companies were able to increase their returns on capital from around 20 percent in the mid-1990s to roughly 30 percent two decades later, despite challenges to traditional brands from new market entrants. One example is the competition faced by Procter & Gamble's Gillette shaving business from challengers such as Harry's and Dollar Shave Club.[4] Consumer goods giants have often reacted to the threat from such "challenger brands" by acquiring them; McKinsey research in 2021 found that such deals accounted for 25 percent of consumer M&A in that year.[5]

In extraction industries, one company's products are the same as another's (iron ore is iron ore, with minor quality differences), so prices are the same across the industry at any point in time. In addition, the companies use the same capital-intensive processes to extract their products. As a result, the median company in the industry doesn't have a competitive advantage, and returns are low, averaging only 9 percent during this 30-year period. It is worth noting that imbalances in supply and demand can lead to cycles in product price and ROIC, as was the case with a long run-up in commodity prices in the years leading up to 2008. In the end, though, competition leads to low ROIC on average.

Industry structure is by no means the only determinant of ROIC, as the significant variation among companies within industries shows. Consider the global automotive industry, which has been plagued by overcapacity for years. Still, the industry's low returns do not deter new entrants, whether from different geographies (such as South Korean automakers' entry into the U.S. market and, more recently, Chinese automakers' entry into European markets) or due to the emergence of new technologies (such as electric-vehicle producers, including Tesla and BYD). Add in the difficulties that some manufacturers encounter in trying to close unionized plants, and it's easy to see how overcapacity keeps returns across the sector low. Only a few manufacturers, such as BMW, can parlay their premium brands and higher quality into higher prices and superior returns on capital compared with other manufacturers. Or consider the highly competitive European airline industry, where most players typically generate returns very close to their cost of capital—and occasionally below it. Nevertheless, Ryanair has consistently earned superior returns over the last three decades, thanks to its strategy of strictly point-to-point connections between predominantly secondary airports at the lowest cost in the industry.

[4] Unilever acquired Dollar Shave Club in 2016 but sold a 65 percent stake in the business to Nexus Capital Management.
[5] H. Atmar, K. Lloyd George, R. Slelatt, and S. Rickert, "Driving Growth in Consumer Goods through Programmatic M&A," McKinsey & Company, March 14, 2023, www.mckinsey.com.

Finally, industry structure and competitive behavior aren't fixed; they're subject to shocks from technological innovation, changes in government regulation, and competitive entry—any or all of which can affect individual companies or an entire industry. We show in this chapter's final section that the software and pharmaceutical industries, for example, consistently earn high returns. However, the leading companies in 20 years may be different from today's leaders, just as many of today's leaders were not major players or didn't even exist 20 years ago.

COMPETITIVE ADVANTAGE

Competitive advantage derives from some combination of ten different sources, defined in Exhibit 8.2. Of these, five allow companies to charge a price premium, four contribute to cost and capital efficiency, and one (often referred to as "network effects") combines price and cost advantages to produce increasing returns to scale. It is important to understand that competitive advantage drawn from these sources is enjoyed not by entire companies but by particular business units and product lines. This is the only level of competition at which the concept of competitive advantage affords you any real traction in strategic thinking; even if a company sells soup or dog food exclusively, it may still have individual businesses and product lines with very different degrees of competitive advantage and therefore different returns on invested capital.

EXHIBIT 8.2 **Sources of Competitive Advantage**

Price premium	Cost and capital efficiency
Innovative products: Difficult-to-copy or patented products, services, or technologies	**Innovative business method:** Difficult-to-copy business method that contrasts with established industry practice
Quality: Customers willing to pay a premium for a real or perceived difference in quality over and above competing products or services	**Unique resources:** Advantage resulting from inherent geological characteristics or unique access to raw material(s)
Brand: Customers willing to pay a premium based on brand, even if there is no clear quality difference	**Economies of scale:** Efficient scale or size for the relevant market
Customer lock-in: Customers unwilling or unable to replace a product or service they use with a competing product or service	**Scalable product/process:** Ability to add customers and capacity at negligible marginal cost
Rational price discipline: Lower bound on prices established by large industry leaders through price signaling or capacity management	

← **Network effects:** Products or services that offer increasing value to customer with scale, at negligible or decreasing costs to scale, possibly combined with customer switching costs →

On balance, price premiums are an effective means for businesses to achieve an attractive ROIC, but they are usually more difficult to pull off than cost efficiencies. Also, the businesses or products with the highest returns are often those that weave together more than one advantage. The biggest potential for superior ROIC comes from increasing network effects, which are even more difficult to achieve and very rare, as we will discuss in this section.

Price Premium Advantages

In commodity markets, companies are typically price takers, meaning they must sell at the market price to generate sales, because the products are hard to differentiate. To sell its products at a price premium, a company must find a way to differentiate its products from those of competitors. We distinguish five sources of price premiums: innovative products, quality, brand, customer lock-in, and rational price discipline.

Innovative Products   Innovative goods and services yield high returns on capital if they are protected by patents or copyrights, difficult to copy, or both. Absent these protections, even an innovative product won't do much to generate high returns.

Pharmaceutical companies earn high returns because they produce innovative products that, although often easy to copy, are protected by patents for up to 20 years. The business can charge a price premium during the protected period, after which generics will enter the market and drive the price down. Even after the patent expires, the holder may enjoy some price "stickiness." Similarly, copyright protection on fictional characters supports the returns of entertainment and games businesses such as Disney and Hasbro.

A classic example of an innovative product line that is not patent protected but still difficult to copy is Apple's iPhone. The core technology of the device has been similar to that of key competitors, such as Samsung's Galaxy series smartphones. But the iPhone generated much higher returns on capital because of its appealing design, ease of use afforded by its user interface, and reputation of superior security and privacy.

Quality   A term used as broadly as *quality* requires definition. In the context of competitive advantage and ROIC, quality means a real or perceived difference between one product or service and another for which consumers are willing to pay a higher price. In the truck manufacturing business, for example, Paccar's key brands Peterbilt and Kenworth enjoy a price premium because customers are convinced that their trucks are better to drive (and live in) than comparable trucks that cost less. The cost of providing the extra quality is less than the price premium. Hence, Paccar has often been able to earn higher returns than many other truck manufacturers. Appliance makers such as Weber can price their products at a premium over those of their competitors because customers perceive their reliability and durability to be superior.

Sometimes the perception of quality lasts significantly longer than any actual difference in quality. This has been the case with Honda and Toyota relative to many automakers (at least until Toyota had to make product recalls in 2009). While American and Japanese cars have been comparable in terms of quantifiable quality measures, such as the J.D. Power survey, Japanese companies have enjoyed a price premium for their products. Even when American and Japanese sticker prices on comparable vehicles were the same, American manufacturers were often forced to sell at a $2,000 to $3,000 discount, whereas Japanese cars sold for nearer the asking price.

Brand   Price premiums based on brand are sometimes hard to distinguish from price premiums based on quality, and the two are highly correlated (as in the example of the iPhone). While the quality of a product may matter more than its established branding, sometimes the brand itself is what matters more—especially when the brand has lasted a very long time, as in the cases of Heineken, Coca-Cola, Perrier, and Mercedes-Benz.

Packaged food, beverages, and durable consumer goods are good examples of sectors where brands earn price premiums for some but not all products. In some categories, such as bottled water and breakfast cereals, customers are loyal to brands such as Perrier and Cheerios despite the availability of high-quality branded and private-label alternatives. In other categories, including meat, branding has not been successful. Because of their strong brands, beverage and cereal companies have earned returns on capital of around 30 percent, while meat processors have typically earned returns of around 15 percent. Beginning in the mid-2010s, consolidation in the U.S. meat industry led to improved returns but also triggered government measures for market regulation.[6]

Customer Lock-In   When replacing one company's product or service with another's is costly (relative to the price of the product) for customers, the incumbent company can charge a price premium—if not for the initial sale, then at least for additional units or for subsequent generations and iterations of the original product. Gillette's shaving products offer a classic example: the manufacturer realizes its margin not on the starter pack but on replacement razor blades. Manufacturers of inkjet and laser printers have adopted a very similar business model, generating more profit from selling ink cartridges than from the printer itself. Some wireless-audio product manufacturers such as Sonos also create a form of lock-in: once customers have one or more of the

[6] See "Fact Sheet: The Biden-Harris Action Plan for a Fairer, More Competitive, and More Resilient Meat and Poultry Supply Chain," White House Briefing Room, January 3, 2022, www.whitehouse.gov.

company's speakers installed, they are not likely to switch to other brands when replacing or adding units, as these would lack compatibility with their existing Sonos units.

High switching costs, relative to the price of the product or service, create the strongest customer lock-in. Medical devices, such as artificial joints, can lock in the doctors who purchase them, because doctors need time to train and become proficient in the procedures for using and/or implanting those devices. Once doctors are up to speed on a device, they won't switch to a competing product unless there is a compelling reason to invest the necessary effort. Similarly, bankers and traders who have invested considerable time in learning how to work with software systems of certain providers are often reluctant to learn another system.

Rational Price Discipline   In commodity industries with many competitors, the laws of supply and demand will drive down prices and ROIC. This applies not just to obvious commodities—say, chemicals and paper—but also to more recently commoditized products and services, such as airline seats. It would take a net increase of only some five percentage points in airline ticket prices to double the return on capital of some of the large European airlines (given their small margins). But each competitor is tempted to get an edge in filling seats by keeping prices low, even when fuel prices and other costs rise for all competitors. In the late 2010s, the airline sector in the United States rapidly consolidated and became more cautious about adding seat capacity. That allowed U.S. airlines to operate at more attractive price levels and earn healthy returns on capital. In contrast, most European airlines still faced strong price competition and have rarely been able to earn returns on capital above their cost of capital.

Occasionally, we find an example such as the U.S. airline industry that manages to overcome the forces of competition and set its prices at a level that earns its companies reasonable returns on capital (though rarely more than 15 percent) without breaking competition law. For example, for many years, almost all real estate agents in the United States charged a 6 percent commission on the price of each home they sold. However, after many decades of fixed commissions, the National Association of Realtors faced a series of lawsuits arguing that its rules forced homeowners to pay excessive fees. In a 2024 settlement, the organization agreed to revise its practices. At the time of this writing, it's unclear how a new system of real estate commissions will develop.

Rational, legitimate pricing discipline typically works when one competitor acts as the leader and others quickly replicate its price moves. In addition, there must be barriers to new entrants, and each competitor must be large enough that a price war will surely reduce the profit on its existing volume by more than any extra profit gained from new sales. If there are smaller competitors with more to gain from extra volume than they would lose from lower prices, then price discipline will be very difficult to maintain.

Most attempts by industry players to maintain a floor price fail. Take the paper industry, for example. Its ROIC averaged less than 10 percent from 1990 to 2020. The industry created this problem for itself because the companies all tended to expand at once, after demand and prices had risen. As a result, a large chunk of new capacity came on line at the same time, upsetting the balance of supply and demand and forcing down prices and returns.

Even cartels (which are illegal in most of the world) find it difficult to maintain price levels, because each cartel member has a great incentive to lower prices and attract more sales. This so-called free-rider issue makes it difficult to maintain price levels over long periods, even for the Organization of Petroleum Exporting Countries (OPEC), the world's largest and most prominent cartel.

Cost and Capital Efficiency Advantages

Theoretically, cost and capital efficiency are two separate competitive advantages. Cost efficiency is the ability to deliver products and services at a lower cost than the competition. Capital efficiency is about delivering more products per dollar of invested capital than competitors. In practice, both tend to share common drivers and are hard to separate. (Is a company's outsourcing of manufacturing a source of cost efficiency or capital efficiency?) Consequently, we treat the following four sources of competitive advantage as deriving from the cost and capital efficiencies they achieve.

Innovative Business Method　A company's business method is the combination of its production, logistics, and pattern of interaction with customers. Sweden's IKEA provides one example of the advantage to be gleaned from an innovative business method. IKEA transformed the home furniture business around the world, driving innovations in all steps of the business chain from design to manufacturing and distribution to sales. Its concept of self-assembly furniture reduces production and storage costs. Close collaboration in design and manufacturing minimizes product development costs and time. Manufacturing costs are kept low by use of a limited range of raw materials. Its automated distribution centers are highly efficient because its product meets standard packaging requirements. Its retail stores are highly standardized and operate at low labor costs because customers pick up their furniture, still in packages, directly from storage. By making sure all these steps in the chain also stay carefully aligned with customer preferences, IKEA has become the largest furniture retailer in the world, operating more than 450 stores in more than 55 markets as of 2023.

Another example is Nestlé's subsidiary Nespresso, which since 1986 has successfully introduced espresso coffee to millions of customers worldwide. Nespresso's business is centered on a patented system of coffee roasting, single-use capsules, and coffee machines that enable customers to prepare high-quality espresso coffee at home. Coffee capsules, machines, and accessories are sold both through Nespresso's direct-to-consumer online channels and in boutiques, with subscription services offered to enhance customer retention (e.g., the Nespresso Club). Strategic partnerships with machine manufacturers such as Krupps, DeLonghi, and Eugster/Frismag, as well as with premium coffee brands such as Starbucks and Blue "Bottle" have helped Nespresso strengthen its market position. Even after some of its capsule and machine patents expired in 2012, customer loyalty has remained strong, thanks to these partnerships, continuing innovation, and consistent brand marketing. All of this has enabled Nespresso to grow into a business with $7.5 billion in revenue and an operating margin of more than 20 percent in 2023.

Unique Resources   Sometimes a company has access to a unique resource that cannot be replicated. This provides a significant competitive advantage. For example, in general, gold miners in North America earn higher returns than those in South Africa because the North American ore is closer to the surface, so extracting it is easier and costs less. These lower extraction costs are a primary driver of higher returns from North American mines (though partially offset by higher investment costs).

Other examples are some of the national oil companies, which own some of the largest oil and gas reserves in the world, which produce among the highest-graded crude oil at the lowest extraction costs in the industry. That places these companies in a position to generate superior returns on their upstream oil activities.

Geography often plays a role in gaining advantage from unique resources. Obviously, most leading seaports and airports owe their success to their specific location. The Port of Rotterdam Authority operates the largest seaport of Europe, benefiting from a location that connects the Rhine River (Europe's busiest waterway) and the continent's largest economy (Germany) to the North Sea and global shipping routes. But geography is important not only for infrastructure companies. In general, whenever the cost of shipping a product is high relative to the value of the product, producers near their customers have a unique advantage. For example, China is the world's largest consumer of iron ore. South American mines, therefore, face a distinct transportation cost disadvantage compared with Australian iron mines, and this contributes to the South American mines' lower returns compared with Australian competitors.

Economies of Scale   The notion of economies of scale is often misunderstood to mean there are automatic economies that come with size. Scale can indeed be important to value, but usually only at the regional or even local level, not in the national or global market. For example, for many retail businesses in dry cleaning, funeral services, or workspace rentals, it's much more important to be large in one city than large across the entire country, because local costs for facilities and advertising are either lumpy or fixed. Buying advertising airtime and space in Chicago is the same whether you have one store or a dozen. Likewise, a key element that determines the profitability of health insurers in the United States is their ability to negotiate prices with providers (hospitals and doctors), who tend to operate locally rather than nationally. The insurer with the highest market share in a local market will be in a position to negotiate the lowest prices, regardless of its national market share. In other words, it's better to have the number-one market share in ten states than to be number one nationwide but number four in every state.[7]

Another aspect of scale economies is that a company derives benefit only if competitors cannot easily achieve similar scale. Sometimes the required investments are large enough to deter competitors. Anyone who wants to compete with United Parcel Service (UPS), for instance, would need to first pay the enormous fixed expense of installing an international network and then operate at a loss for quite some time while drawing customers away from the incumbent. Even though UPS continually must add new costs for planes, trucks, and drivers, these costs are variable—in contrast to the fixed cost of building the international network—and are incurred in stepwise fashion. That does not mean the industry is completely safe from competition. Over the past few years, Amazon has been building its own shipping network, which delivered more than 20 percent of total parcel volume in the United States by 2022.[8] Scale is less effective as a barrier to entry for Amazon: the company can rapidly reach sufficient scale thanks to its internal demand, and it has shown itself prepared and able to incur significant up-front investments.

Scalable Product or Process   Having products or processes that are scalable means the cost of supplying or serving additional customers is very low at almost any level of scale. Businesses with this advantage usually deliver their products and services using information technology (IT). Consider a company that provides standardized software (in other words, a product that requires little customization). Once the software is developed, it can be sold to many customers with no incremental development costs, so the gross margin on incremental sales could be as high as 100 percent. As sales rise, the only costs that increase are typically for selling, marketing, and administration.

---

[7] In recent years, national scale is becoming more important, with increasing investments in new technologies that are expensive and harder to scale for smaller insurers.
[8] *Parcel Shipping Index 2023*, Pitney Bowes, 2023.

For scalable software businesses, the up-front investments are not the only hurdle that competitors must deal with. Customers face costs of switching to other software providers, so competitors cannot easily achieve a scale similar to the incumbent player's. That does not mean such competitive advantages last indefinitely, however; ongoing technological innovations in IT create opportunities for new competitors. For example, in financial and payments services, new entrants such as PayPal or Adyen have secured leading positions by starting new business models built on innovative technology platforms. Incumbent players, such as retail and wholesale banks, as well as traditional payment processors, which are strapped with legacy organizations, systems, and processes, have found it difficult to copy the innovations.

Other examples of scalable businesses include media companies that make and distribute movies or TV shows. Making the movie or show requires an initial outlay for the crew, sets, actors, and so on. But those costs are fixed regardless of how many people end up viewing and paying for the movie or show. There may be some incremental advertising costs and very small costs associated with streaming the movie to customers directly or distributing it to cinemas. But overall, costs do not rise significantly as customer numbers increase. In this case, the access to unique resources—namely, media content—is what holds off competitors from capturing similar scale economies.

Most IT-based or IT-enabled businesses offer some form of scalability, especially given recent developments in cloud-based computing. But what counts is whether all critical elements of a business system are scalable. Take, for example, online food delivery businesses. These businesses can easily scale up in terms of number of registered restaurants, customers, and orders, but they still incur incremental costs for each individual order delivery, if only for transportation (the cost per meal and kilometer does not decrease much with increased scale). As a result, costs still mount with the number of clients, which presents some limits on scalability and reduction of costs to serve as the business grows—similar to the IWG example in the beginning of this chapter.

Network Effects

Some scalable businesses models provide extraordinarily high returns on capital because they exhibit network effects that generate not only decreasing costs but also increasing returns to scale. As the business gains customers and grows, the cost of offering the products decreases, and the products' value to customers increases, triggering even bigger increases in returns on capital (see Exhibit 8.3). The Airbnb example we related at the beginning of this chapter illustrates this. Other examples are online mobility platforms such as Lyft and lodging and travel platforms such as Expedia and Booking.com. These models feature scalable products where the marginal cost of additional transactions is minimal. In addition, with scale, these platform services also become more

EXHIBIT 8.3 **Network Effects Boosting ROIC**

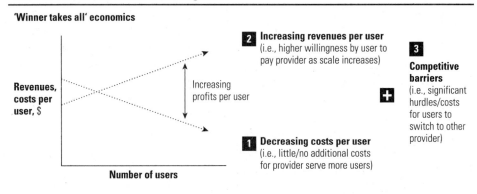

valuable to both end customers and lodging providers. As a result, Expedia and Booking.com can simultaneously realize competitive advantages in price and in cost and capital efficiencies.

Such sources of competitive advantage become even more powerful when customers face high switching costs. For businesses such as Airbnb, Booking. com, Expedia, and Lyft, users can fairly easily switch to competing platforms—and this holds for customers as well as drivers, hotels, and travel operators. In contrast, consider a company such as Microsoft. Its Office software benefits from scalable operations on the cost side because it can supply online products and services at extremely low marginal cost. Office has also become more valuable as the customer base has expanded over time. Microsoft has been able to lock in customers who want to easily exchange documents with other Office users and who are not keen to spend time and effort switching to alternative software. Some social-media business models, such as Facebook's or WhatsApp's, offer similar but milder customer lock-in combined with increasing returns on scale. And most mobility platforms have some form of customer rewards program in place to incentivize customers to return to the same platform for future transactions. However, when competition is strong and switching costs for customers are very small, rewards programs effectively translate to lower pricing and margins.

Although many new digital business models for social media, digital marketplaces, and e-commerce claim to offer increasing and lasting returns to scale, such returns occur only in rare circumstances. Economists Carl Shapiro and Hal Varian popularized this concept in their 1998 book *Information Rules.*[9] The management implication of this insight was that in a business with increasing returns, it is important to get big faster than anyone else. Shapiro and Varian also explained the rare conditions under which it is possible to

[9] C. Shapiro and H. Varian, *Information Rules: A Strategic Guide to the Network Economy* (Boston: Harvard Business School Press, 1998).

increase returns to scale. Sadly, executives who ignored that part of the book and pursued size without the necessary conditions for success faced disaster. For example, many U.S. electric-power producers tried to get big fast in the early 2000s by buying up everything they could. Most collapsed, because there are no increasing returns from scaling electric-power production with a random collection of power plants around the world. In recent years, NextEra has had some success by carefully placing its wind power operations—choosing locations based on criteria such as where it is possible to have a small number of technicians servicing many turbines. Perhaps more important, such scale effects lead to superior lasting returns only if a company can prevent competitors from achieving similar scale.

SUSTAINING RETURN ON INVESTED CAPITAL

The longer a company can sustain a high ROIC, the more value management will create. In a perfectly competitive economy, ROIC higher than the cost of capital gets competed away. Whether a company can sustain a given level of ROIC depends on the length of the life cycles of its businesses and products, the length of time its competitive advantages can persist, and its potential for renewing businesses and products.

Length of Product Life Cycle

The longer the life cycle of a company's businesses and products, the better its chances of sustaining its ROIC. To illustrate, while the products of companies such as Coca-Cola or Mars may not seem as exciting as the latest flashy electronics items or digital services, culturally entrenched branded soft drinks and snacks are likely to have a market for far longer than many new gadgets. Similarly, a unique resource (such as high-quality crude oil with low extraction costs) can be a durable source of advantage if it is related to a long product life cycle but will be less so if it isn't (as appears to be the case for lignite and coal). Note that a product life cycle is not given and fixed. For many products, companies can effectively manage and extend the life cycle. For example, since its release in the early 20th century, the traditional board game Monopoly has been issued in many different affinity versions (including Star Wars, Mario Brothers, and Ted Lasso versions), in versions with electronic features, and in online form—which has helped to maintain the game's best-seller status.

A business model that locks customers into a product with a short life cycle is far less valuable than one that locks customers in for a long time. Once users of Microsoft's Windows have become well versed in the platform, they are unlikely to switch to a new competitor. Even Linux, a low-cost alternative to Windows, has struggled to gain market share as system administrators and end users remain wary of learning a new way of computing. Microsoft's success in extending the life cycle of Windows has been a huge source of value to the company. Contrast this with a company such as BlackBerry, which had an impressive customer base until the life cycle of its early smartphones was cut short by the introduction of the iPhone and other next-generation devices.

Persistence of Competitive Advantage

If a company cannot prevent competition from duplicating its business, high ROIC will be short-lived, and the company's value will diminish. Consider two major cost improvements that airlines implemented in the 2010s. The self-service kiosk and the smartphone app have both allowed passengers to purchase a ticket and then email or download a boarding pass from anywhere in the world without waiting in line. From the airlines' perspective, fewer ground personnel are needed to handle even more passengers. So why has this cost improvement not translated into high ROIC for the airlines? Since every company has access to the technology, any cost improvements are passed directly to the consumer in the form of lower prices. A similar example comes from robotic automation's ongoing effect on productivity improvements in automotive manufacturing: all players adopt the new technology and pass on the cost reductions to customers. In general, advantages that arise from brand and quality on the price side and scalability on the cost side tend to have more staying power than those arising from more temporary sources of advantage, such as innovations that will be adopted by most competitors and tend to be superseded by subsequent innovations.

Potential for Product Renewal

Few businesses or products have life cycles as long as Coca-Cola's. Most companies need to find renewal businesses and products where they can leverage existing advantages or build new ones. This is an area where brands prove their value. Consumer goods companies excel at using their brands to launch new products: think of Apple's success with the iPhone, Bulgari moving into fragrances, Mars entering the ice cream business, Netflix switching from DVD rentals by mail to video streaming online, John Deere offering information services to farmers, and Signify (the former Philips Lighting) developing connected lighting solutions such as Hue. Being good at innovation also helps companies renew products and businesses. Thus, pharmaceutical companies exist because they can discover new drugs, and semiconductor technology players such as ARM, ASML, and Nvidia rely on their technology innovation to launch new products and stay ahead of competitors.

Some companies, such as LVMH, Microsoft, Amazon and Alphabet's Google subsidiary, are able to maintain their primary product lines while simultaneously expanding into new markets. Google built new advertising and subscription businesses around, for example, YouTube and Google Workspace (which comprises Gmail, Calendar, and Drive, among other elements) to complement the original advertising business that its search engine powers. Over the past two decades, Amazon and Microsoft started offering their cloud computing platforms AWS (2006) and Azure (2010), and they have grown into the world's leading platforms for developing and hosting applications and services in the cloud. LVMH has maintained its position as one of the world's leading purveyors of luxury goods by extensive use of M&A to add to its collection of brands, as well as through brand and product development via partnerships and organic growth. Its *maisons* include some brands with centuries of history such as storied French winemaker Chateau d'Yquem, some of which are recent purchases (including the U.S. jeweler Tiffany, acquired in 2021). But others are newer businesses, which LVMH helped fund and grow, such as Fenty Beauty, a cosmetics brand that was started in 2017 and is 50 percent owned by pop star Rihanna.

As the next section of this chapter indicates, empirical studies show that over the past six decades, companies have been generally successful in sustaining their rates of ROIC. It appears that when companies have found a strategy that creates competitive advantages, they are often able to sustain and renew these advantages over many years. This also holds for the relatively new digital business models with which Amazon, Google, Microsoft, and others have retained and renewed their competitive advantages for two decades and more. While competition clearly plays a major role in driving down ROIC, managers can sustain a high rate of return by anticipating and responding to changes in the environment better than their competitors do.

AN EMPIRICAL ANALYSIS OF RETURNS ON INVESTED CAPITAL

Several key findings concerning ROIC emerge from a study of 1963–2023 returns on invested capital at U.S.- and Europe-based nonfinancial companies with (inflation-adjusted) revenues greater than $1 billion[10]:

- Returns on capital have generally been higher in the United States than in Europe since 1995, and the difference has been increasing in recent years.

---

[10] The results come from McKinsey's Value Intelligence database, which relies on financial data provided by Standard & Poor's Compustat and Capital IQ. The European sample includes data over a more limited time frame (1995–2023) for companies from all 27 member states of the European Union plus the United Kingdom and Switzerland. The combined U.S. and European samples include all companies with more than $1 billion in revenues in 2020 real terms, except financial institutions, real estate companies, and industrial companies with significant financial businesses. For most years since 1995, the combined sample contains more than 2,000 companies. Note that results may vary from prior editions due to, for example, changes in industry definitions and accounting standards.

- The median ROIC in the United States was stable at about 10 percent until the turn of the century, increased to 15 percent after 2005, and increased again after the 2020 COVID-19 crisis to around 20 percent. Important drivers of this effect were a general increase in profitability across sectors, combined with a significant shift in the mix of U.S.-based companies to higher-returning sectors in life sciences and technology. These sectors not only significantly increased their ROIC but also grew faster. The increase after 2020 was likely driven by the sharply higher inflation in 2021 and 2022 (see Chapter 26 for more background). In Europe, the long-term trends are similar, but with ROIC lower by around two percentage points over the last ten years, mainly because the sectors in life sciences and technology are smaller than in the United States.

- Returns on invested capital differ by industry in both the United States and Europe—and largely in similar ways. For both regions, industries such as pharmaceuticals and branded consumer goods that rely on patents and brands for their sustainable competitive advantages tend to have high median ROIC, whereas companies in basic industries, such as oil and gas, mining, and utilities, tend to earn low ROIC. For most industries, returns are higher in the United States than in Europe.

- Rates of ROIC vary widely within industries. Some companies, including Ryanair and Walmart, earn attractive returns in industries where the median return is low, and vice versa.

- In both the United States and Europe, relative rates of ROIC across industries are generally stable, especially compared with rates of growth (discussed in the next chapter). Industry rankings by median ROIC do not change much over time; only a few industries make a clear aggregate shift up or down. These shifts typically reflect structural changes, such as the widespread consolidation in the U.S. defense industry and the maturing of the biotech industry over the past decades. Individual company returns gradually tend toward their industry medians over time but are generally persistent. Even the 2008 financial crisis and the 2020 COVID-19 pandemic did not upset this trend in either the United States or Europe.

ROIC Trends and Drivers

Relatively stable ROIC levels from the early 1960s to the early 2000s are evident in Exhibit 8.4, which plots median ROIC between 1963 and 2023 for U.S.-based nonfinancial companies.[11] In that exhibit, the measure of ROIC excludes

---

[11] Some numbers in this section are based on U.S. companies only because longer-term data for non-U.S. companies are not readily available.

EXHIBIT 8.4 **ROIC of U.S.-Based Nonfinancial Companies, 1963–2023**

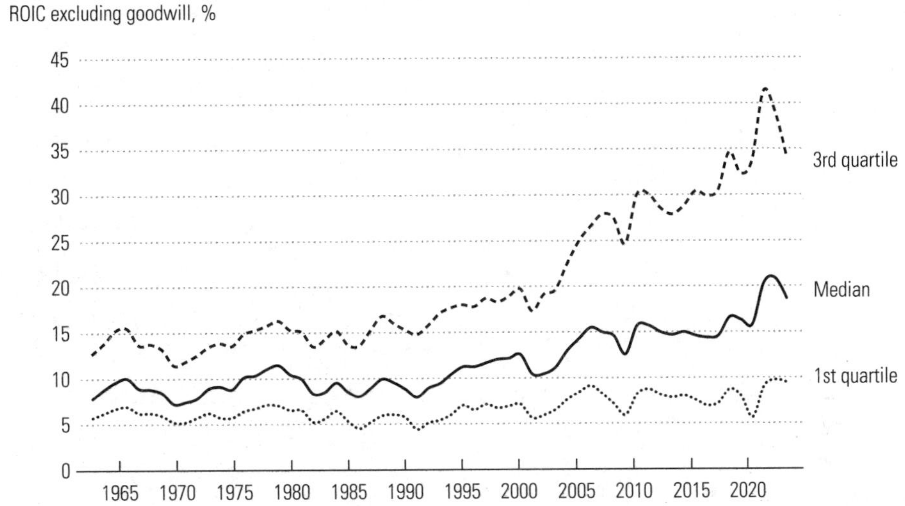

ROIC excluding goodwill, %

Source: McKinsey Value Intelligence database.

goodwill and acquired intangibles, which allows us to focus on the under-lying economics of companies without the distortion of premiums paid for acquisitions (discussed later in the chapter).

Until the 2000s, the median ROIC without goodwill was about 10 percent. Furthermore, annual medians oscillated in a tight range, with higher returns in high-GDP-growth years and lower returns in low-growth years. Since the 2000s, however, median ROIC without goodwill has increased to what appears to be a new level of about 15 percent in 2005 and beyond. Exhibit 8.5 shows the median ROIC for European companies between 1995 and 2022. By and large, the ROIC pattern is similar to that of U.S. companies, with the ten-year average ROIC in 2023 at 14.7 percent in Europe, versus 16.7 percent in the United States.

The recent, sharp ROIC increase in both the United States and Europe is at least partly driven by high inflation in 2021 and 2022, following the COVID-19 pandemic. Because invested capital is generally recorded at historical pur-chase prices while operating profits inflate, ROIC typically increases in times of inflation. These inflationary effects in ROIC should gradually disappear as property, plant, and equipment in invested capital are replaced in future years at higher prices (see Chapter 26).

Notice also that the spread between the first and third quartiles has wid-ened in both regions. This is especially the case in the United States, where the first-quartile company earned around 5 to 10 percent during the entire period, while the third-quartile company's return has increased from the midteens prior to 2000 to over 35 percent in recent years.

EXHIBIT 8.5 **ROIC of Europe-Based Nonfinancial Companies, 1995–2023**

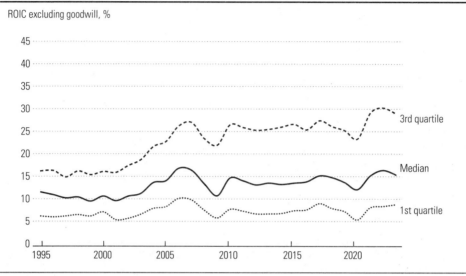

ROIC excluding goodwill, %

Source: McKinsey Value Intelligence database.

In fact, the entire distribution of ROIC has widened as more and more companies earn high returns on capital in both the United States and Europe. Exhibit 8.6 shows the distribution of ROICs for U.S. companies over different eras. In the 1965–1967 period, only 15 percent of companies earned more

EXHIBIT 8.6 **Distribution of ROIC**

% of U.S.-based companies with given annual ROIC excluding goodwill, by time period

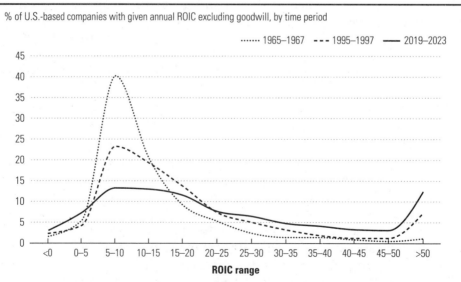

Source: McKinsey Value Intelligence database.

than a 20 percent ROIC, compared with 46 percent in 2019–2023. At the same time, the share of companies earning less than 10 percent has declined from 52 percent to 26 percent.[12]

One factor powering the shift in the median ROIC is the steady increase of operating margins across sectors since the mid-1990s. As shown in Exhibit 8.7, the aggregate operating margin in the United States (total NOPAT over total sales for all companies) has risen by more than four percentage points. When higher margins combine with stable or improving capital productivity (invested capital over sales), returns on capital rise. This has been the case in both the U.S. and the European economies.

What differentiates the U.S. economy is its changing mix of industries, which serves as an even more powerful driver and helps explain the widening dispersion of returns. Among U.S.-based nonfinancial companies, the share of operating profits from companies in the life sciences and technology

EXHIBIT 8.7 **Disaggregating ROIC of U.S.-Based Nonfinancial Companies, 1995–2023**

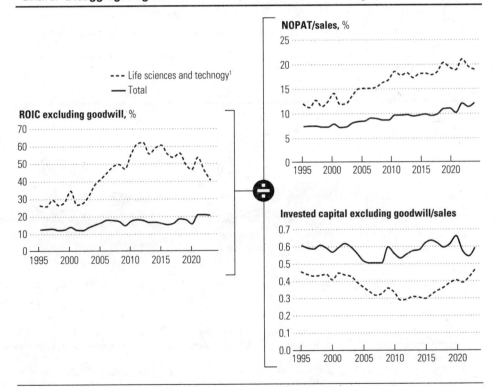

Note: ROIC, NOPAT/sales, and invested capital/sales are aggregate metrics.

[1] Life sciences and technology sectors comprise pharmaceuticals, biotechnology, health care equipment and supplies, information services and software, media, technology hardware, storage, and peripherals.

Source: McKinsey Value Intelligence database.

[12] The analysis of the ROIC distribution changes generated similar results for U.S. and European companies.

sectors increased from 20 percent of total operating profits in 1995 to 38 percent in 2023, with a limited number of very large companies (such as Alphabet, Amazon, Apple, Eli Lilly, Johnson & Johnson, and Microsoft, to name just a few) generating very high returns.[13] This impressive increase has been driven by the faster growth of these sectors relative to the rest of the economy, these sectors' generally higher margins and returns on capital, and increases in these sectors' margins and returns on capital. As a result, the life sciences and technology sectors contributed almost eight percentage points of the total 20 percent aggregate return on capital for the U.S. economy as a whole, compared with only three percentage points of a 12 percent total aggregate return in 1995. (Aggregate ROIC is calculated as total NOPAT divided by total invested capital for the economy.) For the European economy, this effect has been much smaller, with life sciences and technology sectors driving only three percentage points of the total 16 percent aggregate return on capital in 2023 (see Exhibit 8.8).[14] In both Europe and the United States, these sectors make all the difference for return on capital.

EXHIBIT 8.8 **Contribution of Life Sciences and Technology Industries to the Broader Economy, 1995–2023**

Contribution to aggregate ROIC excluding goodwill for total sample, %

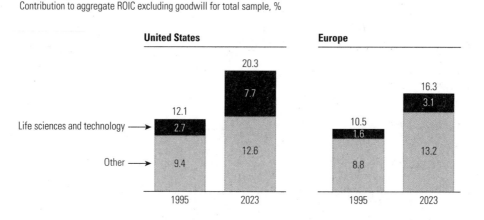

Source: McKinsey Value Intelligence database.

[13] We defined life sciences and technology sectors to comprise pharmaceuticals, biotechnology, health care equipment and supplies, information services and software, media, and technology hardware, storage, and peripherals.

[14] The ROIC contribution is calculated as the total NOPAT of the life sciences and technology sectors divided by the invested capital of all sectors. These sectors contribute eight percentage points to the U.S. aggregate ROIC, which implies that if all other sectors had generated 0 percent ROIC, the U.S. aggregate ROIC would still be 8 percent. Note that the aggregate ROIC for the total sample differs somewhat from the median, depending on the distribution of ROIC across companies of different size (for the U.S., a median ROIC of 11 percent in 1995 and 19 percent in 2023, and for Europe, 12 percent in 1995 and 16 percent in 2023).

ROIC by Industry

To see how differences in ROIC across industries and companies relate to likely differences in drivers of competitive advantage, we examined variations in ROIC by industry over the past two decades. Our findings are in line with results from prior editions of this book, in which we tracked profitability going back to the 1960s. Exhibit 8.9 shows the median returns on invested capital for a range of industries in the United States during the periods 1995–1999 and 2019–2023. The exhibit reveals large differences in median ROIC across industries. Not surprisingly, industries with the highest returns, such as pharmaceuticals, health care equipment, and technology-related businesses, are

EXHIBIT 8.9 **ROIC by Industry for U.S.-Based Companies, 1995–2023**

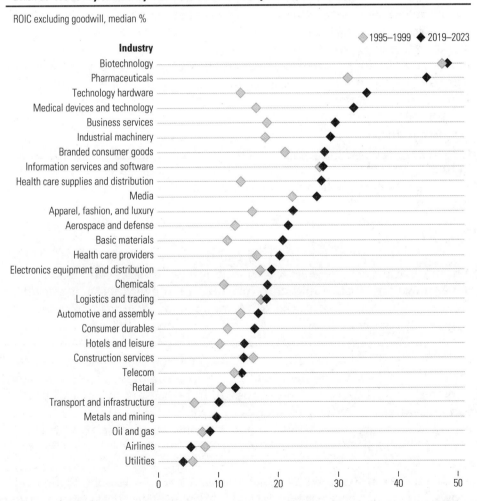

ROIC excluding goodwill, median %

♦ 1995–1999   ♦ 2019–2023

those with sustainable competitive advantages. In the case of pharmaceuticals and health care equipment, this is due to patent-protected innovation. In technology-related businesses, advantage typically flows from increasing returns to scale and customer lock-in. The branded consumer goods sector, for instance, has high returns thanks to customer loyalty based on brand strength. The industries at the bottom of the chart tend to be those where it is difficult to achieve a price premium or cost advantage—often commodity-based industries, including oil and gas, metals and mining.

Industries typically recognized for having higher returns have often been the ones that also deliver the clearest improvements in ROIC over time. The reasons vary by sector. For example, leading aerospace and defense companies tend to focus on government contracts that include advance payments. This keeps the companies' invested capital at low levels relative to revenues. On the other hand, many technology players have benefited from growth and innovation in hardware (via semiconductors, servers, and smartphones) and in software and services. Among the highest-performing industries shown in Exhibit 8.9, only the biotechnology and the information services and software sectors did not significantly improve ROIC between the two periods covered—but they did manage to sustain what were already high ROIC levels in 1995–1999.

Most industries that had lower returns on capital in the mid-1990s have not shown significant improvement over the past three decades. These are industries in which price premiums are difficult to achieve because of, for example, low barriers to entry, commodity products, or regulated returns. For example, health care facilities face ongoing price pressure from the government, insurers, and competition with nonprofits. Retail businesses face similar difficulties, since they too can achieve little price differentiation versus competitors, so as a rule, they realize persistently low returns. While a number of industries have shown very low returns on capital, very few have shown any decline in their return on capital over this same period.

As Exhibit 8.10 shows, the ROIC ranking of European industries is largely consistent with that of U.S. industries, with the pharmaceutical, health care equipment, and branded consumer goods sectors showing up at the high end and transport, metals and mining, and oil and gas appearing at the low end. But while the rankings are similar, levels of ROIC tend to be higher for U.S. companies across all industries, with few exceptions. Some examples of industries that do not follow this pattern are biotechnology and information services and software—but these industries are marked by a high degree of variation in ROIC from company to company, as we discuss next.

Differences in ROIC within industries can be considerable. Exhibit 8.11 shows the variation between the first and third quartiles for the same industries in the United States. Note the wide range of returns in information services and software. Some of the companies in the sector earn low returns because

EXHIBIT 8.10 **ROIC by Industry for U.S.-Based vs. Europe-Based Companies, 1995–2023**

ROIC excluding goodwill, median %

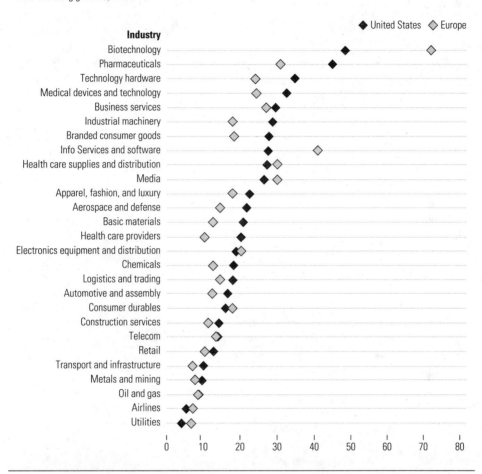

Source: McKinsey Value Intelligence database.

they are capital intensive, and low margins because their business model is not scalable, as in the case of running data centers. Other companies provide services based on standardized and scalable software, where the incremental cost to serve a new customer is small, leading to high ROIC. In some industries, the largest players also generate the highest returns, and median ROIC does not reflect the aggregated ROIC for the sector as a whole (defined as NOPAT for the sector divided by its total invested capital). An example is the technology hardware sector, where players like Apple, Broadcom, Nvidia, and Qualcomm drive the aggregate ROIC to around 125 percent, versus a median of 35 percent in the years 2019–2023.

This chart also shows that the best performers in a weaker or mediocre industry may outperform the median performer in a stronger industry.

EXHIBIT 8.11 **Variation in ROIC within U.S. Industries, 2019–2023**

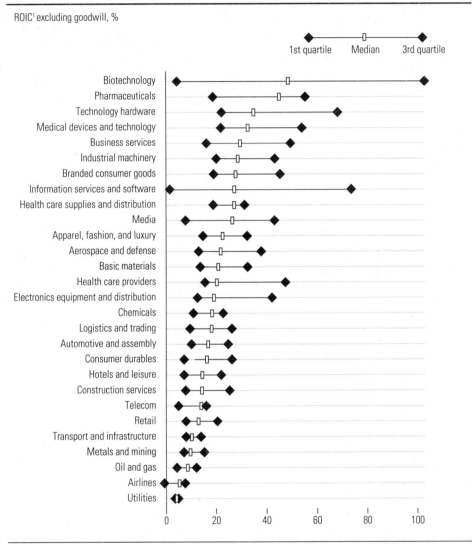

ROIC[1] excluding goodwill, %

Source: Corporate Performance Analytics by McKinsey.

Consider, for example, retail, shown in the bottom half of the chart. The stronger retailers (such as Walmart) outperform the weaker companies in branded consumer goods, which appears in the top half of the chart.

Stability of ROIC

As we have seen in Exhibit 8.9, many industries tend to generate fairly stable or even improving ROIC over time, and very few show declining ROIC. There is similar evidence of sustained rates of return at the company level. For the

U.S. sample, we measured the sustainability of company ROIC in our database of nonfinancial corporations by ranking companies based on their ROIC in each year and dividing the group into four portfolios according to ROIC quartiles. We then tracked the median ROIC for each portfolio over the following 15 years, as shown in Exhibit 8.12. The persistence of the companies' performance over 15 years is striking. The returns of the best-performing companies do *not* decline to the aggregate median. High-performing companies are, in general, remarkably capable of sustaining a competitive advantage in their businesses and/or finding new businesses where they can continue or rebuild such advantages. At the same time, low-performing companies typically do not easily move to median ROIC levels. The pattern is consistent across the United States and Europe, as well as over time—even over the most recent 20 years, which included the 2008 credit crisis and the 2020 pandemic.[15] The crisis years are marked by lower returns across all portfolios without significantly affecting the return differences, let alone the rankings of portfolios.

Since a company's value is highly dependent on long-run forecasts of ROIC and growth, this result has important implications for corporate valuation. For example, basing a continuing value on the economic concept that ROIC will approach the weighted average cost of capital (WACC) is overly conservative for the *typical* company generating high ROIC. (Continuing value is the focus of Chapter 14.)

Keeping this range of performance in mind, it is important when benchmarking the historical decay of company ROIC to segment results by industry,

EXHIBIT 8.12 **ROIC Decay Through Economic Crisis and Recovery**

Median ROIC of portfolios (excluding goodwill),[1] %

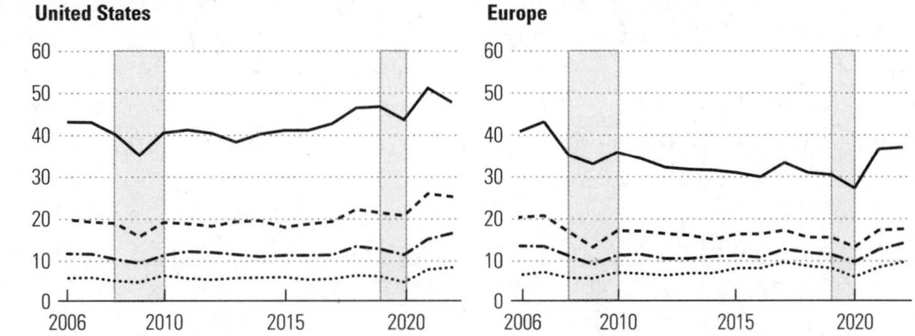

United States

Europe

[1] As of 2006, companies are grouped into one of four portfolios, based on ROIC.

Source: McKinsey Value Intelligence database.

[15] We tracked ROIC quintiles in similar ways from 1965 in prior editions of this book and found very consistent patterns of very limited convergence to median levels across all quintiles.

EXHIBIT 8.13 **ROIC Decay for U.S. Branded Consumer Goods Companies**

Median ROIC of portfolios (excluding goodwill),[1] %

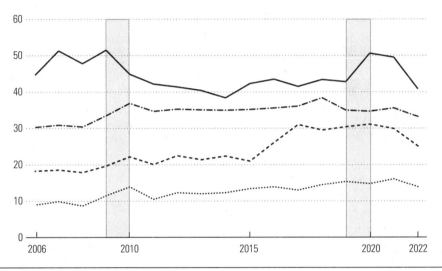

[1] As of 2006, companies are grouped into one of four portfolios, based on ROIC.

Source: McKinsey Value Intelligence database.

especially if industry is a proxy for sustainability of competitive advantage. As an example, Exhibit 8.13 plots the ROIC decay rates for U.S. branded consumer goods, again sorting the companies into four portfolios based on their starting ROICs in 2006. Here, the top-performing companies don't show much reversion to the mean either. Even after 15 years, the original class of best performers still outperforms the bottom portfolio by more than 15 percentage points.

Although decay rates examine the *rate* of regression toward the mean, they present only aggregate results and tell us nothing about the spread of potential future performance. Of course, not every company will follow the ROIC trajectories shown in Exhibit 8.13; some will go on to generate higher returns, while others will generate lower returns. Some top performers will become poor performers and vice versa. But how frequently is this the case? To address this question, we measured the probability that a company will migrate from one ROIC grouping to another in ten years, for both the United States and Europe. The results are presented in Exhibit 8.14. Read across each row from left to right.

Both high and low performers demonstrate significant stability in their performance. Companies with high or low ROIC are most likely to stay in the same grouping—and this holds equally for both regions. For the United States, a company whose ROIC was below 15 percent in 2012 had a 61 percent chance of earning less than 15 percent in 2022, while in Europe, the probability was 69 percent. For U.S. companies with a ROIC above 25 percent, the probability of maintaining

EXHIBIT 8.14 **ROIC Transition Probability**

Probability of achieving ROIC in 2022, by 2012 ROIC

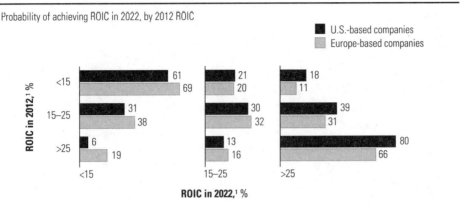

¹ ROIC excluding goodwill.

Source: McKinsey Value Intelligence database.

that high performance was 80 percent, while a similar European company had a 66 percent chance of maintaining such performance. The high percentage for the United States in this category is partly explained by its much larger technology and life sciences sectors, where returns are persistently high across companies (see also Exhibit 8.8). Among companies whose ROIC was between 15 and 25 percent in 2012, there was no clear tendency for companies to increase or decrease their ROIC ten years later.[16]

Effect of Acquisitions on ROIC

While returns on invested capital without goodwill have been increasing, returns on invested capital with goodwill have been flat, as shown for U.S. and European companies in Exhibit 8.15. Furthermore, at around 10 percent, these returns have been fairly close to the typical cost of capital in recent decades, which has been around 7 to 9 percent. Again, the pattern of median returns for Europe is very similar, and the return improvement during the inflation years post-COVID is evident in both regions. Companies paid high prices for their acquisitions, so much of the value the deals created was transferred to the shareholders of the target company. (Acquisitions and value creation are discussed in Chapter 31.) It does not mean that companies have failed to create value from acquisitions: returns on capital including goodwill above the cost of capital, combined with ongoing growth, indicate that they have created value above and beyond the price paid for these acquisitions. Increasing returns without goodwill indicates that companies have captured significant synergies to improve the performance of the acquired businesses.

[16] We did the same analysis using ROIC including goodwill and obtained very similar results, showing little or no convergence of returns across the ranked portfolios.

EXHIBIT 8.15 **ROIC Including and Excluding Goodwill, 1963–2023**

Median ROIC, %

— U.S.-based companies   — Europe-based companies[1]

Excluding goodwill

Including goodwill

[1] For European countries, results are shown for 1995–2023.

Source: McKinsey Value Intelligence database.

For some industries, the differences in return with and without goodwill are even bigger than shown here. For the life sciences and technology sectors, for example, aggregate returns on capital including goodwill were around 17.5 percent, versus more than 50 percent without goodwill over the last ten years. Companies in this sector have created more value than any other sector, but shareholders of acquired companies captured much of it.

SUMMARY

There is much to learn about returns on invested capital, and the lessons apply to Europe as well as to the United States, as returns on capital in both regions follow the same underlying economic logic. First, these returns are driven by competitive advantages that enable companies to realize price premiums, cost and capital efficiencies, or some combination of these. Second, industry structure is an important—but not an exclusive—determinant of ROIC. Certain industries are more likely to earn either high, medium, or low returns, but there is still significant variation in the rates of return for individual companies within each industry. Third and most important, if a company finds a formula or strategy that earns an attractive ROIC, there is a good chance it can sustain that attractive return over time and through changing economic, industry, and company conditions, especially in the case of industries that enjoy relatively long product life cycles. Of course, the converse also is true: if a company earns a low ROIC, that is likely to persist as well.

9

Growth

Growth and its pursuit grip the business world. The popular view is that a company must grow to survive and prosper. There is certainly some truth to this. Companies that are able to continue growing through the economy's ups and downs have a much greater chance of not just surviving but thriving.[1] This is particularly true of companies whose growth is driven by innovation.[2] Slow-growing companies present fewer interesting opportunities for managers and so may have difficulty attracting and retaining talent. They are also much more likely to be acquired than faster-growing firms. Over the past decades, most of the companies that have disappeared from the S&P 500 index were acquired by larger companies or went private.

However, as discussed in Chapters 2 and 3, growth creates value only when a company's new customers, projects, or acquisitions generate returns on invested capital (ROIC) greater than the company's cost of capital. And as companies grow larger and their industries become ever more competitive, finding good, high-value-creating projects becomes increasingly difficult. Striking the right balance between growth and return on invested capital is critically important to value creation. Our research shows that for companies with a high ROIC, shareholder returns are affected more by an increase in revenues than by pushing the ROIC even higher.[3] Indeed, we have found that if such companies let their ROIC drop a bit (though not too much) to achieve higher growth, their returns to shareholders are higher than for companies that maintain or improve their high ROIC but grow more slowly. Conversely,

---

This chapter was coauthored by Rebecca Doherty and Laura Laberge.

[1] R. Doherty and A. Koivuniemi, "Rev Up Your Growth Engine: Lessons from Through-Cycle Outperformers," McKinsey & Company, May 27, 2020, www.mckinsey.com.

[2] M. Banholzer, R. Doherty, A. Morris, et al., "Innovative Growers: A View from the Top," *McKinsey Quarterly*, November 2023, www.mckinsey.com.

[3] See T. Koller and B. Jiang, "How to Choose between Growth and ROIC," *McKinsey on Finance*, no. 25 (Autumn 2007): 19–22.

for companies with a low ROIC, increasing it will create more value than growing the company will.

The previous chapter explored why executives need to understand whether their strategies will lead to high returns on invested capital. Similarly, they also need to know which growth opportunities will create the most value. This chapter discusses the principal drivers of revenue growth, the ways in which growth creates value, and the challenges of sustaining growth. It ends by analyzing the data on corporate growth patterns over the past 60 years.

DRIVERS OF REVENUE GROWTH

When executives plan for growth, a good starting point is for them to disaggregate revenue growth into its three main components:

1. *Portfolio momentum.* This is the organic revenue growth a company enjoys because of overall expansion in the market segments represented in its portfolio.
2. *Market share performance.* This is growth achieved relative to market peers, where companies can gain or lose market share organically through commercial or innovation levers, as well as inorganically through acquisitions.
3. *Expansion into new businesses.* This represents growth into existing or new businesses that are outside the company's current portfolio. Again, the growth can be driven organically by innovative business building, as well inorganically by acquiring existing businesses.

McKinsey research has shown that for large companies, the largest driver of growth is being in fast-growing businesses (or expanding into them). Least important is market share growth. Yet managers tend to focus most of their attention on increasing their share within the product markets they are already in. While it's necessary to maintain and sometimes increase market share, changing a company's exposure to growing and shrinking market segments should be a major focus. In fact, a significant portion of the most value-creating companies worldwide were able to achieve that level of success by creating or rapidly moving into an entirely new market, taking advantage of the high growth potential associated with starting from scratch with limited competition.[4]

To see the effects of portfolio momentum and business expansion, consider how the long-term median growth of the largest U.S. companies

---

[4] See P. Viguerie, S. Smit, and M. Baghai, *The Granularity of Growth* (Hoboken, NJ: John Wiley & Sons, 2008).

(those with revenues of $1 billion or more) from 2013 to 2023 differs by industry (Exhibit 9.1).[5] The fastest-growing sector over this period was biotechnology, which fueled its impressive pace of growth by developing a wave of innovative, blockbuster drugs. Next in line are the information

EXHIBIT 9.1 **Variation in Revenue Growth by Industry: U.S.-Based Companies**

Long-term annualized revenue growth rate,[1] adjusted for inflation, %

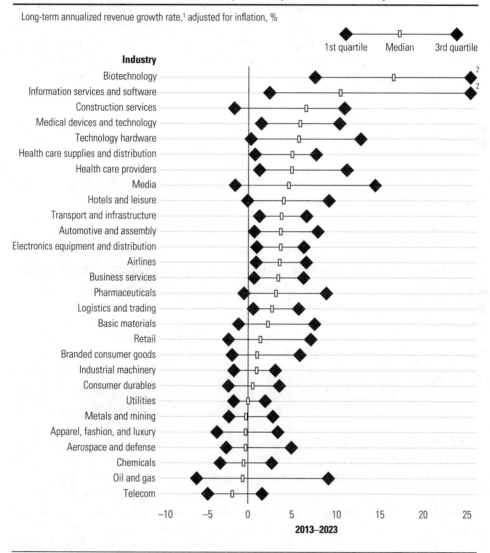

[1] Scale limited to 25 for presentation purposes.

[2] This is where scale is cut off (i.e., 3rd quartile beyond scale maximum).

Source: McKinsey Value Intelligence database.

[5] In this chapter, we are using the same company samples for the United States and Europe as in Chapter 8.

and technology sectors, which also grew thanks to product and service innovations. Health-care-related sectors, such as health care supplies and distribution, have shown strong growth as well, driven both by long-term changes in demographics and by innovations in medical technology (for example, medical devices). However, makers of traditional pharmaceutical products dropped to average growth levels in the past decade as many of the highest-selling drugs from the 1990s came off patent and growth from consolidation slowed down. The construction services industry, traditionally perceived as very cyclical, secured a high place in the growth rankings because underlying demand remained strong over the decade, especially in areas such as energy and infrastructure projects. Airlines, after several years of strong growth from consolidation in the United States, ended up with average revenue growth over the decade, restrained by the COVID-19 pandemic. And telecommunications services companies, which experienced strong growth at the turn of the century, dropped to the bottom of the list as markets matured and customer rates declined.

Exhibit 9.1 also shows widely varied growth within industries over the same period, especially in biotechnology and information services, where a quarter of all companies achieved long-term growth rates of more than 30 percent. In part, this is explained by extremely successful innovations at small and start-up companies that were able to reach revenues of $1 billion within several years. In the U.S. oil and gas sector, levels of growth were highly varied, with local producers attaining strong growth levels as they boosted production from technological innovations, such as horizontal drilling and hydraulic fracturing. But even in sectors without significant innovations, such as branded consumer goods, long-term growth differences among companies can be significant, with around eight percentage points between the lowest and highest quartiles—sizable amounts, given that all these companies have revenues of at least $1 billion.

If a company's growth depends mainly on the dynamics of the sector markets in which it operates, why should there be such big differences in growth among different companies operating in the same sector? The most important reason is that the median growth rate of companies competing in any sector masks big differences in growth across the sector's market segments and subsegments. To understand markets in this fine-grained way and the differences in companies' revenue growth, Baghai, Smit, and Viguerie analyzed market growth at the level of individual product and geographical segments with around $50 million to $200 million in sales, rather than at the company, divisional, or business unit level.[6] Their example of a large European manufacturer of personal-care products shows why such analysis is revealing. The company has three divisions with apparently low prospective growth rates

---

[6] See M. Baghai, S. Smit, and P. Viguerie, "Is Your Growth Strategy Flying Blind?" *Harvard Business Review* (May 2009): 86–96.

ranging from 1.6 percent to 7.5 percent a year. However, the range of forecast growth rates for individual product lines within the divisions is much wider. For instance, the division with the lowest expected growth rate has one product line growing at 24 percent, one of the company's best growth opportunities. At the same time, the division with the highest growth rate has several product lines that are shrinking fast and may warrant divestment.

GROWTH AND VALUE CREATION

While managers typically strive for high growth, the highest growth will not necessarily create the most value. The reason is that the three drivers of growth—portfolio momentum, market share gains, and expansion into new businesses—do not all create value in equal measure. To illustrate, we have ranked several different growth scenarios according to their potential for creating value (see Exhibit 9.2). Each of these scenarios builds on some form of capturing market momentum, gaining market share, or creating new businesses. The ranking may not be exactly the same for all industries, but it works well as a starting point. The scenarios with the highest potential to create value are all

EXHIBIT 9.2 **Value Creation from Alternative Growth Scenarios**

Value created[1]	Growth scenario	Rationale
Above average	• Create new markets through new products or services	• No established competitors; diverts customer spending
	• Innovate business models or ecosystems	• Harder to replicate vs. product or commercial moves, even by similarly placed competitors
	• Convince existing customers to buy more of a product	• All competitors benefit; low risk of retaliation
	• Attract new customers to the market	• All competitors benefit; low risk of retaliation
Average	• Gain market share in fast-growing market	• Competitors can still grow despite losing share; moderate risk of retaliation
	• Make bolt-on acquisitions to accelerate product growth	• Modest acquisition premium relative to upside potential
Below average	• Gain market share from rivals through incremental product or service innovation	• Competitors can replicate and take back customers
	• Gain market share from rivals through product promotion and pricing	• Competitors can retaliate quickly
	• Make large acquisitions	• High premium to pay; significant value diverted to selling companies
	• Increase prices	• Unless demand has low price elasticity, customers likely to reduce or divert consumption

[1] Per dollar of revenue.

variations on creating or entering fast-growing product markets that generate new sources of revenues or take revenues from distant companies, rather than from direct competitors or customers via price increases.

Developing *new products* or services that are so innovative as to create entirely new product categories, or even an entirely new industry, is the scenario with the highest potential for value creation. The stronger the competitive advantage a company can establish in the new-product category, the higher its ROIC will be and the more value it will create. For example, the coronary stent, commercialized in the early 1990s, reduced the need for heart surgery, lowering both the risk and cost of treating cardiac problems. Owing to this innovation's overwhelming competitive advantage over traditional treatments and over subsequent products entering the market,[7] neither type of competitor could retaliate, so the innovators created large amounts of value. As the stent market became highly competitive over the following decades, however, returns on capital declined considerably. Similarly, traditional music retailers have been all but competed away—initially by online sales platforms such as Amazon, then by downloading services such as iTunes, and more recently as consumers have taken up online streaming services for mobile devices offered by Apple Music, Spotify, YouTube, and others. However, competition in the new digital-entertainment category is itself fierce, so the value created per dollar of revenue in this sector is unlikely to reach the levels that coronary stents once generated.

Business model innovation is tied in first place, owing mainly to how difficult it is for competitors to replicate a business model, compared with copying a new product. This type of innovation can deliver growth similar to that generated by a newly created product market. We saw this with online retailers able to gain scale in terms of customers and suppliers, as well as consolidate warehousing costs. Examples in manufacturing include companies such as TSMC, which has achieved long-term growth through business model innovation in disintermediating its supply chain, and Stryker, a maker of medical and surgical equipment, which has adapted its business model to meet the demands of ambulatory surgical centers, which are replacing traditional hospitals for many medical procedures.

Next in the pecking order of value-creating growth tactics comes *persuading existing customers to buy more* of a product or related products. For example, if Procter & Gamble convinces customers to wash their hands more frequently, the market for hand soap will grow faster. Similarly, if antivirus software provider McAfee convinces computer owners that they need better protection against hackers and viruses, total demand for antivirus software and services will grow faster. Direct competitors will not respond, because they benefit as well. The ROIC associated with the additional revenue is likely to be high,

---

[7] Products that entered the market at a later stage were less successful because of high switching costs for customers.

because the companies' manufacturing and distribution systems can typically produce the additional products at little additional cost, as in the aforementioned examples.

Attracting new customers to a market also can create substantial value. Consumer packaged-goods company Beiersdorf accelerated growth in sales of skin care products by convincing men to use its Nivea products, which had previously been used mainly by women. Once again, competitors didn't retaliate because they also gained from the category expansion. Men's skin care products aren't much different from women's, so much of the research and development, manufacturing, and distribution cost could be shared. The major incremental cost was for marketing and advertising.

The value a company can create from increasing market share depends on both the market's rate of growth and the way the company goes about gaining share. There are three main ways to grow market share, and these don't fall next to each other in our pecking order shown in Exhibit 9.3. When a company *gains market share in a fast-growing market*, the absolute revenues of its competitors may still be growing strongly, too, so the competitors may not retaliate. However, gaining share in a mature market is more likely to provoke retaliation by competitors.

Gaining share from *incremental product or service innovation*—for example, through incremental technology improvements that can be copied but do not fundamentally change a product or create an entirely new category—won't create much value. And it is unlikely that a company pursuing this strategy

EXHIBIT 9.3 **Value Creation from Organic Growth vs. Acquisitions**

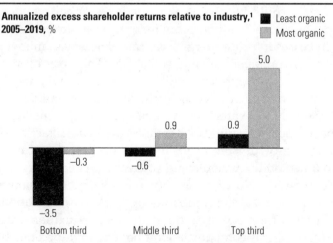

Annualized excess shareholder returns relative to industry,[1] 2005–2019, %

■ Least organic
▨ Most organic

5.0

0.9   0.9

−0.3   −0.6

−3.5

Bottom third   Middle third   Top third

Large European and U.S. companies, ranked by revenue growth rate

[1] Excludes banks, insurance companies, extraction companies and cyclical commodities.
Source: McKinsey Value Intelligence database.

will be able to maintain the advantage for long. From a customer's viewpoint, hybrid and electric vehicles aren't fundamentally different from gas or diesel vehicles, so they cannot command much of a price premium to offset their higher costs. The total number of vehicles sold will not increase, and if one company gains market share for a while, competitors will try to take it back, as competitors can copy each other's innovations before the innovator has been able to extract much value, if any. All in all, auto companies, whether new or incumbent, may not create much value from hybrid or electric vehicles; competition will likely transfer most benefits to consumers.

Gaining share through *product pricing and promotion* in a mature market rarely creates much value, if any. Huggies and Pampers lead the disposable-diaper market and are financially strong, and each can easily respond if the other tries to gain share. Therefore, any growth arising from, say, an intense campaign to reduce prices that hits directly at the other competitor will provoke a response.

In concentrated markets, share battles often lead to a cycle of market share give-and-take but rarely to a permanent share gain for any one competitor, unless that competitor changes the product or its delivery enough to create what is effectively a new product. The possible exception, as with the Amazon example in the preceding paragraph, is stronger companies gaining share from smaller, weaker competitors and forcing the weaker players out of the market entirely.

Price increases, over and above cost increases, can create value as long as any resulting decline in sales volume is small. However, they tend not to be repeatable: if a company or several competitors get away with a price increase one year, they are unlikely to have the same good fortune the next. Furthermore, the first increase could be eroded fairly quickly. Otherwise, you would see some companies increasing their profit margins year after year, while in reality long-term increases in profit margins are rare. There was an exception among packaged-goods companies in the mid-1990s. They passed on increases in commodity costs to customers but did not lower prices when their commodity costs subsequently declined. But the prospect of higher margins made it more attractive for retailers to enter the packaged-goods segments with offerings of private-label brands, sometimes via online sales channels.

The value of growth from acquisitions is hard to characterize, because it depends so much on the benefits and price of the specific acquisition (as discussed in Chapter 31). However, as shown in Exhibit 9.3, a sample of 1,700 of the largest U.S. and European companies by market capitalization reveals that, in general, growth from acquisitions creates less value than organic growth.[8] The main reason is that companies don't have to invest as much up front for organic growth. In growing through acquisitions, companies typically must

[8] See also M. Goedhart and T. Koller, "The Value Premium of Organic Growth," *McKinsey on Finance*, no. 61 (Autumn 2017): 14–15 (similar results for a prior time frame).

pay for the stand-alone value of an acquired business plus a takeover premium. This results in a lower return on invested capital and lower value creation compared with growing organically.[9] The key question is whether the benefits from the acquisition outweigh the price paid up front.

Growth through *bolt-on acquisitions* can create value if the premium paid for the target is carefully calibrated against the benefits generated. Bolt-on acquisitions make incremental changes or enhancements to a business model—for example, by completing or extending a company's product offering or filling gaps in its distribution system. In the 2000s, IBM was very successful in bolting on smaller software companies and subsequently marketing their applications through its existing global sales and distribution system, which could absorb the additional sales without too much extra investment. Because such acquisitions are relatively small, they boosted IBM's growth but added little cost and complexity.

In contrast, creating growth through *large acquisitions*—say, one-third the size or more of the acquiring company—can be less likely to create value: potential benefits can be larger, but the probability of success tends to be lower than for bolt-on acquisitions. For example, many large acquisitions occur when a market has begun to mature and the industry has excess capacity. While the acquiring company shows revenue growth, the combined revenues often do not increase, and sometimes they decrease because customers prefer to have multiple suppliers. Any new value comes primarily from cost cutting, not from growth. Furthermore, integrating the two companies requires significant investments and involves far more complexity and risk than integrating small, bolt-on acquisitions.

In general, underlying product market growth tends to create the most value. Companies should aim to be in the fastest-growing product markets, so they can achieve growth that consistently creates value. If a company is in the wrong markets and can't easily get into the right ones, it may do better by sustaining growth at the same level as its competitors while finding other ways to improve and sustain its ROIC.

WHY SUSTAINING GROWTH IS HARD

Sustaining high growth is much more difficult than sustaining ROIC, especially for larger companies. The math is simple. Suppose your core product markets are growing at the rate of the gross domestic product (GDP)—say, 5 percent nominal growth—and you currently have $10 billion in revenues. Ten years from now, assuming you grow at 5 percent a year, your revenues will be $16.3 billion. Assume you aspire to grow organically at 8 percent a year.

---

[9] Of course, since the scale of growth by acquisitions can be large, the absolute value generated can still be very high, even if the associated return on capital is lower.

In ten years, your revenues will need to be $21.6 billion. Therefore, you will need to find new sources of revenues that can grow to more than $5.3 billion per year by the tenth year. Adjusting for inflation of 1 to 2 percent, you need an extra $4.3 billion to $4.8 billion per year in today's dollars. Another way to think of it is that to find such revenues, you would need to reinvent a business almost half your current size and close to a Fortune 500 company.[10] If your product markets are growing at only 5 percent, how can you possibly achieve that magnitude of growth?

Given this difficulty, the growth targets that some companies embrace are simply unrealistic. One with sales already in excess of $5 billion announced organic growth targets of more than 20 percent a year for the next 20 years. Since annual world economic growth is typically less than 4 percent in real terms and many companies are competing for a share of that growth, such growth targets are hardly achievable.

Sustaining growth is difficult because most product markets have natural life cycles, which means innovation is needed just to avoid company decline. The market for a product—that is, for a narrow product category sold to a specific customer segment in a specific geography—typically follows an S-curve over its life cycle until maturity, as shown on the left side of Exhibit 9.4. The right side shows actual growth curves for various product categories, scaled to their relative penetration of U.S. households. First, a product has to prove itself with early adopters. Growth then accelerates as more people want to buy the product, until it reaches its point of maximum penetration. After this point of maturity, and depending on the nature of the product, either sales growth

EXHIBIT 9.4 **Variation in Growth over Product Life Cycle**

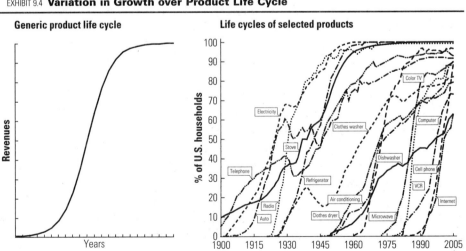

Source: W. Cox and R. Aim, "You Are What You Spend," *New York Times*, February 10, 2008.

[10] The cutoff point for the Fortune 500 in terms of revenues was around $5.5 billion in 2018.

falls back to the same rate of growth as the population or the economy, or sales may start to shrink. Therefore, as products mature and reach the top of the S curve, companies may need to innovate or acquire to continue growing.

While the general pattern of growth is usually the same for every product and service, the amount and pace of growth will vary. For example, autos and packaged snacks have continued to grow in line with economic growth for half a century or more, while videocassette recorders (VCRs) lasted less than 20 years before they started to decline and then disappeared.

As with product life cycles, the growth patterns of companies can also vary significantly, as shown in the comparison of Walmart and eBay in Exhibit 9.5. Walmart's growth did not dip below 10 percent until the end of the 1990s, some 35 years after it was founded. In contrast, eBay saw its growth fall to below 10 percent after only 12 years, having grown very rapidly to reach maturity early. Because eBay is an internet-based auction house, it doesn't need to add many more staff members in order to grow. In contrast, Walmart, as a pre-dominantly physical retailer, must grow its staff as quickly as it adds stores and increases sales. The speed at which Walmart can build stores, hire staff, and train them limits its rate of growth relative to eBay. But Walmart's core market is much larger than eBay's, because it can offer many products that eBay cannot (such as perishable and refrigerated products). In 2023, Walmart generated around $650 billion in revenue, mostly from its core discount and supercenter stores, whereas eBay generated only about $10 billion of revenues because its core addressable market is so much smaller.[11]

EXHIBIT 9.5 **Walmart and eBay: Growth Trajectories**

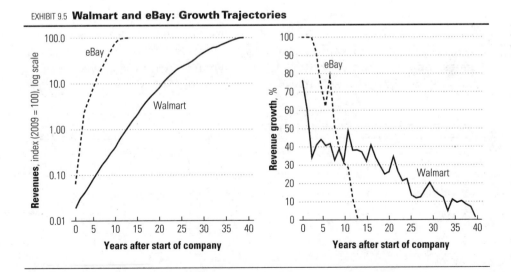

[11] The comparison is somewhat distorted: eBay spun off its subsidiary PayPal in 2012, reducing its revenues by $6 billion from $14 billion at that time.

Sustaining high growth presents major challenges to companies. Given the natural life cycle of products, the only way to achieve consistently high growth is to consistently find new product markets and enter them successfully in time to enjoy their more profitable high-growth phase. Exhibit 9.6 illustrates this by showing the cumulative sales for a company that introduces one new product in one market (geographic or customer segment) in each year. All products are identical in terms of sales volume and growth; their growth rates are very high in the beginning and eventually slow to 3 percent once the market is fully penetrated. Although the company continues to launch new products that are just as successful as their predecessors, aggregate sales growth slows down rapidly as the company gets bigger. In the long term, growth approaches 3 percent, equal to the long-term growth rate of the markets for the company's products. Ultimately, a company's growth and size are constrained by the growth and size of its product markets and the number of product markets in which it competes.

To sustain high growth, companies need to overcome this "portfolio treadmill" effect: for each product that matures and declines in revenues, the company needs to find a similar-size replacement product to stay level in revenues—and even more to continue growing. Think of the pharmaceutical industry, where companies are facing such replacement challenges around patent expiration of successful, so-called blockbuster drugs. Growth will plummet if such drugs come off patent and the next generation of drugs fails to deliver the same level of sales.

Finding sizable new sources of growth requires more experimentation and a longer time horizon than many companies are willing to invest in. Royal Philips's health technology business was a small corporate division in 1998, when it generated around 7 percent of total company revenues. It took 15 years of ongoing investments and acquisitions to become Philips's largest business unit, generating half of its total revenues. After the carve-out of its lighting business and other divestitures, health technology became Philips's

EXHIBIT 9.6 **The Challenge of Sustaining High Growth**

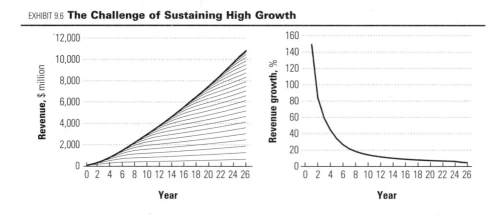

core business after 2016. One way to grow without spending more is to shift resources away from "hobbies" that will never amount to significant sales, or from mature products that don't warrant further investment, and channel those resources instead into the areas with the highest growth and market potential.

EMPIRICAL ANALYSIS OF CORPORATE GROWTH

The empirical research backs up the principles we have been discussing. This section presents our findings regarding the level and persistence of corporate growth for the largest U.S.- and Europe-based nonfinancial companies with revenues greater than $1 billion (inflation-adjusted) from 1963 to 2023.[12] We use real rather than nominal data to analyze all corporate growth results, because even mature companies saw a dramatic increase in revenues during the 1970s and the early 2020s as inflation increased prices. Ideally, we would report statistics on *organic* revenue growth, but current reporting standards do not require companies to disclose the effects of currencies and M&A on their revenues.

The overall findings concerning revenue growth are as follows:

- The median rate of revenue growth for U.S. companies between 1965 and 2023 was 4.5 percent in real (inflation-adjusted) terms. Real revenue growth fluctuated significantly from year to year, ranging from around 0 percent to 9 percent, with significant cyclicality. For European companies, the median growth rate was typically lower by around 0.5 percentage points. Between 1995 and 2023, the median for European companies was at 3.8 percent, with fluctuations in a similar range to U.S. companies.

- Between 2012 and 2023, growth rates were generally lower than in earlier decades, at 2.9 percent for U.S. companies and 2.5 percent for European companies.

- Growth rates show more variation across industries and time than ROIC: rankings and levels of industry growth change significantly over the decades. Nevertheless, some sectors (mostly life sciences and technology industries) were consistently at the highest end of

---

[12] The results come from McKinsey's Value Intelligence Platform, which relies on financial data provided by Standard & Poor's Compustat and Capital IQ. The European sample includes data over a more limited time frame (1995–2023) for companies from all 27 member states of the European Union plus the United Kingdom and Switzerland. The combined U.S. and European samples include all companies with more than $1 billion in revenues in 2020 real terms, except financial institutions, real estate companies, and industrial companies with significant financial businesses. For most years since 1995, the combined sample contains more than 2,000 companies. Results may vary from prior editions of this book, due to, for example, changes in industry definitions and accounting standards.

growth rankings over the two decades from 2003 to 2023, and others (including chemicals, retail, and branded consumer goods) ended up consistently at the lower end.

- High growth rates decay very quickly. For example, half of the U.S.-based companies growing faster than 15 percent in real terms between 2010 and 2012 grew at less than 5 percent within ten years. For Europe, this holds for 46 percent of companies, showing very similar decay patterns.

Growth Trends

Let's begin by examining aggregate levels and trends of corporate growth. Exhibit 9.7 presents median revenue growth rates in real terms for U.S. companies between 1965 and 2023. The average median revenue growth rate for that period equals 4.5 percent per year and oscillates between roughly 0 percent and 9 percent. Median revenue growth demonstrates no consistent trend over time, but over the decade from 2013 to 2023, growth rates declined to just below 3 percent in real terms. For European companies, growth rates are around 0.5 percentage points lower than for U.S. companies (see Exhibit 9.8). Between 1995 and 2023, the median growth rate was at 3.8 percent. During the decade from 2013 to 2023, growth rates declined to 2.5 percent—a drop of around 1.0 to 1.5 percentage points, similar to that for U.S. companies.

Real revenue growth of 4.5 percent for U.S. companies is quite high when compared with real GDP growth in the United States, which was around 2 percent during the same period. A similar difference applies to the growth of European company revenues versus that of GDP. Why the difference? Possible explanations

EXHIBIT 9.7 **Long-Term Revenue Growth for U.S.-Based Companies, 1965–2023**

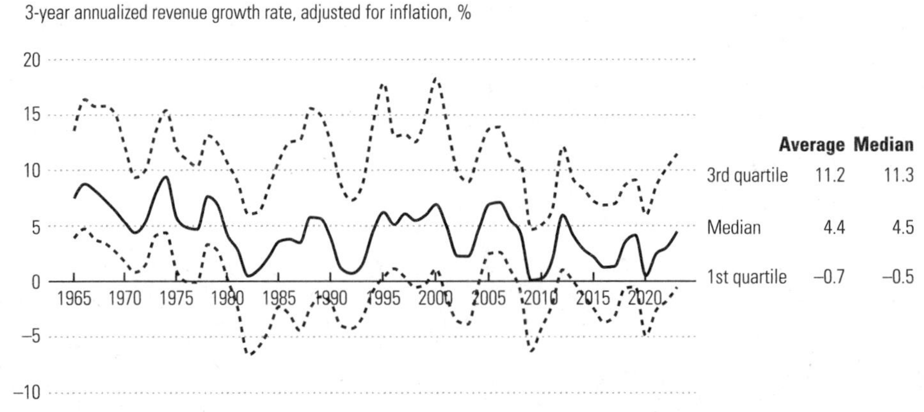

3-year annualized revenue growth rate, adjusted for inflation, %

	Average	Median
3rd quartile	11.2	11.3
Median	4.4	4.5
1st quartile	–0.7	–0.5

Source: McKinsey Value Intelligence database.

EXHIBIT 9.8 **Long-Term Revenue Growth for Europe-Based Companies, 1997–2023**

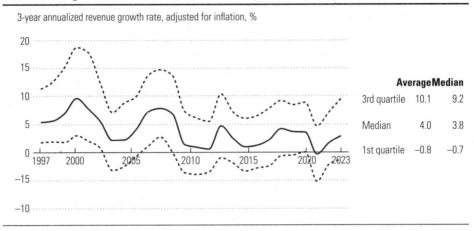

3-year annualized revenue growth rate, adjusted for inflation, %

	Average	Median
3rd quartile	10.1	9.2
Median	4.0	3.8
1st quartile	−0.8	−0.7

Source: McKinsey Value Intelligence database.

abound. The first is self-selection: companies with good growth opportunities need capital to grow. Since public markets are large and liquid, high-growth companies are more likely to be publicly traded than privately held ones. We measure only publicly traded companies, so these growth results are likely to be higher.

Second, as companies become increasingly specialized and outsource more services, firms providing services will grow and develop quickly without affecting the GDP figures. Consider Jabil Circuit, a contract electronics manufacturer. When a company such as Apple or IBM has Jabil manufacture products such as Airpods or components on its behalf, GDP, which measures aggregate output, will not change. Yet Jabil's growth will influence our sample.

A third explanation is global expansion. Many of the companies in the sample create products and generate revenue outside the United States and Europe, so they can grow faster than domestic GDP without gaining sales in their home countries. Finally, although we use rolling averages and medians, these cannot eliminate but only dampen the effects of M&A and currency fluctuations, which do not reflect organic growth.

In addition to mapping median growth, Exhibits 9.7 and 9.8 also reveal that in any given year over the past three to four decades, at least one-quarter of all large U.S. and European companies shrank in real terms. Although most companies project healthy growth over the years ahead in their public communications or even analyst guidance, the reality is that many mature firms will shrink. This underlines the need to exercise caution before projecting strong growth for a valuation, especially for large companies in mature sectors.

Exhibit 9.9 shows the distribution of long-term real revenue growth of U.S. companies over two periods, 2003–2013 and 2013–2023. The distribution shifted somewhat to the left between these two periods, as growth generally

EXHIBIT 9.9 **Distribution of Growth Rates, U.S.-Based Companies**

% of U.S.- based companies with given long-term annualized revenue growth rate, inflation-adjusted, by time period

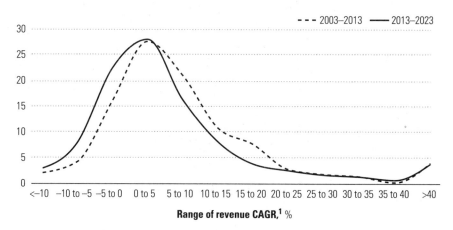

Range of revenue CAGR,[1] %

[1] Compound annual growth rate.

Source: McKinsey Value Intelligence database.

declined in the latter decade. (For European companies, we found a similar pattern.) From 2013 to 2023, around 60 percent of companies in the sample grew at an annualized real rate of less than 5 percent. Only 22 percent grew faster than 10 percent over 10 years. These growth rates include the effect of acquisitions, so fewer companies achieved organic growth rates of more than 10 percent.

Growth across Industries

As Exhibit 9.1 already illustrated, growth rates for U.S. companies vary widely across industries. This also holds for growth in European industries, shown next to U.S. counterparts in Exhibit 9.10. Note that although growth rates were generally lower in Europe, this does not hold for all industries. European growth appears to be lagging especially in industries related to technology and life sciences, which also delivered the highest growth rates overall. European companies outgrow their U.S. counterparts mostly in low-growth industries, such as fashion and luxury, retail, utilities, and consumer durables.

Whereas the ranking of industries according to ROIC tends to be stable, the ranking according to growth rates has varied significantly over time. Exhibit 9.11 shows how the ranking of U.S. companies changed between the decades 2003–2013 and 2013–2023. Some of this variation is explained by structural factors, such as the saturation of markets (the declining growth in branded consumer goods, retail, and chemicals) or the effect of technological

EXHIBIT 9.10 **Revenue Growth by Industry: U.S.-Based vs. Europe-Based Companies**

Long-term annualized revenue growth rate, adjusted for inflation, %

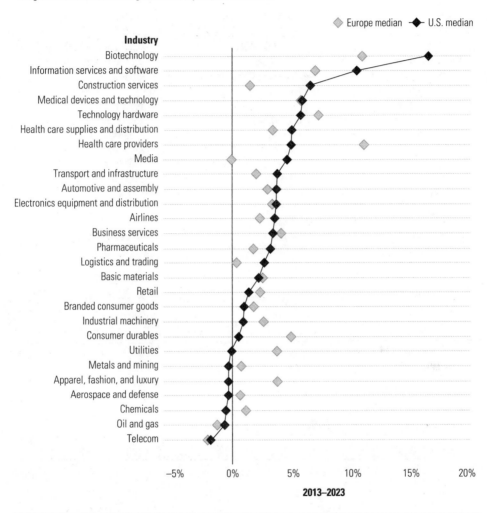

Source: McKinsey Value Intelligence database.

innovation in creating entirely new markets (the strong growth in biotechnology and information services). Of course, for some industries (for example, airlines, hotels, and leisure), growth in the latter decade was affected by the COVID-19 pandemic. In other cases, growth is just more cyclical. Growth in the oil and gas sector varied from more than 15 percent in the first decade to almost –1 percent in the latter, as oil prices plummeted after 2014. Metal and mining companies also faced strong cycles that shifted the industry from middle-of-the-pack to bottom-of-the-range growth levels.

EXHIBIT 9.11 **Volatile Growth by Industry, U.S.-Based Companies**

Long-term annualized revenue growth rate,[1] industry median adjusted for inflation, %

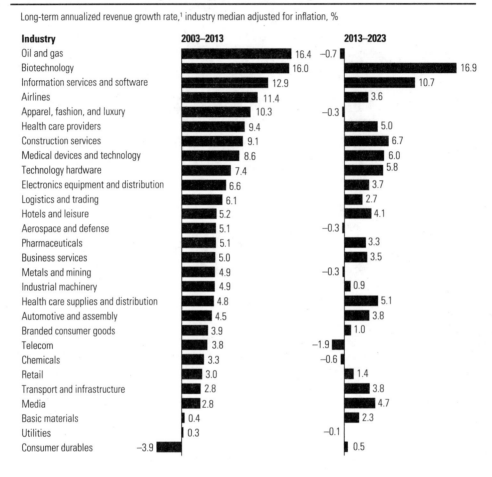

Industry	2003–2013	2013–2023
Oil and gas	16.4	−0.7
Biotechnology	16.0	16.9
Information services and software	12.9	10.7
Airlines	11.4	3.6
Apparel, fashion, and luxury	10.3	−0.3
Health care providers	9.4	5.0
Construction services	9.1	6.7
Medical devices and technology	8.6	6.0
Technology hardware	7.4	5.8
Electronics equipment and distribution	6.6	3.7
Logistics and trading	6.1	2.7
Hotels and leisure	5.2	4.1
Aerospace and defense	5.1	−0.3
Pharmaceuticals	5.1	3.3
Business services	5.0	3.5
Metals and mining	4.9	−0.3
Industrial machinery	4.9	0.9
Health care supplies and distribution	4.8	5.1
Automotive and assembly	4.5	3.8
Branded consumer goods	3.9	1.0
Telecom	3.8	−1.9
Chemicals	3.3	−0.6
Retail	3.0	1.4
Transport and infrastructure	2.8	3.8
Media	2.8	4.7
Basic materials	0.4	2.3
Utilities	0.3	−0.1
Consumer durables	−3.9	0.5

[1] Compound annual growth rate.

Source: McKinsey Value Intelligence database.

Telecommunications service providers achieved almost 4 percent growth in the first decade, when mobile phones were first becoming ubiquitous, but revenue growth rates over the latter decade ended up negative due to ongoing price pressure.

Despite this high degree of variation, some sectors have consistently been among the fastest growing, not only during the two decades covered in this sample but also for earlier periods. These include life sciences and technology, such as information services and software, technology hardware, biotechnology, and medical technology, where demand has remained strong for three decades. Others, such as chemicals, retail, and branded consumer goods, have consistently registered lower growth rates, as most of their markets had already reached maturity well before 2003.

Sustaining Growth

Understanding a company's potential for growing revenues in the future is critical to valuation and strategy assessment. Yet developing reasonable projections is a challenge, especially given the upward bias in growth expectations demonstrated by equity research analysts and the media. Research shows that analyst forecasts of one-year-out aggregate earnings growth for the S&P 500 are systematically overoptimistic, exceeding actual earnings growth by five percentage points or more.[13]

To put long-term corporate growth rates in their proper perspective, we analyzed historical rates of annual growth decay for U.S. and European companies since 2007. Companies were segmented into five portfolios, depending on their growth rate in the year the portfolio was formed. Exhibit 9.12 plots how each portfolio's median company grows over time. As the exhibit shows, the decay patterns are very similar for both regions: annual growth decayed very quickly; high growth is not sustainable for the typical company. Within three years, the difference across portfolios narrowed considerably, and within six years, the highest-growth portfolio outperformed the lowest-growth portfolio by less than five percentage points. Within ten years, this difference dropped to less than three percentage points.

EXHIBIT 9.12 **Revenue Growth Decay Through Crises and Recoveries: U.S.-Based vs. Europe-Based Companies**

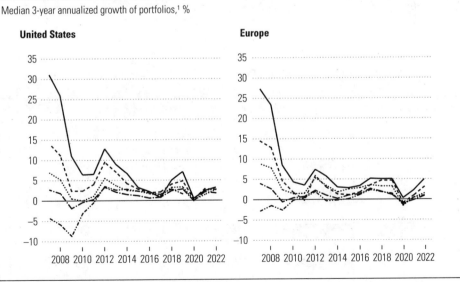

Median 3-year annualized growth of portfolios,[1] %

---

[1] As of 2007, companies are grouped into one of five portfolios, based on their 2005–2007 revenue growth.

Source: McKinsey Value Intelligence database.

[13] See, for example, M. Goedhart, B. Raj, and A. Saxena, "Equity Analysts: Still Too Bullish," *McKinsey on Finance*, no. 35 (Spring 2010): 14–17.

Also note how the 2008 credit crisis and the 2020 COVID-19 pandemic caused a temporary decline of growth rates overall but without changing the long-term decay pattern. These findings are very consistent for companies not only since 2007, but also going as far back as 1965. Comparing the decay of growth to that of ROIC, described in the previous chapter, shows that although companies' rates of return on invested capital generally remain fairly stable over time (top companies still outperform bottom companies by more than 20 percentage points after 15 years), rates of growth do not.

As discussed earlier in this chapter, companies struggle to maintain high growth because product life cycles are finite and growing becomes more difficult as companies get bigger. Do any companies counter this norm? The short answer: very few. Exhibit 9.13 shows what happened to the growth rates of U.S. and European companies grouped by their 2010–2012 growth rates. Reading across each row, the percentages indicate the share of companies in each group that fell into each of the growth categories one decade later. Clearly, maintaining high growth is much less common than being stuck with slow growth. Of the U.S. and European companies reporting less than 5 percent revenue growth from 2010 to 2012, 73 percent continued to report growth below 5 percent ten years later. In contrast, only 25 percent of U.S. high-growth companies (20 percent for European companies) maintained better than 15 percent real growth ten years later. Even more concerning for high-growth companies, 50 percent of the U.S. companies (and 46 percent of European companies) that grew faster than 15 percent from 2010 to 2012 were growing at real rates below 5 percent a decade later.

EXHIBIT 9.13 **Revenue Growth Transition Probability for U.S.-Based vs. Europe-Based Companies**

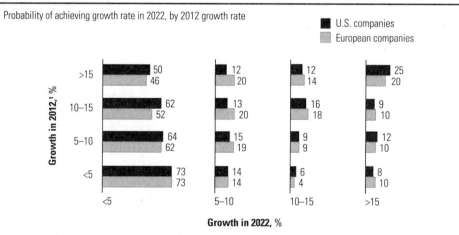

Probability of achieving growth rate in 2022, by 2012 growth rate

■ U.S. companies
▨ European companies

[1] 3-year annualized growth.

Source: McKinsey Value Intelligence database.

It is striking how similar the decay rates and the transition frequencies are across the United States and Europe and how little they have changed over the past four editions of this book. The law of growth convergence appears to hold universally. The conclusion is that sustaining high growth is very difficult—much more difficult than sustaining high ROIC.

SUMMARY

To maximize value for their shareholders, companies should understand what drives growth and how it creates value. For large companies, the growth of the markets in which they operate largely drives long-term revenue growth. Although gains in market share contribute to revenues in the short term, these gains are far less important for long-term growth.

Revenue growth is not all that matters for creating value; the value created per dollar of additional revenues is the crucial point. In general, this depends on how easily competitors can respond to a company's growth strategy. The growth strategy with the highest potential in this respect is true product innovation, because entirely new product categories, by definition, have no established competition. Attracting new customers to an existing product or persuading existing customers to buy more of it also can create substantial value, because direct competitors in the same market tend to benefit as well. Growth through bolt-on acquisitions can add value, because such acquisitions can boost revenue growth with little additional cost and complexity. Typically, revenue growth from market share gains is much less attractive, because it comes at the expense of established direct competitors, who are likely to retaliate, especially in maturing markets.

Sustaining high growth is no less a challenge than initiating it. Because most products have natural life cycles, the only way to achieve lasting high growth is to continue introducing new products at an increasing rate—which is nearly impossible. Not surprisingly, growth rates for large companies decay much faster than do returns on invested capital; growth rates for even the fastest-growing companies tend to fall below 5 percent within ten years.

Part Two

Core Valuation Techniques

10

Frameworks for Valuation

In Part One, we built a conceptual framework to show what drives the creation of value for investors. A company's value stems from its ability to earn a healthy return on invested capital (ROIC) and its ability to grow. Healthy rates of return and growth produce future cash flows, the ultimate source of value.

Part Two offers a step-by-step guide for analyzing and valuing a company in practice, including technical details for properly measuring and interpreting the drivers of value. Among the many ways to value a company (see Exhibit 10.1 for an overview), we focus particularly on two: enterprise discounted cash flow (DCF) and discounted economic profit. When applied correctly, both valuation methods yield the same results; however, each model has certain benefits in practice. Enterprise DCF remains a favorite of practitioners and academics because it relies on the flow of cash in and out of the company, rather than on accounting-based earnings. For its part, the discounted-economic-profit valuation model can be quite insightful because of its close link to economic theory and competitive strategy. Economic profit highlights whether a company is earning its cost of capital and quantifies the amount of value created each year. Given that the two methods yield identical results and have different but complementary benefits, we recommend creating *both* enterprise DCF and economic-profit models when valuing a company.

Both the enterprise DCF and economic-profit models discount free cash flow using the weighted average cost of capital (WACC) under the assumption that the company will maintain a stable capital structure. If a company's debt-to-value ratio is expected to change, WACC-based models can still yield accurate results but are difficult to implement correctly. In such cases, we recommend an alternative to WACC-based models: adjusted present value (APV). APV discounts the same free cash flows as the enterprise DCF model but uses the unlevered cost of equity as the discount rate. It then values the tax benefits associated with debt and adds them to the all-equity value to determine

EXHIBIT 10.1 **Frameworks for DCF-Based Valuation**

Model	Measure	Discount factor	Assessment
Enterprise discounted cash flow	Free cash flow	Weighted average cost of capital	Works best for projects, business units, and companies that manage their capital structure to a target level.
Discounted economic profit	Economic profit	Weighted average cost of capital	Explicitly highlights when a company creates value.
Adjusted present value	Free cash flow	Unlevered cost of equity	Incorporates changing capital structure more easily than WACC-based models.
Capital cash flow	Capital cash flow	Unlevered cost of equity	Combines free cash flow and the interest tax shield in one number, making it difficult to compare operating performance among companies and over time.
Equity cash flow	Cash flow to equity	Levered cost of equity	Difficult to implement correctly because capital structure is embedded within the cash flow. Best used when valuing financial institutions.

the total enterprise value.[1] When applied properly, the APV model results in the same value as the enterprise DCF value.

This chapter also includes a brief discussion of capital cash flow and equity cash flow valuation models. Properly implemented, these models will yield the same results as enterprise DCF. However, given that they mix operating performance and capital structure, we believe they are more prone to implementation errors. For this reason, we avoid capital cash flow and equity cash flow valuation models, except when valuing banks and other financial institutions, where capital structure is an inextricable part of operations (for how to value banks, see Chapter 43).

ENTERPRISE DISCOUNTED CASH FLOW MODEL

The enterprise DCF model discounts free cash flow (FCF), meaning the cash flow available to all investors—equity holders, debt holders, and any other investors—at the weighted average cost of capital, meaning the blended cost of capital for all investor capital. The company's debt and other nonequity claims on cash flow are subtracted from enterprise value to determine equity value.[2] Equity valuation models, in contrast, value directly

---

[1] Leveraged buyouts conducted by private-equity firms often use substantial leverage to finance the acquisition. In these situations, discount free cash flow at the unlevered cost of equity, and evaluate the benefits of financial structure such as interest tax shields and preferential borrowing separately. For more on how to model leveraged buyouts, see Chapter 37.

[2] Throughout this chapter, we refer to debt and other nonequity claims. Other nonequity claims arise when stakeholders other than shareholders have a claim against the company's future cash flow but do not hold traditional interest-bearing debt or common stock. Nonequity claims include debt equivalents (e.g., operating leases and unfunded pension liabilities) and hybrid securities (e.g., convertible debt and employee options).

EXHIBIT 10.2 **Enterprise Valuation of a Single-Business Company**

$ million

Free cash flow

110 140 100 120 180

Discount free cash flow by the weighted average cost of capital.

Enterprise value

427.5

20 70 15 65 110

After-tax cash flow to debt holders

90 70 85 55 70

Cash flow to equity holders

427.5

Debt value[1]
200.0

Equity value
227.5

[1] Debt value equals discounted after-tax cash flow to debt holders plus the present value of interest tax shield.

the equity holders' cash flows. Exhibit 10.2 demonstrates the relationship between enterprise value and equity value. For this example, it is possible to calculate equity holders' value either directly at $227.5 million or by estimating enterprise value ($427.5 million) and subtracting the value of debt ($200.0 million).

The enterprise DCF method is especially useful when applied to a multi-business company. As Exhibit 10.3 shows, the enterprise value equals the summed value of the individual operating units, plus the value of nonoperating

EXHIBIT 10.3 **Enterprise Valuation of a Multi-Business Company**

$ million

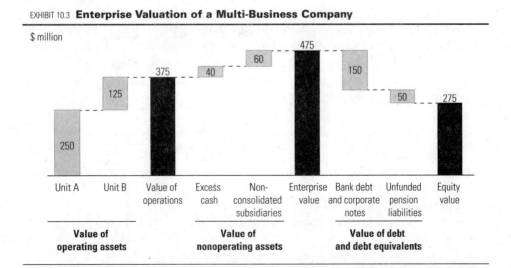

Unit A	Unit B	Value of operations	Excess cash	Non-consolidated subsidiaries	Enterprise value	Bank debt and corporate notes	Unfunded pension liabilities	Equity value
250	125	375	40	60	475	150	50	275

Value of operating assets   **Value of nonoperating assets**   **Value of debt and debt equivalents**

assets such as excess cash or nonconsolidated subsidiaries.[3] You can use the enterprise DCF model to value individual projects, business units, and even the entire company with a consistent methodology.

Valuing a company's equity using enterprise DCF is a four-step process:

1. Value the company's operations by discounting free cash flow at the weighted average cost of capital.

2. Identify and value nonoperating assets, such as excess cash and marketable securities, nonconsolidated subsidiaries, and other nonoperating assets not incorporated into free cash flow. Summing the value of operations and nonoperating assets gives enterprise value.[4]

3. Identify and value all debt and other nonequity claims against the enterprise value. Debt and other nonequity claims include fixed-rate and floating-rate debt, debt equivalents such as unfunded pension liabilities and restructuring provisions, employee options, and preferred stock, which are discussed in Chapter 16.

4. Subtract the value of debt and other nonequity claims from enterprise value to determine the value of common equity. To estimate value per share, divide equity value by the number of current shares outstanding.

Exhibit 10.4 presents the results of an enterprise DCF valuation for GlobalCo, an imaginary international logistics company. GlobalCo is used throughout the chapter to compare valuation methods. While realistic, GlobalCo is a simplified example that ignores some of the complexities of modern companies. In Appendix I, we present a complete valuation of the global retailer Costco Wholesale. We use Costco throughout Part Two to demonstrate in greater detail various parts of the valuation process.

To value GlobalCo, we forecast three years of cash flow. Cash flows generated beyond year 3 are valued using the key value driver formula and reported as continuing value. Next, discount each year's projected free cash flow and the continuing value by the company's weighted average cost of capital. Sum the present values of the annual cash flows and discounted continuing value to determine the present value of operations.[5]

---

[3] Many investment bankers define enterprise value as interest-bearing debt plus the market value of equity minus cash, whereas we define enterprise value as the value of operations plus nonoperating assets. The investment banker's definition of enterprise value resembles our definition of the value of operations, but only for companies that do not own nonoperating assets (e.g., nonconsolidated subsidiaries) or owe debt equivalents (e.g., unfunded pension liabilities). For companies with significant nonoperating assets or debt equivalents, the abbreviated version of enterprise value can lead to distortions in analysis.

[4] Many investment professionals do not include excess cash when estimating enterprise value and instead net excess cash directly against debt. Properly implemented, this should lead to the same value of equity.

[5] To generate identical results across valuation methods, we have not adjusted figures to eliminate rounding errors. Rounding errors occur in most exhibits.

EXHIBIT 10.4 **GlobalCo: Enterprise DCF Valuation**

$ million, except where noted

Forecast year	Free cash flow (FCF)	Discount factor at 7.8%	Present value of FCF
Year 1	(2.0)	0.928	(1.9)
Year 2	22.5	0.861	19.4
Year 3	54.6	0.798	43.6
Continuing value[1]	1,176.2	0.798	938.9
Value of operations			1,000.0
Value of nonoperating assets			–
Enterprise value			1,000.0
Less: Value of debt			(250.0)
Less: Debt equivalents and noncontrolling interests			–
Equity value			750.0
Shares outstanding, millions			12.5
Equity value per share, $			60.00

[1] In the GlobalCo example, all calculations are performed using unrounded data. For example, the present value of the continuing value is derived by multiplying $1,176.2 by $1/(1.078)^3$, which equals $938.9. In this and other exhibits, using the data as presented will lead to small rounding errors.

For simplicity, the first year's projected cash flow is discounted by one full year, the second by two full years, and so on. For the purpose of clear exposition, we assume cash flows occur in lump sums. In actuality, cash flows occur throughout the year, not as a lump sum. You can adjust the discount rate as necessary to better match the timing of cash flows.[6] The resulting present value is known as the value of operations, which equals $1 billion for GlobalCo.

To the value of operations, add nonoperating assets, such as excess cash and any noncontrolling interests in other companies. Since GlobalCo has no nonoperating assets, the value of operations equals enterprise value. To determine equity value, subtract the value of debt and other nonequity claims. GlobalCo has $110 million in short-term debt and $140 million in long-term debt, for a total debt of $250 million. The company has no unfunded pension obligations or noncontrolling interests held by other companies, but if it did, their value would be subtracted as well.[7] Divide the resulting equity value of $750 million by the number of shares outstanding (12.5 million) to estimate a per-share value of $60.

The result from a discounted cash flow model is often referred to as the intrinsic value. An intrinsic value represents the stock's worth based on future

[6] If cash flow occurs smoothly throughout the year, lower each discount factor by half a year. If cash flow is heavily weighted toward the year end, as in retail, a smaller adjustment to the discount factor is required.

[7] A noncontrolling interest arises when an outside investor owns a minority share of a subsidiary. Since this outside investor has a claim on cash flows, the claim's value must be deducted from enterprise value to compute equity value.

performance, discounted at the cost of capital. Thus, an estimate of intrinsic value will reflect one's assessment of these inputs and, as such, can vary among analysts. If the company is publicly traded, compare your estimate of intrinsic value with the market price. If they differ, identify potential reasons for the disparities.

Over the course of the next few sections, we dig deeper into the required inputs and the valuation process. Although this chapter presents the steps in an enterprise DCF valuation sequentially, valuation is an iterative process.

Valuing Operations

The value of operations equals the discounted value of future free cash flow. Free cash flow equals the cash flow generated by the company's operations, less any reinvestment back into the business. As defined at the beginning of this section, free cash flow is the cash flow available to all investors—equity holders, debt holders, and any other investors—so it is independent of how the company is financed. Consistent with this definition, free cash flow must be discounted using the weighted average cost of capital, because the WACC represents rates of return required by the company's debt and equity holders blended together. It is the company's opportunity cost of funds.

Reorganizing the Financial Statements   To begin the valuation process, collect the company's historical financial statements. In Exhibit 10.5, we present

EXHIBIT 10.5 **GlobalCo: Income Statement and Shareholders' Equity Statement**

$ million

| | | Forecast | | | |
| | | | | | Continuing |
	Historical	Year 1	Year 2	Year 3	value
Revenue	200.0	250.0	287.5	301.9	308.5
Operating costs	(120.0)	(150.0)	(172.5)	(181.1)	(185.1)
Depreciation	(20.0)	(25.0)	(28.8)	(30.2)	(30.9)
Operating profit	60.0	75.0	86.3	90.6	92.6
Interest expense	(9.0)	(10.0)	(10.8)	(11.4)	(11.8)
Earnings before taxes	51.0	65.0	75.5	79.1	80.8
Income taxes	(10.2)	(13.0)	(15.1)	(15.8)	(16.2)
Net income	40.8	52.0	60.4	63.3	64.6
Statement of shareholders' equity					
Equity, beginning of year	65.0	98.0	140.0	171.1	
Net income	40.8	52.0	60.4	63.3	
Dividends	(7.8)	(10.0)	(14.3)	(24.1)	
Share issuances (repurchases)	–	–	(15.0)	(30.0)	
Equity, end of year	98.0	140.0	171.1	180.3	

EXHIBIT 10.6 **GlobalCo: Balance Sheet**

$ million

| | Today | Forecast | | |
		Year 1	Year 2	Year 3
Cash	4.0	5.0	5.8	6.0
Accounts receivable	20.0	25.0	28.8	30.2
Inventories	40.0	50.0	57.5	60.4
Current assets	64.0	80.0	92.0	96.6
Property and equipment	200.0	250.0	287.5	301.9
Goodwill and acquired intangibles	100.0	100.0	100.0	100.0
Total assets	364.0	430.0	479.5	498.5
Liabilities and equity				
Short-term debt	110.0	110.0	125.4	134.0
Accounts payable	16.0	20.0	23.0	24.2
Current liabilities	126.0	130.0	148.4	158.2
Long-term debt	140.0	160.0	160.0	160.0
Shareholders' equity	98.0	140.0	171.1	180.3
Total liabilities and equity	364.0	430.0	479.5	498.5

the income statement and statement of shareholders' equity for GlobalCo. Exhibit 10.6 presents the company's balance sheet. For ease of exposition, we present only one historical year of financial statements. In practice, it is best to collect multiple years in order to properly assess the company's long-run performance and future potential.

Although ROIC and free cash flow (FCF) are central to the valuation process, the two measures cannot be computed easily from a company's financial statements, which commingle operating performance and capital structure. Therefore, to calculate ROIC and FCF, first reorganize the accounting financial statements into new statements that clearly separate operating items, nonoperating items, and sources of financing.

This reorganization leads to two new terms: invested capital and net operating profit after taxes (NOPAT). Invested capital represents the investor capital required to fund operations, without distinguishing how the capital is financed. NOPAT represents the total after-tax operating income generated by the company's invested capital, available to all investors. We briefly summarize the reorganization process next, but for a more detailed discussion using Costco, see Chapter 11.

In Exhibit 10.7, we reorganize the income statement to calculate NOPAT. To estimate NOPAT, deduct only operating costs and depreciation from revenue. Neither add nonoperating income nor deduct interest expense; they will be analyzed and valued separately as part of nonoperating assets and debt, respectively. Operating taxes are computed on operating profit and represent the level of taxes that would be paid if the firm were financed entirely by equity and held only operating assets. A robust valuation will

EXHIBIT 10.7 **GlobalCo: Net Operating Profit after Taxes (NOPAT)**

$ million

	Historical	Year 1	Year 2	Year 3	Continuing value
Revenue	200.0	250.0	287.5	301.9	308.5
Operating costs	(120.0)	(150.0)	(172.5)	(181.1)	(185.1)
Depreciation	(20.0)	(25.0)	(28.8)	(30.2)	(30.9)
Operating profit	60.0	75.0	86.3	90.6	92.6
Operating taxes	(12.0)	(15.0)	(17.3)	(18.1)	(18.5)
NOPAT	48.0	60.0	69.0	72.5	74.0
Reconciliation to net income					
Net income	40.8	52.0	60.4	63.3	64.6
Interest expense	9.0	10.0	10.8	11.4	11.8
Interest tax shield	(1.8)	(2.0)	(2.2)	(2.3)	(2.4)
NOPAT	48.0	60.0	69.0	72.5	74.0

reconcile net income to NOPAT. The reconciliation will prevent errors and force explicit choices about how each financial account will be incorporated in the valuation.

In Exhibit 10.8, we reorganize the balance sheet into invested capital and total funds invested. Invested capital includes working capital, property, plant, equipment, and other operating assets, net of other operating liabilities.

EXHIBIT 10.8 **GlobalCo: Invested Capital and Total Funds Invested**

$ million

		Forecast		
	Today	Year 1	Year 2	Year 3
Working capital[1]	48.0	60.0	69.0	72.5
Property, plant, and equipment, net	200.0	250.0	287.5	301.9
Invested capital, excluding goodwill	248.0	310.0	356.5	374.3
Goodwill and acquired intangibles	100.0	100.0	100.0	100.0
Invested capital, including goodwill	348.0	410.0	456.5	474.3
Nonoperating assets	—	—	—	—
Total funds invested	348.0	410.0	456.5	474.3
Reconciliation of total funds invested[2]				
Short-term debt	110.0	110.0	125.4	134.0
Long-term debt	140.0	160.0	160.0	160.0
Debt and debt equivalents	250.0	270.0	285.4	294.0
Equity and equity equivalents	98.0	140.0	171.1	180.3
Total funds invested	348.0	410.0	456.5	474.3

[1] In the case of GlobalCo, working capital equals the sum of operating cash, accounts receivable, and inventories, less accounts payable.

[2] For the purpose of simplicity, GlobalCo does not carry debt or equity equivalents. Debt equivalents include accounts like unfunded pension liabilities, and equity equivalents include items such as deferred taxes.

Measure invested capital both with and without goodwill and acquired intangibles. By analyzing invested capital with and without goodwill, we can assess the impact of acquisitions on past performance. A company with high margins and lean operations can still have a low ROIC with goodwill because of the high prices it paid for past acquisitions.

GlobalCo holds only operating assets, so invested capital equals total funds invested. Since nonoperating assets are typically valued using methods other than DCF, we explicitly distinguish them from operating assets and operating liabilities. Next, reconcile total funds invested with sources of capital: debt, equity, and their equivalents. Examples of debt equivalents include unfunded pension obligations and environmental-remediation liabilities. An example of an equity equivalent is deferred taxes.

To calculate ROIC in year 1, divide NOPAT by the prior year-end invested capital.[8] In year 1, ROIC excluding goodwill equals 24.2 percent ($60/$248), and ROIC including goodwill equals 17.2 percent ($60/$348). Because ROIC is greater than the cost of capital of 7.8 percent, the company is creating value both with and without the effect of acquisition premiums.

Analyzing Historical Performance   Once the company's financial statements are reorganized into NOPAT and invested capital, analyze the company's historical financial performance. By thoroughly analyzing the past, we can understand whether the company has created value, how fast it has grown, and how it compares with its competitors. A good analysis will focus on the key drivers of value: return on invested capital, revenue growth, and free cash flow. Understanding how these drivers behaved in the past will help you make better estimates of future cash flow.

Exhibit 10.9 presents a historical analysis of organic revenue growth and ROIC. GlobalCo has been performing well, with organic growth rates and ROICs without goodwill both above 20 percent. If possible, assess many years—even decades—of past performance. While the company's performance from many years ago may be outdated, understanding how it performs in different phases of the economic cycle will better inform your forecasts. For an in-depth discussion of financial analysis and competitive benchmarking using reorganized financial statements, see Chapter 12.

Projecting Revenue Growth, ROIC, and Free Cash Flow   Based on insights from your historical analysis, as well as forecasts of economic and industry trends, the next step is to create a set of integrated financial statements going forward. In Exhibits 10.5 and 10.6, we present line-by-line forecasts of the income statement, statement of shareholders' equity, and balance

---

[8] In this calculation, we estimate ROIC using prior-year invested capital (that is, measured at the beginning of the year) in order to link our enterprise DCF valuation with an economic-profit valuation presented later in this chapter. When benchmarking performance, use a two-year average of invested capital.

EXHIBIT 10.9 **GlobalCo: Forecast Revenue Growth and ROIC**

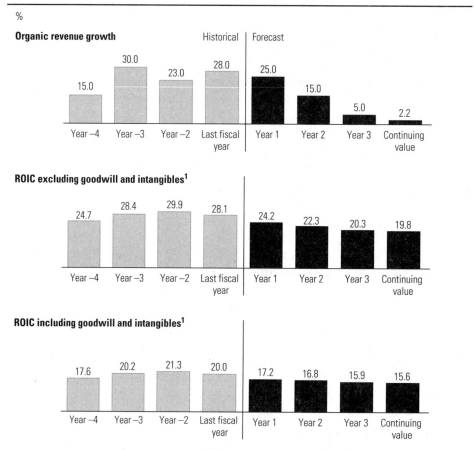

[1] Measured using beginning-of-year capital to match economic-profit models presented later in the chapter.

sheet. The three statements should be integrated in that net income should flow through the statement of equity, which should match the corresponding account in the balance sheet. Use excess cash, debt, dividends, or a combination thereof to ensure that the balance sheet balances. Chapter 13 provides details on the forecasting process.

When building the forecast model, use your judgment to calibrate how much detail to include at various points in the future. Over the short run (the first few years), forecast each financial-statement line item, such as gross margin, selling expenses, accounts receivable, and inventory. This will allow you to incorporate visible trends in individual line items. Moving further out, individual line items become difficult to project, and a high level of detail can obscure the critical value drivers. Therefore, over the medium horizon (5 to 15 years), focus on the company's key value drivers, such as operating margin, the operating tax rate, and capital efficiency.

At some point, projecting even key drivers on a year-by-year basis becomes impractical. To value cash flows beyond this point, use a continuing-value formula, often called the terminal value. Choosing an appropriate point of transition depends on the company and how it is changing over time. A company undergoing significant change may require a long, detailed window, whereas a stable, mature company may require only a short explicit forecast period.

Next, use the reorganized financial statements to calculate free cash flow. Exhibit 10.10 presents the free cash flow for GlobalCo. Defined in a manner consistent with ROIC, free cash flow is derived directly from NOPAT and the change in invested capital. Unlike the accounting statement of cash flows (provided in the company's annual report), free cash flow is independent of nonoperating items and capital structure.

Estimating Continuing Value   At the point when predicting the individual key value drivers on a year-by-year basis becomes impractical, do not vary the individual drivers over time. Instead, use a perpetuity-based continuing value, such that

Value of Operations = Present Value of Free Cash Flow during Explicit
                   Forecast Period + Present Value of Free Cash Flow
                   after Explicit Forecast Period

EXHIBIT 10.10 **GlobalCo: Projected Free Cash Flow**

$ million

	Year 1	Year 2	Year 3
NOPAT	60.0	69.0	72.5
Depreciation	25.0	28.8	30.2
Gross cash flow	85.0	97.8	102.6
Decrease (Increase) in operating working capital	(12.0)	(9.0)	(3.4)
Capital expenditures, net of disposals	(75.0)	(66.3)	(44.6)
Free cash flow	(2.0)	22.5	54.6
Reconciliation of free cash flow			
Interest expense	10.0	10.8	11.4
Interest tax shield	(2.0)	(2.2)	(2.3)
Decrease (Increase) in short-term debt	0.0	(15.4)	(8.6)
Decrease (Increase) in long-term debt	(20.0)	–	–
Flows to (from) debt holders	(12.0)	(6.8)	0.5
Cash dividends	10.0	14.3	24.1
Repurchased (Issued) shares	–	15.0	30.0
Flows to (from) equity holders	10.0	29.3	54.1
Free cash flow	(2.0)	22.5	54.6

Although many continuing-value models exist, we prefer the key value driver formula presented in Chapter 3. The key value driver formula is superior to alternative methodologies because it is based on cash flow and it links cash flow directly to growth and ROIC. The key value driver formula is expressed as follows:

$$\text{Continuing Value}_t = \frac{\text{NOPAT}_{t+1}\left(1 - \frac{g}{\text{RONIC}}\right)}{\text{WACC} - g}$$

The formula requires a forecast of NOPAT in the year following the explicit forecast period, the long-run forecast for return on new invested capital (RONIC) deployed during the continuing value period, the WACC, and long-run growth (g) in NOPAT.

Exhibit 10.11 presents an estimate for GlobalCo's continuing value. Based on a final-year estimate of NOPAT from Exhibit 10.7 of $74.0 million, RONIC excluding goodwill from Exhibit 10.9 of 19.8 percent, and a long-term growth rate from Exhibit 10.9 of 2.2 percent, the continuing value is estimated at $1,176.2 million. The valuation model presented in Exhibit 10.4 discounts this value into today's dollars and adds it to the value from the explicit forecast period to determine GlobalCo's operating value.

Alternative methods and additional details for estimating continuing value are provided in Chapter 14.

Discounting Free Cash Flow at the Weighted Average Cost of Capital   In an enterprise valuation, free cash flows are the cash flows available to all investors. Consequently, the discount factor for free cash flow must represent the risk faced by all investors. The WACC blends the rates of return required by debt holders (k_d) and equity holders (k_e). For a company financed solely with debt and equity, the WACC is defined as follows:

$$\text{WACC} = \frac{D}{D + E}k_d(1 - T_m) + \frac{E}{D + E}k_e$$

EXHIBIT 10.11 **GlobalCo: Continuing Value**

$ million

Key inputs[1]		Calculation[2]
Projected NOPAT in final forecast year	74.0	
NOPAT growth rate in perpetuity (g)	2.2%	$\text{Continuing Value}_t = \dfrac{\text{NOPAT}_{t+1}\left(1 - \frac{g}{\text{RONIC}}\right)}{\text{WACC} - g}$
Return on new invested capital (RONIC)[1]	19.8%	
Weighted average cost of capital (WACC)	7.8%	
		= 1,176.2

[1] RONIC is calculated by dividing the NOPAT estimated in the continuing-value year by the invested capital in year 3, excluding goodwill. For GlobalCo, the calculation is 74.0 divided by 374.3.

[2] $1,176.2 is calculated using unrounded data. The continuing value with rounded inputs would be $1,174.6 million.

where debt (D) and equity (E) are measured using market values. Note how the cost of debt has been reduced by the marginal tax rate (T_m). The reason for doing this is that the tax shield attributable to interest has been excluded from free cash flow. Since the interest tax shield (ITS) has value to the shareholder, it must be incorporated in the valuation. Enterprise DCF incorporates the value of the tax shield by reducing the cost of debt and, ultimately, the weighted average cost of capital.

Why move interest tax shields from free cash flow to the cost of capital? By calculating free cash flow as if the company were financed entirely with equity, one can compare operating performance across companies and over time without regard to capital structure. By focusing solely on operations, it is possible to develop a clearer picture of historical performance, and this leads to better performance measurement and forecasting.

Although applying the WACC is intuitive and relatively straightforward, it has some drawbacks. If you discount all future cash flows with a constant cost of capital, as most analysts do, you are implicitly assuming the company keeps its capital structure constant at a target ratio of debt to equity. But if a company plans, say, to increase (or decrease) its debt-to-value ratio, the current cost of capital will understate (or overstate) the expected tax shields. The WACC can be adjusted to accommodate a changing capital structure. However, the process is complicated, and in these situations, we recommend an alternative method such as adjusted present value (APV).

The weighted average cost of capital for GlobalCo is presented in Exhibit 10.12. GlobalCo's 7.8 percent WACC is based on a cost of equity of 9.3 percent, pretax cost of debt of 4.0 percent, and a debt-to-value ratio of 25 percent.

Identifying and Valuing Nonoperating Assets

Many companies own assets that have value but whose cash flows are not included in revenue, operating costs, or operating profit. As a result, the cash generated by these assets is not part of free cash flow and must be valued separately.

For example, consider equity investments, also known as nonconsolidated subsidiaries. When a company owns a minority stake in another company, it will not record the company's revenue or costs as part of its own. Instead, the company will record only its proportion of the other company's net income as a

EXHIBIT 10.12 **GlobalCo: Weighted Average Cost of Capital**

%

Source of capital	Proportion of total capital	Cost of capital	Marginal tax rate	After-tax cost of capital	Contribution to weighted average
Debt	25.0	4.0	20.0	3.2	0.8
Equity	75.0	9.3		9.3	7.0
WACC	100.0				7.8

separate line item.[9] Including net income from nonconsolidated subsidiaries as part of the parent's operating profit will distort margins, since only the subsidiaries' profit is recognized and not the corresponding revenues. Consequently, nonconsolidated subsidiaries are best analyzed and valued separately.

Other nonoperating assets include excess cash, unused real estate, tradable securities, and customer finance business units, among others. A detailed process for identifying and valuing nonoperating assets appears in Chapter 16.

Identifying and Valuing Debt and Other Nonequity Claims

To convert enterprise value into equity value, subtract debt and other nonequity claims, such as unfunded retirement liabilities, capitalized operating leases, and outstanding employee stock options. Common equity is a residual claimant, receiving cash flows only *after* the company has fulfilled its other contractual claims. Therefore, careful analysis of all potential claims against cash flows is critical.

Debt and other nonequity claims are not always easy to spot. Often, these claims are aggregated under broader categories such as other liabilities. In some instances, they are disclosed only in the company's notes to the financial statements. According to current accounting standards, a claim is only recognized on the balance sheet if it is deemed probable and can be reliably estimated. For example, a lawsuit with a low probability of loss may be mentioned only in the notes. However, economic theory suggests that such claims should be factored into the overall valuation using a probability-weighted average. Therefore, it is crucial to thoroughly examine both the balance sheet and the notes to uncover and properly value all potential claims against a company's cash flows.

Although a comprehensive list of nonequity claims is impractical, here are the most common:

- *Debt.* If available, use the *market* value of all outstanding debt, including fixed- and floating-rate debt. If that information is unavailable, the book value of debt is a reasonable proxy, unless the probability of default is high or interest rates have changed dramatically since the debt was originally issued. Any valuation of debt, however, should be consistent with your estimates of enterprise value.

- *Leases.* Rather than purchase assets outright, many companies lease certain assets for a fixed period. Any portion of lease payments recorded or reclassified as interest expense and not rental expense must be valued separately and deducted from enterprise value. This includes finance leases, operating leases, and variable leases.

[9] For stakes between 20 and 50 percent, the parent company will recognize its proportion of the subsidiary's income. A parent that owns less than a 20 percent stake in another company records only dividends paid as part of its own income. This makes valuation of stakes of less than 20 percent in privately held companies extremely challenging.

- *Unfunded retirement liabilities.* Companies with defined-benefit pension plans and promised retiree medical benefits may have unfunded obligations that should be treated like debt.

- *Preferred stock.* For large, stable companies, preferred stock more closely resembles unsecured debt. For small start-ups, preferred stock contains valuable options. In both situations, value preferred stocks separately from common stock.

- *Employee stock options.* Many companies offer their employees compensation in the form of stock options, stock grants, and stock appreciation rights (SAR). Any future compensation not accounted for in free cash flow, as well as the value of past grants, must be factored into equity value.

- *Noncontrolling interests.* When a company has majority control of a subsidiary but does not own 100 percent, the entire subsidiary must be consolidated on the parent company's balance sheet. The funding other investors provide for this subsidiary is recognized on the parent company's balance sheet as noncontrolling interests (formerly called minority interest). When valuing noncontrolling interests, it is important to realize that the minority interest holder does not have a claim on the company's assets but rather a claim on the subsidiary's assets.

The identification and valuation of nonequity claims are covered in detail in Chapter 16. A detailed discussion of how to analyze leases is presented in Chapter 22. Additional detail on retirement obligations can be found in Chapter 23.

A common mistake made when valuing companies is to double-count nonequity claims already deducted from free cash flow. Consider a company with a pension shortfall. Imagine you have been told the company will make extra payments to eliminate the liability. If you deduct the present value of the liability from enterprise value, do not model the extra payments within free cash flow; that would mean double-counting the shortfall (once in cash flow and once as a debt-like claim), leading to an underestimate of equity value.

Valuing Equity

Once you have identified and valued all nonequity claims, subtract the value of these claims from enterprise value to determine equity value. In Exhibit 10.4, we subtract $250 million in debt, both short-term and long-term debt, from $1 billion in enterprise value. Since GlobalCo has no debt equivalents, this leads to an intrinsic equity value of $750 million.

To determine GlobalCo's share price, divide the intrinsic equity value by the number of *undiluted* shares outstanding. Do not use diluted shares. Convertible debt, convertible preferred stock, and employee stock options should be valued separately. If you were to subtract the value of these claims and use diluted shares, you would double-count the options' value. At the time of GlobalCo's valuation, the company had 12.5 million shares outstanding. Dividing the equity estimate of $750 million by 12.5 million shares generates an estimated value of $60 per share.

Although it may appear at this point that the valuation is complete, the job is not yet done. Compare the intrinsic value with market prices. If the two values differ (and they probably will), search for the cause, such as overly optimistic forecasts or missing liabilities. Next, use the model to explore how changes in key inputs impact the overall valuation, testing the sensitivity of your assumptions to better understand their influence on the results. Determine which inputs lead to the biggest changes, and which lead to negligible differences. Use this analysis to identify opportunities, prioritize operating activities, and identify risks. Chapter 17 offers guidelines for how to assess a completed valuation model.

ECONOMIC-PROFIT-BASED VALUATION MODELS

The enterprise DCF model is a favorite of academics and practitioners because it relies solely on how cash flows in and out of the company. Complex accounting can be replaced with a simple question: Does cash change hands? One shortfall of enterprise DCF, however, is that each year's cash flow provides little insight into the company's competitive position and economic performance. Declining free cash flow can signal either poor performance or investment for the future. The economic-profit model highlights how and when the company creates value. Properly implemented, it leads to a valuation identical to that of enterprise DCF.

Economic profit measures the value created by the company in a single period and is defined as follows:

$$\text{Economic Profit} = \text{Invested Capital} \times (\text{ROIC} - \text{WACC})$$

Since ROIC equals NOPAT divided by invested capital, we can rewrite the equation as follows:

$$\text{Economic Profit} = \text{NOPAT} - (\text{Invested Capital} \times \text{WACC})$$

Exhibit 10.13 presents economic-profit calculations for GlobalCo, using both methods. Not surprisingly, with an ROIC more than double its cost of capital, GlobalCo generates significant economic profits.

To demonstrate how economic profit can be used to value a company—and to demonstrate its equivalence to enterprise DCF—consider a stream of growing cash flows valued using the growing-perpetuity formula:

$$\text{Value}_0 = \frac{\text{FCF}_1}{\text{WACC} - g}$$

EXHIBIT 10.13 **GlobalCo: Economic-Profit Summary**

$ million, except where noted

	Year 1	Year 2	Year 3	Continuing value
Method 1				
Return on invested capital,[1] %	24.2	22.3	20.3	19.8
Weighted average cost of capital, %	(7.8)	(7.8)	(7.8)	(7.8)
Economic spread, %	16.4	14.5	12.5	12.0
× Invested capital, excluding goodwill[1]	248.0	310.0	356.5	374.3
= Economic profit	40.7	44.8	44.6	44.9
Method 2				
NOPAT	60.0	69.0	72.5	74.0
Capital charge	(19.3)	(24.2)	(27.8)	(29.2)
Economic profit	40.7	44.8	44.6	44.9
Capital charge				
Invested capital, excluding goodwill[1]	248.0	310.0	356.5	374.3
× Weighted average cost of capital, %	7.8%	7.8%	7.8%	7.8%
= Capital charge	19.3	24.2	27.8	29.2
Including goodwill				
Economic profit including goodwill	32.9	37.0	36.8	37.1

[1] Invested capital is measured at the beginning of the year, excluding goodwill and acquired intangibles. In year 1, ROIC equals NOPAT of $60 million divided by $248 million in invested capital excluding goodwill.

In Chapter 3, we transformed this cash flow perpetuity into the key value driver model. The key value driver model is superior to the simple cash flow perpetuity model, because it explicitly models the relationship between growth and required investment. Using a few additional algebraic steps (detailed in Appendix A) and the assumption that the company's ROIC on new projects equals the ROIC on existing capital, it is possible to transform the cash flow perpetuity into a key value driver model based on economic profits:

$$\text{Value}_0 = \text{Invested Capital}_0 + \frac{\text{Invested Capital}_0 \times (\text{ROIC}_1 - \text{WACC})}{\text{WACC} - g}$$

Finally, we substitute the definition of economic profit:

$$\text{Value}_0 = \text{Invested Capital}_0 + \frac{\text{Economic Profit}_1}{\text{WACC} - g}$$

As can be seen in the economic-profit-based key value driver model, the operating value of a company equals its book value of invested capital plus the present value of all future value created. In this case, the future economic profits are valued using a growing perpetuity, because the company's economic profits are increasing at a constant rate over time. The formula also demonstrates that when economic profit is expected to be zero, the value of operations will equal invested capital. If a company's value of operations exceeds its invested capital, be sure to identify the sources of competitive advantage that allows the company to maintain superior financial performance.

More generally, a company can be valued as follows:

$$\text{Value}_0 = \text{Invested Capital}_0 + \sum_{t=1}^{\infty} \frac{\text{Economic Profit}_t}{(1 + \text{WACC})^t}$$

Since the economic-profit valuation was derived directly from the free cash flow model, any valuation based on discounted economic profits will be identical to enterprise DCF. To assure equivalence, however, it is necessary to do the following:

- Use beginning-of-year invested capital (i.e., last year's ending value) instead of average or current-year invested capital, which is commonly used in competitive benchmarking.

- Define invested capital the same way for both economic profit and ROIC. For example, ROIC can be measured either with or without goodwill. If you measure ROIC without goodwill, you must also measure invested capital without goodwill. All told, it doesn't matter how you define invested capital, as long as you are consistent.

- Use a constant cost of capital to discount projections.

Exhibit 10.14 presents the valuation results for GlobalCo, using discounted economic profit. Economic profits are explicitly forecast for three years; the remaining years are valued using the economic-profit continuing-value formula.[10] Comparing the equity value from Exhibit 10.4 with that

---

[10] To calculate continuing value, you can use the economic-profit-based key value driver formula, but only if RONIC equals ROIC in the continuing-value year. If RONIC going forward differs from the final year's ROIC, then the equation must be separated into current and future economic profits:

$$\text{Value}_t = \text{IC}_t + \text{Current Economic Profit} + \text{New Economic Profit}$$

$$= \text{IC}_t + \frac{\text{IC}_t(\text{ROIC}_{t+1} - \text{WACC})}{\text{WACC}} + \frac{\text{PV}(\text{Economic Profit}_{t+2})}{\text{WACC} - g}$$

such that

$$\text{PV}(\text{Economic Profit}_{t+2}) = \frac{\text{NOPAT}_{t+1}\left(\frac{g}{\text{RONIC}}\right)(\text{RONIC} - \text{WACC})}{\text{WACC}}$$

To estimate the continuing value of GlobalCo, we sum the present values of current and new economic profits. The present value of current economic profits is derived by dividing $44.9 by 0.078, resulting in $575.0. For the present value of new economic profits, we incorporate the inputs from Exhibit 10.11, including NOPAT$_{t+1}$ of $74.0, NOPAT growth of 2.2 percent, RONIC without goodwill of 19.8 percent, and WACC of 0.078. The ensuing calculation amounts to $226.8. The sum of discounted current and future economic profits equals $801.8. For more on these and other continuing value formulas, see Chapter 14.

EXHIBIT 10.14 **GlobalCo: Valuation Using Discounted Economic Profit**

$ million, except where noted

Year	Invested capital[1]	ROIC,[1] %	WACC, %	Economic profit	Discount factor at 7.8%	Present value of economic profit
Year 1	248.0	24.2	(7.8)	40.7	0.928	37.7
Year 2	310.0	22.3	(7.8)	44.8	0.861	38.6
Year 3	356.5	20.3	(7.8)	44.6	0.798	35.6
Continuing value				801.8	0.798	640.1
Present value of economic profit						752.0
Invested capital[1]						248.0
Value of operations						1,000.0
Nonoperating assets						–
Enterprise value						1,000.0
Less: Value of debt						(250.0)
Less: Value of noncontrolling interest						–
Equity value						750.0

[1] Invested capital measured at the beginning of the year without goodwill and acquired intangibles.

of Exhibit 10.14, we see that the estimate of GlobalCo's DCF value is the same, regardless of the method.

The benefits of economic profit become apparent when we examine the drivers of economic profit, ROIC and WACC, on a year-by-year basis in Exhibit 10.14. Note that for GlobalCo, the valuation assumes that returns on capital exceed the cost of capital but drop over time as new competitors enter and put pressure on operating margins. Explicitly modeling ROIC as a primary driver of economic profit prominently displays expectations of value creation. Conversely, the FCF model fails to highlight when a company creates and destroys value. Free cash flow combines ROIC and growth, two critical but very different value drivers.

Also note how GlobalCo's high ROIC—double its cost of capital—leads to an operating value that exceeds the book value of its invested capital ($1 billion versus $348 million). When investors believe a company will create value, enterprise value will be greater than invested capital.

ADJUSTED-PRESENT-VALUE MODEL

When building an enterprise DCF or economic-profit valuation, most investment professionals discount all future flows at a constant WACC. Using a constant WACC, however, assumes the company manages its capital structure to a target debt-to-value ratio.

In most situations, debt grows with company value. But suppose the company planned to change its capital structure significantly, as in a leveraged buyout. Companies with a high proportion of debt often pay it down as cash flow improves, thus lowering their future debt-to-value ratios. In these cases, a valuation based on a constant WACC would overstate the value of the tax shields. Although the WACC can be adjusted yearly to handle a changing capital structure, the process is complex. Therefore, we turn to the most flexible of valuation models: adjusted present value (APV).

The APV model separates the value of operations into two components: the value of operations as if the company were all-equity financed and the value of tax shields that arise from debt financing[11]:

$$
\begin{array}{ccc}
\text{Adjusted} \\
\text{Present Value}
\end{array}
=
\begin{array}{c}
\text{Enterprise Value as if the} \\
\text{Company Were All-Equity Financed}
\end{array}
+
\begin{array}{c}
\text{Present Value of} \\
\text{Tax Shields}
\end{array}
$$

The APV valuation model follows directly from the teachings of Nobel laureates Franco Modigliani and Merton Miller, who proposed that in a market with no taxes (among other things), a company's choice of financial structure will not affect the value of its economic assets.[12] Only market imperfections, such as taxes and distress costs, affect enterprise value.

When building a valuation model, it is easy to forget these teachings. To see this, imagine a company (in a world with no taxes) that has a 50/50 mix of debt and equity. If the company's debt has an expected return of 5 percent and the company's equity has an expected return of 15 percent, its weighted average cost of capital would be 10 percent. Suppose the company decides to issue more debt, using the proceeds to repurchase shares. Since the cost of debt is lower than the cost of equity, it would appear that issuing debt to retire equity should lower the WACC, raising the company's value.

This line of thinking is flawed, however. In a world without taxes, a change in capital structure would not change the cash flow generated by operations or the risk of those cash flows. Therefore, neither the company's enterprise value nor its cost of capital would change. So why would we think it would? When adding debt, we adjusted the weights, but we failed to properly increase the cost of equity. Since debt payments have priority over cash flows to equity, adding leverage increases the risk to equity holders. When leverage rises, they demand a higher return. Modigliani and Miller postulated that this increase would perfectly offset the change in weights.

In practice, taxes play a role in determining capital structure.[13] Since interest is tax deductible, profitable companies can lower taxes by raising debt.

---

[11] This book focuses on the tax shields generated by interest expense. On a more general basis, the APV values any cash flows associated with capital structure, such as tax shields, issuance costs, preferential borrowing rates, and distress costs. Distress costs include direct costs, such as bankruptcy-related fees, and indirect costs, such as the loss of wary customers and suppliers.

[12] F. Modigliani and M. H. Miller, "The Cost of Capital, Corporation Finance and the Theory of Investment," *American Economic Review* 48(3) (1958): 261–297.

[13] For more on the principles of capital structure design, see Chapter 35.

But if the company relies too heavily on debt, the company's customers and suppliers may fear financial distress and be reluctant to do business with the company, reducing future cash flow (academics call this distress costs or dead-weight costs). Rather than model the effect of capital-structure changes in the weighted average cost of capital, APV explicitly measures and values the cash flow effects of financing separately.

To build an APV valuation, value the company as if it were all-equity financed. Do this by discounting free cash flow by the unlevered cost of equity (what the cost of equity would be if the company had no debt).[14] To this value, add any value created by the company's use of debt. Exhibit 10.15 values GlobalCo using adjusted present value.

Since we assume (for expositional purposes) that GlobalCo will manage its capital structure to a target debt-to-value level of 25 percent, the APV-based valuation leads to the same value for equity as did enterprise DCF (see Exhibit 10.4) and economic profit (see Exhibit 10.14). A simplified proof of equivalence between enterprise DCF and adjusted present value can be found in Appendix B. The following subsections explain adjusted present value in detail.

Valuing Free Cash Flow at Unlevered Cost of Equity

When valuing a company using the APV, explicitly separate the unlevered value of operations (V_u) from any value created by financing, such as tax shields (V_{txa}). For a company with debt (D) and equity (E), this relationship is as follows:

$$V_u + V_{txa} = D + E \tag{10.1}$$

EXHIBIT 10.15 **GlobalCo: Valuation Using Adjusted Present Value**

$ million, except where noted

Year	Free cash flow (FCF)	Interest tax shield (ITS)	Discount factor at 8.0%	Present value of FCF	Present value of ITS
Year 1	(2.0)	2.0	0.926	(1.9)	1.9
Year 2	22.5	2.2	0.857	19.3	1.9
Year 3	54.6	2.3	0.794	43.4	1.8
Continuing value	1,135.6	40.6	0.794	901.5	32.2
Present value				962.3	37.7
Present value of free cash flow					962.3
Present value of interest tax shield					37.7
Value of operations					1,000.0

[14] Free cash flow projections in the APV model are identical to those presented in Exhibit 10.4. Continuing value is computed using the key value driver formula. Only the cost of capital differs.

A second implication of Modigliani and Miller's theories is that the total risk of the company's assets, real and financial, must equal the total risk of the financial claims against those assets. Thus, in equilibrium, the blended cost of capital for operating assets (k_u), which we call the unlevered cost of equity, and financial assets (k_{txa}) must equal the blended cost of capital for debt (k_d) and equity (k_e):

$$\frac{V_u}{V}k_u + \frac{V_{txa}}{V}k_{txa} = \frac{D}{V}k_d + \frac{E}{V}k_e \qquad (10.2)$$

In the corporate-finance literature, academics combine Modigliani and Miller's two equations to solve for the cost of equity (k_e) in order to demonstrate the relationship between leverage and the cost of equity. Appendix C algebraically rearranges Equation 10.2 to solve for the most flexible version of the levered cost of equity:

$$k_e = k_u + \frac{D}{E}(k_u - k_d) - \frac{V_{txa}}{E}(k_u - k_{txa}) \qquad (10.3)$$

As this equation indicates, the cost of equity depends on the unlevered cost of equity, or the cost of equity when the company has no debt, plus a premium for leverage, less a reduction for the tax deductibility of debt. Note that when a company has no debt ($D = 0$) and subsequently no tax shields ($V_{txa} = 0$), k_e equals k_u. This is why k_u is referred to as the unlevered cost of equity.

Unfortunately, k_u cannot be observed directly. In fact, none of the variables on the left side of Equation 10.2 can be observed directly. Only the values on the right—that is, those related to debt and equity—can be estimated using market data. Because there are so many unknowns and only one equation, we must impose additional restrictions to build a usable relationship between the levered (k_e) and unlevered (k_u) cost of equity.

If you believe the company will manage its debt-to-value ratio to a target level (the company's debt will grow with the business), then the value of the tax shields will track the value of the operating assets. Thus, the risk of tax shields will mirror the risk of operating assets ($k_{txa} = k_u$). Setting k_{txa} equal to k_u, Equation 10.3 can be simplified as follows:

$$k_e = k_u + \frac{D}{E}(k_u - k_d) \qquad (10.4)$$

The unlevered cost of equity can now be reverse engineered using the observed cost of equity, the cost of debt, and the market debt-to-equity ratio. (Appendix C shows some alternative versions for deriving k_u from k_e.)

Valuing Tax Shields and Other Capital Structure Effects

To complete an APV valuation, forecast and discount capital structure side effects such as tax shields, security issuance costs, and distress costs. Since GlobalCo has only a small probability of default, we estimated the

EXHIBIT 10.16 **GlobalCo: Forecast of Interest Tax Shields**

$ million

Forecast year	Prior-year net debt[1]	Interest rate, %	Expected interest payment	Marginal tax rate, %	Interest tax shield
Year 1	250.0	4.0	10.0	20.0	2.0
Year 2	270.0	4.0	10.8	20.0	2.2
Year 3	285.4	4.0	11.4	20.0	2.3
Continuing-value forecast	294.0	4.0	11.8	20.0	2.4

[1] Total debt, net of excess cash.

company's future interest tax shields using the company's expected interest payments and marginal tax rate (see Exhibit 10.16). To calculate the expected interest payment in year 1, multiply the prior year's debt of $250 million by the interest rate of 4.0 percent. This results in an expected interest payment of $10 million. Next, multiply the expected interest payment by the marginal tax rate of 20 percent, for an expected interest tax shield of $2 million in year 1. To determine the continuing value of interest tax shields beyond year 3, use a growth perpetuity based on interest tax shields in the continuing-value year, the unlevered cost of capital, and growth in NOPAT.

A company with significant leverage may not be able to fully use the tax shields (it may not have enough profits to shield). If there is a significant probability of default, you must model *expected* tax shields, rather than the calculated tax shields based on promised interest payments.[15] To do this, reduce each promised tax shield by the cumulative probability of default. For more on how to model leveraged buyouts, see Chapter 37.

CAPITAL CASH FLOW MODEL

When a company actively manages its capital structure to a target debt-to-value level, both free cash flow (FCF) and the interest tax shield (ITS) should be discounted at the unlevered cost of equity, k_u, such that enterprise value equals the sum of discounted cash flows plus the sum of discounted interest tax shields:

$$V = \sum_{t=1}^{\infty} \frac{\text{FCF}_t}{(1 + k_u)^t} + \sum_{t=1}^{\infty} \frac{\text{ITS}_t}{(1 + k_u)^t}$$

[15] In the United States, the Tax Cuts and Jobs Act of 2017 placed additional restrictions on the deductibility of interest, even for profitable companies. Only value interest tax shields that meet deductibility guidelines.

In 2002, Richard Ruback of the Harvard Business School argued that there is no need to separate free cash flow from tax shields when both flows are discounted by the same cost of capital.[16] He combined the two flows and named the resulting cash flow (i.e., FCF plus interest tax shields) capital cash flow (CCF):

$$V = \text{PV}(\text{Capital Cash Flow}) = \sum_{t=1}^{\infty} \frac{\text{FCF}_t + \text{ITS}_t}{(1 + k_u)^t}$$

Given that Ruback's assumptions match those of the weighted average cost of capital, the capital cash flow and WACC-based valuations will lead to identical results. In fact, we have now detailed three valuation methods that differ only in how they treat tax shields: WACC (tax shield valued in the cost of capital), APV (tax shield valued separately), and CCF (tax shield valued in the cash flow).

Although free cash flow and capital cash flow lead to the same result when debt is proportional to value, we believe FCF models are superior to CCF models. Because FCF models keep NOPAT and FCF independent of leverage, it is easier to evaluate the company's operating performance over time and against competitors. A clean measure of historical operating performance leads to better forecasts.

CASH-FLOW-TO-EQUITY VALUATION MODEL

Each of the preceding valuation models determined the value of equity indirectly by subtracting debt and other nonequity claims from enterprise value. The equity cash flow model values equity directly by discounting cash flows to equity (CFE) at the cost of equity, rather than at the weighted average cost of capital.[17]

Exhibit 10.17 details the cash flow to equity for GlobalCo. Cash flow to equity starts with net income. To this, add back noncash expenses to determine gross cash flow. Next, subtract investments in working capital, fixed assets, and nonoperating assets. Finally, add any increases in debt and other nonequity claims, and subtract decreases in debt and other nonequity claims.

Unlike free cash flow, cash flow to equity includes operating, nonoperating, and financing items in the calculation. Alternatively, you can compute

---

[16] R. S. Ruback, "Capital Cash Flows: A Simple Approach to Valuing Risky Cash Flows," *Financial Management* (Summer 2002): 85–103.

[17] The equity method can be difficult to implement correctly because capital structure is embedded in the cash flow. For companies whose operations are related to financing, such as financial institutions, the equity method is appropriate. Chapter 43 discusses valuing financial institutions.

EXHIBIT 10.17 **GlobalCo: Equity Cash Flow Summary**

$ million

	Forecast		
	Year 1	Year 2	Year 3
Net income	52.0	60.4	63.3
Depreciation	25.0	28.8	30.2
Gross cash flow	77.0	89.1	93.5
Decrease (Increase) in operating working capital	(12.0)	(9.0)	(3.4)
Capital expenditures, net of disposals	(75.0)	(66.3)	(44.6)
Increase (Decrease) in short-term debt	–	15.4	8.6
Increase (Decrease) in long-term debt	20.0	–	–
Cash flow to equity holders	10.0	29.3	54.1
		–	–
Reconciliation of cash flow to equity			
Cash dividends	10.0	14.3	24.1
Repurchased (Issued) shares	–	15.0	30.0
Cash flow to equity holders	10.0	29.3	54.1

cash flow to equity as dividends plus share repurchases minus new equity issues. The two methods generate identical results.[18]

To value GlobalCo using cash flow to equity holders, discount projected equity cash flows at the cost of equity (see Exhibit 10.18). Unlike enterprise-based models, this method makes no adjustments to the DCF value for non-operating assets or debt. Rather, they are embedded as part of the equity cash flow.

Once again, note how the valuation, derived using equity cash flows, matches each of the prior valuations. This occurs because we have carefully

EXHIBIT 10.18 **GlobalCo: Valuation Using Cash Flow to Equity**

$ million, except where noted

Forecast year	Cash flow to equity (CFE)	Discount factor at 9.3%	Present value of CFE
Year 1	10.0	0.915	9.1
Year 2	29.3	0.837	24.5
Year 3	54.1	0.765	41.4
Continuing value	882.1	0.765	675.0
Present value of equity cash flows			750.0
Less: Value of noncontrolling interest			–
Equity value			750.0

[18] Calculate the continuing value using an equity-based variant of the key value driver formula:

$$V_e = \frac{\text{Net Income}\left(1 - \frac{g}{\text{ROE}}\right)}{k_e - g}$$

modeled GlobalCo's debt-to-value ratio at a constant level. If leverage is expected to change, the cost of equity must be appropriately adjusted to reflect the change in risk imposed on equity holders. Although formulas exist to adjust the cost of equity (as done in the APV section earlier in this chapter), many of the best-known formulas are built under restrictions that may be inconsistent with the way you are implicitly forecasting the company's capital structure via the cash flows. This will cause a mismatch between cash flows and the cost of equity, resulting in an incorrect valuation.

It is quite easy, when using the cash-flow-to-equity model, to change the company's capital structure without realizing it—and that is what makes implementing the equity model so risky. Suppose you plan to value a company with a debt-to-value ratio of 25 percent. You believe the company will pay extra dividends, so you increase debt to raise the dividend payout ratio. Presto! Increased dividends lead to higher equity cash flows and a higher valuation. Even though operating performance has not changed, the equity value has mistakenly increased. What is happening? Using new debt to pay dividends causes a rise in the debt-to-value ratio. Unless you adjust the cost of equity, your estimate of the company's valuation will erroneously increase.

A second shortcoming of the equity cash flow model is how it values non-operating assets. Imagine a company that holds a significant amount of low-risk, low-return excess cash. Since operating and nonoperating cash flows are combined in cash flows to equity, they will both be discounted at the same rate, the cost of equity. Since the cost of equity exceeds the interest earned on cash, it appears as if the nonoperating asset is destroying value, and the asset will be incorrectly valued below its book value, even if the asset in actuality is earning a fair rate of return. Enterprise DCF is superior because it values assets with different risks separately.

A third shortcoming of the cash-flow-to-equity model emerges when valuing a company by business unit. The direct equity approach requires allocating debt and interest expense to each unit. This creates extra work yet provides few additional insights.

One situation where the equity cash flow model leads to the simplest implementation is the analysis and valuation of financial institutions. Since capital structure is a critical part of operations in a financial institution, using enterprise DCF to separate operations and capital structure requires unnecessary assumptions. This is why Chapter 43 uses the cash-flow-to-equity model to value banks and other financial institutions.

What's in a Name? Free Cash Flow versus Cash Flow to Equity

To accurately value a company, it is crucial to discount a given cash flow using the appropriate cost of capital. Specifically, free cash flow should be discounted at the WACC, while cash flow to equity should be discounted at the cost of equity. To prevent confusion, it is necessary to be diligent about using precise terminology.

EXHIBIT 10.19 **The Language of Cash Flow**

Measure	Free cash flow (FCF)	Cash flow to equity (CFE)
Description	FCF represents the cash generated by a company's operations that is available for distribution to all investors, including equity and debt holders.	CFE focuses on the cash available for distribution to equity holders, excluding debt holders.
Corresponding discount factor	WACC	Cost of equity
Examples of alternative terminology	Unlevered free cash flow (UFCF) Free cash flow to firm (FCFF)	Levered free cash flow (LFCF) Free cash flow to equity (FCFE)

In practice, various professionals may use different terms to refer to the same calculation. For instance, free cash flow is alternatively known as unlevered free cash flow or free cash flow to the firm, while cash flow to equity can be referred to as levered free cash flow or free cash flow to equity (see Exhibit 10.19). We prefer the term "cash flow to equity" more than "levered free cash flow" because new modelers often overlook the term "levered," leading to an incorrect discounting of equity-based cash flow using an enterprise-based WACC. Given this common error, never make assumptions about the underlying calculation in another person's model that are based solely on a name.

PROBLEMATIC MODIFICATIONS TO DISCOUNTED CASH FLOW

In this chapter, we valued GlobalCo by discounting nominal cash flows at a nominal cost of capital. An alternative is to value companies by projecting cash flow in real terms, ignoring the rise in prices, and discounting this cash flow at a real discount rate (the nominal rate less expected inflation). But most managers think in terms of nominal rather than real measures, so nominal measures are often easier to communicate. In addition, interest rates are generally quoted nominally rather than in real terms, excluding expected inflation.

A second difficulty occurs when calculating and interpreting ROIC. The historical statements are nominal, so historical returns on invested capital are nominal. But if the projections for the company use real rather than nominal forecasts, returns on new capital are also real. Projected returns on total capital—new and old—are a combination of nominal and real, so they are impossible to interpret. The only way around this is to restate historical performance on a real basis, which is a complex and time-consuming task. The extra insights to be gained from this are rarely worth the effort, except in extremely high-inflation environments, described in Chapter 26.

A second alternative to the enterprise DCF method outlined earlier is to discount pretax cash flows at a pretax hurdle rate (the market-based cost of capital multiplied by 1 plus the marginal tax rate) to determine a pretax value. This method, however, leads to three fundamental inconsistencies. First, the government calculates taxes on profits after depreciation, not on cash flow after capital expenditures. By discounting pretax cash flow at the pretax cost of capital, you implicitly assume capital investments are tax deductible when made, not as they are depreciated. Furthermore, working-capital investments, such as accounts receivable and inventory, are never tax deductible. Selling a product at a profit, rather than holding inventory, is what leads to incremental taxes. By discounting pretax cash flow at the pretax cost of capital, you incorrectly assume that investments in operating working capital are tax deductible. Finally, it can be shown that even when net investment equals depreciation, the result will be downward biased—and the larger the cost of capital, the larger the bias. This bias occurs because the method is only an approximation, not a formal mathematical relationship. Because of these inconsistencies, we recommend against discounting pretax cash flows at a pretax hurdle rate.

ALTERNATIVES TO DISCOUNTED CASH FLOW

To this point, we've focused solely on discounted-cash-flow models. Two additional valuation techniques are using the multiples of comparable companies and real options.

Multiples

One simple way that investors and executives value companies is to triangulate their value in relation to the value of other companies, akin to the way a real estate agent values a house by comparing it with similar houses that have recently sold. To do this, first calculate how similar companies are valued as a multiple of a relevant metric, such as earnings, invested capital, or an operating metric such as barrels of oil. You can then apply that multiple to the company you are valuing. For example, assume the company's NOPAT equals $100 million and the typical enterprise-value-to-NOPAT multiple for companies in the industry with similar growth and ROIC prospects is 13 times. Multiplying 13 by $100 million leads to an estimated value of $1.3 billion.

Multiples, if properly selected and applied, can be a great check on your DCF valuation. Suppose the value estimated by multiples is $1.3 billion but your DCF value is $2.7 billion. This might be a clue that there is something wrong with your DCF valuation model. Alternatively, it could be that the company you are valuing is expected to perform differently than the comparable companies. Or it could be that investors have a different outlook for the entire industry than you do (in which case the multiples of all the comparable companies would be out of line with their DCF value). Of course, it could just be that your multiples valuation wasn't performed properly.

Because of the broad use of multiples and the potential for error, we devote Chapter 18 to valuation using multiples. In a nutshell, to use multiples properly, you need to carefully choose the multiple and the comparable companies. In the case of earnings multiples, we recommend using ratios based on enterprise value, such as enterprise value-to-NOPAT, rather than an equity-based multiple such as the price-to-earnings ratio. We also urge you to be careful when choosing the comparable companies. The comparable companies not only should be in the same industry but also should have similar economic performance, as measured by ROIC and growth.

Real Options and Replicating Portfolios

In 1997, Robert Merton and Myron Scholes won the Nobel Prize in economics for developing an ingenious method to value derivatives that avoids the need to estimate either cash flows or the cost of capital.[19] Their model relies on what today's economists call a "replicating portfolio." They argued that if a portfolio exists of traded securities whose future cash flows perfectly mimic the security you are attempting to value, the portfolio and security must have the same price. This is known as the law of one price. As long as you can find a suitable replicating portfolio, you need not discount future cash flows.

Given the model's power in valuing derivatives such as stock options, there have been many attempts to translate the concepts of replicating portfolios to corporate valuation. This valuation technique, commonly known as real options, is especially useful in situations of great uncertainty. Unlike those for financial options, however, replicating portfolios for companies and their projects are difficult to create. Therefore, although option-pricing models may teach powerful lessons, today's practical applications remain limited. Chapter 40 covers valuation using options-based models.

SUMMARY

Our exploration of the most common DCF valuation models has emphasized the enterprise DCF model and the economic-profit model. Each model has its own rationale, and each has an important place in corporate valuation. The remaining chapters in Part Two describe a step-by-step, detailed approach to valuing a company using enterprise DCF. These chapters explain the technical details of valuation, including how to reorganize the financial statements, analyze return on invested capital and revenue growth, forecast free cash flow, compute the cost of capital, and estimate an appropriate terminal value.

---

[19] Fischer Black would have been named as a third recipient, but the Nobel Prize is not awarded posthumously.

11

Reorganizing the Financial Statements

Traditional financial statements—the income statement, balance sheet, and statement of cash flows—do not provide easy insights into operating performance and value. They simply aren't organized that way. The balance sheet mixes together operating assets, nonoperating assets, and sources of financing. The income statement similarly combines operating profits, interest expense, and other nonoperating items.

To prepare the financial statements for analyzing economic performance, you should reorganize each financial statement into three categories: operating items, nonoperating items, and sources of financing. This often requires searching through the notes to separate accounts that aggregate operating and nonoperating items. This task may seem mundane, but it is crucial for avoiding the common traps of double-counting, omitting cash flows, and hiding leverage that can distort your assessment of performance and value.

This chapter breaks down the process into three sections. The first section presents a simple example demonstrating how to build invested capital, net operating profit after taxes (NOPAT), and free cash flow. The second section applies this method to the financial statements of the global retailer Costco Wholesale, with comments on some of the intricacies of implementation. In the third section, we provide a summary of advanced topics, including how to adjust for restructuring charges, operating leases, pensions, and capitalized expenses. A more comprehensive analysis of each of these topics can be found in the chapters of Part Three.

REORGANIZING THE FINANCIAL STATEMENTS: KEY CONCEPTS

To calculate return on invested capital (ROIC) and free cash flow (FCF), it is necessary to reorganize the balance sheet to estimate invested capital, and to reorganize the income statement to estimate NOPAT. Invested capital represents the investor capital required to fund operations, without regard to how the capital is financed. NOPAT represents the after-tax operating profit (generated by the company's invested capital) that is available to all investors.

ROIC and FCF are both derived from NOPAT and invested capital. ROIC is defined as

$$\text{ROIC} = \frac{\text{NOPAT}}{\text{Invested Capital}}$$

and free cash flow is defined as

$$\text{FCF} = \text{NOPAT} + \text{Noncash Operating Expenses} - \text{Investment in Invested Capital}$$

By combining noncash operating expenses, such as depreciation, with investment in invested capital, it is also possible to express FCF as

$$\text{FCF} = \text{NOPAT} - \text{Increase in Invested Capital}$$

Invested Capital: Key Concepts

To build an economic balance sheet that separates a company's operating assets from its nonoperating assets and financial structure, we start with the company's balance sheet. The balance sheet is bound by the most fundamental rule of accounting:

$$\text{Assets} = \text{Liabilities} + \text{Equity}$$

The balance sheet equation, however, mixes operating liabilities and sources of financing on the right side of the equation.

Assume a company has only operating assets (OA), such as accounts receivable, inventory, and property, plant, and equipment (PP&E); operating liabilities (OL), such as accounts payable and accrued salaries; interest-bearing debt (D); and equity (E). Using this more detailed breakdown of assets, liabilities, and equity leads to an expanded version of the balance sheet relationship:

$$\text{OA} = \text{OL} + \text{D} + \text{E}$$

Moving operating liabilities to the left side of the equation leads to invested capital:

$$\text{OA} - \text{OL} = \text{Invested Capital} = \text{D} + \text{E}$$

This new equation rearranges the balance sheet to reflect more accurately capital used for operations and the financing provided by investors to fund those operations. Note how invested capital can be calculated using either the operating method (that is, operating assets minus operating liabilities) or the financing method (debt plus equity).

For many companies, the previous equation is too simple. Assets consist of not only operating assets but also nonoperating assets (NOA), such as marketable securities, prepaid pension assets, nonconsolidated subsidiaries, and other long-term investments. Liabilities consist of not only operating liabilities and interest-bearing debt but also debt equivalents (DE), such as unfunded retirement liabilities, and equity equivalents (EE), such as deferred taxes and income-smoothing provisions. (We explain debt and equity equivalents in detail later in the chapter.) We can expand our original balance sheet equation to show these:

$$
\underset{\substack{\text{(operating} \\ \text{assets)}}}{\text{OA}} + \underset{\substack{\text{(nonoperating} \\ \text{assets)}}}{\text{NOA}} = \underset{\substack{\text{(operating} \\ \text{liabilities)}}}{\text{OL}} + \underset{\substack{\text{(debt and its} \\ \text{equivalents)}}}{\text{D} + \text{DE}} + \underset{\substack{\text{(equity and its} \\ \text{equivalents)}}}{\text{E} + \text{EE}}
$$

Rearranging leads to total funds invested:

$$
\underset{\substack{\text{(invested} \\ \text{capital)}}}{\text{OA} - \text{OL} +} \underset{\substack{\text{(nonoperating} \\ \text{assets)}}}{\text{NOA}} = \underset{\text{Invested}}{\text{Total Funds}} = \underset{\substack{\text{(debt and its} \\ \text{equivalents)}}}{\text{D} + \text{DE}} + \underset{\substack{\text{(equity and its} \\ \text{equivalents)}}}{\text{E} + \text{EE}}
$$

For a company with debt and equity equivalents, invested capital no longer equals debt plus equity. It equals operating assets minus operating liabilities. From an investing perspective, total funds invested equals invested capital plus nonoperating assets. From the financing perspective, total funds invested equals debt and its equivalents plus equity and its equivalents. Exhibit 11.1 rearranges the balance sheet for a simple hypothetical company into invested capital and total funds invested. The reconciliation at the lower right shows how the amount of total funds invested is identical regardless of the method used.

Net Operating Profit after Taxes: Key Concepts

NOPAT is the after-tax profit generated from core operations, excluding any income from nonoperating assets or financing expenses, such as interest. Whereas net income is the profit available to equity holders only, NOPAT is the profit available to *all* investors, including providers of debt, equity, and any other types of investor financing. It is critical to define NOPAT consistently with your definition of invested capital and to include only those profits generated by invested capital.

EXHIBIT 11.1 **An Example of Invested Capital**

$ million

Accountant's balance sheet			Invested capital			
Assets	**Prior year**	**Current year**		**Prior year**	**Current year**	
Cash	5	15	Cash	5	15	
Inventory	200	225	Inventory	200	225	Operating liabilities
Net PP&E	300	350	Accounts payable	(125)	(150)	are netted against
Equity investments	15	25	Operating working capital	80	90	operating assets
Total assets	520	615				
			Net PP&E	300	350	
Liabilities and equity			Invested capital	380	440	
Accounts payable	125	150				Nonoperating assets
Interest-bearing debt	225	200	Equity investments	15	25	are not included in
Shareholders' equity	170	265	Total funds invested	395	465	invested capital
Total liabilities and equity	520	615				
			Reconciliation of total funds invested			
			Interest-bearing debt	225	200	
			Shareholders' equity	170	265	
			Total funds invested	395	465	

To calculate NOPAT, we reorganize the accounting income statement in three ways (see Exhibit 11.2). First, interest is not subtracted from operating income, because interest is compensation for the company's debt investors, not an operating expense. By reclassifying interest as a financing item, we make NOPAT independent of the company's capital structure.

Second, when calculating NOPAT, exclude income generated from assets that were excluded from invested capital. Mistakenly including nonoperating income in NOPAT without including the associated assets in invested capital will lead to an inconsistent definition of ROIC; the numerator and denominator will include unrelated elements. If one-time items such as a major litigation settlement are reported, exclude them from NOPAT as well. One-time items are important to analyze, but including them makes trends in core performance difficult to identify.

Finally, since reported taxes are calculated after interest and nonoperating income, they are a function of nonoperating items and capital structure. To calculate operating taxes, start with reported taxes, add back the tax shield from interest expense, and remove the taxes paid on nonoperating income. The resulting operating taxes should equal the hypothetical taxes that would be paid by an all-equity, pure operating company. Nonoperating taxes, the difference between operating taxes and reported taxes, are not included in NOPAT but instead treated as part of income available to investors.

EXHIBIT 11.2 **An Example of NOPAT**

$ million

Accountant's income statement	Current year		NOPAT	Current year	
Revenues	1,000		Revenues	1,000	
Operating costs	(700)		Operating costs	(700)	
Depreciation	(20)		Depreciation	(20)	
Operating income	280		EBITA	280	
Interest expense	(20)		Operating taxes[1]	(70)	← Taxes are calculated on operating profits
Income from equity investments	4		NOPAT	210	
Earnings before taxes (EBT)	264				Do not include income from any asset excluded from invested capital as part of NOPAT
			Income from equity investments	4	←
Income taxes	(66)		Tax shield on nonoperating items[2]	4	
Net income	198		Income available to investors	218	
			Reconciliation with net income		
			Net income	198	Treat interest as a financial payout to investors, not an operating expense
			Interest expense	20	←
			Income available to investors	218	

[1] Assumes a marginal tax of 25% on all income.

[2] Interest tax shield less taxes on equity income.

Free Cash Flow: Key Concepts

To value a company's operations, we discount forecast free cash flow at a company's weighted average cost of capital. Free cash flow is the after-tax cash flow available to all investors: debt holders and equity holders. Unlike "cash flow from operations" reported in a company's annual report, free cash flow is independent of financing flows and nonoperating items. It can be viewed as the after-tax cash flow generated for equity holders if the company were to retain only its core operating assets and finance the business entirely with equity. Free cash flow is defined as

$$FCF = NOPAT + \text{Noncash Operating Expenses} - \text{Investments in Invested Capital}$$

As shown in Exhibit 11.3, free cash flow excludes nonoperating flows and items related to capital structure. Unlike the accounting cash flow statement, the free cash flow statement starts with NOPAT (instead of net income). As discussed earlier, NOPAT excludes nonoperating income and interest expense. Instead, interest is classified as a financing cash flow.

Changes in nonoperating assets and the gains, losses, and income associated with these nonoperating assets are not included in free cash flow. Instead, nonoperating cash flows should be analyzed and valued separately.

EXHIBIT 11.3 **An Example of Free Cash Flow**

$ million

Accountant's cash flow statement		**Free cash flow**		
	Current year		**Current year**	
Net income	198	NOPAT	210	
Depreciation	20	Depreciation	20	
Decrease (Increase) in inventory	(25)	Gross cash flow	230	
Increase (Decrease) in accounts payable	25			Subtract investments in operating items from gross cash flow
Cash flow from operations	218	Decrease (Increase) in operating cash	(10)	
		Decrease (Increase) in inventory	(25)	
		Increase (Decrease) in accounts payable	25	
Capital expenditures	(70)	Capital expenditures	(70)	
Decrease (Increase) in equity investments	(10)	Free cash flow	150	
Cash flow from investing	(80)			
				Evaluate cash flow from nonoperating assets separately from free cash flow
Increase (Decrease) in interest-bearing debt	(25)	Nonoperating income	4	
Dividends	(103)	Nonoperating taxes	4	
Cash flow from financing	(128)	Decrease (Increase) in equity investments	(10)	
		Cash flow available to investors	148	
Starting cash	5			
Cash flow from operations	218			
Cash flow from investing	(80)	**Reconciliation of cash flow available to investors**		Treat interest as a financial payout to investors, not an expense
Cash flow from financing	(128)			
Ending cash	15	Interest expense	20	
		Decrease (Increase) in interest-bearing debt	25	
		Dividends	103	
		Cash flow available to investors	148	

Combining free cash flow and nonoperating cash flow leads to cash flow available to investors. As is true with total funds invested and NOPAT, cash flow available to investors can be calculated using two methodologies: one focuses on how the cash flow is generated, and the other focuses on the recipients of free cash flow. Although the two methods seem redundant, checking that both give the same result can help avoid line-item omissions and classification pitfalls.

REORGANIZING THE FINANCIAL STATEMENTS: IN PRACTICE

Reorganizing a company's financial statements can be difficult, even for the savviest analyst. Which assets are operating assets? Which are nonoperating? Which liabilities should be treated as debt? Which count as equity?

In the following pages, we demonstrate how to reorganize financial statements in practice, using Costco Wholesale. (A complete valuation of Costco with commentary is presented in Appendix I.) Costco, the third-largest retailer in the world, is well known for selling everyday items in bulk. The company opened its first store in Seattle in 1983 and now operates more than 800 stores in 14 countries.

Invested Capital: In Practice

To estimate the invested capital for Costco, we reorganize the company's balance sheet. Exhibit 11.4 presents historical balance sheets for Costco, whose fiscal year ends on the Sunday nearest August 31. The version presented is slightly more detailed than the balance sheets reported in Costco's annual reports, because we have searched the notes in each annual report for

EXHIBIT 11.4 **Costco: Balance Sheet**

$ million

Assets	2019	2020	2021	2022	2023
Cash and cash equivalents[1]	9,444	13,305	12,175	11,049	15,234
Receivables, net	1,535	1,550	1,803	2,241	2,285
Merchandise inventories	11,395	12,242	14,215	17,907	16,651
Other current assets	1,111	1,023	1,312	1,499	1,709
Total current assets	23,485	28,120	29,505	32,696	35,879
Property, plant, and equipment	20,890	21,807	23,492	24,646	26,684
Operating lease right-of-use assets	—	2,788	2,890	2,774	2,713
Finance lease assets[2]	—	592	1,000	1,620	1,325
Goodwill[2]	53	988	996	993	994
Deferred income taxes[2]	398	406	444	445	491
Other long-term assets[2]	574	855	941	992	908
Total assets	45,400	55,556	59,268	64,166	68,994
Liabilities and shareholders' equity					
Accounts payable	11,679	14,172	16,278	17,848	17,483
Accrued salaries and benefits	3,176	3,605	4,090	4,381	4,278
Accrued member rewards	1,180	1,393	1,671	1,911	2,150
Deferred membership fees	1,711	1,851	2,042	2,174	2,337
Current portion of long-term debt	1,699	95	799	73	1,081
Current portion of operating leases[3]	—	231	222	239	220
Current portion of finance leases[3]	26	31	72	245	129
Other current liabilities[3]	3,766	3,466	4,267	5,127	5,905
Total current liabilities	23,237	24,844	29,441	31,998	33,583
Long-term debt	5,124	7,514	6,692	6,484	5,377
Long-term operating lease liabilities	—	2,558	2,642	2,482	2,426
Long-term finance leases[4]	395	657	980	1,383	1,303
Deferred income taxes[4]	543	665	754	724	795
Other long-term liabilities[4]	517	613	681	448	452
Total liabilities	29,816	36,851	41,190	43,519	43,936
Costco shareholders' equity	15,243	18,284	17,564	20,642	25,058
Noncontrolling interests	341	421	514	5	—
Total shareholders' equity	15,584	18,705	18,078	20,647	25,058
Liabilities and shareholders' equity	45,400	55,556	59,268	64,166	68,994

Note: Costco's fiscal year ends on the Sunday nearest August 31. For example, the 2023 fiscal year ended on September 3, 2023.

[1] Includes short-term investments.

[2] Aggregated in other long-term assets in original filings.

[3] Aggregated in other current liabilities in original filings.

[4] Aggregated in other long-term liabilities in original filings.

information about accounts that mix operating and nonoperating items. For instance, the notes in Costco's 2023 annual report reveal that the company aggregates finance leases in other liabilities. Since finance leases are a form of debt and must be treated as such, the balance sheet in its original form masks some details that could be important for valuation purposes.

Invested capital sums operating working capital (current operating assets minus current operating liabilities), fixed assets (net property, plant, and equipment), net other long-term operating assets (net of long-term operating liabilities), and when appropriate, intangible assets (goodwill, acquired intangibles, and capitalized software). Exhibit 11.5 demonstrates this line-by-line aggregation for Costco. In the following subsections, we examine each element in detail.

EXHIBIT 11.5 **Costco: Invested Capital and Total Funds Invested**

$ million

	2019	2020	2021	2022	2023
Operating working capital	(4,417)	(6,337)	(7,099)	(5,255)	(6,662)
Property, plant, and equipment	20,890	21,807	23,492	24,646	26,684
Operating lease right-of-use assets[1]	2,147	2,788	2,890	2,774	2,713
Variable lease assets[2]	—	963	1,474	1,466	1,405
Finance lease assets	—	592	1,000	1,620	1,325
Other assets, net other liabilities[3]	57	242	260	544	456
Invested capital, excluding goodwill	18,677	20,055	22,017	25,795	25,921
Goodwill and acquired intangibles	53	988	996	993	994
Invested capital, including goodwill	18,730	21,043	23,013	26,788	26,915
Excess cash[4]	6,390	9,970	8,256	6,510	10,388
Foreign tax credit carryforward[5]	65	101	146	201	250
Total funds invested	25,185	31,114	31,415	33,499	37,553
Reconciliation of total funds invested					
Debt	6,823	7,609	7,491	6,557	6,458
Operating lease liabilities[6]	2,147	2,789	2,864	2,721	2,646
Variable lease liabilities[2,6]	—	963	1,474	1,466	1,405
Finance lease liabilities[6]	421	688	1,052	1,628	1,432
Debt and debt equivalents	9,391	12,049	12,881	12,372	11,941
Deferred income taxes, operating[5]	189	320	518	485	574
Deferred income taxes, nonoperating[5]	21	40	(62)	(5)	(20)
Noncontrolling interests	341	421	514	5	—
Costco shareholders' equity	15,243	18,284	17,564	20,642	25,058
Equity and equity equivalents	15,794	19,065	18,534	21,127	25,612
Total funds invested	25,185	31,114	31,415	33,499	37,553

[1] As reported on the balance sheet, except in 2019. Prior to the adoption of ASC 842 in 2020, it is necessary to estimate the value of operating leases. For more on estimation methodologies, see Chapter 22.

[2] The value of variable leases is estimated using the ratio of operating lease expense to variable lease expense.

[3] Other assets and liabilities are classified as operating because no description is provided by the company.

[4] Operating cash is estimated at 2% of revenues. Remaining cash is treated as excess cash.

[5] Foreign tax credit carryforward and deferred-tax accounts are detailed in Exhibit 11.8.

[6] Includes current portion.

EXHIBIT 11.6 **Costco: Operating Working Capital**

$ million

	2019	2020	2021	2022	2023
Operating cash[1]	3,054	3,335	3,919	4,539	4,846
Receivables, net	1,535	1,550	1,803	2,241	2,285
Merchandise inventories	11,395	12,242	14,215	17,907	16,651
Other current assets	1,111	1,023	1,312	1,499	1,709
Operating current assets	17,095	18,150	21,249	26,186	25,491
Accounts payable	(11,679)	(14,172)	(16,278)	(17,848)	(17,483)
Accrued salaries and benefits	(3,176)	(3,605)	(4,090)	(4,381)	(4,278)
Accrued member rewards	(1,180)	(1,393)	(1,671)	(1,911)	(2,150)
Deferred membership fees	(1,711)	(1,851)	(2,042)	(2,174)	(2,337)
Other current liabilities	(3,766)	(3,466)	(4,267)	(5,127)	(5,905)
Operating current liabilities	(21,512)	(24,487)	(28,348)	(31,441)	(32,153)
Operating working capital	(4,417)	(6,337)	(7,099)	(5,255)	(6,662)

[1] Estimated at 2 percent of revenues. Remaining cash is treated as excess cash.

Operating Working Capital   In Exhibit 11.6, we present an estimate of operating working capital for Costco. Operating working capital is operating current assets minus operating current liabilities. Operating current assets comprise all current assets necessary for the operation of the business, including working cash balances, trade accounts receivable, inventory, and prepaid expenses. Specifically *excluded* are excess cash and marketable securities— that is, cash greater than the operating needs of the business.[1] Excess cash generally represents temporary imbalances in the company's cash position or cash trapped in tax-advantaged countries—more to come on this.[2]

Operating current liabilities include liabilities that are related to the ongoing operations of the firm. The most common operating liabilities are those related to suppliers (accounts payable), employees (accrued salaries), customers (as either prepayments or, in the case of Costco, deferred membership fees), and the government (income taxes payable).[3] If a liability is deemed operating rather than financial, it should be netted from operating assets to determine invested capital and consequently incorporated into free cash flow.

[1] Analyze excess cash separately from operating working capital for two reasons. First, excess cash is more accurately valued using a market value rather than as part of free cash flow. Second, excess cash will have a much lower risk–return profile than operating capital. Commingling assets with different risk profiles can distort your perception of performance.

[2] In a company's financial statements, accountants often distinguish between cash and marketable securities but not between working cash and excess cash. We provide guidance on distinguishing working cash from excess cash later in this chapter.

[3] When analyzing Costco, we treat accrued member rewards as an operating-related current liability and thus part of working capital. While we believe accrued member rewards are no different from other customer prepayments, the member is not paying cash specifically for the reward. One alternative is to use cash accounting for accrued member rewards, treating the liability as an equity equivalent. To convert to cash, add the increase in accrued member rewards to EBITA. Since taxes will not change, compute taxes using original EBITA.

Interest-bearing liabilities are nonoperating and should *not* be netted from operating assets but rather valued separately (the related interest expense is classified as a nonoperating expense).

Some argue that operating liabilities, such as accounts payable, are a form of financing and should be treated no differently than debt. However, this would lead to a definition of NOPAT that is inconsistent with invested capital. NOPAT is the income available to both debt and equity holders, so when you are determining ROIC, you should divide NOPAT by debt plus equity. Although a supplier may charge customers implicit interest for the right to pay in 30 days, the charge is an indistinguishable part of the price, and hence an indistinguishable and inseparable part of the cost of goods sold. Since cost of goods sold is subtracted from revenue to determine NOPAT, operating liabilities must be subtracted from operating assets to determine invested capital. A theoretical but cumbersome alternative would be to treat accounts payable as debt and adjust NOPAT for the implicit interest cost embedded in the cost of goods sold.

Property, Plant, Equipment, and Other Capitalized Investments   Include the book value of property, plant, and equipment net of accumulated depreciation in operating assets. Book value measures the company's ability to create value on past investments. Use market value or replacement cost only when evaluating the sale or replacement of a specific asset.

Some companies, including IBM and UPS, have significant investments in software they have developed for internal use. Under certain restrictions, these investments can be capitalized on the balance sheet rather than immediately expensed. Although it is labeled as an intangible asset, treat capitalized software no differently than property and equipment; treat amortization as if it were depreciation; and treat investments in capitalized software as if they were capital expenditures. (The cash flow statement in the IBM annual report separates "investment in software" from investment in PP&E. In contrast, UPS combines the two accounts within capital expenditures. In this case, attributing reported capitalized expenditures entirely to PP&E would overstate the actual investment.) Only internally generated intangible assets, and not acquired intangibles, should be treated like PP&E. Acquired intangibles require special care and are discussed in a later subsection of this chapter.

Other Operating Assets, Net of Liabilities   If other long-term assets and liabilities are small—and not detailed by the company—we typically assume they are operating. To determine net other long-term operating assets, subtract other long-term liabilities from other long-term assets. This figure should be included as part of invested capital. If, however, other long-term assets and liabilities are relatively large, you will need to disaggregate each account into its operating and nonoperating components before you can calculate other long-term operating assets, net of other liabilities.

For instance, a relatively large other long-term assets account might include nonoperating items such as deferred-tax assets, prepaid pension assets, non-consolidated subsidiaries, or other equity investments. Nonoperating items should not be included in invested capital. Classifying assets as operating or nonoperating requires judgment, especially for obscure accounts. For instance, we treat restricted cash as operating when cash must be set aside to secure third-party guarantees, as is the case with distressed airlines that accept credit card payments with ticket insurance. As a helpful guidepost, operating assets typically scale with revenues.

Long-term liabilities might similarly include operating and nonoperating items. Operating liabilities are liabilities that result directly from an ongoing operating activity. For instance, one manufacturer we analyzed recorded long-term customer advances within other liabilities. In general, however, most long-term liabilities are not operating liabilities but rather what we deem debt and equity equivalents. These include unfunded pension liabilities, unfunded postretirement medical costs, restructuring reserves, and deferred taxes.

Where can you find a breakdown of other assets and other liabilities in the annual report? In some cases, companies provide a comprehensive table in the footnotes. Most of the time, however, you must work through the footnotes, note by note, searching for items aggregated within other assets and liabilities.

Goodwill and Acquired Intangibles   In Chapter 12, return on invested capital is analyzed both with and without goodwill and acquired intangibles. ROIC with goodwill and acquired intangibles measures a company's ability to create value after paying acquisition premiums. ROIC without goodwill and acquired intangibles measures the competitiveness of the underlying business. For example, from the 1960s through the mid-1980s, the median ROIC without goodwill of large consumer packaged goods companies was consistently in the mid-teens. ROIC with goodwill was only slightly lower. Then, beginning in the mid-1980s, the companies were able to use the power of their brands to increase their ROIC without goodwill to a median of about 25 percent in 2023. At the same time, they also stepped up their acquisition activity. In contrast, their median ROIC including goodwill was just 9 percent. The gap between the ROIC with goodwill and ROIC without goodwill was 16 percentage points. When you are analyzing the performance of a company, it's critical to assess ROIC both with and without goodwill.

To evaluate the effect of goodwill and acquired intangibles properly, we recommend two adjustments if applicable. First, subtract deferred-tax liabilities related to the amortization of acquired intangibles from intangible assets.[4] Why? When amortization is not tax deductible, accountants create a

---

[4] Since goodwill is tested regularly for impairment and cannot be amortized, this issue relates only to acquired intangibles. For example, this issue does not apply to Costco, as the company has only disclosed goodwill, not intangible assets, from its acquisitions.

deferred-tax liability at the time of the acquisition that is drawn down over the amortization period (since reported taxes will be lower than actual taxes). To counterbalance the liability, acquired intangibles are artificially increased by a corresponding amount, even though no cash is laid out. Subtracting deferred taxes related to acquired intangibles eliminates this distortion. For companies with significant acquired intangibles—for example, Coca-Cola—the adjustment can be substantial.

Second, add back cumulative amortization and impairment. Unlike other fixed assets, goodwill and acquired intangibles do not wear out, nor are they replaceable. Therefore, you need to adjust reported goodwill and acquired intangibles upward to recapture historical impairments of goodwill and amortization of intangibles. (To maintain consistency, do not deduct amortization of acquired intangibles from revenues to determine NOPAT. This is why NOPAT starts with EBITA.)

Consider FedEx, which wrote down nearly $1 billion in goodwill and acquired intangibles when it converted the acquired brand name Kinko's to FedEx Office. Failing to add back this impairment would have caused a large artificial jump in return on invested capital following the write-down. The money spent on an acquisition is real and needs to be accounted for, even when the investment loses value.

Computing Total Funds Invested

Invested capital represents the capital necessary to operate a company's core operating business. In addition to invested capital, companies can also own nonoperating assets. The combination of invested capital and nonoperating assets leads to total funds invested. Nonoperating assets include excess cash and marketable securities, receivables of financial subsidiaries (for example, credit card receivables), nonconsolidated subsidiaries, overfunded pension assets, and tax loss carryforwards. Costco has two nonoperating assets: excess cash and foreign tax credit carryforwards.

There are two reasons to diligently separate operating and nonoperating assets. First, nonoperating assets can distort performance measures. For example, many nonoperating assets generate income, but companies do not report the income unless certain ownership thresholds are met. Including an asset without its corresponding income distorts performance measurements. Second, there are often better methods than discounted cash flow to value nonoperating assets. You would never discount interest income to value excess cash. For this asset, the book value suffices.

Let's examine the most common nonoperating assets.

Excess Cash and Marketable Securities   Do not include excess cash in invested capital. By its definition, excess cash is unnecessary for core operations. Instead, it is cash that could be returned to shareholders or used to pay down debt. Rather than mix excess cash with the capital required to operate the business, analyze and value excess cash separately. Given its liquidity and low risk, excess cash will earn very small returns. Failing to separate excess cash from core operations will incorrectly depress the company's apparent ROIC.

Companies do not disclose how much cash they deem necessary for operations. Nor does the accounting definition of cash versus marketable securities distinguish working cash from excess cash. Based on past analysis, companies with the smallest cash balances held cash just below 2 percent of sales. If this is a good proxy for working cash, any cash above 2 percent should be considered excess.[5] In 2023, Costco held approximately $15.2 billion in cash and marketable securities and generated $242.3 billion in revenue. At 2 percent of revenue, operating cash equals $4.8 billion. The remaining cash of $10.4 billion is treated as excess. Exhibit 11.5 separates operating cash from excess cash. Excess cash is not included in invested capital but rather is treated as a nonoperating asset.

Nonconsolidated Subsidiaries and Equity Investments Nonconsolidated subsidiaries—also referred to as investments in associates, investments in affiliated companies, and equity investments—should be measured and valued separately from invested capital. When a company owns a minority stake in another company, it will record the investment as a single line item on the balance sheet and will not record the individual assets owned by the subsidiary. On the income statement, only the net income from the subsidiary will be recorded on the parent's income statement, not the subsidiary's revenues or costs. Since only net income, not revenue, is recorded, including nonconsolidated subsidiaries as part of operations will distort margins and capital turnover. Therefore, we recommend separating nonconsolidated subsidiaries from invested capital and analyzing and valuing nonconsolidated subsidiaries separately from core operations.

Financial Subsidiaries Some companies, including General Motors and Siemens, have financing subsidiaries that finance customer purchases. Because these subsidiaries charge interest on financing for purchases, they resemble banks. Since bank economics are quite different from those of manufacturing and service companies, it is necessary to differentiate line items related to the financial subsidiary from the line items for the manufacturing business. Then evaluate the return on capital for each type of business separately. Otherwise,

---

[5] This aggregate figure is not a rule, however. Required cash holdings vary by industry. For instance, one study found that companies in industries with higher cash flow volatility hold higher cash balances. To assess the minimum cash needed to support operations, look for a minimum clustering of cash to revenue across the industry. To better understand the reason behind significant cash holdings in a historical context, see J. Graham and M. Leary, "The Evolution of Corporate Cash," *Review of Financial Studies* 31, no. 11 (November 2018): 4288–4344.

significant distortions of performance will make a meaningful comparison with competitors impossible. For more on how to analyze and assess financial subsidiaries, see Chapter 19.

Overfunded Pension Assets   If a company runs a defined-benefit pension plan for its employees, it must fund the plan each year. And if a company funds its plan faster than its pension expenses dictate or assets grow faster than expected, under U.S. Generally Accepted Accounting Principles (GAAP) and International Accounting/Financial Reporting Standards (IAS/IFRS) the company can recognize a portion of the excess assets on the balance sheet. Pension assets are considered a nonoperating asset and not part of invested capital. Their value is important to the equity holder, so they will be valued later but separately from core operations. Chapter 23 examines pension assets in detail.

Tax Loss Carryforwards   Tax loss carryforwards are government-granted credits related to past losses. (In the case of Costco, they are reported as a foreign tax credit carryforward.) Unless tax loss carryforwards—also known as net operating losses (NOLs)—are small and grow consistently with revenue, do not include them as part of invested capital. Instead, value them separately in a manner consistent with the tax rules of the granting country. Given the complexity of tax credits and deferred taxes more generally, we will discuss these topics in more detail later in this section, in the subsection titled "Equity Equivalents Such as Deferred Taxes."

Other Nonoperating Assets   Other nonoperating assets, such as derivatives, excess real estate, and discontinued operations, also should be excluded from invested capital. For Costco, derivatives were disclosed in the footnotes but were immaterial, so no adjustments were made to the balance sheet accounts.

Reconciling Total Funds Invested

Total funds invested can be calculated as invested capital plus nonoperating assets, as in the previous section, or as the sum of debt, equity, and their equivalents. The totals produced by the two approaches should reconcile. A summary of sources of financing appears in Exhibit 11.7. We next examine each of these sources of capital contributing to total funds invested.

Debt   Debt includes all short-term or long-term interest-bearing liabilities. Short-term debt includes credit line drawdowns, commercial paper, notes payable, and the current portion of long-term debt. Long-term debt includes fixed debt, floating debt, term loans, and convertible debt, all of which have maturities extending beyond one year.

EXHIBIT 11.7 **Sources of Financing**

Source of capital	Description
Debt	Interest-bearing debt from banks and public capital markets
Debt equivalents	Off-balance-sheet debt and one-time debts owed to others that are not part of ongoing operations (e.g., severance payments as part of a restructuring, an unfunded pension liability, or expected environmental remediation following a plant closure)
Equity	Common stock, additional paid-in capital, retained earnings, and accumulated other comprehensive income
Equity equivalents	Balance sheet accounts that arise because of noncash adjustments to retained earnings; similar to debt equivalents but not deducted from enterprise value to determine equity value (e.g., most deferred-tax accounts and income-smoothing provisions)
Hybrid securities	Claims that have equity characteristics but are not yet part of owners' equity (e.g., convertible debt and employee stock options)
Noncontrolling interest by other companies	External investors' minority ownership position in any of the company's consolidated subsidiaries

Debt Equivalents Such as Retirement Liabilities and Restructuring Reserves

If a company's defined-benefit plan is underfunded, the company must recognize the underfunding as a liability. The amount of underfunding is not an operating liability. Rather, treat unfunded pension liabilities and unfunded postretirement medical liabilities as a debt equivalent (and treat the net interest expense associated with these liabilities as nonoperating). It is as if the company must borrow money to fund the plan. As an example, UPS announced in 2012 that it would withdraw from a multiemployer pension fund. To be released from its obligations to the fund, UPS promised to pay $43 million per year for 50 years. This fixed repayment promise, an obligation with seniority to equity claims, is no different from traditional debt.

We discuss other debt equivalents, such as reserves for plant decommissioning and restructuring reserves, in Chapter 21.

Equity   Equity includes original investor funds, such as common stock and additional paid-in capital, as well as investor funds reinvested into the company, such as retained earnings and accumulated other comprehensive income (OCI). In the United States, accumulated OCI consists primarily of currency adjustments, aggregate unrealized gains and losses from liquid assets whose value has changed but that have not yet been sold, and pension plan fluctuations within a certain band. IFRS also includes accumulated OCI within shareholders' equity but reports each reserve separately. Any stock repurchased and held in the treasury should be deducted from total equity. In Exhibits 11.4 and 11.5, we consolidate these accounts into a single account titled Costco shareholders' equity.

Equity Equivalents Such as Deferred Taxes   Equity equivalents are balance sheet accounts that arise because of noncash adjustments to retained earnings.

Equity equivalents are like debt equivalents; they differ only in that they are not deducted from enterprise value to determine equity value. Instead, their value is incorporated into the valuation elsewhere, often through a corresponding account.

The most common equity equivalent, deferred taxes, arises from differences in how businesses and the government account for taxes. For instance, the government typically uses accelerated depreciation to determine a company's taxes, whereas the accounting statements are prepared using straight-line depreciation. This leads to cash taxes being lower than reported taxes during the early years of an asset's life. For growing companies, this difference will cause reported taxes to consistently overstate the company's actual tax payments. To avoid this bias, we typically recommend using cash-based (as opposed to accrual-based) taxes to determine NOPAT. Since we are using cash taxes on the income statement, the corresponding deferred-tax account on the balance sheet is no longer necessary. This is why the deferred-tax account is referred as an equity equivalent. It represents the adjustment to retained earnings that would be made if the company reported cash taxes to investors instead of accrual taxes.

Not every deferred-tax account is operating. Although both operating and nonoperating deferred-tax accounts are equity equivalents, incorporate only deferred-tax accounts associated with ongoing operations into operating cash taxes.[6] In contrast, value nonoperating deferred taxes as part of the corresponding account.[7] For instance, when valuing an underfunded pension, do not use the book value of deferred taxes to value potential tax savings. Instead, reduce the underfunding by the projected taxes likely to be saved when the plan is funded.

Exhibit 11.8 converts deferred-tax assets and liabilities for Costco into operating, nonoperating, and tax loss carryforwards, using the tax footnote in the company's annual report. Although individual operating-related accounts, such as accrued liabilities and reserves, are large, the net amount has been relatively stable. For this reason, operating cash taxes for Costco will not differ significantly from accrual-based taxes.

Hybrid Securities and Noncontrolling Interests   Some sources of financing resist easy classification as debt or equity. These include hybrid securities and noncontrolling interests. Unlike debt, these accounts do not have fixed interest payments. Unlike equity, they are not the residual claim on cash flows.

---

[6] Separating deferred taxes into operating and nonoperating items can be challenging and often requires advanced knowledge of accounting conventions. For an in-depth discussion of deferred taxes, see Chapter 20.

[7] As discussed earlier, deferred-tax assets related to past losses, known as tax loss carryforwards, should be classified as a nonoperating asset and valued separately. Deferred-tax liabilities related to amortization of acquired intangibles should be netted against acquired intangibles. These accounts are not equity equivalents.

EXHIBIT 11.8 **Costco: Reorganized Deferred Taxes**

$ million	As reported			$ million	Reorganized		
	2021	**2022**	**2023**		**2021**	**2022**	**2023**
Deferred-tax assets				**Operating deferred tax assets, net of liabilities**			
Equity compensation	72	84	89	Equity compensation	72	84	89
Deferred income/membership fees	161	302	309	Deferred income/membership fees	161	302	309
Foreign tax credit carryforward	146	201	250	Operating lease assets, net of liabilities	25	26	23
Operating leases	769	727	678	Accrued liabilities and reserves	681	694	761
Accrued liabilities and reserves	681	694	761	Property and equipment	(935)	(962)	(867)
Other	62	5	20	Merchandise inventories	(216)	(231)	(380)
Total deferred-tax assets	1,891	2,013	2,107	Foreign branch deferreds	(92)	(85)	(87)
				Valuation allowance	(214)	(313)	(422)
Valuation allowance	(214)	(313)	(422)	Operating deferred-tax assets, net of liabilities	(518)	(485)	(574)
Total net deferred-tax assets	1,677	1,700	1,685				
				Nonoperating deferred tax assets, net of liabilities[1]			
Deferred-tax liabilities							
Property and equipment	(935)	(962)	(867)	Other assets	62	5	20
Merchandise inventories	(216)	(231)	(380)	Other liabilities	—	—	—
Operating leases	(744)	(701)	(655)	Nonoperating deferred-tax assets, net of liabilities	62	5	20
Foreign branch deferreds	(92)	(85)	(87)				
Other	—	—	—				
Total deferred-tax liabilities	(1,987)	(1,979)	(1,989)	**Tax loss carryforwards**			
				Foreign tax credit carryforward	146	201	250
Deferred-tax assets, net of liabilities	(310)	(279)	(304)	Deferred-tax assets, net of liabilities	(310)	(279)	(304)

[1] We classify other deferred-tax assets and liabilities as nonoperating because they have not scaled consistently with revenue.

Therefore, these accounts should be valued separately and deducted from enterprise value to determine equity value.

- *Hybrid securities.* The three most common hybrid securities are convertible debt, preferred stock, and employee options. Since hybrid securities contain embedded options, they cannot be treated as common stock. Instead, use the market price or, if necessary, option-pricing models to value these claims separately. Failing to do so can undervalue the hybrid security and overstate the value of common stock. This is especially important for venture-capital-backed preferred stock and long-dated employee options.

- *Noncontrolling interests.* A noncontrolling interest occurs when a third party owns a minority holding in one of the company's consolidated subsidiaries, which is a common characteristic of cross-border investments. If a noncontrolling interest exists, treat the balance sheet amount as a source of financing. Treat the earnings attributable to any noncontrolling interest as a financing cash flow similar to dividends. If data are available, value the subsidiary separately, and deduct the noncontrolling interest from the company's enterprise value to determine equity value. To value the subsidiary, discount earnings related to the noncontrolling interest at an appropriate cost of equity.

Chapter 16 presents various methodologies for valuing convertible debt, employee options, and noncontrolling interests. Correctly classifying balance sheet items can be a daunting task. But fret not: perfect classification is not required. You only need to assure that the value of each account is embedded as part of free cash flow or valued separately.

Calculating NOPAT

To determine NOPAT for Costco, we turn to the income statement (see Exhibit 11.9) and convert it into NOPAT, as shown in Exhibit 11.10.

Net Operating Profit (EBITA)   NOPAT starts with earnings before interest, taxes, and amortization of acquired intangibles (EBITA), which equals revenue minus operating expenses, such as cost of goods sold, selling costs, general and administrative costs, and depreciation.

Why use EBITA and not EBITDA? When a company purchases a physical asset such as equipment, it capitalizes the asset on the balance sheet and depreciates the asset over its lifetime. Since the asset wears out over time, any measure of profit (and return) must recognize this loss in value. While depreciation does not match the periodic loss in value perfectly, it is a suitable proxy.

EXHIBIT 11.9 **Costco: Income Statement**

$ million

	2019	2020	2021	2022	2023
Merchandise sales	149,351	163,220	192,052	222,730	237,710
Membership fees	3,352	3,541	3,877	4,224	4,580
Revenues	152,703	166,761	195,929	226,954	242,290
Merchandise costs	(132,886)	(144,939)	(170,684)	(199,382)	(212,586)
Selling, general, and administrative[1]	(13,588)	(14,742)	(16,756)	(17,879)	(19,513)
Depreciation and lease amortization[2]	(1,492)	(1,645)	(1,781)	(1,900)	(2,077)
Operating income	4,737	5,435	6,708	7,793	8,114
Interest expense	(150)	(160)	(171)	(158)	(160)
Interest income[3]	126	89	41	61	470
Other income[3]	52	3	102	144	63
Earnings before taxes	4,765	5,367	6,680	7,840	8,487
Provision for income taxes	(1,061)	(1,308)	(1,601)	(1,925)	(2,195)
Net income, consolidated	3,704	4,059	5,079	5,915	6,292
Net income, noncontrolling interests	(45)	(57)	(72)	(71)	—
Net income, Costco	3,659	4,002	5,007	5,844	6,292

[1] Includes pre-opening expenses.

[2] Aggregated in selling, general, and administrative expenses in original filings; assumes amortization related to acquired intangibles is immaterial.

[3] Aggregated in "Interest income and other, net" in original filings.

EXHIBIT 11.10 **Costco: NOPAT and Its Reconciliation to Net Income**

$ million

	2019	2020	2021	2022	2023
Revenue	152,703	166,761	195,929	226,954	242,290
Merchandise costs	(132,886)	(144,939)	(170,684)	(199,382)	(212,586)
Selling, general, and administrative	(13,588)	(14,742)	(16,756)	(17,879)	(19,513)
Depreciation and lease amortization	(1,492)	(1,645)	(1,781)	(1,900)	(2,077)
EBITA,[1] unadjusted	4,737	5,435	6,708	7,793	8,114
Add: Operating lease interest[2]	112	96	60	65	67
Add: Variable lease interest[2]	—	—	21	33	36
EBITA, adjusted	4,849	5,531	6,789	7,891	8,217
Operating cash taxes[3]	(946)	(1,294)	(1,546)	(2,166)	(2,064)
NOPAT	3,904	4,237	5,243	5,725	6,154
Reconciliation to net income					
Net income, consolidated	3,704	4,059	5,079	5,915	6,292
Operating taxes deferred[3]	228	131	198	(33)	89
Adjusted net income	3,932	4,190	5,277	5,882	6,381
Interest expense	150	160	171	158	160
Operating lease interest[2]	112	96	60	65	67
Variable lease interest[2]	—	—	21	33	36
Interest income	(126)	(89)	(41)	(61)	(470)
Other income[4]	(52)	(3)	(102)	(144)	(63)
Taxes related to nonoperating accounts[5]	(21)	(40)	(27)	(12)	66
Other nonoperating taxes[3]	(92)	(77)	(116)	(196)	(24)
NOPAT	3,904	4,237	5,243	5,725	6,154

[1] Earnings before interest, taxes, and amortization.

[2] Operating lease and variable lease interest is estimated by multiplying the corresponding prior-year liability by the weighted average discount rate for operating leases disclosed by the company.

[3] Operating cash taxes and other nonoperating taxes are detailed in Exhibit 11.12.

[4] Other income consists primarily of foreign-currency transaction gains. It is treated as nonoperating for simplicity of exposition.

[5] Estimated by multiplying the statutory tax rate by the sum of interest expense, operating lease interest, variable lease interest, less the sum of interest income and other income. The statutory tax rates are reported in Exhibit 11.11.

Why use EBITA and not EBIT? After all, the same argument could be made for the amortization of acquired intangibles: they, too, have fixed lives and lose value over time. But the accounting for intangibles differs from the accounting for physical assets. Unlike capital expenditures, internally created intangible assets such as new customer lists and product brands are *expensed* and not capitalized. Thus, when the acquired intangible loses value and is replaced through additional investment internally, the reinvestment is *already* expensed, and the company is penalized twice in the same time period: once through amortization and a second time through reinvestment. Although not perfect, using EBITA is consistent with existing accounting rules.

Choosing which line items to include as operating expenses requires judgment. As a guiding principle, include ongoing expenses related to the company's core operations. One company we recently analyzed included an account for rationalizations on their income statement. Since rationalizations had been a consistent part of the company's expense structure and are likely to continue as the industry continues to mature, we kept them as operating expenses. Had they been a one-time expense, we would not have included them in EBITA and analyzed them separately. Chapter 21 provides a detailed discussion on the impact of one-time items.

Adjustments to EBITA   In some companies, certain nonoperating items may be embedded within operating expenses. To ensure your EBITDA calculation reflects only operating performance, carefully review the notes to identify and exclude any nonoperating items from operating expenses. Common nonoperating items include interest expenses embedded in operating leases and one-time restructuring charges hidden within the cost of sales or general expenses.

In Exhibit 11.10, we adjust EBITA for the interest embedded in operating and variable leases. No other adjustments are required, as Costco did not embed material one-time items in operating expenses.

Although one-time items embedded in operating expenses are not common, they can happen. UPS's decision to withdraw from a multiemployer pension plan in 2012 caused its "compensation and benefits" expense to spike that year. Since the withdrawal was a one-time event, it is better evaluated separately as a nonoperating expense and not embedded in operating income. Choosing whether an expense is one-time or ongoing requires judgment. Separating one-time items from ongoing expenses, however, highlights trends and opens the valuation discussion to future risks.

Operating Cash Taxes   As with other items on the income statement, taxes must be separated into operating and nonoperating components. Given the intricacies of the tax code, this adjustment process can be particularly complex. Chapter 20 goes into more detail about the specifics of the process, the reasoning behind it, and alternative ways to implement it. For now, we summarize the process.

To determine operating taxes, you will need the tax reconciliation table from the company's notes. Some companies report the tax reconciliation table in percent; others report the table in currency. In Chapter 20, we present how to estimate operating taxes using both reporting styles. The tax reconciliation table for Costco, presented in Exhibit 11.11, reports in currency (millions of dollars).

To estimate operating cash taxes, proceed in three steps:

1. Using the tax reconciliation table, determine the statutory tax rate. The statutory tax rate equals the tax rate paid on income. Multiply the statutory tax rate by adjusted EBITA to determine statutory taxes on adjusted EBITA.

EXHIBIT 11.11 **Costco: Tax Reconciliation Table**

$ million

	2019	2020	2021	2022	2023
Federal taxes at statutory rate	1,001	1,127	1,403	1,646	1,782
State taxes, net	171	190	243	267	302
Foreign taxes, net	(1)	92	92	231	160
Employee stock ownership plan (ESOP)	(18)	(24)	(21)	(23)	(25)
Special dividend related to 401(k) plan[1]	—	—	(70)	—	—
2017 tax act	(123)	—	—	—	—
Other	31	(77)	(46)	(196)	(24)
U.S. and foreign tax expense	1,061	1,308	1,601	1,925	2,195
Tax Rates[2], %					
Federal income tax rate	21.0	21.0	21.0	21.0	21.0
State income tax rate	3.6	3.5	3.6	3.4	3.6
Statutory tax rate	24.6	24.5	24.6	24.4	24.6

[1] Aggregated in the ESOP account in original filings.

[2] To determine each tax rate, divide each tax amount by earnings before taxes. Earnings before taxes are reported in Exhibit 11.9.

Source: Costco annual report, 2023, note 8, "Income Taxes."

2. Increase (or decrease) statutory taxes on EBITA by other operating taxes (or credits). To estimate other operating taxes, search the tax reconciliation table for ongoing, operating-related taxes other than statutory taxes. The most common operating tax is the difference between domestic and foreign tax rates. Sum the other rates deemed operating, and if the table is presented in percent, multiply the resulting summation of by earnings before taxes (EBT). Multiplying the percentages by EBT (not EBITA) converts the percentages found in the tax reconciliation table into a dollar-based adjustment.[8]

3. Convert accrual-based taxes into operating cash taxes. For companies that systematically defer taxes, accrual-based taxes will not properly represent cash taxes actually paid by the company. The simplest way to calculate operating cash taxes is to subtract the increase in operating deferred-tax liabilities (net of deferred-tax assets) from operating taxes. While the notes provide information on taxes that have been deferred, they do not separate operating from nonoperating deferred taxes, making the disclosure unusable. Not every company discloses enough information to separate operating deferred taxes, such as accelerated depreciation, from nonoperating deferred taxes, such as those related to prepaid pension assets. When the appropriate information is unavailable, we recommend using operating taxes without an adjustment to cash.

[8] When adjusting statutory taxes on EBITA for other operating items, we prefer to use dollar adjustments rather than percentage adjustments. This is because an artificially low "earnings before taxes" can distort the percentages in a significant way. For instance, when UPS withdrew from the multistate pension plan in 2012, adjustment percentages related to foreign tax savings were uncharacteristically large because of the smaller than usual EBT.

EXHIBIT 11.12 **Costco: Operating Cash Taxes**

$ million

	2019	2020	2021	2022	2023
Adjusted EBITA	4,849	5,531	6,789	7,891	8,217
× Statutory tax rate	24.6%	24.5%	24.6%	24.4%	24.6%
Statutory taxes on EBITA	1,193	1,357	1,673	1,925	2,018
Foreign taxes, net[1]	(1)	92	92	231	160
Employee stock ownership plan (ESOP)[1]	(18)	(24)	(21)	(23)	(25)
Operating taxes	1,174	1,425	1,744	2,133	2,153
Operating taxes deferred[2]	(228)	(131)	(198)	33	(89)
Operating cash taxes	946	1,294	1,546	2,166	2,064
Reported taxes					
Operating taxes	1,174	1,425	1,744	2,133	2,153
Taxes related to nonoperating accounts[3]	(21)	(40)	(27)	(12)	66
Other nonoperating taxes[4]	(92)	(77)	(116)	(196)	(24)
Income taxes, reported	1,061	1,308	1,601	1,925	2,195

[1] Reported in the tax reconciliation table presented in Exhibit 11.11.

[2] Computed as the increase (decrease) in operating deferred-tax assets, net of liabilities. Operating deferred taxes are reported in Exhibit 11.8.

[3] Estimated in Exhibit 11.10.

[4] Other nonoperating taxes include taxes related to the 2017 tax act and "other" taxes, reported in Exhibit 11.11.

To demonstrate the three-step process, we construct operating cash taxes for Costco in Exhibit 11.12. In 2023, the statutory tax rate for Costco was 24.6 percent. This value includes both federal taxes (21.0 percent) and state taxes (3.6 percent). To determine statutory taxes on EBITA, multiply the statutory tax rate (24.6 percent) by EBITA ($8,217 million), which was estimated in Exhibit 11.10. In 2023, statutory taxes on EBITA were $2,018 million.

Next, search the tax reconciliation table for other operating taxes. We classify foreign income taxed at rates different from the U.S. statutory rate ($160 million) and tax savings from the employee stock ownership plan ($25 million) as operating. In contrast, taxes related to the substantial change in U.S. corporate tax rates brought about by the 2017 Tax Cuts and Jobs Act are a one-time event. Therefore, treat them as nonoperating. To determine other operating taxes, sum across operating-related tax adjustments. In 2023, other operating taxes increased Costco's taxes on EBITA by $135 million. Summing statutory taxes on EBITA ($2,108 million) and other operating taxes ($135 million) leads to $2,153 million in operating taxes.

To convert operating taxes into operating cash taxes, add (subtract) the increase in *operating* deferred-tax assets (liabilities). As discussed in the section on invested capital, do not incorporate the change in nonoperating deferred taxes into cash taxes. Instead, value nonoperating deferred taxes as part of your valuation of the corresponding nonoperating account. For instance, future taxes on pension shortfalls should be computed using projected contributions, not the deferred-tax account on the balance sheet.

Exhibit 11.8 separates Costco's operating and nonoperating deferred taxes. Since operating deferred-tax assets net of liabilities decreased in 2023, Costco is paying less in cash taxes than reported using accrual accounting. In 2023, operating deferred-tax assets net of liabilities fell by $89 million. Therefore, operating taxes of $2,153 million are reduced by $89 million to estimate operating cash taxes at $2,064 million, as shown in Exhibit 11.12.[9]

Like other balance sheet accounts, operating deferred-tax accounts rise and fall for reasons other than deferrals, such as acquisitions, divestitures, and revaluations. However, only organic changes in deferred taxes should be included in operating cash taxes, not one-time changes resulting from revaluation or consolidation. For instance, most American companies revalued their 2018 deferred-tax accounts to reflect the 2017 Tax Cuts and Jobs Act. To estimate the organic change in deferred-tax assets and liabilities, estimate what the change would have been if tax rates had remained unchanged. In the case of Costco, the effect was immaterial.

For many companies, a clean measure of operating cash taxes may be impossible to calculate. When this is the case, use operating taxes without converting to cash.

Reconciliation of Reported Taxes   To reconcile NOPAT to net income, it is helpful to first reconcile operating taxes to reported taxes. At the bottom of Exhibit 11.12, we present a reconciliation of reported taxes. The reconciliation includes the taxes related to nonoperating accounts and other nonoperating taxes. Although the two accounts sound similar, they are estimated differently.

The taxes related to nonoperating accounts, which equal $66 million in 2023, are calculated by multiplying the statutory (marginal) tax rate by the sum of nonoperating accounts reported in the reconciliation of NOPAT presented in Exhibit 11.10. For Costco, nonoperating accounts include interest expense, lease interest, interest income, and other income. To determine other nonoperating taxes, search the tax reconciliation table presented in Exhibit 11.11 for nonoperating items, such as one-time audits and write-offs. To reconcile reported taxes in 2023, we classified the "other" tax adjustment as nonoperating because the account demonstrated no predictable pattern.

Note how the reconciliation ties to the reported income taxes on the income statement presented in Exhibit 11.9. Although reconciliation can be time consuming, it assures that the modeling has been carried out correctly.

Reconciliation to Net Income

To ensure that the reorganization is accurate, we recommend reconciling net income to NOPAT (see the lower half of Exhibit 11.10). To reconcile NOPAT, start with net income available to both common shareholders and

---

[9] In Appendix I, we forecast the operating cash tax rate as part of our valuation of Costco. Since the percentage of Costco's taxes that are deferred is volatile, we use a five-year average to estimate the percentage of operating taxes that are likely to be deferred.

noncontrolling interests, and add back the increase (or subtract the decrease) in operating deferred-tax liabilities. We label this amount adjusted net income.

Next, add any nonoperating charges (or subtract any nonoperating income) reported by the company, such as interest expense and other non-operating expenses. After this, include any supplemental adjustments that have been made, including adjustments for the interest embedded in leases and, if required for older statements, the nonoperating portion of the pension expense. Finally, subtract tax shields on the nonoperating expenses calculated previously and add any nonoperating taxes from the tax reconciliation table. Whether NOPAT is estimated using revenues less expenses or alternatively as net income plus nonoperating items and other adjustments, the result should be identical.

Free Cash Flow: In Practice

Once the financial statements are reorganized into NOPAT and invested capital, the next step is to estimate free cash flow. However, this calculation requires more than just the income statement and balance sheet; the statement of shareholders' equity is also necessary. Exhibit 11.13 presents the statement of shareholders' equity for Costco. This statement reconciles the income statement with the balance sheet and presents additional information required to estimate free cash flow and cash flow available to investors. Free cash flow is defined as follows:

$$FCF = NOPAT + Noncash\ Operating\ Expenses - Investments\ in\ Invested\ Capital$$

Exhibit 11.14 presents the free cash flow calculation for Costco and reconciles free cash flow to cash flow available to investors. To create free cash flow, start with NOPAT and add back noncash expenses, such as

EXHIBIT 11.13 **Costco: Statement of Shareholders' Equity**

$ million

	2019	2020	2021	2022	2023
Equity, beginning of year	12,799	15,243	18,284	17,564	20,642
Net income	3,659	4,002	5,007	5,844	6,292
Foreign-currency translation adjustment	(237)	139	160	(686)	24
Comprehensive income	3,422	4,141	5,167	5,158	6,316
Stock-based compensation, net release	326	291	356	365	475
Acquisition of noncontrolling interest	—	—	—	(505)	—
Repurchases of common stock	(247)	(198)	(495)	(442)	(677)
Cash dividends	(1,057)	(1,193)	(5,748)	(1,498)	(1,698)
Equity, end of year	15,243	18,284	17,564	20,642	25,058

Note: Costco shareholders' equity excludes noncontrolling interests

EXHIBIT 11.14 **Costco: Free Cash Flow and Cash Flow to Investors**

$ million

	2020	2021	2022	2023
NOPAT	4,237	5,243	5,725	6,154
Depreciation	1,645	1,781	1,900	2,077
Gross cash flow	5,882	7,024	7,625	8,231
Decrease (Increase) in working capital	1,920	763	(1,845)	1,407
Capital expenditures[1]	(2,810)	(3,588)	(3,891)	(4,323)
Decrease (Increase) in operating leases	(641)	(102)	116	61
Decrease (Increase) in variable leases	(963)	(512)	8	62
Decrease (Increase) in finance leases	(592)	(408)	(620)	295
Decrease (Increase) in goodwill	(935)	(8)	3	(1)
Decrease (Increase) in other assets, net of liabilities	(185)	(18)	(284)	88
Free cash flow	**1,676**	**3,151**	**1,112**	**5,820**
Interest income	89	41	61	470
Other income	3	102	144	63
Taxes related to nonoperating accounts	40	27	12	(66)
Other nonoperating taxes	77	116	196	24
Decrease (Increase) in excess cash	(3,580)	1,713	1,747	(3,878)
Decrease (Increase) in tax credit carryforward	(36)	(45)	(55)	(49)
Unexplained foreign-currency translation[2]	387	282	151	232
Cash flow to investors	(1,343)	5,387	3,368	2,615
Reconciliation of cash flow to investors				
Interest expense	160	171	158	160
Operating lease interest	96	60	65	67
Variable lease interest	—	21	33	36
Decrease (Increase) in debt	(786)	118	934	99
Decrease (Increase) in operating lease liabilities	(642)	(75)	143	75
Decrease (Increase) in variable lease liabilities	(963)	(512)	8	62
Decrease (Increase) in finance lease liabilities	(267)	(364)	(576)	196
Cash flow to debt and debt equivalents	(2,401)	(581)	765	695
Dividends	1,193	5,748	1,498	1,698
Repurchases of common stock	198	495	442	677
Shares issued for stock-based compensation, net[3]	(291)	(356)	(365)	(475)
Payments to (Investments in) noncontrolling interests[4]	(23)	(21)	1,085	5
Nonoperating deferred income taxes	(19)	102	(57)	15
Cash flow to equity and equity equivalents	1,058	5,968	2,603	1,920
Cash flow to investors	(1,343)	5,387	3,368	2,615

[1] Capital expenditures are reported on the statement of cash flows.

[2] In 2023, the unexplained foreign-currency adjustment equals the foreign-currency translation adjustment of $24 million reported in Exhibit 11.13 plus the unexplained changes to property, plant, and equipment (PP&E) of $208 million estimated in Exhibit 11.15.

[3] Includes stock-based compensation and stock options exercised, net of the release of vested restricted stock units.

[4] Equals net income to nonconsolidated interests minus (plus) the increase (decrease) in noncontrolling interests.

depreciation and depletion. From gross cash flow, subtract investments in working capital, capital expenditures, and investments in other long-term operating assets net of liabilities. Each of these components is discussed in detail below.

Gross Cash Flow   Gross cash flow represents the cash operating profits that the company generates. It represents the cash available for investment and investor payout without the company having to sell nonoperating assets, such as excess cash, or to raise additional capital. Gross cash flow has two components:

1. *NOPAT.* As previously defined, net operating profit after taxes is the after-tax operating profit available to all investors.

2. *Noncash operating expenses.* Some expenses embedded in NOPAT are noncash and represent the economic decay of past investments. To convert NOPAT into cash flow, add back depreciation, depletion, and amortization of capitalized assets. Only add back amortization deducted from revenues to compute NOPAT, such as the amortization of capitalized software or purchased customer contracts. Do not add back the amortization from acquired intangibles and impairments to NOPAT; they were not subtracted from revenue in calculating NOPAT. Another major noncash expense is share-based employee compensation. Although noncash, do not add back share-based compensation to NOPAT to determine gross cash flow. Since employees have a new claim on cash flows, this claim must be incorporated into the valuation, either as part of cash flow or as a separate calculation. (Share-based employee compensation is discussed in Chapter 16.)

Investments in Invested Capital   To maintain and grow their operations, companies must reinvest a portion of their gross cash flow back into the business. To determine free cash flow, subtract gross investment from gross cash flow. We segment gross investment into five primary areas:

1. *Change in operating working capital.* Growing a business requires investment in operating cash, inventory, and other components of working capital. Operating working capital excludes nonoperating assets, such as excess cash, and financing items, such as short-term debt and dividends payable.

2. *Capital expenditures, net of disposals.* Capital expenditures represent investments in property, plant, and equipment (PP&E), less the book value of any PP&E sold. One way to estimate net capital expenditures is to add depreciation to the increase in net PP&E.[10] Do not estimate

---

[10] If possible, use capital expenditures reported in the accounting statement of cash flows, but only after reconciling reported capital expenditures with the change of net PP&E plus depreciation. Capital expenditures can differ from net PP&E plus depreciation because of currency translations (discussed later in this section), acquisitions, and impairments. Acquisitions should be analyzed separately, and impairments should be treated as a nonoperating noncash expense in the income statement.

capital expenditures by taking the change in gross PP&E. Since gross PP&E drops when companies retire assets, the change in gross PP&E will often understate the actual amount of capital expenditures.

3. *Change in leases.* To keep the definitions of NOPAT and invested capital consistent with free cash flow, include the change in right-of-use assets, financial leases, and capitalized variable leases in gross investment. Additional details on leases are discussed later in the chapter.

4. *Investment in goodwill and acquired intangibles.* For acquired intangible assets, where cumulative amortization has been added back, you can estimate investment by computing the change in net goodwill and acquired intangibles. For intangible assets that are being amortized, use the same method as for determining net capital expenditures (by adding amortization to the increase in net intangibles).

5. *Change in other long-term operating assets net of long-term liabilities.* Subtract investments in other net operating assets. As with invested capital, do not confuse other long-term operating assets with other long-term non-operating assets, such as equity investments and excess pension assets. Changes in nonoperating assets need to be evaluated—but should be analyzed separately.

For most assets and liabilities, the year-to-year change in a balance sheet account will suitably approximate net investment. This will not always be the case. Currency translations, acquisitions, write-offs, and accounting changes also can impact the change in a financial account across years. For example, companies translate foreign balance sheets into their home currencies, so changes in accounts will capture both true investments (which involve cash) and currency-based restatements (which are merely accounting adjustments and not the flow of cash into or out of the company). If a particular account is a significant part of cash flow, use the cash flow statement and notes from the annual report to better understand the year-to-year change in the account.

Exhibit 11.15 deconstructs the change in property, plant, and equipment for Costco. Capital expenditures and asset dispositions are reported in the accountant's cash flow statement. To estimate depreciation, start with depreciation and amortization from the cash flow statement and subtract amortization of acquired intangibles, often found in the note on goodwill and intangible assets. (In the case of Costco, no information on amortization is presented in their annual report.) The remaining line items either came from the management discussion and analysis section in Costco's annual reports or, when not disclosed, are our estimates.

It is not always possible to eliminate the currency effects for each line item on the balance sheet. If this is the case, adjust aggregate free cash flow for currency effects using the balance sheet account titled foreign-currency translation, which under U.S. GAAP and IFRS is found within the statement

EXHIBIT 11.15 **Costco: Changes in Property, Plant, and Equipment**

$ million

	2019	2020	2021	2022	2023
Property, plant, and equipment, beginning of year	19,681	20,890	21,807	23,492	24,646
Capital expenditures[1]	2,998	2,810	3,588	3,891	4,323
Depreciation[1]	(1,492)	(1,645)	(1,781)	(1,900)	(2,077)
Unexplained changes, including currency translation[2]	(297)	(248)	(122)	(837)	(208)
Property, plant, and equipment, end of year	20,890	21,807	23,492	24,646	26,684

[1] Reported in the statement of cash flows.

[2] Calculated as the unexplained difference between beginning and end of year.

of accumulated other comprehensive income. Unfortunately, the balance sheet account reports the aggregate effect across *all* foreign assets and liabilities, not just operating items. If you believe most currency adjustments are related to operating items, add the increase in the currency translation account to determine free cash flow. Consider the situation where inventory is rising on the balance sheet due to currency changes and not investment. To balance the balance sheet, the company increases the currency translation account within equity. Since the increase in inventory overstates actual investment in inventory, adding the increase in foreign-currency translation back to free cash flow undoes the negative cash flow caused by currency translation. For Costco, we classify the unexplained currency translations as nonoperating.

Cash Flow Available to Investors

Although not included in free cash flow, cash flows related to nonoperating assets are valuable in their own right. They must be evaluated and valued separately and then added to free cash flow to give the total cash flow available to investors:

$$\begin{matrix} \text{Present Value} & & \text{Value of} & & \text{Total Value} \\ \text{of Company's} & + & \text{Nonoperating} & = & \text{of} \\ \text{Free Cash Flow} & & \text{Assets} & & \text{Enterprise} \end{matrix}$$

To reconcile free cash flow with total cash flow available to investors, include the following nonoperating cash flows:

- *Nonoperating income and expenses.* Unless you can simplify your reconciliation by netting the account directly against a change in a corresponding asset or liability (because it is noncash), include nonoperating income and expenses in total cash flow available to investors, not in free cash flow.
- *Nonoperating taxes.* Include nonoperating taxes in total cash flow available to investors. Nonoperating taxes include taxes related to nonoperating items and other nonoperating taxes disclosed in the tax reconciliation table.
- *Cash flow related to excess cash and marketable securities.* Subtract the increase (or add the decrease) in excess cash and marketable securities to compute

total cash flow available to investors. If the company reports unrecognized gains and losses related to marketable securities in its statement of other comprehensive income, net the gain or loss against the change computed previously.

- *Cash flow from other nonoperating assets.* Repeat the process used for excess cash and marketable securities for other nonoperating assets. When possible, combine nonoperating gains and losses from a particular asset with changes in that nonoperating asset.

Reconciling Cash Flow Available to Investors

Cash flow available to investors should be identical to the company's total financing flow. By modeling cash flow to and from investors, you will catch mistakes otherwise missed. Financial flows include flows related to debt, debt equivalents, and equity:

- *Interest expenses.* Interest from both traditional debt and operating leases should be treated as a financing flow.

- *Debt issues and repayments.* The change in debt represents the net borrowing or repayment on all the company's interest-bearing debt, including short-term debt, long-term debt, and leases. All changes in debt should be included in the reconciliation of total funds invested, not in free cash flow.

- *Change in debt equivalents.* Since accrued pension liabilities and accrued postretirement medical liabilities are considered debt equivalents (see Chapter 23 for more on issues related to pensions and other postretirement benefits), their changes should be treated as a financing flow.[11]

- *Dividends.* Dividends include all cash dividends on common and preferred shares. Dividends paid in stock have no cash effects and should be ignored.

- *Share issues and repurchases.* When new equity is issued or shares are repurchased, four accounts will be affected: common stock, additional paid-in capital, treasury shares, and retained earnings (for shares that are retired). Although different transactions will have varying effects on the individual accounts, only the aggregate matters, not how the individual accounts are affected. Exhibit 11.14 refers to the aggregate change as "Repurchases of common stock."

- *Outflows to nonconsolidated subsidiaries.* Income attributable to nonconsolidated subsidiaries, found at the bottom of the income statement, is a financing flow, similar to dividends.

---

[11] Pensions will affect many accounts, including the pension expense on the income statement, pension assets, pension liabilities, and deferred taxes.

ADVANCED ISSUES

In this section, we summarize a set of the most common advanced topics in reorganizing a company's financial statements, including nonoperating charges and restructuring reserves, leases, pensions, and capitalized research and development (R&D). We provide only a brief summary of these topics here, as each one is discussed in depth in the chapters of Part Three, "Advanced Valuation Techniques."

Nonoperating Charges and Restructuring Reserves   Provisions are non-cash expenses that reflect future costs or expected losses. Companies record provisions by reducing current income and setting up a corresponding reserve as a liability (or deducting the amount from the relevant asset).

For the purpose of analyzing and valuing a company, we categorize provisions into one of four types: ongoing operating provisions, long-term operating provisions, nonoperating restructuring provisions, and provisions created for the purpose of smoothing income (transferring income from one period to another). Based on the characteristics of each provision, adjust the financial statements to reflect the company's true operating performance:

- *Ongoing operating provisions.* Operating provisions such as product warranties are part of operations. Therefore, deduct the provision from revenue to determine NOPAT, and deduct the corresponding reserve from net operating assets to determine invested capital.

- *Long-term operating provisions.* For certain liabilities, such as expected plant decommissioning costs, deduct the operating portion from revenue to determine NOPAT, and treat the interest portion as nonoperating. Treat the corresponding reserve as a debt equivalent.

- *Nonoperating provisions.* Unless deemed as ongoing, provisions such as one-time restructuring charges related to severance are nonoperating. Treat the expense as nonoperating and the corresponding reserve as a debt equivalent.

The process of adjusting for provisions is explained in greater detail and illustrated with examples in Chapter 21.

Leases

Starting in 2019, new accounting rules related to leases went into effect, leading to the reclassification of leases into three categories: finance, operating, and variable leases.[12] Previously known as capital leases, finance leases retain their

---

[12] The International Accounting Standards Board (IASB) published IFRS 16, "Leases," in January 2016, and the Financial Accounting Standards Board (FASB) issued Accounting Standards Update (ASU) 2016-02, "Leases" (Topic 842), in February 2016.

existing accounting treatment; their value is capitalized, with rental expenses divided between interest and depreciation.

The most significant rule change affects operating leases. Under both GAAP and IFRS, the present value of lease payments is now recognized on the balance sheet. GAAP mandates that lease payments be expensed as operating items, whereas IFRS reallocates the interest embedded in the rental payment as a financial expense. Variable leases, which adjust based on market conditions, do not appear on the balance sheet; their payments are also expensed as operating items when incurred.

Chapter 22 provides a detailed example of how leases are accounted for in financial statements, how to adjust the financial statements for better comparability, and how to incorporate leases into an enterprise DCF valuation. For now, here's a summary of the reorganization process:

- *Finance leases.* The accounting for finance leases follows the principles for traditional debt, so no special treatment is necessary.

- *Operating leases.* Operating leases are now capitalized as a right-of-use asset, with a corresponding liability titled "operating lease liabilities." These liabilities may be embedded in other accounts, so it is important to consult the notes for their exact location. For companies reporting under GAAP, one should reclassify embedded interest as a financial expense. The appropriate interest rate for leases will be disclosed in the notes.

- *Variable leases.* Disclosure for variable leases remains limited, making capitalization challenging. To determine the value of variable leases relative to that of operating leases, base your estimate on proportional rental expenses. If deciding to capitalize variable leases, reclassify embedded interest as a financial expense and deduct their value from enterprise value to determine equity value.

To assess and value leases for Costco, start by searching the balance sheet and notes for right-of-use assets, finance lease assets, operating lease liabilities, and finance lease liabilities. Because Costco aggregates finance lease assets under other long-term assets in its original filings, searching the notes is required. Exhibit 11.4 displays each account as a separate line item on an expanded balance sheet, while Exhibit 11.5 reorganizes the accounts into categories of invested capital and debt equivalents. To estimate the value of variable lease assets in 2023, multiply the right-of-use assets ($2,713 million) by the ratio of variable lease expense ($160 million) to operating lease expense ($309 million).

Exhibit 11.10 presents an estimate of NOPAT for Costco adjusted for operating and variable leases. To estimate operating profit, increase EBITA by the amount of estimated lease interest. For 2023, we estimate operating lease interest ($67 million) by multiplying 2022 operating lease liabilities ($2,721 million) by the weighted average discount rate for leases (2.47 percent) as provided in the Costco note on leases. This process is repeated for variable leases.

While capitalizing operating leases improves the quality of benchmarking, whether or not you capitalize will not affect intrinsic value as long as it is incorporated correctly in free cash flow, the cost of capital, and debt equivalents. Chapter 22 demonstrates how to incorporate operating leases throughout the valuation. The chapter also discusses alternative models to value operating leases.

Retirement Obligations Such as Pensions

Defined-benefit plans, such as pensions and other retiree benefits, are often underfunded. Companies must report the present value of any pension shortfalls (and excess pension assets) on their balance sheets.[13] Since excess pension assets do not generate operating profits, nor do pension shortfalls fund operations, pension accounts should not be included in invested capital. Instead, pension assets should be treated as nonoperating assets, and pension shortfalls as a debt equivalent (and both should be valued separately from operations). If pension accounts are not explicitly detailed on the company's balance sheet, search the pension footnote to determine where they are embedded. Often excess pension assets are embedded in other assets, and unfunded pension liabilities are in other liabilities.

Reporting rules under IFRS (IAS 19) differ slightly in that companies can postpone recognition of their unfunded pension obligations resulting from changes in actuarial assumptions, but only as long as the cumulative unrecognized gain or loss does not exceed 10 percent of the obligations. For companies reporting under IFRS, search the notes for the current value of obligations.

On the income statement, current accounting rules for pensions dictate that only service cost—the new benefits promised to employees for service rendered in a given year—be included in operating expenses such as cost of goods sold.[14] The remaining items, such as expected return on assets and interest cost on the liabilities, are now included as nonoperating income or expense. For years prior to 2018, an adjustment is still required.

Since Costco does not provide defined-benefit pension plans to employees, we do not adjust the company's historical statements. Chapter 23 provides details on how to adjust NOPAT for pensions and how to factor under- or overfunded pensions into a company's value.

---

[13] From December 2006, FASB Statement 158 eliminated pension smoothing on the balance sheet. Companies are now required to report excess pension assets and unfunded pension obligations on the balance sheet at their current values, not as smoothed values as in the past.

[14] The FASB published ASU 2017-07, "Compensation—Retirement Benefits (Topic 715): Improving the Presentation of Net Periodic Pension Cost and Net Periodic Postretirement Benefit Cost," on March 10, 2017. IFRS already separates service cost from financial performance in pensions.

Capitalized Research and Development

In line with the conservative principles of accounting, accountants expense R&D, advertising, and certain other costs in their entirety in the period when they are incurred, even when economic benefits resulting from such expenses continue beyond the current reporting period.[15] This practice can dramatically understate invested capital and overstate return on capital for some companies. Therefore, you should consider whether it would be effective to capitalize and amortize R&D and other quasi investments in a manner like that used for capital expenditures. Equity should be adjusted correspondingly to balance the invested-capital equation.

If you decide to capitalize R&D, do *not* deduct the reported R&D expense from revenue to calculate operating profit. Instead, deduct the amortization associated with past R&D investments, using a reasonable amortization schedule. Since amortization is based on past investments (versus expense, which is based on current outlays), this approach will prevent reductions in R&D from driving short-term improvements in ROIC.

Since tax laws are constantly changing and vary across countries, review local tax laws to ensure that free cash flow accurately reflects governing tax policy. For example, while financial statements prepared under GAAP necessitate expensing of R&D, U.S. tax law has mandated amortization since 2022. Consequently, taxes will likely be higher than reported, particularly for companies with significant R&D expenses.

Whether or not you capitalize certain expenses will not affect computed value; it will affect only the timing of ROIC and economic profit. Chapter 24 analyzes the complete valuation process for R&D-intensive companies, including adjustments to free cash flow and value.

Other Advanced Adjustments

Some companies may have industry-specific items that require adjustment. These adjustments arise from an uncommon line item on the income statement or balance sheet and, given their rarity, require thoughtful judgment based on the economic principles of this book.

Consider an example from FedEx. In 2013, the company sold aircraft to another company and leased the aircraft back. This transaction is commonly known as a sale-leaseback. If a gain arises from the sale, the company cannot recognize the gain as income but instead must lower the annual rental expense over the life of the contract. Since the gain is collected in cash but retained earnings do not rise, a liability for deferred gains is recognized.

---

[15] One exception to this conservatism is the development of software. Although software is an intangible asset, both GAAP and IFRS accounting allow for certain software investments to be capitalized and amortized over the life of the asset.

Should the liability for deferred gains be treated as operating and deducted from operating assets to determine invested capital, or should it be classified as a debt or equity equivalent? From a valuation perspective, it doesn't matter how you choose to classify the account, as long as it is treated consistently throughout your analysis. It will, however, have an impact on our perceptions about return on invested capital and ultimately value creation. Accounting rules prevent a one-year spike in income caused by a financial transaction, but we believe the downward distortion in future rental expense is worse, since this lower rental expense is noncash and could distort the perceived cost of new leases. Therefore, we would undo the transaction entirely, treat the gain as a one-time item, and recognize the deferred-gain account as an equity equivalent.

Not every advanced issue will lead to material differences in ROIC, growth, and free cash flow. Before collecting extra data and estimating required unknowns, decide whether the adjustment will further your understanding of a company and its industry. An unnecessarily complex model can sometimes obscure the underlying economics that would be obvious in a simple model. Remember, the goal of financial analysis is to provide a strong context for good financial decision making and robust forecasting, not to create an overly engineered model that deftly handles unimportant adjustments.

12

Analyzing Performance

Understanding a company's past is essential to forecasting its future, so a thorough analysis of historical performance is a critical component of valuation. Always begin with the core elements of value creation: return on invested capital (ROIC) and revenue growth. Examine trends in the company's long-run performance and its performance relative to that of its peers, so you can base your forecasts of future cash flows on reasonable assumptions about the company's key value drivers.

Start by analyzing ROIC, with and without goodwill. ROIC with goodwill measures the company's ability to create value over and above premiums paid for acquisitions. ROIC without goodwill is a better like-for-like measure of the company's operating performance compared with that of its peers. In your analysis, be sure to drill down into the components of ROIC—operating margin and capital productivity—to arrive at an integrated view of the company's operating performance and understand which aspects of the business are responsible for its overall performance.

Next, examine what drives revenue growth. Does revenue growth stem, for instance, more from organic growth or from currency effects, which are largely beyond management control and probably not sustainable? Finally, assess the company's financial health to determine whether it has the financial resources to conduct business and make investments for growth. By systematically analyzing these elements, you can develop a solid foundation for valuation that links the company's historical performance to its future potential.

ANALYZING RETURNS ON INVESTED CAPITAL

Always begin the benchmarking process by reorganizing the financial statements into operating, nonoperating, and financial accounts. Chapter 11 showed how to reorganize the income statement into net operating profit after taxes (NOPAT) and the balance sheet into invested capital. ROIC measures the ratio of NOPAT to invested capital:

$$ROIC = \frac{NOPAT}{Invested\ Capital}$$

Since profit is measured over an entire year, whereas capital is measured only at one point in time, we recommend using the average of starting and ending invested capital when benchmarking.[1] If the business is highly seasonal and the amount of capital measured is unrepresentative at the fiscal year-end, consider using quarterly averages.

ROIC is a better analytical tool than return on equity (ROE) or return on assets (ROA) for understanding the company's performance because it focuses solely on a company's operations. ROE mixes operating performance with capital structure, making peer group analysis and trend analysis less insightful. ROA—even when calculated on a pre-interest basis—is an inadequate measure of performance because it includes nonoperating assets and ignores the benefits of accounts payable and other operating liabilities that together reduce the amount of capital required from investors.

As an example of using ROIC to assess performance, Exhibit 12.1 plots ROIC for Costco and the median of a competitive peer group from 2019 to 2023, based on the NOPAT and invested-capital calculations presented in Chapter 11.[2] Costco has consistently earned higher returns on invested capital than its peers. This gap widened in the aftermath of the COVID-19 pandemic, as Costco continued to deliver strong returns while many of its peers struggled to maintain their performance. Later, we'll demonstrate how Costco's superior ROIC stems from its volume-driven strategy, generating a higher level of sales for each dollar of capital deployed.

Analyzing ROIC with and without Goodwill and Acquired Intangibles

ROIC should be computed with and without goodwill and acquired intangibles. In our analysis, we treat goodwill identically to acquired intangibles.[3] Therefore, we often shorten the expression *goodwill and acquired intangibles* to simply *goodwill.*

---

[1] Exercise caution when comparing companies that present their own ROIC calculations. Companies reporting ROIC in their annual reports may compute it using starting invested capital, ending capital, or the average of the two.

[2] Costco's fiscal year ends on the Sunday closest to August 31, so its 2023 fiscal year ended on September 3, 2023. In contrast, members of the peer group close their fiscal year in January or February of the following year.

[3] To be classified as an acquired intangible, the asset must be separable and identifiable, as in the case of patents. Goodwill describes assets that are not separable or identifiable. Acquired intangibles are amortized over the life of the asset, whereas goodwill is impaired if value falls below book value. Since we analyze the two accounts in the same manner, we do not make a distinction.

EXHIBIT 12.1 **Costco vs. Peer Group: Return on Invested Capital**

ROIC,[1] %

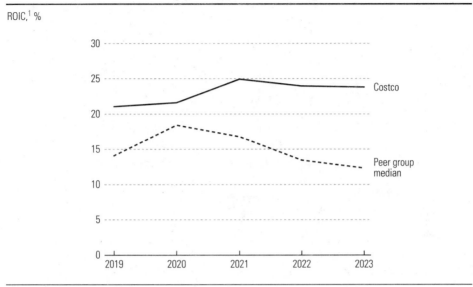

[1] Return on invested capital, measured on average capital without goodwill and acquired intangibles.

The reason to compute ROIC with and without goodwill is that each ratio analyzes different things. ROIC with goodwill measures whether the company has earned adequate returns for shareholders, factoring in the price paid for acquisitions. ROIC without goodwill measures the underlying operating performance of a company. It tells you whether the underlying economics generate ROIC above the cost of capital. It can be used to compare a company's performance against that of peers and to analyze trends. It is not affected by the price premiums paid for acquisitions. ROIC without goodwill is also more relevant for projecting future cash flows and setting strategy. A company does not need to spend more on acquisitions to grow organically, so ROIC without goodwill is a more relevant baseline for forecasting cash flows. Finally, companies that have a high ROIC without goodwill will likely create more value from growth, while companies that have low ROIC without goodwill typically create more value by improving ROIC.

Costco doesn't have much goodwill, having grown mostly organically, but for companies that make significant acquisitions, the difference between ROIC with and without goodwill can be large. Exhibit 12.2 highlights ROIC with and without goodwill for one luxury goods manufacturer that undertook a significant acquisition of another brand between year 1 and year 2. Since both companies had similar returns on capital, the acquirer's ROIC without goodwill remained relatively stable before and after the transaction. However, ROIC with goodwill experienced a sharp decline, falling from 24.2 percent to 12.0 percent after the acquisition.

Does this drop in ROIC with goodwill indicate that the acquisition destroyed value? Not necessarily. The advantages of acquisitions, such as cost

EXHIBIT 12.2 **Return on Invested Capital Following Acquisition**

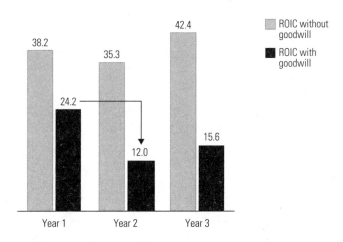

ROIC, %

savings and cross-selling opportunities, often require time to fully materialize. Furthermore, gaining access to the acquired brand's younger customer base could provide a valuable opportunity to drive growth in the acquirer's existing product lines, contributing to long-term value creation.

Accurately evaluating ROIC with goodwill leads to a second challenge: ROIC may increase even without improvements to the underlying business. We've seen situations where a business unit submitted a new strategic plan saying it expected to improve its ROIC over time. On the surface, its forecast looked impressive, but we then discovered that the ROIC included goodwill, and the expected improvement in ROIC would be caused solely by goodwill remaining constant as the business grew profits organically. The management team would earn accolades for improving ROIC purely as a result of the accounting for goodwill, not an underlying improvement to the business.

Decomposing ROIC to Develop an Integrated Perspective of Company Economics

To show how to analyze a company's economics based on decomposition of its ROIC, we return to the example of Costco and its peers. Costco has consistently earned a higher ROIC than its peers. But what caused this difference in performance? To understand which elements of a company's business are driving the company's ROIC, split apart the ratio as follows:

$$\text{ROIC} = (1 - \text{Operating Cash Tax Rate}) \times \frac{\text{EBITA}}{\text{Revenues}} \times \frac{\text{Revenues}}{\text{Invested Capital}}$$

This is one of the most powerful equations in financial analysis. It demonstrates the extent to which a company's ROIC is driven by its ability to maximize profitability (EBITA divided by revenues, or the operating margin), optimize capital turnover (measured by revenues over invested capital), or reduce operating taxes.

Each of these components can be further disaggregated so that each expense and capital item can be analyzed, line item by line item. Exhibit 12.3 shows how the components can be organized into a tree. On the right side of the tree are operational financial ratios, the drivers of value over which managers have the most control. Reading from right to left, each subsequent box for Costco is a function of the boxes to its right. For example, operating margin equals 100 percent less the ratios of cost of sales to revenues and selling and general expenses to revenues. Pretax ROIC equals operating margin times capital turnover (revenues divided by invested capital), and so on.

Once you have calculated the historical drivers of ROIC, compare them with the ROIC drivers of other companies in the same industry. You can then weigh this perspective against your analysis of the industry structure

EXHIBIT 12.3 **Costco vs. Peer Group: ROIC Tree, 2023**

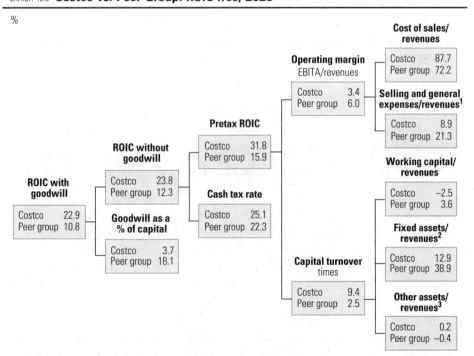

Note: Capital accounts are measured using a 2-year average. Costco's ROIC excluding goodwill and using beginning-of-year capital was 23.9%.

[1] Selling and general expenses include depreciation and add-back for embedded lease interest.

[2] Fixed assets include property, plant, and equipment and leased assets.

[3] Other assets, net of other liabilities.

(opportunities for differentiation, barriers to entry or exit, etc.) and a qualitative assessment of the company's strengths and weaknesses.

To illustrate, let's examine the difference between Costco and its peers. In 2023, Costco's ROIC with goodwill equaled 22.9 percent, compared with its peers' median of 10.8 percent. The difference is somewhat smaller without goodwill. You might ask what drives Costco's higher ROIC. Costco has an unusual business model for a retailer. It doesn't mark up its costs as much as other retailers, leading to a higher cost of sales relative to revenues. It makes up for that with lower selling and general expenses. For example, its cost to stock shelves is lower than that of its peers because it doesn't put items on the shelves individually but instead uses the manufacturers' containers. Costco also sells larger bundles of its products with a smaller assortment to manage. Despite the significantly lower selling and general expenses, it still ends up with a lower operating profit margin (3.4 percent, versus 6.0 percent). It makes up for this with higher capital productivity—primarily much lower fixed assets relative to "sales" due to its volume-driven warehouse format.

Line Item Analysis   A comprehensive valuation model will convert every line item in the company's financial statements into some type of common size ratio. For the income statement, most items are taken as a percentage of sales. (Exceptions exist: operating cash taxes, for instance, should be calculated as a percentage of pretax operating profits, not as a percentage of sales.)

For the balance sheet, each line item can also be taken as a percentage of revenues (or as a percentage of cost of goods sold for inventories and payables, to avoid distortion caused by changing prices). For operating current assets and liabilities, you can also convert each line item into days, using the following formula:

$$\text{Days} = 365 \times \frac{\text{Balance Sheet Item}}{\text{Revenues}}$$

If the business is seasonal, operating ratios such as inventories should be calculated using quarterly data. The differences can be quite substantial.

The use of days lends itself to a simple operational interpretation. How much cash is tied up in the business, and for how long? In 2023, Costco had only 29.7 days of inventory, versus 74.2 for its peers (Exhibit 12.4). In other words, products at Costco move more quickly through distribution and off store shelves than they do at its competitors. Costco also has lower accounts payable days (30.3 versus 44.7 in 2023). This means it pays its suppliers faster, perhaps to get better prices. All told, Costco pays its suppliers and other stakeholders more slowly than it collects from customers, resulting in negative working capital—a key aspect of its lean, volume-driven business model.

EXHIBIT 12.4 **Costco vs. Peer Group: Working Capital in Days**

Number of days in revenue[1]

	Costco			Peer group		
	2021	2022	2023	2021	2022	2023
Operating cash	6.8	6.8	7.1	7.0	6.5	6.1
Accounts receivable, net	3.1	3.3	3.4	2.6	3.0	2.9
Inventory[2]	28.3	29.4	29.7	67.3	72.9	74.2
Other current assets	2.2	2.3	2.4	2.8	2.0	2.4
Operating current assets[3]	36.7	38.1	38.9	59.7	63.2	65.4
Accounts payable[2]	32.6	31.2	30.3	50.9	47.0	44.7
Accrued salaries and benefits	7.2	6.8	6.5	3.8	3.5	3.5
Other current liabilities[4]	13.7	13.8	14.8	11.1	11.1	11.0
Operating current liabilities[3]	49.2	48.1	47.9	50.1	47.7	45.8
Working capital	(12.5)	(9.9)	(9.0)	9.6	15.5	19.6

[1] Measured using a 2-year average of the working capital account.

[2] Days in inventory and accounts payable computed using cost of sales, rather than revenues.

[3] Operating current assets and operating current liabilities do not equal the sum of individual accounts. Instead, they are denoted in days of revenue.

[4] Other current liabilities for Costco includes accrued member rewards and deferred membership fees.

Operating Analysis Using Nonfinancial Drivers

In an external analysis, benchmarking ratios are often confined to financial performance. If you are working from inside a company, however, or if the company releases operating data, you should link operating drivers directly to return on invested capital. By evaluating the operating drivers, you can better assess whether any differences in financial performance between competitors are sustainable.

Take, for example, airlines, which are required for safety reasons to release a tremendous amount of operating data. Exhibit 12.5 presents the financial and operating data for two airlines we'll refer to as Airline A and Airline B. Operating statistics include the number of employees, measured using full-time equivalents, and available seat-miles (ASMs), the standard measurement of passenger capacity for U.S. airlines.

Exhibit 12.6 transforms the data presented in Exhibit 12.5 into the operating-margin branch on the ROIC tree. Both airlines faced substantial challenges during the global pandemic, yet by 2023, only Airline A had achieved a full recovery. With an operating margin of 10.7 percent, Airline A far outpaced Airline B's modest 0.8 percent. To understand the factors driving this disparity, let's delve deeper into the underlying causes.

For airlines, operating margin is driven by three primary accounts: labor expenses, aircraft fuel, and other expenses. At first glance, it appears that Airline A has a significant advantage over Airline B in labor costs. Labor expenses as a percentage of revenues average 27.9 percent for Airline A and 32.2 percent for Airline B. But this statistic is misleading. To

EXHIBIT 12.5 **Airline A and Airline B: Financial and Operating Statistics**

$ million

	Airline A			Airline B		
	2021	2022	2023	2021	2022	2023
Revenues	17,244	31,469	37,602	8,452	12,821	13,461
Salaries and related costs	(6,792)	(8,141)	(10,499)	(3,348)	(3,901)	(4,338)
Aircraft fuel and related taxes	(3,971)	(9,048)	(8,729)	(1,982)	(4,285)	(3,754)
Other operating expenses	(9,317)	(12,171)	(14,361)	(4,292)	(4,748)	(5,267)
Operating profit	(2,836)	2,108	4,013	(1,170)	(112)	102
Operating statistics						
Available seat-miles, millions	128,652	178,458	209,760	77,923	92,844	98,636
Employees, full-time equivalent	56,347	62,176	69,211	23,395	25,172	28,555

EXHIBIT 12.6 **Operating Drivers of Labor Expenses to Revenues, 2023**

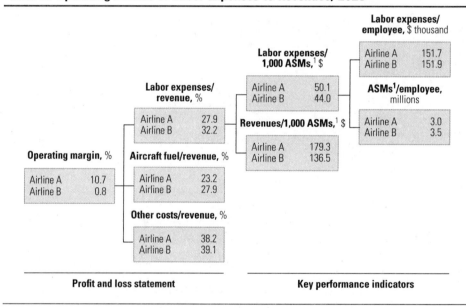

Profit and loss statement	**Key performance indicators**

[1] Available seat-miles (ASMs) are the standard unit of measure in the U.S. airline industry.

see why, disaggregate the ratio of labor expenses to revenues using available seat-miles (ASMs):

$$\frac{\text{Labor Expenses}}{\text{Revenues}} = \left(\frac{\text{Labor Expenses}}{\text{ASMs}}\right) \div \left(\frac{\text{Revenues}}{\text{ASMs}}\right)$$

The ratio of labor expenses to revenues depends on both labor expenses per ASM and revenues per ASM. Labor expenses per ASM refers to the labor cost to fly one seat mile, while revenues per ASM indicates the average price charged per seat mile. Although Airline B has a 12 percent advantage in labor cost per ASM, with $44.0 in labor costs per thousand ASMs, compared with

$50.1 for Airline A, this advantage is offset by Airline A's ability to charge higher prices. Due to its strategic locations and international reach, Airline A can charge $179.3 per thousand ASMs, 31 percent higher than Airline B's $136.5 per thousand ASMs.

But what is driving this differential in labor expenses per ASM? Are Airline B's employees more productive? Or are they paid less? To answer these questions, disaggregate labor expenses to ASMs, using the following equation:

$$\frac{\text{Labor Expenses}}{\text{ASM}} = \left(\frac{\text{Labor Expenses}}{\text{Employees}}\right) \div \left(\frac{\text{ASMs}}{\text{Employees}}\right)$$

Two elements drive labor expenses per ASM: the first term represents the average salary per full-time employee, and the second measures the productivity of each full-time employee (in millions of ASMs flown per employee per year). The boxes on the right side of Exhibit 12.6 report the calculations for this equation. While both companies offer similar average salaries, Airline B outperforms in productivity per mile by 14 percent. This productivity edge is often seen in airlines that operate point-to-point routes rather than relying on hub-and-spoke systems.

As the example of Airline A and Airline B shows, analyzing performance using these operating drivers gives interesting insights into the competitive differences among companies. But the analysis is far from done. In fact, a thoughtful analysis will often raise more questions than it answers. For example, is the difference in employee productivity solely due to route structure, or could other competitive factors, such as a streamlined fleet, explain the disparity? Each of these analyses will provide additional insight into each carrier type's ability to survive and prosper.

ANALYZING REVENUE GROWTH

Chapter 3 showed that ROIC, cost of capital, and growth in cash flows drive a company's value. By analyzing historical revenue growth, you can assess the potential for growth in the future.

The calculation of a company's year-to-year revenue growth is straightforward, but the results can be misleading. Three prime culprits distort revenue growth: fluctuation in currency values, mergers and acquisitions, and changes in accounting policies. To generate a better forecast of organic revenue growth, it's essential to eliminate these distortions and focus on the underlying performance trends.

Exhibit 12.7 demonstrates how misleading raw year-to-year revenue growth figures can be. Compass (based in the United Kingdom) and Sodexo (based in France) are global providers of canteen services for businesses, health systems, schools, and sporting venues. In the run-up to the global pandemic, Compass saw its reported revenue grow by 1.8 percent in 2018 and

EXHIBIT 12.7 **Compass and Sodexo: Revenue Growth Analysis**

%

Compass	2018	2019	2020	2021	2022	2023
Organic growth	5.5	7.7	−18.8	−6.3	37.5	18.8
Currency effects	−4.6	5.9	−1.3	−4.5	5.0	3.1
Portfolio changes	0.9	0.8	0.3	0.6	0.0	−0.3
Reported revenue growth	1.8	14.4	−19.8	−10.2	42.5	21.6

Sodexo	2018	2019	2020	2021	2022	2023
Organic growth[1]	1.6	3.6	−12.0	−5.6	16.9	11.6
Currency effects	−5.8	1.4	−0.8	−4.0	5.5	1.5
Portfolio changes	2.8	2.6	0.8	−0.2	−1.2	−0.8
Reported revenue growth	−1.4	7.6	−12.0	−9.8	21.2	12.3

[1] As reported by Sodexo. Adjusting for 53-week year in 2017, organic growth was 2.0% in 2018.

14.4 percent in 2019, though these gains were heavily skewed by currency fluctuations. Stripping out currency and portfolio effects, organic growth was more consistent, at 5.5 percent and 7.7 percent, respectively. While currency differences remained a factor during and after the pandemic, the distortion was less pronounced, as organic growth experienced broad swings. For this period, a longer perspective is helpful. For instance, in 2022, Compass reached 105 percent of its 2019 level on a constant-currency basis.

The next three sections discuss in detail each of the major sources of distortions—changes in currency values, mergers and acquisitions, and changes in accounting policies. For each, we consider its effect on performance measurement, forecasting, and ultimately valuation.

Currency Effects

Multinational companies conduct business in many currencies. At the end of each reporting period, these revenues are converted to the home currency of the reporting company. If foreign currencies are rising in value relative to the company's home currency, this translation at better rates will lead to higher revenue numbers. Thus, a rise in revenue may not reflect increased prices or greater quantities sold but simply depreciation in the company's home currency.

Compass and Sodexo are both exposed to foreign currency and have similar geographic mixes, with nearly half of each company's revenues coming from North America. But the companies translate U.S. dollars into different currencies for their consolidated financial statements, so exchange rates will affect each company in different ways.

For an example of the impact of exchange rates, consider Compass, which converts U.S. dollars from its North American business into British pounds. In the company's 2022 fiscal year, the exchange rate averaged 1.28 dollars per pound, which then dropped to 1.23 in 2023. As a result, $100 translated to

£78.38 in 2022, while the same $100 translated to £81.63 in 2023. This means that even without growth in its American markets, the company would report higher revenue in 2023. In 2023, Compass reported a 3.1 percent boost in revenue growth across all its markets due to currency effects. Given the volatility of exchange rates and the difficulty in forecasting them, these distortions can obscure the company's true performance in its core markets.

Mergers and Acquisitions

Growth through acquisition can affect value creation differently than internal growth, largely due to the significant premiums often needed to acquire another company. Therefore, when analyzing performance, it is important to understand how companies have historically generated revenue growth, whether through organic means or through acquisition.

Many large companies provide data tables such as the ones for Compass and Sodexo found in Exhibit 12.7. Without voluntary disclosure, stripping the effect of acquisitions from reported revenues can be difficult. Unless an acquisition is deemed material by the company's accountants, company filings do not need to detail or even report the acquisition. For larger acquisitions, a company will report pro forma statements that recast historical financials as though the acquisition were completed at the beginning of the fiscal year. Organic revenue growth, then, should be calculated using the pro forma revenue numbers.[4] If the target company publicly reports its own financial data, you can construct pro forma statements manually by combining revenue of the acquirer and target for the prior year. But beware: the bidder will include partial-year revenues from the target for the period after the acquisition is completed. To remain consistent from year to year, reconstructed prior years also must include only partial-year revenue.

Exhibit 12.8 presents the hypothetical purchase of a target company in the seventh month of year 3. Both the parent company and the target are growing organically at 10 percent per year. Whereas the individual companies are growing organically at 10 percent, consolidated revenue growth is reported at 22.8 percent in year 3 and 18.2 percent in year 4.

To create an internally consistent comparison for years 3 and 4, adjust the prior year's consolidated revenues to match the current year's composition. To do this, add seven months of the target's year 2 revenue (7/12 × $22 million = $12.8 million) to the parent's year 2 revenue ($110.0 million). This leads to adjusted year 2 revenues of $122.8 million, which matches the composition of year 3. To compute an organic growth rate, divide year 3 revenues ($135.1 million) by adjusted year 2 revenues ($122.8 million) to get the 10 percent organic growth of the two companies.

---

[4] For example, in its 2022 annual report, Sodexo disclosed that it "divested from its operations in Russia, sold Rydoo, its Travel & Expenses business, and exited its investments in sports aggregation."

EXHIBIT 12.8 **Effect of Acquisitions on Revenue Growth**

$ million

	Year				
	1	2	3	4	5
Revenue by company					
Acquiring company	100.0	110.0	121.0	133.1	146.4
Target company	20.0	22.0	24.2	26.6	29.3
Consolidated revenues					
Revenue of acquirer	100.0	110.0	121.0	133.1	146.4
Revenue from target			14.1	26.6	29.3
Consolidated revenues[1]	100.0	110.0	135.1	159.7	175.7
Growth rates at acquirer, %					
Consolidated revenues[1]		10.0	22.8	18.2	10.0
Organic growth		10.0	10.0	10.0	10.0

[1] Only consolidated revenues are typically reported in a company's annual report.

Even though the acquisition occurs in year 3, the revenue growth rate for year 4 also will be affected by the acquisition. Year 4 contains a full year of revenues from the target. Therefore, to estimate year 4 organic growth, you must increase year 3 revenue by five months of target revenue (5/12 × $24.2 million = $10.1 million).

Accounting Changes and Irregularities

Each year, the Financial Accounting Standards Board (FASB) in the United States and the International Accounting Standards Board (IASB) make recommendations concerning the financial treatment of certain business transactions through either formal standards or topic notes issued by assigned task forces. Changes in a company's revenue recognition policy can significantly affect revenues during the year of adoption, distorting the one-year growth rate.[5] To understand real historical revenue trends, therefore, you need to eliminate the effects of these distortions.

Consider the new revenue recognition standards that replaced existing IFRS and GAAP revenue rules in 2017.[6] These standards introduced a requirement that companies follow a five-step process to determine the allocation of revenue over the life of a contract. In some cases, initiating this process caused revenues to be delayed to later in the contract, causing a one-time drop in like-for-like revenues. For example, automobile companies that provide free maintenance saw a one-time drop as revenues were delayed. Other industries,

---

[5] Revenue recognition changes can also affect margins and capital turnover ratios. These changes will not, however, affect free cash flow.
[6] ASC 606 and IFRS 15, "Revenue from Contracts with Customers," was issued jointly by the FASB and IASB on May 28, 2014. Implementation began in 2017.

including cell phone providers, experienced a one-time increase in revenue when the new rules allowed them to immediately recognize cell phone equipment sales. Although the standard has been in place since 2017, companies continued to refine their implementation of these standards, particularly in complex areas such as variable consideration, performance obligations, and the treatment of contract modifications.

If an accounting change is material, a company will document the change in its section on management discussion and analysis (MD&A). For instance, Sodexo specifically called attention to an unusual 53-week year in 2017. The longer time period in 2017 artificially raised the reported growth rate in 2017 while lowering the reported growth rate in 2018.

Decomposing Revenue Growth to Develop an Integrated Perspective of Growth Drivers

Once you have removed the effects of mergers and acquisitions, currency translations, and accounting changes your growth numbers, analyze organic revenue growth from an operational perspective. The most standard breakdown is

$$\text{Revenues} = \frac{\text{Revenues}}{\text{Units}} \times \text{Units}$$

Using this formula, determine whether prices or quantities are driving growth. Do not, however, confuse revenue per unit with price; they can be different. If revenue per unit is rising, the change could be due to rising prices, or the company could be shifting its product mix from low-price to high-price items.

The operating statistics that companies choose to report (if any) depend on the industry's norms and competitors' practices. For instance, most retailers provide information on the number of stores they operate, the number of square feet in those stores, and the number of transactions they conduct annually. By relating different operating statistics to total revenues, it is possible to build a deeper understanding of the business.

Consider this retailing standard:

$$\text{Revenues} = \frac{\text{Revenues}}{\text{Stores}} \times \text{Stores}$$

Exhibit 12.9 reports disguised operating statistics for two big-box retailers we'll call Retailer A and Retailer B. Analyzing the data in Exhibit 12.9 reveals that, despite having fewer stores than Retailer B, Retailer A generates more revenue per store, with $65.7 million per store in 2022, compared with $51.0 million per store for Retailer B. As we will examine later, Retailer B has been reducing its store count, but this has failed to close the gap in revenues per store.

Using the data reported in Exhibit 12.9, it is possible to build several insightful operating ratios, including revenues per store, transactions per store, square feet per store, dollars per transaction, and number of transactions per

EXHIBIT 12.9 **Retailer A and Retailer B: Operating Statistics**

	Retailer A			Retailer B		
Reported	2020	2021	2022	2020	2021	2022
Revenues, $ million	79,266	90,694	94,442	71,678	77,000	77,647
Average number of stores	1,422	1,430	1,438	1,620	1,617	1,521
Number of transactions, millions	1,019	1,021	967	816	782	731
Derived						
Revenues per store, $ million	55.7	63.4	65.7	44.2	47.6	51.0
Transactions per store, thousands	716.6	714.0	672.5	503.7	483.6	480.6
Revenues per transaction, $	77.8	88.8	97.7	87.8	98.5	106.2

square foot. Although these operating ratios are powerful in their own right, what can really change one's thinking about performance is how the ratios change over time. Exhibit 12.10 organizes each ratio based on Exhibit 12.9 into a growth tree. Rather than report a calculated ratio, such as revenues per store, however, we report the growth in the ratio over the period analyzed and relate this back to the growth in aggregate revenue.

The exhibit reveals that while Retailer A grew faster overall than Retailer B, the drivers of the two companies' growth differed significantly. Retailer A achieved growth by expanding its store count, whereas Retailer B reduced its number of stores. However, Retailer B outperformed Retailer A in same-store sales, recording a 7.2 percent increase in revenue per store, compared to Retailer A, which achieved only a 3.6 percent increase. This growth in same-store sales is extremely important, to the point that financial analysts have a special name for growth in revenues per store: *comps*, shorthand for compara-bles, or year-to-year same-store sales.[7] Why is this revenue growth important?

EXHIBIT 12.10 **Retailer A and Retailer B: Organic Revenue Growth Analysis, 2022**

Growth rates, %

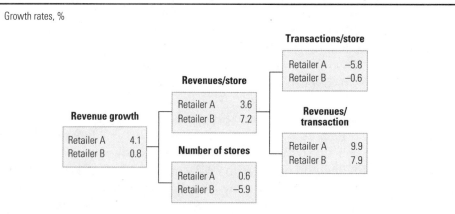

---

[7] In Exhibit 12.10, we present the change in revenues per store. This value differs from comparable-store sales reported by each company, which includes only stores that were open for at least 13 months.

First, the number of stores to open is an investment choice, whereas same-store sales growth reflects each store's ability to compete effectively in its local market. Second, new stores require large capital investments, whereas growth in comps requires little incremental capital. Hence, same-store sales growth comes with higher capital turnover, higher ROIC, and greater value creation.

Moving farther right in the tree, we gain further insight into the drivers behind same-store sales for each company. Both retailers experienced a dip in transactions. However, the rise in revenue per store was largely fueled by higher revenues per transaction. While this increase could stem from various factors, it's likely that a significant portion can be attributed to the inflationary pressures felt across many countries in the wake of the pandemic.

CREDIT HEALTH AND CAPITAL STRUCTURE

To this point, we have concentrated on the operating performance of the company and its ability to create value. In the final step of our financial analysis, we turn our attention to the company's financing strategy. This analysis includes evaluating the sustainability of the capital structure, assessing the company's resilience in the face of an industry downturn, and determining the amount of cash, if any, that has been distributed to shareholders.

To assess a company's credit health, conduct three analyses. Begin with an examination of liquidity using coverage ratios, which gauge the company's ability to meet short-term obligations such as interest expenses and rental payments. Next, evaluate leverage by analyzing debt-to-EBITDA and debt-to-value ratios, incorporating lease obligations into the debt calculation. This analysis provides insight into the company's capacity to fulfill its long-term obligations. Finally, assess the payout by examining how the company has distributed cash. This analysis will reveal the company's approach to returning value to shareholders as part of its overall financial strategy.

This section covers the mechanics of data collection and context setting for evaluating a company's capital structure. Chapter 35 explores how companies can actively integrate capital structure decisions into their operating strategies and plans for returning cash to shareholders.

Measuring Liquidity Using Coverage Ratios

To estimate the company's ability to meet short-term obligations, analysts use ratios that incorporate three measures of earnings:

1. Earnings before interest, taxes, and amortization (EBITA)
2. Earnings before interest, taxes, depreciation, and amortization (EBITDA)
3. Earnings before interest, taxes, depreciation, amortization, and rental expense (EBITDAR)

With the first two earnings measures, you can calculate interest coverage. To do this, divide either adjusted EBITA or adjusted EBITDA by interest, where both profitability figures are computed before the interest expense on debt *and* leases. The first coverage ratio is adjusted EBITA to interest, which measures the company's ability to pay interest using profits without cutting capital expenditures intended to replace depreciating equipment. The second ratio, adjusted EBITDA to interest, measures the company's ability to meet short-term financial commitments using both current profits and the depreciation dollars earmarked for replacement capital. Although EBITDA provides a good measure of the short-term ability to meet interest payments, most companies cannot compete effectively without replacing worn assets.

For companies such as airlines and retailers that lease a significant portion of their asset base, a third ratio—EBITDAR to the sum of interest and rental expenses—is often used. Like the interest coverage ratio, this ratio also assesses the company's ability to meet its future obligations, in this case fully accounting for the impact of operating leases.

Returning to our previous example of Costco and its peers, Exhibit 12.11 presents their financial data and coverage ratios. For 2023, Costco's coverage ratio of EBITA to interest equaled 31.2 times, whereas its peers had an average ratio of just 5.3 times. By most standards, Costco carries very little debt,

EXHIBIT 12.11 **Costco vs. Peer Group: Measuring Coverage**

$ million

	Costco			Peer group		
	2021	2022	2023	2021	2022	2023
Adjusted EBITA[1]	6,789	7,891	8,217			
Depreciation	1,781	1,900	2,077			
Adjusted EBITDA[2]	8,570	9,791	10,294			
Interest expense, debt	171	158	160			
Interest expense, leases	81	98	103			
Interest expense, total	252	256	263			
Short-term and long-term debt	7,609	7,491	6,557			
Finance, operating, and variable leases	4,440	5,390	5,815			
Debt plus leases	12,049	12,881	12,372			
Coverage ratios						
EBITA/total interest expense[1]	26.9	30.8	31.2	7.8	7.1	5.3
EBITDA/total interest expense[2]	34.0	38.2	39.1	10.2	10.4	7.7
EBITDAR/interest plus rental expense[3]	14.9	14.5	16.6	5.4	4.8	4.4
Debt multiples						
Debt plus leases to EBITA[1]	1.8	1.6	1.5	3.6	5.1	5.4
Debt plus leases to EBITDA[2]	1.4	1.3	1.2	2.9	3.4	3.6

[1] EBITA plus lease interest expense.

[2] EBITDA plus lease interest expense.

[3] EBITDA plus rental expense divided by the sum of the interest expense on debt and the rental expense related to operating leases.

as evidenced by its robust A+ rating from Standard & Poor's. In contrast, Costco's peers employ significantly more leverage, primarily through operating leases, which is reflected in their much lower coverage ratios.

Assessing Leverage

During the last 15 years, interest rates dropped to unprecedented lows, making interest coverage ratios uncharacteristically high. To evaluate leverage in a low-interest-rate environment, many analysts shifted to measuring and evaluating debt multiples such as debt plus leases to EBITDA or debt plus leases to EBITA. Given its much larger denominator, debt to EBITDA tends to be more stable in these circumstances, making assessments over time much clearer. The ratio also does a better job of teasing out companies that are exposed to rollover risk and widening default spreads, neither of which is captured when interest rates are extremely low.

A second reason the debt-to-EBITDA measure has gained in popularity involves the increased use of convertible securities. Many convertibles compensate through the potential conversion to equity rather than interest, making interest coverage ratios, especially for technology companies, artificially high. By using the debt-to-EBITDA ratio, one can build a more comprehensive picture of the risk of leverage.

To further assess leverage, also measure the company's (market-based) debt-to-equity ratio over time and against peers. Does the leverage ratio compare favorably with the industry? How much risk is the company taking? Chapter 35 offers in-depth answers to these and other questions about the use of debt to finance operations.

Analyzing Payout to Investors

A company's valuation hinges on its ability to generate cash flow, but understanding its financial health also requires knowing where that cash ultimately goes. To get a full picture, track the distribution of the company's cash flow over an extended window.

For example, consider Costco: between 2019 and 2023, the company generated $25.2 billion in NOPAT, paid $800 million in debt-related interest, and returned $13.3 billion to shareholders through dividends. This kind of analysis reveals not just the company's profitability, but also its priorities in managing and allocating its capital—crucial information for any investor.

BENCHMARKING VALUATION

In Chapter 18, we explore the essential practice of stress-testing your valuation by placing it in context through a multiples analysis. Crafting a robust set of multiples is an art in itself, and Chapter 18 offers a set of best practices

EXHIBIT 12.12 **Costco vs. Peer Group: Operating Value to EBITDA**

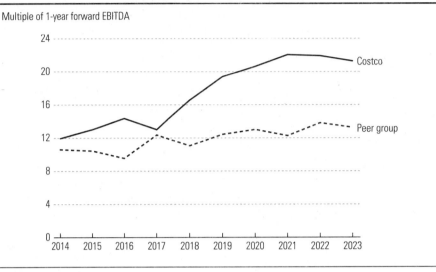

Note: Operating value equals enterprise value less the book value of nonoperating assets.

to master this skill. For now, we focus on one key multiple: the operating-value-to-EBITDA multiple. By tracking this multiple over time, we can assess whether the market is accurately valuing the performance metrics discussed earlier.

Exhibit 12.12 provides a look at the operating-value-to-EBITDA multiples for Costco and its peers from 2014 to 2023, revealing three noteworthy trends. First, the entire industry has seen a rise in the multiple, a trend partially fueled by lower federal tax rates in the United States. Second, we see that Costco consistently trades at a significant premium, driven by stronger revenue growth and superior ROIC. Finally, the valuation gap between Costco and its peers has widened, largely due to Costco's improved financial performance, which its competitors have struggled to match. Whether this shift is permanent remains a key question for analysts and investors. Only time will reveal the answer.

While operating value to EBITDA is the most common measure of valuation, other measures, including operating value to EBITA and operating value to NOPAT, often provide helpful insights as well.

CLOSING THOUGHTS

While there is no one-size-fits-all checklist for analyzing a company's historical financial performance, several key guidelines can help sharpen your analysis. First, look as far back as possible—ideally at least 10 years. A longer time horizon reveals whether the company and industry tend to revert to a normal level of performance, helping you discern whether short-term trends are likely to be permanent.

Next, break down value drivers such as ROIC and revenue growth into as much detail as possible. Linking operational performance measures to each key value driver can provide valuable insights. If you notice any radical changes in performance, it's crucial to identify the source and determine whether the change is temporary, permanent, or simply an accounting anomaly.

For deeper insight, include as much detail as possible in your analysis, focusing not just on the company, but also on individual business units, product lines, and even customers if the data is available. This level of granularity often uncovers important trends that a broader analysis might miss.

With this thorough historical analysis complete, we're now equipped with the necessary context to build a robust set of forecasts—an essential component of any valuation.

13

Forecasting Performance

This chapter focuses on the *mechanics* of forecasting—specifically, how to develop an integrated set of financial forecasts. We'll explore how to build a well-structured spreadsheet model that separates raw inputs from computations, flows from one worksheet to the next, and is flexible enough to handle multiple scenarios. Then we'll discuss the process of forecasting.

Unlike a capital budgeting project, we do not forecast cash flows directly. Instead, to arrive at future cash flow, we first forecast the income statement, balance sheet, and statement of changes in equity. The forecast financial statements provide the information necessary to compute net operating profit after taxes (NOPAT), invested capital, return on invested capital (ROIC), and, ultimately, free cash flow (FCF).

While you are building a forecast, it is easy to become engrossed in the details of individual line items. But we stress the importance of placing your aggregate results in the proper context. You can do much more to improve your valuation by carefully analyzing whether your forecast of future ROIC is consistent with the company's ability to generate value than you can by precisely (but perhaps inaccurately) forecasting an immaterial line item ten years out.

DETERMINE THE FORECAST'S LENGTH AND DETAIL

Before you begin forecasting individual line items on the financial statements, decide how many years to forecast and how detailed your forecast should be. The typical model, described in Chapter 10, is to develop an explicit year-by-year forecast for a set period and then to value the remaining years by using a perpetuity formula, such as the key value driver formula introduced in Chapter 3. Whatever perpetuity formula you choose, all the continuing-value approaches assume steady-state performance. Thus, the explicit forecast period must be long enough for the company to reach a steady state, defined by the following characteristics:

- The company grows at a constant rate by reinvesting a constant proportion of its operating profits into the business each year.
- The company earns a constant rate of return on both existing capital and new capital invested.

As a result, free cash flow for a steady-state company will grow at a constant rate and can be valued using a growth perpetuity. The explicit forecast period should be sufficiently long to ensure that the company's growth rate aligns with or falls below the economy's growth rate. Sustaining a higher growth rate in perpetuity would eventually result in the company becoming unrealistically large relative to the overall economy.

We recommend using an explicit forecast period of 10 to 15 years—perhaps longer for companies subject to industry cycles or those experiencing rapid growth. Using a short explicit forecast period, such as five years, typically results in a significant undervaluation of a company or requires heroic long-term growth assumptions in the continuing value. Even so, a long forecast period raises its own issues—namely, the difficulty of forecasting individual line items 10 to 15 years into the future.

To simplify the model and avoid the error of false precision, we often split the explicit forecast into two periods:

1. A detailed five-year to seven-year forecast, which develops complete balance sheets and income statements with as many links as possible to operating variables such as unit volumes and cost per unit
2. A simplified forecast for the remaining years, focusing on a few important value drivers, such as revenue growth, margins, and capital turnover

Using a simplified intermediate forecast forces you to focus on the business's long-term economics, rather than becoming engrossed in too much detail.

COMPONENTS OF A GOOD MODEL

Combining 15 years of financial forecasts with 10 years of historical analysis makes even the simplest valuation spreadsheet complex. Therefore, you should carefully design and structure your model before forecasting.

EXHIBIT 13.1 **Sample Workbook**

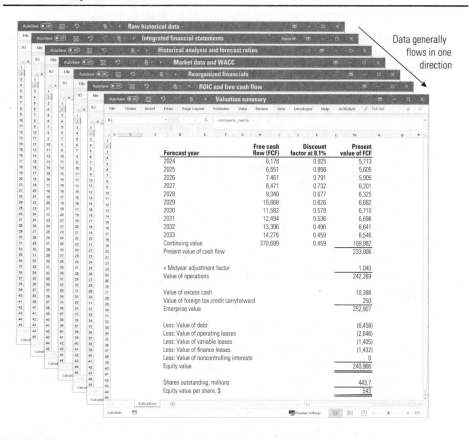

Data generally flows in one direction

In Exhibit 13.1, we structure a valuation model with seven distinct worksheets:

1. *Raw historical data.* Collect raw data from the company's financial statements, footnotes, and external reports in one place.[1] By keeping the raw data together, you can verify information as needed and update data year by year. Report the raw data in their original form.

2. *Integrated financial statements.* Using figures from the raw-data worksheet, create a new set of historical financials that find the right level of detail. Generally, operating and nonoperating items should not be aggregated within the same line item. The income statement should be

[1] For large, established companies, the amount of collected data can be substantial. To analyze and value Costco in Chapter 11 and Appendix I, we created separate worksheets for the company's financial statements, statutory tax table, note on deferred taxes, and note on lease payments.

linked with the balance sheet through retained earnings. This worksheet will contain historical and forecast financial statements.

3. *Historical analysis and forecast ratios.* For each line item in the financial statements, create historical ratios and forecasts of future ratios. These ratios will generate the forecast financial statements contained on the previous sheet.

4. *Market data and the weighted average cost of capital (WACC).* Collect all financial market data on one worksheet. This worksheet will contain estimates of beta, the cost of equity, the cost of debt, the weighted average cost of capital, and historical market values and trading multiples for the company.

5. *Reorganized financial statements.* Once you have built a complete set of financial statements (both historical and forecast), reorganize the financial statements to calculate NOPAT, its reconciliation to net income, invested capital, and its reconciliation to total funds invested.

6. *ROIC and FCF.* Use the reorganized financials to build return on invested capital, economic profit, and free cash flow. Future free cash flow will be the basis of your enterprise valuation.

7. *Valuation summary.* Create a summary worksheet that sums discounted cash flows and converts the value of operations into equity value. The valuation summary includes the value of operations, the value of nonoperating assets, the value of nonequity claims, and the resulting equity value.

Well-built valuation models share a certain set of characteristics. First, original data and user input are collected in only a few places. For instance, limit original data and user input to just three worksheets: raw data (worksheet 1), forecasts (worksheet 3), and market data (worksheet 4). To provide additional clarity, denote raw data and user input in a different color from calculations. Second, a given worksheet should feed into the next worksheet whenever possible. Formulas should not bounce from sheet to sheet without clear direction.[2] Raw data should feed into integrated financials, which in turn should feed into ROIC and FCF. Third, numbers should never be hard-coded into a formula unless specified as data input. Hard-coded numbers are easily forgotten as the spreadsheet grows in complexity. Finally, avoid making much use of the software's built-in formulas, such as the net present value (NPV) formula. Built-in formulas can obscure your model's logic and make it difficult to audit results for accuracy.

MECHANICS OF FORECASTING

The forecast of free cash flow (FCF) is a central component of an enterprise discounted cash flow (DCF) model. However, as noted earlier in this chapter, FCF forecasts should be derived indirectly by first projecting the income

---

[2] Data should always flow in one direction and never loop back to create a circular reference. Unintended circular references will prevent your spreadsheet from calculating results accurately.

statement, balance sheet, and statement of retained earnings. Once a complete set of financial statements is prepared, you can calculate FCF forecasts using the same approach used when analyzing historical performance. (A well-built spreadsheet will use the same formulas for historical and forecast ROIC and FCF without any modification.)

We break the forecasting process into six steps:

1. *Prepare and analyze historical financials.* Before forecasting future financials, examine past performance, using financial ratio analysis. A robust analysis will place your forecasts in the appropriate historical and competitive context.

2. *Build the revenue forecast.* Almost every line item will rely directly or indirectly on revenues. Estimate future revenues by using either a top-down (market-based) or a bottom-up (customer-based) approach. Forecasts should be consistent with the long-run evidence on growth detailed in Chapter 9.

3. *Forecast the income statement.* Use the appropriate economic drivers to forecast operating expenses, depreciation, nonoperating income, interest expense, and taxes.

4. *Forecast the balance sheet: invested capital and nonoperating assets.* On the balance sheet, forecast operating working capital, net property, plant, and equipment, goodwill, and nonoperating assets.

5. *Reconcile the balance sheet with investor funds.* Complete the balance sheet by computing retained earnings and forecasting other equity accounts. Use excess cash, new debt, equity issuances, or share repurchases to ensure that assets equal liabilities and equity.

6. *Calculate ROIC and FCF.* Calculate ROIC on future financial statements to ensure your forecasts are consistent with economic principles, industry dynamics, and the company's ability to compete. To complete the forecast, calculate free cash flow as the basis for valuation.

Out of all these steps, the revenue forecast is especially important. Almost every line item in the spreadsheet will be either directly or indirectly driven by revenues, so you should devote enough time to arrive at a good revenue forecast, especially for rapidly growing businesses.

Step 1: Prepare and Analyze Historical Financials

Before building a forecast, enter the company's historical financials into a spreadsheet. To do this, you can rely on data from a professional service, such as Bloomberg, S&P Capital IQ, Compustat Financials, or LSEG Data & Analytics, or you can use financial statements directly from the company's filings.

Professional services benefit from standardized data (i.e., financial data formatted into a set number of categories). Since data items do not change across companies, a single spreadsheet can quickly analyze any company. However, using a standardized data set carries a cost. Many of the specified categories aggregate important items, hiding critical information. For instance, Compustat groups "advances to sales staff" (an operating asset) and "pension and other special funds" (a nonoperating asset) into a single category titled "other assets." Because of this, models based solely on preformatted data can lead to meaningful errors in the estimation of value drivers, and hence to poor valuations.

For situations that demand extra diligence, use financial data obtained directly from the company's annual report. However, as with data obtained from a professional service, you must still dig. Often, companies aggregate critical information to simplify their financial statements.

Consider, for instance, the financial data for Colgate-Palmolive presented in Exhibit 13.2. On its reported balance sheet, the company consolidates many items into the account titled "other accruals." In the notes that follow the company's financial statements, note 18, titled "Supplemental Balance Sheet Information," details this line item. Some of the components (such as advertising, payroll, and taxes) are operating liabilities, and others (such as restructuring, pension, lease, interest, and derivatives) are debt equivalents. Since the valuation of each of these items requires different treatment, the items must be separated on an expanded balance sheet.

EXHIBIT 13.2 **Colgate-Palmolive: Current Liabilities on the Balance Sheet**

$ million

Balance Sheet	2022	2023
Notes and loans payable	11	310
Current portion of long-term debt	14	20
Accounts payable	1,551	1,698
Accrued income taxes	317	336
Other accruals	2,111	2,377
Total current liabilities	4,004	4,741
From note 18: Supplemental Balance Sheet Information		
Accrued advertising and coupon redemption	774	882
Accrued payroll and employee benefits	329	403
Accrued taxes other than income taxes	133	167
Restructuring accrual	39	11
Pension and other retiree benefits	82	96
Lease liabilities due in one year	108	95
Accrued interest	59	78
Derivatives	15	26
Other	572	619
Total other accruals	2,111	2,377

Source: Colgate-Palmolive Company annual report, 2023.

We prefer to collect raw data on a separate worksheet. On the raw-data sheet, record financial data as originally reported, and never combine multiple data into a single cell. Once you have collected raw data from the reported financials and notes, use the data to build a set of expanded (or simplified) financial statements: the income statement, balance sheet, statement of equity, and statement of accumulated other comprehensive income. Although the statement of equity appears redundant, it will be critical for error checking during the forecasting process, because it links the income statement to the balance sheet. If available, accumulated other comprehensive income will be necessary to complete the free cash flow statement.

As you build the integrated financials, you must decide whether to aggregate immaterial line items. Analyzing and forecasting too many line items can lead to confusion, introduce errors, and cause the model to become unwieldy. Returning to the Colgate-Palmolive example presented in Exhibit 13.2, the income taxes payable account amounts to under 1.0 percent of Colgate-Palmolive's revenues.[3] Therefore, you might simplify a valuation of Colgate-Palmolive by combining income taxes payable with the "other" account. When aggregating, however, make sure never to combine operating and non-operating accounts into a single category. You cannot calculate ROIC and FCF accurately if operating and nonoperating accounts are combined.

Step 2: Build the Revenue Forecast

To build a revenue forecast, you can use a *top-down* forecast to estimate revenues by sizing the total market, determining market share, and forecasting prices. Alternatively, you might opt to use a *bottom-up* approach, which would involve forecasting demand from existing customers, customer turnover, and the potential for new customers. When possible, use both methods to establish bounds for the forecast.

The top-down approach to estimate future revenue can be applied to any company or, if possible, business unit. For companies in mature industries, the aggregate market grows slowly and is closely tied to economic growth and other long-term trends, such as changing consumer preferences. In these situations, you can rely on third-party forecasts of the aggregate market and focus your own efforts on forecasting market share by competitor.[4] To do this, you must determine which companies have the capabilities and resources to compete effectively and capture share. A good place to start, of course, is with historical financial analysis. But more importantly, make sure to address how the company is positioned for the future. Does it have the required products and

---

[3] Contrast this to accrued compensation and employee benefit costs; that account is nearly 15 times as large as taxes payable. Given its size, accrued compensation and employee benefit costs should not be aggregated with other accrued liabilities.

[4] Examples of third-party forecasts include Evaluate Ltd for drug-by-drug revenue forecasts, McCoy Power Reports for power generation equipment, and RBR Data Services for point-of-sale systems.

services to capture share? Do other competitors have products and services that will displace the company's market position? A good forecast will address each of these issues.

Over the short term, top-down forecasts should build on the company's announced intentions and capabilities for growth. For instance, many retailers have well-mapped plans for new store openings, serving as their primary revenue growth driver. Oil and gas companies have proven reserves and relatively fixed amounts of transportation and/or refining capacity. And pharmaceutical companies have a fixed set of drugs under patent and in clinical trials.

In Exhibit 13.3, we present a sample revenue forecast for Costco. In its annual report, Costco provides data on the number of stores opened each year and the average revenue per store, grouped by the year of opening.[5] For instance, stores opened in 2023 averaged $151 million in revenue in their opening year, whereas stores that have been open for more than ten years averaged $268 million. Older stores tend to generate more revenue as they expand their reach into the community. Using year-by-year cohorts, we can forecast at a more granular level, capturing revenue trends for stores at different stages of maturity.

EXHIBIT 13.3 **Costco: Sample Revenue Forecast**

$ million

Year opened	Revenue per store			Forecast		Number of stores	Total revenue	Forecast	
	2021	2022	2023	2024	2025		2023	2024	2025
Before 2015	228	259	268	278	288	663	177,684	184,387	190,996
2015	163	189	199	207	215	23	4,577	4,765	4,950
2016	173	204	212	221	231	29	6,148	6,420	6,691
2017	206	237	247	259	270	26	6,422	6,728	7,032
2018	172	202	214	225	236	21	4,494	4,723	4,951
2019	172	208	216	228	239	20	4,320	4,554	4,788
2020	152	184	193	204	215	13	2,509	2,653	2,798
2021	140	158	172	182	193	20	3,440	3,649	3,859
2022		150	158	168	178	23	3,634	3,867	4,102
2023			151	161	171	23	3,473	3,707	3,944
2024F				169	180	31		5,228	5,579
2025F					172	25			4,300

Stores	216,701	230,679	243,989
53rd week	4,089	0	0
Ancillary businesses[1]	21,500	22,575	23,704
Total revenue	242,290	253,255	267,693

[1] Ancillary businesses include gas stations, pharmacies, optical dispensing centers, food courts, and hearing-aid centers.

[5] Costco refers to its retail stores as "warehouses" in its financial disclosures.

It is important to note that the cohort analysis conducted for Costco in Exhibit 13.3 is possible only because the company disclosed the data; not every company does. Other retailers provide information on revenues per transaction, transaction counts, customer counts, and other operating data. A robust forecast will incorporate operating data in creative ways, depending on the data provided.

In new-product markets, the top-down approach is especially helpful but often requires more work than for established markets. For instance, consider the launch in 2023 of Tesla's Cybertruck, an all-electric pickup truck. The Cybertruck stands out from existing SUVs due to its unique, angular design and stainless-steel exoskeleton. It incorporates advanced technology features, including Tesla's Autopilot, a large touchscreen interface, and over-the-air software updates, which are not commonly found in many conventional SUVs. Given the short history of Tesla's Cybertruck, how do you estimate the potential size and speed of penetration of this new product?

You could start by sizing the more traditional products of companies such as Ford and Chevrolet. Analyze whether the new electric trucks, given their advanced technology, will be adopted by even more users than traditional trucks—or perhaps by fewer, due to their unique design. Next, forecast how quickly electric trucks might penetrate the market. To do this, look at the speed of migration for other products that have gone through a similar transition, such as the four-door sedan. Determine the characteristics that drive conversion in other markets, which will help you to place your forecast in context. Next, assess the Cybertruck's price point and the resulting operating margin. How many companies are developing similar products, and how competitive will the market be? As you can see, there are more questions than answers. The key is structuring the analysis and applying historical evidence from comparable markets to help bound forecasts whenever possible.

A top-down approach begins with the overall market, predicting penetration rates, price changes, and market shares. In contrast, a bottom-up approach focuses on projections of customer-by-customer demand. Start by assessing the current number of customers. By aggregating this data, you can forecast revenues from the existing customer base. Next, estimate the customer turnover rate. If turnover is significant, adjust the revenue estimates accordingly. Finally, project the number of new customers the company will attract and their potential revenue contribution. The resulting bottom-up forecast combines revenues from both new and existing customers.[6]

Regardless of the method, forecasting revenues over long time periods will inevitably be imprecise. Customer preferences, technologies, and corporate strategies change. These often-unpredictable changes can profoundly

---

[6] For more on company valuation using customer acquisition and retention statistics, see D. McCarthy, P. Fader, and B. Hardie, "Valuing Subscription-Based Businesses Using Publicly Disclosed Customer Data," *Journal of Marketing* 81, no. 1 (2018): 17–35.

influence the winners and losers in the marketplace. Therefore, you must constantly reevaluate whether the current forecast is consistent with industry dynamics, competitive positioning, and historical evidence on corporate growth. If you lack confidence in your revenue forecast, use multiple scenarios to model uncertainty. Doing this will not only bound the forecast but also help company management make better decisions. A discussion of scenario analysis can be found in Chapter 17.

Step 3: Forecast the Income Statement

With a revenue forecast in place, forecast individual line items related to the income statement. To forecast a line item, use a three-step process:

1. *Decide what economic relationships drive the line item.* For many line items, forecasts will be tied directly to revenues. Others will be economically tied to a specific asset or liability. For instance, interest income is usually generated by cash and marketable securities; if this is the case, forecasts of interest income should be linked to cash and marketable securities.

2. *Estimate the forecast ratio.* For each line item on the income statement, compute historical values for each ratio, followed by estimates for each of the forecast periods. To get the model working properly, initially set the forecast ratio equal to the previous year's value. We call this an "as-is" forecast. Your forecasts are likely to change as you learn about the company, so at this point, a working model should be your priority. Once the entire model is complete, return to the forecast page and enter your best estimates.

3. *Multiply the forecast ratio by an estimate of its driver.* Since many line items are driven by revenues, most forecast ratios, such as cost of goods sold (COGS) to revenues, should be applied to estimates of future revenues. This is why a good revenue forecast is critical. Any error in the revenue forecast will be carried through the entire model. Ratios dependent on other drivers should be multiplied by their respective drivers.

Exhibit 13.4 presents the historical income statement and partially completed forecast for a hypothetical company. To demonstrate the three-step process, we forecast cost of goods sold. In the first step, calculate historical COGS as a function of revenues, which equals 37.5 percent. To get the model operational, initially set next year's ratio equal to 37.5 percent as well. Finally, multiply the forecast ratio by an estimate of next year's revenues: 37.5 percent × $288 million = $108 million.

Note that we did not forecast COGS by increasing the previous year's costs by 20 percent (the same growth rate as revenues). Although this process leads to the same *initial* answer, it uncouples the model and reduces flexibility. By using a forecast ratio rather than a growth rate, we can either vary estimates

EXHIBIT 13.4 **Partial Forecast of the Income Statement**

Forecast worksheet

%	2024	Forecast 2025
Revenue growth	20.0	20.0
Cost of goods sold/revenues	37.5	37.5
Selling and general expenses/revenues	18.8	
Depreciation$_t$/net PP&E$_{t-1}$ [1]	9.5	

Step 1: Choose a forecast driver, and compute historical ratios.

Step 2: Estimate the forecast ratio.

Step 3: Multiply the forecast ratio by next year's estimate of revenues (or appropriate forecast driver).

Income statement

$ million	2024	Forecast 2025
Revenues	240.0	288.0
Cost of goods sold	(90.0)	(108.0)
Selling and general expenses	(45.0)	
Depreciation	(19.0)	
EBITA	86.0	
Interest expense	(15.0)	
Interest income	2.0	
Nonoperating income	4.0	
Earnings before taxes (EBT)	77.0	
Provision for income taxes	(18.0)	
Net income	59.0	

[1] Net PP&E = net property, plant, and equipment.

of revenues (and COGS will change in step) or vary the forecast ratio (for instance, to value a potential improvement). If we had increased the COGS directly, however, we could only vary the COGS growth rate.

Exhibit 13.5 presents typical forecast drivers and forecast ratios for the most common line items on financial statements. The appropriate choice for a forecast driver, however, depends on the company and the industry in which it competes.

Most valuation models, especially those of public companies, rely on ratios created directly from the company's financial statements. If you have access to other data that improves your forecast, incorporate it. For instance, the external valuation of a delivery company such as UPS will tie fuel costs directly to

EXHIBIT 13.5 **Typical Forecast Drivers for the Income Statement**

	Line item	Typical forecast driver	Typical forecast ratio
Operating	Cost of goods sold (COGS)	Revenue	COGS/revenue
	Selling, general, and administrative (SG&A)	Revenue	SG&A/revenue
	Depreciation	Prior-year net PP&E	Depreciation$_t$/net PP&E$_{t-1}$
Nonoperating	Nonoperating income	Appropriate nonoperating asset, if any	Nonoperating income/nonoperating asset or Growth in nonoperating income
	Interest expense	Prior-year total debt	Interest expense$_t$/total debt$_{t-1}$
	Interest income	Prior-year excess cash	Interest income$_t$/excess cash$_{t-1}$

revenue. A more sophisticated model might link fuel costs to the price of fuel and the number of packages delivered or miles driven. It might also take into account economic issues such as the company's ability to pass on any changes in fuel prices to its customers. Regardless of what sort of model you are using, always be mindful about incorporating new data. While additional data often improves the realism of your model, it will also increase the model's complexity. A talented modeler carefully balances realism with simplicity.

Operating Expenses   For each operating expense on the income statement—such as cost of goods sold; selling, general, and administrative expenses; and research and development—we recommend generating forecasts based on revenues. In most cases, the process for operating expenses is straightforward. However, as outlined in Chapter 11, the income statement sometimes embeds certain nonoperating items in operating expenses. Before you begin the forecasting process, reformat the income statement to properly separate ongoing expenses from one-time charges.

Depreciation   To forecast depreciation, you have three options. You can forecast depreciation as either a percentage of revenues or a percentage of property, plant, and equipment (PP&E), or—if you are working inside the company—you can generate depreciation forecasts based on specific equipment purchases and their related depreciation schedules.

Although one can link depreciation to revenue, you will get better forecasts if you use PP&E as the forecast driver. To illustrate this, consider a company that makes a large capital expenditure every few years. Since depreciation is directly tied to a particular asset, it should increase only following an expenditure. If you tie depreciation to sales, it will incorrectly grow as revenues grow, even when capital expenditures haven't been made.

When using PP&E as the forecast driver, forecast depreciation as a percentage of net PP&E, rather than gross PP&E. Ideally, depreciation would be linked to gross PP&E, since depreciation for a given asset's life (assuming straight-line depreciation) equals gross PP&E divided by its expected life. But linking depreciation to gross PP&E requires modeling asset life and retiring the asset when it becomes fully depreciated. Implementing this correctly is tricky. If you forget to model asset retirements, for example, you would overestimate depreciation (and consequently its tax shield) in the later years.

If you have access to detailed, internal information about the company's assets, you can build formal depreciation tables. For each asset, project depreciation using an appropriate depreciation schedule, asset life, and salvage value. To determine company-wide depreciation, combine the annual depreciation of each asset.

Exhibit 13.6 presents a forecast of depreciation, as well as the remaining line items on the income statement.

EXHIBIT 13.6 **Completed Forecast of the Income Statement**

Forecast worksheet			Income statement		
%	2024	**Forecast** **2025**	$ million	2024	**Forecast** **2025**
Revenue growth	20.0	20.0	Revenue growth	240.0	288.0
Cost of goods sold/revenues	37.5	37.5	Cost of goods sold	(90.0)	(108.0)
Selling and general expenses/revenues	18.8	18.8	Selling and general expenses	(45.0)	(54.0)
Depreciation$_t$/net PP&E$_{t-1}$	9.5	9.5	Depreciation	(19.0)	(23.8)
			EBITA	86.0	102.3
Interest rates			Interest expense	(15.0)	(13.8)
Interest expense	5.4	5.4	Interest income	2.0	1.2
Interest income	2.0	2.0	Nonoperating income	4.0	5.3
			Earnings before taxes (EBT)	77.0	95.0
Nonoperating items					
Nonoperating-income growth	33.3	33.3	Provision for income taxes	(18.0)	(22.2)
			Net income	59.0	72.7
Taxes					
Operating tax rate	23.4	23.4			
Statutory tax rate	24.0	24.0			
Effective tax rate	23.4	23.4			

Nonoperating Income   Nonoperating income is generated by nonoperating assets, such as customer loans, nonconsolidated subsidiaries, and other equity investments. Since nonoperating income is typically excluded from free cash flow and the corresponding nonoperating asset is valued separately from core operations using a variety of techniques, the forecast will not affect the value of core operations. Instead, the primary purposes of nonoperating-income forecasts are cash flow planning and estimating earnings per share.

For nonconsolidated subsidiaries and other equity investments, the forecast methodology depends on how much information is available. For illiquid investments in which the parent company owns less than 20 percent, the company records income only when dividends are received or assets are sold at a gain or loss. For these investments, you cannot use traditional drivers such as the parent company's revenue to forecast nonoperating cash flows; instead, estimate future nonoperating income by examining historical growth in nonoperating income or by examining the revenue and profit forecasts of publicly traded companies that are comparable to the equity investment.

For nonconsolidated subsidiaries with greater than 20 percent ownership, the parent company records income even when it is not paid out. Also, the recorded asset grows as the investment's retained earnings grow. Thus, you can estimate future income from the nonconsolidated investment either by forecasting a nonoperating-income growth rate or by forecasting a return on equity (nonoperating income as a percentage of the appropriate nonoperating asset) consistent with the industry dynamics and competitive position of the subsidiary.

Interest Expense and Interest Income   Interest expense (or income) should be tied directly to the liability (or asset) that generates the expense (or income). For instance, the appropriate driver for interest expense is total debt, including both short-term and long-term debt. To simplify implementation, use *prior-year* debt to drive interest expense, rather than same-year year-end debt. To see why, consider a rise in operating costs. If the company uses debt to fund short-term needs, total debt will rise to cover the financing gap caused by lower profits. This increased debt load will cause interest expense to rise, dropping profits even further. The reduced level of profits, once again, requires more debt. To avoid the complexity of this feedback effect, compute interest expense as a function of the prior year's total debt. This shortcut will simplify the model and avoid circularity.[7]

A forecast of interest expense requires data from the income statement and the balance sheet. The balance sheet for our hypothetical company is presented in Exhibit 13.7. From the income statement presented in Exhibit 13.6, start with the 2024 interest expense of $15 million, and divide by 2023's total debt of $280 million (from the balance sheet, the sum of $200 million in short-term debt plus $80 million in long-term debt). This ratio equals 5.4 percent. To estimate the 2025 interest expense, multiply the estimated forecast ratio (5.4 percent) by 2024's total debt ($258 million), which leads to a forecast of $13.8 million. In this example, interest expense is falling even while revenues rise, as the company uses cash from operations to reduce short-term debt.

Using historical interest rates to forecast interest expense is a simple, straightforward estimation method. And since interest expense is not part of free cash flow, the choice of how to forecast interest expense will not affect the company's valuation (only free cash flow drives valuation; the cost of debt is modeled as part of the weighted average cost of capital).[8] When a company's

EXHIBIT 13.7 **Historical Balance Sheet**

$ million

Assets	2023	2024	Liabilities and shareholders' equity	2023	2024
Operating cash	5.0	5.0	Accounts payable	15.0	20.0
Excess cash	100.0	60.0	Short-term debt	200.0	178.0
Inventory	35.0	45.0	Current liabilities	215.0	198.0
Current assets	140.0	110.0			
			Long-term debt	80.0	80.0
Net PP&E	200.0	250.0	Shareholders' equity	145.0	182.0
Equity investments	100.0	100.0	Total liabilities and equity	440.0	460.0
Total assets	440.0	460.0			

[7] If you are using last year's debt multiplied by current interest rates to forecast interest expense, the forecast error will be greatest when year-to-year changes in debt are significant.

[8] In a WACC-based valuation model, the cost of debt and its associated tax shields are fully incorporated in the cost of capital. In an adjusted present value (APV) model, the interest tax shield is valued separately using a forecast of interest expense.

financial structure is a critical part of the forecast, however, split debt into two categories: existing debt and new debt. Until repaid, existing debt should generate interest expense consistent with contractual rates reported in the company's financial notes. Interest expense based on new debt, in contrast, should be paid at current market rates, available from a financial data service. Projected interest expense should be calculated using a yield to maturity for comparably rated debt at a similar duration.

Estimate *interest income* the same way, with forecasts based on the asset generating the income. But be careful: interest income can be generated by multiple investments, including excess cash, short-term investments, customer loans, and other long-term investments. If a footnote details the historical relationship between interest income and the assets that generate the income (and the relationship is material), develop a separate calculation for each asset.

Income Taxes   Do not forecast the provision for income taxes as a percentage of earnings before taxes (EBT) using the effective tax rate. If you do, ROIC and FCF in forecast years will inadvertently change as leverage and nonoperating income change. Instead, start with a forecast of operating taxes on earnings before interest, taxes, and amortization (EBITA), and adjust for taxes related to nonoperating accounts, such as interest expense. Use this combined number to generate taxes on the income statement.

Exhibit 13.8 presents the forecast process for income taxes. To forecast operating taxes for 2025, multiply EBITA by the *operating* tax rate (23.4 percent). Earlier, we estimated EBITA equal to $102.3 million for 2025. Do not use the statutory tax rate to forecast operating taxes. Many companies pay taxes at rates below their local statutory rate because of low foreign rates and operating

EXHIBIT 13.8 **Forecast of Reported Taxes**

$ million

	2024	Forecast 2025
Operating taxes		
EBITA	86.0	102.3
× Operating tax rate	23.4%	23.4%
= Operating taxes	20.2	24.0
Taxes on nonoperating accounts		
Interest expense	(15.0)	(13.8)
Interest income	2.0	1.2
Nonoperating income	4.0	5.3
Nonoperating income (expenses), net	(9.0)	(7.3)
× Marginal tax rate	24.0%	24.0%
= Taxes on nonoperating accounts	(2.2)	(1.8)
Provision for income taxes[1]	18.0	22.0

[1] The provision for income taxes equals the sum of operating and nonoperating taxes.

tax credits.[9] Failure to recognize operating credits can cause errors in free cash flow forecasts and an incorrect valuation. Also, if you use historical tax rates to forecast future tax rates, you implicitly assume that these special incentives will grow in line with EBITA. If this is not the case, EBITA should be taxed at the marginal rate, and tax credits should be forecast one by one.

Next, forecast the taxes related to nonoperating accounts such as interest expense and nonoperating income. Although such taxes are not part of free cash flow, a robust forecast of them will provide insights about future net income and cash needs. For each line item between EBITA and earnings before taxes, compute the marginal taxes related to that item. If the company does not report each item's marginal tax rate, use the country's statutory rate. In Exhibit 13.8, the cumulative net nonoperating expense ($7.3 million in 2025) was multiplied by the marginal tax rate of 24 percent. It is possible to do this because each item's marginal income tax rate is the same. When marginal tax rates differ across nonoperating items, forecast nonoperating taxes line by line.

To determine the 2025 provision for income taxes, sum operating taxes ($24.0 million) and marginal taxes related to nonoperating accounts (–$1.8 million). You now have a forecast of $22.2 million for reported taxes, calculated such that future values of FCF and ROIC will not change if you adjust leverage.

Step 4: Forecast the Balance Sheet: Invested Capital and Nonoperating Assets

To forecast the balance sheet, start with items related to invested capital and nonoperating assets. Leave out excess cash and financing sources like debt and equity, as these will be addressed in step 5.

One of the first issues you will face when forecasting the balance sheet is whether to forecast line items on the balance sheet directly (in stocks) or indirectly by forecasting the year-to-year changes in accounts (in flows). For example, the stock approach forecasts end-of-year receivables as a function of revenues, while the flow approach forecasts the *change* in receivables as a function of the growth in revenues. We favor the stock approach. The relationship between the balance sheet accounts and revenues (or other volume measures) is more stable than that between balance sheet changes and changes in revenues. Consider the example presented in Exhibit 13.9. The ratio of accounts receivable to revenues remains within a tight band between 9.2 percent and 10.1 percent, while the ratio of changes in accounts receivable to changes in revenues ranges from –1 percent to 16 percent, too volatile for identifying patterns.

Exhibit 13.10 summarizes forecast drivers and forecast ratios for the most common line items on the balance sheet. The three primary operating line items are operating working capital, long-term capital such as net PP&E, and

---

[9] For an in-depth discussion of the difference between statutory, effective, and operating tax rates, see Chapter 20.

EXHIBIT 13.9 **Stock vs. Flow Example**

	Year 1	Year 2	Year 3	Year 4
Revenues, $	1,000	1,100	1,200	1,300
Accounts receivable, $	100	105	121	120
Stock method				
Accounts receivable as a % of revenues	10.0	9.5	10.1	9.2
Flow method				
Change in accounts receivable as a % of change in revenues		5.0	16.0	−1.0

EXHIBIT 13.10 **Typical Forecast Drivers and Ratios for the Balance Sheet**

	Line item	Typical forecast driver	Typical forecast ratio
Operating line items	Operating working capital		
	Accounts receivable	Revenues	Accounts receivable/revenues
	Inventories	Cost of goods sold	Inventories/COGS
	Accounts payable	Cost of goods sold	Accounts payable/COGS
	Accrued expenses	Revenues	Accrued expenses/revenues
	Net PP&E	Revenues or units sold	Net PP&E/revenues
	Goodwill and acquired intangibles	Acquired revenues	Goodwill and acquired intangibles/acquired revenues
Nonoperating line items	Nonoperating assets	None	Growth in nonoperating assets
	Pension assets or liabilities	None	Trend toward zero
	Deferred taxes	Operating taxes or corresponding balance sheet item	Change in operating deferred taxes/operating taxes, or Deferred taxes/corresponding balance sheet item

intangible assets related to acquisitions. Nonoperating line items include non-operating assets, pensions, and deferred taxes, among others. We discuss each category next.

Operating Working Capital   Begin the balance sheet forecast by focusing on items within operating working capital, including accounts receivable, inventories, accounts payable, and accrued expenses. Remember, operating working capital excludes any nonoperating assets (such as excess cash) and financing items (such as short-term debt and dividends payable).

When forecasting operating working capital, estimate most line items as a percentage of revenues or in days' sales.[10] Possible exceptions are inventories

[10] To compute a ratio in days' sales, multiply the percent-of-revenue ratio by 365. For instance, if accounts receivable equals 10 percent of revenues, this translates to accounts receivable at 36.5 days' sales. This implies that, on average, the company collects its receivables in 36.5 days. If the data allows, separate cash sales from credit sales and use credit sales to estimate days receivable.

and accounts payable. Since these two accounts are economically tied to input prices, estimate them instead as a percentage of cost of goods sold (which is also tied to input prices).[11] Look for any other possible links between the income statement and balance sheet. For instance, accrued wages can be calculated as a percentage of compensation and benefits.

Exhibit 13.11 presents a partially completed forecast of our hypothetical company's balance sheet, in particular its operating working capital, long-term operating assets, and nonoperating assets (investor funds will be detailed later). Working-capital items are best forecast in days, most of which are computed using days' sales. Working cash is estimated at 7.6 days' sales, inventory at 182.5 days' COGS, and accounts payable at 81.1 days' COGS. We forecast in days for the added benefit of tying forecasts more closely to the velocity of operating activities. For instance, if management announces its intention to reduce its inventory holding period from 180 days to 120 days, it is possible to compute changes in value by adjusting the forecast directly.

Property, Plant, and Equipment   Consistent with our earlier argument concerning stocks and flows, net PP&E should be forecast as a percentage of revenues.[12] A common alternative is to forecast capital expenditures as a

EXHIBIT 13.11 **Partial Forecast of the Balance Sheet**

Forecast worksheet			Balance sheet			
		Forecast				**Forecast**
	2024	**2025**	**$ million**	**2023**	**2024**	**2025**
Working capital			**Assets**			
Operating cash, days' sales	7.6	7.6	Operating cash	5.0	5.0	6.0
Inventory, days' COGS	182.5	182.5	Excess cash	100.0	60.0	
Accounts payable, days' COGS	81.1	81.1	Inventory	35.0	45.0	54.0
			Current assets	140.0	110.0	
Fixed assets						
Net PP&E/revenues, %	104.2	104.2	Net PP&E	200.0	250.0	300.0
			Equity investments	100.0	100.0	100.0
Nonoperating assets			Total assets	440.0	460.0	
Growth in equity investments, %	0.0	0.0				
			Liabilities and equity			
			Accounts payable	15.0	20.0	24.0
			Short-term debt	200.0	178.0	
			Current liabilities	215.0	198.0	
			Long-term debt	80.0	80.0	
			Shareholders' equity	145.0	182.0	
			Total liabilities and equity	440.0	460.0	

[11] As a practical matter, we sometimes simplify the forecast model by projecting each working-capital item using revenues. The distinction is material only when price is expected to deviate significantly from cost per unit.

[12] Some companies, such as oil refiners, will report number of units. In these cases, consider using number of units instead of revenue to forecast equipment purchases.

percentage of revenues. However, this method too easily leads to unintended increases or decreases in capital turnover (the ratio of PP&E to revenues). Over long periods, companies' ratios of net PP&E to revenues tend to be quite stable, so we favor the following three-step approach for PP&E:

1. Forecast net PP&E as a percentage of revenues.
2. Forecast depreciation, typically as a percentage of gross or net PP&E.
3. Calculate capital expenditures by summing the projected increase in net PP&E plus depreciation.

To continue our example, we use the forecasts presented in Exhibit 13.11 to estimate expected capital expenditures. In 2024, net PP&E equaled 104.2 percent of revenues. If this ratio is held constant for 2025, the forecast of net PP&E equals $300 million. To estimate capital expenditures, compute the increase in net PP&E from 2024 to 2025, and add 2025 depreciation from Exhibit 13.6.

$$
\begin{aligned}
\text{Capital Expenditures} &= \text{Net PP\&E}_{2025} - \text{Net PP\&E}_{2024} + \text{Depreciation}_{2025} \\
&= \$300.0\,\text{million} - \$250.0\,\text{million} + \$23.8\,\text{million} \\
&= \$73.8\,\text{million}
\end{aligned}
$$

For companies with low growth rates and projected improvements in capital efficiency, this methodology may lead to negative capital expenditures (implying asset sales). Although positive cash flows generated by equipment sales are certainly possible, they are unlikely. More likely, there was a write-down of PP&E. In these cases, if capital expenditures are negative, make sure to assess the resulting cash flow carefully.

Goodwill and Acquired Intangibles   A company records goodwill and acquired intangibles when the price it pays for an acquisition exceeds the target's book value.[13] For most companies, we choose not to model potential acquisitions explicitly, so we set revenue growth from new acquisitions equal to zero and hold goodwill and acquired intangibles constant at their current level. We prefer this approach because of the empirical literature documenting how the typical acquisition fails to create value.[14] Since adding a zero-NPV investment will not increase the company's value, forecasting acquisitions is unnecessary. In fact, by forecasting acquired growth in combination with the company's current financial results, you make implicit (and often hidden) assumptions

---

[13] This section refers to acquired intangibles only. Forecast internal investments in intangibles, such as capitalized software and purchased sales contracts, with the methodology used for PP&E.

[14] While acquisitions fail to create value on average, many do succeed. Acquirers, particularly those executing roll-ups of privately held businesses, effectively manage acquisition premiums and capture synergies. In such cases, acquisitions can be viewed similarly to new product launches, with attention to critical factors such as the number, size, and timing of acquisitions, as well as the ability to realize value from them.

about the present value of future acquisitions. For instance, if the forecast ratio of goodwill to acquired revenues implies positive NPV for acquired growth, increasing the growth rate from acquired revenues can dramatically increase the resulting valuation, even when good deals are hard to find.

If you decide to forecast acquisitions, first assess what proportion of future revenue growth they are likely to provide. For example, consider a company that generates $100 million in revenues and has announced an intention to grow by 10 percent annually—5 percent organically and 5 percent through acquisitions. In this case, measure historical ratios of goodwill and acquired intangibles to acquired revenues, and apply those ratios to acquired revenues. For instance, imagine a company historically adds $3 in goodwill and intangibles for every $1 of acquired revenues. Multiplying the expected $5 million of acquired growth by 3, you obtain an expected increase of $15 million in goodwill and acquired intangibles. Make sure, however, to perform a reality check on your results by varying acquired growth and observing the resulting changes in company value. Confirm that your results are consistent with the company's past performance related to acquisitions and the challenges of creating value through acquisition.

Nonoperating Assets, Unfunded Pensions, and Deferred Taxes   After completing a forecast for operating items, forecast nonoperating assets (such as nonconsolidated subsidiaries), debt equivalents (such as pension liabilities), and equity equivalents (such as deferred taxes). Because many nonoperating items are valued using methods other than discounted cash flow (see Chapter 16), any forecasts of these items are primarily for the purpose of financial planning and cash management, not enterprise valuation. For instance, consider unfunded pension liabilities. Assume management announces its intention to reduce unfunded pensions by 50 percent over the next five years. To value unfunded pensions, do not discount the projected outflows over the next five years. Instead, use the current actuarial assessments of the shortfall, which appear in the note on pensions. The rate of reduction will have no valuation implications but will affect the ability to pay dividends or perhaps require additional financing. To this end, model a reasonable time frame for eliminating pension shortfalls.

We are quite cautious about forecasting nonconsolidated subsidiaries and other equity investments for the purpose of valuation. Instead, valuations should be based on an assessment of the investments currently owned, not reached by discounting the forecast changes in their book values and/or their corresponding income. If a forecast is necessary for planning, keep in mind that income from associates is often noncash, and nonoperating assets often grow in a lumpy fashion unrelated to a company's revenues. To forecast equity investments, rely on historical precedent to determine the appropriate level of growth.

Regarding deferred-tax assets and liabilities, those used to occur primarily through differences in depreciation schedules, because investor and tax authorities use different depreciation schedules to determine taxable income. Today, deferred taxes arise for many reasons, including tax adjustments for pensions, stock-based compensation, acquired-intangibles amortization, and deferred revenues. (For an in-depth discussion of deferred taxes, see Chapter 20.)

For sophisticated valuations that require extremely detailed forecasts, be sure to forecast deferred taxes line by line, tying each tax to its appropriate driver. In most situations, forecasting operating deferred taxes by applying a historical deferral rate to estimated taxes provides a reasonable approach. For example, if a company's operating taxes are projected to be 23.4 percent of EBITA and it has historically deferred one-fifth of its tax payments, a common assumption is that it will continue to defer one-fifth of 23.4 percent. Operating-related deferred-tax liabilities will then increase by the amount deferred.

Step 5: Reconcile the Balance Sheet with Investor Funds

To complete the balance sheet, forecast the company's sources of financing. To do this, rely on the rules of accounting. First, use the principle of clean surplus accounting:

$$\text{Equity}_{2025} = \text{Equity}_{2024} + \text{Net Income}_{2025} - \text{Dividends}_{2025} + \text{Net Equity Issued}_{2025}$$

Applying this to our earlier example, Exhibit 13.12 presents the statement of shareholders' equity. To estimate equity in 2025, start with 2024 equity of $182 million from Exhibit 13.11. To this value, add the 2025 forecast of net income: $72.7 million from the income statement in Exhibit 13.6. Next, estimate the dividend payout. In 2024, the company paid out 37.3 percent of net income in the form of dividends. Applying a 37.3 percent payout ratio to estimated net income leads to $27.1 million in expected dividends. Finally, add new equity issued net of equity repurchased, which in this example is zero. Using the clean surplus relationship, we estimate 2025 equity at $227.6 million.

EXHIBIT 13.12 **Statement of Shareholders' Equity**

$ million

	2023	2024	Forecast 2025
Shareholders' equity, beginning of year	120.8	145.0	182.0
Net income	40.2	59.0	72.7
Dividends	(16.0)	(22.0)	(27.1)
Issuance (Repurchase) of common stock	—	—	—
Shareholders' equity, end of year	145.0	182.0	227.6
Dividends/net income, %	39.8	37.3	37.3

At this point, four accounts on the balance sheet remain: excess cash, short-term debt, long-term debt, and a new account titled "newly issued debt." Some combination of these accounts must make the balance sheet balance. For this reason, these items are often referred to as "the plug." In simple models, existing debt either remains constant or is retired on schedule, according to contractual terms.[15] To complete the balance sheet, set one of the remaining two items (excess cash or newly issued debt) equal to zero. Then use the primary accounting identity—assets equal liabilities plus shareholders' equity—to determine the remaining item.

Exhibit 13.13 presents the elements of this process for our example. First, hold short-term debt, long-term debt, and common stock constant. Next, sum total assets, excluding excess cash: cash ($6 million), inventory ($54 million), net PP&E ($300 million), and equity investments ($100 million) total $460 million. Then sum total liabilities and equity, excluding newly issued debt: accounts payable ($24 million), short-term debt ($178 million), long-term debt ($80 million), and shareholders' equity ($227.6 million) total $509.6 million. Because liabilities and equity (excluding newly issued debt) are greater than assets (excluding excess cash), newly issued debt is set to zero. Now total liabilities and equity equal $509.6 million. To ensure that the balance sheet balances, we set the only remaining item, excess cash, equal

EXHIBIT 13.13 **Forecast Balance Sheet: Sources of Financing**

$ million

	2023	2024	Preliminary 2025F	Completed 2025F	
Assets					
Operating cash	5.0	5.0	6.0	6.0	**Step 1:** Determine retained earnings
Excess cash	100.0	60.0		49.6	using the clean surplus relation, forecast
Inventory	35.0	45.0	54.0	54.0	existing debt using contractual terms,
Current assets	140.0	110.0	60.0	109.6	and keep common stock constant.
Net PP&E	200.0	250.0	300.0	300.0	**Step 2:** Test which is higher: (a) assets
Equity investments	100.0	100.0	100.0	100.0	excluding excess cash or (b) liabilities
Total assets	440.0	460.0	460.0	509.6	and equity, excluding newly issued debt.
Liabilities and equity					
Accounts payable	15.0	20.0	24.0	24.0	**Step 3:** If assets excluding excess cash
Short-term debt	200.0	178.0	178.0	178.0	are higher, set excess cash equal to
Current liabilities	215.0	198.0	202.0	202.0	zero, and plug the difference with the
					newly issued debt. Otherwise, plug with
Long-term debt	80.0	80.0	80.0	80.0	excess cash.
Newly issued debt	—	—		—	
Shareholders' equity	145.0	182.0	227.6	227.6	
Total liabilities and equity	440.0	460.0	509.6	509.6	

[15] Given the importance of debt in a leveraged buyout, buyout models often contain a separate worksheet detailing interest and principal repayment by year for each debt contract.

to \$49.6 million. This increases total assets to \$509.6 million, and the balance sheet is complete.

To implement this procedure in a spreadsheet, use the spreadsheet's pre-built If function. Set up the function so it sets excess cash to zero when assets (excluding excess cash) exceed liabilities and equity (excluding newly issued debt). Conversely, if assets are less than liabilities and equity, the function should set short-term debt equal to zero and excess cash equal to the difference.

The Link Between Capital Structure Forecasts and Valuation   When using excess cash and newly issued debt to complete the balance sheet, you will likely encounter one common side effect: as growth drops, newly issued debt will drop to zero, and excess cash will become very large.[16] But what if a drop in leverage is inconsistent with your long-term assessments concerning capital structure? In an enterprise DCF valuation that uses the weighted average cost of capital for discounting, this side effect does not matter. Excess cash and debt are not included as part of free cash flow, so they do not affect the enterprise valuation. Capital structure affects enterprise DCF only through the weighted average cost of capital.[17] Thus, only an adjustment to WACC will lead to a change in valuation.

To bring the capital structure on the balance sheet in line with the capital structure implied by WACC, adjust the dividend payout ratio or amount of share repurchases. For instance, as the dividend payout is increased, retained earnings will drop, and this should cause excess cash to drop as well. By varying the payout ratio (both through dividends and share repurchases), you can also test how robust your FCF model is. Specifically, ROIC and FCF, and hence value, should not change when the dividend rate or amount of share repurchases is adjusted. If it does, this indicates the presence of an inconsistency. For more on capital structure, including a discussion of dividends and share repurchases, see Chapter 35.

How you choose to model the payout ratio depends on the requirements of the model. In most situations, you can adjust the dividend payout ratio or amount of repurchases by hand when needed (remember, the ratio does not affect value but rather brings excess cash and newly issued debt closer to reality). For more complex models, determine net debt (total debt less excess cash) by applying the target net-debt-to-value ratio modeled in the WACC at each point in time. Next, using the target debt-to-value ratio, solve for the required payout. To do this, however, you must perform a valuation in each forecast

[16] Whenever ROIC is greater than revenue growth, a company will generate operating cash flow; that is, the investment rate will be negative. If dividends or share repurchases are not increased to disgorge cash, debt will drop, and/or excess cash will accumulate.

[17] In the APV model, your forecast of debt will affect valuation. Interest tax shields are computed year by year based on the amount of debt, the interest rate, and the tax rate. Models that discount with a constant WACC implicitly assume debt-to-value never changes, such that balance sheet forecasts are ignored.

year and iterate backward—a time-consuming process for a feature that will not affect the final valuation.[18]

Step 6: Calculate ROIC and FCF

Once you have completed your income statement and balance sheet forecasts, calculate ROIC and FCF for each forecast year. This process should be straightforward if you have already modeled ROIC and FCF historically. Since a full set of forecast financials is now available, you can simply copy the two calculations from historical financials to projected financials.

For companies that are creating value, future ROICs should fit one of three general patterns: ROIC should either remain near current levels (when the company has a distinguishable sustainable advantage), trend toward an industry or economic median, or trend to the cost of capital. Think through the economics of the business to decide what is appropriate. For more on long-term trends of ROIC, refer to Chapter 8.

ADVANCED FORECASTING

The preceding sections detail the process for creating a comprehensive set of financial forecasts. However, when forecasting, you may come across three advanced issues: forecasting using nonfinancial operating drivers, forecasting using fixed and variable costs, and handling the impact of inflation.

Nonfinancial Operating Drivers

Until now, the chapter has created forecasts that rely solely on financial drivers. In industries where prices are changing or technology is advancing, forecasts should incorporate nonfinancial, operating-related ratios, such as volume and productivity.

Consider the turmoil in the airline industry during the early 2000s. Fares requiring Saturday-night stays and advance purchases disappeared as competition from low-cost carriers intensified. Network carriers could no longer distinguish business travelers, their primary source of profit, from leisure travelers. As the average price dropped, costs rose as a percentage of sales. But were airlines truly becoming higher-cost businesses or just lower-price businesses?[19] And how would this trend continue? To forecast changes more

---

[18] To value Costco in Appendix I, we modeled a constant leverage ratio year by year and iterated backward. While iteration is not necessary to value a company more generally, it is required to ensure that the enterprise DCF valuation ties to other valuation methodologies, such as cash-flow-to-equity models.

[19] For example, Spirit Airlines dedicates a higher percentage of revenue to labor than American Airlines does. In terms of cost per seat-mile, however, American is the higher-cost airline of the two.

accurately, separate price from volume (as measured by seat-miles). Then, instead of forecasting costs as a percentage of revenues, forecast costs as a function of expected quantity—in this case, seat-miles.

The same concept applies to advances in technology. For instance, rather than estimate labor as a percentage of revenues, you could forecast units per employee and average salary per employee. Separating these two drivers of labor costs allows you to model a direct relationship between productivity improvements from new technology and estimated changes in units per employee.

Fixed Versus Variable Costs

When you are valuing a small project, it is important to distinguish fixed costs (incurred once to create a basic infrastructure) from variable costs (correlated with volume). When you are valuing an individual project, only variable costs should be increased as revenues grow.

At the scale of most publicly traded companies, however, the distinction between fixed and variable costs is often immaterial, because nearly every cost is variable. For instance, consider a mobile-phone company that transmits calls using radio-frequency towers. In spite of the common perception that the tower is a fixed cost, this is true for only a given number of subscribers. As subscribers increase beyond a certain limit, new towers must be added, even in an area with preexisting coverage. (A small company adding 1,000 customers can leverage economies of scale more than a large company adding 100,000 customers.) What is a fixed cost in the short run for small increases in activity becomes variable over the long run even at reasonable growth rates (10 percent annual growth doubles the size of a company in about seven years). Since corporate valuation is about long-run profitability and growth, nearly every cost should be treated as variable.

When an asset, such as cloud-based software or a mobile app, is truly scalable, its development cost should be treated as a fixed cost. Be careful, however. Many technologies, such as computer software, quickly become obsolete, requiring new incremental expenditures for the company to remain competitive. In this case, a cost deemed fixed actually requires repeated cash outflows, just not in traditional ways.

Incorporating Inflation

In Chapter 10, we recommended that financial-statement forecasts and the cost of capital be estimated in nominal currency units (with inflation), rather than real currency units (without inflation). To remain consistent, the nominally based financial forecast and the nominally based cost of capital must reflect the same expected general inflation rate. This means the inflation rate built into the forecast must be derived from an inflation rate implicit in the cost of capital.[20]

To estimate inflation appropriate to your forecast period, do not use the current level of inflation. Instead, derive the expected inflation rate from the term structure of government bond rates. The nominal interest rate on government bonds reflects investor demand for a real return plus a premium for expected inflation. Estimate expected inflation as the nominal rate of interest less an estimate of the real rate of interest, using the following formula:

$$\text{Expected Inflation} = \frac{(1 + \text{Nominal Rate})}{(1 + \text{Real Rate})} - 1$$

To estimate expected inflation, start by calculating the nominal yield to maturity on a ten-year government bond. But how do you find the real rate? Many countries, such as the United States, United Kingdom, and Japan, issue inflation-linked bonds (ILBs). An ILB is a bond that protects against inflation by growing the bond's coupons and principal at the consumer price index (CPI). Consequently, the yield to maturity on an ILB is the market's expectation of the real interest rate over the life of the bond.

In April 2024, the yield on a ten-year U.S. Treasury bond equaled 4.54 percent, and the yield on a U.S. Treasury inflation-protected security (TIPS) bond equaled 2.15 percent.[21] To determine expected inflation, apply the previous formula to the data:

$$\text{Expected Inflation} = \frac{1.0454}{1.0215} - 1 = 0.0234$$

Expected inflation, as measured by the difference in nominal and real bonds, equals 2.34 percent annually over the next ten years.

Exhibit 13.14 presents annualized growth in the U.S. consumer price index (CPI) versus expected ten-year inflation implied by traditional U.S. Treasury bonds and U.S. TIPS bonds. Since the ten-year TIPS bond is based on long-term inflation, the implied inflation rate is much more stable than the one-year change in CPI. This attribute was evident during the COVID-19 pandemic, when inflation in the United States, as measured by the change in the CPI, surged from 1.2 percent to 9.0 percent between 2020 and 2022. Macroeconomists identified the key drivers as supply chain disruptions, a shift from

---

[20] Individual line items may have inflation rates that are higher or lower than the general rate, but they should still derive from the general rate. For example, the revenue forecast should reflect the growth in units sold and the expected increase in unit prices. The increase in unit prices, in turn, should reflect the generally expected level of inflation in the economy plus or minus an inflation rate differential for that specific industry. Suppose general inflation is expected to be 4 percent and unit prices for the company's products are expected to increase at one percentage point less than general inflation. Overall, the company's prices would be expected to increase at 3 percent per year. If we assumed a 3 percent annual increase in units sold, we would forecast 6.1 percent annual revenue growth (1.03 × 1.03 – 1).

[21] 10-Year Treasury Constant Maturity Rate (DGS10) and 10-Year Treasury Inflation-Indexed Security, Constant Maturity (FII10), Federal Reserve Bank of St. Louis.

EXHIBIT 13.14 **Expected Inflation vs. Growth in the Consumer Price Index**

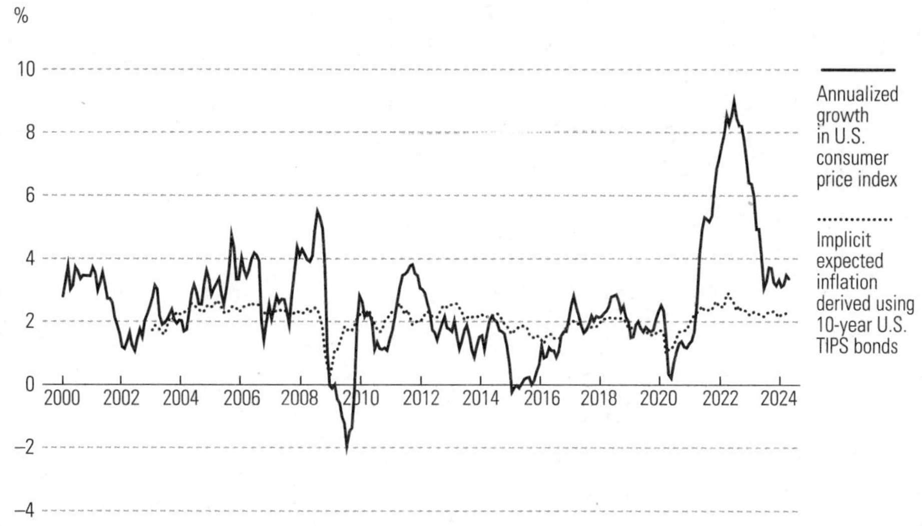

Source: Federal Reserve Bank of St. Louis.

services to goods, and fiscal and monetary stimulus. Many argued that this inflation was transitory and would subside once the world returned to normal activity. This belief was reflected in the implicit inflation rate, which rose from 0.8 percent to only 3.1 percent over the same period. The market turned out to be right, at least during the first few years after COVID, as CPI-based inflation gradually dropped to 3.3 percent by December 2023.

Inflation can distort historical analysis, especially when long-term inflation exceeds 5 percent annually. In these situations, historical financials should be adjusted to reflect operating performance independent of inflation. We discuss the impact of high inflation rates in Chapter 26.

CONCLUDING THOUGHTS

In this chapter, we provided a detailed line-by-line process to create a set of financial forecasts. While it is important that the model reflect the complexities of the business you are analyzing, always keep a close eye on the bigger picture. Make sure resulting value drivers, such as ROIC and growth, are consistent with the past performance of the business and the industry's economics. When the model is complete, use the model to test the importance of various inputs. A what-if analysis can provide insight not only on the valuation but also on the actions management must undertake to capture it.

14

Estimating
Continuing Value

A thoughtful estimate of continuing value is essential to any company valuation. It serves as a useful method for simplifying the valuation process while still incorporating solid economic principles. To estimate a company's value, separate the forecast of expected cash flow into two periods and define the company's value as follows:

$$\text{Value} = \frac{\text{Present Value of Cash Flow}}{\text{during Explicit Forecast Period}} + \frac{\text{Present Value of Cash Flow}}{\text{after Explicit Forecast Period}}$$

The second term is the continuing value: the value of the company's expected cash flow beyond an explicit forecast period. By deliberately making some simple assumptions about the company's performance during this second period—for example, assuming a constant rate of growth and return on capital—you can estimate continuing value by using formulas instead of forecasting and discounting cash flows year by year over an extended period.

Continuing value often accounts for a large percentage of a company's total value. Exhibit 14.1 shows the continuing value as a percentage of the total value for four representative companies in different industries, based on a ten-year explicit forecast period. In these examples, the continuing value ranges from 62 percent to 91 percent of total value. These large percentages do not necessarily mean that most of a company's economic value will be created in the continuing-value period. Often, continuing value is large because profits and other inflows in the early years are offset by outflows for capital spending and working-capital investment—investments that should generate higher cash flow in later years. We discuss the interpretation of continuing value in more detail later in this chapter.

EXHIBIT 14.1 **Continuing Value's Contribution to Total Value**

Representative companies, % of total value

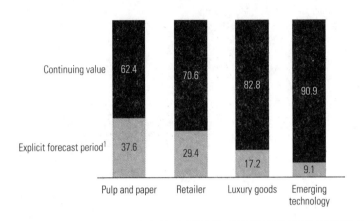

Continuing value

Explicit forecast period[1]

| Pulp and paper | Retailer | Luxury goods | Emerging technology |

[1] 10-year forecast period.

The continuing-value formulas developed over the next few pages are consistent with the principles of value creation and discounted cash flow (DCF). This is important, because too often investment professionals ignore the economics that underpin their estimate of continuing value. For example, we have seen acquirers estimate the continuing value of a target company by applying the same multiple of earnings five years in the future as the multiple they are currently paying for the acquisition target.[1] By doing this, they are implicitly assuming that someone would be willing to pay the same multiple five years from now, regardless of changes in prospects for growth and return on invested capital over that period. This type of circular reasoning leads to inaccurate valuations that are often overly optimistic. Instead, acquirers should estimate what the multiple will be at the end of the forecast period, given the company's potential at that time.

This chapter begins with our recommended continuing-value formulas for DCF and economic-profit valuation models. It then discusses concerns that arise out of common misinterpretations of continuing value, explaining how proper measurement addresses these concerns. Next, we identify common pitfalls in estimation and offer best practices for avoiding them. Finally, we compare the recommended formulas with other common techniques, such as multiples and liquidation values.

---

[1] Typical multiples include enterprise value to EBITA, where EBITA equals earnings before interest, taxes, and amortization, and enterprise value to EBITDA, where EBITDA equals earnings before interest, taxes, depreciation, and amortization.

RECOMMENDED FORMULA FOR DCF VALUATION

If you are using the enterprise DCF model, you should estimate continuing value by using the value driver formula derived in Chapter 3:

$$\text{Continuing Value}_t = \frac{\text{NOPAT}_{t+1}\left(1 - \frac{g}{\text{RONIC}}\right)}{\text{WACC} - g}$$

where NOPAT_{t+1} = net operating profit after taxes in the first year after the explicit forecast period

g = expected growth rate in NOPAT in perpetuity

RONIC = expected rate of return on new invested capital[2]

WACC = weighted average cost of capital

A simple example demonstrates that the value driver formula accurately replicates the process of projecting cash flows and discounting them to the present value. Consider the following cash flow projections:

	Year 1	Year 2	Year 3	Year 4	Year 5
NOPAT	$10.0	$10.6	$11.2	$12.0	$12.6
Net investment	5.0	5.3	5.6	6.0	6.3
Free cash flow	$ 5.0	$ 5.3	$ 5.6	$ 6.0	$ 6.3

Beyond year 5, the company continues to reinvest half its after-tax operating profit at a 12 percent rate of return, driving continued growth at 6 percent. The weighted average cost of capital (WACC) is assumed to be 11 percent.

To compare the methods of computing continuing value, first discount a long forecast—say, 100 years:

$$CV = \frac{\$5.0}{1.11} + \frac{\$5.3}{(1.11)^2} + \frac{\$5.6}{(1.11)^3} + \cdots + \frac{\$50(1.06)^{99}}{(1.11)^{100}}$$

$$CV = \$99$$

Next, use the growth perpetuity formula:

$$CV = \frac{\$5.0}{0.11 - 0.06}$$

$$CV = \$100$$

---

[2] Return on new capital may differ from the return on existing capital, known as return on invested capital (ROIC). The rate of return on existing capital is already incorporated into NOPAT and is thus not explicitly stated in the key value driver formula.

Finally, use the value driver formula:

$$CV = \frac{\$10\left(1 - \frac{0.06}{0.12}\right)}{0.11 - 0.06}$$

$$CV = \$100$$

All three approaches yield virtually the same result. If we were to carry out the discounted cash flow beyond 150 years, the result would be nearly identical.[3]

Although the value driver formula and the cash-flow-based growth perpetuity formula are technically equivalent, applying the cash-flow-based perpetuity formula is tricky, and it is easy to make the common error of ignoring the interdependence between free cash flow and growth. More specifically, if growth in the continuing-value period is forecast to be lower than the growth at the end of the explicit forecast period (as is normally the case), then required reinvestment is likely to be less, leading to higher free cash flow. If the perpetuity's free cash flow is computed using cash flow from the higher-growth explicit forecast period, this cash flow will be too low, and the calculation will underestimate the continuing value. Later in this chapter, an example illustrates what can go wrong when using the cash flow perpetuity formula rather than the key value driver formula.

Because perpetuity-based formulas rely on parameters that never change, use a continuing-value formula only when the company has reached a steady state, with low revenue growth and stable operating margins. Chapters 8 and 9 provide guidance for thinking about return on capital and long-term growth.

In addition, when estimating the continuing-value parameters, keep in mind the following technical considerations:

- *NOPAT.* The level of NOPAT should be based on a normalized level of revenues, sustainable margin, and return on invested capital (ROIC). This is especially important in a cyclical business; revenues and operating margins should reflect the midpoint of the company's business cycle, not its peak or trough.

- *RONIC.* The expected rate of return on new invested capital (RONIC) should be consistent with expected competitive conditions beyond the explicit forecast period. Economic theory suggests that competition will eventually eliminate abnormal returns, so for companies in highly competitive industries, set RONIC equal to WACC. However, for companies

---

[3] The sum of discounted cash flow will approach the perpetuity value as the forecast period is extended. In this example, a 75-year forecast period will capture 96.9 percent of the perpetuity value, whereas a 150-year forecast period will capture 99.9 percent. This is only true, however, when growth is meaningfully less than the cost of capital. If the two variables are of near-equal value, an infinitely lived perpetuity will overstate the value of a company with a limited life. In these situations, either incorporate a probability of failure into your perpetuity, or approximate continuing value with a growth annuity.

with sustainable competitive advantages, such as brands and patents, you might set RONIC equal to the return the company is forecast to earn during later years of the explicit forecast period. Chapter 8 presents data on the long-term returns on capital for companies in different industries.

- *Growth rate.* A company's growth rate typically reverts to industry growth rates very quickly, and few companies can be expected to grow faster than the economy for long periods. The best estimate is probably the expected long-term rate of consumption growth for the industry's products, plus inflation. Sensitivity analyses are useful for understanding how the growth rate affects continuing-value estimates. Chapter 9 presents empirical evidence on historical corporate growth rates.
- *WACC.* The weighted average cost of capital should incorporate a sustainable capital structure and an underlying estimate of business risk consistent with expected industry conditions.

Exhibit 14.2 shows how continuing value, calculated using the value driver formula, is affected by various combinations of growth rate and RONIC. The example assumes a $100 million base level of NOPAT and a 10 percent WACC. For RONIC near the cost of capital, there is little change in value as the growth changes. This is because the company is taking on projects whose net present value is close to zero. At an expected RONIC of 14 percent, however, changing the growth rate from 6 percent to 8 percent

EXHIBIT 14.2 **Impact of Continuing-Value Assumptions**

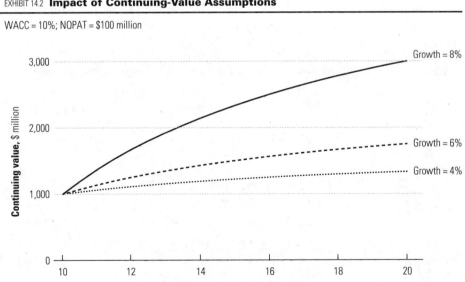

increases the continuing value by 50 percent, from about \$1.4 billion to about \$2.1 billion. The higher the RONIC, the more sensitive the continuing value is to changing growth rates.

Two-Stage Continuing-Value Models

For high-growth companies or companies undergoing long-term structural changes, we recommend extending the explicit forecast period until the company reaches a steady state. If the resulting model and its required forecasts are too cumbersome, use a multistage continuing value that aggregates multiple years into a single formula. In a two-stage model, the continuing value is split into a growth annuity followed by a growth perpetuity. This allows for distinct returns on capital and growth rates for different stages of the company's life, without the burden of year-by-year forecasts. We provide two-stage continuing-value formulas for discounted cash flow and economic-profit models in Appendix H.

CONTINUING VALUE USING ECONOMIC PROFIT

To estimate continuing value in an economic-profit valuation, we again rely on perpetuity-based formulas. With the economic-profit approach, however, the continuing value does not equal the value of the company following the explicit forecast period, as it does for discounted free cash flow. Instead, it is the incremental value over the company's invested capital at the end of the explicit forecast period. Therefore, the key value driver formula from the last section is not appropriate. Today's value of the company is as follows:

$$\text{Value}_0 = \underset{\text{capital}_0}{\text{Invested}} + \underset{\substack{\text{economic profit } during \\ \text{explicit forecast period}}}{\text{Present value of forecast}} + \underset{\substack{\text{economic profit } after \\ \text{explicit forecast period}}}{\text{Present value of forecast}}$$

The continuing value is the last term in the preceding equation.

The formula to estimate continuing value using economic profit is more complicated than that for discounted cash flow. Unlike the key value driver formula used in an enterprise DCF model, the continuing value for economic profit contains two terms. The first term represents the present value of economic profits on capital in place at the end of the forecast period. The second term represents the present value of economic profits for annual investments beyond the explicit forecast period. The formula is as follows:

$$CV_t = \frac{IC_t(ROIC_{t+1} - WACC)}{WACC} + \frac{PV(\text{Economic Profit}_{t+2})}{WACC - g}$$

where

$$PV(\text{Economic Profit}_{t+2}) = \frac{NOPAT_{t+1}\left(\frac{g}{RONIC}\right)(RONIC - WACC)}{WACC}$$

where

IC_t = invested capital at the end of the explicit forecast period

$ROIC_t$ = ROIC on existing capital at the end of the explicit forecast period, measured as $NOPAT_{t+1}/IC_t$

$WACC$ = weighted average cost of capital

g = expected growth rate in NOPAT in perpetuity

$RONIC$ = expected rate of return on new invested capital after the explicit forecast period

According to the formula, total economic profit following the explicit forecast period equals the present value of economic profit in the first year after the explicit forecast in perpetuity plus any incremental economic profit after that year. Incremental economic profit is created by additional growth at returns exceeding the cost of capital. If expected RONIC equals WACC, the third term (economic profits beyond year 1) equals zero, and the continuing economic-profit value is the value of just the first year's economic profit in perpetuity.

MISUNDERSTANDINGS ABOUT CONTINUING VALUE

Properly applied, continuing value can simplify your valuation while incorporating robust economic principles. In practice, however, proper application requires vigilance to avoid three common misunderstandings about continuing value. The first is the perception that the length of the explicit forecast affects the company's value. As we show in this section, only the *split* of value is changing, not the total value. The second is the incorrect belief that value creation stops at the end of the explicit forecast period, when return on *new* invested capital is set equal to WACC in the continuing-value formula. As we demonstrate, since returns from *existing* capital carry into the continuing-value period, aggregate ROIC will only gradually approach the cost of capital. Finally, there is the erroneous view that a large continuing value relative to the company's total value indicates that value creation occurs primarily after the explicit forecast period, which leads to unease about using enterprise DCF. In this section, we show why these concerns are not necessarily justified and why continuing value is more robust than often perceived.

Why Forecast Length Doesn't Affect a Company's Value

While the length of the explicit forecast period you choose is important, it does not affect the value of the company; it affects only the distribution of the company's value between the explicit forecast period and the years that

EXHIBIT 14.3 **Comparison of Total-Value Estimates Using Different Forecast Horizons**

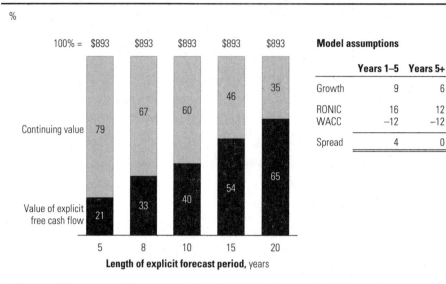

%

100% =	$893	$893	$893	$893	$893

Model assumptions

	Years 1–5	Years 5+
Growth	9	6
RONIC	16	12
WACC	−12	−12
Spread	4	0

Continuing value

Value of explicit free cash flow

Length of explicit forecast period, years

follow. In Exhibit 14.3, the value of the company is $893 million, regardless of how long the forecast period is. With a forecast horizon of five years, the continuing value accounts for 79 percent of total value. With an eight-year horizon, the continuing value accounts for only 67 percent of total value. As the explicit forecast horizon grows longer, value shifts from the continuing value to the explicit forecast period, but the total value always remains the same.

To see how the value shift works, compare Exhibits 14.4 and 14.5. The former details the calculations for the valuation model using a five-year explicit forecast period, whereas the latter repeats the analysis with an eight-year period.

In Exhibit 14.4, NOPAT starts at $100 million. During the first five years, NOPAT grows at 9 percent per year. Following year 5, NOPAT growth slows to 6 percent. Using the definition of free cash flow derived in Chapter 10, we compute gross cash flow by adding depreciation to NOPAT. Free cash flow equals gross cash flow minus gross investment. To compute the company's gross investment, multiply NOPAT by the reinvestment rate, where the reinvestment rate equals the ratio of growth to RONIC (9 percent divided by 16 percent), and then add depreciation. To determine the present value of the company, sum the present value of the explicit forecast period cash flows plus the present value of continuing value. (Since the continuing value is measured as of year 5, the continuing value of $1,246.9 million is discounted by five years, not by six, a common mistake.) The total value equals $892.6 million.

EXHIBIT 14.4 **Valuation Using Five-Year Explicit Forecast Period**

$ million

	Year 1	Year 2	Year 3	Year 4	Year 5	Base for CV
NOPAT	100.0	109.0	118.8	129.5	141.2	149.6
Depreciation	20.0	21.8	23.8	25.9	28.2	
Gross cash flow	120.0	130.8	142.6	155.4	169.4	
Gross investment	(76.3)	(83.1)	(90.6)	(98.7)	(107.6)	
Free cash flow (FCF)	43.8	47.7	52.0	56.7	61.8	
× Discount factor	0.893	0.797	0.712	0.636	0.567	
Present value of FCF	39.1	38.0	37.0	36.0	35.0	

Present value of FCF_{1-5}	185.1
Continuing value	707.5
Total value	892.6

Calculation of continuing value (CV)

$$CV_5 = \frac{NOPAT_{cv}\left(1 - \dfrac{g}{RONIC}\right)}{WACC - g} = \frac{149.6\left(1 - \dfrac{0.06}{0.12}\right)}{0.12 - 0.06} = 1{,}246.9$$

$$CV_0 = \frac{CV_5}{(1 + WACC)^5} = \frac{1{,}246.9}{(1.12)^5} = 707.5$$

Exhibit 14.5 details the calculations for a valuation model that uses an eight-year explicit forecast period and a continuing value that starts in year 9. The structure and forecast inputs of the model are identical to those of Exhibit 14.4. In the first five years, growth is 9 percent, and RONIC equals 16 percent. After five years, growth drops to 6 percent, and RONIC drops to

EXHIBIT 14.5 **Valuation Using Eight-Year Explicit Forecast Period**

$ million

	Year 1	Year 2	Year 3	Year 4	Year 5	Year 6	Year 7	Year 8	Base for CV
NOPAT	100.0	109.0	118.8	129.5	141.2	149.6	158.6	168.1	178.2
Depreciation	20.0	21.8	23.8	25.9	28.2	29.9	31.7	33.6	
Gross cash flow	120.0	130.8	142.6	155.4	169.4	179.6	190.3	201.7	
Gross investment	(76.3)	(83.1)	(90.6)	(98.7)	(107.6)	(104.7)	(111.0)	(117.7)	
Free cash flow (FCF)	43.8	47.7	52.0	56.7	61.8	74.8	79.3	84.1	
× Discount factor	0.893	0.797	0.712	0.636	0.567	0.507	0.452	0.404	
Present value of FCF	39.1	38.0	37.0	36.0	35.0	37.9	35.9	34.0	

Present value of FCF_{1-5}	292.9
Continuing value	599.8
Total value	892.6

Calculation of continuing value (CV)

$$CV_8 = \frac{NOPAT_{cv}\left(1 - \dfrac{g}{RONIC}\right)}{WACC - g} = \frac{178.2\left(1 - \dfrac{0.06}{0.12}\right)}{0.12 - 0.06} = 1{,}485.1$$

$$CV_0 = \frac{CV_8}{(1 + WACC)^8} = \frac{1{,}485.1}{(1.12)^8} = 599.8$$

12 percent. This leads to an explicit forecast value of $292.9 million, which is higher than under the shorter five-year window. Since NOPAT in the continuing value is higher, continuing value also is higher, but since it occurs three years later, its discounted value is lower.

You can see that the amounts under the two valuation methods are identical. Since the underlying value drivers are the same in both valuations, the results will be the same. The length of your forecast horizon should affect only the proportion of total value allocated between the explicit forecast period and continuing value, not the total value.

The choice of forecast horizon will indirectly affect value if it is associated with changes in the economic assumptions underlying the continuing-value estimate. You can unknowingly change the amount of value creation when you change your forecast horizon. Many forecasters assume the company will generate returns above the cost of capital during the explicit forecast period, and they set return on new capital equal to WACC in the continuing value. By extending the explicit forecast period, you increase the number of years the company is creating value. Extending the forecast period indirectly raises the value, even when that is not intended.

So how do you choose the appropriate length of the explicit forecast period? The period should be long enough that the business will have reached a steady state by the end of it. Suppose you expect the company's margins to decline as its customers consolidate. Margins are currently 14 percent, and you forecast they will fall to 9 percent over the next seven years. In this case, the explicit forecast period must be at least seven years, because continuing-value approaches cannot account for the declining margin (at least not without complex computations). The business must be operating at an equilibrium level for the continuing-value approaches to be useful. If the explicit forecast period is more than seven years, there will be no effect on the company's total value.

Why Continuing Value Doesn't Mark the End of Competitive Advantage

A related but subtle issue is the concept of the competitive-advantage period, or that period during which a company earns supernormal returns above the cost of capital. Although counterintuitive, setting RONIC equal to WACC in the continuing-value formula does not imply that the competitive-advantage period will conclude at the end of the explicit forecast period.

Remember, the key value driver formula is based on the return for new capital invested, not company-wide average ROIC. If you set RONIC in the continuing-value period equal to the cost of capital, you are *not* assuming that the return on total capital (old and new) will equal the cost of capital. The *original* capital (prior to the continuing-value period) will continue to earn the returns projected in the last forecast period. In other words, the company's competitive-advantage period has not come to an end once the continuing-value period is reached. Existing capital will continue to earn the final-year

EXHIBIT 14.6 **Gradual Decline in Average ROIC According to Continuing-Value Formula**

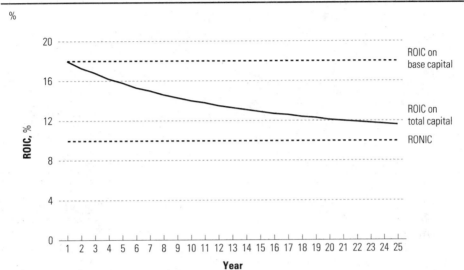

returns in perpetuity. For example, imagine a retailer that opens its initial stores in high-traffic, high-growth, extremely profitable areas. These stores earn a superior rate of return and fund ongoing expansion. But as the company grows, new locations become difficult to find, and the ROIC related to expansion starts to drop. Eventually, the ROIC on the newest store will approach the cost of capital. But does this imply that ROIC on early stores will drop to the cost of capital as well? Probably not. A great location is hard to beat.

Exhibit 14.6 shows the average ROIC based on continuing-value growth of 5 percent. The return on base capital is 18 percent, return on new capital is 10 percent, and WACC is 10 percent. Note how the average return on aggregate capital declines only gradually. From its starting point at 18 percent, it declines to 14 percent (the halfway point to RONIC) after ten years in the continuing-value period. It reaches 12 percent after 21 years and 11 percent after 37 years. How quickly this decay occurs from ROIC in the forecast period to RONIC in the continuing value depends on the growth rate in the continuing value. The higher the growth rate, the more capital there is to be deployed at lower returns, and the faster the decline.

Why Value Isn't Just from Continuing Value

"All the value is in the continuing value" is a comment we've often heard from dismayed executives. Exhibit 14.7 illustrates the problem for a hypothetical company, Innovation Inc. Based on discounted free cash flow, it appears that 80 percent of Innovation's value comes from the continuing value. But there are other interesting ways to interpret the source of value.

EXHIBIT 14.7 **Innovation Inc.: Free Cash Flow Forecast and Valuation**

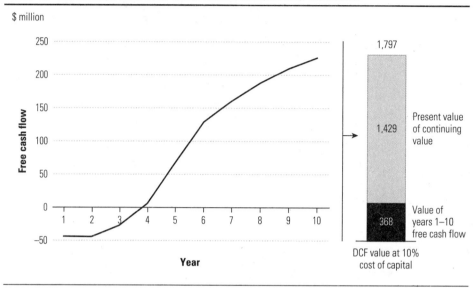

Exhibit 14.8 suggests an alternative: a business components approach. Innovation Inc. has a base business that earns a steady 20 percent return on capital and is growing at 5 percent per year. It also has developed a new product line that will require several years of negative cash flow for development of a new sales channel, which management hopes will lead to organic growth. As shown in Exhibit 14.8, the base business has a value of $1,325 million, or 74 percent of Innovation's total value. In other words, 74 percent of the company's value comes from operations that are currently generating stable,

EXHIBIT 14.8 **Innovation Inc.: Valuation by Components**

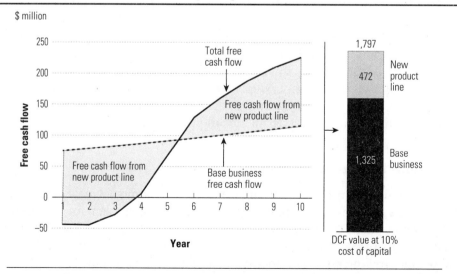

EXHIBIT 14.9 **Innovation Inc.: Comparison of Continuing-Value Approaches**

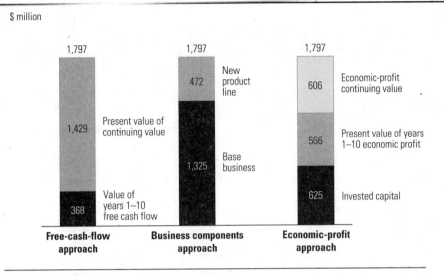

$ million

predictable cash flow. Only 26 percent of total value can be attributed to the unpredictable growth business. When the situation is reframed this way, uncertainty plays only a small role in the total value of the company.

If we use the economic-profit model, we can see yet another possible interpretation of continuing value. Exhibit 14.9 compares the components of value for Innovation Inc., using the discounted-FCF approach, the business components approach, and an economic-profit model. Under the economic-profit model, 35 percent of Innovation's value is simply the book value of invested capital. The rest of the value, $1,172 million, is the present value of projected economic profit. Of that, only 34 percent of total value is generated during the continuing-value period—a much smaller share than under the discounted-FCF model.

COMMON PITFALLS

Estimating a company's performance ten to 15 years out is an imprecise exercise. Common mistakes in continuing-value estimation include erroneously extrapolating base year cash flow, as well as making overly conservative assumptions on capital returns, both naively and purposely.

Erroneous Base Year Extrapolation

Exhibit 14.10 illustrates a common error in forecasting the base level of free cash flow: assuming that the investment rate is constant, so that NOPAT, investment, and FCF all grow at the same rate. From year 9 to year 10 (the last forecast year), the company's earnings and cash flow grow by 10 percent. Revenue growth in the continuing-value period is expected to be 5 percent

EXHIBIT 14.10 **Correct and Incorrect Methods of Forecasting Base FCF**

$ million

| | Year 9 | Year 10 | Year 11, 5% growth | |
			Incorrect	Correct
Revenues	1,000	1,100	1,155	1,155
Operating expenses	(850)	(935)	(982)	(982)
EBITA	150	165	173	173
Operating taxes	(60)	(66)	(69)	(69)
NOPAT	90	99	104	104
Depreciation	27	30	32	32
Gross cash flow	117	129	136	136
Capital expenditures	(30)	(33)	(35)	(35)
Increase in working capital	(27)	(30)	(32)	(17)
Gross investment	(57)	(63)	(67)	(52)
Free cash flow	60	66	69	84
Supplemental calculations				
Working capital, year-end	300	330	362	347
Working capital/revenues, %	30.0	30.0	31.3	30.0

per year. Given these circumstances, a common, yet incorrect, forecast for year 11 (the continuing-value base year) would simply increase every line item from year 10 by 5 percent, as shown in the third column. This forecast is wrong because the current increase in working capital is far too large, given the smaller increase in sales. Since revenues are growing more slowly, the proportion of gross cash flow devoted to working capital requirements should decline significantly, as shown in the last column. In the final column, the increase in working capital should be the amount necessary to maintain the year-end working capital at a constant percentage of revenues.

The erroneous approach continually increases working capital as a percentage of revenues (5 percent) and will significantly understate the value of the company. Note that in the third column, free cash flow is 18 percent lower than it should be. The same problem applies to capital expenditures. To keep the example simple, we limited it to working capital.

To avoid making an error in estimating final-year cash flow, we strongly recommend using the key value driver formula instead of the cash flow perpetuity model. The key value driver model implicitly computes the required investment based on expectations of growth and ROIC.

Naive Overconservatism

Many investment professionals routinely assume that the incremental return on capital during the continuing-value period will equal the cost of capital.

This practice relieves them of having to forecast a growth rate, since growth in this case neither adds nor destroys value. For some businesses, this assumption is too conservative. For example, both Coca-Cola's and PepsiCo's soft-drink businesses earn high returns on invested capital, and their returns are unlikely to fall substantially as they continue to grow, due to the strength of their brands, high barriers to entry, and limited competition.[4] For these businesses, an assumption that RONIC equals WACC would understate their values.[5] This problem applies equally to almost any business selling a product or service that is unlikely to be duplicated, including many pharmaceutical companies, numerous consumer products companies, and some software companies.

However, even if RONIC remains high, growth will drop as the market matures. Therefore, any assumption that RONIC is greater than WACC should be coupled with an economically reasonable growth rate.

Purposeful Overconservatism

Some investment professionals are overly conservative because of the uncertainty and size of the continuing value. But if continuing value is to be estimated properly, the uncertainty should cut both ways: the results are just as likely to be higher than an unbiased estimate as they are to be lower. So conservatism overcompensates for uncertainty. Uncertainty matters, but it should be modeled using scenarios, rather than making conservative assumptions regarding return on capital or growth in the continuing-value formula.

OTHER APPROACHES TO CONTINUING VALUE

Several alternative approaches to estimating continuing value are used in practice. A few of them are acceptable if applied carefully, but in general, these alternatives often produce misleading results. We prefer the value driver methods explored earlier in this chapter, because they explicitly rely on the underlying economic assumptions embodied in the company analysis. The alternative approaches tend to obscure the underlying economic assumptions. Using the example of a sporting goods company, Exhibit 14.11

---

[4] Even the strongest brands face pressure from new technologies and changing customer preferences. For instance, Coca-Cola and PepsiCo have looked to new businesses as consumers have shifted away from carbonated soft drinks to bottled water and energy drinks.

[5] In this example, RONIC equaling WACC is unlikely because of economic reasons. RONIC may also permanently exceed the cost of capital because capital is systematically understated. Under current accounting standards, only physical (or contractual) investment is capitalized on the balance sheet. Companies that have valuable brands, distribution, and intellectual property do not recognize their investment on the balance sheet unless acquired. For more on how to compute invested capital for companies with large intangible assets, see Chapter 24.

EXHIBIT 14.11 **Continuing-Value Estimates for a Sporting Goods Company**

$ million

Technique	Assumptions	Continuing value
Other DCF approaches		
Perpetuity based on final year's NOPAT	Normalized NOPAT growing at inflation rate	582
Perpetuity based on final year's cash flow	Normalized FCF growing at inflation rate	428
Multiples (comparables)		
Price-to-earnings ratio	Industry average of 15 times earnings	624
Market-to-book ratio	Industry average of 1.4 times book value	375
Asset-based valuations		
Liquidation value	80% of working capital	186
	70% of net fixed assets	
Replacement cost	Book value adjusted for inflation	275

illustrates the wide dispersion of continuing-value estimates that these different techniques can yield.

The most common of these techniques can be divided into three categories: other DCF approaches, multiples, and asset-based valuations. This section describes techniques in these categories and explains why we prefer the approaches we recommended earlier.

Other DCF Approaches

The recommended DCF formulas can be modified to create additional continuing-value formulas with more restrictive (and sometimes unreasonable) assumptions.

One variation is the *convergence* formula. For companies in competitive industries, many expect that the return on net new investment will eventually converge to the cost of capital as all the excess profits are competed away. This assumption allows a simpler version of the value driver formula:

$$CV = \frac{NOPAT_{t+1}}{WACC}$$

The derivation begins with the value driver formula:

$$CV = \frac{NOPAT_{t+1}\left(1 - \frac{g}{RONIC}\right)}{WACC - g}$$

Assume that RONIC = WACC (that is, the return on incremental invested capital equals the cost of capital):

$$CV = \frac{NOPAT_{t+1}\left(1 - \frac{g}{WACC}\right)}{WACC - g}$$

$$= \frac{NOPAT_{t+1}\left(\frac{WACC - g}{WACC}\right)}{WACC - g}$$

Canceling the term WACC − g leaves a simple formula:

$$CV = \frac{NOPAT_{t+1}}{WACC}$$

The fact that the growth term has disappeared from the equation does *not* mean that the nominal growth in NOPAT will be zero. The growth term drops out because new investment to drive growth adds nothing to value, as the RONIC associated with growth equals the cost of capital. This formula is sometimes interpreted as implying zero growth (not even with inflation), but this is not an accurate interpretation.

Misinterpretation of the convergence formula has led to another variant: the *aggressive-growth* formula. This formula assumes that earnings in the continuing-value period will grow at some rate, most often the inflation rate. Some investment professionals then conclude that earnings should be discounted at the real WACC rather than at the nominal WACC. The resulting formula is

$$CV = \frac{NOPAT_{t+1}}{WACC - g}$$

Here, g is the inflation rate.

This formula can substantially overstate continuing value, because it assumes that NOPAT can grow without any incremental capital investment. This is unlikely or impossible, because any growth will probably require additional working capital and fixed assets.

To see the critical assumption hidden in the preceding formula, we analyze the key value driver formula as RONIC approaches infinity:

$$CV = \frac{NOPAT_{t+1}\left(1 - \frac{g}{RONIC}\right)}{WACC - g}$$

$$RONIC \rightarrow \infty; \text{ therefore, } \frac{g}{RONIC} \rightarrow 0$$

$$CV = \frac{NOPAT_{t+1}(1 - 0)}{WACC - g}$$

$$= \frac{NOPAT_{t+1}}{WACC - g}$$

Exhibit 14.12 compares the two variations of the key value driver formula, showing how the average return on invested capital (both existing and new investment) behaves under the two assumptions. In the aggressive-growth case, NOPAT grows without any new investment, so the return on invested capital eventually approaches infinity. In the convergence case, the average return on invested capital moves toward the weighted average cost of capital as new capital becomes a larger portion of the total capital base.

EXHIBIT 14.12 **Rates of Return Implied by Alternative Continuing-Value Formulas**

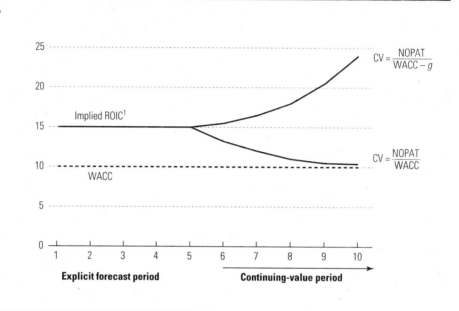

[1] Implied ROIC equals the return on both new and existing capital.

Multiples

Multiples, also known as comparables, assume that a company will be worth some multiple of future earnings or book value in the continuing period. But how do you estimate an appropriate future multiple?

A common approach, especially in private-equity transactions, is to assume that the company will be worth a multiple of earnings or book value based on the multiple for the company today. Suppose we choose today's industry average enterprise-value-to-EBITDA ratio. This ratio reflects the economic prospects of the industry during the explicit forecast period as well as the continuing-value period. In maturing industries, however, prospects at the end of the explicit forecast period are likely to be very different from today's. Therefore, a different EV-to-EBITDA is needed: one that reflects the company's prospects at the end of the forecast period. What factors will determine that ratio? As discussed in Chapter 3, the factors include the company's expected growth, the rate of return on new capital, and the cost of capital—the same factors found in the key value driver formula. Unless you are comfortable using an arbitrary multiple, you are better off with the economic insights of the value driver formula.

When valuing an acquisition, companies sometimes fall into the circular reasoning that the multiple for the continuing value should equal the multiple paid for the acquisition. In other words, if I pay 15 times EBITDA today, I should be able to sell the business for 15 times EBITDA at the end of the explicit forecast period. In most cases, the reason a company is willing to pay a particular multiple for an acquisition is that it plans to improve the target's profitability. So the effective EBITDA multiple it is paying on the improved level of EBITDA will be much less than 15. Once the improvements are in place and earnings are higher, buyers will not be willing to pay the same multiple unless they can make additional improvements beyond those already made. Chapter 18 describes other common mistakes made when using multiples.

Asset-Based Valuations

Unlike the previous methods, which rely on future cash flow or earnings, estimating continuing value using liquidation value or replacement cost is known as an asset-based approach. Since these approaches ignore the future potential of the company, use them only in situations where ongoing operations are in jeopardy.

The liquidation value approach sets the continuing value equal to the estimated proceeds from the sale of the assets, after paying off liabilities at the end of the explicit forecast period. Liquidation value is often far different from the value of the company as a going concern. In a growing, profitable industry, a company's liquidation value is probably well below the going-concern value. In a dying industry, liquidation value may exceed going-concern value. Do not use this approach unless liquidation is likely at the end of the forecast period.

The replacement cost approach sets the continuing value equal to the expected cost to replace the company's assets. This approach has at least two drawbacks. First, not all tangible assets are replaceable. The company's organizational capital can be valued only on the basis of the cash flow the company generates. The replacement cost of just the company's tangible assets may greatly understate the value of the company. Second, not all the company's assets will ever be replaced. Consider a machine used by a particular company. As long as it generates a positive cash flow, the asset is valuable to the ongoing business of the company. But the replacement cost of the asset may be so high that replacing it is not economical. Here, the replacement cost may exceed the value of the business as an ongoing entity.

CLOSING THOUGHTS

The future is inherently unknowable, so it is understandable that many professionals are skeptical about enterprise DCF models that rely on a continuing-value formula. This skepticism may be warranted in some cases, but for many valuations, disaggregating the continuing value into its economic components can show why these concerns are often overstated. Remember, the value of a company is merely its invested capital plus the economic profits it generates on that capital. If most of the value creation occurs during the explicit forecast period, then the continuing value plays a much smaller role than the free cash flow would lead you to believe.

When estimating continuing value, remember to follow a few simple guidelines for successful valuation. First, use the key value driver formula to estimate continuing value. Unlike the free-cash-flow model, the value driver formula implicitly models the correct investment required for growth. Second, carefully assess the value drivers at the time of continuing value. The value drivers should be consistent with the company's potential in the future, rather than today's performance or economic environment. We believe a thoughtful analysis will lead to insights not available with other models.

15

Estimating the Cost of Capital

To value a company using enterprise discounted cash flow (DCF), discount your forecast of free cash flow (FCF) at the weighted average cost of capital (WACC). The WACC represents the returns that all investors in a company—equity and debt—expect to earn for investing their funds in one particular business instead of others with similar risk. The investment return they are forgoing is also referred to as their opportunity cost of capital.

The WACC has three primary components: the cost of equity, the after-tax cost of debt, and the company's target capital structure. Estimating WACC with precision is difficult because there is no way to directly measure an investor's opportunity cost of capital, especially the cost of equity. Moreover, some traditional approaches for estimating WACC that worked well in the past became complicated in the 2010s, when monetary policies pushed government bond yields to historically low levels. Although interest rates have risen since then, they remain relatively low compared with historical norms.

This chapter begins with a summary of the WACC calculation and then presents detailed sections on how to estimate its components: the cost of equity, the after-tax cost of debt, and the target capital structure, which is used to weight the first two components. The chapter concludes with a discussion of WACC estimation for companies whose capital structure is more complex than traditional debt and common stock.

CALCULATING THE WEIGHTED AVERAGE COST OF CAPITAL

In its simplest form, the weighted average cost of capital equals the weighted average of the after-tax cost of debt and cost of equity:

$$\text{WACC} = \frac{D}{V} k_d (1 - T_m) + \frac{E}{V} k_e$$

where

D/V = target level of debt to value using market-based values

E/V = target level of equity to value using market-based values

k_d = cost of debt

k_e = cost of equity

T_m = company's marginal tax rate on income

For companies with other securities, such as preferred stock, additional terms must be added to the cost of capital, representing each security's expected rate of return and percentage of total enterprise value. The cost of capital does not include expected returns of operating liabilities, such as accounts payable. The compensation required for capital provided by customers, suppliers, and employees is embedded in operating expenses and thus already incorporated in free cash flow.

The WACC relies on three key inputs, the cost of equity, the cost of debt, and the company's target capital structure. The cost of equity is determined by estimating the expected return on the market portfolio, adjusted for the risk of the company being valued.[1] In this book, we estimate risk by using the capital asset pricing model (CAPM). The CAPM adjusts for company-specific risk using beta, which measures how a company's stock price responds to movements in the overall market. Stocks with high betas have expected returns that exceed the market return; the converse is true for low-beta stocks. Only beta risk is priced. Any remaining risk, which academics call idiosyncratic risk, can be diversified away by holding multiple securities, as explained in Chapter 4. In practice, measurements of individual company betas are imprecise. Therefore, we recommend using a set of peer company betas to estimate an industry beta.

To approximate the after-tax cost of debt for an investment-grade firm, use the company's after-tax yield to maturity on its long-term debt.[2] For companies whose debt trades infrequently or for nontraded debt, use the company's debt rating to estimate the yield to maturity. Since free cash flow is measured without interest tax shields, use the after-tax cost of debt to incorporate the interest tax shield into the WACC.

Finally, assess the company's practices for setting its capital structure, and use the target levels to weight the after-tax cost of debt and cost of equity. For stable companies, the target capital structure is often approximated by the company's current debt-to-value ratio, using market values of debt and equity. As we'll explain later in this chapter, do not use book values.

---

[1] In this section, we assume the company has a single line of business and therefore discuss risk at the company level. If the company has multiple lines of business, estimate the cost of capital for each business separately.

[2] The yield to maturity is not a good proxy for the cost of debt when a company carries substantial debt. We discuss alternative methods to estimate the cost of debt for highly leveraged companies later in this chapter.

EXHIBIT 15.1 **Costco: Weighted Average Cost of Capital (WACC)**

%

Source of capital	Target proportion of total capital	Cost of capital	Marginal tax rate	After-tax cost of capital	Contribution to weighted average
Debt	4.9	4.6	24.6	3.5	0.2
Equity	95.1	8.3		8.3	7.9
WACC	100.0				8.1

For an example of the WACC calculation, see Exhibit 15.1, which presents the calculation for Costco. We estimate the company's cost of equity at 8.3 percent using the CAPM. To estimate Costco's pretax cost of debt, we use the yield to maturity on a long-dated, liquid Costco bond, which leads to a cost of debt of 4.6 percent. In Chapter 11, we estimated Costco's marginal tax rate at 24.6 percent, so the company's after-tax cost of debt equals 3.5 percent. To weight the after-tax cost of debt and cost of equity, we set the target capital structure equal to the company's current debt-to-value, excluding excess cash. Normally, we net excess cash against gross debt to determine the cost of capital, but since Costco has little net debt compared with its peer group, we assume the company will disgorge excess cash to increase leverage. Adding together the weighted contributions from debt and equity, WACC equals 8.1 percent.

Always estimate the WACC in a manner consistent with the principles of free cash flow. For example, since free cash flow is the cash flow available to all financial investors, the company's WACC must also include the expected return for each investor class. In general, the cost of capital must meet the following criteria:

- It must include the cost of capital for all investors—debt, preferred stock, common stock, and so on—since free cash flow is available to all investors, who expect compensation for the risks they take.

- Any financing-related benefits or costs, such as interest tax shields, not included in free cash flow must be incorporated into the cost of capital or valued separately using adjusted present value.[3]

- WACC must be computed after corporate income taxes (since free cash flow is calculated in after-tax terms).

---

[3] For most companies, discounting forecast free cash flow at a constant WACC is a simple, accurate, and robust method of arriving at a corporate valuation. If, however, the company's target capital structure is expected to change significantly—for instance, in a leveraged buyout (LBO)—WACC can overstate (or understate) the impact of interest tax shields. In this situation, you should discount free cash flow at the unlevered cost of equity and value tax shields and other financing effects separately (as described in Chapter 10).

- It must be based on the same inflation expectations as those embedded in free cash flow forecasts.
- The duration of the securities used to estimate the cost of capital must match the duration of the cash flows.

ESTIMATING THE COST OF EQUITY

The cost of equity is the central building block of the cost of capital. Unfortunately, it is extremely difficult to measure accurately. Academics and practitioners have proposed numerous models to estimate the cost of equity, but none have been reliable, especially at the company level. Even if a model could be agreed upon, accurately measuring the required inputs has also proven elusive. Consequently, deriving the cost of equity is far more difficult in practice than many core finance texts imply. With these hurdles in mind, we estimate the cost of equity in two steps:

1. *Estimate market return.* First, we estimate the expected return on the entire stock market. Although a particular company will not necessarily have the same cost of capital as the market as a whole, the market return provides a critical benchmark for judging how reasonable estimates of the cost of equity for individual companies are.
2. *Adjust for risk.* We next adjust for company risk, using one of two well-known models, the capital asset pricing model (CAPM) and the Fama-French three-factor model. Each model measures company risk by measuring the correlation of its stock price to changes in a market-based portfolio, known as beta. Since beta estimates are at best imprecise, we rely on peer group betas, rather than individual company betas.

Estimating the Market Return

Every day, thousands of investors attempt to estimate the market's expected return. Since the future is unobservable, many practitioners use one of two approaches to estimate it.

The first method calculates the cost of equity implied by the relationship between current share prices and expected future financial performance. By valuing a large sample of companies like the Standard & Poor's (S&P) 500 index, we can reverse engineer the embedded cost of equity. Although the method requires a forecast of future performance, it is quite powerful, since it incorporates up-to-date market prices.

The second method looks backward using historical market returns. However, given that past market returns are heavily influenced by the rate of inflation prevalent at the time, a simple average of past returns isn't helpful in predicting today's market return. Instead, we add to today's interest rate a historical market risk premium (stocks minus bonds) that incorporates today's expectation of future inflation, rather than past inflation rates.

Using Market Prices to Estimate the Cost of Equity   Our first approach for estimating the cost of equity—analyzing current share prices alongside expected corporate performance metrics such as earnings, return on equity (ROE), and growth projections for a large sample of companies—yields striking results. After inflation is stripped out, the expected market return (*not* excess return) is remarkably constant, averaging 7 percent between 1962 and 2022.

To reverse engineer the expected market return, we start with the value driver formula described in Chapter 3. In this case, we've expressed it in terms of equity value rather than enterprise value (substituting the cost of equity for the weighted average cost of capital, return on equity for ROIC, etc.):

$$\text{Equity Value} = \frac{\text{Earnings}\left(1 - \frac{g}{\text{ROE}}\right)}{k_e - g}$$

where

$$\text{Earnings} = \text{equity earnings}$$
$$g = \text{expected growth in earnings}$$
$$\text{ROE} = \text{expected return on equity}$$
$$k_e = \text{cost of equity}$$

Solving for the cost of equity gives the following equation:

$$k_e = \frac{\text{Earnings}\left(1 - \frac{g}{\text{ROE}}\right)}{\text{Equity Value}} + g$$

Earnings divided by equity value is the inverse of the price-to-earnings ratio (P/E), so it is possible to reduce the equation further:

$$k_e = \left(\frac{1}{\text{P/E}}\right)\left(1 - \frac{g}{\text{ROE}}\right) + g$$

We apply this formula to the S&P 500 index, using the long-run return on equity of 14.5 percent and the long-run growth in real gross domestic product (GDP) of 3.5 percent, to convert a given year's S&P 500 median P/E into the cost of equity.[4] Implementing the model is slightly more complex than the formula implies, because we also strip out the effects of inflation to arrive at a real cost

---

[4] R. Dobbs, T. Koller, and S. Lund, "What Effect Has Quantitative Easing Had on Your Share Price?" *McKinsey on Finance*, no. 49 (Winter 2014): 15–18; and M. H. Goedhart, T. M. Koller, and Z. D. Williams, "The Real Cost of Equity," *McKinsey on Finance*, no. 5 (Autumn 2002): 13–15.

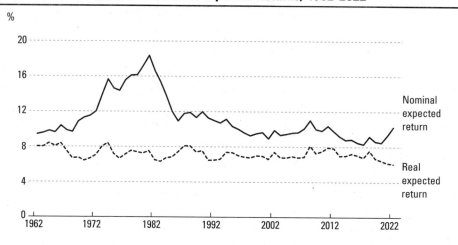

EXHIBIT 15.2 **S&P 500 Real and Nominal Expected Returns, 1962–2022**

of equity. Exhibit 15.2 plots the real expected market returns between 1962 and 2022. As the exhibit demonstrates, the nominal return changes substantially over time, but the real expected return hovers quite close to 7 percent. For the United Kingdom, the real market return is slightly more volatile and averages 6 percent.

Techniques like this date back to Charles Dow in the 1920s, and many authors have tested the concept.[5] One set of studies used analyst forecasts to estimate growth, but many argue that analyst forecasts focus on the short term and are upwardly biased.[6] In 2003, Eugene Fama and Kenneth French used long-term dividend growth rates as a proxy for future growth, but they focused on dividend yields, not on available cash flow.[7] Therefore, we believe our implementation is best.

To convert the real expected return into a nominal return appropriate for discounting, add an estimate of future inflation that is consistent with your cash flow projections. In the United States, the Federal Reserve Bank of Philadelphia provides a long-run forecast of inflation.[8] In December 2023, this equaled 2.4 percent. Alternatively, you can estimate expected long-term inflation by using the spread between inflation-protected and regular government

[5] E. Fama and K. French, "Dividend Yields and Expected Stock Returns," *Journal of Financial Economics* 22, no. 1 (1988): 3–25; R. F. Stambaugh, "Predictive Regressions," *Journal of Financial Economics* 54, no. 3 (1999): 375–421; and J. Lewellen, "Predicting Returns with Financial Ratios," *Journal of Financial Economics* 74, no. 2 (2004): 209–235.

[6] J. Claus and J. Thomas, "Equity Premia as Low as Three Percent? Evidence from Analysts' Earnings Forecasts for Domestic and International Stocks," *Journal of Finance* 56, no. 5 (October 2001): 1629–1666; and W. R. Gebhardt, C. M. C. Lee, and B. Swaminathan, "Toward an Implied Cost of Capital," *Journal of Accounting Research* 39, no. 1 (2001): 135–176.

[7] E. F. Fama and K. R. French, "The Equity Premium," *Journal of Finance* 57, no. 2 (April 2002): 637–659.

[8] See Federal Reserve Bank of Philadelphia, *Survey of Professional Forecasters*, www.philadelphiafed. org.

bonds yield. In December 2023, this spread was approximately 2.2 percent. When you add inflation in the range of 2.2–2.4 percent to a real return of 7 percent, you get an expected market return of 9.2–9.4 percent.

Later in this chapter, we apply the CAPM to adjust the market return for company-specific risk. The CAPM relies on an estimate of the market risk premium—the difference between market returns and those of risk-free bonds. Assuming the stock market continues to deliver a 7 percent return on an inflation-adjusted basis, and subtracting the December 2023 real interest rate of 1.7 percent, we estimate the market risk premium at 5.3 percent—right in the middle of our recommended range of 5.0–5.5 percent.

Historical Estimates of the Market Risk Premium   A second method to estimate the market return starts with a historical estimate of the market risk premium and then adds this estimate to today's long-term government bond rate.

Properly estimating the historical risk premium requires some statistical sophistication. A detailed description of the most relevant issues is available in Appendix F; we offer only a summary here. First, use as long a time period as possible. Our work relies on research by Elroy Dimson, Paul Marsh, and Mike Staunton, who have provided market returns dating back to 1900.[9] Although some argue that market risk premiums have dropped over time, a simple regression analysis does not support this. Therefore, we believe more data improve the quality of estimation.

Second, neither the arithmetic average nor a geometric average of single-year returns will estimate multiyear discount rates well. The best value falls somewhere between the two averages. While the arithmetic average is best for estimating a one-period return, compounding the average return also compounds any estimation error, causing the compounded number to be too high.

Exhibit 15.3 presents the rates of return for the U.S. stock and bond markets between 1900 and 2023. The first two columns present the average returns for various holding periods. For example, the average cumulative return over a ten-year period was 179.7 percent for U.S. stocks and 64.6 percent for bonds. To annualize these figures, the geometric mean is calculated over the respective holding periods. The excess return of stocks over bonds is then determined by taking the difference between the two. For a ten-year holding period, the annualized excess return was 5.6 percent.

Even with the best statistical techniques, however, these numbers are probably too high to estimate future returns because the sample above includes only one country with strong historical returns.[10] Statisticians refer

---

[9] E. Dimson, P. Marsh, and M. Staunton, "The Worldwide Equity Premium: A Smaller Puzzle," in *Handbook of Investments: Equity Risk Premium*, ed. R. Mehra (Amsterdam: Elsevier Science, 2007).

[10] S. Brown, W. Goetzmann, and S. Ross, "Survivorship Bias," *Journal of Finance* (July 1995): 853–873.

EXHIBIT 15.3 **Cumulative Returns for Various Intervals, 1900–2023**

%

	Average cumulative returns		Annualized returns		
Holding period	U.S. stocks	U.S. government bonds	U.S. stocks[1]	U.S. government bonds[1]	Excess returns[2]
1 year	11.5	4.9	11.5	4.9	6.6
2 years	24.3	10.0	11.5	4.9	6.6
4 years	53.2	21.1	11.1	4.9	6.2
5 years	67.7	26.9	11.1	5.0	6.1
10 years	179.7	64.6	10.8	5.1	5.6

[1] Measured as the geometric mean over the holding period.

[2] Measured as the difference between annualized stock returns and annualized bond returns.

Source: Data for 1900–2002 from E. Dimson, P. Marsh, and M. Staunton, "The Worldwide Equity Premium: A Smaller Puzzle," in *Handbook of Investments: Equity.*

to this phenomenon as survivorship bias. Zvi Bodie writes, "There were 36 active stock markets in 1900, so why do we only look at two [the UK and U.S. markets]? I can tell you—because many of the others don't have a 100-year history, for a variety of reasons."[11]

Since the U.S. stock market is unlikely to replicate its performance over the next century, we adjust the historical market risk premium downward. Dimson, Marsh, and Staunton find that the U.S. arithmetic annual return exceeded a 17-country composite return by 0.8 percent in real terms.[12] Subtracting a 0.8 percent survivorship premium from the ten-year holding period of 5.6 percent tells us that the historical risk premium, measured by excess returns, is just under 5 percent. While past returns cannot guarantee future returns, they do offer supporting evidence that the forward-looking estimate calculated earlier in the chapter is reasonable.

Estimating the Risk-Free Rate   With an estimate of the market risk premium in hand, we can now calculate the expected market return by adding the market risk premium to the current risk-free rate. For decades, many practitioners relied on a ten-year government yield as a proxy for the risk-free rate in valuation. However, a new approach became necessary when interest rates fell to unprecedented lows following the 2007–2009 financial crisis.

To combat the financial crisis, the U.S. Federal Reserve reduced short-term rates to almost zero, pulling down long-term rates as a by-product. It also began a policy of repurchasing bonds in the open market (known as quantitative easing), further pushing up prices and driving down yields. At the same time, U.S. government bonds became a haven for investors worldwide, leading to high prices and lower yields for government bonds. Over the next decade,

---

[11] Z. Bodie, "Longer Time Horizon 'Does Not Reduce Risk,'" *Financial Times,* January 26, 2002.

[12] Dimson, Marsh, and Staunton, "The Worldwide Equity Premium."

the yield on ten-year government bonds began a long and volatile decline, reaching an all-time low of 0.5 percent in July 2020.

With interest rates at such low levels, many practitioners realized that valuation models based on these rates didn't lead to sensible results. With government bonds at 0.5 percent, a 5 percent market risk premium implies an expected market return of just 6.5 percent. Compared with expected returns before 2009, this should have caused a dramatic rise in the market's price relative to earnings. Mathematically, every 1 percent decrease in the cost of equity for the S&P 500 index should increase the P/E of the index by roughly 20 to 25 percent. So a 3 percent drop in the cost of equity would have increased the P/E from a typical trading range of 15 times to more than 25 times. Yet no rise occurred. Instead, the median P/E hovered around 16 times over the next decade.[13]

If markets are functioning normally and Treasury yields reflect typical market conditions, the ten-year interest rate will serve as a suitable proxy for the risk-free rate. However, during unusual periods, such as the financial crisis of the late 2000s or the global pandemic in 2020, when governments dramatically lower interest rates to stimulate the economy, we recommend using a synthetic risk-free rate to estimate the expected market return. To build a synthetic risk-free rate, add the expected inflation rate of 2.2 to 2.4 percent presented in the previous section to the long-run average real interest rate of 2 percent; this yields a rate between 4.2 and 4.4 percent.[14]

Matching Cash Flow Duration   In the preceding analysis, we focused on returns from ten-year bonds. But why ten years and not something longer or shorter? The most theoretically sound approach is to discount a given year's cash flow at a cost of capital that matches the maturity of the cash flow. In other words, year 1 cash flows would be discounted at a cost of capital based on a one-year risk-free rate, while year 10 cash flows would be discounted at a cost of capital based on a ten-year discount rate. To do this, use zero-coupon bonds (known as STRIPS),[15] rather than Treasury bonds that make interim payments. The interim payments on Treasury bonds cause their effective maturity to be much shorter than their stated maturity.

---

[13] For more on the market returns and P/E multiples during periods of ultra-low interest rates, see V. Gupta, D. Kohn, T. Koller, and W. Rehm, "Markets versus Textbooks: Calculating Today's Cost of Equity," McKinsey & Company, January 2023.

[14] For ease of implementation, we use a single cost of equity to discount all cash flows. More advanced models split cash flows into two periods: an explicit forecast period and a continuing value. When using two periods, discount the first set of cash flows at observed yields, and create the perpetuity using a synthetic risk-free rate. Although a two-period model uses short-term market data more effectively, the valuation differences between one- and two-period models are relatively small, especially for short forecast windows.

[15] Introduced by the U.S. Treasury in 1985, STRIPS stands for "separate trading of registered interest and principal of securities." The STRIPS program enables investors to hold and trade the individual components of Treasury notes and bonds as separate securities.

Using multiple discount rates, however, is quite cumbersome. Therefore, few practitioners discount each cash flow using its matched bond maturity. Instead, most choose a single rate that best matches the cash flow stream being valued. For U.S.-based corporate valuations, we recommend ten-year government STRIPS. (Longer-dated bonds such as the 30-year Treasury bond might match the cash flow stream better, but they may not be liquid enough to represent the risk-free rate correctly.) When valuing European companies, use ten-year German government bonds, because they trade more frequently and have lower credit risk than the government bonds of other European countries. Always use government bond yields denominated in the same currency as the company's cash flow to estimate the risk-free rate. Also, ensure the inflation rate in your cash flows is consistent with the inflation rate in the government bond rate you are using.

Do *not* use a short-term Treasury bill to determine the risk-free rate. When introductory finance textbooks calculate the CAPM, they typically use a short-term Treasury rate because they are estimating expected returns for the next *month*. Instead, use longer-term bonds, as they better align with the time horizon of corporate cash flows.

Closing Thoughts on Expected Market Returns   Although many in the finance profession disagree about how to measure the market risk premium, we believe a number around 5 percent is appropriate. Historical estimates found in various textbooks (and locked in the minds of many), which often report numbers near 8 percent, are too high for valuation purposes, because they compare the market risk premium versus Treasury bills (very short-term bonds) and are biased by the historical strength of the U.S. market.

Adjust for Industry/Company Risk

Once you've estimated the cost of equity for the aggregate market, adjust it for differences in risk across companies. Keep in mind the discussion from Chapter 4 about the difference between diversifiable and nondiversifiable risk. Only the nondiversifiable risk that investors cannot eliminate by holding a portfolio of stocks is incorporated into the cost of equity.

The most common model used to adjust the cost of equity for differences in risk is the capital asset pricing model (CAPM). Other models include the Fama-French three-factor model and the arbitrage pricing theory (APT). The three models differ primarily in which factors are used to estimate the effect of compensated risk. Despite extensive criticism of the CAPM, we believe it remains the best model to adjust for risk. Even so, a significant degree of judgment is required. A blind application of the model using historical data may result in an unrealistic cost of equity.

Capital Asset Pricing Model   Because the CAPM is discussed at length in modern finance textbooks, we focus only on the key ideas.[16] The CAPM postulates that the expected rate of return on any security equals the risk-free rate plus the security's beta times the market risk premium:

$$E(R_i) = r_f + \beta_i [E(R_m) - r_f]$$

where

$E(R_i)$ = expected return of security

r_f = risk-free rate

β_i = security i's beta

$E(R_m)$ = expected return of the market portfolio

In the CAPM, the risk-free rate and the market risk premium, which is defined as the difference between $E(R_m)$ and r_f, are common to all companies; only beta varies across companies. Beta represents a stock's incremental risk to a diversified investor, where risk is measured as the extent to which the stock moves up and down in conjunction with the aggregate stock market.

Consider General Mills, a cereal and snack foods manufacturer, and Micron Technology, a semiconductor manufacturer that produces memory chips. Basic consumer foods purchases are relatively independent of the stock market's value, so the beta for consumer products companies is quite low; we estimated it at 0.8. Based on a risk-free rate of 4.2 percent and a market risk premium of 5 percent, the cost of equity for General Mills equals 8.2 percent (see Exhibit 15.4). In contrast, technology companies tend to have high betas. When the economy struggles, the stock market drops, and companies stop purchasing new technology. Thus, the value of Micron Technology is highly correlated with the market's value, and so its beta is high. Based on a semiconductor beta of 1.3, Micron's expected rate of return equals 10.7 percent. Since General Mills offers greater protection against market downturns than Micron Technology does, investors are willing to pay a premium for the stock, driving down the stock's expected return. Conversely, since Micron offers little diversification in relation to the market portfolio, the company must earn a higher return to entice investors.[17]

To apply the CAPM in practice, you must estimate each component. The core question for a particular company's cost of equity is its risk relative to

[16] For example, R. Brealey, S. Myers, and F. Allen, *Principles of Corporate Finance*, 14th ed. (New York: McGraw-Hill, 2023); and T. Copeland, F. Weston, and K. Shastri, *Financial Theory and Corporate Policy* (Boston: Pearson Education, 2004).

[17] For technology companies like Micron, neither a high unlevered beta nor its corresponding high expected return is a sign of poor management. Beta is largely dictated by the industry in which a company operates, while expected returns simply represent the premium investors require for taking on risk.

EXHIBIT 15.4 **Cost of Equity Using the Capital Asset Pricing Model (CAPM)**

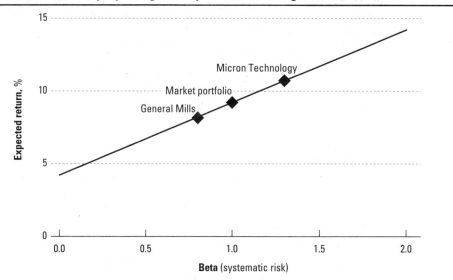

the aggregate market and, consequently, beta. Keep in mind that when you are valuing a company, your objective is not to measure the company's historical beta precisely. Rather, it is to estimate its future beta. Therefore, you must use judgment and common sense, not a purely mechanical approach.

We find that nonrepeatable events can heavily influence individual company betas, so we recommend using an industry peer median rather than the historically measured beta for the company in question. Betas can also be affected by unusual events in the stock market, such as the 2007–2009 financial crisis or the tech surge during the early 2020s. By examining how industry betas have changed over time, you can assess whether current betas are likely to revert to their long-term averages.

The remainder of this section describes how to estimate a company's beta step-by-step. First, use regression to estimate the beta for each company in the peer group. Then convert each company's observed beta into an unlevered beta—that is, what the beta would be if the company had no debt. Once you have a collection of betas, examine the sample for a representative beta, such as the median beta. To ensure that the current beta is representative of risk and not an artifact of unusual data, do not rely on a point estimate. Instead, examine the trend over time. We discuss each step next.

Estimating Beta for Each Company in the Industry Sample Set   To develop an industry beta, you first need the betas of the company's peer set. Since beta cannot be observed directly, you must *estimate* its value. The most common regression used to estimate a company's raw beta is the market model:

$$R_i = \alpha + \beta R_m + \varepsilon$$

EXHIBIT 15.5 **Costco: Stock Returns, 2018–2023**

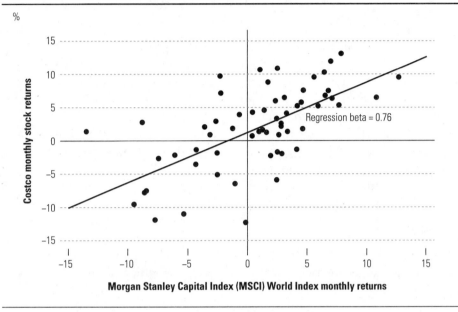

Morgan Stanley Capital Index (MSCI) World Index monthly returns

In the market model, the stock's return (R_i), not price, is regressed against the market's return.

Exhibit 15.5 plots 60 months of Costco stock returns versus 60 months of Morgan Stanley Capital International (MSCI) World Index returns between September 2018 and August 2023. The solid line represents the best-fit relationship between Costco's stock returns and the stock market. The slope of this line is commonly denoted as beta. Costco's raw regression beta (slope) is 0.76.

But why did we choose to measure Costco's returns in months? Why use five years of data? And how precise is this measurement? The CAPM is a one-period model, offering limited guidance on its application for a company valuation. Yet following certain market characteristics and the results of a variety of empirical tests leads to several guiding conclusions:

- The measurement period for raw regressions should include at least 60 data points (e.g., five years of monthly returns). Rolling betas should be graphed to search for any patterns or systematic changes in a stock's risk.

- Raw regressions should be based on monthly returns. Using more frequent return periods, such as daily and weekly returns, leads to systematic biases.[18]

[18] Using daily or even weekly returns is especially problematic when the stock is rarely traded. An illiquid stock will have many reported returns equal to zero, not because the stock's value is constant but because it hasn't traded (only the last trade is recorded). Consequently, estimates of beta on illiquid stocks are biased downward. Using longer-dated returns, such as monthly returns, lessens this effect.

- Company stock returns should be regressed against a value-weighted, well-diversified market portfolio, such as the MSCI World Index, bearing in mind that this portfolio's value may be distorted if measured when some sectors influence the market more than usual.

In the CAPM, the market portfolio equals the portfolio of all assets, both traded (such as stocks and bonds) and untraded (such as private companies and human capital). Since the true market portfolio is unobservable, a proxy is necessary. For U.S. stocks, the most common proxy is the S&P 500, a value-weighted index of large U.S. companies. Outside the United States, financial analysts rely on either a regional index like the MSCI Europe Index or the MSCI World Index, a value-weighted index comprising large stocks from 23 developed countries, including the United States.

Most well-diversified indexes, such as the S&P 500 and MSCI World Index, are highly correlated (the two indexes had a 99 percent correlation between 2018 and 2023). Thus, the choice of index will have only a small effect on beta. Do *not*, however, use a local country index, which some data services provide. Most countries are heavily weighted in only a few industries and, in some cases, a few companies. Consequently, when measuring beta versus a local index, you are not measuring market-wide systematic risk, but often a company's sensitivity to a particular set of industries.

Beta Smoothing   Many academics and beta services also adjust a company's raw beta closer to the mean of all companies, a process called smoothing. Smoothing moves the point estimate of beta toward the overall average. Consider the simple smoothing process used by Bloomberg:

$$\text{Adjusted Beta} = 0.33 + 0.67\,(\text{Raw Beta})$$

This formula smooths raw regression estimates toward 1. For instance, a raw beta of 0.5 leads to an adjusted beta of 0.67, while a raw beta of 1.5 leads to an adjusted beta of 1.34.

Bloomberg's smoothing mechanism dates to Marshall Blume's observation that betas revert to the mean.[19] Today, more advanced smoothing techniques exist.[20] Although the proof is beyond the scope of this book, the following adjustment will reduce beta estimation error:

$$\beta_{\text{adj}} = \left(\frac{\sigma_\varepsilon^2}{\sigma_\varepsilon^2 + \sigma_b^2}\right) 1 + \left(1 - \frac{\sigma_\varepsilon^2}{\sigma_\varepsilon^2 + \sigma_b^2}\right)\beta_{\text{raw}}$$

[19] M. Blume, "Betas and Their Regression Tendencies," *Journal of Finance* 30 (1975): 1–10.

[20] For instance, see P. Jorion, "Bayes-Stein Estimation for Portfolio Analysis," *Journal of Financial and Quantitative Analysis* 21 (1986): 279–292.

where

σ_ε^2 = standard error of the regression beta

σ_b^2 = cross-sectional standard deviation of all betas

The raw regression beta receives the most weight when the standard error of beta from the regression (σ_ε^2) is the smallest. In fact, when the beta is measured perfectly ($\sigma_\varepsilon^2 = 0$), the raw beta receives all the weight. Conversely, if the regression provides no meaningful results (σ_ε^2 is very large), you should set the beta equal to 1.0.

Since we are using an industry peer beta to estimate Costco's cost of equity, we did not smooth regression results.

Creating an Industry Beta   Estimating beta is an imprecise process. We used historical regression to estimate Costco's beta at 0.76. However, the regression's *R*-squared was only 39 percent, and the standard error of the beta estimate was 0.12. Using two standard errors as a guide, a statistician would feel confident Costco's true beta lies between 0.5 and 1.0—hardly a tight range.

To reduce the noise around beta estimates, use industry, rather than company-specific, betas. Companies in the same industry face similar *operating* risks, so they should have similar operating betas. If estimation errors across companies are uncorrelated, overestimates and underestimates of individual betas will tend to cancel, and an industry median beta will produce a superior estimate.

Consider two similarly skilled companies competing for a large customer contract. Depending on which company wins the contract, one company's stock price will rise; the other's will fall. If the market rises during this period, the winning company will have a higher measured beta, and the losing company will have a lower measured beta, even though the contract selection had nothing to do with market performance. Using an industry beta to proxy for company risk lessens the effect of random shocks.

Simply using the median of an industry's raw regression betas, however, overlooks a second important factor: leverage. A company's beta is a function of not only its operating risk but also the financial risk it takes. Shareholders of a company with more debt face greater risks, and this increase is reflected in beta. Therefore, to compare companies with similar operating risks, you must first strip out the effect of leverage. Only then can you compare betas across an industry.

To undo the effect of leverage (and its tax shield), we rely on the theories of Franco Modigliani and Merton Miller, introduced in Chapter 10. According to Modigliani and Miller, the weighted average risk of a company's financial claims equals the weighted average risk of a company's economic assets. In Appendix C, we present this concept algebraically and rearrange the equation to isolate the risk of equity, as measured by beta. The general equation for the beta of equity is as follows:

$$\beta_e = \beta_u + \frac{D}{E}(\beta_u - \beta_d) - \frac{V_{txa}}{E}(\beta_u - \beta_{txa})$$

where

β_u = beta of the company's operating assets

β_d = beta of the company's debt

β_{txa} = beta of the company's interest tax shields

D = market value of the company's debt

E = market value of the company's equity

V_{txa} = present value of the company's interest tax shields

To simplify the formula further, if the company maintains a constant ratio of debt to equity, the value of tax shields will fluctuate with the value of operating assets, and the beta of the tax shields (β_{txa}) will equal the beta of the unlevered company (β_u). Setting β_{txa} equal to β_u eliminates the final term[21]:

$$\beta_e = \beta_u + \frac{D}{E}(\beta_u - \beta_d)$$

Some professionals further simplify by assuming that the beta of debt is zero. Others use a beta of 0.15 for the debt of investment-grade companies, which is the implied beta based on the spread between investment-grade corporate debt and government debt.

Thus, a company's equity beta equals the company's operating beta (also known as the unlevered beta) times a leverage factor. As leverage rises, so will the company's equity beta. Using this relationship, we can convert equity betas into unlevered betas. Since unlevered betas focus solely on operating risk, they can be averaged across an industry, assuming competitors have similar operating characteristics.

To calculate an industry beta, follow these steps. First, calculate the beta for each company in your peer set and unlever each beta at each company's debt-to-equity ratio. Remove any outliers, that is, companies where the beta is unusually far away from those of the other companies; these are typically driven by anomalous events and are unlikely to recur. Calculate a median beta and an average beta of the sample set. Statistically speaking, the sample average will have the smallest estimation error. However, we prefer the median beta because outliers heavily influence small-sample averages. The final step is to plot the median industry beta over a long period. Look to see if the beta is changing in a predictable way and whether the current beta is the best predictor of future beta for the industry.

---

[21] See Appendix C for a comprehensive set of equations with different assumptions for the proportion of debt to equity, the beta of debt, and the beta of the tax shields.

Examining the Long-Term Trend   To determine the cost of equity for Costco, we create an industry peer beta from a set of discount retailers. We start by estimating the beta for each company, using regression analysis (as shown in Exhibit 15.5), and then unlever the results using each company's respective debt-to-equity ratio. Rather than using beta from a single point in time, we look for trends. Unless there is a discernible trend or dramatic change in the industry, we believe the long-run unlevered beta provides a better estimate of a future beta than a single-point estimate. Therefore, use the long-run mean when relevering the industry beta to the company's target capital structure.

Exhibit 15.6 presents estimates of levered betas for a selection of industries, including retail. For Costco, we use an unlevered beta of 0.8, at the low end of the historical range for retailers. We use this value because discount retailers have been trading at a beta well below 1. To estimate the cost of equity for Costco, we relever the unlevered beta to a peer group debt-to-equity ratio. To lever beta, we use the same capital structure used to weight debt and equity in the WACC. The levered beta for Costco equals 0.83 (in practice, we often round to one decimal to avoid misleading precision). Using a 4.2 percent risk-free rate and a 5 percent market risk premium leads to a cost of equity of 8.3 percent.

In some cases, examining the long-term trend will reveal important insight into beta and market prices. During the dot-com boom of the late 1990s, equity markets rose dramatically. Still, this increase was confined primarily to extremely large-capitalization stocks and stocks in the telecommunications, media, and technology (commonly known as TMT) sector. Historically, TMT stocks contributed approximately 15 percent of the market value of the S&P 500. Between 1998 and 2000, this percentage rose to 40 percent. And as the market portfolio changed, so too did industry betas. Exhibit 15.7 presents the median beta over time for stocks outside TMT, such as food companies,

EXHIBIT 15.6 **Unlevered Beta Estimates by Industry**

Industry	Beta range
Electric utilities	0.5–0.7
Health care providers	0.7–0.8
Integrated oil and gas	0.7–0.8
Airlines	0.7–0.9
Consumer packaged goods	0.8–0.9
Pharmaceuticals	0.8–1.0
Retail	0.8–1.0
Telecom	0.8–1.0
Mining	0.9–1.0
Automotive and assemblers	0.9–1.1
Chemicals	0.9–1.1
IT services, hardware	0.9–1.1
Software	0.9–1.1
Banking	1.0–1.1
Insurance	1.0–1.1
Semiconductors	1.0–1.3

EXHIBIT 15.7 **Effect of the Dot-Com Bubble on Beta**

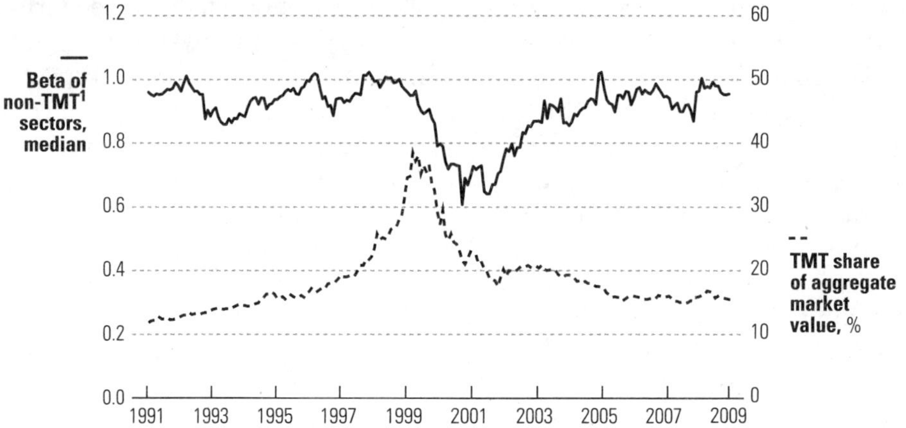

[1] TMT = telecommunications, media, and technology.

airlines, and pharmaceuticals.[22] The median beta dropped from 1.0 to 0.6 as TMT became a dominant part of the overall market portfolio.

With the collapse of the TMT sector in 2001, TMT stocks returned to their original proportion of the overall market. Since beta is computed using 60 months of historical data, however, non-TMT betas still reflected the TMT-heavy market composition. Thus, to value future cash flows in the period immediately after 2001, a more appropriate beta than the one from 2001 would have been the one from 1997, when the market composition last matched the post-2001 composition. Remember, the end goal is not to determine a backward-looking beta but to use historical estimates as a predictive tool for beta going forward.

Alternatives to CAPM: Fama-French Three-Factor Model   In 1992, Eugene Fama and Kenneth French published a paper in the *Journal of Finance* that received a great deal of attention for its authors' conclusion: "In short, our tests do not support the most basic prediction of the SLB [Sharpe-Lintner-Black] Capital Asset Pricing Model that average stock returns are positively related to market betas."[23] Based on prior research and their own comprehensive regressions, Fama and French concluded that equity returns are inversely related to the size of a company (as measured by market capitalization) and positively associated with the ratio of a company's book value to its market value of equity.

---

[22] A. Annema and M. Goedhart, "Better Betas," *McKinsey on Finance*, no. 6 (Winter 2003): 10–13; and A. Annema and M. Goedhart, "Betas: Back to Normal," *McKinsey on Finance*, no. 20 (Summer 2006): 14–16.
[23] E. Fama and K. French, "The Cross-Section of Expected Stock Returns," *Journal of Finance* (June 1992): 427–465.

EXHIBIT 15.8 **Costco: Cost of Equity Using the Fama-French Model, 2023**

Factor	Average monthly premium,[1] %	Average annual premium, %	Regression coefficient[2]	Contribution to expected return, %
Market portfolio		5.0	0.83	4.1
Small-minus-big (SMB) portfolio	0.19	2.3	(0.44)	(1.0)
High-minus-low (HML) portfolio	0.34	4.2	(0.48)	(2.0)
Premium over risk-free rate[3]				1.2
Risk-free rate				4.2
Cost of equity				5.4

[1] SMB and HML premiums based on average monthly returns data, 1926–2023.

[2] Based on monthly returns data, 2018–2023.

[3] Summation rounded to one decimal point.

Given the strength of Fama and French's empirical results, the academic community now measures risk with a model commonly known as the Fama-French three-factor model. With this model, a stock's excess returns are regressed on excess market returns (similar to the CAPM), the excess returns of small stocks over big stocks (commonly referred to as SMB for "small minus big"), and the excess returns of high-book-to-market stocks over low-book-to-market stocks (known as HML for "high minus low").[24] Because the risk premium is determined by a regression on the SMB and HML stock portfolios, a company does not receive a premium for being small. Instead, the company receives a risk premium if its stock returns are correlated with those of small stocks or high-book-to-market companies. The SMB and HML portfolios are meant to replicate unobservable risk factors, factors that cause small companies with high book-to-market values to outperform their CAPM expected returns.

We use the Fama-French three-factor model to estimate Costco's cost of equity in Exhibit 15.8. We regress Costco's monthly stock returns against the excess market portfolio, SMB, and HML to determine the company's three betas. As the exhibit indicates, the Costco beta on the market portfolio of 0.83 is slightly higher in the Fama-French regression than the beta of 0.76 from the market regression presented in Exhibit 15.5, but its levered cost of equity is much lower because Costco is negatively correlated with small companies (remember, small companies outperform big companies on average) and companies with a high book-to-market ratio (high-book-to-market companies outperform low-book-to-market companies on average).

While the Fama-French model outperforms the CAPM in predicting future returns, it is important to use caution when relying on regression results for one company at a point in time. As we discussed earlier in this chapter, regression results for a single company are quite imprecise. To best implement the CAPM, for instance, we recommend using a peer group beta, rather than raw

[24] For a complete description of the factor returns, see E. Fama and K. French, "Common Risk Factors in the Returns on Stocks and Bonds," *Journal of Financial Economics* 33 (1993): 3–56.

regression results. In the Fama-French model, three beta coefficients exist, and their estimation depends on one another. A set of industry betas cannot be created cleanly. Consequently, the Fama-French model works well for controlling company risk in large historical data sets but may not be appropriate for measuring a single company's cost of equity.

The bottom line? It takes a better theory to kill an existing theory, and we have yet to see a better theory. Therefore, we continue to use the CAPM while keeping a watchful eye on new research in the area.

Alternatives to CAPM: Arbitrage Pricing Theory   Another proposed alternative to the CAPM, the arbitrage pricing theory (APT), resembles a generalized version of the Fama-French three-factor model. In the APT, a security's actual returns are generated by k factors and random noise:

$$R_i = \alpha + \beta_1 F_1 + \beta_2 F_2 + \; ... \; + \beta_k F_k + \varepsilon$$

where F_i = return on factor i.

Since investors can hold well-diversified factor portfolios, epsilon risk will disappear. In this case, a security's expected return must equal the risk-free rate plus the cumulative sum of its exposure to each factor times the factor's risk premium (λ)[25]:

$$E(R_t) = r_f + \beta_1 \lambda + \beta_2 \lambda + \; ... \; + \beta_k \lambda_k$$

Otherwise, arbitrage (positive return with zero risk) is possible.

On paper, the theory is extremely powerful. Any deviations from the model result in unlimited returns with no risk. In practice, implementation of the model has been tricky, as there is little agreement about how many factors there are, what they represent, and how to measure them. For this reason, the usefulness of the APT resides primarily in the classroom.

ESTIMATING THE AFTER-TAX COST OF DEBT

To estimate the cost of debt for investment-grade companies, use the yield to maturity of the company's long-term, option-free bonds. Do not use the coupon rate or the coupon yield, as these reflect past funding terms and not current opportunity costs. To calculate the after-tax cost of debt, multiply the cost of debt by 1 minus the marginal tax rate.

Technically speaking, yield to maturity is only a proxy for expected return, because the yield is a *promised* rate of return on a company's debt; it assumes all coupon payments are made on time and the debt is paid in full. An enterprise

[25] For a thorough discussion of the arbitrage pricing theory, see M. Grinblatt and S. Titman, *Financial Markets and Corporate Strategy*, 2nd ed. (New York: McGraw-Hill, 2001).

valuation based on the yield to maturity is, therefore, theoretically inconsistent, as expected free cash flows should be discounted by an expected return, not a promised yield. For companies with investment-grade debt (debt rated at BBB or better), the probability of default is so low that we believe this inconsistency is immaterial, especially when compared with the estimation error surrounding the cost of equity. Thus, yield to maturity is a suitable proxy for estimating the cost of debt for a company with investment-grade debt.

For companies with below-investment-grade debt, we recommend one of two alternatives. If the debt-to-value ratio is uncharacteristically high, estimate the cost of debt using a target capital structure that better reflects the long-term dynamics of the industry. If the company's strategy includes substantial leverage, value the company using adjusted present value (APV) discounted at the unlevered cost of equity, rather than the WACC.

Determining Yield to Maturity

To solve for yield to maturity (YTM), reverse engineer the discount rate required to set the present value of the bond's promised cash flows equal to its price:

$$\text{Price} = \frac{\text{Coupon}}{(1 + \text{YTM})} + \frac{\text{Coupon}}{(1 + \text{YTM})^2} + \cdots + \frac{\text{Face} + \text{Coupon}}{(1 + \text{YTM})^N}$$

Ideally, yield to maturity should be calculated on liquid, option-free, long-term debt. As discussed earlier in this chapter, short-term bonds do not match the duration of the company's free cash flow. If the bond is rarely traded, the bond price will be outdated, or "stale." Using stale prices will lead to an obsolete yield to maturity. Yield to maturity can also be distorted when corporate bonds have attached options, such as callability or convertibility at a fixed price, as their value will affect the bond's price but not its promised cash flows.

In the United States, you can download the yield to maturity for corporate debt free of charge by using the TRACE pricing database.[26] Exhibit 15.9 displays TRACE data for Costco's 1.75 percent coupon bonds due in April 2032 (the longest-duration bond in Costco's August 2023 capital structure). TRACE reports four data items: when the trade occurred, the size of the trade, the bond price, and the implied yield to maturity. When measuring the yield to maturity, use the largest trades available, as smaller trades are unreliable. The largest trade for Costco's 2032 bond on August 31, 2023, was consummated at 4.63 percent (0.5 percent above the yield for a ten-year U.S. Treasury bond).

---

[26] The Financial Industry Regulatory Authority (FINRA) introduced TRACE (Trade Reporting and Compliance Engine) in July 2002. The system captures and disseminates transactions in investment-grade, high-yield, and convertible corporate debt, representing all over-the-counter market activity in these bonds.

EXHIBIT 15.9 **Costco: Trading Data on Corporate Debt, August 2023**

Bond: 1.75% due April 20, 2032

Trade	Trade date	Trade time	Trade volume, thousands	Bond price, $	Yield, %
1	8/31/23	17:03	150.0	79.6	4.64
2	8/31/23	17:03	150.0	79.6	4.64
3	8/31/23	13:06	8.0	79.5	4.67
4	8/31/23	13:06	8.0	79.5	4.67
5	8/31/23	13:06	8.0	79.0	4.74
6	8/31/23	11:57	10.0	79.7	4.63
7	8/31/23	11:57	11.0	79.7	4.63
8	8/31/23	11:57	134.0	79.7	4.63
9	8/31/23	11:57	700.0	79.7	4.63
10	8/31/23	11:57	107.0	79.7	4.63

Costco bond yield	4.6
10-year U.S. Treasury yield	(4.1)
Costco default premium	0.5

Source: Financial Industry Regulatory Authority's Trade Reporting and Compliance Engine (TRACE).

For companies with only short-term bonds or bonds that seldom trade, do not use market-based prices to determine the yield. Instead, use credit ratings. Start by identifying the company's credit rating on unsecured long-term debt. Then look at the average yield to maturity for a portfolio of long-term bonds with the same credit rating. Use this yield as a proxy for the company's implied yield on long-term debt.

To determine a company's bond rating, a rating agency such as S&P or Moody's will examine the company's most recent financial ratios, analyze the company's competitive environment, and interview senior management. Corporate bond ratings are freely available to the public and can be downloaded from rating agency websites. As of August 2023, Costco was rated A+ by S&P and Aa3 by Moody's. Once you have a rating, convert the rating into a yield to maturity. Exhibit 15.10 presents the difference in yields between U.S. corporate bonds and U.S. Treasury bonds. The difference is referred to as the yield spread. All quotes are presented in basis points (hundredths of 1 percent).

EXHIBIT 15.10 **Corporate Yield Spread over U.S. Treasuries by Bond Rating, August 2023**

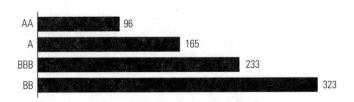

Basis points

AA 96
A 165
BBB 233
BB 323

Source: Bloomberg bond portfolio with 10-year maturity.

To estimate Costco's pretax cost of debt, we rely on its longest-dated bond, maturing in 2032 with a yield of 4.6 percent. Given its frequent trading, this market-based yield serves as a reliable estimate. If Costco didn't have a long-dated, liquid bond, we could turn to its credit rating, which falls between A and AA. In August 2023, similarly rated bonds traded at 140 basis points over Treasuries. Adding this premium to the ten-year Treasury yield of 4.1 percent results in a 5.5 percent cost of debt, closely matching Costco's bond yield.

Using the company's bond ratings to determine the yield to maturity is a good alternative to calculating the yield to maturity directly from bond prices. But never approximate the yield to maturity using a bond's coupon rate. Coupon rates are set by the company at issuance and approximate the yield only if the bond trades near its par value. When valuing a company, you must estimate expected returns relative to *today's* comparable investments. Thus, when you measure the cost of debt, estimate what a comparable investment would earn if bought or sold today.

Cost of Below-Investment-Grade Debt

In practice, few financial analysts distinguish between expected and promised returns. But for debt below investment grade (rated BB or below), using the yield to maturity as a proxy for the cost of debt can significantly overestimate the cost of debt.

To clarify the distinction between expected returns and yield to maturity, consider the following example. You have been asked to value a one-year zero-coupon bond whose face value is $100. The bond is risky; there is a 25 percent chance the bond will default and you will recover only half the final payment. Finally, the cost of debt (not yield to maturity), estimated using the CAPM, equals 6 percent.[27]

Based on this information, you estimate the bond's price by discounting *expected* cash flows by the cost of debt:

$$\text{Price} = \frac{E(\text{Cash Flows})}{1 + k_d} = \frac{(.75)(\$100) + (.25)(\$50)}{1.06} = \$82.55$$

Next, to determine the bond's yield to maturity, place promised cash flows, rather than expected cash flows, into the numerator. Then solve for the yield to maturity:

$$\text{Price} = \frac{\text{Promised Cash Flows}}{1 + \text{YTM}} = \frac{\$100}{1 + \text{YTM}} = \$82.55$$

Solving for YTM, the $82.55 price leads to a 21.1 percent yield to maturity—much higher than the 6 percent cost of debt.

---

[27] The CAPM applies to any security, not just equities. In practice, the cost of debt is rarely estimated using the CAPM, because infrequent trading makes estimation of beta impossible.

Why is there a large difference between the cost of debt and yield to maturity? Three factors drive the yield to maturity: the cost of debt, the probability of default, and the recovery rate after default. When the probability of default is high and the recovery rate is low, the yield to maturity will deviate significantly from the cost of debt. Thus, for companies with high default risk and low ratings, the yield to maturity is a poor proxy for the cost of debt.

When a company is not investment grade, start by assessing the company's financial strategy related to capital structure. If the company has uncharacteristically high levels of debt relative to its peers, use the company's stated target or a peer-based capital structure to determine the WACC. Estimate the debt rating the company is likely to generate based on this target capital structure.

If the company purposely maintains a debt rating below investment grade, we do not recommend using the weighted average cost of capital to value the company. Instead, use adjusted present value. The APV model discounts projected free cash flow at the company's industry-based unlevered cost of equity and adds the present value of tax shields. For more on APV valuation, see Chapter 10.

Incorporating the Interest Tax Shield

To calculate free cash flow (using techniques detailed in Chapters 10 and 11), we compute taxes as if the company were entirely financed by equity. By using all-equity taxes, it is possible to make comparisons across companies and over time, without regard to capital structure. Yet since the tax shield has value, it must be accounted for. In an enterprise DCF using the WACC, the tax shield is valued as part of the cost of capital. To value the tax shield, reduce the cost of debt by the marginal tax rate:

$$\text{After-Tax Cost of Debt} = \text{Cost of Debt} \times (1 - T_m)$$

Chapters 10 and 11 detail how to calculate the marginal tax rate for historical analysis. For use in the cost of capital, calculate the marginal tax rate in a consistent manner, with one potential modification. Multinational companies often borrow money in high-tax countries to lower their tax burden in those countries. Check the annual report for the location of corporate debt, and, if necessary, use the marginal tax rate where the debt was raised, not the statutory tax rate of the company's home country.

For companies with either low or volatile earnings, the statutory tax rate may overstate the marginal tax rate in future years. According to research by John Graham, the statutory marginal tax rate overstates the *future* marginal tax rate because of rules related to tax loss carryforwards, tax loss carrybacks, investment tax credits, and alternative minimum taxes.[28] Graham

---

[28] J. Graham and L. Mills, "Using Tax Return Data to Simulate Corporate Marginal Tax Rates," *Journal of Accounting and Economics* 46 (2009): 366–388; and J. Graham, "Proxies for the Corporate Marginal Tax Rate," *Journal of Financial Economics* 42 (1996): 187–221.

uses simulation to estimate the realizable marginal tax rate on a company-by-company basis. He estimates that the marginal tax rate is, on average, 5 percentage points below the statutory rate, primarily driven by smaller, less profitable companies.

ESTIMATING TARGET CAPITAL STRUCTURE

With our estimates of the cost of equity and after-tax cost of debt in hand, it is now possible to blend the two expected returns to estimate the WACC. To do this, use the target weights of debt (net of excess cash) and equity to enterprise value (net of excess cash) on a market basis:

$$\text{WACC} = \frac{D}{V}k_d(1 - T_m) + \frac{E}{V}k_e$$

That we should use market values rather than book values to weight expected returns follows directly from the formula's algebraic derivation (see Appendix B for a derivation of free cash flow and WACC). But consider a more intuitive explanation: the WACC represents the expected return on a *different* investment with identical risk. Rather than reinvest in the company, management could return capital to investors, who could reinvest elsewhere. To return capital without changing the capital structure, management can repay debt and repurchase shares but must do so at their *market* value. Conversely, book value represents a sunk cost, so it is no longer relevant.

The cost of capital should rely on a forecast of target weights, rather than current weights, because at any point, a company's current capital structure may not reflect the level expected to prevail over the life of the business. The current capital structure may merely reflect a short-term swing in the company's stock price, a swing that has yet to be rebalanced by management. Thus, using today's capital structure may cause you to overestimate (or underestimate) the value of tax shields for companies whose leverage is expected to drop (or rise).

Many companies are already near their target capital structure. If the company you are valuing is not, decide how quickly you will assume that the company will achieve its target. In the simplest scenario, the company will rebalance immediately and maintain the new capital structure. In this case, using the target weights and a constant WACC (for all future years) will lead to a reasonable valuation. If you expect the rebalancing to happen over a longer period of time, you must use a different cost of capital each year, reflecting the capital structure at the time. In practice, this procedure is complex; you must correctly model the weights, as well as changes in the cost of debt and equity caused by increased default risk and higher betas. For extreme changes in capital structure, modeling enterprise DCF using a constant WACC can lead to a notably inaccurate valuation. In this case, do not use WACC. Instead, value the company using adjusted present value.

To estimate the target capital structure from an external perspective, first estimate the company's current market-value-based capital structure. Next, review the capital structure of comparable companies. Finally, examine management's implicit or explicit approach to financing and its implications for the target capital structure. The next section will discuss each of these steps in greater detail.

Current Capital Structure

To determine the company's current capital structure, measure the market value of all claims against enterprise value. For most companies, the claims will consist primarily of traditional debt and equity. (This chapter's final section addresses more complex securities.) If a company's debt and equity are publicly traded, multiply each security's quantity by its most recent price. Most difficulties arise when securities are not traded and prices cannot be readily observed.

Debt and Debt Equivalents, Net of Excess Cash   To value debt and debt equivalents, sum short-term debt, long-term debt, and debt equivalents such as unfunded retirement obligations. From this total, subtract excess cash to determine net debt. For most companies, debt will be recorded on the balance sheet at book value, which may differ from market value.[29] Therefore, use a data service to determine market value when possible. Regarding debt equivalents, the valuation method will depend on the account. We discuss the valuation of debt and debt equivalents next.

Market prices for U.S. corporate bonds are reported on the Financial Industry Regulatory Authority (FINRA) TRACE system. As previously shown in Exhibit 15.9, Costco's 2032 bond traded at $79.7, or 79.7 percent of par value, on August 31, 2023. To determine the bond's market value, multiply 79.7 percent by the bond's book value of $1 billion (found in the Costco annual report); the result is $797 million. Since a bond's price depends on its coupon rate versus its yield, not every Costco bond trades at the same price. For instance, the Costco bond paying 3 percent and maturing in 2027 closed at 94 percent of par on the same day. Consequently, each debt security needs to be valued separately.

If an observable market value is not readily available, value debt securities at book value (referred to as carrying value), or use discounted cash flow. In most cases, the book value reported on the balance sheet reasonably approximates the current market value. However, this will not be

---

[29] Companies can choose to report debt at fair value under the fair value option (FVO), but this is mainly used by financial institutions. Most manufacturing and service companies report debt at book value.

the case if interest rates have changed since the company's last valuation or if the company is in financial distress. In these two situations, the current price will differ from the carrying value because either expected cash flows have changed or the discount rate has changed from its last valuation.[30] In these situations, value each bond separately by discounting promised cash flows at the appropriate yield to maturity. The size and timing of coupons will be disclosed in the notes of a company's annual report. Determine the proper yield to maturity by examining the yields from comparably rated debt with similar maturities.

Next, value debt equivalents, such as operating leases and unfunded retirement obligations. In Chapters 22 and 23, we describe in detail the accounting for operating leases and pensions, including the required adjustments to free cash flow and cost of capital. A consistent application between free cash flow and the cost of capital is paramount. As of December 2019, the value of fixed-payment operating leases is presented directly on the balance sheet; the estimation of these leases is no longer necessary. To find the value of unfunded retirement obligations, search the pension note for the most recent market value. Although accounting authorities require disclosure of unfunded retirement obligations on the balance sheet, it is often embedded in other accounts.

Equity   If the company's common stock is publicly traded, multiply the market price by the number of shares *outstanding*. The market value of equity should be based on shares outstanding in the capital market. Do not use shares issued, as they may include shares repurchased by the company but not retired. For European companies in particular, you need to be careful in determining the correct amount of shares outstanding because of the way companies sometimes account for treasury shares.

At this point, you may be wondering why you are valuing the company if you are going to rely on the market's value of equity in the cost of capital. Shouldn't you be using the estimated equity value? No. Remember, you are only estimating today's market value to frame management's philosophy concerning capital structure. To value the company, use forward-looking *target* weights.

For privately held companies, the equity value is unobservable. In this case, you must determine equity value (for the cost of capital) by either using a multiples approach or through DCF iteratively. To perform an iterative valuation, assume a reasonable capital structure, and value the enterprise using DCF. Using the estimate of debt-to-enterprise value, repeat the valuation. Continue this process until the valuation no longer materially changes.

---

[30] For floating-rate bonds, changes in Treasury rates won't affect value, since coupons float with Treasury yields. Changes in market-based default premiums, however, will affect the market value of floating-rate bonds, since bonds are priced at a fixed spread above Treasury yields.

EXHIBIT 15.11 **Median Debt to Value by Industry, 2023**

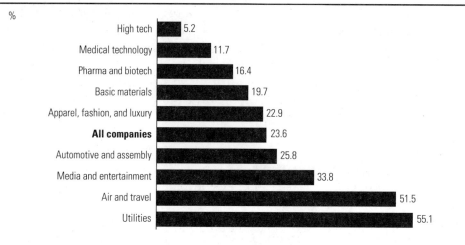

Note: Calculated using S&P 1500 classified by GICS industry. Market values used when available.

Capital Structure of Peer Companies

To place the company's current capital structure in the proper context, compare its capital structure with those of similar companies. Exhibit 15.11 presents the median debt-to-value levels for nine industries. As the exhibit shows, companies in high-growth industries such as technology and pharmaceuticals, especially those with intangible investments, tend to use less debt. In fact, some companies hold more excess cash than debt, causing the net debt ratio to be negative.[31] In industries with heavy fixed investment in tangible assets, such as mining and utilities, companies tend to have higher debt levels. In 2023, the median debt-to-value ratio for S&P 1500 nonfinancial companies was 23.6 percent, and the median debt-to-equity ratio was 30.8 percent.

It is perfectly acceptable for a company's capital structure to differ from that of its industry, but you should understand why. For instance, does the company have a more aggressive or innovative philosophy regarding the use of debt financing, or is the capital structure only a temporary deviation from a more conservative target? Often, companies finance acquisitions with debt they plan to retire quickly or refinance with a stock offering. Alternatively, is there anything different about the company's cash flow or asset intensity that can explain the difference? Determine the cause for any difference before applying a target capital structure.

---

[31] Over the past 15 years, cash balances have grown substantially because companies must pay taxes in their home country on any repatriated earnings. For companies whose home country's tax rate is relatively high, cash will become trapped abroad. Following the change in the U.S. tax code in 2017, the cash balance at American companies was expected to drop as companies repatriated foreign earnings, but many companies still retain significant cash.

Management's Financing Philosophy

As a final step, review management's historical financing philosophy. Even better, ask management outright, if possible. Has the current team been actively managing the company's capital structure? Is the management team aggressive in its use of debt? Or does it take a more cautious approach? Take Costco, for instance. Despite its robust and stable cash flow, the company has taken on very little debt. From a financing perspective, it doesn't need to issue additional securities; investments can be funded with current profits.

ESTIMATING WACC FOR COMPLEX CAPITAL STRUCTURES

The weighted average cost of capital is determined by weighting each security's expected return by its proportional contribution to total value. For a complex security, such as convertible debt, measuring expected return is challenging. Is a convertible bond similar enough to straight debt, enabling us to use the yield to maturity? Or is it like equity, enabling us to use the CAPM? In fact, it is neither, so we recommend an alternative method.

If the treatment of hybrid securities will make a material difference in valuation results,[32] we recommend using adjusted present value (APV). In the APV model, enterprise value is determined by discounting free cash flow at the industry-based unlevered cost of equity. The value of incremental cash flows related to financing, such as interest tax shields, is then computed separately.

In some situations, you may still desire an accurate representation of the WACC. In these cases, split hybrid securities into their individual components. For instance, you can replicate a convertible bond by combining a traditional bond with a call option on the company's stock. You can further disaggregate a call option into a portfolio consisting of a risk-free bond and the company's stock. By converting a complex security into a portfolio of debt and equity, you once again have the components required for the traditional cost of capital. The process of using replicating portfolios to value options is discussed in Chapter 40.

CLOSING THOUGHTS

The cost of capital is one of the most hotly debated topics in the field of finance. While robust statistical techniques have improved our understanding of the issues, a practical measurement of the cost of capital remains elusive.

---

[32] If the hybrid security is out-of-the-money and unlikely to be converted, it can be treated as traditional debt. Conversely, if the hybrid security is well in-the-money, it should be treated as traditional equity. In these situations, errors are likely to be small, and a WACC-based valuation remains appropriate.

Nonetheless, we believe the steps outlined in this chapter, combined with a healthy perspective on long-term trends, will lead to a cost of capital that is reliable and reasonable. Even so, do not let a lack of precision overwhelm you. A company creates value when ROIC exceeds the cost of capital, and for many of our clients, the variation in ROIC across projects greatly exceeds any variation in the cost of capital. Smart selection of strategies and their corresponding investments based on forward-looking ROIC, not a precise measurement of the cost of capital, often generates most of the impact in day-to-day decision making.

16

Moving from Enterprise Value to Value per Share

When you have completed the valuation of core operations, as described in Chapter 10, you are ready to estimate enterprise value, equity value, and value per share. Enterprise value represents the value of the entire company, while equity value represents the portion owned by shareholders.

To determine enterprise value, add nonoperating assets to the value of core operations. The most common nonoperating assets are excess cash, investments in nonconsolidated companies, and tax loss carryforwards.[1] To estimate equity value, subtract all nonequity claims from enterprise value. Nonequity claims include short-term and long-term debt, debt equivalents such as unfunded pension liabilities, and hybrid securities such as convertible securities and employee stock options. Finally, to estimate the intrinsic value per share, divide the resulting equity value by the most recent number of shares outstanding.

While nonoperating assets and nonequity claims may feel like an afterthought, this is not always the case. Many clever investors have discovered substantial value hidden in nonoperating assets, especially in privately held conglomerates. In contrast, other investors have been burned by not accurately identifying and valuing all claims against enterprise value, as happened in the well-publicized case of Enron. It is critical to know who has a claim on cash flow before equity holders do.

This chapter begins by incorporating nonoperating assets into the enterprise-wide valuation. We then determine equity value by adjusting for

---

[1] Throughout the book, we define enterprise value as the value of core operations plus nonoperating assets. Many bankers define enterprise value as debt plus equity minus cash. For a company whose only nonoperating asset is excess cash and that owes only traditional debt, this definition is equivalent to our definition of the value of core operations. This simple definition of enterprise value, however, fails to account for other nonoperating assets and debt equivalents, and if misunderstood, it can lead to errors in valuation.

nonequity claims, such as debt and debt equivalents. Next, we address hybrid securities, which require special consideration because of their connection to enterprise value. Finally, we conclude the chapter with a discussion of the best methods for converting equity value into value per share.[2]

THE VALUATION BUILDUP PROCESS

The valuation buildup begins with a company's core operating value, based on discounted cash flow (DCF)—the top line of the example shown in Exhibit 16.1. This amount plus nonoperating assets equals enterprise value. The equity value—the bottom line in the exhibit—is the value that remains after subtracting from the enterprise value all the nonequity claims. We use the term *nonequity claim* because there are many financial claims against a company's cash flows other than traditional fixed-coupon debt and shareholders' equity.

EXHIBIT 16.1 **Sample Comprehensive Valuation Buildup**

$ million		
DCF value of operations	5,000	
Excess cash and marketable securities	50	
Excess real estate	5	
Investments in nonconsolidated companies	270	
Financial subsidiary	300	Nonoperating assets
Tax loss carryforwards	10	
Discontinued operations	30	
Enterprise value	5,665	
Claims against enterprise value		
Bank loans	(250)	
Bonds	(550)	Interest-bearing debt
Long-term operating provisions	(50)	
Nonoperating provisions	(75)	
Operating leases	(250)	Debt equivalents
Unfunded retirement obligations	(200)	
Contingent liabilities	(40)	
Convertible debt	(200)	
Preferred stock	(100)	Hybrid claims and
Employee stock options	(50)	noncontrolling interests
Noncontrolling interests	(150)	
Equity value	3,750	

[2] Estimating the value per share completes the technical aspect of the valuation, yet the job is not complete. It is then time to revisit the valuation with a comprehensive look at its implications. We examine this process in Chapter 17.

In general, a nonoperating asset is any asset for which the associated cash flow is not incorporated as part of free cash flow. Common nonoperating assets are excess cash, one-time receivables, investments in nonconsolidated companies (also known as equity investments and by other names), excess pension assets, discontinued operations, and financial subsidiaries. Take extra care not to classify an asset required for ongoing operations as nonoperating. For instance, some analysts who follow retailers add the value of real estate to the value of core operations. But since the real estate is required to conduct business, its benefits are already embedded in the value of operations. The value of a retailer's real estate can only be truly realized if the retailer shuts down a store and liquidates the asset.

In contrast to nonoperating assets, nonequity claims are financial claims against enterprise value whose expenses are not included when determining EBITA and consequently are excluded from free cash flow. Traditional debt contracts such as bank debt and corporate bonds are the most common nonequity claims. Other debt-like claims, known as debt equivalents, include the value of operating leases, unfunded pension and other retirement liabilities, and environmental remediation liabilities, among others. Nonequity claims also include hybrid securities that have both debt and equity characteristics, such as convertible debt and preferred stock.

VALUING NONOPERATING ASSETS

This section identifies the most common nonoperating assets and describes how to handle each of them in the valuation. When assessing nonoperating assets, adjust for factors that would affect the company's ability to capture the full value of these assets. For example, if the company has announced it will sell off a nonoperating asset, deduct the estimated capital gains taxes (if any) on the asset from its market value. If ownership of the asset is shared with another company, include only your company's portion of the value.

Excess Cash and Marketable Securities

Companies often hold more cash and marketable securities than they need to run the business. Companies hold excess cash for a number of reasons, often parking it in short-term securities until they can invest it or return it to shareholders. Prior to the change in American tax laws in 2018, American companies held significant amounts of excess cash when they had substantial earnings outside the United States. They were reluctant to repatriate cash because they were required to pay any difference in taxes upon repatriation. With a drop in the corporate tax rate from 35 percent to 21 percent in 2018, many companies committed to repatriating cash, but cash balances, especially in technology companies, remain at historically high levels.[3]

Rather than using the cash and marketable securities reported on a company's balance sheet, estimate how much cash the business needs for operations. Classify the remaining cash and marketable securities as nonoperating. As a rule of thumb, we often assume a company requires about 2 percent of annual revenues in cash to operate the business. The remaining cash and marketable securities are considered excess.

Investments in Nonconsolidated Companies

Companies often invest in other companies without taking control, in which case they do not consolidate the investment's financial statements into their own. Investments in nonconsolidated companies can be found on the balance sheet under many names. For instance, Philips calls them investments in associates, Intel calls them equity investments, and PPG Industries calls them investment in equity affiliates.

Because their financials are not consolidated, these investments must be valued separately from operations. Under U.S. Generally Accepted Accounting Principles (GAAP) and International Financial Reporting Standards (IFRS), nonconsolidated subsidiaries can appear in the parent company's accounts in either of two ways:

1. For equity stakes in which the parent company exerts "significant influence" but lacks control (often between 20 and 50 percent ownership), the equity holding in the subsidiary is reported as a separate line item on the parent's balance sheet at the investment's historical cost plus any reinvested income. The parent company's portion of the subsidiary's profits is shown on the parent's income statement as either a separate line item or part of other income. Accountants refer to this as the equity method.

2. For equity stakes below 20 percent, the parent company is often assumed to have no influence. The equity holdings are shown at historical cost on the parent's balance sheet.[4] The parent's portion of the subsidiary's *dividends* is included as a separate line item or in other income on the income statement.

---

[3] For more on corporate cash holdings, see V. Govindarajan, A. Srivastava, and C. Chatterjee, "Why Are Companies Sitting on Cash Right Now?" *Harvard Business Review*, February 5, 2024, www .hbr.org.

[4] If the parent company is determined to exert significant influence over the investment, the equity method is applied, regardless of the ownership percentage. Conversely, if the parent company does not exert significant influence and the investment is publicly traded, the investment is recorded at fair value and marked to market on the balance sheet.

EXHIBIT 16.2 **Coca-Cola Company: Publicly Traded Equity Investments, December 2023**

$ million

	Book value	Fair value	Valuation of Coca-Cola HBC	
Monster Beverage Corporation	4,837	11,766	Share price, €	26.4
Coca-Cola Europacific Partners	3,858	5,870	× Shares outstanding, millions	366.9
Coca-Cola FEMSA	2,092	5,549	= Market capitalization, € million	9,693.7
Coca-Cola HBC	1,252	2,296 ←		
Coca-Cola Consolidated	473	2,304	× Percent ownership	21.0%
Coca-Cola Bottlers Japan Holdings	367	484	= Ownership stake, € million	2,035.7
Coca-Cola İçecek	228	911		
Embotelladora Andina	90	137	× Currency conversion, $ / €	1.128
Total	13,197	29,317	= Value to Coca-Cola	2,296.0

Source: Coca-Cola Company annual report, 2023; Coca-Cola HBC annual report, 2023; Yahoo Finance.

In response to the accounting and financial scandals of the early 2000s, global accounting moved away from absolute thresholds to consolidation methods that rely on the parent's influence around key activities and exposure to gains and losses. Implementation has been complex, and companies can report under multiple standards. Always investigate the notes to determine which investments contribute to EBITA and which do not.

Investments in Publicly Traded Companies   If the investment in a nonconsolidated company is publicly listed, use the market value to determine the value of the parent company's equity stake. However, in some cases, listed subsidiaries may have a limited free float or low liquidity. In such situations, exercise caution, as the most recent share price may not accurately represent the subsidiary's value.

Exhibit 16.2 presents the equity investments held by Coca-Cola. Since Coca-Cola does not control these companies, their revenue, income, and assets are not consolidated on Coca-Cola's financial statements. Each investment must be valued separately and added to Coca-Cola's value of operations to determine enterprise value.

In the management discussion and analysis section of its 2023 annual report, Coca-Cola reports both book value and fair value for its equity investments.[5] If you are valuing Coca-Cola near its fiscal-year close, the valuation from the annual report will suffice. As the year progresses, however, these data become stale, and each investment must be revalued.

Consider Coca-Cola HBC, Coca-Cola's bottler in much of Europe and parts of Africa. To value this equity stake, start by multiplying the equity value of Coca-Cola HBC, which is €9,693.7 million, by Coca-Cola's 21 percent

[5] Companies will disclose how fair value is determined for each security, using a system of levels. Level 1 inputs are quoted prices of identical securities in liquid markets. Level 2 inputs are quoted prices of identical securities in illiquid markets or similar securities in liquid markets. Level 3 inputs are not observed and are estimated using financial models.

ownership. This gives an ownership stake of €2,035.7 million. Since Coca-Cola reports in U.S. dollars, you need to convert this value to dollars at the prevailing exchange rate. Multiplying €2,035.7 million by 1.128 gives you the value of Coca-Cola's ownership in Coca-Cola HBC, $2,296.0 million.

Although this valuation was accurate as of December 31, 2023, any change in one of the inputs will require an update to the valuation. For instance, during the first quarter of 2024, HBC's stock price rose by approximately 11.7 percent. This increase in value was reflected in Coca-Cola's subsequent quarterly report, but only as part of a summarized estimate of its entire portfolio of equity investments.

Investments in Unlisted Companies   If the nonconsolidated subsidiary is not listed but you have access to its financial statements—for example, through a public bond offering or private disclosure—ideally do a separate DCF valuation of the equity stake. Discount the cash flows at the appropriate cost of capital, which may differ from the parent company's weighted average cost of capital. Also, when completing the parent valuation, include only the value of the parent's equity stake and not the subsidiary's entire equity value.

If the parent company's accounts are the only source of financial information for the subsidiary, we suggest the following alternatives to DCF:

- *Simplified cash-flow-to-equity valuation.* This is a feasible approach when the parent has a 20 to 50 percent equity stake, because the subsidiary's net income and book equity are disclosed in the parent's accounts.[6] Build forecasts for the development of key equity-based value drivers, such as growth in net income and return on equity, to facilitate accurate projections of cash flows to equity. Discount these cash flows at a cost of equity appropriate to the subsidiary in question, not at the parent company's cost of capital.

- *Multiples valuation.* As a second alternative, estimate the partial stake's value using a price-to-earnings and/or market-to-book multiple. If the company owns 20 to 50 percent of the subsidiary, apply an appropriate multiple to reported income.

- *Tracking portfolio.* For parent equity stakes below 20 percent, you may have no information beyond the investment's original cost—that is, the book value shown in the parent's balance sheet and often only disclosed in the notes. Even applying a multiple is difficult, because neither net income nor the current book value of equity is reported. If you know

---

[6] The book value of the subsidiary equals the historical acquisition cost plus retained profits, which is a reasonable approximation of book equity. If goodwill is included in the book value of the subsidiary, it should be deducted.

when the stake was acquired (or last valued), you can approximate its current market value by applying the relative price change for a portfolio of comparable stocks over the same holding period.

With these valuation approaches, triangulate your results as much as possible, given their lack of precision.

Loans to Other Companies

For loans to other companies (including nonconsolidated subsidiaries), use the reported book value. This is a reasonable approximation of market value if the loans were given at fair market terms and if the borrower's credit risk and general interest rates have not changed significantly since issuance. If this is not the case and the investment is substantial, you should perform a separate DCF valuation of the promised interest and principal payments at the yield to maturity for corporate bonds with similar risk and maturity.

Finance Subsidiaries

Some companies, including General Motors and Siemens, have subsidiaries that finance customer purchases. Although they are very different operationally, these subsidiaries are consolidated into the parent company's financial accounts. For valuation, it is best to "deconsolidate," or separate the accounts of the finance subsidiary and value it separately. Otherwise, ROIC, free cash flow, and WACC will be distorted.

Once the finance subsidiary is separated from operations, use the reorganized financial statements to value the subsidiary as if it were a financial institution. Add this value to the value of core operations to determine enterprise value. Since the finance subsidiary's debt will already be incorporated into your valuation of the finance subsidiary, do not subtract total debt from the parent company's enterprise value to determine equity value. Subtract only general obligation debt unrelated to the finance subsidiary.

Detailed guidance on valuing a company with a finance subsidiary is provided in Chapter 19. Bank valuation is covered in Chapter 43.

Discontinued Operations

Discontinued operations are businesses being sold or closed. The earnings from discontinued operations are explicitly shown in the income statement as a separate line item, and the associated net asset position is disclosed as a separate line item on the balance sheet. Because discontinued operations are no longer part of a company's operations, their value should not be modeled as part of free cash flow or included in the DCF value of operations. Under U.S. GAAP and IFRS, the assets and liabilities associated with the discontinued operations are written down to their fair value and disclosed as a net asset on the balance sheet, so the most recent book value is usually a reasonable approximation.[7]

Excess Real Estate

Excess real estate and other unutilized assets are assets no longer required for the company's operations. As such, any cash flows these assets generate are excluded from the free-cash-flow projection, and the assets are not included in the DCF value of operations. Identifying these assets in an outside-in valuation is nearly impossible unless they are specifically disclosed in the company's footnotes. For that reason, only internal valuations are likely to include their value separately as a nonoperating asset.

For excess real estate, use the most recent appraisal value when it is available. Alternatively, estimate the real estate value either by using a multiple, such as value per square meter, or by discounting expected future cash flows from rentals at the appropriate cost of capital. Of course, be careful to exclude any real estate used for business operations, as its value is already implicitly included in the free cash flow projections and the valuation of operations.

We do not recommend a separate valuation for unutilized operating assets unless they are expected to be sold in the near term.

Excess Pension Assets

Surpluses in a company's pension funds show up as net pension assets on the balance sheet and are typically reported at market value.[8] (Small amounts are typically embedded within other assets.) On an after-tax basis, the pension's value depends on management's plans. If pensions are expected to be dissolved soon, subtract liquidation taxes—typically set higher than the statutory tax rate—from the market value of excess pension assets. Otherwise, subtract taxes at the statutory rate, which reflects the need for lower future contributions. For an in-depth discussion of retirement-related accounting and its impact on a company's valuation, see Chapter 23.

Tax Loss Carryforwards

When a company generates losses in a given year, it can accumulate those losses and net them against future income, thereby reducing future taxes.[9]

---

[7] Any upward adjustment to the current book value of assets and liabilities is limited to the cumulative historical impairments on the assets. Thus, the fair market value of discontinued operations could be higher than the net asset value disclosed in the balance sheet.

[8] Under IFRS, companies can still report excess pension assets at book value. If pensions are not marked to market, search the company's pension footnote for the value of excess pension assets.

[9] Tax policy varies widely across countries. Check local tax policy to determine if, how, and when you can net past losses against future income.

This is known as a tax loss carryforward. Since tax savings will increase future cash flows, estimate their value using discounted cash flow, and add your result to the company's value of operations.

A tax loss carryforward is recorded on the balance sheet as a deferred-tax asset.[10] Use the deferred-tax asset as a starting point to value the tax loss carryforwards. If the company is unlikely to use the tax loss carryforward, the company will record a valuation allowance against the deferred-tax asset. Both numbers can be found in the note on taxes that accompanies the company's financial statements. The company's valuation allowance will reflect its current expectations of future profitability, which may be different from your projections, so use caution in adopting the company's calculation. If you develop multiple scenarios to value operations, estimate your own allowance against the deferred-tax asset based on the probability of the asset being realized under each scenario.

Because tax savings are recorded on an undiscounted basis, apply discounted cash flow to estimate their value as of today. Ideally, you would discount tax savings at a cost of capital that perfectly matches their risk. In practice, use the weighted average cost of capital. This will appropriately counter the value of operating taxes embedded in your value of operations.

To estimate the present value, forecast the year-by-year tax savings based on your projected earnings for the company. Unless income by geography is available, year-by-year tax savings will be difficult to assess because tax loss carryforwards must be matched in the country in which they are generated. A pragmatic approach is to assume the tax benefits will be realized over an arbitrary period—say, five years. If your valuation of tax loss carryforwards affects share price in a meaningful way, ask management for additional disclosures regarding the location and timing of tax credits.

Finally, be careful not to double-count future tax savings by also incorporating them into the projected free cash flow. Since we value tax loss carryforwards separately, the tax loss carryforward is classified as a nonoperating asset and not included as part of either net operating profit after taxes (NOPAT) or invested capital. For more on taxes, including tax loss carryforwards, see Chapter 20.

Valuing Interest-Bearing Debt

After determining the enterprise value, the next step is to subtract the value of each nonequity claim to calculate the equity value. The process starts with traditional interest-bearing debt.

---

[10] As detailed in Chapter 11, we classify deferred taxes into tax loss carryforwards, operating deferred taxes, and nonoperating deferred taxes. Only tax loss carryforwards should be valued separately. The other two accounts are either incorporated into free cash flow via cash operating taxes or valued as part of the account that generated the deferral.

Traditional debt comes in many forms: commercial paper, notes payable, fixed and floating bank loans, corporate bonds, and finance leases. For companies with investment-grade debt, the value of debt will be independent of the value of operations and can be assessed separately. However, in highly leveraged or distressed firms, the value of debt will be linked to the value of operations, necessitating a simultaneous evaluation of both.

Investment-Grade Debt   If the debt is relatively secure and actively traded, use the market value of debt.[11] Market prices for U.S. corporate debt are reported on the Financial Industry Regulatory Authority (FINRA) Trade Reporting and Compliance Engine (TRACE) system.[12] If the debt instrument is not traded, estimate current value by discounting the promised interest payments and the principal repayment at a yield to maturity that reflects the riskiness of the debt—typically based on the company's bond rating and current levels of interest rates. The book value of debt is a reasonable approximation for fixed-rate debt if interest rates and default risk have not significantly changed since the debt issuance. For floating-rate debt, value is not sensitive to interest rates, and book value is a reasonable approximation if the company's risk of default is low.

When testing how potential changes in operating performance may affect your valuation model, be sure to evaluate the impact on debt value. A new initiative that boosts margins could influence the company's credit rating. Check leverage ratios, such as the debt-to-EBITDA ratio, to see whether the bond rating might shift under the new forecasts—though often, it won't. A change in the credit rating can trigger a new yield to maturity, prompting a needed reassessment of the debt's valuation. For more on debt ratings and interest rates, see Chapter 35.

Highly Levered Companies   For companies with significant debt or companies in financial distress, valuing debt requires careful analysis. For distressed companies, the intrinsic value of the debt will be at a significant discount to its book value and will fluctuate with the value of the enterprise. Essentially, the debt has become like equity: its value will depend directly on your estimate for the enterprise value.

To value debt in these situations, apply an integrated-scenario approach. Exhibit 16.3 presents a simple two-scenario example for a company with significant debt. In scenario A, the company's management can implement

---

[11] When a bond's yield is below its coupon rate, the bond will trade above its face value. Intuition dictates that, at most, the bond's face value should be deducted from enterprise value. Yet, since enterprise value is computed using the cost of debt (via the weighted average of cost of capital) and not the coupon rate, subtracting face value is inconsistent with how enterprise value is computed.

[12] Developed by FINRA, the TRACE system facilitates the mandatory reporting of over-the-counter market transactions for eligible debt securities in the United States. It is available to the public via FINRA's website. At the time of writing, FINRA provided an online bond search tool on its home page.

EXHIBIT 16.3 **Valuation of Equity Using Scenario Analysis**

$ million

	Enterprise value	Face value of debt	Equity value[1]	Probability of occurrence	Weighted equity value
Scenario A					
New owner successfully implements value improvements.	1,500	1,200	300	50%	150
Scenario B					
Company maintains current performance.	900	1,200	—	50%	—
				Equity value:	150

[1] Equity value equals enterprise value less the face value of debt or zero, whichever is greater.

improvements in operating margin, inventory turns, and so on. In scenario B, changes are unsuccessful, and performance remains at its current level.

For each scenario, estimate the enterprise value conditional on your financial forecasts.[13] Next, deduct the full value of the debt and other nonequity claims from enterprise value. The full value is not the market value but rather the value of debt if the company were default free.[14] If the full value of debt is greater than enterprise value, set the equity value to zero. To complete the valuation, weight each scenario's resulting equity value by its probability of occurrence. For the company in Exhibit 16.3, scenario A leads to an equity valuation of $300 million, whereas the equity value in scenario B is zero. If the probability of each scenario is 50 percent, the probability-weighted value of equity is $150 million.

The scenario valuation approach treats equity as a call option on enterprise value. A more comprehensive model would estimate the entire distribution of potential enterprise values and use an option-pricing model to value equity.[15] However, using an option-pricing model has practical drawbacks. First, to model the distribution of enterprise values, you must forecast the expected change and volatility for each source of uncertainty, such as revenue growth and gross margin. This too easily becomes a mechanical exercise that replaces a thoughtful analysis of the underlying economics of potential scenarios. Second, most options models treat each source of uncertainty as independent of the others. This can lead to outcomes that are economically unrealistic. For these reasons, we believe a thoughtful

[13] All nonequity claims need to be included in the scenario approach for distressed companies. The order in which nonequity claims are paid upon liquidation will make a difference for the value of each nonequity claim but not for the equity value.
[14] If the coupon rate does not equal the yield on comparable bonds, the value of debt will not equal the book value, even if the debt is default free.
[15] Chapter 40 describes option-pricing models.

scenario analysis leads to a better-informed and more accurate valuation than an advanced options model will.

VALUING DEBT EQUIVALENTS

Debt equivalents have the characteristics of debt but are not formal loan contracts. They include operating leases, operating provisions such as plant decommissioning, nonoperating provisions such as restructuring charges, and contingent liabilities such as pending lawsuits. In this section, we will discuss some of the most common of these debt equivalents.

Operating Leases

Since 2019, companies have been required to recognize nearly all leases, including fixed-payment operating leases, on the balance sheet. For companies that report using IFRS, lease-related interest is recorded as a financial expense, and lease-related liabilities are incorporated within debt. Therefore, no special adjustment is required.

For companies reporting under U.S. GAAP, leases are categorized into three types: finance leases, fixed-payment operating leases, and variable-payment operating leases. Finance leases are treated similarly to debt, so you should handle them accordingly. Fixed-payment operating leases are capitalized on the balance sheet, but interest is not recognized. To address this, estimate the interest, remove it from operating costs to determine operating profit, and deduct the operating lease liabilities listed on the balance sheet from the enterprise value. Variable-payment operating leases, however, are not capitalized. You will need to estimate their value and the associated interest expense. Once estimated, treat them similarly to fixed-payment operating leases.

Chapter 22 offers a comprehensive example that details the accounting and valuation process for leases.

Provisions

Certain provisions should be treated as debt equivalents and deducted accordingly. Excluding retirement-related provisions, search for three types of provisions and value them as follows:

1. **Ongoing operating provisions** for accounts such as product warranties are already accounted for in the free cash flows and therefore *should not be deducted* from enterprise value.
2. **Long-term operating provisions** such as those related to asset decommissioning *should be deducted* from enterprise value as debt equivalents.

Because these provisions cover cash expenses payable in the long term, they are recorded at a discounted value in the balance sheet. There is no need to perform a separate DCF analysis; you can use the book value of the liability in your valuation.[16]

3. **Nonoperating provisions** arising from infrequent activities such as a restructuring *should be deducted* from enterprise value as a debt equivalent. These provisions are recorded on the financial statements at an undiscounted value since outlays are typically made in the near term. While a discounted value would be preferable, the book value from the balance sheet often serves as a reasonable approximation.

In Chapter 21, we present a detailed example to illustrate the valuation process for provisions.

Unfunded Retirement Obligations

Unfunded retirement obligations, such as unfunded pensions and post-retirement medical benefits, should be treated as debt equivalents and deducted from enterprise value to determine equity value. Since the future contributions to eliminate unfunded liabilities are tax deductible at the marginal tax rate, multiply unfunded pension liabilities by 1 minus the statutory income tax rate. For details on pension accounting and valuation, see Chapter 23.

Contingent Liabilities

Certain liabilities are not disclosed in the balance sheet but are separately discussed in the notes that accompany the balance sheet. Examples are potential liabilities from pending litigation and loan guarantees. When possible, estimate each liability's expected after-tax cash flows (if the costs are tax deductible), and discount these at the cost of debt. Unfortunately, an external assessment of the probability of such cash flows materializing is challenging, so the valuation should be interpreted with caution. To provide some boundaries on your final valuation, estimate the value of contingent liabilities for a range of probabilities.

VALUING HYBRID SECURITIES AND NONCONTROLLING INTERESTS

For stable, profitable companies, the current values of debt and debt equivalents are typically independent of enterprise value. For hybrid securities and noncontrolling interests, this is not the case. Each must be valued in

---

[16] The company will also recognize a decommissioning asset at the time of initial investment. The decommissioning asset is already incorporated into free cash flow, so no adjustment for the asset is required.

conjunction with estimates of enterprise value. The most common hybrid securities are convertible debt, convertible preferred stock, and employee stock options. We will detail the treatment of all three, as well as noncontrolling interests.

Convertible Securities

Convertible bonds are corporate bonds that can be exchanged for common equity at a predetermined conversion ratio.[17] Convertible preferred stock has the same basic structure as convertible bonds, except convertible stock often comes with other rights of control, such as board seats. Both have become a meaningful source of financing for technology companies.[18] A convertible bond is essentially a package of a straight corporate bond plus a call option on equity, referred to as the conversion option. Because the conversion option can have significant value, this form of debt requires treatment different from that of regular corporate debt.

The value of convertibles depends on the enterprise value. In contrast to valuation of straight debt, neither the book value nor the simple DCF value of bond cash flows is a good proxy for calculating the value of convertibles. Depending on the information available, there are three possible methods to apply:

1. *Fair value.* Companies report the "fair" value of financial instruments, including convertible debt, in the notes to the financial statements. Companies value these investments using quoted market prices or pricing models, and they disclose the methodology used. Use this value if enterprise value has not changed significantly since the last financial report. If the enterprise value has changed, search the TRACE database for the most recent market value of each security.

2. *Option value.* If the fair value is not disclosed or is no longer relevant, we recommend using an option-based valuation for convertible debt.[19] Accurate valuation of convertible bonds with option-based models is not straightforward. That said, by following methods outlined by DeSpiegeleer, Van Hulle, and Schoutens, you can make a reasonable approximation by applying an adjusted Black-Scholes option-pricing model.[20]

[17] For more on convertible bonds, see R. Brealey, S. Myers, F. Allen, and A. Edmunds, *Principles of Corporate Finance*, 14th ed. (New York: McGraw-Hill, 2023), chap. 24.
[18] H. Clarfelt and N. Megaw. "Tech Companies Cash In on "Frothy" Stock Rally with Convertible Bond Sales," *Financial Times*, February 29, 2024, www.ft.com.
[19] If you plan to modify enterprise value because of proposed operating changes, the fair value is no longer appropriate, as the value of convertible debt will change with enterprise value.
[20] For more on the valuation of convertible debt, see, for example, J. DeSpiegeleer, C. Van Hulle, and W. Schoutens, *The Handbook of Hybrid Securities: Convertible Bonds, CoCo Bonds, and Bail-In* (Hoboken, NJ: John Wiley & Sons, 2014).

3. *Conversion value.* The conversion value approach assumes that all convertible bonds are immediately exchanged for equity and ignores the time value of the conversion option. It leads to reasonable results when the conversion option is deep in the money, meaning the bond is more valuable when converted into equity than when held for future coupon and principal payments.

Valuing Convertibles   Exhibit 16.4 illustrates the three valuation methods for a generic tech company, TechCo. In addition to having fixed-rate debt and operating leases, this company issued two convertible bonds: $1.15 billion in convertible bonds due in 2025 and $1.725 billion in convertible bonds due in 2028. Because the coupon rate was below the prevailing yield for nonconvertible debt at the time of offering, the bonds are reported on the balance sheet below their principal due.[21] Unfortunately, the discounts are aggregated across

EXHIBIT 16.4 **TechCo Convertible Debt, December 2023**

$ million

Capital structure	Fair value	Black-Scholes value	Conversion value	Principal due
Enterprise value	142,000.0	142,000.0	142,000.0	
Fixed-rate debt	(9,561.0)	(9,561.0)	(9,561.0)	9,561.0
Operating lease liabilities	(1,740.0)	(1,740.0)	(1,740.0)	1,740.0
→ Convertible debt at 0.0% due 2025	(1,200.0)	(1,193.4)	—	1,150.0
→ Convertible debt at 0.875% due 2028	(1,900.0)	(1,981.3)	—	1,725.0
→ Convertible note hedge	239.1	239.1	—	
Employee options	(535.0)	(535.0)	(535.0)	
Equity value	127,303.1	127,228.4	130,164.0	
Number of shares, millions				
Number of nondiluted shares	2,071.1	2,071.1	2,071.1	
→ New shares issued	—	—	38.0	
Number of diluted shares	2,071.1	2,071.1	2,109.1	
Value per share, $	61.5	61.4	61.7	

[21] When a company issues convertible debt at a coupon rate below the yield on similar nonconvertible debt, it will be recorded on the balance sheet at a discount but may not trade in the public market at a discount. This is because the conversion feature has value. The value of the conversion feature, however, is not recorded as part of debt, but rather as shareholders' equity. Since the book value of equity is not used in DCF valuation, this can lead to a significant underestimation of the convertible's value. For more on the accounting related to convertible debt, see Accounting Principles Board (APB) 14–1, "Accounting for Convertible Debt Instruments That May Be Settled in Cash upon Conversion (Including Partial Cash Settlement)," Financial Accounting Standards Board, May 9, 2008, www.fasb.org.

all bonds, so the balance sheet carrying value on a bond-by-bond basis is not available.

The first column in Exhibit 16.4 values TechCo's equity, based on the fair value of convertible debt reported in its 10-K. In its note on debt, the company rounded this fair value to the nearest $100 million. Notably, the convertible debt trades at a premium compared with the principal amount on the balance sheet. For example, the fair value of the convertible debt due in 2028 is reported at $1,900 million, exceeding the $1,725 million principal amount.

The premium paid by investors can be traced to the bond's conversion feature. According to its note on debt, the bonds maturing in 2028 are convertible at $72.54 per share. At this conversion price, $1.725 billion in outstanding principal can be converted into 23.8 million shares. With TechCo's stock trading at $61.57 2023, the bonds were "out of the money," meaning conversion held no immediate value. However, if the stock price were to rise above $72.54 before 2028, converting the bonds to shares would be more profitable than collecting the principal. For instance, if the share price reached $100, conversion of the 2028 bond into shares would yield approximately $2.4 billion, exceeding the $1.725 billion in principal due.

In contrast to the treatment of investment-grade, nonconvertible debt, any change in enterprise value necessitates revaluing TechCo's convertibles using an option-pricing model. To model the value of TechCo's convertible debt, disaggregate the value of convertible debt into underlying straight debt and the option value to convert. For the bond maturing in 2028, the value of the straight debt is the net present value of a 0.875 percent coupon bond yielding 6.2 percent, the yield on comparable bonds without conversion features, maturing in five years. Without the ability to convert, this bond is valued at 77.7 percent of the $1,725.0 million in principal due, or $1,340.3 million.

To determine the conversion option's value, you need six inputs: the underlying asset value, the strike price, the volatility of the underlying asset, the risk-free rate, the time to maturity, and the dividend rate on the underlying asset. For the option embedded in TechCo's 2028 convertible bond, the underlying asset is 23.8 million shares of its stock, for which the current value equals $1,464.1 million. The strike price, which represents what the investor must pay to receive the shares, equals the current value of straight debt, currently valued at $1,725.0 million. We use a 40.3 percent volatility rate for TechCo shares, as reported in the note on stockholders' equity. The bond's time to maturity is five years, and the five-year risk-free rate is 3.83 percent.[22] TechCo does not pay dividends, so the dividend yield is set at zero.

Plugging the data into a Black-Scholes estimator leads to an option value of $641.0 million. Thus, as shown in the second data column of Exhibit 16.4, the Black-Scholes value of the convertible debt amounts to $1,981.3 million—comprising

---

[22] TechCo's convertible debt is not callable, so the remaining maturity can be used in the options valuation. If the debt is callable, this must be incorporated into the bond's valuation.

the $1,340.3 million in straight debt calculated earlier, plus $641.0 million in option value. This result is contingent on stability of the Black-Scholes inputs, especially volatility. If volatility is expected to drop as the company matures, the historical estimate of volatility will overestimate the option value. The errant valuation is largest for longer-dated options, which is often the case for convertible debt.

A simple alternative to option pricing is the conversion value approach, shown in the third data column of Exhibit 16.4. The method is easier to implement than Black-Scholes but ignores optionality. Under the conversion value approach, convertible bonds are converted immediately into equity. Since TechCo's bonds are convertible into 38.0 million shares (14.2 million from the debt due in 2025 and 23.8 million from the debt due in 2028), diluted shares increase from 2,071.1 million to 2,109.1 million. This approach eliminates convertible debt and divides the equity value by the diluted share count.

Unless the bonds are significantly in-the-money, the immediate conversion approach tends to underestimate the bonds' value while overestimating the share price. Therefore, we recommend using an option valuation model, such as Black-Scholes.

Convertible-Bond Hedges   When a company issues a convertible bond, the bond is sometimes accompanied by a complex derivative transaction to synthetically increase the strike price.[23] Investors prefer strike prices close to the current share price. Issuers, concerned about dilution from conversion into equity, prefer a higher strike price that lowers the odds of conversion. An investment bank can create a hedge to bridge the difference. Increasing the strike price through derivatives requires a cash outlay by the company. Since the 2020 pandemic, with technology companies tightening their belts, these hedges have become less common.[24]

In its annual report, TechCo reports, "In connection with the issuance of the 2028 Convertible Notes, we entered into privately negotiated capped call transactions. ... The initial cap price of the Capped Calls was approximately $95.81 per share." To account for the value of the hedge, we use Black-Scholes to revalue the convertible bond at the higher strike price. The convertible note hedge reported in Exhibit 16.4 equals the difference between the original and synthetic bond price.

Although companies do not typically report the value of the hedge on the balance sheet or in the notes, another company engaged in a similar transaction wrote, "The convertible note hedge and warrant transactions may affect the value of our Class A common stock." Even with the continued improvements

---

[23] In the transaction, the company purchases a call option on its own shares at the original share price and writes a second call option at the preferred conversion price.

[24] A. Or, "More Convertible Bond Issuers Are Saying No to Hedging Their Bets," Bloomberg, August 17, 2023, www.bloomberg.com.

in accounting transparency, a diligent analysis of the notes for claims against cash flow continues to be critical.

Employee Stock Options

Many companies offer their employees stock options as part of their compensation. Options give the holder the right, but not the obligation, to buy company stock at a specified price, known as the exercise price. Since employee stock options have long maturities and the company's stock price could eventually rise above the exercise price, these options can have great value.

Employee stock options affect a company valuation in two ways. First, the value of options that will be *granted in the future* needs to be captured in the free-cash-flow projections or in a separate DCF valuation, following the guidelines in Chapter 11. If captured in the free-cash-flow projections, the value of future options grants is included in the value of operations and should not be treated as a nonequity claim. Second, the value of options *currently outstanding* must be subtracted from enterprise value as a nonequity claim. Note, however, that the value of the options will depend on your estimate of enterprise value. Your option valuation should reflect this.

The following approaches can be used for valuing employee options:

- *Company-disclosed fair value.* Start by searching the annual report for the company's assessment of fair value. For instance, TechCo reports the "aggregate intrinsic value" of employee options at $535 million in the note on stockholders' equity.

- *Option-pricing model.* If the company's enterprise value has changed since the last financial filing, estimate the value using option valuation models such as Black-Scholes or more advanced binomial (lattice) models. Under U.S. GAAP and IFRS, the notes to the balance sheet report the total value of all employee stock options outstanding, as estimated by such option-pricing models. Note that the balance sheet value is a good approximation only if your estimate of share price is close to the one underlying the option values in the annual report. Otherwise, you need to create a new valuation using an option-pricing model.[25] The notes disclose the information required for valuation.

- *Exercise value approach.* The exercise value approach assumes all options are exercised immediately. Upon exercise, both the company's cash balance and the number of shares outstanding increase, and the value per share is calculated accordingly. However, this approach overlooks the time value of the options. Option holders have the right to delay exercise,

---

[25] For more on the valuation of employee stock options, see, for example, J. Hull and A. White, "How to Value Employee Stock Options," *Financial Analysts Journal* 60, no. 1 (January/February 2004): 114–119.

and this flexibility adds value beyond immediate exercise. Since a more accurate valuation is typically disclosed in the annual report, we do not recommend using this method. Despite its limitations, however, it remains a common practice among professionals.

Exhibit 16.5 provides an example of the three valuation methods. The first data column is based on the fair value reported by TechCo, which it calls "aggregate intrinsic value." The second column uses the Black-Scholes option-pricing model to value the outstanding options. The value of outstanding options will be an upper bound on value, because outstanding options include some options that will be lost if the employee leaves the company.

To estimate the value of employee stock options, you need six inputs: the current stock price, the average strike price, the stock's volatility, the risk-free rate, the time to maturity, and the stock's dividend rate. In December 2023, TechCo's shares traded at $61.57. The other inputs are disclosed in its annual report for both outstanding and exercisable options. For outstanding options, the weighted average strike price equals $20.03, the volatility of TechCo's shares is reported at 40.3 percent, and the average time to maturity is reported at 2.79 years. The current risk-free rate over five years is 4.00 percent, and the expected dividend rate is zero. The Black-Scholes estimator prices the average option at $43.94.[26] With 12.8 million options

EXHIBIT 16.5 **TechCo Employee Options, December 2023**

$ million

Capital structure	Fair value	Black-Scholes value[2]	Conversion value
Enterprise value[1]	142,000.0	142,000.0	142,000.0
Fixed-rate debt	(9,561.0)	(9,561.0)	(9,561.0)
Operating lease liabilities	(1,740.0)	(1,740.0)	(1,740.0)
Convertible debt, net of hedges	(2,860.9)	(2,860.9)	(2,860.9)
→ Employee options: Value[2]	(535.0)	(560.8)	—
→ Employee options: Exercise proceeds	—	—	255.7
Equity value	127,303.1	127,277.3	128,093.8
Number of shares, millions			
Number of nondiluted shares	2,071.1	2,071.1	2,071.1
→ New shares issued	—	—	12.8
Number of diluted shares	2,071.1	2,071.1	2,083.9
Value per share, $	61.5	61.5	61.5

[1] Enterprise value is calculated by aggregating the market prices of all claims as of December 2023. No assessment of value has been performed.

[2] The fair value of options is reported in TechCo's 2018 10-K in note 15, "Shareholder's Equity," under "Aggregate Intrinsic Value." The Black-Scholes value is estimated using the Black-Scholes option-pricing model and company-disclosed inputs.

[26] Using Black-Scholes to determine the value of a single option on an average strike price will under-value a portfolio of options with a spread of strike prices. Unless you know the spread of strike prices, you cannot measure the bias.

outstanding, the aggregate value of options is valued at $560.8 million. To estimate share price, deduct the aggregate value of employee stock options from enterprise value, and divide by the number of undiluted shares. Since some outstanding options will go unclaimed, repeat the process for just the options that can be exercised. The actual value will fall somewhere between the two.

The third methodology is the conversion value approach, which assumes employee options are exercised immediately. We illustrate this approach in the third column of Exhibit 16.5. According to TechCo's 2023 annual report, 12.8 million shares can be exercised at an average strike price of $20.03, generating total proceeds of $255.7 million. While the exercise of these options increases the company's equity value through new cash inflows, it also raises the number of shares outstanding from 2,071.1 million to 2,083.9 million. Dividing the adjusted equity value by the diluted share count results in a per-share value of $61.5, matching the value calculated using the Black-Scholes method.

Noncontrolling Interests by Other Companies

When a company controls a subsidiary but does not fully own it, the subsidiary's financial statements must be fully consolidated in the group accounts. The subsidiary's assets and liabilities will be included in the parent company's accounts, but the portion of the subsidiary's equity not owned by the parent company will be separated from other equity accounts as noncontrolling interest.[27] Since the full value of the subsidiary will be incorporated into the value of operations, a valuation adjustment must be made for the portion of the subsidiary *not* owned by the parent company being valued.

Because noncontrolling interests owned by other companies are to a certain extent the mirror image of nonconsolidated assets, the valuation approach for noncontrolling interests is similar to that of nonconsolidated assets, described earlier in this chapter. If the subsidiary is publicly traded, deduct the proportional market value owned by outsiders from enterprise value to determine equity value. Alternatively, you can perform a separate valuation using a DCF approach, multiples, or a tracking portfolio, depending on the amount of information available. Remember, however, that a noncontrolling interest is a claim on a subsidiary, not the entire company. Thus, any valuation should be directly related to the subsidiary and not to the company as a whole.

---

[27] For example, Berkshire Hathaway reported $3.8 billion in noncontrolling interests in 2018. This amount can be found on the company's balance sheet under shareholders' equity.

ESTIMATING VALUE PER SHARE

The final step in a valuation is to calculate the value per share. To do this, divide your estimated equity value by the number of shares. However, the share count you use will depend on the process you used to estimate equity value.

Assuming you used an option-based valuation approach for convertible bonds and employee options, divide the total equity value by the number of undiluted shares outstanding. Use the undiluted (rather than diluted) number of shares because the full values of convertible debt and stock options have already been deducted from the enterprise value as nonequity claims. Also, use the most recent number of undiluted shares outstanding. Do not use the weighted average of shares outstanding, which is reported on the income statement to determine earnings per share.

The number of shares outstanding is the gross number of shares issued, less the number of shares held in treasury. Most U.S. and European companies report the number of shares issued and those held in treasury under shareholders' equity. However, some companies report treasury shares as an investment asset, which is unnecessarily complex and potentially misleading from an economic perspective. Treat them instead as a reduction in the number of shares outstanding.

If you used the conversion and exercise value approach to account for employee options and convertible debt and stock options, divide by the diluted number of shares.

With intrinsic value per share in hand, you have completed the mechanics of your valuation. But the job is not done. The next two chapters discuss how to stress-test your valuation using integrated scenarios and trading multiples.

17

Analyzing the Results

Now that the valuation model is complete, we are ready to put it to work. Start by testing its validity. Even a carefully planned model can have mechanical errors or flaws in economic logic. To help you avoid such troubles, this chapter presents a set of systematic checks and other tools to test the model's sturdiness. During this verification, you should also ensure that key value drivers such as revenue growth and return on invested capital (ROIC) are consistent with the economics of the industry.

Once you are confident that the model works, learn the ins and outs of your valuation by changing each forecast input one at a time. Examine how each part of your model changes, and determine which inputs have the largest effect on the company's valuation and which have little or no impact. Since forecast inputs are likely to change in concert, build a sensitivity analysis that tests multiple changes at a time. Use this analysis to set priorities for strategic actions.

Next, use scenario analysis to deepen the understanding your valuation provides. Start by determining the key uncertainties that affect the company's future, and use these to construct multiple forecasts. Uncertainty can hinge on a question as simple as "Will a product launch be successful?" or a more complex one, such as "Which of several different emerging technologies will dominate the market?" Construct a comprehensive forecast consistent with each scenario, and weight the resulting equity valuations by their probability of occurring. Scenario analysis will not only guide your valuation range but also inform your thinking about strategic actions and resource allocation under alternative situations.

VALIDATING THE MODEL

Once you have a workable valuation model, perform several checks to test the logic of your results, minimize the possibility of errors, and ensure you understand the forces driving the valuation. Start by making sure the model is technically robust—for example, by checking that net income flows through shareholders' equity and that the balance sheet balances in each forecast year. Second, test whether results are consistent with industry economics. For instance, do key value drivers, such as ROIC, evolve in a way that is consistent with the intensity of competition? Finally, compare the model's output with the current share price and trading multiples. Can differences be explained by economics, or is an error possible? We address each of these tasks next.

Is the Model Technically Robust?

Ensure that all checks and balances in your model are in place. Your model should reflect the following fundamental equilibrium relationships:

- In the unadjusted financial statements, the balance sheet should balance every year, both historically and in forecast years. Does net income correctly link to retained earnings, dividends, and share issues or repurchases in changes to equity?
- In the rearranged financial statements, check that the sum of invested capital plus nonoperating assets equals the cumulative sources of financing. Is net operating profit after taxes (NOPAT) identical when calculated top down from sales and bottom up from net income?
- Does the change in excess cash and debt line up with the cash flow statement?

A good model will automatically compute each check as part of the model and flag the user when an issue arises. A technical change to the model that breaks a check can then be clearly noted. To stress-test the model, change a few key inputs in an extreme manner. For instance, if gross margin is increased to 99 percent or lowered to 1 percent, does the balance sheet still balance?

As a final consistency check, adjust the dividend payout ratio. Since payout will change funding requirements, the company's capital structure will change. Because NOPAT, invested capital, and free cash flow are independent of capital structure, these values should *not* change with variations in the payout ratio. If they do, the model has a mechanical flaw.

Is the Model Economically Consistent?

The next step is to check that your results reflect appropriate value driver economics. If the projected returns on invested capital are above the weighted average cost of capital (WACC), the value of operations should be above the book value of invested capital. Moreover, if revenue growth is high, the value of operations should be considerably above book value. If not, a computational error has probably occurred. Compare your valuation results with a back-of-the-envelope value estimate based on the key value driver formula, using long-term average revenue growth and return on invested capital as key inputs.

Make sure that patterns of key financial and operating ratios are consistent with economic logic:

- *Are the patterns intended?* For example, does invested-capital turnover increase over time for sound economic reasons (economies of scale) or simply because you modeled future capital expenditures as a fixed percentage of revenues? Are future cash tax rates changing dramatically because you forecast deferred-tax assets as a percentage of revenues or operating profit?

- *Are the patterns reasonable?* Avoid large step changes in key assumptions from one year to the next, because these will distort key ratios and could lead to false interpretations. For example, a large single-year improvement in capital efficiency could make capital expenditures in that year negative, leading to an unrealistically high cash flow. While possible, selling fixed equipment at its book value is unlikely.

- *Are the patterns consistent with industry dynamics?* In certain cases, a set of reasonable changes in key inputs can lead to unintended consequences. Exhibit 17.1 presents price and cost data for a hypothetical company in a competitive industry. To account for inflation, you may decide to forecast that the company's prices will increase by 3 percent per year. Separately, because of cost efficiencies, operating costs are expected to drop by 2 percent per year. In isolation, each rate appears innocuous. Computing ROIC, however, reveals a significant trend. Between year 1 and year 10, ROIC grows from 9.3 to 39.2 percent—an unlikely outcome in a competitive industry. Since cost advantages are

EXHIBIT 17.1 **ROIC Impact of Small Changes: Sample Price and Cost Trends**

$

	Year 1	Year 2	Year 3	Year 4	Year 5	⋯	Year 10	Growth, %
Price	50.0	51.5	53.0	54.6	56.3	…	65.2	3.0%
Number of units	100.0	103.0	106.1	109.3	112.6	…	130.5	
Revenue	5,000.0	5,304.5	5,627.5	5,970.3	6,333.9	…	8,512.2	
Cost per unit	43.0	42.1	41.3	40.5	39.7	…	35.9	−2.0%
Number of units	100.0	103.0	106.1	109.3	112.6	…	130.5	
Cost	4,300.0	4,340.4	4,381.2	4,422.4	4,464.0	…	4,677.8	
Operating profit	700.0	964.1	1,246.3	1,547.9	1,869.9	…	3,834.4	
Invested capital	7,500.0	7,725.0	7,956.8	8,195.5	8,441.3	…	9,785.8	
Pretax ROIC, %	9.3	12.5	15.7	18.9	22.2	…	39.2	

difficult to protect, competitors are likely to mimic production and lower prices to capture share. A good model will highlight economic inconsistencies like this one.

- *Is the company in a steady state by the end of the explicit forecasting period?* Following the explicit forecasting period, when you apply a continuing-value formula, the company's margins, returns on invested capital, and growth should be stable. If this is not the case, extend the explicit forecast period until a steady state is reached.

Are the Results Plausible?

Once you are confident the model is technically sound and economically consistent, test whether the model's valuation results are plausible. If the company is publicly listed, compare your results with the market value. If your estimate is far from the market value, do not jump to the conclusion that the market price is wrong. If a difference exists, search for the cause. For instance, perhaps not all relevant information has been incorporated in the share price—say, due to a small free float or paucity of trading in the stock. While the largest companies trade every day, many small companies do not.

Also perform a sound multiples analysis. Calculate the implied forward-looking valuation multiples of the operating value over, for example, earnings before interest, taxes, and amortization (EBITA). Compare these with equivalently defined multiples of traded peer-group companies. Chapter 18 describes how to do a proper multiples analysis to triangulate your results. Regardless of where your valuation falls in the competitive set, make sure you can explain the differences with peer-group companies in terms of the companies' value drivers and underlying business characteristics or strategies.

SENSITIVITY ANALYSIS

With a robust model in hand, test how the company's value responds to changes in key inputs. Senior management can use sensitivity analysis to prioritize the actions that have the greatest effect on value. From the investor's perspective, sensitivity analysis can focus on which inputs to investigate further and monitor more closely. Sensitivity analysis also helps bound the valuation range when there is uncertainty about the inputs.

Assessing the Impact of Individual Drivers

Start by testing each input, one at a time, to see which has the largest impact on the company's valuation. Exhibit 17.2 presents a sample sensitivity analysis. Among the alternatives presented, a permanent one-percentage-point reduction

EXHIBIT 17.2 **Sample Sensitivity Analysis**

Driver	Change	Valuation impact, $ million
Margin	1 percentage point permanent reduction in selling expenses	29
Growth	1 percentage point increase in price each year for next 5 years	26
Growth	1 percentage point increase in volume each year for next 5 years	14
Taxes	1 percentage point reduction in operating tax rate	11
Capital	5-day reduction in inventory	8

in selling expenses has the greatest effect on the company's valuation.[1] Such an analysis will also show which drivers have a minimal impact on value. Too often, we find our clients focusing on actions that are easy to measure but fail to move the needle.

Although an input-by-input sensitivity analysis will increase your knowledge about which inputs drive the valuation, its use is limited. First, inputs rarely change in isolation. For instance, an increase in selling expenses should, if managed well, increase revenue growth. Second, when two inputs are changed simultaneously, interactions can cause the combined effect to differ from the sum of the individual effects. Therefore, you cannot compare a one-percentage-point increase in selling expenses with a one-percentage-point increase in growth. If there are interactions in the movements of inputs, the one-by-one analysis would miss them. To capture possible interactions between inputs, analyze trade-offs.

Analyzing Trade-offs

Strategic choices typically involve trade-offs between inputs into your valuation model. For instance, raising prices leads to fewer purchases, lowering inventory results in more missed sales, and entering new markets often affects both growth and margin. Exhibit 17.3 presents an analysis that measures the impact on a valuation when two inputs are changed simultaneously. Based on an EBITA margin of 14 percent and revenue growth of 3 percent (among other forecasts), the company is currently valued at $365 million. The curve drawn through this point represents all the possible combinations of EBITA margin and revenue growth that lead to the same valuation. (Economists call this an isocurve.) To increase the valuation by 25 percent, from $365 million to $456 million, the organization needs to move northeast to the next isocurve. Using this information, management can set performance targets that are consistent with the company's valuation aspirations and competitive environment.

---

[1] Some analysts test the impact of both positive and negative changes to each driver and then plot the results from the largest to smallest variation. Given its shape, the resulting chart is commonly known as a tornado chart.

EXHIBIT 17.3 **Valuation Isocurves by Growth and Margin**

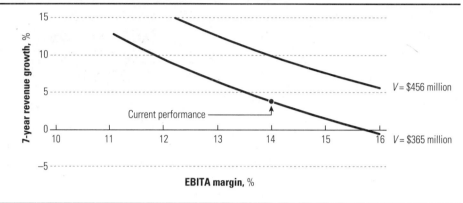

When performing sensitivity analysis, do not limit yourself to changes in financial variables. Check how changes in sector-specific operational value drivers such as transactions per customer affect the final valuation. This is where a best-in-class model's real power lies. For example, if you increase the cancellation rates for a streaming service, does the company's value decrease? Can you explain with back-of-the-envelope estimates why the change is large or small?

CREATING SCENARIOS

Valuation requires a forecast, but the future can take many paths. A government might pass legislation affecting the entire industry. A new discovery could revolutionize a competitor's product portfolio. Since the future is never knowable, consider making financial projections under multiple scenarios.[2] The scenarios should reflect different assumptions regarding future macroeconomic, industry, or business developments, as well as the corresponding strategic responses by industry players. Collectively, the scenarios should capture the future states of the world that would have the most impact on value creation over time and a reasonable chance of occurrence. Assess how likely it is that the key assumptions underlying each scenario will change, and assign to each scenario a probability of occurrence.

[2] Overconfidence is a well-known behavioral bias. Embracing uncertainty through the use of scenario analysis helps mitigate overconfidence. For more on overconfidence and valuation, see M. Grežo, "Overconfidence and Financial Decision-Making: A Meta-analysis," *Review of Behavioral Finance* 13, no. 3 (2021): 276–296.

When analyzing the scenarios, critically review your assumptions concerning the following variables:

- *Broad economic conditions.* How critical are these forecasts to the results? Some industries are more dependent on basic economic conditions than others are. Home building, for example, is highly correlated with the overall health of the economy. Branded food processing is less so.

- *Competitive structure of the industry.* A scenario that assumes substantial increases in market share is less likely in a highly competitive and concentrated market than in an industry with fragmented and inefficient competition.

- *Operating capabilities of the company.* Focus on capabilities that are necessary to achieve the business results predicted in the scenario. Can the company develop a set of competitive products or services within the required range of time, quality, and cost?

- *Financing capabilities of the company.* Financing capabilities are often implicit in the valuation. For each scenario consider the following: If debt or excess marketable securities are excessive relative to the company's targets, how will the company resolve the imbalance? Should the company raise equity if too much debt is projected? Should the company be willing to raise equity at its current market price?

Complete the alternative scenarios suggested by the preceding analyses. The process of examining initial results may well uncover unanticipated questions that are best resolved by creating additional scenarios. In this way, the valuation process is inherently circular. Performing a valuation often provides insights that lead to additional scenarios and analyses.

Exhibits 17.4 and 17.5 provide a simplified example of a scenario approach to a discounted-cash-flow (DCF) valuation. The company being valued faces significant uncertainty because of a new-product launch for which it has spent considerable time and money on research and development (such as when one luxury car company introduced its first all-electric SUV in 2024). If the new product is a top seller, revenue growth will more than double over the next few years. Returns on invested capital will peak above 20 percent and remain above 12 percent in perpetuity. If the product launch fails, however, growth will continue to erode as the company's current products face increased competition. Lower average selling prices will cause operating margins to fall. The company's returns on invested capital will decline to levels below the cost of capital, and the company will struggle to earn its cost of capital in the long term. Exhibit 17.4 presents forecasts on growth, operating margin, and capital efficiency that are consistent with each of these two scenarios.

EXHIBIT 17.4 **Key Value Drivers by Scenario**

%

	Financial forecasts								Scenario assessment
	2024A	2025	2026	2027	2028	2029	2030	Continuing value	
Scenario 1: New product is a top seller									
Revenue growth	5.0	12.0	15.0	14.0	12.0	10.0	5.0	3.5	New-product introduction leads to spike in revenue growth.
After-tax operating margin	7.5	9.0	11.0	14.0	14.0	12.0	10.0	8.0	Margins improve to best in class as consumers pay a price premium for product.
× Capital turnover, times	1.5	1.4	1.3	1.4	1.5	1.6	1.6	1.6	Capital turnover drops slightly during product launch as company builds inventory to meet expected demand.
Return on invested capital	11.3	12.6	14.3	19.6	21.0	19.2	16.0	12.8	
Scenario 2: Product launch fails									
Revenue growth	5.0	3.0	(1.0)	(1.0)	1.5	1.5	1.5	1.5	Revenue growth drops as competitors steal share.
After-tax operating margin	7.5	7.0	6.5	6.0	5.5	5.5	6.5	6.5	Lower prices put pressure on margins; cost reductions cannot keep pace.
× Capital turnover, times	1.5	1.4	1.4	1.4	1.3	1.3	1.3	1.3	Capital efficiency falls as price pressure reduces revenue; inventory reductions mitigate fall.
Return on invested capital	11.3	9.8	9.1	8.4	7.2	7.2	8.5	8.5	

EXHIBIT 17.5 **Example of a Scenario Approach to DCF Valuation**

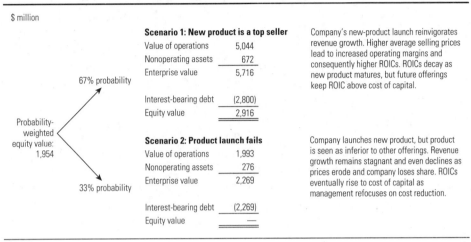

$ million

Probability-weighted equity value: 1,954

67% probability

Scenario 1: New product is a top seller

Value of operations	5,044
Nonoperating assets	672
Enterprise value	5,716
Interest-bearing debt	(2,800)
Equity value	2,916

Company's new-product launch reinvigorates revenue growth. Higher average selling prices lead to increased operating margins and consequently higher ROICs. ROICs decay as new product matures, but future offerings keep ROIC above cost of capital.

33% probability

Scenario 2: Product launch fails

Value of operations	1,993
Nonoperating assets	276
Enterprise value	2,269
Interest-bearing debt	(2,269)
Equity value	—

Company launches new product, but product is seen as inferior to other offerings. Revenue growth remains stagnant and even declines as prices erode and company loses share. ROICs eventually rise to cost of capital as management refocuses on cost reduction.

Next, build a separate free cash flow model for each set of forecasts. Although not presented here, the resulting cash flow models are based on the DCF methodology outlined in Chapter 10. Exhibit 17.5 presents the valuation results. In the case of a successful product launch, the DCF value of operations equals $5,044 million. The nonoperating assets consist primarily of nonconsolidated subsidiaries, and given their own reliance on the product launch, they are valued at the implied NOPAT multiple for the parent company, $672 million. A comprehensive scenario will examine all financial accounts to make sure they are consistent with the scenario's underlying premise. Next, deduct the face value of the debt outstanding at $2,800 million (assuming interest rates have not changed, so the market value of debt equals the face value). The resulting equity value is $2,916 million.

If the product launch fails, the DCF value of operations is only $1,993 million. In this scenario, the value of the nonconsolidated subsidiaries is much lower ($276 million), as their business outlook has deteriorated due to the failure of the new product. The value of the debt is no longer $2,800 million in this scenario. Instead, the debt holders would end up with $2,269 million by seizing control of the enterprise. In scenario 2, the common equity would have no value.

Given a two-thirds probability of success for the product, the probability-weighted equity value across both scenarios amounts to $1,954 million. Since estimates of scenario probabilities are likely to be rough at best, determine the range of probabilities that point to a particular strategic action. For instance, if this company were an acquisition target available for $1.5 billion, any probability of a successful launch above 50 percent would lead to value creation. Whether the probability is 67 percent or 72 percent does not affect the launch decision.

When using the scenario approach, make sure to generate a complete valuation buildup from value of operations to equity value. Do not shortcut the process by deducting the face value of debt from the scenario-weighted value of operations. Doing this would seriously underestimate the equity value, because the value of debt is also different in each scenario. In this case, the equity value would be undervalued by $175 million ($2,800 million face value minus $2,625 million probability-weighted value of debt).[3] A similar argument holds for nonoperating assets.

Creating scenarios also helps you understand the company's key priorities. In our example, reducing costs or cutting capital expenditures in the downside scenario will not meaningfully affect value. Any improvements in a downside scenario in which value is less than $531 million ($2,800 million in face value less $2,269 million in market value) will accrue primarily to the debt holders. In contrast, increasing the odds of a successful launch has a much greater impact on shareholder value. Increasing the success probability from two-thirds to three-fourths would boost shareholder value by more than 10 percent.

THE ART OF VALUATION

Valuation can be highly sensitive to small changes in assumptions about the future. Take a look at the sensitivity of a company with a forward-looking price-to-earnings ratio of 15 to 16. Increasing the cost of capital for this company by half a percentage point will decrease the value by approximately 10 percent. Changing the growth rate for the next 15 years by one percentage point annually will change the value by about 6 percent. For high-growth companies, the sensitivity is even greater. Considering this, it shouldn't be surprising that the market value of a company fluctuates over time. Historical volatilities for a typical stock over the past several years have been around 25 percent per year. Taking this as an estimate for future volatility, the market value of a typical company could well fluctuate around its expected value by 15 percent over the next month.[4]

We typically aim for a valuation range of plus or minus 15 percent, which is similar to the range used by many investment bankers. Even the best professionals cannot generate exact estimates. In other words, keep your aspirations for precision in check. It's what you learn from the model that really matters.

---

[3] Although this approach is typically recommended, deducting the market value of debt from enterprise value will lead to an inconsistent estimate of equity value if your estimate of default does not match market expectations. For more on how to correctly incorporate debt into the valuation, see Chapter 16.

[4] Based on a 95 percent confidence interval for the end-of-month price of a stock with an expected return of 9 percent per year.

18

Using Multiples

While discounted cash flow (DCF) is the most accurate and flexible method for valuing companies, using a relative valuation approach, such as juxtaposing the earnings multiples of comparable companies, can provide insights and help you summarize and test your valuation. In practice, however, multiples are often used in a superficial way that leads to inaccurate conclusions. This chapter explains how to use multiples correctly. Most of the focus will be on earnings multiples, the most commonly used variety. At the end, we'll also touch on some other multiples.

The basic idea behind using multiples for valuation is that similar assets should sell for similar prices, whether they are houses or shares of stock. In the case of a share of stock, the typical benchmark is some measure of earnings, often the price-to-earnings multiple (P/E), which is simply the equity value of the company divided by its net income. Multiples can be used both to see how a listed company is valued relative to peers and to value nontraded companies or business units of traded companies. Again, the same basic idea holds: businesses in the same industry and with similar performance should trade at a similar multiple.

Valuing a company by using multiples may seem straightforward, but arriving at useful insights requires careful analysis. Exhibit 18.1 illustrates what happens if you don't go deep enough in your multiples analysis. The managers of Company A, a producer of packaged foods, looked only at P/Es and were concerned that their company was trading at a P/E of 7.3 times while most of their peers were trading at a P/E of about 14, a discount of 50 percent. The management team believed the market didn't understand Company A's strategy or performance. In fact, management didn't understand the math of multiples. If the managers had looked at the more instructive multiple shown in the exhibit—net enterprise value to earnings before interest, taxes, and amortization (EV/EBITA)—they would have seen that the company was trading right in line with its peers.

EXHIBIT 18.1 **Multiples for Packaged-Foods Companies**

$ billion

| | | | | | Multiples | |
Company	Market value of equity	Enterprise value (equity + debt)	Net income (1 year forward)	EBITA (1 year forward)	Price/ earnings	Enterprise value/EBITA
A	2,783	9,940	381	929	7.3	10.7
B	13,186	16,279	856	1,428	15.4	11.4
C	8,973	11,217	665	1,089	13.5	10.3
D	14,851	22,501	1,053	2,009	14.1	11.2
Median (excluding A)					14.1	11.2

The reason for the difference in P/Es was that their company had much more debt relative to equity than the other companies. We estimated that if the company had had the same relative debt as its peers, its P/E also would have been 14. Except for very-high-growth companies, a company with higher debt relative to peers will have a lower P/E because more debt translates to higher risk for shareholders and a higher cost of equity. Therefore, each dollar of earnings (and cash flow to shareholders) will be worth less to an investor.[1]

To use earnings multiples properly, you should dig into the accounting statements to make sure you are comparing companies on an apples-to-apples basis. You also must choose the right companies to compare. Keep in mind the following five principles for correctly using earnings multiples:

1. *Value multibusiness companies as a sum of their parts.* Even companies that appear to be in a single industry will often compete in subindustries or product areas with widely varying return on invested capital (ROIC) and growth, leading to substantial variations in multiples.

2. *Use forward estimates of earnings.* Multiples using forward earnings estimates typically have much lower variation across peers, leading to a narrower range of uncertainty of value. They also embed future expectations better than multiples based on historical results.

3. *Use the right multiple, usually net enterprise value to EBITA, EBITDA, or NOPAT.* Although the P/E is widely used, it is distorted by capital structure and nonoperating income and expenses. (In this book, when we refer to the enterprise value multiple, including abbreviations such as EV/EBITA, we use "enterprise value" as shorthand for net enterprise value, equal to the value of operations.)

4. *Adjust the multiple for nonoperating items.* Nonoperating items embedded in reported EBITA or EBITDA, as well as balance sheet items such as excess cash and pension items, can lead to large distortions of multiples.

---

[1] The P/E is a function of return on capital, cost of capital, and growth. For very-high-growth companies, whose enterprise multiples are greater than the multiple for debt, the multiple will actually increase with leverage. See also Appendix D.

5. *Use the right peer group, not a broad industry average.* A good peer group consists of companies that not only operate in the same industry but also have similar prospects for ROIC and growth.

VALUE MULTIBUSINESS COMPANIES AS A SUM OF THEIR PARTS

Most large companies, even if they operate in a single industry, have business units in subindustries with different competitive dynamics and therefore differ widely in ROIC and growth. For example, Johnson & Johnson is composed of a pharmaceuticals business and a medical device business, which differ from one another in growth and return on capital and have different peers. Each of the units will therefore have different valuation multiples. For such multibusiness companies, a valuation using multiples requires a sum-of-parts approach, which values each business unit with a multiple appropriate to its peers and performance.

Even companies in more narrowly defined sectors often have units with different economics. For example, oil and gas services companies provide oil and gas companies with equipment and services that might include bottom hole assemblies, drill pipes, pressure-control services, intervention services, pressure pumping, fluid handling, subsea construction, and even temporary housing for workers. Some of these product areas, including bottom hole assemblies and drill pipes, tend to earn much higher returns on capital than others, such as pressure-control services and intervention services. Ideally, you would value units by using as fine-grained an approach as possible, comparing them with companies that have similar units and economics.

For an example of a good sum-of-parts valuation, see Exhibit 18.2. For each unit of this disguised company, we apply a different multiple to its earnings, based on different peers. Then we sum the values of the units to estimate net enterprise value. To estimate equity value, we add nonoperating assets and subtract debt and debt equivalents.

Note that the business unit multiples range from the midteens to less than ten. Without the sum-of-parts approach, it would be impossible to value this company accurately. We also use ranges for the value of each unit, reflecting the imprecision of valuing any business based on the valuation of peers at a single point in time.

USE FORWARD EARNINGS ESTIMATES

When you are building multiples, the denominator should be a forecast of profits, preferably normalized for unusual items, rather than historical profits. Forward-looking multiples are more consistent with the principle that a company's value equals the present value of future cash flows, and should not be based on what

EXHIBIT 18.2 **Sample Sum-of-Parts Valuation**

	NOPAT, 2024, $ million	EV/NOPAT, times		Value, $ million	
		High	Low	High	Low
Business unit 1	410	16.0	14.5	6,568	5,952
Business unit 2	299	13.9	12.5	4,165	3,749
Business unit 3	504	13.1	12.5	6,597	6,306
Business unit 4	587	9.7	9.4	5,681	5,533
Business unit 5	596	9.0	8.0	5,365	4,769
Business unit 6	116	8.0	7.0	931	814
Corporate	(542)	8.0	9.1	(4,339)	(4,917)
Net enterprise value	1,971	12.7	11.3	24,968	22,207

	Post-tax net income, 2023, $ million	Book value, $ million	Earnings multiple, 2023, times	Market value/ book value, times	Value, $ million	
					High	Low
Joint ventures	157	675	12.0	2.5	1,879	1,688
Other investments		1,525			1,525	1,525
Cash and marketable securities		2,879			2,879	2,879
Gross enterprise value					31,251	28,298
Debt		(10,776)			(10,776)	(10,776)
Unfunded retirement liabilities		(2,907)			(2,907)	(2,907)
Noncontrolling interest	(45)	(296)	12.0	2.5	(540)	(738)
Other		(1,940)			(1,940)	(1,940)
Equity value					15,088	11,937
Shares outstanding, millions					500	500
Equity value per share					$30.18	$23.87

happened in the past, nor distorted by nonrecurring items in the past, such as write-offs or the effects of acquisitions or divestitures. Normalized earnings estimates better reflect long-term cash flows by avoiding one-time items. For example, Warren Buffett and other disciples of value-investing guru Benjamin Graham don't use reported earnings. Rather, they rely on a sustainable level of earnings that they refer to as "earnings power."[2]

Forward-looking multiples generally also have lower variation across peer companies. A particularly striking example is the stock market valuation of eight large pharmaceutical companies in 2024. The backward-looking ratio of enterprise value to the previous year's EBITA ranges from about 8 to 23 times (see Exhibit 18.3). When we look ahead to a forecast of earnings four years in the future, the variation across companies is significantly lower, with multiples for all but one of the companies falling in a range of about 9 to 11 times.

The convergence of multiples four years out in the pharmaceuticals industry is extreme. This is most likely due to the market's ability to project near-term earnings well, because drug introductions and patent expirations are well

---

[2] B. C. N. Greenwald, J. Kahn, P. D. Sonkin, and M. van Biema, *Value Investing: From Graham to Buffett and Beyond* (Hoboken, NJ: John Wiley & Sons, 2001).

EXHIBIT 18.3 **Pharmaceuticals: Backward- and Forward-Looking Multiples, 2024**

Enterprise value/EBITA, valuation in 2024[1]

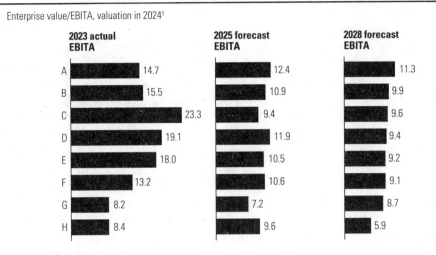

¹ Based on the 8 largest pharmaceutical companies in 2024.

Source: McKinsey Value Intelligence; S&P Global Market Intelligence.

known. By contrast, it is difficult to differentiate long-term success across companies because it depends on an individual company's ability to discover or develop new drugs, which no one has figured out a good way to predict.

Empirical evidence shows that forward-looking multiples are indeed more accurate predictors of value than historical multiples are. One empirical study examined the characteristics and performance of historical multiples versus forward industry multiples for a large sample of companies trading on U.S. exchanges.[3] When multiples for individual companies were compared with their industry multiples, their historical earnings-to-price ratios (E/Ps) had 1.6 times the standard deviation of one-year-forward E/Ps (6.0 percent versus 3.7 percent). Other research, which used multiples to predict the prices of 142 initial public offerings, also found that multiples based on forecast earnings outperformed those based on historical earnings.[4] As the analysis moved from multiples based on historical earnings to multiples based on one- and two-year forecasts, the average pricing error fell from 55.0 percent to 43.7 percent to 28.5 percent, respectively.

To build a forward-looking multiple, choose a forecast year for EBITA that best represents the long-term prospects of the business. In periods of stable growth and profitability, next year's estimate will often suffice. For companies generating extraordinary near-term earnings (either too high or too low) or for companies whose performance is expected to change, use projections further out.

[3] J. Liu, D. Nissim, and J. Thomas, "Equity Valuation Using Multiples," *Journal of Accounting Research* 40 (2002): 135–172.
[4] M. Kim and J. R. Ritter, "Valuing IPOs," *Journal of Financial Economics* 53, no. 3 (1999): 409–437.

USE NET ENTERPRISE VALUE DIVIDED BY ADJUSTED EBITA OR NOPAT

Most financial websites and newspapers quote a price-to-earnings ratio by dividing a company's share price by the prior 12 months' GAAP-reported earnings per share. Yet these days, sophisticated investors and bankers use forward-looking multiples of net enterprise value to EBITA, EBITDA, or NOPAT. They find that these multiples provide a more apples-to-apples comparison of company values.

The reasons for using forward earnings are the same as the ones discussed in the previous section. Using net enterprise value to EBITA, EBITDA, or NOPAT rather than a P/E eliminates the distorting effect of different capital structures, nonoperating assets, and nonoperating income statement items, such as the nonoperating portion of pension expense. Any item that isn't a helpful indicator of a company's future cash-generating ability should be excluded from your calculation of the multiple. For example, one-time gains or losses and nonoperating expenses, such as the amortization of intangibles, have no direct relevance to future cash flows; including them in the multiple would distort comparisons with other companies.

While EBITDA is more commonly used in this multiple than EBITA or NOPAT, we will explain the logic of using each of these measures later in the section.

Why Not Price to Earnings?

This book largely focuses on the drivers of operating performance—ROIC, growth, and free cash flow—because the traditional metrics, such as return on assets (ROA) and return on equity (ROE), mix the effects of operations and capital structure. The same logic holds for multiples. Since the price-to-earnings ratio mixes capital structure and nonoperating items with expectations of operating performance, a comparison of P/Es is a less reliable guide to companies' relative value than a comparison of enterprise value (EV) to EBITA or NOPAT.

To show how capital structure distorts the P/E, Exhibit 18.4 presents financial data for four companies, named A through D. Companies A and B trade at 10 times enterprise value to EBITA, and Companies C and D trade at 25 times enterprise value to EBITA. In each pair, the companies have different P/Es. Companies A and B differ only in how their business is financed, not in their operating performance. The same is true for Companies C and D.

Since Companies A and B trade at typical enterprise value multiples, the P/E drops for the company with higher leverage. This is because the EV-to-EBITA ratio ($1,000 million/$100 million = 10 times) is lower than the ratio of debt value to interest expense ($400 million/$20 million = 20 times). Since the blend of debt at 20 times and pretax equity must equal the enterprise value

EXHIBIT 18.4 **P/E Multiple Distorted by Capital Structure**

$ million

	Company A	Company B	Company C	Company D
Income statement				
EBITA	100	100	100	100
Interest expense	—	(20)	—	(25)
Earnings before taxes	100	80	100	75
Taxes	(40)	(32)	(40)	(30)
Net income	60	48	60	45
Market values				
Debt	—	400	—	500
Equity	1,000	600	2,500	2,000
Enterprise value (EV)	1,000	1,000	2,500	2,500
Multiple, times				
EV/EBITA	10.0	10.0	25.0	25.0
Price/earnings	16.7	12.5	41.7	44.4

at 10 times, the pretax equity multiple must drop below 10 times to offset the greater weight placed on high-multiple debt.[5] The opposite is true when enterprise value to EBITA exceeds the ratio of debt to interest expense (though this is much less common). Company D has a higher P/E than Company C because Company D uses more leverage than Company C. In this case, a high pretax P/E (greater than 25 times) must be blended with the debt multiple (20 times) to generate an EV-to-EBITA multiple of 25 times.

Why Not EV to EBIT?

It's clear that shifting to enterprise-value multiples provides better insights and comparisons across peer companies. The next question is what measure of operating profits to use in the denominator—EBIT, EBITA, EBITDA, or NOPAT? We recommend EBITA, EBITDA, or NOPAT. If you use EBITA or EBITDA, they should be adjusted to exclude nonrecurring items.

The difference between EBIT and EBITA is amortization of intangible assets. Most often, the bulk of amortization is related to acquired intangible assets, such as customer lists or brand names. Chapter 11 explained why we exclude amortization of acquired intangibles from the calculation of ROIC and free cash flow. It is noncash, and unlike depreciation of physical assets, the replacement of these intangible assets is already incorporated in EBITA

[5] Appendix D derives the explicit relationship between a company's actual P/E and its unlevered P/E, that is, the P/E as if the company were entirely financed with equity. For companies with large unlevered P/Es (i.e., companies with significant opportunities for future value creation), P/E systematically increases with leverage. Conversely, companies with small unlevered P/Es would exhibit a drop in P/E as leverage rises.

through line items such as marketing and selling expenses. Using EBITA is preferred, both from a logical perspective and because it leads to more comparable multiples across peers.

To illustrate the distortion caused by amortization of acquired intangible assets, we compare two companies with the same size and underlying operating profitability. The difference is that Company A achieved its current size by acquiring Company B, whereas Company C grew organically. Exhibit 18.5 compares these companies before and after A's acquisition of B.

Concerned that its smaller size might lead to a competitive disadvantage, Company A purchased Company B. Assuming no synergies, the combined financial statements of Companies A and B are identical to Company C's, with two exceptions: acquired intangibles and amortization. Acquired intangibles are recognized when a company is purchased for more than its book value. In this case, Company A purchased Company B for $1,000 million, which is $750 million greater than its book value. If these acquired intangibles are separable and identifiable, as is the case with patents, Company A + B must amortize them over the estimated life of the asset. Assuming an asset life of ten years, Company A + B will record $75 million in amortization each year.

The bottom of Exhibit 18.5 shows enterprise value multiples using EBITA and EBIT, both before and after the acquisition. Since all three companies generated the same level of operating performance, they traded at identical multiples before the acquisition, 10 times EBIT (and EBITA). After the acquisition, the combined Company A + B should continue to trade at a multiple of

EXHIBIT 18.5 **Enterprise-Value-to-EBIT Multiple Distorted by Acquisition Accounting**

$ million

	Before acquisition			After A acquires B	
	Company A	**Company B**	**Company C**	**Company A + B**	**Company C**
EBIT					
Revenues	375	125	500	500	500
Cost of sales	(150)	(50)	(200)	(200)	(200)
Depreciation	(75)	(25)	(100)	(100)	(100)
EBITA	150	50	200	200	200
Amortization	—	—	—	(75)	—
EBIT	150	50	200	125	200
Invested capital					
Organic capital	750	250	1,000	1,000	1,000
Acquired intangibles	—	—	—	750	—
Invested capital	750	250	1,000	1,750	1,000
Enterprise value	1,500	500	2,000	2,000	2,000
Multiple, times					
EV/EBITA	10.0	10.0	10.0	10.0	10.0
EV/EBIT	10.0	10.0	10.0	16.0	10.0

10 times EBITA, because its performance is identical to that of Company C. However, amortization expense causes EBIT to drop for the combined company, so its EV-to-EBIT multiple increases to 16 times. This rise in the multiple does not reflect a premium, however (remember, no synergies were created). It is merely an accounting artifact. In situations like this, using EV-to-EBITA multiples can help you avoid forming a distorted picture of the companies' relative values.

In limited cases, companies will capitalize organic investments in intangible assets. For example, telecommunication service providers capitalize the purchase costs for spectrum licenses and then amortize them over their useful life. In a similar way, development costs for software that is to be sold or licensed to third parties can be capitalized and amortized under IFRS and U.S. GAAP if certain conditions are met. In such cases, the amortization charges are operating costs and should be separated from acquisition amortization. Just like depreciation charges, operating amortization should be included in adjusted EBITA.

Choosing between EBITA and EBITDA

A common alternative to the EBITA multiple is the EBITDA multiple. Many practitioners use EBITDA multiples because depreciation is, strictly speaking, a noncash expense, reflecting sunk costs, not future investment. This logic, however, does not apply uniformly. For many industries, depreciation of existing assets is the accounting equivalent of setting aside the future capital expenditure that will be required to replace the assets. Subtracting depreciation from the earnings of such companies therefore better represents future cash flow and consequently the company's valuation.

To see this, consider two companies that differ in only one aspect: in-house versus outsourced production. Company A manufactures its products using its own equipment, whereas Company B outsources manufacturing to a supplier. Exhibit 18.6 provides financial data for each company. Since Company A owns its equipment, it recognizes significant annual depreciation—in this case, $200 million. Company B has less equipment, so its depreciation is only $50 million. However, Company B's supplier will include its own depreciation costs in the price it charges Company B, and Company B will consequently pay more for its raw materials. Because of this difference, Company B generates EBITDA of only $350 million, versus $500 million for Company A. This difference in EBITDA will lead to differing multiples: 6.0 times for Company A versus 8.6 times for Company B. Does this mean Company B trades at a valuation premium? No, when Company A's depreciation is deducted from its earnings, both companies trade at 10.0 times EBITA.

When computing the EV-to-EBITDA multiple in the previous example, we failed to recognize that Company A (the company that owns its equipment) will have to expend cash to replace aging equipment: $200 million for

EXHIBIT 18.6 **Enterprise-Value-to-EBITDA Multiple Distorted by Capital Investment**

$ million

	Company A	Company B		Company A	Company B
Income statement			**Free cash flow**		
Revenues	1,000	1,000	NOPAT	210	210
Raw materials	(100)	(250)	Depreciation	200	50
Operating costs	(400)	(400)	Gross cash flow	410	260
EBITDA	500	350			
			Investment in working capital	(60)	(60)
Depreciation	(200)	(50)	Capital expenditures	(200)	(50)
EBITA	300	300	Free cash flow	150	150
Operating taxes	(90)	(90)	Enterprise value	3,000	3,000
NOPAT	210	210			
Multiples, times					
EV/EBITA	10.0	10.0			
EV/EBITDA	6.0	8.6			

Company A versus $50 million for Company B (see the right side of Exhibit 18.6). Since capital expenditures are recorded in free cash flow and not NOPAT, the EBITDA multiple is distorted.

In some situations, EBITDA scales a company's valuation better than EBITA. These occur when current depreciation is not an accurate predictor of future capital expenditures. For instance, consider two companies, each of which owns a machine that produces identical products. Both machines have the same cash-based operating costs, and each company's products sell for the same price. If one company paid more for its equipment (for whatever reason—perhaps poor negotiation), it will have higher depreciation and, thus, lower EBITA. Valuation, however, is based on future discounted cash flow, not past profits. And since both companies have identical cash flow, they should have identical values.[6] We would therefore expect the two companies to have identical multiples. Yet, because EBITA differs across the two companies, their multiples will differ as well.

NOPAT Versus EBITA

Analysts and investors often use enterprise value to EBITA instead of NOPAT because there is no need to figure out the operating taxes on EBITA. (Reported taxes are not usually a good predictor of operating taxes, because they include nonoperating items. Therefore, most analysts ignore taxes altogether.) We often use EBITA because it's common practice and works well when all

---

[6] Since depreciation is tax deductible, a company with higher depreciation will have a smaller tax burden. Lower taxes lead to higher cash flows and a higher valuation. Therefore, even companies with identical EBITDAs will have different EBITDA multiples. The distortion, however, is less pronounced.

EXHIBIT 18.7 **Difference between Pre- and Post-tax Earnings Multiples for U.S. Stock Market**

Multiples for 2024, based on 2026 forecast of earnings

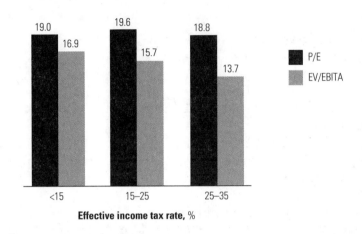

Effective income tax rate, %

Source: McKinsey Value Intelligence.

the companies in the peer group have the same operating tax rate, as when they all operate within a single tax jurisdiction. However, when tax rates are different, NOPAT is a better measure to use.

The difference between a company's post- and pretax earnings valuation multiple simply follows from the company's tax rate. If the stock market correctly reflects taxation in company valuations, we would expect that for companies with higher tax rates, the difference between their pre- and post-tax earnings multiples also would be bigger. This is indeed the pattern we found when examining the market valuations of the largest U.S. companies in 2024. Exhibit 18.7 shows the average difference in pretax earnings multiples (EV/EBITA) and post-tax earnings multiples (P/Es) for companies categorized according to their income tax rates. As predicted, the difference between the multiples steadily increases with the tax rate a company pays. Differences in tax rates clearly matter for market valuation. Thus, when companies face different tax rates, they should not be valued at the same EBITA multiple (or any other pretax earnings multiple).

This is an important consideration for international comparisons, because corporate tax rates vary widely from country to country. For example, as of 2023, the Irish corporate tax rate was one of the lowest, at 12.5 percent; the U.S. tax rate was significantly higher, at 26 percent; and the Brazilian tax rate was one of the highest, at 34 percent.[7] Because of such variations, companies in the same industry with a different geographic mix of operations can have different

---

[7] Tax Foundation, taxfoundation.org. Note that these include estimated state and local income taxes. For example, the U.S. federal rate was 21 percent; state income taxes add another 5 percent on average.

tax rates, which must be factored into their valuation using multiples. If the tax rates differ across peers, use net enterprise value to NOPAT rather than net enterprise value to EBITA.

ADJUST FOR NONOPERATING ITEMS

In a presentation to a group of professional investors, we provided the audience with financial data on two companies. We then asked the audience which company traded at a higher EV multiple. The results were surprising. Upon polling the group, we discovered that there was no common agreement on how to compute the EV multiple. A group of 100 professionals generated nearly a dozen different comparisons. Further investigation revealed that the primary cause of this divergence was inconsistency in defining enterprise value.

Only one approach to building an EV-to-EBITA multiple is theoretically consistent. Enterprise value should include *only* the portion of value attributable to assets and liabilities that generate (adjusted) EBITA. Strictly speaking, it should be referred to as "net" enterprise value, meaning net of nonoperating assets. Including other assets, such as the value of joint ventures, in the numerator without including its corresponding income or loss in the denominator will systematically distort the multiple upward. Conversely, failing to recognize a component of enterprise value will understate the numerator and bias the multiple downward. This occurs, for example, when the value of noncontrolling interest is not added to the value of common equity.

Cisco Systems offers an example of a biased multiple. At the end of June 2023, Cisco had $26 billion in cash and marketable securities. With a market value of equity of $207 billion and $8 billion of total debt, its gross enterprise value was $215 billion. Subtracting cash gives a net enterprise value of $189 billion. With EBITA of $16 billion, its gross enterprise value to EBITA would be 13.4 times, while its net enterprise value to EBITA would be 11.8 times, or 12 percent lower.

A way to think about the difference is to think of Cisco as a portfolio with two components: one is an operating business that sells products and technologies for networking, security, and other areas, and the other is a pile of cash. The operating business is valued at 11.8 times EBITA, while if the cash earned 1.0 percent before taxes, it would be valued at 100 times the earnings on the cash (the inverse of the earnings yield). The company as a whole is valued at the weighted average of the two multiples, 13.4 times. Since the 13.4 times is a weighted average of two very different numbers, it doesn't provide any insight into how to think about Cisco's value.

To see how the math provides additional clarity, Exhibit 18.8 presents three companies—A, B, and C—with identical EV-to-EBITA multiples. Company A

EXHIBIT 18.8 **Enterprise Value Multiples and Complex Ownership**

$ million

	Company A	Company B	Company C
Partial income statement			
EBITDA	100	100	100
Interest income	—	4	—
Interest expense	(18)	(18)	(18)
Earnings before taxes	82	86	82
Gross enterprise value			
Value of core operations	900	900	900
Excess cash	—	100	—
Nonconsolidated subsidiaries	—	200	—
Gross enterprise value	900	1,200	900
Debt	300	300	300
Noncontrolling interest	—	—	100
Market value of equity	600	900	500
Gross enterprise value	900	1,200	900
Multiples, times			
Net EV/EBITA	9.0	9.0	9.0
Debt plus equity minus cash/EBITA	9.0	11.0	9.0
Debt plus equity/EBITA	9.0	12.0	8.0

owns only core operating assets and is financed by traditional debt and equity. Its combined market value of debt and equity equals $900 million. Dividing $900 million by $100 million in EBITA leads to an EV multiple of 9.0 times.

Company B operates a business similar to Company A but also owns $100 million in excess cash and a minority stake in a nonconsolidated subsidiary, valued at $200 million. Since excess cash and nonconsolidated subsidiaries do not contribute to EBITA, do not include them in the numerator of an EV-to-EBITA multiple. To compute a net enterprise value consistent with EBITA, sum the market value of debt and equity ($1,200 million), and subtract the market value of nonoperating assets ($300 million).[8] Divide the resulting net enterprise value ($900 million) by EBITA ($100 million). The result is an EV-to-EBITA multiple of 9.0, which matches that of Company A. Failing to subtract the market value of nonoperating assets will lead to a multiple that is too high. For instance, if you divide debt plus equity by EBITA for Company B, the resulting multiple is 12 times, three points higher than the correct value.

Similar adjustments are necessary for financial claims other than debt and equity. To calculate enterprise value consistently with EBITA, you must include the market value of all financial claims, not just debt and equity.

---

[8] Alternatively, we could adjust the denominator rather than the numerator by adding interest income to EBITA. This definition of EV to EBITA is consistent but is biased upward. This is because the multiple for excess cash typically exceeds that of core operations. The greater the proportion of cash to overall value, the higher the resulting multiple.

For Company C, outside investors hold a noncontrolling interest in a consolidated subsidiary. Since the noncontrolling stake's value is supported by EBITA, you must include it in the enterprise value calculation. Otherwise, the EV-to-EBITA multiple will be biased downward. For instance, when only debt plus equity is divided by EBITA for Company C, the resulting multiple is only 8.0 times.

As a general rule, any nonoperating asset that does not contribute to EBITA should be removed from enterprise value. This includes not only the market value of excess cash and nonconsolidated subsidiaries, as just mentioned, but also excess real estate, other investments, and the market value of prepaid pension assets. Financial claims include debt and equity, but also noncontrolling stakes, the value of unfunded pension liabilities, and the value of employee grants outstanding. A detailed discussion of nonoperating assets and financial claims is presented in Chapter 16.

A trickier adjustment is needed for pensions and other retirement benefits, as explained in Chapter 23. Treat the unfunded liabilities as debt or the excess assets as a nonoperating asset. In addition, exclude the nonoperating parts of pension expense from EBITA.

USE THE RIGHT PEER GROUP

Selecting the right peer group is critical to coming up with a reasonable valuation using multiples. Common practice is to select a group of 8–15 peers and take the average of the multiples of the peers. Getting a reasonable valuation, though, requires judgment about which companies and their multiples are truly relevant for the valuation.

A common approach to identifying peers is to use the Standard Industrial Classification (SIC) codes or the newer Global Industry Classification Standard (GICS) system developed by Standard & Poor's and Morgan Stanley.[9] These may be a good starting point, but they are usually too broad for a good valuation analysis. For example, United Parcel Service (UPS) is included in the air freight and logistics GICS code, which includes dozens of companies, most of which do not compete with UPS in its core business of delivering small parcels. Another approach is to use peers provided by the company being valued. However, companies often provide aspirational peers rather than companies that truly compete head-to-head. It is better to have a smaller number of peers of companies that truly compete in the same markets with similar products and services.

---

[9] Beginning in 1997, SIC codes were replaced by a major revision called the North American Industry Classification System (NAICS). The NAICS six-digit code not only provides for newer industries but also reorganizes the categories on a production/process-oriented basis. The Securities and Exchange Commission (SEC), however, still lists companies by SIC code.

Even if you find companies that compete head-to-head, differences in performance may justify differences in multiples. Remember the value driver formula expressed as a multiple:

$$\frac{\text{Value}}{\text{EBITA}} = \frac{(1-T)\left(1 - \frac{g}{\text{ROIC}}\right)}{\text{WACC} - g}$$

or

$$\frac{\text{Value}}{\text{NOPAT}} = \frac{\left(1 - \frac{g}{\text{ROIC}}\right)}{\text{WACC} - g}$$

As both versions of the formula indicate, a company's EBITA or NOPAT valuation multiple is driven by growth (g), ROIC, and the weighted average cost of capital (WACC). While most peers will have similar costs of capital, the other variables may be different, leading to differences in expected multiples.

A common flaw is to compare a company's multiple with an average multiple of other companies in the same industry, regardless of differences in their performance. Better to use a smaller subsample of peers with similar performance. Exhibit 18.9 shows the multiples of nine disguised companies in the same industry. Assume you are seeking to value one of these companies using multiples based on a peer group. The EV-to-NOPAT multiples for the group of nine range from approximately 10 times to almost 17 times. The company being evaluated, Swallow, had a multiple of 12 times, at the lower end of the range. Does this mean the company is undervalued? Probably not. When you examine the performance of the other companies, you can see that

EXHIBIT 18.9 **Peer Groups by ROIC and Growth**

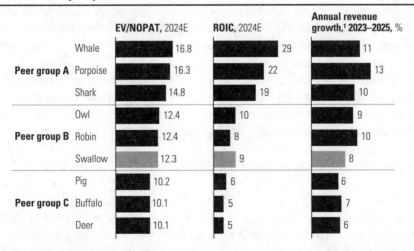

		EV/NOPAT, 2024E	ROIC, 2024E	Annual revenue growth,[1] 2023–2025, %
Peer group A	Whale	16.8	29	11
	Porpoise	16.3	22	13
	Shark	14.8	19	10
Peer group B	Owl	12.4	10	9
	Robin	12.4	8	10
	Swallow	12.3	9	8
Peer group C	Pig	10.2	6	6
	Buffalo	10.1	5	7
	Deer	10.1	5	6

[1] Compound annual growth rate.

they neatly divide into three groups: a top group with multiples of about 15 to 17 times, a middle group with multiples of about 12 times, and a low group with multiples of about 10 times. Note that the ROIC and growth rates line up with the ranges of multiples. Swallow, with a multiple of 12 times, is valued right in line with the other two companies (Owl and Robin) that have similar ROIC and growth. If you didn't know Swallow's multiple, your best estimate would be the average of Owl and Robin, 12 times, not the average of the entire sample or some other sample.

Once you have collected a list of peers and measured their multiples properly, the digging begins. You must answer a series of questions: Why are the multiples different across the peer group? Do certain companies in the group have superior products, better access to customers, recurring revenues, or economies of scale? If these strategic advantages translate to superior ROIC and growth rates, better-positioned companies should trade at higher multiples.

ALTERNATIVE MULTIPLES

Although we have so far focused on enterprise value multiples based on EBITA, EBITDA, or NOPAT, other multiples can prove helpful in certain situations. The EV-to-revenues multiple can be useful in bounding valuations with negative or volatile EBITA. The P/E-to-growth (PEG) ratio, while sometimes used, has serious deficiencies. Nonfinancial multiples can be useful for young companies where current financial information is not relevant. This section discusses each of these alternative multiples.

Enterprise Value to Revenues

In most cases, value-to-revenues multiples are not particularly useful for explaining company valuations, except in industries with unstable or negative profits. We'll use a simple example to illustrate. Companies A and B have the same expected growth, ROIC, and cost of capital; the only difference is that A's EBITA margin is 10 percent, while B's is 20 percent. (B is more capital intensive, so its higher margin is offset by its greater invested capital.) Because the companies have the same ROIC and growth, their value-to-EBITA ratios must be the same (13 times, based on the value driver formula). But the resulting value-to-revenues multiple is 1.3 for A and 2.6 for B. In this case, the value-to-revenues multiple tells us nothing about the valuations of the companies.

EV-to-revenues multiples are useful as a last resort in several situations. One is in the case of start-up industries, where profits are negative or a sustainable margin level can't be estimated. Another is in industries with highly volatile profit margins, where you believe that over the long term the companies will have roughly similar profit margins. You might also come across situations in which a company is periodically spending more on research and development (R&D) or marketing than its peers, so its earnings are temporarily depressed. If investors are confident that the company's profit margins will return to a level similar to that of its peers, an EV-to-revenues multiple in line with peers might prove more relevant than an EV-to-EBITA multiple that is out of line with peers. Finally, a revenue multiple can provide a quick understanding of the potential value a company could generate if it were able to achieve the same levels of growth, operating margins, and capital efficiency as its peer group.

PEG Ratio

Some analysts and investors use a P/E-to-growth (PEG) ratio to assess the value of a company. For example, a company with a P/E of 15 and expected growth of 4 percent would have a PEG ratio of 3.75:

$$\text{PEG ratio} = \frac{\text{P/E}}{\text{Growth} \times 100} = \frac{15}{4\% \times 100} = 3.75$$

The PEG ratio is seriously deficient, however, because it doesn't take into consideration ROIC, which, as seen earlier, has a significant impact on a company's valuation. While the concept of relating P/E to growth is relevant, there is no mathematical derivation that says you can simply divide one by the other and produce a significant result.

Furthermore, there is no standardized approach for PEG ratios, particularly the choice of time horizon for growth. Should it be one year, five years, or a decade? The choice of horizon can make a big difference, as growth tends to flatten out over time. A company with 6 percent expected growth over five years may have only 4 percent expected growth over ten years. Shifting the growth horizon, in this case, would increase a company's PEG ratio by 50 percent. Finally, as you increase the time frame, growth rates in an industry will converge, so you will end up with differences in the PEG ratios just reflecting differences in P/Es.

The bigger problem, though, is ignoring ROIC. Exhibit 18.10 shows a DCF valuation we conducted for two companies. Company A has a higher ROIC (30 percent, versus 14 percent for B), while Company B has higher expected growth over the first ten years (10 percent, versus 5 percent for A). The DCF valuations of both companies at a 9 percent cost of capital and no debt lead to the same earnings multiple: 17 times. But Company A's PEG ratio is 3.4, while Company B's is 1.7. The common interpretation is that Company A is overvalued relative to Company B because its PEG ratio is higher. Yet it's clear that both companies are valued the same when both growth and ROIC are taken into account.

EXHIBIT 18.10 **PEG Ratios Distorted by ROIC Differences**

	Company A	Company B
ROIC, %	30	14
Expected growth in years 1–10,%	5	10
Expected growth after year 10, %	3	3
WACC, %	9	9
P/E = EV/NOPAT, times	17.0	17.0
PEG ratio, times	3.4	1.7

Multiples of Invested Capital

In some industries, multiples based on invested capital can provide better insights than earnings multiples. One example comes from the banking industry. In the years after the 2008 credit crisis, there was tremendous uncertainty about what levels of return on equity banks would be able to earn.[10] Furthermore, earnings forecasts one to three years out were not reliable and were often negative. Many investors resorted to using multiples of book equity. Banks with higher expected long-term returns on equity, based on their mix of businesses and the underlying economics of those businesses, tended to have higher multiples than banks in lower-return businesses. For example, banks whose portfolios emphasized wealth management and transaction processing, which are stable and earn high returns, were valued at higher multiples to equity than banks focused on more volatile and lower-return investment banking and retail banking.

Regulated industries provide another application of invested-capital multiples. Under some regulatory regimes, profits are capped by the allowed return on a company's so-called regulatory asset base (RAB). The RAB is separately reported and represents the invested capital as calculated following certain rules that the regulator sets for qualified capital expenditures. If regulators were to not allow any excess returns above the cost of capital, the enterprise-value-to-RAB multiple of a regulated company should be (close to) 1. In practice, the multiples end up at higher levels because regulators often provide various efficiency incentives allowing companies to generate excess returns. In addition, most companies have growth opportunities; they can expand their RAB by new, approved investment projects. For companies under similar regulatory regimes, many investors and analysts use RAB multiples for comparison and valuation.

Multiples Based on Operating Metrics

Sometimes company valuations are based on multiples of operating metrics. For example, values of oil and gas companies can be expressed as value per barrel of oil reserves. Clearly, the amount of oil reserves in the ground the company has access to will drive the company's value. While the value of

---

[10] As explained in Chapter 43, we use return on equity, rather than return on capital, for banks.

each barrel of oil extracted and sold is roughly the same, the costs to extract those barrels will vary widely and affect profit per barrel, depending on the geology of those reserves and the techniques needed to extract them. Therefore, when you estimate the value of an oil and gas company based on a valuation multiple of the amount of reserves it holds, you must adjust for any differences in the costs of extraction and distribution relative to the companies for which the multiple was estimated.

In other cases, investors and analysts resort to operating multiples when valuing young, fast-growing companies, because of the great uncertainty surrounding potential market size, profitability, and required investments. Financial multiples that normally provide a benchmark for valuation are often useless, as profitability (measured in any form) is often negative. A way to overcome this shortcoming is to apply nonfinancial multiples, comparing enterprise value with operating statistics such as number of users or subscribers. However, this approach works only when companies have virtually identical business models and are at similar stages of maturity.

For example, the market value of audio-streaming companies Spotify and Sirius XM can be expressed per user or subscriber. As of June 2024, Spotify was trading about $86 per user, while Sirius XM traded at $218 per subscriber.[11] The question is whether such multiples offer real insights.

Although the two companies are both in audio streaming, the large difference in their value-per-user multiples reflects very different business models and economics. Spotify streams audio through the internet and has 626 million users worldwide, but its revenue per user per year is only $24. Sirius XM's primary revenue generator is its satellite radio business (though, in 2019, it bought Pandora, which has a business model similar to Spotify's), and it has about 86 million users. For multiple reasons, including the quality of programming it provides, the lack of ads, the variety of different channels, and customers' tendency to listen to satellite radio in their cars, Sirius XM has an impressive level of customer stickiness, allowing the company to earn about $100 per user per year (an average that includes the lower rate for Pandora). When we also consider the differences in the two companies' size, growth, and return on capital, it is hardly surprising that they trade at very different multiples of users.

While using operating multiples can be useful with younger companies and newer industries, research has shown that this becomes less true as an industry matures. When this happens, financial metrics such as gross profit and R&D spending become increasingly predictive, while nonfinancial data tend to lose power.[12]

---

[11] Based on company filings and investor presentations for the second quarter of 2024.

[12] P. Jorion and E. Talmor, "Value Relevance of Financial and Non Financial Information in Emerging Industries: The Changing Role of Web Traffic Data," working paper no. 021, London Business School Accounting Subject Area, March 13, 2001.

SUMMARY

Of the available valuation tools, discounted cash flow continues to deliver the best results. However, a thoughtful comparison of selected multiples for the company you are valuing from a carefully selected group of peers merits a place in your tool kit as well. When that comparative analysis is careful and well reasoned, it not only serves as a useful check of your DCF forecasts but also provides critical insights into what drives value in a given industry. The distinction between operating and nonoperating results, capital, and cash flows should follow the exact same logic as applied in DCF valuation. The most insightful multiples are those that compare operating value to operating results. Operating metrics such as mineral reserve size or number of subscribers can be used when these are clearly related to value creation. In all cases, be sure that you analyze the underlying reasons that multiples differ from company to company, and never view multiples as a shortcut to valuation. Instead, approach your multiples analysis with as much care as you bring to your DCF analysis.

19

Valuation by Parts

Up to this point, our analysis has focused on single-business companies. But many large companies have multiple business units, each competing in segments with different economic characteristics. For instance, Anglo Dutch Unilever competes in food and refreshments, personal products, and home-care products. Amazon is one of the world's largest retailers but also offers cloud computing services and digital streaming. Even so-called pure-play companies, such as Vodafone (mobile telecommunication services) and Heineken (brewing and beverage), often have a wide variety of underlying geographical and category segments. This is not just the case for large companies: consider the local bicycle shop that also has an online sales channel.

If the economics of a company's segments are different, you will gain deeper insights by valuing each segment on its own and adding them up to estimate the value of the entire company. Trying to value the entire company as a single enterprise will not provide much understanding, and your final valuation may be significantly off the mark. Consider a simple case where a faster-growing segment has lower returns on capital than a slower-growing segment. If both segments maintain their return on invested capital (ROIC), the corporate ROIC would decline as the weights of the different segments change, while the corporate growth rate would steadily increase.

Valuing by parts generates more precise valuation estimates and deeper insights into where and how the company is generating value. That is why it is standard practice in industry-leading companies and among sophisticated investors. This chapter explains four critical steps for valuing a company by its parts:

1. Understanding the mechanics of valuing by parts and why it is useful to do so

2. Building financial statements by business unit—based on incomplete information, if necessary

3. Estimating the weighted average cost of capital (WACC) by business unit

4. Testing the value based on multiples of peers

THE MECHANICS OF VALUING BY PARTS

The most effective way to explore the mechanics of valuing by parts and the insights to be gained is by working through an example. Exhibit 19.1 details the key financials, value drivers, valuation results, and multiples for each part of ConsumerCo, a hypothetical business. It consists of four business units, a financial subsidiary, and a nonconsolidated joint venture. To simplify, we kept all future returns and growth rates constant at 2025 levels for each business unit.

All of ConsumerCo's businesses sell products for personal care, but their economics differ widely. The key financials and value drivers in Exhibit 19.1 make this clear. The company's primary business unit, branded consumer products, sells well-known brands in personal care (mainly skin creams, shaving creams, and toothpaste). It generates $2.0 billion in revenues at returns well above its 8.6 percent cost of capital but mainly in slow-growth, mature markets. Private label, the next-largest business, at $1.5 billion in revenues, produces for large discount chains selling products under their own names. This unit is growing faster than the branded-products business but at far lower returns on capital that barely meet its cost of capital.

The devices business, with $1.25 billion in revenues, sells electronic devices for personal care, such as sun beds, shavers, and toothbrushes, at a very healthy 18.1 percent return on capital, paired with high growth rates. The newly developed organic-products business has $750 million in revenues in premium products made with natural materials. It generates both the highest returns and the highest growth. The $83 million in annual costs for running the corporate center are shown as a separate business unit. Finally, internal revenues, earnings before interest, taxes, and amortization (EBITA), and invested capital are eliminated in the consolidation of ConsumerCo's financials, as the branded-products business buys components from the private-label business unit.

The discounted-cash-flow (DCF) valuation results and multiples in Exhibit 19.1 reflect these differences in size, growth, and ROIC across the businesses. Not surprisingly, the branded-products business's high returns and large scale mean that it has the largest valuation ($5,188 million), and the implied multiple of enterprise value (EV) to net operating profit after taxes (NOPAT) is 16.0 times. The private-label business generates almost a third of the company's revenues but contributes only around 10 percent of value ($1,128 million) because of its low returns on capital. Despite its higher growth

EXHIBIT 19.1 **ConsumerCo: Valuation Summary, January 2025**

| | Key financials
$ million | | | Value drivers
% | | | | | | | | | | | | WACC | Valuation
$ million | Multiples | |
| | Revenue | EBITA | Invested capital | Revenue growth | | | | Operating margin | | | | ROIC | | | | | DCF value | EV/
NOPAT | EV/
NOPAT |
	2025	2025	2025	2023	2024	2025	2025–30	2023	2024	2025	2030	2023	2024	2025	2030				Peers
Branded products	2,000	500	1,600	1.5	2.5	3.0	3.0	23.0	24.3	25.0	25.0	19.7	19.9	20.3	20.3	8.6	5,188	16.0	15.6
Private label	1,500	143	900	4.6	4.7	5.0	5.0	7.7	8.5	9.5	9.5	8.5	9.3	10.3	10.3	9.1	1,128	12.2	11.7
Devices	1,250	156	563	7.1	7.3	7.5	7.5	11.2	12.0	12.5	12.5	15.8	17.1	18.1	18.1	10.1	1,474	14.5	14.0
Organic products	750	206	488	9.3	9.5	10.0	10.0	27.6	27.3	27.5	27.5	27.6	27.5	27.5	27.5	8.6	3,440	25.7	24.5
Corporate center[1]	–	(83)	806	4.4	5.0	5.4	5.6									9.1	(1,123)	20.9	–
Eliminations	(500)	(2)	(50)														–	–
Total operations	5,000	920	4,306	4.5	5.1	5.5	5.7	17.7	18.4	18.4	18.3	12.6	13.2	13.9	14.7		10,107	16.9	
Customer finance[2]																10.5	150	12.1	12.0
Cosmetics joint ventures[3]																9.1	609	17.6	17.0
Excess cash																	250		
Gross enterprise value																	11,117		
Debt[4]																	(1,941)		
Equity value																	9,175		

1 For corporate center, growth of headquarters costs is used in place of revenue growth rate.
2 For customer finance, WACC is cost of equity, DCF value is equity value net of debt, and EV/NOPAT is P/E.
3 For cosmetics joint venture, DCF value is equity value of minority stake.
4 Debt excludes $1,038 million debt in customer finance.

rate, its EV/NOPAT multiple of 12.2 is lower than that of the branded-products unit. The devices business, with returns well above cost of capital and growth rates exceeding those of private-label products, is valued at $1,474 million and has a multiple of 14.5 times NOPAT. The organic-products business combines high returns with high growth, achieving a value of $3,440 million, second highest after branded products, but at a much higher implied multiple of 25.7 times NOPAT. With headquarters DCF at a negative $1,123 million and no impact on value from eliminations (see later in this chapter), the value of operations for ConsumerCo totals $10,107 million, corresponding to a weighted average multiple of 16.9 times NOPAT.

ConsumerCo's customer finance subsidiary provides loans for about a quarter of device revenues. It is valued at $150 million (net of $1,038 million of debt), using cash flow to equity discounted at its cost of equity of 10.5 percent (see the next section). The cosmetics joint venture is valued using an enterprise DCF valuation, but only ConsumerCo's 45 percent stake of the equity, valued at $609 million, is included in ConsumerCo's value.

The combined total of ConsumerCo's businesses, including the finance subsidiary, the cosmetics joint venture, and $250 million of excess cash, is $11,117 million. Subtracting $1,941 million of debt (excluding the portion allocated to the finance subsidiary from the company's total debt of $2,980 million) leads to an equity value of $9,175 million.

ConsumerCo's results illustrate why valuation by parts provides better answers. For example, even while all business units are at constant (but different) growth rates and returns on capital, ConsumerCo's overall growth and return continue to change between 2025 and 2030 as the weight of organic products in the portfolio steadily increases. When the economics of business segments differ greatly, a purely top-down approach becomes inadequate for understanding historical patterns or for projecting the future trajectory of a company's returns and growth. If you were to conduct a top-down DCF valuation of ConsumerCo as a single business at a constant 2025 ROIC of 13.9 percent and an ongoing growth rate of 5.5 percent, the resulting value would be 10 percent too low. Also note how large the differences in multiples are across the businesses (from 12.2 to 25.7 times NOPAT) and how the aggregate multiple for the operating enterprise value matches none of the underlying businesses.

The equity value buildup in Exhibit 19.2 illustrates that branded and organic products generate the bulk of the company's value. They also stand out for their market value added—the difference between DCF value and book value of invested capital. For each dollar of invested capital, value creation is the highest in these two business units.

A valuation-by-parts approach offers insights into the sources and drivers of a company's value creation that a purely top-down view cannot reveal. Exhibit 19.3 shows how additional growth or ROIC affects the value of each of the business units. Given the high returns on capital for the organic-products unit, growth through additional investments in that business would create

EXHIBIT 19.2 **ConsumerCo: Equity Value Buildup, January 2025**

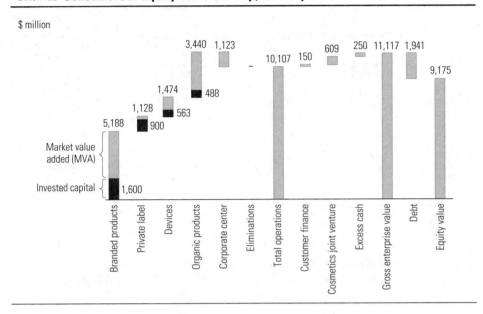

EXHIBIT 19.3 **ConsumerCo: How Changes in ROIC and Growth Affect Value**

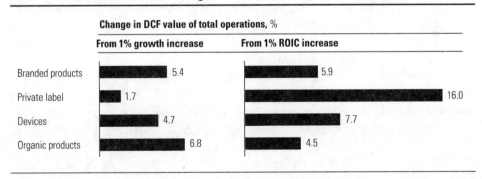

more value for the company than investments in other units. In contrast, the private-label unit creates the least amount of value, due to its low returns on capital, so improving returns is the best way to generate more value from this segment. To maximize value creation, ConsumerCo's management should differentiate priorities for growth and return across its segments, rather than set company-wide targets.

Many companies, ConsumerCo among them, struggle with such differentiation. As the investment map in Exhibit 19.4 shows, ConsumerCo's capital expenditures over the five years from 2020 to 2025 have been more in line with the size of each business than with their returns or growth. Investments

EXHIBIT 19.4 **ConsumerCo: Historical Investments, 2020–2025**

	Cumulative net investments,[1] $ million	Cumulative revenues, $ million	Average ROIC, %	Revenue growth, CAGR, %
Organic products	205	3,620	27.4	9.6
Devices	214	6,343	16.3	7.1
Private label	240	8,070	5.4	4.2
Branded products	334	11,373	20.1	1.8

[1] Capital expenditures plus investments in net working capital minus depreciation.

were largest in the private-label and branded-products businesses, and lowest in organic products. In the typical annual budgeting process, many companies routinely allocate their capital, research and development (R&D), and marketing budgets to the same activities year after year, regardless of their relative contribution to value creation. The cost of such oversight is high, since companies that more actively reallocate resources generate, on average, 30 percent higher total shareholder returns (TSR).[1] Valuation by parts can highlight whether a company's capital budgets (as well as its budgets for product development, sales and marketing, and business development) are aligned with its value creation opportunities.

However, many situations are more complex than the ConsumerCo example, and arriving at the necessary insights sometimes requires an even deeper understanding of how the company's different parts contribute to its value. When we analyzed four divisions within a consumer-durable-goods company, we found that all were generating fairly similar returns, between 12 and 18 percent, well above the company's 9 percent cost of capital (see Exhibit 19.5). But at the next level, business units, returns were much more widely distributed. Even in the company's highest-performing division, a business unit was earning returns below its cost of capital. At the level of individual segments within business units, the return distribution was even larger. Differentiating where to invest in growth and where to improve margins at such granular levels can trigger significant improvements in value creation for the company as a whole.[2]

---

[1] S. Hall, D. Lovallo, and R. Musters, "How to Put Your Money Where Your Strategy Is," *McKinsey Quarterly* (March 2012).
[2] M. Goedhart, S. Smit, and A. Veldhuijzen, "Unearthing the Source of Value Hiding in Your Corporate Portfolio," *McKinsey on Finance* (Fall 2013).

EXHIBIT 19.5 **Breakdown of Return on Invested Capital at Each Level of Analysis**

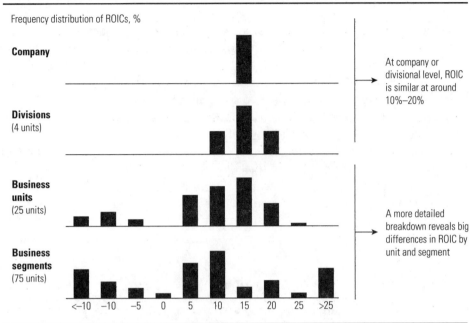

Frequency distribution of ROICs, %

Company

Divisions
(4 units)

At company or divisional level, ROIC is similar at around 10%–20%

Business units
(25 units)

A more detailed breakdown reveals big differences in ROIC by unit and segment

Business segments
(75 units)

<-10   -10   -5   0   5   10   15   20   25   >25

BUILDING BUSINESS UNIT FINANCIAL STATEMENTS

To value a company's individual business units, you need income statements, balance sheets, and cash flow statements. Ideally, these financial statements should approximate what the business units would look like if they were stand-alone companies. Creating financial statements for business units requires consideration of several issues:

- Allocating corporate overhead costs
- Dealing with intercompany transactions
- Understanding financial subsidiaries
- Navigating incomplete public information

We will illustrate each of these issues by extending the ConsumerCo example.

Allocating Corporate Overhead Costs

Most multibusiness companies have shared services and corporate overhead, so you need to decide which costs should be allocated to the businesses and which retained at the corporate level. For services that the corporate center provides, such as payroll, human resources, and accounting, allocate the costs by cost drivers. For example, the aggregate cost of human resources services provided by the corporate parent could be allocated by the number of employees in each business unit.

When costs are incurred only because the units are part of a larger company (for example, the CEO's compensation or the corporate art collection), do not allocate the costs. They should be retained as a corporate cost center and valued separately for two reasons. First, allocating corporate costs to business units reduces your ability to compare them with pure-play business unit peers that don't incur such costs (most business units already have their own chief executives, CFOs, and controllers who are comparable to pure-play competitors). Second, keeping the corporate center as a separate unit reveals how much of a drag it creates on the company's value.

For ConsumerCo, the unallocated corporate costs are estimated at $83 million, around 1.7 percent of revenue, with a present value amounting to about 10 percent of enterprise value. The present value of corporate costs is often in the range of 10 to 20 percent of enterprise value for multibusiness companies.

Dealing with Intercompany Transactions

Sometimes business units provide goods and services to one another, incur intragroup payables and receivables, and borrow and lend funds to a group treasury. To arrive at consolidated corporate results without any double counting, accountants eliminate the internal revenues, costs, and profits, as well as internal assets and liabilities. Only revenues, costs, assets, and liabilities from transactions with external parties remain at the consolidated level. Exhibit 19.6 shows how the 2025 reorganized financials for ConsumerCo's businesses are consolidated with the accounts of the parent company, ConsumerCo Corporation. In this example, ConsumerCo Corporation has no business activities and only holds the equity stakes in the business subsidiaries and most of the group's debt. Note that you typically do not need the full right-hand side of the balance sheet for the subsidiaries in order to perform a DCF valuation by parts—so long as you can calculate the operating invested capital.

Intercompany Sales and Profits   ConsumerCo's private-label segment sells partially finished products to the open market but also to the branded-products unit, generating $500 million of internal sales in 2025 (in Exhibit 19.6, see the first line under Eliminations I). If the branded-products unit would process and resell all transferred materials in the same year, $500 million of internal revenues and internal costs could simply be eliminated in the consolidation. Since one unit's revenues are another unit's costs, overall earnings are unaffected.[3]

---

[3] The cumulative value of business units will equal the aggregate value, but the value split depends on the level of transfer pricing between the two units. The higher the transfer price, the more aggregate value is transferred to the private-label business. To value each business unit accurately, record intercompany transfers at the value that would be transacted with third parties. Otherwise, the relative value of the business units will be distorted.

EXHIBIT 19.6 **ConsumerCo: Eliminations and Consolidation, 2025**

$ million

	Subsidiary companies				Corporate center	Customer finance	ConsumerCo parent company	Eliminations I	Eliminations II	ConsumerCo consolidated
	Branded products	Private label	Devices	Organic products						
NOPAT										
Revenues	2,000	1,500	1,250	750	–	–	–	(500)	–	5,000
Operating costs	(1,500)	(1,358)	(1,094)	(544)	(83)	–	–	498	–	(4,080)
EBITA	500	143	156	206	(83)	–	–	(2)	–	920
Taxes on EBITA	(175)	(50)	(55)	(72)	29	–	–	–	–	(323)
NOPAT	325	93	102	134	(54)	–	–	(2)	–	597
Income from associates and joint ventures	–	–	–	–	–	–	972	–	(942)	30
Interest income	–	–	–	–	–	77	16	–	–	93
Interest expense	–	–	–	–	–	(58)	(118)	–	–	(177)
Taxes on nonoperating items	–	–	–	–	–	(7)	(304)	–	330	19
Net income	325	93	102	134	(54)	12	565	(2)	(612)	563
Invested capital										
Accounts receivable	240	105	25	75	–	–	–	–	–	445
Accounts payable	(216)	(74)	(18)	(5)	–	–	–	–	–	(312)
Inventory	700	375	500	150	–	–	–	(50)	–	1,675
Net PP&E	876	494	55	288	806	–	–	–	–	2,492
Invested capital	1,600	900	563	488	806	–	–	(50)	–	4,306
Excess cash	–	–	–	–	–	–	250	–	–	250
Intercompany receivables	300	–	450	–	–	–	200	–	(950)	–
Loans to customers	–	–	–	–	–	1,154	–	–	–	1,154
Investments in associates and joint ventures	–	–	–	–	–	–	5,097	–	(5,021)	76
Total funds invested	1,900	900	1,013	488	806	1,154	5,547	(50)	(5,971)	5,785
Intercompany payables	–	200	–	–	–	–	750	–	(950)	–
Debt and debt equivalents	–	–	–	–	–	1,038	1,941	–	–	2,980
Adjusted equity	1,900	700	1,013	488	806	115	2,856	(50)	(5,021)	2,806
Total funds invested	1,900	900	1,013	488	806	1,154	5,547	(50)	(5,971)	5,785

But as is often the case for intercompany sales, ConsumerCo's branded-products unit typically does not process and resell all of the private-label deliveries in the same year. Because of the resulting inventory changes of internally supplied materials, one unit's revenues are not necessarily another unit's costs, and some earnings and inventory now must be eliminated in the consolidation as well. ConsumerCo's consolidated financials eliminate $2 million in earnings and $50 million in inventory (see the Eliminations I column of Exhibit 19.6).[4] As in most situations, the earnings impact is small because it is driven by the change in inventory, not the final inventory. Note that in any case, the eliminations cannot affect ConsumerCo's aggregate free cash flow and enterprise DCF valuation, because consolidation adjustments to inventory always offset the changes in NOPAT.

When you build and forecast the financial statements for the business units, treat each unit as if it were a stand-alone company, using total sales (external plus internal). Otherwise, margins and comparisons over time and with peers will be distorted. Prepare separate projections of the consolidation eliminations, similar to the corporate center. The growth rate of intercompany sales can be estimated from the details of how and why these items arise. It is simplest to assume that the eliminations grow at the same rate as the entire group or as the receiving businesses. Remember, however, that the eliminations are used only to reconcile business unit forecasts to the consolidated-enterprise forecasts. They do not affect the value of the company or the individual business units.

Intercompany Financial Receivables and Payables   Multibusiness companies typically manage cash and debt centrally for all business units, which can lead to intercompany receivables from, and payables to, the corporate parent. Sometimes these intercompany accounts are driven by tax considerations. For example, one business unit might lend directly to another unit so that funds don't flow through the parent company, which could trigger additional taxes. Sometimes the accounts have no economic purpose but are simply an artifact of the company's accounting system. Regardless of their purpose, intercompany receivables and payables should not be treated as part of operating working capital but as intercompany equity in the calculation of invested capital.

The Eliminations II column of Exhibit 19.6 shows how this occurs for ConsumerCo. The parent company has $5,097 million of equity investments in its subsidiaries, of which $700 million is in the private-label unit, for example, as reflected in the equity of the subsidiary accounts. This accounting treatment is for internal reports only; since ConsumerCo Corporation owns the private-label business in its entirety, its financial statements are consolidated

---

[4] There is no impact on cash taxes or free cash flow from the accounting consolidation. We abstract from any impact of tax consolidation (fiscal grouping) in this example.

for external reports, eliminating the $700 million of equity investment. The same holds for the other businesses shown. This leads to the elimination of $5,021 million of equity investments in consolidation, leaving only the $76 million stake in the minority-owned cosmetics joint venture as equity investment in the consolidated accounts.

In addition, ConsumerCo Corporation has lent $200 million to the private-label unit, which shows up as an intercompany receivable for the parent company and an intercompany payable for the private-label unit. For the parent company, it represents a nonoperating asset that does not generate operating profits and hence should not be included in its operating working capital. For private label, it represents a financial infusion that is similar to equity. In the consolidated financials, the amounts are eliminated. Similarly, the intercompany receivables for the branded-products and devices businesses are treated as nonoperating assets that are eliminated in the consolidated financials against the $750 million of parent intercompany payables. Failure to handle the intercompany receivables and payables correctly can generate seriously misleading results. In the ConsumerCo example, if the intercompany accounts had been treated as working capital instead of equity, the private-label business's invested capital would have been understated by more than 20 percent, leading to an overstatement of ROIC by roughly the same percentage.

Understanding Financial Subsidiaries

Some firms have financial subsidiaries that provide financing for customers (for example, John Deere Financial and practically all automotive manufacturers). If these subsidiaries are majority owned, they are fully consolidated in the company financial statements. But balance sheets of financial businesses are structured differently from those of industrial or service businesses. The assets tend to be financial rather than physical (largely receivables or loans) and are usually highly leveraged. As detailed in Chapter 43, financial businesses should be valued using cash flow to equity, discounted at the cost of equity. Many companies with significant financial subsidiaries provide a separate balance sheet and income statement for those subsidiaries; the information can be used to analyze and value the financial subsidiaries separately.

Exhibit 19.7 shows that in 2025, ConsumerCo's customer finance unit has $1,154 million in outstanding customer loans. We estimated the ratio of debt to customer loans required to maintain its current BBB credit rating at 90 percent, so that its funding consists of $1,038 million of debt (0.90 × $1,154 million) and $115 million of equity. The loans generate $77 million in annual interest income. After deducting $58 million of interest expenses on debt and taxes of $7 million, after-tax net income of $12 million remains. The return on equity for the customer finance unit is 10.8 percent ($12 million of net income divided by $115 million of equity), just above its 10.5 percent cost of equity (see also Exhibit 19.1). These loans, debt, and financial income streams need to be valued separately from ConsumerCo's business operations. Looking ahead, the customer finance unit's loans are assumed to grow in line with the revenues of the devices business (for which it provides the customer loans). Keeping interest rates and the ratio of debt to customer loans stable at 90 percent, the equity DCF value is estimated at $150 million (see Exhibit 19.1).

Be careful not to double-count the debt of the financial subsidiary in the overall valuation of the company. The equity value of the customer finance subsidiary is already net of its $1,038 million debt, so when we subtracted debt from ConsumerCo's total enterprise value to arrive at the consolidated company's equity value in Exhibit 19.1, we subtracted only the $1,941 million debt not associated with the financing subsidiary.

Navigating Public Information

For our ConsumerCo example, we have the benefit of complete financial statements by business unit. But that will typically not be the case if you are valuing a multibusiness company from the outside in. Exhibit 19.7 shows the disclosure of financial information typical of U.S. Generally Accepted Accounting Principles (GAAP) and International Financial Reporting Standards (IFRS) for a company like ConsumerCo. Companies often disclose revenues, operating profit (or something similar, such as EBITA), depreciation, capital expenditures, and assets by segment. You must convert these items to NOPAT and invested capital.

NOPAT   To estimate NOPAT, start with reported operating earnings by business unit.[5] Next, allocate operating taxes, any pension adjustment (to eliminate the nonoperating effect of pension expense), and operating lease

EXHIBIT 19.7 **ConsumerCo: Public Information for Business Segments, 2025**

Reported financials, $ million	Branded products	Private label	Devices	Organic products	Corporate center	Intersegment eliminations	Consolidated
Revenues	2,000	1,500	1,250	750	–	(500)	5,000
Operating profit	500	143	156	206	(83)	(2)	920
Depreciation[1]	150	59	57	31	42		338
Capital expenditures	208	107	90	79	42		526
Assets	1,872	882	596	531	830	(50)	4,662
Invested capital: Estimate vs. actual							
Assets/total assets,%	40	19	13	11	18		99
Invested capital estimate, $ million	1,711	806	545	486	759		4,306
Invested capital actual, $ million	1,600	900	563	488	806		4,306
Estimation error, %	6.9	(10.4)	(3.1)	(0.4)	(5.9)		

[1] Included in operating profit.

[5] Companies use different names, such as operating profit, underlying profit, or simply earnings before interest and taxes (EBIT), for business unit results.

adjustment (eliminating interest expense embedded in rental expense before new accounting standards were introduced in 2019) to each of the business units. (For more information on these adjustments, see Chapter 11.) Use the overall operating tax rate for all business units unless you have information to estimate each unit's tax rate—for example, if units are in different tax jurisdictions. For the ConsumerCo example, this would have resulted in exactly the right NOPAT per business unit, because no pension, lease, or other adjustments are needed on reported EBITA, though this is not typically the case.

After estimating NOPAT, reconcile the sum of all business unit NOPATs to consolidated NOPAT and net income. This step ensures that all adjustments have been properly made.

Invested Capital   To estimate invested capital, you can use an incremental approach or a proportional approach, depending on the information available. When possible, use both approaches to triangulate your estimates.

In the *incremental* approach, start with total assets by business unit, and subtract estimates for nonoperating assets and non-interest-bearing operating liabilities—if information is available on these items. (Note that many companies will hold nonoperating assets at the corporate level, not the unit level. In that case, no adjustment is necessary.) Nonoperating assets include excess cash, investments in nonconsolidated subsidiaries, pension assets, and deferred tax assets. Non-interest-bearing operating liabilities include accounts payable, taxes payable, and accrued expenses. They can be allocated to the business units by either revenue or total assets. As discussed in the earlier section on intercompany payables and receivables, do not treat intercompany loans and debt as an operating liability.

Then allocate the invested capital for the consolidated entity to all its business units by the amount of total assets minus nonoperating assets and non-interest-bearing liabilities for each business unit. To measure invested capital excluding goodwill,[6] subtract allocated goodwill by business unit. If goodwill is not reported by business unit, you can try to make an estimate from past transactions if these can be aligned with individual business units. However, Exhibit 19.7 does not provide all the information needed for this approach.

Using the *proportional* approach to estimate ConsumerCo's invested capital, you would allocate its total operating invested capital (excluding the customer loans and joint venture, of course) to each of the business units according to their proportion of total assets as reported before intersegment eliminations. Note that the proportional approach in this instance would yield some estimation errors, such as allocating $1,711 million invested capital (calculated as $1,872/$4,712 × $4,306 million) to branded products when its true invested capital is $1,600 million.

---

[6] By goodwill, we mean both goodwill and acquired intangibles.

Once you have estimated invested capital for the business units and corporate center, reconcile these estimates with the total invested capital derived from the consolidated statements.

COST OF CAPITAL

Each business segment should be valued at its own cost of capital, because the systematic risk (beta) of operating cash flows and their ability to support debt—that is, the implied capital structure—will differ by business. To determine an operational business unit's weighted average cost of capital (WACC), you need the unit's target capital structure, its cost of equity (as determined by its levered beta), and its cost of debt. For a financial business, you simply need the cost of equity following from its equity beta. (For details on estimating the cost of equity and WACC, see Chapter 15.) The results for ConsumerCo's segments are summarized in Exhibit 19.8.

First, estimate the target capital structure in terms of the debt-to-equity (D/E) ratio and the cost of debt for each of ConsumerCo's business units. We recommend using the median capital structure of publicly traded peers, especially if most peers have similar capital structures. Most peers for ConsumerCo's businesses have a credit rating close to investment grade (BBB– or better), corresponding to a debt-to-equity ratio of 0.25 to 0.30 and a cost of debt of around 5.5 percent. Next, determine the levered beta, cost of equity, and WACC. To determine a business unit's levered beta, first estimate an unlevered median

EXHIBIT 19.8 **ConsumerCo: WACC Estimates, January 2025**

Business	Debt/ equity[1]	Cost of debt,[2] %	Beta, unlevered	Beta, levered	Cost of equity,[3] %	WACC,[4] %	DCF value, $ million	Implied debt, $ million
Branded products	0.30	5.5	0.9	1.1	10.1	8.6	5,188	1,197
Private label	0.30	5.5	1.0	1.2	10.7	9.1	1,128	260
Devices	0.25	5.5	1.2	1.5	11.8	10.1	1,474	295
Organic products	0.25	5.5	0.9	1.1	9.9	8.6	3,440	688
Corporate center	0.30					9.1	(1,123)	(259)
Eliminations							–	–
Total operations							10,107	2,181
Customer finance								1,038
Total ConsumerCo: Net debt, implied								3,220
Excess cash, actual								(250)
Debt, actual in operations								1,941
Debt, actual in customer finance								1,038
Total ConsumerCo: Net debt, actual								2,730

[1] At targeted BBB credit rating.

[2] Beta of debt equals 0.20, and risk-free rate of interest equals 4.5%.

[3] Assuming market risk premium of 5.0%.

[4] Tax rate set at 35%.

beta for its peer group, being thoughtful about which companies to include, especially outliers. Relever the beta, using the same business unit's target capital structure, and estimate its WACC. For the corporate headquarters cash flows, use a weighted average of the business units' costs of capital. Most of ConsumerCo's businesses have similar betas in a range of 1.1 to 1.2, with resulting WACC estimates between 8.6 and 9.1 percent. An exception is the devices business, which is more cyclical at a beta of around 1.5 and a cost of capital of 10.1 percent. For ConsumerCo's customer finance subsidiary, we directly estimated the equity beta of its peers in retail banking at 1.2, leading to an estimated cost of equity of 10.5 percent.

Finally, using the debt levels based on industry medians, aggregate the business unit debt to see how the total compares with the company's total target debt level.[7] Set the headquarters target D/E at a weighted average of the business units' D/Es, since its negative cash flow reduces the company's overall debt capacity. If the sum of business unit target debt differs from the consolidated company's actual debt, we typically record the difference as a corporate item, valuing its tax shield separately (or its tax cost when the company is more conservatively financed). Remember that the business units' valuations are based on target, not actual, capital structure.

In ConsumerCo's case, the resulting aggregate target debt level for its business units and finance subsidiary is $3,220 million. That amount is above its total current net debt of $2,730 million, or $2,980 million debt net of −$250 million excess cash (see Exhibit 19.8). If ConsumerCo held on to its current leverage, it would realize a loss in value relative to our estimated value of its parts. To estimate this loss, project the lost tax shields from the company's current below-peer-level leverage into perpetuity at the overall revenue growth rate, and discount these at the unlevered cost of equity.[8]

When you value a company by summing the business unit values, there is no need to estimate a corporate-wide cost of capital or to reconcile the business unit betas with the corporate beta. The individual business unit betas are more relevant than the corporate beta, which is subject to significant estimation error

---

[7] The allocation of debt among business units for legal or internal corporate purposes is generally irrelevant to the economic analysis of the business units. The legal or internal debt is generally driven by tax purposes or is an accident of history (cash-consuming units have lots of debt). These allocations rarely are economically meaningful and should be ignored.

[8] Recall from Chapter 15 that using the cost of debt to discount tax shields significantly overestimates their value. In theory, a company's unlevered cost of equity is a complex average of the unlevered cost of equity of its underlying businesses that changes over time. You can use a simple average of the unlevered costs of equity of the underlying businesses as an approximation, as any associated error has very small impact on value. Assuming a tax rate of 35 percent and an interest rate of 6 percent, the tax shields lost from $490 million in debt below target are $10.3 million for 2025. Assuming future tax shield losses would roughly grow in line with overall revenues, and discounting at ConsumerCo's unlevered cost of equity of around 9.5 percent, the loss in value would amount to around $190 million.

and is likely to change over time as the weights of the underlying businesses in the company portfolio change.[9]

TESTING THE VALUE BASED ON MULTIPLES OF PEERS

Whenever possible, triangulate the discounted cash flow results with valuation multiples, following the recommendations made in Chapter 18. For each of the company's segments, carefully select a group of companies that are comparable not only in terms of sector but also in terms of return on capital and growth. Do not simply take an average or median of the peer group multiples. Instead, always eliminate outliers with multiples that are out of line with their underlying economics, and where possible, estimate a median of close peers with similar returns and growth. Furthermore, we recommend using NOPAT-based instead of EBITA-based multiples, as the latter can be distorted by tax differences across companies.

Exhibit 19.9 shows the EV-to-earnings multiples and underlying ROIC and growth for the competitors of ConsumerCo's branded-products business. Eliminated from the sample are two outliers with valuation multiples that are far above all other peers and not justified by their growth and return on capital. Note how the spread in the EBITA multiples is larger than that of the NOPAT multiples because of different company tax rates. NOPAT multiples are therefore a more reliable basis for the valuation.

EXHIBIT 19.9 **ConsumerCo: Multiples for Peer Branded-Product Companies, January 2025**

Company		ROIC 2025, %	Growth, 2020–2025, %	EV/EBITA	EV/NOPAT	
Peer	1	31.0	4.7	16.5	22.0	Top-peer average: 21.0
Peer	2	29.6	4.4	15.8	22.6	
Peer	3	28.5	4.5	14.3	20.4	
Peer	4	27.1	3.9	12.8	19.1	
Peer	5	22.0	3.0	12.0	16.0	Close-peer average: 15.6
Peer	6	21.1	2.8	10.5	15.7	
Peer	7	19.7	2.4	11.0	15.7	
Peer	8	19.0	2.1	10.0	15.4	
Peer	9	18.5	2.2	9.5	15.1	
Peer	10	18.3	4.0	20	26.7	Outliers
Peer	11	9.0	3.4	32	45.7	
Overall average				18.0		Excluding outliers
				21.3		Including outliers

[9] The implied cost of capital for ConsumerCo as a whole for each future year is around 8.8 percent. It can be derived by backing it out from the sum of the underlying business units' free cash flows and the sum of the discounted values of these free cash flows.

The overall average NOPAT multiple across the entire peer group is 18.0 times, which would suggest a significantly higher value than the DCF estimate (which has an implied NOPAT multiple of 16.0). But the peers in this group appear to be clustered in two groups with very different underlying returns and growth rates, making the overall average less meaningful. There is a group of leading players with outstanding returns and growth rates that are valued in the stock market at an average of 21.0 times NOPAT. Based on the multiple for this top-peer group, ConsumerCo's branded-products business would be valued at $6,833 million, which would be a clear overestimation, given its actual performance and growth (see Exhibit 19.10). At best, it could represent what ConsumerCo's business would be worth if it were able to attain the economics of these leading players in the sector. In contrast, the players in the peer group with returns and growth rates closer to ConsumerCo's business have an average multiple of 15.6 times NOPAT, leading to a value estimate of $5,060 million, which is much closer to the DCF results.

Adopting the same approach of using close-peer multiples to value all of ConsumerCo's other segments, including ConsumerCo finance and the cosmetics joint venture, the estimated equity value is $8,774 million (Exhibit 19.10). Note that by using top-peer multiples for the valuation, ConsumerCo's value would be estimated some 30 percent higher than its DCF value, at $11,956 million. Showing the range of value estimates for close-peer and top-peer multiples helps to triangulate the DCF valuation results. In our experience, close-peer multiples typically lead to valuation

EXHIBIT 19.10 **ConsumerCo: Valuation with Multiples, January 2025**

		EV/NOPAT		Multiples-based value				
Business	**NOPAT,** $ million	**Close peers**	**Top peers**	**Close peers,** $ million	**Delta to DCF,%**	**Top peers,** $ million	**Delta to DCF,%**	**DCF value,** $ million
Branded products	325	15.6	21.0	5,060	(2)	6,833	32	5,188
Private label	93	11.7	16.0	1,084	(4)	1,482	31	1,128
Devices	102	14.0	19.5	1,422	(4)	1,980	34	1,474
Organic products	134	24.5	26.5	3,285	(5)	3,553	3	3,440
Corporate center	(54)			(1,123)		(1,123)		(1,123)
Eliminations	(2)	–	–	–		–		–
Total operations	597			9,727	(4)	12,726	26	10,107
Customer finance[1]	12	12.0	12.0	149	(0)	149	(0)	150
Cosmetics joint venture[2]	81	17.0	22.0	589	(3)	772	27	609
Excess cash				250		250		250
Gross enterprise value				10,716	(4)	13,897	25	11,117
Debt				(1,941)		(1,941)		(1,941)
Equity value				8,774	(4)	11,956	30	9,175

[1] For customer finance, net income is used for NOPAT, and P/E is used for EV/NOPAT. Multiples and DCF values are given at equity value, net of debt.

[2] For the cosmetics joint venture, the DCF value is the equity value of the minority stake.

results within 10 to 15 percent of the DCF outcomes—in other words, within the normal margin of error for any valuation.

However, many analysts and other practitioners often base their valuations on top-peer multiples. Valuing a company by parts then easily leads to the conclusion that it suffers from a so-called conglomerate discount, which in turn prompts recommendations that it be broken up into parts to unlock the valuation gap versus its peers.

The conclusion is as wrong as the recommendation. The discount simply reflects the fact that compared with its top peers, the company is at a lower valuation level because of lower performance. Splitting up the company does not automatically fix that performance gap (and might not even be needed).

Over the years, practitioners and academics have debated whether a conglomerate or diversification discount exists. In other words, does the market value conglomerates at less than the sum of their parts? Unfortunately, the results are incomplete. There is no consensus about whether diversified firms are valued at a discount relative to a portfolio of pure plays in similar businesses.[10] Some argue that they may even trade at a premium. Among studies that claim a discount, there is no consensus about whether the discount results from the weaker performance of diversified firms relative to more focused firms or whether the market values diversified firms lower than focused firms.[11] In our experience, however, whenever we have examined a company valued at less than pure-play peers, the company's business units have tended to exhibit lower growth and/or returns on capital relative to those peers. In other words, there was a performance discount, not a diversification or conglomerate discount.

SUMMARY

Many large companies have multiple business units, each competing in segments with different economic characteristics. Valuing such companies by their individual parts is standard practice in industry-leading companies and among sophisticated investors. Not only does it generate better valuation results, but it also produces deeper insights into where and how the company is generating value.

To value a company by its parts, you need statements of NOPAT, invested capital, and free cash flow that approximate what the business units would look like if they were stand-alone companies. In preparing such statements,

---

[10] P. Berger and E. Ofek, "Diversification's Effect on Firm Value," *Journal of Financial Economics* 37 (1995): 39–65; and B. Villalonga, "Diversification Discount or Premium? New Evidence from Business Information Tracking Series," *Journal of Finance* 59, no. 2 (April 2004): 479–506.

[11] A. Schoar, "Effects of Corporate Diversification on Productivity," *Journal of Finance* 57, no. 6 (2002): 2379–2403; and J. Chevalier, "What Do We Know about Cross-Subsidization? Evidence from the Investment Policies of Merging Firms" (working paper, University of Chicago, July 1999).

you likely have to separate out corporate center costs, deal with intercompany transactions, and make a separate equity cash flow valuation of any financial subsidiaries. Estimate the weighted average cost of capital for each business unit separately, based on the leverage and the betas of its most relevant peer companies.

To triangulate your DCF estimate, make a multiples-based valuation estimate for each individual unit. Make sure to use a peer group that closely matches the unit's return on capital and growth. In our experience, conclusions that a corporate group suffers from a so-called conglomerate discount are often the result of selecting a peer group with significantly higher returns on capital and growth.

Part Three

Advanced Valuation
Techniques

20

Taxes

A good valuation begins with good housekeeping. Start by reorganizing the company's income statement and balance sheet into three categories: operating, nonoperating, and financing items. The reorganized statements can then be used to estimate return on invested capital (ROIC) and free cash flow (FCF), which in turn drive the company's valuation.

One particularly complex line item that spans all three categories is taxes. In this chapter, we explore the role of taxes in valuation and discuss how to use the notes in the annual report to estimate operating taxes and the operating tax rate. Since some companies can defer a portion of their reported taxes over long periods, we'll also go through the steps for converting operating taxes to operating cash taxes and, as a result, how to incorporate deferred taxes into a valuation.

ESTIMATING OPERATING TAXES

The operating tax rate represents the tax rate a company would pay if the company generated only operating income and was financed entirely with equity. It is the best tax rate for estimating net operating profit after taxes (NOPAT), a key component of free cash flow. The operating tax rate is better suited for this task than two well-known alternatives, the *statutory* tax rate and the *effective* tax rate. The statutory tax rate, which equals the domestic tax rate on a dollar of income, fails to account for differences in foreign tax rates and ongoing, operating-related tax credits. For a company that actively manages its tax burden, the statutory tax rate will often overestimate the taxes paid. In contrast, the effective tax rate, which equals income taxes divided by pretax income, often includes nonoperating items, such as one-time audit resolutions. Because of these one-time nonoperating items, the effective tax rate can be quite volatile, which makes accurate tax forecasts challenging.

To determine operating taxes, it is necessary to remove the effects of non-operating and financing items from taxes reported on the income statement. This process can be challenging because of the complexity of tax accounting and the need for data not often disclosed. We'll introduce a hypothetical company to show several ways to estimate operating taxes, as each approach requires certain assumptions to fill in gaps left by public financial statements.

To illuminate these trade-offs, we begin by estimating operating taxes when you have complete information, including information that is not typically disclosed to the public. Exhibit 20.1 presents the internal financial statements of a hypothetical global company, TaxCo, for a single year. In that year, TaxCo generated $2.2 billion in operating profits from its domestic operations. From this amount, it deducted $400 million for the amortization of domestically held acquired intangible assets and $600 million for interest on domestically held debt, resulting in $1.2 billion in domestic pretax profit. The company paid a statutory tax rate of 25 percent on this profit.

During the same year, the company generated $600 million in operating income from a foreign subsidiary. It also sold an asset held by the foreign subsidiary, recording a gain of $100 million. This led to $700 million in foreign pretax profit, on which it paid a statutory tax rate of 15 percent.

TaxCo generates $40 million in *ongoing* research and development (R&D) tax credits (credits determined by the amount and location of the company's R&D activities, not by the level of pretax profit), which are expected to grow as the company grows. It also has $24 million in *one-time* tax credits—in this case, a tax rebate from the successful resolution of a historical tax dispute. All told, TaxCo paid an effective tax rate on pretax profits of 17.9 percent, well below its domestic statutory rate of 25 percent.

EXHIBIT 20.1 **TaxCo: Income Statement by Geography**

$ million

	Domestic subsidiary	Foreign subsidiary	R&D tax credits	Resolution of tax dispute	Consolidated
EBITA[1]	2,200	600	—	—	2,800
Amortization of acquired intangibles	(400)	—	—	—	(400)
EBIT[1]	1,800	600	—	—	2,400
Interest expense	(600)	—			(600)
Gains on asset sales	—	100	—	—	100
Pretax profit	1,200	700	—	—	1,900
Income taxes	(300)	(105)	40	24	(341)
Net income	900	595	40	24	1,559
Tax rates, %					
Statutory tax rate	25.0	15.0			
Effective tax rate					17.9

[1] EBITA is earnings before interest, taxes, and amortization; EBIT is earnings before interest and taxes.

EXHIBIT 20.2 **TaxCo: Operating Taxes and NOPAT by Geography**

$ million

	Domestic subsidiary	Foreign subsidiary	R&D tax credits	Resolution of tax dispute	Consolidated
EBITA	2,200	600	—	—	2,800
Operating taxes	(550)	(90)	40	—	(600)
NOPAT[1]	1,650	510	40	—	2,200
Tax rates, %					
Statutory tax rate	25.0	15.0			
Operating tax rate					21.4

[1] Net operating profit after taxes.

As noted earlier, operating taxes are the taxes that would be paid by a company with only operating income and financed entirely with equity. Exhibit 20.2 calculates operating taxes and NOPAT for TaxCo. To determine operating taxes, apply the appropriate statutory tax rate to each jurisdiction's EBITA.

In this case, calculate statutory taxes by multiplying 25 percent by the domestic EBITA of $2.2 billion and 15 percent by the foreign EBITA of $600 million. The sum of these amounts equals statutory taxes of $640 million. Since the $40 million in research and development (R&D) credits are related to operations and are expected to grow as the company grows, they are treated as operating. As a result, the company pays $600 million in operating taxes. To find the operating tax rate, divide operating taxes by global EBITA of $2.8 billion, for a rate of 21.4 percent.

Note how the statutory, effective, and operating taxes differ. The statutory tax rate on domestic income is 25.0 percent, the effective tax rate (shown in Exhibit 20.1) equals 17.9 percent, and the operating tax rate is 21.4 percent. The operating tax rate is the best tax rate for converting EBITA to NOPAT.

Applying a tax rate to EBITA rather than pretax accounting profit seems to overlook the value of tax shields generated by interest and amortization. While the interest tax shield is valuable, it is typically not valued as part of income but rather as part of the weighted average cost of capital. Regarding amortization related to acquired intangibles, most acquisitions are structured such that this amortization is not tax deductible and, therefore, does not generate tax shields. In situations where this is not the case, the tax shields related to amortization must be incorporated into the valuation. We discuss the complex tax accounting related to amortization later in the section on deferred taxes.

Using Public Statements to Estimate Operating Taxes

In practice, companies do not publicly disclose income by country. Instead, you must rely on a company-wide income statement and a tax reconciliation table.

The tax reconciliation table can be found in the notes that accompany the financial statements. It explains why the taxes reported on the income statement do not equal the product of its pretax profit and the statutory rate. At the company's discretion, the table can express amounts in percentages or in the company's reporting currency.

To illustrate how such a table denoted in percentages explains the difference between statutory and effective rates, the left side of Exhibit 20.3 presents the tax reconciliation table for TaxCo. Because foreign income was taxed at 15 percent, TaxCo paid $70 million less in taxes than if it had been taxed at the domestic rate of 25 percent (that is, it paid $105 million in taxes at 15 percent, rather than $175 million at 25 percent). To report this difference as a percentage of pretax profit, the tax reconciliation table divides the $70 million by the company-wide pretax profit of $1.9 billion to obtain 3.7 percent of pretax income. Each of the adjustments is divided by pretax profit to determine the corresponding percentages in the reconciliation table.

The right side of Exhibit 20.3 shows how to use the tax reconciliation table to estimate operating taxes in millions of dollars. Start by calculating statutory taxes on EBITA. Next, work through the table, looking for line items that are ongoing and related to operations. Finally, add the statutory taxes on EBITA to the operating-related adjustments. The following paragraphs take a closer look at these steps.

To calculate statutory taxes on EBITA for TaxCo, multiply EBITA by the statutory tax rate: 25 percent times $2.8 billion equals $700 million.

Next, search the tax reconciliation table for tax adjustments that are ongoing and related to operations. The most common operating adjustments are state and foreign taxes. To determine if other adjustments are operating, look for consistency over time, and use the account description. Some account

EXHIBIT 20.3 TaxCo: Calculating Taxes Using a Tax Table Reported in Percent

Tax reconciliation table %		Operating taxes $ million	
Statutory tax rate	25.0	EBITA	2,800
Foreign-income adjustment	(3.7)	× Statutory tax rate	25.0%
R&D tax credits	(2.1)	= Statutory taxes on EBITA	700
Resolution of tax dispute	(1.3)		
Effective tax rate	17.9	Foreign-income adjustment	−3.7%
		R&D tax credit	−2.1%
		Cumulative adjustments	−5.8%
		× Pretax profit	1,900
		= Operating adjustments	(110)
		Operating taxes	590

descriptions are cryptic; for these, an online search may shed light on the adjustment. For TaxCo, we classify R&D tax credits as operating and the resolution of past tax disputes as nonoperating.

To calculate cumulative operating adjustments for TaxCo, sum the foreign-income adjustment (3.7 percent) and the R&D tax credit (2.1 percent), and multiply the results by pretax profit, not EBITA. (This is because the company's accountants create the tax reconciliation table using pretax profit, rather than EBITA.) For TaxCo, operating adjustments equal $110 million. Subtracting $110 million from $700 million calculates operating taxes of $590 million.[1]

While this method is effective, it is only an estimate. In our example, the calculation of $590 million using public reports does not match the internal results of $600 million shown in Exhibit 20.2. The difference is explained by the $100 million in gains that were taxed at 15 percent, not at the statutory rate of 25 percent. Had gains been taxed at 25 percent, the methodology in Exhibit 20.3 would have estimated operating taxes without error. Our analysis is limited by our lack of access to internal financial statements.

If a company denotes the tax reconciliation table in its home currency, the process for calculating operating taxes follows the same principles but differs slightly in implementation.[2] The left side of Exhibit 20.4 presents the tax reconciliation table for TaxCo in millions of dollars. The first line item

EXHIBIT 20.4 **TaxCo: Calculating Taxes Using a Tax Table Reported in Dollars**

$ million

Tax reconciliation table		Operating taxes	
Pretax profits at the statutory rate	475	Pretax profits at the statutory rate	475
Foreign-income adjustment	(70)	/ Pretax profit	1,900
R&D tax credits	(40)	= Statutory tax rate on EBITA	25.0%
Resolution of tax dispute	(24)		
Income taxes	341	× EBITA	2,800
		= Statutory taxes on EBITA	700
		Foreign-income adjustment	(70)
		R&D tax credit	(40)
		Estimated operating taxes	590

[1] To estimate operating taxes, some professionals add the percentage-based operating adjustments directly to the statutory tax rate. While this method works in simple situations, it is not reliable. When a company has a large nonoperating expense such as an asset write-off, this will depress pretax profit, causing the percentage-based tax reconciliation items to spike. These spikes make historical analysis challenging and forecasting unreliable. As a result, we recommend adjusting statutory taxes using currency-based adjustments.

[2] In 2023, for instance, Walmart presented its tax reconciliation table in percent, Home Depot presented its tax reconciliation table in U.S. dollars, and Costco presented its tax reconciliation table in both percent and U.S. dollars.

represents what the company would pay if pretax profit were taxed at the statutory tax rate. Often the company's statutory tax rate is reported in the text accompanying the table. However, if it is not, divide the line item by pretax profit to estimate the statutory tax rate.

With the statutory tax rate in hand, multiply EBITA by the statutory tax rate to determine statutory taxes on EBITA (see the right side of Exhibit 20.4). Next, work through the tax table for other operating adjustments. Since operating adjustments are already denoted in dollars, they can be transferred directly to the calculation of operating taxes. The process may vary, but our estimate of operating taxes remains unchanged.

Operating Taxes at Costco   For a real-world example of the process, Exhibit 20.5 presents the tax reconciliation table for Costco Wholesale. In addition to federal and state taxes, the company reports taxes on foreign income at higher rates and tax credits related to its employee ownership plans, its 401(k) plan, and the 2017 Tax Cuts and Jobs Act (TCJA). The TCJA lowered the U.S. corporate tax rate from 35 percent to 21 percent. Because tax rates are subject to change, monitor tax laws to keep informed of the relevant rates.

In Exhibit 20.6, we use the tax reconciliation table to estimate operating taxes for "Costco" using the process described earlier in this section. The estimation of EBITA is detailed separately in Exhibit 11.10.

EXHIBIT 20.5 **Costco: Tax Reconciliation Table**

$ million

	2019	2020	2021	2022	2023
Federal taxes at statutory rate	1,001	1,127	1,403	1,646	1,782
State taxes, net	171	190	243	267	302
Foreign taxes, net	(1)	92	92	231	160
Employee stock ownership plan (ESOP)	(18)	(24)	(21)	(23)	(25)
Special dividend related to 401(k) plan[1]	—	—	(70)	—	—
2017 Tax Cuts and Jobs Act	(123)	—	—	—	—
Other	31	(77)	(46)	(196)	(24)
U.S. and foreign tax expense (benefit)	1,061	1,308	1,601	1,925	2,195
Earnings before taxes	4,765	5,367	6,680	7,840	8,487
Tax rates,[2] %					
Federal income tax rate	21.0	21.0	21.0	21.0	21.0
State income tax rate	3.6	3.5	3.6	3.4	3.6
Statutory tax rate	24.6	24.5	24.6	24.4	24.6

[1] Aggregated in employee stock ownership plan in original filings.

[2] While Costco reports the federal and state tax rates in its annual reports, many companies do not. To determine each tax rate, divide each tax amount by earnings before taxes.

Source: Costco annual report, n. 8, "Income Taxes."

EXHIBIT 20.6 **Costco: Estimation of Operating Taxes**

$ million

	2019	2020	2021	2022	2023
EBITA	4,835	5,493	6,789	7,891	8,217
× Statutory tax rate	24.6%	24.5%	24.6%	24.4%	24.6%
Statutory taxes on EBITA	1,189	1,348	1,673	1,925	2,018
Foreign taxes, net[1]	(1)	92	92	231	160
Employee stock ownership plan (ESOP)[1]	(18)	(24)	(21)	(23)	(25)
Operating taxes	1,170	1,416	1,744	2,133	2,153
Operating taxes deferred[2]	(228)	(131)	(198)	33	(89)
Operating cash taxes	942	1,285	1,546	2,166	2,064
Tax Rate on EBITA					
Operating tax rate	24.2%	25.8%	25.7%	27.0%	26.2%
× (1 – percent deferred)	19.5%	9.3%	11.4%	−1.5%	4.1%
Operating cash tax rate	19.5%	23.4%	22.8%	27.5%	25.1%

[1] Reported in the tax reconciliation table presented in Exhibit 20.5.

[2] Computed as the increase (decrease) in operating deferred-tax assets, net of liabilities. Operating deferred taxes are reported in Exhibit 20.9.

To begin, multiply the statutory tax rate by EBITA. In 2023, for example, the statutory tax rate was 24.6 percent, and the statutory taxes on EBITA equaled $2,018 million. Next, adjust statutory taxes for other operating items. The most common adjustment, especially for international companies, is foreign taxes. We also include the tax credit for the employee stock ownership plan. Although Costco does not describe the credit in detail, dividends paid to employee plans to purchase additional shares are generally tax deductible.

On a net basis, the two operating tax adjustments increase taxes on EBITA by $135 million. Therefore, operating taxes, including adjustments, total $2,153 million. To estimate the operating tax rate, divide this amount by the EBITA of $8,217 million. This yields a rate of 26.2 percent, which is higher than the statutory tax rate of 24.6 percent. Therefore, using the U.S. statutory rate would overestimate the company's value, especially considering higher tax rates abroad.

Reconciling Income Taxes In Chapter 11, we highlight the importance of reconciling NOPAT, total funds invested, and cash flow to and from investors. This process ensures a clear and thoughtful classification of each financial account while reducing the risk of omitting or double-counting items. The same approach can be applied to income taxes. The reconciliation of income taxes will include three accounts: operating taxes, taxes related to nonoperating income and expenses, and other nonoperating taxes.

EXHIBIT 20.7 **Costco: Reconciling Income Taxes**

$ million

	2019	2020	2021	2022	2023
Operating taxes[1]	1,170	1,416	1,744	2,133	2,153
Taxes related to nonoperating accounts	(17)	(31)	(27)	(12)	66
Other nonoperating taxes	(92)	(77)	(116)	(196)	(24)
Income taxes, reported	1,061	1,308	1,601	1,925	2,195
Taxes related to nonoperating accounts					
Interest expense	150	160	171	158	160
Operating lease interest	98	58	60	65	67
Variable lease interest	0	0	21	33	36
Interest income	(126)	(89)	(41)	(61)	(470)
Other income	(52)	(3)	(102)	(144)	(63)
Interest expense, net income	70	126	109	51	(270)
× Statutory tax rate	24.6%	24.5%	24.6%	24.4%	24.6%
Taxes related to nonoperating accounts	17	31	27	12	(66)
Other nonoperating taxes[2]					
Special dividend related to 401(k) plan	—	—	(70)	—	—
2017 Tax Cuts and Jobs Act	(123)	—	—	—	—
Other	31	(77)	(46)	(196)	(24)
Other nonoperating taxes	(92)	(77)	(116)	(196)	(24)

[1] Estimated in Exhibit 20.6.

[2] Reported in the tax reconciliation table presented in Exhibit 20.5.

In Exhibit 20.7, we reconcile operating taxes to reported income taxes. In 2023, the reconciliation starts with operating taxes of $2,153 million. To this number, add taxes related to the nonoperating accounts on the income statement. For Costco, nonoperating accounts include interest expense, operating lease interest, variable lease interest, interest income, and other income. To estimate taxes related to nonoperating accounts, we multiply the sum of nonoperating accounts, −$270 million, by the statutory tax rate of 24.6 percent, which equals −$66 million. Finally, we add all taxes from the tax reconciliation table deemed nonoperating. For Costco, this includes the special dividend related to the 401(k) plan, the 2017 tax act, and other taxes, totaling −$24 million in 2023. The sum of the three elements equals $2,195 million, which matches the income taxes reported by Costco in 2023.

CONVERTING OPERATING TAXES TO OPERATING CASH TAXES

In the previous section, we estimated operating taxes on an accrual basis. For most companies, especially growing companies, the taxes reported on the income statement will not reflect the actual cash taxes paid, because of differences in accounting rules versus tax rules. For instance, tax rules allow for accelerated depreciation of physical assets, whereas financial accounting typically uses straight-line depreciation. With higher expenses and lower pretax profits on its tax books, companies can significantly delay or perhaps even perpetually postpone paying accrual-based taxes. For companies that consistently defer or prepay taxes, we recommend using cash-based operating taxes, which we call operating cash taxes.

We recommend using cash taxes when the differences between cash and accrual taxes are consistent and predictable. In the case of low-growth companies, deferred-tax accounts may rise and fall unpredictably. If the operating cash tax rate is volatile and does not show a systematic pattern, do not adjust for deferrals. Instead, use the operating tax rate on an accrual basis.

If you choose to convert operating taxes to operating cash taxes, start with operating taxes and add the increase (or subtract the decrease) in *operating-related* deferred-tax assets net of deferred-tax liabilities.[3] Since deferred taxes on the balance sheet include both operating and nonoperating items, we need to separate them. To do this, search the notes for a detailed listing of deferred taxes.

Exhibit 20.8 presents the deferred-tax table for Costco, found in note 8 of the company's annual report. Deferred-tax assets (DTAs) are presented in the upper portion of the table. Costco recognizes a valuation allowance against tax assets because some tax assets are unlikely to be realized. In the lower portion of the table are deferred-tax liabilities (DTLs). The table concludes by netting deferred-tax liabilities against deferred-tax assets.

Exhibit 20.9 reorganizes deferred-tax assets and liabilities into operating and nonoperating items. Costco has four deferred-tax accounts related to operations: equity compensation, membership fees, operating leases, and accrued liabilities. The membership fees are collected from the customer upfront but recorded as income over the life of the membership. The government recognizes income when the cash is collected, but the accounting statements recognize income over time, so a deferred-tax asset is created. As a result, for Costco and for other growing companies in this situation, cash taxes are higher than reported on the income statement.

Another operating item, property and equipment, is a deferred-tax liability. It is a liability that results from Costco using straight-line depreciation on its financial statements and accelerated depreciation for its tax returns. As a result, for Costco and for other growing companies in this situation, cash taxes are lower than reported on the income statement.

As shown in Exhibit 20.9, operating-related deferred-tax liabilities (such as those associated with accelerated depreciation) should be netted against deferred-tax assets (such as those related to accrued liabilities). This reorganization will

---

[3] Given the complexity of today's deferred-tax accounting, adjusting taxes by the change in aggregate deferred taxes is insufficient for calculating free cash flow. For Coca-Cola in 2018, 85 percent of the increase in deferred-tax assets was attributable to a restatement of their value due to an accounting change, rather than the actual prepayment of taxes.

EXHIBIT 20.8 **Costco: Deferred Taxes, Reported**

$ million

	2019	2020	2021	2022	2023
Deferred-tax assets:					
Equity compensation	74	80	72	84	89
Deferred income/membership fees	180	144	161	302	309
Foreign tax credit carryforward	65	101	146	201	250
Operating leases	—	832	769	727	678
Accrued liabilities and reserves	566	639	681	694	761
Other	—	—	62	5	20
Total deferred-tax assets	885	1,796	1,891	2,013	2,107
Valuation allowance	(76)	(105)	(214)	(313)	(422)
Total net deferred-tax assets	809	1,691	1,677	1,700	1,685
Deferred-tax liabilities:					
Property and equipment	(677)	(800)	(935)	(962)	(867)
Merchandise inventories	(187)	(228)	(216)	(231)	(380)
Operating leases	—	(801)	(744)	(701)	(655)
Foreign branch deferreds	(69)	(81)	(92)	(85)	(87)
Other	(21)	(40)	—	—	—
Total deferred-tax liabilities	(954)	(1,950)	(1,987)	(1,979)	(1,989)
Deferred-tax assets, net of liabilities	(145)	(259)	(310)	(279)	(304)

Source: Costco annual report, note 8, "Income Taxes."

make the components of operating taxes, the reorganized balance sheet, and ultimately the final valuation more transparent and less prone to error.

The remaining items in Exhibit 20.9 are classified as nonoperating. In general, a company will have three nonoperating deferred-tax accounts:

1. *Loss carryforwards net of allowances.* When a company loses money, it does not receive a cash reimbursement from the government (as negative taxes in the income statement would imply) but rather an offset toward future taxes. Given that these offsets are unrelated to current profitability, they should be analyzed and valued separately from operations.

2. *Acquired intangibles.* When a company buys another company, it recognizes intangible assets on its balance sheet for items such as patents and customer lists.[4] Since these assets are amortized on the income statement but are not typically deductible for tax purposes, the company

---

[4] Under current accounting standards, the premium paid in an acquisition is split between goodwill and other intangible assets (acquired intangibles). Acquired intangibles include identifiable and separable assets such as patents, copyrights, product formulas, and customer lists. Unlike goodwill, acquired intangibles are amortized over their estimated lives.

EXHIBIT 20.9 **Costco: Deferred Taxes, Reorganized**

$ million

	2019	2020	2021	2022	2023
Operating deferred-tax assets, net of liabilities					
Equity compensation	74	80	72	84	89
Deferred income/membership fees	180	144	161	302	309
Operating lease assets, net of liabilities	—	31	25	26	23
Accrued liabilities and reserves	566	639	681	694	761
Property and equipment	(677)	(800)	(935)	(962)	(867)
Merchandise inventories	(187)	(228)	(216)	(231)	(380)
Foreign branch deferreds	(69)	(81)	(92)	(85)	(87)
Valuation allowance	(76)	(105)	(214)	(313)	(422)
Operating deferred-tax assets, net of liabilities	(189)	(320)	(518)	(485)	(574)
Nonoperating deferred-tax assets, net of liabilities[1]					
Other assets	—	—	62	5	20
Other liabilities	(21)	(40)	—	—	—
Nonoperating deferred-tax assets, net of liabilities	(21)	(40)	62	5	20
Tax loss carryforwards					
Foreign tax credit carryforward	65	101	146	201	250
Deferred-tax assets, net of liabilities	(145)	(259)	(310)	(279)	(304)

[1] We classify other deferred-tax assets and liabilities as nonoperating because they have not scaled consistently with revenue.

will record a deferred-tax liability during the year of the acquisition and then draw down the liability as the intangible asset amortizes. Since operating taxes already exclude the amortization tax benefit in calculating NOPAT, no adjustment is required for deferrals related to these intangible assets. Instead, treat the change in deferred taxes related to amortization of intangibles as nonoperating.

3. *Other nonoperating assets net of liabilities.* Other examples of nonoperating deferred taxes are deferred taxes related to pensions or convertible debt. Without further disclosure, classifying other accounts is tricky. Since we did not see a consistent pattern in "other" deferred taxes, we treat them as nonoperating.

To convert accrual-based operating taxes into operating cash taxes, add the increase in operating DTAs net of operating DTLs to operating taxes. In most cases, DTLs will exceed DTAs, so this is equivalent to subtracting the increase in operating DTLs net of operating DTAs. For Costco, net operating DTLs grew from $485 million in 2022 to $574 million in 2023, an increase of $89 million (see Exhibit 20.9). Subtracting the $89 million from 2023 operating taxes of $2,153 million (computed in Exhibit 20.6) gives $2,064 million of operating cash taxes:

$ million	2023
Operating taxes	2,153
Decrease (Increase) in net operating DTLs	(89)
Operating cash taxes	2,064

The operating cash tax rate for 2023 equals operating cash taxes of $2,064 million divided by EBITA of $8,217 million (as shown in Exhibit 20.6), resulting in a cash tax rate of 25.1 percent. Due to the operating deferrals, operating cash taxes are approximately 4.1 percent lower than operating taxes computed on an accrual basis. The operating cash tax rate can be used to forecast EBITA when projecting future free cash flow. If the percentage deferred varies each year, consider using a historical average. For instance, the average deferral percentage during the last five years for Costco has been 8.5 percent.

Once the estimation of cash taxes is complete, analyze the results. For instance, while most deferred-tax accounts rose in 2023, the property and equipment account fell. Ask yourself if the decline is sustainable or perhaps the result of a one-time occurrence. Include only ongoing, operating-related differences in your forecast cash taxes and ultimately free cash flow.

DEFERRED TAXES ON THE REORGANIZED BALANCE SHEET

One critical component of a well-structured valuation model is a properly reorganized balance sheet. As outlined in Chapter 11, the accounting balance sheet is reorganized into invested capital, nonoperating items, and sources of financing. Since operating DTAs and DTLs flow through NOPAT via cash taxes, they are considered equity equivalents. Why equity? When we convert accrual taxes to cash taxes, income is adjusted, and the difference becomes part of retained earnings, making it an equity equivalent. As discussed in Chapter 11, equity equivalents are included in the reconciliation of total funds invested and not as part of invested capital. If operating DTAs and DTLs were mistakenly included as part of invested capital, they could be double-counted in free cash flow: once in NOPAT via cash taxes and again when taking the change in invested capital.

Exhibit 20.10 presents a reorganized balance sheet that incorporates the deferred-tax items from Exhibit 20.9. Equity equivalents, which appear in the equity section of total funds invested (the right side of Exhibit 20.10), include all deferred-tax accounts except loss carryforwards and nondeductible intangibles, which appear elsewhere. In 2023, Costco's operating deferred-tax liabilities net of assets equaled $574 million, and its other nonoperating assets equaled –$20 million. Because we record the result in the equity section (and not as an asset), we reverse the sign.

EXHIBIT 20.10 **Costco: Treatment of Deferred Taxes on the Reorganized Balance Sheet, 2023**

$ million

Total funds invested: Uses		Total funds invested: Sources	
Working capital	(6,662)	Current portion of long-term debt	1,081
Property, plant, and equipment	26,684	Current portion of leases	349
Leases	5,443	Long-term debt	5,377
Other assets, net of liabilities	456	Long-term leases	5,134
Invested capital, excluding intangibles	25,921	Debt and debt equivalents	11,941
Acquired intangibles	994	→ Deferred-tax liabilities, operating	574
→ Less: Nondeductible intangibles	0	→ Deferred-tax liabilities, nonoperating	(20)
Acquired intangibles, net of gross-up	994	Noncontrolling interests	0
		Shareholders' equity	25,058
Invested capital, including intangibles	26,915	Equity and equity equivalents	25,612
Excess cash	10,388		
→ Tax loss carryforwards	250	Total funds invested	37,553
Total funds invested	37,553		

Two nonoperating deferred-tax accounts that will *not* be classified as equity equivalents are tax loss carryforwards and deferred taxes related to acquired intangibles. The DTA for tax loss carryforwards is a nonoperating asset and should be valued separately. The deferred-tax liability related to the acquired intangibles is treated as an offset to the intangible asset itself, since the asset was grossed up for nondeductible amortization when the asset was created.

Why deduct deferred taxes for intangible assets from acquired intangibles? When a company buys another company, it typically recognizes as intangible assets those intangibles that are separable and identifiable (such as patents). These intangible assets are amortized over their estimated life on the GAAP income statement. But since, in most countries, the amortization is not deductible for tax purposes, a mismatch will occur. As a result, the company creates a deferred-tax liability when it makes the acquisition. To keep the balance sheet balanced, the company also increases intangible assets (known in accounting as "grossing up") by the size of the new DTL. Since the grossed-up intangible and DTL are purely accounting conventions and do not reflect cash transactions, they should be eliminated from the analysis of intangible assets and deferred taxes.

In Exhibit 20.10, we classify the $250 million tax loss carryforward as a nonoperating asset, to be valued separately. In 2020, Costco acquired Innovel Solutions for $1 billion in cash but did not distinguish goodwill from intangible assets, nor did they report a deferred tax liability for the acquired intangibles. As a result, we do not adjust the value of the acquired intangibles for the tax considerations mentioned above.

Finding Deferred Taxes on the Balance Sheet

One practical difficulty with DTAs and DTLs is finding them. Sometimes they are explicitly listed on the balance sheet, but often they are embedded within other assets and other liabilities. For instance, in the notes to its 2023 annual report, Costco discloses that $491 million in deferred-tax assets are embedded in "other long-term assets."

VALUING DEFERRED TAXES

As noted in the previous section, any deferred-tax assets and liabilities classified as operating are incorporated into operating cash taxes. As such, they flow through NOPAT and free cash flow, so they are already embedded in the value of operations. In contrast, the valuation process for nonoperating deferred taxes depends on the particulars of the account.

The valuation of tax loss carryforwards depends on the information provided. If information allows, apply past losses against projections of future income to estimate the timing of tax savings. Discount these cash flows at an appropriate cost of capital, such as the unlevered cost of equity. Be careful to check with local tax experts, since the statutes governing tax loss carryforwards are complex. Also keep in mind that tax loss carryforwards are country specific. A company with tax loss carryforwards in one country cannot use the benefit against profits in another country.

Deferred-tax liabilities related to acquired intangibles are netted against intangible assets and ignored. As described in the previous section, amortization is noncash and, in many countries, nondeductible. Thus, amortization and its corresponding deferred-tax liability have no effect on cash flow.[5]

To value the remaining deferred-tax accounts, including those related to pensions and convertible debt, turn to their corresponding accounts. How you will do this depends on the nuances of the account. As an example, deferred taxes related to pensions arise when pension expense differs from the cash contribution. But the deferred-tax account recognized on the balance sheet reflects accumulated *historical* differences, not future tax savings. Therefore, to value the tax shield associated with unfunded pensions, multiply the current unfunded liability by the marginal tax rate (that is, the expected tax savings attributable to funding the shortfall). We can do this because under U.S. law, cash contributions to close gaps in funding are tax deductible.

---

[5] Some treat the deferred-tax liability as operating and embed it in free cash flow using the following logic. First, operating taxes are calculated on EBIT, not EBITA. If amortization is not deductible, the resulting estimate for taxes is too low. As the deferred-tax liability declines, this implies a negative cash flow. This decline offsets the amortization tax shield generated by using EBIT. However, since we compute operating taxes on EBITA, we ignore the amortization tax shield and consequently do not apply the offset.

Regardless of the deferred-tax account, never use the book value of the account to approximate value. Deferred-tax accounts reflect past differences between accounting and tax statements. They reflect neither expected cash flows nor the present value of those flows.

CLOSING THOUGHTS

Accounting for taxes is complex and can be daunting, even for seasoned professionals. However, given that many companies have operating tax rates that differ from both statutory and effective tax rates, a careful assessment of the operating tax rate is essential for an accurate valuation.

If you are unsure about whether to make a particular adjustment to the statutory tax rate, rely on the general principles outlined in this book by asking two key questions: First, is the adjustment ongoing and related to the business's operating activities? Second, does your classification choice significantly alter your perception of the company's performance or valuation? It is easy to get caught up in details that will not ultimately alter the overall outcome.

Finally, when converting from operating taxes to cash taxes, always evaluate whether your estimate of the deferral rate is reasonable and sustainable. An acquisition or a write-off may cause an artificial spike in a deferred-tax account, leading to an unusually high deferral rate in a single year. In such cases, avoid relying on any one year; instead, use long-term trends to forecast future deferral rates.

While the intricacies of tax accounting can be overwhelming, applying a structured approach and focusing on broader trends will help you navigate the complexity effectively. Accuracy in tax assessment goes beyond the details: it's about understanding the overall impact on a company's financial health.

21

Nonoperating Items,
Provisions, and Reserves

To project free cash flow, the focus is typically on the costs related to operating activities, such as cost of sales, distribution expenses, selling expenses, and administrative expenses. But what about infrequent, out-of-the-ordinary expenses, such as business realignment expenses, asset write-offs, and other extraordinary items?

These so-called nonoperating expenses are indirectly tied to the company's typical activities and generally not expected to recur. The conventional wisdom is that discounted-cash-flow (DCF) calculations should ignore nonoperating expenses as backward-looking, one-time costs. Yet research shows that the type and accounting treatment of nonoperating expenses can affect future cash flow—and in certain situations must be incorporated into your valuation.

This chapter analyzes the most common nonoperating expenses. These include the amortization of acquired intangibles, restructuring charges, unusual charges such as litigation expenses, asset write-offs, and goodwill impairments. Since many noncash expenses are accompanied by a corresponding provision on the balance sheet, we create a classification system of various provisions and describe the process for reorganizing the income statement and balance sheet to reflect the true effect of such provisions, if any, on company value. Finally, we show how to incorporate provisions in free cash flow and equity valuation.

NONOPERATING EXPENSES AND ONE-TIME CHARGES

Given their infrequent nature, nonoperating expenses and one-time charges can distort a company's historical financial performance and consequently distort our view of the future. It is therefore critical to separate one-time nonoperating expenses from ongoing operating expenses. The idea sounds simple, but implementing it can be tricky. Nonoperating expenses are often spread across the income statement, and some are hidden within other accounts and can be discovered only by searching the company's notes. Even after you've properly identified nonoperating expenses, the job is not done. Each nonoperating expense must be carefully analyzed to determine its impact on future cash flow, and if necessary, forecasts must be adjusted to reflect any information embedded in the expense.

To assess the impact of nonoperating expenses and incorporate their information in cash flow forecasts, we recommend a three-step process:

1. *Separate operating from nonoperating items.* This process requires judgment. As a general rule, treat items that grow in proportion to revenues and are related to running the core business as operating. For line items that are lumpy and only tangentially related to core operations, test the impact of each line item on long-term ROIC.

2. *Search the notes for embedded one-time items.* Not every one-time charge will be separately disclosed on the income statement. Sometimes the management discussion and analysis section of the annual report will disclose additional information on one-time items, particularly if there has been a significant change in the account between years.

3. *Analyze each nonoperating item for its impact on future operations.* Line items not included in earnings before interest, taxes, and amortization (EBITA) will not be included in free cash flow (FCF), so they are not part of core operating value. Therefore, it is critical to analyze each nonoperating line item separately and determine whether the charge is likely to continue in the future, in which case it should be incorporated into FCF projections.

Separating Operating from Nonoperating Expenses

Many companies include a line item on their income statement that reads, "Operating income (loss)" or "Operating profit/loss." For example, in Exhibit 21.1, the income statement for Boston Scientific shows that in 2023 the company reported an operating profit of $2.3 billion. But is this profit an accurate reflection of the company's long-run earnings potential? The accounting definition of operating profit differs from our definition of EBITA, in that the accounting standards for classifying items as nonoperating (i.e., to be recorded below operating profit or loss) are extremely strict. To benchmark core operations effectively, EBITA and net operating profit after taxes (NOPAT) should include only items related to the ongoing core business, regardless of their classification by accounting standards.

EXHIBIT 21.1 **Boston Scientific: Income Statement**

$ million

Accounting income statement[1]	2021	2022	2023	Reorganized income statement	2021	2022	2023
Net sales	11,888	12,682	14,240	Net sales	11,888	12,682	14,240
Cost of products sold	(3,711)	(3,956)	(4,345)	Cost of products sold	(3,711)	(3,956)	(4,345)
Gross profit	8,177	8,726	9,895	Gross profit	8,177	8,726	9,895
SG&A expense	(4,359)	(4,520)	(5,190)	SG&A expense	(4,359)	(4,520)	(5,190)
R&D expense	(1,204)	(1,323)	(1,414)	R&D expense	(1,204)	(1,323)	(1,414)
Royalty expense	(49)	(47)	(46)	Royalty expense	(49)	(47)	(46)
Amortization expense	(741)	(803)	(828)	EBITA	2,565	2,836	3,245
Intangible-asset impairment charges	(370)	(132)	(58)				
Contingent consideration benefit	136	(35)	(58)				
Restructuring charges	(40)	(24)	(69)				
Litigation-related credits (charges)	(430)	(173)	111				
Gain (Loss) on disposals	78	(22)	—				
Operating income (loss)	1,198	1,647	2,343				

[1] As reported in the Boston Scientific 2023 annual report.

Boston Scientific reports several so-called operating expenses that we treat as nonoperating. Amortization of intangibles ($828 million in 2023) and intangible-asset impairment charges ($58 million) are noncash reductions in the value of intangible assets; they differ only in their timing and regularity. Other nonoperating expenses include contingent consideration benefit ($58 million), restructuring charges ($69 million), and litigation-related credits ($111 million). For valuation purposes, such nonoperating expenses should not be deducted from revenue to determine EBITA.

The right side of Exhibit 21.1 presents the calculation of EBITA for Boston Scientific. Only operating expenses that grow in line with revenue—such as cost of products sold; selling, general, and administrative (SG&A) expense; research and development (R&D) expense; and royalty expense—are included in the calculation of EBITA. Note how the accounting definition of operating income grows dramatically, while the growth in EBITA is much more measured.

As noted earlier, judgment is called for in classifying items as operating or nonoperating. Operating expenses tend to be ongoing and tied to revenue, so a long-term perspective is critical. For instance, treat a plant closure that occurs once in ten years as nonoperating. Conversely, for a retailer with hundreds of stores, treat extra expenses related to closing stores each year as operating.

For Boston Scientific, we classify royalty payments as operating because royalties are a fundamental part of the medical-devices industry and grow in line with revenue. In contrast, litigation expenses are sporadic and come in waves. Exhibit 21.2 presents litigation expenses for Boston Scientific between 2004 and 2023. While litigation expenses have been declining over the last three years, this trend does not capture the long-term levels. We could treat the litigation expenses as operating, but this would depress ROIC during

EXHIBIT 21.2 **Boston Scientific: Litigation Expenses by Year**

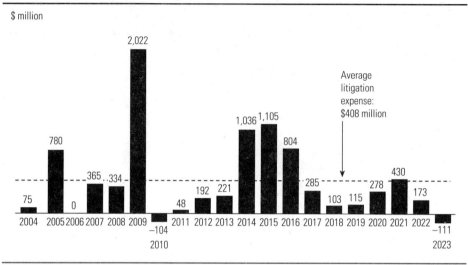

Source: Boston Scientific annual reports.

periods when the expenses were recognized, rather than in the years when the corresponding benefits were reaped. At the same time, litigation expenses are real, so a valuation of Boston Scientific must incorporate them. Although time consuming, a thorough analysis of the company's current exposure to litigation and an analysis of average litigation expenses across all medical-technology companies could provide valuable insights.

When it is unclear how an expense should be classified, measure ROIC with and without it. If the expense is lumpy, smooth the expense over the period in which it was generated.

Searching the Notes for Hidden One-Time Items

The income statement does not always explicitly report every nonoperating expense or one-time charge. Some of these can also be embedded in the cost of sales or selling expenses. To find embedded expenses, read the management discussion and analysis section in the company's annual report. This section details the changes in cost of sales and other expenses from year to year and will sometimes report unusual items. For example, in 2020, Boston Scientific reported an inventory write-off that was aggregated *within* cost of products sold:

> On November 17, 2020, we announced a global, voluntary recall of all unused inventory of our LOTUS Edge Aortic Valve System. During 2020 we recorded $119 million of inventory charges within cost of products sold and $8 million of intangible asset impairment charges associated with the product discontinuation.

Whether you make an adjustment to NOPAT for such an expense depends on whether the charge is large enough to affect perceptions of ongoing performance. If it is not, don't bother. An adjustment could make your analysis unnecessarily complex.

Analyzing Each Nonoperating Item for Impact on Future Operations

Academic researchers have been examining the predictive component of special items and one-time charges for years. Early research pointed to the low persistence of special items, indicating that they are in fact transitory and should not be incorporated into forecasts. However, this research examined persistence only on a year-to-year basis. In 2009, researchers extended the window to multiple years and found persistence in special items for companies with strong core profits.[1] In other words, a highly profitable company that reports a series of, say, restructuring charges is likely to continue with similar charges in the future. Persistence was low for companies with little operating profit.

One reason special items may persist year after year for profitable companies is that management may be shifting ongoing operating costs into special items to meet certain earnings targets, as many academic researchers believe they do. This belief also seems to be common among research analysts, as they decrease their earnings forecasts following the disclosure of a special item.[2] Although the research showing that special items are used to manage earnings is persuasive, it remains unclear how to relate the research results to an individual company. Judgment is required: pay close attention to companies disclosing special items. If the special items seem likely to recur, especially in a challenging economy, adjust your forecasts accordingly.

A comprehensive list of nonoperating items and one-time charges is impractical, but the following items are among the most common: amortization of acquired intangibles; asset write-offs, including write-offs of goodwill and purchased R&D; restructuring charges; litigation charges; and gains and losses on asset sales. Since each of these nonoperating items requires a particular adjustment, we will work through them one by one.

Amortization of Acquired Intangibles   Although accounting standards require amortization of acquired intangibles, in most circumstances you should *not* deduct amortization from operating profit to determine NOPAT. As an alternative to expensing amortization, use EBITA (not EBIT) to determine operating profits. Since amortization is excluded from operating profit,

---

[1] P. M. Fairfield, K. A. Kitching, and V. W. Tang, "Are Special Items Informative about Future Profit Margins?" *Review of Accounting Studies* 14, nos. 2–3 (2009): 204–236.
[2] N. Li, H. Su, W. Dong, and K. Zhu, "The Effect of Non-recurring Items on Analysts' Earnings Forecasts," *China Journal of Accounting Research* 11, no. 1 (2018): 21–31.

remember to include the cumulative excluded amortization in your total for intangible assets on the balance sheet. A corresponding entry should be made to equity (titled "cumulative amortization") to balance total funds invested.

Why not amortize intangibles, particularly since we include depreciation in our calculation of ROIC? The idea of recognizing an intangible asset and then amortizing its use over a useful life is a good one. Yet current accounting standards do not allow companies to take this approach consistently across all intangibles. Today, only *acquired* intangibles are capitalized and amortized, while *internally generated* intangible assets, such as brand and distribution networks, are expensed when they are created. Thus, the EBIT of a company that acquires an intangible asset and then replenishes the asset through internal investment will be penalized twice on its financial statements, once through SG&A expenses and again through amortization. In fact, expensing the creation of new intangible assets while amortizing old intangibles would be tantamount to including both capital expenditures and depreciation on the income statement, which would clearly be undesirable.

For valuation purposes, avoid mixing amortization and expensing by maintaining goodwill and acquired intangibles at their original values. To do this, compute operating profit before amortization, and add cumulative amortization to the current value of goodwill and intangible assets.

Exhibit 21.3 illustrates the impact of amortizing acquired intangibles on the margins of four companies in the medical devices industry. While Company A appears to lead the group based on EBIT margin, this view is skewed by the amortization of acquired intangibles. When Company B was formed through the earlier merger of two different companies, accounting standards required the merged entity to record substantial intangible assets, which must be amortized. Excluding this amortization, it becomes clear that Company B generated the best cash-based margin in 2023. In this case, the amortization expense is distorted by a past transaction and does not provide much insight into future outlays.

EXHIBIT 21.3 **EBIT vs. EBITA Margin, 2023**

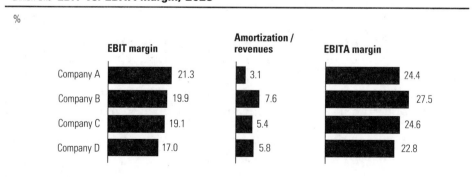

	EBIT margin	Amortization / revenues	EBITA margin
Company A	21.3	3.1	24.4
Company B	19.9	7.6	27.5
Company C	19.1	5.4	24.6
Company D	17.0	5.8	22.8

Source: Annual reports.

One situation in which it is appropriate to deduct amortization is when intangibles can be capitalized (versus expensed) consistently. Consider a company that has no sales force and instead purchases customer contacts from a third party. Since sales outlays are never expensed via SG&A, they should be amortized to arrive at a meaningful measure of operating profitability. Otherwise, the income statement would not accurately reflect the true cost of selling its products and services. Another example is the purchase of frequency rights by telecom companies. Since these assets can be capitalized and amortized without exception, treat them no differently than fixed equipment and depreciation.

Asset Write-Offs   If the value of an asset falls below its book value, accounting standards dictate that the asset should be written down (sometimes entirely) to its fair value. Although write-downs and write-offs give banks and other lenders insight into the diminished value of their collateral, the resulting balance sheet value understates the historical investment made by shareholders. Thus, ROIC can artificially rise following a write-down. To counteract this effect, treat asset write-downs and write-offs as nonoperating, and *add* cumulative write-downs to invested capital. To balance total funds invested, create a corresponding equity equivalent.

Two categories of asset write-offs are common:

1. *Operating assets.* In general, treat the markdown of an operating asset such as property, plant, and equipment as nonoperating. In the rare cases when they occur systematically, treat them as operating. Add back write-downs to the asset, except when you are estimating capital turn- over to project future capital needs. In this case, compute the ratio in a manner that best reflects future capital needs.

2. *Goodwill and intangibles impairments.* Treat goodwill and other intan- gibles impairments as nonoperating, and add back cumulative impairments to goodwill on the balance sheet. Since the purpose of computing ROIC with goodwill is to measure historical performance *including* all past acquisition premiums, goodwill should remain at its original level.

Restructuring Charges   As business changes, companies must adapt. Major changes often require plant closures, employee layoffs, inventory write- downs, asset write-offs, and other restructuring charges. If a restructuring charge is unlikely to recur, treat the charge as nonoperating. If, however, a pattern of ongoing restructuring charges emerges, further analysis is required. Exhibit 21.4 presents the restructuring charges for Boston Scientific between 2014 and 2023. During this period, Boston Scientific's restructuring

EXHIBIT 21.4 **Boston Scientific: Restructuring Charges**

$ million

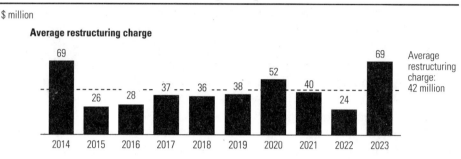

Source: Boston Scientific annual reports.

charges averaged $42 million per year, or 0.4 percent of revenues. These expenses are reported separately from cost of sales and SG&A.

Given the persistence of Boston Scientific's restructuring charges, they should be analyzed to determine what portion represents cash (such as severance payments), whether any cash restructuring charges are likely to continue, and for how long. To this end, a careful reading of the company's notes reveals the following:

> In February 2023, the Board of Directors approved, and we committed to, a new global restructuring program. The implementation of the 2023 Restructuring Plan is estimated to result in total pre-tax charges of approximately $450 million to $550 million, of which approximately $350 million to $450 million is expected to result in cash outlays, and reduce gross annual pre-tax expenses by approximately $225 million to $275 million as program benefits are realized.

Many restructuring charges are recorded before any cash is spent. If this is the case, a corresponding reserve will be recorded in the liabilities section of the balance sheet. In a later section, we describe the appropriate treatment of various reserves, including those related to restructuring charges.

Litigation Charges   When there is likely to be a legal judgment against a company, the company will recognize a litigation charge. If the litigation charge recurs frequently and grows with revenue, treat the charge as operating. For instance, hospital systems frequently defend themselves against malpractice lawsuits. Since these lawsuits are a cost of doing business, the litigation costs should be treated as operating costs for valuation and projected forward. However, if a litigation cost is truly a one-time expense, treat it as nonoperating, and value any claims against the company separately from core operations.

Gains and Losses on Asset Sales   When an asset's sale price differs from its book value, the company will recognize a gain or loss. Since current gains and losses are backward-looking (value has been created or destroyed in the past), treat them as nonoperating. Additionally, double-check to make sure projected free cash flow does not incorporate the asset recently sold. For instance, make sure future depreciation and its related tax shields reflect only the remaining assets.

Although gains and losses should not be included in operating profit, past asset sales may provide insight about the level of cash to be generated by future asset sales. Again, be careful to value future asset sales (and their corresponding gains and losses) only when income from those assets is not incorporated in free cash flow. Otherwise, the resulting double-counting will overstate the company's value.

PROVISIONS AND THEIR CORRESPONDING RESERVES

Provisions are noncash expenses that reflect future costs or expected losses. Companies take provisions by reducing current income and setting up a corresponding reserve as a liability (or deducting the amount from the relevant asset).

For the purpose of analyzing and valuing a company, we categorize provisions into one of four types: ongoing operating provisions, long-term operating provisions, nonoperating provisions such as restructuring provisions, or provisions created for the purpose of smoothing income (transferring income from one period to another). Based on the characteristics of each provision, adjust the financial statements to best reflect the company's operating performance. For example, ongoing operating provisions are treated the same way as any other operating expense, whereas restructuring provisions are converted from an accrual to a cash basis and treated as nonoperating. Exhibit 21.5 summarizes the four types of provisions and how to incorporate them into NOPAT, invested capital, and valuation.

We believe our classification system of reserves leads to better analysis, but the way you adjust the financial statements should not affect the company's valuation. A valuation depends solely on how and when cash flows through a business, not on accounting adjustments.

Adjustments for the Provisions

In Exhibit 21.6, we present the abbreviated financial statements for a hypothetical company that recognizes four provisions: an environmental provision for decommissioning the company's plant, an operating provision for future product defects, a provision for smoothing income, and a restructuring provision for future severance payments. In this example, we reorganize forecast statements instead of historical statements to demonstrate how each type of

EXHIBIT 21.5 **Treatment of Provisions and Reserves**

Classification	Examples	Treatment in NOPAT[1]	Treatment in invested capital	Treatment in valuation
Ongoing operating provisions	Product returns and warranties	Deduct provisions from revenue to determine NOPAT.	Deduct reserve from operating assets to determine invested capital.	Provision is part of free cash flow.
Long-term operating provisions	Plant decommissioning costs and unfunded retirement plans	Deduct operating portion from revenue to determine NOPAT, and treat interest portion as nonoperating.	Treat reserve as a debt equivalent.	Deduct reserve's present value from the value of operations.
Nonoperating provisions	Restructuring charges, such as expected severance due to layoffs	Convert accrual provision into cash provision, and treat as nonoperating.	Treat reserve as a debt equivalent.	Deduct reserve's present value from the value of operations.
Income-smoothing provisions	Provisions for the sole purpose of income smoothing	Eliminate provision by converting accrual provision into cash provision.	Treat reserve as an equity equivalent.	Since income-smoothing provisions are noncash, there is no effect.

[1] Net operating profit after taxes.

EXHIBIT 21.6 **Provisions and Reserves in the Financial Statements**

$ million

	Today	Year 1	Year 2	Year 3	Year 4
Income statement					
Revenue		1,000.0	1,200.0	1,400.0	1,600.0
Operating costs		(750.0)	(900.0)	(1,190.0)	(1,200)
Decommissioning asset, depreciation[1]		(7.7)	(7.7)	(7.7)	—
Decommissioning reserve, accretion[2]		(15.0)	(16.5)	(18.2)	—
Provision for product defects[2]		(100.0)	(120.0)	(140.0)	(160.0)
Income-smoothing provision[2]		(40.0)	(40.0)	80.0	—
Operating profit, as reported		87.3	115.8	124.1	240.0
Provision for restructuring		—	(30.0)	—	—
Net income		87.3	85.8	124.1	240.0
Balance sheet					
Decommissioning asset, gross	77.1	77.1	77.1	77.1	—
Accumulated depreciation	(54.0)	(61.7)	(69.4)	(77.1)	—
Decommissioning asset, net	23.1	15.4	7.7	—	—
Other operating assets	700.0	840.0	980.0	1,120.0	—
Total assets	723.1	855.4	987.7	1,120.0	—
Reserve for decommissioning	150.3	165.3	181.8	—	—
Reserve for product defects	100.0	120.0	140.0	160.0	—
Reserve for restructuring	—	—	30.0	—	—
Reserve for income smoothing	—	40.0	80.0	—	—
Equity	472.9	530.1	555.9	960.0	—
Total liabilities and equity	723.1	855.4	987.7	1,120.0	—

[1] Typically embedded in depreciation and amortization.

[2] Typically embedded in operating costs, such as cost of sales.

provision would be treated from a valuation perspective. Historical statements should be adjusted in the same way as forecast statements. For simplicity, we assume the company pays no taxes and has no debt.

The process for adjusting the financial statements depends on the type of provision. Exhibit 21.7 shows how to reorganize the income statement and balance sheet for each provision for our hypothetical company.

Provisions Related to Ongoing Operations   A company that warranties a product or self-insures a service must create a corresponding liability when that product or service is sold. If the reserve is related to the ongoing operations, the reserve should be treated the same way as other non-interest-bearing liabilities (for example, accounts payable and wages payable). Specifically, the income statement provision should be deducted from revenues to determine EBITA. The corresponding balance sheet reserve ($100 million) should be netted against operating assets ($723.1 million) to measure invested capital ($623.1 million). Since the provision and reserve are treated as operating items, they are integrated directly into free cash flow and should not be valued separately.

EXHIBIT 21.7 **ROIC with Provisions and Reserve**

$ million

	Today	Year 1	Year 2	Year 3	Year 4
NOPAT					
Operating profit, as reported		87.3	115.8	124.1	240.0
Decommissioning reserve, accretion		15.0	16.5	18.2	—
Increase (Decrease) in income-smoothing reserve		40.0	40.0	(80.0)	—
NOPAT		142.3	172.3	62.3	240.0
Reconciliation to net income					
Net income		87.3	85.8	124.1	240.0
Decommissioning reserve, accretion		15.0	16.5	18.2	—
Increase (Decrease) in income-smoothing reserve		40.0	40.0	(80.0)	—
Provision for restructuring		—	30.0	—	—
NOPAT		142.3	172.3	62.3	240.0
Invested capital					
Plant decommissioning, net	23.1	15.4	7.7	—	—
Other operating assets	700.0	840.0	980.0	1,120.0	—
Reserve for product defects	(100.0)	(120.0)	(140.0)	(160.0)	—
Invested capital	623.1	735.4	847.7	960.0	—
Reconciliation of invested capital					
Reserve for plant decommissioning	150.3	165.3	181.8	—	—
Reserve for restructuring	—	—	30.0	—	—
Reserve for income smoothing	—	40.0	80.0	—	—
Equity	472.9	530.1	555.9	960.0	—
Invested capital	623.1	735.4	847.7	960.0	—
ROIC on beginning-of-year capital, %		22.8	23.4	7.3	25.0

Long-Term Operating Provisions   Sometimes, when a company decommissions a plant, it must pay for cleanup and other costs. Assume our hypothetical company owns a plant that will operate for ten years and requires $200 million in decommissioning costs. Rather than expense the cash outflow in a lump sum at the time of decommissioning, a company will instead record the present value of the cost as both an asset and a liability at the time of investment.[3] In this case, the ten-year present value of $200 million at 10 percent equals $77.1 million.[4] It's as if the company borrowed $77.1 million and holds the money in restricted cash to fund the future decommissioning outlay.

Once the decommissioning asset and reserve are recognized, the decommissioning asset is depreciated (somewhat like cash being paid into an outside fund set aside for cleanup), and the reserve is grown (as if the debt accumulates unpaid interest charges). As a result, the decommissioning cost is recognized over the life of the asset, instead of in a lump sum at closing.

If the decommissioning costs are substantial, as with a nuclear power plant or a mine, the costs will be presented in the company's footnotes. We show a sample note in Exhibit 21.8. In Panel A of Exhibit 21.8, the decommissioning asset declines by $7.7 million each year. This expense is computed using straight-line depreciation on the original decommissioning asset.

EXHIBIT 21.8 **Provisions and Reserves in the Notes**

$ million

	Today	Year 1	Year 2	Year 3
Panel A: Change in the asset account				
Decommissioning asset, starting	30.8	23.1	15.4	7.7
Depreciation	(7.7)	(7.7)	(7.7)	(7.7)
Decommissioning asset, ending	23.1	15.4	7.7	—
Panel B: Change in the liability account				
Decommissioning reserve, starting	136.6	150.3	165.3	181.8
Accretion expense at 10%	13.7	15. 0	16.5	18.2
Payout	—	—	—	(200.0)
Decommissioning reserve, ending	150.3	165.3	181.8	—
Panel C: Income statement				
Decommissioning asset, depreciation	7.7	7.7	7.7	—
Decommissioning reserve, accretion	15.0	16.5	18.2	—
Decommissioning expense	22.7	24.2	25.9	—

[3] In the United States, asset retirement obligations (AROs) are governed by SFAS 143. Entities covered by IFRS use IAS 37, where the AROs are called "provisions."

[4] In Exhibit 21.6, the current year represents the seventh year of the plant's expected ten-year life. Consequently, the decommissioning asset and the decommissioning reserve no longer equal their initial value of $77.1 million. Instead, the decommissioning asset has been depreciated seven years to $23.1 million, using straight-line depreciation. Conversely, the decommission reserve grows annually at the discount rate. As a result, the current-year reserve equals $77.1 million $\times (1.10)^7$, which equals $150.3 million.

In Panel B, the decommissioning reserve grows each year by an ever-increasing amount, computed at 10 percent of the prior year's ending reserve. This expense, which mimics interest, is known as accretion. In year 1, the current-year reserve of $150.3 million grows by $15.0 million due to accretion. The income statement presented in Exhibit 21.6 reports both depreciation and accretion as operating items, often embedded within depreciation and operating costs, respectively.

To estimate NOPAT, invested capital, ROIC, and FCF, apply the guiding principles presented in Chapter 11. When reorganizing the income statement, treat depreciation as an operating item. Conversely, since accretion mimics interest, do not include accretion in NOPAT; instead, include it in the reconciliation to net income, next to interest expense. NOPAT and the reconciliation to net income are computed in the top portion of Exhibit 21.7. To reorganize the balance sheet, classify the decommissioning asset (which is comparable to restricted cash) as part of invested capital and the reserve as a debt equivalent. Invested capital and its reconciliation are presented in the bottom half of Exhibit 21.7. To compute free cash flow, start with NOPAT, add back depreciation of the decommissioning asset (since it is noncash), and subtract investments in invested capital. Free cash flow is presented in Exhibit 21.9.

When you treat the plant closure reserve as a debt equivalent, the interest expense and reserve drawdown will not flow through free cash flow. Therefore, subtract the current reported reserve ($150.3 million as of today) from the value of operations ($858.9 million) to determine equity value. The value of operations, which includes this and other deductions, is converted into equity value in Exhibit 21.10.

EXHIBIT 21.9 **Free Cash Flow with Provisions and Reserves**

$ million

	Year 1	Year 2	Year 3	Year 4	
NOPAT	142.3	172.3	62.3	240.0	
Depreciation	7.7	7.7	7.7	—	
Gross cash flow	150.0	180.0	70.0	240.0	
Investment in invested capital	(120.0)	(120.0)	(120.0)	960.0	Present value at
Free cash flow	30.0	60.0	(50.0)	1,200.0	10% = 858.9
Reconciliation of free cash flow					
Provision for restructuring	—	30.0	—	—	
(Increase) Decrease in restructuring reserve	—	(30.0)	30.0	—	Present value at
Cash-based restructuring provision	—	—	30.0		10% = 22.5
Decommissioning reserve, accretion	15.0	16.5	18.2	—	
(Increase) Decrease in decommissioning reserve	(15.0)	(16.5)	181.8	—	
Dividends	40.0	70.0	—	1,120.0	
Equity repurchases (issues)	(10.0)	(10.0)	(280.0)	80.0	
Free cash flow	30.0	60.0	(50.0)	1,200.0	

EXHIBIT 21.10 **Enterprise DCF with Provisions and Reserves**

$ million

Valuation		Methodology
Value of operations	858.9	Summation of discounted cash flow
Value of restructuring provision	(22.5)	Present value at 10% (debt equivalent)
Reserve for plant decommissioning	(150.3)	Reported on balance sheet (debt equivalent)
Equity value	686.1	

One-Time Restructuring Provisions   When management decides to restructure a company, it will often recognize certain future expenses (e.g., severance payments) immediately. We recommend treating one-time provisions as nonoperating and treating the corresponding reserve as a debt equivalent. In year 2, our hypothetical company declared a $30 million restructuring provision, which will be paid in year 3 (see Exhibit 21.6). Since the restructuring is nonoperating, it is not deducted from revenues to determine NOPAT. Rather, it is included in the reconciliation to net income (see Exhibit 21.7). Because we plan to value the provision on a cash basis, the noncash reserve is treated as a debt equivalent and therefore is not netted against operating assets to determine invested capital.

Since nonoperating income and expenses do not flow through free cash flow, the restructuring expense must be valued separately on a cash basis. To convert accrual-based restructuring expenses to cash, start with the restructuring expense, and subtract the increase in the restructuring reserve. This leads to a cash-based restructuring provision of $0 in year 2 and $30 million in year 3 (see Exhibit 21.9 for free cash flow and its reconciliation). The present value of the nonoperating cash flow stream equals $22.5 million, which must be deducted from the value of operations to determine equity value, as shown in Exhibit 21.10.

Income-Smoothing Provisions   Except in limited circumstances, provisions to purposefully smooth earnings are not allowed under International Financial Reporting Standards (IFRS) or U.S. Generally Accepted Accounting Principles (GAAP). To prevent purposeful earnings smoothing or even the perception of it, many companies use a third party to estimate key provisions. The limited situations in which companies can use provisions to smooth earnings include government contractors adjusting the estimated total profit of a long-term contract if there is a change in estimated costs. This adjustment is spread over the remaining life of the project. If the adjustment results in an overall loss for the contract, GAAP requires that the entire loss be recognized immediately.

In Exhibit 21.6, our hypothetical company was able to show a smooth growth in reported EBITA and net income by using a smoothing provision. To make our intentions clear, we choose a straightforward title for the account,

"Income-smoothing provision," but in practice, companies will use subtler wording, such as "Other provisions." For our hypothetical company, a provision was recorded in years 1 and 2 and was reversed in year 3. By using an income-smoothing provision, the company hid its year 3 decline in operating performance (operating costs rose from 75 percent to 85 percent of sales).

To evaluate the company's performance properly, eliminate any income-smoothing provisions. Do this by adding the income-smoothing provision back to reported EBITA (essentially undoing the income-smoothing provision). In this way, we are converting the provision to cash, rather than accounting for it as an accrual, and subsequently need to treat the reserve as an equity equivalent (using a process identical to the one for deferred taxes). Since income-smoothing provisions are entirely noncash, they don't affect free cash flow or valuation.

Provisions and Taxes

In most situations, provisions are tax deductible only when cash is disbursed, not when the provision is reported. Thus, most provisions will give rise to deferred-tax assets. For example, a $30 million noncash restructuring charge would lead to a $30 million restructuring reserve. If the restructuring charge is tax deductible on the GAAP income statement, retained earnings will drop by only $21 million (assuming a 30 percent tax rate). Since the increase in the restructuring reserve does not match the drop in retained earnings, the balance sheet will not balance. To eliminate the difference, a $9 million deferred-tax asset is recognized.

For operating-related provisions, we recommend using cash, rather than accrual taxes. For nonoperating provisions, estimate the tax impact of the corresponding provision. Do not use book values, as they reflect past accounting and not necessarily future cash flow. For an in-depth discussion of deferred taxes, see Chapter 20.

CLOSING THOUGHTS

The accounting definition of nonoperating expense is narrow and limited to interest expense and a few other items. Therefore, the accounting definition of operating profits can include many one-time and other nonoperating items. Always start your financial analysis by separating ongoing operating-related items from nonoperating items on the income statement. This will create a better picture of the company's performance and its potential for generating future cash flow. In some cases, the proper classification of a particular expense will be unclear. But don't let this distract you from the task at hand. A proper valuation will not depend on how the item is treated, as long as you include it somewhere and treat it consistently.

22

Leases

Many companies, especially retailers and airlines, lease assets from other companies rather than purchasing the assets outright. They do this for many reasons, including to increase flexibility and to lower taxes.

In the past, clever use of accounting rules allowed companies to keep certain assets and debts off balance sheets. These included leased assets and their corresponding debts, securitized assets such as receivables, and unfunded retirement obligations. In some cases, this helped companies manage cash flow or take advantage of alternative routes to raise funds. In other instances, off-balance-sheet items were used to artificially boost results such as earnings per share or return on assets.

In response, the International Accounting Standards Board (IASB) and the Financial Accounting Standards Board (FASB) made significant changes to their guidelines. Since 2019, companies have been required to capitalize nearly all asset leases, including fixed-payment operating leases, on their balance sheets.[1] This stands in stark contrast to past guidelines, under which a company could rent an asset, even for long periods, and recognize only the periodic rental expense.

The new accounting guidelines for fixed-payment operating leases bring the treatment of operating leases closer to the underlying principles of this book. Implementation of the new guidelines, however, differs slightly across accounting bodies, so incorporating operating leases into your valuation still requires special care.

This chapter begins with a review of the updated accounting rules, their differences across accounting bodies, and the way they are presented on

---

[1] The International Accounting Standards Board (IASB) published IFRS 16, "Leases," in January 2016, and the Financial Accounting Standards Board (FASB) issued Accounting Standards Update (ASU) 2016-02, "Leases (Topic 842)," in February 2016.

the financial statements. We then outline how to incorporate fixed-payment operating leases into an enterprise valuation. Since operating leases influence every aspect of valuation, their implementation offers an excellent opportunity to review the valuation principles outlined in Part Two. Next, we apply the leasing framework to Costco Wholesale, which employs a mix of finance leases, fixed-payment operating leases, and variable-payment operating leases. The chapter concludes with a discussion of an alternative approach to valuing leases, which can be helpful when benchmarking across companies.

ACCOUNTING FOR OPERATING LEASES

Although both IASB and FASB now require capitalization of operating leases, there are differences in implementing the new standards. For companies that use International Financial Reporting Standards (IFRS), nearly all leases greater than one year are treated as "finance" leases, meaning that leased assets and their corresponding liabilities are capitalized on the balance sheet, and the lease expense is appropriately split between depreciation and interest expense. The enterprise valuation methodology outlined in Part Two will correctly incorporate leases under IFRS without further adjustment.

Capitalizing leases under U.S. Generally Accepted Accounting Principles (GAAP) is more complicated. Companies classify asset leases into either "finance" leases, as described in the previous paragraph, or "operating" leases. A lease is classified as a finance lease if cumulative payments to the lessor exceed certain thresholds.[2] Finance leases are not typically visible on the financial statements, as each element is embedded within another financial statement account. The leased asset is included either in property, plant, and equipment or in other assets, while the corresponding liability is reported within short-term or long-term debt or an "other" account. As under IFRS, finance leases under GAAP do not require special treatment.

In contrast, operating lease expenses under GAAP are not properly disaggregated. Neither fixed-payment nor variable-payment operating leases distinguish between depreciation and interest payments. Instead, the entire expense is incorporated into operating expenses, such as cost of sales or general expenses, depending on the asset type. Although the balance sheet now reflects fixed-payment operating leases, companies reporting under GAAP need to reorganize the income statement to accurately value these expenses.

To illustrate the accounting behind operating leases, we will analyze and value FlightCo, a hypothetical airline that uses operating leases. To avoid the

---

[2] A lease is classified as a finance lease if the lease term is greater than 75 percent of the useful life, if the present value of lease payments is greater than 90 percent of the original cost, if the asset is specialized and has no value to the lessor once returned, or if ownership of the asset is transferred to the lessee at the end of the lease.

EXHIBIT 22.1 **FlightCo: Valuation of the Operating Lease**

$ million

	Lease payment	Discount factor	Discounted cash flow
Year 1	9.0	0.952	8.6
Year 2	9.0	0.907	8.2
Year 3	12.0	0.864	10.4
Present value of operating lease			27.1

unnecessary complexities of continuing value, we assume the company leases only one aircraft and plans to liquidate at the end of the third year. At that point, parts inventory is sold, general obligation debt is retired, and a liquidating dividend is paid. The lease is classified as an operating lease because the contract length is significantly shorter than the life of the underlying asset.

Exhibit 22.1 presents the valuation of FlightCo's operating lease, using discounted cash flow. The lease has payments of $9 million, $9 million, and $12 million in years 1, 2, and 3, respectively. Using discounted cash flow at a cost of debt of 5 percent, the lease has a present value of $27.1 million. Because the contract life is only three years, the present value of lease payments is significantly lower than the asset's actual value. Later in this chapter, under "An Alternative Method for Valuing Operating Leases," we present a valuation method for estimating the full value of leased assets, using data in the annual report. This is helpful when benchmarking two companies that have different financing policies.

Exhibit 22.2 presents the financial statement accounts related to leases for FlightCo and shows how the accounts evolve over time. Although the evolution is neither required for valuation nor disclosed in practice, it will be helpful for explaining the accounting behind leases.

On the income statement, U.S. GAAP requires that the total lease payments of $30 million be spread evenly over the life of the contract, even though the cash payments change over time.[3] The annual lease expense is recorded on the income statement at $10 million per year. The lease payment covers the depreciation of the asset, as well as financial compensation for the lessor.

On the balance sheet, the present value of lease payments is recorded as a right-of-use asset, and the corresponding liability is recorded as an operating lease. Both accounts start at $27.1 million—the present value of the lease. While the two accounts will match when initially recorded, they will not match over time if cash payments vary year to year. That is the case in our FlightCo example. The right-of-use asset will decline $8.6 million in the first year (from $27.1 million to $18.5 million), equal to the lease expense

[3] Some might think the expense accounting for operating leases mirrors that of finance leases; it does not. In a finance lease, the present value is straight-line amortized over the life of the lease. If FlightCo's lease were a finance lease, amortization expense would equal $9.03 million per year for three years. Lease amortization is included in the depreciation and amortization. Lease interest expense is calculated on the liability and included in interest expense.

EXHIBIT 22.2 **FlightCo: Financial Statement Accounts Related to Leases**

$ million

	Year 1	Year 2	Year 3
Income statement			
Lease expense	10.0	10.0	10.0
Assets: Right-of-use asset			
Right-of-use asset, start	27.1	18.5	9.4
Lease expense	(10.0)	(10.0)	(10.0)
Embedded interest[1]	1.4	1.0	0.6
Right-of-use asset, end	18.5	9.4	—
Liabilities: Operating lease			
Lease principal, start	27.1	19.5	11.4
Interest at 5%	1.4	1.0	0.6
Lease payment	(9.0)	(9.0)	(12.0)
Lease principal, end	19.5	11.4	—

[1] Under U.S. GAAP, the interest on the operating lease liability is netted against the lease expense to determine the annual reduction in the right-of-use asset.

of $10.0 million less interest of $1.4 million. (As if this were not confusing enough, interest is calculated on the operating lease *liability*, not the asset.) In the same year, the operating lease liability declines by $7.6 million (from $27.1 million to $19.5 million), equal to the cash payment of $9.0 million less the interest of $1.4 million.

Because of the mismatch described in the previous paragraph, most companies report right-of-use assets that differ from their operating lease liabilities. For example, Costco Wholesale reported $2,713 million in right-of-use assets in 2023. In contrast, their current and long-term operating lease liabilities amounted to $2,646 million, resulting in a $67 million difference. In some companies, the discrepancy between these values can exceed 10 percent.

VALUING A COMPANY WITH OPERATING LEASES

Incorporating operating leases into an enterprise valuation follows the same process outlined in Part Two of this book. We use four steps to value FlightCo:

1. Reorganize the financial statements. During the reorganization, adjust earnings before interest, taxes, and amortization (EBITA) upward by removing the implicit interest in operating lease expense. Adjust operating taxes to determine adjusted net operating profit after taxes (NOPAT).

2. Estimate free cash flow (FCF), using adjusted NOPAT and changes in the right-of-use asset. Liabilities classified as operating leases should be treated as debt and incorporated into the reconciliation of free cash flow.

3. Estimate a weighted average cost of capital (WACC) that includes the value of the operating lease liability as debt.

4. Value the enterprise by discounting free cash flow (based on the adjusted NOPAT) at the WACC, including operating leases. Subtract traditional debt and the value of operating lease liability from enterprise value to determine equity value.

As long as you treat right-of-use assets as purchased equipment and treat the operating lease liability as a form of debt, your results will theoretically be consistent. Only operating profit requires an upward adjustment for implicit lease interest. Failing to adjust operating profit will undervalue equity, because implicit interest would be double-counted: once as part of lease expense and again as part of lease value when subtracting the value of leases from enterprise value to get to equity value.

Reorganizing the Financial Statements

To start the valuation of FlightCo, first reorganize the financial statements. Exhibit 22.3 presents the income statement, balance sheet, and statement of equity for FlightCo.

EXHIBIT 22.3 **FlightCo: Financial Statements**

$ million

	Year 0	Year 1	Year 2	Year 3
Income statement				
Revenue		75.0	75.0	75.0
Operating expenses		(40.0)	(40.0)	(40.0)
Operating lease expense[1]		(10.0)	(10.0)	(10.0)
Operating profit, unadjusted		25.0	25.0	25.0
Interest expense, debt		(0.4)	(0.3)	(0.3)
Earnings before taxes		24.6	24.7	24.7
Income taxes at 20%		(4.9)	(4.9)	(4.9)
Net income		19.7	19.7	19.8
Balance sheet				
Inventory	15.0	15.0	15.0	—
Right-of-use assets	27.1	18.5	9.4	—
Total assets	42.1	33.5	24.4	—
Operating leases	27.1	19.5	11.4	—
Debt	7.8	6.6	5.0	—
Equity	7.2	7.4	8.0	—
Liabilities and equity	42.1	33.5	24.4	—
Statement of equity				
Equity, start		7.2	7.4	8.0
Net income		19.7	19.7	19.8
Dividends and/or share repurchases		(19.5)	(19.1)	(27.8)
Equity, end		7.4	8.0	—

[1] Typically embedded in operating expenses, such as cost of sales.

EXHIBIT 22.4 **FlightCo: NOPAT and Reconciliation to Net Income**

$ million

	Year 1	Year 2	Year 3
EBITA,[1] unadjusted	25.0	25.0	25.0
Operating lease interest	1.4	1.0	0.6
EBITA, adjusted for lease interest	26.4	26.0	25.6
Operating taxes at 20%	(5.3)	(5.2)	(5.1)
NOPAT[2]	21.1	20.8	20.5
Reconciliation to net income			
Net income	19.7	19.7	19.8
Interest expense, debt	0.4	0.3	0.3
Operating lease interest	1.4	1.0	0.6
Interest tax shield at 20%	(0.3)	(0.3)	(0.2)
NOPAT[2]	21.1	20.8	20.5

[1] Earnings before interest, taxes, and amortization.

[2] Net operating profit after taxes.

Using the information from FlightCo's financial statements, Exhibit 22.4 presents a calculation of NOPAT and its reconciliation to net income. The process starts by adding back the implicit interest embedded in the operating lease expense. To estimate implicit interest, multiply the prior year's operating lease liability by the interest rate used to value the operating lease. The company will typically disclose the weighted average discount rate in its note on leases, but if it does not, use the yield to maturity on AA-rated debt.[4] In the first year, embedded interest equals the operating lease liability of $27.1 million multiplied by the interest rate of 5 percent. Estimate implicit interest using the operating lease liability and not the right-of-use asset.

To calculate NOPAT, subtract operating taxes from adjusted operating profit. Operating taxes are estimated by multiplying operating profit by the operating tax rate. The resulting NOPAT for year 1 is $21.1 million. The tax shield for embedded interest will be incorporated into the cost of capital.

We do not present a reorganized balance sheet for FlightCo, as the simplified balance sheet already matches invested capital. In general, include the right-of-use asset as part of invested capital and the operating lease liability as a source of financing.

Estimating Free Cash Flow

Once the financial statements are reorganized, estimate free cash flow. Exhibit 22.5 presents the free cash flow statement and its reconciliation to cash flow to investors for FlightCo. Free cash flow starts with NOPAT. Since FlightCo does

[4] Leased assets are similar to secured debt and therefore present lower risk than unsecured debt. As AAA ratings are typically assigned to financial institutions, we use an AA rating for nonfinancial companies as a proxy for secured debt.

EXHIBIT 22.5 **FlightCo: Free Cash Flow and Its Reconciliation**

$ million

	Year 1	Year 2	Year 3
NOPAT	21.1	20.8	20.5
Decrease (Increase) in inventory	—	—	15.0
→ Decrease (Increase) in right-of-use assets	8.6	9.0	9.4
Free cash flow	29.7	29.8	44.9
Interest tax shield at 20%	0.3	0.3	0.2
Cash flow available for investors	30.1	30.1	45.1
Reconciliation of free cash flow			
Interest, debt	0.4	0.3	0.3
→ Interest, operating leases	1.4	1.0	0.6
Decrease (Increase) in debt	1.2	1.6	5.0
→ Decrease (Increase) in operating leases	7.6	8.0	11.4
Flows to debt holders	10.6	10.9	17.3
Dividends	19.5	19.1	27.8
Cash flow to investors	30.1	30.1	45.1

not own property or equipment, there is no add-back for depreciation.[5] From this value, subtract increases in working capital (inventory) and long-term assets (in this case, the right-of-use assets). Since both accounts are declining over time, they are positive numbers.

Note in Exhibit 22.5 how the sum of operating lease interest plus the decrease in right-of-use assets each year equals the operating lease expense in Exhibit 22.3. Essentially, the valuation process eliminates the entire lease expense for existing assets from free cash flow. At the completion of the valuation, the lease of existing assets will be valued not as part of free cash flow but rather as debt. Consistent with fundamental finance principles, this process separates investing flows from the manner in which they are financed.

When reconciling cash flow to investors, treat embedded interest on operating leases and the change in the operating lease liability as a flow to debt holders. Again, note in Exhibit 22.5 how the total of these two accounts matches the *cash-based* lease payment initially reported in Exhibit 22.1. Financing and its associated taxes should not be part of free cash flow.

Incorporating Operating Leases into Financial Projections

To forecast right-of-use assets, use the forecasting process introduced in Chapter 13. Link right-of-use assets to sales or a quantity-based measure, such as the number of units sold. In the airline industry, units are represented by

[5] To determine free cash flow, we incorporate the change in the right-of-use asset, which for FlightCo is decreasing over time. The positive value generated by the decline mimics the depreciation add-back. Essentially, the cash flows from capitalizing a lease are identical to those from purchasing an asset financed with debt.

the number of available seat-miles, often referred to as ASMs. Make sure the mix of purchased and leased assets is consistent with the amount of capacity necessary to conduct operations.

Set the operating lease liability as a percentage of the right-of-use asset. While this estimation method is far from precise, flows to and from financing do not affect an enterprise-based valuation. Instead, financing affects valuation only through the target capital structure set in the weighted average cost of capital. If helpful, you can model the combination of operating leases and debt to the target capital structure in your financial statements, but it is not required.

Estimating the Cost of Capital

To discount free cash flow, use the weighted average cost of capital inclusive of the value of operating leases. Exhibit 22.6 presents the weighted average cost of capital for FlightCo.

We assume the company will maintain its current capital structure of 40 percent debt to value, inclusive of leases. Total debt equals the sum of the operating lease liability of $27.1 million and traditional debt of $7.8 million, divided by enterprise value, estimated at $87.4 million. When estimating enterprise value, include operating leases as well. For FlightCo, the mix of operating leases and debt will change over time, but we set the combination to be stable at 40 percent of enterprise value. Since operating leases and interest expense are tax deductible, reduce the cost of capital for operating leases and debt by the company's marginal tax rate.[6]

In the calculations for this example, the cost of equity is provided. In practice, the cost of equity must be estimated using beta. Following the principles of Chapter 15, start by estimating an industry unlevered beta. Unlever each company's beta using a debt-to-equity ratio adjusted for operating leases.

EXHIBIT 22.6 **FlightCo: Weighted Average Cost of Capital (WACC)**

%

Source of capital	Value, $ million	Proportion of total capital	Cost of capital	Marginal tax rate	After-tax cost of capital	Contribution to weighted average
Operating leases[1]	27.1	31.0	5.0	20.0	4.0	1.2
Debt	7.8	9.0	5.0	20.0	4.0	0.4
Equity	52.4	60.0	12.0		12.0	7.2
WACC	87.4	100.0				8.8

[1] The present value of operating leases, found in the liabilities section of the balance sheet.

[6] Some governments impose limits on the amount of interest that can be deducted for tax purposes. Consequently, tax professionals often seek alternative financing options that offer deductible expenses. Leasing can provide tax-deductible benefits, even when interest expenses are not deductible.

Next, to determine the target company's beta, relever the unlevered beta to the target company's capital structure, again inclusive of leases.

Moving from Enterprise Value to Equity Value

To calculate enterprise value, discount free cash flow at the weighted average cost of capital, both inclusive of leases. Exhibit 22.7 shows the enterprise DCF valuation for FlightCo.

Since free cash flow excludes future payments related to existing operating leases, the value of operating leases must be deducted from enterprise value to determine intrinsic equity value. For FlightCo, enterprise value is estimated at $87.4 million. Deducting the present value of the operating lease liability ($27.1 million) and debt of $7.8 million leads to an equity value of $52.4 million.

Valuation Using Cash Flow to Equity

In general, we do not recommend a valuation model based on cash flow to equity, because it mixes assets of different risks and commingles operating performance with the capital structure. If implemented properly, however, a cash-flow-to-equity valuation can confirm the accuracy of the enterprise DCF process described in this chapter. It can also provide insight into choices made during the capitalization process.

Exhibit 22.8 presents cash flow to equity for FlightCo. In this exhibit, each line item represents actual cash flowing into or out of the company, from the equity holder's perspective. In the equity model, do not capitalize lease expense. Instead, deduct the cash payments paid to the lessor when they occur. Since leases are expensed and not capitalized, do not include either the change in the right-of-use asset or the change in the operating lease liability in cash flow to equity. This stands in contrast to debt flows, where both

EXHIBIT 22.7 **FlightCo: Enterprise DCF Valuation**

Forecast year	Free cash flow (FCF), $ million	Discount factor at 8.8%	Present value of FCF, $ million
Year 1	29.7	0.919	27.3
Year 2	29.8	0.845	25.2
Year 3	44.9	0.776	34.9
Value of operations			87.4
Less: Operating leases[1]			(27.1)
Less: Debt			(7.8)
Equity value			52.4

[1] The present value of operating leases, found in the liabilities section of the balance sheet.

EXHIBIT 22.8 **FlightCo: Cash Flow to Equity Holders**

$ million

	Year 1	Year 2	Year 3
Revenue	75.0	75.0	75.0
Operating costs	(40.0)	(40.0)	(40.0)
Lease payments[1]	(9.0)	(9.0)	(12.0)
Interest expense, debt	(0.4)	(0.3)	(0.3)
Earnings before taxes	25.6	25.7	22.7
Income taxes	(4.9)	(4.9)	(4.9)
Earnings after taxes	20.7	20.7	17.8
Change in inventory	0.0	0.0	15.0
Increase (Decrease) in debt	(1.2)	(1.6)	(5.0)
Cash flow to equity	19.5	19.1	27.8

[1] Cash-based lease payments.

EXHIBIT 22.9 **FlightCo: Valuation Using Cash Flow to Equity**

Forecast year	Cash flow to equity (CFE), $ million	Discount factor at 12%	Present value of CFE, $ million
Year 1	19.5	0.893	17.4
Year 2	19.1	0.797	15.3
Year 3	27.8	0.712	19.8
Equity value			52.4

interest expense and payoff of debt are included in the calculation, since they represent actual cash flows.

Exhibit 22.9 values cash flow to equity at the cost of equity. The cost of equity used to discount equity cash flows equals the cost of equity used to determine the weighted average cost of capital. Though one might expect that the cost of equity should fall, since the leverage associated with operating leases is being ignored, this is not the case. Merely switching models does not change the risk to equity holders, so the cost of equity should not change either.

Discounting cash flow to equity at a 12 percent cost of equity leads to an equity valuation of $52.4 million. Not surprisingly, this is the same valuation as we calculated by using the enterprise DCF model.

ADJUSTING FOR LEASES IN PRACTICE

To incorporate leases into the valuation of a real company, begin by searching the annual report for relevant lease information. While some details are presented in the company's consolidated financial statements, many are subtly embedded within other accounts. Therefore, it is essential to consult the notes to the financial statements to uncover all necessary details. In the case of Costco

EXHIBIT 22.10 **Costco: Note on Leases, 2023**

Lease assets and liabilities	2022	2023
Assets		
Operating lease right-of-use assets	2,774	2,713
Finance lease assets[1]	1,620	1,325
Total lease assets	4,394	4,038
Liabilities		
Current		
Operating lease liabilities[2]	239	220
Finance lease liabilities[2]	245	129
Long-term		
Operating lease liabilities	2,482	2,426
Finance lease liabilities[3]	1,383	1,303
Total lease liabilities	4,349	4,078

Lease costs	2022	2023
Operating lease costs[4]	297	309
Finance lease costs:		
Amortization of lease assets[4]	128	169
Interest on lease liabilities[5]	45	54
Finance lease costs	173	223
Variable lease costs[4]	157	160
Total lease costs	627	692
Weighted-average discount rate		
Operating leases	2.26%	2.47%
Finance leases	4.47%	3.97%

[1] Included in other long-term assets in the consolidated balance sheets.

[2] Included in other current liabilities in the consolidated balance sheets.

[3] Included in other long-term liabilities in the consolidated balance sheets.

[4] Included in selling, general, and administrative expenses and merchandise costs in the consolidated statements of income.

[5] Included in interest expense and merchandise costs in the consolidated statements of income.

Source: Costco 2023 annual report.

Wholesale, their lease information is detailed in Note 5, "Leases," presented in Exhibit 22.10.

On the left side of Exhibit 22.10, we present Costco's disclosure of assets and liabilities related to leases. Only operating lease right-of-use assets and long-term lease liabilities are reported explicitly on the balance sheet, while other items are embedded within different accounts. For instance, the current portion of operating lease liabilities is included under other current liabilities. It is crucial to separate lease liabilities from other current liabilities, such as wages payable, to avoid underestimating the company's leverage and the interest costs embedded within operating expenses.

In Exhibit 22.11, we use the information disclosed in Exhibit 22.10 to estimate the embedded interest related to operating leases. No adjustment is required for finance leases, as the embedded interest in a finance lease is already separated and included in interest expense. Due to the differences in accounting for fixed-payment and variable-payment operating leases, we separate the calculations accordingly.

A fixed-payment lease is one where the future payments are predetermined. In contrast, a variable-payment lease specifies that payments will depend on an economic or operational metric, such as revenue or growth in the consumer price index (CPI). For the uncertain portion of a variable lease payment, no right-of-use asset or corresponding liability is recognized in the financial statements. As a result, unlike fixed-payment operating leases, the right-of-use asset and related liability for variable-payment leases must be estimated and incorporated into the reorganized balance sheet.

EXHIBIT 22.11 **Costco: Lease Adjustments, 2023**

Fixed-payment operating lease liabilities		Variable-payment operating lease liabilities	
Current liabilities, 2022	239.0	Fixed-payment assets, 2022	2,774.0
Long-term liabilities, 2022	2,482.0	/ Fixed-payment lease cost, 2022	297.0
Operating lease liabilities	2,721.0	Fixed-payment lease multiple	9.3
× Weighted-average discount rate	2.47%	Variable-payment lease cost, 2022	157.0
Interest embedded in SG&A, 2023	67.2	× Fixed-payment lease multiple	9.3
		Variable-payment liabilities, 2022	1,466.4
		× Weighted-average discount rate	2.47%
		Interest embedded in SG&A, 2023	36.2

The left side of Exhibit 22.11 presents the estimation of interest expense related to fixed-payment operating leases, while the right side does the same for variable-payment leases. To estimate the interest for fixed-payment operating leases in 2023, we multiply the aggregate operating lease liabilities in the prior year, both current and long-term, by the weighted average discount rate: $2,721 million times 2.47 percent equals $67.2 million.

To determine the embedded interest for variable leases, we first estimate the value of the right-of-use asset related to variable leases. A proper valuation would discount future cash flows at the weighted average discount rate. However, since companies are not required to disclose variable lease forecasts, we apply a simplified approach. We assume that the ratio of asset value to lease cost, termed the lease multiple, will be the same for both fixed-payment and variable-payment leases. In 2022, the ratio of assets to lease cost for fixed-payment leases was $2,774 million divided by $297 million, or approximately 9.3 times. Applying this multiple to variable lease costs of $157.0 million yields an estimated $1,466 million in right-of-use assets for variable leases in 2022. To calculate the embedded interest in the upcoming year, we multiply $1,466 million by 2.47 percent, which equals $36.2 million in variable lease interest.

In Chapter 11, we reorganized Costco's balance sheet and income statement, including an adjustment for leases. In Exhibit 11.5, we added $1,466 million in variable lease assets to 2022 invested capital and reconciled 2022 total funds invested with $1,466 million in variable lease liabilities.[7] In Exhibit 11.10, we added $67.2 million in fixed-payment operating lease interest and $36.2 million in variable-payment lease interest to 2023 unadjusted EBITA to determine 2023 operating-only EBITA.

---

[7] Some researchers have argued that current accounting standards related to variable leases lead to debt being understated by 7.1 percent on average. For more, see J. Heese, A. Shin, and C. C. Y. Wang, "Variable Leases under ASC 842: First Evidence on Properties and Consequences," May 9, 2024, available at https://ssrn.com/abstract=4266529.

Adjusting Pre-2019 Financial Statements for Operating Leases

As time progresses, distortions caused by operating leases will be forgotten in the same way most investors have forgotten the adjustments required for the long-defunct pooling of interests prior to 2000. Until then, it is important to recognize that historical financial statements will remain unadjusted. To assure consistency in historical analysis prior to 2019, adjust historical statements to match current accounting policy.

Exhibit 22.12 presents the valuation of operating leases for Costco in 2019, the year before Costco adopted the new standard.[8] To value operating leases, we discount future lease payments at the cost of AA-rated debt. Lease commitments are reported in note 5 of Costco's 2019 annual report. The company reports only the first five years of lease payments year by year. Lease payments beyond 2024 are lumped into a single undiscounted number. At the bottom of Exhibit 22.12, we value the lump sum using an annuity formula. In the formula, set the cash flow equal to the 2024 lease payment. To estimate the number of years, divide the undiscounted lump sum by the 2024 rental payment. For Costco, the annuity value equals almost $1.8 billion. Since the annuity values the lump-sum payments beyond 2024 as of 2024, make sure to discount the result back to 2019, as you would any other cash flow.

EXHIBIT 22.12 **Costco: Operating Lease Valuation, 2019**

Forecast year	Rental commitments, $ million	Discount factor at 3.6%[1]	Present value of payments, $ million
2020	239.0	0.965	230.6
2021	229.0	0.931	213.2
2022	202.0	0.898	181.5
2023	193.0	0.867	167.3
2024	181.0	0.837	151.4
Value beyond 2024	1,757.1	0.837	1,470.0
Value of operating leases			2,414.0

Value beyond 2024, $ million

Rental commitments beyond 2024	2,206.0
/ Final-year rental payment	181.0
= Number of years remaining	12.19

Annuity value of $181.0 per year at 3.63% for 12.19 years = $1,757.1

[1] Yield to maturity on 10-year AA-rated debt.

Source: Costco 2019 annual report, note 5.

[8] Companies whose fiscal year ends after December 15 had to implement the new leasing standard in 2019. Since Costco's fiscal year ended on September 1, 2019, it chose to adopt the new standard in 2020.

AN ALTERNATIVE METHOD FOR VALUING OPERATING LEASES

To capitalize operating leases on the balance sheet, the company discounts future lease commitments at the company's borrowing rate. For short-term leases, this methodology will understate the actual value of the asset, since it ignores the residual value of the asset being returned to the lessor. Consider FlightCo, which rented an aircraft for three years of the plane's 40-year life. A new aircraft may cost $125 million, but three years of rental expense will be far lower. Although short-term leases offer strategic flexibility for the borrower, they result in an understatement of invested capital.[9]

While using the present value of lease payments in place of the true asset value will not bias the valuation, it will understate the value of the assets being deployed to run operations. (The error will be largest for short-term leases on long-term assets. In the case of finance leases, the error will be small, since the lease life more closely matches the asset life.) When benchmarking two companies, one that purchases assets and one that rents them, the comparison will not be like-for-like, even under new accounting standards.[10] Distortions to capital turnover will be largest when leased assets are a significant proportion of invested capital.

One way to create a like-for-like comparison for companies with different leasing policies is to estimate each company's asset value by using a perpetuity. To see how, let's examine the determinants of rental expense. To compensate the lessor properly, the rental expense includes compensation for the cost of financing the asset (at the cost of secured debt, denoted by k_d in the following equations) and the periodic depreciation of the asset (for which we assume straight-line depreciation). The following equation solves for periodic rental expense:

$$\text{Lease Expense}_t = \text{Asset Value}_{t-1}\left(k_d + \frac{1}{\text{Asset Life}}\right)$$

To estimate the asset's value, rearrange the equation as follows:

$$\text{Asset Value}_{t-1} = \frac{\text{Lease Expense}_t}{\left(k_d + \frac{1}{\text{Asset Life}}\right)}$$

Lease expense is disclosed in the notes, and the cost of debt can be estimated using AA-rated yields. This leaves only the asset life, which is often

[9] Lessors often charge a premium for the flexibility provided by short-term leasing agreements for long-lived assets. To ensure an accurate comparison between leasing and owning assets, exclude this premium from expenses. Including capital without removing the premium can distort the return on invested capital, particularly when the premium is substantial. Therefore, this alternative analysis is most effective for measuring capital productivity across companies with different financing policies, rather than value creation.

[10] In this section, we focus on the distortions to benchmarking caused by different leasing policies. Companies choose different leasing policies for many reasons, including flexibility and taxes.

unreported. If this is the case, search the notes for the type of asset being leased, and estimate an asset life appropriate to the asset type. As an alternative, Lim, Mann, and Mihov propose using property, plant, and equipment (PP&E) divided by annual depreciation.[11] In their research, they examined 7,000 firms over 20 years and computed the median asset life at 10.9 years.

CLOSING THOUGHTS

Recent changes in lease accounting have brought financial reporting much closer to the core principles of this book. Still, a proper valuation requires special care regarding operating leases. To inform better forecasts, adjust statements created prior to the accounting rules changes to incorporate operating leases. If you do not, apples-to-oranges comparisons may obscure crucial trends. For companies reporting under U.S. GAAP, be sure to remove any interest embedded in operating expenses. Failing to do so may lead to double-counting the embedded interest, which can skew your valuation downward. For companies with significant variable-rate operating leases, ensure these are capitalized to accurately assess ROIC and leverage.

[11] S. C. Lim, S. C. Mann, and V. T. Mihov, "Market Evaluation of Off–Balance Sheet Financing: You Can Run but You Can't Hide," EFMA 2004 Basel Meetings paper, European Financial Management Association (December 1, 2003).

23

Retirement Obligations

To attract and retain talent, most companies offer retirement benefits to employees. These benefits include fixed pension payments, tax-advantaged savings plans, and promises to provide medical benefits when the employee retires. In some countries, companies are required to set up separate funds to pay these benefits, but inconsistencies are common because of differences in regulations and tax policy. For example, in the United States, companies must set up separate funds for pension promises (known as defined-benefit plans) but not for promises of retiree medical benefits. If the value of investments does not fully fund future promises, the company will have unfunded retirement obligations. Since the company is responsible for any shortfalls and these obligations take precedence over equity, any accurate valuation must account for them.

This chapter explores how to analyze and value a company with pension and other retirement obligations. Changes to accounting standards have made the analysis easier, but it still requires careful thinking and reorganizing of financial statements. The challenges include deciding which part of the pension expense is operating versus nonoperating, reorganizing the balance sheet with unfunded or overfunded obligations, estimating the cost of capital for companies with pensions, and adjusting equity value to reflect unfunded (or overfunded) retirement obligations.

REORGANIZING THE FINANCIAL STATEMENTS WITH PENSIONS

Under past standards, accounting for pensions and other retirement obligations severely distorted the income statement and balance sheet, requiring numerous adjustments to correctly measure the impact of retirement obligations on the company's value. In response, accounting policy has changed, gradually bringing the accounting for retirement obligations in line with the underlying doctrines of this text.

For companies that report under U.S. Generally Accepted Accounting Principles (GAAP), the changes occurred over many decades. Under original accounting principles, companies did not recognize unfunded pension liabilities on their balance sheets. Rule changes in the 1980s required companies to record unfunded pension liabilities (though smoothing was allowed) as well as other postretirement obligations, including promised medical benefits. Starting in 2006, additional changes required companies to recognize the actual value of the unfunded (or overfunded) pension liability on the balance sheet without smoothing.[1]

Although the balance sheet reflected the value of unfunded pension liabilities after 2006, the pension expense continued to include both operating and nonoperating items. It included not only new benefits granted to employees, but also interest on the liability, returns on plan assets, and adjustments for actuarial changes. Starting in 2013 for companies that report using International Financial Reporting Standards (IFRS) and in 2018 for those that report under GAAP, nonoperating items were required to be excluded from pension expenses, aligning with the adjustments we recommended in earlier editions of this book.[2] Any new benefits granted to employees are now included in the appropriate operating expense, such as cost of sales or selling, general, and administrative (SG&A) expenses. All other items, such as interest expense, actuarial changes, and earnings, are classified as "other" expense.

Because of this, fewer adjustments to the financial statements for pensions and retirement benefits are needed for periods after the accounting changes—after 2013 for IFRS or 2018 for GAAP. However, if you are evaluating performance over a longer window, you must still adjust financial statements released before those changes.

Throughout the chapter, we will examine pension accounting using the American food manufacturer Kellanova, formerly known as Kellogg, as an example. Kellanova is an interesting case because, even though its pension obligations are almost fully funded, we still must dive into the details to make accurate adjustments for estimating invested capital, ROIC, and free cash flow. The necessary information to analyze pensions for Kellanova is in the footnotes of their financial statements—specifically, note 11, "Pension Benefits," and note 12, "Nonpension Postretirement and Postemployment

---

[1] Statement of Financial Accounting Standards (SFAS) 158 was passed by the Financial Accounting Standards Board (FASB) in September 2006.

[2] Accounting Standards Update (ASU) Number 2017-07 was passed by the FASB in March 2017. IAS 19 was first updated in June 2011, separating service cost from other expenses. A subsequent update to IAS 19, aligned with ASU 2017-07, was issued by the IASB in February 2018 to further enhance consistency in the accounting for employee benefits across different reporting frameworks.

Benefits."[3] These notes provide information on projected benefit obligations, the fair value of plan assets, and a breakout of the annual pension expense.

Reorganizing the Financial Statements

To reorganize the balance sheet, start by locating all the retirement-related assets and liabilities on the balance sheet. If these items are small, companies often include prepaid pension assets in other long-term assets and unfunded pension liabilities as part of other long-term liabilities, but the exact location will be disclosed in the pension note.

Exhibit 23.1 reports the funded status of Kellanova's defined-benefit plans and the location of the company's underfunding on the balance sheet, as reported in the company's notes. In 2023, Kellanova had $139 million in unfunded pension and other postretirement liabilities. This amount does not appear as a single value on the balance sheet. Instead, the net underfunding is disaggregated across four accounts, including $512 million embedded in other assets, $16 million embedded in other current liabilities, a pension liability of $613 million, and $22 million embedded in other liabilities.[4] A company can have both excess pension assets and unfunded pension liabilities, because it may have multiple pension plans, and pension assets from one plan are not netted against underfunding from another.

When reorganizing the balance sheet, separate operating assets from pension assets, and treat excess pension assets as nonoperating. Unfunded pension liabilities (on a gross basis) should be treated as a debt equivalent and, as such, should not be deducted from operating assets to determine invested

EXHIBIT 23.1 **Kellanova: Pension Note in Annual Report, Funded Status, 2023**

$ million

	Pension benefits[1]	Other benefits[2]	Total benefits
Fair value of plan assets at end of year	2,650	587	3,237
Projected benefit obligation at end of year	(3,077)	(299)	(3,376)
Funded status	(427)	288	(139)
Amounts included in the consolidated balance sheet			
Other assets	201	311	512
Other current liabilities	(15)	(1)	(16)
Pension liability	(613)	—	(613)
Other liabilities	—	(22)	(22)
Net amount recognized	(427)	288	(139)

[1] Kellanova 2023 annual report, note 11, "Pension Benefits."

[2] Kellanova 2023 annual report, note 12, "Nonpension Postretirement and Postemployment Benefits."

[3] All the data related to Kellanova in this chapter appear in Kellanova's 2018 through 2023 10-K filings.
[4] Unlike Kellanova, most companies don't fund their "other" retirement obligations, such as promised medical benefits, so this will typically appear only as a liability.

capital. Instead, they will be valued separately during the transition from enterprise value to equity value.

On the income statement, current accounting standards now require separating the costs of granting retirement benefits from investment performance. New retirement benefits are now treated similarly to salaries and included in the relevant operating expenses. In contrast, investment performance and one-time changes to retirement benefits are reported under other income and expenses, below operating profit. Since NOPAT incorporates only operating expenses, no special adjustments for pensions are necessary when analyzing companies under the current standard.

Exhibit 23.2 presents Kellanova's pension expense as detailed in the notes to their annual report. The service cost, which represents benefits granted to employees in return for their service to the company, is a key component. As stated in the notes, "service cost is recorded in COGS [cost of goods sold] and SGA expense."

The remaining components of pension expense are primarily influenced by investment performance. These include interest cost on plan liabilities, expected return on plan assets, and recognized gains and losses, which collectively reflect the changes in plan assets and liabilities over time.[5] Ideally, if the change in plan assets perfectly matched the change in plan liabilities each year, these accounts would offset each other. However, due to market volatility, this is rarely the case, leading to fluctuations that impact pension expense. Kellanova's pension note confirms that "all other components of net periodic benefit cost are included in other income (expense)." Typically, most accounts within other income and expenses are nonoperating and therefore not included in NOPAT.

EXHIBIT 23.2 **Kellanova: Pension and Other Postretirement Expenses**

$ million

	2016	2017	2018	...	2023	
Service cost	119	114	105		20	→ Operating expense
Interest cost	213	201	201		170	
Expected return on plan assets	(442)	(469)	(455)		(234)	Nonoperating, related
Amortization of prior service cost	4	—	(1)		2	→ to plan performance
Recognized net (gain) loss	304	(126)	350		142	and one-time items
Settlements (Curtailments)	1	(151)	(30)		—	
Net periodic (benefit) cost	199	(431)	170		100	→ Information recorded on income statement

Source: Kellogg 2016–2018 and Kellanova 2023 annual reports.

[5] Interest cost represents the present value of service cost growing into the actual retiree payout. Expected return on plan assets equals the expected return based on asset mix. Recognized gains and losses represent the gradual recognition of past gains and losses of the pension fund.

Benchmarking for Periods Prior to Accounting Changes   To benchmark historical performance under IFRS prior to 2013 and GAAP prior to 2018, it is necessary to manually separate employee benefit grants from investment performance. Prior to the update, companies reported the entire pension expense as part of operating expenses. Although not visible on the income statement, the expense was subtly embedded in cost of sales and in SG&A expenses. This meant operating expenses and consequently operating profit were a function of the investment performance of plan assets, leading to distortions in competitive benchmarking.

To better understand potential distortions, let's examine the portion of pension expense titled "recognized net (gain) loss" in Exhibit 23.2. In 2016, Kellanova recognized $304 million in *losses* on plan assets. This increased pension expense relative to other years. In 2017, Kellanova reported recognized *gains* of $126 million. This caused pension expense to convert from a $199 million expense in 2016 to a $431 million benefit in 2017. Since pension expense is embedded within cost of sales, this caused the operating profit as originally reported to rise in 2017. As a result, the unadjusted operating margin rose from 10.7 percent to 15.1 percent in 2017, even though adjusted margins—that is, those that only include service expense—fell from 11.3 percent to 10.8 percent.

To eliminate plan performance from past operating expenses, remove the pension expense—in Kellanova's case, a $431 million gain in 2017—and replace it with the service cost of $114 million. These adjustments are shown in the middle section of Exhibit 23.3. Note how adjustments are made in 2016 and 2017, but no adjustments are made in 2018 and beyond, as operating expenses now exclude the nonoperating portion of the pension expense.

EXHIBIT 23.3 **Kellanova: EBITA Adjusted for Pensions**

$ million

	2016	2017	2018	...	2023
Operating profits, unadjusted					
Revenues	13,014	12,923	13,547		13,122
Operating costs	(11,619)	(10,977)	(11,841)		(11,617)
EBITA, unadjusted	1,395	1,946	1,706		1,505
Operating profits, adjusted					
Revenues	13,014	12,923	13,547		13,122
Operating costs	(11,619)	(10,977)	(11,841)		(11,617)
Add: Net periodic (benefit) cost	199	(431)	—		—
Less: Service cost	(119)	(114)	—		—
EBITA, adjusted	1,475	1,401	1,706		1,505
Operating margin, %					
Operating margin, unadjusted	10.7	15.1	12.6		11.5
Operating margin, adjusted	11.3	10.8	12.6		11.5

Source: Kellogg 2016–2018 and Kellanova 2023 annual reports.

The Pension Expense and Earnings Manipulation   To avoid volatility in the income statement, accounting standards still allow companies to include an "expected return" on pension plan assets as part of pension expense, rather than actual returns. This enables companies to smooth pension returns from year to year, avoiding volatility in net income. Any actual gains and losses are amortized over time.

Since expected return must be estimated, company management has discretion over the rate used—a license that management may sometimes use to manipulate accounting profitability. One research study found that management increases expected rates of return to increase profitability immediately before acquiring other firms and before exercising stock options.[6] They also found that companies with the weakest shareholder protections tend to use the highest estimates for expected return. With nonoperating items now incorporated into other income and expenses, cost of sales and operating profit are no longer affected by expected-return choices. Even so, net income remains susceptible, which is just one of many reasons why NOPAT, and not earnings per share (EPS), remains a central measure of accurate benchmarking and financial forecasting.

Pensions and the Cost of Capital   A key component of valuation is the cost of equity, which is typically estimated using the capital asset pricing model (CAPM) and beta. As discussed in Chapter 15, it is difficult to accurately measure the beta of a single company. Therefore, we recommend using an industry beta derived from multiple competitors estimated over appropriate sample periods.

To create an industry beta, you must remove the effects of leverage to isolate economic risk. This adjustment allows for aggregation across companies in similar lines of business. For most companies without pensions, relying solely on the market values of debt and equity is sufficient. However, if a company has significant exposure to retirement plans, especially unfunded ones, include the impact of pensions and other retiree benefits such as healthcare in your unlevering process.

Exhibit 23.4 presents Kellanova's capital structure, including pension plans and other retiree benefits. The company's plans are well funded, with the current shortfall being less than 5 percent of projected benefit obligations. Therefore, incorporating pensions into the unlevering process for Kellanova will have little effect on the results. However, we will demonstrate the process below for illustrative purposes.

---

[6] D. B. Bergstresser, M. A. Desai, and J. Rauh, "Earnings Manipulation, Pension Assumptions, and Managerial Investment Decisions," *Quarterly Journal of Economics* 121, no. 1 (February 2006): 157–195. For more on shareholder protection indexes, see P. Gompers, J. Ishii, and A. Metrick, "Corporate Governance and Equity Prices," *Quarterly Journal of Economics* 118, no. 1 (2003): 107–155.

EXHIBIT 23.4 **Kellanova: Capital Structure with Pensions**

$ million

	Value	Proportion of total capital, %
Projected benefit obligations[1]	3,376	13.6
Value of plan assets[1]	(3,237)	(13.0)
Unfunded pension liabilities	139	0.6
Debt, net of excess cash	5,599	22.5
Debt and debt equivalents	5,738	23.1
Market value of equity	19,150	76.9
Enterprise value	24,888	100.0

[1] Includes pensions and other retirement obligations.

There are two ways to incorporate pensions into the unlevering process. In the first method, we assume the pension fund manager has successfully matched the beta risk of plan assets to the beta risk of projected benefits. In this case, the funded portion will net out, and only the unfunded portion will affect the equity beta. In the second method, we relax the assumption of a matched beta between assets and liabilities. While the second method is more flexible than the first, it requires an estimate of the beta risk for plan assets, which can be cumbersome to collect.[7]

In the first method, we assume that only the unfunded pension liability affects the equity beta. Since the unfunded pension liability resembles debt, we can use the equation for unlevering beta presented in Chapter 15:

$$b_u = \frac{D}{V}b_d + \frac{E}{V}b_e \qquad (23.1)$$

where b_u equals the unlevered beta, b_d equals the beta of debt, b_e equals the beta of equity, and E equals the market value of equity. The unfunded pension liability is a debt equivalent. Therefore, D equals traditional debt *plus* unfunded pension liabilities less excess cash.

In the top portion of Exhibit 23.5, we summarize the unlevering process when the unfunded portion of retirement liabilities is classified as a debt equivalent. Although debt is a significant component of the company's capital structure, unfunded pensions are negligible compared with the enterprise value and thus do not impact the resulting unlevered beta. If unfunded pensions were substantial, they would influence the calculation.

To illustrate the unlevering process when the portfolio is risk matched, assume Kellanova's betas are 0.17 for debt and 0.80 for equity. The unlevered beta is then calculated by multiplying each security's beta by its respective

---

[7] Since the estimate requires data found only in the notes (versus a professional data provider), as well as a few assumptions regarding asset composition, its use should be limited to situations where pensions play a critical role in company valuation.

EXHIBIT 23.5 **The Unlevering Process with Pensions**

Method 1: Treat unfunded pension as debt equivalent

	Value, $ million	Proportion of total capital, %	Beta[1]	Contribution to unlevered beta
Debt, net of excess cash	5,599	22.5	0.17	0.04
Unfunded pension liabilities	139	0.6	0.17	0.00
Debt plus unfunded pensions, net of cash	5,738	23.1	0.17	0.04
Market value of equity	19,150	76.9	0.80	0.62
Unlevered beta, estimate	24,888	100.0		0.65

Method 2: Allow plan asset beta to differ from liabilities beta

	Value, $ million	Proportion of total capital, %	Beta[1]	Contribution to unlevered beta
Debt, net of excess cash	5,599	22.5	0.17	0.04
Projected benefit obligations	3,376	13.6	0.17	0.02
Debt plus projected benefit obligations	8,975	36.1		0.06
Market value of equity	19,150	76.9	0.80	0.62
Less: Value of plan assets	(3,237)	(13.0)	0.67	(0.09)
Unlevered beta, estimate	24,888	100.0		0.59

[1] In this example, we assume a beta of 0.17 for debt and 0.80 for equity. In practice, estimating a company's unlevered beta should incorporate an industry-wide perspective. For more on how to create industry betas, see Chapter 15.

market weight within the company's capital structure and then summing. Using this method, we obtain an unlevered beta estimate of 0.65. While this example illustrates the unlevering process for a single company in a single year, a comprehensive analysis would involve multiple companies over a relevant period to obtain a more accurate industry-wide measure.

To unlever beta when the beta of pension assets differs from pension liabilities, we separate plan assets from pension liabilities in the capital structure equation and apply the teachings of economists Franco Modigliani and Merton Miller (see Chapter 10) to solve for the beta of operating assets. In Appendix C, we step through the algebraic derivation, leading to the following formula for unlevered beta with mismatched pensions:

$$b_u = \frac{D + V_{pbo}}{V} b_d + \frac{E}{V} b_e - \frac{V_{pa}}{V} b_{pa} \qquad (23.2)$$

where b_u represents the unlevered beta appropriate for free cash flow, b_d represents the beta of debt, b_e represents the equity beta, b_{pa} represents the beta of plan assets, D equals the value of debt less excess cash, V_{pbo} equals the projected benefit obligations, E equals the market value of equity, V_{pa} equals the market value of plan assets, and V equals enterprise value, as measured by the sum of debt, unfunded pension liabilities, and the market value of equity.

To measure the aggregate beta of plan assets, we use the target allocation reported in the pension footnote. In the Kellanova 2023 annual report, the company states, "The current weighted-average target asset allocation reflected by this strategy is: equity securities at 38.0%; debt securities at 40.0%; real estate and other at 22.0%." Following the research of Jin, Merton, and Bodie, we assume debt securities have a beta of 0.17 and other investments have a beta of 1.0.[8] With 40 percent of plan assets dedicated to debt, this leads to an aggregate plan beta of 0.67. Using the data from Exhibits 23.4 and 23.5, we solve for unlevered beta, using equation 23.2. In this example, the resulting unlevered beta equals 0.59. Because the beta of plan assets exceeds that of projected benefits, the resulting estimate of unlevered beta is slightly lower than we obtained using the first method. Had the betas for plan assets and plan liabilities been the same, the two methods would have yielded the same results.

While each method has its benefits, we believe method one, using equation 23.1 inclusive of unfunded pension liabilities, is the easiest and most reliable method for unlevering beta, especially for the large number of companies required to estimate unlevered industry betas.

Estimating Levered Beta   Once you have an unlevered industry beta, relever the industry beta to the company's target capital structure and compute the company's cost of capital. To relever an industry beta, do *not* incorporate unfunded pensions as part of the target capital structure. While this may seem inconsistent for a company with pensions, it is not. We have eliminated pensions from free cash flow and the cost of capital, and there is no reason to reintroduce pensions, or the risk associated with them, into the value of operations. Instead, value pensions separately, and sum the parts.

INCORPORATING PENSIONS INTO THE VALUE OF EQUITY

Pension plans and other obligations, such as promised medical benefits, will affect a company's value in two ways. First, service cost will be embedded within free cash flow. Since only cash contributions and not service costs are tax deductible, make sure to adjust taxes appropriately for companies that systematically underfund their obligations. Not every country provides tax relief on pension contributions, so check local tax law to determine the marginal tax rate for contributions. Second, past over- or underfunding must be incorporated into value as a nonoperating asset or debt equivalent.

For an ongoing enterprise, excess pension assets can be netted against unfunded liabilities to determine net assets (or liabilities) outstanding. If the company is being valued for liquidation or the pension plan is being terminated, net unfunded liabilities cannot be netted against excess pension assets,

[8] L. Jin, R. Merton, and Z. Bodie, "Do a Firm's Equity Returns Reflect the Risk of Its Pension Plan?" *Journal of Financial Economics* 81, no. 1 (2006): 1–26.

as most countries charge a meaningful penalty for withdrawing excess funds from pension plans. Instead, add after-tax excess pension assets at the penalty rate, and deduct after-tax unfunded pension liabilities at the marginal tax savings for pension contributions.

To value companies with net unfunded liabilities, reduce enterprise value by the product of (1 – marginal tax rate) times net pension liabilities. To incorporate pensions for a company with net excess assets, increase enterprise value by the product of (1 – marginal tax rate on pensions) times net pension assets, as excess pension assets will lead to fewer required contributions in the future.

In 2023, Kellanova recognized $427 million in unfunded pension liabilities and $288 million in prefunded other benefits (see Exhibit 23.1), for a net total liability of $139 million. Assuming a marginal tax rate of 24 percent, the after-tax liability equals $106 million. To determine equity value, deduct the after-tax liability from enterprise value.

CLOSING THOUGHTS

The International Accounting Standards Board and the U.S.-based Financial Accounting Standards Board have worked to eliminate the distortions caused by pension accounting. For companies that file under these standards, the income statement now separates service cost from nonoperating pension expenses, and the balance sheet, albeit still complicated, recognizes the market value of unfunded pension obligations. The result is better benchmarking, requiring fewer adjustments, and a valuation that is easier to carry out.

24

Measuring Performance in Capital-Light Businesses

In this book, our primary measure of return on capital is return on invested capital (ROIC). We define ROIC as net operating profit after taxes (NOPAT) divided by invested capital. We derive ROIC from items on a company's financial statements, with some adjustments, such as separating operations from financing and separating operating items from nonoperating items.[1] ROIC correctly reflects return on capital in most cases, but special circumstances require alternative measures. For example, a young biotech company could spend a billion dollars on research and development (R&D) before its product is launched. Since R&D is expensed, not capitalized, the company would show a negative ROIC in its early years and a very high ROIC once the product is launched. The actual economic return on capital over the life of the product would lie at some average level in between.

In this chapter, we show how to deal with such investments in R&D and in marketing and sales that are expensed when they are incurred. Creating pro forma financial statements that capitalize these expenses can provide more insight into the underlying economics of a business. In addition, we discuss businesses with very low capital requirements, where we recommend using economic profit or economic profit scaled by revenues to measure return on capital.

---

[1] In Chapter 11, we explain why we use ROIC instead of other accounting-based metrics such as return on equity (ROE) or return on assets (ROA).

CAPITALIZING EXPENSED INVESTMENTS

When a company builds a plant or purchases equipment, it capitalizes the asset on the balance sheet and depreciates it over time. Conversely, when a company invests in intangible assets such as a new production technology, a brand name, or a distribution network, the entire outlay must be expensed immediately. In sectors such as pharmaceuticals, high technology, and branded consumer goods, failure to recognize such expenses as investments can lead to significantly underestimating a company's invested capital and overstating its return on invested capital.

To get a more accurate measurement of ROIC,[2] it's best to capitalize outlays for intangible investments if they bring benefits over multiple years in the future rather than merely for the current year. Earnings in any given year are supported not by just that year's R&D or brand advertising expenses, but instead by many prior years of these expenses. It has taken companies such as Coca-Cola and PepsiCo many decades and billions of dollars to build their global brand names. Pharmaceutical companies such as Pfizer and Novartis, and high-tech companies such as Intel and ASML, had to invest in technology development projects over many years to build and sustain their current product offerings.

The economics of investments in intangible assets are very similar to those of investments in tangible assets. Their treatment in ROIC should therefore also be the same to ensure that it adequately reflects the internal rate of return (IRR), or true return, of the underlying investments.[3] Failure to do so would lead to ROICs far above the true return of the business. Consider what would happen to ROIC if capital expenditures for net property, plant, and equipment (net PP&E) were not capitalized but were expensed instead.

In addition to improving the measurement of ROIC, capitalizing intangible investments can reduce the manipulation of short-term profits. Under traditional accounting, a manager looking to meet short-term earnings targets can simply reduce R&D spending. With R&D capitalized, however, amortization charges to earnings will remain almost unchanged in the short term.

Capitalizing investments can also provide strategic insights. For example, many companies set R&D budgets at a fixed percentage of revenue. When combined with expensing R&D, this masks the change in performance resulting from any change in revenues, because the earnings margin remains unchanged. But when R&D is capitalized, amortization charges do not change with revenues, and the impact on performance is clearly reflected in earnings.

---

[2] The same applies to return on capital measures such as cash flow return on investment (CFROI), as discussed in the following chapter.

[3] To be truly "value based," the measure for return on capital should reflect the internal rate of return (IRR) of the underlying business from the time investments are made until all the cash flows from that investment have been collected (see also Chapter 25).

Example: Capitalizing R&D Expenses

As an illustration of capitalizing intangible investments and its impact on ROIC, Exhibit 24.1 presents the reorganized financial statements for PharmaCo. This fictional company has experienced rapid growth over the past 25 years, reaching around $1.2 billion in revenues by 2025. The after-tax earnings margin is 11 percent of sales. R&D expenses, to renew the product pipeline, are at around 20 percent of sales. ROIC is at 33 percent, with revenues at three times invested capital as computed directly from the balance sheet. But this ROIC does not represent the company's true economic performance, because the invested capital includes only purchased capital and not the intellectual capital created internally from R&D.

To estimate ROIC with capitalized investments in R&D, use the following three-step process:

1. Capitalize and amortize the R&D asset, using an appropriate asset lifetime.
2. Adjust invested capital upward by the historical cost of the R&D asset, net of cumulative amortization.
3. Adjust NOPAT by replacing R&D expense with R&D amortization. (Do not adjust operating taxes.)

To capitalize the R&D asset, choose a starting year, and begin accumulating R&D expenses. Choose the earliest year feasible, as the model requires accumulated R&D to reach a steady state before the adjusted ROIC

EXHIBIT 24.1 **PharmaCo: Reorganized Financial Statements**

$ million

Partial income statement	2020	2021	2022	2023	2024	2025	
Revenues	1,045	1,077	1,109	1,142	1,176	1,212	Fixed at 60% of revenues
Cost of sales	(627)	(646)	(665)	(685)	(706)	(727)	
R&D expense	(229)	(235)	(242)	(248)	(255)	(262)	
Operating profit	189	195	202	208	215	222	
Taxes	(76)	(78)	(81)	(83)	(86)	(89)	
NOPAT[1]	113	117	121	125	129	133	

Partial balance sheet	2020	2021	2022	2023	2024	2025	
Invested capital	348	359	370	381	392	404	Fixed at 3 times capital turnover

	2020	2021	2022	2023	2024	2025
NOPAT/revenues, %	10.9	10.9	10.9	10.9	11.0	11.0
ROIC, %	32.6	32.7	32.8	32.8	32.9	33.0

[1] Net operating profit after taxes.

calculation becomes meaningful. Exhibit 24.2 starts in 2000, assuming straight-line amortization and an eight-year R&D asset life. PharmaCo spent $22 million on R&D in 2000, which we capitalize and add to invested capital and start to amortize in 2001. By adding R&D expenses to the prior year's net asset value and then deducting amortization charges in each year, we arrive at a capitalized R&D asset base of $1,666 million in 2025.[4]

To adjust invested capital for the intangible investments, add the capitalized R&D asset to invested capital. On this basis, PharmaCo's total capital amounts to $2,070 million in 2025, most of it in the form of capitalized R&D.[5]

Adjust NOPAT by replacing R&D expense ($262 million in 2025) with R&D amortization ($200 million), computed as outlined in Exhibit 24.3. Operating taxes remain unchanged, because capitalization and amortization of R&D expense does not change taxable income for fiscal purposes. For PharmaCo, replacing R&D expense with amortization raises NOPAT in 2025 from $133 million to $195 million. This is quite common for growth firms, as current R&D is typically higher than the amortization of historical R&D. As the company's growth rate tapers off, however, amortization will catch up with expense, and NOPAT adjustments will be small.

Note that for PharmaCo's historical years, free cash flows cannot change when R&D expenses are capitalized (see Exhibit 24.4). The amortization is a noncash charge in NOPAT and is added back to calculate gross cash flow. This

EXHIBIT 24.2 **PharmaCo: Capitalization of R&D**

$ million

Partial income statement	Estimated R&D asset lifetime: 8 years				2023	2024	2025
	2000	2001	2002				
Revenues	10	22	43	...	1,142	1,176	1,212
R&D expense	(22)	(24)	(29)	...	(248)	(255)	(262)
Capitalized R&D asset							
Capitalized R&D, starting	–	22	44	...	1,477	1,541	1,604
R&D expense	22	24	29	...	248	255	262
Amortization	–	(3)	(5)	...	(185)	(193)	(200)
Capitalized R&D, ending	22	44	67	...	1,541	1,604	1,666
Partial balance sheet	**2000**	**2001**	**2002**		**2023**	**2024**	**2025**
Invested capital, unadjusted	3	7	14	...	381	392	404
Capitalized R&D	22	44	67	...	1,541	1,604	1,666
Invested capital, adjusted	25	51	81	...	1,922	1,996	2,070

[4] In this example, for illustration purposes, we approximate amortization at 10 percent of the preceding year's ending balance. More advanced models use straight-line amortization of actual R&D expense.
[5] If we add capitalized R&D to operating assets, total funds invested will no longer balance. To balance total funds invested, add capitalized R&D to equity equivalents. For more on total funds invested and their reconciliation, see Chapter 11.

EXHIBIT 24.3 **PharmaCo: NOPAT Adjusted for R&D Capitalization**

$ million

	2021	2022	2023	2024	2025
Revenues	1,077	1,109	1,142	1,176	1,212
Cost of sales	(646)	(665)	(685)	(706)	(727)
R&D expense	(235)	(242)	(248)	(255)	(262)
Operating profit	195	202	208	215	222
Operating taxes	(78)	(81)	(83)	(86)	(89)
NOPAT	117	121	125	129	133
Add back: R&D expense	235	242	248	255	262
R&D amortization	(168)	(177)	(185)	(193)	(200)
Adjusted NOPAT	184	186	189	192	195
ROIC,%	32.7	32.8	32.8	32.9	33.0
ROIC adjusted for R&D capitalization, %	10.4	10.1	9.8	9.6	9.4

EXHIBIT 24.4 **PharmaCo: Free Cash Flow**

$ million

R&D expensed, unadjusted	2022	2023	2024	2025
NOPAT	121	125	129	133
Depreciation	37	38	39	40
Gross cash flow	158	163	168	174
Capital expenditures	(48)	(49)	(51)	(52)
Free cash flow	**110**	**114**	**118**	**122**

R&D capitalized	2022	2023	2024	2025
Adjusted NOPAT	186	189	192	195
Depreciation	37	38	39	40
Amortization of R&D	177	185	193	200
Gross cash flow	400	412	424	436
Capital expenditures	(48)	(49)	(51)	(52)
Investment in R&D	(242)	(248)	(255)	(262)
Free cash flow	**110**	**114**	**118**	**122**

effectively moves R&D expenses from gross cash flow to investments, leaving free cash flow unchanged.

Based on the new measures for invested capital with capitalized R&D investments and for NOPAT with R&D amortization instead of expenses, we derive an adjusted ROIC. The adjusted ROIC with R&D capitalized represents PharmaCo's return on capital, including intangible investments. It can be compared with an unadjusted ROIC with R&D expensed, as shown in Exhibit 24.5. Because the R&D asset lifetime was estimated at eight years, at least as many years of constant growth must elapse for capital and ROIC to reach a steady state and provide a meaningful indication of true economic returns. As Exhibit 24.5 shows, the adjusted ROIC computed on total capital stabilizes at around 9.5 percent, dramatically lower than the 33 percent ROIC

EXHIBIT 24.5 **PharmaCo: ROIC, 2002–2025**

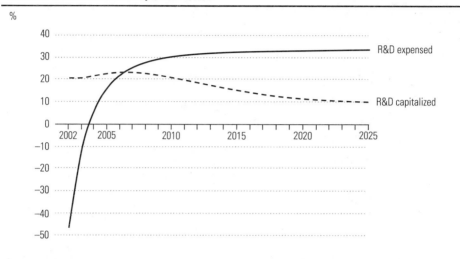

derived from the unadjusted financial statements. As long as the R&D investments needed to support earnings remain unchanged, PharmaCo's adjusted ROIC is the better estimate of its true economic return and underlying performance.[6]

One of the key assumptions made in capitalizing intangible investments is the asset lifetime. Although it may be hard to come up with an accurate estimate, this should not keep you from capitalizing the R&D expenses. Asset lifetime has less impact on ROIC than you might expect. In the PharmaCo example, we assumed an asset life of eight years. In Exhibit 24.6, we stress-test this assumption by varying asset life between two and 12 years. Even an asset life of just two years dramatically reduces PharmaCo's ROIC from 33 percent when R&D is expensed to 16 percent when it is capitalized. Increasing the asset life continues to lower ROIC, but by smaller amounts as asset life increases. Therefore, choosing an asset life of 12 rather than eight years (a reasonable range for the life of most R&D assets) does not materially affect perceptions of performance: for PharmaCo, ROIC would be 8.9 percent for a 12-year life, versus 9.4 percent for an eight-year life. This pattern remains unchanged when R&D spending is much lower—for example, at only 10 percent of revenues. Furthermore, when using ROIC to compare the performance of competing companies, what matters most is that asset lifetime estimates are consistent across all companies. Keep in mind that the lifetimes for tangible assets are also based on rough estimates and accounting conventions. Yet most

[6] That is, ROIC is the better estimate of the investments' value creation, as explained in Chapter 25. R&D expenses shown consist of a fixed amount of $20 million per year plus a variable amount of 10 percent (or 20 percent) of annual revenues. Note that under straight-line amortization of actual R&D expenses, asset lifetime has a somewhat greater impact on ROIC than the under the approximate amortization applied here (but also that the ROIC impact will diminish as the asset lifetime increases).

EXHIBIT 24.6 **PharmaCo: ROIC at Different Estimates of R&D Asset Lifetime, 2025**

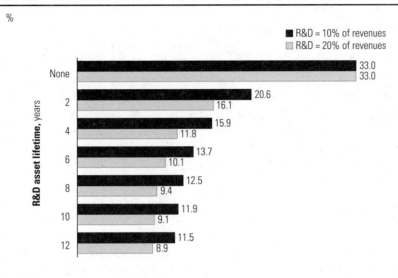

managers and analysts are quite comfortable using tangible-asset book values and depreciation charges as the basis for return on capital and earnings.[7]

Interpreting Return on Capital, Including Capitalized Expenses

In general, capitalizing intangible investments will lead to lower ROIC. For mature companies with stable revenues and investment spending, the amortization charges for intangible assets are likely to be close to the amounts expensed. As a result, capitalizing the expenses may have little impact on NOPAT. But the capital base will always increase when the expenses are capitalized, leading to lower ROIC.

Although the capitalization can never change historical free cash flows, as discussed in the PharmaCo example, the resulting adjustments to capital turnover and ROIC can affect projections of future free cash flows. For PharmaCo, required investments in R&D to achieve growth of 10 percent per year would be estimated at $375 million in 2026, which is $113 million more than the $262 million spent in 2025. This follows from required growth of the net R&D asset base (10 percent, or $167 million) plus an annual amortization charge of $208 million (one-eighth of the 2025 ending balance). If R&D investments going forward are modeled as expenses, the required additional R&D outlay in 2026 would be only 10 percent of the additional 2026 revenues, or $26 million. This is comparable to what

---

[7] Note also that for an alternative measure of ROIC, such as cash flow return on investment (CFROI) with or without resource capitalization, estimates of asset lifetimes are critical—not for book value or depreciation, but for estimating the CFROI itself (see Chapter 25).

happens to investment projections if capital expenditures for tangible assets are derived from a constant ratio to revenues or instead implied from a constant capital turnover (see Chapter 13).

If PharmaCo can increase its revenues by 10 percent as a result of increasing its R&D expenses by 10 percent, the unadjusted ROIC provides the best estimate of the IRR of future investments in its business. In contrast, if achieving that same revenue growth would require PharmaCo to increase its net R&D asset base, rather than its R&D expenses, by 10 percent, the adjusted ROIC is the better estimate. Of course, these R&D investment estimates for PharmaCo are not likely to apply from year to year. What matters is which R&D investments are required for growth over the long term.

More accurately reflecting the economics of intangible investments on ROIC can have major implications for investment decisions, performance assessments, resource allocation, and competitive behavior. For instance, if the cost of capital is 10 percent, PharmaCo is in fact destroying value, and management should question continued investment. Competitors should question the validity of entering the company's product markets. The margins may be high, but required investments in R&D are large.

To illustrate how capitalizing intangibles affects estimates of ROIC and alters our understanding of value creation, we analyzed past spending on research and advertising over a ten-year period for four global companies in branded consumer goods. After the estimated past expenses in R&D and advertising were capitalized and amortized, ROIC for all companies decreased significantly and provided a very different ranking of performance, as shown in the top portion of Exhibit 24.7. A similar analysis of ROIC including capitalized R&D expenses among high-tech hardware manufacturers showed similar shifts in perceived performance levels and rankings (see the bottom portion of Exhibit 24.7).

Capitalizing intangibles can provide a better financial perspective on competitive positions. Think of comparing current budgets on brand advertising between incumbents and new entrants in personal or household products. The comparison is not very useful if the incumbent brands have been built by many years of marketing efforts. Incumbents' current advertising budgets will then underestimate the investments required by new entrants to reach similar levels of brand awareness among customers. A capitalized investment base can provide a more accurate estimate.

While insights from capitalizing resources are valuable, companies must take care. Left unchecked, managers could have an incentive to classify all expenses as investments, even those with no long-term benefits, because this will maximize reported short-term performance. They could also be reluctant to write off investments that prove worthless after they have been capitalized. For instance, a distribution channel may be kept open merely to avoid a write-down on the manager's economic balance sheet.

EXHIBIT 24.7 **Impact of Adjusting ROIC for Intangible Investments**

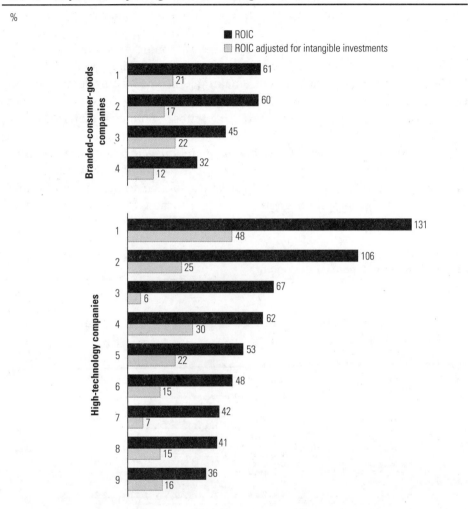

%

- ■ ROIC
- ▨ ROIC adjusted for intangible investments

WHEN BUSINESSES NEED LITTLE OR NO CAPITAL

Some businesses do not require significant amounts of capital—for example, those in the professional services sector, but also consumer electronics companies with outsourced manufacturing. Because of these companies' low or even negative capital base, ROIC can become less meaningful. In such cases, we recommend using economic profit as the key measure of value creation.

Capital-Light Business Models and ROIC

Examples of businesses with an inherently low need for capital include accounting, legal counseling and other professional services, and real estate and other forms of brokerage services. Businesses such as software development and services have limited fixed capital needs, and customer license prepayments and supplier financing often bring their overall invested capital close to zero. In these cases, capital is very low relative to earnings generated, and ROIC accordingly is high. Modest changes in an already small invested-capital base can lead to very large swings in ROIC, making ROIC in any particular year hard to use for performance management or financial planning and target setting.

Consider the example of TradeCo, whose financial statements are summarized in Exhibit 24.8. TradeCo is a trading company in plumbing supplies and tools. It has offices and a warehouse in a low-cost location. Inventories are kept to a minimum: except for the items with the highest turnover, supplies and tools are purchased on customer order. Because TradeCo pays its suppliers after receiving payment on its own customer invoices, working capital is negative.

EXHIBIT 24.8 **TradeCo: Financial Statements**

$ million

NOPAT	2020	2021	2022	2023	2024	2025
Revenues	200.0	209.0	212.1	216.4	214.2	212.1
Cost of goods sold	(160.0)	(165.1)	(169.7)	(175.3)	(171.4)	(170.7)
SG&A	(20.0)	(20.9)	(21.2)	(21.6)	(21.4)	(21.2)
Operating taxes	(7.0)	(8.0)	(7.4)	(6.8)	(7.5)	(7.1)
NOPAT	13.0	14.9	13.8	12.7	13.9	13.1

Invested capital	2020	2021	2022	2023	2024	2025
Net working capital	(12.0)	(8.4)	(10.6)	(2.2)	(4.3)	(6.4)
Net PP&E	10.0	9.5	9.1	9.0	8.7	8.4
Invested capital	(2.0)	1.1	(1.5)	6.8	4.4	2.1

Free cash flow	2020	2021	2022	2023	2024	2025
NOPAT	13.0	14.9	13.8	12.7	13.9	13.1
Net investments	(2.0)	(3.1)	2.6	(8.3)	2.4	2.3
Free cash flow	11.0	11.9	16.3	4.4	16.3	15.4

Key value drivers, %	2020	2021	2022	2023	2024	2025
NOPAT/revenues	6.5	7.2	6.5	5.9	6.5	6.2
Invested capital/revenues	(1.0)	0.5	(0.7)	3.1	2.1	1.0
⟶ ROIC	NM[1]	1,371	NM[1]	186	316	632

Economic profit	2020	2021	2022	2023	2024	2025
NOPAT	13.0	14.9	13.8	12.7	13.9	13.1
Capital charge[2]	0.2	(0.1)	0.1	(0.7)	(0.4)	(0.2)
⟶ Economic profit	13.2	14.8	13.9	12.0	13.5	12.9

[1] Not meaningful.
[2] Cost of capital equals 10%.

As Exhibit 24.8 shows, revenues, earnings, and free cash flow are fairly stable on a year-by-year basis. But as the graph in Exhibit 24.9 shows, ROIC fluctuates wildly and is even unmeasurable in some years, despite stable earnings margins and healthy cash flows. The reason is that TradeCo's invested capital is very small and sometimes even negative, mainly because of movements in working capital. ROIC is not meaningful in 2020 and 2022, for instance, because the company had negative invested capital. ROIC is numerically negative, but it lacks any economic interpretation.[8] Looking at the bottom of Exhibit 24.8, we see that economic profit was positive in 2022, clearly indicating value creation. But the movements in ROIC could distort your assessment of TradeCo's performance. For example, ROIC increased from 316 percent in 2024 to 632 percent in 2025. Yet value creation declined, as the change in economic profit for the same period shows. The change in ROIC was driven by a decline in working capital. Earnings declined simultaneously and pushed down value creation.

Not all businesses with low capital are inherently capital light. Indeed, some capital-intensive businesses have adopted capital-light models by outsourcing their processes that require the most capital—typically manufacturing and distribution. Familiar examples in the high-tech electronics sector include Apple, HP, Samsung, and Sony. In the apparel sector, companies such as Nike have outsourced nearly all of their manufacturing.[9]

EXHIBIT 24.9 **TradeCo: ROIC and NOPAT Margin**

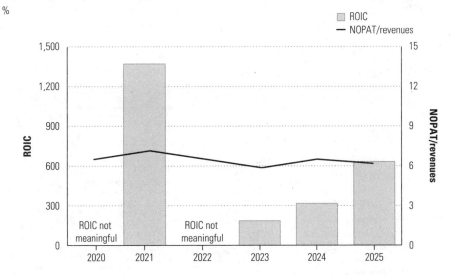

---

[8] Mathematically, ROIC still ties perfectly with cash flow and value, following the fundamental logic described in Chapter 3.

[9] Nike Fiscal 2024 Annual Report (Nike, Inc. Form 10-K, 2024), www.sec.gov.

ROICs for businesses that have aggressively outsourced parts of their business chain can be very high and volatile. In addition, the capital reduction that comes with outsourcing can lead to confusion when ROIC is used to assess whether outsourcing creates any value to begin with. After outsourcing, many businesses end up with much higher ROICs. In some cases, managers even refer to the higher ROIC as one of the main benefits of outsourcing. But the ROIC increase does not necessarily mean that the company has created value for its shareholders.

Consider the companies InhouseCo and ContractCo in Exhibit 24.10. The companies are identical, with one exception: ContractCo has outsourced all its production to a third party. It has no net PP&E and no depreciation charges, but its operating costs are higher than InhouseCo's. Although ContractCo's earnings are lower than InhouseCo's, its ROIC is more than five times larger because it no longer needs PP&E. But ContractCo is not creating more value in its business than InhouseCo. In fact, as the measure of economic profit indicates, the two companies' value creation is identical. In this example, ContractCo has separated out its capital-intensive and low-ROIC production activities from its other activities without creating value. The ROIC for ContractCo goes up simply because it retains only the high-ROIC activities. But that does not

EXHIBIT 24.10 **Impact of Production Outsourcing on ROIC**

$ million

	InhouseCo	ContractCo
NOPAT		
Revenues	100.0	100.0
Operating costs	(85.0)	(94.5)
Depreciation	(3.8)	—
Operating taxes	(3.9)	(1.9)
NOPAT	7.3	3.6
Invested capital		
Net working capital	5.0	5.0
Net PP&E	50.0	—
Invested capital	55.0	5.0
Key value drivers, %		
NOPAT/revenues	7.3	3.6
Invested capital/revenues	55.0	5.0
→ ROIC	13.3	71.2
Economic profit		
NOPAT	7.3	3.6
Capital charge[1]	(4.1)	(0.4)
→ Economic profit	3.2	3.2

[1] Cost of capital equals 7.5%.

say anything about the value creation from outsourcing.[10] Managers should therefore not make decisions to outsource merely on the grounds that it raises ROIC. These decisions need to be supported by an analysis of economic profit or, equivalently, a DCF valuation.

Economic Profit as a Key Value Metric

Although there is no objective way to determine a cutoff point, we believe that ROICs above 50 percent need to be handled with caution when used as a measure of value creation. And special caution is required in businesses where high capital turnover, rather than high earnings margins, drives such ROIC levels.

In such cases, economic profit is a more dependable performance measure, since it is always in line with value creation. (For more details on economic profit, see Chapter 3.) It can be defined in either of the following two equivalent ways:

$$\text{Economic Profit} = (\text{ROIC} - \text{WACC}) \times \text{Invested Capital} \qquad (24.1)$$

$$\text{Economic Profit} = \text{NOPAT} - \text{Capital Charge} \qquad (24.2)$$

In Equation 24.2, the capital charge equals WACC times invested capital.

Because ROIC is multiplied by invested capital, economic profit automatically corrects for any distortion in ROIC for business models with extremely low capital intensity. The TradeCo example in Exhibit 24.8 illustrated this. ROIC shows very large fluctuations over the years, even becoming unmeasurable in some years. In contrast, economic profit is fairly stable, just as TradeCo's cash flows are stable and consistently positive over the years. Economic profit is a much better reflection of TradeCo's underlying business economics. It provides more accurate insights into its historical performance and a useful basis for predicting future performance.

As economic profit is a measure of return on capital in absolute terms, it is very useful for understanding whether value creation in a particular business has increased from one year to the next. But it is harder to use for interpreting differences in economic profit generated by businesses of different sizes. Take, for example, DiversiCo in Exhibit 24.11. DiversiCo is a diversified industrial company with business units in software, hardware, hardware services, and supplies. The business units are very different in size and economics. Hardware, for example, has annual revenues of $2.5 billion, dwarfing the $100 million in revenues generated by software development. The software business has negative invested capital, thanks to customer prepayments, whereas hardware requires $1 billion in capital, mainly for manufacturing

---

[10] Of course, outsourcing in this example could still create real value if it enables ContractCo to realize higher growth because it needs less capital for its business.

EXHIBIT 24.11 **DiversiCo: Economic Profit Scaled by Revenues**

$ million

	Revenues	Invested capital	NOPAT	NOPAT/ revenues, %	ROIC, %	Economic profit[1]	Economic profit/ revenues,[1] %
Software	100	(5)	25	25	NM[2]	25	25
Hardware services	250	10	44	18	438	43	17
Supplies	750	250	94	13	38	73	10
Hardware	2,500	1,000	188	8	19	103	4

[1] Cost of capital equals 8.5%.

[2] Not meaningful.

and distribution facilities and inventories. ROIC is meaningless for comparing performance across DiversiCo's businesses, because software and hardware services have little or negative capital. Economic profit provides an accurate picture of value creation, but comparisons among businesses of such different sizes are difficult. Economic profit is lowest for the software business (at $25 million), not so much because of the business's performance, but because of its size.

To better compare the value creation of DiversiCo's businesses, scale economic profit by revenues, turning it into a measure of value creation per dollar of sales.[11] As graphed in the final column of Exhibit 24.11, it now becomes clear that DiversiCo's software business generates the highest value per dollar of revenues, and its hardware business the lowest. Driving revenue growth in software development would therefore be most beneficial for shareholders.[12] Scaling economic profit in this way provides DiversiCo's management with a better yardstick for decisions on resource allocation and portfolio strategy.

In the same way, the ratio of economic profit over revenues can help in benchmarking performance with peers of different size and capital intensity. Consider the example of a branded-consumer-goods company, which we refer to as ReturnCo, in Exhibit 24.12. ReturnCo is generating a ROIC of 105 percent, far above its international peers' ROIC levels of around 30–40 percent. But this does not necessarily mean ReturnCo creates more value nor that it has some source of competitive advantage over its peers. Following our rule of thumb, ROICs above 50 percent should be interpreted with caution and carefully analyzed. In this case, it turns out that ReturnCo provides its customers with aggressive discounts for early payment. The discount pushes its earnings

[11] See M. Dodd and W. Rehm, "Comparing Performance When Invested Capital Is Low," *McKinsey on Finance* (Autumn 2005): 17–20.

[12] Note how economic profit over revenues is almost identical to NOPAT margin for capital-light businesses, such as software and hardware services in this example. This is easily explained by examining Equation 24.2: when invested capital is 0, the capital charge is 0, and economic profit is equal to NOPAT.

EXHIBIT 24.12 **Better Performance Comparison with Economic Profit over Revenues**

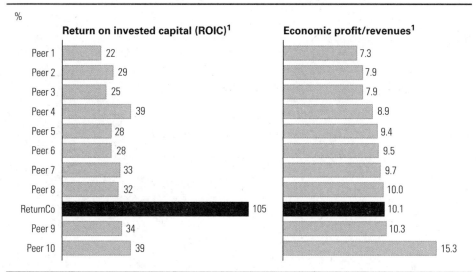

%

Return on invested capital (ROIC)[1]	Economic profit/revenues[1]
Peer 1 — 22	Peer 1 — 7.3
Peer 2 — 29	Peer 2 — 7.9
Peer 3 — 25	Peer 3 — 7.9
Peer 4 — 39	Peer 4 — 8.9
Peer 5 — 28	Peer 5 — 9.4
Peer 6 — 28	Peer 6 — 9.5
Peer 7 — 33	Peer 7 — 9.7
Peer 8 — 32	Peer 8 — 10.0
ReturnCo — 105	ReturnCo — 10.1
Peer 9 — 34	Peer 9 — 10.3
Peer 10 — 39	Peer 10 — 15.3

[1] Excluding goodwill and acquired intangibles.

Source: S&P Capital IQ; McKinsey Value Intelligence database.

margins below peer levels, but the early payments make its net working capital negative and reduce its invested capital. The result is an exceptionally high ROIC. Comparing its ROIC with those of its peers is pointless because of this difference in capital intensity, and absolute economic profit will of course differ with the size of the competitors. Instead, an analysis of economic profit over revenues best reveals how ReturnCo performs relative to its peers in terms of value creation. As the exhibit shows, the increased capital efficiency is roughly offset by the discount provided. ReturnCo's ratio of economic profit to revenues is very similar to those of its peers. At first sight, ReturnCo's ROIC appeared superior, but a closer look has revealed that its value creation is in line with that of its peers.

In general, when you are comparing the performance of businesses with very different capital intensity and size, using economic profit over revenues provides the best insights into performance and value creation.

SUMMARY

For most businesses, ROIC is a good measure of return on capital. However, for businesses that rely on significant investments in intangibles, such as R&D or brands, you should make some adjustments to ROIC to include the capitalized value of these resources. For businesses that use very little or no capital, economic profit is a better measure of value creation. To allow for comparison across businesses of different sizes, you can scale economic profit by revenues.

25

CFROI and Other Ways to Measure Return on Capital

Valuations often assume that historical return on capital is a good starting point for projecting future returns as a company grows. But if historical return on capital is measured in a way that gives us no meaningful information about value creation, decisions about whether to continue investing in a business may be incorrect. Ideally, the measure for return on capital should reflect the internal rate of return (IRR) of the underlying business from the time investments are made until all the cash flows from those investments have been collected. That's not possible in practice, because we can't wait until the end of every project to assess a company's performance; a business is an accumulation of different investments made at different times. We need a proxy that measures how much value a company has created in the recent past and that can help a company with the particularly important task of planning for the future.

Return on invested capital (ROIC), our primary measure of return on capital, correctly reflects value creation in most cases. But ROIC has some imperfections. For example, it doesn't account for the age of assets or the effect that inflation has on its measurement. Analysts have therefore proposed alternatives to overcome some of ROIC's weaknesses. One of these, cash flow return on investment (CFROI), is estimated from cash flows rather than from accounting measures. CFROI is the better measure of value creation in certain rare situations. This chapter explores the conditions under which ROIC accurately reflects the true economic return on capital and when to consider a more complex CFROI measure. We then look at some other alternatives and explain why they are flawed measures of value creation.

As we compare these measures, note that all of them apply this important principle: any measure of return on capital should be based on the amount invested, not the current market value of the company or its assets. Take, for example, the case where the fair value of an asset is based on the intrinsic, discounted-cash-flow (DCF) value of its future cash flows. By definition, the return on capital for the asset at its fair value does not provide any indication of an investment's value creation in such assets. For a growing business, a return on capital measured against the DCF value will always be less than the cost of capital, because the DCF value reflects the value creation of future investments.

WHEN ROIC EQUALS IRR

The simplest approach to measuring return on capital, which works well in most cases, is the one we use throughout this book: ROIC, or operating earnings divided by the net book value of a company's operating capital (purchase cost less accumulated depreciation). To illustrate when ROIC accurately estimates the IRR of an asset and the business activities it supports, we will use a stylized example, shown in Exhibit 25.1. The initial investment is $100, and assume the operating cash flows gradually decline over the asset's five-year lifetime. With linear depreciation charges of $20, the operating profit is proportional to the net invested capital in each year, declining from $15 in the first year to $3 in the last. We define ROIC in a particular year as the operating profit for that year divided by the invested capital at the beginning of the year, net of accumulated depreciation (ignoring taxes for simplicity). In this example, the asset's ROIC is constant over the asset's lifetime at 15 percent. (Note that the exhibit includes several of the alternative measures of return on capital that we will discuss later in this chapter.)

EXHIBIT 25.1 **Returns When Profits Are Proportional to Net Invested Capital**

$

	Individual asset						Business of five assets
	Year						
	0	1	2	3	4	5	
Operating cash flow	(100)	35	32	29	26	23	145
Depreciation		(20)	(20)	(20)	(20)	(20)	(100)
Operating profit		15	12	9	6	3	45
Gross invested capital[1]		100	100	100	100	100	500
Cumulative depreciation[1]		—	(20)	(40)	(60)	(80)	(200)
Net invested capital[1]		100	80	60	40	20	300
IRR, %	15.0						15.0
Cash return on gross invested capital, %		35.0	32.0	29.0	26.0	23.0	29.0
Cash return on net invested capital, %		35.0	40.0	48.3	65.0	115.0	48.3
ROIC, %		15.0	15.0	15.0	15.0	15.0	15.0
CFROI, %		22.1	18.0	13.8	9.4	4.8	13.8

ROIC is constant over asset lifetime.   ROIC = IRR

CFROI decreases over asset lifetime.   CFROI < IRR

[1] At beginning of year.

When ROIC is constant, the asset provides a constant return over the initial investment, net of recovering the initial investment itself. Therefore, this return must also equal the IRR of the cash flows for the asset, or 15 percent. More precisely, the investment's ROIC equals the IRR if the earnings generated from the investment are proportional to the invested capital, net of accumulated depreciation, in each year of the investment's lifetime.

It is possible to generalize the result for a business consisting of a portfolio of five of these individual assets, which have remaining lifetimes of one, two, three, four, and five years, respectively (see the rightmost column in Exhibit 25.1). For this business, the operating cash flow, profit, and invested capital are a straightforward sum of the operating cash flow, profit, and invested capital for each year of the individual asset's lifetime (for example, operating cash flows for the business equal $35 + $32 + $29 + $26 + $23 = $145). What holds for the assets will therefore also hold for the business as a whole, so its ROIC must equal an individual asset's ROIC and IRR of 15 percent. If this business wants to grow its earnings by, say, 10 percent, it will need to expand its net invested capital by 10 percent as well—requiring an investment outlay of $30 in this case. The IRR on that incremental investment for carbon-copy growth equals exactly the business's ROIC of 15 percent.

This means that the ROIC of a business (or company) is equal to the IRR of new investments if the operating earnings for the business are proportional to net invested capital.[1] In these conditions, ROIC is a value-based measure of return on capital, even though it is based on accounting measures of earnings and capital.

WHEN CFROI EQUALS IRR

CFROI is an alternative measure of return on capital based on cash flow rather than profit and book value.[2] For any given year, CFROI is defined as the discount rate for which the present value of that year's operating cash flow (as an N-year annuity) equals gross invested capital at the beginning of the year, where N is the lifetime of the underlying asset. The basic formula for calculating CFROI in a given year T is

$$\text{GIC}_T = \sum_{t=1}^{N} \frac{\text{OCF}_T}{(1 + \text{CFROI})^t}$$

where GIC_T is the gross invested capital at the beginning of year T and OCF_T equals operating cash flow in year T.

[1] The same logic underlies the value driver formula introduced in Chapter 3, which showed that DCF value increases only for earnings growth at a ROIC above the cost of capital.
[2] For more information, see B. Madden, *CFROI Valuation: A Total System Approach to Valuing the Firm* (Oxford: Butterworth-Heinemann, 1999).

Any residual value of the asset should be included as an additional cash flow for year N and discounted at CFROI.

We illustrate CFROI as an alternative measure of returns by showing financial projections for an asset whose economics are different from those of the prior example. In this case, shown in Exhibit 25.2, the operating cash flows are proportional to gross invested capital and constant over the asset's lifetime, at $29 per year. The IRR for the investment is 13.8 percent and exactly equals the CFROI, which is constant over the asset's lifetime. Take, for example, year 2. We estimate the asset's CFROI by solving the following equation:

$$\$100 = \frac{\$29}{(1 + \text{CFROI})^1} + \cdots + \frac{\$29}{(1 + \text{CFROI})^5} \Rightarrow \text{CFROI} = 13.8\%$$

In fact, when the operating cash flow is constant over an asset's lifetime, CFROI must be equal to the IRR, as follows from the preceding formula. We could also say that CFROI equals the IRR of an investment if the operating cash flows generated are proportional to the gross invested capital (before accumulated depreciation).

Let's generalize the results again to a business consisting of five such individual assets, with remaining lifetimes of one, two, three, four, and five years (the right column in Exhibit 25.2). As in the prior example, the business's overall cash flows, earnings, and invested capital derive from those of the underlying five assets. The business's CFROI and IRR therefore equal the CFROI and IRR of each individual asset. If this business wants to grow its cash flows by 10 percent, it must expand its gross invested capital by 10 percent as

EXHIBIT 25.2 **Returns When Cash Flows Are Proportional to Gross Invested Capital**

$

	Individual asset						Business of five assets
	Year						
	0	1	2	3	4	5	
Operating cash flow	(100)	29	29	29	29	29	145
Depreciation		(20)	(20)	(20)	(20)	(20)	(100)
Operating profit		9	9	9	9	9	45
Gross invested capital[1]		100	100	100	100	100	500
Cumulative depreciation[1]		—	(20)	(40)	(60)	(80)	(200)
Net invested capital[1]		100	80	60	40	20	300
IRR, %	13.8						13.8
Cash return on gross invested capital, %		29.0	29.0	29.0	29.0	29.0	29.0
Cash return on net invested capital, %		29.0	36.3	48.3	72.5	145.0	48.3
ROIC, %		9.0	11.3	15.0	22.5	45.0	15.0
CFROI, %		13.8	13.8	13.8	13.8	13.8	13.8

ROIC increases over asset lifetime.

CFROI is constant over asset lifetime.

ROIC > IRR

CFROI = IRR

[1] At beginning of year.

well—an investment outlay of $50. The IRR on that incremental investment is now equal to its CFROI of 13.8 percent. Note that the business ROIC of 15 percent overestimates the IRR in this case. In general, the business (or company) CFROI is exactly equal to the IRR of new investments if operating cash flows for the business are proportional to gross invested capital.

CHOOSING BETWEEN ROIC AND CFROI

To understand when to use ROIC and when to use CFROI, let's now compare the two examples in Exhibits 25.1 and 25.2 in more detail. Note that the businesses (not the individual assets) in both examples have identical ROIC, CFROI, earnings (operating profit), operating cash flow, and invested capital. Nevertheless, the underlying economics and value creation are quite different, as is the "right" measure for return on capital.[3]

For the example in Exhibit 25.1, ROIC is the right measure of return on capital for the asset and the business, equaling the IRR of 15 percent. The reason: the cash flow pattern over the lifetime of the asset leads to *earnings* that are proportional to *net* invested capital in each year. At the asset level, this results in a constant ROIC and a changing CFROI over the asset's lifetime. At the business level, it implies that aggregate earnings and net invested capital grow in line with each other (assuming that growth comes only from adding more assets to the business).[4]

For the example in Exhibit 25.2, CFROI is the right measure and equal to the IRR of 13.8 percent, because now the *operating cash flows* are proportional to *gross* invested capital. At the asset level, CFROI is constant over the asset's lifetime, and ROIC continues to increase as the capital base is depreciated. For the business, this means that aggregate operating cash flows and gross invested capital grow in line with each other.

These two examples illustrate that there is no single right measure of return on capital. Depending on the earnings and cash flow pattern of the investment projects underlying a business, ROIC or CFROI can be equal to IRR—in theory. The fact that CFROI is calculated based on cash components does not mean it is always superior to the accounting-based ROIC.

Theoretical Trade-Offs

Although the examples were stylized, it is possible to derive general insights about the theoretical trade-offs between ROIC and CFROI. CFROI is more appropriate in businesses where investments are very lumpy. As two extreme

---

[3] Even though the cumulative cash flows over the lifetime of the underlying assets are equal, the assets shown in Exhibit 25.1 generate higher cash flows earlier in their lifetimes. As a result, the value creation is higher, as reflected in the assets' IRR of 15.0 percent, versus 13.8 percent for the assets in Exhibit 25.2.
[4] Note that this is in fact the economic model we assumed in deriving the ROIC-growth value driver formula in Chapter 3.

examples, think of infrastructure projects or hydroelectric power plants. These require very substantial up-front investments that generate relatively stable cash flows without significant investments in maintenance or overhauling over many years or even decades. Although accounting conventions may require that the assets be depreciated, their net capital base has little bearing on the capacity to generate cash flows. ROIC often rises to levels that are unrelated to the project's economic return (IRR), but CFROI will be much closer to the IRR because the operating cash flows are very stable.

In contrast, ROIC is likely to be a better estimate of the underlying IRR in businesses where investments occur in a more regular and smoother pattern because they are needed to support the earnings. As an example, think of retail supermarkets or a manufacturing company with many plants and pieces of equipment. These businesses require regular investments as management maintains, upgrades, and renews product lines and shop formats. In the periods between making such investments, pricing and earnings are likely to face pressure from competition with newer products or formats. As a result, the depreciated capital base is a reasonable approximation of the ability to generate earnings, making ROIC a better estimate of underlying IRR. In our experience, this is the case for most companies: maintenance and replacement investments are required on an ongoing basis to support the operating earnings.

Practical Considerations

Apart from these theoretical considerations, some practical trade-offs exist between ROIC and CFROI. First, it is easier to estimate ROIC and its components, such as operating earnings and book value of invested capital, from standard financial reporting statements with some reorganization and adjustments (as described in Chapter 11). Once you have the components, ROIC is a straightforward ratio that most managers are familiar with. In contrast, CFROI requires a more complex, iterative calculation that is not transparent to many managers.[5]

Because of the way CFROI is defined and calculated, interpreting it also is less straightforward than in the case of ROIC. For example, it follows that to double the ROIC, managers would need to double their profit margin or

---

[5] For this reason, practitioners have developed approximations of CFROI that are based on less complex calculations. For the example above, the following approximation can be applied when CFROI is close to the cost of capital:

$$CFROI_T = \frac{OCF_T - EcDep_T}{GIC_T}$$

Where GIC_T = gross invested capital at the beginning of year T
$\quad OCF_T$ = operating cash flow in year T

$\quad EcDep_T$ = economic depreciation, defined as $\dfrac{GIC_T \times k}{(1 + k)^N - 1}$, in year T

$\quad k$ = cost of capital
$\quad N$ = asset lifetime
See, for example, A. Damodaran, *Investment Valuation*, 2nd ed. (New York: Wiley, 2002), chap. 32.

double their capital turnover. With this logic, any reductions in inventory levels or costs of raw materials, for example, translate easily into ROIC improvements. In contrast, doubling capital turnover does not necessarily translate to doubling CFROI, because it is not a simple ratio. For the same reason, deriving the CFROI for a division or corporate group does not easily follow from the CFROI calculations of the underlying business units. A group's ROIC, however, is simply the capital-weighted average of the returns on invested capital of the underlying businesses.

An additional feature of CFROI is that, in its precise definition, it includes an adjustment for the effect of inflation on returns. The gross invested capital is indexed for inflation over the years dating to the initial purchase of the assets involved. For most economies in North America and Western Europe, this usually does not make a big difference. But the impact of the adjustment is significant when inflation is more than a couple of percentage points per year. In some cases, we found that this adjustment was the key source of difference between a company's CFROI and ROIC. However, adjustments for inflation can also be made when calculating ROIC. Basically, the adjustment involves using current-year dollars to express depreciation and property, plant, and equipment (PP&E). Adjusting ROIC for inflation and using CFROI with its inflation adjustment typically lead to similar results across widely different inflation rates and asset lifetimes, as illustrated for a range of stylized examples in Exhibit 25.3. (See Chapter 26 for more details about inflation's impact on ROIC and cash flows.)

EXHIBIT 25.3 **Returns under Inflation: ROIC vs. CFROI**

%

		Return after 20 years		
Inflation rate	Asset life, years	ROIC	CFROI[1]	Inflation-adjusted ROIC
0	5	15	14	15
2	5	17	13	12
4	5	19	13	11
6	5	22	13	10
8	5	24	12	10
10	5	26	12	10
0	10	15	13	15
2	10	19	12	11
4	10	23	12	10
6	10	27	11	10
8	10	31	11	10
10	10	35	11	10
0	20	17	12	17
2	20	21	12	15
4	20	25	12	14
6	20	30	12	13
8	20	35	11	13
10	20	39	11	13

[1] CFROI includes an inflation adjustment.

Differences between ROIC and CFROI could be sizable for specific businesses, depending on their economics, as we saw in the preceding two examples. Nevertheless, when we analyzed 1,000 U.S. companies between 2003 and 2013, we found that, on average, these differences were not very large (see Exhibit 25.4). For all but one of the ten nonfinancial sectors we considered, the spread between the average ROIC and CFROI was three percentage points or less when taking both ROIC and CFROI without inflation adjustments. The difference between the highest- and lowest-quartile ROIC in a sector was typically four times larger than this spread. Thus, your decision whether to

EXHIBIT 25.4 **Pretax ROIC and CFROI per Sector, 2003–2013**

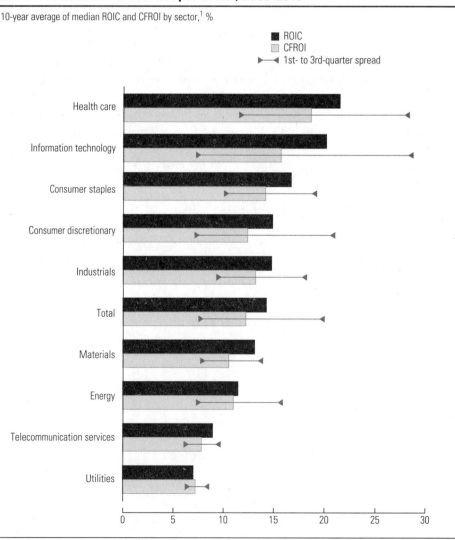

10-year average of median ROIC and CFROI by sector,[1] %

[1] For the 1,000 largest U.S. companies by market capitalization.

measure a business's return on capital by using ROIC or CFROI is unlikely to make a difference in what the result tells you about the company's relative performance versus that of sector peers.

FLAWS OF OTHER CASH RETURNS ON CAPITAL

In practice, we see managers and analysts apply other measures of return on capital, not just ROIC and CFROI. Sometimes the only difference is in the name. For example, most definitions of return on capital employed (ROCE) are fairly similar to ROIC and calculated as operating earnings divided by operating capital employed—although the exact definition of earnings and capital varies across applications.

Another set of measures, based on cash return on capital, is fundamentally different. They appear under various names, such as cash return on capital invested (CROCI), cash return on gross investment (CROGI), and cash return on assets (CashROA). These cash returns are typically calculated as operating cash flow divided by invested capital[6]:

$$\text{Cash Return on Net Invested Capital} = \frac{\text{Operating Cash Flow}}{\text{Net Invested Capital}}$$

$$\text{Cash Return on Gross Invested Capital} = \frac{\text{Operating Cash Flow}}{\text{Gross Invested Capital}}$$

Unfortunately, such cash returns are flawed measures of value creation, as they do not equal the underlying IRR. In Exhibits 25.1 and 25.2, the cash returns on both gross and net invested capital overestimate the true underlying IRR. The main reason is that these cash returns on capital fail to account for the charge of depleting the underlying capital, because they ignore depreciation charges.[7] For the cash return on invested capital net of cumulative depreciation, the error is magnified, as the denominator becomes smaller over the lifetime of the asset. This makes the overestimation of IRR even worse, as indicated by the results for operating cash flow divided by net invested capital in Exhibits 25.1 and 25.2. Because of these variances from IRR, we advise against using cash returns on capital as measures of business performance.

---

[6] See, for example, P. Costantini, *Cash Return on Capital Invested: Ten Years of Investment Analysis with the CROCI Economic Profit Model* (Amsterdam: Elsevier, 2006).

[7] CFROI is also based on operating cash flows, but it includes an implicit charge for the use of the underlying assets, because it is calculated as the IRR over the lifetime of the asset. The simple "cash return" discussed here equals CFROI if the lifetime of the asset is infinite.

SUMMARY

For most businesses, ROIC is a good measure of return on capital. It accurately reflects the economic return, as defined by the internal rate of return of the cash flows that the business generates. In addition, it is derived from information that is readily available from standard financial reports, and it is easy for managers to understand. For businesses with high up-front investments in capital that generate steady cash flows for many years, you can consider whether using CFROI justifies the additional effort and complexity relative to ROIC.

26

Inflation

Over the past three decades, inflation rates have mostly been at very low levels, rarely exceeding three percentage points—at least in the developed economies of North America and western Europe. Many finance practitioners had come to ignore the effects of inflation on the financial performance and value creation of companies. But the dramatic surge of American and European inflation rates in 2021 and 2022 was a strong reminder that inflation should not be completely ignored. High-inflation environments make analyzing and forecasting companies' financial performance a challenge. Inflation distorts the financial statements, adding to the difficulty of year-to-year historical comparisons, ratio analyses, and performance forecasts.

When inflation is high, analysis and valuation depend on insights from both nominal- and real-terms approaches. Sometimes nominal indicators are not useful (say, for capital turnover). In other cases, real indicators are problematic (for example, when determining corporate income taxes). But when properly applied, valuations in real and nominal terms should yield an identical value.

Although all the familiar tools described in Part Two still apply in periods of high inflation, these periods cause certain complications, which need to be dealt with. This chapter discusses the following issues:

- How inflation leads to lower value creation in companies, because it erodes real-terms free cash flow (FCF) if companies don't increase prices enough to overcome higher capital costs and taxation as well as operating costs
- How to evaluate a company's historical performance when inflation is high
- How to prepare financial projections of a company's performance in both nominal and real terms
- How to estimate a cost of capital that is consistent with inflation assumptions underlying these financial projections

INFLATION LEADS TO LOWER VALUE CREATION

Since the 1980s, inflation had generally been mild in the developed economies of Europe and North America, at levels around 2 to 3 percent per year. That changed quite suddenly with the COVID-19 outbreak of 2020 and Russia's invasion of Ukraine in February 2022. Supply chain interruptions and labor shortages triggered by the pandemic, paired with surging energy and food costs due to the ongoing conflict in Ukraine, drove up prices for a wide range of goods. At the same time, pandemic-related government subsidies and stimulus packages had fueled demand in many developed economies. As a result, annual inflation rates for 2022 sharply increased to around 8 percent in the United States and even higher in some European countries (for example, 10 percent in the Netherlands).

Although, as Exhibit 26.1 shows, inflation rates in these economies have come down significantly since 2023 and never reached their peaks from the 1970s, when inflation hovered around 10 to 15 percent for almost a decade, the absence of high inflation can no longer be taken for granted. Furthermore, some of the largest economies in Latin America and Asia (such as, for example, Brazil, China, and India), as well as South Africa, have faced inflation at double-digit levels for intervals of many years. Even Japan, which has experienced extremely low inflation and even deflation since the early 1990s, was not completely immune to the recent price surge: inflation rose to 3.3 percent in 2023.

In contrast to the recent surge, high inflation levels have often persisted for longer periods, stretching over several years as they did during the 1970s and early 1980s. This is because suppressing inflation requires strict and unpopular government measures. For example, curbing inflation caused by overheating in the economy typically requires increasing interest rates and reducing public spending to dampen growth. In 2022, central banks in the United States and Europe quickly intervened with strong step-ups in interest rates that appear to have been effective. Unfortunately, in many cases in the past, such measures were undertaken only when everything else had failed and when inflation had become too high to ignore—making it all the more difficult to fix.

It's necessary to take account of persistent inflation in analysis and valuation, because a large body of academic research clearly shows that inflation is negatively correlated with stock market returns.[1] To illustrate, as inflation increased from around 2 or 3 percent in the late 1960s to around 10 percent in the second half of the 1970s, the median price-to-earnings ratio (P/E) for companies in the United States declined from around 18 to below 10. When inflation finally came down, from 1985 onward, P/Es returned to their historical levels. Perhaps surprisingly, the 2021–2022 inflation surge did not depress market valuation, with median P/Es remaining at around 17 or higher

[1] See, for example, E. Fama and G. Schwert, "Asset Returns and Inflation," *Journal of Financial Economics* 5 (1977): 115–146; and J. Ritter and R. Warr, "The Decline of Inflation and the Bull Market of 1982–1999," *Journal of Financial and Quantitative Analysis* 37, no. 1 (2002): 29–61.

EXHIBIT 26.1 **Historical Inflation Rate in Developed and Emerging Economies**

Annual CPI-based inflation rate, %

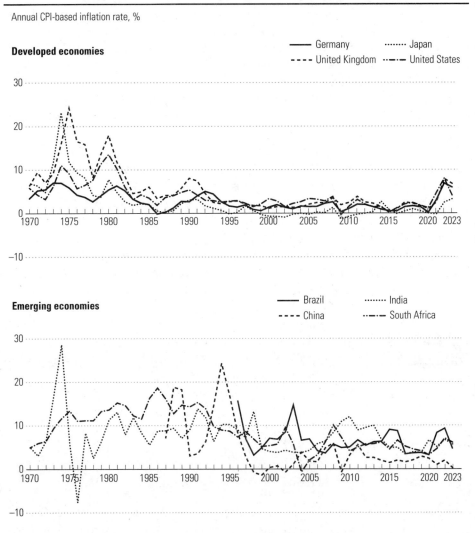

Source: World Development Indicators, World Bank, https://data.worldbank.org/indicator/FP.CPI.TOTL.

(see Chapter 6). One reason is that investors did not expect high inflation levels to last for many years. Another reason is that many companies managed to pass on the inflation effects to their customers and to sustain their real-terms cash flows, as we will discuss in greater detail later in this section.

Persistent inflation has pernicious effects on value creation. Academic research has found evidence that investors often misjudge inflation, which pushes up the cost of capital in real terms and depresses market valuations.[2]

---

[2] See, for example, F. Modigliani and R. Cohn, "Inflation, Rational Valuation, and the Market," *Financial Analysts Journal* 35 (1979): 24–44; and Ritter and Warr, "The Decline of Inflation," who found that in times of high inflation, investors tend to capitalize real cash flows at nominal discount rates.

Inflation creates a one-off loss in value for companies with so-called net monetary assets—that is, asset positions that are fixed in nominal terms.[3] For example, a balance of receivables loses 10 percent in value when inflation unexpectedly increases by 10 percent. The reverse holds for net monetary liabilities, such as fixed-rate debt. Depending on the relative size of a particular company's receivables, payables, and debt, the direct effect could be positive or negative. Companies also can end up paying higher taxes if their depreciation tax shields are not inflation adjusted for tax purposes—and this is typically the case.

Inflation's most severe value-destroying effect is less obvious. Though companies may increase prices, most cannot or do not increase them enough to cover both their higher operating costs (salaries and purchased goods) and the higher cost of future taxation and capital expenditures. As a result, they fail to maintain profitability in real terms.

To understand how significant the challenge of passing on cost increases can be, consider this simple example. Assume a company generates steady sales of $1,000 per year. Earnings before interest, taxes, and amortization (EBITA) are $133. At a tax rate of 25 percent, this results in net operating profit after taxes (NOPAT) of $100. With invested capital at $1,000, this translates to a return on invested capital (ROIC) of 10 percent. Net working capital is 10 percent of sales. Assume the fixed asset base is evenly spread across ten vintages with remaining lifetimes of one to ten years. Gross property, plant, and equipment (PP&E) is $1,636, and annual capital expenditures equal depreciation charges at $164.[4] The company's key financials would be as shown in Exhibit 26.2. If the cost of capital is 10 percent, the discounted-cash-flow (DCF) value at the start of year 1—or any year—equals:

$$DCF = \frac{\$100}{(10\% - 0\%)} = \$1,000$$

Now assume that in year 2, inflation suddenly increases to 15 percent and stays at that level in perpetuity, affecting costs and capital expenditures equally. (We have chosen this exceptionally high value for inflation to more acutely illustrate how inflation affects financial performance.) Assume the company increases prices enough that its EBITA grows with inflation while keeping sales volume and physical production capacity constant. In the process, the company even succeeds in lifting its EBITA margin over sales and its ROIC to 14 percent after 15 years (see Exhibit 26.3).

---

[3] See, for example, H. Hong, "Inflation and the Market Value of the Firm: Theory and Test," *Journal of Finance* 32, no. 4 (1977): 1031–1048.

[4] At the end of each year, after replacement of the asset group that is fully depreciated, the average remaining life of assets is exactly 5.5 years. Annual depreciation is equal to gross PP&E of $1,636 ÷ 10 = $164, and net PP&E equals 5.5 × $164 = $900.

EXHIBIT 26.2 **Financial Projections without Inflation**

$ million

	1	2	3	4	13	14	15
Sales	1,000	1,000	1,000	1,000	1,000	1,000	1,000
EBITDA[1]	297	297	297	297	297	297	297
Depreciation	(164)	(164)	(164)	(164)	(164)	(164)	(164)
EBITA[2]	**133**	**133**	**133**	**133**	**133**	**133**	**133**
Taxes	(33)	(33)	(33)	(33)	(33)	(33)	(33)
NOPAT	**100**	**100**	**100**	**100**	**100**	**100**	**100**
Gross property, plant, and equipment (GPPE)	1,636	1,636	1,636	1,636	1,636	1,636	1,636
Cumulative depreciation	(736)	(736)	(736)	(736)	(736)	(736)	(736)
Net property, plant, and equipment (NPPE)	**900**	**900**	**900**	**900**	**900**	**900**	**900**
Net working capital	100	100	100	100	100	100	100
Invested capital	**1,000**	**1,000**	**1,000**	**1,000**	**1,000**	**1,000**	**1,000**
EBITDA	297	297	297	297	297	297	297
Taxes	(33)	(33)	(33)	(33)	(33)	(33)	(33)
(Increast)/Decrease in working capital	—	—	—	—	—	—	—
Capital expenditures	(164)	(164)	(164)	(164)	(164)	(164)	(164)
Free cash flow (FCF)	**100**	**100**	**100**	**100**	**100**	**100**	**100**
EBITA growth, %		—	—	—	—	—	—
EBITA/sales, %	13.3	13.3	13.3	13.3	13.3	13.3	13.3
Taxes/EBITDA	11.2	11.2	11.2	11.2	11.2	11.2	11.2
Return on invested capital, %	10.0	10.0	10.0	10.0	10.0	10.0	10.0
FCF growth, %		—	—	—	—	—	—

[1] Earnings before interest, taxes, depreciation, and amortization.

[2] Earnings before interest, taxes, and amortization.

Although these results may be impressive at first sight, a closer inspection of the financial performance reveals significant value destruction. Even though EBITA grows at 15 percent per year, annual growth in earnings before interest, taxes, depreciation, and amortization (EBITDA) is at only 7 to 9 percent in the first four years because depreciation is recorded at historical nominal cost. As a result, capital spending should exceed depreciation charges to keep physical capacity constant, leading to an actual decline in free cash flow (FCF) in the first few years.

FCF growth only gradually rises to the rate of inflation in year 13.[5] Combine this with a cost of capital increase to 26.5 percent, and the company's value

[5] Given our assumption of an asset lifetime of 10 years, FCF growth gradually increases from 0 to 15 percent until 11 years after the start of inflation, when a new steady state is reached if inflation remains constant.

EXHIBIT 26.3 **Financial Projections with Inflation and Incomplete Pass-On**

$ million

	1	2	3	4	13	14	15
Sales	1,000	1,125	1,272	1,443	4,914	5,651	6,499
EBITDA[1]	297	317	342	374	1,153	1,326	1,525
Depreciation	(164)	(164)	(166)	(171)	(439)	(505)	(581)
EBITA[2]	**133**	**153**	**176**	**203**	**713**	**820**	**943**
Taxes	(33)	(38)	(44)	(51)	(178)	(205)	(236)
NOPAT	**100**	**115**	**132**	**152**	**535**	**615**	**708**
Gross property, plant, and equipment (GPPE)	1,636	1,661	1,714	1,799	5,053	5,811	6,683
Cumulative depreciation	(736)	(736)	(739)	(747)	(1,710)	(1,966)	(2,261)
Net property, plant, and equipment (NPPE)	**900**	**925**	**975**	**1,052**	**3,343**	**3,845**	**4,422**
Net working capital	100	113	127	144	491	565	650
Invested capital	**1,000**	**1,037**	**1,102**	**1,197**	**3,835**	**4,410**	**5,072**
EBITDA	297	317	342	374	1,153	1,326	1,525
Taxes	(33)	(38)	(44)	(51)	(178)	(205)	(236)
Increase/Decrease in working capital	—	(13)	(15)	(17)	(64)	(74)	(85)
Capital expenditures	(164)	(188)	(216)	(249)	(875)	(1,007)	(1,158)
Free cash flow (FCF)	**100**	**78**	**67**	**57**	**35**	**40**	**46**
EBITA growth, %		15.0	15.0	15.0	15.0	15.0	15.0
EBITA/sales, %	13.3	13.6	13.9	14.0	14.5	14.5	14.5
Taxes/EBITDA	11.2	12.1	12.9	13.5	15.5	15.5	15.5
Return on invested capital, %	10.0	11.1	12.0	12.7	14.0	14.0	14.0
FCF growth, %		(22.1)	(13.7)	(14.6)	15.0	15.0	15.0

[1] Earnings before interest, taxes, depreciation, and amortization.

[2] Earnings before interest, taxes, and amortization.

plummets.[6] An explicit DCF valuation with continuing value estimated as of year 12 would show the value at the start of year 2 being as low as $213.

To pass on inflation to customers in full without losing sales volume, the company must increase its after-tax free cash flows, not its earnings, at 15 percent per year (see Exhibit 26.4). In this case, the DCF value at the start of year 2 is fully preserved:

$$DCF = \frac{\$115}{(26.5\% - 15\%)} = \$1,000$$

But having after-tax free cash flows grow with inflation means earnings must increase much faster than inflation. As the summary financials show, EBITA growth is now almost 55 percent in year 2. In the same year, the sales margin increases from 13.3 percent to 17.9 percent, and ROIC increases from

[6] With inflation at 15 percent, the cost of capital increases from 10 percent to $(1 + 10\%) \times (1 + 15\%) - 1 = 26.5\%$.

EXHIBIT 26.4 **Financial Projections with Full Inflation Pass-On**

$ million

	1	2	3	4	13	14	15
Sales	1,000	1,150	1,323	1,521	5,350	6,153	7,076
EBITDA[1]	297	370	433	504	1,827	2,101	2,417
Depreciation	(164)	(164)	(166)	(171)	(439)	(505)	(581)
EBITA[2]	**133**	**206**	**266**	**333**	**1,388**	**1,596**	**1,835**
Taxes	(33)	(52)	(67)	(83)	(347)	(399)	(459)
NOPAT	**100**	**155**	**200**	**249**	**1,041**	**1,197**	**1,377**
Gross property, plant, and equipment (GPPE)	1,636	1,661	1,714	1,799	5,053	5,811	6,683
Cumulative depreciation	(736)	(736)	(739)	(747)	(1,710)	(1,966)	(2,261)
Net property, plant, and equipment (NPPE)	**900**	**925**	**975**	**1,052**	**3,343**	**3,845**	**4,422**
Net working capital	100	115	132	152	535	615	708
Invested capital	**1,000**	**1,040**	**1,107**	**1,204**	**3,878**	**4,460**	**5,129**
EBITDA	297	370	433	504	1,827	2,101	2,417
Taxes	(33)	(52)	(67)	(83)	(347)	(399)	(459)
(Increase)/Decrease in working capital	—	(15)	(17)	(20)	(70)	(80)	(92)
Capital expenditures	(164)	(188)	(216)	(249)	(875)	(1,007)	(1,158)
Free cash flow (FCF)	**100**	**115**	**132**	**152**	**535**	**615**	**708**
EBITA growth, %		54.5	29.3	24.8	15.0	15.0	15.0
EBITA/sales, %	13.3	17.9	20.1	21.9	25.9	25.9	25.9
Taxes/EBITDA, %	11.2	13.9	15.4	16.5	19.0	19.0	19.0
Return on invested capital, %	10.0	14.9	18.0	20.7	26.8	26.8	26.8
FCF growth, %		15.0	15.0	15.0	15.0	15.0	15.0

[1] Earnings before interest, taxes, depreciation, and amortization.

[2] Earnings before interest, taxes, and amortization.

10.0 percent to 14.9 percent. After ten years of constant inflation, the sales margin and ROIC would end up at 25.9 percent and 26.8 percent, respectively. ROIC needs to rise this far to keep up with inflation and the higher cost of capital.[7]

There are three reasons why the company's nominal financial performance in this stylized example needs to increase that much:

1. *Inflated cash costs and capital expenditures.* This implies that cash earnings (EBITDA, not EBITA) should increase at least with the inflation rate.

[7] The reason is that invested capital and depreciation do not grow with inflation immediately. For example, in year 2, annual capital expenditures increase by 15 percent, but this adds only 15 percent × $164 = $25 to invested capital. Assets are acquired at the end of each year and depreciated for the first time in the next year. Annual depreciation changes in year 3 by only a small amount: $1/10 × 25 = 2.5$ (shown in the exhibit as rounded figures, increasing from 163.6 to 166.1). In each year, the company replaces only 1/10 of assets at inflated prices, so it takes ten years of constant inflation to reach a steady state where capital and depreciation grow at the rate of inflation. As the example shows, sales margin, ROIC, and FCF increase each year until the steady state in year 13.

2. *Investments in net working capital.*[8] In the presence of inflation, the company needs to make additional investments in working capital even when its sales are constant in real terms (compare Exhibits 26.2 and 26.4).

3. *Reduced tax shields on depreciation.* Because depreciation is based on the company's asset purchases over the prior ten years, it does not keep up with inflation until year 13. As a result, the company incurs a loss from lower tax shields that needs to be compensated for with higher cash flows from operations.[9]

Although this example is stylized, the conclusion applies to all companies: for value to remain constant, after each acceleration in inflation, reported earnings should outpace inflation, and the reported sales margin and ROIC should increase—even though, in real terms, nothing has changed.

During the most recent inflation peak in the early 2020s, companies were quite successful in improving their ROIC to compensate for inflation (see Exhibit 8.4). In fact, the median ROIC for U.S.-based companies increased by five percentage points to 21 percent in 2022, with strong ROIC improvements in practically all the sectors we analyzed. This economy-wide pass-on of inflation is one of the reasons why equity markets showed no significant negative price reaction to the inflation surge. In addition, equity markets did not expect high inflation to last, as evidenced by market-derived breakeven rates for long-term inflation that remained around 2.0 to 2.5 percent.[10] (For more on this, see Chapter 15).

Unfortunately, history shows that in periods of prolonged inflation, companies do not always achieve and sustain such big improvements in reported return on invested capital. For example, ROICs remained in the range of 7 to 12 percent in the United States during the 1970s and early 1980s, when inflation was at 10 percent or more. If companies had succeeded in passing on inflation effects, they should have earned much higher ROICs in those years. Instead, they hardly managed to keep returns at pre-inflation levels.

When companies cannot sufficiently improve their financial performance (and this is even more the case for leveraged performance indicators, such as earnings per share), their cash flow in real terms declines. In addition, there is empirical evidence that in times of inflation, investors are likely to undervalue

---

[8] Even for assets held at constant levels in real-terms balance sheets, replacement investments are required at increasing prices in an inflationary environment. In nominal terms, this shows up as an investment in net working capital equal to the inflation rate times the working capital at the beginning of the year. In real terms, this equals the real-terms working capital at the beginning of the year times inflation/(1 + inflation). See also the discussions in the next sections.

[9] The size of the tax shield loss depends on the depreciation schedule for corporate income tax purposes. In this stylized example, we assumed linear depreciation. In case of accelerated depreciation for tax purposes, the tax shield loss would obviously be smaller.

[10] The market-based estimates of long-term inflation, also referred to as breakeven rates, are derived from yield differences for long-term nominal versus inflation-protected government bonds.

stocks as they misjudge inflation's effects.[11] Lower cash flow and higher cost of capital are a proven recipe for lower share prices, just as occurred in the 1970s and 1980s.

HISTORICAL ANALYSIS IN TIMES OF HIGH INFLATION

In countries experiencing extreme inflation (more than 25 percent per year), companies often report in year-end currency. In the income statement, items such as revenues and costs that were booked throughout the year are restated at year-end purchasing power. Otherwise, the addition of these items would have no relevance. The balance sheet usually has adjustments to fixed assets, inventory, and equity; the accounts payable and receivables are already in year-end terms.

In most countries, however, financial statements are not adjusted to reflect the effects of inflation. But when inflation is high (roughly 7.5 to 10 percent or higher) and persistent, it produces distortions in the balance sheet and income statement. In the balance sheet, nonmonetary assets, such as inventories and PP&E, are shown at values far below current replacement value. In the income statement, depreciation charges are too low relative to current replacement costs. Sales and costs in December and January of the same year are typically added as if they represented the same purchasing power. As a result, many financial indicators typically used in historical analyses can be distorted when calculated directly from the financial statements in high-inflation economies, so adjustments are needed for each distortion:

- Growth is overstated in times of inflation, so restate it in real terms by deflating with an annual inflation index if sales are evenly spread across the year. If sales are not spread evenly, use quarterly or monthly inflation indexes to deflate the sales in each corresponding interval.

- Capital turnover is typically overstated because operating assets are carried at historical costs. You can approximate the current costs of long-lived assets by adjusting their reported values with an inflation index for their estimated average asset age. Or consider developing ratios of real sales relative to physical-capacity indicators appropriate for the sector—for example, sales per square meter in consumer retail. Inventory levels also need restating if turnover is low and inflation is very high.

- Operating margins (operating profit divided by sales) can be overstated because depreciation is too low and slow-moving inventories make large nominal holding gains. Corrections for depreciation charges follow

[11] Modigliani and Cohn, "Inflation, Rational Valuation, and the Market"; Ritter and Warr, "The Decline of Inflation."

from adjustments to PP&E. You can estimate cash operating expenses at current-cost basis by inflating the reported costs for the average time held in inventory. Alternatively, use historical EBITDA-to-sales ratios to assess the company's performance relative to peers; these ratios at least do not suffer from any depreciation-induced bias.

• Return on capital is often overstated because of the distortions in capital turnover and margin. Even with indexed capital turnover and operating margins, an adjustment is needed in return on capital for the additional investment requirements in working capital, as illustrated in the example shown in Exhibit 26.5.

• Credit ratios and other indicators of capital structure health become distorted and require cautious interpretation. Distortions are especially significant in solvency ratios such as debt to equity or total assets, because long-lived assets are understated relative to replacement costs, and floating-rate debt is expressed in current currency units. As Chapter 35 advises, use coverage ratios such as EBITDA to interest expense.[12]

EXHIBIT 26.5 **Indexed Historical Financials Under Inflation**

$ million

	1	2	3	4		13	14	15	
Indexed NPPE,[1] beginning of year	900	1,035	1,190	1,369		4,815	5,538	6,368	← ①
Indexed depreciation	(164)	(188)	(216)	(249)		(875)	(1,007)	(1,158)	②
Capital expenditures	164	188	216	249		875	1,007	1,158	
NPPE,[1] end of year	**900**	**1,035**	**1,190**	**1,369**		**4,815**	**5,538**	**6,368**	
Net working capital	100	115	132	152		535	615	708	
Indexed invested capital	**1,000**	**1,150**	**1,323**	**1,521**		**5,350**	**6,153**	**7,076**	
EBITDA	297	370	433	504		1,827	2,101	2,417	← ③
Indexed depreciation	(164)	(188)	(216)	(249)		(875)	(1,007)	(1,158)	
Indexed EBITA	**133**	**182**	**216**	**255**		**952**	**1,095**	**1,259**	
Taxes	(33)	(52)	(67)	(83)		(347)	(399)	(459)	
Indexed NOPAT	**100**	**130**	**150**	**172**		**605**	**696**	**800**	
Depreciation rate[2]	18.2%	18.2%	18.2%	18.2%		18.2%	18.2%	18.2%	
Indexed ROIC,[3] %	10.0%	10.0%	10.0%	10.0%		10.0%	10.0%	10.0%	← ④

Example: Calculation steps for year 2

① End-of-Year NPPE$_1$ × (1 + Inflation Rate) = 900 × (1 + 15%)

② Beginning-of-Year NPPE$_2$ × Depreciation Rate = 1,035 × (18.2%)

③ Indexed invested capital and NOPAT

④ ROIC adjusted for inflation loss on net working capital

[1] Net property, plant, and equipment.

[2] Depreciation/NPPE in real terms.

[3] Return on invested capital, including inflation adjustment for net working capital.

[12] Distortions occur in the ratio of EBITA to interest coverage if operating profit is overstated due to low depreciation charges and low costs of procured materials.

These are less exposed to accounting distortions, because depreciation has no impact on them and debt financing is mostly at floating rates or in foreign currency when inflation is persistent.

One approach to overcoming distortions in capital turnover, margins, and ROIC is to index financial statements. In fact, some companies routinely index their internal management accounts when faced with high inflation. Exhibit 26.5 illustrates how a simple four-step indexation would work for our example company, assuming that the company achieved the financial projections with full inflation pass-on from Exhibit 26.4. We are now in year 15 and analyzing the performance since the start of inflation in year 2, using indexed asset values:

1. In the first step, the net PP&E as of the end of year 1 is increased by 15 percent to obtain the indexed net PP&E for the beginning of year 2 at $1,035.

2. Next, the depreciation charges for year 2 are derived as the real-term depreciation rate of 18.2 percent times the indexed net PP&E of $1,035. The depreciation rate is the real-terms depreciation of $164 divided by beginning-of-year, real-terms net PP&E of $900.[13]

3. Then the nominal net PP&E and depreciation are replaced by the indexed values to calculate indexed invested capital, EBITA, and NOPAT. Note that EBITDA, taxes, and sales figures do not require indexation, so margin and capital turnover follow readily. However, we cannot simply divide indexed NOPAT by indexed invested capital to obtain an estimate of the real-terms ROIC. As discussed in the previous section, inflation leads to an additional investment need that does not follow from the change in real-terms working capital.

4. Finally, we adjust ROIC by an amount equal to the inflation rate times the net working capital position at the beginning of the year. For example, in year 4:

$$\text{Indexed ROIC} = \frac{\$172}{\$1,521} = 11.3\%$$

$$\text{Indexed ROIC*} = \frac{\$172 - (15\% \times \$132)}{\$1,521} = 10.0\%$$

This adjusted ROIC* based on indexed financials is exactly equal to the true, underlying ROIC in real terms.

---

[13] Note that the results are exactly equal to those obtained when applying a price index growing at 15 percent annually to inflate the real-terms net PP&E and depreciation in each year from Exhibit 26.2.

All steps are repeated for each of the following years to provide unbiased estimates of ROIC in real terms, which remains constant at 10 percent over the years (identical to Exhibit 26.2).

The index illustration shown in Exhibit 26.5 is stylized. For example, the indexation starts in the first year of inflation and assumes that the average asset lifetime in the company does not change over time. In practice, you would apply more robust, alternative approaches. When you have access to a company's internal reporting information, you can index individual asset values and depreciation charges in each year to the price level for that year. You typically group assets by year of purchase and use a general price index to inflate each grouping's book values and depreciation to any given year. Of course, this requires detailed information on the company's asset base. When you are doing an outside-in analysis, an alternative, practical approach is to adjust the reported asset values with an inflation index for their estimated average asset age.

FINANCIAL PROJECTIONS IN REAL AND NOMINAL TERMS

When you make financial projections of income statements and balance sheets for a valuation in a high-inflation environment, keep in mind that accounting adjustments should not affect free cash flow. Projections are typically made in either nominal or real terms, but high-inflation environments require a hybrid approach because each single approach has different strengths. On the one hand, projecting in real terms makes it difficult to calculate taxes correctly, as tax charges are often based on nominal financial statements. Furthermore, you need to project explicitly the effects of working-capital changes on cash flow, because these do not automatically follow from the annual change in real-terms working capital. On the other hand, using nominal cash flows makes future capital expenditures difficult to project, because the typically stable relationship between revenues and fixed assets does not hold in times of high inflation. This means it will also be difficult to project depreciation charges and EBITA.

Therefore, to prepare consistent financial projections, you must use elements of both nominal and real forecasts. This section illustrates how to combine the two approaches in a DCF valuation. We continue with our example company, which is now in year 15. It has reached a steady state under 15 percent inflation and zero growth in real terms. Following the historical analysis with indexed asset values, it generates a real-terms ROIC of 10 percent (adjusted for working-capital investments). Going forward, the company plans to accelerate its real-terms growth to 3.5 percent and increase its EBITDA margin from 34 to 40 percent by year 18. Inflation rates are expected to increase to 18 percent in year 18 and then gradually decline to 2 percent in year 25 and thereafter (see Exhibit 26.6).

In practice, financial projections for high-inflation valuations raise many more issues than in this simplified example.[14] Nevertheless, the example is useful for showing how to address some key issues when developing a cash flow forecast in periods of inflation. Using the following step-by-step approach leads to the real and nominal valuation results shown in Exhibit 26.6.

Step 1: Forecast Operating Performance in Real Terms

To the extent possible, convert historical nominal balance sheets and income statements into real terms, using one of the indexation approaches discussed in the previous section. At a minimum, make a real-terms approximation of the historical development of the key value drivers—growth and return on capital—and the underlying capital turnover and EBITA margin, so you can understand the true economics of the business. Based on these indexations or approximations, develop the operating assumptions for your forecasts in real terms, as indicated in the second page of Exhibit 26.6. Then project the operating performance of the business in real terms:

- Project future revenues and cash expenses to obtain EBITDA forecasts.[15]
- Estimate PP&E and capital expenditures from your assumptions for real-terms capital turnover.
- Working capital follows from projected revenues and assumptions about days of working capital required.
- From projected net PP&E and assumptions about the lifetime of the assets, derive the annual depreciation to estimate real-terms EBITA.[16]

Margins, capital turnover, and most other metrics in real-terms projections can be readily interpreted, but unadjusted ROIC in real-terms is distorted by inflation. It needs a correction for the replacement investments in working capital. For ROIC* on beginning-of-year invested capital, the adjusted definition is as follows:

$$\text{ROIC}_t^{R*} = \frac{\text{NOPAT}_t^R - \text{NWC}_{t-1}^R \times \frac{i_t}{(1+i_t)}}{\text{Invested Capital}_{t-1}^R}$$

where NOPAT_t^R is the real-terms NOPAT and i_t is the inflation rate in year t, and where NWC_{t-1}^R and Invested Capital$_{t-1}^R$ are net working capital and invested capital in real terms for year $t-1$.

---

[14] For example, we assume that all cash flows occur at the end of the year. For extremely high, fluctuating levels of inflation, however, this assumption could distort financial projections, because the cash flows that accumulate throughout the year are subject to different inflation rates. In such cases, split the year into quarterly or even monthly intervals, project cash flows for each interval, and discount the cash flows at the appropriate discount rate for that interval.

[15] This step assumes that all expenses included in EBITDA are cash costs.

[16] In this example, depreciation is projected using a fixed ratio of depreciation to net PP&E of 18 percent. Alternatively, you could project depreciation as 10 percent of gross PP&E, which would be more complex and lead to some differences, depending on real-terms growth rates.

EXHIBIT 26.6 **Financial Projections Under Inflation**

$ million

	Indexed	Nominal projections						
	15	16	17	18	19	20	25	40
Sales	7,076	8,422	10,198	12,455	15,083	17,874	29,002	65,393
EBITDA[1]	2,417	3,032	3,773	4,982	6,033	7,150	11,601	26,157
Depreciation	(1,158)	(909)	(1,032)	(1,194)	(1,404)	(1,666)	(3,472)	(9,403)
EBITA[2]	**1,259**	**2,123**	**2,741**	**3,788**	**4,629**	**5,484**	**8,129**	**16,755**
Taxes	(459)	(531)	(685)	(947)	(1,157)	(1,371)	(2,032)	(4,189)
NOPAT	**800**	**1,592**	**2,056**	**2,841**	**3,472**	**4,113**	**6,097**	**12,566**
NPPE[3]	6,368	5,678	6,568	7,722	9,162	10,866	21,091	54,640
Net working capital	708	842	1,020	1,246	1,508	1,787	2,900	6,539
Invested capital	**7,076**	**6,520**	**7,588**	**8,968**	**10,670**	**12,653**	**23,991**	**61,180**
EBITDA		3,032	3,773	4,982	6,033	7,150	11,601	26,157
Taxes		(531)	(685)	(947)	(1,157)	(1,371)	(2,032)	(4,189)
(Increase)/Decrease in working capital[4]		(135)	(178)	(226)	(263)	(279)	(153)	(345)
Capital expenditures		(1,588)	(1,923)	(2,348)	(2,844)	(3,370)	(5,468)	(12,329)
Free cash flow (FCF)		**779**	**988**	**1,461**	**1,769**	**2,130**	**3,947**	**9,294**
Continuing value								140,804
Present value factor		0.791	0.614	0.473	0.368	0.292	0.133	0.026
Present value of FCF		616	607	691	651	622	524	3,729
DCF value, beginning of year		**14,655**						
Operating assumptions								
Sales growth, %	15.0	19.0	21.1	22.1	21.1	18.5	5.6	5.6
EBITDA/sales, %	34.2	36.0	37.0	40.0	40.0	40.0	40.0	40.0
NPPE/sales	0.90	0.67	0.64	0.62	0.61	0.61	0.73	0.84
Net working capital/sales	0.10	0.10	0.10	0.10	0.10	0.10	0.10	0.10
Depreciation/NPPE, beginning of year	0.18	0.18	0.18	0.18	0.18	0.18	0.18	0.18
Financial assumptions								
Inflation, %	15.0	15.0	17.0	18.0	17.0	14.5	2.0	2.0
Inflation index (year 15 = 100)	100	115	135	159	186	213	291	391
Tax rate, %	25.0	25.0	25.0	25.0	25.0	25.0	25.0	25.0
WACC, %		26.5	28.7	29.8	28.7	26.0	12.2	12.2
FCF growth, %		10.0	26.8	47.9	21.1	20.4	8.1	5.6
EBITA/sales, %	17.8	25.2	26.9	30.4	30.7	30.7	28.0	25.6
ROIC, %[4]	10.0	24.4	27.1	31.7	32.5	32.5	25.4	20.5

[1] Earnings before interest, taxes, depreciation, and amortization.

[2] Earnings before interest, taxes, and amortization.

[3] Net property, plant, and equipment.

[4] In real-terms projections: return on invested capital including inflation adjustment for net working capital.

					☐	*Projection assumptions*	

Real-terms projections

16	17	18	19	20	25	40
7,323	7,580	7,845	8,120	8,404	9,981	16,722
2,636	2,804	3,138	3,248	3,361	3,992	6,689
(1,158)	(1,198)	(1,240)	(1,284)	(1,329)	(1,578)	(2,644)
1,479	**1,606**	**1,898**	**1,964**	**2,033**	**2,414**	**4,045**
(462)	(509)	(596)	(623)	(645)	(699)	(1,071)
1,017	**1,097**	**1,301**	**1,341**	**1,388**	**1,715**	**2,974**
6,591	6,822	7,060	7,308	7,563	8,983	15,049
732	758	784	812	840	998	1,672
7,323	**7,580**	**7,845**	**8,120**	**8,404**	**9,981**	**16,722**
2,636	2,804	3,138	3,248	3,361	3,992	6,689
(462)	(509)	(596)	(623)	(645)	(699)	(1,071)
(117)	(132)	(142)	(141)	(131)	(53)	(88)
(1,381)	(1,429)	(1,479)	(1,531)	(1,584)	(1,882)	(3,153)
677	**734**	**920**	**953**	**1,001**	**1,359**	**2,377**
						36,725
0.909	0.826	0.751	0.683	0.621	0.386	0.102
616	607	691	651	622	524	3,729
14,655						
3.5	3.5	3.5	3.5	3.5	3.5	3.5
36.0	37.0	40.0	40.0	40.0	40.0	40.0
0.90	0.90	0.90	0.90	0.90	0.90	0.90
0.10	0.10	0.10	0.10	0.10	0.10	0.10
0.18	0.18	0.18	0.18	0.18	0.18	0.18
31.2	31.7	31.4	31.7	31.7	29.0	26.5
10.0	10.0	10.0	10.0	10.0	10.0	10.0
(4.3)	8.4	25.4	3.5	5.1	6.0	3.5
20.2	21.2	24.2	24.2	24.2	24.2	24.2
12.6	13.1	15.1	15.1	15.3	17.0	17.6

Step 2: Build Financial Statements in Nominal Terms

Based on the financial assumptions shown on the right-hand side of Exhibit 26.6, the real operating projections can be readily converted into nominal terms through the following steps[17]:

- Project nominal revenues, cash expenses, EBITDA, and capital expenditures by multiplying their real-terms equivalents by an estimated inflation index for the year.
- Estimate net PP&E on a year-by-year basis from the prior-year balance plus nominal capital expenditures minus nominal depreciation (which is estimated as a percentage of net PP&E according to the ratio of real-terms depreciation to net PP&E).
- Project working capital by multiplying the real-terms amounts by the inflation index for the year (or derive it from real-terms revenues and days of working capital required).
- Subtract the nominal depreciation charges from EBITDA to obtain nominal EBITA.
- Calculate income taxes on nominal EBITA without inflation corrections, unless tax laws allow for such corrections.

Keep in mind that margins, capital turnover, and ROIC in nominal projections are distorted by inflation. They will not provide meaningful insights in the value creation of the company. Use the real-terms projections and metrics instead—or prepare indexed versions of nominal projections (which should give identical results).

This example did not build a complete balance sheet and income statement. Complete financial statements would be needed for major decisions concerning, for example, dividend policy and capital structure, debt financing, and share repurchase. Developing complete nominal financial statements would require the following additional steps:

- Forecast interest expense and other nonoperating income statement items in nominal terms (based on the previous year's balance sheet).
- Check that equity equals last year's equity plus earnings, less dividends, plus or minus any share issues or repurchases.
- Balance the balance sheet with debt or marketable securities.

---

[17] As noted, these projections are made for valuation purposes and not necessarily in accordance with local or international accounting standards prescribing any inflation or monetary corrections for particular groups of assets and liabilities under, for example, inflation accounting. Free cash flows would not be affected by such adjustments.

Step 3: Build Financial Statements in Real Terms

Most of the operating items for the real-terms income statement and balance sheet were already estimated in step 1. Now include the real-terms taxes on EBITA by deflating the nominal taxes as estimated in step 2 with the inflation index. For full financial statements, use the inflation index to convert debt, marketable securities, interest expense, income taxes, and nonoperating terms from the nominal statements into real terms. The real-terms equity account is a plug to balance the balance sheet. To make sure you have done this correctly, be sure the real equity account equals last year's equity plus earnings, less dividends, plus or minus share issues or repurchases, and plus or minus inflationary gains or losses on the monetary assets and liabilities (such as cash, receivables, payables, and debt).

Step 4: Forecast Free Cash Flows in Real and Nominal Terms

Forecast the future free cash flows in real and nominal terms from the projected income statements and balance sheets. Follow the general approach described in Chapter 10. The only difference is that in the real-terms projections, the investment in net working capital (NWC^R) is equal to the increase in working capital plus the replacement investment needs due to inflation[18]:

$$\text{Investment in } NWC_t^R = \text{Increase in } NWC_t^R + NWC_{t-1}^R \left(\frac{i_t}{1 + i_t} \right)$$

where i_t is the inflation rate in year t.

To check for consistency, use the inflation index to convert the free cash flows from the nominal projections to real terms. These should equal the free cash flows from the real-terms projections in each year.

Step 5: Estimate DCF Value in Real and Nominal Terms

When discounting real and nominal cash flows under high inflation, you must address three key issues.

First, ensure that the weighted average cost of capital estimates in real terms ($WACC^R$) and nominal terms ($WACC^N$) are defined consistently with the assumptions for inflation (i) in each year:

$$1 + WACC_t^N = \left(1 + WACC_t^R \right)(1 + i_t)$$

---

[18] Even for assets held at constant levels in real-terms balance sheets, replacement investments are required at increasing prices in an inflationary environment. These replacement investments represent a cash outflow, also in real terms, but do not show up from real-terms balance sheet differences from year to year. In nominal terms, these replacement investments are automatically included in the working capital differences from year to year and equal to $NWC^{t-1} \times i_t$, as discussed in Exhibit 26.4.

EXHIBIT 26.7 **Nominal and Real WACC Under Inflation**

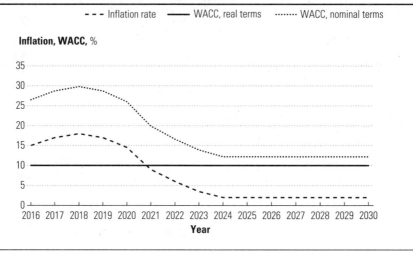

Given the inflation assumptions for years 16 and beyond and the real-terms WACC of 8 percent, the nominal WACC for our example company will vary over the years, as in Exhibit 26.7.

Note that you need to discount the cash flow for any given year with the WACC estimates for that year and all prior years. For example, the present value of the cash flow in year 18 is calculated as

$$PV(FCF_{t=18}) = \frac{FCF_{t=18}}{(1 + WACC_{t=16}) \times (1 + WACC_{t=17}) \times (1 + WACC_{t=18})}$$

$$PV(FCF_{t=18}) = \frac{FCF_{t=18}}{(1 + 8\%)(1 + 15\%) \times (1 + 8\%)(1 + 17\%) \times (1 + 8\%)(1 + 18\%)}$$

$$= \frac{\$1,461}{2.11} = \$691$$

The second issue is the length of the explicit forecast period. Make sure it is long enough for the model to reach a steady state with constant growth rates of free cash flow in the year when you apply the continuing-value formula. Because of the way inflation affects capital expenditures and depreciation, you need a much longer horizon than for valuations with no or low inflation.

Third, the value driver formula as presented in Chapter 14 can be readily applied when estimating continuing value in nominal terms, but it should be adjusted when estimating in real terms in high-inflation environments. As discussed in step 1, the unadjusted return on capital in real-terms projections overestimates the economic returns in the case of positive net working capital. You should use the adjusted $ROIC^{R*}$ on beginning-of-year invested capital in the value driver formula. Also, instead of using real-terms NOPAT in the formula, use the implied NOPAT from adjusted ROIC and invested capital to estimate continuing value in real terms (CV^R)[19]:

$$CV^R = \frac{ROIC_T^{R*} \times InvCap_{T-1}^R \left[1 - \frac{g_T^R}{ROIC_T^{R*}}\right]}{(WACC^R - g_T^R)} = InvCap_{T-1}^R \times \frac{(ROIC_T^{R*} - g_T^R)}{(WACC^R - g_T^R)}$$

where g_T^R is real-terms growth and $ROIC_T^{R*}$ is adjusted real-terms return on capital in perpetuity T, and where $InvCap_{T-1}^R$ is the real-terms invested capital at the beginning of the perpetuity year T. The resulting continuing-value estimate is the same as that obtained from an FCF perpetuity growth formula. After indexing for inflation, it also equals the continuing-value estimates derived from nominal projections.

Of course, the DCF valuations in nominal and real terms should lead to exactly the same result. Combining both approaches not only provides additional insights into a company's economics under inflation but also is a useful cross-check on the validity of the valuation outcomes.

SUMMARY

High and persistent inflation destroys value because companies typically cannot increase prices enough to offset higher capital outlays. To analyze and value companies in the presence of such inflation, we use the same tools and approaches as introduced in Part Two. However, applying them can be somewhat different.

When analyzing a company's historical performance, you should be aware that persistent inflation can distort many familiar financial indicators, such as growth, capital turnover, operating margins, and solvency ratios. Ensure that you make appropriate adjustments to these ratios. When making financial projections, use an approach that combines nominal and real terms, because real-terms and nominal-terms projections offer relevant insights and can be used for cross-checking your results. When discounting cash flows, use inflation assumptions in the weighted average cost of capital that are fully consistent with those underlying your cash flow projections.

---

[19] Prior editions showed a different version of the value-driver formula where the adjustment was not in the return on capital but in the growth rate. We prefer the current, rearranged version because it uses a return on capital that more accurately reflects underlying value creation.

27

Cross-Border Valuation

To value businesses, subsidiaries, or companies in foreign countries, follow the same principles and methods we presented in Part Two. Fortunately, accounting issues in cross-border valuations have diminished. Most of the world's major economies have adopted either International Financial Reporting Standards (IFRS) or U.S. Generally Accepted Accounting Principles (GAAP), and these two standards have become largely aligned. Moreover, if you follow Chapter 11's recommendations for rearranging financial statements, you will obtain identical results regardless of which accounting principles you follow in preparing the financial statements.

Nevertheless, the following issues arise in cross-border valuations and still require special attention:

- Forecasting cash flows, whether in foreign currency (the currency of the foreign entity to be valued) or domestic currency (the home currency of the person performing the valuation)
- Estimating the cost of capital
- Applying a domestic- or foreign-capital WACC
- Incorporating foreign-currency risk in valuations
- Using translated foreign-currency financial statements

This chapter highlights the steps involved in the special analyses required for each of these issues.

FORECASTING CASH FLOWS

A company or business unit valuation should always result in the same value regardless of the currency or mix of currencies in which cash flows are projected. To achieve this, you should use consistent monetary assumptions and one of the two following methods for forecasting and discounting cash flows denominated in foreign currency.

1. *Spot-rate method.* Project foreign cash flows in the foreign currency, and discount them at the foreign cost of capital. Then convert the present value of the cash flows into domestic currency, using the spot exchange rate.

2. *Forward-rate method.* Project foreign cash flows in the foreign currency, and convert these into the domestic currency, using the relevant forward exchange rates. Then discount the converted cash flows at the cost of capital in domestic currency.

Let's use a simple example to illustrate. Assume you want to estimate the value of an Australian subsidiary for its German parent company as of January 2025. The top of the table in Exhibit 27.1 shows the nominal and real-terms cash flow projections for the subsidiary in the foreign currency (Australian dollars).

To value the subsidiary using the spot-rate method, simply discount nominal cash flows in Australian dollars (A$) at the Australian nominal risk-free interest rates (we assume the subsidiary's beta is zero). The resulting present value is 595.5 Australian dollars. Converting this value at the spot exchange rate of 1.600 Australian dollars per euro results in a discounted-cash-flow (DCF) value of €372.2 million:

		Year					
Spot-rate method		**2025**	**2026**	**2027**	**2028**	**2029**	**2030**
Cash flow, A$ million		100.5	104.0	108.2	112.6	117.2	121.9
Discount factor		0.976	0.947	0.915	0.883	0.853	0.824
Present value of cash flow, A$ million		98.0	98.5	99.0	99.5	100.0	100.5
DCF value, A$ million	595.5						
DCF value, € million	372.2						

Note: Numbers may not sum due to rounding.

The forward-rate method for valuation is more elaborate. The projected nominal cash flows in Australian dollars are now converted to euros on a year-by-year basis, using forward exchange rate, and then discounted at nominal euro interest rates. Estimate synthetic forward rates by using interest parity as described in the discussion of forward exchange rates later in this section. You could use market-based forward exchange rates, too, but check for interest rate parity to ensure consistent valuation results across currencies. We obtain a present value of €372.2 million, exactly the same value as obtained under the spot-rate method:

Forward-rate method	Year					
	2025	2026	2027	2028	2029	2030
Cash flow at forward exchange rate, € million	63.1	65.7	69.0	72.5	76.2	80.4
Discount factor	0.971	0.938	0.897	0.858	0.820	0.781
Present value of cash flow, € million	61.3	61.6	61.9	62.2	62.5	62.8
DCF value, € million	372.2					

Note: Numbers may not sum due to rounding.

EXHIBIT 27.1 **Cash Flows Projected and Discounted Under Consistent Monetary Assumptions**

← Consistent assumptions on inflation, interest, and currency rates

Foreign currency, Australian dollars (A$)	2025	2026	2027	2028	2029	2030
Cash flows, A$ million						
Nominal cash flow	100.5	104.0	108.2	112.6	117.2	121.9 ←
Real cash flow	100.0	102.5	105.1	107.7	110.4	113.1
Inflation, %	0.50	1.00	1.50	1.50	1.50	1.50
Interest rates, %						
Real interest rate (yield)	2.00	2.00	2.00	2.00	2.00	2.00
Nominal forward interest rate	2.51%	3.02%	3.53%	3.53%	3.53%	3.53%
Nominal interest rate (yield)	2.51%	2.76%	3.02%	3.15%	3.22%	3.27%
Foreign-exchange rates, €/A$						
Spot exchange rate 1.600						
Forward exchange rate	1.592	1.584	1.569	1.553	1.538	1.516 ←
Domestic currency, euros (€)						
Interest rates, %						
Nominal interest rate (yield)	3.02%	3.27%	3.70%	3.91%	4.04%	4.21%
Nominal forward interest rate	3.02%	3.53%	4.55%	4.55%	4.55%	5.06%
Real interest rate (yield)	2.00	2.00	2.00	2.00	2.00	2.00
Inflation, %	1.00	1.50	2.50	2.50	2.50	3.00
Cash flows, € million						
Real cash flow	62.5	64.1	65.7	67.3	69.0	70.7
Nominal cash flow	63.1	65.7	69.0	72.5	76.2	80.4 ←

The results for the spot-rate and forward-rate valuations are identical because the domestic and foreign cash flows are projected and discounted under consistent monetary assumptions, as shown in Exhibit 27.1. As we explain in more detail in the following sections, you cannot make independent assumptions for inflation, interest rates, and forward exchange rates across currencies:

- Inflation assumptions underlying cash flow projections in a specific currency must be consistent with inflation assumptions underlying interest rates in that currency.
- Forward exchange rates between currencies must be consistent with inflation and interest rate differences between those currencies.
- Conversion of cash flow projections from one currency into another should be done at forward exchange rates.

Inflation and Interest Rates

Inflation and interest rates should be projected in accordance with the Fisher effect.[1] For each currency, the inflation rate i_t in each year should align with the nominal forward interest rate (f_t) and real interest rate (R_t) in that year:

$$(1 + f_t) = (1 + R_t) \times (1 + i_t)$$

For example, in Exhibit 27.1, the Australian forward interest rate in 2026 equals the real interest rate plus the expected inflation rate for that year:

$$3.02\% = (1 + 2.00\%)(1 + 1.00\%) - 1$$

The two-year interest rate (yield) as of January 2025 is the geometric average of the first- and second-year nominal forward interest rates:

$$2.76\% = [(1 + 2.51\%)(1 + 3.02\%)]^{1/2} - 1$$

Forward Exchange Rates

Forward exchange rates should reflect inflation and interest rates following interest rate parity. For currencies with liquid forward markets, arbitrage trading drives forward rates to interest rate parity, but you should always verify that the rates are consistent with inflation and interest rates you are using in your cash flow projections and valuation. The forward foreign-exchange rate

---

[1] See, for example, R. Brealey, S. Myers, and F. Allen, *Principles of Corporate Finance*, 13th ed. (Burr Ridge, IL: McGraw-Hill/Irwin, 2020), chap. 27.

in year t, X_t, should equal the current spot rate, X_0, multiplied by the ratio of nominal interest rates in the two currencies over the forecast interval, t:

$$X_t = X_0 \left(\frac{1 + r^F}{1 + r^D} \right)^t$$

where r^F is the interest rate in foreign currency and r^D is the interest rate in domestic currency. In our example, the four-year nominal interest rate (yield) in Australia, r^F, is 3.15 percent as of January 2025, while the borrowing rate in euros, r^D, is 3.91 percent for the same period. As the spot exchange rate, X_0, is 1.600 Australian dollars per euro, the four-year forward rate, X_4, should be calculated as follows[2]:

$$X_4 = 1.600 \left(\frac{1 + 3.15\%}{1 + 3.91\%} \right)^4 = 1.553$$

The Fisher effect and interest rate parity imply that the ratio of the inflation rates for two currencies over a forecast interval t should also align with the forward exchange rate in year t, X_t, and the current spot rate, X_0:

$$X_t = X_0 \left[\frac{(1 + i_1^F) \times (1 + i_2^F) \times \ldots \times (1 + i_t^F)}{(1 + i_1^D) \times (1 + i_2^D) \times \ldots \times (1 + i_t^D)} \right]$$

where i_t^D = inflation rate in year t in domestic currency

i_t^F = inflation rate in year t in foreign currency

In the example from Exhibit 27.1, the four-year forward rate ties not only with the euro and Australian dollars interest rates but also with the inflation rates:

$$X_4 = 1.600 \left[\frac{1.005 \times 1.010 \times 1.015 \times 1.015}{1.010 \times 1.015 \times 1.025 \times 1.025} \right] = 1.553$$

Conversion of Cash Flows

Conversion of future cash flows should be done only at forward exchange rates that are consistent with the interest and inflation rates used in your valuation. Otherwise, valuation results are likely to differ depending on the currency used in the cash flow projections. Do not rely on "forecast" exchange rates for your projections, as these rates could induce a bias in your valuation if they are not consistent with your assumptions on inflation and discount rates.

---

[2] Interest rate parity implies that whether a company borrows in Australian dollars or euros has no impact on value (unless there are any tax implications). You could borrow 1,600 Australian dollars today at 3.15 percent interest per year, totaling 1,811 Australian dollars to repay in 2029. At the four-year forward exchange rate, this amounts to €1,166 (1,811 ÷ 1.553). Alternatively, you could take up a €1,000 loan today at 3.91 percent annual interest in euros, accruing to an identical payment of €1,166 in 2029.

ESTIMATING THE COST OF CAPITAL

As when you are forecasting cash flows in different currencies, the most important rule for estimating costs of capital for cross-border valuations is to have consistent monetary assumptions. The expected inflation that determines the foreign-currency cash flows should equal the expected inflation to be included in the foreign-currency weighted average cost of capital (WACC) through the risk-free rate. Then estimate the cost of capital, depending on the investor's position.

For investors and companies that face little or no restriction on investing outside their home markets, the cost of capital is best estimated following a global capital asset pricing model (CAPM) that applies equally to foreign and domestic investments.

For investors and companies in markets facing capital controls that prevent them from freely investing abroad, we recommend using a so-called local CAPM. Since they can invest in domestic assets only, they should estimate the cost of capital from a domestic perspective, measuring market risk premium and beta versus a (diversified) domestic portfolio.

Many practitioners make ad hoc adjustments to the discount rate to reflect political risk, foreign-investment risk, or foreign-currency risk. We don't recommend this. As the discussion of emerging markets explains in Chapter 35, political or country risk is diversifiable and best handled by using probability-weighted scenarios of future cash flows.

Finally, keep in mind that estimating a cost of capital is not a mechanical exercise with a precise outcome. You should pair the approach outlined in this chapter with sound judgment on long-term trends in interest rates and market risk premiums (see Chapter 15) to obtain a cost of capital estimate that is sufficiently robust for financial decision making. The following sections and Appendix G provide further background for our recommendations and practical guidelines for estimating the cost of capital in foreign currency.

Global CAPM

For investors and companies able to invest outside their home markets without restrictions, we recommend using a global CAPM. In a global CAPM, there is a single, real-terms risk-free rate, and the market risk premium and beta are measured against a global market portfolio:

$$E(r_j) = r_f + \beta_{j,G}[E(r_G) - r_f]$$

where r_j = return for asset j

r_f = risk-free rate

$\beta_{j,G}$ = beta of asset j versus global market portfolio G

r_G = return for global market portfolio G

Effectively, this means applying the approach described in Chapter 15. The cost of capital for domestic and foreign assets is determined in exactly the same way. What matters is their beta, relative to the global market portfolio, and the market risk premium of that same portfolio, relative to the risk-free rate.

We recommend this approach because capital markets are global. A considerable share of all equity trades is international, and traders, primarily large institutional investors, draw their capital and invest it globally. For example, consider the consumer goods companies Procter & Gamble and Unilever. Both sell their household products around the world and have roughly the same geographic spread. The shares of both are traded in the United States and Europe. The primary difference is that Procter & Gamble is domiciled in the United States and Unilever is domiciled in the United Kingdom. With such similar business profiles and investor bases, it would be odd if the two companies had different costs of capital. In general, we find that the domicile of otherwise-comparable companies does not influence their valuation levels. For example, the EBITA-to-enterprise-valuation multiples of U.S. and European pharmaceutical companies are all in a very narrow range, regardless of the company domicile.

As explained in Appendix G, the global CAPM technically holds only if purchasing power parity (PPP) holds, which is the case in the long run.[3] Although evidence on PPP has been mixed, academic research has converged around the conclusion that on average, deviations from PPP between currencies are reduced to half their value within three to five years. In other words, exchange rates ultimately adjust for differences in inflation between countries, although not immediately and perfectly.

Estimating Market Risk Premium in Global CAPM   In the absence of capital controls for investors, the global market risk premium should be based on a global index that includes most of the world's investment assets. As explained in Chapter 15, the market risk premium for an index can be estimated from its historical returns or from forward-looking models, which by and large lead to similar results. Global indexes rarely go far back in time, so long-term estimates of historical market risk premiums are not readily available. Therefore, we generally resort to specially compiled estimates for the global market or the well-diversified U.S. market as a basis for a global market risk premium. Correlation between the S&P 500 and global market indexes (such as the MSCI World Index) has, so far, been very high, making the S&P 500 a good proxy. Estimates from both sources are typically not far apart, falling in the range of 4.5–5.5 percent (also see Chapter 15).

---

[3] For an overview, see A. M. Taylor and M. P. Taylor, "The Purchasing Power Parity Debate," *Journal of Economic Perspectives* 18, no. 4 (Fall 2004): 135–158.

Estimating Beta across Currencies in Global CAPM   Since we are using a global market risk premium, a global beta also should be used. Follow the guidelines from Chapter 15 on how to estimate beta. There is one special issue to consider when estimating betas for stocks in international markets: the currency in which returns are measured. For example, should a Swiss investor estimate the beta of IBM based on returns in U.S. dollars or Swiss francs? If you use total returns to estimate beta, the results will be different when returns are expressed in U.S. dollars or Swiss francs, because the dollar-to-franc exchange rate fluctuates over time. But a stock's beta should be the same in all currencies, as any difference would imply differences in the real-terms cost of capital across currencies. The solution is to use excess returns over the risk-free rate, rather than total returns.[4] Beta estimates are consistent across currencies when the stock's excess returns are regressed against the excess return of a global market portfolio, as follows for any period ending at time t:

$$\left(r_{j,t}^A - r_{f,t}^A\right) = \beta_j\left(r_{M,t}^A - r_{f,t}^A\right)$$

where $r_{j,t}^A$ = realized return for stock j in currency A

   $r_{f,t}^A$ = risk-free rate in currency A

   $r_{M,t}^A$ = realized return for global market portfolio in currency A

If the international Fisher effect and purchasing power parity would hold, differences in international interest rates would reflect differences in inflation across countries, and differences in inflation across countries would also be reflected in changes in exchange rates. In that case, the risk-free rate for each currency should equal the U.S. dollar risk-free return and the change in the exchange rate:

$$\left(1 + r_{f,t}^A\right) = \left(1 + r_{f,t}^\$\right)\frac{X_{t-1}}{X_t} \tag{27.1}$$

where $r_{f,t}^\$$ = risk-free rate in U.S. dollars

   X_t = exchange rate at time t of currency A expressed in U.S. dollars

If risk-free rates across currencies are tied to changes in exchange rates in this way, beta estimates based on excess returns will be the same whether we use U.S. dollars, Swiss francs, or any other currency. In practice, the relations will not hold perfectly. To avoid any differences in beta estimates, we

---

[4] Most practitioners use the so-called market model, estimating beta from absolute returns instead of excess returns. This is an approximation that produces good results if the risk-free rate is relatively stable. When translating returns from another currency, the approximation no longer holds, as the nominal risk-free rate will fluctuate with exchange rates.

recommend using a synthetic risk-free rate for each currency when calculating a stock's excess returns, based on the U.S. risk-free rate and the U.S. dollar exchange rate as defined in Equation 27.1.

Local CAPM   We recommend using a local CAPM for investors and companies facing restrictions on investing abroad. In that case, the local market portfolio is the right reference to estimate the cost of capital. As a result, valuations in such restricted markets can be out of line with those in global markets—which is what we have encountered in the past for valuations in, for example, the Indian and some Asian stock markets. The local CAPM is similar to the model described in Chapter 15 but stated in terms of a local risk-free rate, a risk premium of the local market portfolio over that risk-free rate, and a local beta measured against that same local market portfolio:

$$E(r_j) = r_{f,L} + \beta_{j,L}\big[E(r_L) - r_{f,L}\big]$$

where r_j = return for asset j

$r_{f,L}$ = local risk-free rate

$\beta_{j,L}$ = local beta of asset j versus local market portfolio L

r_L = return for local market portfolio L

Some practitioners and academic researchers propose always using a local CAPM, regardless of any investment restrictions for investors and companies.[5] Interestingly enough, empirical research finds that the local and global CAPM generate similar results for well-integrated markets (which is in line with theoretical predictions, as explained in Appendix G). For the United States, United Kingdom, Germany, France, and smaller economies such as the Netherlands and Switzerland, cost of capital estimates from a local and a global CAPM are very close to each other.[6]

Nevertheless, we don't recommend the local CAPM approach for integrated markets, for several reasons. When applying the local CAPM for investments in different countries, you need to estimate the local market risk premium and beta for each of these countries instead of only the global market risk premium when applying the global CAPM. Using a local CAPM also means you cannot make a straightforward estimate of a company's beta based on the average of the estimated betas for a sample of industry peers. In Chapter 15, we recommend estimating an industry average beta to reduce its standard error, but if the peers are in different countries, their local betas are not directly comparable.

---

[5] See, for example, R. Stulz, "The Cost of Capital in Internationally Integrated Markets: The Case of Nestlé," *European Financial Management* 1, no. 1 (1995): 11–22.

[6] R. Harris, F. Marston, D. Mishra, and T. O'Brien, "Ex-Ante Cost of Equity Estimates of S&P 500 Firms: The Choice between Domestic and Global CAPM," *Financial Management* 32, no. 3 (2003): 51–66.

Finally, local risk premiums are typically less stable over time than their aggregate, the global risk premium. See Appendix G for more detail.

APPLYING A DOMESTIC- OR FOREIGN-CAPITAL WACC

When cash flows and cost of capital are estimated in a consistent manner, the currency in which the cash flows are denominated will not affect the valuation. This holds regardless of whether you are using the enterprise DCF approach, the adjusted present value (APV) approach, or the cash-flow-to-equity approach.

But you should be aware of some implicit assumptions made when applying the enterprise DCF approach with a weighted average cost of capital (WACC) for cross-border valuations. As explained in Chapter 15, the WACC automatically accounts for the value of interest tax shields in your valuation of free cash flows. When you translate a WACC from one currency into another, you also translate the implied interest tax shields—and the underlying assumptions on debt financing and taxation.[7] As a result, there are two basic choices in applying WACC in cross-border valuations:

1. *Domestic-capital WACC.* Use a domestic-capital WACC if the cross-border business is financed and taxed at domestic interest and tax rates. As international companies tend to borrow in their parent country at parent company currencies, this is the most common approach.[8] To discount foreign cash flows, convert the domestic-capital WACC into a foreign-currency equivalent WACC by adding the inflation-rate difference between the currencies in each year.[9] The valuation result can be converted at the spot rate to obtain a value in domestic currency.

2. *Foreign-capital WACC.* Use a foreign-capital WACC if cross-border businesses are financed and taxed at foreign rates. Discount the foreign cash flows directly at this WACC, and convert the result into domestic currency at the spot rate. Alternatively, you could convert the foreign-capital WACC and cash flows into domestic currency and value the business using the forward-rate approach, which leads to the same result.

Note that even when converted into the same currency, the domestic- and foreign-capital WACCs are not equal and therefore generate different valuation results. For example, consider a WACC estimate for the valuation of a Mexican subsidiary by its German parent company (Exhibit 27.2). For illustration purposes, we assume that the parent and subsidiary have identical business risk

---

[7] This assumption concerns only the taxation of interest charges, not the foreign operating tax rate.
[8] As always, account for the riskiness of the cross-border business in the WACC via the unlevered beta.
[9] That is, by adding to the domestic-capital WACC any forward inflation difference between the domestic and foreign currency, as explained in the first section of this chapter.

EXHIBIT 27.2 **WACC Measures for Mexican Subsidiary of German Parent Company**

Cross-border DCF valuation example

	Domestic-capital WACC	Foreign-capital WACC	
Currency for measuring cash flows	Euros	Mexican pesos	
Cost of debt (k_d),%	5.0	12.3	
Tax rate on interest, %	33.0	33.0	
Debt/(debt + equity),%	33.0	33.0	Difference from tax
Weighted k_d after taxes, %	**1.1**	**2.7** ←	deduction of interest in foreign versus domestic currency
Unlevered cost of equity (k_u), %	**9.0**	**16.6**	
Debt/equity, %	49.3	49.3	
Cost of equity (k_e),%	11.0	18.7	
Equity/(debt + equity),%	67.0	67.0	
Weighted k_e , %	**7.3**	**12.5**	
WACC,%	**8.5**	**15.2**	
€ inflation, %	1.0	1.0	
Peso inflation, %	8.0	8.0	
Equivalent WACC,[1] %	(in Mex$) **16.0**	(in €) **7.7**	

[1] Equivalent WACC in the other currency after adjustment for the difference in inflation.

(k_u = 9.0 percent in euros), tax rates (33 percent), credit quality (k_d = 5.0 percent in euros), and target leverage (debt to value = 33 percent). The domestic-capital WACC for cash flows in euros is 8.5 percent. When we account for the seven-percentage-point inflation difference between the two currencies, the 8.5 percent WACC is equivalent to 16.0 percent in Mexican pesos. Applying this 16.0 percent WACC assumes that the debt financing and taxation of interest are taking place in euros.

The foreign-capital WACC is derived by converting the euro-based cost of debt and unlevered cost of equity into pesos (k_d = 12.3 percent, and k_u = 16.6 percent). The foreign-capital WACC based on cash flow in pesos amounts to 15.2 percent, equivalent to 7.7 percent in euros. The difference from the domestic-capital WACC stems from the after-tax cost of debt: tax shields are larger when the debt is financed and taxed in a higher-inflation currency, everything else being equal.

In practice, financing choices for cross-border business operations are far from straightforward, because companies need to take into account many complicating factors. These include differences in international taxation, the cost of local versus international debt funding, the depth of alternative debt markets, the impact on foreign-currency exposure, and others. How to make such international financing choices is beyond the scope of this book. But you should be careful in properly reflecting the outcome of such financing choices via the cost of capital in cross-border valuations. In practice, a domestic-capital WACC is most common—but beware of exceptions.

INCORPORATING FOREIGN-CURRENCY RISK IN THE VALUATION

Many executives are concerned about the impact that currency fluctuations from foreign investments have on value creation in company results. The analyst community and investors may be wary of the resulting earnings volatility, even though it does not matter for value creation. As a result, many companies still add a premium for currency risk to the cost of capital for foreign investments. This is unnecessary. As we discuss in Appendix G, currency risk premiums in the cost of capital—if any—are likely to be small. There should be no difference between the cost of capital for investments in foreign currency and otherwise identical investments in domestic currency (when you apply consistent monetary assumptions). First, price fluctuations tend to mitigate currency fluctuations because of purchasing power parity. Second, currency risk is largely diversifiable for companies and shareholders. Any remaining risk from currency rate changes is best reflected in the cash flow projections for the investment.

Keep in mind that nominal currency risk is irrelevant if exchange rates immediately adjust to differences in inflation rates. The only relevant currency risk is therefore real currency risk as measured by changes in relative purchasing power. For example, if you held $100 million of Brazilian currency in 1994, by 2024 it would be worth about $20 million in U.S. dollars. Yet if you adjust for purchasing power, the value of the currency has fluctuated much closer to the $100 million mark during the 30-year period. Exhibit 27.3 shows the estimated real effective (inflation-adjusted) exchange rate for the Brazilian currency, which has continued to hover around the 1994 level although the nominal exchange rate to the U.S. dollar plummeted.

EXHIBIT 27.3 **Brazilian Inflation-Adjusted Exchange Rate**

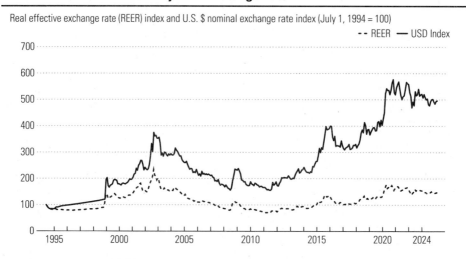

Real effective exchange rate (REER) index and U.S. $ nominal exchange rate index (July 1, 1994 = 100)

- - REER   — USD Index

Source: Banco Central do Brasil.

Analysis of purchasing power parity (PPP) indicates that, in general, currencies indeed revert to parity levels following changes in relative rates of inflation, albeit not immediately.[10] For example, as Exhibit 27.3 shows, the value of the Brazilian currency declined sharply versus the U.S. dollar during the COVID-19 pandemic in 2020. General price levels in Brazil did not adjust immediately to that step change, making the real effective exchange rate deviate from parity levels for subsequent years. In general, these deviations will converge in the long term, as has been the case in the past (note how much flatter the line is for the real exchange rate versus the nominal exchange rate). However, even if short-term, such deviations from exchange rates at purchasing power parity potentially leave corporations exposed to real-terms currency risk.

Shareholders are typically able to diversify this risk. To see how, consider Exhibit 27.4, which shows the monthly volatility of real exchange rates for a selection of Latin American and Asian currencies, as well as the British pound, and compares them with four currency portfolios. Although some of the currencies are highly volatile, holding a regional portfolio already eliminates a lot of the resulting real currency risk, as shown by the lower volatility of the regional portfolios. Combining a developing-markets portfolio with a British-pounds portfolio diversifies the real risk even further. If shareholders can disperse most real currency risk by diversifying, there is no need for a currency risk premium of any significance in the company's cost of capital.

EXHIBIT 27.4 **Diversification of Real Currency Risk**

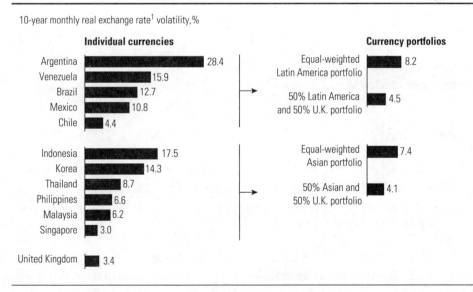

10-year monthly real exchange rate[1] volatility,%

[1] Exchange rates to U.S. dollar.
Source: International Monetary Fund.

[10] See Taylor and Taylor, "The Purchasing Power Parity Debate."

Sometimes currency exchange rates move fast and far from PPP. As Exhibit 27.3 shows, this happened in Brazil not only during the 2020 pandemic, but at several other points in time as well. During a period of just two weeks in 1999, Brazil's currency weakened by more than 50 percent relative to the U.S. dollar in nominal terms. When conducting a valuation in a currency that shows large deviations from PPP, you should account for the risk of a few weeks or even several years passing before the currency moves back toward PPP. Do not adjust the cost of capital, but instead use scenarios to account for this risk, as described in Chapter 4.

If the foreign business being valued has limited international purchases and sales, the impact of any exchange rate convergence toward PPP is likely to be limited as well. In this case, value the business's forecast cash flows using either the spot-rate or forward-rate approach to obtain a valuation in your domestic currency. Apply two different currency scenarios: one using spot and forward rates based on the actual exchange rate, and one based on a deemed convergence of the exchange rate toward PPP. The valuation results in the local currency of the foreign business will be identical for both scenarios. But that won't be the case for the result in your domestic currency, highlighting the exposure to a potential exchange rate change.

If the business has significant cash flows in international currencies, as an oil-exporting company would, exchange rate adjustments toward PPP will affect cash flows in local currency. Prepare the local cash flow forecasts for the business based on two scenarios: one with convergence of the exchange rate toward PPP and one without. Then value the cash flows for both currency scenarios using the spot-rate or forward-rate approach. Ensure that the spot and forward rates correctly reflect your currency scenarios' assumptions about the convergence of the exchange rate. The result will again be a valuation range in domestic currency indicating the potential impact of an exchange rate convergence toward PPP.

USING TRANSLATED FOREIGN-CURRENCY FINANCIAL STATEMENTS

To analyze foreign businesses' historical performance, it's best to use the foreign currency. But this is impossible if you are conducting your analysis on an outside-in basis and the business's statements in foreign currency have been translated into its parent company's domestic currency and consolidated in the parent's accounts.

For example, a British subsidiary of a European corporate group will always prepare financial statements in British pounds, and when the European parent company prepares its financial statements, it will translate the British pounds in the statements of the British subsidiary at the current euro–pound exchange rate. However, if the exchange rate fluctuates from year to year, the European parent company will report the same asset at a different euro amount each year, even if the asset's value in British pounds has not changed. This change in the value of the British asset in the parent's reporting currency would suggest a cash expenditure. But no cash has been spent, because the change is solely due to a change in the exchange rate. Therefore, following the guidelines from Chapter 11, you need to adjust the cash flow estimated from the financial statements by an amount equal to the gains or losses from the currency translation.

Three Approaches

Between them, U.S. GAAP and IFRS sanction three approaches to translating the financial statements of foreign subsidiaries into the parent company's currency: the current method, the temporal method, and the inflation-adjusted current method. Exhibit 27.5 shows the approach recommended by each standard for countries with moderate inflation and for those with hyperinflation.

Current Method   For subsidiaries in moderate-inflation countries, translating the financial statements into the currency of the parent company is straightforward. Both U.S. GAAP and IFRS apply the current method, which requires translating all balance sheet items except equity at the year-end exchange rate. Translation gains and losses on the balance sheet are recognized in the equity account in other comprehensive income (OCI), so they do not affect net income. The average exchange rate for the period is used to translate the income statement.

For subsidiaries in countries with higher inflation rates, IFRS and U.S. GAAP differ in what they define as hyperinflation, whether to adjust statements for inflation, and what approach to use for translating the financial statements. U.S. GAAP defines hyperinflation as cumulative inflation over three years of approximately 100 percent or more. IFRS states that this is one

EXHIBIT 27.5 **Currency Translation Approaches**

	U.S. GAAP	IFRS
Moderate inflation	Current method	Current method
Hyperinflation	Temporal method	Inflation-adjusted current method

indicator of hyperinflation but suggests considering other factors as well, such as the degree to which local investors prefer to keep wealth in nonmonetary assets or stable foreign currencies.

Temporal Method   U.S. GAAP requires companies to use the temporal method for translating into the parent's currency financial statements of subsidiaries in hyperinflation countries. To use this method, you must translate all items in the financial statements at the exchange rate prevailing at the relevant transaction date. This means using historical exchange rates for items carried at historical cost, current exchange rates for monetary items, and year-average or other appropriate exchange rates for other balance sheet items and the income statement. Any resulting currency gains or losses are reported in the equity account of the parent in OCI.

Inflation-Adjusted Current Method   The IFRS approach to currency translation for subsidiaries in hyperinflation countries is like that for moderate-inflation countries. The key difference? IFRS requires that the hyperinflation country statements be restated in current (foreign) currency units based on a general price index before they are translated into the parent company's currency. All except some monetary items need to be restated to account for the estimated impact of very high inflation on values over time. The restatement will result in a gain or loss on the subsidiary's income statement. Because the full statements are restated in current (year-end) foreign-currency units, the year-end exchange rate should be used to translate both the balance sheet and the income statement into the parent company's currency. Any translation gains or losses will be included in the equity account of the parent in OCI.

An Application of the Methods

Exhibit 27.6 shows an example for a U.S. parent company using all three approaches to currency translation. In this example, the exchange rate has changed from 0.95 at the beginning of the year to 0.85 at the end of the year, consistent with 14 percent inflation in the foreign country during the year and U.S. inflation of 2 percent. The average exchange rate for the year is 0.90. As the exhibit illustrates, the three approaches can result in significantly different amounts for net income and equity in the parent company's currency.

Of course, these differences should not affect your estimate of free cash flow for the subsidiary. As a general rule, you should ensure that translation adjustments in components of invested capital are excluded from the investment cash flows. Under IFRS, companies typically specify currency translation adjustments by category of fixed assets, so you can identify the "cash" investments. Under U.S. GAAP, this information is usually not provided; you will have to add back the translation results to the change in invested capital.

EXHIBIT 27.6 **Currency Translation**

	Current method			Temporal method		Inflation-adjusted currency method		
	Local currency	Foreign-exchange rate	U.S. $	Foreign-exchange rate	U.S. $	Adjusted	Foreign-exchange rate	U.S. $
Balance sheet								
Cash and receivables	100	0.85	85	0.85	85	100	0.85	85
Inventory	300	0.85	255	0.90	270	321	0.85	273
Net fixed assets	600	0.85	510	0.95	570	684	0.85	581
	1,000	—	850	—	925	1,105	—	939
Current liabilities	265	0.85	225	0.85	225	265	0.85	225
Long-term debt	600	0.85	510	0.85	510	684	0.85	581
Equity								
Common stock	100	0.95	95	0.95	95	100	0.95	95
Retained earnings	35	—	32	—	95	56	—	48
Foreign-currency adjustment	—	—	(12)	—	—	—	—	(10)
	1,000	—	850	—	925	1,105	—	939
Income statement								
Revenue	150	0.90	135	0.90	135	161	0.85	137
Cost of goods sold	(70)	0.90	(63)	0.93	(65)	(75)	0.85	(64)
Depreciation	(20)	0.90	(18)	0.95	(19)	(23)	0.85	(20)
Other expenses, net	(10)	0.90	(9)	0.90	(9)	(11)	0.85	(9)
Foreign-exchange gain/(loss)[1]	—	—	—	—	66	20	0.85	17
Income before taxes	50	—	45	—	108	72	—	61
Income taxes	(15)	0.90	(13)	0.90	(13)	(16)	0.85	(13)
Net income	35	—	32	—	95	56	—	48

[1] Gain from restatement.

For the analysis of historical performance, ratios such as ROIC, operating margin, and capital turnover typically are not significantly distorted under the current method. You do have to adjust growth rates for currency translation effects (see also Chapter 12). For translated financial statements from hyperinflation countries, we recommend analyzing performance based on the original statements or by reversing translations made for the key operating items (following the analysis recommendations found in Chapters 26 and 41).

SUMMARY

In principle, applying the DCF valuation approach to foreign businesses is the same as applying it to domestic companies. But there are some additional issues to consider. You'll want to reflect local accounting in your analysis, following the general guidelines from Chapter 11. Because IFRS and U.S. GAAP are now the dominant standards, accounting issues have become less of a burden.

You can project and discount cash flows for foreign businesses in foreign or domestic currency if you apply consistent assumptions for exchange rates, interest, and inflation and if you correctly apply the spot-rate or forward-rate method of valuation. The approach for estimating the cost of capital should be the same for any company anywhere in the world. With the global integration of capital markets in mind, we recommend using a single real-terms risk-free rate and market risk premium for companies around the world. For investors and companies facing restrictions on investing abroad, we recommend estimating a local cost of capital. It is not necessary to add separate premiums to the cost of capital to address currency risks. These are best reflected in a scenario-based valuation.

Part Four

Managing for Value

28

Corporate Portfolio Strategy

Applying a management perspective to the science and art of value creation is the focus of the nine chapters that make up Part Four of this book. Specifically, we examine critical top management decisions: What should executives decide to hold in the company's portfolio of businesses? How should they allocate resources across opportunities, including capital expenditures, research and development (R&D), talent management, and more? How can managers best use acquisitions and divestitures to support their decisions around their desired portfolio of business? In addition, this section discusses three how-tos of portfolio strategy: how to maximize value through choosing a supportive capital structure and cash return to shareholders policy, how to measure and manage the impact of the growing focus on sustainability and the innovation of digital technologies, and how to effectively communicate with investors.

We begin in this chapter with the question of what businesses a company should be in, based on the attractiveness of the underlying product markets and whether the company is a better owner of a particular business unit. We also explore why diversification's role in creating value is often misunderstood.

CORPORATE PORTFOLIO: MARKET ATTRACTIVENESS AND BETTER OWNER

Deciding what businesses to own and operate is clearly one of the most important decisions executives make. Research undertaken by our colleagues has shown that it is a critical determinant of a company's destiny.[1] For example, a company that produces commodity chemicals is unlikely ever to earn as

This chapter was coauthored by Jamie Koenig, Paul Morgan, and Justin Sanders.
[1] C. Bradley, M. Hirt, and S. Smit, *Strategy Beyond the Hockey Stick* (Hoboken, NJ: John Wiley & Sons, 2018).

much return on capital as one that makes branded breakfast cereal (although commodity chemicals is still a growing industry, while breakfast cereal consumption is flat to declining). That said, different owners and managers might be able to extract more or less value from the same business. So maximizing value requires that a company identify which businesses it can extract more value from, compared with other potential owners, as well as invest in attractive businesses and reduce exposure to unattractive businesses.

Exhibit 28.1 illustrates an approach to evaluating a company's portfolio of businesses, a step that begins the process of deciding whether and how to change the portfolio. On the vertical axis is the fundamental attractiveness of each product market in which the company competes (or could compete). As described throughout this book, the primary drivers of market attractiveness are the potential return on capital and growth. The horizontal axis measures the degree to which the company is a "better owner" than others. In other words, does it have or can it develop competitive advantages relative to its peers?

Business units in markets with high fundamental attractiveness and ownership potential to create more value are more likely to be ones in which the company should increase its investments. Business units with low market attractiveness and lower ownership quality are ones where a company might reduce resources or consider divestment.

The unit of analysis here should be granular. Too high a level of aggregation could hide important insights about the portfolio of businesses. Assume a large chemical company with four divisions, one of which is coatings (basically various types of paint). One way to disaggregate coatings is into consumer and industrial coatings, each of which has different product requirements and sales channels. Industrial coatings can further be divided into at least seven

EXHIBIT 28.1 **Portfolio Assessment Framework**

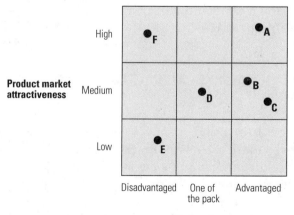

types, based on their raw materials and applications.[2] At this granular level, these product lines are likely to have different fundamental market attractiveness and potential for better ownership.

We don't assign numbers to the two axes in Exhibit 28.1, because market attractiveness or better ownership in a single number is too simplistic, but in the rest of this section, we describe the factors that should be considered in placing a unit on this chart.

Note that we've divided better ownership into three ranges: better owner, one of the pack, and disadvantaged. Of course, the best place to be and potentially invest more resources is the top right of the graph, where market attractiveness is high and ownership is advantaged. A unit with disadvantaged ownership might be a divestiture candidate regardless of industry attractiveness, because someone else might be willing to pay a price for the unit that exceeds the value to its current owner. Being in the middle on ownership (one of the pack) doesn't necessarily mean you should sell a unit. If the market is attractive and the business unit earns attractive returns with reasonable growth, keeping up with the pack may create value. As you can see, this matrix is just a starting point for deciding what to do with each unit.

MARKET ATTRACTIVENESS

The importance of market attractiveness cannot be overstated. Even the best managers cannot make up for a business that is in decline or structurally is unlikely to earn high returns on capital. Warren Buffett made the point in his own unique way: "When a management team with a reputation for brilliance joins a business with poor fundamental economics, it is the reputation of the business that remains intact."

This does not mean companies should always exit businesses they are already in where the economic performance is likely to deteriorate due to factors such as new technology or the entrance of lower-cost competitors from emerging-market countries. They still might be better owners to manage a business as it declines, although they most likely should minimize new investments in these businesses.

Market attractiveness ultimately comes down to the potential for high returns on capital and growth based on the characteristics of the product market. In other words, the question is whether the potential is there for some companies to earn a competitive advantage—not whether any one company has achieved or can achieve a competitive advantage (which will be covered in the next section).

In addition to observing the current growth and returns on capital for the companies competing in a particular product market, you should understand

---

[2] "Seven Common Types of Industrial Coatings and Their Uses," Industrial Inspection, www. indinspect.com.

EXHIBIT 28.2 **Sources of Competitive Advantage**

Price premium	Cost and capital efficiency
Innovative products: Difficult-to-copy or patented products, services, or technologies	**Innovative business method:** Difficult-to-copy business method that contrasts with established industry practice
Quality: Customers willing to pay a premium for a real or perceived difference in quality over and above competing products or services	**Unique resources:** Advantage resulting from inherent geological characteristics or unique access to raw material(s)
Brand: Customers willing to pay a premium based on brand, even if there is no clear quality difference	**Economies of scale:** Efficient scale or size for the relevant market
Customer lock-in: Customers unwilling or unable to replace a product or service they use with a competing product or service	**Scalable product/process:** Ability to add customers and capacity at negligible marginal cost
Rational price discipline: Lower bound on prices established by large industry leaders through price signaling or capacity management	

Network economies: Products or services that offer increasing value to customer with scale, at negligible or decreasing costs to scale, possibly combined with customer switching costs

the drivers of that performance. One way is to use a framework, such as the structure-conduct-performance (SCP) framework discussed in Chapter 8. It's an enduring framework that simply says the competitive structure in a product market influences the conduct of competitors, which in term drives their performance. Michael Porter's *Competitive Strategy* established the SCP model and variations of it as the standard for most analyses of industry structure and conduct.[3]

As we said in Chapter 8, in the Porter model, the intensity of competition in a product market (and the primary driver of ROIC for the competitors in that market) is determined by five forces: the threat of new entry, pressure from substitute products, bargaining power of buyers, that of suppliers, and the degree of rivalry between competitors. In a world of innovation, the last force, rivalry, incorporates innovation as a key sub-driver. These factors ultimately determine whether there is the potential for competitive advantage (which leads to the potential for high ROIC). Chapter 8 identifies ten sources of potential competitive advantage that drive ROIC and market attractiveness, as summarized in Exhibit 28.2.

WHAT MAKES A BETTER OWNER?

A classic example of the better-owner principle is General Mills' 2001 purchase of Pillsbury from Diageo. Shortly after buying Pillsbury for $10.4 billion, General Mills increased the business's pretax cash flows by more than $400 million per year, and its operating profits by roughly 70 percent.

[3] Michael Porter, *Competitive Strategy* (Free Press, 1980).

Diageo's core business was in alcoholic beverages, while General Mills and Pillsbury both sold packaged foods. Under Diageo, Pillsbury had been run entirely separately from Diageo's core business, because the two companies' manufacturing, distribution, and marketing operations rarely overlapped. In contrast, General Mills was able to substantially reduce costs in Pillsbury's purchasing, manufacturing, and distribution, because the two companies' operations duplicated significant costs. On the revenue side, General Mills boosted Pillsbury's revenues by introducing Pillsbury products to schools in the United States, where General Mills already had a strong presence. The synergies worked both ways; for instance, Pillsbury's refrigerated trucks were used to distribute General Mills' new line of refrigerated meals. General Mills was a better owner of Pillsbury than Diageo, unlocking a 70 percent increase in value.

To identify the better owners of a business, you must first understand the sources of value that potential owners might draw upon. Some owners add value by linking a business with other activities in their portfolio—for example, by using the same sales channels to access customers or by sharing manufacturing infrastructure. Others add value by applying distinctive skills such as operational or marketing excellence, by providing better governance and incentives for the management team, or by having better insight into how a market will develop. Still others add value by more effectively influencing a particular market's critical stakeholders—for instance, governments, regulators, or customers. We'll examine these sources of value one at a time, understanding that in some cases, the better owners may be able to draw on two or more sources at once.

Unique Links with Other Businesses

The most direct way owners add value is by creating links between businesses within their portfolio, especially when only the parent company can make such links. For instance, larger consumer packaged goods (CPG) companies sometimes purchase young, small companies that have developed an innovative product but have limited sales and distribution capabilities. A large, global CPG company that acquires such a product can extract substantial value by taking it to new markets through its global sales, marketing, and distribution channels.

Similarly, NextEra—which is both the largest electricity utility in the United States (operating in Florida) and the largest renewable electricity producer in the United States (in Florida and many other parts of the country)—has used its experience in Florida to achieve operating costs for renewables that are lower than 90 percent of its peers throughout the rest of the country. For example, it has only one control center for its power operations in Florida and has used the technology from that center so that it needs only one additional center to control its renewable assets throughout the United States.

In another example, suppose a copper mining company has the rights to develop a copper mine in a remote location far from any rail lines or other infrastructure. Just ten miles away, another mining company already operates a copper mine and has built the necessary infrastructure, including a rail line. The second mining company would be a better owner of the new mine because its incremental costs to develop the mine are much lower than anyone else's. It can afford to purchase the undeveloped mine at a higher price than any other firm in the market and still earn an attractive ROIC.

These sorts of links can be made across the value chain, from R&D to manufacturing to distribution to sales. For instance, a large pharmaceutical company with a sales force dedicated to oncology might be the best owner of a small pharmaceutical company with a promising new oncology drug but no sales force.

Distinctive Skills

Better owners may have distinctive functional or managerial skills from which the new business can benefit. Such skills may reside anywhere in the business system, including product development, manufacturing processes, and sales and marketing. But to make a difference, any such skill must be an important driver of success in the industry. For example, a company with great manufacturing skills probably wouldn't be a better owner of a CPG business, because the latter company's manufacturing costs aren't large enough to affect its competitive position.

In consumer packaged goods, distinctive skills in developing and marketing brands are more likely to make one company a better owner than another. Take Procter & Gamble (P&G), which in 2013 had 180 brands, including 23 billion-dollar brands in terms of net sales—almost all of which ranked first or second in their respective markets—and 14 half-billion-dollar brands. Its brands were spread across a range of product categories, including laundry detergent, beauty products, pet food, and diapers. As of 2013, some brands, including Tide and Crest, had been P&G brands for decades. The company added newer brands to its portfolio in different ways: for example, it acquired Gillette and Oral-B, while it developed Febreze and Swiffer from scratch. In 2014, P&G determined that its distinctive skills were best applied to very large brands. It announced that it would discontinue or divest 90 to 100 of its brands, focusing its energy on the brands that remained. In 2023, P&G was down to fewer than 80 brands.[4]

Another example of distinctive skills is Danaher, a diversified company with revenues of $19 billion. What makes Danaher successful is its well-known Danaher Business System. Danaher makes acquisitions only where it believes it can apply its management approach to substantially improve margins. By applying this

---

[4] P&G website, accessed July 1, 2024.

strategy over the past 25 years, Danaher has consistently increased the margins of its acquired companies. These include Gilbarco Veeder-Root, a leader in point-of-sale solutions, and Videojet Technologies, which manufactures coding and marking equipment and software. Both companies' margins improved by more than 700 basis points after Danaher acquired them. As Danaher's activities grew in size and complexity, the company also began to divest or spin off some of the businesses that were large enough to stand on their own. These divestments—including Fortive (professional instrumentation) in 2016, Envista (dental) in 2019, and Veralto (environmental and applied solutions) in 2023—were of companies where Danaher had already improved performance.

Better Governance

Regardless of whether owners are running day-to-day operations, better owners can add value through their overall governance of a business. They provide better governance through the way they (or their representatives) interact with the management team to create maximum value in the long term. For example, the best private-equity firms don't just recapitalize companies with debt; they improve the companies' performance through better governance.

Two of our colleagues analyzed 60 successful investments by 11 leading private-equity firms. They found that in almost two-thirds of the transactions, the primary source of new value was improvement in the operating performance of the company, relative to peers, through fruitful interaction between the owners and the management team.[5] The use of financial leverage and clever timing of investments, often cited as private-equity firms' most important sources of success, were not as important as improved governance.

Private-equity firms don't have the time or skills to run their portfolio companies from day to day, but the higher-performing private-equity firms do govern these companies very differently from the way exchange-listed companies are governed. This is a key source of their outperformance. Typically, the private-equity firms introduce a stronger performance culture and make quick management changes when necessary. They encourage managers to abandon any sacred cows, and they give managers leeway to focus on a longer horizon—say, five years—rather than the typical one-year horizon for a listed company. Moreover, the boards of private-equity companies spend three times as many days on their roles as do those at public companies. Private-equity firms' boards spend most of their time on strategy and performance management, rather than compliance and risk avoidance, where boards of public companies typically focus.[6]

---

[5] C. Kehoe and J. Heel, "Why Some Private Equity Firms Do Better," *McKinsey Quarterly*, no. 1 (2005): 24–26.

[6] V. Acharya, C. Kehoe, and M. Reyner, "The Voice of Experience: Public versus Private Equity," *McKinsey on Finance* (Spring 2009): 16–20.

Better Insight and Foresight

Companies that act on their insight into how a market and industry will evolve in order to expand existing businesses or develop new ones can be better owners because they capitalize on innovative ideas.

Consider Amazon Web Services (AWS). As the largest e-commerce company in the world, Amazon had developed unique skills running distributed computing systems. In 2006, using those skills and its purposeful focus on innovation, Amazon officially launched AWS, selling cloud computing services to companies, governments, and individuals. By 2012, its revenues were estimated to be $1.8 billion (Amazon didn't disclose AWS's results as a separate unit until 2015). In 2023, AWS generated a whopping $91 billion of revenues and $25 billion of operating profits.

Another example is John Deere's initiatives to use its knowledge of the needs of its farmer customers to develop new product features and new services. For example, its suite of precision agriculture products and services can help farmers improve output at lower costs.

Distinctive Access to Critical Stakeholders

Distinctive access to talent, capital, government, suppliers, and customers primarily benefits companies in some Asian and emerging markets. Several factors complicate running companies in emerging markets: relatively small pools of managerial talent from which to hire, undeveloped capital markets, and governments that are heavily involved in business as customers, suppliers, and regulators.

In such markets, large-scale diversified conglomerates, such as Tata and Reliance in India and Samsung and Hyundai in South Korea, can be better owners of many businesses because they are more attractive employers, allowing them to attract the best talent. Regarding capital, many emerging countries still need to build up their infrastructures; such projects typically require large amounts of capital that smaller companies can't raise. Companies also often need government approval to purchase land and to build factories, as well as government assurances that there will be sufficient infrastructure to get products to and from factories and sufficient electricity to keep them operating. Large conglomerates typically have the resources and relationships needed to navigate the maze of government regulations and to ensure relatively smooth operations.

In more developed markets, access to talent and capital is rarely an issue. In fact, in the United States, smaller, high-growth companies are often more attractive to talent than larger companies. Moreover, capital is readily available in these markets, even for small businesses. Finally, with some exceptions, clout with the government rarely provides an advantage, given the arm's-length government procurement processes more common in these countries.

THE BETTER-OWNER LIFE CYCLE

The definition of *better owner* isn't static, and better owners themselves will change over time as a business's circumstances change. Thus, a business's better owner could at different times be a larger company, a private-equity firm, a government, a sovereign wealth fund, a family, the business's customers, its employees, or (when a business becomes an independent public company listed on a stock exchange) its shareholders.

For many years, businesses making pharmaceuticals for animals were owned by companies that also made pharmaceuticals for people. Then, from 2009 to 2019, an industry-wide restructuring transformed the animal health business. With different economics, sales, and distribution channels, five of the largest pharmaceutical companies—Bayer, Johnson & Johnson, Novartis, Pfizer, and Sanofi—sold or spun off their animal health businesses. Elanco, a division of Eli Lilly, bought six animal health companies during this period and in 2019 was itself spun off as an independent company. The managers of these large, conglomerate pharmaceutical companies recognized they were not the better owners of animal health businesses, essentially creating a new market sector of pure-play animal health companies.

The parties vying to become best owners are continually evolving in different ways in different parts of the world. In the United States, most large companies are either listed or owned by private-equity funds. They tend to go public earlier than companies elsewhere, so they rarely involve the second generation of a founding family. In Europe, government ownership also plays an important role. In Asia and South America, large companies are often controlled for several generations by members of their founding families, and family relationships also create ownership links between different businesses. Capital markets in these regions aren't as well developed, so founders are more concerned about ensuring that their firms stay true to their legacy after the founders have retired.

Consider an example of how the best owner of a company might change with its circumstances. Naturally, a business's founders will almost always be its first best owners. The founders' entrepreneurial drive, passion, and tangible commitment to the business are essential to getting the company off the ground.

As a business grows, it will probably need more capital, so it may sell a stake to a venture capital fund that specializes in helping new companies grow. At this point, it's not unusual for the fund to put in new managers who supplant or supplement the founders, bringing skills and experience better suited to managing the complexities and risks of a larger organization.

To provide even more capital, the venture capital firm may take the company public, selling shares to a range of investors and, in the process, enabling itself, the founders, and the managers to realize the value of the company they created. When the company goes public, control shifts to an independent board of directors, though the founders will still have important influence if they continue to own substantial stakes.

As the industry evolves, the company might find that it cannot compete with larger companies because, for instance, it needs distribution capability far beyond what it can build by itself in a reasonable time to challenge global competitors. Other external factors, such as regulatory or technological changes, also can create a need to change owners. In response to this limitation, the company may sell itself to a larger company that has the needed capability. In this way, it becomes a product line or business within a division of a multibusiness corporation. Now the original company will merge with the manufacturing, sales, distribution, and administrative functions of the division.

As the markets mature for the businesses in the division where the original company now operates, its corporate owner may decide to focus on other, faster-growing businesses. So the corporation may sell its division to a private-equity firm. Now that the division stands alone, the private-equity firm can see how it has amassed an amount of central overhead that is far greater than needed for a slow-growth market. The response: the private-equity firm restructures the division to give it a leaner cost structure. Once the restructuring is done, the private-equity firm sells the division to a large company that specializes in running slow-growth brands.

At each stage of the company's life, each better owner took actions to increase the company's cash flows, thereby adding value. The founder came up with the idea for the business. The venture capital firm provided capital and professional management. Going public provided the early investors with a way to realize the value of the founders' groundwork and raised more cash. The large corporation accelerated the company's growth with a global distribution capability. The private-equity firm restructured the company's division when growth slowed. The company that became the final best owner applied its skills in managing slow-growth brands. All these changes of ownership made sense in terms of creating value.

DYNAMIC PORTFOLIO MANAGEMENT

Applying the better-owner sequence, executives must continually identify and develop or acquire companies where they could be the better owner and must divest businesses where they used to be the better owner but now have less to contribute than another potential owner. Since the best owner for a given business changes with time, a company needs to have a structured, regular corporate strategy process to review and renew its list of development ideas and acquisition targets, and to test whether any of its existing businesses have reached their sell-by date. Similarly, as demand falls off in a mature industry, long-standing companies are likely to have excess capacity. If they don't have the will or ability to shrink assets and people along with capacity, then they're not the best owner of the business anymore. At any time in a business's history, one group of managers may be better equipped to manage the business than another. At moments such as these, acquisitions and divestitures are often the best or only way to allocate resources sensibly.

For acquisitions, applying the best-owner principle often leads potential acquirers toward targets that are very different from those produced by traditional screening approaches. Traditional approaches often focus on finding potential targets that perform well financially and are somehow related to the parent's business lines. But through the best-owner lens, such characteristics might be less important or irrelevant.

Potential acquirers might do better to seek a financially weak company that has great potential for improvement, especially if the acquirer has proven expertise in improving performance. Focusing attention on tangible opportunities to reduce costs or on identifying common customers may be more rewarding in the long run than investigating a target for the vague reason that it is somehow related to your company.

Companies following the better-owner philosophy are as active in divesting as they are in acquiring; they sell and spin off companies regularly and for good reasons. To illustrate, 50 years ago, many pharmaceutical and chemical companies were combined because they required similar manufacturing processes and skills. But as the two industries matured, their research, manufacturing, and other skills diverged considerably, to the extent that they became distant cousins rather than sister companies.

Today the keys to running a commodity chemicals company are scale, operating efficiency, and management of costs and capital expenditures. In contrast, the keys to running a pharmaceutical company are managing an R&D pipeline, a sophisticated sales force, the regulatory approval process, and relations with government in state-run health systems that buy prescription drugs. So while it might once have made sense for the two types of business to share a common owner, it no longer does. This is why nearly all formerly combined chemical-pharmaceutical companies have split up. For instance, the pharmaceutical company Zeneca was split from Imperial Chemical Industries in 1993 and later merged with another pharmaceutical company to form AstraZeneca. Similarly, pharmaceutical company Aventis was split off from the chemical company Hoechst in 1999; it was later purchased by Sanofi Synthelabo to create Sanofi Aventis, forming a bigger pharma-only company. Sanofi Synthelabo was itself formed by a long series of acquisitions and divestitures. In 2011, Sanofi Aventis renamed itself Sanofi. It subsequently made a number of substantial acquisitions, including Genzyme ($20 billion, 2011), Bioverativ ($12 billion 2018), Ablynx ($5 billion, 2018), and several smaller acquisitions. At the end of 2023, it announced that it would separate its consumer health business, which several bankers valued at about $20 billion. As of this writing, the transaction had not been completed.

Dynamic portfolio management has also driven the creation of three of the top four oil-refining companies in the United States, based on refining capacity. Marathon Petroleum, the largest U.S. refiner, was spun off from Marathon

Oil in 2011. Phillips 66, the fourth largest, came into being as a spin-off from ConocoPhillips in 2012. Valero Energy, the number-two refiner, was originally spun off from Coastal States Gas in 1980. Valero grew into its ranking through major acquisitions in 2000, 2001, 2005, and 2011. Valero then spun off its gasoline retailing operations in 2013, to become a pure refining company. In 2021, Marathon Petroleum also sold off its retail operations, for $21 billion.

Executives are often concerned that divestitures look like an admission of failure, will make their company smaller, and will reduce their stock market value. Yet the research shows that, on the contrary, the stock market consistently reacts positively to divestitures, both sales and spin-offs (see Chapter 32). Thus, planned divestitures are a sign of successful value creation, as in the case of Danaher's significant spin-offs of three businesses between 2016 and 2023. In recent years, other prominent companies have decided that shrinking is a good thing. When P&G announced in 2014 that it would discontinue or divest 90 to 100 small brands, the company said it would sell its pet food businesses and spin off its Duracell battery business. This kind of thoughtful shrinking allows disparate businesses to focus on their unique needs and competitive situations. As we mentioned earlier, P&G is now down to fewer than 80 brands.

CONSTRUCTING THE PORTFOLIO: AN EXAMPLE

Executives can apply the principles discussed in this chapter to construct a portfolio of businesses for their company. While there's no single right way to think through this task, we provide an example of how this could be done. This section illustrates a simplified output using a hypothetical company, HexaCorp. Ideally, this analysis would be done at a granular level, looking at each of perhaps 20 to 50 units for a large company. We've used only six units to keep the example from becoming too complex. HexaCorp is a consumer products company with six units: processed meat, cheese, specialty cheese, high-end pet food, energy bars, and nutrition for athletes.

We first assess the market attractiveness of the product market and the relative quality of ownership (the degree to which the company is or could be a better owner), as shown in Exhibit 28.3. Exhibit 28.4 details the output of this assessment, plus other factors including whether the unit's value creation is worth the required time of the management team, for each business unit.

As you can see from the exhibits, the units vary in all areas of this assessment:

- The processed-meat business is highly competitive (customers are not brand loyal), with only a 10 percent market ROIC and low growth. HexaCorp's ROIC is on par with that of peers, benefiting somewhat from high retail penetration. Overall, the processed-meat business rates low on both market attractiveness and better ownership.

EXHIBIT 28.3 **HexaCorp: Summary Portfolio Assessment**

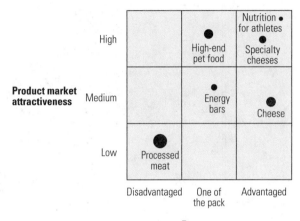

- The cheese business is highly competitive because most consumers aren't brand loyal, but the market does earn a decent 15 percent ROIC, so its market attractiveness is rated medium. However, HexaCorp has a strong retail network and strong manufacturing and distribution capabilities that it shares with the specialty cheese business, so it is a better owner.

- The specialty cheese business, in contrast, has brand-loyal customers and a 25 percent market ROIC. HexaCorp has 40 percent market share, with a strong retail network and strong manufacturing and distribution capabilities. Therefore, its market attractiveness is high, and HexaCorp is a better owner.

- The high-end pet food business has an attractive market ROIC of 22 percent and high growth at 6 percent, with customers loyal to brands and perceived quality differences. HexaCorp's pet food business has a slightly higher ROIC than competitors and higher growth because of its stronger brand and superior product innovation. While the industry is high on the attractiveness scale, HexaCorp is just one of the pack, because customers can be fickle if the next innovation isn't perfect.

- The energy bar business is rated medium on the industry attractiveness scale because its high ROIC and reasonably good growth combine with continual introductions of new products, making it difficult for a company to maintain any advantage. Energy bars are a faddish business. HexaCorp's ownership is rated as one of the pack, with lower market share and lower growth than competitors, given that it hasn't led the latest fads.

- Nutrition for athletes is a new product market with high growth. While competitors aren't earning high returns right now, they have high potential because of the focus on innovation and customer loyalty. HexaCorp has 35 percent market share with higher growth than peers and has the best innovators. It is a better owner of this business.

EXHIBIT 28.4 **HexaCorp: Assessment of Market Attractiveness and Better Ownership**

	Processed meat	Cheese	Specialty cheese	High-end pet food	Energy bars	Nutrition for athletes
Market attractiveness						
Current product market ROIC	10%	15%	25%	22%	20%	Start-up/high potential
Expected long-term growth	2%	2%	4%	6%	5%	10%
Key drivers of structural attractiveness	Retail penetration	Retail penetration, quality	Brand	Brand, quality	Brand, retail distribution	Innovation, brand
Ease of defending advantage	Medium	Medium	High	Medium	Low	High
Current or potential headwinds/tailwinds	Consumers shifting to healthier products	No change	No change	Tailwinds	No change	Tailwinds
Overall assessment	Low	Medium	High	High	Medium	High
Better ownership						
ROIC vs. competitors	Equal	Below	Above	Above	Equal	Potentially higher
Growth vs. competitors	Equal	Equal	Equal	Faster	Below	Above
Market share	25%	10%	40%	25%	10%	35%
Driver of current advantage	High retail penetration	None	Brand	Brand, innovation	Brand	Innovation, distribution
Ability to maintain advantage	High	N/A	High	Moderate	Moderate	High
Corporate value added	Retail network	Retail network, manufacturing, distribution	Retail network, manufacturing, distribution	Distribution	Innovation	Innovation
Overall assessment	Disadvantaged	Better owner	Better owner	One of the pack	One of the pack	Better owner
Other factors						
Size relative to total company	Large	Medium	Medium	Medium	Small	Small
Cash generation	Moderate	High	Very high	High	Moderate	Currently negative
Value potential vs. management time	Moderate	Moderate	High	High	Moderate	Moderate

Next, we incorporate these insights into estimating the value of each business unit from four perspectives:

1. A baseline or momentum DCF value that grows in line with Hexacorp's underlying product markets (or its historical growth rate if below peers)

2. A DCF value based on potential or planned operating improvements, such as increasing margins, accelerating revenue growth, and improving capital efficiency

3. Value to alternative owners if the unit were to be divested (see Chapter 32)

4. Value with additional growth opportunities through innovation or acquisitions (see Chapters 9 and 31)

The final step is to combine the valuations with the assessment of each unit to identify the value-maximizing actions for each unit, as illustrated in Exhibit 28.5. HexaCorp could increase its equity value from $7.1 billion to $9.1 billion if it fully executed the following actions:

- Divest the processed-meat business, since its returns are poor, its growth is limited, and HexaCorp is not a better owner.

- Keep cheese but focus on cost reduction. Returns are reasonable, and HexaCorp is a better owner because of links to its specialty cheese business.

- Specialty cheese is a jewel in a highly attractive market, with HexaCorp a better owner. No changes are necessary.

- High-end pet food's value could be increased by acquiring some poorly managed brands. The market is highly attractive, and despite HexaCorp

EXHIBIT 28.5 **HexaCorp: Summary of Value Creation Opportunities**

$ million

	DCF value of momentum case	DCF value of new actions	Increase in value	Actions
Processed meat	1,500	2,000	500	Divest
Cheese	2,000	2,200	200	Optimize costs
Specialty cheese	1,500	1,500	0	Maintain position
High-end pet food	2,200	2,600	400	Acquire poorly managed brands
Energy bars	1,500	1,800	300	Invest in innovation and branding
Nutrition for athletes	1,000	1,500	500	Acquire new brands and capabilities
Total business units	9,700	11,600	1,900	
Corporate overhead	(900)	(800)	100	
Enterprise value	8,800	10,800	2,000	
Debt	(1,700)	(1,700)	0	
Equity value	7,100	9,100	2,000	

being only one of the pack in ownership, the business creates significant value. Furthermore, HexaCorp could use its position to add value to underperforming brands.

- Energy bars have medium attractiveness, and HexaCorp is one of the pack. Still, there appear to be opportunities to increase value through innovation and better branding.

- HexaCorp is a better owner of nutrition for athletes, a highly attractive market. The company could use its strengths to purchase new brands and capabilities to combine with its own.

- HexaCorp could reduce its corporate overhead by about 10 percent.

THE MYTH OF DIVERSIFICATION

A perennial question in corporate strategy is whether companies should hold a diversified portfolio of businesses. The idea seemed to be discredited in the 1970s, yet today some executives still say things such as, "It's the third leg of the stool that makes a company stable." Our perspective is that diversification is intrinsically neither good nor bad. Which one it is depends on whether the parent company adds more value to the businesses it owns than any other potential owner could, making it a better owner of those businesses in the circumstances.

Smoothing Cash Flow Isn't the Key

Over the years, different ideas have been advanced to encourage or justify diversification, but these theories simply don't add up. Most rest on the idea that different businesses have different business cycles, so cash flows at the peak of one business's cycle will offset the lean cash years of other businesses, thereby stabilizing a company's consolidated cash flows. If cash flows and earnings are smoothed in this way, the reasoning goes, then investors will pay higher prices for the company's stock.

The facts refute this argument. First, we haven't found any evidence that diversified companies actually generate smoother cash flows. Of the 500 largest U.S. companies, we examined the 50 with the lowest earnings volatility from 2013 to 2022. Only six might be considered diversified companies, in the sense of owning businesses in more than two distinct industries. Second, and just as important, there is no evidence that investors pay higher prices for less volatile companies (see Chapter 7). In our regular analyses of diversified companies for our clients, we almost never find that the value of the sum of a diversified company's business units is substantially different from the market value of the consolidated company, once we adjust for the performance of the company's business units.[7]

Another argument is that diversified companies with more stable cash flows can safely take on more debt, thus getting a larger tax benefit from debt. While this may make sense in theory, we've never come across diversified companies that systematically used more debt than their peers.

A more nuanced argument is that diversified companies are better positioned to take advantage of different business cycles in different sectors. They can use cash flows from their businesses in sectors at the top of their cycle to invest in businesses in sectors at the bottom of their cycle (when their undiversified competitors cannot). Once again, we haven't found diversified companies that actually behave that way. In fact, we typically find the opposite: the senior executives at diversified companies don't understand their individual business units well enough to have the confidence to invest at the bottom of the cycle, when none of the competitors are investing. Diversified companies tend to respond to opportunities more slowly than less diversified companies.

Elusive Benefits, Real Costs

While any benefits from diversification are elusive, the costs are very real. Investors can diversify their investment portfolios at lower cost than companies can diversify their business portfolios, because they only have to buy and sell stocks, something they can do easily and relatively cheaply many times a year. In contrast, substantially changing the shape of a portfolio of real businesses involves considerable transaction costs and disruption, and it typically takes many years. Moreover, the business units of diversified companies often perform less well than those of more focused peers, partly because of added complexity and bureaucracy.

Today, many executives and boards in developed markets realize how difficult it is to add value to businesses that aren't connected to each other in some way. As a result, many pairings have largely disappeared. In the United States, for example, by the end of 2010, there were only 22 true conglomerates.[8] Since then, ten have announced that they, too, would split up or divest major businesses.

We examined the performance of these conglomerates versus focused companies. The striking insight was not that average total shareholder returns (TSR) were lower for conglomerates but that the top end of the distribution

---

[7] A. West, T. Koller, and W. Rehm, "Is Your 'Conglomerate Discount' a Performance Discount or a Communication Problem?" McKinsey & Company, October 31, 2024, www.mckinsey.com.

[8] J. Cyriac, T. Koller, and J. Thomsen, "Testing the Limits of Diversification," *McKinsey Quarterly* (February 2012). Conglomerates were defined as a company with three or more business units that do not have common customers, distribution systems, technologies, or manufacturing facilities.

EXHIBIT 28.6 **Distribution of TSR by Levels of Diversification**

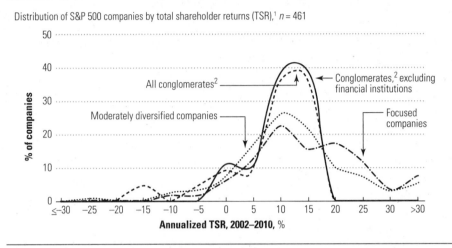

Distribution of S&P 500 companies by total shareholder returns (TSR),[1] n = 461

[1] Includes companies in 2010 S&P 500 that were also publicly listed on Dec. 31, 2002.

[2] Defined as any company with 3 or more business units that do not have common customers, distribution systems, manufacturing facilities, or technologies.

was chopped off. No conglomerate in our study exceeded a TSR of 20 percent, while the TSR of more focused companies topped out above 30 percent (see Exhibit 28.6). Upside gains are limited for conglomerates because it's unlikely that all their diverse businesses will outperform at the same time. The returns of units that do are dwarfed by underperformers. Moreover, conglomerates are usually made up of relatively mature businesses, well beyond the point where they would be likely to generate unexpected high returns. But the downside isn't limited, because the performance of a more mature business can fall a lot further than it can rise. Consider a simple mathematical example: if a business unit accounting for a third of a conglomerate's value earns a 20 percent TSR while other units earn 10 percent, the weighted average will be about 14 percent. But if that unit's TSR is –50 percent, the weighted average TSR will be dragged down to about 2 percent, even before other units are affected. In addition, the poor aggregate performance can affect the motivation of the entire company and the company's reputation with customers, suppliers, and prospective employees.

What Does Matter

What matters in a diversification strategy is whether managers have the skills to add value to businesses in unrelated industries. We found three ways high-performing conglomerates outperform. First, as we discuss in greater depth in Chapter 31, high-performing conglomerates continually rebalance their portfolios by purchasing companies whose performance they can improve.

Second, high-performing conglomerates aggressively manage capital allocation across units at the corporate level. All cash that exceeds what's needed for operating requirements is transferred to the parent company, which decides how to allocate it across current and new business or investment opportunities, based on their potential for growth and returns on invested capital.

Finally, high-performing conglomerates operate in much the same way as better private-equity firms: with a lean corporate center that restricts its involvement in the management of business units to selecting leaders, allocating capital, vetting strategy, setting performance targets, and monitoring performance. At Illinois Tool Works (ITW), for example, business units are primarily self-supporting, with broad authority to manage themselves as long as managers adhere to the company's 80/20 rule (80 percent of a company's revenue is derived from 20 percent of its customers) and innovation principles. The ITW corporate center largely handles taxes, auditing, investor relations, and some centralized human resources functions. Also, just as important as the organization structure, these conglomerates do not create extensive corporate-wide processes or large shared-service centers. For instance, you won't find corporate-wide programs to reduce working capital, because that may not be a priority for all parts of the company.

Conglomerates in Emerging Markets

As mentioned earlier, the economic situation in emerging markets is distinct enough that we are cautious in applying insights gleaned from developed-world companies. Some preliminary, unpublished McKinsey research shows that more diversified companies in emerging markets outperform their less diversified peers. That is not the case in developed markets. While we expect the conglomerate structure to fade away eventually, the pace will vary from country to country and industry to industry.

We can already see the rough contours of change in the role conglomerates play in emerging markets. Infrastructure and other capital-intensive businesses are likely to be parts of large conglomerates as long as access to capital and connections are important. In contrast, companies that rely less on access to capital and connections tend to focus on opportunities that differ from those of large conglomerates. These companies include export-oriented ones, such as those in information technology (IT) services and pharmaceuticals.

The rise of IT services and pharmaceuticals in India is an example that shows that the large conglomerates' edge in access to managerial talent has already fallen. As emerging markets open to more foreign investors, these companies' advantage in access to capital also may decline. That will leave access to government as their last remaining strength, further restricting their opportunities to industries where government influence remains important. Although the time could be decades away, conglomerates' large size and diversification will eventually become impediments rather than advantages.

PRACTICAL CONSIDERATIONS

In practice, changing the corporate portfolio is not as simple as we've described. Challenges abound, and making changes can take years.

One of the primary challenges is the emotional element of selling units. It's not unusual for executives to push back against divesting what was once the crown jewel but now is a drain, or a business unit that was the original business when the company was founded. Another challenge is overcoming the anchoring on a price the company could have received for selling a unit several years ago but no one is willing to pay today. Overcoming these challenges boils down the courage and conviction of the CEO.

Companies sometimes avoid divesting because they want to fix up the business before selling it, so they can get a better price. In our experience, the performance usually doesn't improve and often continues to decline. Rarely is the price they can sell for better in a couple of years.

In some countries, particularly the United States, there may be a large tax bill from selling business units. If the taxes are large enough, the company may have to hold onto an unattractive business. However, the tax can often be avoided by spinning off rather than selling the business.

While it's important to figure out ways to overcome these challenges, companies do have to be realistic about how quickly they can change their portfolio. For example, how much bandwidth does the management team have to execute on multiple acquisitions and divestitures while still managing the ongoing operations of the company? How do you maintain morale? How do you ensure you invest in all your growth opportunities?

SUMMARY

To construct a portfolio of value-creating businesses, managers need to take into consideration both the underlying attractiveness of the product market in which it competes and whether their company is a better owner of its businesses. A rigorous analysis often leads to substantial changes in a company's portfolio, because the attractiveness and better owner changes over time.

The following chapters build on these ideas to continue our study of how managers can contribute to a company's value. Chapters 29 and 30 focus on how companies can be more effective at allocating resources in general, while Chapters 31 and 32 cover acquisitions and divestitures as tools to change a company's portfolio of businesses. Chapter 33 focuses on how companies can think about digital and value creation, and Chapter 34 does the same for sustainability. Chapter 35 explains a company's need to have its strategy supported by the right financial underpinnings, including policies for capital structure, dividends, and share repurchases. Chapter 36 closes this part by discussing some core principles of communicating with investors.

29

Strategic Management: Analytics

Successful strategic management encompasses all the tasks a company undertakes to develop and achieve its strategic goals and create long-term value. Along with talent management, strategic management is arguably the most important job of the CEO and senior management team. The primary elements of strategic management include the following:

- Developing corporate and business unit strategies
- Allocating resources across the business portfolio (including internal investments, acquisitions, and divestitures) and setting long-term financial plans and short-term budgets to achieve strategic targets
- Managing performance by reviewing business unit results and deciding when and how to intervene

As value-minded managers navigate these tasks, obstacles abound. Primary among them is the difficulty of finding the right balance between generating profits in the short term and investing for value creation in the long term. Especially in companies with many businesses, markets, and management layers, decisions tend to be biased toward short-term profit, because it is the most readily available and widely understood performance measure. Investors, equity analysts, supervisory directors, the press, and even internal reporting processes all contribute to this short-term bias.

Overcoming this obstacle requires fluency in two distinct yet interrelated disciplines. The first of these—and the subject of this chapter—is the use of analytics to ferret out sources of value and make the right decisions for value creation. The second is ensuring the execution of strategy to orient the entire management team toward common goals, through the right governance, synchronized planning processes, and effective decision making. We take up the second discipline in Chapter 30.

The analytical discipline of strategic management should adhere to four imperatives:

1. Every initiative (including maintenance and regulatory projects) should have a financial analysis, preferably net present value.

2. Rank the 10 to 30 most important strategic initiatives across the enterprise each year, initially based on financial outcome (ideally, the ratio of present value to investment).

3. Allocate the remaining resources across business units, product categories, or other logical groups at a granular level of 20 to 50 units.

4. For planning and performance monitoring, use not only financial metrics but also nonfinancial value drivers that indicate both short- and long-term performance.

CONDUCT A FINANCIAL ANALYSIS FOR EVERY INITIATIVE

It should go without saying that every initiative a company undertakes, whether a capital expenditure, product development, marketing and sales, or new-business building, should have a financial analysis that management can use to make a go/no-go decision. Yet we find that companies often take short-cuts for so-called maintenance projects or strategic initiatives, which tends to lead to suboptimal decision making. For example, when a company does not require a financial analysis for maintenance projects, operating managers may pad these projects because approval is easy to get, or the company may not consider alternatives. Similarly, the difficulty of measuring the financial impact of strategic projects doesn't mean that shouldn't be done. Even if the only possible estimate is a rough range of outcomes, that is still vastly preferable to a simple hunch. (For ideas on dealing with uncertainty and flexibility, see Chapter 40.)

The best financial analysis, of course, is net present value (NPV) or variations such as internal rate of return. The math is simple and known to almost every businessperson. But this analysis is too often neglected, with the excuse that it requires too much work. This need not be the case. Companies can tailor the amount of detail to the scope of the projects. You shouldn't put as much effort into deciding whether to add a new software feature for customer applications as you would put into analyzing a billion-dollar mine. It should be noted as well that using NPV does not mean that it is permissible to overlook other factors, such as the impact on short-term earnings or the cash flow pattern.

To ensure consistency across the organization, many companies use a standard template, adjusting the amount of work by the size and strategic importance of the investment.

Also be sure to use the proper base case. The estimate of NPV should be driven by the incremental cash flows relative to a base case. The base case is not necessarily business as usual. For example, when considering a strategic project that is necessary to maintain competitiveness and market share, the base case would reflect a decline in cash flows due to a decline in market share. Such a project may show a positive NPV even if it doesn't increase cash flows above the current level, since it avoids a *decline* in cash flow.

RANK THE ENTERPRISE'S TOP STRATEGIC INITIATIVES

Effective strategic management includes a periodic ranking (typically once a year) of all strategic initiatives across the entire enterprise, so they can be considered not just as individual stand-alone decisions or within the context of a division or business unit.[1] Taking the enterprise view means evaluating resource investments from the perspective of how they affect the company as a whole. This approach provides several benefits:

- It ensures that resources are allocated to where they will create the greatest value for the company as a whole, regardless of which division or business unit receives the resources.

- It helps overcome the inertia that leads to allocating resources to the same units from year to year. Research shows that the best predictor of a company's resource allocation is typically the previous year's allocation. Yet companies that more actively reallocate resources create more value, translating into 30 percent higher total shareholder returns, on average.[2]

- It mitigates the negative effects of loss aversion—the tendency to pass on high-risk, high-reward investments because individuals tend to weight losses more heavily than gains. Mid- and lower-level managers are typically too risk averse, attaching much more importance to potential losses than gains from investments. This applies even when the amounts at stake are small and any losses could be easily absorbed by the organization.[3] Combining investment opportunities from different business units and segments typically generates diversification benefits, reducing the risk per dollar invested.[4]

---

[1] This section draws on D. Lovallo, T. Koller, R. Uhlaner, and D. Kahneman, "Your Company Is Too Risk-Averse," *Harvard Business Review* (March/April 2020), hbr.org.

[2] S. Hall, D. Lovallo, and R. Musters, "How to Put Your Money Where Your Strategy Is," *McKinsey Quarterly* (March 2012), www.mckinsey.com.

[3] See T. Koller, D. Lovallo, and Z. Williams, "Overcoming a Bias against Risk," McKinsey & Company, August 2012, www.mckinsey.com.

[4] As noted in Chapter 4, this does not mean that the company's cost of capital is lower. By definition, diversification cannot reduce a project's beta and cost of capital.

Effective strategic management should aim to make allocation decisions for the entire company all at once or at least in groups, using some form of project ranking and prioritization across the company. Ideally, a company would apply a portfolio optimization model that incorporates risk correlations across potential investment projects. In Chapter 4, we discussed the example of a technology company that adopted this approach. Regardless of which division or business unit individual projects belong to, they are combined in alternative portfolios, and the portfolios are ranked by their aggregate return and risk.[5] With this approach, a company can find the portfolio of projects that would provide the best balance between risk and return.

For most companies, the math of this approach is unrealistic. A simpler ranking approach can generate the needed insights without explicit estimates of project risk correlations. Consider the example of a company that operates three business units, each with ten projects seeking investment. In this approach, the business units submit all their project proposals to the enterprise senior management and its staff. Each proposal includes a range of possible present-value outcomes and an assessment of the associated risks. The corporate staff then simply ranks all 30 projects across the company based on their expected return, ignoring risk for the moment. Given a certain investment budget and based on this ranking, the senior management determines which projects should be selected to maximize overall value creation, regardless of which business they belong to (see Exhibit 29.1).

For this preliminary selection, the senior management assesses whether the overall risk profile is acceptable for the company as a whole. If the projects

EXHIBIT 29.1 **Ranking of Investment Projects at Aggregate Portfolio Level**

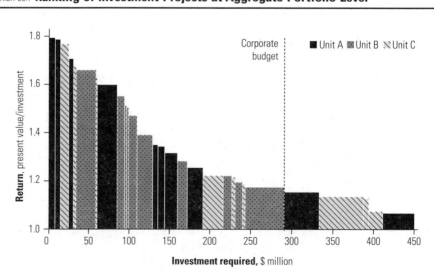

---

[5] We measure return as expected present value divided by investment (PV/I) and risk as the standard deviation of return.

are largely uncorrelated, the aggregate risk per dollar invested for the selected portfolio will be lower than for the individual projects. Depending on the situation, the senior management could exchange parts of the portfolio with less correlated projects from the next-highest-ranked projects, which would reduce aggregate portfolio risk, even though the reduction in risk will come at the expense of overall return.

The approach aims to create the best allocation from a corporate perspective, maximizing value creation with an acceptable risk profile for the company as whole. But it may well allocate investments unevenly from the viewpoint of the business units—for example, when one unit has very few proposals approved relative to others. If uneven allocations are the rule rather than the exception, that can be an important insight. Businesses that are unable to compete successfully for investment resources could be candidates for divestment to a better owner or should focus their strategy on cash generation rather than growth through investments.

Allocating resources through project ranking and prioritizing should be done annually at the very least, though the frequency should depend on the nature of the industry. Of course, doing this at the corporate rather than business level might hamper an organization's ability to react quickly to new opportunities or information. Each organization will have to find the right balance between flexibility and efficiency in resource allocation. For example, some companies set up investment reserves for unforeseen initiatives. Others assign investment funds to projects on a conditional basis, so allocations can be changed during the year if projects don't meet predetermined milestones. One company we know devotes several weeks per year to discussion of resource allocation. Most of the company's investment decisions are made during these weeks, always in the context of the overall portfolio of projects. If certain investment decisions must be made outside this allocation cycle, their impact on the company's overall portfolio is analyzed separately.

When a company is faced with too many projects to assess individually, the approach can be easily modified. Instead of submitting all investment projects separately, the business units could propose tranches of logically grouped projects. For example, the units could submit a tranche of $50 million investments just to "keep the lights on," a second tranche of $100 million projects to maintain market share and growth with their market, and a third tranche that might provide $100 million for some new products or services or enhancements to customer service. The investment proposal for each tranche would include an estimated value and risk profile. Then the corporate staff and senior management would rank and prioritize the tranches (rather than the individual projects) across all business units, following the same logic as described earlier. Some units would receive all three tranches, others only one or two.

A variation is a hybrid approach, where the top 10 to 30 strategic initiatives are separated from the business unit tranches and included alongside them in the overall ranking. This approach ensures that critical strategic projects are highlighted for discussion and funding at the level of the company's executive leadership, rather than by business unit management.

Ranking by financial return is not meant to be a straitjacket for the senior management. Management may have other priorities, such as meeting carbon reduction targets. Management can always downgrade a project that makes it difficult to satisfy these priorities or upgrade a project that helps with them. But starting with a financial ranking provides greater rigor and discipline.

ALLOCATE RESOURCES ACROSS UNITS AT A GRANULAR LEVEL

Many large companies have 10 to 50 or more business units or product lines. In these cases, many individual projects will be too small to warrant attention from senior management. In such cases, the company might allocate resources to individual units rather than projects. Or it could use a hybrid approach, allocating resources to strategic projects and the remaining resources to business units (leaving the leaders of those units to allocate within their unit).

Allocating at a granular level of 20 to 50 units overcomes the scourge of averaging.[6] Often companies have three to five divisions, each with 5 to 15 units. Allocating resources just to the three to five divisions tends to hide the outliers—the strongest and weakest performers, which are the ones most in need of promotion or correction. Exhibit 29.2 shows an example where the four divisions of a diversified industrial company each fell between 5 and 10 percent short of overall economic-profit goals, suggesting only modest underperformance. Yet a closer look found that two-thirds of the company's 150 business segments were underperforming on its economic-profit goals by as much as 40 percent, while the rest were outperforming enough to skew the

EXHIBIT 29.2 **Improvement Opportunity at Different Levels of Review**

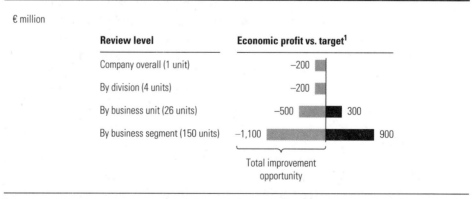

€ million

Review level	Economic profit vs. target[1]
Company overall (1 unit)	−200
By division (4 units)	−200
By business unit (26 units)	−500 ... 300
By business segment (150 units)	−1,100 ... 900

Total improvement opportunity

[1] Economic-profit target: €2,650 million.

[6] This section draws on M. Goedhart, S. Smit, and A. Veldhuijzen, "Unearthing the Sources of Value Hiding in Your Corporate Portfolio," *McKinsey on Finance*, no. 48 (Autumn 2013): 2–9.

averages. As a result, the opportunity for improvement turned out to be much larger than the executives had anticipated.

It's clear from this example that strategy and resource allocation should take place at the level of product category so that senior management clearly sees where value is created, not at the corporate center. However, the management structure of division heads overseeing business units, business unit leaders supervising segment managers, and so on typically gets in the way of value-oriented decision making. Divisional managers like the "averaging" of business unit results, which enables them to achieve short-term targets for their division, possibly at the expense of long-term value creation.

In our experience, for a company earning $10 billion in revenue, strategic management by corporate executives should typically take place at the level of at least 20 to 50 or sometimes more units or projects.[7] One rule of thumb is to dissect businesses as long as underlying subsegments show significant differences in terms of growth and return on capital and are material in value relative to the company as a whole. Wherever managers find that their companies lack the necessary financial data, such as revenue, operating earnings, and capital expenditures, they will probably also find that they rely too heavily on averages when setting strategic priorities, financial targets, and resource budgets.

The finer-grained perspective we recommend offers several important benefits. First, it reveals more value creation opportunities, as it dissects average performance and growth across the portfolio. For example, executives at one global company considered a consumer goods business in Asia to be the most successful in the company's portfolio, because it consistently delivered double-digit top-line growth. But a more detailed analysis revealed that this business was losing market share because the relevant local markets were growing even faster—which would almost inevitably lead to lower value creation in the long term.

Second, taking a finer-grained perspective helps managers understand performance trends for business units that consist of several distinct product or market segments. While a higher number of units might appear to complicate matters for executives and the corporate center, the reverse is often the case. For example, the aggregated growth rate and return on invested capital for a business unit will continuously change over time if its underlying units have different growth rates and returns on capital, even if these are stable for each segment. Unless you analyze performance at the unit level, it will be very difficult to understand and forecast the business unit performance.

Finally, a granular approach offers executives better information for direct and radical interventions at the level of individual units, should stepping in become necessary. This can occur when a division-based structure leads to misaligned management incentives.[8] For example, in one global industrial

[7] These segments are similar to what we have elsewhere called "value cells." See, e.g., M. Giordano and F. Wenger, "Organizing for Value," *McKinsey on Finance*, no. 28 (Summer 2008): 20–25.
[8] Giordano and Wenger, "Organizing for Value."

company, whenever one of the business units needed to achieve its overall profit target, it would cut its research investments in breakthrough renewable-energy technology, although the technology had excellent potential to create long-term value. To remedy the situation, management separated out the renewable-energy project as an independent unit reporting directly to the executive team. Detached from the original business unit's profit goals, the new unit increased and stabilized these value-creating research investments.

This is also the level at which strategic portfolio decisions should be made. There are various analytical tools to help managers make these allocation decisions. For an example of resource allocation across business units, refer to Chapter 28.

APPLYING VALUE DRIVERS TO MANAGE PERFORMANCE

To plan and monitor progress, it is critical to understand what drives long-term performance. Think of a patient visiting the doctor. The patient may be feeling fine, in the sense of meeting requirements for weight, strength, and energy. But if the patient's cholesterol is above the target level that medical science has established as safe, the patient may need to take corrective action now to prevent future heart disease. Similarly, if a company shows strong growth and return on invested capital (ROIC), it still needs to know whether that performance is sustainable. Comparing readings of company health indicators against meaningful targets can tell us whether a company has achieved impressive past financial results at a cost to its long-term health, perhaps crippling its ability to create value in the future. Consider retail chains that sometimes maintain apparently impressive margins by scrimping on store refurbishment or branded consumer packaged goods companies that don't invest enough in product development and brand building, to the detriment of their future competitive strength.

Identifying Value Drivers

We can gain insight into a company's health by examining what drives long-term growth and ROIC, the key drivers of value creation. A systematic method for analytically and visually linking a business's unique value drivers to financial metrics and shareholder value is the value driver tree. It breaks down each element of financial performance into value drivers.

The value driver tree in Exhibit 29.3 illustrates the basic kinds of value drivers. The left side of the exhibit shows the financial drivers of intrinsic value: revenue growth and ROIC.[9] Proceeding to the right, the exhibit calls

[9] Cost of capital is also a driver of company value, but it is largely determined by the company's industry sector and is difficult for management to influence.

EXHIBIT 29.3 **Value Driver Tree with Three Horizons**

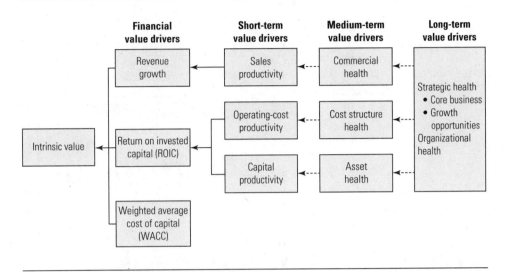

out short-term value drivers, followed by medium- and long-term value drivers. The choice of a particular value driver, along with metrics and targets for testing and strengthening each one, should vary from company to company, reflecting each company's different sectors and aspirations.

Companies should choose their own set of value drivers and metrics, under the generic headings set out here, and tailor their choice to their industry and strategy. Such tailoring is critical for setting the right strategic priorities. For example, product innovation may be important to companies in one industry, while for companies in another, tight cost control and customer service may matter more.

Short-Term Value Drivers   Short-term value drivers are the immediate drivers of ROIC and growth. They are typically the easiest to quantify and monitor frequently (monthly or quarterly). They are indicators of whether current growth and ROIC can be sustained, will improve, or will decline over the short term. They might include cost per unit for a manufacturing company or same-store sales growth for a retailer.

Following the growth and ROIC framework in Exhibit 29.4, short-term value drivers fall into three categories:

1. *Sales productivity* refers to drivers of recent sales growth, such as price and quantity sold, market share, the company's ability to charge higher prices relative to peers (or charge a premium for its product or services), sales force productivity, and for retailers, same-store sales growth versus new-store growth.

2. *Operating-cost productivity* includes drivers of unit costs, such as the component costs for building an automobile or delivering a package.

EXHIBIT 29.4 **Basic Value Driver Tree: Manufacturing Company**

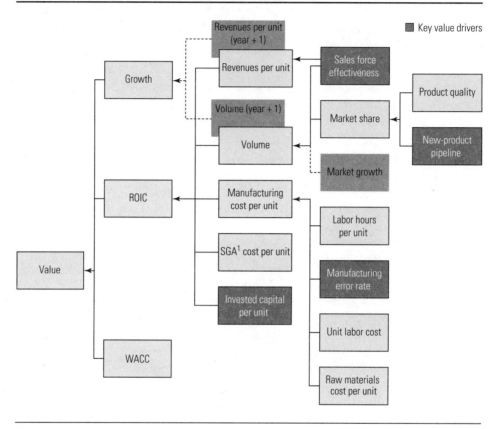

[1] Selling, general, and administrative.

UPS, for example, is well known for charting the optimal delivery path of its drivers to enhance their productivity and for developing well-defined standards on how to deliver packages.

3. *Capital productivity* measures how well a company uses its working capital (inventories, receivables, and payables) and its property, plant, and equipment. Dell revolutionized the personal-computer business in the 1990s by building to order so it could minimize inventories. Because the company kept inventory levels so low and had few receivables to boot, it could on occasion operate with negative working capital.

When assessing drivers of short-term corporate performance, separate the effects of forces outside management's control (both good and bad) from things management can influence. For instance, executives of upstream oil companies shouldn't get much credit for higher profits that result from higher oil prices, nor should real estate brokerage executives be credited for higher real estate prices (and the resulting higher commissions). Oil company performance should be evaluated with an emphasis on new reserves and production growth, exploration costs, and drilling costs. Real estate brokerages should be evaluated primarily on the number of sales, not whether housing prices are increasing or decreasing.

Medium-Term Value Drivers   Medium-term value drivers look forward to indicate whether a company can maintain and improve its growth and ROIC over the next one to five years (or longer for companies such as pharmaceutical manufacturers that have long product cycles). In most cases, there is no clear mathematical relation between these drivers and financial performance in terms of ROIC and growth. These drivers may also be harder to translate into metrics than short-term drivers and are more likely to be measured or assessed annually or over even longer periods.

The medium-term value drivers fall into three categories:

1. *Commercial health* indicates whether the company can sustain or improve its current revenue growth. Drivers in this category include the company's product pipeline quality (talent and technology to bring new products to market over the medium term), brand strength (investment in brand building), and customer satisfaction. Commercial-health metrics vary widely by industry and over time. In branded consumer product sectors, such as packaged food and personal products, minimizing the use of scarce resources and trading fairly with suppliers are becoming more relevant as health indicators of a company's product line in some categories. For a telecom service provider, customer satisfaction and brand strength may be the most important components of medium-term commercial health.

2. *Cost structure health* is a company's ability to manage its costs relative to competitors over three to five years. For an automotive manufacturer, the number of shared platforms and components across its model range is an important driver. Insights in cost health drivers often follow from programs such as Six Sigma, a method to reduce costs continually and maintain a cost advantage relative to competitors across most of the company's businesses.

3. *Asset health* is how well a company maintains and develops its assets. For land transportation and logistics companies, the share of electric or hybrid vehicles in their fleets can indicate the extent of their exposure to potential tax increases on fossil fuels. For an airline, indicators may be the average lifetime of the current fleet and the resale or trade-in value of decommissioned aircraft. For a refining company, it could be the average time between plant turnarounds. For a hotel or restaurant chain, the average time between remodeling projects may be an important driver of asset health.

Long-Term Value Drivers   Long-term value drivers reflect a company's ability to sustain its core business, capture new growth areas, and develop its talent, skills, and culture over the next decade and more. In most cases, these drivers affect ROIC and growth through multiple categories of short- and medium-term value drivers. For example, a company's ability to attract and develop talented employees likely affects its future commercial and cost structure health, with higher sales and cost productivity as a result. In another instance, a track record of trading fairly with suppliers could improve a company's reputation with key stakeholders and enable it to charge a price premium for its products or attract more talented employees.

We distinguish two basic categories of long-term value drivers:

1. *Strategic health* consists of a company's ability to sustain its core business and to identify new growth opportunities. For example, the growth of market share captured by new entrants to the sector can be an insightful measure of a company's strategic health. New entrants often rely on radically different business models that incumbents may find hard to compete with. Even small current market shares for such attackers could translate into significant strategic threats over the longer term. Illustrations are found when looking back at the success of Ayden in the payments sector, Booking.com in the travel sector, or Dollar Shave Club and Harry's in razors and personal grooming. Besides guarding against threats, companies must continually watch for new growth opportunities, whether in related industries or in new geographies. A meaningful indicator can be the number of successful ventures or partnerships in new business areas. Examples are the successes of Alibaba and Apple in building new businesses outside their traditional core, such as Alipay and Apple Pay. In the automotive industry, the share of electric vehicle offerings in the development pipeline of a manufacturer could be a meaningful indicator of long-term growth in premium car categories.

2. *Organizational health* reflects whether the company has the people, skills, and culture to sustain and improve its performance. Diagnostics of organizational health typically measure the skills and capabilities of a company, its ability to retain its employees and keep them satisfied, its culture and values, and the depth of its management talent. Again, what is important varies by a company's sector and life cycle stage. E-commerce businesses need entrepreneurial and innovation capabilities in the start-up phase and require more managers and customer-service-oriented staff as they mature. Semiconductor and biotechnology companies need deep scientific innovation capabilities but relatively few managers. Retailers need lots of trained store managers, a few great merchandisers, and in most cases, store staff with a customer service orientation.

Benefits of Understanding Value Drivers

Clearly understanding a business's value drivers has several advantages. If managers know the relative impact of their company's value drivers on long-term value creation, they can make explicit trade-offs between pursuing a critical driver and allowing performance against a less critical driver to deteriorate. This is particularly helpful for choosing between activities that deliver short-term performance and those that build the long-term health of the business. These trade-offs are material: increasing investment for the long term will cause short-term returns to decline, as management expenses some of the costs, such as R&D or advertising, in the year they occur rather than the year the investments achieve their benefits.

Clarity about value drivers also enables the management team to set priorities so that activities expected to create substantially more value take precedence over others. Setting priorities encourages focus and often adds more to value than efforts to improve on multiple dimensions simultaneously. For example, reducing accounts receivable in telecom services creates value but far less than the value created by improved customer retention. And improvements in customer retention might well require a company to refrain from cutting back on customer credit. Without an explicit discussion of such priorities and trade-offs, members of the management team could interpret and execute the business strategy in numerous and perhaps incompatible ways.

In general, distinctive strategic management promotes a common language and understanding of value drivers that shape the way top management and employees think about creating value at each level of the organization. For example, in a pharmaceutical company, distinctive strategic management would encourage discussion and coordinated action across the organization about specific steps to increase the speed of product launches, thus accelerating value creation. In contrast, strategic management in refining and other commodity-based process industries would focus on operational excellence in terms of capacity utilization and operational expenses.

Creating Actionable Metrics

As in Exhibit 29.3, most value driver trees start on the left side with financial value drivers such as ROIC and growth, and each of these is disaggregated into more specific drivers of business value and operational value, moving from left to right. Where possible, managers and analysts should specify actionable metrics for the value drivers.

The more a value driver tree is tailored to the business, the more insight it yields into a company's key sources of value creation and how to influence them. Exhibit 29.4 shows a basic value driver tree developed for a manufacturing company. In this example, the key drivers for growth turn out to be sales force effectiveness and new-product pipeline, because of low market growth and strong competition. For return on capital, the key drivers of value are capacity utilization (measured as invested capital per unit) and the manufacturing error rate. These are important because invested capital is fixed over the next several years, and labor and raw materials costs per unit are very high.

In contrast, Exhibit 29.5 shows a value driver tree for a grocery retailer. In this very different example, the key value drivers for gross margin are the average basket size (the number of transactions per square foot is important but always has an upper limit) and the markdown percentage on product prices. For operating costs, labor productivity is key, as most other components are fixed in the near term. Similarly, within invested capital, inventory level is one of the key value drivers; again, most other components are fixed in the near term.

How do you tailor the tree to get such insights? Our experience has taught us that developing different initial versions of trees based on different hypotheses and business knowledge will stimulate the identification of

EXHIBIT 29.5 **Basic Value Driver Tree: Grocery Retailer**

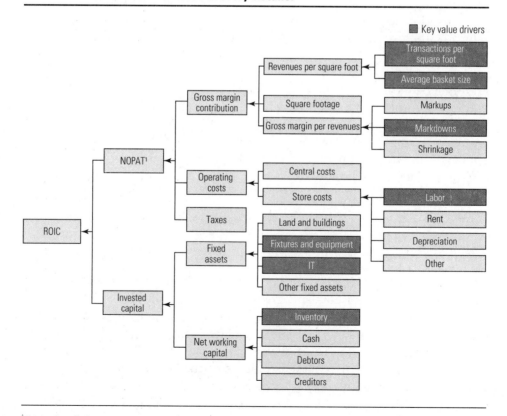

unconventional sources of value. The information from these versions should then be integrated into one tree (or in some cases, a few trees) that best reflects the understanding of the business.

To illustrate this process, we apply it to a hypothetical company running a chain of bicycle repair shops. Exhibit 29.6 shows four different approaches to developing the short-term portion of a value driver tree for this company. We used these trees to develop the summary short-term value driver tree shown in Exhibit 29.7. Adopting the most useful insights provided by the original four approaches, this tree combines the location and customer value driver trees.

Managers often expect that the most natural and easiest-to-complete tree is one based on a profit-and-loss (P&L) structure. Such a tree, however, is unlikely to provide the insight gained by looking at the business from the perspective of a customer, a shop location, or some other relevant vantage point. For example, in most parts of the world, fuel service stations create much more value per customer from selling food and beverage products than from fuel. As a result, the conversion of station visits into food and beverage sales is an even more important value driver than the number of station visits itself.

When you develop value driver trees, pay particular attention to the drivers of growth, because of the lag time between investment in developing a growth opportunity and the eventual payoff. Lag times for opportunities will differ. Continuing the example of the bicycle repair company, Exhibit 29.8 illustrates a value tree created for developing business in a new geographic market. For this opportunity, important value drivers include those associated with building the customer base (such as market share, revenues per customer, customer acquisition costs, and number of shops per customer) and improving employee productivity in the new geography (the number of mechanic hours per dollar of revenues), both of which take time to achieve.

Carefully disaggregating value drivers helps managers identify and set priorities for operating initiatives to improve a company's performance. Exhibit 29.9 shows the value driver tree for a component-manufacturing company. Financial value drivers such as ROIC are cascaded to business value drivers such as gross manufacturing margin and to operating value drivers such as labor productivity and manufacturing error rates. Understanding what is most critical for value creation at the operating or work floor level is important and can be expressed in a range of potential upsides and downsides for ROIC. Carefully aligning various operating initiatives with the value drivers affected enables a systematic comparison and can serve as a basis for deciding which initiatives matter most. For example, initiatives to improve employee effectiveness are linked to sales force effectiveness and thus to sales volume and earnings. Product redesign improves earnings via lowering materials, energy, and/or labor costs.

EXHIBIT 29.6 **Alternative Value Driver Trees for a Bicycle Repair Company**

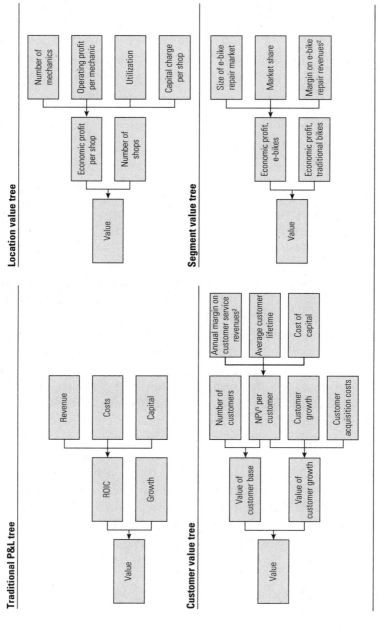

Traditional P&L tree

Location value tree

Customer value tree

Segment value tree

[1] Net present value.
[2] Including capital charge.

EXHIBIT 29.7 **Combined Location and Customer Value Driver Trees: Bicycle Repair Company**

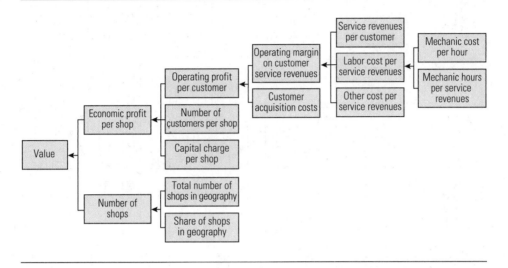

EXHIBIT 29.8 **Value Driver Tree for New Geography: Bicycle Repair Company**

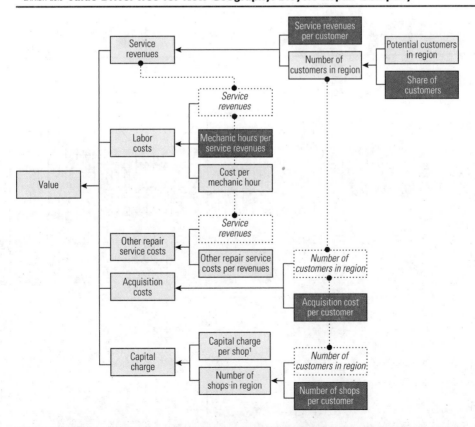

[1] Including other indirect costs.

EXHIBIT 29.9 **Aligning Operating Initiatives and Value Drivers: Manufacturing Company**

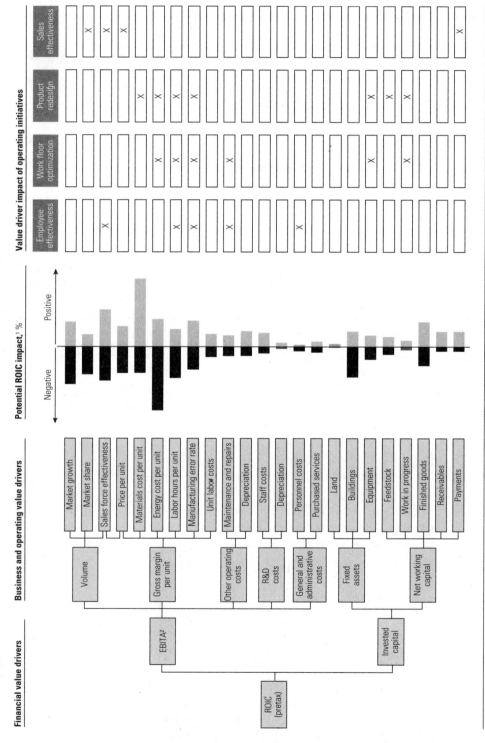

The tip of every branch of a value tree is a potential value driver, so a full dis-aggregation would result in many value drivers and metrics—more than could possibly be helpful for running the company. To be sure performance management remains practical and effective, managers need to decide at this stage which drivers are the most important for value creation and then should focus on these.

Setting Targets

Targets for value drivers should be both challenging and realistic enough that managers can take responsibility for meeting them.

Businesses can identify realistic opportunities and set targets by studying world-class competitors' performance on a particular value metric or milestone and comparing it with their own potential. Alternatively, executives can perform a similar analysis of high-performing firms operating in a different but similar sector. For instance, a petroleum company might benchmark product availability in its service station shops against a grocery retailer's equivalents.

Businesses can also learn from internal benchmarks. This may involve measuring the performance of the same operation at different time periods or studying comparable operations in different businesses controlled by the same parent. These measures may be less challenging than external benchmarks, as they do not necessarily involve world-class players. However, the use of internal benchmarks delivers several benefits. The data are likely to be more readily available, since sharing the information poses no competitive or antitrust problems. Also, unearthing the causes of differences in performance is much easier, as the unit heads can visit the benchmark unit.

After assessing the data, companies typically arrive at performance targets defined as single points, although ranges can be more helpful. Some companies set a range in terms of base and stretch targets. Managers should meet the base target under any circumstance. The stretch target is a statement of the aspiration for the business and is developed by the management team responsible for delivery. Those who meet their stretch targets are rewarded, but those who miss them are seldom penalized. Using base and stretch targets makes a performance management system much more complex, but it allows the managers of the business units to communicate what they aspire to deliver (and what it would take for them to achieve that goal) without committing themselves to delivery.

Choosing the right performance metrics lays the groundwork for discovering new insights into how a company might improve its performance in the future. For instance, a hypothetical pharmaceutical company has the key value drivers listed on the left side of Exhibit 29.10. For each of these value drivers, the exhibit shows the company's current performance relative to best- and worst-in-class benchmarks, its targets for each driver, and the potential value impact from meeting its targets. The greatest value creation would come from three areas: accelerating the rate of release of new products from 0.5 to 0.8 per year, reducing from six years to four the time it takes for a new drug to reach 80 percent of peak sales, and cutting the cost of goods sold from 26 percent to

EXHIBIT 29.10 **Key Value Drivers: Pharmaceutical Company**

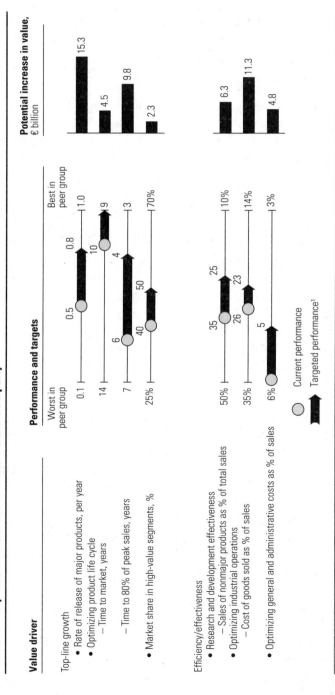

¹ All arrows represent an equivalent implementation effort.

23 percent of sales. Some of the value drivers (such as new-drug development) are long-term, whereas others (such as reducing cost of goods sold) have a shorter-term focus.

Monitoring Results

Focusing on the right performance metrics can reveal what may be driving underperformance. A consumer goods company we know illustrates the importance of having a tailored set of key value metrics. For several years, a business unit showed consistent double-digit growth in economic profit. Since the financial results were consistently strong—in fact, the strongest across all the business units—corporate managers were pleased and did not ask many questions of the business unit. One year, the unit's economic profit unexpectedly began to decline. Corporate management began digging deeper into the unit's results and discovered that for the preceding three years, the unit had been increasing its profit by raising prices and cutting back on product promotion. That created the conditions for competitors to take away market share. The unit's strong short-term performance was coming at the expense of its long-term health. The company changed the unit's management team, but lower profits continued for several years as the unit recovered its position with consumers.

A well-defined and appropriately selected set of key value drivers ought to allow management to articulate how the organization's strategic, marketing, operating, or other initiatives create value. If it is impossible to represent some component of a strategic initiative using the key value drivers, or if some key value driver does not serve as a building block in the initiative, then managers should reexamine the value trees. Similarly, managers must regularly revisit the targets they set for each value driver. As their business environment changes, so will the limits of what they can achieve.

SUMMARY

Strategic management encompasses some of the most important decisions executives make to create value in a company. One critical element of managing strategically is establishing the analytics to assess performance and investment opportunities. To establish the right analytical base, executives should ensure financial rigor in all investment decisions, allocate resources to strategic investments and business units by ranking opportunities across the enterprise at a granular level of insights, and manage performance by reviewing business unit results. To monitor performance, managers should move beyond standard financial and operating metrics to apply an approach that identifies what drives both short- and long-term value.

Another critical element of strategic management is establishing governance and processes to orient the organization toward achievement of long-term value creation. That is the subject of the next chapter.

30

Strategic Management: Governance, Processes, and Decision Making

Even the best strategies won't create long-term value for a company if it can't translate those strategies into action through its planning and resource allocation processes. Chapter 29 described the analytics capabilities required for effective planning and resource allocation. This chapter focuses on the human elements: the governance, processes, and decision-making behaviors that orient and motivate the management team toward its long-term goals.

For all the time managers spend developing strategic plans, they are often ineffective at turning those plans into actions. Budgets and actual spending don't always reflect strategic priorities. In a McKinsey survey of 1,271 executives, only 30 percent of managers said their company's budgets for capital expenditures, research and development (R&D), and sales and marketing were closely aligned with their strategic plans.[1] In another survey, about two-thirds of the respondents said their companies underinvest in product development, and more than half said their companies underinvest in sales and marketing and in new products or new markets. Instead, companies frequently cut back R&D spending or sales and marketing expenditures to meet arbitrary short-term earnings targets.

Durably tying strategy to action requires changing these shortsighted practices. Too often, the processes of planning and resource allocation are

---

This chapter was coauthored by Aaron De Smet, Zuzanna Kraszewska, Dan Lovallo, and Derek Schatz.

[1] T. Koller, D. Lovallo, and Z. Williams, "The Finer Points of Linking Resource Allocation to Value Creation," *McKinsey on Finance*, no. 62 (Spring 2017), www.mckinsey.com. In another survey, conducted in 2023, only a little more than half of respondents said their companies fully funded strategic initiatives. See "Tying Short-Term Decisions to Long-Term Strategy," McKinsey & Company, May 20, 2024, www.mckinsey.com.

siloed: the CEO allocates resources to division heads, who in turn allocate to business units. Along the way, the organization's broad strategic priorities can get lost. Effectively allocating resources means thinking across the entire enterprise, ranking all opportunities according to their strategic importance, and making tough decisions about which units will get a greater or smaller share of resources, which projects will be fully funded or will not get any funding, and how the organization will balance its short- and long-term objectives.

Doing this well requires strong governance, coordinated processes, and objective decision making. This chapter examines all three of these elements in detail:

1. *Strong governance.* The CEO and top team must be fully committed to the company's long-term strategy and willing to invest resources accordingly. They must devote substantial time to planning and resource allocation at an appropriate level of granularity. Finally, they must have the support of an influential corporate staff that can challenge the business units' investment plans.

2. *Synchronized and streamlined processes.* Companies must link more explicitly their strategic planning, resource allocation, budgeting, and other processes to ensure that strategic initiatives are fully funded with a view to maximizing long-term value.

3. *Debiased decision making.* Most organizations are susceptible to a wide range of cognitive and organizational decision-making biases. Companies must make a systematic effort to overcome these biases in order to improve the quality of their decisions.

STRONG GOVERNANCE

It's easy to go along to get along—that is, to give lots of managers an equal say and allot each division its "fair share" of capital. But this approach, while tempting, frequently underserves a corporation's most promising opportunities for growth. High-growth initiatives often don't receive the resources they urgently need, while less promising endeavors receive more than they deserve. Effective resource allocation starts with corporate governance.[2]

Commitment to the Long-Term Vision

To commit to their company's strategy, executives must take a long-term view and avoid becoming preoccupied with the demands of short-term profit. This is often easier said than done. In many cases, incentives for both management

---

[2] This section is adapted from A. De Smet and T. Koller, "Capital Allocation Starts with Governance—and Should Be Led by the CEO," McKinsey & Company, June 22, 2033, www.mckinsey.com.

and employees are tied to short-term performance, and the company's board may focus on short-term measurable results, rather than progress toward long-term goals.

A company's ability to stay committed to its strategy can often depend on whether the CEO and executive team have the courage to defy these pressures, putting the necessary resources and talent behind the most promising initiatives even if doing so causes a dip in short-term profits. The success stories of many companies include a period in which profitability pauses while investment in the next wave of growth takes root.

Investing Significant CEO Time

The CEO should be the decision-maker-in-chief, typically supported by the CFO. Governance achieves the greatest impact in this area when it is marked by a meaningful investment of CEO and CFO time. How much of a CEO's already full calendar should be reserved for capital allocation? While no single answer is right for every company, a good rule of thumb is at least 10 percent—perhaps even 20 percent or higher in certain situations. One effective CEO commits 20 percent of his time; he makes sure to review at least one strategic initiative each week. At the Dutch publishing company Wolters Kluwer, CEO Nancy McKinstry devotes an outsize portion of her time to resource allocation, both organic and through M&A. Under her direction, Wolters Kluwer discontinued funding or divested about $1.0 billion in lower-growth initiatives and acquired $1.5 billion worth of companies that advanced its digital strategy.[3]

Many CEOs believe, understandably, that the bulk of their time should be spent as the face or voice of the company. No one disputes that CEOs have an enormous amount to do, but if they fail to decisively reallocate capital, huge growth opportunities can go unrealized.

A Very Small Decision-Making Committee

The CEO should be the ultimate decision maker on capital allocation but in some situations may lack the information or perspective necessary to do so effectively. As a result, it is often necessary for the CEO to work with a small committee of two to four additional executives. It is important to keep this group small and to avoid placing undue emphasis on consensus. Seeking consensus among a large group can lead to watered-down decisions.

One principle that can trip up even outstanding leaders is the distinction between decisions and debate. Decisions are made when the CEO enacts

[3] C. Dewar, S. Keller, and V. Malhotra, *CEO Excellence: The Six Mindsets That Distinguish the Best Leaders from the Rest* (New York: Scribner, 2022), 61.

one of several possible courses of action. Debate, in contrast, helps inform those decisions, and a robust, meaningful debate often encompasses a wider circle—in many cases, one that extends beyond the small resource allocation committee. While successful decisions are supported by meaningful analyses and data, the quality of team dynamics also can make a huge difference—especially the ability to encourage pushback and avoid groupthink. Healthy debate about capital allocation enables decision makers to understand different implications of an investment and to see both sides of the decision. If the debate starts to sound perfunctory—or worse, like an echo chamber—CEOs should actively seek out individuals with a different view. Business managers and outside experts with demonstrated operational, technology, risk, or country- or demographic-specific knowledge can offer valuable perspectives, especially when uncertainty is high.

Another consideration to weigh is the degree to which division heads should be involved in this small group—whether they should have a voting say, for instance, or even be included as nonvoting participants. Division heads typically wield enormous power and talent, yet they often lack the holistic perspective needed to make optimal capital allocation decisions on an organization-wide basis. Moreover, they are typically incentivized based on the results their own businesses deliver during their tenure, which doesn't necessarily match the long-term performance of the enterprise. This often leads them to seek more capital for their division and more resources for operating results right now, even if this is not what is best for the company as a whole. If a CEO decides to include heads of divisions in the resource allocation committee, the CEO must ensure that the division heads assume the role of enterprise leaders in these deliberations, not the role of siloed division heads.

Most important, the CEO must avoid settling for a compromise allocation that gives every business an equal or proportional amount based on historical revenues. By definition, that's precisely the wrong way to place outsize bets; there is no such thing as a "fair share" when it comes to capital allocation. Rather, to be effective, capital allocation needs to be *unfair*: low-growth, non-strategic businesses should receive fewer resources than the company's future growth engines.

Shifting the Mission from Gatekeeper to Growth

CEOs, the resource allocation committee, and their supporting teams should strive relentlessly to invest for growth. Yet all too often, those who are most involved in capital allocation find themselves adopting the role of gatekeeper. As they come to see it, their duty is to protect and safeguard the company's scarce resources.

Ultimately, it is up to the CEO to dissuade leaders from adopting this mindset and to push them instead to relentlessly seek out opportunities for growth and value creation. Effective resource allocation means ensuring, consistently and proactively, that strategically important businesses receive and keep receiving the capital, talent, and management attention they need, so long as the growth thesis remains robust.

Getting Clear—and Granular—about Resource Allocation

Decisions also need to be made at the right level of granularity. Consider a large health care company that was organized into three divisions, each composed of roughly 20 business units. The company had a culture of decentralized decision making, so executives allocated R&D and sales and marketing spending to the three divisions and let the division leaders decide how to allocate across their business units. The result: spending was aligned not with corporate priorities but with the short-term incentives of the division heads. Even worse, if one business unit was having a difficult year, the division head would frequently ask other units to pull back funding from longer-term investments.

The solution in such a case is for the CEO, often with the CFO, to allocate resources and set performance targets with a far greater degree of detail. As we discussed in Chapter 29, for a company with around $10 billion in annual revenues, resource allocation works well at a level of 20–50 units or projects, though some companies go further.

Allocating resources at a more granular level requires more CEO time. But we believe that careful allocation, as one of the CEO's most important decisions, is well worth the extra time and effort. One large company spent more than $10 billion per year in capital expenditures, but the top corporate executives spent only several hours per year in their final deliberations on how to allocate that spending. After working through a new process, they increased their time spent on resource allocation to two days. The result: a finer-grained capital spending plan more tightly linked to the company's overall strategic priorities.

To make sure the right businesses are receiving sufficient resources, the CEO-led resource allocation committee must heed two imperatives. First, it must be clear about the company's strategic priorities. This means understanding the divisions' businesses at the appropriate level of granularity, which is definitely not a 30,000-foot view. Getting to good decisions requires committees to rank the 10 to 30 most important initiatives across the corporation. These are the initiatives that simply must have the resources they need. Practically, it's impossible for resource allocation committees to rank more than about 30 top initiatives: doing so not only can present a false sense of specificity but also can demoralize business unit heads by limiting their discretion to fund their individual business lines.

Second, the resource allocation committee should make sure it has insight into, and funding authority over, capital allocation at a level of about 20–50 business cells, regardless of the formal organizational structure. In large corporations, the major divisions likely comprise businesses and individual product lines that can have very different economics and potential. Sometimes, the highest-potential initiatives, particularly for innovative products or services, may be housed (rightly) outside a formal line; these "skunkworks" can mature into major breakthroughs or, conversely, shrivel away if they fail to receive sufficient capital and management attention. Transparency is therefore essential.

Of course, micromanagement is neither realistic nor without consequences, the most common of which is a sense of information overload for the decision makers and demoralization for the talented executives below the C-suite. But often, the most compelling cells within a division can get lost when they are aggregated into broader groups. When resource allocation committees are presented with too few businesses or initiatives per division, they lose the opportunity to make decisions at a meaningful level of granularity.

Empowering a Capable, Influential Support Team

To make allocation decisions, CEOs and CFOs need effective staff support. This usually takes the form of a financial planning and analysis (FP&A) team and/or a corporate-strategy team. Despite the importance of this role, many companies have in recent years cut the resources of their FP&A teams to unacceptably low levels in order to demonstrate their commitment to spending reductions. In doing so, however, they are left with no capacity for thoughtful analysis and no means to challenge business units' resource requests.

In contrast, we've observed that companies with stronger FP&A or corporate-strategy teams tend to draw valuable insight and influence from the teams. This appears to make a large difference in the effectiveness of their planning and resource allocation. Common indicators of a strong FP&A capability include an FP&A leader with real stature and influence inside the company, team members with extensive experience in different parts of the company beyond finance, and a team with time to do its own analysis of the current and potential performance and opportunities for different business units.

While the support team doesn't do the deciding, its members shouldn't be gofers or wallflowers. On the contrary, they must do the rigorous prework of digging into capital allocation requests, pushing for higher-quality data, and presenting the information in a usable way. The resource allocation committee's time is precious; every meeting should be action oriented.

SYNCHRONIZED AND STREAMLINED PROCESSES

Most large corporations have annual processes to set financial targets and allocate capital and other resources across business units and for strategic initiatives enterprise-wide.[4] The typical practice is to begin with a strategy or "strategic refresh," develop a long-term (three- to seven-year) financial plan, and finally lay out a highly detailed budget for the first year of the plan. Unfortunately, the processes are often both muddled and rigid; they typically take months to iterate, generate reams of distracting detail, and then fail to allow for sufficient flexibility to adjust resource allocation over the year. The result: a failure to align resources with strategy.

To avoid these problems and ensure that the corporate strategy and resource allocation are implemented soundly, the most effective companies do the following:

- As part of the strategy or strategic refresh, identify the role of each business in realizing the company's strategy (for example, to accelerate growth, improve ROIC, or divest) and the company's 10 to 30 most important initiatives.

- Use a streamlined approach to develop the company's long-term financial plan by employing a value driver model, with only a few line items for each individual business unit or product line.

- Ensure that the long-term financial plan allocates resources to the company's ten to 30 most important initiatives.

- Match the next year's budget to the initial year of the long-term financial plan.

- Keep to a compact planning schedule.

- Create flexibility to continue resource allocation at a regular cadence, year round.

Start with an Actionable Strategy

Every strategic refresh should address two fundamental questions: First, what is the *role* of each business in realizing company strategy (such as to accelerate growth, improve ROIC, or divest)? Second, which *specific initiatives* are the highest priority for the company within each business and across the enterprise?

For example, a company may announce that its strategy is to grow in Latin America. That may be a terrific idea, but without more detail, it isn't actionable. What would a practical Latin America growth strategy look like?

---

[4] This section is adapted from T. Koller with Z. Kraszewska, "Keep Calm and Allocate Capital: Six Process Improvements," McKinsey & Company, June 5, 2024, www.mckinsey.com.

To start, the company should identify the specific countries it will focus on. Next, it should spell out the major considerations, such as whether the company intends to enter a country on its own, partner with an existing player in that market, or make an acquisition. The company should then allocate the capital needed for whichever options it intends to pursue and identify which business or team will be accountable.

The company's strategy need not be on the same rigid schedule as the rest of the planning and performance management process. In fact, some argue that the timing should be separated so that the strategy can be refined and revised as circumstances change and new information becomes available.[5] This also provides more time for introspection and avoids the "all hands on deck" approach that often arises during the formal process and consumes too much time.

Simplify the Long-Term Financial Plan

Most companies' long-term financial plans include too many line items. This kind of detail slows down the process, makes iteration difficult, and can obscure the true drivers of value.

To be effective, a long-term financial plan needs to be concise. For example, there is no need for ten or more items under general and administrative (G&A) expenses; the G&A line can stand alone. In most cases, income statements for each business should include only revenues, cost of goods sold, sales and marketing, R&D, and overhead costs, without disaggregating detail. An enterprise runs on value drivers, not accounting items. An effective financial plan clearly lays out the most important value drivers for each business unit, surfacing the few key elements that are most important for profitable growth, return on capital, and other company imperatives.

What do key value drivers look like? Consider a filmmaking company: a great deal goes into creating successful movies, but ultimately the model could be simplified to producing, say, three blockbusters and five smaller films. The most impactful value drivers might be the average budgets for large and small films, marketing costs, and overhead expenses. A music subscription business would have similarly compact but completely different key drivers: the number of subscribers, revenue per customer, and customer churn.

In many cases, senior leaders may push back on the imperative to "keep it simple," saying it is impossible to distill their businesses into just a few drivers. But it simply isn't possible to always achieve 100 percent certainty in a complex business. Parsing excessive line items takes away time that could be better spent managing issues with more of an impact, and it yields diminishing returns. Often, the extra detail delivers no benefits at all.

[5] C. Bradley, M. Hirt, and S. Smit, *Strategy beyond the Hockey Stick* (Hoboken, NJ: John Wiley & Sons, 2019), 175–177.

While the number of line items should be kept to a minimum, the number of business units or product lines should be sufficiently granular to aid the allocation of resources based on the roles, objectives, and needs of each business unit. For example, a division with a fast-growing business unit and a mature or shrinking business should be divided into two businesses, so top management can ensure that each has the right goals and resources (even if the division leader remains responsible for execution). In practice, a large corporation's long-range financial plan should typically cover 20–50 product lines or business units.

Allocate Resources to the Most Important Priorities

As noted earlier in this chapter, senior leaders tend to report that their organizations are underinvesting in the most important strategic initiatives (especially growth initiatives) and failing to properly allocate resources. For many companies, the long-range financial plan simply states the targets and financial projections for each business unit.

A better approach is to be clear on targets *and* specify in the long-range financial plan which resources are allocated to the highest-priority initiatives in order to make sure those targets are met. This typically requires the company to allocate resources among its business units differently from how it did in prior years.

For example, one major consumer-packaged-goods company took away the "base" level of spending from some of its legacy European operations because of their lack of growth and relatively low returns on capital. Instead, the company allocated those resources to three specific initiatives in Latin America. And at one leading retailer, the CEO personally ensures the full funding and management of the company's top six enterprise initiatives, in addition to spending almost one day per week on those initiatives.

Base the Budget on the Plan's First Year

Remarkably, the financial-planning process usually ends with a year-one budget that does not tie to the long-range financial plan; instead, the year-one budget is often closer to the last year's budget.[6] In the McKinsey survey of 1,271 executives mentioned earlier in this chapter, less than one-third of participants reported that their company's budgets were similar or very similar to their most recent strategic plans.[7]

While the year-one budget should be more detailed than the long-term financial plan, the top-line revenues, profits, and cash flows for each unit should always match year one of the long-term plan. Two techniques are useful for making this happen. First, start building the budget based on the initial

---

[6] Some companies add a step, called the annual operating plan, between the long-term plan and the budget.

[7] Koller et al., "The Finer Points of Linking Resource Allocation to Value Creation."

year of the long-term financial plan, rather than the previous year's budget or current year's results. Second, require that only the CEO and CFO have authority to approve deviations from the long-range plan. Without that rigor, resource allocation decisions tend to get lost in a fog of war.

Compress the Time Frame

Financial planning can be a never-ending story. A senior team starts with a strategic refresh in the first quarter, followed by a long-term financial plan that kicks off in the second quarter, and finishes toward the end of the third quarter. Meanwhile, the budget for the next year begins in the third quarter and wraps up at the turn of the year—or even later. This prolonged timeline invites unnecessary draft turning and complexity.

The planning and resource allocation process should be synchronized and as short as possible, with each step taking a maximum of two months. These steps should be scheduled as late in the year as possible while still allowing ample time for rigorous analysis and meaningful debate. The entire process should also be contiguous.

One retail company's process serves as an example of an *inefficient* resource allocation timeline. The company conducts its annual strategic refresh in April or May, followed by long-term financial planning in September and October. Finally, after about two more months of hiatus, the budgeting process takes place from December until March for the calendar year that has already begun. Each step in the process is excessively time consuming and remarkably disconnected from the others.

A consumer packaged-goods company by contrast, demonstrates a more effective resource allocation timeline. The company initiates its annual strategic refresh in May, which drives the long-term strategic financial plan and resource allocation process conducted from June until September. The long-term strategic financial plan flows into the annual budgeting process, which starts in October and ends in November.

Precise timelines will vary depending on the enterprise, which in turn depends on its industry (technology companies, for example, move much faster). But in most cases, a company should begin its strategic refresh shortly after midyear and complete the refresh before the end of the third quarter, commence its long-term strategic financial plan as soon as the refresh is completed, and then, when the long-term strategic plan is done, immediately turn to its budget for the upcoming year.

Continue the Allocation Process throughout the Year

Budgets are never perfect—which is to be expected, since circumstances change over the course of the year. For many companies, the approach to in-year flexibility is to allocate the resources to each division or unit leader and give them the decision rights to reallocate among lines they control, as they see fit. This, however, creates a perverse incentive for divisions or business units to hoard resources they don't need and spend them on lower-priority items or, even worse, underinvest in strategic initiatives to meet short-term targets.

To prepare for changing circumstances, senior leaders should be the only ones afforded meaningful flexibility in resource allocation at the enterprise level throughout the year. The resource allocation committee should meet monthly to make important in-year investment decisions. These monthly meetings should be focused and address only urgent matters that require a decision, including allocating funds for stage-gated projects or projects that were provisionally approved during the annual planning process, discontinuing projects that aren't likely to meet their objectives, and approving new projects that arose after the annual planning cycle.

Flexibility usually requires setting a reserve of unallocated funds that can be used during the year for new initiatives that were not anticipated during the planning process. Withdrawals from the reserve should be authorized only by the CEO or resource allocation committee and must be used for a strategically vital initiative or covering essential external costs, such as dealing with natural disasters. While there is no universally applicable percentage for the "right" amount to reserve, a general guideline is to set aside 5–10 percent of the corporation's budget.

Certain projects, such as pharmaceutical companies preparing to make significant investments in marketing once regulatory approvals are obtained, are easier to stage-gate during the formal planning cycle. Other allocations of capital may be approved only provisionally because they require further analysis (for example, proof of concept for a new technology or decisions to drill to a gas or petroleum deposit); in those cases, the resource allocation committee should withhold that capital for in-year allocation. The key is to build in flexibility. An effective resource allocation process anticipates change and maintains at least a monthly cadence.

UNBIASED DECISION MAKING

When it comes to making decisions, human beings have built-in biases. So do companies and other organizations. In any number of ways, these biases can stall, skew, or deny the kind of clear-sighted decisions that are at the heart of strategic management. To effectively tie strategy to value creation, management must make tangible efforts to overcome these biases.

Our thinking in this section is inspired by our collaboration with the late Nobel Prize–winning psychologist and economist Daniel Kahneman. His work laid the foundation for what we now call behavioral economics and behavioral finance, and while his focus was primarily on individual decision making, we had the opportunity to ask how it might apply to organizations.

We asked him, "If people don't behave in an economically rational way, is there any hope for organizations?" His response: "I'm much more optimistic about organizations than individuals. Organizations can put systems in place to help them." Managers can develop rules and processes that help overcome inherent decision-making biases.

Drawing on Kahneman's insights, a group of colleagues have proposed (or adopted from others) a number of techniques to help organizations understand and improve their decision making in resource allocation. In this section, we discuss four common biases that can affect organizational decision making, along with some potential remedies.

Groupthink

Groups of decision makers tend to engage in groupthink, an overemphasis on harmony and consensus. This can get in the way of examining all the options objectively, leading to weaker—and sometimes disastrous—decisions. Consider the failed Bay of Pigs invasion of Cuba during U.S. president John F. Kennedy's administration. Arthur Schlesinger Jr., one of Kennedy's advisers, wrote this about his participation in the debate leading up to the humiliating defeat of U.S.-backed Cuban exiles trying to overthrow the regime of Cuban leader Fidel Castro: "In the months after the Bay of Pigs I bitterly reproached myself for having kept so silent in the Cabinet Room ... . I can only explain my failure to do more than raise a few timid questions by reporting that one's impulse to blow the whistle on this nonsense was simply undone by the circumstance."[8]

A variation on this failing occurs when participants don't speak up because they feel the subject under discussion does not fall into their area of responsibility or expertise. At one global agriculture company, the members of the executive committee tended to speak up during strategy conversations only if their area of the business was being discussed. The tacit assumption was that colleagues wouldn't intrude on other colleagues' areas of responsibility—an assumption that deprived the committee of their insights.

The weight of evidence strongly supports that decisions are better when there is rigorous debate. One research effort found that for big-bet decisions, high-quality debate led to decisions that were 2.3 times more likely to be successful.[9] Extensive study has explored the importance of vigorous debate in improving decision making.[10]

Ideally, a company dedicated to pursuing long-term strategic success should have a culture of dissent, where rigorous debate is the norm. But most

---

[8] A. Schlensinger Jr., *A Thousand Days: John F. Kennedy in the White House* (New York: Houghton Mifflin, 1965), 255.

[9] I. Aminov, A. De Smet, G. Jost, and D. Mendelsohn, "Decision Making in the Age of Urgency," McKinsey & Company, April 2019, www.mckinsey.com.

[10] See, for example, A. Duke, *Thinking in Bets: Making Smarter Decisions When You Don't Have All the Facts* (New York: Portfolio/Penguin, 2018).

companies need to take more active steps to stimulate debate. The key ingredient is to depersonalize debate and make it socially acceptable to be a contrarian. Here are some useful techniques:

- *Assigning a devil's advocate.* At a strategy discussion, assign someone the task of taking an opposing point of view. Make sure this contrarian's contribution is more than just offering opinions. The focus should be on calling attention to potential alternate scenarios or highlighting missing information important to the debate.

- *Bringing a diverse group to the discussion.* More than 150 years ago, John Stuart Mill wrote in *On Liberty*, "The only way in which a human being can make some approach to knowing the whole of a subject is by hearing what can be said about it by persons of every variety of opinion." More recent research has proven his point.[11] Diversity means drawing on the opinions of people from different disciplines, roles, genders, and races in important discussions. Bring in more junior people with special expertise, create an environment where it is safe for them to speak up, and ask them for ideas.

- *Encouraging debate with secret ballots.* Use a secret ballot at the beginning of the debate, not the end. Once a proposal has been presented and before it is debated, ask participants to vote on the idea in secret. The request could be for a yes-or-no vote on a project or for a ranking of investment priorities. When the results are revealed, assuming participants discover at least one other person shares their views, the knowledge will likely make them more comfortable expressing their opinion.

- *Setting up a red-team/blue-team activity for large investments.* Arrange two teams to prepare arguments for opposing outcomes. While undertaking the preparatory work and analysis for this approach is expensive, it can make a difference for particularly large decisions with high uncertainty.

Confirmation Bias and Excessive Optimism

Confirmation bias and overoptimism are two distinct biases. However, the same set of techniques applies to both, so we discuss them together.

Confirmation bias is the tendency to look for evidence that supports your hypothesis or to interpret ambiguous data in a way that achieves the same result. For business decisions, this often takes the form of "I have a hunch that investing in *x* would create value. Therefore, let's look for some supporting facts that will back up our hunch." The universal foundation of the scientific approach to addressing a hypothesis is the opposite: you should look for disconfirming evidence.

[11] Ibid.

Overoptimism is the tendency to assume that everything will go right with a project, even though past projects tell us that such smooth outcomes are rare. A classic example is the construction of the famous Sydney Opera House, whose schedule and budget were both overly optimistic. The project was completed ten years late and cost 14 times the original budget.

Some of the techniques used to overcome groupthink, such as the use of opposing red and blue teams, can help here. The simplest approaches are to avoid developing hypotheses too early in the process and to actively look for contrary evidence. Other potential correctives for confirmation bias and overoptimism include the following two methods:

1. *Conducting a pre-mortem.* A "pre-mortem" is an exercise in which, after a project team has developed a proposal, its members purposely imagine that the plan has failed. The very structure of a pre-mortem makes it safe to identify problems.[12]

2. *Taking the outside view.* This is an exercise that involves building a statistical view of a project based on a reference class of similar projects. For instance, a group at a private-equity company was asked to build a forecast for an ongoing investment from the bottom up—tracing its path from beginning to end and noting the key steps, actions, and milestones required to meet proposed targets. The group was then asked to compare that ongoing investment with categories of similar investments, looking at factors such as relative quality of the investment and average return for an investment category. Using this outside view, the group saw that its median expected rate of return was more than double that of the most similar investments.[13]

Inertia (Stability Bias)

Inertia, or stability bias, is the natural tendency of organizations to resist change. One study found that, among the companies it studied, spending allocations across business units were correlated by an average of more than 90 percent from year to year.[14] In other words, the allocation of spending to business units essentially never changed. The same study showed that companies that reallocated more resources—the top third of the sample—earned, on average, 30 percent higher total shareholder returns (TSR) annually than companies in the bottom third of the sample.

---

[12] G. Klein, T. Koller, and D. Lovallo, "Pre-Mortems: Being Smart at the Start," *McKinsey Quarterly*, April 2019, www.mckinsey.com.

[13] T. Koller and D. Lovallo, "Bias Busters: Taking the 'Outside View,'" *McKinsey Quarterly*, September 2018, www.mckinsey.com.

[14] S. Hall, D. Lovallo, and R. Musters, "How to Put Your Money Where Your Strategy Is," *McKinsey Quarterly*, March 2012, www.mckinsey.com.

The solution to inertia bias is relatively straightforward. Rank initiatives across the entire enterprise, as described in Chapter 29. In addition, ensure that the budget you are building is rooted in the current strategic plan, not last year's budget, as described in the "Synchronized and Streamlined Processes" section of this chapter. The essential idea is to ignore as much as possible the influences of past allocations or budgets. In practice, you may not be able to shift resources as quickly or as much as you should. But trying to ignore the past is a starting point and will help you minimize inertia.

Loss Aversion

We previously explored loss aversion in Chapter 4, via survey results showing that most executives are loss averse and unwilling to undertake risky projects with high estimated present values.[15] The primary solution to overcoming loss aversion is to view investment decisions based not on their individual risk but on their contribution to the risk of the enterprise as a whole (see Chapter 29).

That's easy in theory, but executives are typically concerned about the risk of their own projects and the potential impact on their careers. That's why those decisions should be elevated to executives with a broader portfolio of projects whose risks cancel each other out. Often, the decisions must be pushed up to the CEO.

To be most effective, companies also must encourage middle-level managers and other employees to propose risky ideas. Companies can do this by eliminating risks to the employee. Many employees censor themselves because of concerns that their careers will suffer if their idea for a project fails. To overcome this concern, it's important to agree on the various risks up front with the top leadership and conduct post-mortems on projects, particularly to identify causes of failure. If a project fails because the decision to go ahead with the project turns out to be incorrect (which should happen frequently), that failure should not bear on the manager responsible for the project. The responsible manager should only be accountable for the quality of execution of the project.

Jeff Bezos, founder of Amazon, puts it this way: "I always point out that there are two different kinds of failure. There's experimental failure—that's the kind of failure you should be happy with. And there's operational failure. We've built hundreds of fulfillment centers at Amazon over the years. … If we build a new fulfillment center and it's a disaster, that's just bad execution. That's not good failure. But when we are developing a new product or service or experimenting in some way, and it doesn't work, that's okay. That's great failure."[16]

---

[15] For more on overcoming loss aversion, see D. Lovallo, T. Koller, R. Uhlaner, and D. Kahneman, "Your Company Is Too Risk-Averse," *Harvard Business Review*, March–April 2020, hbr.org.

[16] J. Bezos, *Invent & Wander: The Collected Writings of Jeff Bezos* (Brighton: Harvard Business Review Press, 2020), 230–231.

CLOSING THOUGHTS

Executives squander good corporate strategy when they can't overcome the organizational barriers, behavioral biases, weak processes, and plain lack of courage needed to turn ideas into value-creating actions. Long-term value creation through effective planning and resource allocation requires combining strong analytics capabilities with strong governance, synchronized and streamlined processes, and debiased decision making. The list of best practices is long and can be daunting, but executives can begin by focusing on those that are easiest and likely to have the biggest impact on their performance. Adding new refinements over time will move any company closer to the goal of managing strategically for the long term.

31

Mergers and Acquisitions

Mergers and acquisitions (M&A) are an important element of a dynamic economy. At different stages of an industry's or a company's life span, resource decisions that once made economic sense no longer do. For instance, the company that invented a groundbreaking innovation may not be best suited to exploit it. As demand falls off in a mature industry, companies are likely to have built excess capacity. At any time in a business's history, one group of managers may be better equipped to manage the business than another. At moments like these, acquisitions (and their siblings, divestitures, which are covered in the next chapter) are often the best or only way to reallocate resources sensibly and rapidly.

Acquisitions that reduce excess capacity or put companies in the hands of better owners or managers typically create substantial value both for the economy generally and for investors. You can see this effect in the increase in the combined cash flows of many companies involved in acquisitions. Even though acquisitions create value overall, the distribution of any value they create tends to be lopsided, with the selling company's shareholders capturing the bulk.

For companies in growth mode, acquisitions can be an effective way to accelerate their expansion; fill in gaps in products, technologies, or geographies; or create new products or services altogether. Typically, numerous smaller acquisitions can help companies access markets faster or help smaller companies get their products to market faster.

The challenge for executives, therefore, is to ensure that their acquisitions are among those that *do* create value for their shareholders. To that end, this chapter provides a framework for analyzing how to create value from acquisitions and summarizes the empirical research. Next, it discusses the archetypal approaches that are most likely to create value. It provides practical advice on how to estimate and achieve operating improvements and whether to pay in cash or in stock. Finally, it reminds managers that stock markets respond to the expected impact of acquisitions on intrinsic value, not accounting results.

This chapter was coauthored by Patrick McCurdy and Liz Wol with contributions from Riccardo Andreola.

A FRAMEWORK FOR VALUE CREATION

Acquisitions create value when the cash flows of the combined companies are greater than they would have otherwise been. If the acquirer doesn't overpay for the acquisition, some of that value will accrue to the acquirer's shareholders. Acquisitions are a good example of the conservation of value principle (explained in Chapter 3).

The value created for an acquirer's shareholders equals the difference between the value received by the acquirer and the price paid by the acquirer:

Value Created for Acquirer's Shareholders = Value Received − Price Paid

The value received by the acquirer equals the intrinsic value of the target company as a stand-alone company run by its former management team plus the present value of any performance improvements to be achieved after the acquisition, which will show up as improved cash flows for the target's business or the acquirer's business or the combined business. The price paid is the market value of the target plus any premium required to convince the target's shareholders to sell their shares to the acquirer:

Value Created for   = (Stand-Alone Value of Target
Acquirer's Shareholders   + Value of Performance Improvements)
                           − (Market Value of Target
                           + Acquisition Premium)

Exhibit 31.1 uses this framework to illustrate a hypothetical acquisition. Company A buys Company B for $1.3 billion, which includes a 30 percent

EXHIBIT 31.1 **Acquisition Evaluation Framework**

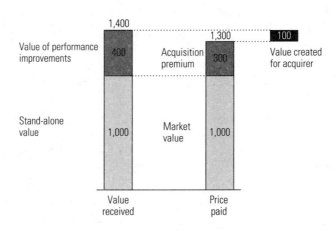

premium over its market value. Company A expects to increase the value of Company B by 40 percent through various operating improvements, so the value of Company B to Company A is $1.4 billion. Subtracting the purchase price of $1.3 billion from the value received of $1.4 billion leaves $100 million of value created for Company A's shareholders.

In the case where the stand-alone value of the target equals its market value, value is created for the acquirer's shareholders only when the value of improvements is greater than the premium paid:

Value Created = Value of Improvements − Acquisition Premium

Examining this equation, it's easy to see why most of the value created from acquisitions goes to the seller's shareholders: if a company pays a 30 percent premium, then it must increase the value of the target by at least 30 percent to create any value.

Exhibit 31.2 shows the value created for the acquirer's shareholders relative to the amount invested in acquisitions at different levels of premiums and operating improvements. For example, Company A, from the example just considered, paid a 30 percent premium for Company B and improved Company B's value by 40 percent, so the value created for the acquirers' shareholders represents 8 percent of the amount Company A invested in the deal.

If we further assume that Company A was worth about three times Company B's worth at the time of the acquisition, this major acquisition would be expected to increase Company A's value by only about 3 percent: $100 million of value creation (see Exhibit 31.1) divided by Company A's value of $3 billion. As this example shows, it is difficult for an acquirer to create a

EXHIBIT 31.2 **Value Creation for Given Performance Improvements and Premium Paid**

Value creation as % of deal value

Premium paid, % of stand-alone target value	10	20	30	40	50
0	10	20	30	40	50
10	0	9	18	27	36
20	−8	0	8	17	25
30	−15	−8	0	8	15

Value of performance improvements,
% of stand-alone target value

EXHIBIT 31.3 **Selected Deals: Significant Improvements**

%

Transaction	Year	Value of improvements relative to target value[1]	Deal premium as share of target value	Net value created relative to price
Baxter/Hillrom	2021	25–30	10	15–20
Goodyear/Cooper Tires	2021	60–75	25	35–50
Abbott Labs/Alere	2016	45–55	35	10–20
Tesoro/Western Refining	2016	45–55	35	10–20
Pfizer/Hospira	2015	45–50	35	5–15
Henkel/National Starch	2007	60–90	55	5–25
Pepsi/Quaker Oats	2000	35–55	10	25–45

Note: Equity value represents target's market capitalization plus value of acquisition premium, 1 month prior to the deal announcement; excludes impact of net debt and residual ownership interest components included within total enterprise/deal value.

[1] The value of improvements relative to the target is based on the NPV of announced run-rate savings.

substantial amount of value from acquisitions without having an extremely compelling value creation thesis and successfully executing on it.

While a 40 percent performance improvement sounds steep, that's what better acquirers often achieve. Exhibit 31.3 presents estimates of the value created from a sample of deals over the past 25 years. To estimate the gross value creation, we discounted the announced actual performance improvements at the company's weighted average cost of capital (WACC). The performance improvements were substantial, typically exceeding 50 percent of the value of the target. In addition, note that several of the companies paid lower premiums to capture more value.

EMPIRICAL RESULTS

Acquisitions and their effects on value creation are a perennial topic of interest to researchers. Empirical studies of acquisitions have yielded useful insights into when they occur, whether they create value, and for whom they create value.

Acquisition activity tends to occur in waves, as shown in Exhibit 31.4. Several factors drive these waves. First, we tend to see more acquisitions when stock prices are rising and managers are optimistic (though to maximize the amount of value created, they should really make acquisitions when prices are low). Low interest rates also stimulate acquisitions, especially heavily leveraged acquisitions by private-equity firms. Finally, one large acquisition in an industry encourages others in the same industry to acquire something, too.

For decades, academics and other researchers have studied the question of whether acquisitions create value. For the most part, the question of whether

EXHIBIT 31.4 **Historical M&A Activity: U.S. and European Transactions**

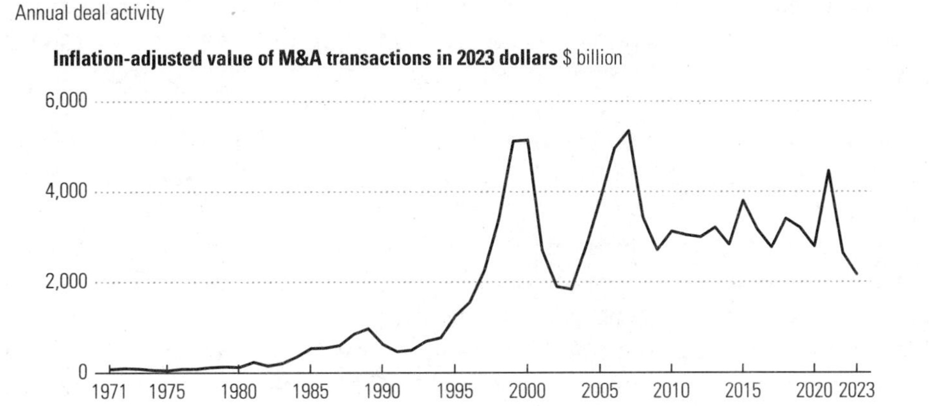

Annual deal activity

Inflation-adjusted value of M&A transactions in 2023 dollars $ billion

acquisitions create value *on average* is largely irrelevant. We know that some do and some don't. For most companies, what matters is whether the acquisitions they make create value for their shareholders, not the averages. But there are some patterns worth mentioning.

Researchers have shown that from the collective perspective of the shareholders of the acquirer and the acquired company, acquisitions do create value. According to McKinsey research on 1,770 acquisitions from 1999 through 2013, the combined value of the acquirer and target increased by about 5.8 percent on average.[1] This also means acquisitions tend to be good for the economy, as a result of cost and revenue synergies.

Given the typical premiums paid for acquisitions, it's clear that sellers regularly benefit from acquisitions. It's much harder to determine whether acquisitions create value for the acquirers. Ninety-five percent of acquisitions by large companies are of targets that are smaller than 5 percent of the acquirer's market capitalization. That means, from the outside, we can't see whether most acquisitions create value for the acquirers.

In the next several paragraphs, we summarize studies that examine the short-term share price reaction to acquisition announcements. Then, we'll look at the track records of companies over longer periods of time.

Empirical studies examining the reaction of capital markets to M&A announcements find that, on average, acquisitions of larger targets (relative to the size of the acquirer) lower the acquirer's stock price between 1 and 3 percent in the weeks around the announcement.[2] Stock returns following the acquisition are no better. Mark Mitchell and Erik Stafford have found that acquirers underperform comparable companies on shareholder returns

[1] D. Cogman, "Global M&A: Fewer Deals, Better Quality," *McKinsey on Finance*, no. 50 (Spring 2014): 23–25.
[2] S. B. Moeller, F. P. Schlingemann, and R. M. Stulz, "Do Shareholders of Acquiring Firms Gain from Acquisitions?" (NBER Working Paper W9523, Ohio State University, 2003).

by 5 percent during the three years following the acquisitions.[3] The United Kingdom has rules requiring a shareholder vote on larger acquisitions. Research by Marco Becht, Andrea Polo, and Stefano Rossi showed that in situations where shareholders voted, the stock price reaction of the acquirer was much more likely to be positive than when shareholders didn't vote. They also showed that in larger transactions in the United States, where shareholders don't vote, the stock price reactions were also more likely to be negative.[4]

While large transactions, on average, tend to have a poor track record when it comes to value creation, looking at the average masks the fact that many acquisitions do create value for the acquirer. Another way to consider the question is to estimate the percentage of deals that create any value at all for the acquiring company's shareholders. McKinsey research using the announcement effect approach with data from 1995 to 2009 found that one-third created value, one-third did not, and for the final third, the empirical results were inconclusive. A more recent analysis published in 2022 looked at the performance of the acquiring companies over a longer time period after the deal and found that they had a 50/50 chance of outperforming peers on total shareholder return (TSR).[5]

It comes as no surprise that most or all of the value creation from large acquisitions accrues to the shareholders of the target company, since the target shareholders are receiving, on average, high premiums over their stock's preannouncement market price—typically about 30 percent.

Although at first glance the success of large deals appears to be a coin flip, important insights can be gained by studying the outperformers. The 2022 study identified four commonalities of companies that successfully created value through large transactions. They each (1) pair a large-deal approach with a programmatic one (discussed next), (2) have a healthy corporate culture, (3) possess a source of competitive advantage, and (4) focus on revenue growth, continually resetting cost baselines to perform better than competitors.

Although studies of announcement effects give useful results for large samples, the same approach cannot be applied to individual transactions.[6]

---

[3] M. L. Mitchell and E. Stafford, "Managerial Decisions and Long-Term Stock Price Performance," *Journal of Business* 73 (2000): 287–329.

[4] M. Becht, A. Polo, and S. Rossi, "Does Mandatory Shareholder Voting Prevent Bad Acquisitions? The Case of the United Kingdom," *Journal of Applied Corporate Finance* 31, no. 1 (Winter 2019): 42–61.

[5] W. Rehm and C. Sivertsen, "A Strong Foundation for M&A in 2010," *McKinsey on Finance*, no. 34 (Winter 2010): 17–22; P. Daume, T. Lundberg, A. Montag, and J. Rudnicki, "The Flip Side of Large M&A Deals," McKinsey & Company, March 25, 2022, www.mckinsey.com.

[6] Many people have criticized using announcement effects to estimate value creation. The evidence on whether announcement effects persist is inconsistent. Sirower and Sahna have shown that the initial market reactions are persistent and indicate future performance for the next year. Some of our colleagues, however, examined a different sample of larger transactions over a two-year period and found inconclusive evidence of persistence. M. Sirower and S. Sahna, "Avoiding the Synergy Trap: Practical Guidance on M&A Decisions for CEOs and Boards," *Journal of Applied Corporate Finance* 18, no. 3 (Summer 2006): 83–95.

While the market may correctly assess the results of transactions on average, that statistic does not mean its initial assessment of a single transaction will always be correct.

To overcome these challenges, several of our colleagues looked at acquisition programs of companies, rather than single acquisitions.[7] In their most recent analysis, they examined 2,000 nonbanking companies from 2013 to 2022 and grouped them into four categories:

1. *Programmatic acquirers* completed an average of two or more acquisitions, often smaller or midsize, per year.
2. *Large-deal acquirers* completed at least one deal that was larger than 30 percent of its value.
3. *Organic companies* conducted almost no M&A.
4. *Selective acquirers* did not fit into the other three categories.

Exhibit 31.5 shows the results, including median TSRs versus peers, along with the 25th and 75th percentiles. Based on medians, programmatic acquirers performed best. That said, the medians conceal important details. Note that the band of 25th to 75th percentiles is very large and overlaps across the different acquisition strategies. Of all the categories, the distribution of the programmatic acquirers has the most positive and tight skewing. The case of organic

EXHIBIT 31.5 **Success Rates of Acquisition Strategies**

1,926 non-banking companies,[1] Jan 2013–Dec 2022, %

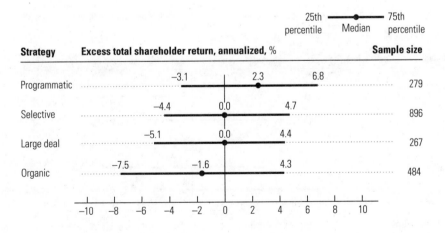

[1] Companies that were among the top 2,000 companies by market cap (>$2.5 billion) as of Dec. 31, 2012, and were still trading as of Dec. 31, 2022. Excludes companies headquartered in Latin America and Africa.

Source: McKinsey Value Intelligence; S&P Capital IQ.

[7] Updated and expanded analysis of W. Rehm, R. Uhlaner, and A. West, "Taking a Longer-Term Look at M&A Value Creation," *McKinsey Quarterly* (January 2012), www.mckinsey.com.

companies is interesting for its very wide distribution of results. This is not surprising, since the sample includes fast-growing, younger companies with high TSRs, as well as declining or troubled companies focused on managing decline.

That idea led us to dig deeper, and the results got more interesting. We separated the programmatic acquirers and organic growers into fast and slow growers, as measured by revenue growth. The results are shown in Exhibit 31.6. As you can see, while fast-growing programmatic acquirers continued to have the highest performance, the slow-growing programmatic acquirers significantly underperformed the fast-growing organic companies. Many fast-growing organic companies aren't yet ready to make acquisitions, nor do they need to.

We also found that the results varied by industry. For example, large acquisitions tended to be more successful in slower-growing, mature industries, where there is great value to reducing excess capacity. By contrast, large deals in faster-growing sectors underperformed significantly. In those companies, the inward focus required to integrate a large acquisition diverted management's attention from the need for continual product innovation. Only the programmatic acquirers tended to outperform across most industries. The results are also consistent with 2017 research by Fich, Nguyen, and Officer, who found that large companies acquiring small companies tend to create more value than when they buy large companies.[8]

EXHIBIT 31.6 **Acquisition Results Depend on Overall Growth**

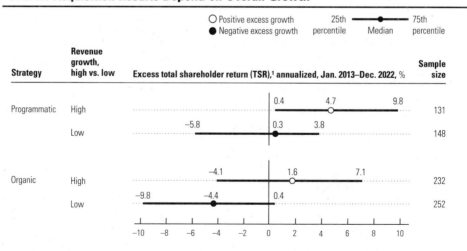

[1] Companies that were among the top 2,000 companies by market cap (>$2.5 billion) as of Dec. 31, 2012, and were still trading as of Dec. 31, 2022; Excludes companies headquartered in Latin America and Africa.

Source: McKinsey Value Intelligence; S&P Capital IQ.

[8] E. M. Fich, T. Nguyen, and M. S. Officer, "Large Wealth Creation in Mergers and Acquisitions" (paper presented at American Finance Association 2013).

Researchers identified specific factors that differentiate successful deals from unsuccessful ones, based on returns to the acquirer's shareholders. This research points to four important characteristics:

1. *Strong operators are more successful.* According to empirical research, acquirers whose earnings and share price grew at a rate above the industry average for three years before the acquisition earn statistically significant positive returns on announcement.[9] Another study found similar results using the market-to-book ratio as a measure of corporate performance.[10]

2. *Low transaction premiums are better.* Researchers have found that acquirers paying a high premium earn negative returns on announcement.[11]

3. *Being the sole bidder helps.* Several studies have found that acquirer stock returns are negatively correlated with the number of bidders; the more companies attempting to buy the target, the higher the price.[12]

4. *Private deals perform better.* Acquisitions of private companies and subsidiaries of large companies have higher excess returns than acquisitions of public companies.[13]

Perhaps it is just as important to identify the characteristics that don't matter. There is no evidence that the following acquisition dimensions are indicative of either value creation or value destruction:

- Whether the transaction increases or dilutes earnings per share
- The price-to-earnings ratio (P/E) of the acquirer relative to the target's P/E
- The degree to which the acquirer and the target are related, based on Standard Industrial Classification (SIC) codes
- Whether deals are made when the economy is strong or weak[14]

---

[9] R. Morck, A. Shleifer, and R. Vishny, "Do Managerial Objectives Drive Bad Acquisitions?" *Journal of Finance* 45 (1990): 31–48.

[10] H. Servaes, "Tobin's *q* and the Gains from Takeovers," *Journal of Finance* 46 (1991): 409–419; and Fich et al., "Large Wealth Creation in Mergers and Acquisitions."

[11] M. L. Sirower, *The Synergy Trap* (New York: Free Press, 1997); and N. G. Travlos, "Corporate Takeover Bids, Methods of Payment, and Bidding Firms' Stock Return," *Journal of Finance* 42 (1987): 943–963. The result was statistically significant in Sirower but not significant in Travlos.

[12] Morck et al., "Do Managerial Objectives Drive Bad Acquisitions?"; and D. K. Datta, V. K. Narayanan, and G. E. Pinches, "Factors Influencing Wealth Creation from Mergers and Acquisitions: A Meta-Analysis," *Strategic Management Journal* 13 (1992): 67–84.

[13] See, for example, L. Capron and J. Shen, "Acquisitions of Private versus Public Firms: Private Information, Target Selection and Acquirer Returns" (INSEAD Working Paper Series, 2005); and P. Draper and K. Paudyal, "Acquisitions: Public versus Private," *European Financial Management* 12, no. 1 (2006): 57–80.

[14] Fich et al., "Large Wealth Creation in Mergers and Acquisitions."

This empirical evidence is important because it shows that there is no magic formula to make an acquisition successful. Like any other business strategy, acquisitions are not inherently good or bad, just as marketing is not inherently good or bad. Each deal must have its own strategic logic, and the company must have the relevant skills to execute single deals or multideal programs. The outperformance of programmatic acquirers does not mean that all companies should pursue lots of acquisitions. Successful acquisition programs require an underlying strategy supported by programmatic M&A (which we sometimes call the M&A blueprint). In other words, programmatic M&A is not a strategy, but rather a way of executing a strategy. Simply carrying out a high volume of acquisitions without a coherent strategy will rarely lead to success. In addition to a solid strategy, companies must satisfy three additional requirements to have the best chance of success in their M&A efforts: they must have the conviction that M&A is an important priority, the financial and operational capacity to successfully execute acquisitions, and clear competitive advantages.

M&A BLUEPRINT

An M&A blueprint articulates exactly *where* and *how* M&A will contribute to the acquirer's corporate strategy.[15] The "where" component must be highly specific—unlike, for example, a European company planning to use M&A to enter the North American market. A better example would be a health care company that realized during the COVID-19 pandemic that it needed to quickly gain the ability to provide telehealth access, so it planned to use M&A to acquire and scale telehealth capabilities. Another would be a rideshare company that plans to use M&A to acquire the tech platform they need to launch a food-delivery business on top of their rideshare business. The specificity of these plans enables the next step, planning for the "how."

In terms of how, a great M&A blueprint lays out the high-level (target-agnostic) business case and preliminary integration plans associated with each M&A theme. It answers questions such as these: What growth expectations must we meet to create value? What synergies are necessary to make these deals work, and what capital would we require, both from an acquisition standpoint and to invest in unlocking the full capability of these assets? Are there existing targets that could potentially fulfill this business case, regardless of whether they are "for sale"? Doing enough up-front work such that the executive team and the board have conviction on the "where" and "how" components of an M&A strategy is a critical first step to take before identifying a potential target or specific deal.

[15] S. Clarke, R. Uhlaner, and L. Wol, "A Blueprint for M&A Success," McKinsey & Company, April 16, 2020, www.mckinsey.com; and R. Uhlaner and L. Wol, "Programmatic M&A: Winning in the New Normal," McKinsey & Company, March 21, 2022, www.mckinsey.com.

For many companies, the link between strategy and a transaction breaks down at each stage of a deal—during, for example, target identification, integration planning, and especially due diligence. By focusing strictly on financial, legal, tax, and operations issues, the due-diligence stage typically fails to bring in data capable of testing whether the strategic vision for the deal is valid.

To validate the strategic impulse behind the deal, companies should bolster the usual financial due diligence with strategic due diligence. This entails testing the value creation rationale for a deal against the more detailed information that becomes available after signing the letter of intent, as well as testing whether the envisioned future operating model is achievable. A strategic due diligence should explicitly confirm the assets, capabilities, and relationships that make a buyer the best owner of a specific target company. It should bolster an executive team's confidence that they are truly an advantaged buyer of an asset. Most importantly, the baseline of a strategic due diligence should be the acquirer's M&A blueprint, ensuring that the potential deal is rooted in the company's strategy and not simply a "shiny object," or distraction.

It is critical for executives to be honest and thorough when assessing their advantages. Ideally, they develop a fact-based point of view on their beliefs—testing them with anyone responsible for delivering value from the deal, including salespeople, R&D engineers, product developers, and their human resources and finance departments. This is not an exercise that can be executed by the corporate development or M&A team alone. Such an approach would have helped, for example, one large financial company whose due diligence focused on auditing existing operations, rather than testing the viability of the future operating models. The advantaged-buyer criteria that the company used in this instance focused on being one of the most effective operators in the industry, supported by strong IT systems and processes. Executives proceeded with the deal without ever learning that the IT team had a different understanding of the eventual end state. Only after close did they learn that the two companies' IT systems could not be integrated.

ARCHETYPES FOR VALUE-CREATING ACQUISITIONS

The empirical analysis is limited in its ability to identify specific acquisition strategies that create value. This is because acquisitions come in a wide variety of shapes and sizes and also because there is no objective way to classify acquisitions by strategy. Furthermore, the stated strategy may not be the real strategy. Companies typically talk up all kinds of strategic benefits from acquisitions that are really all about cutting costs.

As we said earlier, programmatic M&A is not a strategy, it is a means to execute a strategy. The acquisitions that are part of a programmatic approach still need to create value—that is, the parent company still must improve the combined performance of the companies beyond the value of the price paid.

In our experience, the strategic rationale for an acquisition or program of acquisitions that creates value for acquirers typically fits one of the following seven archetypes:

1. Improve the performance of the target company.
2. Consolidate to remove excess capacity from an industry.
3. Create market access for the target's (or, in some cases, the buyer's) products.
4. Acquire skills or technologies more quickly or at lower cost than they could be built in-house.
5. Exploit a business's industry-specific scalability.
6. Pick winners early and help them develop their businesses.
7. Build a new business or capability.

If an acquisition does not fit one or more of these archetypes, it's unlikely to create value.

The strategic rationale for an acquisition should be a specific articulation of one of these archetypes as part of a company's M&A blueprint, not a vague concept such as growth or strategic positioning. While growth and strategic positioning may be important, they need to be translated into something tangible. Furthermore, even if your acquisition conforms to one of these archetypes, it still won't create value if you overpay.

Improve the Performance of the Target Company

One of the most common value-creating acquisition strategies is improving the performance of the target company. Put simply, you buy a company and radically reduce costs to improve margins and cash flows. The best acquirers also focus on accelerating revenue growth, a noticeable trend that has become more common as the sophistication of M&A continually increases.

This acquisition strategy is often employed by the best private-equity firms. Acharya, Hahn, and Kehoe studied successful private-equity acquisitions where the target company was bought, improved, and sold with no additional acquisitions along the way.[16] They found that the operating profit margins of the acquired businesses increased by an average of about 2.5 percentage points more than at peer companies during the private-equity firm's ownership. That means many of the transactions increased operating profit margins even more. For example, we recently came across a transaction where the private-equity owner increased the target's margins by seven percentage points.

---

[16] V. V. Acharya, M. Hahn, and C. Kehoe, "Corporate Governance and Value Creation: Evidence from Private Equity" (working paper, Social Science Research Network, February 17, 2010).

Keep in mind that it is easier to improve the performance of a company with low margins and low return on invested capital (ROIC) than that of a high-margin, high-ROIC company. Consider the case of buying a company with a 6 percent operating profit margin. Reducing costs by three percentage points from 94 percent of revenues to 91 percent of revenues increases the margin to 9 percent and could lead to a 50 percent increase in the value of the company. In contrast, if the company's operating profit margin is 30 percent, increasing the company's value by 50 percent requires increasing the margin to 45 percent. Costs would need to decline from 70 percent of revenues to 55 percent, a 21 percent reduction in the cost base. That expectation might be unreasonable.

Consolidate to Remove Excess Capacity from an Industry

As industries mature, they typically develop excess capacity. For example, in chemicals, companies are constantly looking for ways to get more production out of their plants at the same time as new competitors continue to enter the industry. The combination of higher production from existing capacity and new capacity from new entrants often leads to more supply than demand and lower prices. However, it is in no single competitor's interest to shut a plant. Companies often find it easier to shut plants across the larger combined entity resulting from an acquisition than, absent an acquisition, to shut their least productive plants and end up with a smaller company.

Reducing excess capacity is not limited to shutting factories but can extend to less tangible forms of capacity. For example, consolidation among pharmaceutical companies has reduced their research and development capacity as they have found more productive ways to conduct research, pruned their portfolios of development projects, and faced competition from venture-capital-backed new entrants.

While there is substantial value to be created from removing excess capacity, the bulk of the value nevertheless often accrues to the seller's shareholders, not the buyer's. In addition, all the other competitors in the industry may benefit from the capacity reduction without having to take any action of their own (the free-rider problem).

Accelerate Market Access for Products

Often, relatively small companies with innovative products have difficulty accessing the entire potential market for their products. For instance, small pharmaceutical companies typically lack the large sales forces required to access the many doctors they need to see in order to promote their products. Larger pharmaceutical companies sometimes purchase these smaller companies and use their own large-scale sales forces to accelerate the sales growth of the smaller companies' products. This strategy is often most easily observed when smaller U.S.-based biotech companies are acquired and larger global pharmaceutical companies are able to expand into international markets relatively quickly by leveraging their global market access and commercial footprints.

IBM pursued this strategy in its software and services businesses. Between 2010 and 2013, IBM acquired 43 companies for an average of $350 million each. By pushing the products of these companies through IBM's global sales force, IBM estimated it was able to substantially accelerate the acquired companies' revenues, sometimes by more than 40 percent in the first two years after each acquisition.[17]

In some cases, the target can also help accelerate the acquirer's revenue growth. In Procter & Gamble's acquisition of Gillette, the combined company benefited because P&G had stronger sales in some emerging markets while Gillette had a bigger share in others. Working together, they were able to introduce their products into new markets much more quickly.

Acquire Skills or Technologies Faster or at Lower Cost

Many technology-based companies buy other companies whose technologies the acquirers need to enhance their own products. They do this because they can acquire the technology faster than they can develop it themselves, and they avoid royalty payments on patented technologies. For example, Apple has systematically purchased technologies to supplement its in-house development. Apple bought Siri (the automated personal assistant) in 2010 to enhance its iPhones. In 2014, Apple purchased Novauris Technologies, a speech recognition technology company, to further enhance Siri's capabilities. It purchased Pull String in 2019 to continue enhancing Siri. Apple has also purchased companies to enhance its iPhone cameras, including Linx in 2015 and Spectral Edge in 2019.

Similarly, Alphabet has made more than 200 acquisitions from 2001 through 2024, mostly of smaller companies with technologies Alphabet could use to improve its products and services. Amazon purchased more than 15 companies between 2014 and 2023 just to enhance Amazon Web Services, its cloud computing business.

Exploit a Business's Industry-Specific Scalability

Economies of scale are often cited as a key source of value creation in M&A. While they can be, you have to be very careful in justifying an acquisition by economies of scale, especially for large acquisitions. That's because large companies often are already operating at scale, in which case combining them

---

[17] IBM Investor Briefing website, 2014.

will not likely lead to lower unit costs. Take big package-delivery companies, for example. They already have some of the largest airline fleets in the world and operate them very efficiently. If they were to combine, it's unlikely there would be substantial savings in their flight operations.

Economies of scale can be important sources of value in acquisitions when the unit of incremental capacity is large or when a larger company buys a subscale company. For example, the cost to develop a new car platform is enormous, so auto companies try to minimize the number of platforms they need. The combination of Audi, Porsche, and VW allowed the three companies to share some platforms. For example, the Audi Q7, Porsche Cayenne, and VW Touareg were all based on the same underlying platform.

Companies also find economies of scale in the purchasing function, but such benefits often come with nuances. For example, when health insurance companies combine, they can negotiate better rates with hospital systems— savings they can pass to their customers. However, merging health insurers typically derive these savings in one of two ways: in cities where both insurers are already present, given that most hospital systems are local, so insurers are competitors only if they serve the same local market, or in instances where providers are part of multistate systems in the same states where the insurers operate.

While economies of scale can be a significant source of acquisition value creation, rarely are generic economies of scale, such as back-office savings, significant enough to justify an acquisition. Economies of scale must be unique to be large enough to justify an acquisition.

Pick Winners Early and Help Them Develop Their Businesses

Another winning acquisition strategy involves making acquisitions early in the life cycle of a new product area or industry line, long before most others recognize that the industry will grow. Typical examples come from the medical-device business, where larger companies buy young, innovative companies, help them refine their technology, and accelerate and turbocharge their product launches. It's not unusual in these cases, though, for a payoff to take five or more years. Another example is Unilever's 2020 purchase of Liquid I.V., a powdered water enhancer that hydrates two to three times faster than ordinary water. While Unilever doesn't disclose sales figures, industry publications indicate that, under Unilever's ownership, sales increased from less than $50 million in 2021 to about $1 billion in 2023.[18]

This acquisition strategy requires managers to take a disciplined approach in three dimensions. First, you need to be willing to make investments early,

[18] "Sales of the Leading Sports Drink Mixes Brands in the United States in 2024," Statista, July 2024, www.statista.com; and "Unilever-Owned Liquid I.V. Focused on $1B Brand Status," *Beverage Digest*, March 16, 2023, www.beverage-digest.com.

long before your competitors and the market see the industry's or company's potential. Second, you need to make multiple bets and expect some to fail. Third, you need to have the skills and patience to nurture the acquired businesses.

Build a New Business or Capability

The final acquisitions strategy archetype is to build new businesses, products, technologies, services, or capabilities by acquiring multiple assets and investing significantly to integrate them together and organically build upon them. In this approach, companies unlock value in two distinct yet related ways.

First, they apply the acquired assets' products or capabilities to their own core business to drive additional revenue (for example, sales of new products to existing customers) and/or bring down costs (for example, by applying a newly acquired automation technology to their existing manufacturing process). Often, a company may need to tailor the asset to serve its own needs by adding features or capabilities or investing in scale enhancements.

Second, the acquirer works to attain the acquired assets' full market potential externally. This could mean organically building new features or investing in technology and platform upgrades to best meet the needs of the market or even expand the total addressable market. It also typically entails investing in the integration of several acquired assets to create requisite scale and new go-to-market approaches. For example, the acquirer might move various different acquired assets onto the same technology platform and shared services infrastructure, merge product portfolios, and/or optimize sales teams.

To be successful in this approach, a company needs to follow a strategic, highly proactive, and disciplined program that supports a clear business plan. This is not simply a one-and-done approach; rather, it involves executing multiple closely related acquisitions, engaging in new-business building, and conducting a multi-asset integration. That being said, the complexity of this approach is highly rewarded if executed well. One clear example is United Healthcare, which closed more than 60 deals over a 10 year period to build businesses around pharmacy benefits, diversified health and wellness, and data analytics and technology services, which have contributed to outsize performance compared with peers over the same period.

As an additional example, consider one global retail company's M&A focus: to grow through entry into two emerging markets by acquiring only local companies that are unprofitable yet in the top three of their market. That's a level of specificity few companies exhibit. With their M&A theme defined so precisely, managers were able to narrow the list of potential candidates to a handful of companies.

LONGER-ODDS STRATEGIES FOR CREATING VALUE FROM ACQUISITIONS

Beyond the seven main acquisition archetypes just described, a handful of other acquisition strategies can create value. However, these are more difficult to execute successfully, as we'll now discuss.

Rolling Up

Roll-up strategies are used to consolidate highly fragmented markets, where the current competitors are too small to achieve scale economies. An example is Service Corporation International's roll-up of the U.S. funeral business. Beginning in the 1960s, Service Corporation grew from one funeral home in Houston, Texas, to almost 2,000 funeral homes and cemeteries in 2023. The strategy works when the businesses as a group can realize substantial cost savings or achieve higher revenues than the individual businesses. For example, Service Corporation's funeral homes in a single city can share vehicles, purchasing, and back-office operations. They can also coordinate advertising across a city to reduce costs and realize higher revenues.

Size per se is not what creates a successful roll-up. What matters is the right kind of size. For Service Corporation, having multiple locations in the same city has been more important than simply having many branches spread over many cities, because the cost savings, such as sharing vehicles, can be realized only if the branches are near one another.

Another critical success factor is consistency of approach across deals. Determine early on which set of value creation levers are nonnegotiable across all deals, and apply a consistent approach to the roll-up in order to maximize value created for the enterprise as a whole.

Because roll-up strategies are hard to disguise, they invite copycats. As others tried to copy Service Corporation's strategy, prices for some funeral homes were eventually bid up to levels that made additional acquisitions uneconomic.

Consolidate to Improve Competitive Behavior

Many executives in highly competitive industries hope consolidation will lead competitors to focus less on price competition, thereby improving the industry's ROIC. Besides being potentially illegal, such an approach also fundamentally misunderstands the dynamics at play. The evidence shows that unless an industry consolidates down to just three or four competitors and can keep entrants out, competitor pricing behavior does not change. There's often an incentive for smaller companies or new entrants to gain share through price competition. In an industry with, say, 10 competitors, many deals must be completed before the basis of competition changes.

Enter into a Transformational Merger

A commonly mentioned reason for an acquisition or merger is to transform one or both companies. Transformational mergers are rare, however, because the circumstances must be just right, and the management team needs to execute the strategy well. The best way to describe a transformational merger is by example. One of the world's leading pharmaceutical companies, Novartis of Switzerland, was formed by the $30 billion merger of Sandoz and Ciba-Geigy, announced in 1996. But this merger was much more than a simple combination of businesses. Under the leadership of the new CEO, Daniel Vasella, Sandoz and Ciba-Geigy were transformed into an entirely new company. Using the merger as a catalyst for change, Vasella and his management team not only captured $1.4 billion in cost synergies but also redefined the company's mission and strategy, portfolio and organization, and all key processes from research to sales. In all areas, there was no automatic choice for either the Ciba or the Sandoz way of doing things; instead, a systematic effort was made to find the *best* way of doing things.

Novartis shifted its strategic focus to innovation in its life sciences business (pharmaceuticals, nutrition, and agricultural) and spun off the $7 billion Ciba Specialty Chemicals business in 1997. Later, it also sold or spun off its agricultural and nutrition businesses. Organizational changes included reorganizing research and development worldwide by therapeutic rather than geographic area. Across all departments and management layers, Novartis created a strong performance-oriented culture, supported by a change from a seniority-based to a performance-based compensation system for its managers.

Buy Cheap

The final way to create value from an acquisition is to buy cheap—in other words, at a price below the target's intrinsic value. In our experience, however, opportunities to create value in this way are rare and relatively small.

Although market values revert to intrinsic values over longer periods, there can be brief moments when the two fall out of alignment. Markets sometimes overreact to negative news, such as the criminal investigation of an executive or the failure of a single product in a portfolio of many strong products. Such moments are less rare in cyclical industries, where assets are often undervalued at the bottom of the cycle.[19]

However, while markets do provide occasional opportunities for companies to buy below intrinsic value, we haven't seen many cases. One explanation of why this rarely occurs is that the management and board of a potential target are often loath to sell at or near its low point, as they often are anchored on recent high values.

---

[19] T. Koller and M. de Heer, "Valuing Cyclical Companies," *McKinsey Quarterly*, no. 2 (2000): 62–69.

For targets pursued by multiple acquirers, the premium rises dramatically, creating the so-called winner's curse. If several companies evaluate a given target and all identify roughly the same synergies, the one who overestimates potential synergies the most will offer the highest price. Since the offer price is based on an overestimate of value to be created, the supposed winner overpays—and is ultimately a loser.[20] A related problem is hubris, or the tendency of the acquirer's management to overstate its ability to capture performance improvements from the acquisition.[21]

ESTIMATING OPERATING IMPROVEMENTS

As we've been discussing, the main sources of value created through M&A are the cost, capital, and revenue improvements, often referred to as synergies, that the combined company makes. So estimating the potential improvements is one of the most important success factors for M&A—along with executing on those improvements once the deal is completed.

Before getting into the estimation, it's worth emphasizing that estimating improvements from combining corporate entities is not a one-time event. It's done multiple times: first, before negotiations even begin; second, during negotiations, as the acquirer gets more information; and finally, after the deal closes. Our colleagues found that almost 50 percent of the time, preclosing estimates failed to provide an adequate plan to fully identify improvement opportunities.[22]

We find that companies do a much better job of realizing cost savings than revenue improvements. McKinsey's M&A Practice analyzed 90 acquisitions and found that 86 percent of the acquirers were able to capture at least 70 percent of the estimated cost savings.[23] In contrast, almost half of the acquirers realized *less* than 70 percent of the targeted revenue improvements, and in almost one-quarter of the observed acquisitions, the acquirer realized less than 30 percent of the targeted revenue improvements.

Estimating Cost and Capital Savings

Too often, managers estimate cost savings simply by calculating the difference in financial performance between the bidder and the target. Having an earnings before interest, taxes, and amortization (EBITA) margin 200 basis points higher than the target, however, will not necessarily translate into better

[20] K. Rock, "Why New Issues Are Underpriced," *Journal of Financial Economics* 15 (1986): 187–212.

[21] R. Roll, "The Hubris Hypothesis of Corporate Takeovers," *Journal of Business* 59 (1986): 197–216.

[22] O. Engert and R. Rosiello, "Opening the Aperture 1: A McKinsey Perspective on Value Creation and Synergies" (working paper, McKinsey & Company, June 2010), www.mckinsey.com.

[23] S. A. Christofferson, R. S. McNish, and D. L. Sias, "Where Mergers Go Wrong," *McKinsey Quarterly*, no. 2 (2004): 93–99.

performance for the target. There are no easy rules of thumb in estimating cost and capital savings. The best estimates are based on detailed analysis. Cost and capital reduction should follow a systematic process: estimating a baseline, estimating savings for each category (based on a triangulation of benchmarks, quantitative analysis, and qualitative assessments), and testing the results against benchmarks.

Begin with a detailed baseline for cost and capital as if the two companies remained independent across the different parts of the companies' cost structures. The purpose of the baseline is to ensure that all costs of both the acquirer and target are accounted for, in a common taxonomy, and that you don't run the risk of double-counting when you estimate savings.

Now you can systematically estimate the potential cost and capital savings for each cost category of both the acquirer and the target. While there are some typical types of savings, as Exhibit 31.7 shows, you should ensure that the cost categories and savings ideas are tailored to the company and industry. For example, what is the equivalent head count reduction responsible for the cost savings in selling, general, and administrative (SG&A) expense? What is the resulting revenue per head count? How much will distribution costs fall when trucks are fully loaded, rather than partially loaded? Are revenues sufficient to guarantee fully loaded trucks?

When tying savings to operational drivers, involve experienced line managers in the process. An integrated team that includes both financial analysts and experienced line managers is more likely than a pure finance

EXHIBIT 31.7 **Sample Framework for Estimating Cost Savings**

Function	Example savings initiatives
Research and development	• Stopping redundant projects • Reducing overlap in personnel and key activities • Developing new products through transferred technology
Procurement	• Pooled purchasing • Standardizing vendor contracts and product specifications
Manufacturing	• Eliminating overcapacity • Transferring best operating practices • Optimizing production capacity across combined plant footprint
Supply chain and logistics	• Consolidating/redesigning warehouse and freight network
Sales and marketing	• Using common channels • Transferring best practices • Lowering combined marketing budget
Administrative	• Removing duplicate roles • Exploiting economies of scale in back-office functions • Consolidating leadership roles

team to generate insights on capacity, quality issues, and unit sales not easily found in the public domain. In addition, experienced line managers often will already know details about the target. Together, you can go far beyond poorly tailored benchmarks and greatly improve estimates of cost savings.

Consider an acquisition where the head of operations took the lead in estimating the savings from rationalizing manufacturing capacity, distribution networks, and suppliers.[24] Her in-depth knowledge about the unusual manufacturing requirements for a key product line and the looming investment needs at the target's main plant substantially improved savings estimates. In addition, this manager conducted a due-diligence interview with the target's head of operations, learning that the target did not have an enterprise resource planning (ERP) system. Each of these facts improved negotiations and deal structuring, for example, by permitting management to promise that the target's main European location would be retained while maintaining flexibility about the target's main U.S. facility. Moreover, the involvement of the operations manager ensured that the company was prepared to act quickly and decisively to capture savings following the deal's closure.

After you complete the assessment, always compare the aggregate results for the combined companies with industry benchmarks for operating margins and capital efficiency. Ask whether the resulting ROIC and growth projections make sense, given the overall expected economics of the industry. The more difficult it is to sustain a competitive advantage, the more you need to scale down the performance improvement assumptions over the longer term.

You'll also find that the potential cost savings vary widely by cost category. Exhibit 31.8 presents the cost savings by category for an acquisition in the automotive industry. While the overall estimated cost savings for the automotive acquisition were about 10 percent of total combined costs, the savings varied considerably across category. For example, although procurement costs are the single largest cost category for automotive manufacturers, most companies already have the necessary scale to negotiate favorable contracts. Therefore,

EXHIBIT 31.8 **Automotive Merger: Estimated Cost Savings**

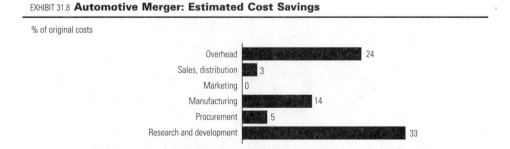

% of original costs

Overhead	24
Sales, distribution	3
Marketing	0
Manufacturing	14
Procurement	5
Research and development	33

[24] This and other examples can be found in Christofferson et al., "Where Mergers Go Wrong."

savings from procurement were estimated at only 5 percent. In contrast, research and development reductions were estimated at 33 percent as the two companies consolidated new-product development, paring down the number of expected offerings.

Estimating Revenue Improvements

Although it is tempting to assume that revenues for the newly combined company will equal stand-alone sales plus new cross-selling, the reality is often quite different. First, the merger is often disruptive and distracting—to existing customer relationships, to the respective sales forces, to operations, and in any number of other ways, leading to a loss of business. Also, smart competitors use mergers as a prime opportunity to recruit star salespeople and product specialists away from both the acquirer and target. In some cases, customers may have used the acquirer and target as dual sources, so they will move part of their business to another company to maintain a minimum of two suppliers. Finally, customers who decide to stay throughout the merger will not be shy in asking for price and other concessions that salespeople may be eager to offer for fear of losing the business.

Make sure to develop estimates of market share increases that are consistent with market growth and competitive reality. As in the process for estimating cost savings, calibrate the pro forma assumptions against the realities of the marketplace. One global financial company estimated that an acquisition would net €1 billion in sales improvements within the next five years, including double-digit profit growth in the first year. However, overall market growth was limited, so the only way to achieve these sales goals was to lower prices. Actual profit growth was a mere 2 percent.

When estimating revenue improvements, be explicit about where any growth in revenues beyond base case assessments is expected to originate. Revenue improvements will typically come from one or more of four sources:

1. Increasing the peak sales level for each company's products
2. Reaching the increased peak sales faster
3. Extending each product's life
4. Adding new products (or features) that could not have been developed if the two companies had remained independent

Don't assume revenue increases could come from higher prices. Antitrust regulations are in place precisely to prevent companies from using this lever. Any increase in price must be directly attributable to an increase in value to the customer.

We also suggest you project revenue improvements in absolute amounts per year or as a percentage of stand-alone revenues, rather than as an increase in the revenue growth rate. With the growth rate approach, you can easily overestimate the true impact of revenue improvements.

Implementation Costs, Requirements, and Timing

Although performance improvements often result from doing more with less, making a change or combining systems always involves some costs. Some are obvious, such as the costs to decommission a plant and the severance that must be paid to employees being let go. Others are more subtle, such as rebranding campaigns when the name of the target is changed, integration costs for different information technology (IT) systems, and employee retraining. But these costs must also be identified and estimated. It is not unusual for total implementation costs to be equivalent to a full year of cost savings or more, especially outside of the United States. Of course, cost savings should be recurring, while implementation costs occur once.

Bear in mind that acquirers often make overly optimistic assumptions about how long it will take to realize improvements. Our experience suggests that improvement initiatives not launched within the first full budget year after consolidation are unlikely to ever be launched. As a result, this potential value is never captured, because the drive and focus needed to do so are diverted to other matters in subsequent events. Persistent management attention matters, as does speed of action. Exhibit 31.9 illustrates the typical timing of synergy realization and the costs incurred to achieve those synergies.

Reassessing Performance Improvement Targets

One of the most common but avoidable pitfalls in any transaction is failure to update expectations for performance improvements as the buyer learns more about the target during pre-integration planning and post-close integration

EXHIBIT 31.9 **Synergy and Cost: Time to Realization**

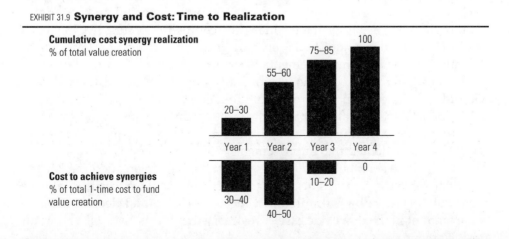

execution. Companies that treat M&A as a project typically build and secure approval for a company's valuation only once, during due diligence, and then build targets based on that valuation into operating budgets. This freezes expectations at a time when information is uncertain and rarely correlated with the real potential of a deal.

Managing this challenge can be complex but worthwhile. One consumer packaged-goods company boosted synergies by 75 percent after managers recognized that the target's superior approach to in-store promotions could be used to improve its base business. A pharmaceutical company raised its synergies by over 40 percent in a very large transaction by actively revisiting estimates immediately after the deal closed, creating a risk-free environment for managers to come up with new ideas. A few years later, it had captured those higher synergies.

HOW TO PAY: WITH CASH OR STOCK?

Should the acquiring company pay in cash or in shares? Research shows that, on average, an acquirer's stock returns surrounding the acquisition announcement are higher when the acquirer offers cash than when it offers shares. We hesitate, however, to draw a conclusion based solely on aggregate statistics; after all, even companies that offer cash can pay too much.

The real issue is whether the risks and rewards of the deal should be shared with the target's shareholders. When the acquiring company pays in cash, its shareholders carry the entire risk of capturing synergies and paying too much. If the companies exchange shares, the target's shareholders assume a portion of the risk.

To show the impact on value of paying in cash rather than shares, Exhibit 31.10 outlines a hypothetical transaction. Assume that the acquirer and the target have market capitalizations of $1 billion and $500 million, respectively. The acquirer pays a total price of $650 million, including a premium of 30 percent. We calculate the estimated discounted-cash-flow (DCF) values after the transaction under two scenarios: (1) a downside scenario in which the value of operating improvements is $50 million lower than the premium paid, and (2) an upside scenario in which the value of these improvements is $50 million higher than the premium. (To simplify, we assume that market value equals intrinsic value for both the target and the acquirer.)

If the payment is entirely in cash, the target's shareholders get $650 million, regardless of whether the improvements are great enough to justify the premium. These shareholders do not share in the implementation risk (or the potential value creation upside). The acquirer's shareholders see the value of their stake increase by $50 million in the upside case and decrease by the same amount in the downside case. They carry the full risk as well as the full upside potential.

EXHIBIT 31.10 **Paying with Cash vs. Stock: Impact on Value**

Value to shareholders after transaction, $ million

Market value before deal

Acquirer	1,000	
Target	500	
Price paid (30% premium)	650	
Ownership ratio (stock deal)	39.4%/60.6%	

	Downside scenario (Synergies = 100)	Upside scenario (Synergies = 200)
Consideration in cash		
Combined value	1,600	1,700
Price paid	(650)	(650)
Value of acquirer postdeal	950	1,050
Value of acquirer predeal	(1,000)	(1,000)
Acquirer value created (destroyed)	(50)	50
Target value created (destroyed)	150	150
Consideration in stock		
Combined value	1,600	1,700
Target's share (39.4%)	(630)	(670)
Value of acquirer postdeal	970	1,030
Value of acquirer predeal	(1,000)	(1,000)
Acquirer value created (destroyed)	(30)	30
Target value created (destroyed)	130	170

Next, consider the same transaction paid for in shares. The target's shareholders participate in the implementation risk by virtue of being shareholders in the new combined entity.[25] In the upside case, their payout from the acquisition increases as improvements increase: they receive $670 million in value, as opposed to $650 million in the cash transaction. In the downside case, the target's shareholders now get less than in the cash transaction but still a nice premium, since their portion of the combined company is worth $630 million, compared with the $500 million market value before the deal.

Two key issues should influence your choice of payment. First, do you think the target and/or your company is overvalued or undervalued? If you believe your shares are more overvalued than the target's, they are valuable in their own right as transaction currency.[26] Second, how confident are you in the ability of the deal to create value overall? The more confident you are, the more you should be inclined to pay in cash.

[25] Target shareholders with small stakes can sell their shares in the public market to avoid implementation risk. Influential shareholders with large stakes, such as company founders and senior executives, will often agree not to sell shares for a specified period. In this case, they share the risk of implementation.
[26] The signaling effect of share consideration is similar to that of share issuance. The capital markets will use this new information (that the shares might be overvalued) when pricing the shares.

FOCUS ON VALUE CREATION, NOT ACCOUNTING

Many managers focus on the accretion and dilution of earnings brought about by an acquisition, rather than the value it could create. They do so despite numerous studies showing that stock markets pay no attention to the effects of an acquisition on accounting numbers but react only to the value that the deal is estimated to create.

But changing accounting doesn't change the economics of the deals. Many acquisitions are earnings accretive but destroy value. Consider the hypothetical deal in Exhibit 31.11. You are deciding whether to purchase a company currently priced in the market at $400 million for $500 million in cash. Your company, the acquirer, is worth $1.6 billion and has a net income of $80 million. For simplicity, assume there are no operating improvements to come from the deal. You decide to finance this deal by raising debt at a pretax interest rate of 6 percent. This deal destroys value: you overpay by $100 million (remember, no improvements). Even so, next year's earnings and earnings per share actually increase because the after-tax earnings from the acquired company ($30 million) exceed the after-tax interest required for the new debt ($19.5 million).

How can a deal increase earnings yet destroy value? The acquirer is borrowing 100 percent of the deal value based on the combined cash flows of both companies. But the acquired business could not sustain this level of debt on its own. Since the acquirer puts an increased debt burden on the existing shareholders without properly compensating them for the additional risk, it is destroying value. Only when the ROIC (calculated as target profits plus improvements divided by the total purchase price) is greater than the weighted average cost of capital are shareholders appropriately compensated. In our hypothetical deal, the investment is $500 million, and the after-tax profit is

EXHIBIT 31.11 **Earnings per Share (EPS) Accretion with Value Destruction**

Assumptions	Acquirer	Target
Net income, $ million	80.0	30.0
Shares outstanding, millions	40.0	10.0
EPS, $	2.0	3.0
Preannouncement share price, $	40.0	40.0
Price-to-earnings ratio	20.0	13.3
Market value, $ million	1,600.0	400.0
Price paid, $ million	—	500.0

Impact on EPS	Cash deal	Stock deal
Net income, $ million		
Net income from acquirer	80.0	80.0
Net income from target	30.0	30.0
Additional interest[1]	(19.5)	—
Net income after acquisition	90.5	110.0
Number of shares, millions		
Original shares	40.0	40.0
New shares	—	12.5
Number of shares	40.0	52.5
Earnings per share, $		
EPS before acquisition	2.00	2.00
EPS accretion	0.26	0.10
EPS after acquisition	2.26	2.10

[1] Pretax cost of debt at 6%, tax ratio of 35%.

$30 million—a mere 6 percent return on invested capital. While this is above the 3.9 percent after-tax cost of financing the debt, it is below the weighted average cost of capital.

Now suppose the same target is acquired through an exchange of shares. The acquirer would need to issue 12.5 million new shares to provide the 25 percent acquisition premium that the target company's shareholders demand.[27] After the deal, the combined company would have 52.5 million shares outstanding and earnings of $110 million. The earnings per share for the new company rise to $2.10, so the deal is again accretive without having created any underlying value. The increase is a result of mathematics rather than value created by the deal.

Conversely, companies sometimes pass up acquisitions that can create value just because they are earnings dilutive in the first several years. Suppose you spend $100 million to buy a fast-growing company in an attractive market, with a P/E of 30 times. Before performance improvements, the earnings from the acquisition will be $3.3 million. If you borrow at 4 percent after taxes, interest expense will be $4.0 million, leading to earnings dilution of $0.7 million. However, if you are able to accelerate the target's growth rate to 20 percent for the next five years and the target earns a 25 percent return on capital, it will probably create value for shareholders, even though the earnings and ROIC will be depressed for a couple of years.

Financial markets understand the difference between creating real value and increasing EPS. In a study of 117 U.S. transactions larger than $3 billion, our colleagues found that earnings accretion or dilution resulting from the deals was not a factor in the market's reaction to the deals (see Exhibit 31.12). Regardless of whether the expected EPS was greater, smaller, or the same two

EXHIBIT 31.12 **Market Reaction to EPS Impact of Acquisitions**

EPS impact in year 1	% of acquirers with positive adjusted market reactions		Number of transactions[1]
	1 month after deal announcement	1 year after deal announcement	
Accretive	41	46	165
Neutral	40	44	25
Dilutive	21	39	83
	Average = 35	Average = 43	

Note: Returns were adjusted with respect to the S&P 500 Index.

[1] The sample set included 273 transactions with deal value greater than $6 billion by public, non-PE, single U.S. acquirers between Jan. 2001 and Dec. 2020.

Source: S&P Capital IQ; company press releases.

[27] The exchange ratio in this hypothetical deal is 1.25 shares of the acquiring company for each share of the target company. We assume that the capital market does not penalize the acquirer and that the exchange ratio can be set in relation to the preannouncement share price plus the 25 percent acquisition premium.

years after the deal, the market's reaction was similar (within the bounds of statistical significance) at one month after the announcement and one year after the announcement.

CLOSING THOUGHTS

Acquisitions are good for the economy when they more efficiently allocate resources between owners. However, most acquisitions create more value for the shareholders of the target company than for those of the buyer, and many destroy value for the buyer's shareholders. This is perhaps not surprising when we recall that acquisitions can create value for acquirers only if the target company's performance improves by more than the value of the premium over the target's intrinsic value that the acquirer had to offer the target to persuade its shareholders to part with it.

Managers should bear in mind that stock markets are interested only in the impact of acquisitions on the intrinsic value of the combined company. Whether an acquisition will increase or decrease earnings per share in the short term has no effect on the direction and extent of movements in the buyer's share price following the acquisition announcement.

Companies are more successful at M&A when they consistently apply the same focus and professionalism to it as they do in other critical disciplines.[28] Managers can help to ensure that their acquisitions are among those that create value for their shareholders by developing a robust M&A blueprint that states exactly where and how M&A will contribute to the acquirer's corporate strategy and by sourcing potential deals that are closely aligned with their M&A blueprint. Success also depends on making realistic estimates of the cost and revenue improvements that the target company can realize under new ownership, taking into account the often substantial cost of implementing those improvements and consistently looking for value creation opportunities beyond those estimated in the deal model. Finally, the best acquirers build systematic institutional skills in tailoring their integration approach to the deal archetype and managing their reputation as an acquirer.

---

[28] Adapted from C. Ferrer, R. Uhlaner, and A. West, "M&A as a Competitive Advantage," *McKinsey on Finance*, no. 47 (Summer 2013): 2–5.

32

Divestitures

As Chapter 28's discussion of corporate portfolio management indicates, any program to create value should include systematically reviewing your portfolio of businesses. In our analyses of the largest global exchange–listed companies, those that endure at the top ranks combine their mergers and acquisitions (M&A) programs with selected divestitures, including shedding businesses that are performing well but could do better under different ownership.

Divestitures, like mergers and acquisitions (covered in Chapter 31), tend to occur in waves, as shown in Exhibit 32.1, which shows the value of divestitures from 1995 through 2023. In the decade following the conglomerate excesses of the 1960s and 1970s, many companies refocused their portfolios. These divestitures were generally sales to other companies or private buyout firms. By the 1990s, divestiture activity included more public-ownership transactions—spin-offs and carve-outs. Such public-ownership transactions have since become an established divestment approach, although most divestitures still take the form of deals between companies.

This chapter first discusses the ways divestitures can create value and the costs of holding on to business units that may be negatively affecting the rest of the company. Next, we discuss why, despite the benefits, executives often shy away from proactively pursuing divestitures. Finally, we provide some guidance on how to choose the specific type of transaction for a divestiture.

HOW DIVESTITURES CREATE VALUE

Divesting a business unit creates value when other owners can extract more value from it than the current owners can. This is the "better owner" principle described in Chapter 28. Often, new owners change the operating model of

This chapter was coauthored by Jamie Koenig and Anna Mattsson with contributions from Raghav Kapur and Mariola Ndrio.

EXHIBIT 32.1 **Value of Divestitures**

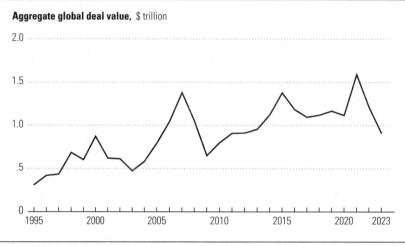

Aggregate global deal value, $ trillion

Source: E.R. Feldman, *Diverstitures: Creating Value Through Strategy, Structure, and Implementation* (New York: McGraw-Hill, 2023), updated by the author for this publication.

both the divested business and the parent company, because large companies often impose mismatched operational requirements on diverse business units. For example, high-growth, high-margin businesses may require different operating models than low-margin, mature ones.[1] The breakup can help both entities develop a fit-for-purpose operating model. Moreover, divesting noncore business units can help free up management attention and allow for better resource allocation decisions within the core businesses. Finally, divestments can improve capital allocation decisions while making it easier for the divested entity to raise capital as a pure-play company, versus competing for funding with all other lines of business.

A value-creating approach to divestitures can result in divesting good and bad businesses at any stage of their life cycle. Clearly, divesting a good business is often not an intuitive choice and may be hard for managers. It therefore makes sense to enforce some discipline in active portfolio management—for example, by holding regular dedicated portfolio review meetings.

Practices such as assigning a future date for each unit to be evaluated for exiting, setting a limit on the number of business units, or targeting a balance between acquisitions and divestitures can promote discipline and help transform divestitures from evidence of failure into shrewd strategies for building value.

An example of a company that has systematically divested is Germany-based Siemens. Its efforts have included a complete portfolio restructuring

[1] J. Koenig, T. Koller, and A. Luu, "When Bigger Isn't Always Better," *McKinsey Quarterly*, December 2021, www.mckinsey.com.

via targeted acquisitions and a series of major divestitures. Siemens put its telecommunication carrier business into a 50–50 joint venture with Nokia in 2006 and sold its joint venture stake to Nokia in 2013. In 2007, it sold its Siemens VDO business (supplying parts and components, as well as software, to carmakers) to Continental. In 2013, it spun off its OSRAM lighting division. Siemens merged its wind power business with Spain's Gamesa in 2017, creating a new industry leader. The health care business was carved out in 2018 as Siemens Healthineers in a minority initial public offering (IPO), one of the largest public offerings in German history. Siemens spun off its gas and power division in 2020 as an independent company. By 2023, Siemens operated in four businesses: Digital Industries (products and services for automation), Smart Infrastructure (products related to building management and operations), Mobility (products for trains and metro systems), and Siemens Healthineers (75 percent owned health care products). Siemens earmarks for divestment not only underperforming businesses (such as gas and power) but also businesses that no longer fit well with its corporate strategy.

The process of systematic divestment is natural and ongoing, as the Siemens example highlights. A divested unit may pursue further separations later in its lifetime, especially in dynamic industries undergoing rapid growth and technological change. For example, in November 2015, Hewlett-Packard split into two publicly traded companies: HP Inc., focusing on personal computer systems and printing, and HP Enterprise (HPE), concentrated on the enterprise products and services, including servers, storage, networking, and financial services. Following the spin-off, HPE divested its software business to Micro Focus International in 2017 and spun off its Enterprise Services business in 2018; the latter business subsequently merged with Computer Sciences Corporation (CSC) to create DXC. The transactions allowed HPE to streamline its operations and focus on high-growth areas such as hybrid IT and intelligent edge solutions.

The value created in a divestment for a parent company equals the price received minus the value forgone minus separation costs incurred by the parent:

$$\text{Value Created} = \text{Price Received} - \text{Value Forgone}$$
$$- \text{Costs of Separation}$$

The value forgone equals the value of the divested business as run by the current management team, plus any synergies with the rest of the parent's businesses. It represents the cash flows that the parent company has given up by selling the business. The costs of separation include the costs the parent incurs to disentangle the business from its other businesses, plus the so-called stranded costs of any assets or activities that have become redundant after the divestment—costs that, as we will see, can often be substantially mitigated by restructuring central and shared services in the parent company. With this further breakdown, we have the following expression for value created:

Value Created = Price Received
 − Stand-Alone Value of Divested Business
 − Lost Synergies
 − Disentanglement Costs
 − Stranded Costs

The remainder of this section discusses these synergies and costs. Also, it examines practical challenges around legal and regulatory issues, as well as pricing and liquidity of the businesses.

Lost Synergies

When a company divests a business unit, it may lose with it certain synergy benefits that come from having that business in its portfolio, even if the company isn't the best owner of the business. For example, a business unit may have cross-selling opportunities with other units. Likewise, a corporation may bundle its procurement for various businesses globally so that it enjoys significant discounts. In other cases, the divested business may have to give up access to shared resources like innovation centers and engineering teams that foster knowledge sharing, promote best practices, and drive efficiencies across business units.

Divestments could also lead to the loss of nonoperating synergies related to taxes and financing, although these tend to be relatively small. For example, an integrated electricity player that divests its (regulated) transmission and/or distribution network business and keeps a portfolio of generation and supply units will have a higher risk profile after the divestiture and, consequently, a lower debt capacity and corresponding value from tax shields.

One-Time Disentanglement Costs

Depending on the extent to which a business unit is integrated within an organization and its operations, disentangling it can incur substantial expenses. These are one-time costs such as expenses for legal and advisory fees, information technology (IT) system replacement or reconfiguration costs, relocation costs, and retention bonuses. Disentanglements can be more complex than the integration processes of large M&A deals.

Taxes triggered by the divestment depend on the details of a proposed deal structure, but they too can have real impact on post-deal economics. Differences in fiscal regimes also play a role. In many European countries, gains on the sale of business units are to some extent exempt from corporate income and withholding taxes. In the United States, however, capital gains from divestitures are often subject to taxes unless the unit is spun off and meets certain tax requirements. Depending on the fiscal regime, executives may therefore prefer different types of transactions, as discussed later in this chapter.

Stranded Costs

Stranded costs can be hard to accurately estimate and harder still to fully address. These are (corporate) costs for assets and activities associated with the business unit but ultimately not transferred with it. Stranded costs can relate to shared services, such as procurement, marketing, and investor relations. They can also refer to IT infrastructure and shared production assets— for example, when a single manufacturing facility consists of production lines of products from different business units. And they can relate to general overhead costs that are allocated to businesses, such as costs for the board of directors, legal counsel, and corporate compliance.

In our experience, divestments often bring to light excessive corporate overhead that cannot be transferred to the divested business unit and is subsumed under stranded costs. Large companies tend to have many layers of management and communication. This easily leads to redundancy and unnecessary costs. For example, sizable business units often have managers in human resources, strategic planning, or financial controlling functions whose primary job is to coordinate and communicate with their counterparts in the corporate headquarters. After a divestiture, such intercompany transaction costs can be largely eliminated in both the parent company and the divested businesses. In fact, successful sellers often use divestitures as a catalyst to reduce overhead and improve efficiency in the remaining business.

Real stranded costs from divestitures take considerable time and effort to unwind. Some stranded costs are fixed and difficult to reduce, as in the case of shared IT systems. Others can be more readily managed over time— for example, by head count reductions in shared service centers. McKinsey research has found that it often takes up to three years for the parent company to recover from stranded costs, leaving it with substantially lower profit margins during this period.[2]

Legal and Regulatory Barriers

The divestment process may be complicated by legal or regulatory issues. These are typically not large enough to distort the value creation potential, but they can seriously slow down the process and add to the amount of work to be done, thereby increasing the time and resources required to come to closure. For example, pharmaceutical companies are required to have a so-called

[2] D. Fubini, M. Park, and K. Thomas, "Profitably Parting Ways: Getting More Value from Divestitures," *McKinsey on Finance* (Winter 2013): 14–21.

marketing authorization to sell an individual product in a specific market, typically a single country. If a pharmaceutical company decides to sell a particular product portfolio (for example, oncology, respiratory, or vaccines) to another pharmaceutical company, it needs to apply for a transfer of the marketing authorization for each individual product in each specific market. The process is time-consuming and requires additional expenses. Asset transactions can be especially complex, because they require extensive documentation and contracts with respect to all the different categories of assets involved.

Contractual issues often come as unpleasant surprises that typically surface after companies have started the divestiture process. Procurement contracts, long-term contracts with customers, and loan agreements, for example, often require the creation of transitional service agreements between buyer and seller to guarantee continuity of the business unit. Or they may include change-of-ownership clauses activated upon divestiture that render the existing contract or agreement invalid when ownership in the business transfers.

Pricing and Liquidity

As discussed in Chapter 6, market valuation levels are generally in line with intrinsic value potential in the long term but can deviate in the short term. A near-term divestiture would seem to be a good idea if the market would price a business above management's estimate of its intrinsic value. The reverse holds as well: Siemens, for example, delayed the spin-off of its lighting business OSRAM for several years because of adverse market conditions, eventually completing the transaction in 2013.

Although external market factors may lower potential proceeds from a divestiture, management should balance this against the (hidden) costs of continuing with the status quo. Alternatively, management could look into transaction types that do not generate cash proceeds and thereby do not lock in an exit price for the company's shareholders. For example, as the credit crunch unfolded in 2008, Cadbury decided against a planned trade sale (in cash) of its American beverages business. Instead, it opted to spin off the business to its shareholders. This left Cadbury shareholders with the option to hold the shares of the American beverage business and sell at some later stage, when prices might be higher.

THE COST OF HOLDING ON

When businesses are underperforming, the clear benefit from divesting lies in avoiding the direct costs of bearing deteriorating results. Companies that hold on to underperforming businesses too long risk bringing down the value of the entire corporation. By the time the company is forced to conduct a fire sale of the assets, it has already destroyed substantial value and generally will receive lower proceeds from the divestiture.

Research has shown that as a business becomes more mature and competitive challenges increase, it loses the potential for ongoing value creation, and its total shareholder returns start to decline relative to the business's industry sector.[3] Ideally, divestment occurs before a business's underlying structural challenges manifest in declining market evaluations. This proactive approach maximizes value realization while mitigating the risk of prolonged underperformance. However, while managers might be best positioned to see the decline coming, they are often blind to the realities of their market or hope a miracle will happen and are often late to divest. We usually find that companies take as long as two years or more between the time they start discussing a potential divestiture and when they decide to move ahead (it takes another year or two to actually make the divestiture). During that time, the business may have declined, or potential buyers will have realized the decline, thus reducing the possible selling price. Sometimes company leaders think they can "fix up" a business before a sale, but that rarely happens.

For profitable and/or growing businesses, divesting can benefit both the parent and the business unit. Well-established, mature businesses provide a company with stability and cash flows, but holding on too long to this can also lead to what we would call corporate inertia. For example, relatively large and stable units may dampen the impetus to innovate—a critical driver of success for smaller businesses in the portfolio. In addition, such large units often absorb a significant share of scarce management time that might be better spent on identifying growth opportunities. Under the ownership of a large multinational health care company, an orthopedic-devices business relied on pricing to grow its revenues. After being spun off, however, it was able to boost growth by investing more aggressively in new technologies, introducing new products, and expanding to new markets. As discussed earlier, no matter how hard managers try, the allocation of scarce resources (capital, personnel, management attention) in an optimal manner to support high-growth opportunities is difficult, highlighting the value opportunity of divestitures.

Other costs include the distortion of economic incentives as a result of cross-subsidization between business units, which can lead to inferior decision making, or situations where being together might impede the growth of one of the businesses. For example, eBay spun off PayPal into a publicly traded company in 2015. Among other reasons, the CEO said eBay and PayPal "will be sharper and stronger, and more focused and competitive as leading standalone companies in their respective markets. As independent companies, eBay and PayPal will enjoy added flexibility to pursue new market and partnership opportunities."[4] Conflicts of interest between business units can also arise from capital structure decisions, which was a key reason for Tyco International's 2006 health care divestiture announcement. As Tyco CFO Chris Coughlin explains, "We were

[3] R. Foster and S. Kaplan, *Creative Destruction* (New York: Doubleday, 2001).
[4] "eBay Inc. to Separate eBay and PayPal into Independent Publicly Traded Companies in 2015," press release, eBay, September 30, 2014, investors.ebayinc.com.

driving the capital structure of all of Tyco on the basis of what a company in the healthcare industry needed, but healthcare was only a quarter of our revenues. The other businesses clearly did not require that kind of a capital structure."[5] In these situations, a divestiture may create value because the subsidiary can become more competitive as a result of greater freedom to tailor financing and investment decisions, improved management incentives, or better focus.

A lack of parent company capabilities can hamper a business unit's performance. All businesses evolve through a life cycle, from start-up through expansion to maturity. Different moments in its life cycle require different skills and capabilities to manage the business effectively: from a focus on innovation in the start-up phase, when a viable business idea and platform are created, to cost management skills at maturity, when efficiency is the key driver of success. Many corporations lack the full breadth and depth of skills. Typically, they excel in only a few capabilities, which also tend to be fairly static over time.

A common misperception about divestments is that they are an easy solution for undervaluation in the stock market. Some managers interpret positive excess returns to divestment announcements as a confirmation that the divestment exposes value the market had overlooked. That interpretation is wrong. It is often based on a misleading sum-of-the-parts analysis showing that the current market value of the company is smaller than the sum of the values of its individual business. It is critical to come at this objectively; often, the lower valuation is due to lower performance of some business units (for more on this, see Chapter 18).

EXECUTIVES SHY AWAY FROM DIVESTITURES

Despite the potential value creation from divestitures, many executives shy away from initiating them, often dispirited by the idea of shrinking the corporate empires they've built. Looking at 1,300 large global companies during the period from 2013 until 2022, almost 60 percent did not execute in any single year divestitures that exceeded 5 percent of their market value. The previously mentioned McKinsey study of 200 U.S. companies found that at least 75 percent of the transactions were made in reaction to some form of pressure, such as underperformance of the corporate parent, the business unit, or both.

Moreover, many divestitures still occur not as an expression of a strategic plan but in reaction to pressure from outside the corporation. For instance, in 2017, AkzoNobel announced the divestiture of its specialty chemicals business when faced with an activist-investor campaign and a takeover attempt by competitor PPG. This trend is on the rise, with a record of 259 activist campaigns globally in 2023. Europe and Asia-Pacific were the regions contributing

---

[5] L. Corb and T. Koller, "When to Break Up a Conglomerate: An Interview with Tyco International's CFO," *McKinsey on Finance* (Autumn 2007): 12–18.

the most to this surge, with two-thirds of campaigns in Europe focused on challenging announced M&A transactions or advocating for sales or divestitures to unlock value.

Several publications have confirmed that parent companies tend to hold on to underperforming businesses too long, waiting until they have to respond to economic, technological, or regulatory shocks.[6]

In our experience, in addition to reducing the size of the company, many managers dislike divestitures because these transactions could reduce the company's earnings per share, price-to-earnings ratio (P/E), or other performance indicators. However, if the business is worth more to an outsider or as an independent company, the divestiture will create value and should be pursued. The example in Exhibit 32.2 illustrates this.

EXHIBIT 32.2 **Earnings Dilution Through Divestitures**

$ million

	Company	Divested business unit	Use of proceeds		
			Hold cash	Debt repayment	Share buyback
Value of operations	2,800	450	2,350	2,350	2,350
Cash	—	—	550	—	—
Enterprise value	2,800	—	2,900	2,350	2,350
Debt	(600)	—	(600)	(50)	(600)
Market value of equity	2,200	—	2,300	2,300	1,750
Shares outstanding	100.0	—	100.0	100.0	76.1
Share price	22.0	—	23.0	23.0	23.0
Invested capital	1,800	150	1,650	1,650	1,650
EBITA	236.0	50.0	186.0	186.0	186.0
Interest income (2%)	—	—	11.0	—	—
Interest expense (6%)	(36.0)	—	(36.0)	(3.0)	(36.0)
Pretax income	200.0	50.0	161.0	183.0	150.0
Taxes (25%)	(50.0)	(12.5)	(40.3)	(45.8)	(37.5)
Net income	150.0	37.5	120.8	137.3	112.5
Earnings per share, $	1.50	—	1.21	1.37	1.48
P/E	14.7	14.7	19.0	16.8	15.6
Earnings yield, %	6.8	6.8	5.3	6.0	6.4
Pretax ROIC, %	13.1	33.3	11.3	11.3	11.3
Operating value/EBITA	11.9	9.0	12.6	12.6	12.6

[6] See, for example, J. Mulherin and A. Boone, "Comparing Acquisitions and Divestitures," *Journal of Corporate Finance* 6 (2000): 117–139; D. Ravenscraft and F. Scherer, *Mergers, Sell-Offs, and Economic Efficiency* (Washington, DC: Brookings Institution, 1987), 167; and M. Cho and M. Cohen, "The Economic Causes and Consequences of Corporate Divestiture," *Managerial and Decision Economics* 18 (1997): 367–374.

The company described in the left side of the exhibit can raise $550 million in cash from divestment of a mature business unit. This unit has a relatively high return on invested capital (ROIC) but limited growth potential. The value of the business to the company is estimated at $450 million, so selling it at $550 million clearly creates value for the company. Any resulting changes in earnings multiples (whether P/E or enterprise value to EBITA) or earnings per share for the company after the transaction are irrelevant. Because divested units are typically the more mature businesses in a company's portfolio (with lower earnings multiples), divestitures often lead to increases in earnings multiples and decreases in earnings per share. But this does not indicate anything about value creation. For example, this divestment would increase the company's P/E multiple even when carried out at a price below $450 million (which would clearly destroy value).

In addition, changes in earnings per share and the earnings multiple depend on how the company decides to use the cash proceeds from the divestment:

- *Holding cash.* If the parent holds on to the proceeds, it will dilute its earnings per share. The reason is straightforward: the interest rate earned on the cash (1.5 percent, calculated as 2 percent less taxes at 25 percent) is lower than the so-called earnings yield (earnings relative to the value of sales proceeds, 6.8 percent after taxes) of the divested business unit. This is just simple mathematics. However, the equity value increases because the divestiture creates value, and the company's P/E is higher than before.

- *Repaying debt.* If the parent uses the proceeds to repay debt, earnings per share will still be diluted; the interest rate on the debt, at 4.5 percent after taxes (calculated as 6 percent less taxes at 25 percent), is also lower than the earnings yield of the divested business. Dilution is less than in the scenario where the parent holds the cash, because the interest rate on debt is higher than on cash. Again, the company's P/E goes up as earnings per share go down, but less so than in the prior scenario. Takeda Pharmaceutical, a global biopharma leader, undertook a series of divestitures to raise cash to pay down debt following the acquisition of Shire in 2019, which significantly increased the company's debt burden. Among the key divestitures were Xiidra and TachoSil. In addition, Takeda sold 21 real estate properties, its coffee and tea business, and several noncore assets in emerging markets in Latin America and Europe, with total proceeds reaching up to $7.7 billion.

- *Buying back shares.* If the parent uses the proceeds to buy back shares, earnings per share will be diluted because the earnings yield of the remaining business (the inverse of the P/E, 6.4 percent) is lower than the earnings yield of the divested business unit (6.8 percent), but the dilution is less than in the other scenarios. The P/E increases but ends up below the P/E in the other two scenarios. In the example shown, for the divestment to become earnings accretive, the sale proceeds and amount used for buybacks would have to increase to more than $583 million.

- *Investment for growth.* A company could also use the proceeds to make acquisitions, thus maintaining its size. This might make sense if the company has already identified an acquisition target and is actively working on it but needs the proceeds to finance the acquisitions. The sequence is important; the company is unlikely to create value if it starts searching for acquisitions just to increase the size of the company. As we discussed in Chapter 31, success at acquisitions requires that they be part of a strategy, not just a way to deploy cash. Investment decisions and divestiture decisions should be kept separate, as much as possible.

Even though the divestment causes the size of the company to be smaller (in terms of revenues and market capitalization) and its earnings per share to be lower, shareholders still benefit from this divestment. What matters is that the company generates more value from selling this business than from running it. Shareholders care about value, not size.

DECIDING ON TRANSACTION TYPE

Once a corporation has identified businesses for divestiture, it must decide what transaction structure to use. Its choices will depend on the availability of strategic or financial buyers, the need to raise cash, the benefits of retaining some level of control during the first phase of the separation, and fiscal implications for the company and/or its shareholders.

The remainder of this chapter provides a brief overview of different transaction types and discusses the trade-offs among alternative forms of public-ownership transactions, their impact on long-term performance, and the dynamics of ownership structures over time.

Private Transactions

Private transactions, or trade sales, are a company's sale of a business unit to another company (often referred to as a strategic buyer) or a financial investor. These transactions typically create the most value if other parties are better owners of the business. Private transactions allow the company to sell the business unit at a premium and capture value immediately.

However, an outright sale may result in taxable gains that will put this alternative at a disadvantage. In the United States and some other countries, for example, a company must pay income tax on gains from a business sale. Businesses with relatively high ROIC or low capital intensity may therefore be less attractive candidates for an outright sale unless the premium offered justifies paying the capital gains tax. In many European countries, the so-called participation exemption makes the sale of the parent's shares in a subsidiary exempt from taxes.

Public Transactions

If the company cannot identify another company as a better owner, it can consider public restructuring alternatives, the most common of which are the following:

- *Spin-off (or demerger):* distribution of all shares in a subsidiary to existing shareholders of the parent company
- *Split-off:* an offer to existing shareholders of the parent company to exchange their shares in the parent company for shares in the subsidiary
- *Carve-out (IPO of a minority stake):* sale of part of the shares in a subsidiary to new shareholders in the stock market
- *Initial public offering (IPO):* sale of all shares of a subsidiary to new shareholders in the stock market
- *Tracking stock:* a separate class of parent shares that is distributed to existing shareholders of the parent company

All the public transactions in the preceding list involve the creation of a new public security, but not all of them actually result in cash proceeds. Full IPOs and carve-outs result in cash proceeds as securities are sold to new shareholders. In spin-off and split-off transactions, new securities are offered to existing shareholders, sometimes in exchange for other existing shares (split-offs). The feasibility of these options depends on several factors, including the size and attractiveness of the business unit. Larger, well-established businesses with strong brands may be better suited for an IPO or carve-out. Conversely, smaller business units may face challenges in meeting listing requirements of public exchanges. Additionally, antitrust regulations can limit the pool of strategic buyers, making a trade sale difficult.

In public transactions, shareholders do not earn a premium from the divestiture itself, but significant value may be created for shareholders in the future. For example, if industry consolidation is expected, a public transaction may be more beneficial for the shareholders in the long term if the newly floated business unit would drive the consolidation or would be a takeover candidate.

Spin-Offs   The most common form of public-ownership transaction is a spin-off. In the case of a spin-off, the parent company gives up control over the business unit by distributing the subsidiary shares to the parent's shareholders, typically as a dividend. This full separation maximizes the strategic flexibility of the subsidiary, provides the greatest freedom to improve operations, and avoids conflicts of interest between the parent company and the business unit.

Depending on the jurisdiction, spin-offs can also offer tax benefits over alternatives such as trade sales and IPOs. In the United States, United Kingdom, and several countries of continental Europe, spin-offs can be structured as tax-free transactions. Such benefits can make a spin-off more value-creating for shareholders than a trade sale at a sizable premium in countries such as the United States, where gains from a trade sale are taxed. Consider a hypothetical example in which a business with a tax book value of $200 million can be sold for $1.2 billion or spun off at an expected market capitalization of $1 billion. At a tax rate of 25 percent, the sale would leave the parent company with after-tax proceeds of $950 million that it could return to its shareholders. In a spin-off, the parent company would distribute shares in the business with an expected value of $1 billion to its shareholders.

Sometimes spin-offs are executed in two steps: a minority IPO (carve-out) followed by a full spin-off relatively shortly thereafter. Some advocates claim that a two-step spin-off has benefits: the initial minority listing establishes dedicated equity coverage, creates market making in the shares, and may reduce the risk of price pressure from flow-back by developing an interested investor base.[7] However, in most situations, these potential issues are rarely material and can be well managed in a one-step spin-off. For example, when one technology conglomerate spun off a business division, some analysts and investors were concerned about flow-back because they considered it to be one of the conglomerate's least attractive businesses. But the flow-back was effectively handled in a so-called balancing book that was used to match supply and demand for the business's shares. No price pressure occurred. A one-step spin-off has the benefit of being less complex and does not depend on market circumstances, as no shares need to be sold to investors.

Split-Offs   Split-offs differ from spin-offs in that shareholders surrender some of their shares in the parent company to receive shares in the newly formed entity. This effectively reduces the parent company's outstanding shares, increasing earnings per share (EPS) for remaining shareholders. A split-off can be seen as a form of share buyback, as shareholders exchange

---

[7] In a spin-off, all parent shareholders receive shares of the spun-off subsidiary. When parent shareholders subsequently sell these shares in the stock market, this gives rise to flow-back.

their ownership in the parent company for ownership in a different company. This structure can appeal to shareholders who have a strong preference for one company over the other.

Split-offs are rare because of their complexity. In a spin-off, the parent company simply distributes shares in the spin-off company to shareholders in proportion to their existing ownership. In a split-off, a company must actively solicit shareholders to exchange some of their shares for shares in the company to be spun off, incurring higher transaction costs.

Carve-Outs   In a carve-out, a company sells a portion of the shares in a business unit to investors in an initial public offering and typically lists the unit on an exchange. Parent companies use carve-outs if they do not want to give up control over a business. Another reason to consider a carve-out is that the parent needs cash for an acquisition or recapitalization. Carve-outs were popular in the late 1990s during the boom in the telecom, media, and technology (TMT) sector. Since then, the allure of carve-outs has faded, and the need for cash propels most decisions to pursue one. Carve-outs have become rare in the last two decades except as part of a two-step spin-off.

In general, carve-outs are not a permanent structure. Because of the inherent inefficiencies of carve-outs, it is rare to see a company owning a majority stake in another listed company. Carve-outs lead to loss of synergies because the two companies have separate management teams and boards of directors, who have fiduciary duties only to their own shareholders. Every transaction between the two companies, even transferring employees, must be at arm's length.

In our research on more than 200 transactions completed in the carve-out boom of the 1990s, the majority of the carve-out entities did not last.[8] Only 8 percent of the carve-out subsidiaries analyzed remained majority-controlled by the parent. Only the carve-outs that gained independence from the parent delivered positive returns to shareholders. Those that were reacquired or remained parent-controlled showed negative shareholder returns. Academic research has found similar results.[9]

The track record of carve-outs leads to the conclusion that executives thinking about partially separating ownership of a business unit through a carve-out should plan for full separation and independence. The arc toward independence should be clear from the start. For example, Philips publicly committed to gradually selling down its remaining stake in its lighting business (Signify) after the IPO of that business in 2016. In September 2019, Philips sold its last remaining shares in Signify.

---

[8] A. Annema, W. Fallon, and M. Goedhart, "Do Carve-Outs Make Sense?," *McKinsey on Finance* (Fall 2001): 6–10.

[9] See, for example, J. Madura and T. Nixon, "The Long-Term Performance of Parent and Units Following Equity Carve-Outs," *Applied Financial Economics* 12 (2002): 171–181; and A. Vijh, "Long-Term Returns from Equity Carveouts," *Journal of Financial Economics* 51 (1999): 273–308.

Initial Public Offering of Business Unit   An initial public offering of a business unit is the same as a carve-out except that all the shares of the business unit are sold to investors, and the parent company retains no stake. A 100 percent IPO raises the most cash, but these sales are rare because it is difficult to raise that much cash for a sizable business unit (anything over $1 billion or even less, depending on market conditions).

Tracking Stock   Tracking stock offers a parent the advantage of maintaining control over a separated subsidiary, through the separate issuance of a special class of shares. Typically, investors don't like tracking stock, for several reasons. First, there is no formal, legal separation between the subsidiary and the parent, so a single board of directors needs to decide on potentially competing needs of common and tracking stock shareholders. Second, tracking stocks cause both entities to be liable for each other's debt, which precludes flexible capital raising. Finally, tracking stocks are hard to value because it's not clear what the shareholders actually own.

After an initial burst of excitement about tracking stock, reality set in, and tracking stocks have disappeared.

EVIDENCE ON VALUE CREATION FROM DIVESTITURES

We can analyze the performance of divestitures and spin-offs in two ways: based on the immediate stock market reaction to the announcement of the transaction and based on the long-term performance of the companies involved.

The immediate stock market reaction is clear: the stock market's immediate reaction to the announcement of a spin-off or divestiture is typically positive. Recent academic research examining the stock price reaction to divestiture announcements from 1995 to 2021 showed significant positive returns relative to the overall market.[10] This confirms decades of earlier research.[11] Our own research analyzing the announcement of spin-offs from 2000 to 2023 showed similar results. From one week before to one week after the announcement,

---

[10] E. R. Feldman, *Divestitures: Creating Value through Strategy, Structure and Implementation* (New York: McGraw-Hill, 2023).

[11] See, for example, B. Eckbo and K. Thornburn, "Corporate Restructuring," *Foundations and Trends in Finance* 7 (2012): 159–288; Mulherin and Boone, "Comparing Acquisitions and Divestitures"; J. Miles and J. Rosenfeld, "The Effect of Voluntary Spin-Off Announcements on Shareholder Wealth," *Journal of Finance* 38 (1983): 1597–1606; K. Schipper and A. Smith, "A Comparison of Equity Carve-Outs and Seasoned Equity Offerings: Share Price Effects and Corporate Restructuring," *Journal of Financial Economics* 15 (1986): 153–186; K. Schipper and A. Smith, "Effects of Recontracting on Shareholder Wealth: The Case of Voluntary Spin-Offs," *Journal of Financial Economics* 12 (1983): 437–468; J. Allen and J. McConnell, "Equity Carve-Outs and Managerial Discretion," *Journal of Finance* 53 (1998): 163–186; and R. Michaely and W. Shaw, "The Choice of Going Public: Spin-Offs vs. Carve-Outs," *Financial Management* 24 (1995): 5–21.

66 percent of companies outperformed their peers, and the median outperformance was 3.3 percent during that period.[12]

Examining longer time frames after the announcement found mixed results depending on the period examined. Over the next three years after the announcement, there was a roughly 50/50 chance of beating peers. The reason may be simply that, over three years, other factors outweigh the impact of the spin-off. Also, the results varied depending on the time frame examined.

We and others have also examined the financial results of parent companies and spun-off businesses following the divestiture transaction. Prior work by us and by academics found that both parent companies and spun-off businesses improved their operating margins during the five years after the transaction. Spun-off businesses also increased their growth rates.[13] However, our research in more recent years has not shown the same outperformance.

SUMMARY

As businesses develop through their life cycles, they pose new challenges to the parent company. Parent companies therefore should continually reevaluate which businesses to keep and which to divest. However, most corporations divest businesses only after resisting shareholder pressure. In delaying, they risk forgoing potentially significant value.

Senior executives should prepare the organization for the cultural shift to a more active approach. They should deliver the message that their new approach will entail divesting good businesses, and such divestitures should not be considered failures. Because managers may find it difficult to divest good businesses, corporations should build forcing mechanisms into their divestiture programs.

There is no guarantee that divestitures will create value. The best divestitures indeed outperform the market, but those at the bottom fall even further behind. To increase the chances of a successful divestiture, executives should thoroughly identify the implications for the economics of the remaining businesses and consider these implications when structuring the divestiture agreement. Executives should also take care not to underestimate the time and effort required to complete a divestiture.

---

[12] These results are consistent over different time periods.
[13] See B. Huyett and T. Koller, "Finding the Courage to Shrink," McKinsey & Company, August 1, 2011, www.mckinsey.com; and P. Cusatis, J. A. Miles, and J. R. Woolridge, "Some New Evidence that Spinoffs Create Value," *Journal of Applied Corporate Finance* 7, no. 2 (Summer 1994).

33

Digital Initiatives and Companies

As we write this book in 2024, the transformative effects of technological improvements building on digitization, robotization, machine learning, and other forms of artificial intelligence (AI)—including generative AI—are high-ranked items on any executive's agenda.

At the same time, exactly what digital means remains fuzzy. Some view it simply as an extension of IT functions. Others focus on digital marketing and sales, providing digital services to customers, or connecting devices. Still others see it as an entirely new, often disruptive model for conducting business based on digital technologies. In recent years, many have started to include various forms of AI in the definition, such as generative AI (gen AI). For our purposes, the applications of digital technology involve all these definitions and probably others that haven't been thought of yet. For example, several of our colleagues examined a typical consumer packaged-goods company to see how many ways digitization and digital applications could be used to improve performance. They identified dozens of possibilities, including digital marketing, optimization of trade spending, improvement of sales force coverage, predictive maintenance, supply chain planning, and robotic process automation in the back office.

Given the wide scope of potential digital initiatives, it is no surprise that most companies are launching them. In a 2022 survey of 1,331 managers, about nine in 10 said their organizations had begun a digital transformation. However, less than a third said their efforts had made and sustained the targeted performance improvements, a clear sign that digital is an area where management discipline is needed.[1]

---

[1] K. Smaje, L. LaBerge, and R. Zemmel, "Three New Mandates for Capturing a Digital Transformation's Full Value," McKinsey & Company, June 2022, www.mckinsey.com.

Digital initiatives can create value in numerous ways, helping to capture opportunities and manage threats. The first, most common way is through *digital performance initiatives*: companies use digital technology to do the things they are already doing, only better. Digital strategies can be applied in mundane but important ways, including cost reduction, improved customer experience, new revenue sources, and better decision making. The second way digital initiatives can create value is by radically modifying existing businesses or creating entirely new businesses—*digital businesses*—that can sometimes fundamentally change an entire industry. The line between existing businesses and new digital initiatives can blur, such as when clothing retailers integrate their physical and online sales. The retailer is still selling clothes, but the customer's experience has changed, and the retailer must substantially retool its business.

While the technologies and sometimes the business models are new, the same fundamental valuation principle applies: digital initiatives, projects, or businesses should be evaluated based on the cash flow they are expected to generate. This chapter discusses how to apply scenario-based approaches for the valuation of digital initiatives. In addition, it presents some specific tools to analyze the value creation from underlying customer growth and returns in digital businesses.

DIGITAL PERFORMANCE INITIATIVES

Our recommendation sounds simple: evaluate digital projects based on the cash flow they are expected to generate. Sometimes executives argue that digital initiatives are "strategic" and that their benefits can't be measured. In our experience, this is rarely the case.

The logical error in this line of thinking often originates in an improper definition of the base case. Ideally, all investment decisions should be analyzed against an alternative course of action. For digital projects, the alternative may be to do nothing. But the do-nothing case doesn't mean there will be no change in a company's cash flows. Banks have faced this challenge several times over the past 40 years. In the 1970s and 1980s, banks introduced automated teller machines. In the 2000s, banks set up online banking. In the 2010s, banks developed mobile-banking apps. In hindsight, it seems obvious that banks needed to introduce all these innovations. But these innovations probably didn't generate new revenues, because they were adopted by all banks. Thus, although a mobile-banking app makes strategic sense, it appears to create a negative present value due to its additional costs with no added revenues.

Here's where the importance of the base case comes in. If the bank doesn't build a mobile app, it will likely lose market share and revenues over time. In this case, the cash inflows are the avoidance of lost revenues, which could be substantial. So this "strategic" digital project likely does have a positive present value.

Digital performance initiatives typically fall into one of four categories based on their intended benefits: cost reduction, improved customer experience, new revenue sources, and better decision making. We discuss each of these in the following sections.

Cost Reduction

Many digital initiatives can help companies reduce their operating costs. Predictive maintenance on factory equipment reduces both maintenance costs and lost production from downtime. Another example is the grandly named robotic process automation (RPA). This doesn't refer to physical robots, but rather to software that automates processes such as accounts-payable processing. As this software become more sophisticated, it can take on even more difficult tasks, handling exceptions in addition to plain-vanilla accounts payable.

Some examples show great progress for this kind of cost reduction. One mining company saved over $360 million per year from process automation in the field that gave managers more insight into what exactly was happening, enabling them to make adjustments and anticipate needs. Fossil-fuel power generators are able to improve a plant's heat rate (how efficiently the plant uses fuel) by up to 3 percent by using sensors and actuators for remote monitoring and automated operations, as well as smart valves that self-report and repair leakages. They have also used automated work order generation, remote expert support using virtual-reality devices, and automated warehouses to reduce operating costs by 5–20 percent. At the same time, they have improved safety by using robots for tasks in confined spaces, as well as advanced analytics to prevent accidents caused by fatigue or distraction.[2]

Understanding the economics of cost reduction is not as straightforward as it may seem. You might be tempted to estimate the present value by simply discounting the expected savings and subtracting the investments required. But you also must examine the second-order effects. Are your competitors pursuing the same initiatives? In a competitive industry such as the chemicals business, those cost reductions might simply be passed through to customers as price reductions. Chemical companies typically find ways to reduce costs by around 2 percent per year, but their margins don't increase, because industry players pass the savings on to customers.

In a situation like this, where the present value of cost reduction efforts is zero because the savings are passed on to customers, the alternative, do-nothing case becomes important. If your competitors are pursuing digital initiatives to reduce costs and you are not, you'll still have to reduce your prices in line with your competitors'. The alternative to the digital initiative would be a decline in cash flows due to lower prices without reduced costs. So the present value

[2] G. Guzman, A. Prasanna, P. Safarik, and P. Tanwar, "Unlocking the Value of Digital Operations in Electric-Power Generation," McKinsey & Company, October 2019, www.mckinsey.com.

of the initiative may turn positive when you compare your initiative with the appropriate base case. Note that a positive present value might not increase a company's share value if investors expect savings to be passed on to customers in order to keep up with the company's peers. In practice, whether the savings are passed on to customers will vary by industry, but it's critical to think carefully through the alternative case.

Improved Customer Experience

Consumers have benefited tremendously from the digital actions of companies. Many retailers have become "omnichannel," giving consumers a high degree of flexibility. Consumers can purchase an item of clothing in a store or online, to be shipped to the buyer's home or to a local store. If the local store doesn't have the right size for an in-store shopper, the customer can order it on the spot and have it delivered to the customer's home. A customer who decides to return an item can return it to any store or mail it back, regardless of how it was purchased. Consumers can also track in real time the progress of shipments heading their way.

Using digitization to improve customer experience can add value to the business in a variety of ways. One leading manufacturer of agricultural products was struggling with low customer satisfaction scores and an erosion of its customer base. Using digital solutions, the company created a seamless online process for ordering, tracking, and query management. This increased the company's customer satisfaction score by 24 percentage points and improved throughput by 20 percent.[3] In some cases, improved customer service also reduces costs. An electricity distribution company fully redesigned its customer interfaces in a "digital first" way that made a priority of the customer's online interaction. Customer satisfaction rose 25 percentage points, employee satisfaction increased by ten percentage points, and customer service costs fell 40 percent.

As is the case with applying digital solutions to reduce costs, it's critical to think through the competitive effects of investing in digital to provide a superior customer experience. Recall our earlier example of the mobile-banking app. The value proposition boils down to cash flow, but special considerations emerge. Does the improved customer service lead to higher market share because your customer service is better than that of your competitors? Or does it maintain your market share or avoid losing market share because your competitors are doing the same thing?

In many situations, a company that adopts a digital initiative of this kind will see its competitors adopt similar initiatives, leading customers to expect an improved experience without paying extra for it. In the case of omnichannel

---

[3] J. Boringer, B. Grehan, D. Kiewell, S. Lehmitz, and P. Moser, "Four Pathways to Digital Growth That Work for B2B Companies," McKinsey & Company, October 2019, www.mckinsey.com.

retailers, today's customers routinely expect seamless transactions across channels from many retailers, but for the retailers, providing omnichannel services is expensive. The cost to ship online orders often makes these sales unprofitable, while in-store sales may be declining, leading to lower margins, as some costs are fixed. Even so, retailers have no choice but to provide omnichannel services despite lower profitability. If they don't, they'll lose even more revenue and profits.

New Revenue Sources

Some companies have been able to create new revenue sources through digital initiatives. In these cases, the economic analysis versus the base case is more straightforward, because at least for a while, you (and maybe your competitors) are making the pie bigger for the whole industry. However, genuinely new revenue sources can be hard to find and difficult to convince customers to pay for.

Imagine you are sitting at home with an urge for some ice cream but don't want to go out to the local convenience store. In several European and North American markets, Ben & Jerry's has set up centralized ice-cream freezers where a delivery company picks up the ice cream and delivers it to the customer within a short time. These centralized freezers generate superior sales volume when compared with convenience store freezers—sales that would, for the most part, not happen otherwise, because without the convenient delivery, many customers would simply skip the ice cream.

Or consider farm equipment manufacturer John Deere's introduction of precision farming services. The company has created a suite of add-on, data-driven offerings that include the analysis of soil samples and weather patterns to help farmers optimize crop yields. Sensors in tractors and other machinery provide data for predictive maintenance, automated sprinkler systems synchronize with weather data, and an open-software platform lets third parties build new service apps.[4]

In a similar way, Ford Motor Company offers software services to its commercial vehicle owners to monitor and analyze in real time their fleet locations, efficiency, and maintenance needs. Then there's one transportation company's digital solution to help its customers improve fleet maintenance. That solution helped generate more than $10 million of additional revenue through software subscriptions and aftermarket parts sales.[5]

These new revenue sources can create value because they don't involve just keeping up with the competition. In two of the examples, digital innovations

[4] J. Bughin, T. Catlin, M. Hirt, and P. Willmott, "Why Digital Strategies Fail," *McKinsey Quarterly* (January 2018), www.mckinsey.com.

[5] M. Banholzer, M. Berger-de Leon, S. Narayanan, and M. Patel, "How Industrial Incumbents Create New Businesses," McKinsey & Company, September 2019, www.mckinsey.com.

created an overall increase in the revenue pool for the industry. In the case of Ben & Jerry's, the overall consumption of ice cream increased. In John Deere's case, a new product offering also increased overall demand.

Better Decision Making

Finally, some executives are pairing the trove of data being generated and new advanced analytics techniques to enable managers to make better decisions about a broad range of activities, including how they fund marketing, utilize assets, and retain customers.

Consider two examples. A maker of high-tech hardware implemented a partially automated solution to improve pricing for thousands of product configurations. Key features included configuration-based price benchmarking, analysis of price trends and automated pricing recommendations with weekly updates of up to 200,000 price points for up to 20,000 products. Separately, a consumer products company used advanced analytics to improve the design of its planograms. A planogram is a model of how a consumer packaged-goods company allocates its limited space on retail shelves. It describes which products will be included and how to display them. Analytics showed decision makers at the company that they could dramatically improve effectiveness. At the same time, they reduced the number of people required to design planograms from ten to just two.

Advanced analytics to improve decision making can generate additional revenues, reduce costs, or both. In the planogram example, the improvement can increase total customer spending by getting customers to upgrade to more profitable products. In this case, because the change involves only choices within the company's product mix, the improvement can create value without necessarily inviting a competitive response. In other cases, the benefits may be diluted because competitors take similar actions, but the investment in analytics still may create value by maintaining competitive parity.

DIGITAL BUSINESSES

In some cases, digital initiatives create new businesses or radically modify existing businesses. For the purposes of this book, we define these digital businesses as businesses that do not typically provide physical goods but instead focus on providing services that are digitally enabled or significantly enhanced—such as, software, electronic payments, content streaming, e-commerce, social media, marketplaces, mobility and delivery platforms, and many others. Some of these new digital businesses have driven out existing companies and upended entire industries. The internet changed the way consumers research and purchase airline tickets and hotel rooms, disintermediating many traditional travel agents. The introduction of audio- and video-streaming services has disrupted the economics of traditional broadcast and cable TV channels. Digital also has created enormous new businesses, such as workspace videoconferencing services, which have largely replaced traditional telephone conferencing services. One of the leading players, Zoom Video Communications, grew its revenues from $60 million in 2017 to more than $4.5 billion in 2024. Similarly, cloud computing services generate around $500 billion of revenues in 2024, up from less than $10 billion 15 years earlier. The rise of cloud computing also disrupted several other industries. First, the standardization of servers by leading players disrupted the manufacturers of mainframe computers and servers. Second, it disrupted the IT services business that ran companies' data centers. Third, it made the software development industry shift from device-specific to cloud-based applications that offer their users scalability and cost-efficiency.

Value Creation in Digital Businesses

With varying rates of success, digital businesses appear in many different sectors, adopting many different commercial models. Consider the wide range of sectors that faced disruption by players such as Amazon and Alibaba (retail), Alphabet (advertising), Spotify and Netflix (media and entertainment), PayPal and Adyen (payments), Airbnb and Booking.com (travel and lodging), Arlo and Ring (residential surveillance), Just Eat Takeaway, Grubhub, and Deliveroo (food delivery), Lyft (mobility services), or Uber (mobility and food delivery). The commercial models adopted by these players also show a wide variety: transaction-based revenues (for example, in e-commerce and mobility services), subscription models (for example, in entertainment), the sale of advertising (for example, ad-supported entertainment), revenue generation from hidden sources (for example, selling user data), or some combination of these (for example, so-called freemium models).

Besides combining elements of different commercial models, digital businesses can operate in different categories. For example, Amazon not only has an e-commerce business in online retail but also offers platform services to other retailers and is a large player in cloud-based computing (Amazon Web Services).

Disruption successes are far from guaranteed in digital business and depend on technological as well as commercial innovation. For example, AI has been widely applied by existing businesses to improve customer service and predict equipment maintenance needs. Gen AI applications have demonstrated impressive productions of text, images, music, and videos. But as of 2024, the first breakthrough commercial AI or gen AI application capable of driving a new digital business had yet to appear.

To value these new businesses, use the standard DCF approach driven by estimates of ROIC and revenue growth. As a practical matter, for new digital businesses, you will typically have to estimate how large revenues will be able to grow at a point in the future when growth stabilizes—as well as what the ROIC might be at that time, based on the fundamental economics of the business. For example, outline one or more scenarios for the type of services the business will be offering, the share of total demand it could capture for such services, the expected intensity of the competition, and the revenues, margins, and returns all these factors would produce. In other words, start in the future and work back to the present, rather than the other way around (for more on this, see Chapter 39).

When estimating the potential size and ROIC of an early-stage digital business, carefully test the underlying economics to determine whether the business might in fact be a "capital light" or "winner takes all" business. Some new digital business models are indeed capital-light, involving only small amount of property, plant, and equipment relative to the revenues generated. In these cases, applying alternative measures to return on capital, such as economic-profit margin or capitalization of research and developments costs, might be useful (for more on this, see Chapter 24). But do not automatically assume that all digital businesses are capital-light. Many leading digital businesses have spent heavily to build expensive data centers or chip factories. For companies such as Alphabet, Amazon, Microsoft, and Oracle, the average ratio of capital expenditures to revenues has increased from around 5 percent in the early 2010s to around 12 percent in 2022.

Claims for a digital business to have winner-takes-all potential are typically based on so-called network effects. As described by Carl Shapiro and Hal Varian in 1998, the basic idea of network effects is as follows.[6] In certain situations, as companies grow, they can earn higher margins and return on capital because their product becomes more valuable with each new customer (see also Chapter 8, particularly Exhibit 8.3). In most industries, competition eventually forces the margins and returns back to reasonable levels. But in some cases, which turn out to be quite rare, competition is kept at bay if customers of the market leader need to overcome certain hurdles or incur costs when switching to competitive offerings (hence the tag "winner takes all"). However, as pointed out by Shapiro and Varian, this is more the exception than the rule, even for digital businesses.

Many early-stage digital businesses, especially so-called platform businesses, are too easily assumed to benefit from network effects. Platform businesses use a digital infrastructure to facilitate interactions between large groups of users, generating revenues through transaction fees, advertising, data monetization, or some combination of these.[7] A classic example is eBay, which has been connecting sellers and buyers from all over the world via

---

[6] C. Shapiro and H. Varian, *Information Rules: A Strategic Guide to the Network Economy* (Boston: Harvard Business School Press, 1998).
[7] F. Zheng and M. Iansinti, "Why Some Platforms Thrive and Others Don't," *Harvard Business Review* 97, no. 1 (January–February 2019): 118–125.

online marketplaces since 1995. For platform business, network effects often seem to be even stronger because they have "customers" on multiple sides. For example, a marketplace such as eBay becomes more valuable to both buyers and sellers as it attracts more transactions to the platform. The principle sounds compelling: more customers means more transactions, which attracts more suppliers, which leads to more offerings and lower costs per transaction, which attracts more customers, leading to a virtuous cycle of increasing competitive advantage. With ever-increasing value to customers and efficiency in costs, the largest player will ultimately drive its competitors out of business. However, very few digital platforms are truly such winner-takes-all businesses.

As noted by Feng Zheng and Marco Iansinti, "It is often easier for a digital platform to achieve scale than to sustain it," as several threats to the success of platform businesses are not easily detected from the outside and apply regardless of platform scale.[8] For example, even a large-scale network can be vulnerable to much smaller-scale, local competitors if it is itself merely a collection of more isolated, local clusters. Consider the example of a large, international food delivery platform. It essentially consists of multiple, fragmented networks of local restaurants and customers that do not particularly value being in an international network. Small-scale local networks could easily compete, as the delivery operations don't benefit much from scale beyond the region serviced. Another example is so-called multi-homing, in which users of the platform business work simultaneously with competitive networks. The threat to the food delivery platform arises when restaurants can offer their products via competing platforms, looking for the lowest transaction fees (if restaurants do not face significant switching costs because of, for example, long-term platform contracts or dependency on platform-provided booking systems). Customers are likely to use multiple food delivery platforms anyway, and any loyalty and membership programs ultimately represent costs to the platform business. To make the business a true winner-takes-all candidate, such threats would need to be mitigated by some user captivity caused by high switching costs, overriding quality offered for users, or long-term contracts.

The history of innovation shows how difficult it is to earn monopoly-size returns on capital for any length of time except in very special circumstances. Many companies and investors didn't realize how rare this was during the dot-com bubble of 1999–2000. More recently, investors again may have gone overboard with the number of "unicorns," typically defined as start-up companies with values above $1 billion (usually still private) and negative profits. As some unicorns went public or tried to, there was a renewed realization that not all these companies could earn extraordinary returns from network effects, and values fell considerably. It's unlikely that companies offering

[8] Ibid.

analytics services, selling e-cigarettes, or renting out short-term office space will achieve long-term network effects. What holds for any business holds for disruptive digital businesses as well: the key is to understand in depth the underlying drivers of long-term ROIC and growth. Subtle differences in business models can have significant impact on their value creation potential, as we discussed with the examples of Regus and Airbnb in Chapter 8.

ANALYTICAL TOOLS FOR DIGITAL BUSINESS VALUATION

Some analytical tools can contribute to an understanding of the underlying economics and trajectory toward value creation for early-stage, fast-growing digital businesses. Achieving scale is key, and you need to analyze more than top-line revenue growth to understand how the business is progressing toward scale and whether its returns are improving with scale. This will be important for understanding the potential size, profitability, and value of the business in the long term. In digital businesses, these analyses are all the more worthwhile, given the high pace of growth, the wide availability of underlying data on customer growth and economics, and the flexibility to adjust customer offerings if needed (at least when compared with customer offerings in physical products).

Growth Analysis: Attrition and Retention

The first step is to disaggregate revenue growth in growth of average revenue per user (or customer)—commonly abbreviated ARPU—and growth of number of users (or customers). For early-stage businesses, it is probably more important to expand the customer base and achieve scale. For later-stage businesses, demonstrating the potential to extract more revenues from existing customers (ARPU) becomes more relevant as customer growth is declining.

In a second step, separate the customer growth rate in the rate of customer additions minus the rate of customer losses. The rate of customer losses is the so-called attrition or churn rate. Its flip side is the customer retention rate, defined as one minus the attrition rate. For early-stage businesses that need to reach scale, understanding attrition is especially important. First, attracting new customers is costly. Customer acquisition costs (CAC) include discounts or vouchers for new customers, additional sales force costs, increased marketing efforts, or any combination of these. That means the cost to reach a certain scale will be higher for a business with high customer churn. Second, attrition is an important indicator of the market share an early-stage business could achieve—in fact, more so than customer growth rates. The reason is that the attrition rate essentially reflects the share of the addressable market the company is losing each year.

EXHIBIT 33.1 **How Attrition Affects Net Revenues and Market Share**

LoChurn	Year 1	2	3	....	18	19	20
Customers, beginning of year	100	115	132		850	838	832
Churn at 5.0%	(5)	(6)	(7)		(42)	(42)	(42)
Additions at 20.0%	20	23	26	....	31	35	41
Customers, end of year	115	132	152	::::	838	832	831
Revenues,[1] $	1,150	1,323	1,521		8,381	8,316	8,307
Customer acquisition costs (CAC),[2] $	(100)	(115)	(132)	....	(154)	(177)	(203)
Net revenues, $	1,050	1,208	1,389	::::	8,227	8,139	8,104
Share of total customer pool,[3] %	12	13	15		84	83	83

HiChurn	Year 1	2	3	....	18	19	20
Customers, beginning of year	100	115	132		611	612	625
Churn at 15.0%	(15)	(17)	(20)		(92)	(92)	(94)
Additions at 30.0%	30	35	40	....	92	105	98
Customers, end of year	115	132	152	::::	612	625	629
Revenues,[1] $	1,150	1,323	1,521		6,120	6,248	6,290
Customer acquisition costs (CAC),[2] $	(150)	(173)	(198)	....	(461)	(523)	(490)
Net revenues, $	1,000	1,150	1,323	::::	5,659	5,725	5,800
Share of total customer pool,[3] %	12	13	15		61	62	63

[1] At $10 per customer.

[2] At $5 per customer.

[3] Total market pool is 8,000 customers.

For example, as shown in Exhibit 33.1, companies LoChurn and HiChurn are both growing their customer base at 15 percent per year but in separate markets with a stable total customer pool. HiChurn loses 15 percent of its customers each year as they switch to competitors with better offerings. For LoChurn, the rate is only 5 percent. Once customers switch, they won't return for at least three years. Customer acquisition costs (CAC) are 50 percent of first-year customer revenues for both companies. Although stylized, the example illustrates two important points. First, HiChurn generates much lower net revenues than LoChurn because it needs to spend three times as much on CAC in every year. Second, the projected maximum share of the total customer pool is 63 percent for HiChurn, much lower than the 83 percent for LoChurn.[9]

Of course, growth and attrition analysis can provide useful insights for any customer-based business. But this is especially true for early-stage digital businesses, where the required customer data should be readily available. For example, meal kit delivery service Blue Apron reduced its

[9] The underlying logic is that, in the long-term, HighChurn will not be able to serve the same share of the total customer pool as LoChun because each year a higher fraction of HighChurn's customers will switch to competitor offerings and not return within three years (on average). As a result, HighChurn will be missing out on a larger share of the total pool than LoChurn.

2017 IPO target price amid investor concerns after publications reported about its high attrition rates, even though its revenues were growing at triple-digit rates.[10]

Cohort Analysis

Analysis of attrition rates at the company (or even business) level has short-comings. Company attrition rates are averages of what can be very diverse patterns of attrition among different customer groups. As a result, these rates can provide false signals of improving or deteriorating customer loyalty. For better insights, cohort analysis tracks growth and attrition by year of first transaction (also known as vintage), by geographic region, by product or service category, or any combination of these.

Exhibit 33.2 illustrates the additional insights that can be derived from even a basic cohort analysis. In this example, customers are grouped in vintage cohorts according to the year in which they made their first transaction. The top of the table shows the company's total number of active customers and its overall growth and attrition rates from the start of business in 2015 to 2025. Based on the overall figures, it appears that the company has impressively managed to grow at double-digit rates while continuously improving its customer loyalty.

EXHIBIT 33.2 **Cohort Analysis Revealing Trends Underlying Corporate Attrition Rates**

Number of customers by calendar year

	2015	2016	2017	2018	2019	2020	2021	2022	2023	2024	2025
Total	10.0	19.0	27.9	37.1	47.0	57.9	70.0	83.4	98.5	115.4	134.5
Growth, %		90%	47%	33%	27%	23%	21%	19%	18%	17%	17%
Attrition, %		25%	23%	21%	20%	20%	19%	19%	19%	19%	19%

Number of customers by vintage and calendar year

Vintage	2015	2016	2017	2018	2019	2020	2021	2022	2023	2024	2025
2015	10.0	7.5	6.1	5.2	4.7	4.3	4.1	3.9	3.7	3.7	3.6
2016		11.5	8.6	6.9	5.9	5.3	4.8	4.6	4.3	4.2	4.1
2017			13.2	9.8	7.8	6.7	5.9	5.4	5.1	4.9	4.7
2018				15.2	11.1	8.9	7.5	6.7	6.1	5.7	5.4
2019					17.5	12.7	10.0	8.5	7.5	6.8	6.4
2020						20.1	14.4	11.4	9.6	8.4	7.7
2021							23.1	16.4	12.9	10.8	9.4
2022								26.6	18.7	14.5	12.1
2023									30.6	21.3	16.4
2024										35.2	24.2
Total	10.0	19.0	27.9	37.1	47.0	57.9	70.0	83.4	98.5	115.4	134.5

[10] See E. Brown, "Stir Fry on Sale? Blue Apron Turns to Deals to Draw Customers," *Wall Street Journal*, June 27, 2017, www.wsj.com.

However, the bottom table reveals a far less favorable pattern. Each row represents a vintage cohort and tracks how many customers have been active in any year from their first year of transaction until 2025. For example, the cohort for vintage 2017 represents the 13,200 customers with their first transaction in 2017, of whom 4,700 are still active customers in 2025. In each column, the customer numbers for each vintage are added to find the total customers in the given year.

The retention rates for the vintage cohorts are shown in Exhibit 33.3. Within all cohorts, the curve flattens over time, indicating that the annual retention rate improves over time. In other words, longer-standing customers are less likely to leave than newly acquired customers. For example, first-year retention for the 2015 vintage cohort is 75 percent and increases to 95 percent in the seventh year. But retention rates across cohorts decrease over the vintage years—so, for example, the first-year retention rate is only 70 percent for the vintage cohort of 2023, a decrease of 5 percent from the 2015 cohort. This indicates that the company has not been able to improve customer loyalty over the years at all. Instead, the reason that overall attrition rates improved is that the share of longer-standing customers (who tend to have better retention rates) inevitably increased as the company expanded.[11] The deterioration in underlying cohort attrition rates will ultimately affect the company's overall attrition, and this needs to be factored in when assessing its value creation potential.

EXHIBIT 33.3 **Retention Rates Show Decreasing Customer Loyalty Over Time**

Retention rates across cohorts

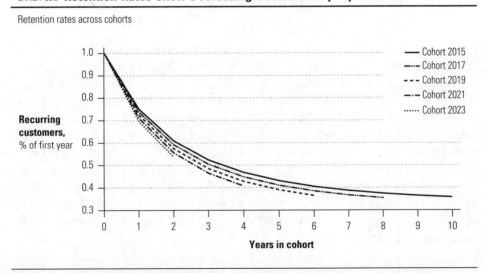

Years in cohort

---

[11] For further reading on customer retention and other customer base analyses, see, for example, P. S. Fader and B. G. S. Hardie, "Probability Models for Customer Base Analysis," *Journal of Interactive Marketing* 23, no. 1 (2009): 61–69; P. S. Fader and B. G. S. Hardie, "Customer-Base Valuation in a Contractual Setting: The Perils of Ignoring Heterogeneity," *Marketing Science* 29, no. 1 (2010): 85–93.

Cohort analysis can be extended to include not only the number of customers but also, for example, the average number of orders per customer and the average revenues per customer. Some companies report underlying data about cohort retention and transactions. One example is meal-delivery service platform Just Eat Takeaway (JET), which regularly publishes data on the number and size of customer orders by vintage year to demonstrate underlying improvements in customer retention and spending.

Customer-Based DCF Valuation

For many digital business models, the source of value creation lies with the business's customers: how much they spend, how long they remain customers, how costly it is to acquire new customers. When these businesses are still aggressively growing their customer base to reach sufficient scale, the associated marketing and sales costs can be overwhelming and drive earnings and free cash flow to negative numbers. Standard analyses of revenue growth, operating margin, and return on capital do not easily reveal how much value for shareholders the business is creating (if at all). A so-called customer-based or user-based analysis can provide the insights in a straightforward manner.

Building on the concepts of average customer revenue (ARPU), attrition rates, and customers cohorts, a customer-based DCF valuation derives the enterprise value (value of business operations) by separately valuing the company's existing customers, future new customers, and corporate overhead:

$$\text{Enterprise Value} = \text{Value of Existing Users} + \text{Value of New Users} \\ + \text{Value of Corporate Overhead}$$

Of course, the results should be fully consistent with standard enterprise DCF valuation, as we will discuss later in this section.

Consider a stylized illustration of digital start-up company GolDigCo in Exhibit 33.4. GolDigCo serves 2.5 million paying users, generating $43.8 million in total revenues in 2025. User loyalty is high, with an average retention rate of 90 percent per year. The company is growing its user base at 15 percent per year and expects to sustain that rate over the next ten years, after which growth declines to a constant 2 percent. Customer acquisition costs (CAC) are $45 of promotion and sales costs per new customer. To keep calculations straightforward, we abstract from taxation and assume retention (attrition) rates, CAC, and ARPU are constant over the years. The valuation is done in three steps:

1. *Valuation of existing users.* To project how many of the existing customers in 2025 survive in each future year, multiply the prior year's number of surviving customers with the retention rate. To obtain expected future revenues, multiply the number of surviving customers by ARPU. In this

EXHIBIT 33.4 **User-Based DCF Valuation of GolDigCo**

		2025	2026	2034	2035	Continuing value	
1. Value of existing users							
Cumulative retention		100%	90%	39%	35%		
Net revenues per user (ARPU), $		17.5	17.5	17.5	17.5		
Existing user base, beginning of year, millions		2.50	2.25	0.97	0.87		Expected user base × ARPU
Net revenues from user base, $ million		43.8	39.4	16.9	15.3	68.6 ◄—	at $17.5
Discount factor @ WACC of 10%		0.909	0.826	0.386	0.350	0.350	
PV(FCF), $ million		39.8	32.5	6.5	5.3	24.1	
Present value, $ million	**219** ◄						─ PV per user = PV/number of users = 219/2.5
2. Value of new users							= 87.5
Total users, beginning of year, millions		2.5	2.9	8.8	10.1		
Users lost @ 10%, millions		(0.3)	(0.3)	(0.9)	(1.0)		
Users added, millions		0.6	0.7	2.2	1.2		Number of users
Total users, end of year, millions		2.9	3.3	10.1	10.3		added ×
							NPV/user =
NPV of users added, $ million		26.6	30.5	93.4	51.6	657.7 ◄—	number added ×
PV(NPV of users added), $ million		24.1	25.2	36.0	18.1	230.5	(PV/user −
Present value, $ million	**545.9**						CAC/user)
3. Value of corporate overhead							Growing at
Overhead cash flow, $ million		(21.3)	(21.7)	(25.4)	(25.9)	(330.3) ◄—	2.0% per year
PV(overhead cash flow), $ million		(19.3)	(17.9)	(9.8)	(9.1)	(115.8)	
Present value, $ million	**(265.6)**						
Enterprise value, $ million	**499.1**						
Key ratios and indicators							
Attrition, %		10.0%	10.0%	10.0%	10.0%		Step-down from
Total user growth, %		15.0%	15.0%	15.0%	2.0% ◄		15.0% to 2.0%
Acquisition costs of users added, $ million		(28.1)	(32.3)	(98.9)	(54.6) ◄		Step-down in
Overhead cash flow growth, %		2.0%	2.0%	2.0%	2.0%		acquisition costs

example, revenues are equal to future cash flows, assuming variable costs per customer are zero. Using a perpetuity formula after ten years of forecasting, discount the cash flows from existing users at a WACC of 10 percent to obtain a present value of $219 million, equivalent to $87.5 per user (equivalent to five times ARPU and three times CAC). Note that the perpetuity growth rate for the existing users' cash flow is negative and equal to the attrition rate because ARPU growth is zero.

2. *Valuation of new users.* Building on the value per existing customer from the step 1 estimates, and given customer acquisition costs of $45 per customer, derive the net present value (NPV) of a new customer:

$$\text{NPV(New Customer)} = \text{Present Value/Existing Customer} - \text{CAC/Customer}$$
$$= \$87.5 - \$45.0$$
$$= \$42.5$$

Project the future total customer base to grow at 15 percent. Based on an attrition rate of 10 percent, project the number of customers lost in each year. Then find the total number of customers added each year, which will include some lost to attrition. The number of new customers added equals the total customer growth plus the number of customers lost (15 percent growth plus 10 percent attrition equals 25 percent customer additions).

Multiply the number of customers added in each year by the NPV per new customer to obtain the annual NPV generated by customer additions (note that this is not cash flow but value added). Discount the annual NPVs at the WACC, using a perpetuity growth equal to GolDigCo's long-term growth rate of 2 percent. The present value of new users equals $595 million, more than 2.5 times the value of the existing user base.

3. *Valuation of corporate overhead.* The first two steps did not include any corporate overhead costs and investments. These could include, for example, brand marketing, research and development, administrative costs, and investments. For GolDigCo, corporate overhead only consists of investments in server capacity and equipment, office space, and some working capital. Total overhead spend amounts to $21.3 million in 2025. GolDigCo believes it can benefit from future scale efficiencies and projects growth of all overhead spend at 2 percent. Discounting the future overhead cash flows at the WACC results in a present value of corporate overhead of −$266 million.

The enterprise value of GolDigCo equals the sum of the value of existing users, new users, and corporate overhead that we estimated in the three steps:

$$\$499 \text{ million} = \$219 \text{ million} + \$546 \text{ million} - \$266 \text{ million}$$

This user-based DCF valuation is quite stylized, but it offers some interesting insights. First, it shows how critical customer growth is: more than 100 percent of the enterprise value is driven by customers that GolDigCo still needs to acquire and keep on serving. Second, it shows that the current customer base does not even cover the cost of running the corporate entity, even at 90 percent retention rates. Third, the value per new user emphasizes the importance of controlling customer acquisition costs: a 10 percent permanent increase in acquisition costs would imply a decline of around 10 percent in the value of new users and in enterprise value.

The user-based approach does not include projections of enterprise-wide cash flows, operating margins, and returns on capital for GolDigCo. That makes it difficult to assess or benchmark its current and projected performance: Are the implied margins and returns on capital reasonable when compared with mature sector peers for GolDigCo, taking into account the attractiveness and

EXHIBIT 33.5 **Enterprise DCF Valuation of GolDigCo**

	2025	2026	2034	2035	Continuing value	
Operating income, $ million						Total users ×
Net revenues	43.8	50.3	153.9	177.0 ←		ARPU @ $17.5
Customer acquisition cost (CAC)	(28.1)	(32.3)	(98.9)	(54.6) ←		Step-down
Depreciation	(8.5)	(9.8)	(17.6)	(18.4)		in 2035
Overhead costs	0.0	0.0	0.0	0.0		
NOPAT	**7.1**	**8.2**	**37.4**	**104.0**	**105.7**	
Operating invested capital, $ million						At constant
Invested capital, beginning of year	85.0	97.8	176.0	183.8		percentage of
Depreciation	(8.5)	(9.8)	(17.6)	(18.4) ←		capital
Add: Capital expenditures	21.3	21.7	25.4	25.9 ←		Overhead
Invested capital, end of year	**97.8**	**109.7**	**183.8**	**191.3**		cash flow
Operating free cash flow, $ million						
NOPAT	7.1	8.2	37.4	104.0		
(Increase)/Decrease in Invested capital	(12.8)	(11.9)	(7.8)	(7.5)		
Free cash flow (FCF)	**(5.6)**	**(3.7)**	**29.6**	**96.5**		
Enterprise DCF valuation, $ million						
Free cash flow (FCF)	(5.6)	(3.7)	29.6	96.5	1,230.0	
Discount factor @ WACC = 10%	0.9	0.8	0.4	0.4	0.4	
PV(FCF)	(5.1)	(3.1)	11.4	33.8	431.1	
Enterprise value	**499.1**					
Key ratios						Step-down
Net revenue growth, %		15.0%	15.0%	15.0%	2.0% ←	in 2036
CAC/revenues, %	64.3%	64.3%	64.3%	30.9% ←		Step-down in
EBITDA/revenues, %	35.7%	35.7%	35.7%	69.1%		acquisition costs
NOPAT/revenues, %	16.3%	16.3%	24.3%	58.8%		Improvement
Revenues/invested capital, beginning of year	0.51	0.51	0.87	0.96 ←		over time
ROIC, beginning of year	**8.4%**	**8.4%**	**21.2%**	**56.6%**	**55.3%** ←	Step-up in 2035 (growth decline)

competitiveness of its markets? We therefore recommend running a standard enterprise-based DCF valuation in parallel (see Exhibit 33.5).

The enterprise valuation model shown translates all user-based projections into net operating profit after taxes (NOPAT), invested capital, and free cash flows. Obviously, with consistent assumptions, both valuation approaches lead to identical results. But combining the approaches avoids some common mistakes and adds to the insights into what drives value, even in this simplified example:

- The user-based projections show that when customer growth declines from 15 to 2 percent in 2035, NOPAT and ROIC almost triple because of the step-down in customer acquisition costs. The user-based model explicitly ties acquisition costs to customer additions (instead of total revenues, for example). When customer acquisition costs are high relative to customer revenues, this implies that changes in growth have a significant and immediate effect on operating earnings and cash flow. Note that revenue growth declines in 2036 rather than 2035 as revenues in each year are driven by the customer base at the beginning of the year.

- The enterprise-based projections show that for constant growth in overhead spend, the company's capital turnover will almost double over the next ten years. As a result, ROIC increases from 8.4 percent in 2025 to 21.2 percent in 2034, even while the EBITDA margin remains constant.[12] The enterprise-based model provides better tracking of implicit assumptions on corporate investments (and overhead costs, although not included in this example) for overall value creation.

In this case, one could question whether these scale efficiencies in invested capital are justified. For example, one could test how much efficiency gains GolDigCo realized in the past or what capital turnover is realized by more mature and larger players (and similarly for corporate overhead). An enterprise-based valuation easily reveals how much value creation is implied by the constant 2 percent growth rate of corporate overhead. For example, just keeping the capital turnover constant at 2025 levels would lower the enterprise value of GolDigCo by one-third, to $328 million!

The GolDigCo example could be made more realistic by including customer cohorts, varying retention (attrition) rates over the cohorts and years, varying ARPU over the years from offering changes or price increases, and including variable costs and taxes.[13] Such refinements would add a great deal of complexity and would likely obscure the key message. User-based DCF can provide some relevant insights on sources of value creation, but it should be accompanied by enterprise-based DCF to generate a buttoned-up valuation result.

CLOSING THOUGHTS

Executives and investors alike often struggle to oversee the implications of technological advancements in digitization, robotization, and AI. Indeed, some companies that have built a business model on these digital technologies have seen valuations in the stock markets that seem to defy fundamental economics. Some of these companies have also experienced significant stock market declines.

---

[12] Note that the ROIC increase in 2035 is driven by the decline in customer acquisition costs as growth declines.

[13] Note that including some of these refinements would significantly increase the complexity of the valuation. For example, any increases in ARPU in future years should increase the value per new user in future years as well. Assuming varying attrition rates over customer lifetimes would mean the projected overall attrition rates depend on past growth rates and cannot be assumed constant.

Still, as new as these topics may seem, existing valuation principles can help with framing executive decisions on digital strategies and investments. Follow the same principles that apply to all investment decisions. That is, evaluate digital projects and strategies based on the cash flows they are expected to generate, making sure to factor in do-nothing or base case scenarios, as well as the overarching objectives of the digital project or strategy being proposed. Additional tools can support the valuation of early-stage digital businesses that are customer facing. To better understand the business's value creation over the short term, consider the analysis of growth and attrition, of customer cohorts and customer-based value. And always ensure that value creation over the long term aligns with reasonable enterprise-based projections.

34

Sustainability

Corporate sustainability—also called environmental, social, and governance (ESG)—refers to a company's practices in relation to issues including its effect on the environment, treatment of its employees, and impact on the local community. This chapter provides a systematic framework for taking these issues into account when valuing a company. Companies can also use the framework to identify threats and opportunities and inform their strategic actions.

Consistent with the rest of this book, companies should approach sustainability with a focus on long-term value creation (or the minimization of long-term value destruction) by maximizing long-term cash flows. This includes avoiding short-term superficial actions that don't create value but may create a perception that the company is committed to sustainability. Some companies, like those in the consumer packaged-goods or steel manufacturing industries, might identify opportunities to create value through sustainable actions—by, for instance, making products in a way that is more appealing to customers and requires fewer carbon emissions. We can think of these as offensive actions: the companies are working to get ahead of their peers and create additional value while addressing sustainability issues. Other companies, like those in extractive industries, will need to take defensive actions to avoid value destruction—focusing, for example, on lowering carbon emissions to meet changing customer requirements or regulations.

PITFALLS IN VALUING SUSTAINABILITY STRATEGY

The measurement of how sustainability issues affect a company's value must avoid several traps, which include improperly measuring the base case, incorrectly assessing the cost of sustainability upgrades, and approaching these issues with an overly optimistic or overly conservative outlook.

This chapter was coauthored by Robin Nuttall, Werner Rehm, and Claudia Rexhausen with contributions from Alex Harman.

Improperly Measuring the Baseline

In today's changing market and regulatory environment, one important question to consider when analyzing the value implications of any sustainability action is what to measure against. One straightforward answer is that any action should be considered in comparison to what would happen to cash flows if no action is taken.

A clear example can be found in the automotive industry. Sales of internal combustion engine cars are likely to decline as demand shifts to electric vehicles. Governments and companies alike are investing in infrastructure to make EVs more attractive to customers, and regulators have started to demand a transition to EV sales. Given these trends, it is very likely that without an EV portfolio, a car company will shrink radically over time. The proper baseline for assessing the impact of the shift to electric vehicles is not today's sales but what would happen to the company's sales without electric vehicles.

Incorrectly Assessing the Cost of Sustainability Upgrades

Technology has made it possible for companies to make sustainability investments that don't cost materially more in present-value terms than the status quo. Examples include reducing the amount of water usage, deploying LED lighting, and eliminating excess packaging. For example, Amazon started to ship some smaller products in the manufacturer's packaging instead of an additional box, which contributes to Amazon's sustainability goals without any additional cost.

Nevertheless, it would be a mistake to assume that all sustainability investments will be so painless. To reach net-zero carbon emissions by 2050 will require about $275 trillion in cumulative spending—approximately 7.5 percent of global GDP every year.[1] However, to arrive at a meaningful understanding of the investments required of any one company, it is necessary to look deeper than the up-front cost of upgrades. For example, achieving net zero by 2050 will require automakers to make significant investments in battery manufacturing for EVs, but those companies will also be able to forgo capital expenditures that otherwise would have gone toward developing the next generation of automated manufacturing for internal combustion engines. When analyzing the impact of sustainability issues, it is crucial to avoid any flawed assumptions that could lead to an incorrect assessment of the cost of necessary upgrades.

Being Overly Optimistic

Another common misjudgment companies make is to optimistically assume that new, sustainability-oriented products will achieve straight-line growth. While costs related to sustainability are rising and likely to

---

[1] "The Economic Transformation: What Would Change in the Net-Zero Transition," McKinsey, January 25, 2022, www.mckinsey.com.

continue rising (as a result of regulatory penalties, litigation judgments, reputational risks, or other factors), it is not obvious whether customers will pay a corresponding premium for goods that are produced with lower carbon emissions. Therefore, companies must develop insights into their customer base. What are customers willing to pay more for? How many of them are willing to pay more? And to what extent do customers' actual spending habits contradict their professed commitments to sustainability?

Another type of overoptimism is forgetting about how the competition will react to any sustainability-oriented moves. When new businesses develop innovative sustainability strategies, competition often erodes all or a part of their first-mover advantage. Many products become commoditized, even if they are, for a time, protected by patents or other intellectual-property rights. The first environmentally friendly laundry detergents, for example, were sold at a significant premium, but the high price points could not be sustained indefinitely. Today, green detergents compete with traditional ones that use essentially the same ingredients. The same pattern is playing out with the high-end electric vehicles of recent years: the electric-car maker Tesla has been forced by market dynamics to lower the prices on its vehicles.

Being Overly Conservative

While overoptimism is an important concern, executives must also avoid being too conservative in their estimation of the opportunities posed by sustainability investments. In fact, over a recent five-year period, consumer products marketed as "sustainable" averaged 28 percent cumulative growth, versus 20 percent for products without such positioning.[2]

Green price premiums can vary enormously. In industrial products, for instance, the difference ranges from less than 1 percent for ferronickel to 300 percent for sustainable aviation fuel, though this will likely change over time. On the consumer side, premiums for beverages and packaged products range from 0 to 20 percent, while fresh meat and dairy can command a premium of up to 30 percent.[3] To take another example, demand for green steel currently far outstrips supply and is forecast to continue doing so for at least a decade. New opportunities will emerge across industries (as they always have before), and companies will compete to capture more of the value.

[2] J. Bar Am, V. Doshi, A. Malik, et al., "Consumers Care about Sustainability—and Back It Up with Their Wallets," McKinsey, February 6, 2023, www.mckinsey.com.
[3] V. Doshi and S. Noble, "Consumers Are in Fact Buying Sustainable Goods: Highlights from New Research," McKinsey, May 18, 2023, www.mckinsey.com.

Assuming Sustainability Reduces the Cost of Capital

Despite a lot of hype in the media, there is simply no conclusive evidence that sustainability efforts reduce the cost of capital by an amount meaningful for strategic decisions. Some studies claim that green financing might result in a somewhat lower cost of debt. For example, in an April 2024 report, J.P. Morgan suggested that green bonds might enjoy a yield advantage of two to six basis points.[4] However, this advantage would not affect the weighted average cost of capital (WACC) of an industrial corporation. Even at the extreme of a 20-basis-point advantage for cost of debt, a 20 percent tax rate, and 30 percent debt in the capital structure, this would affect a typical corporate WACC by less than ten basis points—well within the margin of error of any WACC estimate. Assuming a lower cost of capital can lead to value-destroying strategic decisions.

Another issue to consider is access to capital. Don't assume that having a lot of capital available to invest carries an advantage. Most large corporations fund their investments with a combination of retained cash flow, borrowing, and (rarely) raising new equity. Also, large amounts of capital are flowing into sustainability projects to finance the energy transition. In contrast, access to capital for large fossil fuel projects might be difficult in the future, as might insuring projects with a large carbon footprint. This might force some companies to reconsider their strategic plans if they heavily depend on such a project.

In some businesses, of course, access to capital could matter. Most notably, if you finance a solar farm project with 80 percent of debt, you will see different financing cost than for a fossil fuel power plant. However, these are extreme cases. For a typical corporation, do not focus your time on this. Strategic and operational decisions have a far greater impact.

A SYSTEMATIC FRAMEWORK TO ASSESS VALUE FROM SUSTAINABILITY

To assess the impact of corporate sustainability on value, you can apply the framework shown in Exhibit 34.1, which structures the value impact into three areas: business as usual, defensive actions, and offensive actions. Business as usual starts with the momentum value of the company and subtracts the negative impact of doing nothing. That creates a base case against which a company can take defensive and offensive moves. Playing defense means guarding against the risks that can arise from continuing with business as usual, recognizing that some companies may not be able to fully mitigate

---

[4] V. Juvyns, "Green Bonds: Is Doing Good Compatible with Doing Well in Fixed Income?" J.P. Morgan Asset Management, February 22, 2024, am.jpmorgan.com.

EXHIBIT 34.1 **Framework for Analyzing Value Impact of Sustainability Levers**

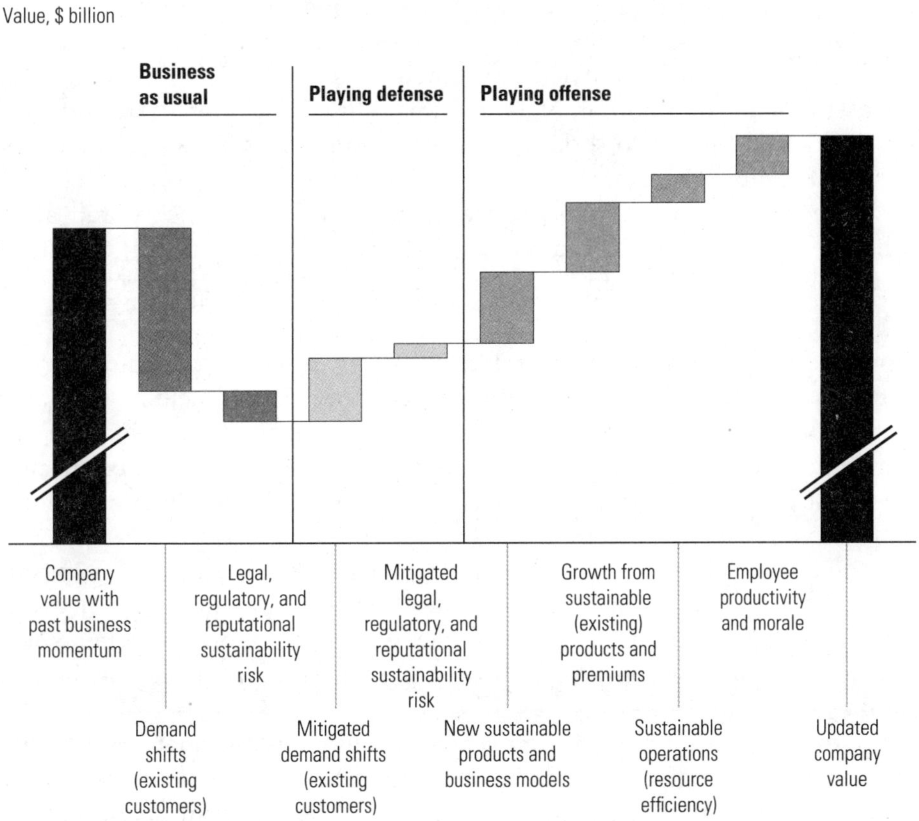

Value, $ billion

these losses. Playing offense means creating value by achieving a true competitive advantage through sustainability—for example, by becoming an industry leader in sustainability efforts or creating new and distinctive sustainable products.

Separating offense and defense can help you ensure you've thought through all the potential value creation levers. In practice, some actions may be both defensive and offensive. Don't get hung up on the classification of individual levers.

Business as Usual

The business-as-usual value of a company is its value from past momentum minus the impact of sustainability risks and costs—particularly the potential for demand decline and the costs of dealing with legal, regulatory, and reputational risk.

To calculate the business-as-usual value, you project, based on past momentum, how the company's value would grow if sustainability were not a factor and its historical performance levels were to hold steady. It is not worth spending much time on this estimate, since it serves only as an anchor point, not a real value or aspiration. Still, the business-as-usual value serves as a forecast against which all future impacts are estimated, so make sure you understand the assumptions built into it. Note that this estimate is different from the current market value, which should already have investors' views on the impact of sustainability priced in.

Once you have created this projection, the next step is to incorporate all the different sustainability-related factors that may affect its value in the future, including demand shifts and legal, regulatory, and reputational risk.

Demand Shifts   A number of factors can drive down the demand for products that don't meet sustainability expectations. These include regulatory changes, changes in customer behavior, low switching costs, and an increasing number of green alternatives. While the overall market might still be strong, if a company's products are not aligned with these shifts, the company will lose a portion of its market share.

The consumer sector is one example of a sector likely to be significantly affected by demand shifts, largely because of these same factors. However, it is not yet clear how significant the impact will be, since only a certain subset of consumers will be able and willing to pay a premium for truly sustainable products.

To estimate sustainability's impact on demand, it is essential to start with a solid understanding of customer behavior in the company's industry. This can be more complex than it appears at first glance. Take the chemical industry, for example. In the past, this industry sold clearly defined molecules at a market price to anybody who would pay this price, and it sold them literally by the boatload. Today, companies are obliged to provide at least three variations of their product: one with low carbon impact, another with medium carbon impact, and the standard product. The molecules have not changed, but customer demand has. Some customers do not care about the carbon content of the chemical products they buy, but others do.

Companies in many other industries face the same customer segments and must do their best to understand them while anticipating how the demand for their products will shift in the future. In analyzing these potential shifts, remember to measure against the baseline of what would happen if the company were to simply continue with business as usual. It may be useful to pose some of the following questions:

- How are the company's product volume and revenue likely to be affected by competing products that are more sustainable? In other words, how big will the market for the company's current products be in 10 or 20 years without change? Consider that some industries and products will be more insulated from these shifts than others will. For example, it is unlikely that enough sustainable airline fuel will be produced in the next decade to support the expected growth in transatlantic and transpacific flights, so "traditional" fuel will need to play a role. Therefore, such fuel is unlikely to be competed out of existence.

- How much could demand shift to replacement products? For example, in the United States, per capita consumption is declining for products such as beef and beer, which are being replaced with other meats, meat alternatives, and other beverages.

- Will regulatory actions change demand directly? One example is the lighting sector, which was obliged by new efficiency standards that took effect in 2023 to discontinue sales of most incandescent light bulbs. The sector has moved to selling LED bulbs almost exclusively. Another example is the automotive sector, which has seen significant shifts in demand as some countries have passed laws requiring that 100 percent of new cars be EVs within a decade.

By analyzing these effects, you should be able to estimate a long-term forecast of revenue, profit, and cash flow for the company's products. Do not forget to account for operational adjustments to changing circumstances. For example, if a product's volume declines by 50 percent, the company would likely close some production sites and get rid of fixed costs. While these estimates will be, by their nature, highly uncertain (and should be done in ranges), try to show a realistic picture of how shrinking demand will affect the company's economics.

Legal, Regulatory, and Reputational Risk   Apart from contending with potential declines in customer demand, companies that opt to stick with business as usual will also face rising legal, regulatory, and reputational risks.

The most obvious regulatory impact comes from carbon taxes. These taxes, along with emission trading schemes (ETS), have grown so much in recent years that, as of 2024, they cover 24 percent of global greenhouse gas (GHG) emissions worldwide.[5] As a result of these policies, heavy GHG emitters like oil, gas, and chemical companies, as well as those in the construction, electricity, and transportation industries, are likely to see significant cash flow deterioration in the years ahead. Regulatory changes may affect customer demand in certain situations—if, for example, companies might try to pass the cost of carbon taxes on to their customers in the form of higher prices. These effects can be complex, and their consequences difficult to predict. For

---

[5] State and Trends of Carbon Pricing Dashboard, World Bank, carbonpricingdashboard.worldbank.org, accessed August 12, 2024.

example, a round-trip business class flight from New York to Delhi in the fall of 2024 cost around $11,000 and emitted about six tons of carbon.[6] A carbon tax of $100 per ton would increase the price for this ticket by about 5 percent. Given that this is a luxury product, a carbon tax might be easily passed on to customers. But for budget flights, the cost cannot be passed on as easily. The impact of such a tax on an economy ticket from Newark to Chicago would be a price increase of between 10 and 25 percent, which might prompt budget-conscious travelers to reconsider the trip altogether. Consider also that not all companies within an industry will be affected equally by carbon taxes. For example, an early-moving steel purchaser might gain an advantage by contracting for low-carbon steel at lower prices than would be possible for a later mover.

Beyond carbon taxes, regulations might have direct impact on demand for your product. For example, heavily regulated industries like banking and insurance might see pressure from regulators to stop selling certain products or to change their business practices in other ways—by, for example, no longer providing financing for new refineries.

Another significant risk of continuing with business as usual is the risk posed to a company's reputation. When some oil and gas players have suffered major accidents affecting both employee and environmental safety, the damage to the companies' reputation has hurt both the business and the share price. Companies that fail to act on issues such as discrimination and labor practices also may face reputational risks. These risks are compounded by the need to attract and retain highly educated employees, who are likely to be sensitive to a company's reputation.[7]

Lastly, reporting requirements will add costs to a business in the form of information technology investments, investor relations functions, and top management time.

Assessing how legal, regulatory, and reputational issues will affect cash flows can be tricky. Estimating the impact of carbon taxes is one thing, but weighing effects of other issues—such as employee and labor relations, as well as customer pressure—can be unpredictable and involve complexities that are difficult to account for.

To estimate cash flows, we recommend a scenario approach: Which regulatory interventions could affect the business? What are the different scenarios that could affect *how much* they affect the business, and what is the respective likelihood of each scenario? Probabilities are difficult to estimate. In some industries, you could use statistics from past instances (e.g., airline workforce strikes). In others, you may be obliged to guess or simply assume a downside scenario.

---

[6] According to information provided by the United Airlines app in October 2024 for a January 2025 flight.
[7] See "ESG Not Making Waves with American Public," Gallup, May 22, 2023, news.gallup.com.

Playing Defense

Playing defense is figuring out how to mitigate the demand shifts and regulatory risks described for business as usual.

Mitigating Demand Shifts   In many ways, the demand shifts occurring as we shift to a low-carbon world are not as extreme as the shifts when, for example, cars replaced the horse and buggy. Most products are not being entirely replaced, but simply reimagined. The change is more akin to the shift from desktop PCs to laptops in the early 2000s, which required a significant rethinking of product lines by the manufacturers but no radically new invention.

For many companies, a first line of defense is adapting their current product line to customer or regulatory demand while minimizing the development effort. For example, a U.S. supplier to pharmaceutical labs quickly identified that the company's largest sources of carbon emissions were the plastic tubes and bags they produced, as well as the sheet metal they used for equipment enclosure. The company worked with suppliers to identify a way to create and transition to lower-carbon tubes and bags, setting a clear timeline and incremental benchmarks. Their customers were happy to pay a marginally higher price for the new lower-carbon products. Similarly, based on feedback from customers, shoe manufacturer Allbirds is using shoelaces made from recycled plastic and outsoles made from a sugarcane-based material. Food companies are responding to their customers' changing preferences by using more sustainable ingredients.[8] Some chocolate manufacturers, for example, have proactively mitigated against consumer concerns about environmental harm from palm oil production by shifting to sustainable palm oil, and some are shifting to more sustainable cocoa. In contrast, other companies will seek to mitigate demand shifts by doubling down on affordability, even if it means becoming more carbon intensive, in order to serve customers who are more price conscious than sustainability conscious.

Many other companies take different actions to address sustainability risks. Chemical player LyondellBasell, for example, is fundamentally exposed to carbon on the product side and includes climate-related risks and opportunities in its enterprise risk management (ERM) program, including measuring and mitigating more than 30 prioritized CO_2 risks. Pharma company Novartis was heavily hit by compulsory licensing, and in response, it has pursued an access-to-medicine strategy focused on risk mitigation, combined with increasing impact on society and providing self-sustaining ROI. The strategy includes new business models and pricing measures, parallel brands for low- and middle-income countries, as well as donations. For example, its

---

[8] See, e.g., Bar Am et al., "Consumers Care about Sustainability"; K. Heiny and D. Schneider, *It Takes Two*, Zalando, April 19, 2021, corporate.zalando.com; and "What Do Consumers Really Think about Sustainable Home Appliances?" BSH Home Appliances, February 17, 2022, stories.bsh-group.com.

Novartis Access program offers 15 drugs priced at $1 per treatment per month to low-income households. In 2020, it launched new access targets, stringently embedded their reporting, and issued a sustainability bond linked to those targets.

Regardless of what strategy companies choose for mitigating demand shifts, properly understanding their value will require a detailed analysis that estimates the net present value (NPV) of mitigation actions against the baseline of business as usual. For example, as in the baseline scenario, it may seem that a company would be obliged to close one of its factories due to lower demand for current products, but in fact, it might make more sense *not* to close the plant and instead to refurbish it, which requires a lower level of investment than a new, greenfield plant.

Mitigating Legal, Regulatory, and Reputational Sustainability Risk   As discussed with regard to business as usual, the most common regulatory risk is the threat of carbon taxes. All companies, but especially those that emit large amounts of carbon, need to carefully monitor regulatory developments and continuously evaluate their strategic options for mitigating in the various possible regulatory scenarios. These options could include, for example, buying emission certificate forwards, upgrading technological equipment, and even exiting specific product lines.

Of course, there are legal, regulatory, and reputational risks beyond those posed by GHG emissions. These include everything from plastic taxes and restrictions on single-use plastic bags or virgin materials to data privacy and human rights issues. Health player CVS, for its part, faced criticism from key stakeholders over its sales of tobacco products. In response, the CEO began a process of strategic repositioning that eventually led the company to articulate that part of its purpose is "to help people on their path to better health." In keeping with this purpose, CVS exited the tobacco market and began an initiative to combat youth smoking.

In the pharma industry, companies have faced fines over issues such as safety violations, government contracting offenses, and unapproved promotion of products. Over a recent ten-year period, these fines eroded pharma companies' EBITDA by an average of 0.75 percent. In the years to come, these companies could face additional concerns on issues such as data privacy, animal rights (insofar as animals are used in product testing), and waste from manufacturing and packaging. Pharmaceutical companies are mitigating these risks in multiple ways. Pfizer, for example, uses only approved animal vendors, which are contractually bound to certain standards and are regularly audited by the company for appropriate animal welfare and care.

It can be difficult to assess how much of an effect mitigating these risks will have on the valuation of a company. While the likelihood that any of them will cause substantial harm is low, the potential damages still need to be accounted for. Because it is often impossible to predict the likelihood or timing of a damaging event, we suggest estimating these factors as well as the potential repercussions of the financial and reputational damage. Potential countermeasures also should be evaluated, depending on the value at stake and taking into account the company's risk-bearing ability.

In some cases, a good sustainability record is merely a prerequisite for participating in a given business. For example, governments that grant access to mining companies to develop deposits of minerals typically scrutinize a company's record on environmental issues, as well as how the company supports the local community and its workers.

Playing Offense

Playing offense means finding new revenue sources or cost reduction opportunities that promote sustainability and provide a competitive advantage at the same time. Every market shift creates opportunity for new products and services. Compare the transcontinental business class seats offered by airlines today with the products available in the late 1990s: the actual seat and the service shifted as a result of competition for high-paying customers. Similarly, many companies today are creating new and reimagined products as they compete for customers who are willing to pay a premium for sustainable products.

Revenue Growth from New Sustainable Products and Business Models   Many companies will find opportunities to grow revenues by creating entirely new products that cater to sustainability-conscious customers. The retailer H&M, for example, launched an initiative to sell secondhand clothes and accessories at its flagship store in London. ASOS, a British-based fashion and cosmetics company, has similarly embarked on building a vintage (used) clothing business. As we mentioned earlier, sustainable consumer products have grown much faster than non-sustainable products. In some cases, companies have been able to bring new sustainable products to market relatively quickly, but in other cases, these products can take a long time to roll out. Developing a brand-new line of electric vehicles, for example, would obviously involve a long and intensive R&D process. Another example would be the long period of time required to build a new power plant or a solar farm.

Some examples of new sustainable products in the industrial and technology sectors include mechanical and electrical gear for wind turbines, electronic equipment for distributed grid operations, and software for carbon accounting. American food producer Cargill is betting on the trend away from animal protein and has invested in increasing the supply of peas as an alternative source of protein, as well as in several companies that develop cell-cultured meat.

New products and offerings can contribute to sustainability goals in other ways, as well. Consider drug manufacturer Civica's efforts to bring competition to generic drugs that are frequently in short supply: Civica partners with health care organizations for volume and other manufacturers for fulfillment. Many innovative fintech companies are bringing banking solutions to world populations that lack access to even the simplest financial tools. All these are new businesses and services that both promote sustainability and create new opportunities for growth.

Growth in Sustainable Products and Premiums for Existing Products In addition to new businesses, the demand for sustainable products can help companies in historically commoditized industries achieve product differentiation, as with the rise of "green" chemicals. The chemical producer BASF, for example, contributed CO_2 capture technology to Japan's first demonstration of blue hydrogen and ammonia production from domestically produced natural gas.[9] Providing green materials can yield price premiums, which reflect the excess demand for such materials beyond the (often nascent) supply levels at present. Though they vary across materials and time frames, these premiums can be substantial, ranging from 2 to 4 percent in aluminum and 8 to 25 percent in steel to more than 50 percent for specific recycled plastics and biopolymers.

Cost Reductions from Sustainable Operations (Resource Efficiency) Many companies are good at identifying opportunities to reduce costs in general but miss valuable opportunities to do so while increasing efficiency and promoting sustainability. One reason could be that cost reduction is often seen as a "no investment" action. Most sustainability actions that lower cost, however, require upfront investment. For example, switching from high-energy-using lights to LEDs would be a tremendously effective investment for many companies, likely paying for itself in less than two years, yet in practice, a large number of companies have hesitated to do this because of the upfront cost.

Companies that fully embrace the cost reduction opportunities from sustainable operations can see impressive results. Consider retailer 7-Eleven, which implemented a global energy management system to monitor, control, and optimize energy use. Or take Google DeepMind, which implemented, among other measures, an AI recommendation system that made its data centers more energy efficient. Another example is the retailer Aldi South, which built a circular, greener packaging ecosystem with the aim of making sustainability affordable to customers. In so doing, the company is securing greater access to more sustainable and recycled materials at a competitive price while also reducing plastic packaging by about 15 percent.

One tool that can help you assess these opportunities is a marginal abatement cost curve, a type of graph that plots the amount of carbon emissions

---

[9] "BASF Contributes CO_2 Capture Technology to Japan's First Demonstration of Blue Hydrogen and Ammonia Production from Domestically Produced Natural Gas," BASF, February 28, 2023, BASF.com.

EXHIBIT 34.2 **Marginal Abatement Cost Curve**

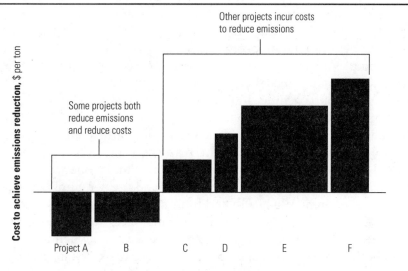

avoided (abated) on the horizontal axis and the cost of the abatement on the vertical axis (Exhibit 34.2). For most companies, the graph starts with the projects for which the cost is negative; the first tons of carbon abated tend to have a positive impact on cash flows. But over time, the cost climbs. From a graph such as this, you can derive the impact of a portfolio of initiatives addressing operating cost from a sustainability angle, put them in a new plan, and estimate the net present value.

Often, sustainability-oriented cost reduction initiatives overlap with the defensive actions described earlier, since they are frequently focused on increasing the sustainability footprint of existing products. Don't spend too much time debating which category an initiative belongs to, but do make sure you avoid double-counting.

Employee Productivity Uplift   Another way companies can play offense on sustainability is by purposefully investing in employees, which tends to increase productivity. This might mean, for example, building employees' leadership capabilities, fostering a sense of belonging at work, and providing opportunities for training and internal advancement.[10] Companies can see improvement from these actions both in direct measures of productivity, such as revenue per employee, and in indirect measures, like employee turnover and safety records. In many cases, these investments can take a long time to come to fruition, and it can be difficult to directly link them to productivity

[10] W. Henisz, "The Value of Corporate Purpose," *Harvard Business Review*, November 2, 2023, hbr.org.

increases. But in the long term, there is clear evidence that they can produce concrete results. For instance, research has shown that companies ranked among *Fortune* magazine's 100 Best Companies to Work For have substantially outperformed their peers.[11]

Examples of companies investing in employees include Walmart's Live Better U program, which supports employees' educational aspirations through reduced tuition, coaching, and college credit. Walmart's hourly associates participating in the program leave the company at one-fourth the rate of nonparticipants, and they are twice as likely as nonparticipants to be promoted.[12] Pharmaceutical companies also are realizing some notable improvements in employee productivity. Among others, GlaxoSmithKline (GSK) and Novartis have reported higher employee retention and greater employee effectiveness as a result of employee health and training programs.

Some companies have seen increased employee productivity simply because of their broader sustainability strategy, not necessarily tied to investments in specifically employee-focused programs. One bank, for instance, committed to a sustainability mission defined by three pillars: support of local start-ups, financial learning initiatives, and tackling climate change. The bank set up tangible goals and interventions for each of the pillars and fully incorporated climate targets into executive remuneration. As a result, over 90 percent of employees said in a survey that they are proud of the bank's social contribution and find the purpose meaningful—attitudes that have been shown to improve productivity.

For valuation purposes, you need to estimate the potential impact of programs such as these. You could start by looking at the productivity numbers for industry peers that have already implemented employee well-being programs, using their example to estimate an upside for turnover, retention, and issues like sales productivity. The impact on cash flow is easily estimated based on assumptions, but these assumptions can be difficult to verify. Do not be surprised, finally, if this impact is less than the impact from growth. Many companies already have excellent productivity benchmarks.

COMPETITIVE ADVANTAGE STILL MATTERS

Many companies will be tempted to jump right in and immediately pursue the offensive actions for sustainable growth, but keep in mind that the competition will be stiff. Large companies and venture-capital-backed new companies will be weighing the same opportunities. Before investing in new areas, companies

---

[11] A. Edmans, *Grow the Pie: How Great Companies Deliver Both Purpose and Profit* (Cambridge University Press, 2020). The 100 Best Companies to Work For list is produced by the Great Place to Work Institute and, since 1998, has been published every year in *Fortune* magazine.
[12] "Live Better U: Walmart and Sam's Club Education Program," Walmart, updated August 17, 2023, corporate.walmart.com.

must make sure they have a competitive advantage that will allow them to earn an attractive return on capital.

For example, private equity, venture capital, pension funds, and sovereign-wealth funds are investing billions of dollars in renewable energy, alternative fuels, carbon capture, and other new technological solutions aimed at fighting climate change. It is not a foregone conclusion that a company from a traditional industry will have the expertise, incentives, employee capabilities, and organizational agility to beat the competition in these fields. If companies find they cannot reinvest their excess cash flows to achieve a competitive advantage through sustainability, they can release that unused cash back to their investors. In that way, the money can flow to those who do have a competitive advantage in new value-creating low-carbon solutions.

For example, governments and other entities have encouraged large oil and gas companies to invest in renewable energy, particularly wind and solar. But in a market like the United States, these companies typically don't have any competitive advantage when it comes to wind and solar. They tend to have different skill sets and capital structures than would be required to succeed against specialized firms. If there were a shortage of capital to invest in solar and wind, there would be a stronger case in favor of oil and gas companies making the investments. But there is no shortage. In fact, there is likely a surplus of capital chasing these investments. That said, if oil and gas companies simply returned the excess cash to shareholders to be recycled, that cash would ultimately make its way to companies that are better positioned to compete in wind and solar.

The point is not that oil and gas companies should never invest in renewables. Rather, they—like all companies—should focus on where they might have a competitive advantage, such as in carbon capture or hydrogen. Nor should companies necessarily avoid investing in areas that benefit the climate simply because those areas are outside of their core focus. For example, HP has made an attractive business of recycling and refurbishing used equipment: they make a nice profit, and buyers of the refurbished equipment get a substantial discount. Likewise, Occidental Petroleum has made substantial investments in carbon capture and as of 2023 had acquired access to over 300,000 acres of pore space, with the intention of developing five sequestration hubs. In May 2023, the company began the construction of Stratos, the world's largest direct air capture plant. These projects, along with leading investments in carbon capture technology, have positioned Occidental for leadership in the area.[27] Finally, Neste, the Finnish oil and gas company, has been a pioneer in developing technology to make sustainable aviation fuel and diesel fuel using renewable raw materials, such as animal fat waste, used cooking oil, and various wastes and residues from vegetable oil processing. These fuels can reduce greenhouse gas emissions by up to 80 percent for aviation fuels and 75 to 95 percent for renewable diesel over the life cycle of the fuel.

SUSTAINABILITY RATINGS

Notably absent from the framework in Exhibit 34.1 are sustainability ratings (also known as ESG ratings), a commonly used measure of companies' sustainability commitments. We have chosen not to focus on these for a simple reason: the purpose of this chapter is to explore how sustainability figures in valuation. For measuring value, cash flows are what matter—not ratings, which are based on a rating firm's assessment. Investors don't value ratings points.

In recent years, these ratings have proliferated, and many data providers have taken advantage of the business opportunity to sell their ratings. However, in contrast to debt ratings, providers tend to assess the business in different ways, using different criteria, weighing the various factors differently, and measuring outcomes differently. It is therefore not uncommon for different ratings providers to have radically different assessments of the same company, and this creates confusion among managers and investors alike.

ESG ratings, like financial ratings, are an outcome of behavior and position, so they are an indirect measure of the company's future value potential. It is easy to imagine a company with extremely high ESG ratings but low cash flow, given that the cash is being invested in sustainability projects. The ratings don't tell us whether these investments will pay off later in the form of a new value-creating business. Conversely, late movers who have a bad rating today might find a faster, cheaper way to achieve the same sustainability results at some later time.

As of this writing, there is no consensus on how ratings influence shareholder returns.[13] Our own research suggests that a good ESG rating cannot rescue a company from bad strategy or performance.[14] Regardless of the rating, companies that have lower return on capital or growth than their peers have in recent years generally underperformed on total shareholder returns (TSR). In contrast, companies with not only the highest ESG ratings but also the highest revenue growth and return on capital outperformed their peers by approximately 2 percent in TSR. These companies were growing faster than even the best of their peers, indicating there is an upside for companies that grow sustainable businesses that result in good cash flows.

A good sustainability assessment can help companies identify where they need to improve. Some frameworks (for example, SbTi) have started to stand

[13] F. Berg, A. W. Lo, R. Rigobon, M. Singh, and R. Zhang, "Quantifying the Returns of ESG Investing: An Empirical Analysis with Six ESG Metrics," MIT Sloan Research Paper no. 6930–23, last revised June 16, 2023, papers.ssrn.com; S. Bhagat, "An Inconvenient Truth about ESG Investing," *Harvard Business Review*, March 31, 2022, hbr.org.

[14] R. Doherty, C. Kampel, A. Koivuniemi, et al., "The Triple Play: Growth, Profit, and Sustainability," McKinsey, August 9, 2023, www.mckinsey.com.

out and might become a standard.[15] However, for corporate valuation, you should focus on the actions, strategy, and cash flow impact. Ratings should be understood as an outcome, not an input.

SUMMARY

Many companies today face challenges on the topic of sustainability, which can affect their cash flows both negatively (from declining demand for current products and regulatory risk) and positively (for companies that can create additional value while mitigating these risks). This is true not just of sustainability but of any major shift in regulatory attention and consumer demand. Sustainability is the most recent of these shifts, but it neither is the first nor is likely to be the last. Consequently, the methodology for analyzing this market shift should resemble those used to analyze past shifts.

Understanding the value impact of sustainability requires a thorough understanding of customer demand and regulatory changes. First, establish a baseline, "business as usual" scenario that reflects what would happen if the company in question were to stick with its present strategy, incurring regulatory penalties and standing by as the demand for its current products erodes. This will be the value against which all possible sustainability investments should be measured. Once you have done this, determine what will be needed to successfully mitigate the risks and to reverse any decrease in customer demand, judging whether defensive or offensive actions are necessary.

In all of this, the basics of valuation described in this book's earlier chapters still apply: you estimate the cash flow impact of the risks and the opportunities rigorously by assessing investments, growth opportunities, margins, and cash flow.

---

[15] The SBTi (Science Based Target Initiative) defines and promotes best practice in science-based target setting of environmental initiatives. Offering a range of target-setting resources and guidance, the SBTi independently assesses and approves companies' targets in line with its strict criteria. As of 2024, over 5,000 companies are participating. SBTi home page, sciencebasedtargets.org.

35

Capital Structure, Dividends, and Share Repurchases

Shaping a modern corporation's financial profile might appear to be an infinitely complex task. But in practice, it typically boils down to just three decisions: how much to invest, how much debt to carry, and how much cash to return to shareholders. In this book, we devote most of our attention to exploring the first of these topics, but the others are also important. It's not so much that making the right decisions about capital structure will create a great deal of value; it's that making the wrong calls can destroy tremendous amounts of it.

The primary objective of a company's decisions to structure its capital, pay dividends, and repurchase shares should be to ensure that the company has enough capital to pursue its strategic objectives and to weather any cash shortfalls along the way. If a company doesn't have enough capital, it will either pass up opportunities or, worse, fall into financial distress or even bankruptcy. When a company holds too much capital, the consequences are not as grave and the remedy is easy: it can always increase its cash distributions to shareholders.

This chapter explores managers' options for choosing an appropriate capital structure for their company and how they should develop a supporting policy for returning cash to shareholders or raising new capital. In the first two sections, we discuss some practical guidelines and a four-step approach to deciding on a company's capital structure, payout, and financing. The remainder of the chapter discusses key theoretical and empirical findings on capital structure and payout that form the basis for our guidelines and approach.

PRACTICAL GUIDELINES

Finance theory has much to say about capital structure and payout—for example, about the costs and benefits of leverage, the way markets react to shareholder payouts, and the ability of managers to time their buying back of shares.[1] But it does not tell us how to set an effective capital structure and payout policy for a given company. Building on insights from finance theory (explored later in this chapter), we offer the following practical guidelines to help executives make the right choices on capital structure and payout:

- *Decisions about capital structure, dividends, and share repurchases should be an integral part of overall cash deployment.* When deciding to deploy cash (for example, by using it for share repurchases), companies should consider all alternative uses of cash and set priorities for the uses according to their potential to create value, as laid out in Exhibit 35.1. The greatest opportunity to create value comes from investing cash in the business at returns above the cost of capital.[2] The returns are typically higher for organic growth, making it the first choice for deploying cash. One level below is using cash for growth by acquisitions, where returns on capital tend be somewhat lower because acquiring assets usually requires paying a premium.[3] Financing—that is, using (or raising) cash to adjust a company's capital structure—should assume a lower priority. This does not mean capital structure decisions are unimportant; rather, they are a necessary means of ensuring that sufficient funding is available to capture attractive investment opportunities and withstand cash shortfalls. At the bottom of the list of cash alternatives are payout decisions. These don't drive value directly but should aim to return cash to shareholders when a company has insufficient opportunities to reinvest at returns above the cost of capital.

- *For their capital structure, large companies should target investment-grade credit ratings between A+ and BBB– to maintain adequate flexibility for difficult times.* Most large exchange-listed companies worldwide have capital structures in this range of credit ratings. Lower ratings typically lead to a significant loss of flexibility, due to restrictive covenants built into loan agreements for sub-investment-grade companies. Higher credit ratings offer little or no additional benefits, as a company typically has enough flexibility to pursue investment opportunities once it reaches a solid investment-grade rating.

[1] For an overview of the literature, see M. Barclay and C. Smith, "The Capital Structure Puzzle: The Evidence Revisited," *Journal of Applied Corporate Finance* 17, no. 1 (2005): 8–17.
[2] Following the conservation of value principle in Chapter 4, this is the primary source of value creation for companies.
[3] See M. Goedhart and T. Koller, "The Value Premium of Organic Growth," *McKinsey on Finance*, no. 61 (2017): 14–15.

EXHIBIT 35.1 **Cash Deployment: Value Creation Hierarchy**

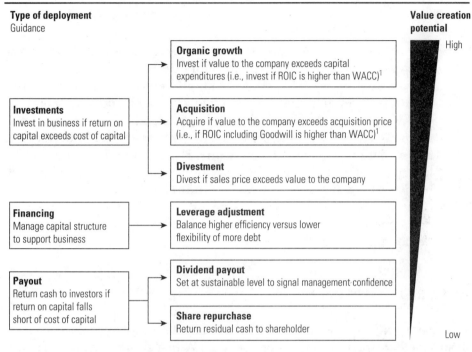

Type of deployment
Guidance

Value creation potential

High

Organic growth
Invest if value to the company exceeds capital expenditures (i.e., invest if ROIC is higher than WACC)[1]

Investments
Invest in business if return on capital exceeds cost of capital

Acquisition
Acquire if value to the company exceeds acquisition price (i.e., if ROIC including Goodwill is higher than WACC)[1]

Divestment
Divest if sales price exceeds value to the company

Financing
Manage capital structure to support business

Leverage adjustment
Balance higher efficiency versus lower flexibility of more debt

Payout
Return cash to investors if return on capital falls short of cost of capital

Dividend payout
Set at sustainable level to signal management confidence

Share repurchase
Return residual cash to shareholder

Low

[1] ROIC is return on invested capital; WACC is weighted average cost of capital.

- *Payout decisions should consider their short-term impact on stock prices.* Dividends and share repurchases are value neutral over the long term but can lead to earlier recognition of value creation in a company's share price. Although long-term value creation comes from business operations and investments that generate returns above the cost of capital, not from a company's payouts to shareholders, short-term price increases can result from increased payouts that signal management discipline in the use of capital and confidence in the company's outlook. In applying this guideline, keep in mind that such increases in share price reflect higher expectations of future value creation. If the company fails to meet these expectations, the price will drop again.

- *Dividends should be set at a level a company can sustain under plausible adverse conditions—for example, during the bottom of the earnings cycle.* Most shareholders expect that regular dividends (or dividend payout ratios) will be cut from customary levels only in cases of severe setbacks.[4] Investors almost always perceive the cutting of regular

---

[4] A small number of companies have a variable dividend policy that targets a fixed payout ratio (or range) of dividends relative to earnings.

dividends as a signal of significantly lower future value creation, so these cuts generally lead to sharp declines in share price and increases in share price volatility.

- *Share repurchases should be used to return excess cash over and above dividend levels to shareholders.* Investors do not consider share buy-backs to be the same long-term commitment as regular dividends. As a result, repurchases are a flexible way to pay out cash amounts that vary from year to year. Unlike dividends, share repurchases typically increase a company's earnings per share, but that does not mean share repurchases create value. Keep in mind that repurchasing shares, like paying regular dividends, is value neutral. In fact, both types of payouts could even indirectly destroy value if they come at the expense of attractive investments; that is why these decisions need to be part of planning a company's broader cash deployment.

A FOUR-STEP APPROACH

With these guidelines in mind, we recommend a sequential approach to establishing capital structure and payout policies. With a clearly defined corporate strategy in place, the approach itself consists of four stages:

1. Project and stress-test the operating cash flows.
2. Develop a capital structure target based on the company's risk profile and risk appetite.
3. Estimate the surplus or deficit cash flow to shareholders by combining the operating cash flow and the capital structure target.
4. Decide on the payout of cash flow surplus and financing of cash flow deficit, including tactical measures, such as share repurchases, dividend payouts, share issuances, and measures to adjust the company's debt to the specified target levels.

To illustrate the approach, we can apply it to a hypothetical company in international branded consumer products. In the past, the company, which we call MaxNV, has generated annual operating earnings before interest, taxes, depreciation, and amortization (EBITDA) of around $1 billion, with some fluctuations resulting from movements in raw-materials prices and currency rates. MaxNV has held little debt, but acquisitions have driven up its ratio of net debt to EBITDA from 1.5 in 2020 to 2.8 at the beginning of 2025 (calculated as net debt at beginning of year over expected EBITDA for the year, which for 2025 would equal $2.8 billion divided by $1.0 billion).

Step 1: Project and Stress-Test Operating Cash Flows

MaxNV's strategic plan under a base case scenario foresees annual EBITDA growth of 5 percent, from $1.0 billion in 2025 to $1.2 billion in 2029 (see Exhibit 35.2). Growth derives in part from planned bolt-on acquisitions of around $0.2 billion per year, with some revenue lost to minor divestments. In the base case, MaxNV generates around $3.0 billion in free cash flow from operations over the next five years.

We tested some of the most important business risks for MaxNV's key market and product segments by developing two downside scenarios. In a competitive-disruption scenario, new entrants with direct-to-customer sales will be more successful than anticipated. Beyond 2026, this will start to depress price and volume levels and require MaxNV to accelerate acquisitions and investments in its own direct-to-customer channels. Compared with the base case, annual EBITDA will be around $200 million lower and capital expenditures around $50 million higher by 2029. Including an additional $500 million spent on acquisitions, MaxNV will generate about $1.0 billion less in after-tax cash flow from operations than in the base case. The second downside scenario sees this competitive disruption aggravated by a major economic downturn, depressing revenues and earnings across the sector. EBITDA will now be $300 million lower in 2029 compared with the base case.

EXHIBIT 35.2 **MaxNV: Projections of Operating Cash Flows**

$ million		Projections					Cumulative
		2025	2026	2027	2028	2029	2025–2029
EBITDA[1]	Base	1,000	1,050	1,103	1,158	1,216	5,526
	Competitive-disruption impact	—	—	(100)	(200)	(200)	(500)
	Economic-downturn impact	—	(100)	(150)	(100)	(100)	(450)
Capital expenditures	Base	(100)	(105)	(110)	(116)	(122)	(553)
	Competitive-disruption impact	—	(50)	(50)	(50)	(50)	(200)
Acquisitions	Base	(200)	(200)	(200)	(200)	(200)	(1,000)
	Competitive-disruption impact	—	—	(500)	—	—	(500)
Divestments	Base	—	25	50	—	—	75
	Competitive-disruption impact	—	—	—	25	25	50
Operating taxes	Base	(188)	(197)	(207)	(217)	(228)	(1,036)
	Competitive-disruption impact	—	—	25	50	50	125
FCF[2] from operations	Base	513	573	636	625	666	3,012
	Competitive-disruption impact	—	(50)	(625)	(175)	(175)	(1,025)
	Economic-downturn impact	—	(150)	(775)	(275)	(275)	(1,475)

[1] Earnings before interest, taxes, depreciation, and amortization.
[2] Free cash flows.

For companies in industries where price and volume risks are greater, such as commodities, you might replace the use of scenarios with a more sophisticated approach: modeling future cash flows by using stochastic simulation techniques to estimate the probability of financial distress at the various debt levels.

Step 2: Develop a Capital Structure Target

Next, we set a target credit rating and estimated the corresponding coverage ratios to develop a capital structure target. Although MaxNV's operating performance is normally stable (as it is with most branded-consumer-goods players), we targeted the high end of a BBB credit rating because of the company's currency risk as an exporter. We translated the target credit rating to a target net-debt-to-EBITDA coverage ratio of 2.5 times.[5] This coverage ratio was applied in all scenarios.

Step 3: Estimate Surplus or Deficit

Based on the target coverage ratio and projections of operating cash flows, we estimated MaxNV's target capital structure and cash surpluses (or deficits) for each of the next five years. The detailed calculations are shown in Exhibit 35.3. For example, in the base case scenario, $1.0 billion of EBITDA in 2025 and a target coverage ratio of 2.5 times result in a target debt level of $2.5 billion for the end of the year. Starting with $2.8 billion of debt at the beginning of 2025, deducting $513 million of free cash flow from operations and adding $105 million of after-tax interest expenses leave MaxNV with surplus cash of $108 million that could be distributed to shareholders in 2025. With the same calculation through the remaining years of the forecast, the cumulative cash surplus for distribution amounts to around $2.7 billion over the five-year period. Exhibit 35.3 also shows the cumulative surplus for the competitive-disruption scenario ($1.2 billion) and the economic-downturn scenario ($552 million).

For both downside scenarios, a cash deficit occurs in some individual years. For these years, MaxNV could decide to simply exceed target debt levels and return to target levels later, as it generates a cumulative cash surplus over the next five years. Alternatively, it could build up excess debt capacity in prior years to ensure target debt levels are met in each year. Of course, if a cumulative deficit occurred for the entire planning horizon, MaxNV would need to consider issuing equity or find other financing opportunities, such as additional divestitures or cost savings.

---

[5] As discussed later in this chapter, empirical analysis shows that approximate credit ratings can be estimated well with three factors: industry, size, and interest or debt coverage.

EXHIBIT 35.3   **MaxNV: Estimates of Cash Surplus and Deficit**

$ million

	Projections					Cumulative
Base case scenario	2025	2026	2027	2028	2029	2025–2029
EBITDA[1]	1,000	1,050	1,103	1,158	1,216	5,526
Net debt, beginning of year	(2,800)	(2,500)	(2,625)	(2,756)	(2,894)	(2,800)
FCF[2] from operations	513	573	636	625	666	3,012
Interest, after-tax	(105)	(94)	(98)	(103)	(109)	(509)
Add: Target net debt, end of year @ 2.5x EBITDA[1]	2,500	2,625	2,756	2,894	3,039	3,039
Cash surplus paid out to equity (cash deficit funded with debt)	108	604	668	659	702	2,742
Target net debt, end of year	(2,500)	(2,625)	(2,756)	(2,894)	(3,039)	
Excess debt	—	—	—	—	—	
Net debt, end of year	(2,500)	(2,625)	(2,756)	(2,894)	(3,039)	
Competitive-disruption scenario						
EBITDA[1]	1,000	1,050	1,003	958	1,016	5,026
Net debt, beginning of year	(2,800)	(2,500)	(2,625)	(2,713)	(2,394)	(2,800)
FCF[2] from operations	513	523	11	450	491	1,987
Interest, after-tax	(105)	(94)	(98)	(102)	(90)	(489)
Add: Target net debt, end of year @ 2.5x EBITDA[1]	2,500	2,625	2,506	2,394	2,539	2,539
Cash surplus paid out to equity (cash deficit funded with debt)	108	554	(207)	29	546	1,237
Target net debt, end of year	(2,500)	(2,625)	(2,506)	(2,394)	(2,539)	
Excess debt	—	—	(207)	—	—	
Net debt, end of year	(2,500)	(2,625)	(2,713)	(2,394)	(2,539)	
Economic-downturn scenario						
EBITDA[1]	1,000	950	853	858	916	4,576
Net debt, beginning of year	(2,800)	(2,500)	(2,375)	(2,604)	(2,351)	(2,800)
FCF[2] from operations	513	423	(139)	350	391	1,537
Interest, after-tax	(105)	(94)	(89)	(98)	(88)	(474)
Add: Target net debt, end of year @ 2.5x EBITDA[1]	2,500	2,375	2,131	2,144	2,289	2,289
Cash surplus paid out to equity (cash deficit funded with debt)	108	204	(472)	(207)	240	552
Target net debt, end of year	(2,500)	(2,375)	(2,131)	(2,144)	(2,289)	
Excess debt	—	—	(472)	(207)	—	
Net debt, end of year	(2,500)	(2,375)	(2,604)	(2,351)	(2,289)	

[1] Earnings before interest, taxes, depreciation, and amortization.
[2] Free cash flows.

Step 4: Decide on a Surplus Payout and Deficit Financing

The final step is to decide what payout and financing over the ensuing years
will move the company to its target capital structure. Consider Exhibit 35.4,
which summarizes the cumulative cash flows associated with the four steps

EXHIBIT 35.4 **MaxNV: Deciding on Payout**

$ million

	Cumulative cash flows, 2025–2029				
	Base case	Competitive disruption		Economic downturn	
	Scenario	Disruption impact	Scenario	Downturn impact	Scenario
Step 1					
Project operational cash flows					
EBITDA[1]	5,526	(500)	5,026	(450)	4.576
Capital expenditures	(553)	(200)	(753)		(753)
Acquisitions	(1,000)	(500)	(1,500)		(1,500)
Divestments	75	50	125		125
Operating taxes	(1,036)	125	(911)		(911)
Free cash flow from operations	3,012	(1,025)	1,987	(450)	1,537
Step 2					
Develop capital structure target					
Net debt/EBITDA[1] target	2.5		2.5		2.5
Step 3					
Estimate surplus (deficit)					
Net debt, beginning of year 2025	(2,800)		(2,800)		(2,800)
Free cash flow from operations	3,012		1,987		1,537
Interest, after-tax	(509)		(489)		(474)
Add: Target net debt, end of year 2029 @ 2.5x EBITDA	3,039		2,539		2,289
Cash surplus paid-out to equity	2,742		1,237		552
Step 4					
Decide on payout (financing)					
Dividend payout	450		450		450
Share buybacks	2,292		787		102
Cash surplus paid out to equity	2,742		1,237		552
Dividend per year, average	90		90		90
Buyback per year, average	458		157		20

[1] Earnings before interest, taxes, depreciation, and amortization.

for each of the three scenarios. Over the next five years under all scenarios, MaxNV can easily return $450 million ($90 million per year) in the form of regular dividends. Taking an aggressive stance, MaxNV could even consider a dividend payout of about $1 billion ($200 million per year), although it would need to cut back in the case of a downturn scenario—and that would not be well received by investors. If the new dividend payout represents an increase from current levels, its announcement would send a strong signal to the stock market that MaxNV is confident about its business outlook and its ability to sustain this dividend level.

In each of the scenarios, any remaining cash could be returned to shareholders over the next several years through share repurchases or extraordinary dividends. The amount based on a conservative $450 million dividend payout would be almost $2.3 billion under the base case, about $800 million under the disruption scenario, and about $100 million under the downturn scenario. Like a dividend increase, share repurchases and extraordinary dividends signal confidence, but they have the advantage that investors won't see them as a commitment to additional payouts in future years. This gives MaxNV valuable flexibility to change the amount of cash paid out over the next years in accordance with business results and market developments. It might increase its share repurchases, for example, as management becomes more certain that the company will achieve the base case projection, or it could withhold most of the cash as long as it considers a downturn scenario more likely.

SETTING A TARGET CAPITAL STRUCTURE

Financing instruments vary widely, offering many options, from traditional common equity and straight debt to more exotic instruments, among them convertible preferred equity and convertible and commodity-linked debt. But the essential choice remains between straight debt and common equity. In this balancing act, tilting toward equity gives managers more flexibility to work through unexpected downturns or take advantage of unforeseen opportunities, such as acquisitions. Taking on more debt delivers higher efficiency from tax benefits and enhances management discipline over investment spending.

Empirical research shows that companies actively manage their capital structure around certain leverage boundaries.[6] That is to say, they make adjustments to regain their target capital structure after they have missed it for one or two years, rather than immediately after each change in leverage. Continual adjustment would be impractical and costly, due to share price volatility and transaction costs.[7]

Fundamental Debt/Equity Trade-Offs

For decades, academic researchers have sought to learn which debt-to-equity ratio represents the best trade-off between flexibility and efficiency while maximizing value for shareholders. Unfortunately, a clear model remains elusive.[8]

The most obvious benefit of debt over equity is a reduction in taxes. Interest charges for debt are typically tax deductible; payments to shareholders as dividends and share repurchases are not.[9] Reducing taxes by replacing

---

[6] P. Marsh, "The Choice between Equity and Debt: An Empirical Study," *Journal of Finance* 37, no. 1 (1982): 121–144.

[7] See, for example, M. Leary and M. Roberts, "Do Firms Rebalance Their Capital Structures?," *Journal of Finance* 60, no. 6 (2005): 2575–2619.

[8] For an overview, see Barclay and Smith, "The Capital Structure Puzzle."

[9] Interest charges are not always deductible in full. Many countries have "thin capitalization rules" that limit interest deductibility for taxes. For example, as of 2018, corporations in the United States can deduct interest charges only up to 30 percent of EBITDA.

equity with debt increases a company's aggregate cash flow and its value.[10] That said, this advantage does not necessarily make 100 percent debt funding the most tax-efficient approach. More debt funding may reduce corporate taxes but could actually lead to higher taxes for investors. In many countries, investors pay higher taxes on interest income than on capital gains from equity holdings. Under these circumstances equity funding could prove more attractive than debt, depending on the relevant tax rates for corporations and investors.[11]

Private-equity firms have known for decades that debt can also impose investment discipline on managers.[12] Especially in companies with strong cash flows and few growth opportunities, managers may be tempted to increase corporate spending on investment projects and acquisitions that will boost growth but do not earn an attractive return on capital. If share ownership is widely dispersed, it is difficult and costly for shareholders to assess when managers are engaging in such overinvestment. Debt restrains such behavior by forcing the company to pay out free cash flow according to scheduled interest and principal obligations before managers can make any additional investments.

However, higher levels of debt reduce financial flexibility for companies. This can give rise to costs from business erosion and investor conflicts.[13] Highly leveraged companies have less flexibility to pursue investment opportunities or free up budgets for research and development (R&D), since they need cash available to repay debts on time. These companies' loan agreements typically include covenants that limit borrowers' freedom of action. When credit is tight, they may also have limited access to new borrowing, especially if their debt is not investment grade. This was the case during the 2008 financial crisis and for some companies during the 2020 COVID-19 pandemic.

As a result, these companies may miss significant opportunities to create value. They are also more likely to lose customers, employees, and suppliers because of their greater risk of financial distress. For example, suppliers to highly indebted retailers typically demand up-front payment, sometimes creating a negative cycle of lower inventories that lead to a decline in sales, which then leads to more difficulty in meeting debt schedules, and so on. The risk of losing customers is particularly high when the products require long-term

---

[10] For an overview, see M. Grinblatt and S. Titman, *Financial Markets and Corporate Strategy*, 2nd ed. (New York: McGraw-Hill, 2002), chap. 14; and R. Brealey, S. Myers, F. Allen, and A. Edmans, *Principles of Corporate Finance*, 14th ed. (New York: McGraw-Hill, 2023), chap. 17.

[11] M. Miller, "Debt and Taxes," *Journal of Finance* 32, no. 2 (1977): 261–275.

[12] M. Jensen, "Agency Costs of Free Cash Flow, Corporate Finance and Takeovers," *American Economic Review* 76, no. 2 (1986): 323–339.

[13] We prefer the term *business erosion* to the more often used *financial distress* because the associated costs arise very gradually and long before there may be an actual distress event, such as nonperformance on debt.

service and maintenance. For example, during the 2008 credit crisis, when Chrysler and General Motors faced financial distress, they lost considerable market share to Japanese and European competitors. Ultimately, such business erosion can even lead to bankruptcy.

Higher leverage may cause additional value destruction related to conflicts of interest among debt holders, shareholders, and managers. For example, when companies come close to defaulting on their debt, shareholders will prefer to take out cash or invest it in high-risk opportunities, at debt holders' expense.[14] Of course, debt holders anticipate such conflicts and try to protect themselves with restrictive covenants and other costly measures.

Evidence on Debt/Equity Trade-Offs

Although finance theory is clear about the sources of costs and benefits of leverage, it does not tell specifically how to measure the best capital structure for a given company. Fortunately, it turns out that capital structure has less impact on value than many practitioners think. In addition, evidence from academic research provides some guidance on leverage profiles for companies, depending on their characteristics, as one would expect from fundamental debt/equity trade-offs.[15]

Leverage should be higher for companies with higher returns on capital, lower growth and risk, or larger and more fungible assets. Indeed, the most highly leveraged industries are typically mature and asset intensive (think infrastructure and utilities). Their stable profits enable high tax savings from interest deductibility, and their low growth calls for strong management discipline, given the likelihood of overinvesting. Because such companies have assets that can serve as collateral and be redeployed after bankruptcy, their expected costs of business erosion are lower. This also explains why airlines can sustain high leverage: in spite of their low returns and high risk, airplanes are easily deployed for use by other airline companies in the event of a bankruptcy.[16] Note that direct bankruptcy costs are relatively small—around 3 percent of a company's market value before the company became distressed.[17]

Leverage should be lower for companies with lower returns on capital, higher growth potential and risk, or highly specific assets and capabilities.

---

[14] In finance theory, these effects from high leverage are called corporate underinvestment (taking out cash rather than investing at low risk) and asset substitution (exchanging lower-risk assets for higher-risk assets). See, for example, S. Ross, R. Westerfield, J. Jaffe, and B. Jordan, *Corporate Finance*, 12th ed. (New York: McGraw-Hill, 2019), chap. 17.

[15] R. Rajan and L. Zingales, "What Do We Know about Capital Structure? Some Evidence from International Data," *Journal of Finance* 50, no. 5 (1995): 1421–1460.

[16] Specifically, leverage is high when the operating leases of aircraft are taken into account.

[17] See, for example, L. Weiss, "Bankruptcy Resolution: Direct Costs and Violation of Priority of Claims," *Journal of Financial Economics* 27, no. 2 (1990): 285–314.

This is the case in sectors such as software, biotechnology, and high-tech start-ups. Potential tax savings are small, because the companies' taxable profits are low in the near term. Management needs more financial freedom, because investments are essential to capture future growth. In contrast, the costs of business erosion are high, because these companies would quickly lose valuable growth opportunities, and any remaining assets have very little value to third parties. For the same reasons, companies with more volatile earnings and higher advertising and R&D costs are generally financed with less debt.[18] Leverage also tends to be low for companies producing durable goods, such as machinery and equipment, requiring long-term maintenance and support. The highly specific capabilities of these companies make financial distress costly for their customers.[19]

Although some finance textbooks show a high potential tax benefit from higher leverage, the benefit is usually limited for large, investment-grade companies. To illustrate, consider a simple example. Exhibit 35.5 shows how the multiple of enterprise value over earnings before interest, taxes, and amortization (EBITA) for an average company in the S&P 500 would change along with the amount of the company's debt financing, as measured by the EBITA-to-interest coverage ratio. The EBITA multiple is estimated using the basic value driver formula, presented in Chapter 3, and applied using an adjusted-present-value (APV) methodology.[20] We assume a long-term ROIC of 17.5 percent and an unlevered cost of capital of 9 percent—typical scores for a middle-of-the-road S&P 500 company. As the exhibit shows, tax-related benefits from debt do not change enterprise value dramatically, except at very low levels of interest coverage (below 2) rarely seen for large,

---

[18] M. Bradley, G. Jarell, and E. Kim, "On the Existence of an Optimal Capital Structure: Theory and Evidence," *Journal of Finance* 39, no. 3 (1984): 857–878; and M. Long and I. Malitz, "The Investment-Financing Nexus: Some Empirical Evidence," *Midland Corporate Finance Journal* 3, no. 3 (1985): 53–59.

[19] See Barclay and Smith, "The Capital Structure Puzzle"; and S. Titman and R. Wessels, "The Determinants of Capital Structure Choice," *Journal of Finance* 43, no. 1 (1988): 1–19.

[20] Applying the APV methodology to the value driver formula and discounting the tax shield on interest at the unlevered cost of equity results in the following formula:

$$\text{Value} = \text{NOPAT}\left(\frac{1 - \frac{g}{\text{ROIC}}}{k_u - g}\right) + \sum_{t=1}^{\infty} \frac{k_D \times T \times D_t}{(1 + k_u)^t}$$

where k_u is the unlevered cost of equity, D_t is the debt in year t, k_D is the cost of debt, T is the tax rate, and all other symbols are as defined in Chapter 3.

If we make the additional assumption that companies finance with debt while maintaining a stable interest coverage ratio, the formula can be simplified as follows:

$$\text{Value} = \text{NOPAT}\left(\frac{1 - \frac{g}{\text{ROIC}} + \frac{T}{1-T}\left[\frac{\text{Interest}}{\text{EBITA}}\right]}{k_u - g}\right)$$

where EBITA/interest is the target coverage ratio.

EXHIBIT 35.5 **Capital Structure's Limited Impact on Enterprise Value**

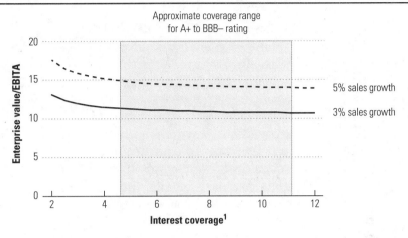

---

[1] EBITA/interest, EBITA is earnings before interest, taxes, and amortization.

investment-grade companies.[21] Compare that with the much bigger impact on shareholder value of key value drivers such as return on invested capital (ROIC) and growth.

In contrast, losses in flexibility from higher leverage do translate to significant value destruction. John Graham and others examined listed U.S. companies over a period of more than 25 years and analyzed the loss in a company's value due to deviations of its leverage from what was estimated as its theoretical optimum.[22] The analysis offers two key insights, illustrated in Exhibit 35.6. First, it confirms our analysis that value at stake is limited to no more than a couple of percentage points for a fairly wide range of leverage around the theoretical optimum. Second, it shows that there is a lot more downside from having too much debt than from having too little. In other words, the losses due to diminished flexibility tend to outweigh the gains from tax benefits and management discipline.

Credit Ratings and Target Capital Structure

Difficult as it may be to determine an *optimal* capital structure, it is much easier to find an *effective* structure—that is, one that cannot clearly be improved upon in terms of shareholder value creation because it is somewhere in the relatively flat range of the valuation curves of Exhibits 35.5 and 35.6.

---

[21] Note that at such low levels of coverage, the expected value of any tax savings will itself decline because of the growing probability that the company will not capture these savings in the first place. As a result, the true curve would be even flatter than shown here.

[22] See J. Van Binsbergen, J. Graham, and J. Yang, "The Cost of Debt," *Journal of Finance* 65, no. 6 (2010): 2089–2136.

EXHIBIT 35.6 **More to Lose Than to Gain from Capital Structure Management**

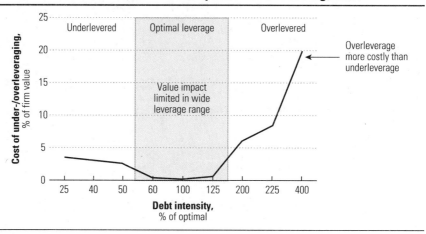

Source: J. Van Binsbergen, J. Graham, and J. Yang, "The Cost of Debt," *Journal of Finance* 65, no. 6 (2010).

Exhibit 35.7 shows the distribution of credit ratings for U.S. and Europe-based private and public companies with revenues in 2022 over $1 billion, according to Standard & Poor's. The ratings, which serve as indicators of a company's credit quality, range between AAA (highest quality) and D (defaulted). Ratings of BBB– and higher indicate so-called investment-grade quality. Half of the companies in Exhibit 35.7 are in the rating categories of A+ to BBB–; a significantly larger share (70 percent) fall in this range when we consider only companies with a market capitalization over €5 billion. This is apparently an effective rating level: credit ratings are fairly stable over time, so most companies probably do not move in and out of this range. Few large

EXHIBIT 35.7 **Credit Ratings for Large Companies: Mostly between A+ and BBB–**

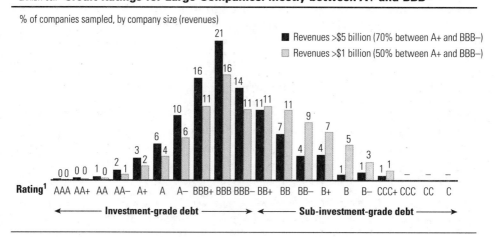

[1] Standard & Poor's credit ratings for all private and public U.S. and Europe-based companies with 2022 revenues exceeding $1 billion.

Source: S&P Capital IQ; McKinsey Value Intelligence database.

companies are at rating levels of AA– and higher, because too little leverage would leave too much value on the table in the form of tax savings and management discipline. At the other extreme, below the rating level of BBB–, the costs of business erosion and investor conflicts associated with high leverage become too onerous. At these ratings, the opportunities for debt funding are also much smaller, because many investors are barred from investing in sub-investment-grade debt.

Over the past decade, credit ratings for these large companies have declined on average, shifting the distribution in Exhibit 35.7 to the right.[23] However, this does not necessarily mean companies have taken on too much debt. First, the decline in ratings was driven not so much by existing corporations being downgraded as it was by the inclusion of newly rated corporations, which typically have higher growth but are smaller and less profitable, so they have lower ratings.[24] Second, even in the wake of the COVID-19 pandemic, key credit ratios are similar to those of the prior ten-year period. In 2023, the most recent year for which we have data as of this writing, the median net debt-to-EBITDA ratios were around 2.0–2.5 across industries in the United States and Europe. Although there are always outliers, this means that most companies are still at healthy levels of debt financing.

To translate an investment-grade (AAA to BBB–) rating into a capital structure target for a company, you must understand what a company's credit rating represents and what goes into determining it. Empirical evidence shows that credit ratings are primarily related to two financial indicators.[25] The first indicator is *size* in terms of sales or market capitalization. However, this indicator makes a difference only for very large or very small companies. For example, as of 2023, the only two industrial companies with AAA ratings, Microsoft and Johnson & Johnson, had market capitalizations above $350 billion. One possible explanation: larger companies are more likely to diversify their risk.

The second indicator is *coverage* in terms of EBITA or EBITDA relative to interest expense or debt, defined as follows:

$$\text{Debt Coverage} = \frac{\text{Net Debt}}{\text{EBITA}} \text{ or } \frac{\text{Net Debt}}{\text{EBITDA}}$$

$$\text{Interest Coverage} = \frac{\text{EBITA}}{\text{Interest}} \text{ or } \frac{\text{EBITDA}}{\text{Interest}}$$

---

[23] See for example: "Carry the Weight: Should the World Worry about America's Corporate-Debt Mountain?" *The Economist*, March 14, 2019, www.economist.com.

[24] See T. Khurana, W. Rehm, and A. Srivastava, "Is a Leverage Reckoning Coming?" *McKinsey on Finance*, no. 70 (May 2019): 1–6.

[25] For an overview, see R. Cantor, "An Introduction to Recent Research on Credit Ratings," *Journal of Banking and Finance* 28, no. 11 (2004): 2565–2573; E. Altman, "Financial Ratios, Discriminant Analysis, and the Prediction of Corporate Bankruptcy," *Journal of Finance* 23, no. 4 (1968): 589–609; and J. Pettit, C. Fitt, S. Orlov, and A. Kalsekar, "The New World of Credit Ratings," UBS research report (September 2004).

A similar indicator that is widely used by credit analysts is based on so-called funds from operations (FFO) instead of EBITA or EBITDA. FFO is defined as EBITDA minus interest and tax charges.

Coverage is more relevant than size when you are setting a capital structure target. Basically, it represents a company's ability to comply with its debt service obligations. For example, EBITA interest coverage measures how many times a company could pay its interest commitments out of its pretax operational cash flow if it invested only an amount equal to its annual depreciation charges to keep the business running (or, for EBITDA coverage, if it invested nothing at all). In a low-interest-rate environment, however, debt coverage is a better measure of a company's long-term ability to service its debt. Interest coverage ratios might then appear strong for some companies simply because they attracted debt at low interest rates. If these companies need to re-fund the debt at higher rates in the future, their interest coverage will plummet.

Exhibit 35.8 shows how interest coverage and debt coverage relate to rating differences for a sample of large U.S. companies rated by Standard & Poor's (excluding financial institutions). Obviously, we could further refine the analysis by including more explanatory ratios, such as funds from operations (FFO) to interest, solvency, and more. However, these ratios are often highly correlated, so calculating them does not always produce a clearer explanation.

EXHIBIT 35.8 **Credit Rating vs. Interest and Debt Coverage**

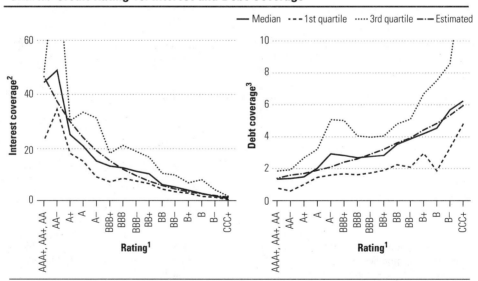

[1] Standard & Poor's credit ratings for all private and public U.S. and Europe-based companies with 2015–2022 revenues exceeding $1 billion and positive debt coverage ratio.

[2] EBITDA/interest. EBITDA is earnings before interest, taxes, depreciation, and amortization.

[3] Net debt/EBITDA.

Source: S&P Capital IQ; McKinsey Value Intelligence database.

For a given credit rating, the coverage will typically differ by industry. This is because of differences in underlying business risk. Companies in industries with more volatile earnings need higher coverage to attain a given credit rating, because their cash flow is more likely to fall short of their interest commitments.[26] For example, companies in basic materials—say, steel companies—will need better levels of debt coverage than food and beverage companies to attain the same credit rating. By taking into account these differences in coverage requirements across industries, we can translate a company's targeted credit rating into a target coverage ratio. Based on the company's estimated future operating profit (and interest rate), we can derive its maximum debt capacity for the chosen credit rating and, thereby, its target capital structure. For example, companies aiming for an investment-grade rating in the food and beverage sector would typically need to have a net-debt-to-EBITDA ratio of around 3 or lower. Given projections of near-term EBITDA, you can derive a first estimate of the target amount of net debt for such a company to reach an investment-grade rating. A definitive rating estimate would require more in-depth analysis of specific financial and business risks that the company is facing. A place to start is, for example, with the websites for Standard & Poor's (www.spratings.com) or Moody's (www.moodys.com).

It is important to compare a target capital structure for a company against that of its industry peer group. The key determinants of value trade-offs in designing capital structure—growth, return, and asset specificity—are largely industry specific, so any large differences in capital structure would require further investigation. It also makes sense from a competitive perspective: as long as your capital structure is not too different, you have at least not given away any competitive advantage derived from capital structure (nor have you gained any).[27] Since the 1960s, a body of evidence has built up showing company credit ratios clustered around industry-specific averages, further indicating that each industry has its own effective capital structure.[28]

From a company's credit rating, you can also estimate the interest rate payable on its debt funding. The difference between the yields on corporate bonds and risk-free bonds—the credit spread—is greater for companies with lower credit ratings, because their probability of default is higher. Exhibit 35.9 plots cumulative default probabilities against the credit ratings

[26] Earnings volatility is measured here as the average standard deviation of relative annual changes in EBITDA for companies in each sector.

[27] For example, there is academic evidence that high-leverage companies sometimes fall victim to price wars started by financially stronger competitors. See P. Bolton and D. Scharfstein, "A Theory of Predation Based on Agency Problems in Financial Contracting," *American Economic Review* 80, no. 1 (1990): 93–106.

[28] E. Schwarz and R. Aronson, "Some Surrogate Evidence in Support of the Concept of Optimal Financial Structure," *Journal of Finance* 22, no. 1 (1967): 10–18.

EXHIBIT 35.9 **Default Probability and Credit Spread**

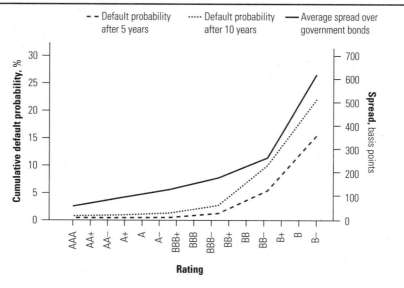

Source: S&P Capital IQ; McKinsey Value Intelligence database.

over five and ten years and the average credit spread for each rating. The credit spread clearly reflects the increasing default probability. For ratings below the investment-grade benchmark of BBB–, default probabilities increase more sharply, which prevents some institutional investors from investing. As a result, the debt market is considerably smaller for below-investment-grade debt.

PAYOUTS TO SHAREHOLDERS

Most successful companies, at some point, find it virtually impossible to reinvest all the cash they generate. In that case, there is little alternative but to return surplus cash to shareholders. Although some executives might consider that a failure to find value-creating investments, it is actually an inevitable consequence for maturing companies with high returns on capital and moderate growth. For example, a company with $1 billion of net operating profit after taxes (NOPAT), a return on invested capital of 25 percent, and annual revenue growth of 5 percent needs net investments of only $200 million per year to continue its growth at that rate. That leaves $800 million of surplus cash flow for additional investments or payouts to shareholders (see Exhibit 35.10). Finding $800 million of new investment opportunities at attractive returns in every year is a challenge in many industries. Reinvesting all its surplus cash

EXHIBIT 35.10 **Surplus Cash Flow, Given Earnings of $1 Billion**

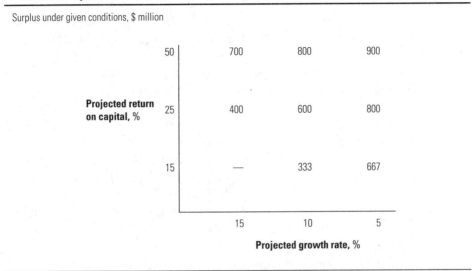

Surplus under given conditions, $ million

			Projected growth rate, %		
			15	10	5
Projected return on capital, %	50		700	800	900
	25		400	600	800
	15		—	333	667

flow in new opportunities at its current return on capital of 25 percent would imply that the company grows revenues by 20 percent each year.

The payout levels for different combinations of return and growth in Exhibit 35.10 indicate that for most successful companies, even those with double-digit growth rates, the implications will eventually be similar: there is no choice but to return substantial amounts of cash to shareholders. Between 2010 and 2023, half of the large industrial companies in the United States and Europe paid out more than 50 percent of their cumulative net earnings over these years. Some companies with high returns on capital were well above that level: Procter & Gamble returned $192 billion in dividends and share repurchases to its shareholders, representing around 120 percent of its cumulative net earnings. Even for a company such as Procter & Gamble, it would have been close to impossible to reinvest that amount of cash, given that it had already spent some $2 billion per year on R&D and $8 billion on advertising.

Companies with cash surpluses have three basic alternatives for paying out the surpluses to shareholders: dividend increases, share repurchases, and extraordinary dividends. All three provide a positive signal to the capital market about a company's prospects. The potential negative signal that a cash payout could send is that the company has run out of investment opportunities. This assumes that investors did not already know that the company was generating more cash flow than it could reinvest. However, such cases are extremely rare; investors typically anticipate payouts long before managers make that decision, as illustrated by the simple math in our example in Exhibit 35.10.

Dividends

Companies that increase their dividends receive positive market reactions averaging around 2 percent on the day of announcement.[29] For companies that initiate dividend payments, the impact is even greater.[30] This holds for even some of the highest-valued and best-known companies: the share price of Meta jumped by 20 percent on February 2, 2024, after the parent company of Facebook and Instagram announced its first-ever dividend (and favorable financial results). In general, investors interpret dividend increases as good news about the company's long-term outlook for future earnings and cash flows. On average, they are right, according to the evidence. Most companies that increase their dividend payout usually do so after strong earnings growth and when they are able to maintain such high levels of earnings in the year following the dividend increase. Companies that start paying dividends for the first time typically continue to experience high rates of earnings growth.

The drawback of increasing dividends is that investors interpret this action as a long-term commitment to higher payouts. Companies, especially in the United States, have created expectations among shareholders that dividends will be cut only in case of severe setbacks. The stock market greatly penalizes companies for cutting dividends from customary long-term levels, which makes companies quite reluctant to do so. Large, stable corporations almost never cut their dividends voluntarily. Between 1995 and 2022, more than 70 percent of U.S. listed companies were clearly committed to a stable dividend policy, without a single significant dividend cut. Less than 30 percent did reduce dividends at least once, but only when faced with an economic crisis (in 2008 or 2020) or a decline in profit of at least 20 percent—or both. Virtually no company since 1995 made a significant dividend cut out of choice rather than need.[31]

A few companies do not commit to dividends or dividend growth rates that are supposed to be upheld even in the face of adverse events or declining business conditions. Instead, they have variable dividend policies and try to manage investor expectations of future payouts by explicitly relating the dividend payouts to business results. For example, in 2016, major resources companies BHP and Rio Tinto adopted a dividend payout policy in which dividends are more closely related to underlying business results. BHP switched to a minimum dividend payout ratio equal to 50 percent of underlying attributable profit, with additional payouts made in the form of special dividends or share repurchases if and when the company's financial position

[29] See, for example, S. Benartzi, R. Michaely, and R. Thaler, "Do Changes in Dividends Signal the Future or the Past?," *Journal of Finance* 52, no. 3 (1997): 1007–1034; and J. Aharony and I. Swarey, "Quarterly Dividends and Earnings Announcements and Stockholders," *Journal of Finance* 35, no. 1 (1980): 1–12.

[30] P. Healey and K. Palepu, "Earnings Information Conveyed by Dividend Initiations and Omissions," *Journal of Financial Economics* 21, no. 2 (1988): 149–175.

[31] P. Catarino, M. Goedhart, T. Koller, and R. Kotsev, "Big Companies Cut Dividends to Grow?," *McKinsey on Finance*, no. 84 (2023): 44–47.

allows (for example, to pay out divestment proceeds).[32] From a value creation perspective, a variable dividend policy is not better or worse than a fixed (or progressive) dividend policy. But it does create more financial flexibility, saving managers from feeling compelled to uphold dividends even if that means forgoing attractive investment opportunities or divesting assets.

Share Repurchases

In the early 1980s, share repurchases represented less than 10 percent of cash payouts to shareholders. Since then, they have gained notable importance as an alternative way to distribute cash to shareholders, mainly because key regulatory limits for corporations to purchase their own shares were removed in the United States in 1982.[33] By 1999, for example, share repurchases totaled $181 billion, close to the $216 billion in regular dividend payments for companies listed on the New York Stock Exchange.[34] The shift from dividend payments to share repurchases persisted in the subsequent decades. Major companies in different sectors adopted share repurchase programs on a large scale; examples include Apple, ExxonMobil, GSK, Pfizer, Shell, and Unilever. In 2023, about 60 percent of cash distributions to shareholders in the United States were share repurchases.

Investors typically interpret share repurchases positively, for several reasons. First, a share buyback shows that managers are confident that future cash flows are strong enough to support future investments and debt commitments. Second, it signals that the company will not spend its excess cash on value-destroying investments. Third, buying back shares indicates to investors that management believes the company's shares are undervalued. If management itself buys back shares, this effect is reinforced. Research appears to suggest that because of this signaling, share prices historically increased 2–3 percent on average on the day of announcement for smaller repurchase programs (in which less than 10 percent of shares outstanding were acquired through open-market transactions).[35] However, these results were mostly driven by share price increases for smaller companies.

---

[32] BHP's new dividend policy was announced in the release of the second-half results for 2015 on February 23, 2016. Rio Tinto's dividend policy states that it expects to pay out dividends in a range of 40–60 percent of aggregate underlying profit through the cycle. *2015 Full Year Results*, Rio Tinto, February 11, 2016, www.riotinto.com.

[33] Following Rule 10b-18 of the U.S. Securities and Exchange Commission.

[34] See Pettit, "Is a Share Buyback Right for Your Company?"

[35] In smaller programs, companies typically buy their own shares at no premium or a limited premium in so-called open-market purchases. Larger programs are often organized in the form of tender offers in which companies announce that they will repurchase a particular number of shares at a significant premium. See, for example, R. Comment and J. Jarrell, "The Relative Signaling Power of Dutch-Auction and Fixed Price Self-Tender Offers and Open-Market Repurchases," *Journal of Finance* 46, no. 4 (1991): 1243–1272; and T. Vermaelen, "Common Stock Repurchases and Market Signaling: An Empirical Study," *Journal of Financial Economics* 9, no. 2 (1981): 138–183.

In addition, repurchases have become a regular payout instrument, so their signaling effect has declined over the years.

These signaling effects should not be confused with value creation for shareholders, as they only reflect higher market expectations of future performance. If the company does not deliver against these higher expectations, the share price will come down again. As is the case for all cash payouts to shareholders, repurchases do not create value for shareholders, because they do not increase the company's cash flows from operations. This is confirmed by empirical evidence that earnings multiples are not related to the amount or the form of the cash returns, whether in dividends or via share buybacks (see Exhibit 35.11).[36]

Nevertheless, two myths about share repurchases seem to persist among analysts and managers. The first is that managers can create value by repurchasing shares when they are undervalued.[37] Managers have inside information and could be in a better position than investors to assess when the company's shares are undervalued in the stock market and to buy these at the right time. Buying the undervalued shares would create value for those shareholders who hold on to them. However, the empirical evidence shows that companies rarely pick the right time to buy back shares.[38] For 2001 through

EXHIBIT 35.11 **Valuation Unrelated to Payout Level or Payout Mix**

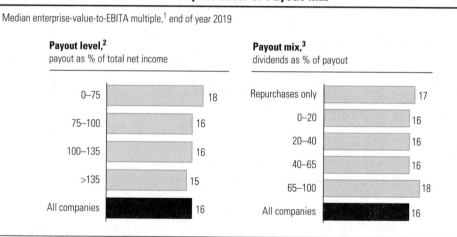

Median enterprise-value-to-EBITA multiple,[1] end of year 2019

Payout level,[2]
payout as % of total net income

0–75	18
75–100	16
100–135	16
>135	15
All companies	16

Payout mix,[3]
dividends as % of payout

Repurchases only	17
0–20	16
20–40	16
40–65	16
65–100	18
All companies	16

[1] Median multiple of nonfinancial companies in the S&P 500 index.
[2] Payout defined as dividends paid plus share repurchases, 2015–2019.
[3] Average proportional share of dividends in total payout, 2015–2019.
Source: S&P Capital IQ; McKinsey Value of Intelligence database.

[36] See B. Jiang and T. Koller, "Paying Back Your Shareholders," *McKinsey on Finance*, no. 39 (2011): 2–7.
[37] See B. Jiang and T. Koller, "The Savvy Executive's Guide to Buying Back Shares," *McKinsey on Finance*, no. 41 (2011): 14–17.
[38] Some academic studies have concluded that companies do, in fact, time their repurchases well. Those findings, however, are driven primarily by smaller companies that make a one-time decision to repurchase shares. Once those smaller companies are excluded, the smart-timing effect disappears.

2010, a majority of the S&P 500 companies bought back shares when prices were high, and few bought shares when prices were low. In fact, the timing of share repurchases by more than three-quarters of S&P 500 companies resulted in lower shareholder returns than a simple strategy of equally distributed repurchases over time would have generated (see Exhibit 35.12).

The second myth is that repurchases create value simply because they increase earnings per share (EPS). The implicit assumption is that the price-to-earnings ratio (P/E) remains constant. As explained in Chapter 3, the logic is flawed: when share repurchases are financed with excess cash or new debt, a company's EPS indeed goes up, simply because the P/E for cash or debt is higher than for the company's equity.[39] However, after the repurchase, the equity P/E will be lower because the company's leverage has increased.[40] The increase in EPS does not lead to value creation for shareholders, because it is exactly offset by the decline in P/E. Of course, in a large sample of companies and over long periods of time, there is always an apparent correlation between EPS growth and total shareholder returns (TSR), but that is entirely

EXHIBIT 35.12 **Relative Performance of Timing Share Repurchases**

Number of companies per TSR cohort,[1] 2004–2010

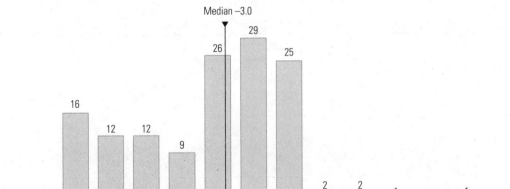

TSR cohorts based on 3-year TSR vs. TSR if shares purchased evenly across periods, percentage points

[1] Based on 135 S&P 500 companies that repurchased shares from 2004 to 2010.
Source: McKinsey Corporate Performance Analysis Tool.

[39] We define the P/E here in general terms as the market value of an asset or liability divided by its after-tax earnings contribution. The P/Es for cash and debt are the inverse of their after-tax interest rates and are typically higher than for the company's equity.
[40] The P/E for a company's equity is a weighted average of the P/Es for its operations, cash, and debt. Paying out cash reduces the weight of the relatively high P/E for cash and therefore lowers the P/E for a company's equity. Attracting debt increases the negative weight of its relatively high P/E and lowers the equity P/E as well.

attributable to revenue growth and return on capital. After controlling for these value drivers, there is no correlation between a company's share repurchase intensity and its shareholder returns.[41]

The real value creation from share repurchases can only be assessed in comparison with alternative cash deployments, such as business investments, debt repayments, cash holdings, or dividend payments. Contrary to common beliefs, EPS and P/Es provide no guidance in making the assessment. Alternative deployments of cash have a mechanical impact on these metrics that does not necessarily correlate with value creation. This is illustrated in Exhibit 35.13 with a hypothetical company that generates net operating profit after taxes (NOPAT) of $100, which translates to an enterprise value of $1,500 (at an enterprise-value-to-NOPAT multiple of 15 times). The company has an excess-cash position of $100, no debt, and 100 shares outstanding. It can decide to hold on to the cash or use it to repurchase shares, pay dividends, or invest in operations.

EXHIBIT 35.13 **Value Creation from Share Repurchases vs. Alternatives for Cash Deployment**

$	Hold cash	Repurchase shares	Pay dividends	Invest
Earnings per share				
NOPAT[1]	100.0	100.0	100.0	115.0
After-tax interest income (expense)[2]	2.0	—	—	—
Net income	102.0	100.0	100.0	115.0
Number of shares	100.00	93.75	100.00	100.00
Earnings per share	1.02	1.07	1.00	1.15
Enterprise and equity value				
Enterprise value/NOPAT[2]	15	15	15	15
Enterprise value	1,500.0	1,500.0	1,500.0	1,725.0
Cash	100.0	—	—	—
Equity value	1,600.0	1,500.0	1,500.0	1,725.0
Payout: Dividends			100.0	
Payout: Share repurchases		100.0		
Equity value including payouts	1,600.0	1,600.0	1,600.0	1,725.0
Value per share				
Value per share	16.00	16.00	15.00	17.25
Dividend per share	—	—	1.00	—
Value per share including dividends	16.00	16.00	16.00	17.25
Price/earnings	15.7	15.0	15.0	15.0

[1] Net operating profit less adjusted taxes.

[2] After-tax interest rate on cash is assumed to be 2% per year.

[41] See O. Ezekoye, T. Koller, and A. Mittal, "How Share Repurchases Boost Earnings without Improving Returns," *McKinsey on Finance*, no. 58 (2016): 15–24.

Shareholder value increases for the investment alternative because the return on capital exceeds the cost of capital. But it remains unchanged for the other three alternatives, even though the associated changes in EPS or P/E appear to indicate otherwise. Exhibit 35.13 compares all four alternative cash deployments in detail:

1. *Hold cash.* In this case, the company keeps the excess cash, and net income for the upcoming year is $102 (assuming the after-tax interest rate on the $100 cash is 2 percent). The company's value per share is $16, EPS is $1.02, and the P/E is 15.7.

2. *Repurchase shares.* The company uses its $100 in cash to buy back 6.25 units of its own shares (equal to $100 divided by a share price of $16). The value per share is unchanged at $16 (the remaining equity value of $1,500 divided by 93.75 remaining shares). But the EPS increases to $1.07, even though no value is created. This is simply because the P/E for cash is higher than for shares.[42] After the share buyback, the company's equity has a lower P/E because leverage is now higher. The decline in P/E cancels out the increase in EPS, keeping shareholder value unchanged.

3. *Pay dividends.* The company pays a $1 dividend on each of its 100 shares outstanding. Although the value per share declines from $16 to $15, each shareholder still ends up with a total value including dividends of $16 per share. Again, there is no value creation, but now the EPS declines to $1.00 because the interest-generating cash has been paid out to the shareholders. The P/E for the company's equity also declines, because leverage increases due to the cash payout. The lower EPS and P/E tie with the decline in value per share of $1, which is exactly equal to the dividend paid per share.

4. *Invest.* The value for shareholders does change when the company can invest the $100 in the business at an after-tax return (ROIC) of 15 percent. At a constant enterprise-value multiple of 15 times, the enterprise and equity value will increase to $1.725 (as NOPAT increases to $115 from $100). Because of the high return on investment, the EPS increases to $1.15, clearly above any other scenario. The value per share is now $17.25, higher than in all other scenarios, because the business investment creates $125 additional value for shareholders ($1.25 per share).

The erratic pattern of EPS changes across the alternative allocations demonstrates that it does not move in line with value creation. Even though it is highest for the alternative with the highest value creation, this does not mean

---

[42] The P/E for cash in this example is 50 times (equal to the inverse of the after-tax interest rate of 2 percent).

EPS is a reliable indicator of value creation. For example, assume the investment would not produce operating earnings in the upcoming year but only after several years. Of course, the investment would still create value.[43] But now the EPS would not increase to $1.15; it would instead decline to $1.00. Also, changes in the P/E would send the wrong signal. Delayed earnings would further increase the P/E for the investment alternative, not because more value is created but simply because the company's earnings for the upcoming year would be lower. Exhibit 35.13 also shows that share repurchases can destroy value if they prevent the company from pursuing attractive investment opportunities. This underlines that payout decisions, whether repurchases or dividends, always need to be considered as part of a company's overall cash deployment.

When a company then decides to pay out cash to shareholders, there are some good reasons to use share repurchases. In contrast to dividend increases, repurchases offer companies more flexibility in adapting their payouts to unexpected investment needs in a volatile economy. Share buyback programs are not seen as long-term commitments and can be adjusted without influencing investor expectations as much as adjustments to regular dividends would. In addition, they offer investors the flexibility to participate or not. For institutional investors, this means they can choose to uphold the amount invested in a stock—for example, because of a client mandate or because they are tracking an index—without having to reinvest dividends and incur any transaction costs. Finally, share buybacks can result in lower taxes than dividend payments for investors in countries where capital gains are taxed at lower rates. In some countries, individuals have the option to defer taxes on any capital gains and realize such gains in a more tax-efficient manner, potentially years later. Because of their flexibility, share repurchases are a very effective way to pay out any cash surpluses that exceed the level of regular dividends.

Extraordinary Dividends

As an alternative to share repurchases, a company could declare an extraordinary dividend payout, as Microsoft did in 2004 as part of its $75 billion, four-year cash return program. Microsoft paid out a significant portion in the form of an extraordinary dividend because of its concern that the share repurchase was so massive that it would swamp the liquidity in the market for Microsoft stock. The drawback of extraordinary dividends, compared with share repurchases, is that they offer no flexibility to shareholders and force the cash payout on all of them, regardless of their preferences for capital gains or dividends.

---

[43] Assuming the same 15 percent ROIC and 15 times enterprise value multiple.

EQUITY FINANCING

If a company is facing a cash deficit and has already reached its long-term leverage target, it has little choice (other than selling noncore businesses, as discussed later in this chapter) but to raise equity or cut its dividends. As with all payout and financing decisions, this does not create or destroy value in itself. But raising equity and—especially—cutting dividends will send negative signals to investors.

Share prices on average decline around 9 percent on the day a company announces dividend cuts or omissions.[44] Furthermore, some investor groups count on dividends being paid out every year. Skipping these dividends will force these investors to liquidate parts of their portfolios, leading to unnecessary transaction costs. Finally, the amount of funds freed up by cutting dividends is often limited, so dividend cuts alone are unlikely to resolve more substantial funding shortages. As noted, most corporations therefore consider dividend cuts only as a measure of last resort.

Issuing equity is also likely to lead to a short-term drop in share prices. Typically, share prices decline by around 3 percent on announcements of so-called seasoned equity offerings.[45] Because investors assume managers have superior insights into the company's true business and financial outlook, they believe managers will issue equity only if a company's shares are overvalued in the stock market. Therefore, the share price will likely decrease in the short term on the announcement of an equity issuance, even if it is not actually overvalued. A similar price reaction can be expected for various equity-like instruments, such as preferred stock, convertibles, warrants, and more exotic hybrid forms of capital.

DEBT FINANCING

In contrast to equity financing, issuing or redeeming debt typically does not send strong signals to investors about the company's future cash flows.

When issuing debt, companies commit to fixed future interest payments that can be withheld only at considerable cost. Investors also know that debt is more likely to be issued when management perceives a company's share price to be undervalued. As a result, the issuance of debt typically meets with more favorable share price reactions than the issuance of new equity. Empirical evidence shows that the price reaction is typically flat.[46]

---

[44] Healey and Palepu, "Earnings Information Conveyed by Dividend Initiations and Omissions."

[45] See, for example, B. Eckbo, R. Masulis, O. Norli, "Security Offerings," in *The Handbook of Corporate Finance: Empirical Corporate Finance*, vol. 1, ed. B, Eckbo, Amsterdam: Elsevier / North-Holland (2007), 330–50; and C. Smith, "Investment Banking and the Capital Acquisition Process," *Journal of Financial Economics* 15, nos. 1/2 (1986): 3–29.

[46] See, for example, W. Mikkelson and M. Partch, "Valuation Effects of Security Offerings and the Issuance Process," *Journal of Financial Economics* 15, nos. 1/2 (1986): 31–60; and Smith, "Investment Banking and the Capital Acquisition Process."

Redeeming debt does not meet with significant stock market reactions, either, unless the company is in financial distress. In that case, buying back bonds can send a positive signal to the equity markets. For distressed companies, bond prices go up and down with the enterprise value, just as share prices do. A bond buyback could therefore be a credible signal that management believes the bonds are undervalued (and because, in this case, bonds are similar to equity, this must also mean that shares are undervalued). For example, when the Swiss Swedish engineering company ABB announced a €775 million bond buyback in July 2004, its share price increased 4 percent on the day of the announcement. The stock market apparently saw the buyback as further evidence that the company was on a trajectory to recover from an earlier financial crisis.

DIVESTITURES OF NONCORE BUSINESSES

As discussed in Chapter 28, companies should regularly monitor whether there are businesses in their portfolio for which they are no longer the best owner. Such businesses could generate more value in the hands of new owners—for example, because of a buyer's distinctive skills, better governance, superior insight and foresight, or strong synergies with their existing businesses. Ideally, portfolio monitoring should form an integral part of a cash deployment process where companies match investment needs across business with funding opportunities from debt, equity financing, and divestitures, also keeping in mind payouts to shareholders.

In the last decade, BP, General Electric, and other companies have divested more than $40 billion in noncore assets, restructuring their corporate portfolios as well as strengthening their balance sheets. Similarly, Royal Philips divested significant parts of its portfolio, such as its lighting business, freeing up cash for investments in organic growth and acquisitions in its core health care businesses. Such examples underline the importance of always considering divestitures in cash deployment because they form an important source of funds as well as value creation.

CREATING VALUE FROM FINANCIAL ENGINEERING

Managing a company's capital structure with financial instruments beyond straight debt and equity—our definition of financial engineering—typically involves complex and sometimes even exotic instruments such as synthetic leasing, mezzanine finance, securitization, commodity-linked debt, commodity and currency derivatives, and balance sheet insurance. In general, capital markets do a good job of pricing even complex financial instruments, and companies will have difficulty boosting their share prices by accessing so-called cheap funding, no matter how complex the funding structures are. Nevertheless, financial engineering can create shareholder value under specific conditions, both directly (through tax savings or lower costs of funding) and indirectly (for example, by increasing a company's debt capacity so it can raise funds to capture more value-creating investment opportunities). However, such benefits need to outweigh any potential unintended consequences that inevitably arise with the complexity of financial engineering.

This section considers three of the more common tools of financial engineering: derivative instruments, off-balance-sheet financing, and hybrid financing.

With derivative instruments, such as forwards, swaps, and options, a company can transfer particular risks to third parties that can carry these risks at a lower cost. For example, some airlines hedge their fuel costs with derivatives to be less exposed to sudden changes in oil prices. Of course, this does not make airlines immune to prolonged periods of high oil prices, because the derivative positions must be renewed at some point. But derivatives at least give the airlines some time to prepare business measures such as cost cuts or price increases. Derivatives are not relevant to all companies, and there are many examples where the complexity around the use of derivatives has been badly managed.[47] In general, they are useful tools for financial managers when risks are clearly identified, derivative contracts are available at reasonable prices because of liquid markets, and the total risk exposures are so large that they could seriously harm a corporation's health.

A wide range of instruments fall under the umbrella of so-called off-balance-sheet financing. These include, for example, real estate investment trusts (REITs), securitization, project finance, synthetic leases, and operating leases. Although the variety of these instruments is huge, they have a common element: companies effectively raise debt funding without carrying all the debt on their own balance sheets. Although they are still referred to as off-balance-sheet financing, new standards for U.S. Generally Accepted Accounting Principles (U.S. GAAP) and International Financial Reporting Standards (IFRS) require that most of these instruments be recognized in the balance sheet, as is also the case since 2019 for operating leases and rentals. In most cases, off-balance-sheet financing is used to capture tax advantages. For example, many of the largest hotel companies in the United States have transferred their hotels into partnerships or REITs. This eliminates an entire layer of taxation and thereby lowers overall income taxes. In other cases, off-balance-sheet financing aims primarily at enabling a company to attract debt funding on terms that would have been impossible to realize for traditional forms of debt. Examples include the use of

---

[47] In the 1990s, some high-profile scandals—for example, at Metallgesellschaft and Orange County, California—underlined the need for such caution.

project financing for building and running large infrastructure projects such as wind and solar power generators, gas pipelines, toll bridges, and tunnels. The interest and principal for the project financing are repaid to the lender directly from the cash flows from the project's revenues, which are often quite predictable and stable. In this way, debt financing can be attracted for the investments even when the project owner-operator has very limited debt capacity. Some managers find off-balance-sheet financing more attractive because it reduces the amount of assets shown on the balance sheet and increases the reported return on assets. That is not a good reason to do it. Investors will see through accounting representations, as discussed in Chapter 7. Furthermore, following U.S. and international accounting standards, most forms of off-balance-sheet financing are fully recognized on the balance sheet.

Hybrid financing involves forms of funding that share some elements of both equity and debt to offer new risk/return financing combinations. Examples are convertible debt, convertible preferred stock, and callable perpetual debt. In particular, issuance of convertible debt has seen strong growth over the past decades. Over the last decade, average issuance of convertible bonds in the United States was around \$35 billion per year, with peaks during the COVID crisis in 2020 and 2021 at around \$80 billion. Convertible debt is an efficient form of debt financing when investors or lenders differ from managers in their assessment of the company's credit risk.[48] The key reason is that higher credit risk makes the straight-debt component of the convertible less attractive and the warrant component more attractive, so the two components balance each other to an extent. Overall, convertible debt is less sensitive to differences in credit risk assessment and may therefore facilitate agreement on credit terms that are attractive to both parties. This also explains why high-growth companies use this instrument much more than other companies; they usually face more uncertainty about their future credit risk. Do not issue convertible debt just because it has a low coupon. The coupon is low because the debt also includes a conversion option. It is a fallacy to think that convertible debt is cheap funding. This holds regardless of whether it is straight convertible debt, mandatory convertible debt, convertible debt with or without call spread overlays, or any other of the many variations possible. Also avoid issuing convertible debt simply because it is a way to issue equity against the current share price at some point in the future when share prices will be much higher. That future value is already priced into the conversion options. Furthermore, if the company's share price does not increase sufficiently, the convertible debt will not be converted to equity, and the company will end up with interest-bearing debt instead.

---

[48] See M. Brennan and E. Schwartz, "The Case for Convertibles," *Journal of Applied Corporate Finance* 1, no. 2 (1988): 55–64.

SUMMARY

Although a poorly managed capital structure can lead to financial distress and value destruction, capital structure is not a key value driver. For companies whose leverage is already at reasonable levels, the potential to add value is limited, especially relative to the impact of improvements in returns on invested capital and growth. Managers should refrain from fine-tuning for the optimal capital structure and from simply giving in to any shareholder demands for higher payouts. Instead, they should make sure capital structure and payout decisions are integral parts of a cash deployment that ensures the company has enough financial flexibility to support its strategy while at the same time minimizing the risk of financial distress.

36

Investor Communications

The value of investor communications is a subject of considerable controversy. Some executives, practitioners, and academics argue that actively handling relations with investors is a waste of management time and has no effect on a company's share price. Others have unrealistic expectations, assuming that you can talk up your company's stock, and if your investor relations staff is really sharp, it can tell you why the share price went down by 1.2 percent yesterday when there was no real news about the company.

We fall somewhere in between. It's virtually impossible to interpret short-term price movements with any useful insights. And even if you could talk up your share price beyond its intrinsic value, you probably shouldn't. Nevertheless, good investor communications can ensure that your share price doesn't get out of line with its intrinsic value. You also can build a base of loyal investors and protect executives from making poor strategic decisions based on misunderstanding what investors are saying to them. Too often, however, executives don't know how to interpret what they are hearing from investors, because they are listening to the wrong investors.

The point of good investor communications is to build relationships with the right kinds of investors and communicate with them at their level. It also entails being selective about which sell-side analysts to focus on, not being overly concerned with investors who have a short-term orientation, and not being overly occupied with media coverage of your company. Finally, it's as much about executives listening to the right investors as it is about delivering the company's message to investors.

This chapter also deals with two questions linked to investor communications. First, should companies provide earnings guidance? There is no evidence that companies benefit from the practice. Similarly, should companies be concerned about meeting or beating consensus earnings forecasts? Again,

This chapter was coauthored by John Evers and Werner Rehm.

the evidence shows that performance—return on invested capital (ROIC) and growth—is more important than whether a company meets the consensus earnings forecast.

OBJECTIVES OF INVESTOR COMMUNICATIONS

Good investor communications must be founded on the right objectives. Achieving the highest-possible share price is not one of them. Instead, the overriding objective of investor communications should be to align a company's share price with what the company should be worth, given its fundamental outlook and opportunities.

When a gap forms between a company's market value and its intrinsic value, all the company's stakeholders are put at a disadvantage. If the share price rises too high and exceeds the company's intrinsic value, the company's real performance will eventually become evident to the market, and the price will fall. When that decline occurs, employee morale will suffer, and management will have to face a concerned board of directors who may not understand why the price is falling so far and so fast. A share price that's too high may also encourage managers to keep it high by adopting short-term tactics, such as deferring investments or maintenance costs, which will hamper value creation in the long run. A share price that is too low also has drawbacks, especially the threat of takeover or attack by an activist investor. Furthermore, an undervalued stock makes paying for acquisitions with shares unattractive and may demoralize managers and employees.

A second objective of investor communications is to develop support from a group of sophisticated intrinsic investors who thoroughly understand the company's strategies, strengths, and weaknesses and can better distinguish between the shorter and longer term. These investors will also be likely to purchase shares on short-term dips in the share price and are more likely to be supporters of management's strategy if activist investors propose alternatives aggressively.

A final objective is to learn what your investors like and don't like about your company as an investment. Investors have many different investing strategies, and you can't please them all. You should therefore separate the concerns of the shorter-term investors from those of the long-term investors who own your shares or follow you but don't own your shares. These investors are a source of feedback for you and a source of intelligence about your customers, competitors, and suppliers. The best investor relations (IR) managers will speak regularly with these groups and may give senior management information that is more objective than the results of the company's own research efforts.

INTRINSIC VALUE VERSUS MARKET VALUE

Senior executives often claim the stock market undervalues or "doesn't appreciate" their company. They say this not just in public, where you would expect them to, but also in private. They truly believe that if only they had different investors, or if only the investors or analysts understood their company better, the company's share price would be higher. Yet often these senior executives have not performed an objective outside-in valuation of their company, viewing it through the lens of a sophisticated investor. Their optimistic belief is based on a superficial comparison of price-to-earnings ratios (P/Es) or a stray comment by an analyst that the shares are undervalued.

Any good strategy must begin with an honest assessment of the situation, and a plan for investor communications is no different. Start with an estimate of the size of the gap, if any, between management's view of the company's intrinsic value and the stock market value. In practice, we typically find that no significant gap exists or that any gap can be explained by the company's historical performance relative to peers or by the way the market is valuing the entire industry. Let's illustrate with a disguised example.

A large apparel manufacturer we'll call Fashion Co. earns a return on invested capital (ROIC) of about 20 percent, but its product lines are in slow-growth segments, so its revenue growth has been low. Fashion Co. recently adopted a strategy to buy small companies in faster-growing areas of the industry with higher ROIC, intending to apply its manufacturing and distribution skills to improve the performance of the acquired companies. Eighteen months after the company made its first acquisitions under this strategy, Fashion Co. derived 5 percent of its revenues from the fast-growth segments.

Fashion Co.'s managers were concerned that the company's P/E trailed the P/Es of many companies with which it compared itself. They wondered whether the low value resulted from such factors as the company's old-fashioned name or the small number of analysts covering the industry.

We began analyzing the apparent discrepancy by assessing Fashion Co.'s value relative to companies it considered peers. Some of the supposed peers were 100 percent involved in the fast-growth segments, far exceeding Fashion Co.'s 5 percent revenue stream from them. When we segmented Fashion Co.'s peers by growth rates, we found that its earnings multiple—enterprise value divided by earnings before interest, taxes, and amortization (EBITA)—was in line with those of its close peers but behind those of the companies in the fast-growing segment (see Exhibit 36.1). Fashion Co. and its closest peers also had lower ROIC than the fast-growth companies. A third set of companies, also shown in Exhibit 36.1, had high multiples because of current low earnings due to restructuring. So based on recent performance, Fashion Co.'s value was aligned with its performance relative to its closest peers.

EXHIBIT 36.1 **Fashion Co.: Valuation in Line with Close Peers**

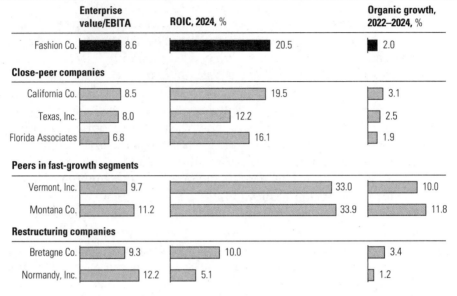

Next, we reverse engineered the share price of Fashion Co. and its peers by building a discounted-cash-flow (DCF) model for each company and estimating what levels of future performance would be consistent with the current share price. We found that if Fashion Co. increased its revenues at 2 percent per year and maintained its most recent level of margins and capital turnover, its DCF value would equal its current share price. This growth rate was in line with the implicit growth of its closest peers and lower than the companies in the fast-growing segment.

Discrepancies between a company's intrinsic value and its market value present both challenges and opportunities for the company's management. So, what can you do if a gap between a company's intrinsic value and market value really exists? If there is a clear undervaluation, a good place to start is to identify where the disconnect between management and investors is—whether it involves growth, margins, aspirations, or a different perspective on the industry or a particular product line. Such an effort shows management what to talk about. Conversely, if there is a clear overvaluation, management would be wise to think strategically about how to address it—not just in terms of capitalizing on market deviations (by using shares to pay for acquisitions when those shares are overvalued by the market, for example) but also managing investors' expectations about the discrepancy.

WHICH INVESTORS MATTER?

Does it matter who your investors are? It is not clear whether one investor base is better than another in the sense of helping to align the share price with a company's intrinsic value. But understanding a company's investor base can give managers insights that might help them anticipate how the market will react to important events and strategic actions, as well as help managers improve the effectiveness and efficiency of their IR activities.

One way to begin seeking an answer to this question is by acknowledging that retail investors do not qualify for consideration in our examination. They rarely matter when it comes to influencing a company's share price. Despite collectively holding around 20–25 percent of U.S. equity, they do not move prices, because they typically do not trade very much.[1]

The real drivers of share prices are institutional investors, which manage hedge funds, mutual funds, or pension funds and can hold significant positions in individual companies for a longer period of time.[2]

When trying to identify these investors, we do not get much help from the common approaches to understanding institutional investors, because they don't look at how investors make decisions. For example, investors are often labeled as growth or value investors, depending on the type of stocks or indexes they invest in. However, most growth and value indexes, such as that of Standard & Poor's, use P/Es or market-to-book ratios to categorize companies as either value or growth: companies with high P/Es and market-to-book ratios are labeled growth companies, and those with low P/Es and market-to-book ratios are value companies. However, growth is only one factor driving differences in P/Es and market-to-book ratios. In fact, as we discussed in more detail in Chapter 6, we found a large overlap in the growth rates between so-called value and growth stocks. In a recent analysis, we found that although "growth" companies have marginally higher median growth than "value" companies (5.1 percent versus 3.4 percent, respectively), "growth" companies had a much higher return on capital than "value" companies (median of 48 percent, versus 29 percent), and more than 40 percent of

---

[1] One rebuttal to this point occurred in January 2021, when retail investors on the messaging platform Reddit started to invest en masse in the American video game retailer GameStop and other securities, in response to short positions taken by hedge funds and short sellers. On January 27, 2021, they drove the share price as high as $86 after these same shares had been trading for closer to $4 for much of the prior year. By 2023, the share price went back down to between $12 and $13. This worked because the retail investors acted together as one big block, not as individual investors holding small shares, a situation that modern communication methods make possible but is unlikely to be sustained over the long-term.

[2] Robert Palter, Werner Rehm, and Jonathan Shih, "Communicating with the Right Investors," *McKinsey on Finance* (Spring 2008): 1–4.

"value" stocks had growth rates higher than the median of "growth" stocks. As a result, almost half the difference between the estimated multiples actually comes from a difference in return on capital, and modestly growing companies with a high ROIC, such as the consumer packaged-goods company Clorox, end up on the growth-stock list, making the classification at best misleading.

Many executives still mistakenly believe they can increase their share price (and valuation multiple) by better marketing their shares to growth investors, because growth investors tend to own shares with higher valuation multiples. But the causality runs in reverse. When we analyzed companies whose stock prices have recently increased enough to shift them from the value classification to the growth classification, the rise in their market value was clearly not driven by an influx of growth investors. Rather, growth investors responded to higher multiples, moving into the stock only after the share price had already increased.

Consequently, neither this growth-versus-value segmentation nor segmentations using legal definitions such as "hedge fund" are helpful for understanding why your company is valued the way it is.

Investor Segmentation by Strategy

A more useful way to categorize and understand investors is to classify them by their investment strategy. Do they develop a view on the value of a company, or do they look for short-term price movements? Do they conduct extensive research and make a few big bets, or do they make lots of small bets with less information? Do they build their portfolios from the bottom up, or do they mirror an index?

Using this approach, we classify institutional investors into four types: intrinsic investors, traders, mechanical investors, and closet indexers.[3] These groups differ in their investment objectives and the way they build their portfolios. As a result, their portfolios vary along several important dimensions, including turnover rate, number of positions held, and positions held per investment professional (see Exhibit 36.2).

Intrinsic Investors   Intrinsic investors take positions only after undertaking rigorous due diligence of a company's inherent ability to create long-term value. This scrutiny typically takes more than a month. The depth of the intrinsic investor's research is evidenced by the fact that such investors typically hold fewer than 80 stocks at any time and each of their investment professionals manage only a few positions, usually between five and ten. Portfolio turnover is low, as intrinsic investors typically accept that price-to-value discrepancies

[3] Palter et al., "Communicating with the Right Investors."

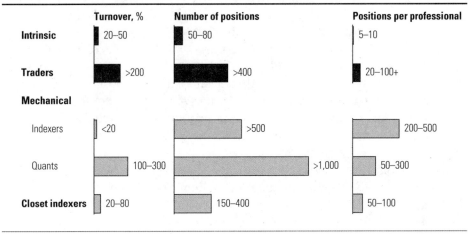

EXHIBIT 36.2 **Investors Segmented by Investment Strategies**

	Turnover, %	Number of positions	Positions per professional
Intrinsic	20–50	50–80	5–10
Traders	>200	>400	20–100+
Mechanical			
Indexers	<20	>500	200–500
Quants	100–300	>1,000	50–300
Closet indexers	20–80	150–400	50–100

may persist for up to three or four years before disappearing. We estimate that these investors hold around 15 to 20 percent of institutional U.S. equity, a decline from 20 to 25 percent prior to 2008,[4] and contribute 10 percent of the trading volume in the U.S. stock market.[5]

We should note here that by "investor," we mean an investment fund. Most large investment houses have many funds with different strategies. Examples of intrinsic investors include the William Blair Growth Fund, which in February 2024 held shares in 53 companies and had a turnover rate of 36 percent. From the hedge fund world, examples of intrinsic investors include Pzena and Hermes Capital. One prominent hedge fund manager, Lee Ainslie of Maverick Capital, describes Maverick as holding only five positions per investment professional, with many staff members having followed a single industry for ten years or more.[6]

Traders   Traders seek profits by betting on short-term movements in share prices, typically based on announcements about the company or technical factors, such as the momentum of the company's share price. The typical investment professional in this segment has 20 or more positions to follow and trades in and out of them quickly to capture small gains over short periods—as short as a few days or even hours. We estimate that traders own

---

[4] The decline in intrinsic holdings among S&P 500 companies is largely the result of an increase in ownership by index funds. However, the degree of the decline in the share of intrinsic investors in S&P 500 companies is less stark when Magnificent 7 stocks (Alphabet, Amazon, Apple, Meta, Microsoft, Nvidia, Tesla), which have a disproportionate share of index and retail investors, are excluded from the analysis.

[5] McKinsey Ownership Platform; McKinsey analysis.

[6] R. Dobbs and T. Koller, "Inside a Hedge Fund: An Interview with the Managing Partner of Maverick Capital," *McKinsey on Finance*, no. 19 (Spring 2006): 6–11.

about 30 to 35 percent of institutional equity holdings in the United States, down from 35 to 40 percent in 2010.

Traders don't need to develop a point of view on a company's intrinsic value, just on whether its shares will go up or down in the very short term. For example, traders may develop a view that a drug company is about to announce good news about a product trial that will boost the company's share price. The trader would buy the shares, wait for the announcement and the subsequent rise in the share price, and then immediately unwind the position. Some traders are in and out of the same stock many times during the year.

Traders follow the news about these companies closely and often approach companies directly, seeking nuances or insights that could matter greatly in the short term. Often, they are the main source of calls into your investor relations department to seek an informational advantage. However, they don't take a view on companies' long-term strategies and business performance.

Mechanical Investors   Mechanical investors (including closet indexers, described below) control about 40 to 45 percent of institutional equity in the United States. They make decisions based on strict criteria or rules. The prototypical mechanical investors are index funds, which merely build their portfolios by matching the composition of an index such as the S&P 500.

Another group of mechanical investors are the so-called quantitative investors, or "quants," which use mathematical models to build their portfolios. Quants make no qualitative judgments about a company's intrinsic value.

Closet Indexers   Finally, closet indexers, often promoted as active managers, have portfolios that largely look like an index. Basing their portfolio on an index and making some adjustments, they hold a great many stocks and don't have the time and resources to do in-depth research on them.[7] By contrast, intrinsic investors know every company in their portfolios in depth and build their portfolios from scratch, without taking their cue from any index.

The extent to which an investment fund might be considered a closet indexer is now measured, and often published, using a metric called active share. Active share is a measure of how much an investment portfolio differs from its benchmark index, based on a scale of 0 percent (complete overlap with the index) to 100 percent (no overlap). An index fund would have an active share of 0 percent. Funds with active shares below 60 percent are often considered closet indexers. For example, Putnam Investors Fund typically has an active share of about 40 percent. In contrast, the William Blair Growth

---

[7] For more on closet index funds, see M. Cremers and A. Petajisto, "How Active Is Your Fund Manager? A New Measure That Predicts Performance" (paper presented at American Finance Association 2007 Chicago Meetings, January 15, 2007); and E. Khusainova and J. Mier, *Taking a Closer Look at Active Share*, Lazard Asset Management, September 2017, www.lazardassetmanagement.com.

Fund, mentioned earlier as an intrinsic investor, typically has an active share above 70 percent.

Antti Petajisto, a researcher and fund manager who taught at the Yale School of Management, has estimated that the percentage of funds that might be considered closet indexers increased from 1 percent in 1980 to almost 30 percent in 2009.[8]

Targeting Communications

Which of these investors matter most for the stock price? Analyzing the trading behavior of all four investor groups in more detail, we find support for the idea that intrinsic investors are the ultimate drivers of share prices over the long term.

Exhibit 36.3 helps make the case, setting aside the inherently short-term-focused mechanical investors and closet indexers. At face value, traders might seem to be the most likely candidates for influencing share price in the market. They own 30 to 35 percent of the institutional U.S. equity base, and as the first two columns show, they trade much more than intrinsic investors. Their overall transaction volume is made up of many more trades, of which many are trades in the same stock within relatively short time periods. The average trader fund bought and sold over $80 billion worth of shares in 2006, more than 12 times the amount traded by the typical intrinsic investor. Similarly, as shown in the third column, the typical trader also buys or sells around $277 million in each equity stock he or she holds—far more per stock than the average intrinsic investor.

But the last column in the exhibit, which shows the value of effective daily trading per investment on the days that an investor traded at all, is the figure that discloses the real impact of each investor group on share prices in the

EXHIBIT 36.3 **Intrinsic Investors Have Greatest Impact on Share Price**

	Total trading per year			Effective trading per day[1]
	Per segment, $ trillion	Per investor,[2] $ billion	Per investment,[1] $ million	Per investment,[3] $ million
Intrinsic	3	6	72	7–30
Trader	11	88	277	1

[1] Trading activity in segment per day that trade is made.

[2] Per investor in segment.

[3] Per investor in segment per investment.

Source: R. Palter, W. Rehm, and J. Shih, "Communicating with the Right Investors," *McKinsey on Finance*, no. 27 (Spring 2008): 1–5.

[8] A. Petajisto, "Active Share and Mutual Fund Performance," December 2010, available at ssrn.com/abstract=1685942 or dx.doi.org/10.2139/ssrn.1685942.

712 INVESTOR COMMUNICATIONS

market. Effective daily trading is higher by far among intrinsic investors: *when intrinsic investors trade, they buy or sell in much larger quantities than traders do.* Although they trade much less frequently than the traders group, they hold much larger percentages of the companies in their portfolios, so when they do trade, they can move the prices of these companies' shares. Ultimately, therefore, intrinsic investors are the most important investor group for setting prices in the market over the longer term.

Furthermore, a recent unpublished McKinsey study shows a correlation between changes in intrinsic-investor holdings and TSR over a ten-year period. We should not infer any causation from this; we cannot know, for instance, whether intrinsic investors are good at picking stocks likely to increase in value or simply tend to invest in companies whose value has increased. The results do, however, reinforce the idea that intrinsic investors play a unique role.

Based on this analysis of investor behavior and impact, companies should focus their investor narrative on intrinsic investors. If intrinsic investors' view of your company's value is consistent with your own view, the market as a whole is likely to value your company as you do, because of the role intrinsic investors play in driving share prices. Their understanding of long-term value creation also means they're more likely than other investors to hold on to a stock, supporting the management team through periods of short-term volatility (so long as they believe these periods do not reflect a material change in the underlying value of the company).

Given the substantial demands on their time, CEOs and CFOs must decide which investors will get their time. Our investor segmentation makes clear that CEOs and CFOs should focus their time on a small set of intrinsic investors and delegate interactions with trading investors and closet indexers to their investor relations executives. In fact, one of the key roles of the IR department should be to determine analytically which investors CEOs and CFOs should develop relationships with, facilitate those relationships, and be the gatekeeper who handles low-priority investors on behalf of the CEO or CFO. The gatekeeper role may not be popular with investors, but it's essential. This would include decisions about how to treat closet indexers, which may be some of a company's largest investors. Remember, a closet indexer is likely to have more than 200 different companies in its portfolio, and most of this investor's holdings are in proportion to the company's size in an index such as the S&P 500. We recommend examining whether the closet indexer is significantly over- or underweight in any company or industry. If the answer is yes, we treat that investor as an intrinsic investor with respect to that company or industry. If not, we keep the investor categorized with the closet indexers.

One company segmented its interactions with investors and analysts into three tiers. Tier 1 included the company's top intrinsic investors, prospective intrinsic investors, those who had bought or sold large volumes of company stock, and select intrinsically focused sell-side analysts. This tier was where management focused its effort. Tier 2—smaller intrinsic investors, indexers and closet indexers, and core sell-side analysts—were delegated to the company's IR team. With tier 3, which included all other investors and the remaining sell-side analysts, the company took a passive approach to interactions. Using frameworks like these, management and IR teams can better structure their time.

In this example, the company considered not only the investor segments but also sell-side analysts.[9] As with closet investors, companies need to evaluate these analysts' impact on a case-by-case basis. An analyst's most important clients are those who generate the most trading commissions, so analysts tend to focus on short-term events and near-term earnings in order to be first to pass the news to their clients. That said, it is common for one to three sell-side analysts to have a deep understanding of the industry dynamics and the company's strategies, opportunities, and risks. These sell-side analysts resemble intrinsic investors in their approach. To address these distinctions, segment sell-side analysts based on their interests and approach, and then devote the most attention to those that tend to mimic intrinsic investors.

COMMUNICATING WITH INTRINSIC INVESTORS

Intrinsic investors are sophisticated and have spent considerable effort to understand your business. They want transparency about results, management's candid assessment of the company's performance, and insightful guidance about the company's targets and strategies. Their role in determining stock prices makes it worth management's time to address intrinsic investors' desire for clear, well-informed communication.

What Investors Want

It's worth remembering that investors aren't just external stakeholders for publicly listed companies. They're the owners. Understood in this light, investors want what anyone who owns part of a company would want: transparency on strategy, performance, and material changes to the business.

In 2015, McKinsey and the Aspen Institute Business and Society Program surveyed and interviewed intrinsic investors to find out what was important to

---

[9] The number of equity analysts covering a particular company can vary significantly and is often determined by external factors based on the analysts' research decisions and the interests of their clients. Companies generally have little control over how many analysts choose to cover them; it is typically a function of the company's size, the industry it operates in, its stock liquidity, and its relevance to the investment community. While there is no mandated minimum number of analysts for S&P 500 companies, larger and more prominent companies typically enjoy broader analyst coverage due to their market significance and investor interest.

them.[10] One highlight from the survey was intrinsic investors' overwhelming support of companies' efforts to pursue long-term value, even at the expense of short-term earnings. This finding was confirmed in a subsequent McKinsey survey in 2022, which showed overwhelming support for management teams that demonstrate willingness to take long-term risks.[11] A second highlight was that intrinsic investors expressed a desire for managers to educate them about companies' strategies and the dynamics of their industries.

McKinsey's follow-up survey with intrinsic investors in 2022 found that the most important criteria they use when deciding whether to hold a company's stock are the presence of a demonstrated competitive advantage resulting in profit margins expected to exceed those of peers, a management team with a track record of delivering results, and an efficient capital allocation program.[12]

Intrinsic investors understand that a long-term focus involves short-term trade-offs. The McKinsey–Aspen survey presented respondents with an investment scenario for a company that earns 70 percent of its revenues and profits abroad and experiences a major decline in short-term profits when foreign-exchange rates shift dramatically. Realizing that companies can't control or predict exchange rates, 19 of 24 investors surveyed said they would be neutral if the company took no action and simply reported lower profits. Nearly two-thirds said they would take a negative view of across-the-board cost reductions to compensate for an exchange rate shift. Responding to another scenario, 17 of 24 investors expressed a negative view of a CEO continuing to operate a legacy unit that is losing money with no expectation of turning profitable, while 20 of 24 were neutral or positive about the company shutting down the unit despite the one-time hit to earnings.

More generally, intrinsic investors favor companies with executive teams that confidently tell their companies' stories. This can be understood as a form of education, which covers topics such as the company's competitive advantages, how its strategy builds on those advantages, what external and competitive forces the company faces, and what concrete actions it is taking to realize its aspirations. As one investor put it in an interview, "I just need to be educated. Help me understand your business and strategy. If I disagree, I don't have to invest."

Investors interviewed as part of this research also identified management credibility as a top factor when considering investments. To assess credibility, they want to understand how CEOs make decisions, whether the company's approach is aligned with long-term value creation, and whether the management team is open and transparent in times of difficulty.

[10] This section is adapted from R. Darr and T. Koller, "How to Build an Alliance against Corporate Short-Termism," *McKinsey on Finance*, no. 61 (2017): 2–9.
[11] McKinsey & Company Investor Survey, third quarter 2022 ($n = 19$).
[12] Ibid.

Another common theme from the interviews was that managers should ensure the long-term view is addressed during every investor engagement. Messages about short-term results can start with the long term and then zoom in on the details as needed. As one investor said, "It's all about the horizon. Long-term investors don't need a lot of detailed guidance about quarterly numbers. They need clarity, consistency, and transparency from managers in communicating strategic priorities and their long-term expectations."

What of intrinsic investors' preferred *communications channels*? Our survey found that they especially value investor days or capital markets days, since, as one equity analyst put it, "you can read body language and get a better read on what's happening with the company." They also assigned great importance to one-on-one or small-group meetings. In contrast, industry conferences and quarterly earnings calls were rated as less important.[13]

Benefits of Transparency

Many companies are reluctant to provide a detailed discussion of results, issues, and opportunities. Their rationale is that this kind of disclosure reduces their flexibility to manage reported profits or will reveal sensitive information to competitors. But transparency of a company's results, opportunities, and issues—including, importantly, an honest assessment of its successes and failures—builds credibility with investors.

Moreover, in our experience, a company's competitors, customers, and suppliers already know more about any business than its managers might expect. For example, there's a cottage industry of photographers dedicated to searching for and publicizing new car models that automotive manufacturers have not yet formally acknowledged. In addition, a company's competitors will be talking regularly to the company's customers and suppliers, who won't hesitate to share information about the company whenever that's in their interest. Therefore, revealing details about yourself is unlikely to affect your company as adversely as you might expect. Managers should keep that in mind as they assess the competitive costs and benefits of greater transparency.

In some situations, companies might even be able to gain an advantage over their competitors by being more transparent. Suppose a company has developed a new technology, product, or manufacturing process that management feels sure will give the company a lead over competitors. Furthermore, managers believe competitors will be unable to copy the innovation. At a strategic level, disclosing the innovation might discourage competitors from even trying to compete, if they believe the company has too great a lead. From an

---

[13] Although industry conferences are generally not considered as valuable as investor days or smaller group meetings, some more prominent, industry-specific investor conferences, such as those held by the Consumer Analyst Group of New York (CAGNY) and J.P. Morgan's annual Healthcare Conference, present an opportunity for interaction with investors.

investor's perspective, disclosure of the innovation could increase the company's share price relative to its competitors, thus making it more attractive to potential partners and key employees, as well as reducing the price of stock-based acquisitions.

Sophisticated investors build up their view of a company's overall value by summing the values of its discrete businesses. They're not much concerned with aggregate results: these are simply averages, providing little insight into how the company's individual businesses might be positioned for future growth and returns on invested capital. At many companies, management teams that desire a closer match between their company's market value and their own assessment might achieve this by disclosing more about the performances of their individual businesses.

Ideally, companies should provide an income statement for each business unit, down to the level of EBITA at least. They should also provide all operating items in the balance sheet—such as property, plant, and equipment (PP&E) and working capital—reconciled with the consolidated reported numbers. Providing the minimum required by both International Financial Reporting Standards (IFRS) and U.S. Generally Accepted Accounting Principles (GAAP) is not enough to allow investors to assess value across business units.

Even companies with a single line of business can improve their disclosures without giving away strategically sensitive information. In the period when Whole Foods Market was growing quickly and before it was acquired by Amazon in 2017, the U.S. natural-foods supermarket chain provided investors with its ROIC numbers by age of store, as well as a detailed table explaining how it calculated its returns. Such openness gives investors deeper insights into the company's economic life cycle.

Deciding What to Disclose

Concerning operational data, what to disclose depends on the key value drivers of a business or business unit. Ideally, these should be the metrics that management uses to make strategic or operational decisions. For example, each quarter, the leading research and advisory firm Gartner discloses a narrow but highly relevant set of metrics for each of its three business units. As Gartner's CFO explains, the firm publishes only the most important of the metrics that management uses to examine the performance of the business. Most importantly, Gartner has done this consistently for over a decade, no matter what the performance indicators showed. Similarly, companies in some industries, such as steel and airlines, regularly disclose volumes and average prices, as well as the use and cost of energy, which are the key drivers of value in these sectors. And home improvement retailer Lowe's provides helpful information about key value drivers such as the number of transactions and the average ticket size, as shown in Exhibit 36.4.

EXHIBIT 36.4 **Lowe's: Operating Statistics and ROIC**

	2019	2020	2021	2022
Comparable sales increase, %	2.6	26.1	6.9	(0.9)
Customer transactions, millions	921	1,046	1,002	937
Average ticket, $	78.36	85.67	96.09	103.64
Number of stores	1,977	1,974	1,971	1,738
Sales floor square feet, millions	208	208	208	195
Average store size, selling square feet, thousands	105	105	106	112
Return on invested capital, %	19.9	27.7	35.3	30.4

Source: Company SEC filings (Form 10-K).

Choosing transparency can be difficult. Some companies that prefer greater discretion hesitate to increase openness. These are often strong performers with good track records. Over many years, that performance record (frequently in the form of steady earnings increases) has provided leverage to rebuff investors' demands for more transparency. But it is the nature of every business's life cycle that growth will slow, even after years of success, as the business matures or markets become more competitive. At that juncture, the company needs new strategies to keep creating value for shareholders, and these changes should be communicated to investors; doing so ensures that the market share price continues to reflect the company's true worth.

In a more positive example, an executive vice president at a multinational chemical and consumer goods company demonstrated openness about the shortcomings of his company's integration efforts. This approach built credibility with the company's analysts and investors, who were looking to see whether management would provide an honest assessment of past performance.

Legislation and accounting rules have been requiring ever-greater transparency. Even so, results that are transparent enough to meet today's regulatory requirements may fail to meet the standard of transparency on operating metrics that satisfies intrinsic investors. In some industries, this has shifted in response to the investors' explicit demands or the leadership of one or more industry pioneers. For example, the petroleum industry has for many years published detailed fact books that describe oil production and reserves by geography. In pharmaceuticals, companies provide detailed information about their product pipelines at every stage of research and development. In these industries, any company that failed to disclose what others disclose would likely lose the market's trust.

In most industries, however, the level of disclosure and transparency has been less standardized, so management must choose how transparent it wants to be. The need to build trust should make management resist fears that a detailed discussion of the issues and opportunities facing their company will reveal sensitive information to competitors or make it harder to put the best gloss on their results. Consider a U.S. media conglomerate that provides detailed information by business unit on the income statement but leaves it to investors to sort out the balance sheet by business unit. Omitting such information risks giving investors the impression that management is trying to obscure underlying performance issues.

LISTENING TO INVESTORS

The final element of effective investor communications is listening to investors. Listening to gain competitive intelligence is, of course, a no-lose proposition. But to what extent should executives be influenced by investors' opinions about what strategies the company should pursue (expressed either as opinions or by the nature of the questions the investors ask)? The question of influence is difficult when investors' opinions run counter to what the senior executives believe is the best strategy for creating long-term value.

Once again, it is helpful to segment investors and interpret their input in light of their strategies. For example, trading investors, who tend to be the most vocal and frequent voices, base their trading strategies on *events*, so they prefer frequent announcements and short-term actions to create trading opportunities. Intrinsic investors are more concerned with longer-term strategic initiatives and the broader forces driving the company and industry. Segmenting investor input helps executives sort through the competing views. We typically find that when executives segment the input they receive from investors, the input from the intrinsic investors is the most helpful.

In the end, though, executives have more information than investors about their company and its capabilities, opportunities, and threats. They need to be confident about their strategic choices and convey that confidence to investors. You can't expect to please all investors. You must do what's right for long-term value creation.

EARNINGS GUIDANCE

For many executives, the ritual of issuing guidance on their company's likely earnings per share (EPS) in the next quarter or year is a necessary, if sometimes onerous, part of communicating with financial markets. In a survey, we found that they saw three primary benefits of issuing earnings guidance: higher valuations, lower share price volatility, and improved liquidity. Yet several analyses have found no evidence that those expected benefits materialize.[14] Therefore, instead of EPS guidance, we believe executives should provide investors with the broader operational measures shaping company performance, such as volume targets, revenue targets, and initiatives to reduce costs.

---

[14] P. Hsieh, T. Koller, and S. Rajan, "The Misguided Practice of Earnings Guidance," *McKinsey on Finance* (Spring 2006): 1–5; and A. Babcock and S. Williamson, *Moving beyond Quarterly Guidance: A Relic of the Past*, FCLTGlobal, October 2017, www.fcltglobal.org.

No Payoff for Earnings Guidance

It's a myth that quarterly EPS guidance is necessary and that almost everyone does it. In 2002, Coca-Cola became one of the earliest large companies to stop issuing guidance. Its executives had concluded that providing short-term guidance prevented management from concentrating on strategic initiatives to build its businesses over the long term. Gary Fayard, CFO at that time, believed that, rather than indicating weak earnings, the move signaled a renewed focus on long-term goals. The market seemed to agree and did not react negatively: Coke's share price held steady.[15] Since then, many other companies have stopped providing guidance entirely or have shifted the focus of their guidance away from EPS and toward broader indicators of performance. In 2022, only 21 percent of S&P 500 companies provided quarterly EPS guidance, while 35 percent gave only annual guidance.[16] In Europe, the share of companies providing quarterly EPS guidance is much lower: only 1 percent of the Eurostoxx 300.

To test whether companies providing EPS guidance are rewarded with higher valuations, we compared the earnings multiples of companies that provided guidance with the multiples of those that did not, industry by industry. For most industries, the underlying distributions of the two sets of companies were statistically indistinguishable. Similar results were found by researchers at the Harvard Business School and KKS Advisors.[17]

Companies that decide to begin offering guidance may hope the effort will boost total shareholder returns (TSR). Yet in the year companies begin to offer guidance, their TSR on average is no different from that of companies not offering guidance at all. Returns to shareholders are just as likely to be above the market as below the market in the year a company starts providing guidance.

On the issue of share price volatility, we found that when a company begins to issue earnings guidance, the likelihood of volatility in its share price increasing or decreasing is the same as it is for companies that don't issue guidance. Finally, we found that when companies begin issuing earnings guidance, they do indeed experience an increase in trading volumes relative to companies that don't provide it, as their management anticipates. However, the effect wears off the next year. The same results were found by the Harvard Business School researchers and KKS Advisors.[18]

When we asked executives about ceasing earnings guidance, many feared their share price would decline and its volatility would increase. But when we analyzed 126 companies that had discontinued issuing guidance, we found

---

[15] D. M. Katz, "Nothing but the Real Thing," *CFO*, March 2003, cfo.com.

[16] A. He and M. Mei, *A Look at Long-Term Guidance Trends in 2022*, FCLT Global, art. 27, July 2023 (www.fcltglobal.org/resource/a-look-at-long-term-guidance-trends-in-2022/).

[17] Babcock and Williamson, *Moving beyond Quarterly Guidance*.

[18] Ibid.

they were just about as likely as the rest of the market to see higher or lower shareholder returns. Of the 126 companies, 58 had higher returns than the overall market in the year they stopped issuing guidance, and 68 had lower returns. Furthermore, our analysis showed that the lower-than-market returns of companies that discontinued guidance resulted from poor underlying performance, not from the act of ending guidance. For example, two-thirds of the companies that halted guidance and experienced lower returns on capital saw lower TSR than the market. For companies that increased ROIC, only about one-third had delivered lower TSR than the market.

Our conclusion was that issuing guidance offers companies and investors no real benefits. On the contrary, it can trigger real costs and unfortunate unintended consequences. The difficulty of predicting earnings accurately, for example, frequently causes management teams to endure the painful experience of missing quarterly forecasts. That, in turn, can be a powerful incentive for management to focus excessive attention on the short term, at the expense of longer-term investments, and to manage earnings inappropriately from quarter to quarter to create the illusion of stability. Moreover, our research with intrinsic investors indicates they realize that earnings are inherently unpredictable. Consequently, they prefer that companies not issue quarterly EPS guidance. Only 20 percent of intrinsic investors surveyed by McKinsey and the Aspen Institute said they would see a company's announced intention to discontinue earnings guidance one year from the announcement as a "yellow flag."[19] In a survey by the Rivel Research Group's Intelligence Council, just 7 percent of investors said they want companies to offer guidance on any metrics at all (financial and operational) for periods less than one year.[20]

An Alternative to Earnings Guidance

As an alternative, we believe executives will gain advantages from providing guidance on the real short-, medium-, and long-term value drivers of their businesses, providing ranges rather than point estimates. For example, some companies, including JPMorgan Chase and Maersk, provide target ranges for returns on capital over a three- to five-year period.[21] Other companies, such as Lowe's, provide a range of possibilities for revenue growth under a variety of assumptions about inflation, and they discuss the growth of individual business units when that matters. Some companies also provide information on value drivers that can help investors assess the sustainability of growth. Humana, for example, provides guidance on estimated membership in its health products, both those that will grow and those that will decline.

---

[19] Darr and Koller, "How to Build an Alliance."
[20] "Evolving Guidance Preferences: Attitudes and Practices of the Global Buy Side," Intelligence Council, Rivel Research Group, September 2017.
[21] Because JPMorgan Chase is a bank, it uses ROE rather than ROIC.

The value drivers a business chooses to publicize will depend on the unique characteristics of the business. For example, a leading project-based company provides details on the performance of individual current projects plus the timing and expected returns of potential projects. One European company provides investors with a tax estimation tool, which uses the investors' assessments of regional growth rates to provide a best guess on the tax rates the company will face.

Ideally, a company would provide the kind of information that would help investors make their own projections of the company's performance based on their assessment of external factors. For example, in resource industries, prices are volatile for extracted commodities such as gold, copper, or oil. For such companies, a management team's view on future prices is not necessarily better than that of their investors. Investors would therefore find production targets more useful than revenue targets in these industries. Similarly, exchange rates are unpredictable, yet they can affect the profits of multinationals by 5 percent or more in a given year. Companies should therefore avoid predicting exchange rates and locking them into EPS targets. Rather, they should discuss their targets at constant currency rates and provide a view on sensitivity. For example, steel company Alcoa has a large exposure to the U.S.-dollar-to-Australian-dollar exchange rate and provides guidance not only on what rate has been used for the EBITDA guidance but also on how much the EBITDA would change if the exchange rate moved. This kind of analysis gives investors a much clearer picture of expected performance.

MEETING CONSENSUS EARNINGS FORECASTS

Whether or not a company provides guidance, there will be an analyst consensus forecast of earnings per share (EPS), which the company will want to meet or beat.[22] The conventional wisdom, mistaken though it is, is that missing the consensus earnings forecast, even by a small amount, means your share price will drop. Conversely, many executives believe that consistently beating the consensus leads to a premium share price. Thus, a common reason given for choosing to provide earnings guidance is to influence the consensus.

Besides trying to influence the consensus, executives often go to some lengths to meet or beat consensus estimates—even acting in ways that could damage the longer-term health of the business. It's not uncommon, for example, for companies to offer customers steep discounts in the final days of a reporting period in order to stoke sales numbers, in effect borrowing from the next quarter's sales. As other researchers have shown, executives may forgo

[22] The section is adapted from T. Koller, R. Raj, and A. Saxena, "Avoiding the Consensus Earnings Trap," *McKinsey on Finance*, no. 45 (Winter 2013).

value-creating investments in favor of short-term results,[23] or they might manage earnings inappropriately to create the illusion of stability.

Yet our analysis of large U.S. companies shows that these fears are unfounded.[24] In the near term, falling short of consensus earnings estimates is seldom catastrophic. Nor does consistently beating or meeting consensus estimates over several years matter, once differences in companies' growth and operating performance are considered. In fact, a company's performance relative to consensus earnings seems to matter only when the company consistently misses earnings estimates over several years.

This doesn't mean companies should ignore consensus estimates, which can hint at what is on investors' minds and why. For example, how does the industry growth outlook of investors compare with that of executives? The consensus can also be used to assess how well analysts and investors understand the drivers of a company's performance. Our findings demonstrate that when investors are valuing a company, they consider more indicators of financial health than whether the company meets its consensus earnings estimates. Thus, companies need not go to extremes to meet or beat analysts' expectations if it means damaging the company's long-term prospects.

When Companies Fall Short

Most executives haven't experienced many catastrophic drops in share price after minor earnings misses, so they conclude that such misses are rare. The mechanics of earnings estimates lend some support to that perception. After all, analysts' estimates typically are overly optimistic at the beginning of the financial year, but by the third quarter, it's reasonable to expect them to fall roughly in line with the eventual reported earnings—a pattern borne out by previous research.[25] According to standard practice, a company has beaten the consensus estimate if its actual earnings are greater than the last available estimate for the year (almost always projected after the year is over). Consequently, one would expect analyst estimates at that stage to be accurate. Moreover, executives tend to focus on dramatic press accounts of earnings mishaps that are among the most extreme outliers.

In fact, falling short is common, but the effect is benign. More than 40 percent of companies generate earnings below consensus estimates, whether those estimates are compiled an entire year or just three days before an earnings announcement. Although some academics have documented a correlation

---

[23] J. R. Graham, C. Harvey, and S. Rajgopal, "Value Destruction and Financial Reporting Decisions," *Financial Analysts Journal* 62 (2006): 27–39, which found that a majority of CFOs would "avoid initiating a positive NPV project if it meant falling short of the current quarter's consensus earnings."

[24] This conclusion is based on analysis of the largest U.S.-based nonfinancial companies with a December 31 fiscal year-end, a sample of 266 companies.

[25] M. Goedhart, B. Russell, and Z. Williams, "Prophets and Profits," *McKinsey on Finance*, no. 2 (Autumn 2001): 11–14.

between the change in a company's share price before and after the announcement of earnings and the degree to which it meets the consensus earnings estimate, the size of the effect is small. Indeed, our analysis suggests that missing the consensus by 1 percent would lead to a share price decrease of only 0.2 percent in the five days after the announcement. In other words, missing the consensus estimate by a penny or so usually doesn't matter.

Executives concerned about their company's performance relative to consensus estimates should also consider that 40 percent of companies that saw their earnings miss the consensus estimate also saw their share price, adjusted for the market, move in the opposite direction. For example, when PPG Industries, a global supplier of paints, coatings, and chemicals, announced earnings for 2010 that were 4 percent below the consensus, the market reacted positively with an excess return of 7 percent. Why? On digging deeper, investors saw that the long-term outlook had improved. Sales were stronger than expected in nearly all business segments. The CEO also announced some investment initiatives that investors viewed as having the potential to create value in the longer term.

In general, EPS forecasts are too far removed to be meaningful for investors and don't forecast performance well. They inevitably result in a systemic overestimation of corporate earnings. More useful are medium- to long-term forecasts about revenue and EBITDA, which are linked much more closely to actual performance. A recent analysis also showed that analysts are much better at estimating revenue and EBITDA than EPS, supporting the view that guidance closer to operating financials might have a place.[26]

When Companies Meet or Beat the Consensus Forecast

Similarly, meeting or exceeding the consensus estimate is less important than how the earnings were reached. That's because investors are continually assessing other news, such as whether the company met the consensus estimate for revenues as well as earnings. When North American brewing company Molson Coors beat the consensus estimate by 2 percent in 2010, the market nevertheless reacted negatively, with an excess return of –7 percent. Investors saw that the company's sales volume had declined by 2 percent and that margins also were down; the company beat the consensus only because of a lower-than-expected tax rate. The market reacted to the fundamental drivers of performance—volume and margin—rather than EPS itself.

Investors are also able to see through cases where one-off items are responsible for meeting the consensus estimate. Meanwhile, earnings announcements themselves often include information that helps investors reassess a company's long-term performance outlook. Our research has shown that the

---

[26] W. Rehm and R. Kotsev, "Another Nail in the Coffin: Analyst EPS Forecasts Are Basically Useless," LinkedIn, January 2, 2024, www.linkedin.com.

market reaction at the time of an earnings announcement is influenced more by changes in analysts' expectations for longer-term earnings than by whether the most recent results met the consensus estimate (see Exhibit 36.5). A company might fall short of current-year earnings estimates and still see its share price increase if analysts revised their earnings estimates upward for the next two years.

Just as critical, the notion that markets reward companies with higher share prices when they consistently beat the earnings consensus turns out to be wrong. Here again, while some researchers have found this to be true, their analysis doesn't take into consideration the underlying performance of companies as measured by revenue growth and return on capital.[27] Once adjusted for performance, the apparent effect of beating the consensus consistently (which we define as four or more years out of seven) disappears. Companies with strong growth or ROIC had high shareholder returns regardless of whether they consistently beat the consensus. Only the companies that missed it consistently—again, in four years out of seven—showed a statistically significant negative effect from doing so (see Exhibit 36.6).

EXHIBIT 36.5 **Impact of Change in Two-Year EPS Estimate Revision vs. Short-Term Earnings Surprise**

Median excess return,[1] %

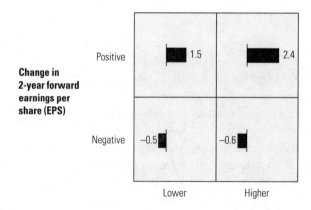

Change in 2-year forward earnings per share (EPS)

Positive — 1.5   2.4

Negative — −0.5   −0.6

Lower   Higher

Actual EPS vs. consensus estimate

[1] Excess return over market return.

Source: Analysis of announcements of 2007 fiscal-year earnings of 590 European companies (n = 127 positive and lower, 203 positive and higher, 118 negative and lower, 142 negative and higher).

[27] See, for example, R. Kasznik and M. McNichols, "Does Meeting Earnings Expectations Matter? Evidence from Analyst Forecast Revisions and Share Prices," *Journal of Accounting Research* 40, no. 3 (June 2002): 727–759.

EXHIBIT 36.6 **Fundamentals vs. Consensus Estimates**

Median excess return vs. sector return,[1] 2005–2011, %

		Relative financial performance[3]			
		High growth + high ROIC	High growth + low ROIC	Low growth + high ROIC	Low growth + low ROIC
Actual earnings vs. consensus estimate[2]	Consistently beating	4	3	0	−2
	Inconsistent	2	0	0	−3
	Consistently missing	0	−5	−5	−6

[1] Company's total shareholder returns (TSR) minus median TSR of the sector. Sample is 243 nonfinancial S&P 500 companies with December fiscal year-end.

[2] Difference between actual earnings per share and consensus estimate 30 days prior to earnings announcement. "Consistently beating" defined as beating expectations by >2% at least 4 out of 7 years. "Consistently missing" defined as missing expectations by >2% at least 4 out of 7 years. Companies consistently meeting expectations (by ± 2% at least 4 out of 7 years) are not shown due to small sample size.

[3] Growth is compound annual growth rate of revenue for 2004–2011; ROIC is return on invested capital for 2005–2011. Companies categorized as high ROIC or high growth exceeded the absolute reference points of 15% for ROIC and 7% for growth or the median of the respective sector in the sample.

Source: S&P Capital IQ.

SUMMARY

At the extremes, there are two views on investor relations: one that you can talk up your share price and one that companies shouldn't spend much time or effort on investor communications at all, because it won't make any difference to their market value. Our view is, first, that investors can more accurately value a company if they have the right information and, second, that a market value aligned with the true value of your company is the best outcome of your investor communications strategy. Moreover, even if you do manage to talk up the stock in the short term, this is unlikely to be the best thing for the company in the long run.

You can better align your company's stock market value with its intrinsic value by applying an analytical approach for identifying value, understanding your current and potential investors, and communicating with the sophisticated investors who ultimately drive a company's share price. These principles also can help managers use their scarce time for investor communications more efficiently and effectively.

We also believe investors need more transparency than what is typically given today. Executives should always remember that investors are the *owners* of the company. Owners deserve to know what managers do with their money in as much detail as possible, given the competitive environment.

Moreover, rather than providing precise earnings guidance or taking actions to achieve consensus earnings forecasts, managers should focus on driving return on invested capital (ROIC) and growth to create maximum value for shareholders. Managers should not be distracted from these efforts by any short-term price volatility—that is, any temporary deviation in their share price from its intrinsic value—because such deviations are likely to occur from time to time, even in the most efficient stock market.

Part Five

Special Situations

37

Leveraged Buyouts

In a leveraged buyout (LBO), private equity (PE) firms, backed by institutional investors and high-net-worth individuals, acquire companies, collaborate with management to improve performance, and eventually exit through public offerings or the sale of the company. These transactions often rely on substantial debt financing, which can amplify returns but also introduces considerable risk.

This chapter outlines how to model an LBO.[1] We begin by analyzing the financing required to complete the purchase, using metrics such as debt-to-EBITDA[2] and equity-to-value ratios. We then forecast debt, covering key LBO-specific terms such as term loans, floating interest rates, and payment-in-kind interest. Finally, we project the company's future operating performance, incorporating anticipated improvements, and evaluate performance metrics such as internal rate of return (IRR). In practice, modelling the debt financing and operating performance is an iterative process, rather than a sequential one.

In the final section of this chapter, we link the LBO model to the fundamental principles of value creation. This connection is essential, as the most successful PE firms achieve superior returns not through leverage or high exit multiples, but by improving operating performance—that is, by increasing revenue, hastening growth, streamlining costs, and optimizing resource allocation.

---

[1] This chapter focuses on LBO modeling. For further insights into the purpose and process of LBOs, see S. N. Kaplan and P. Strömberg, "Leveraged Buyouts and Private Equity," *Journal of Economic Perspectives* 23, no. 1 (2009): 121–146; and P. Gompers, S. N. Kaplan, and V. Mukharlyamov, "What Do Private Equity Firms Say They Do?" *Journal of Financial Economics* 121, no. 3 (2016): 449–476.

[2] Debt to earnings before interest, taxes, depreciation, and amortization.

PROPOSED LBO OF AXELEDGE PARTS COMPANY

To illustrate the modeling for a leveraged buyout, we examine the acquisition of AxelEdge Parts Company, a hypothetical parts manufacturer serving the auto industry. AxelEdge generates approximately $200 million in operating profit on $1.2 billion in revenue. Despite steady revenue growth, the company's returns on capital have rarely exceeded its cost of capital. The partners at the PE fund LBO LLP believe AxelEdge offers significant potential for operational improvements, including streamlining production workflows, implementing lean manufacturing techniques, and renegotiating supplier contracts.

AxelEdge's shares are publicly traded, and its board of directors has indicated a willingness to consider going private if presented with a compelling offer. Exhibit 37.1 provides an overview of the company's current capital structure. In a standard LBO, the buyer acquires all outstanding shares, typically offering a premium above the prevailing stock price. Acquisition premiums generally range from 20 to 40 percent. For AxelEdge, underwriters estimate that a 20 percent premium would be sufficient to secure board approval, resulting in an equity purchase price of $2,180 million.

An LBO buyer will rely heavily on leverage to finance the acquisition.[3] The acquiring firm, also referred to as the financial sponsor, structures the purchase by combining equity contributed by its investors with borrowed

EXHIBIT 37.1 **AxelEdge: Proposed Deal Structure**

$ million

Current capital structure		Proposed capital structure	
Debt		**Debt**	
Debt due in year 5, at 6% coupon	120	Credit facility at SOFR[2] + 3%	0
Debt due in year 15, at 4% coupon	200	Term loan at SOFR[2] + 4%	525
Total debt	320	Subordinated bond at 12%	925
		Total debt	1,450
Equity			
Pre-announcement share price, $	27.92	**Equity**	
× Number of shares, millions	65.00	Private-equity sponsor	1,000
Market capitalization	1,815	Management team	50
		Equity contribution	1,050
× Acquisition premium[1]	1.20		
= Equity offer	2,180		
Required financing	2,500	Required financing	2,500

[1] To finalize the AxelEdge transaction, the underwriter estimates that a 20% premium over the pre-announcement market capitalization will be necessary. This translates to an offer price per share of $33.50.

[2] The 3-Month Secured Overnight Financing Rate (SOFR) is a benchmark interest rate that reflects the cost of borrowing cash overnight, secured by U.S. Treasury securities. It has gradually replaced the London Interbank Offered Rate (LIBOR) as a benchmark rate.

[3] For more on analyzing and designing a capital structure strategy, refer to Chapter 35.

funds. This change in the company's capital structure is commonly known as a recapitalization. Achieving the high debt levels typical of LBOs requires the buyer to retire AxelEdge's existing debt, even if it carries favorable interest rates. This step is necessary because the covenants tied to existing debt often restrict the company's ability to assume additional leverage. By removing these constraints, the buyer gains the flexibility to create a new financing structure aligned with the acquisition's strategic objectives.

Given leverage's central role in an LBO, the buyer will work with debt underwriters to determine the maximum sustainable debt level. Exhibit 37.2 highlights several key metrics relevant to this analysis. Before the transaction, AxelEdge's debt-to-EBITDA ratio stood at 1.3 times, which is within the typical range of one to three times for investment-grade companies.[4] By contrast, LBOs often involve much higher debt levels, ranging from five to eight times EBITDA. Companies with high enterprise-value-to-EBITDA multiples can sometimes sustain even higher leverage ratios.

Lenders will also evaluate the ratio of contributed equity to enterprise value. In current markets (as of 2025), LBOs usually require an equity contribution of at least 35 percent, though this benchmark increases with higher enterprise-value-to-EBITDA multiples. Not surprisingly, both the maximum debt-to-EBITDA

EXHIBIT 37.2 **AxelEdge: Capital Structure Analysis**

$ million

	Value	Forward EBITDA[1]	Debt-to-EBITDA[1]	EV-to-EBITDA[1]	% of value
Current capital structure					
Debt	320	240	1.3×		15.0%
Market capitalization[2]	1,815				85.0%
Enterprise value[2]	2,135	240		8.9×	100.0%
Acquisition premium	365				
Required financing	2,500	240		10.4×	
Proposed structure					
Debt	1,450	240	6.0×		58.0%
Equity contribution	1,050				42.0%
Required financing	2,500	240		10.4×	100.0%

[1] Earnings before interest, taxes, depreciation, and amortization. EBITDA is estimated in Exhibit 37.4.

[2] Enterprise value measured prior to the acquisition announcement.

[4] While lenders consider various financial ratios, debt to EBITDA is the widely accepted benchmark for assessing a company's use of debt. For more on leverage assessment and the role of different financial metrics, refer to Chapter 12.

ratio and the minimum ratio of equity to enterprise value are heavily influenced by prevailing market conditions.[5]

Following discussions with debt underwriters and potential lenders, LBO LLP secures $1,450 million in debt financing to support the acquisition. This financing includes $525 million in term loans from a PE lender and $925 million in subordinated tradeable bonds issued to a range of investors underwritten by an investment bank. Based on AxelEdge's $240 million in EBITDA, this financing structure results in a post-transaction debt-to-EBITDA ratio of 6.0 times. The remaining $1,050 million required to finalize the transaction will be provided through equity, representing approximately 42 percent of the total capitalization.

The equity contribution will come from both the PE sponsor and AxelEdge's management team. This shared financial stake allows management to benefit from the company's upside potential, further incentivizing them to meet ambitious financial targets in partnership with the sponsor.

MECHANICS OF DEBT FINANCING

To finance the acquisition, the PE buyer will rely heavily on debt, which is a foundational element of the LBO financial model. Traditionally, LBO debt financing has been structured across multiple tranches, each with distinct maturities, interest rates, and seniority levels.[6] However, the growth of large private lenders has popularized "unitranche" financing, where a single term loan funds the entire debt requirement.[7] Although this streamlined approach has become common in recent LBOs, it may not represent a permanent shift. Thus, for the AxelEdge example, we assume the company will obtain three types of debt: a credit facility with a maximum limit of $250 million, a

---

[5] Axelson, Jenkinson, Strömberg, and Weisbach analyze how debt market conditions impact leverage and pricing in LBOs, finding that buyout leverage depends more on the availability and cost of credit than on target company characteristics. When credit is cheap and plentiful, LBOs typically feature higher leverage and increased purchase prices, with higher debt levels driving up purchase multiples and resulting in more aggressive valuations. For further details on leverage patterns in LBOs, see U. Axelson, T. Jenkinson, P. Strömberg, and M. S. Weisbach, "Borrow Cheap, Buy High? The Determinants of Leverage and Pricing in Buyouts," *Journal of Finance* 68, no 6 (July 26, 2013): 2223–2267.
[6] Debt markets have a unique, and sometimes cryptic, language. For example, a *tranche*—from the French word for "slice"—refers to a specific segment of a larger debt deal, with each tranche carrying distinct risk levels, interest rates, and repayment priorities. Investors also refer to the capital structure as a "stack," a metaphorical hierarchy of claims, where senior debt holders are repaid first, followed by junior debt, preferred equity, and finally, common equity at the base, which offers the highest returns but also the greatest risk.
[7] Research by Colla, Ippolito, and Li finds that companies with higher growth opportunities and more volatile cash flows tend to prefer term loans from private lenders over issuing bonds in public markets. The authors argue that private lenders provide greater flexibility and the option for renegotiation, which is particularly advantageous for firms facing unpredictable cash flows. For further details, see P. Colla, F. Ippolito, and K. Li, "Debt Specialization," *Journal of Finance* 68, no. 5 (October 2013): 2117–2141.

$525 million term loan from a private lender, and a $925 million subordinated bond. Each debt type has unique characteristics, which we examine next.

Credit Facilities

The credit facility functions as a line of credit that the company can draw on as needed, similar to using a personal credit card. This facility is particularly useful for addressing short-term financing needs, such as seasonal working capital requirements, without requiring the company to access the credit markets repeatedly. Like a credit card balance, any amount drawn from the facility can be repaid and subsequently borrowed again, offering the company a financial cushion and the flexibility to manage temporary funding gaps. The credit facility will not finance the initial acquisition; the $250 million quote is the maximum credit limit.

Term Loans

A term loan is a loan with a fixed maturity. In PE transactions, term loans typically have a fixed maturity of five to eight years, a duration that slightly exceeds the expected timeline of a PE investment.[8] This extended maturity provides the sponsor with added flexibility before refinancing becomes necessary. Term loans also have several distinctive features compared with the corporate bonds that large, investment-grade companies commonly issue. Notable differences include floating rather than fixed interest rates, the option for payment-in-kind interest, required amortization, and prepayment penalties.

To illustrate how a term loan evolves over time, we model a typical loan in Exhibit 37.3. In this example, detailed in the following paragraphs, the term loan has a seven-year maturity, pays a coupon rate that floats, requires only 60 percent of interest payments to be paid in cash, and amortizes at a rate of 2 percent per year.[9]

Floating Interest Rates   Unlike fixed-rate coupon bonds, term loans generally carry floating interest rates, which adjust periodically based on a benchmark

---

[8] Term loans are often designated by letters, such as TLA (term loan A) and TLB (term loan B). TLA loans typically have an amortizing structure, requiring regular principal and interest payments throughout their five- to seven-year maturities. These loans are syndicated to banks and traditional lenders, offering lower interest rates because of their reduced risk profile. In contrast, TLB loans feature minimal amortization, with small annual principal payments and a large bullet payment at maturity, generally over seven to eight years. TLB loans are frequently used in LBO transactions and are primarily marketed to institutional investors.

[9] A term loan typically includes either PIK interest or amortization, but not both. However, loans featuring both components do exist, as individual terms are often negotiated separately. In this example, we model both PIK interest and amortization to demonstrate their impacts on cash flow.

EXHIBIT 37.3 **AxelEdge: Term Loan Forecast Model**

$ million

	Year 1	2	3	4	5	6
Principal, beginning of year	525.0	533.4	543.0	553.8	505.6	397.2
Payment-in-kind interest[1]	18.9	20.3	21.6	22.9	21.7	17.6
Mandatory amortization at 2%	(10.5)	(10.7)	(10.9)	(11.1)	(10.1)	(7.9)
Discretionary paydown	0.0	0.0	0.0	(60.0)	(120.0)	(140.0)
Principal, end of year	533.4	543.0	553.8	505.6	397.2	266.8
Interest rate						
Forward SOFR[2]	5.0%	5.5%	6.0%	6.4%	6.7%	7.0%
+ Loan spread	4.0%	4.0%	4.0%	4.0%	4.0%	4.0%
LBO loan rate	9.0%	9.5%	10.0%	10.4%	10.7%	11.0%
Interest expense						
PIK interest, 40% of total	18.9	20.3	21.6	22.9	21.7	17.6
Cash interest, 60% of total	28.4	30.4	32.4	34.4	32.5	26.3
Interest expense	47.3	50.7	54.0	57.3	54.2	43.9

[1] Payment-in-kind (PIK) interest is a type of interest payment where instead of paying cash, the borrower pays interest with additional debt or equity securities.

[2] Although the term loan is a floating-rate loan, the expected SOFR rate can be modeled using a forward curve.

rate, most commonly the three-month Secured Overnight Financing Rate (SOFR).[10] This floating-rate structure minimizes the lender's exposure to interest rate risk, enabling it to focus primarily on default risk. Lenders are generally reluctant to lock in interest rates on risky loans over extended periods, so floating rates are essential for maintaining liquidity in longer-term lending markets. However, borrowers should recognize that an unexpected rise in interest rates presents a substantial risk—not only to value creation but also potentially to the company's viability.

To forecast interest expense, use forward SOFR curves, which provide projections of future rates. In Exhibit 37.3, we add a negotiated spread of 4 percent to each year's forward rate. For example, in year 1, the forward rate is 5 percent, so the loan's interest rate would be 9 percent for that year. Applying this rate to the beginning principal of $525 million results in interest expense of $47.3 million. By year 6, the forward curve projects a SOFR of 7 percent, raising the loan rate to 11 percent. Despite the increase, AxelEdge plans to use free cash flow to reduce the principal, lowering the overall interest expense relative to earlier years.

Payment-in-Kind (PIK) Interest   A common feature of term loans is the option for payment-in-kind (PIK) interest, where some interest is not paid in cash but is instead added to the loan's principal balance, compounding

[10] SOFR, or the Secured Overnight Financing Rate, has replaced the London Interbank Offered Rate (LIBOR) as the preferred benchmark.

over time. This arrangement enables the buyer to conserve cash, which can be especially valuable during periods of tight cash flow. However, because unpaid interest is capitalized into the loan balance, the debt owed grows over time, and this can lead to challenges later. Borrowers benefit from deferring cash outflows, while lenders see increased returns as the principal accrues with each deferred-interest addition.

PIK interest and cash interest are not necessarily mutually exclusive; the borrower and lender can negotiate a split. In Exhibit 37.3, for example, we assume a split of 40 percent PIK and 60 percent cash interest. While this split has no impact on the income statement, it does affect cash flow to equity. The PIK portion is added back to net income when calculating gross cash flow. Also, notice that the principal rises by $18.9 million in year 1, with the deferred portion added to the loan balance.

Loan Amortization   Term loans typically amortize over time, which means the borrower must repay a portion of the principal each year. Today's LBO term loans follow an extremely modest amortization schedule, with annual payments representing only a small percentage of the principal. For example, in Exhibit 37.3, the lender requires 2 percent of the principal to be repaid each year, gradually reducing the outstanding balance. In year 1, the mandatory amortization is 2 percent of the $525 million principal, which equals a payment of $10.5 million.

While these small amortization payments give borrowers financial flexibility, they also leave the bulk of the loan repayment due at maturity. This back-loaded structure introduces rollover risk—the possibility that the borrower will not be able to refinance the debt at maturity. In the past, lenders mitigated this risk by requiring higher amortization payments to steadily reduce the principal over time. However, recent trends have shifted toward smaller amortization schedules, often just a few percent of the principal.[11] This approach increases the final repayment burden, so careful planning for refinancing is crucial as the loan nears maturity.

Prepayment Penalties   Given the high interest rates associated with significant leverage, borrowers often use free cash flow to pay down debt when possible. Term loans frequently include provisions for early repayment, but these typically carry small penalties that apply only during the initial years. These penalties are generally limited; for instance, a borrower repaying the loan early might be required to pay 102 percent of the outstanding principal if repaid within the first year or two. Over time, these penalties usually decline and may disappear entirely, allowing borrowers greater flexibility to refinance or repay without additional cost. In our AxelEdge example, we assume no prepayment penalties.

---

[11] It might seem odd to have a small amortization and PIK interest at the same time. This is rare and typically caused by regulatory constraints that discourage interest-only loans.

Subordinated Bonds

Although fixed-rate bonds are less common for financing LBOs today, they remain a valuable source of capital for large transactions. Unlike term loans, these bonds carry a fixed interest rate, require cash interest payments, do not amortize, and may or may not allow early repayment. With a fixed rate, prepayment risk becomes significant for lenders; borrowers tend to refinance when rates fall but hold onto the debt when rates rise, creating an asymmetry that makes lenders cautious about issuing large long-term bonds. Consequently, the bond markets don't always have the depth needed for substantial funding requirements.

Typically subordinated within the capital structure, these bonds carry higher coupon rates to offset their lower repayment priority in bankruptcy.[12] Despite the higher coupon payments, they provide borrowers with predictable cash flow obligations. Underwriters often enlist rating agencies to set the coupon rate by evaluating credit risk, with debt-to-EBITDA ratios as a key metric. Higher leverage typically drives up the coupon rate to account for the added risk.

In our example, AxelEdge issues $925 million in subordinated bonds with a seven-year maturity and a 12 percent coupon rate. This results in $111 million in annual interest, translating to $55.5 million in semiannual payments, a common structure in U.S. markets. For simplicity, we ignore the semiannual payment of coupons in our forecasts.

MODELING THE FINANCIAL STATEMENTS

While some professionals may simplify the forecasting process for efficiency, we believe developing a comprehensive set of financial forecasts is crucial for accurately evaluating potential investments. This process includes detailed projections of the income statement, balance sheet, and statement of retained earnings, following the methodology outlined in Section II of this book. For this analysis, forecasts have been prepared for all three statements, although only the income statement projection is included in the exhibits.

Exhibit 37.4 presents a sample income statement forecast for AxelEdge. While it follows a traditional format, there are two special considerations. First, we include a distinct line item for EBITDA, a critical metric for assessing both leverage (debt to EBITDA) and valuation (enterprise value to EBITDA). Second, we provide a detailed breakdown of interest expense by bond type and, where possible, by individual bond, given the importance of interest expense to the transaction's success. This approach contrasts with an enterprise DCF

---

[12] Lenders may occasionally negotiate an equity sweetener as an alternative to a high coupon rate. Typically structured as warrants or options, these sweeteners grant lenders a potential stake in the company's equity if its value increases. For a detailed discussion on valuing bonds with embedded options, see Chapter 16.

EXHIBIT 37.4 **AxelEdge: Income Statement Forecast**

$ million

	Year 1	2	3	4	5	6	7
Revenue	1,200.0	1,260.0	1,323.0	1,375.9	1,431.0	1,473.9	1,518.1
Operating costs	(960.0)	(982.8)	(992.3)	(1,004.4)	(1,001.7)	(1,031.7)	(1,062.7)
EBITDA	240.0	277.2	330.8	371.5	429.3	442.2	455.4
Depreciation	(30.0)	(31.5)	(33.1)	(34.4)	(35.8)	(36.8)	(38.0)
Operating profit	210.0	245.7	297.7	337.1	393.5	405.3	417.5
Interest expense	(158.3)	(164.2)	(168.6)	(168.3)	(165.2)	(154.9)	
Pretax profit	51.8	81.5	129.1	168.8	228.3	250.4	
Taxes	(12.9)	(20.4)	(32.3)	(42.2)	(57.1)	(62.6)	
Net income	38.8	61.1	96.8	126.6	171.2	187.8	
Interest expense							
Credit facility	0.0	2.6	3.6	0.0	0.0	0.0	
Term loan	47.3	50.7	54.0	57.3	54.2	43.9	
Subordinated bond	111.0	111.0	111.0	111.0	111.0	111.0	
Total interest	158.3	164.2	168.6	168.3	165.2	154.9	
Operating margin, %	17.5	19.5	22.5	24.5	27.5	27.5	27.5

model for investment-grade companies, which models the valuation impact of leverage through the cost of capital and often consolidates financial expenses into a single line item for ease of exposition.

A critical aspect of the forecasting process is evaluating how operational improvements can enhance financial performance. Value creation occurs when a company improves margins and ROIC or accelerates revenue growth with returns that exceed its cost of capital. In the case of AxelEdge, the partners at LBO LLP anticipate that internal changes could boost margins from 17.5 percent in year 1 to 27.5 percent in years 5 through 7.

However, translating such projections into an operational reality is often more challenging than it appears. Raising margins through price increases often reduces volumes, while cost-cutting measures are frequently replicated by competitors, who may then lower prices to gain market share. When modeling improvements, you must consider them within the broader strategic and competitive context.

ESTIMATING CASH FLOW TO EQUITY

A central principle of this book is that the enterprise DCF method provides the most robust approach to valuation. By clearly separating operating performance from financial structure, enterprise DCF enables a more accurate assessment of the company's competitive strength in its product markets, without the systematic distortions leverage can introduce.

In contrast, the LBO model evaluates investments using cash flow to equity, partly because that is the tradition but mainly because LBO transactions are finite investments from the PE firm's perspective. Therefore, the emphasis is not the asset's intrinsic value but the returns the equity holders can achieve over the investment horizon.

Later in this chapter, we examine the limitations of evaluating investments using cash flow to equity; for now, however, we present the typical process. Exhibit 37.5 shows a cash-flow-to-equity forecast for AxelEdge. Cash flow to equity starts with net income, which is calculated net of interest expense. To determine gross cash flow, we add back noncash expenses, such as depreciation and amortization, as well as PIK interest.

From gross cash flow, subtract investments in working capital, fixed assets, and other assets, net of any changes in other liabilities. Lastly, deduct mandatory debt amortization. While many refer to the resulting figure as "levered free cash flow," to avoid confusion with other definitions, we label the result "cash flow available for repayment."

With the high coupon rates associated with leverage, many buyers are keen to use internally generated cash to reduce debt, rather than payout to equity. For AxelEdge, however, this is not feasible in the first year; with negative cash flow, the company must draw on its credit line. By year 3, revenue growth and improved margins produce sufficient cash to repay the credit line and initiate discretionary term loan repayments. Unlike other forecasts that depend on the company's competitive performance, discretionary payments are a strategic decision, allowing management to choose whether to pay down debt, issue dividends to equity holders, or build cash reserves.

EXHIBIT 37.5 **AxelEdge: Cash Flow to Equity**

$ million

	Year 1	2	3	4	5	6
Net income	38.8	61.1	96.8	126.6	171.2	187.8
Depreciation	30.0	31.5	33.1	34.4	35.8	36.8
Payment-in-kind interest	18.9	20.3	21.6	22.9	21.7	17.6
Gross cash flow	87.7	112.9	151.5	183.9	228.7	242.2
Change in working capital	(25.0)	(26.3)	(22.1)	(22.9)	(17.9)	(18.4)
Capital expenditures	(80.0)	(84.0)	(77.2)	(80.3)	(71.5)	(73.7)
Term loan mandatory amortization	(10.5)	(10.7)	(10.9)	(11.1)	(10.1)	(7.9)
Cash flow available for repayment	(27.8)	(8.0)	41.4	69.6	129.1	142.2
Change in credit facility	30.0	10.0	(40.0)	0.0	0.0	0.0
Term loan discretionary repayment	0.0	0.0	0.0	(60.0)	(120.0)	(140.0)
Cash flow to equity	2.2	2.0	1.4	9.6	9.1	2.2

MEASURING RETURNS IN AN LBO TRANSACTION

With cash flow projections prepared, the next step is to evaluate AxelEdge's potential returns. A PE firm typically calculates a transaction-based internal rate of return (IRR), which has three primary components: the purchase price, holding-period dividends, and exit proceeds. This calculation helps determine whether the transaction meets return targets and compares favorably with alternative investments.

Purchase Price

In a leveraged buyout, the buyer typically acquires the entire company. For publicly traded targets, this requires paying the prevailing market price plus an acquisition premium. Research indicates that acquisition premiums commonly range from 20 to 40 percent above the target's pre-announcement stock price, though these figures can vary based on industry, market conditions, and strategic goals. For instance, Moeller, Schlingemann, and Stulz found an average premium of 23 percent for U.S. acquisitions, with significant variation across sectors and transaction types.[13] More recently, Agrawal, Varma, and West analyzed 1,640 deals over seven years, discovering that premiums often exceeded 40 percent of the target's market value.[14]

Before the acquisition announcement, AxelEdge's stock traded at $27.92 per share. Applying a 20 percent premium raises the price to $33.50 per share. With 65 million shares outstanding, the acquisition premium would be $365 million above the stand-alone value.

Prudence regarding acquisition premiums is critical for executing a successful LBO. Any value created through operational improvements or financial restructuring must first offset this premium before yielding returns to the buyer.

Holding-Period Dividends

During the holding period, surplus cash flow is typically allocated to debt reduction. However, PE buyers may also extract value through payments to equity holders or a dividend recapitalization.

When cash flows exceed obligations—such as debt service, capital expenditures, and working capital requirements—excess funds may be distributed as dividends. If cash flow consistently surpasses projections, buyers may implement regular dividends to distribute the surplus to equity holders.

[13] S. B. Moeller, F. P. Schlingemann, and R. M. Stulz, "Firm Size and the Gains from Acquisitions," *Journal of Financial Economics* 73, no. 2 (2004): 201–228.
[14] A. Agrawal, R. Varma, and A. West, "Making M&A Deal Synergies Count," McKinsey & Company, October 2017, www.mckinsey.com.

In a dividend recapitalization, the company raises additional debt to fund a special dividend to equity holders, allowing the buyer to recover part of its initial investment before the exit. For example, if EBITDA growth supports increased leverage, the company might secure $100 million in new debt to finance a dividend, reducing the buyer's financial exposure while maintaining control.

For AxelEdge, cash flows to equity (outlined in Exhibit 37.5) are assumed to fund modest dividend payments. While companies typically retain small cash flows to strengthen their financial position, this assumption illustrates how dividends factor into performance calculations.

Exit Value

After implementing strategic changes, the PE firm seeks an exit to realize returns. Common options include initial public offerings (IPOs), trade sales to strategic buyers, and secondary buyouts to another PE firm.

To estimate equity value *at exit*, the LBO model first calculates enterprise value using an enterprise value multiple, then deducts expected debt outstanding. For example, will AxelEdge sell at eight times EBITDA or 12 times EBITDA? While cash flow generated during the holding period adds value, the exit multiple on improved EBITDA is what ultimately determines success, so accurate assessment is essential.

Chapter 18 provides best practices for estimating enterprise value multiples. For LBOs, we focus on three key considerations:

1. *Choose peer multiples aligned with performance.* To determine an appropriate exit multiple, practitioners typically analyze a set of comparable companies, derive each company's enterprise value-to-EBITDA multiple, and then apply the average or median multiple. This approach works best when multiples are closely aligned, but if there is a wide variation across comparable companies, identify the economic factors driving this spread. For instance, companies with higher ROICs, faster growth, or lower tax rates tend to trade at higher multiples. Then, instead of using the average, identify the comparable company whose economic performance most closely aligns with the target company's expected performance at the time of exit.

2. *Select a multiple that reflects future performance.* The chosen multiple should account for anticipated improvements or challenges. For example, a higher exit multiple may be justified if the company is expected to increase ROIC through sustainable operational efficiencies. Conversely, if revenue growth is expected to decline as the company matures, a lower exit multiple may be more realistic.

3. *Be cautious of the target company's current trading multiple.* One questionable approach to determining an exit multiple is applying the target company's current multiple to its projected performance at exit. Struggling

companies often trade at higher multiples that reflect investors' expectations of restructuring or improvement. However, these inflated multiples are rarely sustainable. As profitability improves, the multiple often contracts, aligning more closely with the company's long-term economic fundamentals.

For AxelEdge, operating margins are expected to increase from 17.5 percent in year 1 to 27.5 percent at exit. Over the same period, ROIC is expected to improve from 10.5 percent to 22 percent, while revenue growth is expected to decline from 5.0 percent to 3.0 percent as the company matures. Given these projections, the PE firm's partners expect the multiple to expand from the current pre-announcement level of 8.9 times EBITDA to 10.7 times EBITDA at exit.

IRR Calculation for the AxelEdge Transaction

To evaluate performance at both the investment and fund level, PE funds commonly use the internal rate of return. The IRR allows PE firms to estimate the annualized percentage return of an investment, considering the timing and magnitude of cash flows, thus providing LPs with a common measure of performance.

Exhibit 37.6 illustrates the IRR calculation for the AxelEdge transaction. The initial cash flow represents the equity contributed by LBO LLP to acquire AxelEdge, including the acquisition premium. Cash flows to equity holders are accounted for over the subsequent six years, with the final year also incorporating the projected exit value. This exit value is determined by applying the improved EBITDA to the anticipated multiple, based on the company's expected post-improvement economic performance. The IRR, calculated using the IRR function in spreadsheet software, is 23.5 percent—an impressive return, but one that hinges on achieving financial projections.

The Pitfalls of Internal Rate of Return

While the IRR for the AxelEdge transaction is impressive, the IRR's limitations as a metric for comparing investments cannot be ignored. These shortcomings are particularly significant in private equity, where cash flow timing and strategic decision making are critical to creating long-term value.

Although extensively discussed in finance textbooks,[15] two pitfalls are worth exploring here. First, IRR is unreliable for comparing investments when cash flow patterns differ across opportunities. Second, it can incentivize value-destructive behavior by prioritizing accelerated cash flows, even when those returns fall below the cost of capital.

---

[15] For an in-depth discussion of internal rate of return, see J. Berk and P. DeMarzo, *Corporate Finance*, 5th ed. (Boston: Pearson, 2020).

EXHIBIT 37.6 **AxelEdge: Internal Rate of Return**

$ million

	Today	Year 1	2	3	4	5	6
EBITDA	240.0						455.4
× EBITDA multiple	10.4						10.7
Enterprise value	2,500.0						4,874.4
Total debt	(1,450.0)						(1,191.8)
Equity value	1,050.0						3,682.6
Cash flow to equity	0.0	2.2	2.0	1.4	9.6	9.1	2.2
Cash flow to equity, total	(1,050.0)	2.2	2.0	1.4	9.6	9.1	3,684.8
Internal rate of return, %	23.5						
Debt to EBITDA							
Debt outstanding	1,450.0	1,488.4	1,508.0	1,478.8	1,430.6	1,322.2	1,191.8
/ EBITDA	240.0	277.2	330.8	371.5	429.3	442.2	455.4
Debt to EBITDA	6.0	5.4	4.6	4.0	3.3	3.0	2.6

Note: All multiplies calculated using forward EBITDA (i.e., EBITDA projected 1 year forward).

Using IRR to Compare Investments

To understand why IRR can be unreliable for comparing investments, it's helpful to briefly review how it's calculated and then explore its appropriate uses. IRR is defined as the discount rate that makes the net present value (NPV) of an investment's cash flows equal to zero. Consider two hypothetical investments, Quick Flip and Patient Capital, with the following cash flows:

Investment	Today	Year 1	Year 2	Year 3	IRR
Quick Flip	(1,000)	1,100	300	100	37.2%
Patient Capital	(1,000)	50	700	1,100	27.5%

To calculate IRR, discount rates are tested iteratively until the NPV equals zero. While Quick Flip appears more attractive based solely on its higher IRR, this conclusion can be misleading. Exhibit 37.7 charts the NPV of each investment across discount rates from 0 to 50 percent, with each IRR indicated where the NPV curve intersects zero. However, these intersection points are not relevant when comparing the two investments. What ultimately matters is the NPV of each cash flow stream evaluated at the appropriate cost of capital. For example, at a 12 percent cost of capital, Patient Capital outperforms Quick Flip in terms of NPV, despite having a lower IRR, because it delivers more total cash—$1,850 compared with $1,500. At lower discount rates, the larger total cash flow takes precedence over the time value of money, exposing a fundamental limitation of IRR.

EXHIBIT 37.7 **Valuation of Two Investments by Discount Rate**

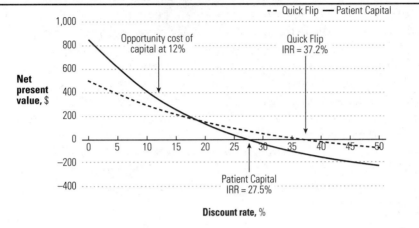

When evaluating the performance of a PE fund, most limited partners (LPs)—the investors who provide capital for PE funds, such as pension funds, endowments, and high-net-worth individuals—still rely on IRR, despite concerns about its shortcomings. Some LPs also look at cash-on-cash returns, calculated as cash returned divided by cash invested. For Patient Capital, this is 1,850/1,000, or 1.85 times, while for Quick Flip, it's 1.5 times. However, these numbers are typically undiscounted, so they introduce their own limitations. As we will discuss later, a better measure is cash-on-cash return discounted at the cost of capital, which some textbooks call the present value index.

Pressure to Accelerate Cash Flows   The limitations of IRR not only affect investment comparisons but also create incentives to accelerate cash flows, even when doing so may destroy value. Consider the example in Exhibit 37.8, where a PE fund raises $170 million and deploys it into an investment that generates distributions of $115 million annually over the next two years. The funds, whose

EXHIBIT 37.8 **Impact on IRR from Accelerating Cash Flows**

$ million

Private-equity fund	Internal rate of return	Cash flow		
		Today	Year 1	Year 2
Structure A	22.8%	(170)	115	115
Structure B	23.5%	(170)	210	
Investor, structure B				
Distribution to investor			210	
Reinvestment by investor			(95)	109
Cash flow			115	109

investors could be pension funds or university endowments, might use these distributions to meet obligations such as retiree benefits or scholarship funding.

In this scenario, the IRR is a respectable 22.8 percent. However, suppose the PE fund accelerates cash flows by selling the rights to the year 2 distribution for $95 million to a third party in year 1. This allows the fund to distribute $210 million in year 1, boosting the IRR to 23.5 percent.

While this acceleration increases IRR, it creates a dilemma for the fund's investors. Since the investors only need $115 million in year 1 to meet their obligations, the excess $95 million must be reinvested. Assuming the investors can reinvest at a 15 percent return, the proceeds will fall short of replicating the original year 2 cash flow. Despite the higher IRR, the fund's investors are ultimately worse off because the cash flow timing is misaligned with reinvestment opportunities.

THE COMPONENTS OF VALUE IN AN LBO TRANSACTION

Thus far, we have outlined the conventional approach to LBO modeling. But while calculating the IRR on cash flows to and from equity holders may seem straightforward, it can lead to a distorted perspective. To ensure a more accurate and meaningful analysis, it is essential to also consider the fundamental drivers of value creation.

The success of any acquisition, including those involving substantial leverage, fundamentally relies on three key factors: the value diminished by acquisition premiums and transaction costs (as discussed above), the value generated through performance improvements, and the net benefits derived from financial structuring. The goal is to disentangle these components and carefully assess the impact of each. Exhibit 37.9 highlights these elements and demonstrates the overall value generated by the transaction.

Valuing Operating Improvements

To isolate the impact of operating improvements, apply the adjusted present value (APV) framework discussed in Chapter 10. Start by calculating the stand-alone value by discounting the baseline free cash flow estimates at the unlevered cost of equity. For AxelEdge, this results in a valuation of $2,074 million, slightly below the pre-announcement enterprise value of $2,135 million, because it excludes $61 million in value from interest tax shields.

Next, reestimate the operating value of the company after incorporating performance improvements, using an exit multiple on EBITDA consistent with baseline performance. Discounting the improved cash flows and applying an 8.9-times multiple to the exit year EBITDA results in $1,004 million in incremental value. However, given AxelEdge's improved returns on capital, a higher multiple—estimated at 10.7 times EBITDA—is more realistic. Applying

EXHIBIT 37.9 **AxelEdge: Sources of Value Creation**

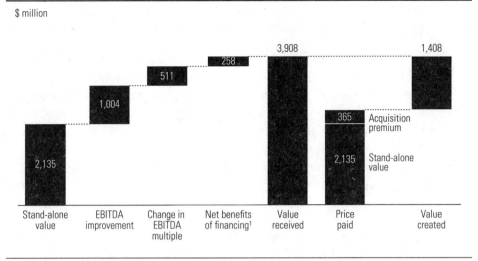

$ million

^{1} Value of additional tax shields and favorable financing options, balanced against transaction costs and increased distress risks.

this higher multiple to the exit year EBITDA adds another $511 million in value. While these results are promising, remain cautious: if either the anticipated performance improvements or the higher multiple fails to materialize, the projected value creation will decline.

In the AxelEdge example, the analysis focuses on improvements from increased operating margins. In practice, a comprehensive valuation should also account for other sources of value creation, such as optimizing invested capital, selling noncore assets, and repositioning the business from mature to growth markets. To prioritize these actions, value each one separately to understand its relative contribution.[16]

Valuing the Net Benefits of Financing

To assess the financial impact of the transaction—considering both its benefits and drawbacks—begin by calculating the incremental value of interest tax shields. As discussed in Chapter 10, expected tax shields are typically discounted at the cost of debt. However, since higher leverage is expected to be temporary, the $258 million increase in value from tax shields is modest compared with the potential gains from operating improvements.[17]

[16] For more on attribution analysis in both IRR and present value terms, see M. Goedhart, C. Levy, and P. Morgan, "A Better Way to Understand Internal Rate of Return," McKinsey & Company, November 1, 2015, www.mckinsey.com.

[17] In the AxelEdge model, we assume the target debt-to-value ratio will increase from its current level of 15 percent to a long-term level of 24 percent. This increase in the target capital structure contributes to roughly half of the incremental value derived from tax shields.

It is also crucial to consider the risks associated with tax shields. While valuable, their realization depends on factors such as the company's ability to meet interest obligations, restrictions imposed by tax laws, and the use of a fair, market-based interest rate.

- *Utilization of tax shields.* Do not assume the company will always fully utilize its interest deductions. Instead, use scenario analysis to assess whether sufficient pretax profits and cash flow will be available to meet interest obligations. If either condition is unmet, the tax shield may not materialize.

- *Limitations on interest deductions.* Recent changes, such as the 2017 Tax Cuts and Jobs Act (TCJA) in the United States, have capped deductible interest at 30 percent of EBITDA, tightened to EBIT in 2022, significantly reducing the potential value of tax shields. Similar reforms globally, including in the European Union and other OECD countries, have imposed stricter limitations on interest deductibility as part of broader initiatives to combat tax base erosion and profit shifting (BEPS). These changes collectively reduce the attractiveness of high-leverage financing structures.

- *Market-based interest rates.* Only include tax shields generated by a market-based interest rate. If a company incurs above-market interest costs, deduct the excess interest on an after-tax basis from enterprise value.

In addition to tax shields, consider other incremental cash flows from financing, such as preferred financing, transaction costs, and potential distress costs. While access to lower borrowing rates can add value, this benefit should be modeled by comparing reduced interest expenses with the expected cost of debt, rather than embedding it directly into the cost of capital. These benefits must be balanced against transaction costs—such as advisory, legal, and underwriting fees—which can significantly erode value in complex deals. Furthermore, high leverage amplifies the risk of financial distress, potentially resulting in operational disruptions, weakened supplier or customer confidence, or bankruptcy. When distress costs are difficult to quantify, qualitative assessments can still provide valuable insights. For example, companies reliant on long-term contracts are often more vulnerable to distress than those in transactional markets.

Evaluating the LBO Transaction

To evaluate the net value created by a potential LBO, subtract the required purchase price from the combined value of operating and financial synergies. A positive net value indicates that the transaction creates value and merits consideration. In the context of a PE fund, however, equity capital is often

EXHIBIT 37.10 **AxelEdge: Investment Analysis Using the Relative Value Index**

$ million

	Value received	Required financing	Relative value index[1]
Enterprise value	3,908	2,500	1.6×
Debt raised	(1,450)	(1,450)	
Equity value	2,458	1,050	2.3×

Internal rate of return = 23.5%

[1] Value received ÷ required financing.

constrained by the fund's size, requiring prioritization of investments. A fund may even reject a value-creating transaction if a more attractive opportunity is anticipated.

A useful tool for comparing investments under such constraints is the relative value index, also known as the present value index. This calculation, illustrated in Exhibit 37.10, involves dividing the post-LBO enterprise value by the required financing to compute the unlevered index. For AxelEdge, the relative value index equals 1.6 times. A value above 1.0 indicates that the transaction creates value.

A levered version of the index, calculated by using equity value instead of enterprise value, results in a value of 2.3 times for AxelEdge. However, exercise caution when comparing levered indexes across companies with varying leverage levels. Higher leverage increases the risk of failure, a factor not captured in the levered index, which focuses solely on synergies created.

CONCLUDING THOUGHTS

Leveraged buyouts have become a significant force in the global economy, reshaping businesses and creating value through strategic changes and operational improvements. While leverage amplifies returns, long-term success hinges on meaningful operating improvements, such as accelerating revenue growth, reducing costs, and optimizing capital deployment. Historically, declining interest rates and multiple expansion have produced strong past results, but future success will depend on enhancing the fundamental operating value drivers such as organic revenue growth and return on invested capital—principles emphasized throughout this book.

Finally, metrics such as the internal rate of return remain essential for evaluating performance but must be applied carefully and in conjunction with thorough value creation analysis. By combining rigorous financial discipline with meaningful operational improvements, PE firms can deliver competitive returns while contributing to the broader efficiency and resilience of the global economy.

38

Venture Capital

This chapter examines the valuation methods that venture capitalists use to assess early-stage investments. These techniques are particularly valuable when start-ups are little more than a promising idea and lack the financial data needed for more traditional approaches. There are three essential methods, summarized in Exhibit 38.1: the post-money valuation method, the venture capital (VC) valuation method, and scenario-based discounted cash flow (DCF). This chapter explores the first two; the scenario-based DCF method, which was introduced in Chapter 4, will be covered more fully in Chapter 39. As start-ups mature and generate meaningful performance data, their valuation methods often evolve to align more closely with the DCF methods discussed throughout this book.

The post-money valuation method, our starting point, is the simplest of the three. It focuses on determining the cash needed to achieve the next milestone and the equity stake required to exert meaningful control. Otherwise known as the "sweet spot" method, it is especially suitable for seed-stage companies characterized by high uncertainty and limited data. While effective for early-stage investments, this method does not explicitly model a company's long-term potential, relying instead on investor enthusiasm to establish a valuation.

The VC valuation method, by contrast, incorporates elements of DCF analysis but tailors them to the unique dynamics of early-stage investing. Rather than modeling all cash flows, this approach centers on projecting an exit value, accounting for potential future dilution, and discounting the exit value using a target rate of return instead of the cost of capital.

Scenario-based DCF is the most theoretically rigorous method. But while we advocate for scenario-based DCF when applicable, simpler methods such as post-money and venture capital valuations remain practical tools. Each has its merits, and selecting the appropriate method depends on the specific stage and context of the investment.

EXHIBIT 38.1 **Venture-Capital Valuation Methodologies**

Post-money method	Venture capital (VC) valuation method	Scenario-based DCF
Early-stage investors focus primarily on two key valuation inputs: the investment required to reach the next milestone and the ownership percentage necessary to exert sufficient control.	The VC method adapts principles from DCF analysis, but unlike DCF, which considers every cash flow, the VC valuation method focuses on an exit value, considers the potential for additional dilution, and discounts the exit value using a target rate of return.	In a scenario-based DCF model, multiple scenarios are constructed based on key uncertainties. An enterprise DCF is then calculated for each scenario and weighted by the probability of occurrence.
Requires the least amount of data; valuation is ultimately based on investor demand.		Most theoretically robust and flexible but requires significant time and data.

POST-MONEY VALUATION AND THE VC SWEET SPOT

In rapidly evolving markets centered on new technologies, potential investments often arise faster than they can be thoroughly analyzed. While enterprise DCF remains the gold standard for evaluating investments, it is both data intensive and time-consuming. For companies with limited financial history and an unproven value proposition, many early-stage investors turn to a simpler, more pragmatic tool: the post-money valuation method, which we call the sweet-spot method. This method emphasizes practicality and is driven by three factors: the amount of investment the company will need to reach its next milestone, an ownership percentage that aligns the interests of investors with those of the company, and eventually the level of interest from other investors.

Investment Amount and Ownership Percentage

Unlike traditional valuation models, the post-money approach does not focus on intrinsic value. Instead, it centers on how much an investor is willing to invest and the percentage of ownership they will receive in return. The implied valuation is derived from these terms, which are shaped by negotiation and, often, competition among investors.

Input 1: Investment Amount   Due to the inherent uncertainty surrounding new technologies and emerging businesses, investors often mitigate risk by staging their investments through multiple financing rounds. They typically begin by estimating the funding required to achieve the next proof point. For instance, developing a working prototype might require $1 million, while assembling a sales team may require $3 million. A sweet-spot valuation starts with an estimate of the company's cash requirements.

Input 2: Ownership Percentage   Although all investors technically own part of the company, not every owner wields the same degree of control or has the same access to information. These are determined by the ownership percentage. For instance, investors with the most shares will often be granted seats on the board of directors, whereas smaller investors may have access only to financial updates.

With these two inputs, an investor can calculate the implied transaction price. For example, if the investor and the company agree that $3 million is required to reach the next milestone and the investor will receive a 25 percent ownership stake, the implied valuation is $12 million. This is calculated as

$$25\% \times Value = \$3.0 \text{ million}$$

$$Value = \$3.0 \text{ million} / 25\% = \$12.0 \text{ million}$$

In general, the formula is

$$Value = Investment / Ownership \ Percentage$$

The resulting value, known as the post-money valuation (illustrated on the left side of Exhibit 38.2), is a standard metric used by venture capitalists. This figure represents the company's value after the investment has been made. To calculate the pre-money valuation, which reflects the company's value before the investment, subtract the amount of the cash injection from the post-money valuation. In this example, the pre-money valuation is $9 million, calculated by subtracting the $3 million investment from the $12 million post-money valuation, as shown on the right side of Exhibit 38.2.

Factoring in Investor Interest

If the valuation process stopped at this point, this straightforward methodology could lead to significantly flawed outcomes. For instance, imagine a scenario

EXHIBIT 38.2 **Pre-money and Post-money Valuation**

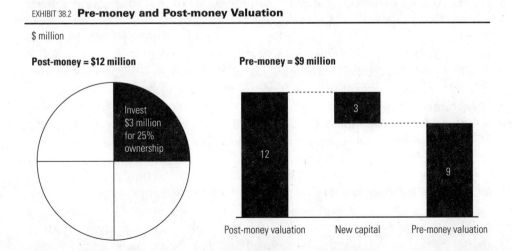

$ million

Post-money = $12 million

Pre-money = $9 million

Invest $3 million for 25% ownership

3

12

9

Post-money valuation   New capital   Pre-money valuation

Note: The post-money valuation reported within venture capital term sheets assumes that each owner has identical cash flow rights. However, venture capital shares often have preferences that enhance their value relative to common stock, thereby distorting the post-money valuation.

in which investors believe a company has developed a cure for cancer but only requires $3 million to reach its next milestone. Would such a groundbreaking innovation truly be valued at just $12 million? Almost certainly not. This highlights the need for one additional critical factor in the valuation process: the level of investor interest.

In vibrant venture communities, such as those in Silicon Valley, Boston, and Berlin, numerous investors scout for deals. An investor will often gauge the level of interest through discussions with the entrepreneur and consultations with other investors. Much as investment banks assess interest levels among potential investors in the IPO market, VC investors typically interpret higher interest as a suggestion that the valuation is likely to exceed the initial estimates.

If a company targets a sizable market, possesses differentiated technology, and is led by a skilled management team with relevant experience, investor interest will likely be substantial. A few conversations with potential coinvestors can quickly confirm this. When interest is high, experienced venture capitalists understand that the transaction cannot proceed at the valuation derived from the initial formula. To secure their participation, they may need to invest more capital at a lower ownership percentage than originally anticipated, driving the post-money valuation higher than initially estimated.

Many VC firms focus on specific investment amounts and ownership levels, creating a preferred zone for investment, which we call their "sweet spot." These boundaries arise from practical constraints: a venture capitalist managing a $50 million portfolio cannot write dozens of $100,000 checks while remaining actively involved in each investment or allocate 60 percent of their fund to a single $30 million investment. For company founders, these limits directly influence the post-money valuation. For instance, raising $3 million for 25 percent of the company would close the transaction at $12 million, potentially undervaluing a groundbreaking innovation.

While the sweet-spot method is straightforward and practical, it reflects the parties' judgment and investor interest more than the company's long-term financial potential. Its use is best suited for situations with high uncertainty, limited data, or challenges in gathering information. However, when available, reliable data on matters such as market size or likelihood of success should inform a more robust valuation approach. For example, while technical uncertainty may exist in biotechnology, the number of potential patients for a specific disease is often well documented. In such cases, a method such as the VC valuation model, discussed next, would be more appropriate.

VC VALUATION METHOD

Unlike the sweet-spot methodology, which emphasizes next-phase funding, ownership constraints, and subjective adjustments based on investor interest, the VC valuation method incorporates projections about a company's long-term

EXHIBIT 38.3 **The Five Steps of the Venture Capital Method**

Step	Task	Description
1	Choose an investment window	Select a single exit point that aligns with the likely duration of the investment, based on the characteristics of the company.
2	Estimate the exit valuation	Similar to the terminal value in a discounted cash flow analysis, the exit value estimates the company's worth at the time of exit.
3	Estimate dilution	If a company is depleting its cash reserves and is unlikely to reach the exit date without additional funding, it is necessary to estimate the required cash infusion and the likely level of dilution.
4	Discount the exit valuation for time and risk	The venture capital method discounts the success outcome by a target return rate, incorporating the probability of failure into the discount rate.
5	Compare the result to required investment	Value the security by discounting the investor's share of the exit value by the target rate of return. If the value exceeds the investment, the net present value is positive.

potential. This approach is more closely aligned with enterprise DCF analysis but is adapted to address the lack of detailed data and the need for venture firms to exit their investments within a fixed time frame. For instance, while traditional DCF evaluates cash flows year by year, the VC method handles negative cash flows through ownership dilution rather than reductions in enterprise value.

The VC valuation method follows a structured five-step process, listed in Exhibit 38.3. First, an investment window is defined to align with the expected exit timeline. The second step is to estimate an exit valuation, akin to the continuing value in enterprise DCF, representing the company's projected value at the exit point. Third, dilution is estimated by calculating the additional funding required before reaching the planned exit date. Fourth, the exit valuation is discounted using a target rate of return, factoring in the probability of failure. Finally, the discounted exit value is compared with the required investment to determine if the net present value is positive, signaling a viable investment opportunity. We discuss each step next.

Step 1: Choose an Investment Window

Venture capital funds have a limited life span, often ten years. Investors must, therefore, carefully strategize when and how they will exit the investment, whether by selling the company or going public opportunity. We discuss each step next. Unlike traditional DCF models that forecast cash flows year-by-year, the venture capital method selects a single exit point based on the investment's expected duration and the company's specific characteristics. For instance, an investment into a software company that can scale easily might last only a few years. In contrast, investing in a biotechnology firm could require a much longer time frame.

Several studies have indicated that the average time from first-round financing to an exit is approximately six years. For relatively short time frames like this, it is not reasonable to expect the company to be in a steady state by the time of exit, as would be required for a perpetuity-based continuing value. Instead, it's important to ensure that the exit valuation corresponds to the company's stage of development and prevailing market conditions at that time.

Step 2: Estimate the Exit Valuation

Similar to the continuing value in a discounted cash flow analysis, the exit value estimates the company's worth at the time of the venture capital fund's exit from the investment. Since the company is unlikely to be in a steady state at this point, valuing it as a perpetuity is not feasible. Instead, investors use multiples from precedent transactions that reflect a similar level of maturity.

Determining an exit value does not follow a prescribed method, but a common approach is to start with a market-wide perspective, translate that into a company perspective, and then apply it to a valuation framework. Exhibit 38.4 provides a sample analysis of a hypothetical company that markets a software package to primary-school teachers.

Determine the Size of the Target Market   Start by estimating the total addressable market (TAM) for the chosen exit date. TAM represents the universe of potential customers for the company's products and services. Next, estimate the serviceable available market (SAM), which is limited by the company's distribution network, marketing efforts, or geographical presence. For instance, our hypothetical software company might have a TAM that includes all students, including secondary-school students, but its serviceable market is smaller because it is only targeting primary-school students.

EXHIBIT 38.4 **Estimating the Exit Value**

$ million

Action	Sample analysis	
1. Size the total addressable market in 5 years	Number of users, millions	3.0
	× Revenue per user, $	96.0
	Market size	288.0
2. Estimate the company's market share	× Market share	33.3%
	Company revenue	96.0
3. Estimate expected operating margins	× Operating margin	20.0%
	Operating profits	19.2
4. Apply a multiple based on precedent transactions	× Industry multiple	12.0
	Enterprise value	230.4

In Exhibit 38.4, we assume that three million teachers will use one of the industry's software packages at an average fee of $8 per month, or $96 per year. Thus, the market's annual revenue is estimated at $288 million.

Estimate the Company's Market Share   Next, estimate the company's market share in the target market, based on competition, market positioning, and the relative advantages of the company's offerings. Some refer to this as the serviceable obtainable market (SOM). In our hypothetical example, we assume there are three companies with similar products, resulting in an expected market share of 33.3 percent per company. If the market is $288 million, the company's estimated revenue at 33.3 percent of the market is $96 million. Sometimes the market will not be split, and one winner may take it all. If the company competes in such a market, the market share can be interpreted as the probability of winning.

Estimate Operating Profit   With exit year revenues in hand, next forecast a simple income statement, including gross profit and operating profit. Gross profit accounts for the direct costs of production, while operating profit includes selling and administrative expenses. To do this, evaluate how gross margins and operating margins have evolved for more established companies with similar products and services. Remember that, unlike a traditional enterprise DCF model, this represents profitability at the time of exit, not today or when the company reaches stability. In Exhibit 38.4, we apply a 20 percent operating margin to $96 million in revenue, which results in operating profits of $19.2 million.

Analyze Exit Multiples for Comparable Companies   Since most venture-backed companies will not be in a steady state at the time of exit, a multiple is typically used. To determine an appropriate multiple, start by assembling a set of comparable companies. If you are working only with public data, limit your data set to companies at a similar stage; mature companies with high margins and low growth rates will not trade at the same multiples as companies still experiencing rapid growth. If possible, include data from private sales. This substantially expands the universe of potential comparables, but since the information will not be publicly available, it requires private data from a VC firm or an investment bank.

If the company is expected to be profitable at exit, use an enterprise-value-to-EBITDA[1] multiple. If EBITDA is negative at the time of exit, use a multiple based on gross profit or revenue. Regardless, ensure the multiple is consistent with your expectations of the company's underlying value drivers. In Chapter 18, we present best practices for estimating multiples.

[1] EBITDA is earnings before interest, taxes, depreciation, and amortization.

In Exhibit 38.4, the median enterprise value multiple for the company's comparable peers is 12 times operating profit. Multiplying 12 by $19.2 million results in an exit valuation of $230.4 million.

Step 3: Estimate Ownership Dilution Based on Required Fundraising

If a company is burning through cash and unlikely to reach an investment exit without new capital, it becomes necessary to estimate the additional capital required. In a traditional DCF model, negative cash flows are modeled year by year and included in the final summation to value operations. In contrast, the VC method estimates ownership dilution by determining what percentage of ownership the company must sell to raise the necessary cash to fund operations.

A best-in-class financial model would forecast each required cash infusion and determine the necessary dilution based on the expected valuation at the time of the expected offering. In practice, many investors instead rely on observed data from similar, recent transactions. For instance, some law firms publish deal statistics, including the percentage ownership offered and cash raised by transaction round.[2]

For example, if a follow-on financing for similar companies averages $8 million in cash for 22 percent ownership and the VC firm owns 25 percent of the current company being valued, the resulting ownership after the second round is calculated as follows:

$$\text{Ownership} = 25\% \times (1 - 22\%) = 19.5\%$$

The drop in ownership from 25 percent to 19.5 percent is known as dilution. After a second round of financing, the first investor will have a claim to only 19.5 percent of the exit proceeds. However, dilution is not limited to the new capital raised. In early rounds, new investors also request that a separate allocation of additional shares be set aside to hire new employees. The amount of this allocation can be negotiated between the investors and the founder, but a common allocation is 15 percent of the post-money number of shares. After including an employee allocation, the ownership is calculated as follows:

$$\text{Ownership} = 25\% \times (1 - 22\% - 15\%) = 15.8\%$$

This process continues for each expected round of new financing. For instance, our hypothetical start-up plans to raise $3 million in the first round and expects to raise $8 million in the second round. The company may not need to raise additional capital if the $11 million of infused cash provides the necessary resources to reach the exit valuation. However, if the $11 million is insufficient, a third round of financing will be required.

Exhibit 38.5 presents the evolution of ownership for approximately 1,000 U.S.-based start-ups. While founders initially own 100 percent of the company

---

[2] For instance, Wilson Sonsini produces *The Entrepreneurs Report* quarterly. The report provides summary statistics on the venture-backed transactions they advise.

EXHIBIT 38.5 **Evolution of Ownership in U.S. Start-Ups**

%

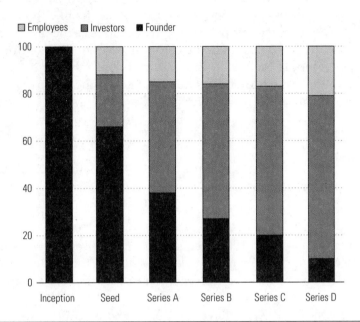

Source: *Rewarding Talent: The Founder's Guide to Stock Options, Index Ventures,* 2018, www.indexventures.com.

at its inception, their ownership typically drops to just 10 percent after five rounds of fundraising. Investors and employees own the remainder. For founders and early investors alike, the dilution caused by additional fundraising is an important consideration.

Step 4: Estimate the Target Rate of Return

Traditional DCF methods typically discount expected cash flows at an expected rate of return, where "expected" represents a probability-weighted average across various scenarios. Conversely, the VC method discounts a success outcome by a target return rate, incorporating the probability of failure into the discount rate.

To clarify the difference between expected returns and target returns, let's analyze the valuation of a late-stage investment with two potential outcomes: it could either grow into a $100 million entity within one year or falter and become valueless. Assume, for ease of exposition, that there is a 90 percent chance of success. We'll use a 14 percent discount rate, roughly the average return for venture capital over the past 40 years. The company can be valued using a probability-weighted DCF approach:

$$\text{Value} = \frac{(.9)100 + (.1)0}{1.14} = 78.9$$

The table on the left side of Exhibit 38.6 reports the present value of a $100 million upside at varying probabilities of success and durations until exit. Unsurprisingly, the company's valuation declines as the likelihood of success diminishes. Moreover, the company's worth decreases as the time required for exit lengthens, in accordance with the core principles of discounting.

Next, let's compute the anticipated return for the investor if the company is procured at the fair price of $78.9 million. Should the company realize the $100 million, the rate of return is determined as follows:

$$\text{Success Return} = \frac{100 - 78.9}{78.9} = 26.7\%$$

whereas the rate of return on failure equals −100 percent. To compute the expected return for the investor, weight the two potential returns by probability:

$$\text{Expected Return} = (.9)(26.7\%) + (.1)(-100\%) = 14\%$$

Note how the expected return equals the cost of capital. This result is a cornerstone of modern finance. An investor will earn the cost of capital when they pay the "fair" price for an asset, where the fair price equals the DCF value.

The VC method takes a different approach to discounting. Instead of discounting the expected cash flow at the expected return, it discounts the "success" cash flow at the target return (TR). For example:

$$78.9 = \frac{100}{1 + \text{TR}}$$

Solving for the target return (TR) yields 26.7 percent. But what does this figure represent? The target return is the rate of return from successful investments that are required to offset the losses from unsuccessful ones. Unlike traditional investments, a successful venture cannot simply achieve the expected cost of capital. Rather, it must deliver an exceptional return on successful investments to compensate for the high failure rate on other investments in its portfolio.

EXHIBIT 38.6 **Converting Expected Return into Target Return**

		Present value of $100 million, $ million							Required target return, %			
		Probability of positive exit							**Probability of positive exit**			
		10%	30%	50%	70%	90%		10%	30%	50%	70%	90%
	1	8.8	26.3	43.9	61.4	78.9	1	1,040.0	280.0	128.0	62.9	26.7
Years	3	6.7	20.2	33.7	47.2	60.7	3	145.6	70.3	43.6	28.4	18.1
until	5	5.2	15.6	26.0	36.4	46.7	5	80.7	45.0	31.0	22.4	16.4
exit	7	4.0	12.0	20.0	28.0	36.0	7	58.4	35.4	25.9	20.0	15.7
	9	3.1	9.2	15.4	21.5	27.7	9	47.2	30.3	23.1	18.6	15.3

The table on the right side of Exhibit 38.6 analyzes the required returns based on varying probabilities of success and investment durations. For example, an investment with only a 30 percent chance of success and a five-year expected duration to exit must deliver an annual return of 45 percent in order to achieve an overall 14 percent cost of capital. This underscores the heightened performance expectations placed on start-ups in high-risk portfolios.

Step 5: Putting the Pieces Together

With all the essential components established, the value of the investment can be determined. Exhibit 38.7 outlines the valuation process. In step 1, we choose an investment window of five years. In step 2, the total serviceable market in year 5 is calculated at $288 million. Assuming the company captures one-third of this market and maintains a 20 percent operating margin, the operating profit is estimated at $19.2 million. Since similar transactions are valued at 12 times operating profit, the enterprise value is projected at $230.4 million.

In step 3, the plan incorporates one additional round of future financing, which includes the allocation of new shares for employee option pools. This dilution reduces the venture capitalist's ownership stake from 25.0 percent to 15.8 percent. Consequently, the future worth of the security is estimated at 15.8 percent of $230.4 million, or $36.3 million. However, this value is projected for five years in the future, not the present day. Therefore, the valuation process concludes by discounting this future amount at an annual rate of 45.0 percent over five years, resulting in the investment being valued today at $5.7 million.

To decide whether to invest, the venture capital firm must compare the security's value with the required cash investment. In this case, the estimated value of $5.7 million exceeds the $3.0 million investment, so the VC valuation method suggests this is a good trade, and the investment should be made.

EXHIBIT 38.7 **Putting the Pieces Together**

$ million

Enterprise value	230.4
× Expected ownership	0.158
Exit value	36.3
× Discount factor	0.156
Security value	5.7
Versus	
Required investment	3.0

ADVANCED ISSUES IN VENTURE-BACKED VALUATION

The VC valuation method values the company at an expected exit point, determines the remaining ownership after additional financing rounds, and adjusts for time and risk. Although the VC method as presented remains quite prevalent, some investors are beginning to incorporate additional, important complexities into their models. This section briefly summarizes three key issues: the value of optionality in preferred stock, the impact of fees and carried interest, and the implications of a fixed fund size.[3]

Embedded Options

When VC firms invest in start-ups, they typically purchase preferred stock rather than common stock. Preferred stock contains embedded options, such as the ability to convert either into common stock or redeem shares at a predetermined dollar value, commonly referred to as a liquidation preference.[4]

Such liquidation preferences can have a significant impact on the payout structure. For example, consider a scenario where a venture capitalist invests $3 million in a start-up, acquiring 25 percent of the fully diluted shares. If this investment includes a two-times liquidation preference, the venture fund is entitled to the first $6 million from any exit proceeds. In the case of a $10 million sale to a strategic buyer, the venture capitalist would opt to redeem the $6 million liquidation preference rather than convert their shares, effectively claiming 60 percent of the proceeds—substantially more than the 25 percent implied by their common stock ownership.

This dynamic illustrates why converting equity value to share price is not as straightforward as dividing by the number of fully diluted shares, and why option-pricing models become essential. To value preferred stock accurately, one should start by sketching a payoff diagram that illustrates the payout structure implied by the specific terms of the preferred stock. Following this, construct a portfolio of call options that replicate the payoff diagram. Lastly, apply an option-pricing model, such as the Black-Scholes model, to value each call option and sum the values across the portfolio. Depending on the terms of the preferred shares, the options component can represent a substantial portion of the shares' overall value.

---

[3] For a detailed examination of these topics, see A. Metrick and A. Yasuda, *Venture Capital and the Finance of Innovation*, 3rd ed. (Wiley, 2021).

[4] Nonparticipating redeemable convertible preferred stock allows for either liquidation or conversion, but not both. In contrast, participating convertible preferred stock permits both redemption and subsequent participation in the proceeds as if converted.

Fees and Carry

A VC firm charges its limited partners (LPs) a management fee to administer the fund and earns additional compensation through carried interest, often referred to as "carry." A typical fee structure is "two and 20," representing an annual management fee of 2 percent of committed capital and 20 percent of fund profits.

In practice, start-up valuations are typically calculated on a gross basis, excluding the impact of fees and carry. However, from the LPs' perspective, what truly matters is the net return—that is, the return after accounting for these costs. Consequently, a more accurate and meaningful analysis should be conducted on a net basis to reflect the actual returns received by the LPs.

Unfortunately, an analysis net of carry is not straightforward, because carry is usually computed on an aggregate whole-fund basis, not on an individual deal-by-deal basis. Therefore, to estimate the impact of carry, one must first estimate the expected performance of the fund based on performance to date. Consider a $100 million fund expected to return $250 million in distributions, so the gross value multiple is 2.5 times. If carry equals 20 percent of the profit, this amounts to 20 percent times $150 million in fund profit, or $30 million. Thus, $30 million of the $250 million in potential distributions will be lost to carry—approximately 12 percent of the proceeds of a typical transaction, ex ante. The investor in a deal must consider this loss in value.

Fixed Fund Size

When a VC firm raises a new investment fund, it secures a fixed amount of committed capital. Once the fund closes, no additional capital can be raised. The firm then invests this capital into a portfolio of companies. However, unlike mutual funds, which can continuously recycle capital, VC funds can invest their capital only once.[5] After the capital is deployed, it must be returned to the limited partners at exit and cannot be reinvested into new companies.

When investors are capital constrained, they may opt not to accept every investment with a positive net present value (NPV) that is offered to them.[6] For instance, if a fund is 90 percent deployed and the venture capitalist experiences an unexpected increase in deal flow, they might hesitate to invest in a company if the NPV of the transaction is positive but small. They may prefer to wait for a potentially better deal. Research shows that venture capitalists are more likely to require a justified premium above the cost of capital when their remaining funds are limited, deal flow is robust, and the quality of deals is volatile.

---

[5] Some funds include recycle provisions that permit the recycling of capital for a fixed period, typically during the initial two years of the fund's operation. Evergreen funds, which allow for continuous recycling of capital, are less common.

[6] Although capital constraints hold over the short term, they will not hold over the long term. If deal flow is strong, a venture capitalist can raise a new fund, even before the current fund is fully deployed.

SUMMARY

Two pragmatic approaches to valuing an emerging business are the post-money valuation (or sweet-spot) method and the venture capital valuation method. While both methods have their limitations, they focus the investor on essential issues related to value creation. For the sweet-spot method, cash burn and control are paramount, while with the VC method, the focus is on what the company must become in order to create value at a portfolio level.

In the next chapter, we explore a third approach: high-growth valuation using scenarios. Rather than being constrained by a single outcome, scenario-based valuation allows investors to assess potential outcomes by modeling a range of possible future states, helping to identify and prepare for critical risks. This approach enables a more thoughtful valuation and the flexibility to handle the unpredictability that often accompanies emerging businesses.

39

High-Growth Companies

Putting a value on a high-growth, money-losing business is no simple task. These companies often operate in highly dynamic and unpredictable environments and frequently lack the stable financial metrics that are typically used in valuation.

In the previous chapter, we explored two common approaches used by venture capitalists: post-money valuation and the venture capital method. While simple and data-efficient, these models often rely on simplifying assumptions, such as equating failure with liquidation, thereby overlooking other potential outcomes, such as the possibility that the company would achieve moderate returns. A deeper assessment requires a more flexible and comprehensive framework.

This chapter introduces a scenario-based discounted cash flow (DCF) model tailored to valuing high-growth businesses operating in uncertain markets. Unlike traditional approaches, which begin with the present and project forward, our method starts with the company's envisioned future state and works backward to the present. The process begins by defining the company's mature-state economics, including its market size, market share, operating margins, and capital intensity. From this envisioned endpoint, we outline the necessary investments and milestones required to realize that vision. To account for uncertainty, we develop multiple scenarios—from best case to worst case—and assign probabilistic weights to each. This approach captures both upside potential and downside risk, providing a more comprehensive valuation framework for high-growth businesses.

A VALUATION PROCESS FOR HIGH-GROWTH COMPANIES

When valuing an established company, the first step is to analyze historical performance. For high-growth businesses, however, past financial results provide limited insights into future prospects. Instead, the valuation process should begin with the future. Start by sizing the potential market, estimating the company's market share, forecasting sustainable operating margins, and determining the investments required to achieve scale. Focus on a point in the future when the company's performance is expected to stabilize, and use that as the foundation for your forecasts.

To bridge this future vision back to the present, incorporate insights from empirical data on customer adoption and market penetration. Understanding how quickly similar companies have captured market share can offer valuable benchmarks. For instance, does the business require large, fixed investments in areas such as infrastructure or product development before achieving profitability? Or is it designed to become profitable early, with margins that scale alongside revenue growth? These factors help refine assumptions about the timeline and capital intensity required to reach steady-state operations.

Since high-growth companies face significant uncertainty, relying on a single long-term forecast is rarely sufficient. Instead, construct multiple scenarios to capture a range of potential outcomes. Develop scenarios that account for variations in market size, competitive dynamics, and strategic execution. For each scenario, ensure that forecasts for revenue growth, profit margins, and capital requirements align with the underlying assumptions. Assign probabilistic weights to these scenarios, drawing on historical evidence of corporate growth rates to enhance realism.

To illustrate these principles, we profile Aurora Elements, a fictitious company that distributes healthy-lifestyle kitchen products such as web-enabled juicers, air fryers, and food processors. Drawing inspiration from companies profiled in past editions of this book—Amazon, Yelp, and Farfetch—Aurora's evolution reflects the trajectory of a modern technology-driven start-up, providing a robust framework for applying valuation principles across diverse contexts.

Aurora begins its journey much as Amazon did, selling niche products online to digitally savvy consumers. Over time, the company introduces a companion app that provides personalized recipes and usage insights, generating new revenue streams. These can be modeled similarly to the way we analyzed Yelp, utilizing a cohort-by-cohort analysis. Then Aurora, like Farfetch, expands into physical stores and launches a secondhand marketplace, adopting a multichannel strategy.[1] These phases highlight the importance of

---

[1] We allow Aurora to expand into multiple products and channels to examine various models and their inputs. In practice, however, a high-growth company must carefully prioritize the right mix of products, geographies, and channels to avoid overextension and maintain focus on its core strengths.

granular analysis—digging into the details of a business's various components—to identify the key drivers of long-term value.

Start from the Future

To begin the valuation process, start by selecting a point that is far enough in the future that key trends will have had time to fully materialize.[2] Start by assessing the potential market size, which provides a foundation for analysis. From there, delve into more complex and speculative factors, such as market penetration, pricing strategies, and customer churn rates. These elements are critical to understanding the company's growth trajectory and potential value.

For Aurora Elements, these assumptions might include the extent to which direct-to-consumer channels will drive adoption or how its secondhand marketplace might compare with other product categories in terms of size. For example, examining consumer behavior in secondhand markets for clothing or luxury goods can offer insights into the likely trajectory of pre-owned kitchen products.

Translating potential revenue into cash flow requires making clear assumptions about where key value drivers will ultimately stabilize. These drivers include operating margins and capital efficiency, which in turn determine return on invested capital (ROIC). When mature comparable businesses are available, their financial performance can serve as a valuable benchmark to inform these assumptions.

If direct comparables are unavailable, looking to analogous businesses with similar economic drivers can provide meaningful context. For example, when we valued OpenTable in 2010, there were no clear comparables providing restaurant reservations. So we turned instead to travel booking platforms such as Expedia, which was founded 15 years earlier, to guide much of our analysis, since these companies were also involved in matching supply and demand within a market moving online.

Sizing the Market   Many high-growth companies develop innovative solutions to address well-known customer needs, often disrupting established markets in the process. For example, a new pharmaceutical product might revolutionize treatment for atrial fibrillation (AFib), a condition that affects millions of adults. Similarly, electric vehicles are reshaping the auto industry, offering sustainable, high-performance alternatives to gas-powered cars.

---

[2] This distinction underscores a fundamental difference between the scenario-based DCF approach and the venture capital method discussed in the previous chapter. The venture capital method is a transaction-oriented model, focusing on the expected exit year for the investor rather than the point at which the business achieves long-term stability. Unlike the DCF approach, which emphasizes the underlying long-term economics of the business, the venture capital method estimates what a future investor might be willing to pay, often using recent market transactions as a benchmark.

In the entertainment sector, audiences are increasingly opting for streaming short series at home, disrupting the traditional theater experience.

Understanding the impact of these trends requires a foundation in aggregate market data, which is now more accessible and detailed than ever. For example, a publicly available study of California hospital patients found that 7 percent had AFib, indicating that approximately 11 million U.S. adults live with the condition. Meanwhile, a recent article noted that U.S. theaters sold about 850 million tickets in 2023, while in the area of automobiles, an industry association reported 16.5 million passenger vehicle sales in 2024.[3] These data points offer helpful context for assessing the market opportunities available to new companies entering these markets.

To illustrate the process of market sizing and estimating penetration, Exhibit 39.1 presents synthesized data on Aurora's target market, which is generating $3.2 billion in revenue in 2024 and is projected to grow at an annual rate of 5.0 percent. Industry analysts forecast that this growth will drive the market to $5.1 billion over the next decade.[4] These projections highlight the steady expansion of demand for healthy-lifestyle kitchen products, providing a solid foundation for assessing Aurora's growth potential as a direct-to-consumer online retailer.

EXHIBIT 39.1 **Aurora Elements: Target Market Revenues**

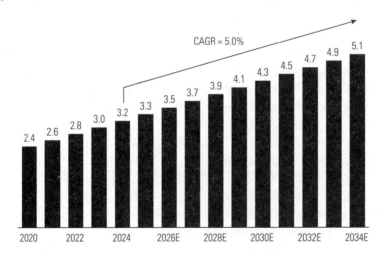

$ billion

CAGR = 5.0%

Note: In this chapter, we value a recently launched fictitious company: Aurora Elements, a digitally native retailer of high-end kitchen products, such as web-enabled juicers.

[3] Sources include Lisa O'Mary, "Atrial Fibrillation Much More Common than Previously Thought," WebMD, September 12, 2024; Wolf Richter, "US Movie Ticket Sales −46 percent in 2023 from 21 Years Ago: AMC and the Movie Theater Meltdown," Wolf Street, January 22, 2024; and the National Automobile Dealers Association, respectively.
[4] While these figures are representative of the juicer market, data throughout the chapter has been synthesized for the purpose of exposition and to illustrate key instructional points.

Estimating Market Penetration   While the overall market is growing at a steady and predictable pace, significant uncertainty remains regarding the shift to direct-to-consumer sales and Aurora's ability to capture market share in this transition. The key questions are what percentage of the market will purchase online by 2034 and, within that digital segment, what share Aurora can realistically claim.

Addressing these uncertainties requires creative approaches to data collection, complemented by economic principles to refine the analysis. Exhibit 39.2 presents forecasts from Cowen and Company, which has been tracking trends in online market penetration for more than a decade. As the exhibit illustrates, online penetration varies widely by product category, from just 5 percent for garden equipment to 80 percent for media-related products and services such as gaming. This stark variability highlights the importance of a nuanced approach to estimating Aurora's potential within its product categories.

One widely recognized framework for assessing technology adoption is Everett Rogers's ACCORD model, which outlines six key factors influencing uptake: relative advantage, compatibility, complexity, trialability, observability, and divisibility.[5] For web-enabled kitchen products, relative advantage measures how features such as automated recipes and smart integration improve on traditional alternatives. Compatibility examines how well the product fits within existing systems, such as smart-device ecosystems. Complexity evaluates ease of use, including setup and app functionality. Trialability assesses the role of demonstrations or trials in encouraging adoption, while observability

EXHIBIT 39.2 **Online Penetration by Industry, 2024**

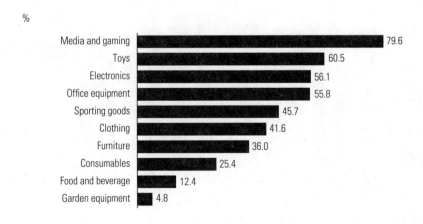

%

Media and gaming	79.6
Toys	60.5
Electronics	56.1
Office equipment	55.8
Sporting goods	45.7
Clothing	41.6
Furniture	36.0
Consumables	25.4
Food and beverage	12.4
Garden equipment	4.8

Source: Cowen and Company.

[5] E. M. Rogers, *Diffusion of Innovations*, 5th ed. (Free Press, 2003). For a modern adaptation of Rogers's work, see G. A. Moore, *Crossing the Chasm: Marketing and Selling Disruptive Products to Mainstream Customers*, 3rd ed. (Harper Business, 2014).

focuses on how clearly the product's benefits can be perceived through use or customer feedback. Divisibility, the final factor, considers whether a product can be adopted incrementally rather than requiring a full-scale commitment. This principle explains why many apps offer free versions initially, allowing users to explore basic features before upgrading to more advanced, paid options.

When applied to web-enabled juicers, the ACCORD model underscores the segment's strong adoption potential compared with categories such as furniture or clothing. Health-conscious, tech-savvy consumers—already familiar with purchasing kitchen gadgets online—are a natural fit for Aurora's offerings. Exhibit 39.3 projects that online penetration of Aurora's target market will reach 68 percent by 2034, matching the trajectory of more established markets such as toys and electronics.

Within the digital market, the next step is estimating the share Aurora is likely to capture. Adoption models provide a valuable framework for comparing Aurora with competitors, including established brands such as Breville and niche players such as Hurom and Kuvings. Based on the strength of its products compared with those of other players, we assume Aurora's direct-to-consumer business could eventually secure 20 percent of the digital market, equal to 13 percent of the aggregate market (see Exhibit 39.3).

However, given the uncertainties surrounding the market's evolution and Aurora's competitive positioning, how can we confidently project online penetration and market share? The short answer is that we can't—at least not yet. This is why constructing multiple scenarios isn't just helpful—it's essential. As more

EXHIBIT 39.3 **Aurora's Target Market: Online Penetration and Company Market Share**

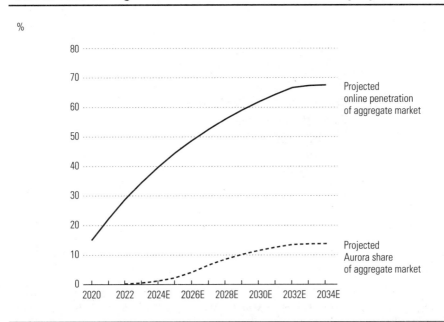

data emerges about Aurora's performance and shifts in market dynamics, the range of potential outcomes will narrow. In the early stages, however, accounting for a broad range of possibilities is not just advisable but imperative.

Customer-Based Revenue Models   When a customer pays cash for a basket of products in a retail store, there is little opportunity to learn about their behavior or preferences. In contrast, a digital platform generates a wealth of data, enabling detailed customer analysis. Metrics such as customer acquisition costs, purchase frequency, and churn rates offer valuable insights that can enhance the valuation process.

To build on our example, imagine Aurora has announced plans to invest in a complementary app aimed at deepening customer engagement and unlocking new revenue streams. The app will feature a free version, allowing users to access recipes and tutorials, supported by limited advertising. For those seeking more advanced features, a premium version—offering tools such as personalized weight management plans and additional capabilities—will be available through a monthly subscription.

To develop a revenue model for the company's app business, we use a cohort-by-cohort approach. In a cohort model, customers acquired during a specific time frame, such as a month or quarter, are grouped into cohorts, enabling their behavior to be tracked over time. This approach evaluates key metrics, including retention rates, upgrades to premium tiers, and customer spending patterns throughout their life cycle.

Exhibit 39.4 introduces the first step: tracking customer movement between tiers. Customers may begin with a free version of the app and later upgrade to the premium tier, which generates higher revenue. For example, assume the free tier starts with 100 customers.[6] Over time, some customers upgrade to premium (five upgrade in the first quarter, nine in the second), while others churn due to attrition. By the end of the third quarter, only 58 of the original 100 free-tier customers remain active on that tier, owing to the combination of attrition and upgrade patterns. Simultaneously, premium-tier customers grow from none in the first quarter to 20 by the beginning of the fourth as upgrades accumulate. By structuring customer flows in this way, the model captures essential dynamics: retention, churn, and movement between tiers, which can be used to estimate customer lifetime value.

The second step, illustrated in Exhibit 39.5, connects customer growth directly to projected revenue. Each cohort's revenue contribution is a function of the number of active customers, which reflects the penetration rates forecast in our earlier analysis, and their spending patterns over time. In this example scenario, we assume that a first cohort begins in the first quarter with 1,500 new customers,

---

[6] Customers join a cohort only at its inception, after which their journey is tracked over time. Future cohorts will include new customers as they join. The layering of multiple cohorts is illustrated in Exhibit 39.5.

EXHIBIT 39.4 **Cohort Model: Sample Customer Life Cycle Model**

Number of customers[1]

	Quarter 1	2	3	4	5	6
Free tier						
At start of quarter	100.0	90.0	74.8	58.0	49.5	44.0
Downgrading from premium	0.0	0.5	2.0	3.0	2.0	0.9
Upgrading to premium	(5.0)	(9.0)	(11.2)	(5.8)	(2.5)	0.0
Attrition	(5.0)	(6.8)	(7.5)	(5.8)	(4.9)	(4.4)
At end of quarter	90.0	74.8	58.0	49.5	44.0	40.6
Premium tier						
At start of quarter	0.0	5.0	13.0	20.3	20.0	18.5
Upgrading from free model	5.0	9.0	11.2	5.8	2.5	0.0
Downgrading to free model	0.0	(0.5)	(2.0)	(3.0)	(2.0)	(0.9)
Attrition	0.0	(0.5)	(2.0)	(3.0)	(2.0)	(0.9)
At end of quarter	5.0	13.0	20.3	20.0	18.5	16.6
Total at start of quarter	100.0	95.0	87.8	78.3	69.5	62.5

[1] Customer counts are estimated based on factors such as upgrade rates and churn rates, and are presented without rounding.

EXHIBIT 39.5 **Cohort Model: Sample Revenue Projection**

	Customers acquired	Quarter 1	2	3	4	5	6
Number of customers							
Quarter 1	1,500	1,500	1,425	1,250	979	680	425
Quarter 2	2,580		2,580	2,451	2,151	1,685	1,170
Quarter 3	4,066			4,066	3,863	3,390	2,655
Quarter 4	5,940				5,940	5,643	4,952
Quarter 5	8,129					8,129	7,723
Quarter 6	10,527						10,527
Total customers		1,500	4,005	7,767	12,933	19,527	27,452
Revenue, $ thousand							
Quarter 1		22.5	22.0	20.4	17.1	12.3	7.9
Quarter 2			38.7	37.9	35.1	29.4	21.2
Quarter 3				61.0	59.7	55.3	46.3
Quarter 4					89.1	87.2	80.7
Quarter 5						121.9	119.4
Quarter 6							157.9
Total revenue		22.5	60.7	119.3	201.0	306.1	433.5

generating $22,500 in revenue. As churn reduces the number of active customers, revenue from this cohort declines to $17,100 by the fourth quarter.

The addition of new cohorts—such as the 2,580 customers acquired in the second quarter—offsets these declines, fueling overall revenue growth. By the fourth quarter, total revenue from all cohorts reaches $201,000, with continued growth projected as larger cohorts are added in subsequent periods. This clear connection between penetration modeling and customer dynamics demonstrates how Aurora's growing customer base translates into revenue.

By combining customer life cycle insights from Exhibit 39.4 with the revenue growth trends in Exhibit 39.5, it is possible to build a more comprehensive picture of the company's expected performance. Cohort analysis not only simplifies revenue forecasting but also serves as the foundation for calculating customer lifetime value, a key measure of long-term profitability. Whether a business sells app subscriptions, kitchen tools, or both, understanding these models is essential for identifying growth opportunities and optimizing financial outcomes.

Projecting Long-Term Margins and ROIC   With a revenue forecast in hand, estimate long-term operating margins, capital productivity, and return on invested capital. To project operating margins, start by triangulating between expected pricing, the cost to serve, and margins achieved by established players in similar industries. Chapter 8 provides a comprehensive overview of ROIC across industries, explaining the factors that affect these returns and the market conditions—such as network effects—that enable businesses to achieve and sustain high ROIC levels.

Our company, Aurora Elements, has largely focused on its direct-to-consumer business but has also made strategic investments in a handful of luxury retail stores to bolster brand awareness in key markets.[7] The company has further broadened its presence by launching a third-party marketplace, facilitating transactions between buyers and sellers of pre-owned equipment and extending its reach within the industry.

Because the underlying economics of Aurora's business segments vary significantly, it is important to analyze each segment separately, as shown in Exhibit 39.6. Consider, for example, Aurora's third-party marketplace, which facilitates transactions between buyers and sellers of pre-owned kitchen tools, as well as its app-based sales. Aurora neither manufactures nor holds inventory for these segments, so it has a low cost of sales, minimal capital requirements, and strong scalability. To forecast steady-state margins and capital intensity, we look to established technology marketplace operators, which have achieved operating margins between 20 and 30 percent.[8]

---

[7] In a strategic shift known as "clicks to bricks," online brands are expanding into physical retail to enhance the customer experience, boost brand awareness, and drive sales. Notable examples include eyewear retailer Warby Parker, sustainable footwear company Allbirds, and jewelry brand Mejuri. For more, see: N. DeMarco, "Why All Your Favourite Indie Designers Are Opening Stores Right Now," *Vogue Business*, December 12, 2024.

[8] Context for our long-term margin forecasts: in 2023, the upscale kitchen retailer Williams-Sonoma posted a 16.1 percent operating margin, the online marketplace eBay achieved a 19.4 percent margin, and the dating app company Match Group recorded a 28.7 percent margin.

EXHIBIT 39.6 **Key Value Drivers: Long-Run Economics**

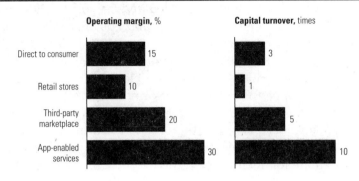

However, while these benchmarks provide a starting point, careful judgment is necessary to account for differences in business mix and strategy when making direct comparisons.

By contrast, Aurora's first-party sales, whether online or in physical stores, operate more like those of a traditional retailer. In these two segments, Aurora sells products directly to customers, which entails purchasing inventory, holding stock, and potentially investing in warehouses or retail spaces as the business grows. As a result, margins for first-party sales will more closely resemble those of online retailers or specialty retailers, often between 5 and 15 percent. Growth in this segment depends on significant working capital investments to scale inventory while increasing sales volumes.

This segmented approach allows for a more accurate forecast of long-term value creation and highlights how differences in business economics shape the company's operating margins and returns on invested capital.

Work Backward to Current Performance

Once you have completed a forecast for total market size, market share, operating margin, and capital intensity, the next step is to reconnect those long-term projections to the company's current performance. This requires assessing the speed of transition from today's performance to the long-term steady state. The transition must align with economic principles and industry characteristics to ensure the forecast is both realistic and internally consistent.

Start by evaluating key dynamics such as operating margins and capital turnover. For operating margins, consider how long fixed costs will dominate variable costs, keeping margins low in the near term. At what point will the business scale enough for variable costs to decline as a percentage of revenue? Similarly, analyze capital turnover: How much scale is required before revenues begin to grow faster than capital investments? As the business reaches scale, will competition intensify and drive down prices, slowing margin expansion? Often, examining these issues will only reveal more uncertainty, rather than providing clear answers—which is yet another reason why forecasting a company's trajectory can be so challenging.

To gauge the likely speed of transition, look to the historical progression of similar companies, because the historical financial performance won't be of much use. High-growth companies typically make significant long-term investments, especially in intangible assets such as technology, brand building, or customer acquisition. Under current accounting rules, intangible investments are expensed rather than capitalized. This treatment understates both early profits and invested capital, so as soon as these companies turn profitable, their ROIC often appears unreasonably high, owing to the limited formal capital base.

Understanding these distortions is critical to making a realistic transition forecast. By carefully accounting for the role of intangible investments and recognizing how fixed costs and capital intensity evolve with scale, you can more accurately determine the path from current performance to long-term targets. While the uncertainties of high-growth businesses cannot be eliminated, a well-reasoned transition forecast provides the necessary bridge to connect short-term performance with long-term value creation.

Exhibit 39.7 illustrates this process by presenting free cash flow calculations for Aurora's two core segments: direct-to-consumer and third-party marketplace.

In the direct-to-consumer business, as digital penetration of the product category stabilizes and Aurora's market share gains level off, growth slows to a steady-state rate of about 4 percent. At the same time, operating margins

EXHIBIT 39.7 **Aurora Elements: Free Cash Flow by Business**

$ million

	Direct-to-consumer					Third-party marketplace			
	2024	2025E	2026E	2033E	2034E	2025E	2026E	2033E	2034E
Company revenue	37.6	74.4	146.8	676.5	705.9	1.6	5.9	47.5	49.6
Cost of sales	(56.4)	(89.3)	(168.8)	(575.0)	(600.0)	(2.1)	(6.8)	(38.0)	(39.7)
Operating profit	(18.8)	(14.9)	(22.0)	101.5	105.9	(0.5)	(0.9)	9.5	9.9
Operating taxes	4.7	3.7	5.5	(25.4)	(26.5)	0.1	0.2	(2.4)	(2.5)
NOPAT	(14.1)	(11.2)	(16.5)	76.1	79.4	(0.4)	(0.7)	7.1	7.4
Growth capital	(11.5)	(12.3)	(24.1)	(12.5)	(9.8)	(0.3)	(0.9)	(0.5)	(0.4)
Free cash flow	(25.6)	(23.4)	(40.6)	63.6	69.6	(0.7)	(1.5)	6.6	7.0
Key drivers									
Revenue growth, %	145.4	98.0	97.2	5.9	4.4	n/a	260.3	5.6	4.3
Operating margin, %	−50.0	−20.0	−15.0	15.0	15.0	−30.0	−15.0	20.0	20.0
Capital turnover, times	3.0	3.0	3.0	3.0	3.0	5.0	5.0	5.0	5.0

Note: This exhibit reflects data exclusively from Aurora's direct-to-consumer and third-party marketplace units. Aurora also generates free cash flow from its retail stores, as well as app-based advertising and digital purchases.

improve with scale and stabilize within five years. Capital turnover, however, remains constant throughout the forecast period.

The marketplace segment follows a similar trajectory but with its own dynamics. While smaller than the direct-to-consumer business, the marketplace segment is more efficient at converting revenue into profit and profit into cash flow, because of its stronger margins and higher capital turnover. These free cash flows form the foundation for our valuation in the next section.

Develop Scenarios

A straightforward approach to addressing the uncertainty of high-growth companies is to use probability-weighted scenarios. Unlike more complex techniques, such as real options or Monte Carlo simulations, scenario analysis provides a clear and practical framework for modeling a range of outcomes while making critical assumptions and their interactions more transparent. This method ensures that the valuation process remains grounded in thoughtful analysis while accounting for uncertainty.

To develop probability-weighted scenarios, estimate financial performance across a range of outcomes, from optimistic to pessimistic. For Aurora Elements, Exhibit 39.8 outlines value drivers for four scenarios as of 2034, shaped by market conditions, competition, and consumer behavior:

1. *Optimistic scenario (A).* In the optimistic scenario, Aurora thrives as online penetration in the kitchen market accelerates to 85 percent, mirroring trends seen in digitally dominant categories such as media and gaming. Aurora captures 25 percent of the digital segment, translating to 21 percent of the total market, and generates nearly $1.4 billion in revenue with 20 percent operating margins. This performance is driven by Aurora's category leadership and agility in meeting evolving consumer preferences.

2. *Moderate scenario (B).* The moderate scenario anticipates steady growth, with online penetration reaching 68 percent and Aurora capturing 14 percent of the total market. Revenue climbs to $897 million, while margins stabilize at 15 percent, in line with other premium retailers, delivering healthy returns on capital.

3. *Conservative scenario (C).* In the conservative scenario, online penetration and Aurora's market share remain consistent with the moderate scenario, but intensified competition and operational challenges compress margins to 10 percent.

4. *Pessimistic scenario (D).* The pessimistic scenario reflects weak online adoption, plateauing at 45 percent, similar to the experience of less digitally inclined categories, such as clothing. Aurora's market share stagnates at 6 percent, with revenue stalling at $395 million and margins held at 10 percent due to pricing pressures needed to maintain scale.

EXHIBIT 39.8 **Aurora Elements: Key Value Drivers by Scenario, 2034 Forecast**

	Online penetration of kitchen, %	Company market share,[1] %	Total revenue,[2] $ million	Operating margin, %	Description
Scenario A: Optimistic	85	21	1,356	20	Online penetration of the kitchen market accelerates, market share expands significantly, and operating margins remain strong as the company maintains its leadership position.
Scenario B: Moderate	68	14	897	15	Online penetration progresses at a steady rate, market share stabilizes, and operating margins align with expectations amid consistent performance.
Scenario C: Conservative	68	14	897	10	Online penetration progresses, but market share growth underperforms; operating margins remain under pressure, failing to meet moderate expectations.
Scenario D: Pessimistic	45	6	395	10	Online penetration and market share fail to meet expectations; margin pressure intensifies due to large-scale entrants and increased omnichannel presence from traditional retailers.

[1] Market share is calculated as the company's direct-to-consumer revenue divided by the total market, which includes both online and retail sales.

[2] Total revenue comprises the company's direct-to-consumer, retail, third-party marketplace, and app segments.

Once the scenarios are defined, the next step is to assign probabilities to each and calculate a probability-weighted equity valuation. Exhibit 39.9 demonstrates this process by combining the intrinsic valuation of each scenario with its assigned probability. For example, scenario A, with a 5 percent probability, contributes $87.0 million, while scenario B, at 40 percent, adds $322.7 million. Scenario C, with a 30 percent likelihood, contributes

EXHIBIT 39.9 **Aurora Elements: Probability-Weighted Expected Value**

Scenario	Intrinsic equity valuation,[1] $ million	×	Probability,[2] %	=	Contribution to equity valuation, $ million
A	1,740.0		5		87.0
B	806.9		40		322.7
C	508.5		30		152.5
D	236.9		25		59.2
			100		621.5
			Shares outstanding, million		45.0
			Value per share, $		13.8

[1] Aurora Elements has no nonoperating assets or debt, so its enterprise value equals its equity value. The company is financed solely with common shares and does not have the preferred stock typically seen in venture-backed companies.

[2] The probabilities assigned to this set of scenarios reflect a high-growth company with meaningful revenues. In contrast, companies with unproven value propositions typically face failure rates ranging between 50 and 70 percent.

$152.5 million, and scenario D, at 25 percent, accounts for $59.2 million. Together, these weighted contributions result in a total equity valuation of $621.5 million, or $13.8 per share, based on 45 million shares outstanding.

This scenario-based approach compels decision makers to confront the full range of potential outcomes while explicitly linking assumptions to financial projections. For example, dividing each scenario's intrinsic equity valuation by the number of shares outstanding results in a wide range of potential share prices, from $5 to $39 per share—far from a narrow band.

UNCERTAINTY IS HERE TO STAY

Even with an adaptable discounted cash flow (DCF) approach, valuing companies in fast-changing markets—particularly those tied to new technologies or complex ecosystems—remains a significant challenge. Both investors and companies face the difficulty of predicting financial outcomes in highly volatile environments. Consider an investor who purchased Aurora Elements stock in 2024 and held it for five years under the four scenarios outlined earlier.

If the optimistic scenario (A) materializes, the investor would see a 35 percent annual return, making the original valuation appear highly conservative. In the conservative scenario (C), however, the return drops to just a few percent annually, failing to meet the cost of capital. In the most pessimistic case, scenario D, the investor incurs a 10 percent annual loss, suggesting the stock was overvalued at the outset. These wide-ranging potential outcomes highlight the inherent uncertainty in high-growth investments. Yet, this variability doesn't necessarily mean the stock was irrationally priced at purchase; it simply reflects the difficulty of forecasting the future in a fast-moving market.

When a company goes public, investors are constantly processing new information, which fuels the volatility seen in young companies' share prices. Such sharp price swings are typical: young companies often experience stock volatility much greater than that of the broader market. For instance, one study conducted by our colleagues examined more than 800 initial public offerings (IPOs) since 2010 and found that only 13 percent delivered annualized returns between 7 and 12 percent, a range widely considered a reasonable equity return. Most IPOs fell far outside this range, with nearly 10 percent either gaining or losing more than 50 percent of their value within the first few years of trading.[9]

The difficulty of identifying winners in a crowded and competitive market adds to this uncertainty. A handful of companies achieve outsize success, but the majority struggle to gain traction. Predicting which ones will thrive

---

[9] The results come from Corporate Performance Analytics by McKinsey, which relies on financial data provided by Standard & Poor's Compustat and Capital IQ.

is inherently speculative. This is why financial advisers recommend portfolio diversification and why acquiring companies often preserve flexibility in the face of uncertainty by using stock rather than cash when buying young, high-growth firms.

CONCLUDING THOUGHTS

The dramatic rise of social networks, online marketplaces, and other high-growth, scalable businesses has created extraordinary value for investors. These successes, however, continue to fuel ongoing debates about the rationality of market valuations. Investors often assign soaring price tags to companies even as their losses mount, believing in the transformative potential of their business models. Even today, similar debates surround artificial intelligence software companies, many of which command multibillion-dollar valuations despite limited evidence of their ability to generate cash flow.[10]

Amid this uncertainty and volatility, scenario-based discounted cash flow remains a powerful tool for valuing high-growth companies. But in these contexts, applying DCF requires a shift in perspective. Rather than starting with the present, forecasts must be anchored in the future, incorporating assumptions about how the business will evolve over time. Developing probability-weighted scenarios can help account for inherent uncertainty, while comparing the economics of the business model with proven benchmarks provides additional grounding.

Although volatility cannot be eliminated, understanding its drivers provides a crucial edge in evaluating high-growth companies operating in rapidly changing markets. By adapting valuation approaches to account for uncertainty and variability, investors and analysts can make more informed judgments—balancing the transformative potential of technology with the reality of financial fundamentals.

---

[10] J. Glasner, "Putting OpenAI's Crazy High $100B Valuation into Context," *Crunchbase News*, August 29, 2024.

40

Flexibility and Options

Properly managing a modern business is about making choices to create value. All these choices take place against a backdrop of uncertainty about the potential outcomes of alternative courses of action.[1] However, in some cases, you can face decisions where not only uncertainty is present, but so is flexibility.

Managerial flexibility and uncertainty are not the same. In cases of uncertainty, the future of a company or a project may be extremely difficult to predict and may depend on a single management decision—for example, the decision to launch a new product line or to invest in a new production facility. Flexibility, in contrast, refers to choices managers may make between alternative plans in response to events. This is especially relevant when you are conducting valuations of investment projects.

The difference is important in deciding your approach to valuation. Whatever the degree of uncertainty, it is possible to value the asset in question by using a *standard* discounted-cash-flow (DCF) approach combined with either different scenarios or a stochastic simulation (see, for example, Chapter 17). But suppose management has planned to stage its investments in a business start-up. In that case, the managers may decide at each stage whether to proceed, depending on information arising from the previous stage. Where managers expect to respond flexibly to events, they need so-called *contingent* valuation approaches. These forecast, implicitly or explicitly, the future free cash flows, depending on the future states of the world and management decisions, and then discount these to today's value. For such decisions, the contingent approaches provide more accurate valuation results and, perhaps even more important, deeper insights into what creates value.

---

[1] See Chapters 4 and 13 for ideas on handling uncertainty—for example, with scenario-based approaches.

This chapter concentrates on the basic concepts of valuing managerial flexibility in businesses and projects. It focuses on the following topics:

- Fundamental concepts behind uncertainty, flexibility, and value (when and why flexibility has value)
- Managing flexibility in terms of real options to defer investments; making follow-on investments; and expanding, changing, or abandoning production
- Comparison of decision tree analysis (DTA) and real-option valuation (ROV) to value flexibility, including situations in which each approach is more appropriate
- A four-step approach to analyzing and valuing real options, illustrated with numerical examples using ROV and DTA

A HIERARCHY OF APPROACHES

It is possible to illustrate a hierarchy of standard and contingent approaches to valuation under situations of uncertainty and flexibility and to suggest when it is best to apply each (Exhibit 40.1). When a flexible response is neither expected nor required, you can choose from the following three variations of a standard DCF approach, depending on the level of uncertainty:

- *Single-path DCF valuation.* When little uncertainty exists about future outcomes or when uncertainty is evenly spread around the expected outcomes, use a standard, single-path DCF analysis based on point estimates of future cash flows.
- *Scenario-based DCF.* When significant uncertainty exists, especially when there is a possibility of much more upside than downside (or vice versa) in future cash flows, it is best to model future outcomes in two or more scenarios that capture the variation in the paths of future cash flow. This approach is easy to apply in, for example, valuing corporate or business strategies.
- *Stochastic simulation DCF.* If you have reliable estimates about the underlying probability distributions of cash flows into the future, such as mean, standard deviation, and possibly skewness, it may be worthwhile to use a stochastic simulation DCF approach. In this approach, future cash flow paths are explicitly modeled and valued in a stochastic simulation. Because this approach is complex and requires voluminous data, applications are mostly restricted to specific industries, such as the valuation of insurance companies and commodity-based businesses.

EXHIBIT 40.1 **Valuation under Uncertainty: Approaches**

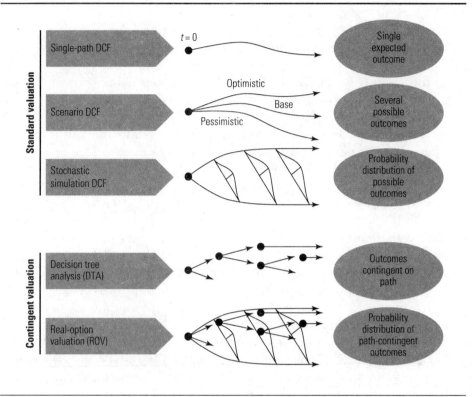

When managerial flexibility is called for, you need one of the following contingent valuation approaches, selected according to the amount of information available:

- *Decision tree analysis (DTA).* If there is limited information about the distribution of future cash flow paths and the decisions that management can take depending on these cash flows, use a decision tree analysis. As the following sections discuss, it builds on scenario DCF valuation and is straightforward and transparent. DTA is especially effective for valuing flexibility related to technological risks that are not priced in the market, such as investments in research and development (R&D) projects, product launches, and plant-decommissioning decisions.

- *Real-option valuation (ROV).* If you have reliable information about the underlying probability distributions of future cash flow paths, such as those required for stochastic simulation, ROV could provide better results and insights. However, it requires sophisticated, formal option-pricing models that are harder for managers to decipher than DTA.

The ROV approach is best suited to decisions in commodity-based businesses, such as investments in oil and gas fields, refining facilities, chemical plants, and power generators, because the underlying commodity risk is priced in the market.[2]

In theory, ROV is more accurate than DTA. But it is not the right approach in every case. It cannot replace traditional discounted cash flow, because valuing an option using ROV still depends on knowing the value of the underlying assets. Unless the assets have an observable market price, you will have to estimate that value using traditional DCF.

Company-wide valuation models rarely take flexibility into account. To analyze and model flexibility accurately, you must be able to describe the set of specific decisions managers could make in response to future events and include the cash flow implications of those decisions. In valuing a company, flexibility therefore becomes relevant only in cases where management responds to specific events that may change the course of the whole company. For example, to value internet or biotech companies with a handful of promising new products in development, you could project sales, profit, and investments for the company as a whole that are conditional on the success of product development.[3] Another example is a company that has built its strategy around buying up smaller players and integrating them into a bigger entity, capturing synergies along the way. The first acquisitions may not create value in their own right but may open opportunities for value creation through further acquisitions.

Flexibility is typically more relevant in the valuation of individual businesses and projects, as it mostly concerns detailed decisions related to production, capacity investment, marketing, research and development, and other factors.

UNCERTAINTY, FLEXIBILITY, AND VALUE

To appreciate the value of flexibility and its key value drivers, consider a simple example.[4] Suppose you are deciding whether to invest $6,000 one year from now to produce and distribute a new pharmaceutical drug already under development. In the upcoming final development stage, the product

[2] See, for example, E. S. Schwartz and L. Trigeorgis, eds., *Real Options and Investment under Uncertainty: Classical Readings and Recent Contributions* (Cambridge, MA: MIT Press, 2001); T. Copeland and V. Antikarov, *Real Options: A Practitioner's Guide* (New York: Texere, 2003); or L. Trigeorgis, *Real Options: Managerial Flexibility and Strategy in Resource Allocation* (Cambridge, MA: MIT Press, 1996).

[3] See, for example, E. S. Schwartz and M. Moon, "Rational Pricing of Internet Companies," *Financial Analysts Journal* 56, no. 3 (2000): 62–75; and D. Kellogg and J. Charnes, "Real-Options Valuation for a Biotechnology Company," *Financial Analysts Journal* 56, no. 3 (2000): 76–84.

[4] The example is inspired by A. Dixit and R. Pindyck, *Investment under Uncertainty* (Princeton, NJ: Princeton University Press, 1994), 26.

will undergo clinical tests on patients for one year, for which all investments have already been made. These tests involve no future cash flows. The trials could have one of two possible outcomes. If the drug proves to be highly effective, it will generate an annual net cash inflow of $500 in perpetuity. If it is only somewhat effective, the annual net cash inflow will be $100 in perpetuity. These outcomes are equally probable.

Based on this information, the expected future net cash flow is $300, the probability-weighted average of the risky outcomes ($500 and $100). To keep it simple, we assume that success in developing the new product and the value of the new product are unrelated to what happens in the overall economy, so this risk is fully diversifiable by the company's investors. Therefore, the beta for this product is zero, and the cost of capital equals the risk-free rate—say, 5 percent. Assuming the company will realize its first year's product sales immediately upon completing the trials and at the end of each year thereafter, the net present value (NPV) of the investment is estimated as follows:

$$NPV = \frac{-\$6,000}{1.05} + \sum_{t=1}^{\infty} \frac{\$300}{(1.05)^t} = \$286$$

To apply the NPV approach, we discount the incremental expected project cash flows at the cost of capital. Any prior development expenses are irrelevant, because they are sunk costs. Alternatively, if the project is canceled, the NPV equals $0. Therefore, management should approve the incremental investment of $6,000.

In this example of the NPV decision rule, undertaking development creates value. But there are more alternatives than deciding *today* whether to invest. Using an approach like the scenario approach described in Chapter 17, we can rewrite the previous NPV calculation in terms of the probability-weighted values of the drug, discounted to today:

$$NPV = 0.5 \left[\frac{-\$6,000}{1.05} + \sum_{t=1}^{\infty} \frac{\$500}{(1.05)^t} \right] + 0.5 \left[\frac{-\$6,000}{1.05} + \sum_{t=1}^{\infty} \frac{\$100}{(1.05)^t} \right]$$

$$= 0.5(\$4,286) + 0.5(-\$3,714)$$

$$= \$286$$

(40.1)

Here, the NPV is shown as the weighted average of two distinct results: a positive NPV of $4,286 following a favorable trial outcome and a negative NPV of –$3,714 for an unfavorable outcome. If the decision to invest can be deferred until trial results are known, the project becomes much more attractive. Specifically, if the drug proves to be less effective, the project can be halted, avoiding the negative NPV. You invest only if the drug is highly effective, and the annual cash flow of $500 more than compensates for the investment required. In practice, an upfront investment would likely be needed for the trial, regardless of its outcome, but we have abstracted from such costs to keep the example simple.

EXHIBIT 40.2 **Value of Flexibility to Defer Investment**

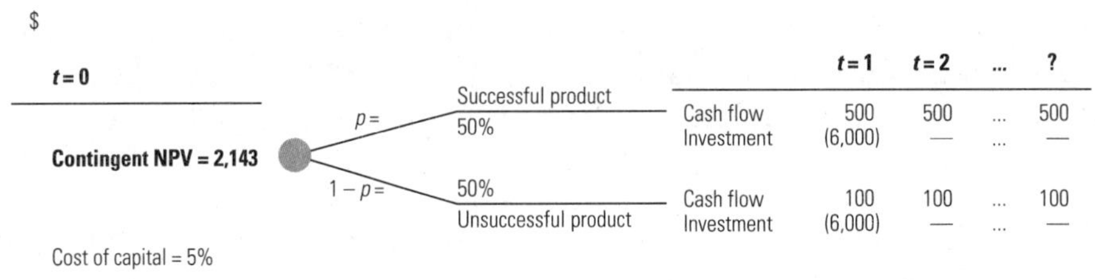

Note: t = time, in years; p = probability.

This flexibility is an option to defer the investment decision. To value the option, a contingent NPV approach can be used, working from right to left in the payoff tree shown in Exhibit 40.2.

$$
\begin{aligned}
\text{NPV} = {} & 0.5 \times \text{Max}\left[\left(\frac{-\$6{,}000}{1.05} + \sum_{t=1}^{\infty}\frac{\$500}{(1.05)^t}\right), 0\right] \\
& + 0.5 \times \text{Max}\left[\left(\frac{-\$6{,}000}{1.05} + \sum_{t=1}^{\infty}\frac{\$100}{(1.05)^t}\right), 0\right] \\
= {} & 0.5(\$4{,}286) + 0.5(0) = \$2{,}143
\end{aligned}
$$

The contingent NPV of $2,143 is considerably higher than the $286 NPV of committing today. Therefore, the best alternative is to defer a decision until the trial outcomes are known. The value of the option to defer investment is the difference between the value of the project with flexibility and its value without flexibility: $2,143 – $286 = $1,857.

Based on this example, it is possible to summarize the distinction between the standard and contingent NPVs. The standard NPV is the maximum, decided today, of the expected discounted cash flows or zero:

$$
\text{Standard NPV} = \text{Max}_{t=0}\left(\frac{\text{Expected (Cash Flows)}}{\text{Cost of Capital}}, 0\right)
$$

The contingent NPV is the expected value of the maximums, decided when information arrives, of the discounted cash flows in each future state or zero:

$$
\text{Contingent NPV} = \text{Expected}_{t=0}\left[\text{Max}\left(\frac{\text{Cash Flows Contingent on Information}}{\text{Cost of Capital}}, 0\right)\right]
$$

These two NPV approaches use information quite differently. Standard NPV forces a decision based on today's expectation of future information, whereas contingent NPV permits the flexibility of making decisions after the

EXHIBIT 40.3 **When Is Flexibility Valuable?**

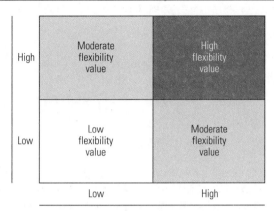

information arrives. Unlike standard NPV, it captures the value of flexibility. A project's contingent NPV will always be greater than or equal to its standard NPV.

The value of flexibility is related to the degree of uncertainty and the room for managerial reaction (see Exhibit 40.3). It is greatest when uncertainty is high and managers can react to new information. In contrast, if there is little uncertainty, managers are unlikely to receive new information that would alter future decisions, so flexibility has little value. Similarly, if managers cannot act on new information that becomes available, the value of flexibility is low.

Including flexibility in a project valuation is most important when the project's standard NPV is close to zero—that is, when the decision whether to go ahead with the project is a close call. Sometimes senior management intuitively overrules standard NPV results and accepts an investment project for "strategic reasons"—for example, because the project creates an initial market position that can be expanded at a later stage if and when the company has the competitive products or services to offer. In these cases, the flexibility recognized in contingent valuation fits better with strategic intuition than do the rigid assumptions of standard NPV approaches.

What Creates Flexibility Value

To identify and value flexibility, you must understand where its value comes from. Consider what happens if the range of possible annual cash flow outcomes (originally $500 versus $100 per year) increases to $600 versus $0. Since expected cash flows and cost of capital remain unchanged, the standard NPV is the same ($286).[5] However, the contingent NPV increases from its prior level of $2,143:

$$\text{NPV} = 0.5 \times \text{Max}\left[\left(\frac{-\$6,000}{1.05} + \sum_{t=1}^{\infty}\frac{\$600}{(1.05)^t}\right), 0\right]$$

$$+ 0.5 \times \text{Max}\left[\left(\frac{-\$6,000}{1.05} + \sum_{t=1}^{\infty}\frac{\$0}{(1.05)^t}\right), 0\right]$$

$$= 0.5(\$6,286) + 0.5(0)$$

$$= \$3,143$$

The contingent NPV of $3,143 is almost 50 percent greater at this higher level of uncertainty. Why? As in the original case, only the cash flows from the favorable outcome affect the contingent valuation. Since these cash flow projections have increased by 20 percent and the required investment has not changed, the contingent NPV increases substantially. The value of the deferral option rises from $1,857 to $2,857 (computed as $3,143 − $286).

We can formally derive the key value drivers of real options from the pricing theory of financial options such as call and put options on equity shares. In our original example, the deferral option is identical to a call option with an exercise price of $6,000 and a one-year maturity on an underlying risky asset that has a current value of $6,000 and a variance determined by the cash flow spread of $400 across outcomes.[6] As with financial options, the value of a real option depends on six drivers, summarized in Exhibit 40.4.

These drivers of option value show how allowing for flexibility affects the valuation of a particular investment project. Holding other drivers constant, option value decreases with higher investment costs and more cash flows lost while holding the option. Option value increases with higher value of the underlying asset's cash flows, greater uncertainty, higher risk-free interest rates, and a longer lifetime of the option. With higher option values, a standard DCF calculation that ignores flexibility will more seriously underestimate the true value of an investment project.

Be careful how you interpret the impact of value drivers when designing investment strategies to exploit flexibility. The impact of any individual driver described in Exhibit 40.4 holds only when all other value drivers remain constant. In practice, changes in uncertainty and interest rates not only affect the value of the option but usually change the value of the underlying asset as well. When you assess the impact of these drivers, you should assess all their effects on the option's value, both direct and indirect. Take the case of higher

---

[5] We assume that the trial outcome risk is uncorrelated with the overall economy.
[6] The current value of the underlying risky asset is the present value of expected annual cash flows of $300 into perpetuity, discounted at a 5 percent cost of capital.

EXHIBIT 40.4 **Drivers of Flexibility Value**

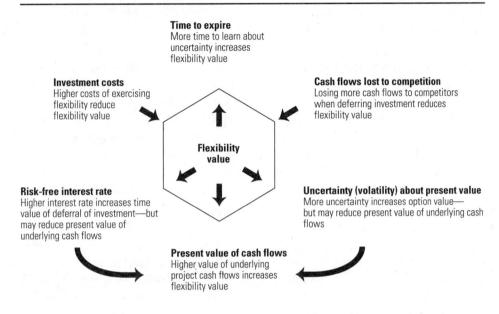

uncertainty. In our example, we increased the uncertainty of future cash flows by widening the gap between future cash flows in the favorable and unfavorable scenarios from $400 to $600. But we kept the expected value of the future cash flows unchanged at $300 so that their present value remained constant. However, if greater uncertainty lowers the expected level of cash flows or raises the cost of capital, the value of the underlying asset declines so that the impact on the value of the option could be negative.

MANAGING FLEXIBILITY

Contingent valuation is an important tool for managers trying to make the right decisions to maximize shareholder value when faced with strategic or operating flexibility. In actual practice, however, flexibility is never as well defined and straightforward as in the preceding examples. Much depends on management's ability to recognize, structure, and manage opportunities to create value from operating and strategic flexibility. A detailed discussion is beyond the scope of this book,[7] but we provide some basic guidelines here.

---

[7] For a more in-depth discussion, see, for example, Copeland and Antikarov, *Real Options*; or Trigeorgis, *Real Options*.

To *recognize* opportunities for creating value from flexibility when assessing investment projects or strategies, managers should try to be as explicit as possible about the following details:

- *Events.* What are the key sources of uncertainty? Which events will bring new information and when? A source of uncertainty is important only if relevant new information about it is likely to trigger a decision change. For example, investing in a pilot project for a product launch makes sense only if there is a chance that the pilot outcome would actually change the launch decision. Similarly, options to switch inputs for manufacturing processes are valuable only if the input prices can be expected to diverge significantly.

- *Decisions.* What decisions can management make in response to events? It is important that managers have some discretion to react to a relevant event. For example, intense competition among manufacturers of domestic appliances makes it unattractive for managers to defer a decision to include innovative internet connection features until there is more information about potential consumer demand for such features.

- *Payoffs.* What payoffs are linked to these decisions? Bear in mind that there should be a positive NPV to be captured in some realistic future state of the world. This NPV should be derived from sustainable competitive advantages. For example, some investors attribute high value to certain digital platforms because they believe these represent "options for future growth," a belief that is often based on multiples of enterprise value over unique website visitors per month. But website visits alone do not create value: the value of e-commerce start-ups depends upon their future cash flows. Start-ups can represent valuable options only if they build sustainable, competitive business models in some plausible future scenarios. Valuing start-ups as options requires articulating what the scenarios are, as well as predicting their likelihood of success and associated businesses cash flows.

With regard to *structuring* flexibility, some projects or strategies have predefined, built-in flexibility. Take, for example, research and development (R&D) investments in pharmaceutical products where the outcomes of clinical or patient trials provide natural moments to decide whether to stop or proceed with investments. But in many other cases, flexibility can be incorporated into a project to create maximum value. One example would be redesigning infrastructure investments in ports or airfields in stages such that future expansion takes place only if and when needed. Another would be reshaping a growth strategy in such a way that it explicitly includes options to redirect resources as more information becomes available.

In the end, flexibility has value only if managers actually *manage* it—that is, use new information to make appropriate changes to their decisions. Therefore, companies should ensure that their managers face proper incentives to capture potential value from flexibility. For example, the option to pull out of a staged-investment project when intermediate results are disappointing has no value if managers do not act on the information. As is sometimes the case, managers will point to nothing more than large sunk costs as the rationale for their inaction. But they forget that value is determined only by future cash flows, so sunk costs are always irrelevant. In the case where a company bases its strategy on creating growth options through a string of acquisitions, those options generate maximum value only if the company delays further acquisitions until new, positive information about their potential arrives. The company leaves the option value on the table if it proceeds with additional acquisitions in the dark.

To help managers recognize, structure, and manage opportunities for capturing value from flexibility, we segment options into the categories described in Exhibit 40.5 and provide some examples.

EXHIBIT 40.5 **Classification of Real Options**

Option type	Financial equivalent	Definitions	Example(s)
Option to defer investment	Call option	The option to defer an investment until the present value of an asset rises above the development costs	The ability of a leaseholder of an undeveloped oil reserve to defer development and investment until oil prices have elevated the value of the reserves above their development costs
Abandonment option	Put option	The option to abandon a project if its present value falls below its liquidation value	Long-term rental leases of airplanes that give the lessee the flexibility to prematurely dissolve the contract and return the plane to the lessor at a prespecified termination fee
Follow-on (compound) option	Series of options on options	The option to invest in stages, contingent on performance	A factory, R&D program, new-product launch, or oil field built so that management can continue the project at each stage by investing additional funds (an exercise price) or abandon it for whatever they can fetch
Option to expand or contract	Call or put option	The option to resize an investment depending on performance	A production facility built so that it can be easily expanded or contracted if a product is more or less successful than anticipated
Option to extend or shorten	Call or put option	The option to shorten or extend the life of an asset or contract	Real estate leases with clauses that allow lessors to extend or shorten the term of the lease
Option to increase scope	Call option	The ability to increase or decrease the number of activities in the future	A hotel designed so that the owner can easily diversify beyond lodging services, such as by adding conference facilities
Switching options	Portfolio of call and put options	The ability to switch the operation of a project on and off—or to switch operations between 2 distinct locations	A flexible manufacturing system that can produce 2 or more different products, peak-load power generation, or the ability to exit and reenter an industry

METHODS FOR VALUING FLEXIBILITY

As mentioned earlier in this chapter, the two methods for contingent valuation are decision tree analysis (DTA) and real-option valuation (ROV) using formal option-pricing models. We will illustrate each method with a simple example: the opportunity to invest $105 at the end of one year in a mining project that has an equal chance of returning either $150 or $50 in cash flow, depending on the mineral price. The risk-free rate, r_f, is 5 percent, and the weighted average cost of capital (WACC) for the project is 10 percent. The present value (PV) of the cash flows today is

$$PV = \frac{0.5(\$150) + 0.5(\$50)}{1.10} = \$90.9$$

The standard NPV of the mining project equals the discounted expected cash flow of $90.90 minus the present value of the investment outlay of $105 next year. Since the level of investment is certain, it should be discounted at the risk-free rate of 5 percent:

$$\text{Standard NPV} = \$90.9 - \frac{\$105}{1.05} = \$90.9 - \$100 = -\$9.1$$

If an investment decision were required immediately, the project would be declined. The answer changes if management has flexibility to defer the investment decision for one year, allowing it to make the decision after observing next year's mineral price and the associated cash flow outcome (see Exhibit 40.6). The net cash flows in the favorable state are $150 – $105 = $45. In the unfavorable state, management would decline to invest, accepting net cash flows of $0.

EXHIBIT 40.6 **Contingent Payoffs for Investment Project, Twin Security, and Risk-Free Bond**

		Project without flexibility	Project with flexibility	Twin security	Risk-free bond
$t=0$	$t=1$				
Successful project 50%	Cash flow	150	150		
$p=$	Investment	(105)	(105)		
	Net cash flow	**45**	**45**	**50**	**1.05**
Unsuccessful project 50%	Cash flow	50	50		
$1-p=$	Investment	(105)	(105)		
NPV = ?	**Net cash flow**	**(55)**	**—**	**16.7**	**1.05**

Risk-free rate = 5%
WACC = 10%

Note: $t =$ time, in years; $p =$ probability.

Real-Option Valuation

Option pricing models constitute the most theoretically correct approach to valuing flexibility, but as you'll see, decision tree analysis has some practical advantages. Option-pricing models use a *replicating portfolio* to value the project. The basic idea of a replicating portfolio is straightforward: if you can construct a portfolio of priced securities that has the same payouts as an option, the portfolio and option should have the same price. If the securities and the option are traded in an open market, this identity is required; otherwise arbitrage profits are possible. The interesting implication is that the ROV approach lets you correctly value complex, contingent cash flow patterns.

Returning to our $105 investment project, assume there exists a perfectly correlated security (or commodity, in this example) that trades in the market for $30.30 per share (or unit).[8] Its payouts ($50 and $16.70) equal one-third of the payouts of the project, and its expected return equals the underlying project's cost of capital.

This twin security can be used to value the project, including the option to defer, by forming a replicating portfolio.[9] Consider a portfolio consisting of N shares of the twin security and B risk-free bonds with a face value of $1. In the favorable state, the twin security pays $50 for each of the N shares, and each bond pays its face value plus interest, or $(1 + r_f)$. Together, these payouts must equal $45. Applying a similar construction to the unfavorable state, we can write two equations with two unknowns:

$$\$50.0N + \$1.05B = \$45$$
$$\$16.7N + \$1.05B = 0$$

The solution is $N = 1.35$ and $B = -21.43$. Thus, to build a replicating portfolio, buy 1.35 shares and short 21.43 bonds (shorting a bond is common language for selling a bond, or borrowing money).

This position produces the same cash flow as the investment project under both states. Therefore, the value of the project, including the ability to defer, should equal the value of the replicating portfolio:

$$\text{Contingent NPV} = N(\text{Price of Twin Security}) - B(\$1)$$
$$= 1.35(\$30.3) - 21.43(\$1)$$
$$= \$19.5$$

---

[8] You could also use this twin security to value the investment project without flexibility by means of a replicating portfolio. Because the twin security's cash flows are always exactly one-third of the project cash flows, the project without flexibility should be worth three times as much as the twin security, or $90.90 (= 3 × $30.30). The twin security is a basic concept that is implicitly used in standard DCF as well; you derive the beta of a project by identifying a highly correlated traded security and use that security's beta as input for the cost of capital in the DCF valuation.

[9] If the project itself were traded, you would not need a twin security but would construct a replicating portfolio with the traded value of the project itself, as in the case of financial options on traded stocks.

The value of the deferral option is the difference between the total contingent NPV of the project and its standard NPV without flexibility: $19.50 − (−$9.10) = $28.60 (remember, the standard NPV was negative).

Contingent NPV can also be determined with an alternative ROV approach called *risk-neutral valuation*. The name is somewhat misleading because a risk-neutral valuation does adjust for risk, but as part of the scenario probabilities rather than the discount rate. To value an option, weight the future cash flows by risk-adjusted (or so-called risk-neutral) probabilities instead of the actual scenario probabilities. Then discount the probability-weighted average cash flow by the risk-free rate to determine current value. The risk-neutral probability of the favorable state, p^*, for the future value (FV) of the twin security is defined as follows[10]:

$$p^* = \frac{1 + r_f - d}{u - d} = 0.45$$

where

$$u = \frac{FV(\text{Favorable State})}{PV} = \frac{\$50.0}{\$30.3} = 1.65$$

$$d = \frac{FV(\text{Unfavorable State})}{PV} = \frac{\$16.7}{\$30.3} = 0.55$$

Solve by substituting:

$$p^* = 0.45$$
$$1 - p^* = 0.55$$

These probabilities implicitly capture the risk premium for investments perfectly correlated with the twin security. We discount the future cash flows weighted by the risk-neutral probabilities at the risk-free rate of 5 percent, arriving at exactly the same value determined using the replicating portfolio:

$$\text{Contingent NPV} = \frac{0.45(\$45) + 0.55(0)}{1.05} = \$19.5$$

It is no coincidence that the replicating portfolio and risk-neutral valuation lead to the same result. They are mathematically equivalent, and both rely on the price of the twin security to derive the value of an investment project with an option to defer.

Valuation Based on Decision Tree Analysis

A second method for valuing a project with flexibility is to use DTA. This leads to the right answer in principle, but only if we apply the correct cost of capital for a project's contingent cash flows.

---

[10] See, for example, Trigeorgis, *Real Options*, 75–76.

One DTA approach is to discount the project's contingent payoffs net of the investment requirements. Unfortunately, we can only derive the correct cost of capital for these cash flows from the ROV results. Given the project's contingent NPV of $19.50 with equal chances of paying off $45 or $0, the implied discount rate from the ROV analysis is 15.5 percent.[11] This is significantly above the underlying asset's 10 percent cost of capital, because the contingent cash flows are riskier. The contingent NPV has an equal chance of increasing by 131 percent or decreasing by 100 percent. The value of the underlying asset ($90.90) has a 50–50 chance of going up only 65 percent (to $150) or down 45 percent (to $50). If the underlying asset's cost of capital of 10 percent were used, the DTA results would therefore be too high relative to the correct ROV result:

$$\text{Contingent NPV} = \frac{0.5(\$45) + 0.5(0)}{1.10} = \$20.5$$

A better DTA approach separately discounts the two components of the contingent cash flows. The contingent payoffs from the underlying asset are discounted at the cost of capital of the underlying asset. The investment requirements are discounted at the risk-free rate:

$$\text{Contingent NPV} = 0.5\left(\frac{\$150}{1.10} - \frac{\$105}{1.05}\right) + 0.5(0) = \$18.2$$

The next section discusses how this second DTA approach leads to the exact ROV outcome if the underlying risk is either diversifiable or nondiversifiable but too small to influence the future investment decision (that is, if the project value would exceed the investment requirements even in the unfavorable state).

Comparing ROV and DTA Approaches

As summarized in Exhibit 40.7, the standard NPV approach undervalues our mining project at –$9.10. The ROV approach generates a correct value (NPV = $19.50) because it captures the value of flexibility by using a replicating portfolio or risk-neutral valuation. The DTA approach at $18.20 is quite close in this example, capturing almost the entire gap between the standard NPV valuation and the more granular ROV result. But the DTA results might be further off or closer to the ROV mark, depending on the project's payoffs and risks.

This example does not mean ROV is always the best approach to valuing managerial flexibility. The stylized example did not take into account two important aspects of real-life investment decisions: the type of prevailing risk

---

[11] In this simplified example, there is one value for the cost of capital. In general, the cost of capital for the contingent cash flows is not constant. It changes with the risk of the option across time and states of the world.

EXHIBIT 40.7 **Valuation Result: Standard vs. Contingent NPV**

$

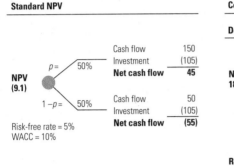

Standard NPV

		Cash flow	150
		Investment	(105)
$p =$ 50%		**Net cash flow**	**45**
NPV (9.1)			
$1 - p =$ 50%		Cash flow	50
		Investment	(105)
Risk-free rate = 5%		**Net cash flow**	**(55)**
WACC = 10%			

Contingent NPV

Decision tree analysis[1]

		Cash flow	150
		Investment	(105)
$p =$ 50%		**Net cash flow**	**45**
NPV 18.2			
$1 - p =$ 50%		Cash flow	50
		Investment	(105)
		Net cash flow	—

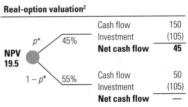

Real-option valuation[2]

		Cash flow	150
		Investment	(105)
p^* 45%		**Net cash flow**	**45**
NPV 19.5			
$1 - p^*$ 55%		Cash flow	50
		Investment	(105)
		Net cash flow	—

Note: t = time, in years; p = probability; p^* = binomial (risk-neutral) probability.

[1] Discounting cash flows at the project's cost of capital of 10% and investments at the risk-free rate of 5%.

[2] Using risk-neutral valuation.

EXHIBIT 40.8 **Application Opportunities for Real-Option Valuation vs. Decision Tree Analysis**

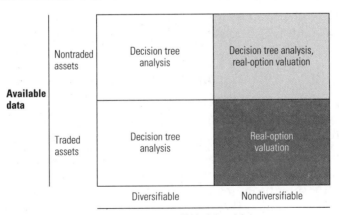

		Diversifiable	Nondiversifiable
Available data	Nontraded assets	Decision tree analysis	Decision tree analysis, real-option valuation
	Traded assets	Decision tree analysis	Real-option valuation

Underlying risk

and the availability of data on the value and variance of cash flows from the underlying asset. Exhibit 40.8 identifies when each method is most suitable. As we explain next, the more straightforward DTA is often the better approach because in practice (most of) the underlying risk is diversifiable or because only rough estimates are available for required inputs such as the underlying asset value and variance. In addition, DTA is easier to use and understand. ROV works best only when the future cash flows are closely linked to traded commodities, securities, or currencies. Not surprisingly, real-option valuations are most often used for commodity-linked investments, such as in the mining and oil industries.

Prevailing Risk: Diversifiable and Nondiversifiable   Investment projects can be exposed to a wide range of risks, such as product price and demand risk, interest and currency risks, technological risk, and political risk. The question is which particular risk (or group of risks) is *prevailing*—in other words, which risk could affect a project's cash flow to such an extent that it would change management's future decisions. The following examples of prevailing risks describe whether the risks are diversifiable and how this affects the choice of a valuation tool:

- If commodity prices (as in mining, the oil industry, or power generation) or currency and interest rates are keys to future investment decisions, the prevailing risk *is not diversifiable*, and only ROV leads to the theoretically correct valuation. This was illustrated in the previous example in this chapter, where the difference in mining payoffs stemmed from changes in the mineral price. The DTA approach could not provide a correct value, although it was quite close in that particular case.

- If technological risks (including customer preferences, technological innovations, drug trial outcomes, or geological survey results) are critical to future investment decisions, the prevailing risk *is diversifiable*, and both ROV and DTA are effective tools for valuing flexibility. The pharmaceutical drug investment case presented near the beginning of the chapter is a case in which DTA and ROV provide identical results (see Equation 40.1).[12]

Let's illustrate how you can apply ROV and DTA, depending on which group of risks dominates in a more complex version of the mining example from the previous section. In addition to price risk, there is now also uncertainty about the size of the reserves found (see Exhibit 40.9, Example 1). The mine is either very large, with reserves at 2.50 times the expected level, or

---

[12] To value the same drug development investment with an ROV approach, we build a replicating portfolio. Assume a twin security exists whose payoffs are perfectly correlated with the outcome of the drug trial, generating $52.50 when the outcome is favorable and $10.50 when it is unfavorable. Because its cash flows are driven by technological risk only, the security's market beta is zero, and its present value must be $30. A replicating portfolio consists of a long position of 107.1 of these securities and a short position of $1,071.40 in risk-free bonds. The ROV is therefore 107.1($30) – $1,071.4(1) = $2,143. See also Dixit and Pindyck, *Investment under Uncertainty*, 30–32, for a similar proof.

EXHIBIT 40.9 **Valuation Result for Mixed Price and Quantity Risk**

● Price risk event ■ Quantity risk event

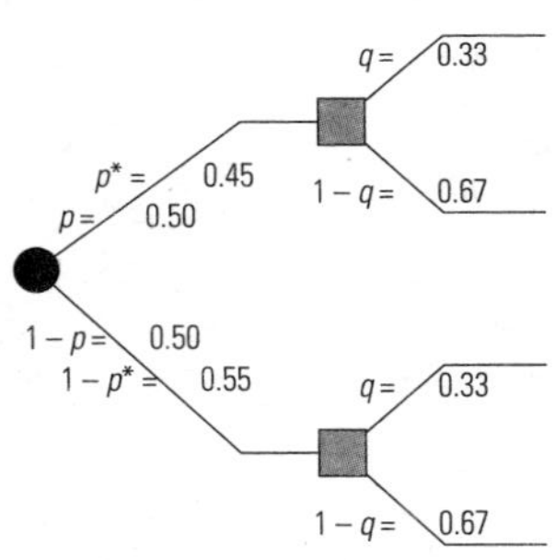

Example 1: High technology risk

Price	Size	Cash flow	Investment	Net cash flow	ROV[1]	DTA[2]
150	2.50	375	(105)	270	38.6	39.8
150	0.26	39	(105)	—	—	—
50	2.50	125	(105)	20	3.4	2.3
50	0.26	13	(105)	—	—	—
				Value	42.0	42.0

Example 2: Low technology risk

Price	Size	Cash flow	Investment	Net cash flow	ROV[1]	DTA[2]
150	1.50	225	(105)	120	17.1	17.3
150	0.75	113	(105)	8	2.3	0.9
50	1.50	75	(105)	—	—	—
50	0.75	38	(105)	—	—	—
				Value	19.5	18.2

Note: p = probability of mineral price being high; p^* = binomial (risk-neutral) probability; q = probability of mine size being large.
[1] Real-option valuation.
[2] Decision tree analysis.

very small, at 0.26 times the expected level. The probability of very large mining reserves is 33 percent, versus a probability of 67 percent for very small
reserves. This implies there are not just two but four possible outcomes to the
initial investment, with cash flows ranging from $375 in the large-mine and
high-mineral-price scenario ($150 × 2.50) to $13 in the small-mine and low-
price scenario ($50 × 0.26). As the conditional payoffs in the exhibit reflect,
the rational decision is to start production only if the mine turns out to be
large, regardless of the commodity price. For a small mine, even the high-price
scenario does not justify production, as the investment requirements ($105)
exceed the cash flow ($39 = $150 × 0.26).

To use the ROV approach to derive the valuation results, multiply the
conditional payoffs by the risk-neutral (pseudo-)probabilities for the price
scenarios and the normal probabilities for the quantity scenarios, and then
discount at the risk-free rate.[13] For example, for the large-mine, high-price
scenario:

$$\frac{0.45 \times 0.33 \times \$270}{1 + 5\%} = \$38.6$$

Summing these values over all possible scenarios leads to an ROV of $42.0.[14]

Taking a DTA approach instead, we would multiply the conditional payoffs
by the normal probabilities for price and quantity scenarios and then separately discount the cash inflows at the mine's cost of capital and the investment cash flow at the risk-free rate. For the large-mine, high-price scenario,
for example:

$$0.50 \times 0.33 \times \left(\frac{\$375}{1 + 10\%} - \frac{\$105}{1 + 5\%} \right) = \$39.8$$

Similarly, summing the results over all scenarios, we obtain a DTA value of
$42.0, which is exactly equal to the ROV result. The reason is that the decision
is driven entirely by the diversifiable, technological risk related to the size of
mine. The nondiversifiable price risk leads to different cash flows but does not
matter for the investment decision.[15]

Now consider Example 2 in Exhibit 40.9 with the same numerical illustration as before, but with smaller quantity risk: the mine now has reserves at

[13] We can use the risk-neutral probabilities from the original example because the mineral price risk
has not changed. For the quantity risk, no risk adjustment to the probabilities is needed because it is
diversifiable. We used the risk-neutral probability approach for the ROV valuation because it is more
straightforward to apply here; of course, the replicating-portfolio approach leads to an identical value.
[14] Note that this value is higher than in the original example, because we now develop the mine only if
the reserves are large; we have introduced additional flexibility.
[15] If the probability distribution of the commodity price were continuous rather than discrete as in this
example, there would always be some price outcome overturning the production decision. But the
point remains that if the probability of reaching such price levels is small, the difference between the
ROV and DTA outcome would be small, too.

either 1.50 times or 0.75 times the expected level. As shown in the exhibit, the variation in price becomes the prevailing risk that drives the decision to start production in the case of lower variation in potential mine size outcomes. For example, if the price turns out to be high, production is started whether the mine size ends up at the higher or lower end of its new range. As a result, the DTA approach now provides only an approximation ($18.2) of the correct ROV value ($19.5).[16]

As illustrated in these two examples, the DTA and ROV approaches both provide the theoretically correct answer when the contingent decisions are (predominantly) driven by diversifiable underlying risk. In our experience, this is the more common case for prevailing risk. Examples are geological risks, such as the size of an undeveloped mine or oil field, and even some forms of marketing risk, such as consumer acceptance of a new product. As in the numerical illustration, these risks often have more impact on value than nondiversifiable risks. For example, the driver of the decision to invest in drug development is whether the drug passes the trials, not whether the drug—once successfully developed—is worth more or less, depending on general economic conditions.

Data Availability: Traded vs. Untraded Assets   The results of any contingent valuation critically depend on well-grounded estimates for the value and the variance of cash flows from the underlying asset.

If the estimate for the *underlying asset value* is inaccurate, the flexibility value also will be inaccurate. Returning to our first example, if we estimate incorrectly the future cash flows generated by a highly effective drug, the value of the option to defer will be inaccurate. In practice, you would have to estimate the value with a full-fledged DCF model projecting sales growth, operating margins, capital turnovers, and so on. All ROV and DTA approaches build on this valuation of the underlying asset.

A similar argument holds for estimates of the variance of the underlying asset's cash flows (called *volatility* in the option-pricing literature). Volatility can have a great impact on value, because real options typically have long lifetimes and are often at-the-money or close to it,[17] meaning the decision of whether to undertake the project is a close call.[18] Still, for many managers and practitioners, volatility remains an abstract concept: How do you reasonably

---

[16] For the ROV result, the present value of the large-mine and high-price scenario would now be $(0.45 \times 0.33 \times \$120)/(1 + 5\%) = \$17.1$. Adding this to the present value for the small-mine and high-price scenario, or $(0.45 \times 0.67 \times \$7.5)/(1 + 5\%) = \$2.3$, leads to total ROV of $19.5 when rounded.

[17] It follows from option-pricing theory that the sensitivity of option value to changes in variance (referred to as vega) increases as the option's lifetime increases and as the option is closer to the money. An option is at-the-money if its exercise price equals the value of the underlying asset.

[18] If the investment decision were a clear go or no-go, there would be little value in flexibility in the first place, and no need to consider the option value.

estimate the range of cash flow outcomes from the sale of a product that has yet to be released?[19]

Sometimes the underlying asset value and variance can be derived from traded assets. Examples include options to shut down gas-fueled power generation, abandon a copper mine, or defer production of an oil field. In such cases, because you can estimate the key inputs with reasonable accuracy, ROV could be more accurate than DTA. When estimates for the underlying asset valuation and variance (volatility) cannot be derived from traded assets and are largely judgmental, a DTA approach is more appropriate. It is more straightforward and transparent to decision makers than the ROV approach. Transparency is especially important when critical valuation assumptions require the decision maker's judgment. DTA captures the essence of flexibility value, and the theoretical advantage of ROV is less important if required inputs are unavailable.

FOUR STEPS TO VALUING FLEXIBILITY

To value flexibility, use the four-step process illustrated in Exhibit 40.10. In step 1, conduct a valuation of the investment project without flexibility, using a traditional discounted-cash-flow model. In step 2, expand the DCF model into an event tree, mapping how the value of the project evolves over time, using (unadjusted) probabilities and the weighted average cost of capital. At this stage, the model does not include flexibility, so the present value of the project, based on discounting the cash flows in the event tree, should still equal the standard DCF value from the first step.

EXHIBIT 40.10 **Four-Step Process for Valuing Flexibility**

	Estimate NPV without flexibility	Model uncertainty in event tree	Model flexibility in decision tree	Estimate contingent NPV
Objectives	Compute base case present value without flexibility	Understand how present value develops with respect to changing uncertainty	Analyze event tree to identify and incorporate managerial flexibility to respond to new information	Value total project using decision tree analysis or real-option valuation
Comments	Standard NPV approach is used for valuation of underlying asset	No flexibility modeled; valuation following event tree should equal standard NPV	Flexibility is incorporated into event tree, transforming it into decision tree	Under high uncertainty and managerial flexibility, contingent NPV will be significantly higher than standard NPV

[19] The range needs to include the associated probabilities to provide a variance estimate.

In step 3, turn the event tree into a decision tree by identifying the types of managerial flexibility that are available. Build the flexibility into the nodes of the tree. Multiple sources of flexibility are possible at a single decision node, such as the option to abandon or expand, but it is important to have clear priorities among them. Be careful in establishing the sequence of decisions regarding flexibility, especially when the decision tree has compound options.

Finally, step 4 entails recognizing how the exercise of flexibility alters the project's risk characteristics. If the prevailing risk affecting the contingent cash flows is fully diversifiable, you need no special modeling; you can use DTA, discounting investment cash flows at the risk-free rate and the underlying project's cash flows at the weighted average cost of capital, as in the pharmaceutical example in the upcoming section on ROV and DTA. If the prevailing risk is nondiversifiable and priced in the market, the appropriate risk-adjusted discount rate for the project's cash flows is no longer the weighted average cost of capital used in step 1. In that case, apply an ROV approach for the project with flexibility, using risk-neutral valuation or a replicating portfolio.

Real-Option Valuation: A Numerical Example

Using the four-step process, we illustrate the ROV approach with a straightforward binomial lattice for valuing flexibility that is assumed to be driven by nondiversifiable risk. The results are identical to alternative option-pricing models that use more complicated mathematics such as stochastic calculus or Monte Carlo simulation.

Step 1: Estimate Net Present Value without Flexibility   Assume that an investment in a project to build a factory generates cash flows whose present value (PV) equals $100, and its expected rate of return and cost of capital (k) equal 8 percent. The risk-free rate is 5 percent per year, and the cash outflow necessary to undertake the project, if we invest in it immediately, is $105. Thus, the standard NPV is –$5, equal to the expected present value of $100 less the investment of $105, and we would not undertake the project if we had to commit today.

Step 2: Model Uncertainty Using Event Tree   The lattice that models the potential values of the underlying risky asset is called an event tree. It contains no decision nodes and simply models the evolution of the underlying asset. Exhibit 40.11 illustrates potential values the factory might take for each of the next five years, assuming a volatility of 15 percent per year.[20] Defining T as the number of years per upward movement and σ as the annualized volatility

---

[20] The standard deviation of the rate of change of the factory value.

EXHIBIT 40.11 **Event Tree: Factory Without Flexibility**

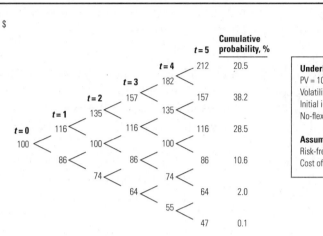

$

					$t=5$	Cumulative probability, %

Underlying asset
PV = 100
Volatility = 15%
Initial investment = 105
No-flexibility NPV = 100 – 105 = (5)

Assumptions
Risk-free rate = 5%
Cost of capital (k) = 8%

Note: t = time, in years.

of the underlying factory value, determine the up and down movements by using the following formulas[21]:

$$\text{Up Movement} = u = e^{\sigma\sqrt{T}}$$
$$\text{Down Movement} = d = \frac{1}{u}$$

Substitute numerical values into these formulas:

$$u = e^{0.15\sqrt{1}} = 1.1618$$
$$d = \frac{1}{1.1618} = 0.8607$$

Based on the 8 percent cost of capital used in the DCF valuation of the factory, the probability of an up movement is 72.82 percent, and the probability of a down movement is 27.18 percent.[22] As can be verified, the present value of any branch in the event tree equals the expected payout discounted at the 8 percent cost of capital. For example, take the uppermost branch in the fifth time period. Its present value is:

$$PV_{t=4} = \frac{E(PV_{t=5})}{(1+k)} = \frac{0.7282(\$211.7) + 0.2718(\$156.8)}{1.08} = \$182.2$$

[21] J. Cox, M. Rubinstein, and S. Ross, "Option Pricing: A Simplified Approach," *Journal of Financial Economics* 7, no. 3 (1979): 229–263. As T becomes smaller, the binomial lattice results converge to the true value of the option. In this example, we have chosen $T = 1$ for ease of illustration.
[22] See the previous note for the derivation of the formula for estimating the upward probability:

$$\frac{(1+k)^T - d}{u - d} = \frac{(1+8\%) - 0.8607}{1.1618 - 0.8607} = 0.7282$$

A similar calculation will produce any of the values in the event tree, resulting in a PV of the project of $100 at $t = 0$. That present value equals the result in step 1, so we know the tree is correct.

Step 3: Model Flexibility Using a Decision Tree

When you add decision points to an event tree, it becomes a decision tree. Suppose the factory can be expanded for an additional $15. The expansion increases the factory's value at that node by 20 percent. The option can be exercised at any time during the next five years—but only once.

Exhibit 40.12 shows the resulting decision tree. To find the payouts at a given point on the tree, start with the final branches. Consider the uppermost branch in period 5. On the upward limb, the payout absent expansion would be $211.70, as Exhibit 40.11 shows. But with expansion, it is $1.20 \times \$211.70 - \$15 = \$240.00$. Since the value with expansion is higher, we would decide to expand. On the lower limb of that same node, the payout with expansion is $1.20 \times \$156.80 - \$15 = \$173.20$, versus $156.80 without expansion, so again we would expand. In this way, complete the payoff estimates for all final branches.

Step 4: Estimate Contingent Net Present Value

To determine the value of the project with the flexibility to expand, work backward through the decision tree, using the replicating-portfolio method at each node. For the node highlighted in Exhibit 40.12, you can replicate the payoffs from the option to

EXHIBIT 40.12 **Decision Tree: Option to Expand Factory**

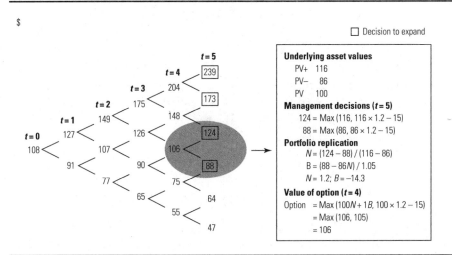

Note: t = time, in years; PV = present value; N = number of replicating securities; B = number of risk-free bonds; incremental investment: $15; incremental payoff: 20%.

expand in $t = 5$, using a portfolio of N units of the underlying project and B units of $1 risk-free bonds[23]:

$$116.2N + \$1.05B = \$124.4$$
$$86.1N + \$1.05B = \$88.3$$

Solving the equations, we find that $N = 1.2$, and $B = -14.3$. Therefore, a replicating portfolio consists of 1.2 units of the project without flexibility (at that node, valued at $100 in the event tree of Exhibit 40.11) plus a short position of 14.3 bonds worth $1. As shown in the calculations in Exhibit 40.12, the value of the option in the node at $t = 4$ is then:

$$PV = \$100N + \$1B = \$105.7$$

Work backward from right to left, node by node, to obtain a present value of $108.40 for a project that has an option to expand. As a result, the net present value of the project increases from –$5.00 to $3.40, so the option itself is worth $8.40. Note that the analysis also provides the value-maximizing decision strategy: management should expand the factory only after five years and only if the factory is worth $75 or more as indicated by the boxed nodes in Exhibit 40.12.[24]

If, instead, management had the option to abandon the factory at any node for a fixed liquidation value of $100, the valuation would be as shown in Exhibit 40.13. Determine the contingent payoffs for final branches. Then work again from right to left through the decision tree. For the highlighted node at $t = 4$, the value of the underlying factory is $116.20 in the upward branch and $86.10 in the downward branch (see in the event tree of Exhibit 40.11). Given the ability to do so, the company would abandon the project for $100 in the downward branch, so the payoffs in the decision tree are $116.20 in the upward branch and $100 in the downward branch. Using risk-neutral valuation this time, the abandonment option can be valued in the node at $t = 4$ at $104.90, as shown in Exhibit 40.13 (the same result a replicating portfolio would have generated). Working backward through time, the value for a factory with the ability to abandon is $106.40, so the abandonment option is worth $6.40. Now the value-maximizing decision strategy is to abandon the factory immediately in any year in which its value drops below $100.

---

[23] If the project itself is not traded but a traded twin security exists, we can construct the portfolio in a similar way with units of the twin security and risk-free bonds.

[24] This is analogous to a call option on a stock that does not pay dividends: it is never exercised prematurely. For example, in the node highlighted in Exhibit 40.12, the value in year 4 of deferring the expansion of the factory to year 5 is $105.70, as calculated in the preceding equation. The value of expanding in year 4 is $100 \times 1.20 - \$15 = \$105$. It is therefore optimal to defer expansion, as is the case for all nodes before year 5.

EXHIBIT 40.13 **Decision Tree: Option to Abandon Factory**

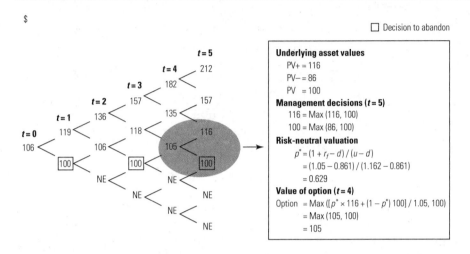

Note: t = time, in years; NE = nonexistent state; PV = present value; p^* = binomial (risk-neutral) probability; rf = risk-free rate; d = downward movement of value; u = upward movement of value; liquidation value: $100.

EXHIBIT 40.14 **Decision Tree: Option to Expand or Abandon Factory**

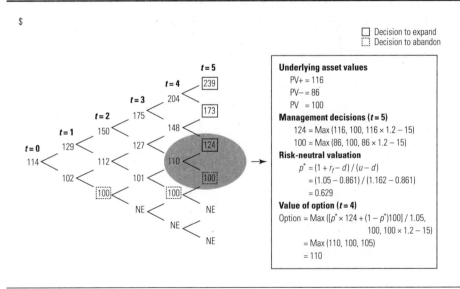

Note: t = time, in years; NE = nonexistent state; PV = present value; p^* = binomial (risk-neutral) probability; rf = risk-free rate; d = downward movement of value; u = upward movement of value; liquidation value: $100; incremental investment: $15; incremental payoff: 20%.

Multiple sources of flexibility can be combined within a single decision tree, as illustrated in Exhibit 40.14, using risk-neutral valuation. The value of the project, including the options to abandon and expand, would be $113.50 rather than $100, its stand-alone value without flexibility. With these options, the correct decision would be to accept the project. Note that the value of the combined expansion-abandonment flexibility, $13.50, is less than the sum of the individual flexibility values ($8.40 + $6.40 = $14.80) but greater than either of them individually. The values of both options are not additive, because they interact in complex ways (for example, you cannot expand the factory once you have abandoned it). As indicated in Exhibit 40.14, the best decision strategy is to abandon the factory whenever its value[25] drops below $100 and to expand only in year 5 if its value exceeds $75.

REAL-OPTION VALUATION AND DECISION TREE ANALYSIS: A NUMERICAL EXAMPLE

Our next example applies both the DTA and the ROV approaches in the valuation of a research and development project. Assume a company needs to decide whether to develop a new pharmaceutical drug. In our simplified example,[26] the first step in development is a research phase of three years, in which the most promising chemical compounds are selected. The probability of success in the research phase is estimated at 15 percent. This is followed by a three-year testing phase, during which the compounds are tested in laboratory and clinical settings. The chance of successfully completing the testing phase is 40 percent. If there are successful results, the drug can be released in the market. Upon failure in any phase, the company terminates development, and the product dies worthless.

DTA Approach: Technological Risk

The DTA approach presented next follows the four steps for the valuation of flexibility as described in the previous section. In the DTA valuation of the research and development project, we consider only the prevailing technological risk relating to the research and testing outcomes. The commercial risk concerning the future profitability of the drug and the technological risk are taken into account jointly in the ROV approach discussed in the next section.

Step 1: Estimate Present Value without Flexibility   If the development process succeeds, the drug will deliver substantial value in six years' time. Margins in the pharmaceutical industry are high because patents protect drugs against competition. A successful drug is expected to generate annual

---

[25] Note that this is the value of the factory including the option to expand. Therefore, abandonment occurs only in more unfavorable states of the world than those triggering abandonment in Exhibit 40.13.

[26] Pharmaceutical R&D is much more complex and consists of more phases than shown in this example. For a more extensive example of valuing flexibility in pharmaceutical research and development, see Kellogg and Charnes, "Real-Options Valuation for a Biotechnology Company."

sales of $2,925 million and 45 percent earnings before interest, taxes, deprecia-tion, and amortization (EBITDA) margin on sales until its patent expires, ten years after its market launch. (Because prices decline drastically after a patent expires, we do not count cash flows beyond that time.) Assuming a 30 percent tax rate and a 7 percent cost of capital, a marketable drug's present value at the launch date would therefore be $6,475 million. Unfortunately, the odds of suc-cessful development are small. The cumulative probability of success over the research and testing phase is only 6 percent (0.15 for research times 0.40 for testing). In addition, the investments needed to develop, test, and market a drug are high: $100 million in the research phase, $250 million in the testing phase, and $150 million in marketing.

If we had to commit to all three investments today, we should not proceed, because the NPV would be negative:

$$\text{Standard NPV}_0 = \text{PV}_0(\text{Expected Cash Flows}) - \text{PV}_0(\text{Investments})$$
$$= 0.06\left[\frac{\$6,475}{(1.07)^6}\right] - \$100 - \frac{\$250}{(1.05)^3} - \frac{\$150}{(1.05)^6}$$
$$= -\$169$$

However, if we take into account management's ability to abandon the project before completion, the value is significantly higher.

Step 2: Model Uncertainty Using an Event Tree   For this development proj-ect, you can model the prevailing technological risk using a straightforward event tree (see Exhibit 40.15). The expected value of a marketable drug after successful development is shown at its DCF value of $6,475 million as of $t = 6$.

EXHIBIT 40.15 **Event Tree: R&D Option with Technological Risk**

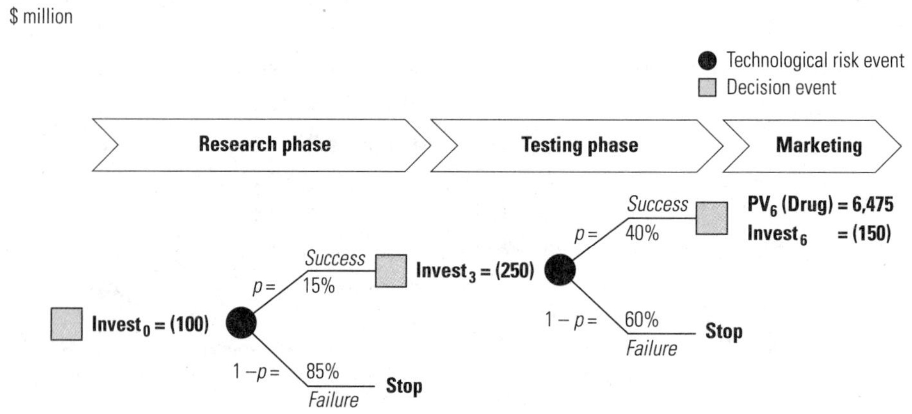

Note: PVt = present value of marketable drug as of year t; p = probability of technological success.

Step 3: Model Flexibility Using a Decision Tree   Next, include decision flexibility in the tree, working from right to left. At the end of the testing phase, we have the option to invest $150 million in marketing to launch the product. We should invest only if testing has produced a marketable product. At the end of the research phase, we have the option to proceed with the testing phase. We proceed to testing only if the payoffs justify the incremental investment of $250 million.

Step 4: Estimate Value of Flexibility   Because the technological risk is fully diversifiable, apply a straightforward DTA approach for the valuation of flexibility. Again, work from right to left in the tree (see Exhibit 40.16). After six years, at the end of the testing phase, we proceed with launching the product only if there is a marketable product. The value in millions at this point in time is therefore $NPV_6 = Max[(\$6,475 - \$150), 0] = \$6,325$. At the end of the research phase, we continue to the testing phase if the future payoffs outweigh the required investments. The value of the project at this point, after three years is:

$$NPV_3 \text{ (Option)} = Max[PV_3(\text{Testing}) - Inv_3(\text{Testing}), 0]$$

In this equation, PV_3(Testing) equals the probability-weighted future payoffs discounted by three years at the cost of capital of 7 percent:

$$PV_3(\text{Testing}) = 0.40\left[\frac{\$6,475 - \$150}{(1.07)^3}\right] + 0.60(0) = \$2,065$$

EXHIBIT 40.16 **Decision Tree: R&D Option with Technological Risk**

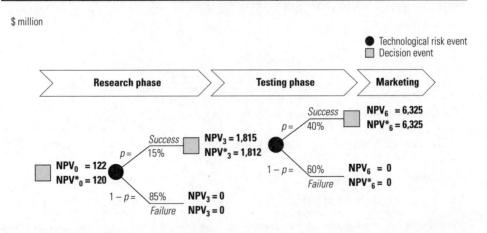

Note: NPVt = net present value as of year t; NPV* = contingent NPV; p = probability of technological success.

With Inv_3(Testing) equal to the $250 million investment requirement for the testing phase, the project value prior to the testing phase amounts to:

$$\text{NPV}_3(\text{Option}) = \text{Max}\,[\,(\$2{,}065 - \$250),\, 0] = \$1{,}815$$

Working further from right to left in the tree, we find the contingent NPV for the entire project prior to the research phase:

$$\text{NPV}_0\,(\text{Option}) = \text{Max}\,[\text{PV}_0(\text{Research}) - \text{Inv}_0(\text{Research}),\, 0]$$
$$= \text{Max}\left[0.15\left(\frac{\$1{,}815}{(1.07)^3}\right) + 0.85(0) - \$100{,}0\right]$$
$$= \$122$$

This value including flexibility is significantly higher than the standard NPV of –$169 million. Note that we discounted all contingent payoffs at the underlying asset's cost of capital, so the $122 million only approximates the true contingent value. But the result is close, as we show in the calculations immediately following, and this approach is straightforward to apply and easy to explain.

The true contingent value turns out to be $120 million and follows from a refined DTA approach that separately discounts the asset cash flows at the cost of capital of 7 percent and the investment cash flows at the risk-free rate of 5 percent.[27] The value of proceeding with testing now becomes[28]

$$\text{P}\,\text{V}_3^*(\text{Testing}) = 0.40\left(\frac{\$6{,}475}{(1.07)^3} - \frac{\$150}{(1.05)^3}\right) + 0.60(0) = \$2{,}114 - \$52 = \$2{,}062$$

The value of the option to proceed with the testing phase is then

$$\text{NPV}_3^*(\text{Option}) = \text{Max}\big[(\$2{,}062 - \$250),\, 0\big] = \$1{,}812$$

Working from right to left but now separately discounting asset and investment cash flows in each step, we obtain the contingent NPV* per $t = 0$:

$$\text{NPV}_0^*(\text{Option}) = \text{Max}\,[\text{PV}_0^*(\text{Research}) - \text{Inv}_0(\text{Research}),\, 0]$$
$$= \text{Max}\left[0.15\left(\frac{\$2{,}114}{(1.07)^3} - \frac{\$302}{(1.05)^3}\right) + 0.85(0) - \$100,\, 0\right]$$
$$= \$120$$

To illustrate, we obtain the same value of $120 million with yet another approach: the ROV method. In this approach, project the future value of the

[27] See the example in Exhibit 40.7. The assumption to discount investment outlays at the risk-free rate is also implicitly made in ROV approaches.
[28] In prior editions of this book, we adopted an alternative but equivalent decision tree where all values of asset and investment cash flows were discounted to $t = 0$ before deriving the contingent value by working from right to left in the tree. The contingent NPV results are identical.

underlying asset under "risk-neutral" return assumptions, and then discount all contingent payoffs at the risk-free rate. The risk-neutral future value of a successfully developed drug is its value as of today, compounded at the risk-free rate for six years:

$$PV_6^{**}(\text{Drug}) = \$4{,}314\,(1.05)^6 = \$5{,}781$$

This means that the risk-neutral value of proceeding with testing is

$$PV_3^{**}(\text{Testing}) = 0.40\left(\frac{\$5{,}781 - \$150}{(1.05)^3}\right) + 0.60(0) = \$1{,}946$$

The risk-neutral value of the option to proceed with testing as of $t = 3$ is

$$NPV_3^{**}(\text{Option}) = \text{Max}\,[\$1{,}946 - \$250,\,0] = \$1{,}696$$

Working from right to left while discounting all cash flows at the risk-free rate gives us the contingent NPV at $t = 0$, which is \$120 million:

$$NPV_0^{**}(\text{Option}) = \text{Max}\,[\,PV_0^{**}(\text{Research}) - \text{Inv}_0(\text{Research}),\,0]$$
$$= \text{Max}\left[0.15\left(\frac{\$1{,}696}{(1.05)^3}\right) + 0.85(0) - \$100,\,0\right]$$
$$= \$120$$

ROV Approach: Technological and Commercial Risk

Our analysis thus far has not included the other source of uncertainty in the development project: the commercial risk concerning the future cash flow potential of the successfully developed and marketed drug. ROV is necessary to handle both technological and commercial risk.

Step 1: Estimate Present Value without Flexibility   The first step, estimating present value without flexibility, is identical for the DTA and ROV approaches.

Step 2: Model Uncertainty Using an Event Tree   Both risks can be modeled in a combined event tree (see Exhibit 40.17). For simplicity, we have chosen a one-step binomial lattice to describe the evolution of the drug value over each three-year period.[29] Assuming an annual volatility of 15 percent, we can derive the upward and downward movements, u and d, as follows:

$$u = e^{\sigma\sqrt{T}} = e^{0.15\sqrt{3}} = 1.30$$
$$d = \frac{1}{u} = \frac{1}{1.30} = 0.77$$

---

[29] With more nodes, the tree quickly becomes too complex to show in an exhibit, because it does not converge in the technological risk. We carried out the analysis with ten nodes and found that doing so did not affect the results for this particular example.

EXHIBIT 40.17   **Event Tree: R&D Option with Technological and Commercial Risk**

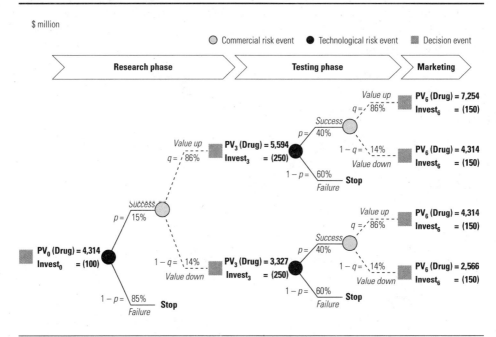

Note: $PV_t(\text{Drug})$ = present value of marketable drug as of year t; Invest$t$ = investment as of year t; p = probability of technological success; q = probability of drug value increase.

The probability of an upward movement is 86 percent, and the probability of a downward movement is 14 percent.[30] The value of a marketable drug at the start of the research phase is \$4,314 million. At the end of the research phase, there are three possible outcomes: success combined with an increase in the value of a marketable drug to \$5,594 million, success combined with a decrease in the value of a marketable drug to \$3,327 million, and failure leading to a drug value of \$0. Following the same logic, there are six possible outcomes after the testing phase.

Step 3: Model Flexibility Using a Decision Tree   The logic underlying the decision tree including commercial risk (see Exhibit 40.18) is the same as under the DTA approach. For example, the payoff at the end of the testing phase in the top branch equals Max[(\$7,254 − \$150), 0] = \$7,104. The primary difference is that the ROV version of the tree recognizes the ability to abandon development if the value of a marketable drug drops too much.

---

[30] The formula for estimating the upward probability is $\dfrac{(1+k)^T - d}{u - d} = \dfrac{1.07^3 - 0.77}{1.30 - 0.77} = 0.86$, where k is the expected return on the asset.

EXHIBIT 40.18   **Decision Tree: R&D Option with Technological and Commercial Risk**

$ million

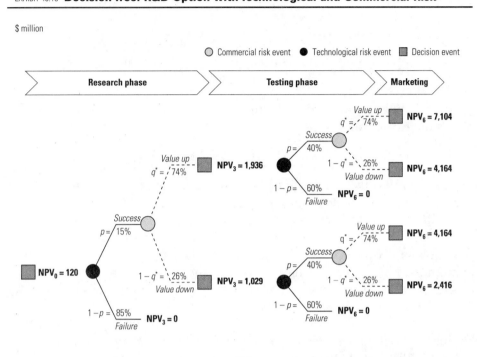

Note: NPVt = net present value of project as of year t; q^* = binomial (risk-neutral) probability of an increase in marketable drug value; p = probability of technological success.

Step 4: Estimate Contingent NPV

The commercial risk regarding the drug's future cash flows is not diversifiable,[31] so you need to use an ROV approach to include it in your valuation. This example uses risk-neutral valuation. Therefore, risk-adjust all probabilities of the upward and downward movements for the drug's value:

$$q^* = \frac{(1 + r_f)^T - d}{u - d} = \frac{1.05^3 - 0.77}{1.30 - 0.77} = 0.74$$

Having applied the risk-neutral probabilities, discount all contingent payoffs at the risk-free rate, working from right to left in the tree. Because the technological risk is fully diversifiable, there is no need to adjust the probabilities for success and failure in research or testing.

For example, from Exhibit 40.18, the value of the option at the end of the research phase showing a drop in the value of the drug is expressed as follows:

$$NPV_3(\text{Option}) = \text{Max}[PV_3(\text{Testing}) - \text{Inv}_3(\text{Testing}), 0]$$

[31] Recall that we assumed the cost of capital for a marketed drug is 7 percent. Given our assumption for a risk-free rate of 5 percent, its beta must be different from zero.

In this equation, PV_3(Testing) represents the value of proceeding with testing at this node. It equals the value of the future payoffs weighted by risk-neutral probabilities and discounted at the risk-free rate:

$$PV_3(\text{Testing}) = \frac{0.40[0.74(\$4,164) + 0.26(\$2,416)] + 0.60(0)}{(1.05)^3} = \$1,279$$

Inv_3(Testing) equals $250 million, so the value of the development project at this node is as follows:

$$NPV_3(\text{Option}) = \text{Max}[(\$1,279 - \$250), 0] = \$1,029$$

Solve for the other nodes in the same way. Working backward through the tree gives us an estimate of the contingent NPV: $120 million, the same result as obtained in the DTA approach without commercial risk.

This is not surprising. A closer look at the decision tree reveals that uncertainty about the future value of the drug if it is marketable is not significant enough to influence any of the decisions in the development process. In this example, the commercial risk makes no difference, even if we assume volatility as high as 50 percent (an amount that exceeds the volatility of many high-tech stocks). As noted earlier, when nondiversifiable risk (the drug's commercial risk as measured by its beta) does not influence investment decisions, the DTA and ROV results are equivalent.

Moreover, in real situations, the prevailing uncertainty in drug development is whether the drug proves to be an effective disease treatment without serious side effects. The commercial risk is far less relevant, because a truly effective drug almost always generates attractive margins. The example illustrates how in such cases it is more practical to focus on the technological risk entirely, using a DTA approach. Explicitly modeling the nondiversifiable (for example, commercial) risk requires an ROV approach that is more complex and may not even affect the valuation results.

In general, when faced with multiple sources of underlying risk, carefully assess whether all these possible risks are important or whether one prevails. Sometimes you can focus the valuation approach on just one or two sources of uncertainty and greatly simplify the analysis.

SUMMARY

Managerial flexibility lets executives defer or change investment decisions as a business or project develops. It can substantially alter the value of a business or project. Rigidly applying standard DCF analysis fails to account for the impact that exercising flexibility can have on present value.

Flexibility takes many forms, such as the option to defer, expand, contract, or abandon projects or to switch them on and off. This chapter has illustrated only a few applications. Contingent NPV analysis, in the form of decision tree analysis (DTA) or real-option valuation (ROV) models, correctly captures flexibility's impact on value. The ROV approach is theoretically superior to DTA, but applying it is more complicated. So ROV is often limited to valuing flexibility in commodity-based industries where prices are measurable, making its application more straightforward. In most other cases, a careful DTA approach delivers results that are reasonably solid and can provide more valuable insights.

41

Emerging Markets

The world's emerging economies, home of 86 percent of the population, accounted for about 60 percent of global GDP in 2024 and are growing faster than most of the developed economies.[1] As emerging markets become more important to the global economy and to investors, sound methods are needed for analyzing and valuing companies and business units in these markets.

Chapters 26 and 27 discussed general issues related to forecasting cash flows, estimating the cost of capital in a foreign currency, and incorporating high inflation rates into cash flow projections. This chapter focuses on additional issues that arise in emerging markets, such as the potential for extreme economic contractions or unexpected government actions such as asset appropriation. It is impossible to generalize about these risks, as they differ by country and may affect businesses in different ways. Academics, investment bankers, and industry practitioners subscribe to different methods and often make arbitrary adjustments based on intuition and limited empirical evidence.

For accurate valuation of companies in emerging markets, we recommend using a scenario discounted-cash-flow (DCF) approach as described in Chapter 16 to prepare multiple cash flow scenarios reflecting the outcomes of different risks that a company could face. These scenarios are each discounted and then weighted by probabilities assigned to each. You can supplement this method by comparing the results with two secondary approaches: a DCF valuation with a country risk markup (country risk premium, as it is often called) added to the cost of capital and a valuation based on the multiples of comparable companies.

This chapter includes contributions from Anuj Gupta.

[1] China's and India's shares of global GDP, at purchasing power parity (PPP), were 19 and 8 percent, respectively, and each country's population was about 18 percent of global population. "GDP Based on PPP, Share of World," International Monetary Fund, IMF DataMapper, imf.org.

COUNTRY RISK IS DIVERSIFIABLE

Compared with developed economies, emerging markets can present additional risks for a business, ranging from potential hyperinflation and devaluation to economic contraction, regime change, nationalization, or even armed conflict. Of course, keep in mind that these risks do not apply to all emerging markets and that developed economies are not immune to some of these risks either. When present, such risks are all very relevant from a manager's perspective. They can make or break financial results for a given business in a given country. If extreme, they could even create financial risks (from business disruption to bankruptcy) for the company as a whole.

As explained in Chapter 4, what matters most for shareholders is whether these risks are diversified away in a larger portfolio of investments. In other words, is emerging-market risk diversifiable or not? If it is not, shareholders would require additional returns on emerging-market investments, which translate into a higher cost of capital. If the risks are diversifiable, there would be no impact on costs of capital—much like, for example, technological risks in the development of a new airplane or geological risks in the development of an offshore oil field.[2]

Looking at the long-term returns in equity markets and business portfolios in emerging markets, we find that emerging market risks are largely diversifiable and ultimately disappear in larger portfolios. We constructed series of portfolios of equity market indexes from randomly selected emerging markets and measured the volatility of the portfolio returns over the past ten years. The individual market indexes often had volatilities more than double those of U.S. or European stock markets. But when we combined just five of these emerging-market indexes, the resulting portfolio volatilities were always radically reduced and typically similar to the US or European stock markets.

We found these diversification effects for business results as well. Consider the returns on invested capital of an international consumer goods player (Exhibit 41.1).[3] Over a 20-year time frame, its returns were highly volatile for individual emerging markets. Taken together, however, these markets were hardly more volatile than developed markets; the corporate portfolio diversified away most of the risks.

Not surprisingly, our empirical research also shows that not much of a premium for emerging-market risk is built into the valuation of stocks. If there were a substantial premium in the cost capital, we would expect price-to-earnings ratios (P/Es) in these markets to be much smaller than they are.

---

[2] In other words, following the capital asset pricing model, diversifiable risk does not affect the beta for an investment object and does not lead to a higher expected (and required) return for investors.
[3] M. H. Goedhart and P. Haden, "Are Emerging Markets as Risky as You Think?" McKinsey & Company, March 2003, www.mckinsey.com.

EXHIBIT 41.1 **Returns on a Diverse Emerging-Market Portfolio**

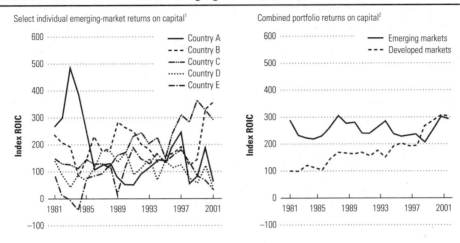

Select individual emerging-market returns on capital[1]

Legend:
— Country A
- - - Country B
—··— Country C
······ Country D
—·— Country E

Combined portfolio returns on capital[2]

Legend:
— Emerging markets
- - - Developed markets

[1] In stable currency and adjusted for local accounting differences.
[2] Combined portfolio includes additional countries not reflected here.
Source: Company information.

Consider Brazil. Many valuations we've seen have incorporated so-called country risk premiums of 3 to 5 percent, plus an inflation differential versus U.S. companies of about 2 to 3 percent. That leads to a cost of equity of 15 to 18 percent for the Brazilian market, versus around 9 percent for the U.S. market. From 2016 to 2022, the P/E for the major Brazilian market index has been in a wide range, from 10 to 17 times. Going back to the value driver formula derived in Chapter 3, we can solve for the expected growth in earnings, given the P/E ratio and estimates for the other values:

$$\frac{P}{E} = \left(1 - \frac{g}{\text{ROE}}\right)/(k_e - g)$$

where g is the growth rate of earnings, ROE is return on equity, and k_e is the cost of equity.

Exhibit 41.2 shows all combinations of growth and return on equity that result in a midrange Brazilian P/E of 13 times, for a cost of equity of 15 percent (dashed line) and 11 percent (solid line). For example, assuming a cost of equity of 15 percent and a marginal return on equity of 20 percent (above a historical average of 14 percent), the implied growth rate of earnings in perpetuity would have to be about 12 percent nominal, or about 8 percent in real terms (assuming 4 percent inflation, based on 2 percent in the United States and two percentage points higher inflation in Brazil). But 8 percent real growth in perpetuity is unrealistic (historical growth was at 3 percent). It's impossible to come up with a set of reasonable growth and return assumptions that ties together a P/E of 13 times and a 15 percent cost of equity.

However, if we eliminate the country risk premium and use a cost of equity of 11 percent, our results work—mathematically and economically.

EXHIBIT 41.2 **No Country Risk Premium for Brazilian Equity Market**

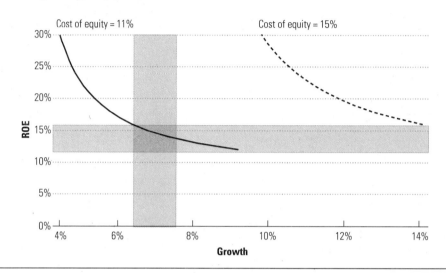

ROE and growth supporting P/E for Brazil

Assuming 3.5 percent long-term real growth plus 4 percent inflation and a 14 percent ROE results in a 13 times P/E. Subtracting inflation at 4 percent gives us a 7 percent real cost of equity, not very different from the real cost of equity of the United States (see Chapter 15).

We did similar analyses for other emerging markets with similar results. Consider, for example, the Indian stock market, which was priced at a P/E ratio of around 26 times between 2016 and 2022. Return on equity was around 16 percent over these years. At a cost of equity of 15 percent, future nominal growth would have to be 15 percent into perpetuity. For India, with inflation rates of around 4 percent, that translates into unrealistic real-terms growth of 11 percent. But when using 11 percent cost of equity without risk premium, nominal growth would need to be around 9.5 percent, close to historical real-terms growth levels of around 6 percent.

Of course, these results are highly sensitive to small changes in some of the assumptions. The key point is that it is very difficult to reconcile current P/Es in large emerging markets such as Brazil and India with a country risk premium of 3 percent or more. An implied country risk premium for Brazil or India is more likely to be closer to 1 percent (or less). Furthermore, most of us underestimate the impact that even a small country risk premium has on valuations, as we will show in the next sections.

APPLYING THE SCENARIO DCF APPROACH

Finance theory clearly dictates that the cost of capital should not reflect risk that can be diversified. This does not mean diversifiable risk is irrelevant for a valuation: the possibility of adverse future events will affect the level of

expected cash flows rather than the cost of equity. But once this has been factored in, there is no need for an additional markup of the cost of capital if the
risk is diversifiable. However, many practitioners do not discount expected
cash flows but rather some form of cash flows from business plans, which are
closer to business-as-usual or even best-case cash flows.

That's where the scenario DCF approach proves its advantages. It allows
you to assess the risk of each company based on company-specific risk
factors and to explicitly include that risk in your cash flow projections. At
a minimum, model two scenarios. The first should assume that cash flow
develops according to conditions reflecting business as usual (that is, without
major economic distress). The second should reflect cash flows assuming one
or more emerging-market risks materialize.

Exhibit 41.3 compares the valuation of a company with a European
factory and an emerging-market factory with a similar outlook except for the
emerging-market risk. In the example, the cash flows for the European factory
grow steadily at 3 percent per year into perpetuity. For the factory in the
emerging market, the cash flow growth is the same under a business-as-usual
scenario, but there is a 25 percent probability of economic distress resulting
in a cash flow that is 55 percent lower into perpetuity. The emerging-market
risk is reflected in the lower expected value of future cash flows from weighting both scenarios by the assumed probabilities. The resulting value of the
emerging-market factory (€1,917) is clearly below the value of its European
sister factory (€2,222), using a WACC of 7.5 percent.

We assumed for simplicity that if adverse economic conditions develop
in the emerging market, they will do so in the first year of the plant's
operation. In reality, of course, the investment will face a probability of
domestic economic distress in each year of its lifetime. Modeling risk over
time would require more complex calculations yet would not change the
basic results. We also assumed that the emerging-market business would
face significantly lower cash flows in a local crisis but not wind up entirely
worthless.

From an operational viewpoint, using scenarios forces managers to discuss
emerging-market risks and their effect on cash flows, thereby gaining more
insights than they would secure from an arbitrary addition to the discount
rate. By identifying specific factors with a large impact on value, managers can
plan to mitigate these risks.

While estimating probabilities of economic distress for the base case and
downside scenarios is ultimately a matter of management judgment, there
are indicators to suggest reasonable probabilities. Historical data on previous
crises can give some indication of the frequency and severity of country
risk and the time required for recovery. We analyzed the changes in GDP
of 20 emerging economies since 1985 and found that they had experienced
economic distress, defined as a real-terms GDP decline of more than 5 percent,
about once every five years. This would suggest a 20 percent probability for a
downside scenario.

EXHIBIT 41.3 **Scenario DCF vs. Country Risk Premium DCF**

Net present value for identical facilities, €

European market

Scenario approach

Cash flows in perpetuity[1]

	Probability	Year 1	2	3	4	...
"As usual"	100%	100	103	106	109	
"Distressed"	0%					

Expected cash flows

	Year 1	2	3	4	...
	100	103	106	109	
Cost of capital		7.5%			
Net present value	2,222				

Country risk premium approach

Cash flows in perpetuity[1]

	Year 1	2	3	4	...
"As usual"	100	103	106	109	
Cost of capital		7.5%			
Net present value	2,222				

Emerging market

Scenario approach

Cash flows in perpetuity[2]

	Probability	Year 1	2	3	4	...
"As usual"	75%	100	103	106	109	
"Distressed"	25%	45	46	48	49	

Expected cash flows

	Year 1	2	3	4	...
	86	89	92	94	
Cost of capital		7.5%			
Net present value	1,917				86% of European NPV

Country risk premium approach

Cash flows in perpetuity[2]

	Year 1	2	3	4	...
"As usual"	100	103	106	109	
Cost of capital		7.5%			
Country risk premium		0.7%			
Adjusted cost of capital		8.2%			
Net present value	1,917				86% of European NPV

[1] Assuming perpetuity cash flow growth of 3%.

[2] Assuming perpetuity cash flow growth of 3% and recovery under distress of 45% of cash flows "as usual."

Another source of information for estimating probabilities is prospective data from current government bond prices.[4] Academic research suggests that government default probabilities in emerging markets such as Argentina five years into the future were around 30 percent in non-distress years.[5]

With such indications of economic distress or default probabilities, the key question is then: To what extent do such events affect business results, and what mitigation measures could be taken? That is what you would need to carefully think through and reflect in the downside scenario. In our experience, the impact on business results can differ widely across sectors.

WHY THE COUNTRY RISK PREMIUM APPROACH IS NOT ADEQUATE

As Exhibit 41.3 shows, there is an alternative way to estimate the value of the emerging-market factory. Instead of probability-weighting future cash flows, you could simply discount the business plan cash flows at an elevated discount rate. By adding a markup of 0.7 percent to the cost of capital, we arrive at exactly the same valuation result. (In this example, the markup is estimated by reverse engineering the valuation and solving for the discount rate based on the base case cash flows.)

Adding a markup to the discount rate to account for the higher risks has been common practice in emerging-market valuations. The markup is typically referred to as the "country risk premium," and it is probably the most vigorously debated issue about valuing companies in emerging markets. The name adds to the confusion in the debate because the markup is, strictly speaking, not a risk premium in the cost of capital but rather a correction of the business plan cash flows.[6] Nevertheless, because the term is so widespread, we will also refer to the markup as the country risk premium.

In our previous example, we could simply reverse engineer the country risk premium, because the true value of the plant was already known from the scenario approach. But for practical purposes, there is no agreed-upon approach to estimate the premium. Estimates from different analysts usually fall into a wide range because of the different methods used.

---

[4] See, for example, D. Duffie and K. Singleton, "Modeling Term Structures of Defaultable Bonds," *Review of Financial Studies* 12 (1999): 687–720; and R. Merton, "On the Pricing of Corporate Debt: The Risk Structure of Interest Rates," *Journal of Finance* 29, no. 2 (1974): 449–470.

[5] See J. Merrick, "Crisis Dynamics of Implied Default Recovery Ratios: Evidence from Russia and Argentina," *Journal of Banking and Finance* 25, no. 10 (2001): 1921–1939.

[6] As finance theory prescribes, we should discount *expected* cash flows at the cost of capital. In the CAPM setting that we use throughout this book, the cost of capital should only include a risk premium for risks that are not diversifiable by shareholders, as measured by beta. The markup approach has a different logic, discounting *promised* instead of expected cash flows at a discount rate that is *not* the cost of capital. Applied carefully, both approaches lead to the same valuation result. This is analogous to the discount rate for a risky corporate bond: its yield to maturity (which is a promised return) does not equal its cost of capital (which is an expected return).

Unfortunately, we can see from our example how easy it is to overestimate the country risk premium. Despite the 25 percent chance that the cash flows would be 55 percent lower than the base case, the equivalent country risk premium is only 0.7 percent. If we had used a country risk premium of 3 percent, the implied probability of economic distress would be 70 percent, versus 25 percent in the example.

Exhibit 41.4 gives a more general indication of the premium required for different combinations of the probability and size of an investment's permanent cash flow reduction. The premium is easily overestimated. For example, if there is a probability of 50 percent that future cash flows will be permanently lower by 40 percent, the risk premium should be just 1.5 percent. Actual premiums will also vary depending on the underlying cash flow profile and cost of capital.[7] Nevertheless, the table allows for some calibration of premiums and risks.

Some practitioners simply base the country risk premium on the local government's borrowing rate relative to a benchmark, such as the borrowing rates for the U.S. government.[8] A major problem with this approach is that the riskiness of lending to a government may have little to do with the risk of investing in a business. It is possible for a company to have a cost of equity lower than the interest rate on the government debt in the country. This seems counterintuitive, but compare the riskiness of a consumer packaged-goods (CPG) producer in an emerging market versus the government debt of that country. The CPG producer may experience a large drop in earnings during an economic crisis, but it typically springs back relatively quickly.

EXHIBIT 41.4 **Probability of Economic Distress Given Small Variations in Risk Premium**

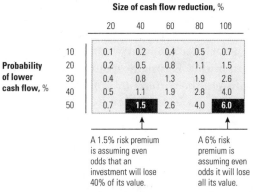

Risk premium that reflects given conditions, %

		Size of cash flow reduction, %				
		20	40	60	80	100
	10	0.1	0.2	0.4	0.5	0.7
Probability	20	0.2	0.5	0.8	1.1	1.5
of lower	30	0.4	0.8	1.3	1.9	2.6
cash flow, %	40	0.5	1.1	1.9	2.8	4.0
	50	0.7	**1.5**	2.6	4.0	**6.0**

A 1.5% risk premium is assuming even odds that an investment will lose 40% of its value.

A 6% risk premium is assuming even odds it will lose all its value.

Note: Chart assumes a smooth cash flow profile, 8% weighted average cost of capital, 2% terminal growth, binomial outcome.

Source: R. Davis, M. Goedhart, and T. Koller, "Avoiding a Risk Premium That Unnecessarily Kills Your Project," *McKinsey Quarterly* (August 2012).

[7] The higher the cash flow's growth rate, the stronger is the impact of a risk premium on the DCF value.
[8] T. Keck, E. Levengood, and A. Longfield, "Using Discounted Cash Flow Analysis in an International Setting: A Survey of Issues in Modeling the Cost of Capital," *Journal of Applied Corporate Finance* 11, no. 3 (1998): 82–99.

And in contrast to the political environment facing banks and mining or energy companies, CPG businesses face little risk of appropriation by the government. With regard to government debt, however, it's not unusual for governments to default. Since 1990, Russia and Argentina have each defaulted. Even Greece required bailout loans from the International Monetary Fund and European Central bank in 2010, 2012, and 2015. It's also possible that the cost of debt for some companies is lower than that of their government, as is the case in Brazil, where a number of companies' debt is rated investment grade while the government's is not.

Furthermore, it's illogical to apply the same country risk premium across all industries. CPG producers generally survive economic disruptions, while banks may go bankrupt. For example, over the period 2013–2018, Brazilian ten-year government bonds were more volatile than beverage company Ambev and less volatile than the major Brazilian banks. Some companies (raw-materials exporters) might benefit from a currency devaluation, while others (raw-materials importers) will be damaged.

We've found that the country risk premiums used in practice are too high and lead to overcompensation in the company's projected performance. Analysts using high premiums frequently compensate by making aggressive forecasts for growth and return on invested capital (ROIC). An example is the valuation we undertook of a large Brazilian chemicals company. Using a local weighted average cost of capital (WACC) of 10 percent, we reached an enterprise value of 4.0 to 4.5 times earnings before interest, taxes, depreciation, and amortization (EBITDA). A second adviser was asked to value the company and came to a similar valuation—an EBITDA multiple of around 4.5—despite using a very high country risk premium of 11 percent on top of the WACC. The result was similar because the second adviser made performance assumptions that were far too aggressive: real sales growth of almost 10 percent per year and a ROIC increasing to 46 percent in the long term. Such long-term performance assumptions are unrealistic for a commodity-based, competitive industry such as chemicals. In another, broader set of analyst forecasts from 2015 to 2018, 30 percent of industries were expected to achieve growth rates more than 20 percent, while in the United States, only 5 percent were expected to achieve similar results. It's hard to imagine 30 percent of industries growing more than 20 percent per year.

ESTIMATING COST OF CAPITAL IN EMERGING MARKETS

Calculating the cost of capital in any country can be challenging, but for emerging markets, the challenge is an order of magnitude greater. This section provides our fundamental beliefs, background on the important issues, and a practical way to estimate the components of the cost of capital.

General Guidelines

Our analysis adopts the perspective of a global investor—either a multinational company or a global investor with a diversified portfolio. Of course, some emerging markets are not yet well integrated with the global market. In China, for example, local investors may face barriers to investing outside their home market. As a result, local investors in such markets cannot always hold well-diversified portfolios, and their cost of capital may be considerably different from that of a global investor. Unfortunately, there is no established framework for estimating the capital cost for local investors. However, if the local stock market is fully integrated into the global markets (investors both in and out of the country can freely trade both locally and internationally), local prices will more likely be linked to an international cost of capital (see Chapter 27 and Appendix E).

From the perspective of the global investor, most country risks are diversifiable. Therefore, when discounting expected cash flows in the scenario DCF approach, we need no additional risk premiums in the cost of capital for the risks encountered in emerging markets. Of course, if you choose to discount the promised cash flow from the business-as-usual scenario only, you should add a separate risk markup ("country risk premium") to the cost of capital, as discussed earlier in this chapter.

The cost of capital in emerging markets should generally be close to a global cost of capital adjusted for local inflation and capital structure. It is also useful to keep some general guidelines in mind:

- *Use the capital asset pricing model (CAPM) to estimate the cost of equity in emerging markets.* The CAPM may be less robust for the less integrated emerging markets than for developed markets, but there is no better alternative model today.

- *Be sure monetary assumptions are consistent.* Ground your model in a common set of monetary assumptions to ensure the cash flow forecasts and discount rate are consistent. If you are using local nominal cash flows, the cost of capital must reflect the local inflation rate embedded in the cash flow projections. For real-terms cash flows, subtract inflation from the nominal cost of capital.

- *Allow for changes in cost of capital.* The cost of capital in an emerging-market valuation may change, based on evolving inflation expectations, changes in a company's capital structure and cost of debt, or foreseeable reforms in the tax system. For example, in Argentina during the economic and monetary crisis of 2002, the short-term inflation rate was 30 percent. This could not have been a reasonable rate for a long-term cost of capital estimate, because such a crisis could not be expected to last forever.[9] In such cases, estimate the cost of capital on a year-by-year basis, following the underlying set of basic monetary assumptions.

[9] Annual consumer price inflation came down to around 5 percent in Argentina in 2004.

When applying these guidelines, don't mix approaches. Use the cost of capital to discount the cash flows in a scenario DCF approach. Do not add any premium for country risk, because you would then be double-counting risk. If you are discounting only future cash flows in a business-as-usual scenario, add a risk markup to the discount rate. Finally, keep in mind there is no one right answer, so be pragmatic. In emerging markets, there are often significant gaps in information and data (for example, in estimating betas). Be flexible as you assemble the available information piece by piece to build the cost of capital.

Estimating the Cost of Equity

To estimate the components of the cost of equity, use the approach described in Chapter 15, with the following considerations for the risk-free rate, market risk premium, and beta.

In emerging markets, it is harder than in developed markets to estimate the risk-free rate from government bonds. Three main problems arise. First, most of the government debt in emerging markets is not, in fact, risk free; the ratings on much of this debt are often well below investment grade. Second, it is difficult to find long-term government bonds that are actively traded with sufficient liquidity. Finally, the long-term debt traded is often in U.S. dollars or euros, so it is not appropriate for discounting local nominal cash flows.

We recommend a straightforward approach. Start with a risk-free rate based on the ten-year U.S. government bond yield, as in developed markets (or based on a synthetic risk-free rate as discussed in Chapter 15). Add to this the projected difference over time between U.S. and local inflation, to arrive at a nominal risk-free rate in local currency.[10] For emerging-market bonds with relatively low risk, you can derive this inflation differential from the spread between local bond yields denominated in local currency and those denominated in U.S. dollars.

Sometimes practitioners calculate beta relative to the local market index. This is not only inconsistent from the perspective of a global investor but also potentially distorted by the fact that the index in an emerging market will rarely be representative of a diversified economy. Instead, estimate industry betas relative to a well-diversified or global market index, as recommended in Chapter 15.

Excess returns of local equity markets over local bond returns are not a good proxy for the market risk premium. This holds even more so for emerging markets, given the lack of diversification in the local equity market. Furthermore, the quality and the length of available data on equity and bond market returns usually make such data unsuitable for long-term estimates.

---

[10] Technically, we should also model the U.S. term structure of interest rates, but it will not make a large difference in the valuation.

To use a market risk premium that is consistent with the perspective of a global investor, use a global estimate (as discussed in Chapter 15) of 4.5 to 5.5 percent.

Estimating the After-Tax Cost of Debt

In most emerging economies, there are no liquid markets for corporate bonds, so little or no market information is available to estimate the cost of debt. However, from a global investor's perspective, the cost of debt in local currency should simply equal the sum of the dollar (or euro) risk-free rate, the systematic part of the credit spread (which depends on the debt's beta; see the section titled "Estimating the After-Tax Cost of Debt" in Chapter 15), and the inflation differential between local currency and dollars (or euros). Most or all of the country risk can be diversified away in a global bond portfolio. Therefore, the systematic part of the default risk is probably no larger than that of companies in international markets, and the cost of debt should not include a separate country risk premium.[11] Furthermore, companies in countries such as Brazil often hold large amounts of cash to provide liquidity and minimize their net debt.

The marginal tax rate in emerging markets can be very different from the effective tax rate, which often includes investment tax credits, export tax credits, taxes, equity or dividend credits, and operating loss credits. Few of these arrangements provide a tax shield on interest expense, and only those few should be incorporated in the after-tax-cost-of-debt component of the WACC. Other taxes or credits should be modeled directly in the cash flows (see also the example in Exhibit 27.2 on how to include foreign tax shields in the WACC estimate).

Estimating Capital Structure and WACC

Having estimated the cost of equity and after-tax cost of debt, we need debt and equity weights to derive an estimate of the weighted average cost of capital. In emerging markets, many companies have capital structures unlike those of their international peers. One reason is, of course, the country risk: even though it is diversifiable, the possibility of macroeconomic distress makes companies more conservative in setting their leverage. Another reason could be anomalies in the local debt or equity markets. In the long run, when the anomalies are corrected, the companies should expect to develop a capital structure similar to that of their global competitors. You could forecast explicitly how the company evolves to a capital structure that is more like global standards. In that case, you should consider using the adjusted-present-value (APV) approach, discussed in Chapter 10.

---

[11] This explains why multinationals with extensive emerging-market portfolios—companies such as Coca-Cola, Colgate-Palmolive, and Unilever—have a cost of debt that is no higher than that of their mainly U.S.-focused competitors.

OTHER COMPLICATIONS IN VALUING EMERGING-MARKETS COMPANIES

Other complications that should be considered in valuing emerging-markets companies include consistent macroeconomic parameters, accounting differences, nonoperating assets, and inefficient capital markets.

Every forecast of a company's financial performance is based on assumptions about real GDP growth, inflation rates, interest and exchange rates, and whatever other parameters, such as energy prices, are relevant. In emerging markets, these parameters can fluctuate wildly from year to year. It becomes all the more important that forecasts be based on an integrated set of economic and monetary assumptions of future inflation, interest rates, exchange rates, and cost of capital (see Chapters 26 and 27 for more details). For instance, make sure that the same inflation rates underlie the financial projections and cost of capital estimates for the company.

One parameter deserves special attention: exchange rates. Although exchange rates converge to purchasing power parity (PPP) in the long run,[12] short-term deviations can be sizable and last for several years, especially in the case of emerging markets. In Chapter 27, Exhibit 27.3 shows how even on an inflation-adjusted basis, the exchange rate of Brazil's currency, the real (plural: reais), has fluctuated strongly over the past three decades versus the U.S. dollar. If the long-term average real exchange rate is indicative of PPP,[13] the Brazilian currency could have been overvalued or undervalued versus the U.S. dollar and other currencies in many of the years since 1995. Any exchange rate convergence to PPP would not be likely to affect the cash flows and value generated by a retailer, as its revenues and costs are mainly determined in Brazilian reais. But an exchange rate change would affect its cash flow and value measured in foreign currency. Because predicting exchange rates is virtually impossible, a range estimate of the impact on a company's value measured in foreign currency is more meaningful. For primarily local companies, like retailers, it would therefore be best to perform the DCF valuation in Brazilian reais and—if needed—translate the result at both the actual and the PPP exchange rates to obtain a value range in foreign currency.

Fortunately, many of the complications arising from different accounting standards have been resolved over the past decades. Almost all countries outside the United States have adopted IFRS accounting standards, with the notable exceptions of China and India. This has reduced the complexity of adjusting their financial statements for valuation purposes. Even in China and India, the vast majority of accounting standards have been converging with IFRS and are now substantially the same.

---

[12] For an overview, see A. M. Taylor and M. P. Taylor, "The Purchasing Power Parity Debate," *Journal of Economic Perspectives* 18, no. 4 (Fall 2004): 135–158.
[13] See Chapter 27 for more details on PPP and exchange rates.

Nonoperating assets remain a challenge, however. Companies in emerging markets—which are often conglomerates with a wide range of businesses—frequently have a large amount of nonoperating assets, including unconsolidated equity investments and real estate.

The capital markets in which emerging-markets companies trade may have inefficiencies. In many cases, these companies may have limited float because controlling shareholders may hold large stakes. The presence of controlling shareholders (often founding families) may also raise concerns about governance and whether there are potential conflicts between the interests of public shareholders and the controlling shareholders. This could lead to a lower share price than otherwise warranted. Some countries also have restrictions on investors, or the governments actively intervene in the markets, causing deviations in share prices from intrinsic values. Finally, companies in emerging markets often have complex corporate structures with voting and nonvoting shares. This often leads to a small group of investors controlling the company even though they own less than 50 percent. In some countries with weak governance, public market investors will discount the value of these companies if they don't believe the controlling shareholders make decisions in the interests of all shareholders.

TRIANGULATING VALUATION

We recommend triangulating the results of the scenario DCF approach with a comparable multiples approach and DCF using a markup for country risk. We'll illustrate with the example of a Brazilian retail company we'll call ConsuCo.

We constructed two scenarios, a business-as-usual case (the base case) and a downside case reflecting performance under adverse economic conditions. Exhibit 41.5 shows the ROIC projections. Brazil has experienced several severe economic and monetary downturns, including an inflation rate that topped 2,000 percent in 1993. Judging by its key financial indicators, such as EBITDA to sales and real-terms sales growth, the impact on ConsuCo's business performance was significant. ConsuCo's cash operating margin was negative for four years, at around –10 to –5 percent, before recovering to its pre-downturn levels. In the same period, sales in real terms declined by 10 to 15 percent per year but grew sharply after the crisis. For the downside scenario projections, we assumed similar negative cash margins and a decline in sales, in real terms, for up to five years, followed by a gradual return to the long-term margins and growth assumed under the business-as-usual scenario.

We discounted the free cash flows for ConsuCo under the base case and the downside scenario. The resulting present values of operations are shown

EXHIBIT 41.5 **ConsuCo: ROIC and Financials, Base Case vs. Downside Scenario**

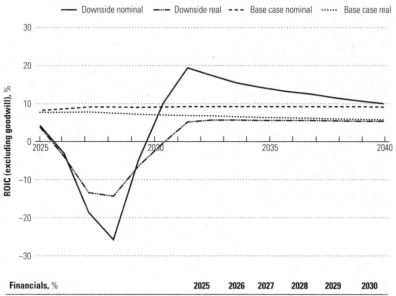

—— Downside nominal   —·—· Downside real   - - - Base case nominal   ······ Base case real

Financials, %	2025	2026	2027	2028	2029	2030
Nominal indicators: Base case						
Sales growth	15.3	14.5	13.6	12.6	11.7	10.8
Adjusted EBITA/sales	6.1	6.2	6.4	6.4	6.4	6.4
Invested capital (excluding goodwill)/sales	54.1	52.6	51.4	50.6	50.1	49.2
ROIC (excluding goodwill)	8.1	8.5	9.0	9.0	8.9	9.0
Free cash flow, reais million	(63)	(136)	(94)	(91)	(85)	113
Nominal indicators: Downside scenario						
Sales growth	10.0	25.0	66.3	66.3	25.0	11.3
Adjusted EBITA/sales	3.1	−2.2	−8.0	−7.6	−1.1	3.3
Invested capital (excluding goodwill)/sales	55.1	47.0	31.2	22.4	21.3	22.2
ROIC (excluding goodwill)	4.2	−3.2	−18.6	−25.7	−5.0	9.9
Free cash flow, reais million	(149)	(777)	(2,533)	(4,504)	(2,677)	(558)

Note: Chart assumes a smooth cash flow profile, 8% weighted average cost of capital, 2% terminal growth, binomial outcome.

Source: R. Davis, M. Goedhart, and T. Koller, "Avoiding a Risk Premium That Unnecessarily Kills Your Project," *McKinsey Quarterly* (August 2012).

in Exhibit 41.6. Note that we conducted the analysis in both nominal and real cash flows to show that the results were identical. We then weighted the valuation results by the scenario probabilities to derive the present value of operations. Finally, we added the market value of the nonoperating assets and subtracted the financial claims to arrive at the estimated equity value. The estimated equity DCF value obtained for ConsuCo is about 32 reais per share, given a 30 percent probability of economic distress. This is somewhat lower than ConsuCo's share price in the stock market of around 37 reais at the time of valuation.

EXHIBIT 41.6 **ConsuCo: Scenario DCF Valuation**

Reais, million

Base case

Probability	70%		2025	2026	2027	2028	2029	2034	2039
DCF value	14,451	Free cash flow (real-terms)	(60)	(125)	(83)	(77)	(68)	171	266
Nonoperating assets	1,139	Free cash flow	(63)	(136)	(94)	(91)	(85)	264	511
Debt and debt equivalents	(5,605)	WACC	11.1%	9.5%	9.3%	9.2%	9.1%	9.0%	9.0%
Equity value	9,985								
Value per share	42.4								

Downside

Probability	30%		2025	2026	2027	2028	2029	2034	2039
DCF value	6,313	Free cash flow (real-terms)	(142)	(593)	(1,105)	(1,123)	(534)	22	105
Nonoperating assets	1,139	Free cash flow	(149)	(777)	(2,533)	(4,504)	(2,677)	136	822
Debt and debt equivalents	(5,605)	WACC	11.1%	29.4%	76.7%	76.4%	28.7%	9.0%	9.0%
Equity value	1,847								
Value per share	7.9								

Probability-weighted value per share	32

To triangulate with multiples, we applied Chapter 18's guidance on how to perform a best-practice multiples analysis to check valuation results. For the ConsuCo example, we compared the implied multiple of enterprise value over EBITDA with those of peer retail companies. All multiples are forward-looking multiples over EBITDA. As Exhibit 41.7 illustrates, the implied multiple from our ConsuCo valuation is significantly higher than for U.S. and European peers, which is not surprising, given its higher growth outlook in the Brazilian market compared with that of large established chains in the U.S. and European markets. ConsuCo's valuation is at the low end of the range for Latin American peers, which also is not unreasonable. Relative to regional peers, ConsuCo could have been expected to have fewer growth opportunities, as it was already very well established and geographically widespread. It also had somewhat more exposure than listed peers had to the lower-growth food segment.

The last part of the triangulation consisted of valuing ConsuCo using a country risk premium approach. In this approach, we added a markup (country risk premium) to the the ConsuCo WACC to discount the cash flows under the business-as-usual scenario. Using a markup of around 0.5 percent generates

EXHIBIT 41.7 **ConsuCo: Multiples Analysis vs. Peers**

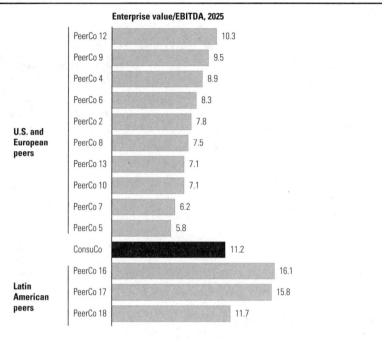

Enterprise value/EBITDA, 2025

U.S. and European peers	PeerCo 12	10.3
	PeerCo 9	9.5
	PeerCo 4	8.9
	PeerCo 6	8.3
	PeerCo 2	7.8
	PeerCo 8	7.5
	PeerCo 13	7.1
	PeerCo 10	7.1
	PeerCo 7	6.2
	PeerCo 5	5.8
	ConsuCo	11.2
Latin American peers	PeerCo 16	16.1
	PeerCo 17	15.8
	PeerCo 18	11.7

a value per share of 32 reais, equal to the result obtained in the scenario DCF approach. The markup is small because ConsuCo still retains a lot of its value in the downward scenario. Although its cash flows significantly decline during an economic downturn, they recover after several years. Note that the markup is lower than the 1 percent level that the table in Exhibit 41.4 would suggest for a 30 percent downside probability and a 50 percent reduction in cash flows. The reason is that ConsuCo has future growth at a much higher level than the 2 percent underlying the table. At higher growth rates of projected cash flows, lower markups should be used.

Note that a risk premium of 3 to 5 percent (as is typically used in emerging markets) would have either resulted in unrealistically low valuations relative to current share price and peer group multiples or else required an unrealistically bullish forecast of future performance.

SUMMARY

To value companies in emerging markets, we use concepts similar to the ones applied to developed markets. However, it's necessary to incorporate into valuations the unique risks of emerging markets, such as macroeconomic or political crises, by following the scenario DCF approach. This approach develops alternative scenarios for future cash flows, discounts the cash flows at the cost of capital without a country risk premium, and then weights the DCF values by the scenario probabilities. The cost of capital estimates for emerging markets build on the assumption of a global risk-free rate, market risk premium, and beta, following guidelines similar to those used for developed markets.

Since company values in emerging markets are often more volatile than values in developed markets, we recommend triangulating the scenario DCF results with two other valuations: one based on discounting cash flows developed in a business-as-usual projection but using a cost of capital that includes a country risk markup, and another based on multiples.

42

Cyclical Companies

A cyclical company is one whose earnings demonstrate a repeating pattern of significant increases and decreases. The earnings of cyclical companies, including those in the steel, mining, paper, and chemical industries, fluctuate because the prices of their products change dramatically as demand and/or supply varies. The companies themselves often create too much capacity. Volatile earnings within the cycle introduce additional complexity into the valuation of these cyclical companies. For example, historical performance must be assessed in the context of the cycle. A decline in recent performance does not necessarily indicate a long-term negative trend, but rather may signal a shift to a different part of the cycle.

This chapter explores the valuation issues particular to cyclical companies. It starts with an examination of how the share prices of cyclical companies behave. This leads to a suggested approach for valuing these companies, and finally to a discussion of possible implications for managers.

SHARE PRICE BEHAVIOR

Suppose you were using the discounted-cash-flow (DCF) approach to value a cyclical company and had perfect foresight about the industry cycle. Would the company's value and earnings behave similarly? No. A succession of DCF values would exhibit much lower volatility than the earnings or cash flows. DCF reduces future expected cash flows to a single value. As a result, any single year is unimportant. For a cyclical company, the high cash flows cancel out the low cash flows. Only the long-term trend really matters.

To illustrate, suppose the business cycle of Company A is ten years. Exhibit 42.1, part 1, shows the company's hypothetical cash flow pattern. It is highly volatile, containing both positive and negative cash flows. Discounting

This chapter includes contributions from Marco De Heer.

833

EXHIBIT 42.1 **The Long-Term View: Free Cash Flow and DCF Volatility**

Free cash flow pattern, Company A, $ million

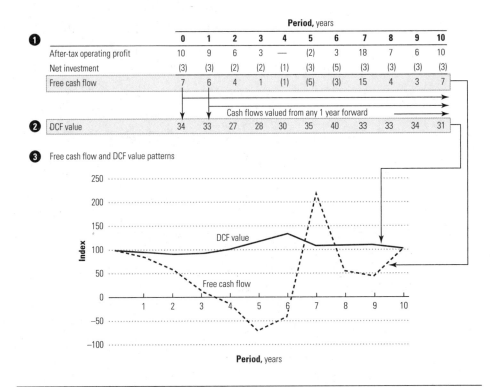

		Period, years										
❶		**0**	**1**	**2**	**3**	**4**	**5**	**6**	**7**	**8**	**9**	**10**
	After-tax operating profit	10	9	6	3	—	(2)	3	18	7	6	10
	Net investment	(3)	(3)	(2)	(2)	(1)	(3)	(5)	(3)	(3)	(3)	(3)
	Free cash flow	7	6	4	1	(1)	(5)	(3)	15	4	3	7
				Cash flows valued from any 1 year forward								
❷	DCF value	34	33	27	28	30	35	40	33	33	34	31

❸ Free cash flow and DCF value patterns

the future free cash flows at 10 percent produces the succession of DCF values in part 2 of the exhibit. Part 3 compares the cash flows and the perfect-foresight DCF values (the values are indexed for comparability). It shows that the DCF value is far less volatile than the underlying cash flow because no single year's performance has a significant impact on the value of the company.

In the real world, the share prices of cyclical companies are less stable than the example in Exhibit 42.1. Exhibit 42.2 shows the earnings per share (EPS) and share prices, both indexed, for 15 companies with a four-year cycle. The share prices are more volatile than the DCF approach would predict, which suggests that market prices exhibit the bias of anchoring on current earnings.

What might explain this pattern? We examined equity analysts' consensus earnings forecasts for cyclical companies, looking for clues to these companies' volatile stock prices. Consensus earnings forecasts for cyclical companies appeared to ignore cyclicality entirely. The forecasts invariably showed an upward-sloping trend, whether the companies were at the peak or trough of the cycle.

What became apparent was not that the DCF model was inconsistent with the facts but that the analysts' projections of earnings and cash flow were to blame (assuming the market followed the analysts' consensus). This conclusion was based on an analysis of 36 U.S. cyclical companies during the period

EXHIBIT 42.2   **Share Prices and Earnings per Share: 15 Cyclical Companies**

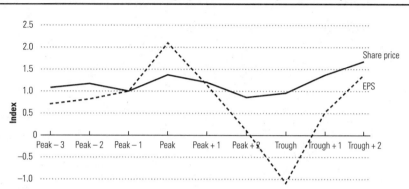

from 1985 to 1997. We divided them into groups with similar cycles (e.g., three, four, or five years from peak to trough) and calculated scaled average earnings and earnings forecasts. We then compared actual earnings with consensus earnings forecasts over the cycle.[1]

Exhibit 42.3 plots the actual earnings and consensus earnings forecasts for the set of 15 companies with four-year cycles in primary metals and manufacturing transportation equipment. The consensus forecasts do not predict the earnings cycle at all. In fact, except for the next-year forecasts in the years following the trough, the earnings per share are forecast to follow an upward-sloping path with no future variation.[2]

One explanation could be that equity analysts have incentives to avoid predicting the earnings cycle, particularly the down part. Academic research has shown that earnings forecasts have a positive bias that is sometimes attributed to the incentives facing equity analysts.[3] Pessimistic earnings forecasts may damage relations between an analyst's employer and a particular company. In addition, companies that are the target of negative commentary might cut off an analyst's access to management. From this evidence, we could conclude that analysts as a group are unable or unwilling to predict the cycles for these companies. If the market followed analyst forecasts, that behavior could account for the high volatility of cyclical companies' share prices.

We know it is difficult to predict cycles, particularly their inflection points. So it is unsurprising that the market does not get them exactly right. However,

---

[1] Note that we have already adjusted downward the normal positive bias of analyst forecasts to focus on just the cyclicality issue. V. K. Chopra, "Why So Much Error in Analysts' Earnings Forecasts?" *Financial Analysts Journal* (November/December 1998): 35–42.

[2] Similar results were found for companies with three- and five-year cycles.

[3] The following articles discuss this hypothesis: M. R. Clayman and R. A. Schwartz, "Falling in Love Again: Analysts' Estimates and Reality," *Financial Analysts Journal* (September/October 1994): 66–68; J. Francis and D. Philbrick, "Analysts' Decisions as Products of a Multi-Task Environment," *Journal of Accounting Research* 31, no. 2 (Autumn 1993): 216–230; K. Schipper, "Commentary on Analysts' Forecasts," *Accounting Horizons* (December 1991): 105–121; B. Trueman, "On the Incentives for Security Analysts to Revise Their Earnings Forecasts," *Contemporary Accounting Research* 7, no. 1 (1990): 203–222.

EXHIBIT 42.3   **Actual EPS and Consensus EPS Forecasts: 15 Cyclical Companies**

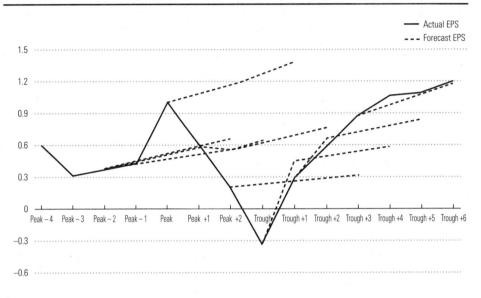

we would be surprised if the stock market entirely missed the cycle, as the analysis of consensus forecasts suggests. To address this issue, we returned to the question of how the market should behave. Should it be able to predict the cycle and therefore exhibit little share price volatility? That would probably be asking too much. At any point, the company or industry could break out of its cycle and move to one that is higher or lower, as illustrated in Exhibit 42.4.

Suppose you are valuing a company that seems to be at a peak in its earnings cycle. You will never have perfect foresight of the market cycle. Based on past cycles, you expect the industry to turn down soon. However, there are signs that the industry is about to break out of the old cycle. A reasonable valuation approach, therefore, would be to build two scenarios and weight their values. Suppose you assumed, with a 50 percent probability, that the cycle will follow the past and that the industry will turn down in the next year or so. The second scenario, also with a 50 percent probability, would be that the industry will break out of the cycle and follow a new long-term trend based on current improved performance. The value of the company would then be the weighted average of these two values.

We found evidence that this is, in fact, the way the market behaves. We valued the four-year cyclical companies three ways:

1. With perfect foresight about the upcoming cycle

2. With zero foresight, assuming current performance represents a point on a new long-term trend (essentially the consensus earnings forecast)

3. With a 50/50 forecast: 50 percent perfect foresight and 50 percent zero foresight

EXHIBIT 42.4 **When the Cycle Changes**

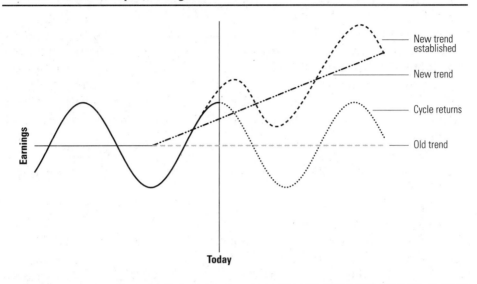

Exhibit 42.5 summarizes the results, comparing them with actual share prices. As shown, the market does not follow either the perfect-foresight or the zero-foresight path; it follows a blended path, much closer to the 50/50 path. So the market has neither perfect foresight nor zero foresight. One could argue that this 50/50 valuation is the right place for the market to be.

EXHIBIT 42.5 **Market Values of Cyclical Companies: Forecasts with Three Levels of Foresight**

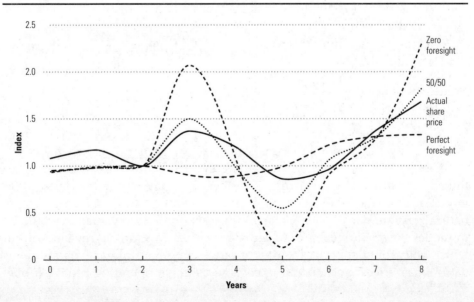

AN APPROACH TO VALUING CYCLICAL COMPANIES

No one can precisely predict the earnings cycle for an industry, and any single forecast of performance must be wrong. Managers and investors can benefit from following explicitly the multiple-scenario probabilistic approach to valuing cyclical companies, similar to the approach used in Chapter 17 and the high-growth-company valuation in Chapter 39. The probabilistic approach avoids the traps of a single forecast and allows exploration of a wider range of outcomes and their implications.

Here is a two-scenario approach for valuing cyclical companies in four steps (of course, this approach would also work with more than two scenarios):

1. Construct and value the normal cycle scenario, using information about past cycles. Pay particular attention to the long-term trend lines of operating profits, cash flow, and return on invested capital (ROIC), because they will have the largest impact on the valuation. Make sure the continuing value is based on a normalized level of profits (i.e., a point on the company's long-term cash flow trend line), not a peak or trough.

2. Construct and value a new trend line scenario based on the company's recent performance. Once again, focus primarily on the long-term trend line, because it will have the largest impact on value. Do not worry too much about modeling future cyclicality (although future cyclicality will be important for financial solvency).

3. Develop the economic rationale for each of the two scenarios, considering factors such as demand growth, companies entering or exiting the industry, and technology changes that will affect the balance of supply and demand.

4. Assign probabilities to the scenarios and calculate their weighted values. Use the economic rationale and its likelihood to estimate the weights assigned to each scenario.

This approach provides an estimate of the value as well as scenarios that put boundaries on the valuation. Managers can use these boundaries to improve their strategy and respond to signals about which scenario is likely to occur.

Another consideration when valuing cyclical companies in commodity-linked industries is that starting with revenues may not be the best way to model performance. Consider a polyethylene manufacturer, which processes natural gas into polyethylene. The traditional approach to valuation would be to model sales volumes and polyethylene prices to estimate revenues, from which you would subtract the cost of purchasing natural gas (volume times natural-gas prices) and operating costs to estimate operating profits. It may be simpler, however, to model only volumes and the "crack spread"—the difference between polyethylene prices and the cost of natural gas—and then subtract operating costs. What ultimately matters is the crack spread, not the revenues. The crack spread will often be set by the demand–supply balance for polyethylene, not the level of natural-gas prices. For example, during a decline in natural-gas prices, the crack spread might remain constant as producers pass on the reduction in natural-gas prices to customers by lowering polyethylene prices. If volumes were stable, so would be operating profits, despite a decline in revenues.[4]

IMPLICATIONS FOR MANAGING CYCLICAL COMPANIES

Is there anything managers can do to reduce or take advantage of the cyclicality of their industry? Evidence suggests that, in many cyclical industries, the companies themselves are what drive cyclicality. Exhibit 42.6 shows the ROIC and net investment in commodity chemicals from 1980 to 2013. The chart shows that, collectively, commodity chemical companies invest large amounts when prices and returns are high. But since capacity comes on line in very large chunks, utilization plunges, and this places

EXHIBIT 42.6   **ROIC and Investment Rate: Commodity Chemicals, 1980–2013**

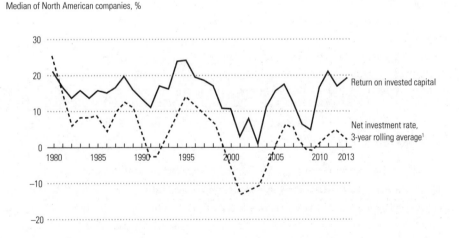

Median of North American companies, %

¹ Change in net property, plant, and equipment adjusted for inflation.

[4] The analysis is more complicated than this example suggests, because some polyethylene producers use naphtha rather than natural gas as their raw material.

downward pressure on price and ROIC. The cyclical investment in capacity is the driver of the cyclical profitability. Fluctuations in demand from customers do not cause cyclicality in profits. Producer supply does.

Managers who have detailed information about their product markets should be able to do a better job than the financial market in figuring out the cycle—and then take appropriate actions. We can only speculate as to why they do not. Still, based on conversations with these executives, we believe the herding behavior is caused by three factors: First, it is easier to invest when prices are high, because that is when cash is available. Second, it is easier to get approval from boards of directors to invest when profits are high. Finally, executives are concerned about their rivals growing faster than their company is, and investments are a way to maintain market share.

This behavior also sends confusing signals to the stock market. Expanding when prices are high tells the financial market that the future looks great (often just before the cycle turns down). Signaling pessimism just before an upturn also confuses the market. Perhaps it should be no surprise that the stock market has difficulty valuing cyclical companies.

How could managers exploit their superior knowledge of the cycle? The most obvious action would be to improve the timing of capital spending. Companies could also pursue financial strategies, such as issuing shares at the peak of the cycle or repurchasing shares at the cycle's trough. The most aggressive managers could take this one step further by adopting a trading approach, making acquisitions at the bottom of the cycle and selling assets at the top. Exhibit 42.7 shows the results of a simulation of optimal cycle timing. The typical company's returns on investment could increase substantially.

Can companies really behave this way and invest against the cycle? It is actually very difficult for a company to take the contrarian view. The CEO must convince the board to expand when the industry outlook is gloomy and competitors are retrenching. In addition, the CEO has to hold back while competitors build at the top of the cycle. Breaking out of the cycle may be possible, but it is the rare CEO who can do it.

EXHIBIT 42.7 **Relative Returns from Capital Expenditure Timing**

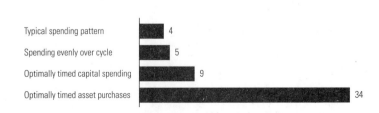

Internal rate of return, %

Typical spending pattern	4
Spending evenly over cycle	5
Optimally timed capital spending	9
Optimally timed asset purchases	34

SUMMARY

At first glance, the share prices of cyclical companies appear too volatile to be consistent with the DCF valuation approach. This chapter shows, however, that share price volatility can be explained by the uncertainty surrounding the industry cycle. Using scenarios and probabilities, managers and investors can take a systematic DCF approach to valuing and analyzing cyclical companies.

43

Banks

Banks are among the most complex businesses to value, especially from the outside in. Published accounts give an overview of a bank's financial performance but often lack vital information about its underlying economics, such as the extent of its credit losses or any mismatch between its assets and liabilities. Moreover, banks are highly levered, making bank valuations even more vulnerable to changing economic circumstances than are valuations in other sectors. Finally, most banks are in fact multibusiness companies, requiring separate analysis and valuation of their key business segments. So-called universal banks today engage in a wide range of businesses, including retail and wholesale banking, investment banking, and asset management.

In the view of some academics, managers, and regulators, the size, complexity, and lack of transparency of universal banks in the United States and Europe has led to undesirable systemic risks, among them that some banks have become "too big to fail."[1] During the 2008 credit crisis, the threat of collapse by some large universal banks led governments to bail out these institutions, triggering an ongoing debate about whether such institutions should be split into smaller and separate investment and commercial banks.[2] These concerns have continued even well after the financial crisis, and in 2023, the U.S. Acting Comptroller of the Currency acknowledged concern that some banks may be "too big to manage."[3]

This chapter provides a general overview of how to value banks and highlights some of the most common valuation challenges peculiar to the sector.

This chapter was co-authored by Alok Bothra and Zane Williams.

[1] See M. Egan, "Too-Big-to-Fail Banks Keep Getting Bigger," *CNNMoney*, November 21, 2017, money.cnn.com. Also see "Universal Banking: Together, Forever?" *The Economist*, August 12, 2012, www.economist.com.

[2] For analyses of the costs and benefits of large universal banks, see *Global Financial Stability Report 2014*, International Monetary Fund, April 2014, www.imf.org; and *Large Bank Holding Companies: Expectations of Government Support*, GAO-14-621, U.S. Government Accountability Office, July 2014, www.gao.gov.

[3] Acting Comptroller of the Currency Michael J. Hsu Remarks at Brookings Institution, "Detecting, Preventing, and Addressing Too Big to Manage," January 17, 2023, www.occ.gov.

After first discussing the economic fundamentals of banking and trends in performance and growth, we describe how to apply the equity cash flow approach for valuing banks, using a hypothetical, simplified example. We conclude by offering some practical recommendations for valuing universal banks in all their real-world complexity.

ECONOMICS OF BANKING

After years of strong profitability and growth in the U.S. and European banking sectors, the crisis in the mortgage-backed securities market in 2007 sent many large banks spiraling into financial distress. Many large institutions on both sides of the Atlantic went bankrupt or were kept afloat only with costly government bailouts. The fallout in the real economy from what was originally a crisis in the banking sector ultimately brought economic growth to a halt worldwide in 2008.

Since then, the sector has gone through years of restructuring, involving mergers, government bailouts, nationalizations, and bankruptcies. Regulation has intensified, leading to stricter capital requirements, restrictions on trading operations, and—in some European countries—caps on bonus payments for bank employees and executives. By 2018, banks in the United States were seeing stronger economic growth domestically, rebounding loan demand, and a reduction in bad debts—all of which allowed them to regain and even surpass their pre-crisis profit levels. In contrast, many European banks, even today, are still below their pre-crisis profit levels, mainly due to lower economic growth across the European Union and the 2010 euro sovereign-debt crisis. In addition, the sector has had returns on equity (ROEs) below the cost of equity for most of the period from 2008 to 2023, resulting in negative economic profit during that time. Only with rate increases in 2022 did ROEs rise above the cost of equity.[4]

The credit crisis demonstrates the extent to which the banking industry is both a critical and a vulnerable component of modern economies. Banks are vulnerable because they are highly leveraged and their funding depends on investor and customer confidence. This can disappear overnight, sending a bank plummeting into failure (as happened with Silicon Valley Bank and First Republic in 2023). As a result, more uncertainty surrounds the valuation of banks than the valuation of most industrial companies. Therefore, it is all the more important for anyone valuing a bank to understand the business activities undertaken by banks, the ways in which banks create value, and the drivers of that value creation.

Universal banks may engage in any or all of a wide variety of business activities, including lending and borrowing, underwriting and placement

---

[4] For more, see "Global Banking Annual Review 2024: Attaining escape velocity," McKinsey & Company, October 17, 2024, www.mckinsey.com.

of securities, payment services, asset management, proprietary trading, and brokerage. For the purpose of financial analysis and valuation, we group these activities according to the three types of income they generate for a bank: net interest income, fee and commission income, and trading income. "Other income" forms a fourth and generally smaller residual category of income from activities unrelated to the main banking businesses.

Net Interest Income

In their traditional role, banks act as intermediaries between customers or investors with excess cash and customers with cash deficits. They attract funds in the form of customer deposits and debt to provide funds to customers in the form of mortgages, credit card loans, and corporate loans. The difference between the interest income a bank earns from lending and the interest expense it pays to borrow funds is its net interest income. For the regional retail banks in the United States and retail-focused universal banks such as ING Group, net interest income is typically the biggest component of total net revenues.

As we discuss later in this chapter, it is important to understand that not all of a bank's net interest income creates value. Most banks have a maturity mismatch as a result of using short-term deposits as funding to back long-term loans and mortgages. In this case, the bank earns income from holding positions on different parts of the yield curve. Typically, deposits are a low-cost and predictable form of funding, so borrowing for the short term costs a bank less than what it can earn from long-term lending.

The presence of deposit insurance makes deposits both lower-cost (since they are risk free to the depositor) and stickier than other forms of financing. In essence, the industry is a beneficiary of an indirect government subsidy that lowers their borrowing costs.

Fee and Commission Income

For services such as transaction advisory, underwriting and placement of securities, managing investment assets, and securities brokerage, banks typically charge their customers a fee or commission. For investment banks (such as Morgan Stanley and Goldman Sachs), such commissions and fees typically make up around half of total net revenues and around one-third or more for universal banks with large investment-banking activities (among them HSBC and Bank of America). Fee income is usually easier to understand than net interest income, as it is independent of financing. However, some forms of fee income are highly cyclical, such as fees from underwriting and transaction advisory services. In addition, many of the activities that generate fee income require less capital than lending, resulting in much higher ROEs for fee-based businesses.

Trading Income

Proprietary trading is a third, albeit smaller category of income for the banking sector as a whole. This can involve not only a wide variety of instruments traded on exchanges and over the counter, such as equity stocks, bonds, and foreign exchange, but also more exotic products, such as credit default swaps and asset-backed debt obligations, traded mostly over the counter.

Trading profits tend to be highly volatile: gains made over several years may be wiped out by large losses in a single year, as the credit crisis painfully illustrated. These activities have also attracted considerable attention in the wake of the crisis. In 2010, the United States adopted legislation preventing banks from engaging in proprietary trading for their own profit.[5] This resulted in steeply lower overall trading income, as the law permits only trading related to serving the bank's customers, including market-making activities. In Europe, restrictions on trading activities also were adopted—for example, through the 2017 Markets in Financial Instruments Directive II (MiFID II). Trading income for European banks has sharply declined since 2008.

Other Income

Some banks also generate income from a range of nonbanking activities, including real estate development, minority investments in industrial companies, and distribution of investment, insurance, and pension products and services for third parties. Typically, these activities make only small contributions to overall income and are unrelated to the bank's main banking activities.

As Exhibit 43.1 shows, the relative importance of these four income sources has changed radically for the European banking sector over past decades. During the 1990s, European banks shifted away from interest income and toward commission and trading income. However, trading income collapsed during the credit crisis. Despite recovering somewhat since then, it has not regained pre-crisis levels.

As the banks have shifted their sources of income, the cyclicality of their profitability and market valuations has increased. This is measured by their return on equity and their market-to-book ratios (see Exhibit 43.2). These measures for the sector in both the United States and Europe rose sharply after 1995 to reach historic peaks in 2006. But they fell sharply during the credit crisis, with European banks suffering a second decline during the 2010 euro bond crisis. In 2024, profitability and valuation levels remained well below their peak levels on

---

[5] The 2010 Dodd-Frank Wall Street Reform and Consumer Protection Act aimed to improve the stability of the U.S. financial system through increased regulation and supervision. For example, it established restrictions on proprietary trading by banks through the so-called Volcker Rule and new government agencies such as the Financial Stability Oversight Council.

EXHIBIT 43.1 **Income Sources for European Banks, 1988–2022**

Income streams/total net revenues,[1] %

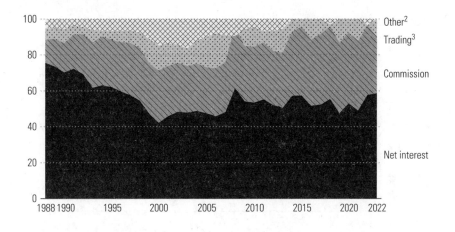

[1] For 1988–2007, based on a sample of 113 EU banks, of which 109 were active in 2007. For 2008–2013, based on a sample of 211 EU banks active in 2013. For 2014–2023, based on a sample of largest 80 EU banks in 2014.

[2] Other income was negative from 2014 to 2017; 2019 to 2021 and 2023.

[3] Trading income was –9% in 2008.

Source: Bloomberg; Compustat; Datastream, S&P Capital IQ.

both sides of the Atlantic, though American banks were much more successful than their European counterparts in regaining some ground.

BANK BALANCE SHEETS

A bank's balance sheet summarizes its financial position: assets include cash, loans, securities, and property, while liabilities consist of deposits, borrowings, and other obligations. Shareholders' equity reflects the bank's net worth. Asset-liability management (ALM) strategies aim to manage the mismatch between the timing and nature of assets and liabilities, mitigating risks and enhancing the bank's ability to meet its obligations. Regulatory requirements govern the composition and quality of assets and liabilities, ensuring financial stability. Overall, effective management of assets and liabilities is crucial for a bank's stability and profitability.

Loans and Advances

Lending is at the core of banking. Banks provide credit to borrowers in exchange for interest payments and the repayment of principal. Typically, consumer loans offer higher interest yields than commercial loans, as the former are usually uncollateralized.

EXHIBIT 43.2 **Increased Cyclicality in Banking**

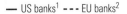

— US banks[1] --- EU banks[2]

Market value of equity/book value of equity

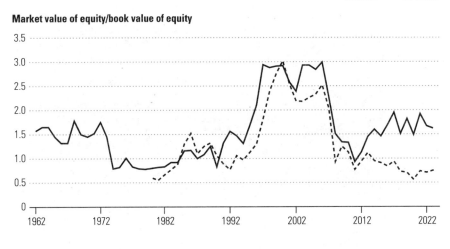

Return on equity, %

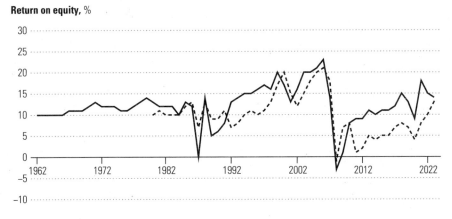

[1] U.S. banks: For 1962–2007, based on aggregate financials and valuation of 957 U.S. banks, of which 346 were active in 2007. For 2006–2013, based on a sample of 509 U.S. banks active in 2013. For 2014–2023, based on a sample of largest 156 US banks in 2014. Book value excludes goodwill.

[2] EU banks For 1988–2007, based on aggregate financials and valuation of 113 EU banks, of which 109 were active in 2007. For 2008–2013, based on a sample of 211 EU banks active in 2013. For 2014–2023, based on a sample of largest 80 EU banks in 2014. Book value excludes goodwill.

Source: Bloomberg; Compustat; Datastream; S&P Capital IQ.

Banks are mandated to establish accounting reserves to cover potential losses from loans that may not be fully repaid. The current expected credit loss (CECL) standard introduced by the Financial Accounting Standards Board (FASB) after the 2008 financial crisis requires banks to estimate expected credit losses over the life span of a loan portfolio, rather than waiting for losses to be realized before acknowledging them. Nonperforming loans (NPLs) denote loans that are either in default or nearing default, usually characterized by a failure to meet scheduled payments for a specified period, often 90 days or more. The total amount of the reserve is reported as an offset to the total loans on the asset side of the balance sheet.

Central Bank Reserves

Banks maintain central bank reserves—funds held in accounts with central banks—for various purposes. These include meeting reserve requirements, facilitating settlements and clearing between banks, and managing liquidity. Such balances ensure efficient payments, regulatory compliance, effective liquidity management, and access to central bank facilities when needed.

Securities and Trading Assets

Investment securities are financial assets held by banks for long-term returns, including bonds and equities. Trading assets are primarily held for market-making activities and to facilitate transactions on behalf of customers. Investment securities provide interest income and portfolio diversification, while trading assets capitalize on market fluctuations for immediate gains. Both contribute to the bank's investment portfolio and income strategies, managed differently due to varying regulatory requirements and accounting treatments.

Risk-Weighted Assets and Equity Risk Capital

Banks are required to hold a minimum level of equity capital that can absorb potential losses to safeguard the bank's obligations to its customers and financiers. In December 2010, new regulatory requirements for capital adequacy were specified in the Basel III guidelines, replacing the 2007 Basel II accords, which were no longer considered adequate in the wake of the 2008 and 2010 financial crises.[6] Banks across the world have been gradually implementing the new guidelines since 2013.

Basel III specifies rules for banks regarding how much equity capital they must hold, based on the bank's so-called risk-weighted assets (RWA).[7] The level of RWA is driven by the riskiness of a bank's asset portfolio and its trading book. Banks have some flexibility to choose either internal risk models or standardized Basel approaches to estimate their RWA. All such models rest on the general principle that the total RWA is the sum of separate RWA estimates for credit risk, market risk, and operational risk. However, banks do not publish the risk models they use. If you are conducting an outside-in valuation, you need an approximation of a bank's future equity risk capital needs. Because banks typically provide information on total RWA but not on

---

[6] The Basel accords are recommendations on laws and regulations for banking and are issued by the Basel Committee on Banking Supervision (BCBS).

[7] In addition, Basel III sets requirements for liquidity and restrictions on leverage in the form of a minimum liquidity coverage ratio (LCR), net stable funding ratio (NSFR), and threshold leverage ratio (LR). We focus here on capital adequacy, as that is typically the most critical requirement to take into account when valuing a bank.

the risk weighting for their asset groups, trading book, and operations, you must approximate the key categories' contribution to total RWA for the bank in order to project RWA and risk capital for future years.[8]

Basel III defines requirements for the bank's so-called common-equity Tier 1 (CET1), additional Tier 1, and Tier 2 capital levels, relative to RWA. Of these capital ratios, CET1 to RWA is typically the most stringent. The total minimum CET1 requirements for a bank consist of different layers that add up to a total of 8.0 to 10.5 percent of RWA:

Basel III CET1 capital requirements

% of risk-weighted assets	
Legal minimum	4.5
Capital conservation buffer	2.5
G-SIB countercyclical buffer	1.0–3.5
Total	8.0–10.5

The first 4.5 percent is the so-called legal minimum that applies to any bank in any given year. The second layer of 2.5 percent is the capital conservation buffer, which can be drawn down in years of losses and then rebuilt in profitable years. The third, or countercyclical, layer can be up to 3.5 percent of RWA but applies only to so-called global systemically important banks (G-SIBs). These banks are identified by the Financial Stability Board (FSB) as sources of systemic risk to the international financial system because of their size and complexity.[9] In November of each year, the FSB publishes the additional capital charge for each G-SIB, which depends on the FSB's assessment of the risk that the bank represents. Among these largest global banks, JPMorgan Chase faced a surcharge of 2.5 percent in 2023, while Citigroup, Bank of America, and HSBC were assigned a surcharge of 2.0 percent. For other G-SIBs, such as ING Bank, Bank of New York, and Morgan Stanley, the surcharge amounted to 1.0 percent.[10]

Many of the larger banks nowadays already target CET1 at around 13 percent of RWA or higher, reflecting not only stricter regulations but also increased investor requirements. According to the Bank for International Settlements (BIS), the worldwide average CET1 for large international banks was at 12.9 percent of RWA in June 2023, well above the 2013 level of 9.5 percent.[11]

---

[8] Without RWA estimates by business line, you could only project the bank's risk capital for a scenario in which all business lines grow at the same rate.

[9] The FSB is an international body monitoring the stability of the international financial system. It was established by the G20 Leaders' Summit of April 2009.

[10] "2023 List of Global Systemically Important Banks (G-SIBs)," Financial Stability Board, November 27, 2023, www.fsb.org.

[11] *Basel III Monitoring Report*, Bank for International Settlements, March 2019, p. 2 (available at www .bis.org).

Using your RWA forecasts and the targeted CET1 ratio, you can estimate the required Tier 1 capital in each future year. From the projected CET1 capital requirements, you can estimate the implied shareholders' equity requirements by applying an average historical ratio of CET1 capital to shareholders' equity excluding goodwill and deferred-tax assets. Historical Tier 1 capital is reported separately in the notes to the bank's financial statements and is typically close to straightforward shareholders' equity excluding goodwill and deferred-tax assets.

Deposits

Deposits serve as a primary source of funding for banks. When customers deposit money into their accounts, banks can use these funds to extend loans to borrowers. Typically, deposits are a low-cost and predictable form of funding, so borrowing for the short term costs a bank less than what it can earn from long-term lending. Cost of deposits drives the interest expense incurred by the bank and ultimately banking profitability and valuation. Lower-cost deposits, such as demand deposits and savings accounts, typically have lower interest rates, reducing the bank's interest expense and improving profitability. Banks carefully manage their deposit mix and pricing strategies to optimize profitability. Examples of banks that have managed to keep their cost of funds low include Regions and M&T. For U.S. banks, typically 75 percent of their funding is from customer deposits.

Banks need to manage their liquidity effectively to meet withdrawal demands from depositors while also funding new loan opportunities. Banks maintain a portion of their assets in highly liquid investments, such as cash reserves, short-term securities, and liquid assets to meet unexpected deposit withdrawals. Deposits generally tend to be short-term in nature while loans have longer-term maturities; banks aim to effectively manage the maturity mismatch between deposits and loans through ALM techniques to match the maturity profiles of their assets (loans) and liabilities (deposits). This involves monitoring and adjusting the duration and maturity of assets and liabilities to manage the maturity gap and reduce liquidity and interest rate risks. Maintaining an appropriate balance between deposits and loans is essential for ensuring liquidity and financial stability.

Both the subprime crisis in 2008 and the deposit crisis in 2023 were linked to a decrease in the value of underlying assets. In 2008, the subprime crisis stemmed from the collapse of mortgage-backed securities, which were tied to subprime mortgages. When the housing bubble burst, the value of these assets plummeted, causing widespread financial turmoil. Similarly, in 2023, the deposit crisis occurred when the value of investment securities held by financial institutions declined due to rising interest rates, leading to a loss of confidence among depositors and a run on banks. In both cases, the erosion of asset values triggered systemic instability and financial distress.

The loan-to-deposit ratio is a key indicator of a bank's lending activity relative to its deposit base. A high ratio suggests the bank is using a significant portion of deposits for lending, potentially posing liquidity challenges if depositors withdraw funds unexpectedly or if loan repayments are not received as anticipated. Conversely, a low ratio may indicate excess liquidity, suggesting underutilization of deposit funds for lending purposes.

Wholesale Funding

Wholesale funding allows banks to diversify their funding base beyond traditional retail deposits. This diversification reduces dependency on a single funding source and enhances the bank's ability to access a broader pool of capital markets and institutional investors. Wholesale funding provides banks with additional liquidity to support lending activities and meet short-term funding needs. It offers flexibility in managing liquidity by providing access to funds on shorter notice compared with longer-term retail deposits, which may be subject to withdrawal restrictions. However, this source of funding tends to be 300–400 basis points more expensive than cost of deposits. U.S. banks, on average, receive about 25 percent of their funding from wholesale funding sources.

PRINCIPLES OF BANK VALUATION

Throughout most of this book, we apply the enterprise discounted-cash-flow (DCF) approach to valuation. Discounting free cash flows is the appropriate approach for nonfinancial companies, where operating decisions and financing decisions are separate. For banks, however, we cannot value operations separately from interest income and expense, since these are the main categories of a bank's core operations. It is necessary to value the cash flow to equity, which includes both the operational and financial cash flows. For valuation of banks, we therefore recommend the equity DCF method.[12]

To understand the principles of the equity DCF method, let's explore a stylized example of a retail bank. ABC Bank attracts customer deposits to provide funds for loans and mortgages to other customers. ABC's historical balance sheet, income statement, and key financial indicators are shown in Exhibit 43.3.

At of the end of 2024, the bank has $1.173 billion of loans outstanding with customers, generating 6.5 percent interest income. To meet regulatory requirements, ABC must maintain an 8 percent ratio of Tier 1 equity capital to loan assets, which we define for this example as the ratio of equity divided by total assets. This means that 8 percent, or $94 million, of its loans are funded by equity capital, and the rest of the loans are funded by $1.079 billion of deposits. The deposits carry 4.3 percent interest, generating total interest expenses of $45 million.

[12] See Chapter 10 for a comparison of the enterprise and equity DCF methods.

EXHIBIT 43.3 **ABC Bank: Historical Financial Statements**

$ million

	2020	2021	2022	2023	2024
Balance sheet[1]					
Loans	1,030.0	1,063.5	1,097.5	1,133.7	1,173.4
Total assets	1,030.0	1,063.5	1,097.5	1,133.7	1,173.4
Deposits	988.8	999.7	1,009.7	1,043.0	1,079.5
Equity	41.2	63.8	87.8	90.7	93.9
Total liabilities	1,030.0	1,063.5	1,097.5	1,133.7	1,173.4
Income statement					
Interest income	70.0	72.1	74.4	71.3	73.7
Interest expense	(48.0)	(47.5)	(47.0)	(45.4)	(44.9)
Net interest income	22.0	24.6	27.5	25.9	28.8
Operating expenses	(11.2)	(13.1)	(14.3)	(12.2)	(13.0)
Operating profit before taxes	10.8	11.6	13.2	13.7	15.9
Income taxes	(3.2)	(3.5)	(4.0)	(4.1)	(4.8)
Net income	7.5	8.1	9.2	9.6	11.1
Key ratios, %					
Loan growth	3.0	3.3	3.2	3.3	3.5
Loan interest rate	7.0	7.0	7.0	6.5	6.5
Deposit growth	3.0	1.1	1.0	3.3	3.5
Deposit interest rate	5.0	4.8	4.7	4.5	4.3
Cost/income	51.0	53.0	52.0	47.0	45.0
Tax rate	30.0	30.0	30.0	30.0	30.0
Equity/total assets	4.0	6.0	8.0	8.0	8.0
Return on equity[2]	18.9	19.7	14.5	10.9	12.2

[1] Book value per end of year.
[2] Return on beginning-of-year equity.

Net interest income for ABC amounted to $29 million in 2024, thanks to the higher rates received on loans than paid on deposits. All capital gains or losses on loans and deposits are included in interest income and expenses. Operating expenses such as labor and rental costs are $13 million, which brings ABC's cost-to-income ratio to 45 percent of net interest income. After subtracting taxes at 30 percent, net income equals $11 million, which translates into a return on equity of 12.2 percent.

As discussed in Chapter 10, the equity value of a company equals the present value of its future cash flow to equity (CFE), discounted at the cost of equity, k_e:

$$V_e = \sum_{t=1}^{\infty} \frac{\mathrm{CFE}_t}{(1 + k_e)^t}$$

We can derive equity cash flow from two starting points. First, equity cash flow equals net income minus the earnings retained in the business:

$$CFE_t = NI_t - \Delta E_t + OCI_t$$

where CFE is equity cash flow, NI is net income, ΔE is the increase in the book value of equity, and OCI is noncash other comprehensive income.

Net income represents the earnings theoretically available to shareholders after payment of all expenses, including those to depositors and debt holders. However, net income by itself is not cash flow. As a bank grows, it will need to increase its equity; otherwise, its ratio of debt plus deposits over equity would rise, which might cause regulators and customers to worry about the bank's solvency. Increases in equity reduce equity cash flow, because the bank setting aside earnings that could otherwise be paid out to shareholders. The last step in calculating equity cash flow is to add noncash other comprehensive income, such as net unrealized gains and losses on certain equity and debt investments, hedging activities, adjustments to the minimum pension liability, and foreign-currency translation items. This cancels out any noncash adjustment to equity.[13]

Exhibit 43.4 shows the equity cash flow calculation for ABC Bank. Note that in 2020, ABC's other comprehensive income included a translation gain on its overseas loan business, which was discontinued in the same year. ABC's cash flow to equity was negative in 2021 and 2022 because it raised new equity to lift its Tier 1 ratio from 4 percent to 8 percent.

Another way to calculate equity cash flow is to sum all cash paid to or received from shareholders, including cash changing hands as dividends, through share repurchases, and through new share issuances. Both calculations arrive at the same result. Note that equity cash flow is not the same as dividends paid out to shareholders, because share buybacks and issuance can also form a significant part of cash flow to and from equity.

EXHIBIT 43.4 **ABC Bank: Historical Cash Flow to Equity**

$ million

	2020	2021	2022	2023	2024
Cash flow statement					
Net income	7.5	8.1	9.2	9.6	11.1
(Increase) Decrease in equity	(1.2)	(22.6)	(24.0)	(2.9)	(3.2)
Other comprehensive income (loss)	0.2	—	—	—	—
Cash flow to equity	6.5	(14.5)	(14.8)	6.7	7.9

[13] Of course, you can also calculate equity cash flow from the changes in all the balance sheet accounts. For example, equity cash flow for a bank equals net income plus the increase in deposits and reserves, less the increase in loans and investments, and so on.

Analyzing and Forecasting Equity Cash Flows

The generic value driver tree for a retail bank, shown in Exhibit 43.5, is conceptually the same as one for an industrial company. Following the tree's branches, we analyze ABC's historical performance as laid out in Exhibit 43.3.

Over the five years analyzed, ABC's loan portfolio has grown by around 3.0 to 3.5 percent annually. Since 2020, ABC's interest rates on loans have been declining from 7.0 percent to 6.5 percent in 2024, but this was offset by an even stronger decrease in rates on deposits from 5.0 percent to 4.3 percent over the same period. Combined with the growth in its loan portfolio, this lifted ABC's net interest income from $22 million in 2020 to $29 million in 2024. The bank also managed to improve its cost-to-income ratio significantly from a peak level of 53 percent in 2021 to 45 percent in 2024.

Higher regulatory requirements for equity risk capital forced ABC to double its Tier 1 ratio (equity to total assets) from 4 percent to 8 percent over the period. The combination of loan portfolio growth and stricter regulatory requirements has forced ABC to increase its equity capital by some $50 million since 2020. As a result, ABC's return on equity declined significantly in 2024 to 12 percent, from nearly 20 percent in 2021.

Exhibit 43.6 shows the financial forecasts for ABC Bank, assuming its loan portfolio growth rate increases to 4.5 percent in the short term and settles at 3.5 percent in perpetuity. Interest rates on loans and deposits are expected to decrease to 6.1 and 3.9 percent, respectively. Operating expenses will decline to 43 percent of net interest income. As a result, ABC's return on equity increases somewhat to 12.8 percent in 2026 and stays at that level in perpetuity.

EXHIBIT 43.5 **Generic Value Driver Tree for Retail Banking**

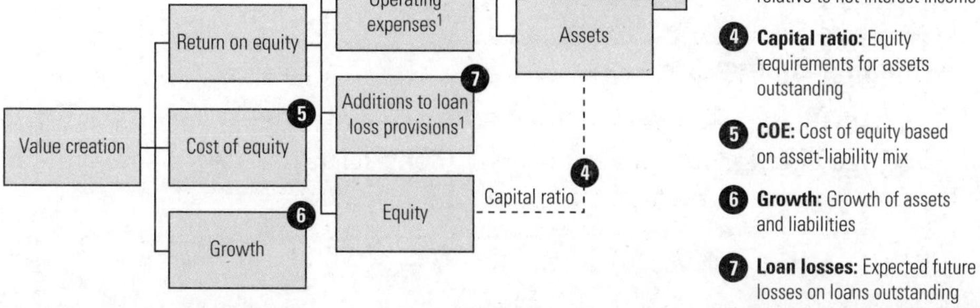

EXHIBIT 43.6 **ABC Bank: Financial Forecast**

$ million

	2025	2026	2027	2028	2029	2030
Balance sheet[1]						
Loans	1,226.2	1,281.4	1,332.6	1,379.3	1,427.6	1,477.5
Total assets	1,226.2	1,281.4	1,332.6	1,379.3	1,427.6	1,477.5
Deposits	1,128.1	1,178.9	1,226.0	1,268.9	1,313.4	1,359.3
Equity	98.1	102.5	106.6	110.3	114.2	118.2
Total liabilities	1,226.2	1,281.4	1,332.6	1,379.3	1,427.6	1,477.5
Income statement						
Interest income	71.6	74.8	78.2	81.3	84.1	87.1
Interest expense	(41.6)	(43.4)	(45.4)	(47.2)	(48.9)	(50.6)
Net interest income	30.0	31.4	32.8	34.1	35.3	36.5
Operating expenses	(13.5)	(13.5)	(14.1)	(14.7)	(15.2)	(15.7)
Operating profit before taxes	16.5	17.9	18.7	19.4	20.1	20.8
Income taxes	(5.0)	(5.4)	(5.6)	(5.8)	(6.0)	(6.2)
Net income	11.6	12.5	13.1	13.6	14.1	14.6
Cash flow statement						
Net income	11.6	12.5	13.1	13.6	14.1	14.6
(Increase) decrease in equity	(4.2)	(4.4)	(4.1)	(3.7)	(3.9)	(4.0)
Other comprehensive (income) loss	—	—	—	—	—	—
Cash flow to equity	7.3	8.1	9.0	9.9	10.2	10.6
Key ratios, %						
Loan growth	4.5	4.5	4.0	3.5	3.5	3.5
Loan interest rate	6.1	6.1	6.1	6.1	6.1	6.1
Deposit growth	4.5	4.5	4.0	3.5	3.5	3.5
Deposit interest rate	3.9	3.9	3.9	3.9	3.9	3.9
Cost/income	45.0	43.0	43.0	43.0	43.0	43.0
Tax rate	30.0	30.0	30.0	30.0	30.0	30.0
Equity/total assets	8.0	8.0	8.0	8.0	8.0	8.0
Return on equity[2]	12.3	12.8	12.8	12.8	12.8	12.8

[1] Book value per end of year.
[2] Return on beginning-of-year equity.

Discounting Equity Cash Flows

To estimate the cost of equity, k_e, for ABC Bank, we use a beta of 1.1 (based on the average beta for its banking peers), a long-term risk-free interest rate of 4.5 percent, and a market risk premium of 5 percent[14]:

$$k_e = r_f + (\beta \times \text{MRP}) = 4.5\% + (1.1 \times 5.0\%) = 10.0\%$$

[14] See Chapter 15 for more details on estimating the cost of capital.

where r_f is the risk-free rate, β is the equity beta, and MRP is the market risk premium. (There is no need to adjust any estimates of equity betas of banking peers for leverage when deriving ABC's equity beta, assuming that banking peers have similar target capital ratios.)

For the continuing value in the equity DCF approach, we use an adapted version of the value driver formula presented in Chapter 3, replacing return on invested capital (ROIC) and return on new invested capital (RONIC) with return on equity (ROE) and return on new equity investments (RONE), and replacing net operating profit after taxes (NOPAT) with net income[15]:

$$CV_t = \frac{NI_{t+1}\left(1 - \frac{g}{RONE}\right)}{k_e - g}$$

where CV_t is the continuing value as of year t, NI_{t+1} is the net income in year $t + 1$, g equals growth, and k_e is the cost of equity.

Assuming ABC Bank continues to generate a 12.8 percent ROE on its new business investments in perpetuity while growing at 3.5 percent per year,[16] its continuing value as of 2030 is as follows:

$$CV = \frac{\$15.1 \ \text{million}\left(1 - \frac{3.5\%}{12.8\%}\right)}{10.0\% - 3.5\%} = \$168.4 \ \text{million}$$

The calculation of the discounted value of ABC's cash flow to equity is presented in Exhibit 43.7. The present value of ABC's equity amounts to $134.2 million, which implies a market-to-book ratio for its equity of 1.4 and a price-to-earnings ratio (P/E) of 11.6. As for industrial companies, whenever possible, you should triangulate your results with an analysis based on multiples (see Chapter 18). Note that the market-to-book ratio indicates that ABC is creating value over its book value of equity, which is consistent with a long-term return on equity of 12.8 percent (which is above the cost of equity of 10.0 percent).

Pitfalls of Equity DCF Valuation

The equity DCF approach as illustrated here is straightforward and theoretically correct. However, the approach involves some potential pitfalls. These concern the sources of value creation, the impact of leverage and business risk on the cost of equity, and the tax penalty on holding equity risk capital.

---

[15] Net income may need to be adjusted for nonoperating items like amortization of acquired intangibles.
[16] If the return on new equity investments (RONE) equals the return on equity (ROE), the formula can be simplified as follows:

$$CV_t = \frac{NI_{t+1}\left(1 - \frac{g}{ROE}\right)}{k_e - g} = E_t\left(\frac{ROE - g}{k_e - g}\right)$$

where E is the book value of equity.

EXHIBIT 43.7 **ABC Bank: Valuation**

$ million

	Cash flow to equity (CFE)	Discount factor	Present value of CFE
2025	7.3	0.909	6.7
2026	8.1	0.826	6.7
2027	9.0	0.751	6.7
2028	9.9	0.683	6.7
2029	10.2	0.621	6.3
2030	10.6	0.564	6.0
Continuing value	168.4	0.564	95.0
Value of equity			134.2
Market-to-book ratio			1.4
P/E ratio[1]			11.6

[1] Forward price-to-earnings ratio on 2020 net income.

Impact of Leverage and Business Risk on Cost of Equity   As with industrial companies, the cost of equity for a bank such as ABC should reflect its business risk and leverage. Its equity beta is a weighted average of the betas of all its loan and deposit businesses. So when you project significant changes in a bank's asset or liability composition or equity capital ratios, you cannot leave the cost of equity unchanged.

For instance, if ABC were to decrease its equity capital ratio, its expected return on equity would go up. But in the absence of taxes, this by itself should not increase the intrinsic equity value, because ABC's cost of equity would also rise, as its cash flows would now be riskier. It will increase ABC's value only to the extent that the bank is creating value on the deposit business that it is growing as a result of the leverage increase (see the next section, on economic-spread analysis).[17]

The same line of reasoning holds for changes in the asset or liability mix. Assume ABC raises an additional $50 million in equity and invests this in government bonds at the risk-free rate of 4.5 percent, reducing future returns on equity. If you left ABC's cost of equity unchanged at 10.0 percent, the estimated equity value per share would decline. But in the absence of taxation, the risk-free investment cannot be value-destroying, because its expected return exactly equals the cost of capital for risk-free assets. There is no impact on value creation if we assume that the bank has no competitive (dis)advantage in investing in government bonds. The assumption seems reasonable, as it

[17] Note that leverage has a different impact on the value of banks than on the value of industrial companies. An industrial company's value is not affected by leverage in the absence of corporate income taxes, because it is assumed that there is no value creation in the issuance of corporate debt raised at market rates (see Chapter 10).

implies that the bank does not obtain the government bonds at a premium or discount to their fair market value. As a result, if you accounted properly for the impact of the change in its asset mix on the cost of equity and the resulting reduction in the beta of its business, ABC's equity value would remain unchanged.

Tax Penalty on Holding Equity Risk Capital Holding equity risk capital represents a cost for banks, and it is important to understand what drives this cost. Consider again the example of ABC Bank issuing new equity and investing in risk-free assets, thereby increasing its equity risk capital. In the absence of taxation, this extra layer of risk capital would have no impact on value, and there would be no cost to holding it. But interest income *is* taxed, and that is what makes holding equity risk capital costly; equity, unlike debt or deposits, provides no tax shield. In this example, ABC will pay taxes on the risk-free interest income from the $50 million of risk-free bonds that cannot be offset by tax shields on interest charges on deposits or debt, because the investment was funded with equity, for which there are no tax-deductible interest charges.

The true cost of holding equity capital is this so-called tax penalty, the present value of which equals the equity capital times the tax rate. If ABC Bank were to increase its equity capital by $50 million to invest in risk-free bonds, holding everything else constant, this would effectively destroy $15 million of present value (30 percent times $50 million) because of the tax penalty. As long as the cost of equity reflects the bank's leverage and business risk, the tax penalty is implicitly included in the equity DCF.[18]

COMPLICATIONS IN BANK VALUATIONS

When you value banks, significant challenges arise in addition to those discussed in the hypothetical ABC Bank example. In reality, banks have many interest-generating business lines, including credit card loans, mortgage loans, and corporate loans, all involving loans of varying maturities. On the liability side, banks could carry a variety of customer deposits as well as different forms of straight and hybrid debt. Banks need to invest in working capital and in property, plant, and equipment, although the amounts are typically small fractions of total assets. Obviously, this variety makes the analysis of real-world banks more complex, but the principles laid out in the ABC example remain generally applicable. This section discusses some practical challenges in the analysis and valuation of banks.

[18] Note that the taxes on the matched capital and the maturity mismatch are included as charges in the economic spread.

Loan Loss Provisions

For our ABC Bank valuation, we did not model any losses from defaults on loans outstanding to customers. In real life, your analysis and valuation must include loan loss forecasts, because loan losses are among the most important factors determining the value of retail and wholesale banking activities. For estimating expected loan losses from defaults across different loan categories, a useful first indicator would be a bank's historical additions to loan loss provisions or sector-wide estimates of loan losses (see Exhibit 43.8). As the exhibit shows, these losses increased sharply during the 2008 credit crisis but recovered to pre-crisis levels by 2013. Credit cards typically have the highest losses, and mortgages the lowest, with business loans somewhere in between. All default losses are strongly correlated with overall economic growth, so use through-the-economic-cycle estimates of additions to arrive at future annual loan loss rates to apply to your forecasts of equity cash flows.

To project the future interest income from a bank's loans, deduct the estimated future loan loss rates from the future interest rates on loans for each year. You should also review the quality of the bank's current loan portfolio to assess whether it is under- or overprovisioned for loan losses. Any required increase in the loan loss provision translates into less equity value.

Value Drivers for Different Banking Activities

Given that many banks have portfolios of different business activities, ranging in some cases all the way from consumer credit card loans to proprietary trading, their businesses can have very distinct risks and returns, making the

EXHIBIT 43.8 **Annual Losses for U.S. Banks by Loan Category**

Write-off charges as % of loans outstanding

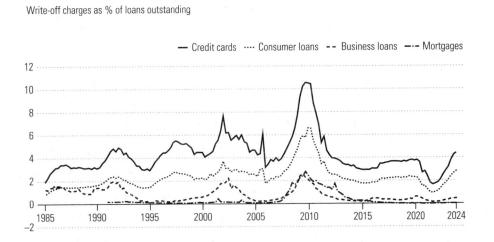

Source: Federal Reserve, "Charge Off and Delinquency Rates on Loans and Leases at Commercial Banks." www.federalreserve.gov.

bank's consolidated financial results difficult to interpret, let alone forecast. The businesses are best valued separately, as in the case of multibusiness companies, discussed in Chapter 19. Unfortunately, financial statements for multibusiness banks often lack separately reported income statements and balance sheets for different business activities. When that is the case, you must construct separate statements following the guidelines described in Chapter 19.

Interest-Generating Activities   Retail banking, credit card services, and whole-sale lending generate interest income from large asset positions and risk capital. These interest-generating activities can be analyzed using the economic-spread approach and valued using the equity DCF model, as discussed for ABC Bank in the previous section.

Trading Activities   Like a bank's interest-generating activities, its trading activities also generate income from large asset positions and significant risk capital. However, trading incomes tend to be far more volatile than interest incomes. Although peak income can be very high, the average trading income across the cycle generally turns out to be limited. The key value drivers are shown in Exhibit 43.9, a simplified value driver tree for trading activities.

You can think of a bank's trading results as driven by the size of its trading positions, the risk taken in trading (as measured by the total value at risk, or VaR), and the trading result per unit of risk (measured by return on VaR). The ratio of

EXHIBIT 43.9 **Value Drivers: Trading Activities**

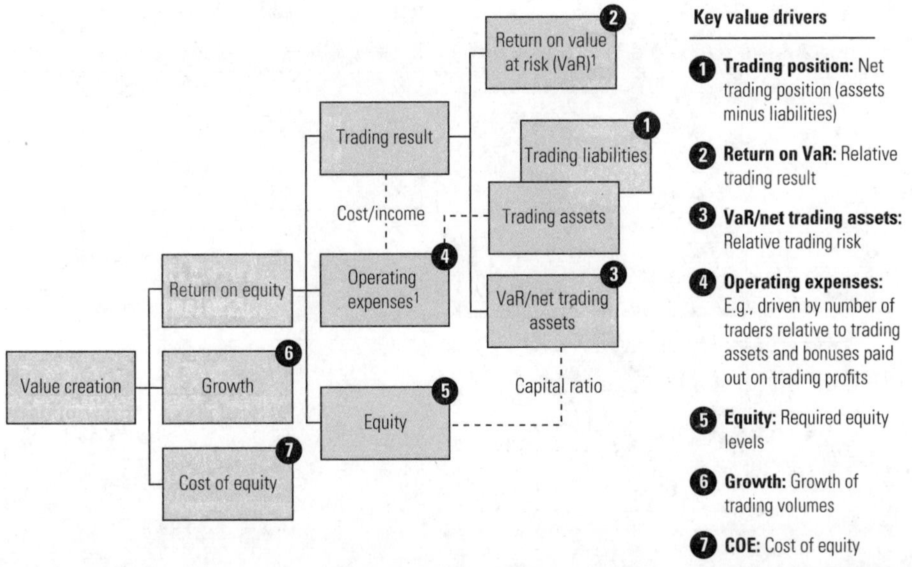

VaR to net trading position is an indication of the relative risk taking in trading. The more risk a bank takes in trading, the higher the expected trading return should be, as well as the required risk capital. The required equity risk capital for the trading activities follows from the VaR (and RWA), as discussed earlier in the chapter. Operating expenses, which include information technology (IT) infrastructure, back-office costs, and employee compensation, are partly related to the size of positions (or number of transactions) and partly related to trading results (for example, employee bonuses).

Fee- and Commission-Generating Activities   A bank's fee- and commission-generating activities, such as brokerage, transaction advisory, and asset management services, have different economics, based on limited asset positions and minimal risk capital. The value drivers in asset management, for example, are very different from those in the interest-generating businesses, as the generic example in Exhibit 43.10 shows. Key drivers are the growth of assets under management and the fees earned on those assets, such as management fees related to the amount of assets under management and performance fees related to the returns achieved on those assets.

Along with these variables in activities, remember that banks are highly leveraged and that many of their businesses are cyclical. When performing a bank valuation, you should not rely on point estimates but should use scenarios for future financial performance to understand the range of possible outcomes and the key underlying value drivers.

EXHIBIT 43.10 **Value Drivers: Asset Management**

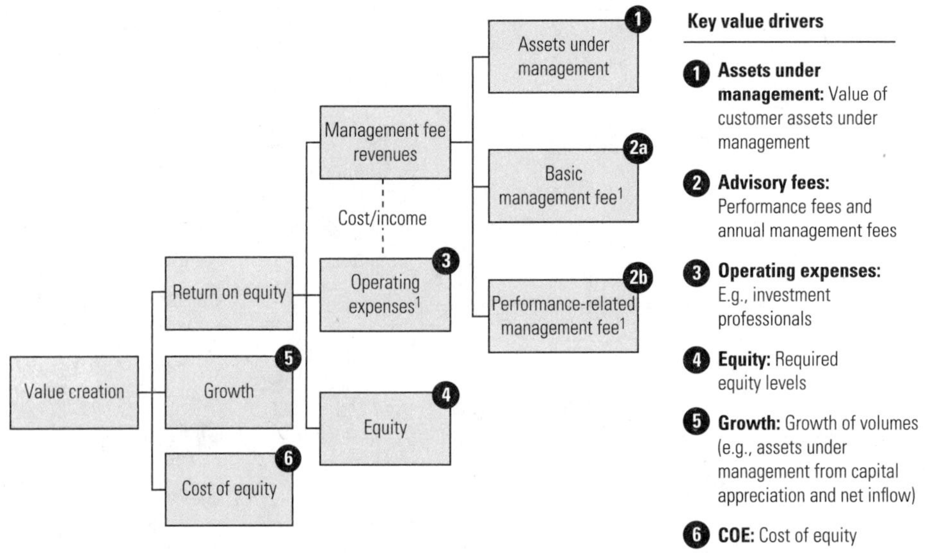

Key value drivers

1 **Assets under management:** Value of customer assets under management

2 **Advisory fees:** Performance fees and annual management fees

3 **Operating expenses:** E.g., investment professionals

4 **Equity:** Required equity levels

5 **Growth:** Growth of volumes (e.g., assets under management from capital appreciation and net inflow)

6 **COE:** Cost of equity

[1] After taxes.

SUMMARY

The fundamentals of the discounted-cash-flow (DCF) approach laid out in this book apply equally to banks. The equity cash flow version of the DCF approach is most appropriate for valuing banks, because the operational and financial cash flows of these organizations cannot be separated, given that banks are expected to create value from funding as well as lending operations.

Valuing banks remains a delicate task because of the diversity of the business portfolio, the cyclicality of many bank businesses (especially trading and fee-based business), and high leverage. Because of the difference in underlying value drivers, it is best to value a bank by its key parts according to the source of income: interest-generating business, fee and commission business, and trading. When forecasting a bank's financials, handle the uncertainty surrounding the bank's future performance and growth by using scenarios that capture the cyclicality of its key businesses.

Discounted Economic Profit Equals Discounted Free Cash Flow

This appendix demonstrates algebraically the equivalence between discounted cash flow and discounted economic profit. In the first section, we convert the key value driver formula presented in Chapter 3 into a value driver formula based on economic profit. This formula is used in Chapter 10 to estimate continuing value in the economic-profit valuation. The second section of this appendix generalizes the proof to any set of cash flows.

PROOF USING PERPETUITIES

To convert the key value driver formula into an economic-profit-based formula, start with the growing cash flow perpetuity:

$$V = \frac{\text{FCF}_{t=1}}{\text{WACC} - g}$$

where
V = value of operations
$\text{FCF}_{t=1}$ = free cash flow in year 1
WACC = weighted average cost of capital
g = growth in NOPAT

In Chapter 3, we convert the growing perpetuity into the key value driver formula:

$$V = \frac{\text{NOPAT}_{t=1}\left(1 - \frac{g}{\text{RONIC}}\right)}{\text{WACC} - g}$$

where NOPAT$_{t=1}$ = net operating profit after taxes

RONIC = return on new invested capital

The key value driver formula can be rearranged further into a formula based on economic profit. We do this to demonstrate that discounted cash flow is equivalent to the book value of invested capital plus the present value of future economic profit.

To begin, start with the key value driver formula, and replace NOPAT with invested capital times return on invested capital (ROIC):

$$V = \frac{\text{Invested Capital}_0 \times \text{ROIC} \times \left(1 - \frac{g}{\text{RONIC}}\right)}{\text{WACC} - g}$$

If we assume that the return on new invested capital (RONIC) equals the return on existing invested capital (ROIC), it is possible to simplify the preceding equation by distributing ROIC in the numerator[1]:

$$V = \text{Invested Capital}_0 \left(\frac{\text{ROIC} - g}{\text{WACC} - g}\right)$$

To complete the transformation to economic profit, add and subtract WACC in the numerator:

$$V = \text{Invested Capital}_0 \left(\frac{\text{ROIC} - \text{WACC} + \text{WACC} - g}{\text{WACC} - g}\right)$$

Separate the fraction into two components, and then simplify:

$$V = \text{Invested Capital}_0 \left(\frac{\text{ROIC} - \text{WACC}}{\text{WACC} - g}\right) + \text{Invested Capital}_0 \left(\frac{\text{WACC} - g}{\text{WACC} - g}\right)$$

$$= \text{Invested Capital}_0 + \text{Invested Capital}_0 \left(\frac{\text{ROIC} - \text{WACC}}{\text{WACC} - g}\right)$$

---

[1] This equation highlights two requirements for using the key value driver formula: both WACC and ROIC must be greater than the rate of growth in cash flows. If WACC is less than the cash flow growth rate, cash flows grow faster than they can be discounted, and value approaches infinity. (Perpetuity-based formulas should never be used to value cash flows whose growth rates exceed WACC.) If ROIC is lower than the growth rate, cash flows are negative, producing a negative value. In actuality, this situation is unlikely; investors would not finance a company that is never expected to generate or enable positive cash flow.

Economic profit is defined as invested capital times the difference of ROIC minus WACC. Substituting this definition into the previous equation leads to our final equation:

$$V = \text{Invested Capital}_0 + \frac{\text{Economic Profit}_1}{\text{WACC} - g}$$

According to this formula, a company's operating value equals the book value of its invested capital plus the present value of all future economic profits. (The final term is a growing perpetuity of economic profits.) If future economic profits are expected to be zero, the intrinsic value of a company equals its book value. In addition, if future economic profits are expected to be less than zero, then enterprise value should trade at less than the book value of invested capital—an occurrence observed in practice.

GENERALIZED PROOF

The previous section limited our proof to a set of cash flows growing at a constant rate. This section generalizes the proof to any set of cash flows. To demonstrate equivalence, start by computing the present value of a periodic stream of cash flows:

$$V = \sum_{t=1}^{\infty} \frac{\text{FCF}_t}{(1 + \text{WACC})^t}$$

where V = value of operations

FCF_t = free cash flow in year t

WACC = weighted average cost of capital

To this value, add and subtract the cumulative sum of all current and future amounts of invested capital (IC):

$$V = \sum_{t=0}^{\infty} \frac{\text{IC}_t}{(1 + \text{WACC})^t} - \sum_{t=0}^{\infty} \frac{\text{IC}_t}{(1 + \text{WACC})^t} + \sum_{t=1}^{\infty} \frac{\text{FCF}_t}{(1 + \text{WACC})^t}$$

where IC_t = invested capital for year t.

Next, adjust the preceding equation slightly to restate the same value using terms that can be canceled later. First, strip invested capital at time zero from the first cumulative sum. Then modify the second cumulative sum to $t = 1$ to infinity, by changing each t inside the second cumulative sum to $t - 1$. This new representation is identical to the original representation but will allow us to cancel terms later. The new representation is as follows:

$$V = \text{IC}_0 + \sum_{t=1}^{\infty} \frac{\text{IC}_t}{(1 + \text{WACC})^t} - \sum_{t=1}^{\infty} \frac{\text{IC}_{t-1}}{(1 + \text{WACC})^{t-1}} + \sum_{t=1}^{\infty} \frac{\text{FCF}_t}{(1 + \text{WACC})^t}$$

Multiply the second cumulative sum by $(1 + WACC)/(1 + WACC)$. This action converts the exponent $t - 1$ in the denominator of the cumulative sum to t. Also substitute for free cash flow in the third cumulative sum, using its definition, NOPAT less the increase in invested capital:

$$V = IC_0 + \sum_{t=1}^{\infty} \frac{IC_t}{(1 + WACC)^t} - \sum_{t=1}^{\infty} \frac{(1 + WACC)IC_{t-1}}{(1 + WACC)^t}$$
$$+ \sum_{t=1}^{\infty} \frac{NOPAT_t - (IC_t - IC_{t-1})}{(1 + WACC)^t}$$

Because there is now a consistent denominator across all three cumulative sums, combine them into a single cumulative sum:

$$V = IC_0 + \sum_{t=1}^{\infty} \frac{IC_t - (1 + WACC)IC_{t-1} + NOPAT_t - IC_t + IC_{t-1}}{(1 + WACC)^t}$$

In the second term of the numerator, distribute $(1 + WACC)IC_{t-1}$ into its two components, IC_{t-1} and $WACC(IC_{t-1})$:

$$V = IC_0 + \sum_{t=1}^{\infty} \frac{IC_t - IC_{t-1} - WACC(IC_{t-1}) + NOPAT_t - IC_t + IC_{t-1}}{(1 + WACC)^t}$$

Simplify by collecting terms:

$$V = IC_0 + \sum_{t=1}^{\infty} \frac{NOPAT_t - WACC(IC_{t-1})}{(1 + WACC)^t}$$

The numerator is the definition of economic profit, so the result is a valuation based on economic profit:

$$V = IC_0 + \sum_{t=1}^{\infty} \frac{Economic\ Profit_t}{(1 + WACC)^t}$$

The enterprise value of a company equals the book value of its invested capital plus the present value of all future economic profits. To calculate the value correctly, you must calculate economic profit using last year's (i.e., beginning-of-year) invested capital—a subtle but important distinction.

The interdependence of invested capital, economic profit, and free cash flow is not surprising. Think of discounted cash flow this way: a portion of future cash flows is required to cover the required return for the investor's capital. The remaining cash flow is either used to grow invested capital (to generate additional future cash flows) or returned to investors as an extra bonus. This bonus is valuable, so investors are willing to pay a premium for cash flows above the amount required. Subsequently, companies with positive economic profits will trade at a premium to the book value of invested capital.

APPENDIX B

Derivation of Free Cash Flow, Weighted Average Cost of Capital, and Adjusted Present Value

Chapter 10 numerically demonstrated the equivalence of three valuation methods—enterprise discounted cash flow (DCF), adjusted present value (APV), and cash flow to equity—under the assumption of a constant debt-to-value ratio. This appendix derives the key inputs of each model—namely, free cash flow (FCF) and the weighted average cost of capital (WACC)—and demonstrates their equivalence algebraically.

To simplify the analysis, we assume cash flows to equity are growing at a constant rate, g. This way we can use growth perpetuities to analyze the relationship between methods.[1]

ENTERPRISE DISCOUNTED CASH FLOW

By definition, enterprise value equals the market value of debt plus the market value of equity:

$$V = D + E$$

---

[1] For an analysis that applies to more complex situations (i.e., when cash flows can follow any pattern), see J. A. Miles, and J. R. Ezzell, "The Weighted Average Cost of Capital, Perfect Capital Markets, and Project Life: A Clarification," *Journal of Financial and Quantitative Analysis* 15 (1980): 719–730 (for a discussion of enterprise DCF and WACC); and S. C. Myers, "Interactions of Corporate Financing and Investment Decisions: Implications for Capital Budgeting," *Journal of Finance* 29 (1974): 1–25 (for a discussion of adjusted present value).

To examine the components of enterprise value, multiply the right side of the equation by a complex fraction equivalent to 1 (the numerator equals the denominator, an algebraic trick we will use many times):

$$V = (D + E)\left(\frac{D(1 - T_m)k_d + CF_e - D(g)}{D(1 - T_m)k_d + CF_e - D(g)}\right) \tag{B.1}$$

where

$$T_m = \text{marginal tax rate}$$
$$k_d = \text{cost of debt}$$
$$CF_e = \text{cash flow to equity holders}$$
$$g = \text{growth in cash flow to equity holders}$$

Over the next few steps, the fraction's numerator will be converted to free cash flow (FCF). We will show later that the denominator equals the weighted average cost of capital. Start by defining FCF:

$$FCF = D(1 - T_m)k_d + CF_e - D(g)$$

If the market value of debt equals the face value of debt, the cost of debt will equal the coupon rate, and D times k_d will equal the company's interest expense. Therefore,

$$FCF = \text{Interest}(1 - T_m) + CF_e - D(g)$$

By definition, cash flow to equity (CF_e) equals earnings before interest and taxes (EBIT) minus interest minus taxes minus net investment plus the increase in debt. Assuming the ratio of debt to equity is constant, the annual increase in debt will equal $D(g)$. Why? Since cash flows to equity are growing at g, the value of equity also grows at g. Since the ratio of debt to equity remains constant (a key assumption), the value of debt must also grow at g. Substitute the definition of cash flow to equity into the preceding equation:

$$FCF = \text{Interest}(1 - T_m) + \text{EBIT} - \text{Interest} - \text{Taxes} - \text{Net Investment} + D(g) - D(g)$$

Next, distribute the after-tax interest expression into its two components, and cancel $D(g)$:

$$FCF = \text{Interest} - T_m(\text{Interest}) + \text{EBIT} - \text{Interest} - \text{Taxes} - \text{Net Investment}$$

Simplify by canceling the interest terms and rearranging the remaining terms:

$$FCF = \text{EBIT} - [\text{Taxes} + T_m(\text{Interest})] - \text{Net Investment}$$

Chapter 11 defines operating taxes as the taxes a company would pay if the company were financed entirely with equity. Operating taxes therefore equal reported taxes plus the interest tax shield (as interest is eliminated, taxes would rise by the interest tax shield). This leads to the definition of free cash flow we use throughout the book:

$$FCF = EBIT - \text{Operating Taxes} - \text{Net Investment}$$

Next, focus on the denominator. To derive the weighted average cost of capital (WACC), start with equation B.1, and multiply CF_e by 1, denoted as $(k_e - g)/(k_e - g)$:

$$V = (D + E)\left(\frac{FCF}{D(1 - T_m)k_d + \frac{CF_e}{k_e - g}(k_e - g) - D(g)}\right)$$

where k_e = cost of equity.

If equity cash flows are growing at a constant rate, the value of equity equals CF_e divided by $(k_e - g)$. Therefore, the growing perpetuity in the denominator can be replaced by the value of equity (E) and distributed:

$$V = (D + E)\left(\frac{FCF}{D(1 - T_m)k_d + E(k_e) - E(g) - D(g)}\right)$$

In the denominator, collapse $E(g)$ and $D(g)$ into a single term:

$$V = (D + E)\left(\frac{FCF}{D(1 - T_m)k_d + E(k_e) - (D + E)g}\right)$$

To complete the derivation of WACC in the denominator, divide the numerator and denominator by $(D + E)$. This will eliminate the $(D + E)$ expression on the left and place it in the denominator as a divisor. Distributing the term across the denominator, the result is the following equation:

$$V = \frac{FCF}{\frac{D}{D+E}(k_d)(1 - T_m) + \frac{E}{D+E}(k_e) - \frac{D+E}{D+E}(g)}$$

The expression in the denominator is the weighted average cost of capital (WACC) minus the growth in cash flow (g). Therefore, equation B.1 can be rewritten as:

$$V = \frac{FCF}{WACC - g}$$

such that:

$$WACC = \frac{D}{D+E}(k_d)(1 - T_m) + \frac{E}{D+E}(k_e)$$

Note how the after-tax cost of debt and the cost of equity are weighted by each security's *market* weight to enterprise value. This is why you should use market-based values, and not book values, to build the cost of capital. This is also why you should discount free cash flow at the weighted average cost of capital to determine enterprise value. Remember, however, that you can use a constant WACC over time only when leverage is expected to remain constant (i.e., debt grows as the business grows).[2]

ADJUSTED PRESENT VALUE

To determine enterprise value using adjusted present value, once again start with $V = D + E$ and multiply by a fraction equal to 1. This time, however, do not include the marginal tax rate in the fraction:

$$V = (D + E)\left(\frac{D(k_d) + CF_e - D(g)}{D(k_d) + CF_e - D(g)}\right)$$

Following the same process as before, convert each cash flow in the denominator to its present value times its expected return, and divide the fraction by $(D + E)/(D + E)$:

$$V = \frac{D(k_d) + CF_e - D(g)}{\frac{D}{D+E}(k_d) + \frac{E}{D+E}(k_e) - g}$$

Appendix C shows that if the company's interest tax shields have the same risk as the company's operating assets (as one would expect when the company maintains a constant capital structure), the fraction's denominator equals k_u, the unlevered cost of equity, minus the growth in cash flow (g). Make this substitution into the previous equation:

$$V = \frac{D(k_d) + CF_e - D(g)}{k_u - g}$$

Next, focus on the numerator. Substitute the definitions of cash flow to debt and cash flow to equity, as we did earlier in this appendix:

$$V = \frac{\text{Interest} + \text{EBIT} - \text{Interest} - \text{Taxes} - \text{Net Investment} + D(g) - D(g)}{k_u - g}$$

[2] To see this restriction applied in a more general setting, see Miles and Ezzell, "Weighted Average Cost of Capital."

In this equation, the two interest terms cancel, and the two $D(g)$ terms cancel, so simplify by canceling these terms. Also insert T_m(Interest) − T_m(Interest) into the numerator of the expression:

$$V = \frac{\text{EBIT} - \text{Taxes} + T_m(\text{Interest}) - T_m(\text{Interest}) - \text{Net Investment}}{k_u - g}$$

Aggregate reported taxes and the negative expression for T_m(Interest) into all-equity taxes. Move the positive expression for T_m(Interest) into a separate fraction:

$$V = \frac{\text{EBIT} - [\text{Taxes} + T_m(\text{Interest})] - \text{Net Investment}}{k_u - g} + \frac{T_m(\text{Interest})}{k_u - g}$$

At this point, we once again have free cash flow in the numerator of the first fraction. The second fraction equals the present value of the interest tax shield. Thus, enterprise value equals free cash flow discounted by the unlevered cost of equity plus the present value of the interest tax shield:

$$V = \frac{\text{FCF}}{k_u - g} + \text{PV(Interest Tax Shield)}$$

This expression is commonly referred to as adjusted present value.

In this simple proof, we assume tax shields should be discounted at the unlevered cost of equity. This need not be the case. Some financial analysts discount expected interest tax shields at the cost of debt. If you do this, however, free cash flow discounted at the traditional WACC (defined earlier) and adjusted present value will lead to different valuations. In this case, WACC must be adjusted to reflect the alternative assumption concerning the risk of tax shields.

Levering and Unlevering the Cost of Equity

This appendix derives various formulas that can be used to compute unlevered beta and the unlevered cost of equity under different assumptions. Unlevered betas are required to estimate an industry beta, as detailed in Chapter 15. We prefer using an industry beta rather than a company beta to determine the cost of capital because company betas cannot be estimated accurately. As discussed in Chapter 10, the unlevered cost of equity is used to discount free cash flow to compute adjusted present value. For companies with substantial postretirement obligations, the appendix concludes by incorporating pensions and other postretirement benefits into the unlevering process.

UNLEVERED COST OF EQUITY

Franco Modigliani and Merton Miller postulated that the market value of a company's economic assets, such as operating assets (V_u) and tax shields (V_{txa}), should equal the market value of its financial claims, such as debt (D) and equity (E):

$$V_u + V_{txa} = \text{Enterprise Value} = D + E \qquad (C.1)$$

A second result of Modigliani and Miller's work is that the total risk of the company's economic assets, operating and financial, must equal the total risk of the financial claims against those assets:

$$\frac{V_u}{V_u + V_{txa}}(k_u) + \frac{V_{txa}}{V_u + V_{txa}}(k_{txa}) = \frac{D}{D+E}(k_d) + \frac{E}{D+E}(k_e) \qquad (C.2)$$

where

$$k_u = \text{unlevered cost of equity}$$
$$k_{txa} = \text{cost of capital for the company's interest tax shields}$$
$$k_d = \text{cost of debt}$$
$$k_e = \text{cost of equity}$$

The four terms in this equation represent the proportional risk of operating assets, tax assets, debt, and equity, respectively.

Since the cost of operating assets (k_u) is unobservable, it is necessary to solve for it using the equation's other inputs. The required return on tax shields (k_{txa}) also is unobservable. With two unknowns and only one equation, it is therefore necessary to impose additional restrictions to solve for k_u. If debt is a constant proportion of enterprise value (i.e., debt grows as the business grows), k_{txa} equals k_u. Imposing this restriction leads to the following equation:

$$\frac{V_u}{V_u + V_{txa}}(k_u) + \frac{V_{txa}}{V_u + V_{txa}}(k_u) = \frac{D}{D + E}(k_d) + \frac{E}{D + E}(k_e)$$

Combining terms on the left side generates an equation for the unlevered cost of equity when debt is a constant proportion of enterprise value:

$$k_u = \frac{D}{D + E}(k_d) + \frac{E}{D + E}(k_e) \tag{C.3}$$

Since most companies manage their debt to value to stay within a particular range, we believe this formula and its resulting derivations are the most appropriate for standard valuation.

Unlevered Cost of Equity When k_{txa} Equals k_d

Some financial analysts set the required return on interest tax shields equal to the cost of debt. In this case, equation C.2 can be expressed as follows:

$$\frac{V_u}{V_u + V_{txa}}(k_u) + \frac{V_{txa}}{V_u + V_{txa}}(k_d) = \frac{D}{D + E}(k_d) + \frac{E}{D + E}(k_e)$$

To solve for k_u, multiply both sides by enterprise value:

$$V_u(k_u) + V_{txa}(k_d) = D(k_d) + E(k_e)$$

and move $V_{txa}(k_d)$ to the right side of the equation:

$$V_u(k_u) = (D - V_{txa})k_d + E(k_e)$$

To eliminate V_u from the left side of the equation, rearrange equation C.1 to $V_u = D - V_{txa} + E$, and divide both sides by this value:

$$k_u = \frac{D - V_{txa}}{D - V_{txa} + E}(k_d) + \frac{E}{D - V_{txa} + E}(k_e) \tag{C.4}$$

Equation C.4 mirrors equation C.2 closely. It differs from equation C.2 only in that the market value of debt is reduced by the present value of expected tax shields.

Measurement Methods

Exhibit C.1 summarizes three methods to estimate the unlevered cost of equity. The two formulas in the top row assume that the risk associated with interest tax shields (k_{txa}) equals the risk of operations (k_u). When this is true, whether debt is constant or expected to change, the formula remains the same.

The bottom-row formulas assume that the risk of interest tax shields equals the risk of debt. On the left, future debt can take on any value. On the right, an additional restriction is imposed that debt remains constant—in absolute terms, not as a percentage of enterprise value. In this case, the annual interest payment equals $D(k_d)$, and the annual tax shield equals $D(k_d)(T_m)$. Since tax shields are constant, they can be valued using a constant perpetuity:

$$\text{PV(Tax Shields)} = \frac{D(k_d)(T_m)}{k_d} = D(T_m)$$

Consequently, V_{txa} in the formula in the bottom left corner is replaced with $D(T_m)$. The equation is simplified by converting $D - D(T_m)$ into $D(1 - T_m)$. The resulting equation is presented in the bottom right corner.

EXHIBIT C.1 **Unlevered Cost of Equity**

	Dollar level of debt fluctuates	Dollar level of debt is constant
Tax shields have same risk as operating assets $k_{txa} = k_u$	$k_u = \dfrac{D}{D+E} k_d + \dfrac{E}{D+E} k_e$	$k_u = \dfrac{D}{D+E} k_d + \dfrac{E}{D+E} k_e$
Tax shields have same risk as debt $k_{txa} = k_d$	$k_u = \dfrac{D - V_{txa}}{D - V_{txa} + E} k_d + \dfrac{E}{D - V_{txa} + E} k_e$	$k_u = \dfrac{D(1 - T_m)}{D(1 - T_m) + E} k_d + \dfrac{E}{D(1 - T_m) + E} k_e$

Note: k_e = cost of equity
  k_d = cost of debt
  k_u = unlevered cost of equity
  k_{txa} = cost of capital for tax shields
  T_m = marginal tax rate
  D = debt
  E = equity
  V_{txa} = present value of tax shields

LEVERED COST OF EQUITY

In certain situations, you will have already estimated the unlevered cost of equity and need to relever the cost of equity to a new target structure. In this case, use equation C.2 to solve for the levered cost of equity, k_e:

$$\frac{V_u}{V_u + V_{txa}}(k_u) + \frac{V_{txa}}{V_u + V_{txa}}(k_{txa}) = \frac{D}{D + E}(k_d) + \frac{E}{D + E}(k_e)$$

Multiply both sides by enterprise value:

$$V_u(k_u) + V_{txa}(k_{txa}) = D(k_d) + E(k_e)$$

Next, subtract $D(k_d)$ from both sides of the equation:

$$V_u(k_u) - D(k_d) + V_{txa}(k_{txa}) = E(k_e)$$

and divide the entire equation by the market value of equity, E:

$$k_e = \frac{V_u}{E}(k_u) - \frac{D}{E}(k_d) + \frac{V_{txa}}{E}(k_{txa})$$

To eliminate V_u from the right side of the equation, rearrange equation C.1 to $V_u = D - V_{txa} + E$, and use this identity to replace V_u:

$$k_e = \frac{D - V_{txa} + E}{E}(k_u) - \frac{D}{E}(k_d) + \frac{V_{txa}}{E}(k_{txa})$$

Distribute the first fraction into its component parts:

$$k_e = \frac{D}{E}(k_u) - \frac{V_{txa}}{E}(k_u) + k_u - \frac{D}{E}(k_d) + \frac{V_{txa}}{E}(k_{txa}) \tag{C.5}$$

Consolidating terms and rearranging leads to the general equation for the cost of equity:

$$k_e = k_u + \frac{D}{E}(k_u - k_d) - \frac{V_{txa}}{E}(k_u - k_{txa}) \tag{C.6}$$

If debt is a constant proportion of enterprise value (i.e., debt grows as the business grows), k_u will equal k_{txa}. Consequently, the final term drops out:

$$k_e = k_u + \frac{D}{E}(k_u - k_d)$$

We believe this equation best represents the relationship between the levered cost of equity and the unlevered cost of equity.

The same analysis can be repeated under the assumption that the risk of interest tax shields equals the risk of debt. Rather than repeat the first few steps, we start with equation C.5:

$$k_e = \frac{D}{E}(k_u) - \frac{V_{txa}}{E}(k_u) + k_u - \frac{D}{E}(k_d) + \frac{V_{txa}}{E}(k_{txa})$$

To solve for k_e, replace k_{txa} with k_d:

$$k_e = \frac{D}{E}(k_u) - \frac{V_{txa}}{E}(k_u) + k_u - \frac{D}{E}(k_d) + \frac{V_{txa}}{E}(k_d)$$

Consolidate like terms and reorder:

$$k_e = k_u + \frac{D - V_{txa}}{E}(k_u) - \frac{D - V_{txa}}{E}(k_d)$$

Finally, further simplify the equation by once again combining like terms:

$$k_e = k_u + \frac{D - V_{txa}}{E}(k_u - k_d)$$

The resulting equation is the levered cost of equity for a company whose debt can take any value but whose interest tax shields have the same risk as the company's debt.

Exhibit C.2 summarizes the formulas that can be used to estimate the levered cost of equity. The top row in the exhibit contains formulas that assume k_{txa} equals k_u. The bottom row contains formulas that assume k_{txa} equals k_d. The formulas on the left side are flexible enough to handle any future capital structure but require valuing the tax shields separately. The formulas on the right side assume the dollar level of debt is fixed over time.

EXHIBIT C.2 **Levered Cost of Equity**

	Dollar level of debt fluctuates	Dollar level of debt is constant
Tax shields have same risk as operating assets $k_{txa} = k_u$	$k_e = k_u + \frac{D}{E}(k_u - k_d)$	$k_e = k_u + \frac{D}{E}(k_u - k_d)$
Tax shields have same risk as debt $k_{txa} = k_d$	$k_e = k_u + \frac{D - V_{txa}}{E}(k_u - k_d)$	$k_e = k_u + (1 - T_m)\frac{D}{E}(k_u - k_d)$

Note: k_e = cost of equity
k_d = cost of debt
k_u = unlevered cost of equity
k_{txa} = cost of capital for tax shields
T_m = marginal tax rate
D = debt
E = equity
V_{txa} = present value of tax shields

LEVERED BETA

Similar to the cost of capital, the weighted average beta of a company's assets, both operating and financial, must equal the weighted average beta of its financial claims:

$$\frac{V_u}{V_u + V_{txa}}(\beta_u) + \frac{V_{txa}}{V_u + V_{txa}}(\beta_{txa}) = \frac{D}{D + E}(\beta_d) + \frac{E}{D + E}(\beta_e)$$

Since the form of this equation is identical to the cost of capital, it is possible to rearrange the formula using the same process as previously described. Rather than repeat the analysis, we provide a summary of levered beta in Exhibit C.3. As expected, the first two columns are identical in form to Exhibit C.2, except that the beta (β) replaces the cost of capital (k).

By using beta, it is possible to make one additional simplification. If debt is risk free, the beta of debt is 0, and β_d drops out. This allows us to convert the following general equation (when β_{txa} equals β_u):

$$\beta_e = \beta_u + \frac{D}{E}(\beta_u - \beta_d)$$

into the following:

$$\beta_e = \left(1 + \frac{D}{E}\right)\beta_u$$

EXHIBIT C.3 **Levered Beta**

	Dollar level of debt fluctuates	Dollar level of debt is constant and debt is risky	Debt is risk free
Tax shields have same risk as operating assets $\beta_{txa} = \beta_u$	$\beta_e = \beta_u + \frac{D}{E}(\beta_u - \beta_d)$	$\beta_e = \beta_u + \frac{D}{E}(\beta_u - \beta_d)$	$\beta_e = \left(1 + \frac{D}{E}\right)\beta_u$
Tax shields have same risk as debt $\beta_{txa} = \beta_d$	$\beta_e = \beta_u + \frac{D - V_{txa}}{E}(\beta_u - \beta_d)$	$\beta_e = \beta_u + (1 - T_m)\frac{D}{E}(\beta_u - \beta_d)$	$\beta_e = \left[1 + (1 - T_m)\frac{D}{E}\right]\beta_u$

Note: β_e = beta of equity
β_d = beta of debt
β_u = unlevered beta of equity
β_{txa} = beta of capital for tax shields
T_m = marginal tax rate
D = debt
E = equity
V_{txa} = present value of tax shields

This last equation is an often-applied formula for levering (and unlevering) beta when the risk of interest tax shields (β_{txa}) equals the risk of operating assets (β_u) *and* the company's debt is risk free. For investment-grade companies, debt is near risk free, so any errors using this formula will be small. If the company is highly leveraged, however, errors can be large. In this situation, estimate the beta of debt, and use the more general version of the formula.

UNLEVERED BETA AND PENSIONS

Since stockholders are responsible for future pension payments and other retirement obligations, the risks associated with these employee benefits can affect a company's beta. If a company has significant pensions, especially unfunded pensions, make sure to include them in the unlevering process.

If you believe the risk of pension assets matches the risk of future obligations, only the unfunded portion of benefit obligations affects the equity beta. In this case, use the unlevering equations in the preceding sections, but treat any unfunded benefit obligations identically to debt.

If you believe the risk of pension assets does not match the risk of future obligations, the unlevering formulas can be reworked such that the risk of pension assets and risk of benefit obligations are evaluated separately. To do this, start with the portfolio equation for beta:

$$\frac{V_u}{V}\beta_u + \frac{V_{pa}}{V}\beta_{pa} = \frac{V_{pbo}}{V}\beta_{pbo} + \frac{D}{V}\beta_d + \frac{E}{V}\beta_e$$

where

$$V_{pa} = \text{value of pension assets}$$
$$V_{pbo} = \text{present value of pension benefit obligations}$$
$$\beta_{pa} = \text{beta of pension assets}$$
$$\beta_{pbo} = \text{beta of pension benefit obligations}$$
$$V = D + V_{pbo} + E$$

Next, multiply both sides by V:

$$V_u\beta_u + V_{pa}\beta_{pa} = V_{pbo}\beta_{pbo} + D\beta_d + E\beta_e$$

Subtract the term related to pension assets from both sides of the equation:

$$V_u\beta_u = V_{pbo}\beta_{pbo} + D\beta_d + E\beta_e - V_{pa}\beta_{pa}$$

To isolate β_u, divide both sides by V_u. This leads to the general equation for estimating unlevered beta, inclusive of pensions:

$$\beta_u = \frac{V_{pbo}}{V_u}\beta_{pbo} + \frac{V_d}{V_u}\beta_d + \frac{V_e}{V_u}\beta_e - \frac{V_{pa}}{V_u}\beta_{pa}$$

If debt and pension liabilities have the same beta, simplify the last equation by combining terms:

$$\beta_u = \frac{D + V_{pbo}}{V_u}\beta_d + \frac{E}{V_u}\beta_e - \frac{V_{pa}}{V_u}\beta_{pa}$$

Chapter 23 discusses how to incorporate pensions into a valuation. In Exhibit 23.5, we use the equation above to unlever beta for Kellanova. Given the small size of the company's pension relative to the company's market value of equity, the difference in unlevered beta with and without the pension adjustment is minor. We therefore recommend adjusting beta for pensions only when pension assets and liabilities are substantial. In most situations, the unlevering equations including the unfunded portion of pensions as debt will suffice.

Leverage and the
Price-to-Earnings Multiple

This appendix demonstrates that the price-to-earnings multiple (P/E) of a levered company systematically depends on its unlevered (all-equity) P/E, its cost of debt, and its debt-to-value ratio. When the unlevered P/E is less than $1/k_d$ (where k_d equals the cost of debt), the P/E falls as leverage rises. Conversely, when the unlevered P/E is greater than $1/k_d$, the P/E rises with increased leverage.

In this proof, we assume the company faces no taxes and no distress costs. We do this to avoid modeling the complex relationship between capital structure and enterprise value. Instead, our goal is to show that there is a systematic relationship between the debt-to-value ratio and the P/E.

STEP 1: DEFINING UNLEVERED P/E

To determine the relationship between P/E and leverage, start by defining the unlevered P/E (PE_u). When a company is entirely financed with equity, its enterprise value equals its equity value, and its net operating profit after taxes (NOPAT) equals its net income:

$$PE_u = \frac{V_{\text{ENT}}}{\text{NOPAT}_{t+1}}$$

where

$$V_{\text{ENT}} = \text{enterprise value}$$
$$\text{NOPAT}_{t+1} = \text{net operating profit after taxes in year } t + 1$$

This equation can be rearranged to solve for the enterprise value, which we will use in the next step:

$$V_{\text{ENT}} = \text{NOPAT}_{t+1}(\text{PE}_u) \tag{D.1}$$

STEP 2: LINKING NET INCOME TO NOPAT

For a company partially financed with debt, net income (NI) equals NOPAT less after-tax interest payments. Assuming the value of debt equals its face value, the company's interest expense will equal the cost of debt times the value of debt, which can be defined by multiplying enterprise value by the debt-to-value ratio:

$$\text{NI}_{t+1} = \text{NOPAT}_{t+1} - V_{\text{ENT}}\left(\frac{D}{V}\right)k_d$$

Substitute equation D.1 for the enterprise value:

$$\text{NI}_{t+1} = \text{NOPAT}_{t+1} - \text{NOPAT}_{t+1}(\text{PE}_u)\left(\frac{D}{V}\right)k_d$$

Factor NOPAT into a single term:

$$\text{NI}_{t+1} = \text{NOPAT}_{t+1}\left[1 - \text{PE}_u\left(\frac{D}{V}\right)k_d\right] \tag{D.2}$$

STEP 3: DERIVING LEVERED P/E

At this point, we are ready to solve for the company's price-to-earnings ratio. Since P/E is based on equity values, first convert enterprise value to equity value. To do this, once again start with equation D.1:

$$V_{\text{ENT}} = \text{NOPAT}_{t+1}(\text{PE}_u)$$

To convert enterprise value into equity value, multiply both sides by 1 minus the debt-to-value ratio:

$$V_{\text{ENT}}\left(1 - \frac{D}{V_{\text{ENT}}}\right) = \text{NOPAT}_{t+1}(\text{PE}_u)\left(1 - \frac{D}{V_{\text{ENT}}}\right)$$

Distribute V_{ENT} into the parentheses:

$$V_{\text{ENT}} - D = \text{NOPAT}_{t+1}(\text{PE}_u)\left(1 - \frac{D}{V_{\text{ENT}}}\right)$$

Replace enterprise value (V_{ENT}) minus debt (D) with equity value (E):

$$E = \text{NOPAT}_{t+1}(\text{PE}_u)\left(1 - \frac{D}{V_{ENT}}\right)$$

Next, use equation D.2 to eliminate NOPAT_{t+1}:

$$E = \frac{\text{NI}_{t+1}(\text{PE}_u)\left(1 - \frac{D}{V}\right)}{1 - \text{PE}_u\left(\frac{D}{V}\right)k_d}$$

Divide both sides by net income to find the levered P/E:

$$\frac{E}{\text{NI}_{t+1}} = \frac{\text{PE}_u - \text{PE}_u\left(\frac{D}{V}\right)}{1 - \text{PE}_u\left(\frac{D}{V}\right)k_d}$$

At this point, we have a relationship between equity value and net income, which depends on the unlevered P/E, the debt-to-value ratio, and the cost of debt. Debt-to-value, however, is in both the numerator and the denominator, so it is difficult to distinguish how leverage affects the levered P/E. To eliminate the debt-to-value ratio in the numerator, use a few algebraic tricks. First, multiply both the numerator and denominator by k_d:

$$\frac{E}{\text{NI}_{t+1}} = \frac{\text{PE}_u(k_d) - \text{PE}_u\left(\frac{D}{V}\right)(k_d)}{k_d\left[1 - \text{PE}_u\left(\frac{D}{V}\right)(k_d)\right]}$$

Next, subtract and add 1 (a net difference of 0) in the numerator:

$$\frac{E}{\text{NI}_{t+1}} = \frac{[\text{PE}_u(k_d) - 1] + \left[1 - \text{PE}_u\left(\frac{D}{V}\right)(k_d)\right]}{k_d\left[1 - \text{PE}_u\left(\frac{D}{V}\right)(k_d)\right]}$$

After separating the numerator into two distinct terms, you can eliminate the components of the right-hand term by canceling them with the denominator. This allows you to remove debt-to-value from the numerator:

$$\frac{E}{\text{NI}_{t+1}} = \frac{\text{PE}_u(k_d) - 1}{k_d\left[1 - \text{PE}_u\left(\frac{D}{V}\right)(k_d)\right]} + \frac{1}{k_d}$$

To simplify the expression further, divide both the numerator and denominator of the complex fraction by k_d:

$$\frac{E}{\text{NI}_{t+1}} = \frac{1}{k_d} + \frac{\text{PE}_u - \frac{1}{k_d}}{1 - \text{PE}_u\left(\frac{D}{V}\right)(k_d)}$$

Finally, multiply the numerator and denominator of the second term by –1:

$$\frac{E}{NI_{t+1}} = \frac{1}{k_d} + \frac{\frac{1}{k_d} - PE_u}{\left(\frac{D}{V}\right)k_d(PE_u) - 1}$$

As this final equation shows, a company's P/E is a function of its unlevered P/E, its cost of debt, and its debt-to-value ratio. When the unlevered P/E equals the reciprocal of the cost of debt, the numerator of the second fraction equals zero, and leverage has no effect on the P/E. For companies with large unlevered P/Es, P/E systematically increases with leverage. Conversely, companies with small unlevered P/Es would exhibit a drop in P/E as leverage rises.

APPENDIX **E**

Other Capital Structure Issues

This appendix discusses alternative models of capital structure and credit rating estimations. These models offer some interesting insights but tend to be less useful in practice for designing a company's capital structure. Finally, the appendix shows the similarities and differences between widely used credit ratios such as leverage, coverage, and solvency.

PECKING-ORDER THEORY

An alternative to the view that there are trade-offs between equity and debt is a school of thought in finance theory that sees a pecking order in financing.[1] According to this theory, companies meet their investment needs first by using internal funds (from retained earnings), then by issuing debt, and finally by issuing equity. One of the causes of this pecking order is that investors interpret financing decisions by managers as signals of a company's financial prospects. For example, investors will interpret an equity issue as a signal that management believes shares are overvalued. Anticipating this interpretation, rational managers will turn to equity funding only as a last resort, because it could cause the share price to fall. An analogous argument holds for debt issues, although the overvaluation signal is much smaller because the value of debt is much less sensitive to a company's financial success.[2]

According to the theory, companies will have lower leverage when they are more mature and profitable, simply because they can fund internally and do

---

[1] See G. Donaldson, "Corporate Debt Capacity: A Study of Corporate Debt Policy and the Determination of Corporate Debt Capacity" (Harvard Graduate School of Business, 1961); and S. Myers, "The Capital Structure Puzzle," *Journal of Finance* 39, no. 3 (1974): 575–592.
[2] An exception is, of course, the value of debt in a financially distressed company.

not need any debt or equity funding. However, evidence for the theory is not conclusive. For example, mature companies generating strong cash flows are among the most highly leveraged, whereas the pecking-order theory would predict them to have the lowest leverage. High-tech start-up companies are among the least leveraged, rather than debt loaded, as the theory would predict.[3] Empirical research shows how the signaling hypotheses underlying the pecking-order theory are more relevant to financial managers in selecting and timing specific funding alternatives than for setting long-term capital structure targets.[4] Surveys among financial executives confirm these findings.[5]

MARKET-BASED RATING APPROACH

Alternative metrics to credit ratings have been developed based on the notion that equity can be modeled as a call option on the company's enterprise value, with the debt obligations as the exercise price.[6] Using option valuation models and market data on price and volatility of the shares, these approaches estimate the future probability of default—that is, the probability that enterprise value will be below the value of debt obligations.[7] The advantage is that all information captured by the equity markets is directly translated into the default estimates. Traditional credit ratings tend to lag changes in a company's performance and outlook because they aim to measure credit quality "through the cycle"[8] and are less sensitive to short-term fluctuations in quality.

The disadvantage of market-based ratings is that no fundamental analysis is performed on the company's underlying business and financial health. If equity markets have missed some critical information, the resulting estimates of default probability do not reflect their omission. As discussed in Chapter 6, markets reflect company fundamentals most of the time, but not always. When they do not, the market-based rating approaches would incorrectly estimate default risk as well.[9]

---

[3] See M. Barclay and C. Smith, "The Capital Structure Puzzle: The Evidence Revisited," *Journal of Applied Corporate Finance* 17, no. 1 (2005): 8–17; and M. Baker and J. Wurgler, "Market Timing and Capital Structure," *Journal of Finance* 52, no. 1 (2002): 1–32.

[4] See also A. Hovakimian, T. Opler, and S. Titman, "The Debt-Equity Choice," *Journal of Financial and Quantitative Analysis* 36, no. 1 (2001): 1–24, for evidence that the pecking-order theory predicts short-term movements in corporate debt levels but that long-term changes are more in line with the trade-offs discussed earlier in this section.

[5] J. Graham and H. Campbell, "How Do CFOs Make Capital Budgeting and Capital Structure Decisions?" *Journal of Applied Corporate Finance* 15, no. 1 (2002): 8–23.

[6] This is because equity is a residual claim on the enterprise value after payment of principal and interest for debt. It has value only to the extent that enterprise value exceeds debt commitments. See R. Merton, "On the Pricing of Corporate Debt: The Risk Structure of Interest Rates," *Journal of Finance* 29 (1974): 449–470; or for an introduction, R. Brealey, S. Myers, F. Allen, and A. Edmans, *Principles of Corporate Finance*, 14th ed. (New York: McGraw-Hill, 2023), Chap. 17.

[7] See P. Crosbie and J. Bohn, "Modeling Default Risk" (Moody's KMV white paper, December 2003).

[8] See E. Altman and H. Rijken, "How Rating Agencies Achieve Rating Stability," *Journal of Banking and Finance* 28, no. 11 (2004): 2679–2714.

[9] See Crosbie and Bohn, "Modeling Default Risk," 23.

LEVERAGE, COVERAGE, AND SOLVENCY

The leverage measure used in the academic literature is typically defined as the market value of debt (D) over the market value of debt plus equity (E):

$$\text{Leverage} = \frac{D}{D + E}$$

This ratio measures how much of the company's enterprise value is claimed by debt holders and is an important concept for estimating the benefits of tax shields arising from debt financing. It is therefore also a crucial input in calculating the weighted average cost of capital (WACC; see Chapter 15 on capital structure weights).

Compared with coverage ratios such as earnings before interest, taxes, and amortization (EBITA) to interest, leverage ratios suffer from several drawbacks as a way to measure and target a company's capital structure. First, companies could have very low leverage in terms of market value but still be at a high risk of financial distress if their short-term cash flow is low relative to interest payments. High-growth companies usually have very low levels of leverage, but this does not mean their debt is low risk. A second drawback is that market value can change radically (especially for high-growth, high-multiple companies), making leverage a fast-moving indicator. For example, during the stock market boom of the late 1990s, several European telecom companies had what appeared to be reasonable levels of debt financing in terms of leverage. Credit providers appeared willing to provide credit even though the underlying near-term cash flows were not very high relative to debt service obligations. But when the companies' market values plummeted in 2001, leverage for these companies shot up, and financial distress loomed. Thus, it is risky to base a capital structure target on a market-value-based measure.

This does not mean that leverage and coverage are fundamentally divergent measures. Far from it: they actually measure the same thing but over different time horizons. For ease of explanation, consider a company that has no growth in revenues, profit, or cash flows. For this company, it is possible to express the leverage and coverage as follows[10]:

$$\text{Leverage} = \frac{D}{D + E}$$

$$= \frac{\text{Interest}_1 + \text{PV}(\text{Interest}_2) + \cdots + \text{PV}(\text{Interest}_\infty)}{\text{NOPAT}_1 + \text{PV}(\text{NOPAT}_2) + \cdots + \text{PV}(\text{NOPAT}_\infty)}$$

$$\text{Coverage} = \frac{\text{EBITA}}{\text{Interest}} = \frac{1}{(1 - T)} \times \frac{\text{NOPAT}}{\text{Interest}}$$

---

[10] The simplifying no-growth assumption is for illustration purposes only. For a growing company, the same point holds.

where
$$D = \text{market value of debt}$$
$$E = \text{market value of equity}$$
$$\text{NOPAT}_t = \text{net operating profit after taxes in year } t$$
$$\text{Interest}_t = \text{interest expenses in year } t$$
$$T = \text{tax rate}$$

The market value of debt captures the present value of all future interest payments, assuming perpetual rollover of debt financing. The enterprise value ($E + D$) is equal to the present value of future NOPAT, because depreciation equals capital expenditures for a zero-growth company. A leverage ratio therefore measures the company's ability to cover its interest payments over a very long term. The problem is that short-term interest obligations are what mainly get a company into financial distress. Coverage, in contrast, focuses on the short-term part of the leverage definition, keeping in mind that NOPAT roughly equals EBITA $\times$ (1 − T). It indicates how easily a company can service its debt in the near term.

Both measures are meaningful, and they are complementary. For example, if market leverage were very high in combination with strong current interest coverage, this could indicate the possibility of future difficulties in sustaining current debt levels in, for example, a single-product company faced with rapidly eroding margins and cash flows because the product is approaching the end of its life cycle. Despite very high interest coverage today, such a company might not be given a high credit rating, and its capacity to borrow could be limited.

Solvency measures of debt over book value of total assets or equity are seldom as meaningful as coverage or leverage. The key reason is that these book value ratios fail to capture the company's ability to comply with debt service requirements in either the short term or the long term. Market-to-book ratios can vary significantly across sectors and over time, making solvency a poor proxy for long-term ability to service debt.

Solvency becomes more relevant in times of financial distress, when a company's creditors use it as a rough measure of the available collateral. Higher levels of solvency usually indicate that debt holders stand better chances of recovering their principal and interest due—assuming that asset book values are reasonable approximations of asset liquidation values. However, in a going concern, solvency is much less relevant for deciding capital structure than coverage and leverage measures.

Technical Issues in
Estimating the Market
Risk Premium

In its simplest form, the historical market risk premium can be measured by subtracting the return on government bonds from the stock returns on a large sample of companies over some time frame. However, this requires many choices that will affect the results. For the best measurement of the risk premium using historical data, follow the guidelines presented in this appendix.

CALCULATE PREMIUM RELATIVE TO LONG-TERM GOVERNMENT BONDS

When calculating the market risk premium, compare historical market returns with the return on ten-year government bonds. Long-term government bonds match the duration of a company's cash flows better than short-term bonds.

USE THE LONGEST PERIOD POSSIBLE

A long observation window is most effective for estimating expected returns when the distribution of returns is stable. If the distribution shifts over time, a shorter time frame may be justified. As we have seen no compelling evidence of such a shift, we recommend using the longest available window to assess the market risk premium. This conclusion is further supported by a simple analysis described below.

To test for the presence of a long-term trend, we regress the U.S. market risk premium against time. Between 1900 and 2023, no statistically significant trend is observable.[1] Based on regression results, the average excess return has risen by less than one basis point per year, but this result cannot be statistically distinguished from zero. Premiums calculated over shorter periods are too volatile to be meaningful. For instance, U.S. stocks outperformed bonds by 18 percent in the 1950s but offered no premium in the 1970s. Given the lack of any discernible trend and the significant volatility of shorter periods, use the longest time series possible.

USE AN ARITHMETIC AVERAGE OF MULTIYEAR RETURNS

Financial data providers often report the stock market's average one-year return, but the figures vary depending on whether they use an arithmetic or geometric average. Unfortunately, neither approach is suitable for multiyear valuation purposes. Instead, we recommend using a multiyear average—for example, over a ten-year span—to mitigate bias from measurement errors. This section explores the underlying principles of arithmetic and geometric averages, the distortion caused by compounding, and techniques for correcting this bias.

Annual returns can be calculated using either an arithmetic or geometric average. An arithmetic (simple) average sums each year's observed premium and divides the sum by the number of observations:

$$\text{Arithmetic Average} = \frac{1}{T} \sum_{t=1}^{T} \frac{1 + R_m(t)}{1 + r_f(t)} - 1$$

where T = number of observations

$R_m(t)$ = market return in year t

$r_f(t)$ = risk-free rate in year t

A geometric average compounds (takes the product of) each year's excess return and takes the (Tth) root of the resulting product:

$$\text{Geometric Average} = \left(\prod_{t=1}^{T} \frac{1 + R_m(t)}{1 + r_f(t)} \right)^{1/T} - 1$$

[1] Some authors, such as Jonathan Lewellen, argue that the market risk premium does change over time and can be measured using financial ratios, such as the dividend yield. We address these models separately. J. Lewellen, "Predicting Returns with Financial Ratios," *Journal of Financial Economics* 74, no. 2 (2004): 209–235.

The choice of averaging methodology will affect the results. For instance, between 1900 and 2023, U.S. stocks outperformed long-term government bonds by 6.9 percent per year when averaged arithmetically. Using a geometric average, the outperformance drops to 4.9 percent. This difference is not random; arithmetic averages always exceed geometric averages when returns are volatile. (See arithmetic-geometric mean inequality on the web for more details.)

So which averaging method on historical data best estimates the *expected* rate of return? Well-accepted statistical principles dictate that the arithmetic average is the best unbiased estimator of the mean (expectation) for any random variable. Therefore, to determine a security's expected return for *one period*, the best unbiased predictor is the arithmetic average of many one-period returns. A one-period risk premium, however, can't value a company with many years of cash flow. Instead, long-dated cash flows must be discounted using a compounded rate of return. But when a single-year is compounded multiple times, the arithmetic average will generate a discount factor that is biased upward (too high).

The cause of the bias is quite technical, so we provide only a summary here. There are two reasons why compounding the historical arithmetic average leads to a biased discount factor. First, the arithmetic average is measured with error. Although this estimation error will not affect a one-period forecast (the error has an expectation of zero), squaring the estimate—as you do in compounding—in effect squares the measurement error, causing the error to be positive. This positive error leads to a multiyear expected return that is too high. Second, several researchers have argued that stock market returns are negatively autocorrelated over time. Suppose positive returns are typically followed by negative returns (and vice versa). In that case, squaring the average will lead to a discount factor that overestimates the two-period return, again causing an upward bias.

We have two choices to correct for the bias caused by estimation error and negative autocorrelation in returns. First, we can calculate multiyear returns directly from the data, rather than compound single-year averages. Using this method, a cash flow received in ten years will be discounted by the average ten-year market risk premium, not by the annual market risk premium compounded ten times.[2]

---

[2] Jay Ritter writes, "There is no theoretical reason why one year is the appropriate holding period. People are used to thinking of interest rates as a rate per year, so reporting annualized numbers makes it easy for people to focus on the numbers. But I can think of no reason other than convenience for the use of annual returns." J. Ritter, "The Biggest Mistakes We Teach," *Journal of Financial Research* 25 (2002): 159–168.

Alternatively, researchers have used simulation to show that an estimator proposed by Marshall Blume best adjusts for problems caused by estimation error and autocorrelation of returns[3]:

$$R = \left(\frac{T-N}{T-1}\right) R_A + \left(\frac{N-1}{T-1}\right) R_G$$

where T = number of historical observations in sample

N = forecast period being discounted

R_A = arithmetic average of historical sample

R_G = geometric average of historical sample

Blume's estimator depends on the length of time you plan to discount. The first year's cash flow should be discounted using the arithmetic average ($T = 124$, $N = 1$), whereas the tenth year's cash flow should be discounted based on a return constructed with a 92.7 percent weighting on the arithmetic average and a 7.3 percent weighting on the long-term geometric average ($T = 124$, $N = 10$).

Even with the best statistical techniques, however, these estimates are probably too high, because our sample includes only U.S. data, representing the best-performing market over the past century. Since the U.S. stock market is unlikely to replicate its performance over the next century, we adjust the historical market risk premium downward. Research shows that the U.S. arithmetic annual return exceeded a 17-country composite return by 0.8 percent in real terms.[4] If we subtract a 0.8 percent survivorship premium from observed returns near 6 percent, the resulting expected return falls within our recommended range of 5.0 percent to 5.5 percent.

[3] D. C. Indro and W. Y. Lee, "Biases in Arithmetic and Geometric Averages as Estimates of Long-Run Expected Returns and Risk Premia," *Financial Management* 26, no. 4 (Winter 1997): 81–90; and M. E. Blume, "Unbiased Estimators of Long-Run Expected Rates of Return," *Journal of the American Statistical Association* 69, no. 347 (September 1974): 634–638.

[4] E. Dimson, P. Marsh, and M. Staunton, "The Worldwide Equity Premium: A Smaller Puzzle," in *Handbook of Investments: Equity Risk Premium*, ed. R. Mehra (Amsterdam: Elsevier Science, 2007).

Global, International, and Local CAPM

The standard capital asset pricing model (CAPM), introduced in Chapter 15, for estimating the cost of capital, does not explicitly account for foreign assets, foreign investors, or currencies. This raises the question whether such a model can provide the right cost of capital for investments in foreign currencies. If foreign-currency rates are changing, the same investment will generate different returns to investors from different countries. Take the case of a German government bond denominated in euros. From the perspective of a German or Dutch investor, this bond generates a risk-free return (assuming there is no inflation), because the euro is also the investor's domestic currency. But the bond's return is not risk free for investors in the United States, because the return measured in U.S. dollars will vary with the dollar-to-euro exchange rate.

As a general rule, investors from countries with different currencies are likely to disagree about an asset's expected return and risk. In theory, this means that the standard CAPM no longer holds, and a more complex, international CAPM is required. In practice, however, we find that the CAPM-based approach as laid out in Chapter 15 is still valid for estimating the cost of capital for cross-border investments. This appendix provides further background for our recommendations and practical guidelines for estimating the cost of capital in foreign currency.

GLOBAL CAPM

Investors' disagreement about the return and risk of international investments disappears if purchasing power parity (PPP) holds across all currencies. In that case, changes in exchange rates perfectly match differences in inflation between currencies[1]:

$$X_t = X_{t-1}\left(\frac{1 + i_A}{1 + i_B}\right)$$

where

X_t = exchange rate of currency B expressed in units of currency A at time t

i_A, i_B = inflation rate for currency A, B

As a result, the expected return and risk in real terms for any asset will be the same for all investors, regardless of their domestic currency. In the German bond example, any appreciation of the U.S. dollar relative to the euro would make the nominal bond return for U.S. investors lower. But if PPP holds, the inflation rate in the United States would be lower by exactly the same amount, so the payoff in real terms for U.S. and German investors would be equal. In real terms, there is no currency risk for investors. They will all hold the same global market portfolio of risky assets and face the same real risk-free rate as if there were only a single currency.

The resulting so-called global CAPM is in fact the standard CAPM with a global market portfolio. It expresses the expected real return for an asset j as follows:

$$E(r_j) = r_f + \beta_{j,G}[E(r_G) - r_f]$$

where

r_j = return for asset j

r_f = risk-free rate

$\beta_{j,G}$ = beta of asset j versus global market portfolio G

r_G = return for global market portfolio G

According to the global CAPM, the cost of capital for domestic as well as foreign assets follows from the asset's beta relative to the global market portfolio and the market risk premium of that market portfolio relative to the risk-free rate.

[1] Technically, this is called relative purchasing power parity, referring to changes in prices and exchange rates. Absolute purchasing power parity requires that prices be the same across currencies; see, for example, R. Brealey, S. Myers, F. Allen, and A. Edmans, *Principles of Corporate Finance*, 14th ed. (New York: McGraw-Hill, 2023), Chap. 28.

Technically, the global CAPM is valid only if PPP holds. Evidence on PPP has been mixed, but academic research appears to conclude that deviations from PPP between currencies are typically reduced to half their value within three to five years.[2] In other words, exchange rates do adjust for differences in inflation between countries, although not immediately and perfectly.

For investors and companies able to invest outside their home markets without restrictions, we recommend using the global CAPM to estimate the cost of capital for foreign as well as domestic investments. Effectively, this means applying the approach described in Chapter 15. Although the alternative, international CAPM (discussed next), may be theoretically superior, it is far more complex and does not lead to materially different results in practice.

INTERNATIONAL CAPM

If PPP does not hold, real returns from foreign assets are no longer free from currency risk, because changes in exchange rates are not offset by differences in inflation. The greater the correlation between the return on a foreign asset and the relevant currency rate, the higher the risk for an investor. Take, for example, a Dutch company whose stock returns, measured in euros, tend to be higher when the euro appreciates against the U.S. dollar and vice versa (for instance, because the company imports components from the United States and sells end products in Europe). The stock's returns will be riskier for an American investor than for a European investor, because the exchange rate tends to amplify the returns when translated into U.S. dollars. The absence of PPP means that disparities between dollar and euro inflation will not offset this difference in returns when measured in real terms.

To hold foreign assets, rational investors will require some compensation in the form of a higher expected return for an asset, depending on its exposure to currency risk. As a result, what matters for an asset's expected return is no longer only the asset's beta versus the global market portfolio (as in the case of the global CAPM). The international CAPM captures the additional return requirements by also including asset betas versus currency exchange rates. For example, in a world consisting of three countries, each with its own currency, the international CAPM would define the expected return on asset j in a given home currency as follows[3]:

$$E(r_j) = r_f + \beta_{j,G}[E(r_G) - r_f] + \beta_{j,A}\mathrm{CRP}_A + \beta_{j,B}\mathrm{CRP}_B \qquad \text{(G.1)}$$

---

[2] For an overview, see A. M. Taylor and M. P. Taylor, "The Purchasing Power Parity Debate," *Journal of Economic Perspectives* 18, no. 4 (Fall 2004): 135–158.

[3] This is a simplified version of the Solnik-Sercu international CAPM; see, for example, P. Sercu, *International Finance* (Princeton, NJ: Princeton University Press, 2009), Chap. 19; and S. Armitage, *The Cost of Capital* (Cambridge: Cambridge University Press, 2005), Chap. 11.

where

$$r_j = \text{return for asset } j$$
$$r_f = \text{risk-free rate}$$
$$\beta_{j,G} = \text{beta of asset } j \text{ versus global market portfolio } G$$
$$\beta_{j,A}, \beta_{j,B} = \text{beta of asset } j \text{ versus currency rate } X_A, X_B$$
$$\text{CRP}_A, \text{CRP}_B = \text{risk premium for currency } A, B$$

The currency risk premiums are defined as follows:

$$\text{CRP}_n = \frac{E(X_{n1}) - F_{n1}}{X_{n0}} \tag{G.2}$$

where

X_{nt} = exchange rate of home currency expressed in units of currency n at time t where $n = A, B$

F_{n1} = forward rate for $t = 1$ of home currency expressed in units of currency n

Although theoretically correct, the international CAPM is probably too cumbersome for practical use. In particular, it is not clear how many of the world's currencies to include in estimating the cost of capital. Even taking only a handful of leading global currencies would require that you estimate as many currency risk premiums. Further, in addition to an asset's market beta, you would need to estimate its beta versus each of these currencies.

Another reason not to use the international CAPM is that empirical research has shown that the currency risk premiums are typically too small to matter when estimating a cost of capital.[4] According to research that compared cost of capital estimates from a global and an international CAPM for large U.S. companies, differences are probably less than half a percentage point.[5] As we can see from Equations G.1 and G.2, the international CAPM simplifies to the global CAPM when currency risk premiums are negligible. In other words, PPP apparently holds sufficiently well for the global CAPM to lead to the same cost of capital as the international CAPM. Expressed either way, this evidence reinforces our recommendation to use the global CAPM.

[4] Sercu, *International Finance*, Chap. 19.

[5] See W. Dolde, C. Giaccotto, D. Mishra, and T. O'Brien, "Should Managers Estimate Cost of Equity Using a Two-Factor International CAPM?" *Managerial Finance* 38, no. 8 (2012): 708–728; and D. Mishra and T. O'Brien, "A Comparison of Cost of Equity Estimates of Local and Global CAPMs," *Financial Review* 36, no. 4 (2001): 27–48.

LOCAL CAPM

Some practitioners and academic researchers propose estimating the cost of capital for an investment opportunity in a particular country by using a local CAPM. The investment's beta is then estimated versus the market portfolio of the country, and the market risk premium follows from the excess return of that same market portfolio over the local risk-free rate. The approach is theoretically correct if stocks are correlated to the global market portfolio only through the local market[6]:

$$\beta_{j,G} = \beta_{j,L} \times \beta_{L,G} \tag{G.3}$$

where

$\beta_{j,G}$ = beta of asset j versus global market portfolio G

$\beta_{j,L}$ = beta of asset j versus local market portfolio L

$\beta_{L,G}$ = beta of local market portfolio L versus global market portfolio G

This implies that any international risk factors influencing the returns of companies in a given country are fully captured by the local market portfolio of that country. You can then indirectly estimate any asset's global beta by multiplying its local beta by the global beta of the local market. If the local stock market is fully integrated and correctly priced in the global market, its expected return is

$$E(r_L) = r_f + \beta_{L,G}[E(r_G) - r_f] \tag{G.4}$$

where

r_L = expected return for local market portfolio L

r_f = risk-free rate

r_G = return for global market portfolio G

Combining Equations G.3 and G.4 shows that the expected return for a stock j estimated via the local and global CAPM should be equal as well. Following the global CAPM, this return is given by

$$E(r_j) = r_f + \beta_{j,G}[E(r_G) - r_f]$$

Substituting the asset's global beta by the indirect beta defined previously in Equation G.3 leads to:

$$E(r_j) = r_f + \beta_{j,L} \times \beta_{L,G}[E(r_G) - r_f]$$

[6] See R. Stulz, "The Cost of Capital in Internationally Integrated Markets: The Case of Nestlé," *European Financial Management* 1, no. 1 (1995): 11–22.

This can be rearranged to show equivalence with the local CAPM:

$$E(r_j) = r_f + \beta_{j,L} [E(r_L) - r_f]$$

Although the assumptions may not seem very realistic at face value, there is evidence that the local and global CAPM generate similar results. Empirical research finds that the cost of capital estimated for U.S. companies with a local CAPM is very close to the estimate based on a global CAPM.[7] For U.S. stocks, this may not be surprising, as the U.S. market portfolio is well diversified and highly correlated with the global market portfolio. But supporting evidence also comes from nine developed economies, including not only the United States but also the United Kingdom, Germany, France, and smaller economies such as the Netherlands and Switzerland. An analysis of beta estimates for companies versus a local and global market portfolio has shown that for these countries, the betas are typically related, as indicated by Equation G.3.[8]

However, the local CAPM approach, when compared with the global CAPM, has some practical drawbacks. First is that when you apply the local CAPM to investments in different countries, you should estimate the local market risk premium and beta for each of these countries, instead of only the global market risk premium, as you would do when applying the global CAPM. Also, with a local CAPM, you cannot make a straightforward estimate of a company's beta based on the average of the estimated betas for a sample of industry peers (which Chapter 15 recommends to reduce the standard error of the company's beta). The reason is that if the peers are in different countries, their local betas are not directly comparable. Finally, local risk premiums are typically less stable over time than their aggregate, the global risk premium. For example, Exhibit G.1 compares the realized premiums on local stock market indexes with government bond returns for several countries and a globally diversified portfolio, using data from Dimson, Marsh, and Staunton's analysis of long-term average returns on equities and corporate and government bonds.[9] The individual countries' risk premiums vary considerably, depending on the time period over which they are measured, while the global premium remains almost unchanged.

Note that the risk premium differences shown in Exhibit G.1 do not mean that the price for risk varies across these countries. These differences are driven by several factors. First, levels of economic development and,

[7] R. Harris, F. Marston, D. Mishra, and T. O'Brien, "Ex-Ante Cost of Equity Estimates of S&P 500 Firms: The Choice between Domestic and Global CAPM," *Financial Management* 32, no. 3 (2003): 51–66.

[8] See C. Koedijk, C. Kool, P. Schotman, and M. van Dijk, "The Cost of Capital in International Financial Markets: Local or Global?," *Journal of International Money and Finance* 21, no. 6 (2002): 905–929.

[9] E. Dimson, P. Marsh, and M. Staunton, *Triumph of the Optimists: 101 Years of Global Investment Returns* (Princeton, NJ: Princeton University Press, 2002); and E. Dimson, P. Marsh, M. Staunton, and J. Wilmot, *Credit Suisse Global Investment Returns Yearbook 2016* (London: Credit Suisse Research Institute, 2016).

EXHIBIT G.1 **Comparing Risk Premiums Across Countries and over Time**

Annualized market risk premium over 1-year Treasury bills, %

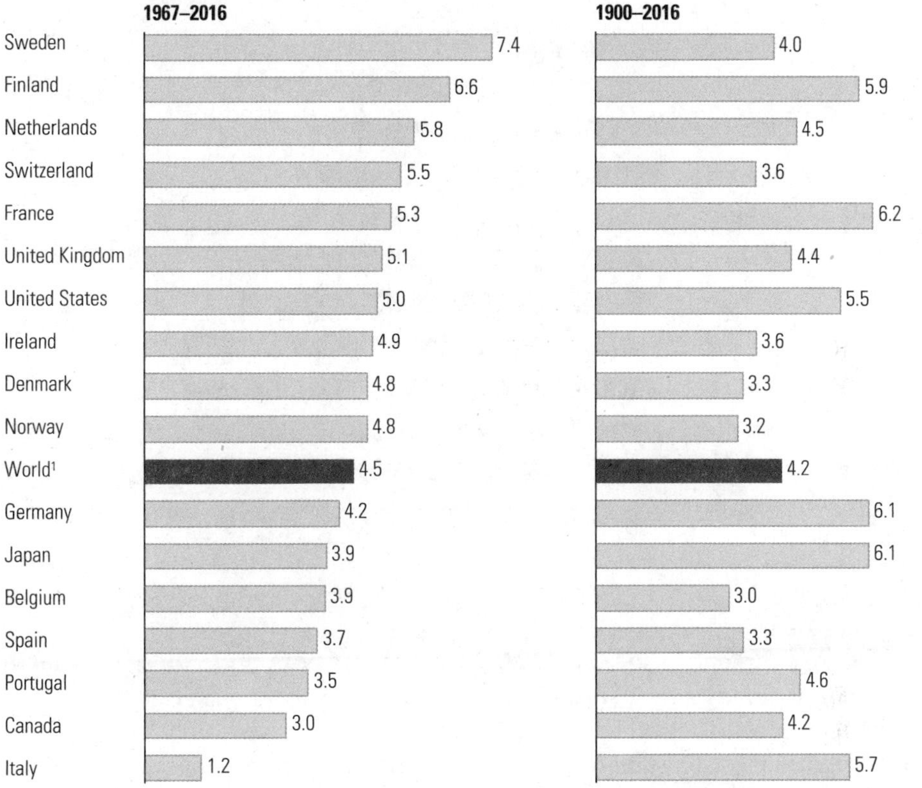

	1967–2016	1900–2016
Sweden	7.4	4.0
Finland	6.6	5.9
Netherlands	5.8	4.5
Switzerland	5.5	3.6
France	5.3	6.2
United Kingdom	5.1	4.4
United States	5.0	5.5
Ireland	4.9	3.6
Denmark	4.8	3.3
Norway	4.8	3.2
World[1]	4.5	4.2
Germany	4.2	6.1
Japan	3.9	6.1
Belgium	3.9	3.0
Spain	3.7	3.3
Portugal	3.5	4.6
Canada	3.0	4.2
Italy	1.2	5.7

[1] Globally diversified portfolio.

Source: E. Dimson, P. Marsh, and M. Staunton, *Triumph of the Optimists: 101 Years of Global Investment Returns* (Princeton, NJ: Princeton University Press, 2002); E. Dimson, P. Marsh, M. Staunton, and J. Wilmot, *Credit Suisse Global Investment Yearbook 2016* (London: Credit Suisse Research Institute, February 2016).

therefore, profit growth have varied over the past century among the countries. Second, capital markets were less integrated in the past, so prices across countries may not have been equalized. The main reason, though, is that many of the stock market indexes used had different levels of diversification and beta. Therefore, their performance was skewed by different industry concentrations. In most European countries, the key stock market indexes, which account for the majority of their stock markets' total capitalization, typically include only 25 to 40 companies, often from a limited range of industries. Indeed, research has shown that a large fraction of the variation in returns on European market indexes could be explained by their industry composition (see Exhibit G.2).[10]

[10] R. Roll, "Industrial Structure and the Comparative Behavior of International Stock Market Indexes," *Journal of Finance* 47, no. 1 (1992): 3–42.

Exhibit G.2 **Share of Equity Returns Explained by Industry Composition of Index**

Adjusted R^2, %

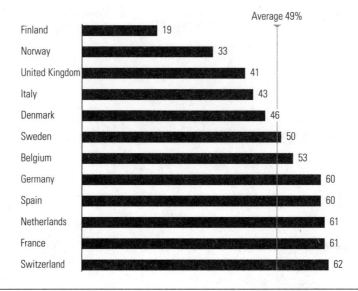

Source: R. Roll, "Industrial Structure and the Comparative Behaviour of International Stock Market Indexes," *Journal of Finance* 47, no. 1 (1992): 3–42.

We recommend a local CAPM only for investors and companies facing restrictions on investing abroad. In that case, the local market portfolio is the right reference to estimate the cost of capital. As a result, valuations in such restricted markets can be out of line with those in global markets—which is what we have encountered in the past for valuations in, for example, Asian stock markets.

Two-Stage Formula for Continuing Value

In certain situations, you may want to split the continuing-value (CV) period into two periods with different assumptions for growth and return on invested capital (ROIC). In a situation such as this, you can use a two-stage variation of the value driver formula for discounted cash flow (DCF) valuations. The first stage is based on a limited-life annuity formula, and the second stage is based on a perpetuity:

$$CV = \text{Annuity Stage} + \text{Perpetuity Stage}$$

such that

$$\text{Annuity Stage} = \left[\frac{NOPAT_{t+1}\left(1 - \frac{g_A}{RONIC_A}\right)}{WACC - g_A} \right]\left[1 - \left(\frac{1 + g_A}{1 + WACC}\right)^N\right]$$

$$\text{Perpetuity Stage} = \frac{1}{(1 + WACC)^N} \times \frac{NOPAT_{t+1}(1 + g_A)^N\left(1 - \frac{g_B}{RONIC_B}\right)}{(WACC - g_B)}$$

where

$NOPAT$ = net operating profit after taxes

g_A = expected growth rate in the first stage of the CV period

$RONIC_A$ = expected return on new invested capital during the first stage of the CV period

$WACC$ = weighted average cost of capital

N = number of years in the first stage of the CV period

g_B = expected growth rate in the second stage of the CV period

$RONIC_B$ = expected return on new invested capital during the second stage of the CV period

Note that g_A can take any value; it does not have to be less than the weighted average cost of capital. Conversely, g_B must be less than WACC for this perpetuity formula to be valid. Otherwise the formula goes to infinity, and the company eventually becomes the entire world economy.

A two-stage variation can also be used for the economic-profit continuing-value formula[1]:

$$
\begin{aligned}
CV = {} & \frac{\text{Economic Profit}_{t+1}}{\text{WACC}} \\
& + \left[\frac{\text{NOPAT}_{t+1}\left(\frac{g_A}{\text{RONIC}_A}\right)(\text{RONIC}_A - \text{WACC})}{\text{WACC}(\text{WACC} - g_A)} \right]\left[1 - \left(\frac{1 + g_A}{1 + \text{WACC}}\right)^N \right] \\
& + \frac{\text{NOPAT}(1 + g_A)^N\left(\frac{g_B}{\text{RONIC}_B}\right)(\text{RONIC}_B - \text{WACC})}{\text{WACC}(\text{WACC} - g_B)(1 + \text{WACC})^N}
\end{aligned}
$$

These formulas always assume that the return on the base level of capital remains constant at the level of the last year of the explicit forecast. If you want to model a decline in ROIC for all capital, including the base level of capital, it is best to model this into the explicit forecast.

It is difficult to model changes in average ROIC with formulas, because the growth rate in revenues and NOPAT will not equal the growth rate in free cash flow (FCF), and there are multiple ways for the ROIC to decline. You could model declining ROIC by setting the growth rate for capital and reducing NOPAT over time (in which case NOPAT will grow much more slowly than capital). Or you could set the growth rate for NOPAT and adjust FCF each period (so FCF growth again will be slower than NOPAT growth). The dynamics of these relationships are complex, and we do not recommend embedding the dynamics in continuing-value formulas, especially if the key value drivers become less transparent.

---

[1] Thanks to Pieter de Wit and David Krieger for deriving this formula.

APPENDIX ▌

A Valuation of Costco Wholesale

This appendix shows a typical outside-in valuation model, using Costco Wholesale as an example. Our historical analysis is based on Costco's published income statements and balance sheets from its 2019 to 2023 annual reports. Companies rarely restate financial statements more than one or two years back in time, so when appropriate, we use data from original filings to avoid confusion. The line item names and references to footnotes are worded according to the conventions of the 2023 annual report.

The valuation process we apply here is detailed in Part Two of the book. The following commentary provides an informal guide to each of the exhibits, including clarification of items that may not be apparent. We hope our references to specific chapters will help readers connect the exhibits to the general principles explored throughout the book.

MODELING THE FINANCIAL STATEMENTS

The valuation process begins by replicating the financial statements in a spreadsheet, including the income statement, balance sheet, statement of stockholders' equity, and tax reconciliation table. The first three statements for Costco are presented in the annual report immediately following the auditor's letter. The company's tax reconciliation table is found in the notes to the financial statements.

Exhibit I.1: Income Statement. We present the income statement as reported by the company, with two exceptions. First, the exhibit separates depreciation and amortization from selling, general, and administrative expenses. Costco reports depreciation and amortization in its statement of cash flows. Second, we separate interest income from other income to facilitate the modeling of income generated from potential future balances of excess cash. Costco provides details on interest and other income in Item 7 of its annual report, within the "Results of Operations" section.

For each of the financial statements, we provide the company's historical values and forecasts of future performance. The final year is denoted by CV, which represents the base year used in continuing value. We discuss continuing value later in this appendix.

Exhibit I.2: Balance Sheet. We present the balance sheet as reported by the company, with three exceptions. First, we aggregate cash and short-term investments into a single account.

Second, we extract finance lease assets, goodwill, and deferred income taxes from other long-term assets. This allows us to estimate cash taxes, identify tax loss carryforwards, and reclassify remaining amounts as equity equivalents during reorganization. Extracting goodwill allows us to measure ROIC with and without goodwill. Costco reports goodwill in Note 1, Summary of Significant Accounting Policies; finance lease assets in Note 5, Leases; and deferred taxes and their location on the balance sheet in Note 8, Taxes.

Third, because leases are a form of debt financing, we separate them from other current liabilities and other liabilities. In our experience, most companies embed finance leases within debt, but this is not the case for Costco. The company reports finance leases and their location on the balance sheet in Note 5, Leases.

Exhibit I.3: Statement of Costco Stockholders' Equity. The statement of stockholders' equity explains the change in equity from one year to the next. The statement includes the translation adjustment for foreign operations, stock-based compensation, repurchases of common stock, and dividends. These accounts are required for reconciling free cash flow to cash flow available to investors. For some accounts, such as dividends, the account appears directly in the reconciliation of cash flow. In other cases, an account will reverse a non-cash change in a balance sheet account, such as the foreign-currency translation adjustment.

Exhibit I.4: Tax Reconciliation Table. The tax reconciliation table is required to estimate operating taxes and reconcile net operating profit after taxes (NOPAT) to net income. Costco reports the tax reconciliation table in Note 8, Taxes. While most companies report the table in either their home currency or percentages, Costco reports both versions.

REORGANIZING THE FINANCIAL STATEMENTS

With financial statements in hand, we next reorganize them into NOPAT, operating taxes, invested capital, and total funds invested. Here we briefly describe the reorganization; Chapter 11 presents a comprehensive description of how to reorganize the financial statements.

Exhibit I.5: NOPAT and Its Reconciliation to Net Income. This exhibit reorganizes the income statement into NOPAT and reconciles NOPAT to net income. In the case of Costco, unadjusted EBITA matches operating profit as reported on the company's income statement. This is not always the case. As discussed in Chapter 21, many companies include nonrecurring items such as restructuring costs as part of operating profit on their financial statements. For the purpose of valuation, only ongoing operating expenses should be deducted from revenue to estimate EBITA.

As outlined in Chapter 11, reclassify interest from fixed-payment and variable operating leases as financial expenses, rather than including it in operating expenses. To calculate lease-related interest, multiply the previous year's lease liability (found in Exhibit I.9) by the weighted-average discount rate for operating leases. Do not add back interest expense from finance leases, as it is already included in interest expense. In 2023, Costco's weighted-average discount rate for operating leases was 2.47 percent, as reported in Note 5, Leases.

To determine net operating profit after tax, subtract operating cash taxes from adjusted EBITA. Operating cash taxes are discussed next.

Exhibit I.6: Operating Cash Taxes. To calculate NOPAT and its reconciliation to net income, it is necessary to disaggregate the provision for income taxes into operating taxes, taxes related to nonoperating accounts such as interest expense, and other nonoperating taxes such as IRS audits. Exhibit I.6 estimates operating cash taxes, using the three-step method introduced in Chapter 11 and discussed in detail in Chapter 20. To start, multiply EBITA by the statutory tax rate presented in Exhibit I.4. The statutory tax rate equals the sum of the federal and state income tax rates.

Next, adjust statutory taxes on EBITA by any items in the tax reconciliation table that you consider to be ongoing and related to operating activities. For Costco, we adjust statutory taxes on EBITA by two items: the foreign tax differential and taxes related to the employee stock ownership plan. In contrast, we treat adjustments related to special dividends and the 2017 tax act as nonoperating, given their one-time nature. Finally, to convert operating taxes into operating cash taxes, subtract the increase in operating-related deferred-tax liabilities, net of deferred-tax assets. An increase in deferred-tax liabilities means the company paid less in taxes than reported on its income statement.

Exhibit I.7: Deferred Taxes. To create the inputs needed for the cash tax rate, reorganize the deferred-tax table into tax loss carryforwards; operating deferred-tax assets, net of operating liabilities; and nonoperating deferred-tax assets, net of nonoperating liabilities. As with the tax reconciliation table, classifying an account as operating or nonoperating requires judgment. Ask yourself which accounts are operating related and likely to scale with revenue. To convert operating taxes into cash taxes, subtract the increase (or add the decrease) in operating deferred tax liabilities, net deferred tax assets from (to) operating taxes.

For more on the concepts underpinning the operating tax rate and the treatment of deferred taxes, see Chapter 20.

Exhibit I.8: Invested Capital and Total Funds Invested. To estimate invested capital, pull each account directly from the balance sheet, except two: operating cash and variable-rate leases. Operating cash, sometimes called working cash, is estimated at 2 percent of revenues. Cash in excess of 2 percent of revenues is classified as excess cash and reported as a nonoperating asset to be valued separately.

Since December 2019, new accounting standards have mandated that companies capitalize fixed-rate operating leases on their balance sheets. The asset, reported as a "right-of-use asset," is treated similarly to property, plant, and equipment (PP&E). Under the new standards, variable-rate leases are not capitalized and require estimation. As detailed in Chapter 11, we estimate the value of variable-rate leases for Costco by multiplying the right-of-use asset value by the ratio of variable-rate rental expense to fixed-rate rental expense.

Exhibit I.9: Reconciliation of Total Funds Invested. To better understand how the business is financed and to assure accuracy through a second set of calculations, recalculate total funds invested, but this time use sources of investor capital. Exhibit I.9 calculates debt and debt equivalents, which include fixed-rate leases, variable-rate leases, and finance leases. Equity includes common stock and retained earnings. Equity equivalents include deferred-tax accounts except tax loss carryforwards. For Costco, the deferred-tax accounts are negative in some years and act as an offset to equity because deferred-tax assets are larger than the corresponding liabilities.

Costco's total funds invested are financed mostly by equity. For more on how to evaluate and create an appropriate capital structure to support the operations of a business, see Chapter 35.

FORECASTING THE FINANCIAL STATEMENTS

For each financial statement, we present a ten-year forecast. Chapter 13 demonstrates how to create a set of integrated forecasts, link your forecasts to the financial statements, and avoid common pitfalls.

Exhibit I.10: Income Statement Forecast Ratios. To estimate Costco's revenue growth and cost of sales, we use analyst reports from September 2023. While these provide only aggregate results, future revenue is projected by modeling new store openings and revenue growth per store. Exhibit 13.3 summarizes this approach. For other accounts, we forecast using financial ratios based on either the most recent fiscal year or a five-year average, depending on the account's stability.

Membership fees are modeled separately from merchandise sales. Given the high margin associated with membership fees, the shift in the mix from merchandise to membership will increase the operating margin.

To forecast the interest expense on debt, we estimate interest expense as a percentage of prior-year debt. Since we value operations using free cash flow, the forecast of interest expense will not affect the value of operations. We create a forecast solely for the purpose of cash flow planning and to create an integrated set of financial statements. A complete set of financials reduces the likelihood of modeling errors.

In the bottom half of Exhibit I.10 under "Results: Operating margins," we present each operating expense as a percentage of sales, rather than in relation to its forecast driver, as shown in the top half. We also include return on invested capital, both with and without goodwill, to deepen our understanding of the implications of our forecasts.

Exhibit I.11: Balance Sheet Forecast Ratios—Invested Capital. Exhibit I.11 presents forecast ratios for key operating items on the balance sheet, including working capital, long-term operating assets, and other long-term operating liabilities. Working capital is further broken down into operating current assets, such as inventories, and operating current liabilities, such as payables, with each account measured in days. For instance, in 2023, Costco held inventory for an average of 28.6 days. Using days as a metric to forecast working capital accounts better aligns the analysis with the company's operating velocity: the faster assets move through the business, the less investor capital is needed to fund operations.

Long-term assets, however, are held over multiple years, so measuring them in days is not meaningful. Instead, operating-related long-term assets and liabilities are expressed as a percentage of sales. An exception is made for goodwill and acquired intangibles, which are fixed at 2023 levels.

Exhibit I.12: Balance Sheet Forecast Ratios—Sources of Financing. To fund the business, we assume Costco will maintain its 2023 debt-to-value ratio, including leases. This assumption allows us to calculate total leverage year by year. We then subtract projected lease obligations from total debt to determine the required level of corporate debt, which is further allocated between short-term and long-term debt, based on the five-year historical average.

For equity-related items, stock-based compensation is forecast as a percentage of revenues, while dividends are projected as a percentage of net income. Excess cash is gradually returned to shareholders over a five-year period through share repurchases. During the remaining forecast period, share repurchases act as the balancing item to ensure the balance sheet remains in equilibrium.

While these capital structure forecasts have an impact on the income statement and balance sheet, they do not affect enterprise value in a DCF analysis, as capital structure influences valuation only through the weighted average cost of capital (WACC).

Exhibit I.13: Free Cash Flow and Cash Flow to Investors. Exhibit I.13 shows how free cash flow is estimated. Most accounts, such as operating working capital, equal the change in the corresponding invested-capital account.

Historical capital expenditures are reported on the statement of cash flows. Because of currency translations, capital expenditures do not equal the change in net property, plant, and equipment plus depreciation. The link between capital expenditures and the change in net PP&E is detailed in Exhibit 11.15. Unexplained currency translations are treated as a nonoperating cash flow.

Exhibit I.14: Reconciliation of Cash Flow to Investors. To reconcile cash flow to investors, we aggregate the changes in debt and equity accounts. Debt includes traditional debt as well as finance, variable, and operating leases. Equity includes stock-based compensation, common stock repurchases, dividends, and proceeds from the sale of noncontrolling interests.

ESTIMATING CONTINUING VALUE

Next, use a continuing-value formula to estimate the value of cash flows beyond the explicit forecast period. Start using the continuing-value formula only at the point when the company has reached a steady state.

Exhibit I.15: Continuing Value. We use the key value driver formula to estimate continuing value. The formula requires a forecast of NOPAT in 2034 (known as the continuing-value year, abbreviated as CV in Exhibits I.1, I.5, I.6, I.10, and I.18) to determine the continuing value as of 2033. We do not generate continuing-value forecasts for invested capital or free cash flow in the continuing-value year; they are unnecessary for the calculation.

One critical forecast in the continuing value is long-run revenue growth. Given the historical strength of Costco's ability to grow, we use a growth rate of 4 percent to estimate the long-run growth rate. For a comprehensive discussion of how to estimate continuing value, see Chapter 14.

ESTIMATING THE WEIGHTED AVERAGE COST OF CAPITAL

To value operations, discount cash flow at the weighted average cost of capital. The WACC incorporates the required return from all sources of capital into a single number.

Exhibit I.16: Weighted Average Cost of Capital. Because of a purposeful financial policy, Costco uses less debt than any of its industry peers. With this in mind, we assume Costco will disgorge excess cash and set its target debt-to-value ratio to its current debt-to-value as measured on a gross basis.

Likewise, when we estimate the levered cost of equity, we use the same debt-to-value ratio. For a comprehensive discussion of the cost of capital, see Chapter 15.

VALUING THE ENTERPRISE AND ESTIMATING VALUE PER SHARE

To value Costco, we use both enterprise DCF and discounted economic profit. Free cash flow (FCF) models measure how cash flows in and out of the company, regardless of the accounting treatment. Economic profit links better to value creation. Implemented correctly, both models will lead to the same valuation result.

Exhibit I.17: Enterprise DCF Valuation. To arrive at the present value of cash flow, we sum each year's discounted FCF with the discounted value of continuing value. Then we adjust the resulting value by half a year to estimate the value of operations, reflecting that cash flows are generated throughout the year, not just at year end. To the value of operations, we add nonoperating assets that are excluded from free cash flow—in this case, excess cash and the value of tax loss carryforwards. For simplicity, we value tax loss carryforwards at book value less the valuation allowance.

Do not add other deferred-tax assets, such as those related to equity compensation or deferred membership fees, to the value of operations. The value of these tax assets is already incorporated into NOPAT by using cash-based taxes. Consequently, they are classified as an equity equivalent and ignored.

To estimate intrinsic equity value, subtract debt and debt equivalents—including all debt, leases, and noncontrolling interests—from enterprise value. Although Costco repurchased its noncontrolling interests in 2022, we retain this placeholder for clarity. Also, while we use the book values for ease of exposition, use the market value of each account when available. Dividing equity value by the number of shares outstanding leads to a value of almost $543 per share, which matches the share price in August 2023. For more on converting enterprise value into equity value by adding nonoperating assets and subtracting debt equivalents, see Chapter 16.

Exhibit I.18: ROIC and Economic Profit. A robust valuation will focus not only on the resulting share price but also on the critical value drivers that result from the model. Exhibit I.17 presents ROIC and economic profit by year. When benchmarking across companies or over time, we usually calculate ROIC using a two-year average of invested capital. In this situation, we calculate ROIC using invested capital from the beginning of the year, in order to create an economic-profit valuation that matches the results from enterprise DCF. In this exhibit, we present only a high-level analysis of performance. For more on how to disaggregate and assess ROIC in depth, see Chapter 12.

Exhibit I.19: Valuation Using Economic Profit. To determine the value of operations, add discounted economic profit to invested capital from year-end 2023. As expected, an economic-profit-based valuation leads to the same value of operations as an enterprise DCF valuation.

PUTTING THE MODEL TO WORK

While the valuation model is complete, a good financial analyst or investor will now put it to work. Ask yourself several questions: Which variables are the most critical to value? What is the value if performance remains unchanged? How does this value differ from one based on other forecasts? What is the value of the proposed improvements? Are there scenarios that may provide additional insights into various strategies?

Exhibit I.20: Costco: Value per Share Sensitivity to Key Inputs. Exhibit I.20 presents a sensitivity table illustrating the value per share (in dollars), based on a range of forecast assumptions. Operating margins, ranging from 3.5 to 6.5 percent, are presented incrementally from left to right in the table. For reference, operating margins in 2023 stood at 3.9 percent. Rather than assuming an immediate margin shift, the model phases in these changes gradually over five years.

The table also analyzes varying growth rates, mainly driven by store expansions. For instance, the top row projects an annual growth rate of 5.8 percent, based on the opening of 268 new stores over the next decade and a 3.0 percent increase in same-store sales. Like margin, the increase in store count happens gradually. Each subsequent row assumes an increase of roughly 60 stores. Notice that while growth does affect projections, margin improvements yield a much more substantial effect. With such narrow margins, the added value from new stores is relatively modest.

It's essential to remember that a model's true worth goes beyond the final valuation. As discussed in Chapter 17, the most valuable insights come from exploring alternatives and building scenarios to test different assumptions.

EXHIBIT I.1 **Costco: Income Statement**

$ million

	Historical					Forecast										CV[4]
	2019	2020	2021	2022	2023	2024	2025	2026	2027	2028	2029	2030	2031	2032	2033	
Merchandise sales	149,351	163,220	192,052	222,730	237,710	248,605	265,011	282,772	302,014	323,206	346,218	368,730	390,426	410,985	430,088	447,421
Membership fees	3,352	3,541	3,877	4,224	4,580	4,815	5,408	6,066	6,794	7,270	7,788	8,295	8,783	9,245	9,675	10,065
Revenues	152,703	166,761	195,929	226,954	242,290	253,420	270,419	288,837	308,808	330,477	354,007	377,024	399,208	420,231	439,763	457,485
Merchandise costs	(132,886)	(144,939)	(170,684)	(199,382)	(212,586)	(221,449)	(235,720)	(251,152)	(267,851)	(286,228)	(305,711)	(325,588)	(344,746)	(362,900)	(379,768)	(395,072)
Selling, general, and administrative[1]	(13,588)	(14,742)	(16,756)	(17,879)	(19,513)	(20,409)	(21,778)	(23,262)	(24,870)	(26,615)	(28,510)	(30,364)	(32,151)	(33,844)	(35,417)	(36,844)
Depreciation and lease amortization[2]	(1,492)	(1,645)	(1,781)	(1,900)	(2,077)	(1,908)	(1,996)	(2,128)	(2,270)	(2,425)	(2,595)	(2,780)	(2,960)	(3,135)	(3,300)	(3,453)
Operating income	4,737	5,435	6,708	7,793	8,114	9,653	10,925	12,296	13,816	15,209	17,191	18,292	19,351	20,352	21,279	22,116
Interest expense	(150)	(160)	(171)	(158)	(160)	(463)	(551)	(628)	(713)	(808)	(894)	(1,018)	(1,085)	(1,148)	(1,209)	(1,265)
Interest income[3]	126	89	41	61	470	104	83	62	42	21	—	—	—	—	—	—
Other income[3]	52	3	102	144	63	—	—	—	—	—	—	—	—	—	—	—
Earnings before taxes	4,765	5,367	6,680	7,840	8,487	9,293	10,457	11,730	13,144	14,421	16,297	17,274	18,267	19,204	20,070	20,851
Provision for income taxes	(1,061)	(1,308)	(1,601)	(1,925)	(2,195)	(2,444)	(2,729)	(3,042)	(3,389)	(3,703)	(4,163)	(4,403)	(4,647)	(4,877)	(5,090)	(5,282)
Net income, consolidated	3,704	4,059	5,079	5,915	6,292	6,850	7,727	8,688	9,755	10,718	12,134	12,871	13,620	14,327	14,980	15,569
Net income, noncontrolling interests	(45)	(57)	(72)	(71)	—	—	—	—	—	—	—	—	—	—	—	—
Net income, Costco	3,659	4,002	5,007	5,844	6,292	6,850	7,727	8,688	9,755	10,718	12,134	12,871	13,620	14,327	14,980	15,569

[1] Includes pre-opening expenses.
[2] Aggregated in selling, general, and administrative expenses in original filings; assumes amortization related to acquired intangibles is immaterial.
[3] Aggregated in "Interest income and other, net" in original filings.
[4] Continuing value (CV) forecast.

EXHIBIT I.2 **Costco: Balance Sheet**

$ million

	Historical					Forecast									
	2019	2020	2021	2022	2023	2024	2025	2026	2027	2028	2029	2030	2031	2032	2033
Assets															
Cash and cash equivalents[1]	9,444	13,305	12,175	11,049	15,234	13,379	11,641	9,932	8,254	6,610	7,080	7,540	7,984	8,405	8,795
Receivables, net	1,535	1,550	1,803	2,241	2,285	2,390	2,547	2,718	2,903	3,107	3,328	3,544	3,753	3,951	4,134
Merchandise inventories	11,395	12,242	14,215	17,907	16,651	17,345	18,463	19,672	20,980	22,419	23,945	25,502	27,003	28,425	29,746
Other current assets	1,111	1,023	1,312	1,499	1,709	1,787	1,905	2,033	2,171	2,324	2,489	2,651	2,807	2,955	3,092
Total current assets	23,485	28,120	29,505	32,696	35,879	34,901	34,557	34,355	34,308	34,459	36,842	39,238	41,547	43,734	45,767
Property, plant, and equipment	20,890	21,807	23,492	24,646	26,684	27,907	29,749	31,742	33,902	36,281	38,865	41,392	43,827	46,135	48,279
Operating lease right-of-use assets	—	2,788	2,890	2,774	2,713	2,837	3,025	3,227	3,447	3,689	3,951	4,208	4,456	4,691	4,909
Finance lease assets[2]	—	592	1,000	1,620	1,325	1,386	1,477	1,576	1,683	1,802	1,930	2,055	2,176	2,291	2,397
Goodwill[2]	53	988	996	993	994	994	994	994	994	994	994	994	994	994	994
Deferred income taxes[2]	398	406	444	445	491	663	856	1,072	1,313	1,577	1,874	2,189	2,522	2,871	3,236
Other long-term assets[2]	574	855	941	992	908	950	1,012	1,080	1,154	1,235	1,322	1,408	1,491	1,570	1,643
Total assets	45,400	55,556	59,268	64,166	68,994	69,638	71,670	74,047	76,801	80,036	85,778	91,485	97,013	102,286	107,226
Liabilities and shareholders' equity															
Accounts payable	11,679	14,172	16,278	17,848	17,483	18,212	19,386	20,655	22,028	23,539	25,142	26,776	28,352	29,845	31,232
Accrued salaries and benefits	3,176	3,605	4,090	4,381	4,278	4,474	4,769	5,089	5,435	5,817	6,231	6,636	7,026	7,396	7,740
Accrued member rewards	1,180	1,393	1,671	1,911	2,150	2,249	2,397	2,558	2,732	2,923	3,131	3,335	3,531	3,717	3,890
Deferred membership fees	1,711	1,651	2,042	2,174	2,337	2,444	2,605	2,780	2,969	3,178	3,404	3,625	3,838	4,041	4,228
Current portion of long-term debt	1,699	95	799	73	1,081	863	995	1,142	1,307	1,451	1,668	1,777	1,882	1,981	2,073
Current portion of operating leases[3]	—	231	222	239	220	230	245	262	280	299	320	341	361	380	398
Current portion of finance leases[3]	26	31	72	245	129	135	144	153	164	175	188	200	212	223	233
Other current liabilities	3,766	3,466	4,267	5,127	5,905	6,176	6,583	7,024	7,502	8,029	8,600	9,160	9,699	10,209	10,684
Total current liabilities	23,237	24,844	29,441	31,998	33,583	34,782	37,124	39,663	42,416	45,411	48,685	51,850	54,901	57,793	60,479
Long-term debt	5,124	7,514	6,692	6,484	5,377	7,029	8,106	9,307	10,644	11,822	13,590	14,475	15,329	16,138	16,890
Long-term operating lease liabilities	—	2,558	2,642	2,482	2,426	2,537	2,705	2,886	3,082	3,299	3,533	3,763	3,985	4,194	4,389
Long-term finance leases[4]	395	657	980	1,383	1,303	1,363	1,453	1,550	1,655	1,772	1,898	2,021	2,140	2,253	2,358
Deferred income taxes[4]	543	665	754	724	795	1,074	1,386	1,736	2,126	2,553	3,034	3,544	4,083	4,649	5,240
Other long-term liabilities	517	613	681	448	452	473	504	538	574	615	658	701	742	781	818
Total liabilities	29,816	36,851	41,190	43,519	43,936	47,258	51,278	55,679	60,498	65,472	71,398	76,355	81,180	85,808	90,173
Costco shareholders' equity	15,243	18,284	17,564	20,642	25,058	22,380	20,392	18,367	16,303	14,565	14,381	15,129	15,833	16,478	17,052
Noncontrolling interests	341	421	514	5	—	—	—	—	—	—	—	—	—	—	—
Total shareholders' equity	15,584	18,705	18,078	20,647	25,058	22,380	20,392	18,367	16,303	14,565	14,381	15,129	15,833	16,478	17,052
Liabilities and shareholders' equity	45,400	55,556	59,268	64,166	68,994	69,638	71,670	74,047	76,801	80,036	85,778	91,485	97,013	102,286	107,226

Note: Costco's fiscal year ends on the Sunday nearest August 31. For example, the 2023 fiscal year ended on September 3, 2023.

[1] Includes short-term investments.

[2] Aggregated in other long-term assets in original filings.

[3] Aggregated in other current liabilities in original filings.

[4] Aggregated in other long-term liabilities in original filings.

EXHIBIT 1.3 **Costco: Statement of Shareholders' Equity**

$ million

	Historical					Forecast									
	2019	2020	2021	2022	2023	2024	2025	2026	2027	2028	2029	2030	2031	2032	2033
Equity, beginning of year	12,799	15,243	18,284	17,564	20,642	25,058	22,380	20,392	18,367	16,303	14,565	14,381	15,129	15,833	16,478
Net income	3,659	4,002	5,007	5,844	6,292	6,850	7,727	8,688	9,755	10,718	12,134	12,871	13,620	14,327	14,980
Foreign-currency translation adjustment	(237)	139	160	(686)	24	—	—	—	—	—	—	—	—	—	—
Comprehensive income	3,422	4,141	5,167	5,158	6,316	6,850	7,727	8,688	9,755	10,718	12,134	12,871	13,620	14,327	14,980
Stock-based compensation, net of releases	326	291	356	365	475	497	530	566	605	648	694	739	783	824	862
Acquisition of noncontrolling interest	—	—	—	(505)	—	—	—	—	—	—	—	—	—	—	—
Repurchases of common stock	(247)	(198)	(495)	(442)	(677)	(8,176)	(8,160)	(8,935)	(9,792)	(10,213)	(9,737)	(9,388)	(10,023)	(10,639)	(11,225)
Cash dividends declared	(1,057)	(1,193)	(5,748)	(1,498)	(1,698)	(1,849)	(2,085)	(2,345)	(2,633)	(2,893)	(3,274)	(3,473)	(3,676)	(3,866)	(4,043)
Equity, end of year	15,243	18,284	17,564	20,642	25,058	22,380	20,392	18,367	16,303	14,565	14,381	15,129	15,833	16,478	17,052

Note: Costco shareholders' equity excludes noncontrolling interests.

EXHIBIT I.4 **Costco: Tax Reconciliation Table**

$ million

	2019	2020	2021	2022	2023
Federal taxes at statutory rate	1,001	1,127	1,403	1,646	1,782
State taxes, net	171	190	243	267	302
Foreign taxes, net	(1)	92	92	231	160
Employee stock ownership plan (ESOP)	(18)	(24)	(21)	(23)	(25)
Special dividend related to 401(k) plan[1]	—	—	(70)	—	—
2017 tax act	(123)	—	—	—	—
Other	31	(77)	(46)	(196)	(24)
U.S. and foreign tax expense	1,061	1,308	1,601	1,925	2,195
Tax rates,[2] %					
Federal income tax rate	21.0	21.0	21.0	21.0	21.0
State income tax rate	3.6	3.5	3.6	3.4	3.6
Statutory tax rate	24.6	24.5	24.6	24.4	24.6

Note: Reported in Costco's annual report, note 8, Income Taxes.

[1] Aggregated in the ESOP account in original filings.

[2] To determine each tax rate, divide each tax amount by earnings before taxes. Earnings before taxes are reported in Exhibit I.1.

EXHIBIT I.5 **Costco: NOPAT and Its Reconciliation to Net Income**

$ million

	Historical					Forecast										
	2019	2020	2021	2022	2023	2024	2025	2026	2027	2028	2029	2030	2031	2032	2033	CV
Revenues	152,703	166,761	195,929	226,954	242,290	253,420	270,419	288,837	308,808	330,477	354,007	377,024	399,208	420,231	439,763	457,485
Merchandise costs	(132,886)	(144,939)	(170,684)	(199,382)	(212,586)	(221,449)	(235,720)	(251,152)	(267,851)	(286,228)	(305,711)	(325,588)	(344,746)	(362,900)	(379,768)	(395,072)
Selling, general, and administrative	(13,588)	(14,742)	(16,756)	(17,879)	(19,513)	(20,409)	(21,778)	(23,262)	(24,870)	(26,615)	(28,510)	(30,364)	(32,151)	(33,844)	(35,417)	(36,844)
Depreciation and lease amortization	(1,492)	(1,645)	(1,781)	(1,900)	(2,077)	(1,908)	(1,996)	(2,128)	(2,270)	(2,425)	(2,595)	(2,780)	(2,960)	(3,135)	(3,300)	(3,453)
EBITA,[1] unadjusted	4,737	5,435	6,708	7,793	8,114	9,653	10,925	12,296	13,816	15,209	17,191	18,292	19,351	20,352	21,279	22,116
Add: Operating lease interest[2]	112	96	60	65	67	122	127	136	145	155	165	177	189	200	210	220
Add: Variable lease interest[2]	—	—	21	33	36	65	68	72	77	82	88	94	100	106	112	117
EBITA, adjusted	4,849	5,531	6,789	7,891	8,217	9,839	11,120	12,504	14,038	15,446	17,444	18,564	19,640	20,658	21,601	22,453
Operating cash taxes[3]	(946)	(1,294)	(1,546)	(2,166)	(2,064)	(2,471)	(2,773)	(3,098)	(3,459)	(3,791)	(4,261)	(4,525)	(4,778)	(5,018)	(5,240)	(5,440)
NOPAT	3,904	4,237	5,243	5,725	6,154	7,368	8,347	9,405	10,578	11,655	13,183	14,039	14,862	15,640	16,361	17,013
Reconciliation to net income																
Net income, consolidated	3,704	4,059	5,079	5,915	6,292	6,850	7,727	8,688	9,755	10,718	12,134	12,871	13,620	14,327	14,980	15,569
Operating taxes deferred[3]	228	131	198	(33)	89	107	120	134	149	163	184	195	206	216	226	235
Adjusted net income	3,932	4,190	5,277	5,882	6,381	6,956	7,847	8,822	9,904	10,882	12,317	13,066	13,826	14,543	15,206	15,804
Interest expense	150	160	171	158	160	463	551	628	713	808	894	1,018	1,085	1,148	1,209	1,265
Operating lease interest[2]	112	96	60	65	67	122	127	136	145	155	165	177	189	200	210	220
Variable lease interest[2]	—	—	21	33	36	65	68	72	77	82	88	94	100	106	112	117
Interest income	(126)	(89)	(41)	(61)	(470)	(104)	(83)	(62)	(42)	(21)	—	—	—	—	—	—
Other income[4]	(52)	(3)	(102)	(144)	(63)	—	—	—	—	—	—	—	—	—	—	—
Taxes related to nonoperating accounts[5]	(21)	(40)	(27)	(12)	66	(134)	(163)	(190)	(219)	(252)	(282)	(317)	(337)	(357)	(376)	(394)
Other nonoperating taxes[3]	(92)	(77)	(116)	(196)	(24)	—	—	—	—	—	—	—	—	—	—	—
NOPAT	3,904	4,237	5,243	5,725	6,154	7,368	8,347	9,405	10,578	11,655	13,183	14,039	14,862	15,640	16,361	17,013

[1] Earnings before interest, taxes, and amortization.

[2] Operating lease and variable lease interest is estimated by multiplying the corresponding prior-year liability by the weighted average discount rate for operating leases disclosed by the company.

[3] Operating cash taxes are detailed in Exhibit I.6.

[4] Other income consists primarily of foreign-currency transaction gains and is treated as nonoperating for simplicity of exposition.

[5] Estimated by multiplying the statutory tax rate by the sum of interest expense, operating lease interest, variable lease interest, less the sum of interest income and other income. Statutory tax rates are reported in Exhibit I.4.

EXHIBIT I.6 **Costco: Operating Cash Taxes**

$ million

	Historical					Forecast										CV
	2019	2020	2021	2022	2023	2024	2025	2026	2027	2028	2029	2030	2031	2032	2033	
EBITA	4,849	5,531	6,789	7,891	8,217	9,839	11,120	12,504	14,038	15,446	17,444	18,564	19,640	20,658	21,601	22,453
× Statutory tax rate	24.6%	24.5%	24.6%	24.4%	24.6%	24.6%	24.6%	24.6%	24.6%	24.6%	24.6%	24.6%	24.6%	24.6%	24.6%	24.6%
Statutory taxes on EBITA	1,193	1,357	1,673	1,925	2,018	2,416	2,730	3,070	3,447	3,793	4,283	4,558	4,823	5,073	5,304	5,513
Foreign taxes, net[1]	(1)	92	92	231	160	192	192	192	192	192	192	192	192	192	192	192
Employee stock ownership plan (ESOP)[1]	(18)	(24)	(21)	(23)	(25)	(30)	(30)	(30)	(30)	(30)	(30)	(30)	(30)	(30)	(30)	(30)
Operating taxes	1,174	1,425	1,744	2,133	2,153	2,578	2,892	3,232	3,609	3,954	4,445	4,720	4,984	5,234	5,466	5,675
Operating taxes deferred[2]	(228)	(131)	(198)	33	(89)	(107)	(120)	(134)	(149)	(163)	(184)	(195)	(206)	(216)	(226)	(235)
Operating cash taxes	946	1,294	1,546	2,166	2,064	2,471	2,773	3,098	3,459	3,791	4,261	4,525	4,778	5,018	5,240	5,440
Tax rates, % of EBITA																
Statutory tax rate	24.6	24.5	24.6	24.4	24.6	24.6	24.6	24.6	24.6	24.6	24.6	24.6	24.6	24.6	24.6	24.6
Other operating taxes	(0.4)	1.2	1.0	2.6	1.6	1.6	1.5	1.3	1.2	1.0	0.9	0.9	0.8	0.8	0.7	0.7
Operating tax rate	24.2	25.8	25.7	27.0	26.2	26.2	26.0	25.8	25.7	25.6	25.5	25.4	25.4	25.3	25.3	25.3
% deferred[3]	19.4	9.2	11.4	(1.5)	4.1	4.1	4.1	4.1	4.1	4.1	4.1	4.1	4.1	4.1	4.1	4.1
Operating cash tax rate[3]	19.5	23.4	22.8	27.5	25.1	25.1	24.9	24.8	24.6	24.5	24.4	24.4	24.3	24.3	24.3	24.2

[1] Reported in the tax reconciliation table presented in Exhibit I.4.
[2] Estimated in Exhibit I.9.
[3] The operating cash tax rate equals the operating tax rate times 1 minus the percent of operating taxes deferred.

EXHIBIT I.7 **Costco: Reorganized Deferred Taxes**

$ million

	As reported		
	2021	**2022**	**2023**
Deferred-tax assets			
Equity compensation	72	84	89
Deferred income/membership fees	161	302	309
Foreign tax credit carryforward	146	201	250
Operating leases	769	727	678
Accrued liabilities and reserves	681	694	761
Other	62	5	20
Total deferred-tax assets	1,891	2,013	2,107
Valuation allowance	(214)	(313)	(422)
Total net deferred-tax assets	1,677	1,700	1,685
Deferred-tax liabilities			
Property and equipment	(935)	(962)	(867)
Merchandise inventories	(216)	(231)	(380)
Operating leases	(744)	(701)	(655)
Foreign-branch deferreds	(92)	(85)	(87)
Other	—	—	—
Total deferred-tax liabilities	(1,987)	(1,979)	(1,989)
Deferred-tax assets, net of liabilities	(310)	(279)	(304)

	Reorganized		
	2021	**2022**	**2023**
Operating deferred-tax assets, net of liabilities			
Equity compensation	72	84	89
Deferred income/membership fees	161	302	309
Operating lease assets, net of liabilities	25	26	23
Accrued liabilities and reserves	681	694	761
Property and equipment	(935)	(962)	(867)
Merchandise inventories	(216)	(231)	(380)
Foreign-branch deferreds	(92)	(85)	(87)
Valuation allowance	(214)	(313)	(422)
Operating deferred-tax assets, net of liabilities	(518)	(485)	(574)
Nonoperating deferred-tax assets, net of liabilities[1]			
Other assets	62	5	20
Other liabilities	—	—	—
Nonoperating deferred-tax assets, net of liabilities	62	5	20
Tax loss carryforwards			
Foreign tax credit carryforward	146	201	250
Deferred-tax assets, net of liabilities	(310)	(279)	(304)

[1] We classify other deferred-tax assets and liabilities as nonoperating because they have not scaled consistently with revenue.

EXHIBIT I.8 **Costco: Invested Capital and Total Funds Invested**

$ million

	Historical					Forecast									
	2019	2020	2021	2022	2023	2024	2025	2026	2027	2028	2029	2030	2031	2032	2033
Operating cash[1]	3,054	3,335	3,919	4,539	4,846	5,068	5,408	5,777	6,176	6,610	7,080	7,540	7,984	8,405	8,795
Receivables, net	1,535	1,550	1,803	2,241	2,285	2,390	2,547	2,718	2,903	3,107	3,328	3,544	3,753	3,951	4,134
Merchandise inventories	11,395	12,242	14,215	17,907	16,651	17,345	18,463	19,672	20,980	22,419	23,945	25,502	27,003	28,425	29,746
Other current assets	1,111	1,023	1,312	1,499	1,709	1,787	1,905	2,033	2,171	2,324	2,489	2,651	2,807	2,955	3,092
Operating current assets	17,095	18,150	21,249	26,186	25,491	26,591	28,324	30,200	32,230	34,459	36,842	39,238	41,547	43,734	45,767
Accounts payable	(11,679)	(14,172)	(16,278)	(17,848)	(17,463)	(18,212)	(19,386)	(20,655)	(22,028)	(23,539)	(25,142)	(26,776)	(28,352)	(29,845)	(31,232)
Accrued salaries and benefits	(3,176)	(3,605)	(4,090)	(4,381)	(4,278)	(4,474)	(4,769)	(5,089)	(5,435)	(5,817)	(6,231)	(6,636)	(7,026)	(7,396)	(7,740)
Accrued member rewards	(1,180)	(1,393)	(1,671)	(1,911)	(2,150)	(2,249)	(2,397)	(2,558)	(2,732)	(2,923)	(3,131)	(3,335)	(3,531)	(3,717)	(3,890)
Deferred membership fees	(1,711)	(1,851)	(2,042)	(2,174)	(2,337)	(2,444)	(2,605)	(2,780)	(2,969)	(3,178)	(3,404)	(3,625)	(3,838)	(4,041)	(4,228)
Other current liabilities	(3,766)	(3,466)	(4,267)	(5,127)	(5,905)	(6,176)	(6,583)	(7,024)	(7,502)	(8,029)	(8,600)	(9,160)	(9,699)	(10,209)	(10,684)
Operating current liabilities	(21,512)	(24,487)	(28,348)	(31,441)	(32,153)	(33,554)	(35,740)	(38,106)	(40,666)	(43,486)	(46,508)	(49,532)	(52,446)	(55,208)	(57,774)
Operating working capital	(4,417)	(6,337)	(7,099)	(5,255)	(6,662)	(6,964)	(7,416)	(7,906)	(8,436)	(9,026)	(9,666)	(10,294)	(10,900)	(11,474)	(12,007)
Property, plant, and equipment	20,890	21,807	23,492	24,646	26,684	27,907	29,749	31,742	33,902	36,281	38,865	41,392	43,827	46,135	48,279
Operating lease right-of-use assets[2]	2,147	2,788	2,890	2,774	2,713	2,837	3,025	3,227	3,447	3,689	3,951	4,208	4,456	4,691	4,909
Variable lease assets[3]	—	963	1,474	1,466	1,405	1,469	1,566	1,671	1,785	1,910	2,046	2,179	2,307	2,429	2,542
Finance lease assets	—	592	1,000	1,620	1,325	1,386	1,477	1,576	1,683	1,802	1,930	2,055	2,176	2,291	2,397
Other assets, net of other liabilities[4]	57	242	260	544	456	477	508	542	579	620	664	707	749	788	825
Invested capital, excluding goodwill	18,677	20,055	22,017	25,795	25,921	27,113	28,909	30,853	32,961	35,275	37,790	40,247	42,616	44,860	46,945
Goodwill and acquired intangibles	53	988	996	993	994	994	994	994	994	994	994	994	994	994	994
Invested capital, including goodwill	18,730	21,043	23,013	26,788	26,915	28,107	29,903	31,847	33,955	36,269	38,784	41,241	43,610	45,854	47,939
Excess cash[1]	6,390	9,970	8,256	6,510	10,388	8,311	6,233	4,155	2,078	—	—	—	—	—	—
Foreign tax credit carryforward	65	101	146	201	250	250	250	250	250	250	250	250	250	250	250
Total funds invested	25,185	31,114	31,415	33,499	37,553	36,667	36,386	36,253	36,282	36,519	39,034	41,491	43,860	46,104	48,189

1 Operating cash is estimated at 2% of revenues. Remaining cash is treated as excess cash.
2 As reported on the balance sheet, except in 2019. Prior to the adoption of ASC 842 in 2020, it is necessary to estimate the value of operating leases. For more on estimation methodologies, see Chapter 22.
3 The value of variable leases is estimated using the ratio of operating lease expense to variable lease expense.
4 Other assets and liabilities are classified as operating because no description is provided by the company.

EXHIBIT I.9 **Costco: Reconciliation of Total Funds Invested**

$ million

	Historical					Forecast									
	2019	2020	2021	2022	2023	2024	2025	2026	2027	2028	2029	2030	2031	2032	2033
Debt	6,823	7,609	7,491	6,557	6,458	7,892	9,101	10,449	11,950	13,273	15,258	16,252	17,210	18,119	18,963
Operating lease liabilities[1]	2,147	2,789	2,864	2,721	2,646	2,767	2,950	3,148	3,362	3,598	3,854	4,104	4,346	4,575	4,787
Variable lease liabilities[1,2]	0	963	1,474	1,466	1,405	1,469	1,566	1,671	1,785	1,910	2,046	2,179	2,307	2,429	2,542
Finance lease liabilities[1]	421	688	1,052	1,628	1,432	1,498	1,596	1,703	1,819	1,947	2,086	2,221	2,352	2,476	2,591
Debt and debt equivalents	9,391	12,049	12,881	12,372	11,941	13,626	15,213	16,971	18,916	20,728	23,244	24,757	26,215	27,598	28,883
Deferred income taxes, operating[3]	189	320	518	485	574	681	800	934	1,083	1,246	1,430	1,625	1,831	2,048	2,274
Deferred income taxes, nonoperating[3]	21	40	(62)	(5)	(20)	(20)	(20)	(20)	(20)	(20)	(20)	(20)	(20)	(20)	(20)
Noncontrolling interests	341	421	514	5	0	0	0	0	0	0	0	0	0	0	0
Costco stockholders' equity	15,243	18,284	17,564	20,642	25,058	22,380	20,392	18,367	16,303	14,565	14,381	15,129	15,833	16,478	17,052
Equity and equity equivalents	15,794	19,065	18,534	21,127	25,612	23,041	21,172	19,281	17,366	15,791	15,791	16,735	17,644	18,506	19,306
Total funds invested	25,185	31,114	31,415	33,499	37,553	36,667	36,386	36,253	36,282	36,519	39,034	41,491	43,860	46,104	48,189

[1] Including current portion.

[2] The value of variable leases is estimated using the ratio of operating lease expense to variable lease expense.

[3] Deferred taxes are detailed in Exhibit I.7.

EXHIBIT I.10 **Costco: Income Statement Forecast Ratios**

%

	Historical					Forecast											Forecast ratio
	2019	2020	2021	2022	2023	2024	2025	2026	2027	2028	2029	2030	2031	2032	2033	CV	
Revenue growth	7.9	9.2	17.5	15.8	6.8	4.6	6.7	6.8	6.9	7.0	7.1	6.5	5.9	5.3	4.6	4.0	% of prior-year revenues
Revenue split																	
Merchandise sales	97.8	97.9	98.0	98.1	98.1	98.1	98.0	97.9	97.8	97.8	97.8	97.8	97.8	97.8	97.8	97.8	% of total revenues
Membership fees	2.2	2.1	2.0	1.9	1.9	1.9	2.0	2.1	2.2	2.2	2.2	2.2	2.2	2.2	2.2	2.2	% of total revenues
Revenues	100.0	100.0	100.0	100.0	100.0	100.0	100.0	100.0	100.0	100.0	100.0	100.0	100.0	100.0	100.0	100.0	% of total revenues
Operating expenses, forecast ratios																	
Merchandise costs	89.0	88.8	88.9	89.5	89.4	89.1	88.9	88.8	88.7	88.6	88.3	88.3	88.3	88.3	88.3	88.3	% of merchandise sales
Selling, general, and administrative	8.9	8.8	8.6	7.9	8.1	8.1	8.1	8.1	8.1	8.1	8.1	8.1	8.1	8.1	8.1	8.1	% of total revenues
Depreciation	7.6	7.9	7.1	6.9	7.2	7.2	7.2	7.2	7.2	7.2	7.2	7.2	7.2	7.2	7.2	7.2	% of net PP&E$_{t-1}$
Nonoperating items																	
Interest expense	2.3	2.3	1.6	1.5	1.7	5.0	5.1	5.2	5.2	5.2	5.2	5.3	5.3	5.3	5.3	5.3	% of total debt$_{t-1}$
Interest income	2.8	1.4	0.4	0.7	7.2	1.0	1.0	1.0	1.0	1.0	n/a	n/a	n/a	n/a	n/a	n/a	% of excess cash$_{t-1}$
Other income	0.0	0.0	0.1	0.1	0.0	—	—	—	—	—	—	—	—	—	—	—	% of total revenues
Results: Operating margins[1]																	
Total revenue	100.0	100.0	100.0	100.0	100.0	100.0	100.0	100.0	100.0	100.0	100.0	100.0	100.0	100.0	100.0	100.0	
Merchandise costs	(87.0)	(86.9)	(87.1)	(87.9)	(87.7)	(87.4)	(87.2)	(87.0)	(86.7)	(86.6)	(86.4)	(86.4)	(86.4)	(86.4)	(86.4)	(86.4)	
Selling, general, and administrative[2]	(8.8)	(8.8)	(8.5)	(7.8)	(8.0)	(8.0)	(8.0)	(8.0)	(8.0)	(8.0)	(8.0)	(8.0)	(8.0)	(8.0)	(8.0)	(8.0)	
Depreciation	(1.0)	(1.0)	(0.9)	(0.8)	(0.9)	(0.8)	(0.7)	(0.7)	(0.7)	(0.7)	(0.7)	(0.7)	(0.7)	(0.7)	(0.8)	(0.8)	
Operating margin	3.2	3.3	3.5	3.5	3.4	3.9	4.1	4.3	4.5	4.7	4.9	4.9	4.9	4.9	4.9	4.9	
Results: Return on invested capital[3]																	
ROIC without goodwill	21.9	22.7	26.1	26.0	23.9	28.4	30.8	32.5	34.3	35.4	37.4	37.1	36.9	36.7	36.5	36.2	
ROIC with goodwill	21.9	22.6	24.9	24.9	23.0	27.4	29.7	31.5	33.2	34.3	36.3	36.2	36.0	35.9	35.7	35.5	

[1] Operating expenses and operating margin measured as a percentage of total revenues.
[2] Selling, general, and administrative as reported, less lease-related interest expense.
[3] Return on invested capital measured using beginning-of-year capital.

EXHIBIT I.11 **Costco: Balance Sheet Forecast Ratios—Invested Capital**

	Historical					Forecast										Forecast ratio
	2019	2020	2021	2022	2023	2024	2025	2026	2027	2028	2029	2030	2031	2032	2033	
Working capital, days																
Operating cash	7.5	7.5	7.4	7.4	7.4	7.3	7.3	7.3	7.3	7.3	7.3	7.3	7.3	7.3	7.3	Days in merchandise sales
Receivables, net	3.8	3.5	3.4	3.7	3.5	3.5	3.5	3.5	3.5	3.5	3.5	3.5	3.5	3.5	3.5	Days in merchandise sales
Merchandise inventories	31.3	30.8	30.4	32.8	28.6	28.6	28.6	28.6	28.6	28.6	28.6	28.6	28.6	28.6	28.6	Days in merchandise cost
Other current assets	2.7	2.3	2.5	2.5	2.6	2.6	2.6	2.6	2.6	2.6	2.6	2.6	2.6	2.6	2.6	Days in merchandise sales
Operating current assets[1]	40.9	39.7	39.6	42.1	38.4	38.3	38.2	38.2	38.1	38.1	38.0	38.0	38.0	38.0	38.0	
Accounts payable	32.1	35.7	34.8	32.7	30.0	30.0	30.0	30.0	30.0	30.0	30.0	30.0	30.0	30.0	30.0	Days in merchandise cost
Accrued salaries and benefits	7.8	8.1	7.8	7.2	6.6	6.6	6.6	6.6	6.6	6.6	6.6	6.6	6.6	6.6	6.6	Days in merchandise sales
Accrued member rewards	2.9	3.1	3.2	3.1	3.3	3.3	3.3	3.3	3.3	3.3	3.3	3.3	3.3	3.3	3.3	Days in merchandise sales
Deferred membership fees	4.2	4.1	3.9	3.6	3.6	3.6	3.6	3.6	3.6	3.6	3.6	3.6	3.6	3.6	3.6	Days in merchandise sales
Other current liabilities	9.2	7.8	8.1	8.4	9.1	9.1	9.1	9.1	9.1	9.1	9.1	9.1	9.1	9.1	9.1	Days in merchandise sales
Operating current liabilities[1]	51.4	53.6	52.8	50.6	48.4	48.3	48.2	48.2	48.1	48.0	48.0	48.0	48.0	48.0	48.0	
Working capital	(10.6)	(13.9)	(13.2)	(8.5)	(10.0)	(10.0)	(10.0)	(10.0)	(10.0)	(10.0)	(10.0)	(10.0)	(10.0)	(10.0)	(10.0)	
Long-term assets and liabilities, %																
Property, plant, and equipment	14.0	13.4	12.2	11.1	11.2	11.2	11.2	11.2	11.2	11.2	11.2	11.2	11.2	11.2	11.2	% of merchandise sales
Operating lease right-of-use assets	n/a	1.7	1.5	1.2	1.1	1.1	1.1	1.1	1.1	1.1	1.1	1.1	1.1	1.1	1.1	% of merchandise sales
Variable lease assets	n/a	0.6	0.8	0.7	0.6	0.6	0.6	0.6	0.6	0.6	0.6	0.6	0.6	0.6	0.6	% of merchandise sales
Finance lease assets	n/a	0.4	0.5	0.7	0.6	0.6	0.6	0.6	0.6	0.6	0.6	0.6	0.6	0.6	0.6	% of merchandise sales
Other assets	0.4	0.5	0.5	0.4	0.4	0.4	0.4	0.4	0.4	0.4	0.4	0.4	0.4	0.4	0.4	% of merchandise sales
Other liabilities	0.3	0.4	0.4	0.2	0.2	0.2	0.2	0.2	0.2	0.2	0.2	0.2	0.2	0.2	0.2	% of merchandise sales
Goodwill, $ million	53	988	996	993	994	994	994	994	994	994	994	994	994	994	994	Straight-lined

[1] Cumulative totals are expressed in days of sales, so they will not equal the summation of the lines above the total.

EXHIBIT I.12 **Costco: Balance Sheet Forecast Ratios—Sources of Financing**

%

	Historical					Forecast										Forecast ratio
	2019	2020	2021	2022	2023	2024	2025	2026	2027	2028	2029	2030	2031	2032	2033	Using market values
Debt-to-value, inclusive of leases	7.0	7.7	6.2	5.2	4.9	4.9	4.9	4.9	4.9	4.9	4.9	4.9	4.9	4.9	4.9	Using market values
Leases																
Operating leases, current	n/a	8.3	7.7	8.6	8.1	8.1	8.1	8.1	8.1	8.1	8.1	8.1	8.1	8.1	8.1	% of operating lease right-of-use assets
Operating leases, long-term	n/a	91.8	91.4	89.5	89.4	89.4	89.4	89.4	89.4	89.4	89.4	89.4	89.4	89.4	89.4	% of operating lease right-of-use assets
Long-term variable lease liabilities	n/a	100.0	100.0	100.0	100.0	100.0	100.0	100.0	100.0	100.0	100.0	100.0	100.0	100.0	100.0	% of variable lease assets
Finance leases, current	n/a	5.2	7.2	15.1	9.7	9.7	9.7	9.7	9.7	9.7	9.7	9.7	9.7	9.7	9.7	% of finance lease assets
Finance leases, long-term	n/a	111.0	98.0	85.4	98.3	98.3	98.3	98.3	98.3	98.3	98.3	98.3	98.3	98.3	98.3	% of finance lease assets
Debt																
Short-term debt	1.4	24.9	1.2	10.7	1.1	16.7	10.9	10.9	10.9	10.9	10.9	10.9	10.9	10.9	10.9	% of total debt, excluding leases
Long-term debt	98.6	75.1	98.8	89.3	98.9	83.3	89.1	89.1	89.1	89.1	89.1	89.1	89.1	89.1	89.1	% of total debt, excluding leases
Equity																
Stock-based compensation	0.2	0.2	0.2	0.2	0.2	0.2	0.2	0.2	0.2	0.2	0.2	0.2	0.2	0.2	—	% of total revenues
Cash dividends declared and other	29.8	114.8	25.6	27.0	27.0	27.0	27.0	27.0	27.0	27.0	27.0	27.0	27.0	27.0	—	% of net income

EXHIBIT I.13 **Costco: Free Cash Flow and Cash Flow to Investors**

$ million

	Historical				Forecast									
	2020	2021	2022	2023	2024	2025	2026	2027	2028	2029	2030	2031	2032	2033
NOPAT	4,237	5,243	5,725	6,154	7,368	8,347	9,405	10,578	11,655	13,183	14,039	14,862	15,640	16,361
Depreciation	1,645	1,781	1,900	2,077	1,908	1,996	2,128	2,270	2,425	2,595	2,780	2,960	3,135	3,300
Gross cash flow	5,882	7,024	7,625	8,231	9,276	10,343	11,533	12,849	14,079	15,778	16,819	17,823	18,775	19,661
Decrease (Increase) in working capital	1,920	763	(1,845)	1,407	301	453	490	530	590	639	628	606	574	533
Less: Capital expenditures[1]	(2,810)	(3,588)	(3,891)	(4,323)	(3,131)	(3,838)	(4,121)	(4,430)	(4,804)	(5,178)	(5,307)	(5,396)	(5,443)	(5,444)
Decrease (Increase) in operating leases	(641)	(102)	116	61	(124)	(187)	(203)	(220)	(242)	(263)	(257)	(248)	(235)	(218)
Decrease (Increase) in variable leases	(963)	(512)	8	62	(64)	(97)	(105)	(114)	(125)	(136)	(133)	(128)	(122)	(113)
Decrease (Increase) in finance leases	(592)	(408)	(620)	295	(61)	(91)	(99)	(107)	(118)	(128)	(125)	(121)	(115)	(106)
Decrease (Increase) in goodwill	(935)	(8)	3	(1)	0	0	0	0	0	0	0	0	0	0
Decrease (Increase) in other assets, net of liabilities	(185)	(18)	(284)	88	(21)	(31)	(34)	(37)	(41)	(44)	(43)	(42)	(39)	(37)
Free cash flow	1,676	3,151	1,112	5,820	6,176	6,551	7,461	8,471	9,340	10,668	11,582	12,494	13,396	14,276
Interest income	89	41	61	470	104	83	62	42	21	0	0	0	0	0
Other income	3	102	144	63	0	0	0	0	0	0	0	0	0	0
Taxes related to nonoperating accounts	40	27	12	(66)	134	163	190	219	252	282	317	337	357	376
Other nonoperating taxes	77	116	196	24	0	0	0	0	0	0	0	0	0	0
Decrease (Increase) in excess cash	(3,580)	1,713	1,747	(3,878)	2,078	2,078	2,078	2,078	2,078	0	0	0	0	0
Decrease (Increase) in tax credit carryforward	(36)	(45)	(55)	(49)	0	0	0	0	0	0	0	0	0	0
Unexplained foreign-currency translation[2]	387	282	151	232	0	0	0	0	0	0	0	0	0	0
Cash flow to investors	(1,343)	5,387	3,368	2,615	8,492	8,875	9,791	10,810	11,690	10,949	11,898	12,831	13,753	14,652

[1] Capital expenditures are reported on the statement of cash flows.

[2] In 2023, the unexplained foreign-currency adjustment equals the foreign-currency translation adjustment of $24 million reported in Exhibit I.3 plus the unexplained changes to property, plant, and equipment (PP&E) of $208 million.

EXHIBIT I.14 **Costco: Reconciliation of Cash Flow to Investors**

$ million

	Historical				Forecast									
	2020	2021	2022	2023	2024	2025	2026	2027	2028	2029	2030	2031	2032	2033
Interest expense	160	171	158	160	463	551	628	713	808	894	1,018	1,085	1,148	1,209
Operating lease interest	96	60	65	67	122	127	136	145	155	165	177	189	200	210
Variable lease interest	—	21	33	36	65	68	72	77	82	88	94	100	106	112
Decrease (Increase) in debt	(786)	118	934	99	(1,434)	(1,208)	(1,349)	(1,501)	(1,323)	(1,985)	(994)	(958)	(908)	(844)
Decrease (Increase) in operating leases	(642)	(75)	143	75	(121)	(183)	(198)	(214)	(236)	(256)	(251)	(242)	(229)	(213)
Decrease (Increase) in variable leases	(963)	(512)	8	62	(64)	(97)	(105)	(114)	(125)	(136)	(133)	(128)	(122)	(113)
Decrease (Increase) in finance leases	(267)	(364)	(576)	196	(66)	(99)	(107)	(116)	(128)	(139)	(136)	(131)	(124)	(115)
Cash flow to debt and debt equivalents	(2,401)	(581)	765	695	(1,036)	(841)	(923)	(1,009)	(767)	(1,368)	(223)	(85)	72	246
Dividends	1,193	5,748	1,498	1,698	1,849	2,085	2,345	2,633	2,893	3,274	3,473	3,676	3,866	4,043
Repurchases of common stock	198	495	442	677	8,176	8,160	8,935	9,792	10,213	9,737	9,388	10,023	10,639	11,225
Shares issued for stock-based compensation, net[1]	(291)	(356)	(365)	(475)	(497)	(530)	(566)	(605)	(648)	(694)	(739)	(783)	(824)	(862)
Payments from (Investments in) nonconsolidated interests[2]	(23)	(21)	1,085	5	—	—	—	—	—	—	—	—	—	—
Nonoperating deferred income taxes	(19)	102	(57)	15	—	—	—	—	—	—	—	—	—	—
Cash flow to equity and equity equivalents	1,058	5,968	2,603	1,920	9,527	9,715	10,713	11,819	12,457	12,318	12,122	12,916	13,681	14,406
Cash flow to investors	(1,343)	5,387	3,368	2,615	8,492	8,875	9,791	10,810	11,690	10,949	11,898	12,831	13,753	14,652

[1] Includes stock-based compensation and stock options exercised, net of the release of vested restricted stock units.
[2] Equals net income to nonconsolidated interests minus (plus) the increase (decrease) in noncontrolling interests.

EXHIBIT I.15 **Costco: Continuing Value**

$ million

Key inputs

Projected NOPAT in final forecast year	17,012.7
NOPAT growth rate in perpetuity (g)	4.0%
Return on new invested capital (RONIC)	36.2%
Weighted average cost of capital (WACC)	8.1%

$$\text{Continuing Value}_t = \frac{\text{NOPAT}_{t+1}\left(1 - \frac{g}{\text{RONIC}}\right)}{\text{WACC} - g}$$

$$= 370{,}699.3$$

Note: Continuing value of $370,699.3 million is calculated from unrounded data. Rounded inputs calculate to $369,093.7 million.

EXHIBIT I.16 **Costco: Weighted Average Cost of Capital (WACC)**

%

Source of capital	Target proportion of total capital	Cost of capital	Marginal tax rate	After-tax cost of capital	Contribution to weighted average
Debt	4.9	4.6	24.6	3.5	0.2
Equity	95.1	8.3		8.3	7.9
WACC	100.0				8.1

EXHIBIT I.17 **Costco: Enterprise DCF Valuation**

$ million, except where noted

Forecast year	Free cash flow (FCF)	Discount factor at 8.1%	Present value of FCF
2024	6,176	0.925	5,713
2025	6,551	0.856	5,605
2026	7,461	0.791	5,905
2027	8,471	0.732	6,201
2028	9,340	0.677	6,325
2029	10,668	0.626	6,682
2030	11,582	0.579	6,710
2031	12,494	0.536	6,696
2032	13,396	0.496	6,641
2033	14,276	0.459	6,546
Continuing value	370,699	0.459	169,982
Present value of cash flow			233,006
× Midyear adjustment factor			1.040
Value of operations			242,269
Value of excess cash			10,388
Value of foreign tax credit carryforward			250
Enterprise value			252,907
Less: Value of debt			(6,458)
Less: Value of operating leases			(2,646)
Less: Value of variable leases			(1,405)
Less: Value of finance leases			(1,432)
Less: Value of noncontrolling interests			0
Equity value			240,966
÷ Shares outstanding, millions			443.7
Equity value per share, $			543

EXHIBIT I.18 **Costco: ROIC and Economic Profit**

$ million, except where noted

	Historical					Forecast										
	2019	2020	2021	2022	2023	2024	2025	2026	2027	2028	2029	2030	2031	2032	2033	CV
Method 1																
Return on invested capital,¹ %	21.9	22.7	26.1	26.0	23.9	28.4	30.8	32.5	34.3	35.4	37.4	37.1	36.9	36.7	36.5	36.2
Weighted average cost of capital, %	(8.1)	(7.5)	(7.8)	(8.3)	(8.4)	(8.1)	(8.1)	(8.1)	(8.1)	(8.1)	(8.1)	(8.1)	(8.1)	(8.1)	(8.1)	(8.1)
Economic spread, %	13.8	15.2	18.4	17.7	15.4	20.3	22.7	24.4	26.2	27.3	29.3	29.0	28.8	28.6	28.4	28.1
× Invested capital¹	17,804	18,677	20,055	22,017	25,795	25,921	27,113	28,909	30,853	32,961	35,275	37,790	40,247	42,616	44,860	46,945
Economic profit	2,464	2,830	3,683	3,894	3,984	5,266	6,149	7,061	8,076	8,982	10,322	10,974	11,598	12,185	12,723	13,206
Method 2																
Invested capital¹	17,804	18,677	20,055	22,017	25,795	25,921	27,113	28,909	30,853	32,961	35,275	37,790	40,247	42,616	44,860	46,945
× Weighted average cost of capital, %	8.1%	7.5%	7.8%	8.3%	8.4%	8.1%	8.1%	8.1%	8.1%	8.1%	8.1%	8.1%	8.1%	8.1%	8.1%	8.1%
Capital charge	1,440	1,407	1,560	1,831	2,169	2,102	2,199	2,344	2,502	2,673	2,860	3,064	3,264	3,456	3,638	3,807
NOPAT	3,904	4,237	5,243	5,725	6,154	7,368	8,347	9,405	10,578	11,655	13,183	14,039	14,862	15,640	16,361	17,013
Capital charge	(1,440)	(1,407)	(1,560)	(1,831)	(2,169)	(2,102)	(2,199)	(2,344)	(2,502)	(2,673)	(2,860)	(3,064)	(3,264)	(3,456)	(3,638)	(3,807)
Economic profit	2,464	2,830	3,683	3,894	3,984	5,266	6,149	7,061	8,076	8,982	10,322	10,974	11,598	12,185	12,723	13,206

¹ Invested capital measured at the beginning of the year, without goodwill.

EXHIBIT I.19 **Costco: Valuation Using Economic Profit**

$ million, except where noted

Forecast year	Invested capital[1]	ROIC,[1] %	WACC, %	Economic profit	Discount factor at 8.1%	Present value of economic profit
2024	25,921	28.4	8.1	5,266	0.925	4,871
2025	27,113	30.8	8.1	6,149	0.856	5,261
2026	28,909	32.5	8.1	7,061	0.791	5,589
2027	30,853	34.3	8.1	8,076	0.732	5,912
2028	32,961	35.4	8.1	8,982	0.677	6,082
2029	35,275	37.4	8.1	10,322	0.626	6,466
2030	37,790	37.1	8.1	10,974	0.579	6,358
2031	40,247	36.9	8.1	11,598	0.536	6,216
2032	42,616	36.7	8.1	12,185	0.496	6,040
2033	44,860	36.5	8.1	12,723	0.459	5,834
Continuing value				323,754	0.459	148,456
Present value of economic profit						207,085
Invested capital in 2023						25,921
Invested capital and economic profit						233,006
× Midyear adjustment factor						1.040
Value of operations						242,269
Value of excess cash						10,388
Value of foreign tax credit carryforward						250
Enterprise value						252,907
Less: Value of debt						(6,458)
Less: Value of operating leases						(2,646)
Less: Value of variable leases						(1,405)
Less: Value of finance leases						(1,432)
Less: Value of noncontrolling interests						0
Equity value						240,966

[1] Invested capital measured at the beginning of the year, without goodwill.

EXHIBIT I.20 **Costco: Value per Share Sensitivity to Key Inputs**

Value per share in $

		Peak operating margin							New stores[2]
		3.5%	4.0%	4.5%	5.0%	5.5%	6.0%	6.5%	
Revenue growth[1]	5.8%	412	467	523	578	633	688	743	268
	6.3%	428	485	543	601	658	716	774	324
	6.9%	444	504	564	625	685	745	806	383
	7.4%	460	523	586	650	713	776	839	444
	7.9%	478	544	609	675	741	807	873	507
	8.4%	496	564	633	702	771	840	909	573
	8.9%	514	586	658	730	802	874	946	642

[1] Compounded annual growth rate between 2023 and 2033.

[2] Net stores added between 2023 and 2033.

Index